Contemporary Authors®

ISSN 0010-7468

Contemporary

Authors®

A Bio-Bibliographical Guide to Current Writers in Fiction, General Nonfiction, Poetry, Journalism, Drama, Motion Pictures, Television, and Other Fields

volume 195

GALE GROUP

THOMSON LEARNING

Detroit • New York • San Diego • San Francisco
Boston • New Haven, Conn. • Waterville, Maine
London • Munich

Staff

Scot Peacock, *Managing Editor, Literature Product*

Mark W. Scott, *Publisher, Literature Product*

Frank Castronova, Lisa Kumar, *Senior Editors*; Katy Balcer, Sara Constantakis, Kristen A. Dorsch, Marie Lazzari, Thomas F. McMahon, *Editors*; Alana Joli Foster, Arlene M. Johnson, Jennifer Kilian, Michelle Poole, Thomas Wiloch, *Associate Editors*; Karen Abbott, Madeline Harris, Anita Sundaresan, Maikue Vang, Denay L. Wilding, *Assistant Editors*; Anna Marie Dahn, Judith L. Pyko, *Administrative Support;* Joshua Kondek, Mary Ruby, *Technical Training Specialist*s

Dwayne Hayes, Joyce Nakamura, *Managing Editors*

Susan M. Trosky, *Content Director*

Victoria B. Cariappa, *Research Manager*

Tamara C. Nott, *Research Associate*; Nicodemus Ford, *Research Assistant*

Library of Congress Catalog Card Number 62-52046
ISBN 0-7876-4590-7
ISSN 0010-7468
Printed in the United States of America

10 9 8 7 6 5 4 3 2 1

Contents

Preface vii

Product Advisory Board xi

International Advisory Board xii

CA Numbering System and
Volume Update Chart xiii

Authors and Media People
Featured in This Volume xv

Acknowledgments xvii

Author Listings 1

Indexing note: All *Contemporary Authors* entries are indexed in the *Contemporary Authors* cumulative index, which is published separately and distributed twice a year.

As always, the most recent *Contemporary Authors* cumulative index continues to be the user's guide to the location of an individual author's listing.

Preface

Contemporary Authors (CA) provides information on approximately 100,000 writers in a wide range of media, including:

- Current writers of fiction, nonfiction, poetry, and drama whose works have been issued by commercial publishers, risk publishers, or university presses (authors whose books have been published only by known vanity or author-subsidized firms are ordinarily not included)

- Prominent print and broadcast journalists, editors, photojournalists, syndicated cartoonists, graphic novelists, screenwriters, television scriptwriters, and other media people

- Authors who write in languages other than English, provided their works have been published in the United States or translated into English

- Literary greats of the early twentieth century whose works are popular in todays high school and college curriculums and continue to elicit critical attention

A *CA* listing entails no charge or obligation. Authors are included on the basis of the above criteria and their interest to *CA* users. Sources of potential listees include trade periodicals, publishers' catalogs, librarians, and other users.

How to Get the Most out of *CA*: Use the Index

The key to locating an author's most recent entry is the *CA* cumulative index, which is published separately and distributed twice a year. It provides access to *all* entries in *CA* and *Contemporary Authors New Revision Series (CANR)*. Always consult the latest index to find an authors most recent entry.

For the convenience of users, the *CA* cumulative index also includes references to all entries in these Gale literary series: *Authors and Artists for Young Adults, Authors in the News, Bestsellers, Black Literature Criticism, Black Literature Criticism Supplement, Black Writers, Children's Literature Review, Concise Dictionary of American Literary Biography, Concise Dictionary of British Literary Biography, Contemporary Authors Autobiography Series, Contemporary Authors Bibliographical Series, Contemporary Dramatists, Contemporary Literary Criticism, Contemporary Novelists, Contemporary Poets, Contemporary Popular Writers, Contemporary Southern Writers, Contemporary Women Poets, Dictionary of Literary Biography, Dictionary of Literary Biography Documentary Series, Dictionary of Literary Biography Yearbook, DISCovering Authors, DISCovering Authors: British, DISCovering Authors: Canadian, DISCovering Authors: Modules* (including modules for Dramatists, Most-Studied Authors, Multicultural Authors, Novelists, Poets, and Popular/Genre Authors), *Discovering Authors 3.0, Drama Criticism, Drama for Students, Feminist Writers, Hispanic Literature Criticism, Hispanic Writers, Junior DISCovering Authors, Major Authors and Illustrators for Children and Young Adults, Major 20th-Century Writers, Native North American Literature, Novels for Students, Poetry Criticism, Poetry for Students, Short Stories for Students, Short Story Criticism, Something about the Author, Something about the Author Autobiography Series, St. James Guide to Children's Writers, St. James Guide to Horror, Ghost, and Gothic Writers, St. James Guide to Science Fiction Writers, St. James Guide to Young Adult Writers, Twentieth-Century Literary Criticism, 20th Century Romance and Historical Writers, World Literature Criticism,* and *Yesterday's Authors of Books for Children.*

A Sample Index Entry:

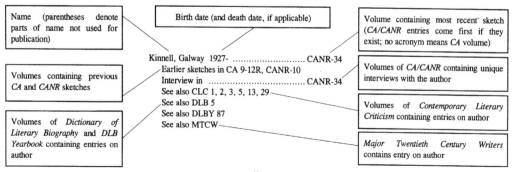

vii

How Are Entries Compiled?

The editors make every effort to secure new information directly from the authors; listees' responses to our questionnaires and query letters provide most of the information featured in *CA*. For deceased writers, or those who fail to reply to requests for data, we consult other reliable biographical sources, such as those indexed in Gale's *Biography and Genealogy Master Index*, and bibliographical sources, including *National Union Catalog, LC MARC,* and *British National Bibliography*. Further details come from published interviews, feature stories, and book reviews, as well as information supplied by the authors' publishers and agents.

An asterisk (*) at the end of a sketch indicates that the listing has been compiled from secondary sources believed to be reliable but has not been personally verified for this edition by the author sketched.

What Kinds of Information Does An Entry Provide?

Sketches in *CA* contain the following biographical and bibliographical information:

- **Entry heading:** the most complete form of author's name, plus any pseudonyms or name variations used for writing

- **Personal information:** author's date and place of birth, family data, ethnicity, educational background, political and religious affiliations, and hobbies and leisure interests

- **Addresses:** author's home, office, or agent's addresses, plus e-mail and fax numbers, as available

- **Career summary:** name of employer, position, and dates held for each career post; resume of other vocational achievements; military service

- **Membership information:** professional, civic, and other association memberships and any official posts held

- **Awards and honors:** military and civic citations, major prizes and nominations, fellowships, grants, and honorary degrees

- **Writings:** a comprehensive, chronological list of titles, publishers, dates of original publication and revised editions, and production information for plays, television scripts, and screenplays

- **Adaptations:** a list of films, plays, and other media which have been adapted from the author's work

- **Work in progress:** current or planned projects, with dates of completion and/or publication, and expected publisher, when known

- **Sidelights:** a biographical portrait of the author's development; information about the critical reception of the author's works; revealing comments, often by the author, on personal interests, aspirations, motivations, and thoughts on writing

- **Interview:** a one-on-one discussion with authors conducted especially for *CA*, offering insight into authors' thoughts about their craft

- **Autobiographical Essay:** an original essay written by noted authors for *CA*, a forum in which writers may present themselves, on their own terms, to their audience

- **Photographs:** portraits and personal photographs of notable authors

- **Biographical and critical sources:** a list of books and periodicals in which additional information on an author's life and/or writings appears

- **Obituary Notices** in *CA* provide date and place of birth as well as death information about authors whose full-length sketches appeared in the series before their deaths. The entries also summarize the authors' careers and writings and list other sources of biographical and death information.

Related Titles in the *CA* Series

Contemporary Authors Autobiography Series complements *CA* original and revised volumes with specially commissioned autobiographical essays by important current authors, illustrated with personal photographs they provide. Common topics include their motivations for writing, the people and experiences that shaped their careers, the rewards they derive from their work, and their impressions of the current literary scene.

Contemporary Authors Bibliographical Series surveys writings by and about important American authors since World War II. Each volume concentrates on a specific genre and features approximately ten writers; entries list works written by and about the author and contain a bibliographical essay discussing the merits and deficiencies of major critical and scholarly studies in detail.

Available in Electronic Formats

GaleNet. *CA* is available on a subscription basis through GaleNet, an online information resource that features an easy-to-use end-user interface, powerful search capabilities, and ease of access through the World Wide Web. For more information, call 1-800-877-GALE.

Licensing. *CA* is available for licensing. The complete database is provided in a fielded format and is deliverable on such media as disk, CD-ROM, or tape. For more information, contact Gale's Business Development Group at 1-800-877-GALE, or visit us on our website at www.galegroup.com/bizdev.

Suggestions Are Welcome

The editors welcome comments and suggestions from users on any aspect of the *CA* series. If readers would like to recommend authors for inclusion in future volumes of the series, they are cordially invited to write the Editors at *Contemporary Authors*, Gale Group, 27500 Drake Rd., Farmington Hills, MI 48331-3535; or call at 1-248-699-4253; or fax at 1-248-699-8054.

Contemporary Authors Product Advisory Board

The editors of *Contemporary Authors* are dedicated to maintaining a high standard of excellence by publishing comprehensive, accurate, and highly readable entries on a wide array of writers. In addition to the quality of the content, the editors take pride in the graphic design of the series, which is intended to be orderly yet inviting, allowing readers to utilize the pages of *CA* easily and with efficiency. Despite the longevity of the *CA* print series, and the success of its format, we are mindful that the vitality of a literary reference product is dependent on its ability to serve its users over time. As literature, and attitudes about literature, constantly evolve, so do the reference needs of students, teachers, scholars, journalists, researchers, and book club members. To be certain that we continue to keep pace with the expectations of our customers, the editors of *CA* listen carefully to their comments regarding the value, utility, and quality of the series. Librarians, who have firsthand knowledge of the needs of library users, are a valuable resource for us. The *Contemporary Authors* Product Advisory Board, made up of school, public, and academic librarians, is a forum to promote focused feedback about *CA* on a regular basis. The five-member advisory board includes the following individuals, whom the editors wish to thank for sharing their expertise:

- **Barbara C. Chumard**, Reference/Adult Services Librarian, Middletown Thrall Library, Middletown, New York.

- **Eva M. Davis**, Teen Services Librarian, Plymouth District Library, Plymouth, Michigan.

- **Adam Janowski, Jr.**, Library Media Specialist, Naples High School Library Media Center, Naples, Florida.

- **Robert Reginald**, Head of Technical Services and Collection Development, California State University, San Bernadino, California.

- **Barbara A. Wencl**, Media Specialist, Como Park High School, St. Paul, Minnesota.

International Advisory Board

Well-represented among the 100,000 author entries published in *Contemporary Authors* are sketches on notable writers from many non-English-speaking countries. The primary criteria for inclusion of such authors has traditionally been the publication of at least one title in English, either as an original work or as a translation. However, the editors of *Contemporary Authors* came to observe that many important international writers were being overlooked due to a strict adherence to our inclusion criteria. In addition, writers who were publishing in languages other than English were not being covered in the traditional sources we used for identifying new listees. Intent on increasing our coverage of international authors, including those who write only in their native language and have not been translated into English, the editors enlisted the aid of a board of advisors, each of whom is an expert on the literature of a particular country or region. Among the countries we focused attention on in 2000 are Mexico, Puerto Rico, Germany, Luxembourg, Belgium, the Netherlands, Norway, Sweden, Denmark, Finland, Taiwan, Singapore, and Japan, as well as England, Scotland, Wales, Ireland, Australia, and New Zealand. The nine-member advisory board includes the following individuals, whom the editors wish to thank for sharing their expertise:

- **Lowell A. Bangerter**, Professor of German, University of Wyoming, Laramie, Wyoming.

- **David William Foster**, Regent's Professor of Spanish, Interdisciplinary Humanities, and Women's Studies, Arizona State University, Tempe, Arizona.

- **Frances Devlin-Glass**, Associate Professor, School of Literary and Communication Studies, Deakin University, Burwood, Victoria, Australia.

- **Hosea Hirata**, Director of the Japanese Program, Associate Professor of Japanese, Tufts University, Medford, Massachusetts.

- **Linda M. Rodríguez Guglielmoni**, Associate Professor, University of Puerto Rico—Mayagüez, Puerto Rico.

- **Sven Hakon Rossel**, Professor and Chair of Scandanvian Studies, University of Vienna, Vienna, Austria.

- **Steven R. Serafin**, Director, Writing Center, Hunter College of the City University of New York, New York City.

- **Ismail S. Talib**, Senior Lecturer, Department of English Language and Literature, National University of Singapore, Singapore.

- **Mark Williams**, Associate Professor, English Department, University of Canterbury, Christchurch, New Zealand.

CA Numbering System and Volume Update Chart

Occasionally questions arise about the *CA* numbering system and which volumes, if any, can be discarded. Despite numbers like "29-32R," "97-100" and "194," the entire *CA* print series consists of only 224 physical volumes with the publication of *CA* Volume 195. The following charts note changes in the numbering system and cover design, and indicate which volumes are essential for the most complete, up-to-date coverage.

CA First Revision

- 1-4R through 41-44R (11 books)
  Cover: Brown with black and gold trim.
  There will be no further First Revision volumes because revised entries are now being handled exclusively through the more efficient *New Revision Series* mentioned below.

CA Original Volumes

- 45-48 through 97-100 (14 books)
  Cover: Brown with black and gold trim.
- 101 through 195 (95 books)
  Cover: Blue and black with orange bands.
  The same as previous *CA* original volumes but with a new, simplified numbering system and new cover design.

CA Permanent Series

- *CAP*-1 and *CAP*-2 (2 books)
  Cover: Brown with red and gold trim.
  There will be no further Permanent Series volumes because revised entries are now being handled exclusively through the more efficient *New Revision Series* mentioned below.

CA New Revision Series

- CANR-1 through CANR-102 (102 books)
  Cover: Blue and black with green bands.
  Includes only sketches requiring significant changes; **sketches are taken from any previously published *CA*, *CAP*, or *CANR* volume.**

If You Have: / You May Discard:

If You Have:	You May Discard:
CA First Revision Volumes 1-4R through 41-44R and *CA Permanent Series* Volumes 1 and 2.	*CA* Original Volumes 1, 2 ,3, 4 Volumes 5-6 through 41-44
CA Original Volumes 45-48 through 97-100 and 101 through 195	**NONE:** These volumes will not be supeseded by corresponding revised volumes. Individual entries from these and all other volumes appearing in the left column of this chart may be revised and included in the various volumes of the *New Revision Series*.
CA New Revision Series Volumes *CANR*-1 through *CANR*-101	**NONE:** The *New Revision Series* does not replace any single volume of *CA*. Instead, volumes of *CANR* include entries from many previous *CA* series volumes. All *New Revision Series* volumes must be retained for full coverage.

A Sampling of Authors and Media People Featured in This Volume

Douglas Southall Freeman

Freeman is recognized as one of the leading biographers and military historians of the twentieth century. His many volumes on Robert E. Lee and the Confederate officers who served under him are considered definitive books on the American Civil War. *R. E. Lee*, which was published as a four-volume work during 1934 and 1935, received widespread critical acclaim, won the 1935 Pulitzer Prize, and established Freeman's reputation as a preeminent biographer and historian. He is also the author of the three-volume history *Lee's Lieutenants: A Study in Command* and the seven-volume biography *George Washington*.

Him Mark Lai

Lai is a leading historian whose writings, in both English and Chinese, are read by international audiences. He has accumulated a vast amount of information about his passion, Chinese-American history, much of it during his long career as an engineer. Decades before Asian-American studies programs became available on campuses, Lai was offering access to his huge collection to students, researchers, and writers who sought to understand and record the details of the lives of Chinese immigrants who had settled in America. In 1982, he received the American Book Award for *Island: Poetry and History of Chinese Immigrants on Angel Island 1910-1940.*

Graciela Limón

Limón is an educator and author whose novels address the issues of multiculturalism, national identity, feminism, and social justice. Her fiction includes *María de Belén: The Autobiography of an Indian Woman* and *In Search of Bernabé,* a novel critical of U.S. involvement in El Salvador during the 1980s. *In Search of Bernabé* was awarded the Chicano Literature award, the Before Columbus Foundation Book Award, and the *New York Times Book Review*'s critics's choice award.

Tim Lott

Lott is a British author who has achieved success in many arenas but whose personal life has been diminished by bouts of depression, an illness he shared with his mother, Jean, who committed suicide by hanging. In the autobiographical volume *The Scent of Dried Roses*, Lott details his life, describing both his accomplishments and the hardships he endured. *The Scent of Dried Roses* was awarded the J. R. Ackerly Prize for autobi-

ography in 1996, while Lott's next offering, *White City Blue*, won the 1999 Whitbread Prize for first novel.

John Rechy

Rechy is an award-winning novelist whose works focus on gay themes. His first book, *City of Night*, was published in 1963 to critical acclaim and quickly became a best-seller. The novel is now regarded as a modern classic and is taught in modern literature courses, although the book's controversial subject matter—tracing the journey of a sexual adventurer through the night life of urban America—has drawn attention away from what Rechy considers more important aspects of his work: the structure of the novel and the craftsmanship of Rechy's art, aspects the author continues to emphasize in his more recent fiction. An autobiographical essay by Rechy is included in this volume of *CA.*

M. Night Shyamalan

Shyamalan, a Hollywood phenomenon, is the writer/director of the film *The Sixth Sense*, the 1999 Academy Award-winning thriller starring Bruce Willis as a doctor treating a little boy with troubling psychic abilities. *The Sixth Sense*, along with Shyamalan's next film, *Unbreakable*, brought in over $1 billion in box-office receipts and have allowed the filmmaker to make movies free of executive interference. His other films include *Praying with Anger*, *Wide Awake*, and the screenplay for *Stuart Little.*

Lemony Snicket (Daniel Handler)

Lemony Snicket, the alter ego of novelist Daniel Handler, is the author of a popular series of children's novels. Subtitled "A Series of Unfortunate Events," the books feature the orphaned Baudelaire siblings, Violet, Klaus, and Sunny, who not only lose their parents, but are then set upon by the vile Count Olaf, whose one goal in life, it seems, is to bilk the children out of their fortune. After a close encounter with this dastardly villain in the opening novel of the series, *The Bad Beginning*, the children make their painful way from one relative to the next, each more hideous than the last.

Judd Winick

A former cast member of the reality-based TV show *The Real World*, Winick is a popular cartoonist, author, and illustrator of the comic strip "Frumpy the Clown," which follows the trail of a chain-smoking, cynical clown, and "The Adventures of Barry Ween, Boy Genius," a series of comic books dealing with the misadventures of a cranky, obnoxious, brilliant, and foul-mouthed ten-year-old. In 2000 Winick published *Pedro and Me: Friendship, Loss, and What I Learned*, a moving and honest graphic-novel account of his friendship with *Real World* co-star Pedro Zamora, an AIDS activist who died from the disease.

Acknowledgements

Grateful acknowledgment is made to those publishers, photographers, and artists whose work appear with these authors' essays. Following is a list of the copyright holders who have granted us permission to reproduce material in this volume of *CA*. Every effort has been made to trace copyright, but if omissions have been made, please let us know.

Photographs/Art

Franny Billingsley: Billingsley, photograph. © Richard Pettengill. Reproduced by permission.

Sylvia Louise Engdahl: All photographs reproduced by permission of the author.

Him Mark Lai: Lai, photograph. AP/Wide World Photos. Reproduced by permission.

John Rechy: Photograph of Rechy leaning against adobe wall, © Cynthia Farah. Reproduced by permission of Cynthia Farah. All other photographs reproduced by permission of the author.

M. Night Shyamalan: Shyamalan, photograph. Corbis. Reproduced by permission.

John A. Williams: Williams, photograph by Lynda Koolish. Reproduced by permission of Lynda Koolish. All other photographs reproduced by permission of John A. Williams.

Judd Winick: Winick, photograph by Duane Cramer. Reproduced by permission.

A-B

ABEL, Lionel 1910-2001

OBITUARY NOTICE—See index for CA sketch: Born November 28, 1910, in New York, NY; died April 19, 2001, in New York, NY. Professor and author. Abel, the authorized translator for the works of Jean-Paul Sartre, spent his life working with words, whether it was writing novels, essays or plays. He grew up in New York City and left home at a young age for the excitement of Greenwich Village. There he became a contemporary of many of the intellectuals and artists of that time, and pursued his own writing career. His first play, *The Death of Odysseus,* was produced in 1953, but it is his play *Absalom* that brought him to the attention of critics. *Absalom* told the story of King David's dilemma over which of his sons should succeed him. The production won the 1956 Obie for best Off-Broadway play as well as the Show Business Award and resulted in Abel's talents coming to the attention of the theater world.

Other plays by Abel include *The Pretender* and *The Wives.* In addition to his work for the stage, Abel translated numerous books by others, including Jean Nicholas Arthur Rimbaud's *Some Poems of Rimbaud,* Camille Pissarro's *Letters to His Son Lucien,* and Sartre's *Three Plays.* In 1958 Abel received a Guggenheim fellowship and although he did not graduate from any college, Abel's skill as a writer garnered him a post in the English department at the State University of New York at Buffalo. He stayed there from 1967 until the early 1980s. In 1984 Abel's autobiography *The Intellectual Follies* was published. He also wrote *Important Nonsense,* essays about writers including Sartre and Dostoyevsky, which was published in 1987.

OBITUARIES AND OTHER SOURCES:

PERIODICALS

New York Times, April 25, 2001, p. A21.
Washington Post, April 27, 2001, p. B8.

*   *   *

ACREDOLO, Linda P. 1947-

PERSONAL: Surname pronounced "a-cre'-do-lo"; born September 24, 1947, in Buffalo, NY; daughter of George (an accountant) and Marjorie Dohn Potter; married Curtis Acredolo, June 17, 1972 (marriage ended); married Larry Stark, February 14, 1997; children: (first marriage) Kate, Kai. *Ethnicity:* "White." *Education:* Bucknell University, B.A., 1967; University of Minnesota, Ph.D., 1974. *Politics:* Democrat. *Religion:* Unitarian.

ADDRESSES: *Home*—22 Darby Ct., Woodland, CA 95776. *Office*—Department of Psychology, University of California, Davis, CA 95616. *Agent*—Miller Agency, 1650 Broadway, Suite 406, New York, NY 10019. *E-mail*—lpacredolo@ucdavis.edu.

CAREER: University of California, Davis, professor of psychology, 1976—.

MEMBER: Society for Research in Child Development (secretary, 1991-98).

AWARDS, HONORS: Distinguished Teacher Award, University of California at Davis.

WRITINGS:

Baby Signs, NTB/Contemporary, 1996.
Baby Minds, Bantam (New York, NY), 2000.

WORK IN PROGRESS: Research on infant development.

* * *

ANDERSSON, Claes 1937-

PERSONAL: Born May 30, 1937, in Helsinki, Finland; married; children: six. *Education:* University of Helsinki, M.D., 1962.

ADDRESSES: Office—Ministry of Culture, Youth, Universities, and Sciences, Meritullinkatu 10, P.O. Box 293, FIN-00171 Helsinki, Finland.

CAREER: Tammiharju Hospital, senior ward physician, 1962-67; Hasperia Hospital, senior ward physician, 1967-69; Veikkola Sanatorium, medical superintendent, 1969-73; Loviisa Mental Health Clinic, physician, 1975—. Member of Finnish Parliament, 1987—; Finnish minister of culture, youth, universities, and sciences, 1995—. Member of Espoo City Council, 1988—. Also performs as a jazz pianist.

WRITINGS:

IN SWEDISH, EXCEPT WHERE NOTED

Ventil (poems; in Finnish), H. Schildt (Helsinki, Finland), 1962.
Som om ingenting hänt (poems), H. Schildt (Helsinki, Finland), 1964.
Staden heter Helsingfors (poems), H. Schildt (Helsinki, Finland), 1965.
Samhället vi dör i, illustrated by Christian Andersson, Bonnier (Stockholm, Sweden), 1967.
Det är inte lätt att vara villaägare i dessa tider (poems), Bonnier (Stockholm, Sweden), 1969.
Bli, tillsammans, Söderström (Stockholm, Sweden), 1970.
Bakom bilderna, Bonnier (Stockholm, Sweden), 1972.
Rumskamrater (poems; in Finnish), Söderström (Helsinki, Finland), 1974.
Den fagraste vår, Söderström (Stockholm, Sweden), 1976.
Jag har mött dem: Dikter, 1962-74 (poems), Söderström (Stockholm, Sweden), 1976.
Genom sprickorna i vårt ansikte, Söderström (Stockholm, Sweden), 1977.

Trädens sånger (poems), Alba (Stockholm, Sweden), 1979.
Tillkortakommanden (poems; title means "Shortcomings"), Söderström (Stockholm, Sweden), 1981.
The Family, English translation by Philip Binham, Centre hongrois de l'I.I.T. (Budapest, Hungary), 1981.
En mänska borjär likna sin själ (novel; title means "A Person Begins to Resemble His Soul"), Alba (Stockholm, Sweden), 1983.
Under (poems), Söderström (Stockholm, Sweden), 1984.
(Editor with Bo Carpelan) *Modern finlandssvensk lyrik: En antologi,* Forum (Stockholm, Sweden), 1986.
Det som blev ord i mig, Alba (Stockholm, Sweden), 1987.
Mina bästa dagar: Dikter & prosadikter (poems), Alba (Stockholm, Sweden), 1987.
Som lyser mellan gallren (poems), Alba (Stockholm, Sweden), 1989.
Huden där den är som tunnast, Söderström (Stockholm, Sweden), 1991.
Dikter från havets botten (poems), Bonnier Alba (Stockholm, Sweden), 1993.
Kaksi kansaa (essays; in Finnish), [Espoo, Finland], 1993.
Poems in Our Absence, English translation by Lennart Bruce and Sonja Bruce, Bonne Chance Press (Cleveland, SC), 1994.
What Became Words, English translation by Rika Lesser, Sun and Moon Press (Los Angeles, CA), 1996.
En lycklig mänska, Bonnier Alba (Stockholm, Sweden), 1996.

Author of stage and radio plays. Translator of poetry from Finnish into Swedish. Work represented in anthologies, including (in translation) *Territorial Song,* edited by Herbert Lomas, 1982. Contributor to periodicals, including (in translation) *Books from Finland, Grand Street, Poetry East, Seneca Review,* and *Scandinavian Review.* Editor-in-chief, *FBT,* 1965-68.

BIOGRAPHICAL/CRITICAL SOURCES:

PERIODICALS

Books from Finland, Volume 13, number 3, 1979, Thomas Warburton, "Claes Andersson: The Poet as a Progressive."*

AOS, Foel
See ter BALKT, H(erman) H(endrik)

*   *   *

ARDOIN, John (Louis) 1935-2001

OBITUARY NOTICE—See index for CA sketch: Born January 8, 1935, in Alexandria, LA; died March 18, 2001, in San José, Costa Rica. Music critic, editor, and author. Ardoin was music editor and critic for the Dallas Morning News from 1966 to 1998 and the author of a number of books on those subjects; some of these works include The Stages of Menotti and The Furtwangler Record. In particular, the 1974 work Callas, which Ardoin wrote with Gerald Fitzgerald, was one of four about the life and work of soprano singer Maria Callas he wrote. He served for a time as music correspondent for the Times of London, England, though Ardoin began his career as an assistant editor for Musical America in 1959. Beginning in 1997, he had become a music consultant for PBS Online.

OBITUARIES AND OTHER SOURCES:

PERIODICALS

New York Times, March 20, 2001, p. A27.

*   *   *

AYLETT, Steve 1967-

PERSONAL: Born 1967, in Bromley, South London, England. Education: Left school at age seventeen.

ADDRESSES: Agent—MBA Literary Agents Ltd., 62 Grafton Way, London W1P 5LD, England.

CAREER: Writer, c. 1994—. Also worked in a book warehouse and in trade and law publishing. Also toured in the "Shroud" show, as a silent impersonator of the Shroud of Turin.

AWARDS, HONORS: Philip K. Dick Award finalist, 1998, for Slaughtermatic.

WRITINGS:

The Crime Studio (novel), Serif (London, England), 1994.

Bigot Hall: A Gothic Childhood (novel), Serif (London, England), 1995.
Slaughtermatic (novel), Four Walls Eight Windows (New York, NY), 1998.
Toxicology (short stories), Four Walls Eight Windows (New York, NY), 1999.
The Inflatable Volunteer, Orion (London, England), 1999.
Atom, Four Walls Eight Windows (New York, NY), 2000.
Only an Alligator, Orion (New York, NY), 2001.

Also contributor of stories to anthologies, including Disco Biscuits.

Aylett's work has been translated into Spanish, Czech, Italian, French, Japanese, German, Russian, and Greek.

SIDELIGHTS: Steve Aylett is an English writer who is known for his quirky, unsettling fiction, which includes both novels and short stories. His first book, The Crime Studio, is an episodic novel that relates disturbing events in Beerlight, a dangerous, futuristic metropolis replete with unlikely criminals. The Crime Studio won praise from David V. Barrett, writing in New Statesman & Society, for its "sharpness" and "cohesion."

Aylett's second novel, Bigot Hall: A Gothic Childhood, was acknowledged by Barrett as "gloriously appalling." Bigot Hall exposes the tension, violence, and sexuality of seemingly mundane domestic life, and the novel's host of oddball characters include an incestuous brother and sister, a mother who cooks mysterious meals, a father who regularly dispenses banal insights, and a twisted, bothersome uncle.

Aylett followed Bigot Hall with the novel Slaughtermatic, in which he returns to Beerlight, the setting of the earlier Crime Studio, to chronicle a wrongheaded burglary and the chaos that ensues. In Slaughtermatic, bank robber Dante Cubit and his pill-popping companion, the Entropy Kid, conduct a heist in which Cubit, who masterminded the ultimately bungled caper, must resort to time travel as a means of avoiding capture. This time-travel escapade in turn leads to the duplication of Cubit, and this event results in still further complications, including the eventual necessity of destroying Cubit's second self. Plans go further awry, however, when the duplicate Cubit dodges death and triggers a chase that involves a pair of racist police officers, a hired assassin, a conniving attorney, and Cubit's gun-wielding lover, Rosa Control. A critic at Complete Review claimed that Slaughtermatic "doesn't quite fit together as a novel," and a Kirkus Reviews critic described the novel as "a baffling exercise in virtual reality storytelling." The *Complete Review* critic conceded, however, that the novel is nonetheless "a hell of a ride, and worthwhile for all that," and even the *Kirkus Reviews* critic summarized the story as "droll, convoluted gamesmanship." John Mort, meanwhile, regarded *Slaughtermatic,* in his *Booklist* assessment, as "a mockery of a novel." But Michael Porter wrote in the *New York Times Book Review* that *Slaughtermatic* constitutes a "hyperkinetically violent, hilarious time-traveling crime caper." Porter added, "While the body count is high, the tone is anything but grim, thanks to Aylett's wickedly funny commentary." *Slaughtermatic* received attention as a finalist for the Philip K. Dick Award in 1998.

Among Aylett's other publications is *Toxicology,* a collection of short stories in a range of genres and experimental forms. The volume includes "If Armstrong Was Interesting," which lists various antics—donning Mickey Mouse ears, confessing to a crime—that astronaut Neil Armstrong might have initiated while becoming the first human being to step onto the surface of the moon, and "Gigantic," wherein mankind's heinous deeds—including the nuclear bombings of Japan—are punished by a storm in which corpses fall to earth like drops of rain. Daniel Reitz, writing in the *New York Times Book Review,* declared that Aylett showed himself guilty of "preening cleverness" with *Toxicology.* In addition, Reitz contended that "the banality of these stories defeats any points [Aylett] is trying to make."

Aylett told *CA:* "It's less insulting to the reader to say something in a few words, like 'Progress accelerates downhill,' rather than spend an entire book saying that. I've seen *Toxicology* described as a liquid concentrate, which you're not supposed to drink without dilution, which is nice. Though I thought there were a few lighter stories in there too. I still just write the kind of books I'd like to read, that I'd like to find out there, and luckily enough people share that taste to be into them.

"Placing your head inside the reaction out there will certainly rot your brain, it's a displacement of energy. Stay in your own body, you see? People may read one of my things and think it's all a particular way, for good or ill. But there's *Slaughtermatic,* which is fairly conventional old-time satire which nobody else does these days. Then there's *The Inflatable Volunteer,* which has no satire and is this big splurge of funny poetics. And later there's stuff that's unlike any of that because I've hardly started yet. So I have to disregard all this. My head stays here.

"I certainly don't think in words. I'm not sure that anyone does, really. Does anyone really think in sentences, like in films when you see someone thinking and you hear a voice-over? I don't anyway. I see stuff visually, as shapes, colours, textures and mechanisms sort of hanging there in space. If there's a hole in someone's argument I visually see a hole in it, in the armature and mass of the thing. Although it may take time to translate it all back into words and express them. And in writing I'll see the shape and colour of a sentence before I know what the words are in it. I'll see the shape of a whole book that way before it's written, and so far, the books have all ended up the way I saw them originally.

"I often feel people don't see past all the fireworks to what I'm talking about. Maybe sometime I'll do something with all the fireworks stripped out, no jokes, for the hard-of-reading—so they'll see what's always been there from the beginning.

"For postmodernist bullshit, the law is streets ahead. Anyone who's sat in on an adversarial court case, seen the mechanisms of the law, the subjectivity, the basic disengagement from fact, truth thrown to the wind, it really is like being in the mouth of madness. The person who's in the right might win the case, but not because he's in the right—just for other, quite surreally disassociated reasons. Reality gets the kiss-off at the start. The lawyer Harpoon Specter is great to write, he's a monster who operates in that totally unanchored, mutable alternate dimension. He says right at the start of *The Crime Studio,* 'The law is where reality goes to die'—he knows this."

BIOGRAPHICAL/CRITICAL SOURCES:

PERIODICALS

Booklist, February 15, 1998, John Mort, review of *Slaughtermatic,* p. 990.

Kirkus Reviews, February 15, 1998, review of *Slaughtermatic,* p. 208.

New Statesman & Society, August 18, 1995, David V. Barrett, "Myths and Mirrors," p. 334.

New York Times Book Review, June 21, 1998, Michael Porter, "Pulp Fiction"; December 26, 1999, Daniel Reitz, review of *Toxicology,* p. 15.

OTHER

Complete Review, http://www.complete-review.com/ (May 9, 2001), review of *Slaughtermatic.*

BAILEY, Cornelia Walker 1945-

PERSONAL: Born June 12, 1945, in GA; daughter of Hicks (a netmaker) and Hettie Bryant Walker; married Julius F. Bailey (a businessman), August 3, 1963; children: Stanley, Teri, Julius, Greg (deceased), Maurice, Tory, Janetta. *Ethnicity:* "Black, Indian, & White." *Politics:* Democrat. *Religion:* Baptist.

ADDRESSES: Home—#1 Main Rd., P.O. Box 34, Sapelo Island, GA 31327. *E-mail*—sapelowagontour@ webtv.net and cornelia@gacoast.com.

CAREER: The Pig Pen (gift shop), owner; Dup Lin Risingi (not-for-profit organization), founder; operator of a small bed & bath. Girl Scouts organizer.

WRITINGS:

(With Christina Blesdoe) *God, Dr. Buzzard, and the Bolito Man: A Saltwater Geechee Talks about Life on Sapelo Island,* Doubleday (New York, NY), 2000.

Contributor to *High Tides Travel Magazine.*

WORK IN PROGRESS: A cookbook and a children's storybook.

SIDELIGHTS: Cornelia Walker Bailey told *CA:* "[I wrote because] I felt I had a story to tell and all the old people told me to do it. Bless them. My ancestors and true friends [influence my work]. I write in the form of telling a story and it really makes sense; and it stays with me and the reader longer. My people [inspired me to write on the subjects I have chosen.] They gave me the needed stories of life and how it was dealt to you. I felt I was given the job of carrying and passing these stories of life along to others."

*   *   *

BALKT, H. H. ter
  See ter BALKT, H(erman) H(endrik)

*   *   *

BANKS, William M(aron III) 1943-

PERSONAL: Born September 22, 1943, in Thomasville, GA; son of W. S .M. (a retired professor) and Hattie L. (a former teacher) Banks; children: two twin daughters. *Education:* Dillard University, B.A., 1963; University of Kentucky, Ed.D., 1967. *Politics:* "Independent but left of center." *Religion:* "No religious affiliation." *Avocational interests:* "Musing and scribbling about jazz and American culture."

ADDRESSES: Home—837 Santa Ray Ave., Oakland, CA 94610. *Office*—University of California—Berkeley, African American Studies, 660 Barrows Hall, #2572, Berkeley, CA 94720-2572.

CAREER: Psychologist, consultant, and writer. Attebury Job Corps Center, counselor and psychologist, 1967; Howard University, counselor and psychologist, 1967-70, associate director for Community Studies, 1968-70, department chairperson, 1972-75; University of California—Berkeley, Berkeley, CA, professor of African American Studies, 1972—, chair of department, 1972-75, provost, 1988-89.

MEMBER: Society for the Psychological Study of Social Issues, Society for the Study of Social Problems, American Personnel & Guidance Association, Association of Black Psychologists.

AWARDS, HONORS: Summer Scholars Award, U.S. Civil Service Commission; University of California Regents Fellowship; American Book Award, 1996, for *Black Intellectuals: Race and Responsibility in American Life;* Outstanding African American Faculty Member on the Berkeley Campus award, 2001.

WRITINGS:

Black Intellectuals: Race and Responsibility in American Life, Norton (New York, NY), 1996.

Also author of articles on black nationalism, black Muslims, and black periodicals and newspapers for the *Dictionary of American History,* seventh edition, 2002.

WORK IN PROGRESS: "Essays on the cultivation and erosion of African American intellectuals," for 2002.

SIDELIGHTS: A former psychologist, William M. Banks is an American author and educator. He teaches African American studies at the University of California—Berkeley, where he has been since 1972. He lives in Oakland, California.

Banks's acclaimed first work, *Black Intellectuals: Race and Responsibility in American Life,* explores the role of black intellectuals in shaping black American culture and their place in the social, political, and economic fabric of American society over time. The scholarly historical work covers approximately 250 years of black history, beginning in the slave era and concluding with a discussion of modern black intellectuals, covering such notable African American thinkers as Frederick Douglass, Anna Cooper, W. E. B. DuBois, Alain Locke, and Toni Morrison. The work provides a "much-needed, overarching historical context," explained Angela D. Dillard in *World and I.*

Critics were largely positive in their assessment of *Black Intellectuals.* Jerry G. Watts in the *New York Times Book Review* found the work "an important book, significant because it highlights the diversity and richness of Afro-American intellectual life throughout our nation's history." Ann Douglas in the *Washington Post Book World* lauded Banks for including significant figures from the years prior to 1930, and for including black women as well, but felt that *Black Intellectuals* "surprises as often by its omissions as by its insights." A *Publishers Weekly* critic called the work "solid and discerning," and found it a "useful introduction to a rich field." Dillard concluded: "While Banks' attention to race often eclipses the dynamics of gender (his handling of the role of black women and feminism is surprisingly perfunctory at times), sexuality, and other forms of identity, the book's merits far outweigh its occasional shortcomings. *Black Intellectuals* is a book that should be read by everyone struggling for a clearer understanding of the impact of race on African-American and American intellectual history." Banks received the American Book Award in 1997 for *Black Intellectuals.*

Banks told *CA:* "I am a single parent with twin daughters born in 1990. The daughters likely account for my growing interest in literature for children. I recently consulted with Children's Book Press on the publication, *I See The Rhythm,* by Toyomi Igus with illustrations by Michelle Wood, Children's Book Press, San Francisco, 1998. The experience convinced me that I could author something credible for young people."

BIOGRAPHICAL/CRITICAL SOURCES:

PERIODICALS

New York Times Book Review, November 10, 1996, Jerry G. Watts, review of *Black Intellectuals: Race and Responsibility in American Life,* p. 21.
Publishers Weekly, September 2, 1996, review of *Black Intellectuals,* p. 103.
Washington Post Book World, November 17, 1996, Ann Douglas, review of *Black Intellectuals,* p. 9.

World and I, April, 1997, Angela D. Dillard, review of *Black Intellectuals,* p. 276.

*   *   *

BARASH, Susan Shapiro

PERSONAL: Born in New York, NY; daughter of Herbert L. (a real estate developer and bank chairperson) and Selma Meyerson Shapiro; married Richard Ripps (marriage ended); married Gary Barash, November 8, 1997; children: Jennie Rebecca Ripps, Michael James Ripps, Elizabeth Jerome Ripps. *Education:* Sarah Lawrence College, B.A.; New York University, M.A. *Avocational interests:* "Women's issues, art, theatre, film."

ADDRESSES: Home—1075 Park Ave, New York, NY 10128.

CAREER: Marymount Manhattan College, New York, NY, professor of critical thinking/gender studies and screenwriting; public relations coordinator.

MEMBER: Authors Guild, Writers Guild, PEN, American Society of Journalists and Authors, Women's National Book Association.

WRITINGS:

A Passion for More: Wives Reveal the Affairs that Make or Break Their Marriages, St. Martin's (New York, NY), 1993.
Sisters: Devoted or Divided, Kensington (New York, NY), 1994.
(With Michele Kasson) *The Men Out There: A Woman's Little Black Book,* Routledge, 1997.
Second Waves: The Pitfalls and Rewards of Marrying Widowers and Divorced Men, New Horizon Press, 2000.
(With Joanne Lara) *Inventing Savannah* (fiction), 1st Books Library, 2001.
Mothers in Law and Daughters in Law: Love Hate Rivalry and Reconciliation, New Horizon Press, 2001.

*   *   *

BARRON, Jonathan N.   1962-

PERSONAL: Born May 20, 1962, in Washington, DC; son of Jerome A. (a law professor) and Myra H. (an attorney) Barron; married Ellen M. Weinauer (an English professor), June 8, 1991; children: Liana, Raphael. *Education:* Tufts University, B.A., 1984; Indiana University, M.A., 1987, Ph.D., 1990. *Politics:* Democrat. *Religion:* Jewish.

ADDRESSES: Home—114 Lesley Lane, Hattiesburg, MS 39402. *Office*—Department of English, Box 5037, University of Southern Mississippi, Hattiesburg, MS 39406. *E-mail*—Jonathan.Barron@usm.edu.

CAREER: Marquette University, Milwaukee, WI, post-doctoral fellow, 1990-92; St. Olaf College, Northfield, MN, assistant professor of English, 1992-94; University of North Carolina, Charlotte, NC, assistant professor of English, 1994-95; University of Southern Mississippi, Hattiesburg, MS, associate professor of English, 1995—.

MEMBER: Robert Frost Society (director), Modern Language Association.

WRITINGS:

(Editor, with Eric Murphy Salinger) *Jewish American Poetry,* Brandeis/University Press of New England, 2000.
(Editor, with Earl J. Wilcox) *Roads Not Taken: Rereading Robert Frost,* University of Missouri Press, 2000.

Editor-in-chief, *Robert Frost Review.*

WORK IN PROGRESS: Research on Jewish American poetry, contemporary American poetry, and mass media.

*   *   *

BARUAH, Sanjib (Kumar)   1951-

PERSONAL: Born 1951. *Education:* Cotton College, Gauhati, India, B.A.; University of Delhi, M.A.; University of Chicago, Ph.D.

ADDRESSES: Office—Graduate School of Environmental Studies, Bard College, Annandale-on-Hudson, NY 12504.

CAREER: Bard College, Annandale-on-Hudson, NY, professor of political studies and faculty member, Graduate School of Environmental Studies, 1983—.

Also taught at University of Wisconsin—Madison and Syracuse University; University of Chicago, associate of Committee on Southern Asian Studies, 1985-87; Syracuse University, research associate at South Asia Center, 1989—.

AWARDS, HONORS: Fellow of Social Science Research Council.

WRITINGS:

The Right to Development and Its Implications for Development Strategy, Anti-Slavery Society (London, England), 1979.
India Against Itself: Assam and the Politics of Nationality, University of Pennsylvania Press (Philadelphia, PA), 1999.

Author of *Getting a Fair Share: Politics and the Poor in Rural India,* 1983. Contributor of articles and reviews to scholarly journals, including *Asian Survey, Socialism and Democracy, Modern Asian Studies, Cultural Survival Quarterly, Development and Change,* and *South Asia Bulletin,* and to newspapers.*

*   *   *

BAUMANN, Charly   1928-2001

OBITUARY NOTICE—See index for *CA* sketch: Born September 14, 1928, in Berlin, Germany; died January 2001, in Sarasota, FL. Animal trainer and author. Baumann was a trainer of tigers. Educated in training lions, Baumann first acquired and began training tigers in 1957. His tigers were used in such circus performances as the Ringling Brothers and Barnum and Bailey Circus, from 1964 to 1984. Beginning in 1984 he served as Ringling Brothers' performance director, where he remained until his retirement in 1991. In 1975, he related his experiences in the circus world in his autobiography, *Tiger, Tiger: My Twenty-Five Years With the Big Cats.* Ringling Museum honored Baumann by giving him their Circus Celebrity 2001 Award for his Bengal Royal Tiger Act, one of the longest-running acts in Ringling history.

OBITUARIES AND OTHER SOURCES:

PERIODICALS

New York Times, March 4, 2001, p. A23.
Sarasota Herald Tribune, January 29, 2001.
Times (London, England), March 12, 2001, p. 21.

BECHER, Ronald E. 1943-

PERSONAL: Born February 1, 1943, in Columbus, NE; son of Hugo A. (a carpenter) and June (Meyer) Becher. *Ethnicity:* "Anglo-Saxon." *Education:* Concordia Teachers College, B.S. Ed., 1965, M. Ed., 1973; University of Kansas, certification work in special education, 1986-88. *Politics:* "Independent." *Religion:* Lutheran. *Avocational interests:* "History."

ADDRESSES: Home—P.O. Box 247, Valparaiso, NE 68065.

MEMBER: American Guild of Organists, Oregon-California Trails Association.

WRITINGS:

Massacre Along the Medicine Road: A Social History of the Indian War of 1864 in Nebraska Territory, Caxton (Caldwell, ID), 1999.

Contributor to *Overland Journal.*

WORK IN PROGRESS: Book of twelve related short stories.

SIDELIGHTS: Ronald E. Becher told *CA:* "Growing up in Nebraska in the 1950s, the stories of the Indian wars in our local history were still very much alive and formed a part of my informal education. In addition, my great-great grandmother lost her first husband in the 1864 raids. I was under no illusion that *Massacre Along the Medicine Road* would ever be a best seller, but I had wanted to ferret out the true details and write the complete story for many years. Having done a great deal of academic writing, I was determined that this book be written for the history buff, the local people who, while not trained as historians, nevertheless possess a wide knowledge of state and local history.

"The initial research required about four years and continued even while the manuscript was being written. My usual method of writing was to begin work on a short episode, usually an average of twelve pages, in the morning. After lunch I went for a five or six mile walk while I thought over what had just been written. Late in the afternoon I began typing my miserable handwriting and making a few corrections here and there. The rough draft for that day was thus finished in the early evening, after which the sources from which the next episodes were to be written would be laid out on my desk, ready for the next day's work.

"A fiction work, still to be title and reworked, was written differently. For several weeks in 1994, while awaiting back surgery, I found that the only relief from the constant pain came when I sat in my swivel chair at my desk. So, unable to do anything else, I sat all day and wrote twelve short stories about a dreadful little town where I began my teaching career, something like Steinbeck's *Pastures of Heaven*. It's amazing how pain sharpens one's memory, and the details simply flowed out onto the paper as fast as I could write."

*   *   *

BECKFORD, Ruth 1925-

PERSONAL: Born December 7, 1925, in Oakland, CA. *Ethnicity:* "African American." *Education:* Attended University of California—Berkeley, 1944-47; studied acting at Oakland Ensemble Theatre. *Politics:* Democrat. *Avocational interests:* "Movie actor/playwright."

ADDRESSES: Office—c/o Author Mail, Pilgrim Press, 700 Prospect Ave. E, Cleveland, OH 44115-1100. *Agent*—Sheryl Fullerton, Berkeley, CA.

CAREER: Dancer and master dance teacher/choreographer. Anna Halprin/Welland Lathrop dance company, San Francisco, CA, member, 1945-55; Oakland Parks and Recreation Department, Oakland, CA, founder, recreational modern dance department, 1947-67; African-Haitian dance schools, Oakland, CA and San Francisco, CA, founder, 1953-75. Affiliated with National Endowment for the Arts, 1972-75; African American Museum/Oakland Library Coalition, president; Private Industry Council, life skills counselor; actress; speaker.

AWARDS, HONORS: Numerous awards associated with dance career and acting, including charter member, Isadora Duncan Dancers Hall of Fame, 1985; service award, San Francisco Foundation Community, 1998.

WRITINGS:

Katherine Dunham: A Biography (authorized biography), Marcel Dekker, 1979.
Still Groovin': Affirmations for Women in the Second Half of Life, Pilgrim Press (Cleveland, OH), 1999.

Also author, with Ron Stacker Thompson, of *'Tis the Morning of My Life* (romantic comedy performance), produced in Oakland, CA, and Off-Broadway, and two sequels of *'Tis the Morning of My Life,* 1984-89. Also author of *Girl You've Got Choices* (for adolescents), 1999; *A Little of This and Some of That* (cookbook); and *The Dance Lady* (autobiography).

WORK IN PROGRESS: Love Dance, nine short stories of romance.

SIDELIGHTS: Ruth Beckford told *CA:* "I have always mentored girls and women in my many years as a dance teacher. My answering unit always gives an affirmation instead of the standard 'leave a number, etc.' I was encouraged by several friends to put them into a book. I believe that if you are in control of your health, empowerment, inner peace and romance, you are having a groovy, good life, hence *Still Groovin': Affirmations for Women in the Second Half of Life.* My seventy-five years and very successful career gives me the wisdom to share with my readers. I am happy to say both the hardback and paperback are doing very well."

Beckford told *CA* that, at age three, she was the first black student at Flarelle Batsford's dance studio. She indicated that she was also the first black modern dance student at the University of California—Berkeley, and the first black member of the school's Orchesis Modern Dance Honor Society. In addition, Beckford told *CA* that she was the first black member of the Anna Halprin/Welland Lathrop dance company in San Francisco. She also noted that her work with the Oakland Parks and Recreation Department marks her as the founder of the first recreational modern dance department in the United States.

*   *   *

BECKWITH, Carol 1945-

PERSONAL: Born 1945, in Cambridge, MA. *Education:* Attended Goucher College, 1963-65; attended Boston Museum School, 1965-68 and 1969-70; attended Skowhegan School of Painting and Sculpture, 1966-67.

ADDRESSES: Office—c/o H. N. Abrams, Author Mail, 100 Fifth Ave., New York, NY 10011.

CAREER: Photographer and painter; writer. Massachusetts Institute of Technology, teacher of Chinese calligraphy brush painting, beginning 1972.

AWARDS, HONORS: Traveling Fellowship, Boston Museum, 1971, for travel in Japan, Thailand, Burma,

and New Guinea; Wolf Book Award in Race Relations, 1980, for photography in *Maasai.;* Award of Excellence (with Angela Fisher), United Nations Society of Writers and Artists, 1999.

WRITINGS:

(Photographer) *Maasai,* by Tepilit Ole Saitoti, H. N. Abrams (New York, NY), 1980.
(Photographer) *Nomads of Niger,* by Marion van Offelen, H. N. Abrams (New York, NY), 1983.
(Photographer, with Angela Fisher) *African Ark: People and Ancient Cultures of Ethiopa and the Horn of Africa,* by Graham Hancock, H. N. Abrams (New York, NY), 1990.
(With Angela Fisher) *African Ceremonies,* H. N. Abrams (New York, NY), 1999.
(With Angela Fisher) *Passages: Photographs in Africa,* H. N. Abrams (New York, NY), 2000.

SIDELIGHTS: American photographer Carol Beckwith gained notoriety in 1980 when she received the Wolf Book Award in Race Relations for her photography in Tepilit Ole Saitoti's book *Maasai.* Collaboration with the Maasai author produced a "beautiful volume," according to Maidel Cason, a reviewer in *Library Journal,* that "will enable readers to understand . . . the dilemma . . . facing the Maasai and others in their nation." Genevieve Stuttaford, a reviewer in *Publishers Weekly,* emphasized that Beckwith "spent two years recording the Maasai way of life." Cason described the illustrations as "handsome" and the text "distinguished."

Beckwith teamed with anthropologist author Marion Van Offelen in the book *Nomads of Niger.* This is a chronicle of the Wodaabe people who are cattle herders. Paul Zweig, a reviewer in the *New York Times Book Review,* claimed that Beckwith's camera "gives us [the readers] not static tableaux but intensely living scenes. The photographs seem to surround us [the readers] with irrepressible movement." Zweig recommended this "startling, beautiful and moving book." John A. Broussard, a reviewer in *Science Books and Films,* called the book "a loving and intimate portrait of life among one of the last nomadic peoples in the world." Elizabeth A. Widenmann, a reviewer in *Library Journal,* considered Beckwith's color photographs "stunning" and recommended the book for libraries "where there is an interest in the decorative arts of traditional societies."

According to Jon Carroll, a reviewer in *Los Angeles Times Book Review,* Bechwith's collaboration with Angela Fisher titled *African Ark: People and Ancient Cultures of Ethiopia and the Horn of Africa* is a "passionate and careful book, rich with love and melancholy." Patrick T. Reardon, a reviewer in the *Chicago Tribune,* asserted that some of the photography "has the feel of fashion" in which subjects are "presented" at "moments of great attractiveness and sensuousness." Michelle Green, a reviewer in *People Weekly,* applauded her effort. "Mesmerized by traditional African cultures," Green claimed, both Beckwith and Fisher "have grown accustomed to the rigors and delights of traveling to outposts where Europeans are seldom seen." Genevieve Stuttaford, a reviewer in *Publishers Weekly,* noted how the book includes approximately 200 "magnificent color photos." Timothy Foote, a reviewer in *Book World,* described the book as "an often dazzling blend of anthropology and art."

Beckwith again collaborates with Fisher for the book *African Ceremonies.* A reviewer in *Publishers Weekly* commended the two volumes for "represent[ing] an important anthropological achievement." A reviewer in *Economist* called the book a "true culmination of two lives' work." K. Anthony Appiah, a reviewer in *New York Times Book Review,* applauded Beckwith and Fisher's work, saying "these are sumptuous photographs . . . and they reflect both the photographers' gift for gaining the trust of their subjects and the reciprocal generosity of all sorts of African men and women." Appiah insists that "the Africa . . . presented here is not just a fantasy," but rather a chronicle of how "alive" so many of the African ceremonies are.

BIOGRAPHICAL/CRITICAL SOURCES:

PERIODICALS

The Atlantic, December, 1983, Phoebe-Lou Adams, review of *Nomads of Niger,* p. 117.
Booklist, December 15, 1999, Bonnie Smothers, review of *African Ceremonies,* p. 741.
Book World, December 2, 1990, Timothy Foote, "Close-Ups and Long Shots," pp. 10-12.
Chicago Tribune, December 2, 1990, Patrick T. Reardon, "Going the Easy Way," p. 5.
Economist, October 9, 1999, "Africa's Vanishing Ceremonies," p. 106.
Library Journal, October 15, 1980, Maidel Cason, review of *Maasai,* p. 2225; December 15, 1983, Elizabeth A. Widenmann, review of *Nomads of Niger,* pp. 2341-2342.
Los Angeles Times Book Review, November 25, 1990, Jon Carroll, "Fantasy Factor Meets the Bloat Quotient," p. 6.

New York Times Book Review, December 4, 1983, Paul Zweig, review of *Nomads of Niger,* pp. 15, 70; December 5, 1999, K. Anthony Appiah, "The Rite Stuff," p. 13.
People Weekly, November 12, 1990, Michelle Green, "Strangers in a Strange Land: Two Daring Photographers Brave Heat and Danger in the African Bush," pp. 159-160.
Publishers Weekly, August 22, 1980, Genevieve Stuttaford, review of *Maasai,* p. 40; August 31, 1990, Genevieve Stuttaford, review of *African Ark: People and Ancient Cultures of Ethiopa and the Horn of Africa,* p. 55; October 25, 1999, review of *African Ceremonies,* p. 57.
Science Books and Film, January-February, 1985, John A. Broussard, review of *Nomads of Niger,* p. 132.*

*   *   *

BEVINGTON, Helen Smith   1906-2001

OBITUARY NOTICE—See index for *CA* sketch: Born April 2, 1906, in Afton, NY; died March 16, 2001, in Chicago, IL. Educator and writer. Bevington was a poet, essayist, and professor of English at Duke University from 1943 to 1976, when she retired with professor emeritus status. Writing her poetry from life experience, Bevington penned such light verse poetry collections as *Dr. Johnson's Waterfall, and Other Poems* and *A Change of Sky, and Other Poems,* which earned her the Roanoke-Chowan award for poetry in 1956. Bevington also authored a small number of nonfiction works, such as a collection of essays entitled *Beautiful Lofty People* and her memoirs, *The Third and Only Way: Reflections on Staying Alive.* Bevington's autobiographical *Charley Smith's Girl* was banned in her native region of Worcester, New York, due to descriptions of her father's infidelity.

OBITUARIES AND OTHER SOURCES:

PERIODICALS

Chicago Tribune, March 25, 2001, section 4, p. 7.
Los Angeles Times, March 26, 2001, p. B4.
New York Times, March 22, 2001, p. A20.

*   *   *

BIBBY, T(homas) Geoffrey   1917-2001

OBITUARY NOTICE—See index for *CA* sketch: Born October 14, 1917, in Heversham, England; died February 6, 2001, in Denmark. Archaeologist and author. Bibby was an archaeologist who led the discovery of a 4,000-year-old city called Dilmun on the island of Bahrain off the Saudi Arabian coast. The author of four books, Bibby wrote his works based on the Danish Archaeological Expeditions he completed during his career. His first work, *Testimony of the Spade,* published in 1956, was followed by *Four Thousand Years Ago* in 1961. His later works include *Looking for Dilmun* and *Preliminary Survey in East Arabia.* Bibby served for a time as curator at the Moesgaard Museum in Aarhus, Denmark.

OBITUARIES AND OTHER SOURCES:

PERIODICALS

Chicago Tribune, February 16, 2001, section 2, p. 11.
New York Times, February 20, 2001, p. A24.
Times (London, England), February 13, 2001.
Washington Post, February 16, 2001, p. B7.

*　　*　　*

Franny Billingsley

BILLINGSLEY, Franny　1954-

PERSONAL: Born July 3, 1954; daughter of Patrick and Ruth Billingsley; married Richard Pettengill, June 18, 1988; children: Miranda, Nathaniel. *Education:* Tufts University, B.A. (summa cum laude), 1976; Boston University Law School, J.D. (cum laude), 1979.

ADDRESSES: Home—5630 South Kimbark Ave., Chicago, IL 60637. *E-mail*—rhpetten@midway. uchicago.edu.

CAREER: Author of children's books, 1983—. Practicing lawyer, 1979-83; worked as a children's bookseller in Chicago, IL, 1987-99. Creative writing teacher, Columbia College, Chicago, IL, and Graham School of General Studies, University of Chicago; speaker at schools, libraries, and teacher conferences.

MEMBER: Phi Beta Kappa.

AWARDS, HONORS: School Library Journal Best Book of the Year designation, and *Booklist*'s Top Ten First Novels for Youth citation, both 1997, Anne Spencer Lindbergh Prize honor book for best fantasy written in the English language, 1997-98, Georgia Children's Book Award nomination, 1999, and Utah Children's Book Award nomination, 2001, all for *Well Wished;*

Booklist Editors' Choice citation, *School Library Journal* Best Book citation, *Bulletin* Blue Ribbon Book citation, and *Publishers Weekly* Best Book of the Year, all 1999, American Library Association Notable Books for Children citation, Mythopoeic Fantasy Award for Children's Literature, and *Boston Globe-Horn Book* Award, all 2000, and Dorothy Canfield Fisher Children's Book Award nomination, and Maine Student Book Award nomination, both 2001, all for *The Folk Keeper.*

WRITINGS:

Well Wished, Atheneum (New York, NY), 1997.
The Folk Keeper, Atheneum (New York, NY), 1999.

ADAPTATIONS: The Folk Keeper has been recorded on audio cassette by Listening Library, 2000.

SIDELIGHTS: Although Franny Billingsley's body of work included only two titles by 2000, she has gained recognition as an important figure in the world of juvenile fantasy. With *Well Wished* and *The Folk Keeper* Billingsley has established a solid reputation as a writer of young adult fiction; her second novel, 1999's *The Folk Keeper,* won the *Boston Globe-Horn Book* Award and the Mythopoeic Fantasy Award for Children's Literature, and was nominated for the Dorothy Canfield Fisher Children's Award in 2000. Fantasy, Billingsley once commented, is an ideal genre through which to explore abstract concepts. "The reason I write fantasy is because of issues of identity," she stated. "Identity, for example, is abstract, but in fantasy you can take a problem that exists only as a mental reality and give it a concrete form. In my books I can take the abstraction and make it real. For example in *The Folk Keeper,* I give my heroine a skin that belongs to her—a real, physical skin that she can try on and decide whether it fits. The skin symbolizes her decision about her identity: if she accepts the skin, she will be making a choice about who she is and how she is to live her life. The skin becomes a tangible as well as an abstract symbol of the decision she has to make."

Billingsley's fascination with fantasy began when she was a child. Because she tended toward being shy, reading played an important role in her life. "I was a huge reader, and often read to the exclusion of doing anything else—my homework, for instance!," the author once admitted. "I used to look forward to bedtime, because then, as l lay there waiting for sleep, I would think up the next installment in the story I was working out in my head." Her reading interests tended toward richly romantic novels like *Jane Eyre* and *Rebecca,* as well as more standard juvenile fare: *Black and Blue Magic; Harriet the Spy; A Wrinkle in Time; Mara, Daughter of the Nile;* and works by A. A. Milne. She also discovered an early love of music, an interest that still plays a part in the lyrical tone of her novels. "My father sang me two songs every night—often long, melancholy Scottish ballads," Billingsley added, "and I have him to thank for giving me such a rich reservoir of vocabulary, a peek at wonderful narrative structures (often these are songs that tell stories), and my love of somewhat haunting, melancholy literature and music."

After graduating from college, Billingsley began a career as a lawyer rather than as a writer, a decision she later attributed to a profound lack of self-knowledge. "It was probably not a bad thing for me to do—it taught me a tremendous amount about organizing and analyzing and writing," she noted of her experience in the legal field. In 1983, after five years of practicing law, she burned out and sought refuge from the legal profession by going to stay with a sister in Barcelona, Spain. On her Web site, Billingsley stated that she "brought all her favorite children's books with [her], intending to do nothing but read and eat tapas, but . . . got hooked on writing instead." After returning to the United States, Billingsley divided her time between working at a prominent Chicago book store and writing her own books. "When I left the law," she once explained, "I was reading children's books as an antidote to those

legal tomes. But when I started to read them, I thought, 'This is where I belong. How could I have gotten so far away from what I truly loved?' " In 1988 she began the manuscript for her first book; in 1997 *Well Wished* finally saw publication.

Well Wished is the story of Nuria, an "energetic, quick-witted, and vibrant" eleven-year-old, according to Susan Dove Lempke in *Booklist,* who discovers that her grandfather's town, Bishop Mayne, has a genuine wishing well—one that will grant one wish per person per lifetime. However, the well also has a pernicious habit of making the wishes it grants go awry. At one point, for instance, someone's wish caused the town's children to disappear. When Nuria's grandfather uses his wish to ask for the return of the children, only one reappears: Catty Winter. "Wheelchair-bound Catty is not exactly the kind of friend Nuria was wishing for—she's selfish and duplicitous," stated a *Publishers Weekly* contributor. "In response to her new friend's manipulative appeals," continued *Horn Book* contributor Anne Deifendeifer, "Nuria wishes 'that Catty had a body just like mine'—whereupon the girls switch bodies." Nuria, used to an active, energetic body, has to learn to adjust to Catty's impairment—and she also has to find a way to get her deceitful friend to agree to switch bodies back. "Billingsley wraps an intriguing fantasy around a convincing and endearing character," Lempke concluded, "using the fantasy elements to explore the very earthly question, What makes me, me?"

Although several critics have singled out the character of Nuria for special praise in their reviews of *Well Wished,* Billingsley explained that the story did not grow out of the protagonist's character. "I tend to have the idea for the plot—the complication—first," the author noted. "*Well Wished* was inspired, for example, by an experience I had in the summer of 1985 when I went to a blood bank to donate blood. There I met a young woman who was receiving blood for an illness that made her very weak (so weak, for example, that she couldn't even unscrew the lid of a jar of peanut butter), and I thought, 'What would it be like for an active person (like me) to be stuck in a body like that?' That was the genesis of my story: I decided to create two characters, one active and one who can't even walk, and I'll have them switch bodies. And then came the hard part: I had to figure out what the magical device was that would permit them to switch bodies." The next step in the story came when Billingsley, who was working as a book buyer at the time, overheard kids talking about books they'd read. She suddenly realized how important books about friendships were to them, and decided then and there that she'd make Nuria want desperately to have a friend. When her protagonist does find that friend, the friend will try to make Nuria do something she knows is wrong but feels she must do to keep the friendship alive . . . like make a dangerous wish on a malevolent wishing well. "It's the plot mechanism that makes it work," Billingsley went on. "The idea of a wishing well and wishes going wrong came quite late. Once I had the idea for the vehicle, that made it easier."

"In the beginning my characters were sort of amorphous," Billingsley explained. "They were too beautiful and too politically correct, and I had to make them into real human beings. And the more I worked on them, the more I discovered their little faults. In *Well Wished* Nuria was originally a goody-two shoes, and I didn't like her. But after several years of writing I began to ask, 'What happens if she breaks a rule, like Little Red Riding Hood or Sleeping Beauty do in their stories?' It was only after Nuria became the kind of character who breaks the rules that she began to speak to me," Billingsley added. "I started to understand who she was. . . . It was after that, after I understood what the demands of the plot were, that she really began to speak to me." The same sort of developmental process would happen after Billingsley went to work on her second novel, *The Folk Keeper.*

The Folk Keeper is told in the form of a series of journal entries written by Corin Stonewall. Corin is an orphan who serves as a "Folk Keeper": a person whose primary responsibility it is to keep the malevolent underground Folk at bay and away from the human community. "The main targets of the Folk are crops, herds and food-related efforts such as baking or brewing," explained contributor Eleanor M. Farrell in *Mythprint,* "and their focus can be diverted or channeled through the Keeper's talents." But Corin is concealing secrets—she is actually Corinna Stonewall, and has been disguising herself as a boy because of the freedom it brings. She has never been formally trained as a Keeper, and she suspects she may herself not be fully human: her silvery hair grows two inches a night! "When Lord Merton calls Corinna to his deathbed and requests that she become the Folk Keeper of his vast estate and live there as a lady," Anne St. John explained in her *Horn Book* assessment of the novel, "she believes that the power she has craved and fought for all her life is now within her grasp."

When Corinna arrives at Marblehaugh Park, the late Lord Merton's estate on the northern isle of Cliffsend, she finds the Folk are quite different from those she had met before; they are more aggressive and less responsive to her powers. While dealing with them, Corinna

also discovers her true nature and history. She is a selkie, a creature from Celtic mythology that can cast off its skin and become human, although the loss of that skin dooms the creature to a life on land. At Marblehaugh Park, which now belongs to the widowed Lady Alicia Merton, Corinna "thrives and mellows in the north, close to the sea," noted Sally Estes in *Booklist,* "as she slowly learns about her heritage; for example, why the sea calls to her, why she has an internal clock . . . and who her parents were." "The plot thickens as Corinna struggles to keep her gender and special powers a secret," explained a *Publishers Weekly* contributor, a task that becomes more complex when she realizes she is attracted to Lady Alicia's son, Finian.

Calling *The Folk Keeper* a "carefully nuanced tale," *Bulletin of the Center for Children's Books* reviewer Janice M. Del Negro noted the value of the work as a coming-of-age story. Billingsley's spunky protagonist "changes from an adolescent girl with a single-minded determination to ensure her own survival at any cost to a young woman who, in spite of herself, responds to the only kindness she has ever known." Romance between Corin/Corinna and Finian develops on a mature footing, held firm by the young woman's developing sense of self.

Billingsley's original idea was to "capture the reader's interest by creating a mystery, a mysterious connection between Corinna and the sea, hoping that the reader would be curious enough about why that they'd keep reading," as she once explained. "But those early drafts were static; there was little narrative tension. So I added the Folk to give Corinna a job, which she hadn't had before. It gave her something to do, something dangerous that would make the reader worry about her and keep turning the pages to find if she's going to survive."

With two novels under her belt, Billingsley has only recently discovered the best way to organize her life as a writer. "I found a way that ideas present themselves to me. It's like being in the middle of a dark sea and not knowing where to swim. I get a plot idea and I jump in feet first, and I say, 'Where do I begin?' It's only after splashing around in the sea for a long time that the sun rises. I'm still in the middle of the ocean, but now I know in what direction to swim.

"I write books that I would like to read," Billingsley continued. "I want to write the things that I love—for me, who I am now, because I honestly love to read children's books. I want my readers to be so caught up in the heroine's adventures that they *must* continue to turn the pages. These are the kinds of books I would have loved to have read when I was thirteen."

BIOGRAPHICAL/CRITICAL SOURCES:

PERIODICALS

Booklist, June 1, 1997, Susan Dove Lempke, review of *Well Wished,* p. 1694; November 15, 1998, review of *Well Wished,* p. 585; September 1, 1999, Sally Estes, review of *The Folk Keeper,* p. 126; April 15, 2000, Sally Estes, review of *The Folk Keeper,* p. 1546.

Bulletin of the Center for Children's Books, October 1, 1999, Janice M. Del Negro, review of *The Folk Keeper.*

Horn Book, May-June, 1997, Anne Deifendeifer, review of *Well Wished,* p. 314; November, 1999, Anne St. John, review of *The Folk Keeper,* p. 734; January, 2001, Kristi Beavin, review of *The Folk Keeper* (audio edition), p. 120.

Mythprint, June, 2000, Eleanor M. Farrell, review of *The Folk Keeper.*

New York Times, January 16, 2000, Betsy Hearne, review of *The Folk Keeper.*

Publishers Weekly, April 7, 1997, review of *Well Wished,* p. 92; October 18, 1999, review of *The Folk Keeper,* p. 83; September 11, 2000, review of *The Folk Keeper* (audio edition), p. 37.

OTHER

Authors Online Tab Reading Circle, http://www.teacher.scholastic.com/ (December 19, 2000).

Cynthia Leitich Smith's Children's Literature Resources, http://www/cynthialeitichsmith.com/ (February 21, 2001), interview with Franny Billingsley.

Franny Billingsley Web site, http://www.franny billingsley.com/ (May 15, 2001).

*   *   *

BINGEL, Horst 1933-

PERSONAL: Born 1933, in Korbach, Hesse, Germany.

ADDRESSES: Office—c/o Philipps-Universitat Marburg, Biegenstrasse 10, D-35032 Marburg, Germany; telephone: 49(0)6421/296-144; fax: 49(0)5421/296-252. *E-mail*—bingel@mailer.uni-marburg.de.

CAREER: Poet and writer, c. 1956—.

WRITINGS:

Kleiner Napoleon: Gedichte, Eremiten-Presse (Stierstadt im Taunus, Germany), 1956.

Junge Schweizer Lyrik, Eremiten-Presse (Stierstadt im Taunus, Germany), 1958.

Deutsche Lyrik: Gedichte seit 1945, Deutscher Taschenbuch Verlag (Munich, Germany), 1961.

Die Koffer des Felix Lumpach, Insel-Verlag (Frankfurt am Main, Germany), 1962.

Zeitgedichte: Deutsche politische Lyrik seit 1945, Piper (Munich, Germany), 1963.

Deutsche Prosa: Erzählungen seit 1945, Deutsche Taschenbuch Verlags (Munich, Germany), 1963.

Wir suchen Hitler: Gedichte, Scherz (Munich, Germany), 1965.

Deutsche Lyrik: Gedichte seit 1945, Deutscher Taschenbuch Verlag (Munich, Germany), 1966.

Herr Sylvester wohnt unter dem Dach: Erzählungen, Deutscher Taschenbuch-Verlag (Munich, Germany), 1967.

Literarische Messe 1968: Handpressen, Flügblätter, Zeitschriften der Avantgarde, Frankfurt am Main, Römerhallen, 10. Mai-5. Juni, Frankfurter Forum Für Literatur, Klingspor Museum (Offenbach/Main, Germany), 1968.

Tandem: ein buch, Pawel-Pan-Presse (Dreichenhain, Germany), 1974.

Phantasie und Verantwortung: Dokumentation des dritten Schrisftstellerkongresses des Verbandes deutscher Schriftsteller (VS) in der I G Druck und Papier, Fischer Taschenbuch (Frankfurt am Main, Germany), 1975.

Lied für Zement: Gedichte, Suhrkamp (Frankfurt am Main, Germany), 1975.

SIDELIGHTS: Horst Bingel lived in the midst of the avant-garde literary movement in Frankfurt in the late 1950s and 1960s. At that time, all of Europe was experiencing a powerful surge of creative energy in art, literature, music, and theatre, and Frankfurt was particularly important. In 1958, Bingel edited *Streit-Zeit-Schrift,* in which he included three experimental poems by Ernst Jandl; these poems later ended up in Landl's *Laut und Luise.* From 1966, he used the Frankfurter Forum für Literatur (Frankfurt Literature Forum) to introduce authors from Bulgaria, Yugoslavia, Poland, Romania, Czechoslovakia, and Hungary.

In 1967, Frankfurt was the site of creation for authors including Witold Wirpsza, Ernst Jandl, Zbigniew Herbert, Michel Butor, and many others. In May of 1968, Bingel presented in the Frankfurter Römerhallen an exciting scenario of artistic, literary, and political turbulence of the present, focusing on the gray market and the underground. Rebellion and revolution were the buzzwords of the day (published as *Main, Römerhallen, 10. Mai-5. Juni*). Bingel himself produced some controversial avant-garde works, such as the poem "Wir suchen Hitler." His most frequently published works are his two anthologies of German literature, *Deutsche Lyrik. Gedichte seit 1945,* and *Deutsche Prosa. Erzählungen seit 1945.*

BIOGRAPHICAL/CRITICAL SOURCES:

OTHER

Bibliographie zum Thema "Phantasie an die Macht"-Literatur und Popkultur um 1968, http://www.ruhr-uni-bochum.de/ (April 11, 2001).
Horst Bingel, http://www.geocities.com/üaristipp/litlinks/bingel.htm (April 11, 2001).
Fortunecity, http://www.fortunecity.de/ (July 14, 2000), "Kunst ist die höchste Form der Politik, Politick ist dies höchste form der Kunst."
Philipps-Universität Marburg, http://www.uni-marbug.de/, (April 3, 2001).
Universität Stuttgart, http://www.uni-stuttgart.de/ (April 3, 2001), Ernst Jandl, "Wie kommt man zu einem Verlag?"
Universität Stuttgart, http://www.uni-stuttgart.de/ (September 25, 2001), Reinhard Döhl, "Wie konkret sind ernst Jandls Texte oder Ernest Jandl und Stuttgart (Ein Exkurs)."
Wohnen-main, http://www.uni-marburg.de/stw/wohnen/main.html (April 11, 2001).*

*   *   *

BIX, Herbert P(hilip)   1938-

PERSONAL: Born September 21, 1938, in Boston, MA; son of James and Francis (Shapiro) Bix; married Toshie Watanabe, 1961; children: Mark, Deborah, Meriam. *Education:* University of Massachusetts, Amherst, B.A., 1960; Harvard University, M.A., 1968, Ph.D., 1972.

ADDRESSES: Office—Faculty of Social Science, Hitotsubashi University, Kaka 2-1, Kunitachi, Tokyo 186-8601, Japan. *E-mail*—CS0359@srv.cc.hit-u.ac.jp.

CAREER: Research associate, University of Massachusetts, Boston, MA, 1970-77, Hosei University, Tokyo, Japan, 1977-78, State University of New York, Bing-

hamton, NY, 1988-89, and E. O. Reischauer Institute for Japanese Studies, Harvard University, Cambridge, MA, 1992—. Hitotsubashi University, Graduate School of Social Sciences, Tokyo, Japan, professor of international relations and Japanese studies. *Military service:* United States Naval Reserve, served in Japan, 1962-64.

MEMBER: Association of Asian Studies, History of Science Society (Japan).

AWARDS, HONORS: National Defense University fellow, 1965-69; Fulbright-Hayes postdoctoral fellow, 1977-78; research grant, U.S.-Japan Education Commission, 1992-93; National Book Critics Circle award for biography, 2000, and Pulitzer Prize for general nonfiction, 2001, both for *Hirohito and the Making of Modern Japan.*

WRITINGS:

Peasant Protest in Japan, 1590-1884, Yale University Press (New Haven, CT), 1986.
(Translator, with Derek Brown) Nakamura Masanori, *The Japanese Monarchy, 1931-1991: Ambassador Joseph Grew and the Making of the Symbol Emperor System,* Sharpe (New York, NY), 1997.
Hirohito and the Making of Modern Japan, HarperCollins (New York, NY), 2000.

Contributor to periodicals, including *Journal of Japanese Studies* and *Diplomatic History.*

SIDELIGHTS: Herbert P. Bix is an American nonfiction author and educator. His works typically focus on aspects of Japanese history. He is a research fellow at the E. O. Reischauer Institute for Japanese Studies at Harvard University and professor of international relations and Japanese studies at the Hitotsubashi University Graduate School in Social Sciences in Tokyo, Japan.

Hirohito and the Making of Modern Japan received the National Book Critics Circle award for autobiography and the Pulitzer Prize for general nonfiction. The work explores the role that Emperor Hirohito played during and after World War II, and is based on extensive research, including many documents released after Hirohito's death in 1989. "Bix presents one of the first complete biographies of the emperor in English," explained Ronald Spector in the *New York Times Book Review.* "Bix's Hirohito," the critic continued, "is neither a Hitler nor a pacifist but a deeply flawed statesman. Above all, he was no passive symbolic monarch but a behind-the-scenes wheeler-dealer whose words could make or break cabinets." Steven Butler in *U.S. News & World Report* summarized the truth behind Bix's Hirohito: "Hirohito was a full and active participant in the planning and prosecution of the war. He personally delayed the inevitable surrender for months essentially to protect his own skin and his divine imperial rule, while hundreds of thousands of Japanese citizens and soldiers died. Afterward, he lied about his role and sacrificed his chief lieutenants to the hangman."

The work received mixed reviews from critics, but most agreed that the work would stimulate a great deal of discussion. Some critics, like Steven I. Levine in *Library Journal*, felt the work was revisionist history. Levine argued that Bix's evidence does not support his own thesis and that he "ruins his case as prosecutor by pressing it beyond the limits of the evidence." Butler did not consider the work revisionist, but rather argued that it was a "pathbreaking study." Still other critics found the work a balanced account of the leader. A critic for *Time International* wrote that Bix "offers up a balanced account that neither paints Hirohito as a villain nor a saint, but as a flawed individual who nonetheless played a larger role in the war than has been officially recognized." Lucian W. Pye in *Foreign Affairs* felt that the work turned the established account of Hirohito "upside down," and called it a "rare achievement." A critic for *Business Week* called the book "a startling work—awesomely ambitious, faultlessly researched, daring in its thesis, and profound in its implications."

BIOGRAPHICAL/CRITICAL SOURCES:

PERIODICALS

American Historical Review, April, 1988, Stephen Vlastos, review of *Peasant Protest in Japan,* p. 480.

Business Week, October 16, 2000, review of *Hirohito and the Making of Modern Japan,* p. 28.

Economist (U.S.), September 2, 2000, review of *Hirohito and the Making of Modern Japan,* p. 77.

English Historical Review, July, 1988, James McMullen, review of *Peasant Protest in Japan,* p. 686.

Foreign Affairs, September-October, 2000, Lucian W. Pye, review of *Hirohito and the Making of Modern Japan,* p. 128.

Journal of Asian Studies, November, 1988, Roger Bowen, review of *Peasant Protest in Japan,* p. 821.

Journal of Japanese Studies, winter, 1989, James W. White, review of *Peasant Protest in Japan,* p. 159.

Library Journal, November 1, 2000, Steven I. Levine, review of *Hirohito and the Making of Modern Japan,* p. 88.

Newsweek International, September 4, 2000, George Wehrfritz, review of *Hirohito and the Making of Modern Japan,* p. 64.

New York Times Book Review, November 19, 2000, Ronald Spector, review of *Hirohito and the Making of Modern Japan,* p. 14.

Publishers Weekly, July 31, 2000, review of *Hirohito and the Making of Modern Japan,* p. 81.

Time International, September 4, 2000, review of *Hirohito and the Making of Modern Japan,* p. 20.

U.S. News & World Report, August 28, 2000, Steven Butler, review of *Hirohito and the Making of Modern Japan,* p. 51.*

*   *   *

BLAKE, Ann   1941-

PERSONAL: Born 1941, in Birmingham, England; daughter of Eric William (a cabinet maker) and Sybil Pauline (a research biochemist; maiden name, Luckett) James; married William Richard Blake (a medical practitioner and researcher), 1966 (deceased, 1981); married Derick Marsh (a professor of English), 1984; children: (first marriage) Thomas, William, Julian. *Education:* Lady Margaret Hall, Oxford, B.A., 1963 (with honors), B.Litt., 1966.

ADDRESSES: Office—School of English, La Trobe University, Bundoora 3083, Australia. *E-mail*—a.blake@latrobe.edu.au.

CAREER: Writer. University of London, Extra-Mural Department, tutor, 1967-69; University of Melbourne, senior tutor, 1969; La Trobe University, Bundoora, lecturer, then senior lecturer, 1970-99, associate dean—faculty of humanities, 1996-98.

WRITINGS:

Christina Stead's Politics of Place, University of Western Australia Press (Nedlands), 1999.

(With Leela Gandhi and Sue Thomas) *England through Colonial Eyes in Twentieth-Century Fiction,* Palgrave (New York City), 2001.

Contributor to *Menu for Murder: Food, Feminism and Felony* (stories), Sisters in Crime (Melbourne), 1994, and to *Cambridge Guide to Writing by Women,* edited by Lorna Sage, Cambridge University Press, 1999. Also contributor of essays to several works on William Shakespeare, including *Shakespeare: Readers, Audi-*

ences, Players, edited by R. S. White, Charles Edelman, and Christopher Worthen, University of Western Australia Press, 1998. Has contributed articles to numerous periodicals, including *Meridian, Review of English Studies, Yearbook of English Studies, Theatre Notebook,* and *Australian Literary Studies.*

WORK IN PROGRESS: Current research: an essay on literary indebtedness, "Why do people say Jane Austen is 'Shakespearean'?"; and a book on Shakespeare and children.

SIDELIGHTS: Writer Ann Blake examines the life of the expatriate author in *Christina Stead's Politics of Place.* Kerryn Goldsworthy noted in *Australian Book Review* that Hazel Rowley's biography of Stead is "generally accepted . . . as definitive," but that a criticism of Rowley's book, particularly by Michael Wilding, was that she had not covered the political aspects of Stead's work. Goldsworthy called the title of Blake's work "misleading," saying that Blake concentrates primarily on Stead's portrayal of England and its people in Stead's fiction. However, Goldsworthy noted that Blake's book is appropriate for the general reader and that Blake is generous in crediting others, particularly Rowley, Wilding, and Diana Brydon, whose works she acknowledges as being the basis of her own. And Goldsworthy praised the "useful" chronology, bibliography, and index, and said the book, "while it does only a limited amount of justice to its own promising thesis, should be of considerable interest." A reviewer for *Australian* said Blake shows readers that Stead's post-war residence in England was largely due to her husband's political beliefs, which required the move from the United States. However, the reviewer noted of Stead: "England and the English are familiars with whom her ties, like those of fellow expatriate writer Jack Lindsay, are circumstantial rather than preferential." The reviewer called *Christina Stead's Politics of Place* an "excellent study."

Blake told *CA:* "My interests as a writer precisely reflect where I've lived. My interest in Shakespeare and the plays on the stage began with going to the theatre at Stratford-upon-Avon at the age of eight. My first husband's being an Australian explains to a great extent why I've spent half my time in Melbourne, and why I've thought and written about emigration, post-Imperial relations, and belonging. This led to Christina Stead, one of the greatest Australian novelists, herself an expatriate and a penetrating critic of the English and of British colonialism."

BIOGRAPHICAL/CRITICAL SOURCES:

PERIODICALS

Australian, February 2, 2000, review of *Christina Stead's Politics of Place,* p. 41.
Australian Book Review, November, 1999, Kerryn Goldsworthy, "Stead's Place," p. 20.

*   *   *

BLAKE, Michelle
   See SIMONS, Michelle Blake

*   *   *

BLASBAND, Philippe   1964-

PERSONAL: Born 1964, in Teheran, Iran.

ADDRESSES: Home—12, rue Henri Wafelaers, 1060 Bruxelles, Belgium.

CAREER: Novelist and screenwriter.

WRITINGS:

De cendres et des fumées, Gallimard (Paris, France), 1990.
Les mangeuses de chocolat, Editions Lansman (Carnières-Morlanwelz, Belgium), 1996.
Zalmans Album, S. Fischer, 1999.
Quand j'étais sumo (short stories), Castor Astral (Bordeaux, France), 2000.

NOVELS

L'effet cathédrale, Gallimard (Paris, France), 1994.
Max et Minnie, Gallimard (Paris, France), 1996.
Le livre des Rabinovich, Castor Astral (Bordeaux, France), 1998.

SCREENPLAYS

W. C., 1993.
Max and Bobo, 1998.
Cha cha cha, 1999.
Une liaison pornographique, Les Productions Lazennec, 1999.
Thomas in Love, 2001.

Contributor to books, including *Feueurs* (short stories), Eperonniers (Brussels), 1992.

SIDELIGHTS: Belgian novelist Philippe Blasband often collaborates as a screenwriter with a countryman, film director Frederic Fonteyne. The two have produced several short films and two feature films based on Blasband's stories. The full-length *Max and Bobo,* filmed in 1998, was followed in 1999 with the French-language feature released in Europe as *Une liaison pornographic.* Though the title translates to "A Pornographic Affair," the movie did not hold to that provocative title outside the Continent: In England the film was released as *An Intimate Affair,* and in the U.S. it was marketed as *An Affair of Love.*

The minimalist plot revolves around Parisians Elle (played by France's Nathalie Baye) and Lui (Spanish actor Sergi Lopez). Each is interviewed about the affair the two conducted—an affair based solely on fulfilling sexual fantasies. Notably, Baye gives the image of a mature woman engaging in purely physical pleasure from a younger man, a notion that Ginette Vincendeau, in a *Sight and Sound* article, felt "makes the idea that sexual equality for women is incompatible with an emotional relationship."

For a movie conceived as a pornographic affair, declared *New York Times* critic A. O. Scott, the finished product to him "is more like 'When Harry Met Sally' remade as a panel discussion." For all its "earnest intellectualism," Scott added, "this film tells you everything you already knew about sex but wouldn't have bothered to ask in the first place." *New Republic* reviewer Stanley Kauffmann had a more positive reaction to the film, saying it shows "finesse, perception, [and] reticent control." David Rooney, in *Variety,* called it "a classy date movie for discerning adults." Rooney felt that the screenplay "develops its themes intelligently, particularly the latter part," and "musters a quiet poignancy."

In 2001, Blasband wrote the screenplay for *Thomas in Love,* "a low-budget, scruffy Belgian equivalent of 'Rear Window,' where the hero, who is never seen, spends all of his days—and, seemingly, most of his nights—connecting with people via a 24-hour video telephone," wrote Kirk Honeycutt in the *Hollywood Reporter.* Honeycutt found *Thomas in Love,* which is set in the future, to be "clever science fiction," with a "witty script."

BIOGRAPHICAL/CRITICAL SOURCES:

PERIODICALS

Hollywood Reporter, August 9, 2001, Kirk Honeycutt, review of "Thomas in Love," p. 18.

New Republic, August 28, 2000, Stanley Kauffmann, "On Films—Questions Large and Small," p. 28.
New York Times, March 24, 2000, A. O. Scott, "Sex Out of Sight but Not Mind," p. E26.
Sight and Sound, July 2000, Ginette Vincendeau, review of "Une liaison pornographique," p. 48.
Variety, September 20, 1999, David Rooney, "A Pornographic Affair," p. 89.*

* * *

BONDESON, Jan 1962-

PERSONAL: Born December 17, 1962, in Malmoe, Sweden; son of Sven and Greta Bondesson. *Education:* Lund University, M.D., 1988; Ph.D., 1996. *Avocational interests:* Sports cars, wine, book collecting.

ADDRESSES: Home—202 Stow Hill, Newport, Gwent NP20 8NE, Wales. *Office*—Department of Rheumatology, University of Wales, College of Medicine, Health Park, Cardiff CF14 4XN, Wales. *E-mail*—bondesonj@cf.ac.uk.

CAREER: Physician and writer. Malmoe University Hospital, Malmoe, Sweden, resident, 1988-90, registrar, 1990-1995, senior registrar, 1995-96; Kennedy Institute of Rheumatology, London, England, research fellow, 1996-2000; University of Wales, College of Medicine, Cardiff, Wales, senior lecturer and consultant rheumatologist, 2000—. *Military service:* Lieutenant, Swedish Army Reserve.

MEMBER: Royal Society of Medicine (fellow), TVR Car Club, Morgan Sports Car Club.

AWARDS, HONORS: Hennerlof Scholarship, Swedish Society of Medicine, 1987; Rheumatology Scholarship, Astra-Boots, 1993.

WRITINGS:

(With Arie Molenkamp) *The Prolific Countess,* (The Hague, Netherlands), 1996.
A Cabinet of Medical Curiosities, Cornell University Press (Ithaca, NY), 1997.
The Feejee Mermaid and Other Essays in Natural and Unnatural History, Cornell University Press (Ithaca, NY), 1999.
The Two-Headed Boy and Other Medical Marvels, Cornell University Press (Ithaca, NY), 2000.
The London Monster: A Sanguinary Tale, University of Pennsylvania Press (Philadelphia, PA), 2000.

Buried Alive: The Terrifying History of Our Most Primal Fear, Norton (New York, NY), 2001.

Bondeson's books have been translated into Swedish, Spanish, Portuguese, German, Japanese, Chinese, Dutch, and Korean.

WORK IN PROGRESS: A book on historical cases of imposture and mistaken identity, to be published by Norton in 2003.

SIDELIGHTS: Jan Bondeson is a physician and writer who presently lives in Wales. His book *A Cabinet of Medical Curiosities* surveys a wide range of medical "monstrosities," or genetic and medical anomalies, inspired by his reading of an old medical book, Gould and Pyle's *Anomalies and Curiosities of Medicine,* published in 1897. Selma Harrison Calmes noted that people have a general fascination with such anomalies, and wrote in the *Lancet* that the book is "Well-researched and extensively illustrated with items from his personal collection, it covers a wide range of medical monstrosities, and there is something for everyone." She also praised Bondeson's historical research, as he draws on material from Europe, the United States, and China. In the book, Bondeson discusses a wide range of medical oddities, including people with tails, spontaneous human combustion, people with hairy faces like those of apes, and conjoined twins. Each chapter ends with a description of the modern medical explanation for the phenomenon, whether it is genetic or caused by disease. In *Journal of the American Medical Association,* Alfred Jay Bollet wrote that the book is "well-written" and "thoroughly researched" and noted that its strength is in its "detailed stories of human gullibility. . . . As such, it is sometimes disturbing but always informative." And a *Publishers Weekly* reviewer remarked that the book is "entertaining in the simultaneously creepy and amusing way of a carnival sideshow."

The Feejee Mermaid and Other Essays in Natural and Unnatural History examines beliefs people had in the past about fantastic creatures, such as, mermaids, toads that are found encased in solid rock, animals with killing vision, lambs that grew on stalks in the garden, and other bizarre forms of life, as well as real creatures, such as Marocco the Dancing Horse, Chunee, an elephant who was executed in London in 1826, and locusts who were put on trial for devouring crops. The ten essays in the book describe biological hoaxes, misinformed beliefs, and other natural and unnatural oddities. The book draws from literature and poetry of the eighteenth century and is illustrated with figures from the same time period. According to a *Publishers Weekly*

reviewer, Bondeson "successfully couples a wealth of historical material with the latest biological information."

Bondeson continues to examine unusual slices of history in his most recent books: *The London Monster: A Sanguinary Tale* and *Buried Alive: The Terrifying History of Our Most Primal Fear.* In *The London Monster,* Bondeson presents the case of a serial slasher who terrified London 100 years before Jack the Ripper as well as the questions that still surround the man who was tried and convicted. "Sound, informative and interesting," wrote the *Washington Post*'s Jonathan Yardley of Bondeson's account. "Working with incomplete and often misleading evidence," Yardley continued, "he has reconstructed the tale with what gives every evidence of being authority, and it is difficult to imagine that a more thorough account of it can or will be written." Calling *The London Monster* a "fascinating account," a reviewer for *Publishers Weekly* further noted that Bondeson "portrays in tart specifics a city plagued by class stratification, street crime and vice, and that was served by barely rudimentary policing."

Buried Alive is a characteristically thorough, and surprisingly witty, foray into the history of the fear and the facts of premature burial. In a *Booklist* review, William Beatty found the book "a trove of information, enlivened by excellent illustrations." A "weird and wonderful little tome," observed Gary Kamiya, in his *Salon* review, noting that Bondeson "ranges with authority from [his subject's] folkloric roots to its wacky historical applications to its literary text to its medical realities, and he backs everything up with voluminous citations." Kathy Arsenault summed up in *Library Journal,* "Although claustrophobics should beware, readers in most libraries will find this book both unusual and fascinating."

Bondeson told *CA:* "In addition to my six books, I have written more than sixty articles published in scholarly periodicals. I think *Buried Alive* and *The London Monster* are my best books, and the reading public seems to agree. My next book will be about historical cases of imposture and mistaken identity, like the false Dauphins of France, Kaspar Hauser, and the Tichborne Claimant. Other book ideas include a biography of the eighteenth-century surgeon John Hunter and a book about the unsolved murder of Olof Palme, the late prime Minister of Sweden."

BIOGRAPHICAL/CRITICAL SOURCES:

PERIODICALS

Bloomsbury Review, September, 1997, p. 24; May-June, 2001, Lily Leath, review of *The Two-Headed Boy, and Other Medical Marvels.*

Booklist, June 1, 2000, William Beatty, review of *The Two-Headed Boy, and Other Medical Marvels,* p. 1825; February 1, 2001, William Beatty, review of *Buried Alive: The Terrifying History of Our Most Primal Fear,* p. 1029.

Contemporary Review, July, 2001, review of *Buried Alive,* p. 64.

Forbes, March 5, 2001, Susan Adams, "A Fate Worse Than Death," review of *Buried Alive,* p. 193.

Globe and Mail, May 15, 1999, p. D14.

Journal of the American Medical Association, April 1, 1998, p. 1041; June 6, 2001, William A. Sodeman, review of *Buried Alive,* p. 2789.

Journal of the History of Medicine, April 2001, John Parascandola, review of *The Two-Headed Boy, and Other Medical Marvels.*

Kirkus Reviews, June 15, 2000, review of *The Two-Headed Boy, and Other Medical Marvels;* November 1, 2000, review of *The London Monster: A Sanguinary Tale;* January 1, 2001, review of *Buried Alive.*

Lancet, April 18, 1998, p. 1216.

Library Journal, February 1, 2001, Kathy Arsenault, review of *Buried Alive,* p. 118.

Los Angeles Times Book Review, October 25, 1998, p. 3.

New England Journal of Medicine, January 4, 2001, Michael Berkwits, review of *The Two-Headed Boy, and Other Medical Marvels,* p. 71.

New Scientist, November 15, 1997, p. 52; May 15, 1999, p. 45.

New York Times Book Review, February 18, 2001, Lynn Karpen, review of *The London Monster,* p. 20.

Publishers Weekly, October 13, 1997, p. 67; May 15, 1999, p. 45; May 29, 2000, review of *The Two-Headed Boy, and Other Medical Marvels,* p. 72; November 20, 2000, review of *The London Monster,* p. 58; January 29, 2001, review of *Buried Alive,* p. 76.

SciTech, June, 1998, p. 59.

Virginia Quarterly Review, Volume 77, number 1, review of *The Two-Headed Boy, and Other Medical Marvels.*

Washington Post, December 21, 2000, Jonathan Yardley, "Stalking a Slasher," review of *The London Monster,* p. C2.

OTHER

Salon, http://www.salon.com/(March 7, 2001), Gary Kamiya, review of *Buried Alive.*

*   *   *

BOON, Kevin A(lexander) 1956-

PERSONAL: Born October 13, 1956, in Tampa, FL; son of Robert Edwin and Robin (a civil servant; maiden name, McCarthy) Boon; married Nancy Stephen, November 2, 1984 (divorced, 1987); married Leslie Marie Janos (a teacher), April 10, 2000; children: Simon McCarthy. *Education:* University of South Florida, B.A., 1983, M.A., 1991, Ph.D., 1995. *Religion:* "Neo-Taoist."

ADDRESSES: Office—Pennsylvania State University, Mont Alto, Department of Humanities, 1 Campus Drive, Mont Alto, PA 17237-9700. *Agent*—Esmond Harmsworth, Zachary Shuster Agency, 45 Newbury St., Boston, MA 02116. *E-mail*—Kevin@Boon.net.

CAREER: Pasco-Hernando Community College, Dade City, FL, instructor, 1991-92; Hillsborough Community College, Tampa, FL, instructor, 1992-94; University of South Florida, Tampa, FL, instructor in world literature, 1995-96; University of Alabama, instructor in American literature, 1996-97; State University of New York Maritime College, Bronx, NY, assistant professor of American studies, 1997-2000; Pennsylvania State University, University Park, PA, assistant professor of English, 2000—. St. Leo College, instructor, 1994-98; Columbia University, New York, NY, visiting scholar and guest lecturer, 1999. Fort Schuyler Press, managing editor, 1998-2000, editor, 2000—. Musician and actor; gives readings from his works; judge of essay contests.

MEMBER: New York College English Association (member of executive board, 1998—).

AWARDS, HONORS: Anspaugh Fiction Award, 1993.

WRITINGS:

Yours for a Song: A Technical Guide for the Craft of Songwriting, Alexander Publications (Tampa, FL), 1993.

The Magic Glass (musical play), produced at Fine Arts Theater, 1996.

Chaos Theory and the Interpretation of Literary Texts: The Case of Kurt Vonnegut, Edwin Mellen (Lewiston, NY), 1997.

The Audience (one-act play), first produced in Alabama, at Allen Bales Theater, 1997.

An Interpretative Commentary on Virginia Woolf's "The Waves," Edwin Mellen (Lewiston, NY), 1998.

Reading the Sea: New Essays on Sea Literature, Fort Schuyler Press (Bronx, NY), 1999.

Absolute Zero (novel), Fort Schuyler Press (Bronx, NY), 1999.

(Editor and contributor) *At Millennium's End: New Essays on the Work of Kurt Vonnegut,* foreword by Vonnegut, State University of New York Press (Albany, NY), 2000.

The Human Genome Project, Enslow Publishers (Hillside, NJ), 2002.

Author of the screenplays *Good Fortune,* 1992, and *Wittgenstein's Lost Book of Love,* 1995; author of the script for the film *Five Vignettes: American Red Cross Video Project,* Zoom Photographics, 1992. Musical composer, including scores for the live-action short films *The House,* 1976, and *Witches Tree,* 1992. Contributor of stories, poems, and articles to periodicals, including *Poetry Motel, Sandhill Review, Creative Screenwriting, Notes on Contemporary Literature,* and *Los Angeles Literary Review.* Newsletter editor, New York College English Association, 2000—.

BIOGRAPHICAL/CRITICAL SOURCES:

PERIODICALS

Publishers Weekly, March 19, 2001, review of *At Millennium's End,* p. 86.

OTHER

Kevin Boon Web site, http://kevin.boon.net (September 1, 2001).*

*   *   *

BORDEN, Iain   1962-

PERSONAL: Born November 9, 1962, in Oxford, England; son of Anthony Ian and Shelagh Mary (Birus) Borden; married Claire Haywood (an architect), July, 2001. *Ethnicity:* "English." *Education:* University of Newcastle Upon Tyne, B.A., 1985; The Bartlett, University College London, M.Sc., 1986; University of California—Los Angeles, M.A., 1989; University of London, Ph.D., 1998.

ADDRESSES: Home—25 Hatfield House, Baltic St. W., Golden Lane Estate, London EC1Y 0ST, England. *Office*—The Bartlett, University College London (UCL), Wates House, 22 Gordon St., London WC1H 0QB, England. *E-mail*—i.borden@ucl.ac.uk.

CAREER: The Bartlett, University College London, lecturer, 1989-96, senior lecturer and sub-dean, Faculty of the Built Environment, 1996-99, director, Architectural History and Theory and reader in architecture and urban culture, 1999—, vice dean of academic affairs, Faculty of the Built Environment, 2000-01. Oslo School of Architecture, visiting professor, 1997; visiting examiner at various institutions, 1995—, including Middlesex University, University of Nottingham, and University of East London; consultant for various organizations, 1989—, including Building Use Studies Ltd., Arts Council of England, and RIBA Architecture Gallery.

Organizer of, and presenter at, many conferences; curator of, and exhibitor at, exhibitions; visiting and public lecturer at more than thirty-five institutions, including Museum of London, National Taiwan University, University of Michigan, and University of Sydney; visiting design tutor and critic; has appeared on television and radio.

WRITINGS:

EDITOR

(With David Dunster) *Architecture and the Sites of History: Interpretations of Buildings and Cities,* Butterworth, 1995.

(With Jane Rendell, Joe Kerr and Alicia Pivaro) *Strangely Familiar: Narratives of Architecture in the City,* Routledge (New York, NY), 1996.

(With Jane Rendell and Barbara Penner) *Gender Space Architecture: An Interdisciplinary Introduction,* Routledge (New York, NY), 1999.

(With Jane Rendell) *InterSections: Architectural Histories and Critical Theories,* Routledge (New York, NY), 2000.

(With Malcolm Miles and Tim Hall) *The City Cultures Reader,* Routledge (New York, NY), 2000.

(With Rendell, Kerr, and Alicia Pivaro; and contributor) *The Unknown City: Contesting Architecture and Social Space,* MIT (Cambridge, MA), 2000.

Guest editor, *Architectural Design,* 2001.

OTHER

(With Katerina Rüedi) *The Dissertation: An Architecture Student's Handbook,* Architectural Press, 2000.
Skateboarding, Space and the City: Architecture and the Body, Berg (Oxford, England), 2001.

Author of more than twenty-five chapters in various publications, including *The Cambridge General Encyclopedia,* edited by David Crystal, Cambridge University Press, 1990; *City A-Z: Urban Fragments,* edited by Steve Pile and Nigel Thrift, Routledge, 2000; and *Constructions of Urban Space,* edited by Ray Hutchison, JAI (Stamford, CT), 2000. Also author of published reports, including *Research Innovation in the Construction Industry,* Stanhope Properties, 1991. Contributor to publications, including *Building Design, Blueprint, New Architecture, Archis, Journal of Architectural and Planning Research, Public Art Journal, Adrenalin, Architect's Journal,* and *Architectural Design.*

WORK IN PROGRESS: DoubleDecker: Architecture through History, Poetics and Politics, with Jane Rendell; *The Architecture of Motility: Practices, Conceptions and Experiences of Movement.*

*   *   *

BOUAZZA, Hafid   1970-

PERSONAL: Born 1970, in Morocco. *Avocational interests:* Composing classical music.

ADDRESSES: Office—c/o Prometheus/Bert Bakker Melvenhoff & Co., Post bus 1662, 1000 BR, Amsterdam, Netherlands.

CAREER: Author of short stories, novellas, and plays, c. 1996—.

AWARDS, HONORS: E. du Perron Prize, 1997, for *De voeten van Abdullah.*

WRITINGS:

De voeten van Abdullah (title means "Abdullah's Feet"), Arena (Amsterdam, Netherlands), 1996, translated by Ina Rilke, Review (London, England), 2000.
Momo Prometheus (Amsterdam, Netherlands), 1998.
Apollien: een toneelstuk Prometheus (Amsterdam, Netherlands), 1998.

SIDELIGHTS: Hafid Bouazza was born in Morocco in 1970, but moved to the Netherlands at the age of seven. He learned Arabic in order to read *1001 Nights* in its original language and made it a point to write in that style, focusing not on the subject of the stories but how they are told. Islam, for example, takes on bizarre, humorous, and irreverent forms in his stories, and strange, surprising situations arise without any fanfare. However, he has a closer affinity with the Dutch language and wishes to write in that tradition. He plays with common as well as archaic Dutch words and creates new ones, and his writing style is ornate. Bouazza composes classical music and uses it to improve his writing technique.

BIOGRAPHICAL/CRITICAL SOURCES:

OTHER

Bouaz, http://www.coenp.cistron.nl/ (May 7, 2000).
Het OCenW-plein-Nieuw-Toespraken, http://www.min ocw.nl/ (May 7, 2000).
Interview: Hafid Bouazza, http://www.groene.nl/ (May 7, 2000).
Schrijvers en dichters B, http://www.xs4all.nl/ (May 7, 2000).
SchrijversNet-Hafid Bouazza, http://www.schrijvers net.nl/ (May 7, 2000).*

*   *   *

BOURKE, Joanna

PERSONAL: Born in Blenheim, New Zealand; naturalized British citizen, 2001.

ADDRESSES: Office—School of History, Classics and Archeology, Birbeck College, Malet Street, London, England, WC1E 7HX. *E-mail*—j.bourke@bbk.ac.uk.

CAREER: Educator and historian.

AWARDS, HONORS: Fraenkel Prize in Contemporary History, 1998, and Wolfson Prize for History, W. H. Smith Literary Prize shortlist, both 2000, all for *An Intimate History of Killing. An Intimate History of Killing.*

WRITINGS:

Husbandry to Housewifery: Women, Economic Change, and Housework in Ireland, 1890-1914, Oxford University Press (New York, NY), 1993.

Working Class Cultures in Britain, 1890-1960: Gender, Class, and Ethnicity, Routledge (New York, NY), 1994.

Dismembering the Male: Men's Bodies, Britain and the Great War, University of Chicago Press (Chicago, IL), 1996.

An Intimate History of Killing: Face-to-Face Killing in Twentieth-Century Warfare, Basic Books (New York, NY), 1999.

(Editor) *The Misfit Soldier,* Cork University Press (Cork, Ireland), 1999.

The Second World War: A People's History, Oxford University Press (Oxford, England), 2001.

Also contributor to numerous periodicals.

SIDELIGHTS: Professor of History, Classics, and Archeology at Birbeck College, London, Joanna Bourke is interested in British and Irish history since 1750. She has taught courses in Irish history from the famine to partition. Bourke's first publication titled *Husbandry to Housewifery: Women, Economic Change, and Housework in Ireland (1890-1914),* describes how many women who had the opportunity to work out of the home often returned to their "house-work" when factory job demands slowed or the men returned to work. J. W. Auld, a reviewer in *Choice,* asserted that the book "is extensively researched and filled with . . . tables and analysis." Auld "recommend[ed]" the book for libraries with holdings of Irish History. Cormac O'Grada, a reviewer in *Times Literary Supplement,* commended Bourke's "dissertation-derived book" as "a rich fruit-cake of statistical detail and anecdotal evidence." O'Grada stated that Bourke "vigorously and impressively marshals her sources in support of her argument that the 1890-1914 period constituted a sharp break in Irish rural history." Although "living standards . . . rose, . . . the change" according to Bourke, "meant a loss in women's autonomy." Mary E. Daly, a reviewer in *The English Historical Review,* claimed that Bourke "focuses on the female labour market in rural Ireland." Bourke professes that "by the turn of the century both voluntary bodies and government agencies had begun to promote the importance of scientific housekeeping as an (unpaid) occupation for unemployed women and as a means of achieving economic progress."

Joanna Bourke's *Working-Class Cultures in Britain, 1890-1960: Gender, Class and Ethnicity,* is a "general text" according to Paul Thompson, a reviewer in *The English Historical Review,* "which is both unusual in structure and . . . lively in detail." Thompson considered the portions on "masculinity and workplace, . . .

domestic roles and power, . . . sex within marriage . . . effective and lively." John Tosh, a reviewer in *History Today,* insisted that "what distinguishes the book is the originality of its argument and structure."

Bourke turns her attention to the psychological effects of "shell-shock" on soldiers during World War I in her book *Dismembering the Male: Men's Bodies, Britain and the Great War.* Sarah Benton, a reviewer in *New Statesmen and Society,* asserted that Bourke's "mission is to retrieve the tenderness, fear and loneliness of men at war." Francis Spufford, a reviewer in *Times Literary Supplement,* pointed to Bourke's use of "several experts" to illustrate the terrors of combat and how soldiers "react" in the aftermath. A reviewer in *The Economist* considered Bourke's book a "survey of how the first world was affected British perception of masculinity."

Bourke's book *An Intimate History of Killing: Face-to-Face Killing in 20th Century Warfare,* focuses on human behavior at its most primal, in other words, on the battlefield fighting "the enemy." Eliot A. Cohen, a reviewer in *Foreign Affairs,* recommended the book as "useful" on the history of military psychology for "it reflects wide reading in the enormous literature on the war." A reviewer in *Publishers Weekly* stated that Bourke "makes the disturbing and convincing argument that soldiers can kill, and even enjoy it, while retaining their senses of self and society, right and wrong." Jason Epstien, a reviewer in the *New York Review of Books,* explained that Bourke "confronts directly the murderous nature of human beings in wartime." He also stated that although the book "is an indictment compiled from the recollections of Allied veterans of the two World Wars and Vietnam, she [Bourke] does not suggest that the warriors she cites were uniquely bloodthirsty." Brian Holden Reid, a reviewer in *History Today,* described *An Intimate History of Killing* "a fascinating book." Reid stated that Bourke "explores with insight the emotional relationships that develop among soldiers in wartime." He recommended that the book "be widely read." Brian Bethune and John Bemrose, reviewers in *Maclean's,* said that Bourke "writes perceptively of how virtually all veterans use psychological stratagems to preserve their moral integrity."

A reviewer in *Bookseller* commented about Bourke's book *The Second World War: A People's History* stating, "Even for those who have read a great deal about the Second World War, [the book] will bring the whole campaign vividly to life, by looking at specific events through individual experiences. It is essential and distressing reading that implores us not to forget or sanitize brutality."

BIOGRAPHICAL/CRITICAL SOURCES:

PERIODICALS

Bookseller, July 20, 2001, review of *The Second World War: A People's History,* p. 40.

Choice, June, 1994, J. W. Auld, review of *Husbandry to Housewifery: Women, Economic Change, and Housework in Ireland, 1890-1914,* p. 1637.

The Economist, May 18, 1996, review of *Dismembering the Male: Men's Bodies, Britain and the Great War,* p. S3-4.

English Historical Review, June, 1996, Mary E. Daly, review of *Husbandry to Housewifery: Women, Economic Change, and Housework in Ireland, 1890-1914,* pp. 781-783; June, 1996, Paul Thompson, review of *Working Class Cultures in Britain, 1890-1960: Gender, Class, and Ethnicity,* pp. 795-796.

Foreign Affairs, November-December, 1999, Eliot A. Cohen, "Recent Books on International Relations: Military, Scientific, and Technological," p. 139.

History Today, September, 1996, John Tosh, review of *Working Class Cultures in Britain, 1890-1960: Gender, Class, and Ethnicity,* p. 57; June, 1999, Brian Holden Reid, review of *An Intimate History of Killing: Face-to-Face Killing in Twentieth-Century Warfare,* p. 53.

Maclean's, October 11, 1999, Brian Bethune and John Bemrose, "The Literary Art of War: Military Historians Bring Little-Known Conflicts of Life and Tackle Controversial Aspects of the Wars Canadians Fought," p. 72+.

New Statesman and Society, March 29, 1996, Sarah Benton, "Gone for a Soldier," pp. 33-35.

New York Review of Books, November 4, 1999, Jason Epstein, "Always Time to Kill," pp. 57-64.

Publishers Weekly, October 25, 1999, review of *An Intimate History of Killing: Face-to-Face Killing in Twentieth-Century Warfare,* p. 60.

Times Literary Supplement, April 1, 1994, Cormac O'Grada, review of *Husbandry to Housewifery: Women, Economic Change, and Housework in Ireland, 1890-1914,* p. 22; March 22, 1996, Francis Spufford, "The War That Never Stopped," pp. 11-12.

OTHER

Birbeck University of London, http://www.bbk.ac.uk/ (February 4, 2000).

BOYD, Melba Joyce 1950-

PERSONAL: Born April 2, 1950, in Detroit, MI; daughter of John P., Sr. (a postal supervisor) and Dorothy (a school administrator; maiden name, Wynn) Boyd; married Herb Boyd (a writer; divorced, 1985); children: (first marriage) John P. III, Maya Wynn. *Ethnicity:* "African American." *Education:* Western Michigan University, B.A., 1971, M.A., 1972; University of Michigan, D.Arts, 1979. *Politics:* Independent. *Religion:* Presbyterian.

ADDRESSES: Home—15703 Grandville, Detroit, MI 48223. *Office*—Department of Africana Studies, Wayne State University, Detroit, MI 48202; fax: 313-577-3407. *E-mail*—ab6993@wayne.edu.

CAREER: Substitute teacher at public schools in Detroit, MI, 1971, high school English teacher, 1972; Wayne County Community College, Detroit, instructor in English composition, black studies, and women's studies, 1972-79; W.I.C. Magnet School Project for the Gifted and Talented, curriculum specialist in English and film, 1979-80; Wayne County Community College, instructor in English composition, black studies, and women's studies, 1980-82; University of Iowa, Iowa City, IA, visiting professor, 1982-83, assistant professor of English and African-American world studies, 1983-88; Ohio State University, Columbus, OH, associate professor of black studies and at Center for Women's Studies, 1988-89; University of Michigan, Flint, MI, associate professor of African-American studies and director of African-American Studies Program, 1989—. Shaw College, Detroit, MI, instructor, 1975-76; Wayne State University, instructor, 1976 and 1977, associate professor of Africana studies, 1993—, professor and head of department, 1996—; University of Michigan, Ann Arbor, MI, adjunct associate professor, 1992-93, adjunct professor at Center for Afro-American and African Studies, 1999. University of Bremen, senior Fulbright lecturer, 1983-84; Colgate University, visiting professor, 1986. Eastside Street Academies, English teacher, 1974; lecturer at colleges and universities in the United States and abroad, including Columbia University, University of Notre Dame, University of Pennsylvania, University of Houston, Mississippi State University, Universities of Hannover and Osnabruck, University of Colorado, Sinte Gleska College, and Grinnell College; lecturer at film presentations and poetry readings. Broadside Press, assistant editor, 1972-76, associate editor, 1980-84; Wayne State University Press, member of editorial board, 1996—; consultant to City of Detroit, Ohio Arts Council, and Michigan Foundation for the Arts.

AWARDS, HONORS: Literature Award, Michigan chapter, National Conference of Artists, 1978; grants from Michigan Council for the Arts, 1981 and 1994; Old Gold summer research fellow, University of Iowa, 1985, 1987, and 1988; grant from College of Humanities, Ohio State University, 1989; recognition, Society of the Culturally Concerned, 1990, for major contributions to African-American culture; President's Affirmative Action Award, Wayne State University, 1995; award from Ann Arbor chapter, Links Inc., 1995, for literary contributions to African-American culture; grant from Arts Foundation of Michigan and Detroit Council of the Arts, 1995-96; award from Frances E. W. Harper Literary Society, 1996, for outstanding achievements in the literary arts.

WRITINGS:

Cat Eyes and Dead Wood (poems), Fallen Angel Press (Detroit, MI), 1978.
Song for Maya (poems), Broadside Press (Detroit, MI), 1983.
Thirteen Frozen Flamingoes (poems), Die Certel (Bremen, Germany), 1984.
The Inventory of Black Roses (poems), Past Tents Press (Detroit, MI), 1989.
Discarded Legacy: Politics and Poetics in the Life of Frances E. W. Harper, 1825-1911, Wayne State University Press (Detroit, MI), 1994.
Letters to Che (poems), Ridgeway Press (Detroit, MI), 1996.
(Editor, with M. L. Liebler) *Abandon Automobile: Detroit City Poetry 2001,* Wayne State University Press (Detroit, MI), 2001.

Contributor to books, including *Missions in Conflict: U.S.-Mexican Relations and Chicano Culture,* edited by Bruce-Novoa Bardeleben and Gunter Narr Verlag Briesmeister (Tuebingen, Germany), 1986; *Protest, Rebellion, and Dissent within the Black Community,* edited by Berndt Ostendorf and Maria Diedrich, Gunter Narr Verlag Briesmeister (Tuebingen, Germany), 1991; *The Canon in the Classroom: The Pedagogical Implications of Canon Revision in American Literature,* edited by John Alberti, Garland Publishing (New York, NY), 1995; *Poetry Criticism: Excerpts from Criticism of the Works of the Most Significant and Widely Studies Poets of the World,* Volume 21, Gale (Detroit, MI), 1998; *Sing the Sun Up: Creative Writing Ideas from African American Literature,* edited by Lorenzo Thomas, Teachers and Writers Collaborative (New York, NY), 1998; *Dispatches from the Ebony Tower,* edited by Manning Marable, Columbia University Press (New York, NY), 2000; *Poetry from Detroit's Black Bottom:*

The Tension between Belief and Ideology in the Words of Robert Hayden in the Mourning Time; Essays on Robert Hayden, edited by Robert Chrisman and Larry Goldstein, University of Michigan Press, in press.

Author, director, and producer of the documentary film *The Black Unicorn: Dudley Randall and the Broadside Press,* 1995. Work represented in anthologies, including *Adam of Ife: Black Women in Praise of Black Men,* edited by Naomi Madgett, Lotus Press (Detroit, MI), 1992; *In Defense of Mumia,* edited by Tony Medina and S. E. Anderson, Writers and Readers (New York, NY), 1996; and *Black Imagination and the Middle Passage,* edited by Diedrich, Carl Pedersen, and Henry Louis Gates, Jr., Oxford University Press (New York, NY), 1999. Coeditor, "African American Life Series," Wayne State University Press (Detroit, MI), 1997—. Contributor of poems, articles, and reviews to periodicals, including *Eyeball, Race and Reason, Journal of the Fantastic in Arts, City Arts Quarterly,* and *Against the Current.* Member of editorial board, *Black Scholar,* 1991—.

SIDELIGHTS: Melba Joyce Boyd told *CA:* "I think like a poet, which alters my view of the ordinary. I am inspired to write by whatever catches my eye or ear or heart. I am especially attracted to history, or what I feel is of historical interest. As a black person living in America, I am concerned about the conditions and circumstances of oppressed people in this country and elsewhere. I am interested in bringing attention to what is too often ignored or belittled in this fast-paced society driven by greed and materialism. I am also interested in the beauty of life, and in finding beauty that is distinct in its own being. Although I often write on difficult and painful subjects that reflect suffering and injustice, I still believe that humanity is capable of greatness that contradicts the severity of its most ugly moments."

BIOGRAPHICAL/CRITICAL SOURCES:

PERIODICALS

AB Bookman's Weekly, February, 1995, William Dunn, review of *Discarded Legacy.*
African American Review, fall, 1996, Margaret Bacon, review of *Discarded Legacy.*
Black Scholar, November-December, 1980, Conyus, "The Best Black Books of the Seventies;" November-December, 1980, Conyus, "The Poet's Corner;" winter, 1995, Frances Smith Foster, review of *Discarded Legacy.*
City Arts Quarterly, winter, 1985, review of *Thirteen Frozen Flamingoes.*

Detroit Free Press, April 1, 1979, Betty Deremus, "Detroit Turns Pain into Poetry."

First World, spring, 1979, review of *Cat Eyes and Dead Wood.*

Library Journal, June, 1994, Gayle S. Leach, review of *Discarded Legacy.*

Michigan Quarterly Review, winter, 1985, Dorothy H. Lee, "Black Voices in Detroit."

SOHO News, February, 1982, "Sturdy Black Bridges."

Women's Review of Books, autumn, 1994, Ann duCille, review of *Discarded Legacy.**

* * *

BRETT, Lily

PERSONAL: Born in Germany; emigrated to Australia with her parents in 1948; married David Rankin (an artist). *Religion:* Jewish.

ADDRESSES: Office—c/o Picador, Pan Macmillan Australia, Level 18, St. Martin's Tower, 31 Market St., Sydney, New South Wales 2000, Australia.

CAREER: Writer.

AWARDS, HONORS: Victorian Premier's award for poetry, 1987, for *The Auschwitz Poems;* National Steel award, 1992, for *What God Wants.*

WRITINGS:

The Auschwitz Poems, Scribe (Brunswick, New South Wales, Australia), 1986.

After the War: Poems, Melbourne University Press (Melbourne, Victoria, Australia), 1990.

Things Could Be Worse, Melbourne University Press (Melbourne, Victoria, Australia), 1990.

What God Wants, University of Queensland Press (St. Lucia, Queensland, Australia), 1991.

Unintended Consequences, Paper Bark Press (Sydney, New South Wales, Australia), 1992.

In Her Strapless Dresses, Picador (Sydney, New South Wales, Australia), 1994.

Just Like That, Pan Macmillan (Sydney, New South Wales, Australia), 1994.

In Full View, Pan Macmillan (Sydney, New South Wales, Australia), 1997.

Mud in My Tears, Picador (Sydney, New South Wales, Australia), 1997.

Too Many Men, Picador (Sydney, New South Wales, Australia), 1999.

SIDELIGHTS: Lily Brett was born in a Polish Displaced Person's camp and came to Australia with her parents in the aftermath of World War II, and has since moved to Manhattan. Her first book of poems, *The Auschwitz Poems,* won critical acclaim and also won the Victorian Premier's award for poetry.

What God Wants is a collection of sixteen intertwined stories about middle-aged people, all children of Holocaust survivors who live in Melbourne, Australia. In the *Australian Book Review,* George Papaellinas wrote of the characters in these stories, "Their meetings, their embraces and even their collisions, their struggles and cruelties, are just as clumsy, just as bruised or bruising, just as recognisable and, importantly, just as funny." The stories can all be read separately, but all are also part of the larger story of this community of people, in which everyone knows everyone else and no secret is kept for long. Brett combines pathos and humor in the telling. As Papaellinas wrote, "Brett is a serious comic. Her surgical bent, her dissection of superficially well-ordered, mundane suburban life and the pedestrians that make their way through it, is tempered by an eye for the absurd and for the plain funny." According to a *Publishers Weekly* reviewer, the stories "explore layers of guilt and fear, and above all the need for belonging."

In *Unintended Consequences,* Brett presents poems exploring the heritage of the Holocaust and her own, and her parents', experiences in a Nazi concentration camp. In one poem, she explains to a dentist who remarks on her bad teeth and tells her that she must not have had enough milk in childhood, that in Auschwitz, milk was not on the menu. In another, she describes the list of dead family members, killed in the camps, that her parents kept. Kevin Brophy wrote in the *Australian Book Review,* "We are never far from the past, and the past usually means her mother's past," and "There is the sense that these poems are written for survival—in the way that Blake, Dickinson or Plath wrote."

In Her Strapless Dresses is another collection of poems, but fewer of these are about the Holocaust. Many of them explore her childhood in Australia and other memories. Phil Brown wrote in the *Australian Book Review,* "The poems are never really black—because of her inherent optimism—but they are often sad."

In Brett's novel *Just Like That,* Esther Zipler, daughter of Holocaust survivors, is an obituary writer for newspapers. She is in her forties, and filled with worries about the state of the world, about her parents' suffering during World War II, about her daughter and her daughter's terrible boyfriend, and about her friend Sonia's pregnancy. James Griffen wrote in the *Australian Book Review,* "There are no big upheavals. It's a comedy of manners that plugs into a very strong New York tradition" of food, affairs, and parties, but this comedy of manners is underlaid by reminders of the horrors of the Holocaust. Griffen commented, "It serves as a song of praise to the modern world in all its pathos, bathos, silliness, tragedy and heroism."

In Full View is a collection of essays about Brett's obsession with weight and thinness. "A frivolous subject, you might think, but you'd be wrong," wrote Marion Halligan in the *Australian Book Review.* The essays tell the story of Brett's struggle with weight and body image, and how her concerns with them grew out of her heritage as a daughter of Holocaust survivors.

BIOGRAPHICAL/CRITICAL SOURCES:

PERIODICALS

Australian Book Review, October, 1991, p. 45; August, 1992, p. 57; August, 1994, p. 15; November, 1994, p. 54; October, 1997, p. 10, 50.
Ms., January 28, 1994, p. 68.
Publishers Weekly, July 19, 1993, p. 236; July 30, 2001, review of *Too Many Men,* p. 59.*

*   *   *

BRONSTEIN, Jamie L.   1968-

PERSONAL: Born March 4, 1968; daughter of Ronald (an attorney) and Susan G. (a teacher) Bronstein; married Michael J. Zigmond (an engineer), August 22, 1998; children: Evan B. Zigmond. *Education:* Tufts University, B.A., 1990; Fletcher School of Law & Diplomacy, M.A.L.D., 1991; Stanford University, M.A. and Ph.D., 1996. *Politics:* "Yellow Dog Democrat." *Religion:* Jewish.

ADDRESSES: Office—Box 30001, Department 3H, Department of History, New Mexico State University, Las Cruces, NM 88003; fax: 505-646-8148. *E-mail*—jbronste@nmsu.edu.

CAREER: New Mexico State University, Las Cruces, professor of history, 1996—.

MEMBER: North American Conference on British Studies, American Historical Association, Royal Historical Society (fellow).

AWARDS, HONORS: Fellowship, National Endowment for the Humanities, 1998.

WRITINGS:

Land-Reform and Working-Class Experience, Stanford University Press (Stanford, CA), 1999.

WORK IN PROGRESS: Writing on "workplace accidents and injured workers in Britain and the U.S., 1800-1880."

SIDELIGHTS: Jamie L. Bronstein told *CA:* "My primary motivation for writing is that I love to craft a good story. As it turns out I am a historian, not an author of fiction, but there are many historical subjects whose lives and experiences would be ignored if labor and working-class historians did not seek to rescue them from the allegation of insignificance. I admire E. P. Thompson, whose *Making of the English Working Class* has shaped both my research agenda and my personal goals.

"In order to write, I immerse myself in the archives and read, read, read. The notes I take there seem to grow organically into research questions and chapters. This is surely not the most coherent way to craft a historical monograph but it has the benefit of letting the material speak for itself to a great extent. My own personal biases are less able to drive the work than they would be had I chosen a fixed hypothesis from the beginning."

*   *   *

BROOKS, Barbara   1947-

PERSONAL: Born December 9, 1947, in Surfers Paradise, Queensland, Australia; daughter of Thomas Ronald and Diana Frances Joyce (maiden name, Machin) Brooks; married, 1967; divorced, 1973. *Education:* Attended University of Queensland, 1965-69. *Avocational interests:* Walking, traveling.

ADDRESSES: Home—Sydney, Australia. *Agent*—c/o Curtis Brown, 27 Union St., Paddington, New South Wales 2021, Australia.

CAREER: Writer. Worked as librarian and lecturer/teacher, writer in residence, and facilitator of community writing and oral history projects.

MEMBER: Sydney Women Writer's Workshop, Australian Society of Authors, Eleanor Dark Foundation.

WRITINGS:

Leaving Queensland (fiction; published with *The Train* by Anna Couani), Sea Cruise Books (Sydney, New South Wales, Australia), 1983.
(With Judith Clark) *Eleanor Dark: A Writer's Life,* Pan Macmillan (Sydney, New South Wales, Australia), 1998.

Work represented in anthologies, including *Mother, I'm Rooted,* Outback, 1975; *Frictions,* Sybylla, 1983; *Transgressions,* Penguin, 1986; *Faber Book of Contemporary Australian Short Stories,* Faber, 1988; *Inner Cities,* Penguin, 1989; *My Looks Caress,* Local Consumption Books, 1990; *Streets of Desire,* Virago/St. Martin's, 1993; *Picador New Writing,* Picador, 1994; *Family Pictures,* HarperCollins, 1994; *Passeport pour Sydney,* Actes du Sud, 2000; and *No Regrets 1, 2, and 3,* Sydney Women Writer's Workshop, various dates.

Author of introductions (with Judith Clark) to Eleanor Dark, *Return to Coolami,* Imprint, 1990, and *Storm of Time* and *No Barrier,* Imprint, 1991. Also author of afterword for Eleanor Dark, *Prelude to Christopher,* Halstead, 1999.

Editor of *You Live and Learn and I'm Still Learning,* Marrickville Community Arts, 1988, and *The Heart of a Place: Stories of Women from the Liverpool Area,* Liverpool Council, 1992 (both with Colleen Burke).

WORK IN PROGRESS: A novel set in Australia.

SIDELIGHTS: Barbara Brooks is an Australian writer whose publications include *Eleanor Dark: A Writer's Life,* a biography written in collaboration with Judith Clark. The novelist Eleanor Dark is described by Ann Skea, writing in *Australian Book Review,* as "an important figure in Australian literary history." The book recounts Dark's entire life, and it provides a record of both her artistic development and her notoriety as a Cold War leftist. In addition, Brooks and Clark consider Dark's ten novels within the socio-political contexts in which they were produced, and the coauthors note Dark's influence within the field of Australian literature.

Upon publication in 1998, *Eleanor Dark* won praise as an important consideration of its subject. Among the volume's enthusiastic reviewers is Clement Semmler, who wrote in *Quadrant* that *Eleanor Dark* constitutes "a work of considerable scholarship." Semmler concluded his review by declaring that "this splendid biography should rekindle interest in one of Australia's

foremost writers." Paul Gillen, meanwhile, wrote in *Meanjin,* "So finely done is the . . . intercutting of Dark's youth with extracts from the novelist's published and unpublished fiction that in places [*Eleanor Dark*] almost reads like autobiography." Gillen added, "Social history, Dark's writing and her powerful but elusive personality are all held together by a dense weaving of themes and imagery, by modulated and varied leitmotifs." Even Skea, who contended in *Australian Book Review* that *Eleanor Dark* "fails to bring [its subject] to life," conceded that the book serves as "an accurate and painstaking record of Eleanor Dark's life and work."

In addition to producing *Eleanor Dark,* Brooks has published fiction, including *Leaving Queensland,* and has seen her work represented in various anthologies, including both the *Faber Book of Contemporary Australian Short Stories, Streets of Desire,* and *Family Pictures.*

Brooks told *CA:* "Writing is about asking questions; it can't be divorced from the social and political but it must be free to subvert everything. I'm interested in writing that crosses boundaries between fiction and nonfiction, prose and poetry, story and essay. In Australia, opportunities for publication and awareness of writers and writing have expanded over the last two decades; but although writers have a larger potential audience, opportunities to read or speak about one's work have become marketing opportunities rather than the debates and discussions of a lively and engaged writing community."

BIOGRAPHICAL/CRITICAL SOURCES:

PERIODICALS

Australian Book Review, December, 1998-January, 1999, Ann Skea, " '. . . But Where Are the Stories and Symphonies?,' " p. 17.
Meanjin, number 4, 1998, Paul Gillen, review of *Eleanor Dark: A Writer's Life,* pp. 840-842.
Quadrant, March, 1999, Clement Semmler, review of *Eleanor Dark: A Writer's Life.*

* * *

BURLEIGH, Nina

PERSONAL: Born in Chicago, IL; married Erik Freeland (a photographer); children: one. *Education:* MacMurray College, B.A.; University of Chicago, M.A.

ADDRESSES: Home—New York and Paris. *Office*—c/o Bantam Doubleday, 1540 Broadway, New York, NY 10036. *E-mail*—ndbur@aol.com.

CAREER: Contributing editor, *New York* magazine.

WRITINGS:

A Very Private Woman: The Life and Unsolved Murder of Presidential Mistress Mary Meyer, Bantam (New York, NY), 1998.

Contributor to *Chicago Tribune, Chicago Magazine, Time, George, Washington Post,* and *Spy.*

WORK IN PROGRESS: A book about James Smithson, for Morrow; a novel "about the adventures of two troublesome girls in the 1970s."

SIDELIGHTS: In 1998, journalist Nina Burleigh published a biography of the life and death of a controversial woman of the 1960s . . . and generated her own furor. The *Time* White House correspondent wrote what she described as a "lighthearted" article for the magazine *Mirabella* in which she told Howard Kurtz, *Washington Post*'s media columnist, that she would perform a sexual act on President Clinton "just to thank him for keeping abortion legal." As columnist Arianna Huffington wrote in an online article, that statement "traveled from the [*Washington Post*] to [the talk show] 'Politically Incorrect'—the equivalent to 'passing go' for a scandal player—with the speed of light."

Burleigh's remark, just as reports of the president's marital infidelities were surfacing, sparked a frenzy among Burleigh's news-industry peers. "I have been told," she wrote in the *New York Observer,* "that by admitting that the president is attractive to some women, I have tainted the image of the objective female scribes who are above such observations." To Huffington, "perhaps Burleigh's heinous crime was that she blew the whistle on the fact that if you share the president's ideology, and resonate his sex appeal . . . you are predisposed to do nice things for him . . . even if it breaks the feminist canon of respect for women, especially in the workplace."

The remark flap nearly eclipsed the occasion of Burleigh's book, *A Very Private Woman: The Life and Unsolved Murder of Presidential Mistress Mary Meyer.* This recounting of an episode from the shadowy files of the Kennedy administration sheds light on both the woman in question and the handling of scandal in the early 1960s. Mary Pinchot Meyer, born into an influen-

tial Philadelphia family, was the divorced wife of Cord Meyer, a Central Intelligence Agency division chief and JFK confidant. The book reveals what many in the presidential inner circle had known—and kept secret—for years: that Meyer had an affair with JFK and possibly introduced him to marijuana and LSD. Christine Carr, reviewing the work for *Rocky Mountain News,* commended Burleigh, stating, "To Burleigh's credit, she devotes only one chapter to Meyer's affair with Kennedy—because 'there was more to the woman than a relationship with one man, even if he was the president.' "

The affair ended by late 1962, and in 1964, nearly a year after Kennedy's assassination, Meyer was shot dead along a wooded path in the Georgetown section of Washington. A black laborer, Ray Crump, was discovered in the vicinity and arrested; *A Very Private Woman* covers his trial and acquittal. No one else was ever charged in the death.

Meyer's killing "sent shudders through the power circles of the capital," Patricia O'Brien wrote in a *New York Times* review, in part because the victim had kept a diary, which was turned over to the CIA. O'Brien found that Burleigh "brings a rich array of real-life characters to [her book], some of whom could have tumbled out of a John Le Carré novel. This was a time when CIA agents, White House operatives and journalists mingled routinely," so "it's hardly surprising that Mary Meyer's death became a peculiar footnote to the conspiracy theories surrounding Kennedy's assassination." *San Francisco Chronicle* reviewer Jim Doyle praised Burleigh's "investigative portrait of Meyer" for being a "superbly crafted, evocative glimpse of an adventurous spirit whose grisly murder remains a mystery."

Some critics said the most memorable characters in the book are Crump and his attorney, Dovey Roundtree, who was "worth a book of her own," according to O'Brien. Roundtree, a black woman who worked through school as a domestic, challenged the traditional legal practices, creating a compelling defense based on circumstantial evidence "while clearly not forgetting for a minute that liberal whites in the rapidly changing civil rights environment were afraid of appearing to be part of a lynch mob."

Overall, reaction to *A Very Private Woman* was mixed. While a *Kirkus Reviews* writer dismissed it as just "another 'I Slept With JFK' scenario," a *Publishers Weekly* reviewer called the book "an excellent study of both its subject and its time." David Bowman, in the *New York*

Observer, called the book a "provocative, erudite biography" of Meyer. A *Booklist* critic recommended the volume as one "conspiracy theorists will love." Doyle observed that "inevitably, given the unique circumstances of Meyer's remarkable life and sudden death, the author raises more questions than she can ever hope to answer." Evan Thomas, in *Washington Post,* maintained that Burleigh "doesn't have the answers and, mercifully, she doesn't try to guess or make them up. She is skeptical of the more sinister or lurid scenarios. . . . *A Very Private Woman* succeeds less as a murder mystery or spy thriller than as a portrait of the age. . . . Burleigh is not, and does not claim to be, a true insider. But she offers a revealing peek through the salon window. . . . She sifts carefully through the available evidence and writes about the living and the dead with sympathy. Unfortunately, Burleigh never quite penetrates the heart and mind of her heroine, who was at once outlandish and reserved." But Thomas pointed out that considering the "limits of her sources, . . . [Burleigh] makes good use of the ones she has." Carr concluded that Burleigh "depicts an enigmatic era in American history and tells the story of a woman who embodied both its grace and its secret turbulence. Through meticulous research, she is able to uncover the essence of a life that nearly got lost in the sands of time."

Burleigh told *CA:* "I believe my famous quote exposed the people in my business who take themselves way too seriously. The media were obsessed (inappropriately in my view) with the president's sex life, and I thought it was time for someone to provide a quote that highlighted the cartoonish aspect of what was underway. I am still trying to digest the fact that we live in such a literal society that even some of my esteemed peers missed the point."

BIOGRAPHICAL/CRITICAL SOURCES:

PERIODICALS

Booklist, October 15, 1998, Vanessa Bush, review of *A Very Private Woman: The Life and Unsolved Murder of Presidential Mistress Mary Meyer,* p. 393.
Insight on the News, March 15, 1999, John Elvis, review of *A Very Private Woman,* p. 14.
Kirkus Reviews, August 15, 1998, p. 1166.
Library Journal, October 1, 1998, Sandra K. Lindheimer, review of *A Very Private Woman,* p. 115.
New York Observer, October 19, 1998, David Bowman, "Presidential Squeeze on Acid: Sexy, Chic, Smart—Very Dead," p. 33.
New York Times, December 20, 1998, Patricia O'Brien, "When History Had Secrets," p. 30.
Publishers Weekly, August 24, 1998, review of *A Very Private Woman,* pp. 34-35.
Rocky Mountain News, October 25, 1998, Christine Carr, "The Mysterious Mistress of JFK," p. 3E.
San Francisco Chronicle, December 13, 1998, Jim Doyle, "The Mysterious Killing of a JFK Mistress/ Mary Meyer May Have Known About the President's Assassination," p. 4.
Washington Post, October 11, 1998, Evan Thomas, "The Woman Who Knew Too Much," p. X05.

OTHER

Arianna Online, http://www.ariannaonline.com/ (July 16, 1998).

*   *   *

BUTLER, (Frederick) Guy   1918-2001

OBITUARY NOTICE—See index for *CA* sketch: Born January 21, 1918, in Cradock, Cape Province, South Africa; died April 26, 2001, in Grahamstown, South Africa. Professor and poet. A lifelong scholar, Butler grew up in South Africa and graduated from Rhodes University there, receiving first a bachelor's then a master's in 1939. He followed that with another bachelor's and a second master's degree, this time from Brasenose College at Oxford University. World War II interrupted his educational career, and Butler served in the South African Army from 1940 until 1945. After Oxford Butler returned to South Africa and a post at the University of the Witwatersrand, where he stayed until 1950. Then he joined the English faculty of Rhodes and there he remained until retirement. At Rhodes, Butler established the journalism, linguistics and speech and drama departments, but he really concentrated on promotion of writers from his homeland who wrote in English. This was not always a popular view and resulted in Butler being reproached by some critics for failing to acknowledge the talent of native South Africans. His skills as an author and intellectual capability were noted by all, however. He edited many books such as *A Book of South African Verse,* and was the author of more than a dozen of his own. Among his books of poetry are *Stranger to Europe* and *Pilgrimage to Dias Cross: A narrative poem by Guy Butler.* Other writings include the novel *A Rackety Colt: The Adventures of Thomas Stubbs,* and three volumes of autobiography: *Karoo Morning, Bursting World* and *A Local Habitation.* His plays include *Take Root or Die* and *Demea.*

OBITUARIES AND OTHER SOURCES:

PERIODICALS

Independent (London, England), May 4, 2001, p. 6.
Times (London, England), May 29, 2001, p. 15.

C

CAESAR, Adrian (David) 1955-

PERSONAL: Born January 25, 1955, in Bowden, Cheshire, England; immigrated to Australia, 1982; son of Gordon and Ethel Irene (Young) Caesar; married Claire Allert, December 6, 1984; children: Damian, Ellen-Marie. *Education:* University of Reading, England, B.A. (honors), 1976, Ph.D., 1981.

ADDRESSES: Office—School of English, University College, Australian Defence Force Academy, Canberra 2600, Australia. *E-mail*—caesar@adfa.edu.au.

CAREER: Educator, author, and poet. Wellcome Institute for the History of Medicine, England, librarian; University of New England, Armidale, Australia, English tutor, 1985-87; University College of New South Wales Australian Defence Academy, Canberra, lecturer, 1988-92, senior lecturer, 1992-99, associate professor of English, 1999—.

MEMBER: Association for the Study of Australian Literature.

AWARDS, HONORS: Postgraduate fellow in humanities at the Flinders University of South Australia, Adelaide, 1982-83; Nettie Palmer Prize for Nonfiction, Victorian Premier's Literary Awards, and Australian Capital Territory (ACT) Book of the Year award, both 2000, both for *The White.*

WRITINGS:

Dividing Lines: Poetry, Class, and Ideology in the 1930s, distributed by St. Martin's (New York, NY), 1991.

Taking It Like a Man: Suffering, Sexuality, and the War Poets: Brooke, Sassoon, Owen, Graves, St. Martin's (New York, NY), 1993.

Kenneth Slessor, Oxford University Press (New York, NY), 1995.

Hunger Games (poems), Polonius Press (Cook, Australian Capital Territory, Australia), 1996.

Life Sentences (poems; "Press Pocket" series), Molonglo Press (Woden, Australian Capital Territory, Australia), 1998.

The White, Picador (Chippendale, New South Wales, Australia), 1999.

SIDELIGHTS: Adrian Caesar was born in England but immigrated to Australia in 1982 after completing his education. He is an associate professor of English at the University College of New South Wales Australian Defence Academy in Canberra, and his research interests include twentieth-century poetry, war literature, and the literature of exploration. Caesar has written several books of literary criticism and poetry.

Review of English Studies contributor Stan Smith explained of *Dividing Lines: Poetry, Class, and Ideology in the 1930s* that Caesar "wants, somewhat quixotically, to demolish the 'myth' of Auden's hegemony in the 1930s." Smith said Caesar reinvents MacSpaunday and "rightly attacks Samuel Hynes's 'reductive and tautological' generational mythology for perpetuating the Movement premise that Neo-Romanticism was a 1940s reaction to the Auden-dominated 1930s. Such mythical periodization leads to the over-valuation of a few upper-class public schoolboys playing at revolution, and the neglect of what he sees as . . . lower-middle-class and/or unpolitical poets." John Morris wrote in the *Journal of European Studies* that Caesar's book "challenges well-established and accepted literary views and interpretations concerning the 1930s." Morris continued that Caesar "effectively set himself an impossible task. . . . Yet despite the reservations I have expressed about this book I have to say that it reads well, is enjoyable, and raises, even though it rarely answers, interesting questions."

Ian Gregson said in the *Times Literary Supplement* that "the most interesting product of Caesar's scholarship is the insight into the influence of social class on 1930s poetry which arises from his discussion of poets' backgrounds. He is not reductive about this, and it is partly through its subtlety that the case Caesar makes for the differences between the Auden group and others less socially elevated is a convincing one."

In *Taking It Like a Man: Suffering, Sexuality, and the War Poets: Brooke, Sassoon, Owen, Graves,* Caesar studied the work of World War I trench poets Rupert Brooke, Siegfried Sassoon, Wilfred Owen, and Robert Graves. "Because of their upbringing and because of various dominant ideological influences, these men could not help but see suffering as a good," wrote Matthew C. Stewart in *College Literature*. Each of the four writers had grappled with homosexuality prior to the war, and Owen and Brooke had both suffered from nervous breakdowns because of their sexual confusion. The war provided the four with the opportunity to love other men in a socially acceptable manner. "It was a chance to live an outdoor, martial, and self-sacrificing life," wrote Stewart, "while at the same time finding theme and outlet for the supposedly feminine act of aesthetic creation." Stewart held that Caesar "excels in his examination of the causes and effects of their sexual repressions and confusions, which he says should not be thought of as unusual, but rather as 'endemic to English society.' " Stewart concluded by calling Caesar's primary theses "both original and compelling."

Caesar's 1995 title *Kenneth Slessor,* an analysis of Slessor's life in light of his poetry, theorizes that Slessor was influenced both by his class and by the cultural attitudes of Australia during his life, as well as a literary heir of both romanticism and symbolism. *Australian Book Review* contributor Thomas Shapcott complained that Caesar censures the Australian poet "for not being a 1990s Marxist-Feminist-New-Age-Sensitive male with the obligatory political correctness to appease the thought police of the new academe." Shapcott continued, "Caesar is rather like a Headmaster who not only brings down his cane on the romantic excesses of the young poet . . . but who has to wrap this all round with a rather salacious replay of Slessor's uncomfortable marriage(s) and attempts at 'psychoanalysing' the

poet's sexual shortcomings." Julian Croft, however, in a review for *Australian Literary Studies,* found the book "refreshing." The critic explained, "Caesar has brought a new perspective to Slessor's poetry in stressing the political nature of his subject. . . . He writes with the same passion and iconoclasm as he does of British poetry of the same period, and he brings to Australian writing a tradition of criticism which is not heard as often as it should be."

Hunger Games is a collection of forty-six of Caesar's poems, some biographical, and many of which had previously appeared in literary journals or were produced on radio. Michael Costigan wrote in *Australian Book Review* that "Glass Houses" is Caesar's humorous look at the evolution of his relationship with his partner, "from trendy anarchism to a state of bourgeois conformity ('married, mortgaged, monogamous')." In "The Pledge" Caesar writes of his response to his young daughter's opposition to his drinking, and in "Accents" he reflects on leaving England for Australia at the age of thirty. Costigan commented that "an old Bogart classic supplies the inspiration for four of the best-executed poems in the collection." They are written under the title, "Casablanca Variations." Costigan concluded by saying that "Caesar's admirable collection surely earns him a place among his adopted country's many fine poets."

In the collection, *Life Sentences,* Caesar's poems reflect his feelings about leaving England and his familiar life for Australia and the unknown. The book is part of the Molonglo Press Pocket series. Each volume comes with a greeting card that features the cover of the book.

BIOGRAPHICAL/CRITICAL SOURCES:

PERIODICALS

Australian Book Review, August, 1995, Thomas Shapcott, "Fashioning Slessor," pp. 49-50; August, 1996, Michael Costigan, "Poetry by Consenting Adults," pp. 59-60; April, 1999, Christopher Bantick, "A New Imprint," pp. 37-38.

Australian Literary Studies, Volume 17, no. 3, 1996, Julian Croft, review of *Kenneth Slessor,* pp. 317-319.

Choice, November, 1993, L. K. MacKendrick, review of *Taking It Like a Man,* p. 452.

College Literature, February, 1995, Matthew C. Stewart, review of *Taking It Like a Man,* p. 223.

Journal of European Studies, December, 1992, John Morris, review of *Drawing Lines,* p. 345.

Review of English Studies, November, 1993, Stan Smith, review of *Dividing Lines,* pp. 617-619.

Times Literary Supplement, November 1, 1991, Ian Gregson, "Class Divisions"; October 1, 1993, review of *Taking It Like a Man,* p. 18.

* * *

CANTOR, Arthur 1920-2001

OBITUARY NOTICE—See index for *CA* sketch: Born March 12, 1920, in Boston, MA; died of a heart attack, April 8, 2001, in New York, NY. Broadway producer and author. Cantor was a good judge of what would make a hit play, and his career as a producer began in 1959 when he worked on *The Tenth Man* by Paddy Chayefsky. The play was not an obvious choice for the theater, as it concerned a demon-possessed Jewish girl, but Cantor was interested and pursued funding for the project, which netted the Pulitzer Prize for drama that year. He also co-produced the 1961 Pulitzer-winning *All the Way Home.* Cantor grew up in Boston and graduated from Harvard University in 1940. After serving in the Air Force during World War II, he got his first job in the theater as a publicist for Playwright's Company in New York City. He stayed there for four years, and became president of Advance Public Relations in 1953. Shortly after he became a press representative and worked on productions of smash hits like *Inherit the Wind,* later producing plays outright including hits like *The Music Man,* although he had said musicals were too expensive to produce. In 1970 Cantor and Stuart W. Little wrote *The Playmakers,* a look at the increasingly high costs of producing Broadway shows. Over his career he produced about 100 plays, more than half of which were in London due to lower production costs and reduced ticket prices.

OBITUARIES AND OTHER SOURCES:

PERIODICALS

Chicago Tribune, April 10, 2001, sec. 2, p. 9.
Los Angeles Times, April 11, 2001, p. B6.
New York Times, April 10, 2001, p. A21.
Washington Post, April 21, 2001, p. B7.

* * *

CARAS, Roger A(ndrew) 1928-2001
(Roger Sarac)

OBITUARY NOTICE—See index for *CA* sketch: Born May 24, 1928, in Methuen, MA; died February 18,

2001, in Towson, MD. Advocate and author. Caras was an animal rights and welfare advocate who wrote nearly 100 books on the lives and lifestyles of animals. A motion picture executive for the early portion of his career, it was in 1964 that he turned to animal welfare issues and began making regular appearances on the *Today Show* as house naturalist. Caras' early works include *Antarctica: Land of Frozen Time* (1962) and *Dangerous to Man* (1964). Some of his later writings include *Private Lives of Animals* and *Roger Caras Pet Book,* which was published in 1977. Caras served as president of the American Society for the Prevention of Cruelty to Animals from 1991 to 1999, when he was named president emeritus.

OBITUARIES AND OTHER SOURCES:

PERIODICALS

Chicago Tribune, February 20, 2001, section 2, p. 8.
Los Angeles Times, February 21, 2001, p. B6.
New York Times, February 20, 2001, p. A25.
Washington Post, February 20, 2001, p. B7.

* * *

CIOFFI, Frank Louis 1951-

PERSONAL: Born September 5, 1951, in Brooklyn, NY; son of Louis Frank and Agnes (Russell) Cioffi; married Kathleen McCutcheon, January 5, 1974. *Education:* Northwestern University, B.A., 1973; Indiana University, M.A., 1976, Ph.D., 1980. *Avocational interests:* Classic cars, biking, swimming, running, weight-lifting.

ADDRESSES: Office—Central Washington University, English Department, Ellensburg, WA 98926.

CAREER: English educator. Indiana University, Bloomington, IN, associate instructor of English, 1976-78; prison education development project, Bloomington, IN, 1978-80; Eastern New Mexico University, assistant professor, 1980-84; University of Gdansk, Poland, Fulbright senior lecturer, 1984-87; Central Washington University, assistant professor, 1987—.

MEMBER: Modern Language Association, Northern Pacific Popular Culture Association.

AWARDS, HONORS: Pilot grantee, National Endowment for the Humanities, 1979.

WRITINGS:

(Editor) *Unlocking Shackled Minds,* 1980.
Formula Fiction? An Anatomy of American Science Fiction, 1930-1940, Greenwood Press (Westport, CT), 1982.

Also contributor of articles to professional journals.

SIDELIGHTS: Frank Cioffi's *Formula Fiction? An Anatomy of American Science Fiction, 1930-1940* is a critical examination of science fiction and its origins in the pulp magazines popular in the 1930s and 1940s. Cioffi describes tensions between editors and writers, as well as innovations in the genre, and provides a history for this particular branch of literature. He notes that the writing from that era is the least complex and the easiest to read. He asks whether there was a difference in quality or importance in this early science fiction, as compared to later, more literary works, or as compared to works by European writers, who had different notions of what science fiction was and how it should be written. Donald M. Hassler wrote in *Modern Fiction Studies* that Cioffi's intelligent analysis of science fiction provides readers with a better understanding of the unspoken rules of the genre, and also "witnesses . . . to the artistic vitality of the fiction as literature." Cioffi focuses mostly on the pulp magazine *Astounding Stories Science Fiction,* in which many of the genre's most famous early writers were published. He noted that this magazine was the first to give science fiction a wide exposure, the first to take science fiction seriously, and had the widest circulation of any of the pulp magazines of that era. A reviewer in *Choice* praised the book for being "largely free of the critical jargon that has invaded recent [science fiction] criticism" and for Cioffi's balanced portrayal of the pulp magazines.

BIOGRAPHICAL/CRITICAL SOURCES:

BOOKS

Reginald, Robert, *Science Fiction & Fantasy Literature, 1975-1991,* Gale (Detroit, MI), 1992.

PERIODICALS

Analog Science Fiction-Science Fact, September 15, 1983, p. 111.
Modern Fiction Studies, summer, 1985, p. 465.
Star, winter, 1983, p. 44.*

CLADIS, Mark S. 1958-

PERSONAL: Born May 20, 1958, in Palo Alto, CA; son of John B. (a physicist) and Genevieve I. (a department manager) Cladis. *Ethnicity:* "Greek-American." *Education:* University of California, Santa Barbara, B.A., 1980; Princeton University, M.A., 1985, Ph.D., 1988. *Politics:* "Progressive." *Avocational interests:* Civil rights, environmental issues.

ADDRESSES: Office—Department of Religion, Vassar College, Box 228, 124 Raymond Ave., Poughkeepsie, NY 12604-0228. *Agent*—Erin Edmison, 83 Vanderbilt Ave., #3, Brooklyn, NY 11205.

CAREER: Stanford University, Stanford, CA, visiting assistant professor of religious studies and philosophy, 1988-90; Vassar College, Poughkeepsie, NY, assistant professor, 1990-95, associate professor of religion and chairperson of department, 1995—.

AWARDS, HONORS: Grant from National Endowment for the Humanities, 1992; senior Fulbright fellow in Paris, France, 1992-93; Rockefeller Foundation fellow at Bellagio Study Center, 1998.

WRITINGS:

A Communitarian Defense of Liberalism, Stanford University Press (Stanford, CA), 1992, published as *A Communitarian Defense of Liberalism: Durkheim and Contemporary Social Theory,* 1994.
(Editor) *Durkheim and Foucault: Perspectives on Education and Punishment,* Durkheim Press (Oxford, England), 1999.
Public Vision, Private Lives, Oxford University Press (New York, NY), in press.
(Editor) Emil Durkheim, *The Elementary Forms of the Religious Life,* Oxford University Press (Oxford, England), 2001.

Contributor to periodicals, including *Interdisciplinary Studies in Literature and Environment, Journal of Religious Ethics, Journal of the History of the Behavioral Sciences, Philosophy and Social Criticism, Journal of the History of Ideas,* and *Journal of Religion.*

WORK IN PROGRESS: Religion Gone Wild: Spirituality and the Environment.

SIDELIGHTS: Mark Cladis once commented in *CA:* "My work has been influenced by Charles Dickens, Zora Neale Hurston, Ludwig Wittengenstein, and Simone Weil—and also by the landscape of the Hudson

River Valley. I write to learn about myself, my community, and the land. I invite others to 'listen in.' I wrote my most recent essay during a pause in the middle of working on a thorny problem in political philosophy. I was trying to figure out why the eighteenth-century philosopher, Rousseau, insisted on using a religious vocabulary even while articulating his most secular projects. I needed a break, I looked up, and there were my chickens. A week later the essay was completed: 'On the Importance of Owning Chickens: Lessons in Nature, Community, and Transformation.' How do I work? Every morning, with coffee, and with chickens nearby—just in case."

*　*　*

CLARE, Baxter
See TRAUTMAN, Victoria B.

*　*　*

CLEMENT, Russell T. 1952-

PERSONAL: Born July 15, 1952, in Sacramento, CA; son of Ted (an economist) and Jean (a schoolteacher) Clement; married Rebecca Schiro (a graphic artist); children: Esther, Jonathan, Samuel, Benjamin. *Education:* Brigham Young University, B.A., 1976, M.L.S., 1977, M.A., 1983; University of Hawaii—Manoa, attended Master's program in English, 1979-81.

ADDRESSES: Office—Art Collection, Northwestern University Library, Northwestern University, 1935 Sheridan Rd., Evanston, IL 60201.

CAREER: Brigham Young University, bibliographic researcher, 1975-77, Brigham Young University—Hawaii, special collections/instruction librarian, 1977-81, head of bibliographic/acquisitions department, 1981-86, fine arts librarian, 1986-95; University of Tennessee, Knoxville, TN, humanities coordinator and professor, 1995-2000; Northwestern University, Evanston, IL, head of art collection, 2000—. Also taught humanities and English courses, 1983—.

MEMBER: American Library Association, Art Libraries Society of North America, Association of Architectural Librarians.

AWARDS, HONORS: Outstanding academic book citation, *Choice,* and best art history reference book cita-

tion, *Lingua Franca,* both 1994, both for *Les Fauves: A Sourcebook; research grant from the National Endowment for the Humanities, 1992.*

WRITINGS:

(Coeditor) *Who's Who in Oceania, 1980-81,* Institute for Polynesian Studies (Laie, HI), 1981.
Mormons in the Pacific: A Bibliography, Institute for Polynesian Studies (Laie, HI), 1981.
Mutiny on the Bounty: An Exhibition Commemorating the Two-Hundredth Anniversary of the Mutiny, Friends of BYU Library (Provo, UT), 1989.
Paul Gaugin: A Bio-Bibliography, Greenwood Press (Westport, CT), 1991.
The Age of Exploration, Friends of BYU Library (Provo, UT), 1992.
Henri Matisse: A Bio-Bibliography, Greenwood Press (Westport, CT), 1993.
Georges Braque: A Bio-Bibliography, Greenwood Press (Westport, CT), 1994.
Les Fauves: A Sourcebook, Greenwood Press (Westport, CT), 1994.
Four French Symbolists: Pierre Puvis de Chavannes, Gustave Moreau, Odilon Redon, Maurice Denis, Greenwood Press (Westport, CT), 1996.
(Coauthor) *Neo-Impressionist Painters: A Sourcebook on Georges Seurat, Camille Pissarro, Paul Signac, Theo Van Rysselberghe, Henri Edmond Cross, Charles Angrand, Maximilien Luce, and Albert Dubois-Pillet,* Greenwood Press (Westport, CT), 1999.
(Coauthor) *The Women Impressionists: A Sourcebook,* Greenwood Press (Westport, CT), 2000.
(Coeditor) *Great Smoky Mountains Regional Bibliography to 1934,* University of Tennessee Press (Knoxville, TN), 2002.

Contributor to books, including *Historical Dictionary of Oceania,* Greenwood Press (Westport, CT), 1981; *Dictionary of Artists' Models,* Fitzroy Dearborn (London, England), 2001; *Encyclopedia of Appalachia,* University of Tennessee Press (Knoxville, TN), 2002.

Contributor of articles and reviews to periodicals, including *Journal of Academic Librarianship, Electronic Library, Mormon History Association Newsletter, Wilson Library Bulletin, Utah Access, Library Journal, Serials Review, Dialogue: A Journal of Mormon Thought, Hawaiian Journal of History, Journal of American Folklore,* and *Friends of the BYU Library Newsletter.*

SIDELIGHTS: "Laboring under the lash of promotion, tenure, and now post-tenure review," Russell Clement told *CA,* "I produce dry academic art bibliographies and research guides to fin-de-siècle avant-garde French colorist painters." But many critics find Clement's works anything but dry. Clement, head of the art collection at Northwestern University Library and a former coordinator of research and reference services at the University of Tennessee, is an authority on French impressionistic art—and "a one-man research dynamo on early twentieth-century colorists," according to an *American Reference Books Annual* review.

Clement is well regarded for his expertise on the short-lived French art movement known as the *Fauves,* which began in 1905 as a scandalous display of striking hues and clashing harmonies that led one critic to label the paintings as "fauves," or wild animals. Just a few years later, Cubism would eclipse Fauvism as the movement of choice. But in its brief lifetime, Fauvism produced "an impact [that] is still felt," as *RQ* reviewer Shannon Paul notes. After reading Clement's reference work *Les Fauves: A Sourcebook,* Paul declared: "I cannot imagine a fine arts library, maybe even a general reference library, functioning without a copy."

Les Fauves includes a chronology, bibliography, and biographical sketch on eleven French artists including Raoul Dufy and Louis Valtat (famous Fauvist Henri Matisse is covered in a separate volume). A *Choice* critic cited the volume's "user-friendly" nature in declaring *Les Fauves* "an invaluable asset to scholars researching the Fauve movement." To Stephanie C. Sigala in *American Reference Book Annual,* "the Clement sourcebook brings together a mass of information on these radical artists, and it may stimulate new thought, or at least higher-quality term papers."

With *Four French Symbolists,* Clement provides a wide-ranging sourcebook on Pierre Puvis de Chavannes, Gustave Moreau, Odilon Ridon, and Maurice Denis—giving his readers "research on the late nineteenth-century beginnings of modern art," in the view of *American Reference Books Annual.* Clement also has compiled bio-bibliographies on individual painters of the era, including Paul Gaugin, Georges Braque, and Henri Matisse. Of the latter book, *American Reference Book Annual* declares that the author "provides the Matisse researcher with an invaluable tool . . . a concise yet information-rich biographical sketch of the artist." Clement's 2000 offering, *The Women Impressionists: A Sourcebook,* earned similarly favorable reviews from *American Reference Book Annual;* Elizabeth A. Ginno commented that the text "offers a rich bibliographic tool for scholars and the four women detailed," adding

that "the greatest strength of this resource lies in its chapters on Gonzales and Bracquemond."

The reviews of Clement's books are often short pieces created specially for library and reference publications. As a reviewer himself for such periodicals, Clement calls creating these short assessments "the most challenging, vexing, and intense writing I do. Capturing a book's thesis," he told *CA,* as well as "content, level of treatment, approach, accuracy, authoritativeness, evaluating its significance, and suggesting which libraries should purchase it—all within a few sentences—is no easy feat. Writing short and tight helps in all other writing."

BIOGRAPHICAL/CRITICAL SOURCES:

BOOKS

American Reference Book Annual, Libraries Unlimited, 1995, 1997, 2001.

PERIODICALS

Choice, December, 1991; June, 1994; October, 1994; March, 1997.
Reference and Research Book News, August, 1997, review of *Georges Braque: A Bio-bibliography,* p. 35; September, 1994, review of *Les Fauves: A Sourcebook,* p. 34.
RQ, winter 1981, Chad J. Flake, review of *Mormons in the Pacific,* pp. 201-202; Shannon Paul, review of *Les Fauves: A Sourcebook.*

*   *   *

CLIFTON, Harry 1952-

PERSONAL: Born August 15, 1952, in Dublin, Ireland; married Deirdre Madden (a writer). *Education:* University College, Dublin, B.A., 1974, M.A., 1975, H.Dip., 1976.

ADDRESSES: Home—6 rue du Pierre Brossolette, 92320 Châtillon, Paris, France.

CAREER: Poet. Government Teacher's College, Keffi, Nigeria, teacher, 1976-78; Blackrock College, Dublin, Ireland, teacher, 1979-80; Irish Civil Service, member of staff, 1980-88; worked with refugee aid programs in Thailand, 1980-82; Robert Frost Place, New Hampshire, writer in residence, 1986; The New School, Assisi, Italy, teacher, 1989-91; St. Charles Sixth Form College, London, England, teacher, 1992-93; University of Bremen, Bremen, Germany, lecturer, 1994; University of Bordeaux, Bordeaux, France, writer in residence, 1996.

AWARDS, HONORS: Patrick Kavanagh Award, 1981; Arts Council bursaries in literature, 1982, 1987; Iowa International Writers Program, fellow, 1985; Foundation Binz 39 Scuol (Switzerland), fellowship, 1991; Atelierhaus Worpswede (Germany), fellowship, 1993-94.

WRITINGS:

POETRY

Null Beauty, Honest Ulsterman (Belfast, Northern Ireland), 1975.
The Walls of Carthage, Gallery (Dublin, Ireland), 1977.
Office of the Salt Merchant, Gallery (Dublin, Ireland), 1979.
Comparative Lives, Gallery (Dublin, Ireland), 1982.
The Liberal Cage, Gallery (Oldcastle, County Meath, Ireland), 1988.
The Desert Route: Selected Poems, 1973-1988, Gallery (Oldcastle, County Meath, Ireland), 1992.
At the Grave of Silone: An Abruzzo Sequence, Honest Ulsterman (Northern Ireland), 1992.
Night Train through the Brenner, Gallery (Oldcastle, County Meath, Ireland), 1994.

OTHER

On the Spine of Italy: A Year in the Abruzzi (memoir), Macmillan (London, England), 1999.

SIDELIGHTS: After Irish poet Harry Clifton completed his education in Dublin in 1976, he traveled to Africa, where he taught English and English literature in Nigeria for two years. In *Contemporary Poets,* he called this experience "a raw, vivifying reality after the cerebral hush of graduate studies, an awakening to sex and death and the violence and innocence of political change." Clifton has also taught in Dublin, England, Italy, Germany, and France. From 1980 to 1982 he worked in the administration of aid programs for hundreds of thousands of Cambodian refugees camped inside the borders of Thailand.

The Desert Route: Selected Poems, 1973-1988, which draws from collections published in Ireland over a period of fifteen years, reflects his experiences in a great variety of settings. It contains one of his best known

poems, "Monsoon Girl." "I hope," said Clifton, "the African, and more particularly the Asian, poems included here convey some sense of a Western consciousness enlarged and threatened by these new psychic spaces. In between, of course, there has always been Ireland—the 'distaff side' to the wanderings. A home to come back to albeit temporarily, and consolidate before sallying forth again."

Sheila Haney Drain and Jeanne Colleran wrote in *Contemporary Poets* that Clifton has "a particular affinity for the poetry of place, a genre, as Seamus Heaney has described it, that is known in Irish poetry as 'dinnseanchas.' This fascination with the actual, psychic, and mythical dimensions of locale allow Clifton to use place in his poetry to negotiate the extremes of experience deftly and quietly amid the problematic terrain of the human heart in joy and despair, in and out of love, anywhere." Drain and Colleran found that Clifton's poems about exile and return "are insufficiently known in some of the places—the United States preeminently—that he describes so acutely. They are extraordinary works, small masterpieces of concrete description and philosophical rumination, and are deserving of a wider readership." *School Librarian* reviewer Audrey Baker commented that Clifton "can create a mood with deceptive simplicity."

Clifton and his wife spent time in a village in the Abruzzi mountains south of Rome. They had planned a one-month vacation, but the month stretched into a year, during which they left only twice, for brief periods. They lived in a vacant visiting priest's house, an old stone place without modern conveniences or links to the outside world. They had come to write. They had no car and caught rides between the villages. The one in which they stayed had a population of ninety. They came to know the people well, and the local priest often brought food to them.

On the Spine of Italy is Clifton's memoir of that year. *Times Literary Supplement* reviewer Caroline Moorehead called it "a poet's book, full of lyrical descriptions of the world in which the couple found themselves, the changing seasons, the intense cold of the snowy winter, the gradual trust of their neighbours." Clifton connects time to seasonal events—the availability of new vegetables in the gardens, the perfect time for picking meadow mushrooms and wild strawberries, and the traditional killing of a pig for Christmas. "From Clifton's description it is easy to imagine the slow, deliberate pace of the villagers, broken by the infrequent excitement of the arrival of the postwoman, or a solitary passing car," added Moorehead, who concluded by calling *On the Spine of Italy* "a quiet and charming book."

BIOGRAPHICAL/CRITICAL SOURCES:

BOOKS

Contemporary Poets, 6th edition, St. James (Detroit, MI), 1996.

PERIODICALS

Irish Literary Supplement, fall, 1995, review of *Night Train through the Brenner,* p. 9.
School Librarian, November, 1992, Audrey Baker, review of *The Desert Route,* p. 155.
Times Literary Supplement, July 30, 1999, Caroline Moorehead, "No change but decay," p. 10.*

*   *   *

CLOWSE, Barbara Barksdale   1937-

PERSONAL: Born March 6, 1937, in Atlanta, GA; daughter of Henry Franklin (an electrical engineer) and Elizabeth Cranford (a homemaker) Barksdale; married Converse Dilworth Clowse (a historian), June 19, 1964 (died, November 18, 1997); children: Stephen, Martin. *Education:* Duke University, A.B., 1958; University of North Carolina, M.A., 1963, Ph.D., 1977. *Politics:* Democrat. *Religion:* Presbyterian.

ADDRESSES: Office—c/o Author Mail, Mercer University Press, 6316 Peake Rd., Macon, GA 31210.

CAREER: University of North Carolina, Greensboro, member of faculty, 1963-65, 1967, 1979, and 1981-83; University of North Carolina, Chapel Hill, member of faculty, 1984-85; North Carolina School of the Arts, Winston-Salem, member of faculty, 1985-86; North Carolina A&T State University, Greensboro, NC, member of faculty, 1987-88.

WRITINGS:

Brainpower for the Cold War, Greenwood Press (Westport, CT), 1981.
Women, Decision Making, and the Future, Westminster/JKP, 1985.
Ralph McGill: A Biography, Mercer University Press (Macon, GA), 1998.

Contributor of short story to *Under Twenty-Five: Duke Narrative and Verse, 1945-1962,* Duke University Press, 1963.

WORK IN PROGRESS: In the Name of Justice, "book relating social reform in U.S. history to trends in the American religious experience."

SIDELIGHTS: Barbara Barksdale Clowse told *CA:* "Being a writer is not something I do; it's what I am. I realize that I've been a writer for most of my life. Cleaning out my parents' home, I found a cache of stories, poems, and fragments of impressions that went far back into childhood. Some of these were scribbled under the covers by flashlight after I'd been sent to bed at night. I've never really needed any particular inspiration to write or suffered from 'block.' I write every day in some form, however mundane. The level of effort is somewhere between breathing and walking around.

"When I discovered that college professors were encouraged to write and rewarded for making that part of their job, I decided it was the occupation for me. Writing history is now as much fun as writing fiction was when I was young. Practicing this craft for decades and exploring different ways to explain research findings have strengthened my expertise. I love the challenge of expressing ideas creatively yet always abiding by the norms and structure of the history profession.

"Doing the McGill biography—looking at an individual's life story in totality—was inspiring. Following the twists and turns, failures and success of his life drove home the truth of the cliche that 'it's not over 'til it's over.' His career taught me anew to keep working and never give up.

"My field, recent U.S. history, allows me to investigate current trends and changes which, I think, baffle and trouble many Americans. When I offer an explanatory framework that reaches deep into the American past, I hope to help students and readers who are unaware of or have forgotten such history. It's an opportunity to provide a bridge between my own times and the past."

*   *   *

COHEN, Naomi W(iener)   1927-

PERSONAL: Born November 13, 1927, in New York, NY. *Education:* Hunter College, B.A. (summa cum laude); Jewish Theological Seminary, B.H.L.; Columbia University, Ph.D.

ADDRESSES: Office—Department of History, Hunter College of the City University of New York, 695 Park Ave., New York, NY 10021.

CAREER: Hunter College, and the Graduate Center of the City University of NY, retired professor of American and American Jewish history; Jewish Theological Seminary, adjunct distinguished service professor.

AWARDS, HONORS: Akiba Award, American Jewish Committee, for scholarship and teaching; Jewish Cultural Achievement Award in History, 1997; National Federation for Jewish Culture laureate in Historical Studies, 1997; *Encounter with Emancipation* and *Jews in Christian America: The Pursuit of Religious Equality* were recipients of the National Jewish Book Award for Jewish History. Honorary degrees from Hebrew Union College and the Jewish Theological Seminary.

WRITINGS:

A Dual Heritage: The Public Career of Oscar S. Straus, Jewish Publication Society, 1969.
Not Free to Desist: The American Jewish Committee, 1906-1966, Jewish Publications Society, 1972.
American Jews and the Zionist Idea, Ktav, 1975.
The Year After the Riots: American Responses to the Palestine Crisis of 1929-1930, Wayne State University Press (Detroit, MI), 1988.
(Editor) *Essential Papers on Jewish-Christian Relations in the United States: Imagery and Reality,* New York University Press (New York, NY), 1990.
Jews in Christian America: The Pursuit of Religious Equality, Oxford University Press (New York, NY), 1992.
Jacob H. Schiff: A Study in American Jewish Leadership, University Press of New England (Hanover, NH), 1999.

SIDELIGHTS: Born and educated in New York City, the 1997 National Foundation for Jewish Culture laureate, Naomi W. Cohen, holds honorary degrees from Hebrew Union College and the Jewish Theological Society, and has received the Akiba Award for Scholarship and Teaching from the American Jewish Committee. Always vigilant and committed to Jewish society, Cohen has written books on the topic of Oscar S. Straus, the American Jewish Committee, and Zionism.

Cohen's book *Jews in Christian America: The Pursuit of Religious Equality,* according to Robert M. Seltzer,

a reviewer in *Commentary,* is a "highly original and lucid study turning on crucial constitutional issues of both practical and symbolic importance." Seltzer comments that Cohen's "angle on the Jewish presence in America shows . . . the long-range impact that Jews and the Jewish tradition have had on American public life."

Cohen then tackled the "myth" that "Jews generally believe[d] that until . . . after World War II American Jewry was afraid to exert political power," according to Deborah H. Lipstadt, a reviewer in *New York Times Book Review,* commenting on Cohen's book *Jacob H. Schiff: A Study in American Jewish Leadership.* Lipstadt called Cohen's work "a useful corrective to this mistaken idea." Lipstadt emphasized that Cohen "demonstrates in her well-written and well-researched book," that Schiff "did what he believed was right and he expected others to follow." Vanessa Bush, a reviewer in *Booklist,* called the book "very interesting and informative" while bringing attention to Schiff's efforts to "advocate assimilation of Jewish immigrants" while encouraging the "distinct Jewish religious and cultural heritage."

BIOGRAPHICAL/CRITICAL SOURCES:

PERIODICALS

Booklist, November 15, 1999, Vanessa Bush, review of *Jacob H. Schiff: A Study in American Jewish Leadership,* p. 581.
Commentary, August, 1993, Robert M. Seltzer, review of *Jews in Christian America: The Pursuit of Religious Equality,* pp. 45-50; February, 2000, Elliott Abrams, review of *Jacob H. Schiff: A Study in American Jewish Leadership,* p. 64.
Journal of American Ethnic History, spring, 2001, Daniel Soyer, review of *Jacob H. Schiff: A Study in American Jewish Leadership,* p. 157.
New York Times Book Review, December 12, 1999, Deborah E. Lipstadt, "Good For the Jews," p. 36.

OTHER

National Foundation for Jewish Culture, http://www.shamash.org/ (February 14, 2000).*

*   *   *

COHEN, Seymour Jay   1922-2001

OBITUARY NOTICE—See index for *CA* sketch: Born January 30, 1922, in New York, NY; died April 9,

2001, in Lakeview, IL. Rabbi, activist and author. Cohen graduated with special honors from City College (now the City College of the City University of New York) in 1942 and then from the Jewish Theological Seminary of America, later completing graduate study at the Hebrew University of Jerusalem. In 1949 he received a master's in economics from Columbia University and a doctorate, also in economics, from the University of Pittsburgh in 1953. While working on his doctorate Cohen was the rabbi of the Patchogue, NY, Jewish Center and served at B'nai Israel Synagogue in Pittsburgh, from 1951 to 1960. From there he moved to Anshe Emet Synagogue in Chicago, where he stayed until retiring in 1991. It was in Chicago that Cohen began pioneering efforts to improve Jewish-Christian relations as well as racial equality, and it was he who introduced Dr. Martin Luther King Jr. at the 1963 National Conference on Religion and Race. Other community efforts in which he was involved include the Interreligious Committee Against Poverty, which he cochaired from 1966 to 1968, and the Chicago Board of Rabbis, which he president of from 1968 to 1970. Cohen was a member of the board of directors of his alma mater, the Jewish Theological Seminary, and president of the Synagogue Council of America. Cohen wrote the book *Negro-Jewish Dialogue* as well as *A Time to Speak* and *Holy Letter: A Study in Medieval Jewish Sexual Morality.* He translated *The Book of Righteous* with Sefer Ha Yasher, as well as *The Holy Letter* and *Ways of Righteous.* His last book, *How to be a Jew: Ethical Teachings of Judaism,* which he cowrote with Byron L. Sherwin, was published in 2001.

OBITUARIES AND OTHER SOURCES:

PERIODICALS

Chicago Tribune, April 13, 2001, sec. 2, p. 11.

*   *   *

COLAPINTO, John

PERSONAL: Male; married; children: one son.

ADDRESSES: Home—New York, NY. *Office*—c/o Author Mail, Harper Collins, 10 East 53rd Street, 20th Floor, New York, NY 10022.

CAREER: Journalist and author.

AWARDS, HONORS: National Magazine Award, for *Rolling Stone* article, "The True Story of John/Joan."

WRITINGS:

As Nature Made Him: The Boy Who was Raised as a Girl, HarperCollins (Toronto, Canada), 2000.
About the Author: A Novel, HarperCollins (New York, NY), 2001.

Contributor to publications, including *Us, Esquire, New Yorker, Vanity Fair, Mademoiselle,* and *Rolling Stone.*

ADAPTATIONS: As Nature Made Him: The Boy Who was Raised as a Girl, audio cassette, Simon & Schuster, 2000.

WORK IN PROGRESS: A novel.

SIDELIGHTS: John Colapinto is an award-winning journalist and the author of *As Nature Made Him: The Boy Who Was Raised as a Girl.* Until the publication of this book, the identity of its main subject had been known only as John/Joan. Early references to John/Joan included a 1997 report published by biologist Milton Diamond of the University of Hawaii and psychiatrist Keith Sigmundson of Victoria, British Columbia, as well as a long article Colapinto wrote for *Rolling Stone,* for which he received a National Magazine Award. In the article, Colapinto slightly changed the details and used pseudonyms, preserving the anonymity of the man whose life was changed forever by a botched procedure. In the book, with the consent of those concerned, the facts and names are real.

Bruce and Brian were eight months old when their parents took them to St. Boniface Hospital in Winnipeg, Manitoba, to be circumcised on the advice of their pediatrician. The boys had phimosis, a common condition in which a closed foreskin at the end of the penis causes painful urination. Bruce was to go first. What should have been a simple procedure turned into tragedy when the general practitioner cut off his entire penis. Doctors told the parents that their baby boy was now defective and incomplete, and they turned to sex researcher John Money of Johns Hopkins University for a solution. Bruce was castrated and given a cosmetic vagina. At age six, he and his twin brother were forced to simulate sex by Money during their office visits, with Bruce, now Brenda, playing the role of a female. Their parents never knew about these games, which Money photographed. Brenda was dressed and treated as a girl and given estrogen to produce female breasts. Money, who felt that sex was a result of nurture rather than nature, pronounced the transformation a success, but Brenda suffered horribly, ridiculed in school by both boys and girls, and did poorly in her schoolwork. Both children made suicide attempts, Brian because he resented the attention his "sister" was receiving. Alcoholism, depression, and destructive behavior were tearing the family apart.

Simon LeVay wrote in *Psychology Today* that "rarely has a prominent living scientist been portrayed as such a villain as Money is in this book." LeVay explained that Bruce "was the ideal test case for [Money's] theory—especially because Bruce had an identical twin brother, Brian, whose penis was still intact. Thus Brian was the 'control,' whose psychosexual development could reveal how 'Brenda' would have ended up if she had remained Bruce." LeVay did point out that because Money has failed to respond to Colapinto's charges, "our view of the case may be one-sided."

Bruce was treated by therapists suggested by Money, but rejected the pressure to become female. He reclaimed his male identity as a teenager and also changed his name to David. Through plastic surgery a penis was constructed for him, and he later married and adopted his wife's three children. He and his family cooperated with Colapinto so that others might be saved from undergoing a similar experience. Natalie Angier claimed in the *New York Times Book Review* that David's case "is not merely of macabre and isolated interest. An estimated one in 2,000 babies is born with anomalous genitals—an enlarged clitoris, a tiny penis, labia fused into something resembling a scrotum. By current practice, the great majority of those infants receive cosmetic surgery in an attempt to 'fix' their genitals, in part as a result of Money's proclamations that a child's psychic and physical sexual identity can—and must—be molded to conform unambiguously to one gender or the other."

Angier noted that advocacy groups, including the Intersex Society of North America, are working to change the practice of altering babies' genitalia. Angier considered that "one of the most startling of Colapinto's finds was a paper written in the 1950s, describing the lives of 250 adults who had been born with unusual genitalia but had not been fixed, surgically or otherwise. Despite 'sexual ambiguity of no mean proportions,' the study said, the adults expressed great satisfaction with their lives. They seemed normal, self-confident, with a 'conspicuously low' rate of neuroses and psychoses. The author of the report was a young doctoral candidate named John Money."

School Library Journal contributor Carol DeAngelo deemed *As Nature Made Him* "a compelling story that will educate teens about some serious physical, psycho-logical, and scientific issues." A *Publishers Weekly* reviewer judged it "illuminating, frightening, and moving." In a *Booklist* review, Donna Seaman described Colapinto as "a writer of striking lucidity and compassion" and reflected that David "emerges as a genuine hero who reminds us that we are far more than the sum of our reproductive parts."

Colapinto next issued a novel, *About the Author,* a tale centered around the book's author-protagonist, Cal Cunningham. Cal's debut work is, in reality, a stolen manuscript written by his now-dead roommate, Stewart. Because the manuscript is based on Cal's own life, he rationalizes the theft. The book is published to instant acclaim, and Cal "lands a monetary and media windfall," noted a reviewer for *Publishers Weekly.* The same review lauded *About the Author* as a "fine first effort from an emerging voice in fiction."

BIOGRAPHICAL/CRITICAL SOURCES:

PERIODICALS

Booklist, January 1, 2000, Donna Seaman, review of *As Nature Made Him,* p. 830; September 1, 2000, Whitney Scott, audio review of *As Nature Made Him,* p. 142.

Library Journal, August, 2001, Sheila Riley, review of *About the Author,* p. 160.

New York Times Book Review, February 20, 2000, Natalie Angier, "X + Y = Z," p. 10.

New England Journal of Medicine, May 11, 2000, Peggy T. Cohen-Kettenis, review of *As Nature Made Him,* p. 1457.

People Weekly, March 6, 2000, Hope Reeves, review of *As Nature Made Him,* p. 55.

Psychology Today, May, 2000, Simon LeVay, review of *As Nature Made Him,* p. 76.

Publishers Weekly, January 17, 2000, review of *As Nature Made Him,* p. 51; May 1, 2000, audio review of *As Nature Made Him,* p. 32; July 9, 2001, review of *About the Author,* p. 42.

School Library Journal, June, 2000, Carol DeAngelo, review of *As Nature Made Him,* p. 174.

Rolling Stone, December 11, 1997, John Colapinto, "The True Story of John/Joan," p. 54.*

*　　*　　*

COMAN, Carolyn

PERSONAL: Born in Evanston, IL. *Education:* Graduated from Hampshire College, Amherst, MA.

ADDRESSES: Office—c/o Author Mail, Front Street Books, 20 Battry Park Ave., Asheville, NC 28801. *E-mail*—coman@frontstreetbooks.com.

CAREER: Writer, 1988—. Studied bookbinding with Arno Werner; practiced bookbinding in partnership with Nancy Southworth, 1975-84. Worked as an editor for Heinemann Educational, and as a writing instructor for Harvard Extension and Harvard Summer School; faculty member, Vermont College MFA Writing for Children program.

AWARDS, HONORS: Newbery Honor Award, and National Book Award finalist, both 1996, Dorothy Canfield Fisher Children's Book Award nomination, 1997, and Iowa Teen Award nomination, 1999, all for *What Jamie Saw;* National Book Award finalist, *School Library Journal* Best Books of the Year citation, *Book Links* Lasting Connections citation, and *Booklist* Top of the List citation, all 2000, and Michael L. Printz Honor Book, Best Book for Young Adults selection, and Young Adult Library Services Association, both 2001, all for *Many Stones.*

WRITINGS:

(With Judy Dater) *Body and Soul: Ten American Women,* photographs by Judy Dater, Hill & Co. (San Francisco, CA), 1988.
Losing Things at Mr. Mudd's (picture book), illustrated by Lance Hidy, Farrar, Straus (New York, NY), 1992.
Tell Me Everything, Farrar, Straus (New York, NY), 1993.
What Jamie Saw, Front Street (Asheville, NC), 1995.
Bee and Jacky, Front Street (Asheville, NC), 1998.
Many Stones, Front Street (Asheville, NC), 2000.

SIDELIGHTS: Carolyn Coman writes books in which young adults face difficult choices in their lives and then deal with the consequences of those choices. In works ranging from the National Book Award-nominated *Many Stones* to the Newbery Honor Book *What Jamie Saw,* Coman explores the darker side of growing up: dealing with a parent's abandonment through death in *Tell Me Everything,* child abuse by a stepparent in *What Jamie Saw,* sibling incest in *Bee and Jacky,* and a sister's death during a political assassination in *Many Stones.* Many of her main characters are damaged in some way; some have been the victims of abuse or neglect, while others, driven by their inner demons, inflict abuse on those they love. "As with the people in my life," Coman wrote in an online essay posted to the Front Street Books Web site, "some char-acters are easier to know and love than others. It's necessary for me to love them because as a writer I am often called upon to look at and say hard things. And the only way to do that without being cruel or disdainful is to have an understanding of and compassion for the wide range of what it means to be a human being."

Coman was born in Evanston, Illinois, and was trained in the art of bookbinding before turning to writing books for teens. Her first two works, *Body and Soul: Ten American Women* and *Losing Things at Mr. Mudd's,* are less angst-ridden than her later efforts. *Body and Soul,* cowritten with photographer Judy Dater, looks at modern Americans who share a commitment to the active and enthusiastic pursuit of life. The subjects range from a Utah housewife whose husband was killed in a battle with police because of his refusal to send his children to a public school, to a poverty-stricken Massachusetts woman who has had to overcome a history of sexual abuse. "Although their personal circumstances differ," explained a *Publishers Weekly* contributor, "these individuals all demonstrate notable integrity." *Losing Things at Mr. Mudd's,* on the other hand, is a picture book intended for children under the age of ten. Six-year-old Lucy meets with continual frustration while visiting the museum-like home of her relative Mr. Mudd—she cannot even sit in the chairs in his house for fear of damaging them. "A ruby ring and a 'lost' tooth," the *Publishers Weekly* reviewer stated, "prove the catalysts for a confrontation between the girl and her host—an encounter that brings greater tolerance and understanding to both participants."

With *Tell Me Everything,* Coman began exploring the problems and potentials of teenaged life. Her protagonist is Roz Jacoby, recently orphaned at the age of twelve. Roz has had a difficult life: she is a child of rape, fathered in an act of violence by a man her mother never knew. She has seen her mother suffer disdain and rejection at the hands of their community because of her unorthodox religious beliefs. Since her mother's death—she was killed in a hiking accident while trying to rescue a boy who had been entombed by an avalanche—Roz "is being raised by her uncle, a Vietnam veteran who is suffering post-traumatic stress disorder and wakes the household when frightened by recurring nightmares," explained *New York Times Book Review* contributor Erin Kelly. In an effort to come to terms with her loss, Roz begins to obsess about the boy her mother died trying to save. She makes phone calls to his home in the dead of night. "When this proves ultimately unsatisfying," Nancy Vasilakis explained in *Horn Book,* "she recalls the story of doubting Thomas and, sensing the need to put a tangible, human face to the inexplicable, goes in search of this stranger." "In the end," Kelly concluded, "Roz buries her mother's ashes and creates for herself a 'regular life,' just what every teen-ager wants." "Coman's narrative skills are made bold by the unimpeachable truths of grief," declared a *Publishers Weekly* reviewer in an assessment of Coman's first work, "and she distills the process of accepting death into an act of discovery."

Coman's Newbery Honor Book, *What Jamie Saw,* also focuses on the issue of character, both in its development and in its realization. The novel begins with a direct, vivid image of child abuse. Nine-year-old Jamie watches as his stepfather, Van, picks up his baby sister Nin, and throws her against a wall in their house. Nin is rescued by her mother Patty, who, remarkably, "steps into the room," stated Janet Bode in the *New York Times Book Review,* "just in time to 'raise up her arms and catch her flying baby.'" Jamie, Patty, and Nin escape into the night, finding refuge in New Hampshire with Patty's friend Earl. "The horrifying incident seems to put this fragile family into suspended animation," declared *Horn Book* contributor Nancy Vasilakis: Jamie stops attending third grade and Patty gives up her job as a grocery bagger. The two of them only begin to turn their lives around through the intervention of Jamie's teacher Mrs. Desrochers. "After that, he has to go to school," Vasilakis continued, "and his mother attends some meetings with 'a group of women who were trying real hard and needed to talk,'" according to Coman's narrative.

Coman's realization of the characters of Jamie and Patty are among the strongest elements of *What Jamie Saw.* Patty is a mother who puts the safety and comfort of her children ahead of her own feelings. She even returns to Van's house to retrieve Nin's toys and Jamie's favorite book of magic tricks. "She also knows in her bones why her son has his own flashes of violence. She senses his unspoken fears of abandonment and his panicky need for stability," explained Bode. "Put simply, 'he liked knowing what was next.' And in his unsettled, disoriented life this wish is often impossible to fulfill." When Van finally tracks the three of them down in their refuge, Patty and Jamie are able to confront him and force him to go away. "Coman depicts with visceral clarity the reactions of both Jamie and his mother," Susan Dove Lempke noted in a *Booklist* assessment, "capturing their jitteriness and the love that carries them through the moments when they take their fear out on each other." She "so deftly slips into the skin of her main character," wrote a *Publishers Weekly* critic, "that he seems almost to be dictating to her." "I don't create characters so much as I make room inside my mind and

heart for them to come and get me," Coman explained in her essay on characterization. "I spend a lot of time with them over the course of writing a story. . . . When they are finally willing to speak to me, I listen carefully to the sounds of their voices, and to what they are trying to say."

In *Bee and Jacky,* Coman moves on to an even more difficult subject: serial sexual abuse between brother and sister. When thirteen-year-old Bee and seventeen-year-old-Jacky are left alone by their parents on Memorial Day weekend, they take the opportunity to reenact a game they began in the woods some years before—a game haunted by their father's service in Vietnam and their mother's inability to deal with his mental and physical scars. The original game, which had begun as a "search-and-rescue" of Bee by Jacky ended with him attacking and raping her. "What was a dark game for young Bee," declared Susan P. Bloom in *Horn Book,* "was actually sexual release for Jacky." The reenactment of the game awakens Bee's suppressed memories, causing her to lose control of herself: she hallucinates, propositions her brother, and removes her clothes before she goes outside. "Jacky finds her standing naked in their yard and treats her with tender solicitousness," explained *School Library Journal* contributor Miriam Lang Budin. "Having passed through the worst of the crisis, Bee reaches a new understanding of the fear and anger her family has harbored."

As they had with *What Jamie Saw,* critics commented on Coman's capacity to create and maintain understanding for all her characters, perpetrators as well as victims. "With clearer vision," said a *Kirkus Reviews* contributor, "Bee sees, and makes readers see too, that Jacky is no monster, just a soul tortured by fear." *Booklist* contributor Stephanie Zvirin celebrated "Coman's . . . remarkable ability to elicit sympathy for all the characters—even Jacky, vicious and angry on the one hand, yet clearly horrified at what he's done to his vulnerable sister." "Coman's most stunning scene, in fact," Zvirin continued, "shows Jacky broken and sobbing after he's tried to force Bee to have sex." A *Publishers Weekly* critic calls the novel "the literary equivalent of a Diane Arbus photograph: it presents a sharp, shocking picture of pathology, but leaves it to the audience to imagine the world beyond the frame."

In *Many Stones,* Coman confronts an overtly political issue—the killing of an American girl working in South Africa—in the context of a damaged family relationship. Laura Morgan had been working as a volunteer at a school near Cape Town when she was murdered in an apparently senseless act of violence. A year later,

Laura's younger sister Berry and her estranged father have come to South Africa to view the unveiling of a monument in Laura's honor. Berry has resented her father ever since he divorced her mother years before and began associating with a series of other women. "Not only are the two unable to provide comfort for each other in this painful situation," wrote a *Horn Book* magazine contributor, "they can't even have a simple conversation without it turning into a minefield." In order to make sense of Laura's death and finally connect with her father, Berry must come to understand both the dark and bloody history of apartheid in South Africa and the family dynamics that have brought her to her present state of mind. But "Coman makes no slick parallels between the political reconciliation and Berry's personal struggle with her father, except, perhaps, to show that both are difficult, incomplete," stated Hazel Rochman in *Booklist*. "Far from the glossy tourist-in-primitive-Africa panoramas, this story says what is." "Part coming-of-age, part tragedy, this realistic novel is not a light read," *School Library Journal* critic Angela J. Reynolds concluded; "it is a solid and powerful exploration into the mind of a grieving teen."

Many Stones, in fact, blends the story of post-apartheid South Africa with that of the grieving Americans on several levels. The work was inspired, Coman said in a *Booklist* interview with Hazel Rochman, by the murder of Amy Biehl, a Fulbright scholarship recipient working in South Africa. "Before I wrote the novel," Coman declared, "I contacted the Biehls and asked them if they would mind if I drew on their family's story. I said I would acknowledge it in the book. They were so gracious and encouraging. They said, 'By all means, go ahead. It's nice of you to ask, but you needn't.'" The images of the places Berry and her father visit on their trip and the people they meet reflect the political reality in which the historical Amy Biehl and the fictional Laura Morgan worked: Robben Island, where Nelson Mandela and many other political opponents of apartheid were imprisoned; Suzanne, the bright young—and racist—woman who flirts with Berry's father and treats her servants as less than human; and Philip, the Xhosa restaurant waiter, who lost his brothers in the struggle against apartheid. Overall, however, is the image of the South African Truth and Reconciliation Commission (TRC), which investigates crimes against humanity perpetrated in the name of the apartheid regime. "I wanted to do a story that somehow connected the personal and the political," Coman told *Booklist* interviewer Rochman. "And I do remember the first time I realized what the TRC was, what it was trying to do, I couldn't believe it. I thought, 'Oh, my God, a country could try to do this, come to terms.'"

"In the simplest words, as hard as stones," commented Rochman in an article for the *New York Times Book Review*, "Carolyn Coman connects a white American family's anguish with a nation's struggle to come to terms with its savage past."

"I'm happy to be writing books that are considered young adult," Coman explained in an interview posted on the Penguin Putnam Web site. "I've written enough now to know that I come back over and over to childhood and adolescent issues. It's something that really interests and concerns me, so when I get an idea for a story, I just go with it. I couldn't have been more graciously and more warmly received, and if all my books end up being in that genre, wonderful."

BIOGRAPHICAL/CRITICAL SOURCES:

PERIODICALS

Booklist, September 15, 1993, Jeanne Triner, review of *Tell Me Everything*, p. 150; December 15, 1995, Susan Dove Lempke, review of *What Jamie Saw*, p. 703; October 1, 1998, Stephanie Zvirin, review of *Bee and Jacky*, p. 324; December 1, 2000, Stephanie Zvirin, review of *Many Stones*, p. 692; January 1, 2001, Hazel Rochman, "The *Booklist* Interview: Carolyn Coman," pp. 938-939.

Book Report, May-June, 1994, Margaret Zinz Jantzen, review of *Tell Me Everything*, pp. 42-43.

English Journal, September, 1994, Lois Stover, review of *Tell Me Everything*, p. 87.

Horn Book, January-February, 1994, Nancy Vasilakis, review of *Tell Me Everything*, p. 72; March-April, 1996, Nancy Vasilakis, review of *What Jamie Saw*, p. 194; November, 1998, Susan P. Bloom, review of *Bee and Jacky*, p. 726; January, 2001, review of *Many Stones*, p. 89.

Kirkus Reviews, September 15, 1998, review of *Bee and Jacky*, pp. 1381-1382.

New York Times Book Review, January 16, 1994, Erin Kelly, review of *Tell Me Everything*; February 11, 1996, Janet Bode, review of *What Jamie Saw*, p. 25; November 19, 2000, Hazel Rochman, "Truth and Reconciliation."

Publishers Weekly, March 11, 1988, review of *Body and Soul*, pp. 92-93; June 15, 1992, review of *Losing Things at Mr. Mudd's*, p. 101; September 20, 1993, review of *Tell Me Everything*, p. 73; August 28, 1995, review of *What Jamie Saw*, p. 114; August 31, 1998, review of *Bee and Jacky*, p. 77; October 30, 2000, review of *Many Stones*, p. 76.

Riverbank Review, spring, 2001, Jenny Sawyer, review of *Many Stones*, p. 44.

School Library Journal, September, 1988, Dorcas Hand, review of *Body and Soul,* p. 212; November, 1998, Miriam Lang Budin, review of *Bee and Jacky,* p. 119; November, 2000, Angela J. Reynolds, review of *Many Stones,* p. 150.

Times Educational Supplement, December 6, 1996, Geraldine Brennan, "Tulip the Battered Flower," p. 17.

Voice of Youth Advocates, December, 1998, Cynthia L. Blinn, review of *Bee and Jacky,* p. 353.

OTHER

Front Street Books Web site, http://www.frontstreet books.com/ (December 1, 2000), "Carolyn Coman on Character."

Penguin Putnam Catalogue Biography, http://www.penguinputnam.com/ (December 1, 2000), interview with Carolyn Coman.

* * *

COMBS, Maxine 1937-
(Ruth Solow)

PERSONAL: Born June 14, 1937, in Dallas, TX; daughter of Eugene Maxwell and Sayd Frances (Travis) Solow; married Edouard Gauthier, December 27, 1959 (divorced); married Bruce Combs, June, 1967 (divorced); married Martin Bernstein, February 20, 1992; children: Bella, Wayne. *Education:* Mills College, B.A., 1958; Wayne State University, M.A., 1961; University of Oregon, Ph.D., 1967.

ADDRESSES: Home—2216 King Pl. N.W., Washington, DC 20007.

CAREER: Idaho State University, Pocatello, ID, instructor in English, 1963-65; Lane Community College, Eugene, OR, instructor in English, 1966-69; American University, Washington, DC, assistant professor of English, 1970-74; University of the District of Columbia, Washington, DC, assistant professor of English, 1972-77, 1981-88; Howard University, Washington, DC, instructor in English, 1988-89; University of the District of Columbia, Washington, DC, assistant professor of English, 1990—. George Mason University, assistant professor, 1979-88.

AWARDS, HONORS: Fiction Award, Slough Press, 1989, for *The Foam of Perilous Seas.*

WRITINGS:

Swimming Out of the Collective Unconscious (poetry chapbook), Wineberry Press, 1989.

The Foam of Perilous Seas (stories), Slough (Austin, TX), 1990.

Handbook of the Strange (novella and stories), Signal Books (Carrboro, NC), 1995.

The Inner Life of Objects (novel), Calyx Books (Corvallis, OR), 2000.

Other writings include *Letters from Burning Buildings* (poetry chapbook), 1989. Work represented in anthologies. Contributor of poems, stories, and reviews to periodicals, including *Piedmont Literary Review, Wooster Review, Far Point, Poet Lore, Habersham Review, Iris,* and *Kalliope.*

SIDELIGHTS: Poet and novelist Maxine Combs offers a "fascinating examination of the nature of belief and how it colors perception" in *The Inner Life of Objects,* according to a reviewer for *Publishers Weekly.* The novel centers on Opal Kirschbaum, who works for an organization that researches paranormal phenomena but who has begun to have doubts about such matters. Also playing significant roles Abel Moore, a widower who worries that he may be losing his psychic powers; Poppy Greengold, a young goddess-worshipper; and Geneva Lamb, a disaffected academic looking for insight into Yeats's mysticism. The reviewer observed that Combs reveals "the heart of human loneliness" in the novel.

BIOGRAPHICAL/CRITICAL SOURCES:

PERIODICALS

Publishers Weekly, October 4, 1999, review of *The Inner Life of Objects,* p. 65.*

* * *

COMBS, Maxine Solow
See COMBS, Maxine

* * *

COQUILLETTE, Daniel R(obert) 1944-

PERSONAL: Born May 23, 1944, in Boston, MA; son of Robert M. (an executive) and Dagmar B. Coquillette;

married Rosamund Judith Courtenay, July 5, 1969; children: Anna, Sophie, Julia. *Education:* Williams College, A.B. (summa cum laude), 1966; Oxford University, B.A., 1969, M.A., 1980; Harvard University, J.D. (magna cum laude), 1971.

ADDRESSES: Home—12 Rutland St., Cambridge, MA 02138. *Office*—Boston College Law School, 885 Centre St., Newton, MA 02459-1163.

CAREER: Supreme Judicial Court of Massachusetts, law clerk, 1971-72; U.S. Supreme Court, Washington, DC, law clerk to the chief justice, 1972-73; Palmer & Dodge, Boston, MA, associate, 1973-75; Boston University, Boston, MA, associate professor of law, 1975-78; Palmer & Dodge, partner, 1980-85; Boston College, Boston, MA, professor of law and dean of Law School, 1985-93 and 1994-96, currently J. Donald Monan University Professor and Esren Kissel visiting professor, Harvard Law School, Cambridge, MA; Cornell University, Ithaca, NY, visiting professor, 1977 and 1984; Harvard University, Cambridge, MA, visiting professor at Harvard Law School, beginning in 1979, Elihu Root Lecturer, 1983 and 1985; Princeton University, Princeton, NJ, Mellon Lecturer, 1987; Claremont College, Francis Bacon Memorial Lecturer, 1993; University of North Carolina, Chapel Hill, NC, Dan K. Moore Lecturer, 1993; Suffolk University, Donahue Lecturer, 1996; guest lecturer at educational institutions in the United States and abroad, including McGill University, University of Barcelona and University of Genoa. Judicial Conference of the United States, reporter, Committee on Rules of Practice and Procedure; Supreme Judicial Court of Massachusetts, member of Committee on Model Rules of Professional Conduct, 1994-1998. Massachusetts Continuing Legal Education, Inc., member of board of trustees, 1985-88. Ames Foundation, member of board of trustees, 1976—, secretary and treasurer, 1978—; Robert K. Byron Memorial Fund, treasurer, 1979—; Boston Athenaeum, proprietor, 1980—, member of board of trustees, 1987—.

MEMBER: American Bar Association, American Law Institute, American Bar Foundation (fellow), American Society of Legal History (member of board of directors, 1986-88), Selden Society, American Antiquarian Society, Massachusetts Bar Association (chairperson of Committee on Professional Ethics, 1977-81; chairperson of Task Force on Unauthorized Practice of Law, 1978), Massachusetts Historical Society, Colonial Society of Massachusetts (vice-president; member of council, 1985—), Boston Bar Association, American Friends of University College, Oxford (vice-president

and member of board of directors, 1977—), Curtis Club (president, 1984), Phi Beta Kappa.

AWARDS, HONORS: Sentimental of the Republic Prize in political science and Kaufman Prize in English, Williams College; Francis Session Hutchins Scholar, Williams College; Fulbright scholar, Oxford University, England, 1966-68; Sir Thomas More Award, Boston College; Alumni Association, Founder's Medal, Barton College Law School.

WRITINGS:

(Editor and contributor) *Law in Colonial Massachusetts,* University Press of Virginia (Charlottesville, VA), 1984.
Comparative Studies in Continental and Anglo-American Legal History, Volume III: *The Civilian Writers of Doctors' Commons, London,* [Berlin, Germany], 1988.
Francis Bacon, Stanford University Press (Stanford, CA), 1992.
Lawyers and Fundamental Moral Responsibility, Anderson Publishing (Cincinnati, OH), 1995.
(With Mary Beth Basile) *Incipit Lex Mercatoria: The Treatise on the Lex Mercatoria in the Little Red Book of Bristol,* translated by Basile, Ames Foundation, 1996.
Anglo-American Legal Heritage, Carolina Academic Press (Durham, NC), 1999.
(With McMorrow) *Federal Law of Attorney Conduct,* Matthew Bender (New York, NY), 2000.

Contributor to *The International Library of Essays in Law and Legal Theory,* edited by T. D. Campbell, Dartmouth Publishing (England), 1992.

Contributor to professional journals. Member of board of editors, *Boston Bar Journal,* 1984-88; member of editorial board, *New England Quarterly,* 1986—; past editor, *Harvard Law Review.*

WORK IN PROGRESS: Editing *Quincy's Reports,* with Mark Walsh, University of Virginia (Charlottesville, VA), completion expected in 2001; *A History of Harvard Law School.*

*   *   *

CRANE, Nicholas

PERSONAL: Married Annabel Huxley, 1991; children: one daughter, one son. *Education:* London University, B.A. (with honors).

ADDRESSES: Home—London, England. *Agent*—c/o Viking Penguin, 375 Hudson St., New York, NY 10014-3657.

CAREER: Writer, 1979—.

MEMBER: Royal Society of Literature, Society of Authors, Royal Geographical Society (fellow).

AWARDS, HONORS: Mungo Park Medal, Royal Scottish Geographical Society, 1993; Thomas Cook/*Daily Telegraph* Travel Writing Award, 1997, for *Clear Waters Rising.*

WRITINGS:

(Editor) *International Cycling Guide,* Tautivy (London, England), 1980.
(With Christa Gausden) *The CTC Route Guide to Cycling in Britain and Ireland,* Oxford Illustrated Press (Sparkford, England), 1980.
Cycling in Europe, Oxford Illustrated Press, 1984.
(With Richard Crane) *Bicycles up Kilimanjaro,* Oxford Illustrated Press, 1985.
(With Crane) *Journey to the Centre of the Earth,* Bantam (New York, NY), 1987.
The Great Bicycle Adventure, Oxford Illustrated Press, 1987.
(With Charles Kelly) *Richard's Mountain Bike Book,* Ballantine (New York, NY), 1988.
Nick Crane's Action Sports, Oxford Illustrated Press, 1989.
Atlas Biker: Mountainbiking in Morocco, Oxford Illustrated Press, 1990.
Clear Waters Rising: A Mountain Walk across Europe, Penguin (New York, NY), 1997.
Two Degrees West: A Walk along England's Meridian, Viking (New York, NY), 1999.

Contributor to periodicals, including *Daily Telegraph, Sunday Times* (London, England), and *Guardian.*

SIDELIGHTS: Nicholas Crane has published various works on bicycling and hiking. In 1984 he produced *Cycling in Europe,* and in 1987 he collaborated with his brother, Richard Crane, in writing *Journey to the Centre of the Earth.* He followed that volume with *The Great Bicycle Adventure,* another 1987 publication, wherein he relates his experiences bicycling up Mount Kilamanjaro and other formidable peaks. Bob Lancaster, writing in the *Times Educational Supplement,* proclaimed *The Great Bicycle Adventure* "delightful reading." The next year, Crane teamed with Charles Kelly in issuing *Richard's Mountain Bike Book.*

Nearly ten years passed before Crane produced *Clear Waters Rising: A Mountain Walk across Europe.* In this volume, he recounts his hike from Cape Finisterre in western Spain to Istanbul. Crane spent more than five hundred days on his trek, and he traveled ten thousand kilometers. The hike took him through various mountain regions, including the Alps, the Carpathians, and the Balkans, and it led him through areas varying from teeming ski resorts to remote villages. Philip Marsden described *Clear Waters Rising,* in his *Times Literary Supplement* review, as "the account of a journey which far surpasses most of today's stunt-like jaunts." Marsden affirmed that Crane's book is "written with charm, assurance and considerable powers of description," and he summarized it as "very impressive."

In 1999 Crane published *Two Degrees West: A Walk along England's Meridian,* an account of his trek across the middle of England. His journey took him through hill towns, industrial plains, villages, and rural regions. Adam Nicolson, in his *Times Literary Supplement* assessment, contended that *Two Degrees West* "is a curiously cold and even lonely book," though he conceded that Crane proves "clearly engaging." A more favorable appraisal came from Paul Routledge, who wrote in *Spectator* that Crane possesses "an original and cultured mind." Routledge added that Crane's sense of purpose "has the great merit of slicing through the country like an excavator exposing hidden strata."

BIOGRAPHICAL/CRITICAL SOURCES:

PERIODICALS

Booklist, September 15, 2000, Mary Frances Wilkens, review of *Two Degrees West,* p. 263.
Geographical Magazine, August, 1999, Sophie Ransom, review of *Two Degrees West,* p. 93.
Spectator, June 26, 1999, Paul Routledge, "The Glory of a Straight Line," p. 40.
Times Educational Supplement, September 11, 1987, Bob Lancaster, "Classics," p. 60; October 4, 1996, Philip Marsden, "From Cape Finisterre to the Carpathians," p. 44.
Times Literary Supplement, July 30, 1999, Adam Nicolson, "In the Swim," p. 8.*

* * *

CRICKILLON, Jacques 1940-

PERSONAL: Born September 13, 1940, in Brussels, Belgium. *Education:* Earned a degree in Romance philology.

ADDRESSES: Office—c/o Royal Academy of Language & Lit., 1 Ducal Street, 1000, Brussels, Belgium.

CAREER: Professor of literature.

MEMBER: Académie royale de langue et de littérature françaises (Belgium), Académie royale d'archéologie de Belgique.

AWARDS, HONORS: Grand prix triennal de poésie du Govt. belge, 1978; Palmier d'or, International Festival of Nice, 1979.

WRITINGS:

La défendue, A. de Rache (Brussels, Belgium), 1968.

L'Œuvre romanesque d'Albert Ayguesparse, A. de Rache (Brussels, Belgium), 1970.

L'ombre du prince, A. de Rache (Brussels, Belgium), 1971.

Portrait-frontière du poème d'Alain Bosquet, Centre d'études poétiques (Brussels, Belgium), 1974.

La barrière blanche (poems), A. de Rache (Brussels, Belgium), 1974.

La guerre sainte (poems), A. de Rache (Brussels, Belgium), 1975.

A visage fermé (poems), A. de Rache (Brussels, Belgium), 1976.

(Author of criticism and interpretation) *André Miguel* (poems), Editions Subervie (Rodez, France), 1977.

Colonie de la mémoire, La Renaissance du livre (Brussels, Belgium), 1979.

(With Philippe Lefebvre and Pierre Sterckx) *Bruxelles à mur ouvert,* illustrated by Michel Huisman, Vokaer (Brussels, Belgium), 1980.

Supra-coronada: Récits, La Renaissance du livre (Brussels, Belgium), 1980.

Nuit la neige, illustrated by "Ferry C.," Vérités (Belgium, Belgium), 1981.

Sommeil blanc [and] *Le cobra noir* (dramas), RTBF centre de production de Bruxelles (Brussels, Belgium), 1981.

Retour à Tawani (poems), P. Belfond (Paris, France), 1983.

La nuit du seigneur: Récits, P. Legrain (Brussels, Belgium), 1983.

Avec ramses, Théâtre de l'Atelier (Brussels, Belgium), 1984.

L'Indien de la Gare du Nord, P. Belfond (Paris, France), 1985.

Le tueur birman (novel), P. Belfond (Paris, France), 1987.

Grand Paradis, L'Âge d'homme (Lausanne, Switzerland), 1987.

Sphère, L'Âge d'homme (Lausanne, Switzerland), 1991.

Neuf royaumes (poems), Maison de la poésie d'Amay (Amay, Belgium), 1991.

Vide et voyageur (poems), L'Âge d'homme (Lausanne, Switzerland), 1993.

Ténébrées (poems), Maison de la poésie d'Amay (Amay, Belgium), 1993.

Elégies d'Evolène, L'Âge d'homme (Lausanne, Switzerland), 1995.

Talisman, Maison de la poésie d'Amay (Amay, Belgium), 1995.

Ballade de Lorna de l'Our, with music by Xavier Riis, Maison de la poésie d'Amay (Amay, Belgium), 1996.

Au bord des fonderies mortes (poetical novel), L'Âge d'homme (Lausanne, Switzerland), 1998.

L'Indien de la gare du Nord, L'Âge d'homme (Lausanne, Switzerland), 2000.

Babylone Demain—Le Tueur birman—Parcours 109—Supra-Coronada, Renaissance du Livre (Brussels, Belgium), 2001.

Contributor to periodicals, including *Marginales* and *Revue-Generale.**

*   *   *

CROFTS, Freeman Wills   1879-1957

PERSONAL: Born June 1, 1879, in Dublin, Ireland; died April 11, 1957; married Mary Bellas Canning, in 1912. *Education:* Attended Methodist and Campbell Colleges in Belfast, Ireland.

CAREER: Belfast and North Countries Railway, Ireland, junior assistant engineer, 1899, district engineer in Coleraine, beginning 1900, chief assistant engineer in Belfast, 1923-29; full-time writer, 1929-57.

AWARDS, HONORS: Fellow, Royal Society of Arts, 1939.

WRITINGS:

CRIME NOVELS

The Cask, Collins (London, England), 1920, Seltzer (New York, NY), 1924.

The Ponson Case, Collins (London, England), 1921, Boni (New York, NY), 1927.

The Pit-Prop Syndicate, Collins (London, England), 1922, Seltzer (New York, NY), 1925.

The Groote Park Murder, Collins (London, England), 1924, Seltzer (New York, NY), 1925.

Inspector French's Greatest Case, Collins (London, England), 1925, Seltzer (New York, NY), 1925.

Inspector French and the Cheyne Mystery, Collins (London, England), 1926, Boni (New York, NY), 1926.

Inspector French and the Starvel Tragedy, Collins (London, England), 1927, published as *The Starvel Hollow Tragedy,* Harper (New York, NY), 1927.

The Sea Mystery: An Inspector French Detective Story, Collins (London, England), 1928, Harper (New York, NY), 1928.

The Box Office Murders: An Inspector French Case, Collins (London, England), 1929, published as *The Purple Sickle Murders,* Harper (New York, NY), 1929.

Sir John Magill's Last Journey: An Inspector French Case, Collins (London, England), 1930, Harper (New York, NY), 1930.

Mystery in the Channel, Collins (London, England), 1931, published as *Mystery in the English Channel,* Harper (New York, NY), 1931.

Sudden Death, Collins (London, England), 1932, Harper (New York, NY), 1932.

Death on the Way, Collins (London, England), 1932, published as *Double Death,* Harper (New York, NY), 1932.

The Hog's Back Mystery, Hodder & Stoughton (London, England), 1933, published as *The Strange Case of Dr. Earle,* Dodd, Mead (New York, NY), 1933.

The 12.30 from Croydon, Hodder & Stoughton (London, England), 1934, Penguin (Baltimore, MD), 1953, published as *Willful and Premeditated,* Dodd, Mead (New York, NY), 1934.

Mystery on Southampton Water, Hodder & Stoughton (London, England), 1934, published as *Crime on the Solent,* Dodd, Mead (New York, NY), 1934.

Crime at Guildford, Collins, 1935, published as *The Crime at Nornes,* Dodd, Mead (New York, NY), 1935.

The Loss of the "Jane Vosper," Collins (London, England), 1936, Dodd, Mead (New York, NY), 1936.

Man Overboard!, Collins (London, England), 1936, Dodd, Mead (New York, NY), 1936, published and abridged as *Cold-Blooded Murder,* Avon (New York, NY), 1947.

Found Floating, Hodder & Stoughton (London, England), 1937, Dodd, Mead (New York, NY), 1937.

The End of Andrew Harrison, Hodder & Stoughton (London, England), 1938, published as *The Futile Alibi,* Dodd, Mead (New York, NY), 1938.

Antidote to Venom, Hodder & Stoughton (London, England), 1938, Dodd, Mead (New York, NY), 1939.

Fatal Venture, Hodder & Stoughton (London, England), 1939, published as *Tragedy in the Hollow,* Dodd, Mead (New York, NY), 1939.

Golden Ashes, Hodder & Stoughton (London, England), 1940, Dodd, Mead (New York, NY), 1940.

James Tarrant, Adventurer, Hodder & Stoughton (London, England), 1941, published as *Circumstantial Evidence,* Dodd, Mead (New York, NY), 1941.

The Losing Game, Hodder & Stoughton (London, England), 1941, published as *A Losing Game,* Dodd, Mead (New York, NY), 1941.

Fear Comes to Chalfont, Hodder & Stoughton (London, England), 1942, Dodd, Mead (New York, NY), 1942.

The Affair at Little Wokeham, Hodder & Stoughton (London, England), 1943, published as *Double Tragedy,* Dodd, Mead (New York, NY), 1943.

Enemy Unseen, Hodder & Stoughton (London, England), 1945, Dodd, Mead (New York, NY), 1945.

Death of a Train, Hodder & Stoughton (London, England), 1946, Dodd, Mead (New York, NY), 1947.

Silence for the Murderer, Dodd, Mead (New York, NY), 1948.

Dark Journey, Dodd, Mead (New York, NY), 1951, published as *French Strikes Oil,* Hodder & Stoughton (London, England), 1952.

Anything to Declare?, Hodder & Stoughton (London, England), 1957.

CRIME SHORT STORIES

The Hunt Ball Murder, Todd (London, England), 1943.

Mr. Sefton, Murderer, Vallancey (London, England), 1944.

Murderers Make Mistakes, Hodder & Stoughton (London, England), 1947.

Many a Slip, Hodder & Stoughton (London, England), 1955.

The Mystery of the Sleeping Car Express (and Other Stories), Hodder & Stoughton (London, England), 1956.

OTHER

Bann and Lough Neagh Drainage, His Majesty's Stationery Office (Belfast, Northern Ireland), 1930.

Chief Inspector's Cases (radio play series), BBC, 1943.

Young Robin Brand, Detective (for children), University of London Press, 1947, Dodd, Mead (New York, NY), 1948.

The Four Gospels in One Story: Written as a Modern Biography, Longmans, Green (London, England), 1949.

Also author of plays *The Nine-Fifty Up Express,* 1942; *Mr. Pemberton's Commission* (based on his own story), 1952; *The Greuze,* 1953; and *East Wind,* 1953. Contributor of crime stories to books, including *The Floating Admiral,* Hodder & Stoughton (London, England), 1931, Doubleday, Doran (Garden City, NY), 1932; *The Anatomy of Murder: Famous Crimes Critically Considered by Members of the Detection Club,* Lane (London, England), 1936; *Six against the Yard,* Selwyn & Blount (London, England), 1936, published as *Six against Scotland Yard,* Doubleday, Doran (Garden City, NY), 1936; and *Double Death: A Murder Story,* Gollancz (London, England), 1939.

SIDELIGHTS: After beginning his career as a writer of detective stories rather late in his life, Freeman Wills Crofts found literary success with his first book, *The Cask,* and continued writing crime stories for thirty-seven years afterwards. Best known for the character "Mr. French," Crofts began writing as a way to pass the time during an illness, never suspecting that he had embarked upon a new career. After *The Cask* was published, Crofts began writing for a living and enjoyed a long and fruitful career. Today he is remembered as one of the authors who were part of the "Golden Age" of English detective fiction.

Born in Dublin, Ireland, on June 1, 1879, Crofts attended school in Belfast at the Methodist and Campbell College until 1896, when his uncle Berkeley D. Wise gave him a position as an apprentice in his department of civil engineers. After being promoted to Coleraine as the chief engineer, Crofts married Mary Bellas Canning in 1912. Another promotion came in 1923, and the Crofts relocated to Belfast. Crofts had been confined indoors after a serious illness in 1919, and it was during this time that he began writing *The Cask* as a way to pass the time. When he was well again, Crofts returned to his regular job. Reading his manuscript some time later, he believed it had potential and began to make revisions.

When he felt his book was ready, Crofts sent it to the literary agency of A. P. Watt, and Collins published it in 1920. The book tells the tale of Detective Georges La Touche and his quest to find the murderer of a young female whose body had been discovered in England inside a cask sent from France. The cask then vanishes, until Inspector Burnley locates it at the home of Felix Leon. Leon appears to recognize the body in the cask,

and in the next part of the tale Inspector Burnley works with Lefarge, another detective, to try and discover the truth. Leon appears to be the killer, but he does not have a motive for the crime. The probable murderer is taken into custody, but it is up to Detective La Touche to uncover the real killer, who has an alibi for the crime. However, La Touche proves that this alibi is false and catches the actual perpetrator. Although it is a more prolonged tale than similar stories at the time, Crofts' first novel was a huge success, and by 1939 it had sold one hundred thousand copies. As a critic for the *New York Times Book Review* stated in 1924, "[T]hat reader will be strong-minded, indeed, who can lay the book down until the very last page is reached." This achievement prompted Crofts to begin work on his second book, *The Ponson Case.*

The second novel became as popular as the first, and in 1929 Crofts left his position with the Belfast & Northern Counties Railway to write full time. Moving to southern England, he and his wife went from Blackheath to Worthing, where they settled permanently. During this time, besides writing, Crofts explored his talents as a carpenter, organist, and gardener.

After the initial Inspector French detective stories appeared, it became clear that he would become a favorite with readers. Crofts shared credit with Dorothy Sayers and Agatha Christie for establishing what is often called the "Golden Age" of detective novels in England, which began around 1918. As part of the Detection Club, Crofts was an influential participant and contributed to several volumes the group put out together, such as *The Anatomy of Murder* in 1936 and *Double Death* in 1939. The BBC also produced several of his brief detective dramas, the "Chief Inspector French's Cases" series, during World War II. These were later redone in story form in 1947 for inclusion in *Murderers Make Mistakes.*

After Crofts' initial four books, Inspector French became the linchpin of his detective stories. Inspector Joseph French of Scotland Yard is a reassuringly normal person, with no distinguishing physical characteristics or social status to cause him to stand out in a crowd. Generally a genial sort, he can be daunting should his work require it. Convinced that nothing happens without a reason, French doggedly solves his cases with unwavering persistence. A key feature of Crofts' work is that the cases are never solved without the investigation of several possible paths of inquiry. Inspector French is believable because he is not omniscient, though he picks up on possible solutions very rapidly. He is human in that he has enemies and desires to get ahead in his job.

Throughout the span of the Inspector French novels, it is possible to trace his career and achievements as he works his way through the ranks from inspector to chief superintendent. Although little is known about French's home life, it is revealed that he has a wife, Em, who is seen in various novels. French is not infallible, and he has made near-fatal errors at times, as in *The Hog's Back Mystery,* when he does not move quickly enough to stop another homicide. While the action in Crofts' novels varies, the endings are consistent in that the reader is told what occurred by the narrator after the case has been solved.

From his career with the Belfast & Northern Counties Railway, Crofts gathered his knowledge of train schedules that he put to frequent use in his novels. The injection of such realism into his novels is part of what made Crofts so popular in his day. He also paid particular attention to the details of the locations in his work. H. Douglas Thomson commented in his 1931 book, *Masters of Mystery: A Study of the Detective Story,* "Mr. Crofts's writing derives much if its effectiveness from the introduction of local colour. His novels have their setting in some precise district. Thus, to those who already know that particular district, there is an added charm."

Crofts likewise thought out his plots carefully, with solutions to the mysteries coming bit by bit as French unravels each criminal's plans. Crofts felt that the reader should have as hard a time solving the case as his fictional detectives did. While his use of timetables may have taxed his readers' knowledge a bit too much, it nevertheless made for a challenging read. By demanding his readers' full attention and participation in solving his mysteries, Crofts became one of the foremost detective fiction writers in England. Some of his books remain in print today and are a testament to the entertainment he provided readers through the years.

BIOGRAPHICAL/CRITICAL SOURCES:

BOOKS

Dictionary of Literary Biography, Volume 77: *British Mystery Writers, 1920-1939,* Gale (Detroit, MI), 1989.

Haycraft, Howard, *Murder for Pleasure: The Life and Times of the Detective Story,* Biblio & Tannen, 1968.

Henderson, Lesley, editor, *Twentieth-Century Crime and Mystery Writers,* third edition, St. James (Detroit, MI), 1991.

Routley, Erik, *The Puritan Pleasures of the Detective Story: A Personal Monograph,* Gollancz, 1972.

Symons, Julian, *Bloody Murder: From the Detective Story to the Crime Novel: A History,* Viking, 1984.

Thomson, H. Douglas, *Masters of Mystery: A Study of the Detective Story,* Collins, 1931.

Twentieth-Century Literary Criticism, Volume 55, Gale, 1995.

PERIODICALS

New York Times Book Review, December 21, 1924, review of *The Cask,* p. 17.*

*   *   *

CROOK, (Peter Michael) John 1946-

PERSONAL: Born June 30, 1946, in Hastings, England; son of Peter Howe (an architect) and Mary Elizabeth (Frewer) Crook. *Ethnicity:* "White." *Education:* Attended Eastbourne College, 1960-65; St. Catherine's College, B.A. and M.A., 1969; University of Bristol, certificate in education, 1970; Hertford College, D. Phil., 1995. *Politics:* "Conservative." *Religion:* Church of England. *Avocational interests:* "Foreign travel, modern languages, yachting, cycling, mountain walking, music."

ADDRESSES: Home—52 Canon St., Winchester, Hantshire SO23 9JW, England; fax: 01962-864392. *E-mail*—jcrook@netcomuk.co.uk.

CAREER: Lycée de Grand Air, Arcachon, France, English assistant, 1967-68; Université de Pau, France, English Lecteur, 1970-72; Eton College, Eton, England, assistant master, 1972-75; The Pilgrims' School, Winchester, England, assistant master, 1975-86; independent architectural historian, lecturer and photographer, 1985—. Dean and Chapter of Winchester, archaeological consultant, 1990—; University of Reading, honorary research fellow, 1997—, research fellow, 1998-99; St. Cross Hospital, archaeological consultant, 2000—.

MEMBER: British Archaeological Association, Athenæum.

AWARDS, HONORS: Fellow, Society of Antiquaries of London and Royal Asiatic Society.

WRITINGS:

A History of the Pilgrims' School, Winchester, and Earlier Choir-Schools, Phillimore, 1981, revised edition, 1991.

(With Ian T. Henderson) *The Winchester Diver,* Henderson and Stirk, 1984.

The Wainscot Book of Winchester Cathedral, 1660-1800, Hampshire Record Series, Volume VI, 1984.

Winchester Cathedral, Pitkin Pictorials (Andover), 1990, revised edition, 1998.

City of Winchester, Pitkin Pictorials, 1991.

Tile and Timber, Stone and Glass: The Craftsmen of Winchester Cathedral, Pitkin Pictorials, 1992.

(Editor and author) *Winchester Cathedral—Nine Hundred Years,* Phillimore, 1993.

The Architectural Setting of the Cult of Saints in the Early Christian West, c. 300-c. 1200 (Oxford Historical monographs series), Oxford University Press (New York, NY), 2000.

Contributor of more than forty articles to various books and periodicals, including *The Blackwell Encyclopaedia of Anglo-Saxon England,* edited by M. Lapidge, J. Blair, S. Keynes, and D. Scragg, Oxford University Press (New York, NY), 1999, *Medieval Archaeology, Antiquaries Journal, Proceedings of the Hampshire Field Club and Archaeological Society, Journal of the Society of Architectural Historians,* and *Archaeologia.* Editor, *Winchester Cathedral Record,* 1986-93.

WORK IN PROGRESS: Fifteenth-Century Chroniclers of Winchester Cathedral, for Oxford Medieval Texts series; *Winchester Cathedral Close,* "a long-term project intended as a companion volume to *Winchester Cathedral—Nine Hundred Years;*" *English Shrines,* for Boydell and Brewer; and *The Income Book of the Dean and Canons of Windsor: The Post-Medieval Canons' Houses,* for Friends of St. George's Windsor monograph series.

*   *   *

CROSLEY, Reginald O. 1937-

PERSONAL: Born July 10, 1937, in Petit-Goave, Haiti; immigrated to U.S., 1967; son of Leonard Gustave Crosley (a business administrator) and Suzanne Bichotte; married Bernadette Carré Crosley, October 22, 1966; children: Beatrice Regina Shields, Pascal George. *Ethnicity:* "Haitian-American." *Education:* Studied painting with painter Cédor at l'École des Beaux Arts, 1955; studied painting, perspective and art history with Expressionist painter Ernst Louisor; studied music with saxophonist Marcel Bichotte; Lycée Pétion, baccalaureate, Section A (Classe de lettres), 1957, Second part, 1958; studied theology, Group Biblique Universitaire, 1960-64; Faculté de Medecine, M.D. 1965. *Politics:* "Independent." *Religion:* Baptist. *Avocational interests:* "Poetry, philosophy, theology, metaphysics, sciences."

ADDRESSES: Home—4940 Pale Orchis Ct., Columbia, MD 21044. *Office*—1235 East Monument St., Baltimore, MD 21202; fax: 410-730-3924. *E-mail*—RegCrosley@aol.com.

CAREER: University Hospital, Port-au-Prince, Haiti, specialist in internal medicine, 1965-67; Queens Hospital Center, NY, residency in internal medicine, 1968-71, fellowship in nephrology (kidney disease), 1971-73; Brookdale Hospital, NY, attending physician in community medicine, 1973; private medical practice, Baltimore, MD, internal medicine and nephrology, 1974-2001; Provident Hospital, Baltimore, MD, assistant chief of medicine, 1974-75, director of Nephrology Division, 1975-85, psychiatric service internist, 1979-82. Group Biblique Universitaire, general secretary, 1959-65; First Baptist Church, prédicateur and Sunday school teacher, 1960-67.

MEMBER: AMHE (Haitian physicians in U.S. and Canada), American Medical Association, Haïte Littéraire (founding member), Monumental Medical Society, American Academy of Pain Management, Institute of Noetic Science, La Foundation Mémoire, Santa Barbara Congress, Haitian Studies Association, Med-Chi (Maryland Medical Society), Haitian Institute of Washington, DC (vice president).

WRITINGS:

Immanences (poetry), Cidihca (Montreal, Canada), 1988.

The Second Coming of Christ (nonfiction), Vantage (New York, NY), 1991.

The Vodou Quantum Leap (nonfiction), Llewellyn (Minneapolis, MN), 2000.

Secrets of Miracles, Llewellyn (Minneapolis, MN), 2001.

WORK IN PROGRESS: Deep Secrets of Miraculous Healings: A Theory of Miracles, In Search of Black Eurydice, novel; *Dark Splendor, Ivory Lust,* novel; *Black Master Races in the Bible.*

CUHULAIN, Kerr
  See ENNIS, Charles A(lbert)

D

DALLAL, Alberto 1936-

PERSONAL: Born June 6, 1936, in Mexico City, Mexico. *Education:* Attended National University.

ADDRESSES: Office—National University of Mexico, Catalogo de Revistas de Arte y Cultura, South Insurgents #3744, Tlalpan D.F., CP 14000, Mexico; fax:(52-5)665 47 40.

CAREER: Writer. Escuela Nacional Preparatoria, professor. Assistant to director, National School of Architecture's Grupo de Teatro; Institute of Aesthetic Investigations. Literary and dance critic; actor in various productions.

AWARDS, HONORS: Madga Donato Award, 1979, for *La danza contra la muerte;* Prize Xavier Villaurrutia, 1982, for *El "dancing" Méxicano.*

WRITINGS:

El capitán queda inmóvil (one-act play; title means "The Captain Stays Still"), in *La Palabra y el Hombre,* 1961.
El hombre debajo del agua (three-act play; title means "The Man Under Water"), Universidad Veracruzana (Xalapa, Mexico), 1962.
El poder de la urraca (novel; title means "The Power of the Magpie"), Organizacíon Editorial Novaro (Mexico), 1969.
Las ínsulas extrañas (novel; title means "The Strange Isles"), Organizacíon Editorial Novaro (Mexico), 1970.
Siete piezas para la escena (plays; title means "Seven Plays for the Stage"), 1970.
El amor por las ciudades, Universidad Nacional Autónoma de México (Mexico City, Mexico), 1972.

Geminis (short stories), Arte y Libros (Mexico), 1974.
La danza moderna, Fondo de Cultura Económica (Mexico City, Mexico), 1975.
Efectos, rastros, definiciones, Arte y Libros (Mexico), 1977.
La danza contra la muerte (title means "Dance Against Death"), Universidad Nacional Autónoma de México (Mexico City, Mexico), 1979.
(With Rafael Doniz) *Louis Falco,* Arte y Libros (Mexico), 1979.
(With Rafael Doniz) *Tres actores mexicanos: Rosenda Monteros, Alejandro Camacho, Claudio Obregón* (title means "Three Mexican Actors: Rosenda Monteros, Alejandro Camacho, Claudio Obregón"), Arte y Libros (Mexico), 1979.
El "dancing" Méxicano, Oasis (Mexico), 1982.
Fínina, Universidad Nacional Autónoma de México (Mexico City, Mexico), 1985.
La danza en situacióne, Gernika, 1985.
Fémina-danza (biographies), Universidad Nacional Autónoma de México (Mexico City, Mexico), 1985.
Periodismo y literaturi, Universidad Nacional Autónoma de México (Mexico City, Mexico), 1985.
La danza en México (title means "Dance in Mexico"), Universidad Nacional Autónoma de México (Mexico City, Mexico), Volume 1: *Panorama crítico,* 1986, Volume 2, 1989, Volume 3: *La danza escénica popular, 1877-1930,* 1994, Volume 4: *La Danza escáica,* 1995.
Todo el hilo, Plaza & Jánes (Mexico City, Mexico), 1986.
Cómo acercarse a la danza, Querétaro/Plaza & Valdés (Mexico City, Mexico), 1988.
Lenguajes periodisticos, Universidad Nacional Autónoma de México (Mexico City, Mexico), 1989.

El aura de cuerpo (articles; title means "The Aura of the Body"), Universidad Nacional Autónoma de México (Mexico City, Mexico), 1990.

Actas referenciales, Editorial Aldus (Mexico), 1996.

Más, Universidad Autónoma Metropolitana (Mexico), 1996.

La abolición del arte, Universidad Nacional Autónoma de México (Mexico City, Mexico), 1998.

Also contributor to various publications. Contributor to periodicals, including *La Palabra y el Hombre, Cuadernos Americanos, La Cultura en México, Cuadernos del Viento,* and *Revista Mexicana de Literatura.* Editor, *Universidad de México.*

SIDELIGHTS: Alberto Dallal is a Mexican writer whose works include drama, fiction, and various articles and essays on dance. Dallal studied architecture at Mexico's National University, and he subsequently worked as a professor and an actor. His earliest books include *El hombre debajo del agua,* a three-act drama that he published in 1962. In *El hombre debajo del agua,* Dallal questions the value of good deeds derived from individual, as opposed to group, efforts.

Dallal followed his plays with two novels, *El poder de la urraca* and *Las ínsulas extrañas,* another play, *Siete piezas para la escena,* and a short-story collection, *Geminis.* These works show Dallal to be a writer of wide-ranging interests and abilities. *El poder de la urraca,* for example, serves to demonstrate Dallal's affinity for both radical storytelling techniques, including methods derived from filmmaking, and the subject of human relationships. The stories in *Geminis,* meanwhile, show Dallal striving to articulate the nature of love.

Dallal's many writings on dance include *El aura del cuerpo,* a collection of articles earlier featured in various periodicals; *La danza en México,* a four-volume chronicle ranging from the pre-Columbian era to the twentieth century; and *La danza contra la muerte,* a collection of assorted materials produced by Dallal over two decades of writing.

BIOGRAPHICAL/CRITICAL SOURCES:

BOOKS

Brushwood, John S., *México en su novela,* FCE, 1966, pp. 118-119.*

DALTON, Pamela
  See JOHNSON, Pamela

*   *   *

DASH, Mike

PERSONAL: Male. *Education:* Attended Cambridge University.

ADDRESSES: Office—c/o Crown/Random House, 201 East 50th Street, New York, NY 10022.

CAREER: Professional historian, writer and magazine publisher. Appears regularly on British radio and television.

WRITINGS:

Borderlands: The Ultimate Exploration of the Surrounding Unknown, Overlook Press (Woodstock, NY), 1999.

Tulipomania: The Story of the World's Most Coveted Flower and the Extraordinary Passions It Aroused, Crown (New York, NY), 2000

SIDELIGHTS: Mike Dash, who is characterized by reviewers as a rationalist skeptic, spent a great deal of time investigating accounts of UFOs, spontaneous human combustion, phone calls from beyond the grave, and other spooky phenomena. As chief researcher for the *Fortean Times,* a periodical devoted to strange phenomena, Dash says, "If half of one percent of such phenomena turn out to be true, science will be revolutionized, history rewritten, and . . . we are likely to learn much about the nature of perception, memory, and belief."

In addition, Dash notes, belief in such phenomena has changed history. For example, in 1856, a young African girl—a member of the Xhosa tribe—had a vision in which two beings told her that sinful people should slaughter all their cattle. Her people believed in the vision, and killed 400,000 cattle, which led to the death of 40,000 Xhosa people and the absorption of their territory by South Africa. Dash believes that many of bizarre phenomena are the result of biochemical factors, such as epilepsy, oxygen starvation, and other problems, but not all of the events he mentions have an explanation.

In *Tulipomania,* Dash examines the "tulip mania" of 1633-67, when Dutch society was overtaken by a passion for the flowers. Bulbs were sold for huge prices—often for as much as the cost of two houses. Some flowers, which were gaudily striped, were ironically the result of a virus that weakened the plants, making them more rare. At the height of the mania, even average flowers were sold for huge prices. The market collapsed almost overnight after reaching this peak of frenzy, and a wave of bankruptcy and despair among tulip speculators ensued.

Junny Uglow wrote in the *Times Literary Supplement* that Dash "has the story-teller's knack of making his readers feel present in the sweaty, smoke-filled taverns of [the Dutch city of] Haarlem, where the trade took place in an alcoholic haze. Dash's skill is to make the madness and its aftermath not merely plausible, but almost inevitable."

BIOGRAPHICAL/CRITICAL SOURCES:

PERIODICALS

New Scientist, October 4, 1997, p. 42.
Publishers Weekly, November 15, 1999, p. 50.
Times Literary Supplement, October 15, 1999.*

* * *

DAVIES, Merton E(dward) 1917-2001

OBITUARY NOTICE—See index for *CA* sketch: Born September (some sources say March) 13, 1917, in St. Paul, MN; died after complications from surgery, April 17, 2001, in Santa Monica, CA. Engineer, space cartographer and author. Davies was a pioneer in the aerospace industry, getting into the field in 1940 when he was hired by Douglas Aircraft. A native of the Midwest, Davies moved to the West Coast when he was accepted at Stanford University, from which he graduated in 1938. He worked briefly as a math instructor at the University of Nevada at Reno, but then joined Douglas, figuring the math necessary for flying fighter planes. In 1948 he transferred to its subsidiary, the Rand project, where he stayed for fifty years. During the 1950s at Rand, Davies worked on technical projects and designed satellite vehicles, becoming integrally involved with cameras for reconnaissance satellites. Davies' knowledge of the satellites and images they collected was of interest to the government, and for several years he analyzed photos for the Pentagon, interpreting weapons systems from countries like the Soviet Union and doing highly classified work for the Air Force. All the

while working at Rand, Davies also helped NASA with its program to explore other planets. He and fellow staffers made maps of the skies and helped plan space missions including Galileo, Mariner and Voyager. Davies co-wrote a trio of books: *The View From Space: Photographic Exploration of the Planets,* with Bruce C. Murray; *Atlas of Mercury,* with Stephen E. Dwornick, Donald E. Gault, and Robert G. Strom; and *RAND's Role in the Evolution of Balloon and Satellite Observation Systems and Related U.S. Space Technology.*

OBITUARIES AND OTHER SOURCES:

PERIODICALS

Los Angeles Times, April 21, 2001, p. B6.
New York Times, April 21, 2001, p. A11.
Washington Post, April 22, 2001, p. C6.

* * *

DAVIES, Pete 1959-

PERSONAL: Born 1959.

ADDRESSES: Office—c/o Author Mail, Henry Holt, 115 W. 18th St., New York, NY 10011.

CAREER: Author.

WRITINGS:

The Last Election (novel), A. Deutsch (London, England), 1986, reprinted, Vintage (New York, NY), 1987.
Dollarville (novel), Random House (New York, NY), 1989.
All Played Out: The Full Story of Italia '90, Mandarin (London, England), 1991.
Storm Country: A Journey Through the Heart of America, Random House (New York, NY), 1992.
Twenty-Two Foreigners in Funny Shorts: The Intelligent Fan's Guide to Soccer and World Cup '94, Random House (New York, NY), 1994.
I Lost My Heart to the Belles, Heinemann (London, England), 1996.
This England, Little, Brown (London, England), 1997.
Mad Dogs and Englishwomen: The Story of England at the 6th Women's Cricket World Cup in India, Abacus (London, England), 1998.
Catching Cold: 1918's Forgotten Tragedy and the Scientific Hunt for the Virus That Caused It, Michael

Joseph (London, England), 1999, reprinted as *The Devil's Flu: The World's Deadliest Influenza Epidemic and the Scientific Hunt for the Virus That Caused It,* Henry Holt (New York, NY), 2000.

Inside the Hurricane, Henry Holt (New York, NY), 2000.

SIDELIGHTS: Welsh author Pete Davies's first novel, *The Last Election,* was published in 1986 and is set in the 1990s. *Times Literary Supplement* contributor J. K. L. Walker wrote that the book "has an underlying, if simplistic moral concern which might be seen as justifying its terrorist tactics." Britain is ruled by the Money Party and Nanny, the prime minister. There is social and moral breakdown, with the poor and unemployed being manipulated by mind-controlling music, drugs, and televised snooker. The rich and powerful are safe in their fortified offices and homes, while the masses roam garbage-filled and dangerous streets and are treated for illness in state-controlled hospitals under slum-like conditions. They have nothing to look forward to but state-offered free cremation at death, which is hurried along to eliminate the elderly who burden the system.

Young club owner Grief discovers the plot to reduce the aging population. Another resister is Bludge, a female police inspector. The narrator, Wally Wasted, is a television personality under the influence of hashish. The government allows him his on-air drug-induced ramblings to alleviate the boredom of the masses. Patrick McGrath wrote in the *New York Times Book Review* that "one is inevitably reminded of Orwell, and also of the early Waugh, whose rage at the passing of an old order provoked him to kill off lightly sketched characters with all the grim relish we find here. Like Waugh, Pete Davies employs a mordant humor to mask his nostalgia, though unlike Waugh what he mourns is the demise of democracy, for his is the anger of a dispossessed and disillusioned generation that sees itself condemned to inherit merely the moribund remnants of a once vigorous political culture."

A *Kirkus Reviews* contributor called Davies's *Dollarville* (1989) "a rambunctious trip down Apocalypse Lane, written with high intensity and humor. Davies understands how ludicrous modern life has become, and his fine second novel . . . gleefully highlights its absurdities." The people of the Third World are manipulated by the rich and powerful Western countries of Dollarville with American-style sports, sex, and religion, all provided by the cable networks who rule over all. The president of the United States is more interested in these diversions than in governing. There may be no

hope for a world mired in political, economic, and environmental devastation, but most people are resigned to their fate. Charlie Fish, who works in public relations, meets Melinda Isenhope, a rhinoceros expert who, due to AIDS paranoia, is prohibited from returning to the United States because she was given African blood after a rhino crushed her legs. The plot includes a friendly alien, doper astronauts, black marketeers, mercenaries, and a civil war.

Publishers Weekly reviewer Sybil Steinberg commented, "That's the bare bones." Steinberg compared Davies's humor, plot, and dialogue to that of Burgess's *A Clockwork Orange,* and called *Dollarville* "an amazingly funny, believably bleak vision of an awful world—awfully similar to ours." Roz Kaveney, writing in the *Times Literary Supplement,* maintained, "Some of the time this is a satire, and occasionally it is funny; more often it is a dark SF thriller in which there is no guarantee that anyone gets out alive." Beth Levine concurred in the *New York Times Book Review,* averring that Davies "possesses a mischievous, wry wit and a wonderful eye for the illuminating detail. One's pleasure in his energetic and unruly tale is dimmed only by the fact that his bleak predictions for our future seem uncomfortably on target."

In writing *All Played Out: The Full Story of Italia '90,* Davies spent nearly a year before and during the 1990 World Cup event, following England's team from Sweden to Turin. Andrew Clifford remarked in *Listener* that Davies concentrated "on the wider cultural and human aspects of the event—the media village, the class system, the press gang, the moral and psychological values of the footballers. All these are examined in what is an excellent and entertaining book." Davies provides interviews with the players and criticizes those who sell stories to the tabloids. Clifford added that the book "is weakest during Davies's narration of the crucial England games, where he is perhaps understandably reduced to a tackle-by-tackle account. This leaves the last 100 pages, which deal with these matches, without a sense of climax. Together with Davies's failure to stun with analysis, this robs the book of a really powerful heart." John Lanchester wrote in the *London Review of Books* that "there are one or two moments in *All Played Out* when Davies's blokily street-wise rhetoric starts to grate, but that's hardly surprising in a book of this length written at what must have been considerable speed. There certainly won't be a better book written about what was, after all, the most engrossing cultural event of 1990."

Storm Country: A Journey Through the Heart of America documents Davies's 7,500-mile road trip during which he covered thirteen states, starting from Coffeyville, Kansas, in a 1981 Ford pickup. *Times Literary Supplement* reviewer John Williams called the book "a decent, unpretentious addition to travel writing about America." Davies fills the book with his experiences and stories of the people he met. He describes the tornadoes and storms of the Midwest, and his many stops at bars, stores, gas stations, diners, a rodeo, a baseball game, even a wedding where he gave away the bride. A *Kirkus Reviews* contributor felt that "although Davies looks with gusto at all the right places . . . he sees only America's surface, never its beating heart." Francis X. Clines contended in the *New York Times Book Review* that each story is "pretty much told . . . to the point of Chaucerian overdrive." But Douglas Kennedy opined in *New Statesman & Society* that "what makes Davies's variations on this 'get your kicks on Route 66' theme so refreshing is his unjaundiced foreign eye for the nuances of Americanness. Indeed, he is an unapologetic romantic when it comes to such wide-open country."

New York Times Book Review contributor Christopher Clarey reviewed *Twenty-Two Foreigners in Funny Shorts: The Intelligent Fan's Guide to Soccer and World Cup '94,* calling it "long on energy, wit and soccer wisdom, . . . [including] a memorable chapter on how cultural differences manifest themselves on the field." *Aethlon* reviewer David C. Ward criticized the title, complaining that "there's nothing especially funny about soccer shorts." Ward felt the book "doesn't really work. . . . One suspects that the format of this book was a publisher's brainstorm." Davies addresses both the World Cup and his team's (Wrexham) struggle in 1993 to get to the Second Division. "Introducing all the players on the team and having them describe what they do, Davies gives the reader a playing-field view of soccer, concisely describing the rules of the game without bogging the reader down in basics," averred Matthew Yeomans in the *Village Voice.* Davies wrote about women's soccer in *I Lost My Heart to the Belles* (1996). He was so fascinated by the Doncaster Belles that he moved to Yorkshire to write the book, which had begun as an article.

Times Literary Supplement contributor Tony Gould noted that *This England,* a "breathless account of last year's general election campaign in the Calder Valley in Yorkshire . . . already has a dated feel about it. . . . The hopes and fears chronicled here have yet to be realized one way or the other." Gould said of Davies's style that "the influence of Tom Wolfe and the New Journalism is a little too pervasive. . . . It is clear from very

early on that this is not going to be a detached, neutral account of the political process at a local level, but a fan's book. . . . Politics isn't football, and to write about it as though it were is to demean it still further at a time when, heaven knows, it is lacking enough in dignity."

Observer reviewer Peter Preston claimed that most modern British post-election books "are psephological analyses pavilioned in statistics. They tell you why what happened happened. Davis tries to explain how it felt while it was happening." Preston continued that "the core of the book—the de facto plot—rests, blow by blow, with the Labour campaign and with Christine McCafferty, a formidably dedicated welfare worker. She's the heroine of the piece: nervy, exhausted, gauche, always battling. But Davies obviously reveres her—and her second husband, Donald Tarlo—too much. They, like all their team, are admirable cyphers. They do nothing but toil devotedly and win."

Carol Cooper noted in *Lancet* that the short title of Davies's *Catching Cold: 1918's Forgotten Tragedy and the Scientific Hunt for the Virus That Caused It,* isn't appropriate, since the cold and influenza are not the same thing. The book was reprinted in the United States as *The Devil's Flu: The World's Deadliest Influenza Epidemic and the Scientific Hunt for the Virus That Caused It.* Davies opens with an account of the 1997 outbreak of avian flu that mutated in Hong Kong to become a human disease. After the death of a child, a local lab found that the cause of death was from a flu virus, but not one of the two human strains. A sample was diagnosed in Holland as a bird virus. A million birds were killed to avoid the kind of pandemic that occurred in 1918. This near catastrophe highlighted the need to uncover the virus responsible for the 1918 outbreak.

The "Spanish" flu epidemic of 1918 took the lives of forty million people. In India corpses filled the rivers, when firewood for burning the bodies was depleted. In Philadelphia, 7,500 died in less than two weeks, and there weren't enough coffins to bury the dead. United States troop carriers became ghost ships as entire crews died, and in Alaska, families were devoured by their dogs. During the late 1990s, virologists exhumed bodies in the United States, as well as others frozen since that time in the Arctic Circle. Pathologist Johan Hultin offered to return to Alaska to continue the work of his 1951 investigation, conducted before modern methods for processing tissue samples had been developed. Hultin was in his seventies when he returned. Alex Butterworth wrote in the *Observer* that "having concluded his 'unfinished business,' Hultin crafts by hand the wooden crosses that dignify the reburied dead, and offers us some glimmer of hope that ours is a species worth saving." Butterworth called *Catching Cold* "rich in interest and truly alarming in its prognosis." The 1918 flu was eventually identified as one of the human strains.

Cooper said Davies "has quite a knack for the kind of language that many a thriller writer might envy. . . . Throughout, Davies peppers his story with lively descriptions of the virologists involved and quotes some as saying that a particular flu strain is 'like an alien' or that viruses behave 'like terrorists.' " Anne Hardy wrote in the *Times Literary Supplement* that "the interest of his readable book lies less in the stories of past tragedy and of present adventure in the permafrost than in its account of the scientific influenza community, of scientific cooperation and competition, and of the crucial influence of money."

Hardy pointed out that influenza does not constitute a research priority. Considerable money is spent to manufacturer vaccines, but little on research. Hardy also noted that the new neuraminidase inhibitors, drugs that will halt the flu if taken within thirty-six hours of infection, will be beneficial only to people in the developed countries who can afford them. Tony Gould commented in *Spectator* that "as Davies writes, 'science is a cut-throat trade'; scientists may be working for the good of humanity, but they are also human beings, subject to the same pressures and ambitions as the rest of us, so it is hardly surprising that 'impressively large brains come housed in depressingly small minds.' "

BIOGRAPHICAL/CRITICAL SOURCES:

PERIODICALS

Aethlon, spring, 1995, David C. Ward, review of *Twenty-Two Foreigners in Funny Shorts* and *All Played Out,* p. 190.

Booklist, October 1, 1989, review of *Dollarville,* p. 261; March 15, 1993, Gilbert Taylor, review of *Storm Country,* p. 1292.

Books, January, 1990, review of *Dollarville,* pp. 4, 18; summer, 1998, review of *Mad Dogs and Englishwomen,* p. 22.

Books & Bookmen, March, 1986, review of *The Last Election,* p. 36.

British Book News, March, 1986, review of *The Last Election,* p. 176.

Kirkus Reviews, August 15, 1989, review of *Dollarville,* p. 1185; April 1, 1993, review of *Storm Country,* p. 423.

Lancet, October 9, 1999, Carol Cooper, "Waiting for the big one," p. 1310.

Library Journal, October 1, 1989, Albert E. Wilhelm, review of *Dollarville,* p. 116.

Listener, November 22, 1990, Andrew Clifford, "Two Halves," p. 31.

Locus, November, 1989, review of *Dollarville,* p. 54.

London Review of Books, December 6, 1990, John Lanchester, "Born of the age we live in," pp. 17-18.

New Statesman, January 31, 1986, John Clute, review of *The Last Election,* p. 29; August 1, 1997, Decca Aitkenhead, "Scoundrel's last refuge," pp. 44-45.

New Statesman & Society, November 23, 1990, Adrianne Blue, review of *All Played Out,* p. 35; July 3, 1992, Douglas Kennedy, "The real America," pp. 36-37.

New York Times Book Review, March 22, 1987, Patrick McGrath, "Offing the Oldies," p. 21; November 19, 1989, Beth Levine, "In short; fiction," p. 24; May 9, 1993, Francis X. Clines, "They See America Rolling," p. 1; June 19, 1994, Christopher Clarey, "Just for Kicks," p. 14.

Observer, January 26, 1986, review of *The Last Election,* p. 51; July 20, 1997, Peter Preston, "Round the May poll," p. 16; August 29, 1999, Alex Butterworth, "An uncommon cold," p. 14.

Publishers Weekly, September 1, 1989, Sybil Steinberg, review of *Dollarville,* p. 73; March 22, 1993, review of *Storm Country,* p. 62.

Punch, November 21, 1990, Jasper Rees, "Terrace firma," pp. 46-47.

Spectator, August 14, 1999, Tony Gould, "Virushunting in the Arctic Circle," pp. 35-36.

Times Higher Education Supplement, November 5, 1999, Christopher Wills, review of *Catching Cold,* p. 25.

Times Literary Supplement, February 14, 1986, J. K. L. Walker, "Disimproving prospects," p. 162; March 9, 1990, Roz Kaveney, "Last things and after," p. 258; December 25, 1992, John Williams, "Middle men," p. 25; February 13, 1998, Tony Gould, "Tightly closed mind at work," p. 33; September 3, 1999, Anne Hardy, "Hard to shake off," p. 31.

Tribune Books (Chicago), February 22, 1987, Clarence Petersen, "Words worth reading: Petersen's paperback picks," p. 5.

Village Voice, May 17, 1994, Matthew Yeomans, "Goal-Oriented," p. 62.*

DAVIS, Timothy G.   1958-

PERSONAL: Born August 12, 1958, in Sioux Falls, SD; son of William G. Davis and Beverly J. Kittelson; married Elia E. Cano (a bank consultant), February 8, 1980; children: David Cano (stepson), Gissel A., Andrea A. *Ethnicity:* "Caucasian." *Education:* Attended various military service academies; awarded Trainer's Certification from the United States Federal Government, 1982. *Politics:* Republican. *Religion:* Lutheran. *Avocational interests:* "Writing, history buff, international travel."

ADDRESSES: Home—5000 South Nevada Ave., Sioux Falls, SD 57108. *E-mail*—panama@dakota.net.

CAREER: QVC Network, Inc., Plymouth, MN, assistant call center manager, 1987-91; Carlson Marketing Group, Maple Plain, MN, call center consultant, 1991; Gage Marketing Group, Maple Plain, MN, supervisor, 1991-92; Lawrence & Schiller, Sioux Falls, SD, supervisor and account executive, 1993-95; Gateway, Sioux Falls, SD, sales consultant, 1995-99; TeleSpectrum Worldwide, Inc., Milbank, SD, general manager, 1999-2000; Trader Publishing, Sioux Falls, SD, sales manager, 2000; KSFY TV, Sioux Falls, SD, internet sales coordinator, 2000—. *Military service:* U.S. Army, 1976-83, served as airborne ranger in Special Operations Units primarily in the Americas and Europe; became E-6(P).

WRITINGS:

The Southern Cross (suspense novel), Writers Club, 2000.

WORK IN PROGRESS: Day of the Ranger, "a suspense novel that takes place in Africa and South America;" *Cooper Penny,* novel; research on "street life in Panama."

SIDELIGHTS: Timothy G. Davis told *CA:* "I love writing. I always have. I was the kid in school that wanted more writing assignments. I love to tell a good story. If I had been born centuries ago, I'd be the guy at the campfire that would keep you awake with a good tale. I like to move people through my writing, to make you think.

"Daily events from around the world [influence my work]. All you have to do is open the newspaper or log on to the web and find a story. I get a lot of ideas about political intrigue from today's headlines."

"I like to write at night, typically every night, for three to four hours. First, I develop a rough outline of the story. Then, the fun part. I write. I don't worry about editing or polishing at this point. Just good, raw writing. Then, I go back and revise my outline, I firm it up more. Then I start the process of going through the whole story and polishing it, getting rid of words that aren't working, and rewriting as necessary.

"As far as writers go, Ernest Hemmingway had a big influence on me. After my years in the army and seeing the world from a very unique perspective, I felt that there were things that needed to be remembered, to be told and passed on to others. I love to write about political intrigue, espionage and suspense."

*   *   *

DAWES, Kwame   1962-

PERSONAL: Born July 28, 1962, in Ghana; emigrated to the United States; son of Neville (a writer) and Sophia (an artist and social worker; maiden name Tevi) Dawes; married Lorna (a librarian), July 14, 1990; children: Sena, Kekeli, Akua. *Education:* University of the West Indies, B.A. (Honors), 1983; University of New Brunswick, Ph.D., 1992. *Ethnicity:* "African-Caribbean." *Religion:* Christian.

ADDRESSES: Home—4 Doral Court, Columbia, SC 29229. *Office*—Department of English, College of Liberal Arts, University of South Carolina, Columbia, SC 29208. *Agent*—Melanie Abrahams, Renaissance One, P.O. Box 22004, London SW2 5ZS, England. *E-mail*—dawesk@gwm.sc.edu.

CAREER: Poet, storyteller, musician, and arts consultant. University of South Carolina, Sumter, SC, assistant professor of English, 1992-96, chairman of the Division of Arts and Letters, 1993-96; University of South Carolina, Columbia, SC, guest lecturer, 1994, associate professor, 1996—, director of M.F.A. program, 2001—. Associate fellow, Centre for Caribbean Studies, Warwick University, 1996; visiting fellow, University of Wisconsin, Eau Claire, WI, 1999. Founder and artistic director, Christian Graduate Theatre Company, Kingston, Jamaica, c. 1982; former lead singer in Ujamaa, a reggae band. Has appeared on radio and television in the Caribbean, the United Kingdom, Canada, Sweden, and the United States.

MEMBER: National Book Critics Circle.

Kwame Dawes

AWARDS, HONORS: Writing Fellow, International Writing Program, University of Iowa, 1986; grant award, "Alternative Roots Collaborative Arts Project," 1994; research and productive scholarship award, University of South Carolina, 1994; Forward Poetry Prize for best first collection, 1994, for *Progeny of Air;* Hugh T. Stoddard, Sr. Award for Distinguished Service as a faculty member, University of South Carolina—Sumter, 1994; two Multicultural Grants, South Carolina Arts Commission, 1995; Individual Artist Award, South Carolina Arts Commission, 1996; Poetry Business Prize, Smith/Doorstop Press, 2000, for *Mapmaker;* Hollis Summers Poetry Prize, Ohio University Press, 2000, for *Midland;* Pushcart Prize, 2001, for poem "Inheritance."

WRITINGS:

POETRY

Progeny of Air, Peepal Tree Press (Leeds, England), 1994.

Resisting the Anomie, Goose Lane Editions (Fredericton, Canada), 1995.

Prophets, Peepal Tree Press (Leeds, England), 1995

Requiem, Peepal Tree Press (Leeds, England), 1996.

Jacko Jacobus, Peepal Tree Press (Leeds, England), 1996.

Shook Foil: A Collection of Reggae Poems, Peepal Tree Press (Leeds, England), 1997.

(Editor) *Wheel and Come Again: An Anthology of Reggae Poems,* Peepal Tree Press (Leeds, England), 1998.

Mapmaker (chapbook), Smith/Doorstop (Westgate, England), 2000.

Midland, Ohio University Press (Athens, OH), 2001.

PLAYS

In the Warmth of the Cold, produced at the Little Theatre, Kingston, Jamaica, 1982.

And the Gods Fell, produced at the Dramatic Theatre, Kingston, Jamaica, 1983.

The Martyr, produced at Bethlehem Teachers' College, Jamaica, 1985.

In Chains of Freedom, produced at the Dramatic Theatre, Kingston, Jamaica, 1984.

The System, produced at the College of Arts, Science, and Technology, Kingston, Jamaica, 1984.

It Burns and It Stings, produced as part of Island Tour, Jamaica, 1985.

Even Unto Death, produced at the Creative Arts Centre, Kingston, Jamaica, 1985.

Charity's Come, produced at the Jamaica School of Drama, Island Tour, 1985, and at the Sumter Little Theater, Sumter, SC, 1998.

Friends and Almost Lovers, produced at the University of the West Indies, Antigua, 1986.

Dear Pastor, produced at the Jamaica School of Drama, Island Tour, 1986.

Confessions, produced at the Dramatic Theatre, Island Tour, Jamaica, 1986.

Brown Leaf and Other Plays, produced at the University of New Brunswick, Fredericton, Canada, 1987.

Coming in from the Cold, produced at the University of New Brunswick, Fredericton, Canada, 1988.

Song of an Injured Stone (musical), produced at the University of the West Indies, Antigua, 1988.

Charades, produced at the Enterprise Theatre, Fredericton, Canada, 1990.

Stump of the Terebinth, produced at the University of South Carolina at Sumter, 1994.

A Celebration of Struggle, produced at the University of South Carolina, Sumter, SC, 1995.

One Love (inspired by the novel *Brother Man* by Roger Mais; produced at the Bristol Old Vic and at the Lyric Theatre, Hammersmith, London, England, 2001), Methuen (London, England), 2001.

Also author of radio plays *Samaritans,* produced for CBC Morningside, 1992, 1993, 1994; *Salut Haiti,* produced for CBC Atlantic Airwaves, 1993; *New World A-Comin',* produced for CBC Morningside, 1994.

OTHER

Natural Mysticism: Towards a New Reggae Aesthetic in Caribbean Writing (nonfiction), Peepal Tree Press (Leeds, England), 1997.
(Editor) *Talk Yuh Talk: Interviews with Anglophone Caribbean Poets,* University of Virginia Press (Charlottesville, VA), 2000.
A Place to Hide (short stories), Peepal Tree Press (Leeds, England), 2001.
Bivouac (novel), Peepal Tree Press (Leeds, England), 2002.

Work represented in anthologies, including *Poems for the Beekeeper: An Anthology of Modern Poetry,* edited by Robert Gent, Five Leaves Press, 1996; *Step into a World: A Global Anthology of the New Black Literature,* edited by Kevin Powell, J. Wiley, 2000; and *Brown Sugar: A Collection of Erotic Black Fiction,* edited Carol Taylor, Plume Books, 2001. Contributor of fiction, essays, and book reviews to numerous journals and periodicals, including *African American Review, Critical Quarterly, Poetry Review, Journal of West Indian Studies, Washington Post Book World, London Review of Books, Emerge, World Press Review,* and *World Literature Today.* Criticism editor, *Obsidian,* 2000—; series editor, Caribbean Play Series, Peepal Tree Press, 1999—.

WORK IN PROGRESS: In Sepia, and Other Writings: A Retrospective on the Writing of Neville Dawes, for Peepal Tree Press; *A Far Cry from Plymouth: A Memoir; The Art of Bob Marley: Essays on the Literary Value of Marley's Lyrics; Arabna and the Fish* (children's novel); several collections of poetry.

SIDELIGHTS: Kwame Dawes was born in Ghana but moved to Jamaica as a child, and has also lived in England, Canada, and the United States. He is a writer and teacher of English who, according to Sudeep Sen in *World Literature Today,* "is young, highly original, and intelligent, possessing an poetic sensibility that is rooted and sound, unshakable and unstoppable, in both its vibrancy and its direction." Sen also wrote that Dawes's first collection of poems, *Progeny of Air,* was "a tremor that is hard to get away from, a shift that is unobtrusive and quiet but powerful, an impact that leaves us stirred, that jolts the imagination and thought dramatically." The poems, many of which use two- and three-line structures, vividly explore issues of colonization and emigration, relationships between teachers and students, and cross-cultural encounters.

In *Resisting the Anomie,* Dawes takes on the character of an explorer who examines the spiritual connections between Africa and all the Africans in the world who have left their home continent, whether willingly or unwillingly, and come to the Caribbean. Adele S. Newson wrote in *World Literature Today* that the poems "draw the reader into worlds of sexuality, loss, celebration, and discovery" and summed up the collection as "dynamic . . . disturbing . . . linguistically engaging . . . [and] expansive." Rita Donovan wrote in *Books in Canada* that Dawes's background as a reggae musician is evident in the poems, and Roger Nash, noting this same musical quality, remarked that like reggae musician Bob Marley, Dawes knows "how to fuse physical grace with emancipator energy."

In *Prophets,* Dawes continues his pattern of using a three-line structure in poetry, and also continues his use of musical reggae-inspired elements and themes. As Sudeep Sen wrote in *World Literature Today,* Dawes mingles "charisma and comment, imagination and documentary, invoking elements from the genre of popular culture, subculture, Jamaican ethos and song, effectively and lyrically."

Shook Foil draws on the work of Caribbean poet Derek Walcott, and the work of T. S. Eliot and Lorna Goodison and, as Dawes notes, "attempts to define reggae and the major personality behind the success of the music, Bob Marley." As reviewer Geoffrey Philp wrote in *Caribbean Writer,* "It was Marley who taught my generation how to be Jamaican and pan-African . . . how to honor ourselves and others, and finally how to love." In the poems, Dawes works to reconcile the western, Judeo-Christian tradition of shame in the body and sexuality with the open-hearted passion and joy of reggae. Like Marley, Dawes works to reconcile the split between body and spirit, and as Philp commented, "To really enjoy the music, you must believe."

Of *Shook Foil,* Dawes wrote on his Web site, "[It] was written as a way to realize a truth that has haunted my poetry for a long time: that my poems and my very imagination have been shaped significantly by a spiritual, intellectual and emotional engagement with reggae music. In this poem I recount the moment when I learned of the death of Bob Marley, an artist of especial importance to me. The weight of that loss, the legacy of his art and its impact on my imagination all form part of the aesthetic that under girds this poem."

Dawes told *CA* that his research into folk life in the South, the Caribbean and Africa has provided him with fodder for his poetry and his storytelling. Dawes is also engaged in research into post-colonial literature and theory and writing from Africa and the African Diaspora.

BIOGRAPHICAL/CRITICAL SOURCES:

PERIODICALS

Books in Canada, September, 1995, Rita Donovan, review of *Resisting the Anomie,* p. 46.
Canadian Book Review Annual, 1996, Roger Nash, review of *Resisting the Anomie,* p. 199.
Canadian Literature, July, 1999, Clara Joseph, review of *Wheel and Come Again: An Anthology of Reggae Poetry.*
Caribbean Writer, Volume 12, 1998, Geoffrey Philp, review of *Shook Foil: A Collection of Reggae Poems,* pp. 276-277.
World Literature Today, autumn, 1995, Sudeep Sen, review of *Progeny of Air,* pp. 850-851; spring, 1996, Adele S. Newson, review of *Resisting the Anomie,* p. 454; autumn, 1996, Sudeep Sen, review of *Prophets,* pp. 1016-1017; spring, 1998, Peter Nazareth, review of *Jacko Jacobus,* p. 440.

OTHER

Kwame Dawes Web site, http://www.state.sc.us/arts/kwame—dawes/(February 21, 2000).

*   *   *

DAYTON, Arwen Elys   1974-

PERSONAL: Born January 3, 1974, in CA. *Avocational interests:* "Snowboarding, yoga."

ADDRESSES: Agent—Matt Bialer, Trident Media Group, 488 Madison Ave., 17th Floor, New York, NY 10022. *E-mail*—author@arwenelysdayton.com.

WRITINGS:

Sovereign's Hold (science fiction), Windstorm Creative, 2000.
Resurrection (science fiction), Roc (New York, NY), 2001.

WORK IN PROGRESS: Research on "witchcraft, string theory, and minor Hindu gods."

de BALKER, Habakuk II
  See ter BALKT, H(erman) H(endrik)

*   *   *

DENTON, Kady MacDonald   1942-

PERSONAL: Born 1942, in Canada.

ADDRESSES: Home—Manitoba, Canada. *Office*—c/o Kingfisher Publishing, P.O. Box 267, Quathiaski Cove, BC, Canada V0P 1N0.

CAREER: Writer and illustrator of children's books.

AWARDS, HONORS: Mr. Christie's Award for Illustration (Great Britain), 1990, for *The Story of Little Quack;* Amelia Frances Howard-Gibbon Award, 1990, for *Til All the Stars Have Fallen.* Governor General's Award for Illustration (English Language), 1998, for *A Child's Treasury of Nursery Rhymes.*

WRITINGS:

SELF-ILLUSTRATED CHILDREN'S BOOKS

The Picnic, Dutton (New York, NY), 1988.
Granny Is a Darling, M. K. McElderry Books, 1988.
Dorothy's Dream, M. K. McElderry Books, 1989.
The Christmas Boot, Little, Brown (New York, NY), 1990.
Janet's Horses, Walker (London, England), 1990, Clarion (New York, NY), 1991.
Would They Love a Lion?, Kingfisher (New York, NY), 1995.
Watch Out, William, Kingfisher (New York, NY), 1997.

ILLUSTRATOR

Pam Zinnemann-Hope, *Find Your Coat, Ned,* M. K. McElderry Books, 1987.
Pam Zinnemann-Hope, *Let's Play Ball, Ned,* M. K. McElderry Books, 1987.
Pam Zinnemann-Hope, *Let's Go Shopping, Ned,* M. K. McElderry Books, 1987.
Pam Zinnemann-Hope, *Time for Bed, Ned,* M. K. McElderry Books, 1987.
David Booth, editor, *Til All the Stars Have Fallen: Canadian Poems for Children,* Kids Can Press (Toronto, Canada), 1989, Viking (New York, NY), 1990.
Betty Gibson, *The Story of Little Quack,* Kids Can Press (Toronto, Canada), 1990.

(Reteller) Ann Pilling, *Before I Go to Sleep: A Collection of Bible Stories, Poems, and Prayers for Children,* Crown (New York, NY), 1990.

David Wynn Millward, *Jenny and Bob,* Delacorte Press (New York, NY), 1991.

(Reteller) P. K. Page, *The Travelling Musicians of Bremen,* Kids Can Press (Toronto, Canada), 1991, Joy Street Books (Boston, MA), 1992.

(Reteller) Ann Pilling, *The Kingfisher Children's Bible: Stories from the Old and New Testaments,* Kingfisher (New York, NY), 1993.

Ann Pilling, *Realms of Gold: Myths and Legends from Around the World,* Kingfisher (New York, NY), 1993.

Shen Roddie, *Toes Are to Tickle,* Tricycle, 1997.

Janet Lunn, *The Umbrella Party,* Douglas & McIntyre (Vancouver, Canada), 1998.

Philip Pullman, *Detective Stories,* Kingfisher (New York, NY), 1998.

A Child's Treasury of Nursery Rhymes, Kingfisher (New York, NY), 1998.

Margaret Park Bridges, *If I Were Your Mother,* Morrow Junior Books (New York, NY), 1999.

Margaret Park Bridges, *If I Were Your Father,* Morrow Junior Books (New York, NY), 1999.

Robert Heidbreder, *I Wished for a Unicorn,* Kids Can Press (Toronto, Canada), 2000.

(Reteller) Ann Pilling, *A Kingfisher Treasury of Bible Stories, Poems, and Prayers for Bedtime,* Kingfisher (New York, NY), 2000.

Clare Masural, *Two Homes,* Candlewick Press (Cambridge, MA), 2001.

Sam McBratney, *In the Light of the Moon and other Bedtime Stories,* Kingfisher (New York, NY), 2001.

SIDELIGHTS: Kady MacDonald Denton is the illustrator of a number of picture books for preschool-age readers and has also authored several titles herself. Her work has won steady praise for the whimsical, cozy world depicted in her art; "charming" is an oft-repeated adjective used in reviews. Her self-illustrated books have also earned commendation for their brief but enchanting storylines.

As Sarah Ellis noted in an essay on Denton for *Children's Books and Their Creators,* "she invariably chooses to illustrate the one delicate gesture that speaks volumes." Though she is a parent herself, Denton says she tries to remember her own imaginative landscape of youth when writing or drawing her books. "I think of how it was for me as a child, not as it is now for me as a parent," Denton told *Children's Books and Their Creators.* Her career as an illustrator began with Pam

Zinnemann-Hope's series of books about an irrepressible little boy and his world: *Find Your Coat, Ned* and *Time for Bed, Ned* were just two of the titles illustrated by Denton published in the late 1980s.

Denton's first two books that she both wrote and illustrated were *The Picnic* and *Granny Is a Darling,* both of which appeared in 1988. The latter title captures in pastel watercolors a young boy's excitement at the pending visit of his grandmother to his household. Billy is afraid of the dark and looks forward to having to share his room with Granny. He thinks the imaginary monsters that torment him at night will then vanish, but instead he now hears a new and ominous noise—Granny's snoring—and believes it to be a large monster about to attack her. When Billy discovers that the noise is emanating from Granny herself, he decides that the monsters can recognize her fearsome power and flee forever.

The bedtime world was again a topic for humor in Denton's 1989 picture book *Dorothy's Dream.* Dorothy is a little girl who wants to stay awake forever lest she miss out on all the fun, and she cavorts and plays until her family becomes worried. But when Dorothy does fall asleep finally, she has bad dreams—a gray, cheerless landscape that looks like pictures of the moon "littered with objects that are frustratingly, terrifyingly semirecognizable, the stuff of childhood nightmare," wrote Ellis in *Children's Books and Their Creators,* who deemed Denton an especially adept illustrator of the dream and make-believe worlds. But towards the end of her sleep cycle, Dorothy gets a glimpse of a golden dream world where she is the star, and so resolves to get to bed early the next night in order to return to that place. A *Books for Keeps* reviewer praised Denton for the title's "attractive, fluid watercolors."

Denton has continued to work with other writers on books for young readers and is at home in a number of different genres, from cozy domestic scenes to fable worlds of pure fantasy. She has illustrated *Til All the Stars Have Fallen: Canadian Poems for Children,* a retelling of the German fairy tale *The Travelling Musicians of Bremen,* and has worked with author Ann Pilling on her *Kingfisher Children's Bible: Stories from the Old and New Testaments* and *A Kingfisher Treasury of Bible Stories, Poems, and Prayers for Bedtime.* With Pilling, Denton also created a visual world for another of her 1993 books, *Realms of Gold: Myths and Legends from Around the World.* The fourteen folktales presented here range from the West African "Iyadola's Babies" to the Norse myth "The Death of Balder." Also included are Pacific Islander, Chinese, and Russian fables, as well as the heartwarming story of a loyal dog in the Welsh classic "Bedd Gelert."

"Lucid, luminous watercolors enliven every page," noted *School Library Journal* critic Patricia Dooley in her assessment of *Realms of Gold,* and Denton's copious illustrations also won particular praise from *Publishers Weekly,* whose reviewer found that the artist was able to "display an intriguing amalgam of styles reflective of the tales' countries of origin."

Denton's list of books that she both wrote and illustrated continued to grow with *The Christmas Boot* and *Janet's Horses.* For her 1995 title *Would They Love a Lion?,* Denton won special praise from reviewers for her talents. When little Anna's life is disrupted with the arrival of a new sibling, this imaginative child tries on a series of "guises" in an attempt to win her preoccupied family's attention. With the help of her reversible bathrobe, Anna becomes a bird, a dinosaur, and a rabbit, but finally it is the roar of her lion that breaks the spell. In the end, everybody has a story and a nap.

Would They Love a Lion? earned commendatory words for both its text and illustration. "Denton brings an abundance of charm to a familiar scenario," declared a commentator in *Publishers Weekly,* while Susan Dove Lempke, critiquing the title for *Bulletin of the Center for Children's Books,* noted that Denton adequately "captures the spirit of a day of imaginary play." *Quill & Quire's* Fred Boer found *Would They Love a Lion?* in possession of "all the elements of a classic."

Denton also drew whimsical images for Shen Roddie's 1997 book for preschoolers, *Toes Are to Tickle.* The text follows a youngster and her infant brother through their day, and presents all the objects familiar to them and their ostensible reasons for being. "A mirror is for making faces," states the text, with Denton's impish siblings sticking out their tongues at their reflections; "a cat is to love." Denton's "breezy, colorful watercolors," as Amelia Kalin of *School Library Journal* described them, were executed in tones of orange. "The palette balances the impish spirit of the compositions," remarked a *Publishers Weekly* reviewer, who noted that Denton's energetic visual composition provides "texture and drive."

Denton's 1998 offering, the self-illustrated *A Child's Treasury of Nursery Rhymes,* includes a range of poems and folk rhymes designed to appeal to very young readers. *Teacher Librarian* reviewer Shirley Lewis praised the "broad, enticing selection" of rhymes, while *Booklist's* Hazel Rochman characterized the author's illustra-

tions as "light and joyful, wild and funny, expressing the mischief, farce, and tenderness of the verses we all love."

In addition to her own books, Denton continues to illustrate works by other authors, including Margaret Park Bridges' companion stories *If I Were Your Mother* and *If I Were Your Father,* and Robert Heidbreder's *I Wished for a Unicorn.* In the former titles, boys and girls imagine switching places with their parents—with humorous results. Both the parents and the children trade ideas about what life might be like with the kids in charge. Reviewing the titles in *Booklist,* Carolyn Phelan asserted that "the playful banter highlights the live and trust of the parent-child relationship," and complimented Denton for her "fresh depictions of familiar activities and childhood fantasies." A *Publishers Weekly* critic concurred that "the lightness and warmth of Denton's watercolors complement the softness of the text." In Heidbreder's *I Wished for a Unicorn,* a girl's wish for the mythical beast is fulfilled by the appearance of a unicorn who looks much like her pet dog. The text follows the girl and the dog/unicorn through numerous adventures, until the pair wakes up in the backyard where the fantasy began. While a *Booklist* reviewer felt that story is "fairly clichéd," the critic noted that Denton's "lovely gouache paintings extend the action, adding emotional subtleties, magic, and humor" to the tale.

BIOGRAPHICAL/CRITICAL SOURCES:

BOOKS

Children's Books and Their Creators, edited by Anita Silvey, Houghton Mifflin, 1995, p. 195.

PERIODICALS

Booklist, August, 1993, p. 2056; August, 1995, p. 1955; June 1, 1997, p. 1721; November 1, 1998, Hazel Rochman, review of *A Child's Treasury of Nursery Rhymes,* p. 496; March 15, 1999, Hazel Rochman, review of *A Child's Treasury of Nursery Rhymes,* p. 134; August, 1999, Carolyn Phelan, review of *If I Were Your Father/If I Were Your Mother,* p. 2064; April 15, 2000, Gillian Engberg, review of *I Wished for a Unicorn,* p. 1545.
Books for Keeps, September, 1990, p. 6; July, 1991, review of *Dorothy's Dream,* p. 7.
Bulletin of the Center for Children's Books, July-August, 1995, Susan Dove Lempke, review of *Would They Love a Lion?,* p. 381.
Canadian Materials, January, 1989, p. 34.

Childhood Education, winter, 2000, Catherine Laubach, review of *I Wished for a Unicorn,* p. 108.

Junior Bookshelf, December, 1989, p. 260.

Kirkus Reviews, August 15, 1989, p. 1243.

Publishers Weekly, April 19, 1993, review of *Realms of Gold: Myths and Legends from Around the World,* p. 62; April 24, 1995, review of *Would They Love a Lion?,* p. 70; May 26, 1997, review of *Toes Are to Tickle,* p. 84; May 24, 1999, review of *If I Were Your Mother/If I Were Your Father,* p. 77.

Quill & Quire, September, 1995, Fred Boer, review of *Would They Love a Lion?.*

School Library Journal, February, 1989, p. 69; December, 1989, pp. 77-78; July, 1995, p. 55; May, 1993, Patricia Dooley, review of *Realms of Gold: Myths & Legends from Around the World,* p. 120; September, 1997, Amelia Kalin, review of *Toes Are to Tickle,* p. 192; November 1, 1998, Joan Zaleski, review of *A Child's Treasury of Nursery Rhymes,* p. 105; May, 1999, Dawn Amsberry, review of *If I Were Your Mother* and *If I Were Your Father,* p. 86; August, 2000, Sharon McNeil, review of *I Wished for a Unicorn,* p. 156.

Teacher Librarian, September, 1998, Shirley Lewis, review of *A Child's Treasury of Nursery Rhymes,* p. 47.*

*   *   *

des PRÉS, Josquin 1954-

PERSONAL: Born July 29, 1954, in St. Tropez, France; son of François (an author and painter) and Marguerite (a painter) Turenne des Prés; married, wife's name Chantal, 1979; children: Chloé Turenne des Prés, Julien Turenne des Prés. *Ethnicity:* "French-American-Italian." *Education:* Beau-Arts School (Bordeaux, France).

ADDRESSES: Home—P.O. Box 3824, La Mesa, CA 91944-3826. *Office*—7242 University Ave., La Mesa, CA 91941; fax: 619-697-7836. *E-mail*—josquindespres@home.com.

CAREER: Track Star Entertainment, La Mesa, CA, former owner and producer; Warner Chappell Publishers, Santa Monica, CA, former writer. Producer and engineer; projects include musical releases by Lisa Sanders, The Young Dubliners, Mary Dolan, Carly Hennessy, Bastard Sons of Johnny Cash; songwriter, including collaborations with Bernie Taupin, work as Warner Bros. songwriter, and Sunset Blvd Entertainment staff writer; bass player, including performances with Jeff Porcaro, Steve Lukather, Vinny Colaiuta, Alex Acuna, David Garibaldi, Jerry Goodman, Fred Tackett, Richie Hayward, Jerry Donahue, Billy Sheehan, Fred Mandel, Bernie Taupin, Ron Wikso, Jimmy Crespo, and Scott Gorham.

WRITINGS:

(With Mark Landsman) *Creative Careers in Music,* Allworth/Billboard, 2000.

Also author, with Landsman and Jack Scovil, of *Reality Check,* Scovil, Chikak & Galen, and of instruction books, including *Bass Fitness,* Hal Leonard, and *J. S. Bach for Bass,* Mel Bay.

SIDELIGHTS: Josquin des Prés told *CA* that "helping others" is his primary motivation for writing; that "everyday situations" particularly influences his work; and that "the lack of books on the subject of music and musician" inspired him to write on his chosen subjects. He described his writing process as "brainstorming with co-writer."

*   *   *

DEUTSCH, Xavier 1965-

PERSONAL: Born February 9, 1965, in Louven, Belgium; father, (a professor of physics); mother (teacher). *Education:* Earned D.Letters.

ADDRESSES: Office—c/o Le Cri Editions, 43 rue Guilaume Stocq, 1050, Brussels, Belgium.

CAREER: Writer.

AWARDS, HONORS: Nominated for Prix Rossel, 1990, for *Les garçons.*

WRITINGS:

(With Anne-Marie Mercier) *Marie Gevers,* Editions Labor (Brussels, Belgium), 1987.

La nuit dans les yeux, Gallimard (Paris, France), 1989.

Les garçons, L'École des loisirs (Paris, France), 1991.

Les foulards bleus, L'École des loisirs (Paris, France), 1992.

Too much sur la terre comme au ciel (novel), Volume I: *Too Much,* Volume II: *Sur la terre,* Volume III:

Comme au ciel: Liverpool 1994, Le Cri (Brussels, Belgium), 1994.

La petite rue Claire et Nette, L'École des loisirs (Paris, France), 1995.

La petite soeur du Bon Dieu, L'École des loisirs (Paris, France), 1995.

Pas de soleil en Alaska (novel), Editions Labor (Brussels, Belgium), 1996.

Allez! Allez!, L'École des loisirs (Paris, France), 1997.

Le grand jeu des courages de l'ours en Alaska (novel), Le Cri (Brussels, Belgium), 1997.

Victoria Bauer!, Le Cri (Brussels, Belgium), 2000.

Le Tilleul de Stalingrad, Le Castor Astral, 2001.

BIOGRAPHICAL/CRITICAL SOURCES:

OTHER

Xavier Deutsch, http://www.multimania.com/agam/atel96/biodeuts/ (September 26, 2001).*

* * *

de VALOIS, Ninette   1898-2001

OBITUARY NOTICE—See index for *CA* sketch: Born June 6, 1898, in Baltiboys, Ireland; died March 8, 2001, in London, England. Choreographer, dancer, and author. De Valois was a world-renowned choreographer, director, and ballet dancer who not only performed with numerous companies during her early years, but also went on to found and lead three of her own ballet troupes. With a highly experimental style rooted in classical ballet elements, the first performance of her choreographed ballet came in 1928 with Les Petits Riens at the Old Vic Theatre in London. De Valois had a keen interest in writing, though she only published four works during her long life. These books include *Invitation to the Ballet,* an autobiography entitled *Come Dance With Me, Step by Step,* and finally, a collection of her poetry called *The Cycle.* De Valois was showered with awards throughout her life; in addition to receiving such esteemed accolades as the Albert Medal of the Royal Society, which she earned in 1964, de Valois was granted membership to the Order of the Companions of Honor by Queen Elizabeth II.

OBITUARIES AND OTHER SOURCES:

PERIODICALS

Chicago Tribune, March 9, 2001, section 2, p. 10.
Los Angeles Times, March 9, 2001, p. B6.

New York Times, March 9, 2001, p. A15.
Times (London, England), March 9, 2001.
Washington Post, March 9, 2001, p. B6.

* * *

DICK, Bruce Allen   1953-

PERSONAL: Born 1953. *Education:* Earned B.A., M.A., Ph.D.

ADDRESSES: Office—c/o Greenwood Press, 88 Post Road W., P. O. Box 5007, Westport, CT 06881-5007.

CAREER: Florida State University, Tallahassee, associate professor of English, 1989—.

WRITINGS:

(Editor, with Amritjit Singh) *Conversations with Ishmael Reed,* University Press of Mississippi (Jackson, MS), 1995.

(Editor, with Silvio Sirias) *Conversations with Rudolfo Anaya,* University Press of Mississippi (Jackson, MS), 1998.

(Editor, with Pavel Zemliansky) *The Critical Response to Ishmael Reed,* Greenwood Press (Westport, CT), 1999.*

* * *

DICKINS, Barry   1949-

PERSONAL: Born 1949, in Regent, Australia; married Sarah Mogridge; children: Louis. *Education:* Trained as a teacher.

ADDRESSES: Agent—c/o Random House Australia, 20 Alfred Street, Milsons Point, New South Wales, Australia 2061.

CAREER: Writer. Set painter, Australian Channel 7; completed teacher training; became part of the La Mama writing and performance group, Carlton, Australia, early 1970s; first play, *Ghosts,* performed by La Mama, 1975; journalist, storyteller, English teacher, actor; writes regularly for the *Age* and *Sunday Age* newspapers.

AWARDS, HONORS: Victorian Premier's award, Louis Esson Prize for Drama, for stage play *Remember Ronald Ryan* (1995).

WRITINGS:

The Banana Bender; The Death of Minnie, Currency (Sydney, New South Wales, Australia), 1981.

One Woman Shoe, Yackandandah Playscripts (Montmorency, Victoria, Australia), 1984.

The Bridal Suite; and, Mag and Bag: Two Plays, Yackandandah Playscripts (Montmorency, Victoria, Australia), 1985.

I Love to Live, Ringwood (Victoria, Australia), published as *The Fabulous Life of Barry Dickins,* Penguin (New York, NY), 1991.

(With Paul Cox) *A Woman's Tale* (screenplay), Orion, 1992.

Post Office Restaurant and Other Stories, Pascoe (Apollo Bay, Australia), 1992.

The House of the Lord, Vintage (Sydney, New South Wales, Australia), 1999.

Also author of *Remember Ronald Ryan, Ron Truffle: His Life and Bump-out, My Grandmother,* and *Heart and Soul: Personal Recollections of Life in the Police Force.* Author, with Paul Cox, of *The Golden Braid,* a screenplay.

SIDELIGHTS: Described as a "poet, historian, playwright, actor, screenwriter, novelist, essayist and incessant bloody talker" by *CitySearch,* Barry Dickins has worked as a journalist and English teacher in Melbourne, Australia. He is one of the most prolific writers in Australia today.

Dickins's *The House of the Lord* is a coming-of-age story about two boys, one of whom, Johnny, has been brutally sexually abused at a Catholic school. When Johnny is brutally killed, his friend Bertie must grieve not only for Johnny's death but for the death of his own ideals. In the *Australian Book Review* Kevin Brophy wrote, "*The House of the Lord* is not merely a novel of loving recreation of [the past] . . . for it takes us, clear-eyed and crazy, into the cruelties and terrors of childhood and out into the contradictions, slipperiness and dangers of trying to live actual lives according to fixed ideas."

Dickins wrote the book in four-hour shifts, at night, while his family was asleep. He stressed the importance of regular writing to an interviewer from the *Age:* "You've got to write to get the plot formed. You're writing the plot as you're inventing. You've got to work to get it invented."

He also noted that as a writer, he listens to internal creative voices, which often reflect the voices of his own family; most of his books, he said, have to do with family. "You go into this willing and contemplative state, almost like a daydream," Dickins said, "which has no bearing on industry. It's not work at all. It's the sweetest thing if you love to write." He commented that although a writer's life may not be as financially rewarding as those of people with more stable careers, it is deeply satisfying in an emotional sense.

Dickins is the sole judge of the Alan Marshall Short Story Award, a national Australian competition.

BIOGRAPHICAL/CRITICAL SOURCES:

PERIODICALS

Age (Melbourne), May 22, 1999, Andrew Bock, "Authors in Search of a Character."

Australian Book Review, April, 1999, p. 27.

OTHER

ABC Australia, http://www.abc.net.au/ (February 8, 2001).

CitySearch, http://theage.citysearch.com.au/ (February 8, 2001), "My Mysterious Melbourne."*

* * *

DIEHM, Floyd L(ee) 1925-

PERSONAL: Born May 1, 1925, in OK. *Education:* Northwest Christian College, B.Th., 1951; Phillips University, M.Div., 1954; School of Theology, Claremont, CA, D.Rel., 1970.

ADDRESSES: Office—St. Andrew's United Methodist Church, 2045 Southeast Green Oaks Blvd., Arlington, TX 76018; fax: 817-465-3043. *E-mail*—SA-UMC.org.

CAREER: Ordained minister of Christian Church (Disciples of Christ), 1950; national evangelist until 1955; served as pastor of Christian churches in Roanoke, VA, 1958-63, Modesto, CA, 1963-70, and Midwest City, OK, beginning in 1970; senior minister of Christian church in Alhambra, CA; served at Christian church in Wichita, KS; St. Andrew's United Methodist Church, Arlington, TX, associate minister. Member of board of directors, California Christian Home and National Evangelism Workshop.

WRITINGS:

How to Be Fully Alive, Abingdon (Nashville, TN), 1976.

Winning with Word Power: How to Ignite the Force of Wonder-Working Words, Baker Book (Grand Rapids, MI), 1988.

Author of the books *Good News for You* and *How to Evangelize Effectively.**

*   *   *

DIMITROVA, Blaga   1922-

PERSONAL: Born January 2, 1922, in Byala Slatina, Bulgaria; married Yordan Vasilev (a literary critic and scholar), 1967; children: Ha (adopted, Vietnamese girl). *Education:* Sofia University, B.A., 1945; Maksim Gorky Institute for Literature, Ph.D., 1950; studied piano with Andre Stoyanov.

ADDRESSES: Office—Bulgarski pisatel, ul 6 Septemvri 35, 1000, Sofia, Bulgaria.

CAREER: Novelist, poet, and translator, beginning early 1940s; *Septemvri,* editor, 1950-55; construction worker in Rhodope Mountains, 1952-53; editor at Bulgarski pisatel and Narodna kultura, beginning 1962; deputy of parliament, 1991; vice president of Bulgaria, 1992.

MEMBER: Club for Democracy (founding member), Bulgarian Writers' Union, Order People's Republic of Bulgaria.

AWARDS, HONORS: Decorated Order of Red Banner of Labor, U.S.S.R.; recipient of Vecherni Novini Silver ring, 1962; Polish PEN Club award, 1978; Lundkvist Prize in Stockholm, 1980s; Herder Prize for poetry, 1992.

WRITINGS:

Stikhove za vozhda (title means "Verses on the Leader"), Bulgarski pisatel (Sofia, Bulgaria), 1950.

S Nazum Khikmet v Bulgaria. Putepis, Bulgarski pisatel (Sofia, Bulgaria), 1952.

Pesni za Rodopite (title means "Songs of the Rhodopa Mountains"), Profizdat (Sofia, Bulgaria), 1954.

Na otkrito. Stikhotvoreniya, Bulgarski pisatel (Sofia, Bulgaria), 1956.

Do utre. Lirika (title means "Until Tomorrow"), Bulgarski pisatel (Sofia, Bulgaria), 1959.

Liyana. Poema, Narodna mladezh (Sofia, Bulgaria), 1959.

Svetut v shepa. Stikhotvoreniya, Bulgarski pisatel (Sofia, Bulgaria), 1962.

Ekspeditsiya kum idniya den. Kiricheski poemim, Narodna kultura (Sofia, Bulgaria), 1964.

Obratno vreme. Stikhotvoreniya, Bulgarski pisatel (Sofia, Bulgaria), 1965.

Putuvane kum sebe si. Roman (title means "Journey to Oneself"), Narodna mladezh (Sofia, Bulgaria), 1965.

Osudeni na lyubov. Stikhotvoreniya (title means "Condemned to Love"), Narodna mladezh (Sofia, Bulgaria), 1967.

Otklonenie. Roman (title means "Detour"), Bulgarski pisatel (Sofia, Bulgaria), 1967.

Migove. Poeziya, Bulgarski pisatel (Sofia, Bulgaria), 1968.

Strashniya sud. Roman-putepis (title means "Judgment Day"), Narodna kultura (Sofia, Bulgaria), 1969.

Ime. Stikhove, Durzhavno izdatelstvo (Varna, Bulgaria), 1971.

Lavina. Roman-poema (title means "Avalanche"), Khristo G. Danov (Plovdiv, Bulgaria), 1971.

Impulsi. Izbrana poeziya, Bulgarski pisatel (Sofia, Bulgaria), 1972.

Podzemno nebe. Vietnamski dnevnik 72 (title means "Subterranean Heaven: A Vietnam Diary"), Partizdat (Sofia, Bulgaria), 1972.

Kak. Stikhotvoreniya (title means "How"), Narodna mladezh (Sofia, Bulgaria), 1974.

(With Yordan Vasilev) *Mladostta na Bagryana i neynite sputuitsi* (title means "Bagryanan's Youth,") Khr. G. Danov (Plovdiv, Bulgaria), 1975.

(With Vasilev) *Dni cherni i beli. Elisaveta Bagryana-nabyudeniia i razgovori,* Nauka i izkustvo (Sofia, Bulgaria), 1975.

Gong. Stikhotvoreniya (title means "Gong"), Narodna mladezh (Sofia, Bulgaria), 1976.

Zabraneno more. Poema, G. Bakalov (Varna, Bulgaria), 1976.

Prostranstva. Stikhotvoreniya (title means "Expanses"), Bulgarski pisatel (Sofia, Bulgaria), 1980.

Litse. Roman (title means "Face"), Bulgarski pisatel (Sofia, Bulgaria), 1981.

Izbrani tvorbi, 2 volumes, Bulgarski pisatel (Sofia, Bulgaria), 1982.

Glas. Stikhove (title means "Voice"), Khr. G. Danov (Plovdid, Bulgaria), 1985.

Labirint. Stikhotvoreniya (title means "Labyrinth"), Bulgarski pisatel (Sofia, Bulgaria), 1987.

Otvud Iyubovta. Lyubovna lirika, Narodna mladezh (Sofia, Bulgaria), 1987.

Mezhdu. Stikhotvoreniya (title means "Between"), Bulgarski pisatel (Sofia, Bulgaria), 1990.

Tranzit. Poema, K. Kadi'ski (Sofia, Bulgaria), 1990.

Predizvikatelstva. Politicheski etiudi, Institut po kultura (Sofia, Bulgaria), 1991.

Klyuch. Poemi (title means "The Key"), Galaktika (Varna, Bulgaria), 1991.

Noshten dnevnik. Stikhove. 1988-1992. I. K. Nov Zlatorog (Sofia, Bulgaria), 1992.

Otsam i otwud. Silueti na priyateli, Kotar (Sophia, Bulgaria), 1992.

Pomen za Topolata, Kotar 88 (Sofia, Bulgaria), 1992.

Hobiada: Hobioda za Hobimoda, Kotar 88 (Sofia, Bulgaria), 1992.

Ctikhove, Sofia Press (Sofia, Bulgaria), 1993.

Uraniya, Roman, Tsuyat (Sofia, Bulgaria), 1993.

I Pak Otnachalo, Stikhove, 1993-94, Nov Zlatorog (Sofia, Bulgaria), 1994.

Do Ruba, Stikhotvoreniya, 1994-95, Universitetsuo Izdatelstvo St. Kliment Okhridski (Sofia, Bulgaria), 1996.

Cherna Kotka v Tunela: Zagadki, Dogadki. Otvoreno Obshtestvo (Sofia, Bulgaria), 1996.

Raznoglasitsi. Eseta, Universitetsko Izdatelstvo St. Kliment Okhridski (Sofia, Bulgaria), 1996.

Gluharcheto, Nov Zlatorog (Sofia, Bulgaria), 1996.

EDITIONS IN ENGLISH

Journey to Oneself, translated by Radost Pridham, Cassell (London, England), 1969.

Because the Sea Is Black: Poems of Blaga Dimitrova, selected and translated by Niko Boris and Heather McHugh, Wesleyan University Press (Middletown, CT), 1989.

Forbidden Sea: A Poem of Blaga Dimitrova, translated by Elizabeth A. Socolow and Ludmilla G. Popova-Wightman, Ivy Press, 2000.

TRANSLATIONS

Aleksandur Tvardovskiy, *Vasiliy T'orkin,* Bulgarska Rabotnicheska Partiya [komunisti] (Sofia, Bulgaria), 1946.

Adam Mickiewicz, *Pan Tadeucz,* Narodna kultura (Sofia, Bulgaria), 1959.

(With Aleksandur Milev) Homer, *Iliada,* Narodna kultura (Sofia, Bulgaria), 1969.

(With Antoaneta Primatarova-Milcheva) Edit Sdergran, *Prustenut na vechnostta,* Narodna kultura (Sofia, Bulgaria), 1984.

(With Primatarova-Milcheva) Iosten Sjstrand, *Chuvam pulsirasht vsemir,* Narodna kultura (Sofia, Bulgaria), 1984.

Wislawa Szymborska, *Obmislyam sveta,* Narodna kultura (Sofia, Bulgaria), 1989.

SIDELIGHTS: Blaga Dimitrova is best known for her searching, linguistically sophisticated poetry and her political leadership of Bulgaria. She has written of the human condition in terms at once abstract and specific; in much of her writing, she attempts to preserve tradition while forging new paths. As Charles Moser wrote in the *Encyclopedia of World Literature in the 20th Century:* "She is sustained, not constricted, by her links with past generations. She incorporates the legacy of the past into her own personality, which she will transmit to others in its entirety only when she dies." In the 1980s, Dimitrova became one of Bulgaria's great poets; in the 1990s, she became one of its political leaders. As Christina Protokhristova suggested in an article for *Dictionary of Literary Biography:* "Dimitrova is one of the most outstanding personalities in contemporary Bulgarian social and political life. An author of strong moral concern, she creates works that are predominantly reflexive, but the intellectual quest in them is never allowed to overwhelm the artistic vision." As Protokhristova also suggested, Dimitrova's poetry authorship relates to her political leadership; she believes, Protokhristova maintained, in "the Word—its magic, its creative potentials, and its ability to build up its own universe that coexists with reality."

Dimitrova, raised in Turnova, studied philosophy at the renowned Sophia University; she was graduated in 1945. During her youth and undergraduate education, Dimitrova published poetry in various student and professional journals: *Blgarska rech, Prometey, Uchenicheski podem, Izkustovo i kritika* and *Literaturen zhivot.* She earned a Ph.D. at the Maksim Gorky Institute for literature in Moscow. After graduating, Dimitrova explored her country and the literary world; she worked as an editor for *Septemvri* and did construction work in the Rhodopa Mountains. Her mountain work seems to have shaped her sense of labor and womanhood. Moser suggested that the experience "found romanticized expression in the moderately modernist novel *Putuvane kum sebe si,* a story of a woman who wishes to do a man's work in this world without ceasing to be a woman."

Putuvane kum sebe si tells of a young woman who does construction work in the Rhodopa Mountains; though little happens, the novel traces the woman's shifts in perception and feeling as she works. Dimitrova finds a feminine model of development that is nonetheless linked to efficient, even masculine, work. Much of Dimitrova's early work attempts to place an interior, feminine perception in a masculine sphere. Protokhristova suggested: "The first collection showing her development was *Do utre* in which the poems reveal an intimate female world of personal experience and private feeling . . . [Later poems also] represent her attempt to realize her place in the world, to come to terms with the vast dimensions of the universe, and to find a female approach to eternal issues."

Thus, in novels such as *Lavina,* Dimitrova approaches physical hardship emotionally and philosophically. In *Lavina,* she chronicles the accidental deaths of a group of mountaineers; though the deaths are brutal, Dimitrova "goes beyond the factual plane," as Protokhristova wrote, "into the realm of philosophical reasoning about the issues of life, juxtaposing what may be considered the 'everyday' morals of human relations, love, and friendship, and duty and responsibility to more abstract, existential problems." Dimitrova's poetry, too, attempts to locate transient, philosophical musings in physical realities—often, this leads Dimitrova to a focus on words themselves. As Protokhristova remarked: "She reaches to the kernel of words to explore the secrets of their designations and thus gain control of a language that is capable of expressing the complexity of existence."

In 1967, Dimitrova married literary scholar Yordan Vasilev, with whom she later adopted a Vietnamese girl, Ha. Dimitrova continued to write, however; in the 1980s she rose to eminence as Bulgaria's greatest female poet. In her novels and poetry, Dimitrova attempts to locate spirit in the real world; as Protokhristova put it: "The novel[s] give expression to the most essential themes and motives in the author's poetry: the problem of moral choice and individual responsibility and the theme of the human face as a symbol of personality." In one of Dimitrova's most famous novels, *Litse,* she tells of a Marxist professor, Bora Naydenova, who helps a student who is persecuted politically. The two fall in love, but Bora eventually realizes the student actually killed her first love. The novel describes political complexities within emotional events, or perhaps the emotional valences of political situations. In this novel, as in much of Dimitrova's work, the inner, emotional life is within the political sphere.

Dimitrova won the Lundkvist Prize in Stockholm in the 1980s for her translations of Swedish literature, and also received the Herder Prize for poetry in 1992. As Moser suggested: "D[imitrova] is now something of an elder 'statesman' of Bulgarian culture." Her most significant appreciation came from her people, who in the 1990s elected her to public office.

Dimitrova was deputy of parliament in 1991 and, months later, became Bulgaria's vice president. She became a pre-eminent supporter of democracy, and one of its architects in Bulgaria. As Protokhristova remarked: "Dimitrova not only contributes to the best achievements of contemporary Bulgarian literature, but she also offers, through her public image, an essential representation of Bulgaria's current political emancipation."

BIOGRAPHICAL/CRITICAL SOURCES:

BOOKS

Dictionary of Literary Biography, Volume 181: *South Slavic Writers Since World War II,* Gale (Detroit, MI), 1997.
Contemporary World Writers, St. James Press (Detroit, MI), 1993.
Encyclopedia of World Literature in the 20th Century, St. James Press (Detroit, MI), 1999.*

*   *   *

DONAHUE, Brian 1955-

PERSONAL: Born 1955. *Education:* Brandeis University, B.A., Ph.D.

ADDRESSES: Office—Department of American Studies, Brandeis University, 415 South St., Waltham, MA 02454-9110.

CAREER: Brandeis University, Waltham, MA, professor of American environmental studies, assistant professor of American environmental studies on the Jack Meyerhoff Chair, chair of Environmental Studies program. Cofounder of Land's Sake community farm, Weston, MA, served as director for 12 years; director of education, the Land Institute, Salina, KS.

WRITINGS:

Reclaiming the Commons: Community Farms and Forests in a New England Town, Yale University Press (New Haven, CT), 1999.

SIDELIGHTS: For twenty-five years Brian Donahue has helped operate community farms in Weston, Massachusetts, a suburb of Boston. In *Reclaiming the Commons: Community Farms and Forests in a New England Town* he suggests that other suburban communities do the same, for the benefits they provide to residents and the local land's well-being, as well as for the positive impact such projects have on the environment as a whole. To this end, Donahue presents agricultural history, his own experiences at the Land's Sake community farm, and the many advantages of maintaining common lands.

Donahue knows that community farms can succeed and recommends that community-owned commons be used for food production or forestry. He advocates organic methods for raising vegetable, fruits, and flowers, including modern techniques as well as older ones. Such farming projects are ideal for involving children, but should also make money. In Weston community farm operators found that while they could not match the price of produce from commercial farms, they were harvesting a superior quality product for which shoppers were willing to pay more.

The book suggests a myriad of benefits from community lands. One is that they are a way to link residents with their hometowns, rather than living in "rootless bedroom communities." Another is giving individuals who have been passively pro-environment an opportunity to act on their convictions. Donahue believes that it is more important to improve general land use than be concerned about wilderness areas. He encourages protecting lands on the fringe of suburbia against urban sprawl as a means of preserving local private farming. Using locally raised foods can result in better products, energy conservation, lower pollution levels, and aid climatic stability.

Yet another aspect of the book is its use of agricultural history as a pattern book. Increased reliance on local farming mirrors the market farms that once surrounded Boston. In response to critics who view the concept of community farms as socialist, Donahue explains that the practice is thoroughly American, descended from the colonial New England practice of common land ownership

A number of critics found *Reclaiming the Commons* to be persuasive and engaging. *Library Journal* writer Marianne Stowell Bracke judged that Donahue offered "hard-won knowledge" and "poignant" ideas on how to involve kids. She described the book as "a lush and persuasive narrative that makes even lambing in the middle of a cold spring night seem charming." *Booklist* contributor Vanessa Bush commended the book as "an engaging look at environmental issues and what can be done beyond hand-wringing." Donahue's ideas were called a "visionary, green blueprint" by a *Publishers*

Weekly reviewer, who concluded, "His radically conservative manifesto offers new approaches to make suburbia economically healthy, more livable and ecologically balanced." The plausibility of Donahue's concept was addressed in a *New York Times Book Review* article by Paul Raeburn: "His aim is to encourage a land ethic that will lead naturally to a desire to protect more remote areas. . . . It's difficult to know whether his proposals for productive use of suburban land can engender that kind of land ethic. But his case that we should try to reconnect with the land is made more powerful because, in one town, he has shown it can work."

BIOGRAPHICAL/CRITICAL SOURCES:

PERIODICALS

Booklist, June 1, 1999, Vanessa Bush, review of *Reclaiming the Commons: Community Farms and Forests in a New England Town,* p. 1752.
Library Journal, June 15, 1999, Marianne Stowell Bracke, review of *Reclaiming the Commons,* p. 99.
New York Times Book Review, Paul Raeburn, "Walden Pond vs. the Mall," p. 29.
Publishers Weekly, May 24, 1999, review of *Reclaiming the Commons,* p. 55.*

* * *

DOWNING, Taylor

PERSONAL: Male. *Education:* Christ's College, Cambridge, B.A.

ADDRESSES: Office—c/o Little, Brown & Company, 1271 Avenue of the Americas, New York, NY 10020.

CAREER: British film maker and author.

WRITINGS:

(With Maggie Millman) *Civil War,* Collins & Brown (London, England), 1991.
Olympia, BFI Publishing (London, England), 1992.
(With Jeremy Isaacs) *Cold War: An Illustrated History, 1945-1991,* Little, Brown & Co. (Boston, MA), 1998.

Also author of *The Troubles,* a made-for-television movie, 1981.

SIDELIGHTS: Taylor Downing documents history for a television audience: he has made accessible television documentaries about topics as varied as the nineteenth-century Luddite movement, the Cold War, and the struggles of Irish nationalists. He has also written about the task of the documentarian, and about the various pressures that shape his or her work. Throughout his career, Downing has questioned the relative value of entertainment and accuracy in popularized television histories.

One of Downing's early works, *The Troubles,* appeared as both a book and as a broadcast on Thames TV. Critics approved the documentary's efforts to provide a historical framework for the difficult subject, though they railed against the documentary's elementary style. Roy Foster, in an article for the *Times Literary Supplement,* commented: "Though marred by inaccuracies and over-simplifications uncharacteristic of the accompanying programmes, it makes a worthwhile addition to the pathetically small body of accessible general literature on the Ulster background." Tom Corfe, in a more politically opinionated review published in the *Times Educational Supplement,* shrugged: "*The Troubles* is neatly packaged, sensible, lucid; a collective work with no visible seams. . . . English mistakes must bear their share of blame. Where *The Troubles* fails is in applying similar critical judgment to Gaelic Irishmen. . . . [The documentary's] cautious and colourless approach to nationalism leaves its proponents as somewhat shadowy and insubstantial figures in what is otherwise a very good book."

Downing, for his part, seems interested only in making his historical understanding broadly available. In an article describing the making of his 1988 documentary, *The Luddites,* he explains: "In making the dramatized documentary *The Luddites,* director Richard Broad and myself imagined we were film makers in 1812 going out with a current affairs crew to report on the disturbances in the woolen industry. We asked ourselves how would we cover such events if they were happening today? And so in our imaginary 'This Week' or 'Panorama' of 1812 we dramatized some of the secret meetings of the Luddites with the men masked to prevent their identities from being known." But though his chief aim was to make the program appealing to television viewers, he insists: "Whilst the film relies upon the central 'deceit' of being reported by an imaginary film unit of the time, everything in the film is derived from historical fact."

In a book about Nazi documentary film making, Downing insists again that aesthetic considerations can outweigh the documentarian's political concerns. In *Olympia* Downing argues that Leni Riefenstahl's work may be appreciated despite its propaganda for the Nazi party—a troubling argument for many. John Fell described the work: "Himself a documentary film maker, Downing details problems faced by Riefenstahl and her crew in a time before Arriflex cameras and Zoomar lenses. Drawing on Riefenstahl's memoirs (soon to be published in English), he itemizes strategies that included pits beneath runways, an immersible camera, and cameras attached to athletes during training." Some critics, however, suggest that Downing ignores political undertones by focusing on the aesthetic aspects. J. Belton explained in *Choice:* "Downing is particularly good at explaining how certain shots were made. Though he acknowledges the political nature of the film, he argues that it transcends the political context which led to its creation, refusing to see that its celebration of physical beauty and athletic prowess is integral to a fascist aesthetic."

Downing again worked to make political history accessible in his "television series and coffee table book" combination, *The Cold War.* Some critics found the series and its accompanying picture book airy; Michael Harrington sneered in *Times Literary Supplement:* "*Cold War* very much belongs in the category of something commissioned by a publisher to accompany a television production, with its dutiful, broadly reliable narrative and its absence of passion or engagement. It will hold a place at the back of the reference shelves."

BIOGRAPHICAL/CRITICAL SOURCES:

PERIODICALS

American Spectator, January 1999, Joseph Shattan, "How Anti-Americanism Won the Cold War," pp. 71-74.

Booklist, September 1, 1998, Mary Carroll, review of *The Cold War,* p. 62.

Choice, September 1993, J. Belton, review of *Olympia,* p. 132.

Economist, December 12, 1998, review of *The Cold War,* p. 6.

Film Quarterly, Summer 1993, John Fell, review of *Olympia,* p. 61.

History Today, March 1988, "Television's Luddites," pp. 18-22.

Nation, October 19, 1998, Harvey Wasserman, review of *The Cold War,* p. 25.

Times Educational Supplement, December 27, 1985, Tom Corfe, "Active and Passive Violence," p. 17.

Times Literary Supplement, February 13, 1981, Roy Foster, "Irish History: Revised and Unrevised Versions," p. 165; January 22, 1999, Michael Harrington, review of *The Cold War*, p. 33.*

*   *   *

DOXIADIS, Apostolos (C.) 1953-

PERSONAL: Born 1953, in Brisbane, Australia. *Education:* Columbia University, B.A., 1968; Paris University, M.A., 1974.

ADDRESSES: E-mail—info@apostolosdoxiadis.com.

CAREER: Writer. Director of stage productions and motion pictures.

AWARDS, HONORS: First Feature Award, American Student Film Festival, 1968, for *The Call;* International Center for Artistic Cinema Prize, Berlin Film Festival, 1988, for *Terirem;* First Feature Award, Thessalonniki Festival, for *Underground Passage.*

WRITINGS:

Makavettas, Hestia (Athens), 1988.
Ho theios Petros kai he eikasia tou gkolntmpach: Mythistorema, Ekdoseis Kastaniote (Athens), 1992.
Ta tria anthropakia: Mythistorema, Ekdoseis Kastaniote, 1997.
Uncle Petros and Goldbach's Conjecture, Bloomsbury, 2000.

SCREENPLAYS; AND DIRECTOR

The Call, 1968.
Underground Passage, 1983.
Terirem, 1988.

SIDELIGHTS: Apostolos Doxiadis is a stage director, filmmaker, and writer. He was born in 1953 in Brisbane, Australia, and he studied mathematics at Columbia University, from which he graduated in 1972, and Paris University, where he earned a master's degree in 1974. He made his first film, *The Call,* when he was still in high school. This film won a prize at the first American Student Film Festival, which was held in 1968. Doxiadis's ensuing films include *Underground Passage,* which appeared in 1983, and *Terirem,* which was completed five years later.

Doxiadis is the author of various Greek-language publications, including *Makavettas, Ho theios Petros kai he eikasia tou gkolntmpach: Mythistorema,* and *Ta tria anthropakia: Mythistorema.* He is also the author of *Uncle Petros and Goldbach's Conjecture,* originally published in Greek, in which a young man develops a relationship with his uncle, a reclusive mathematician branded as a failure. After the nephew reveals his own enthusiasm for mathematics, the uncle encourages him to tackle Goldbach's Conjecture, a mathematical problem which suggests it is possible to prove that all even numbers greater than two are the sum of two primes. The nephew futilely devotes his summer to Goldbach's Conjecture, only to learn from his uncle that the problem as been unsolved for more than two centuries. The uncle also reveals his previously destructive obsession with the problem, which he ultimately abandoned in favor of chess. When the nephew encourages his uncle to renew his interest in the conjecture, trouble develops. *Booklist* reviewer Gilbert Taylor called *Uncle Petros and Goldbach's Conjecture* a "delightful and original diversion," and a *Publishers Weekly* critic deemed it "captivating."

BIOGRAPHICAL/CRITICAL SOURCES:

PERIODICALS

American Scientist, November, 2000, p. 547.
Booklist, February 1, 2000, Gilbert Taylor, review of *Uncle Petros and Goldbach's Conjecture.*
New Scientist, April 1, 2000, "Beans in Their Prime," p. 49.
New Statesman, March 13, 2000, James Hopkin, "Maths Mad," p. 56.
Publishers Weekly, January 10, 2000, review of *Uncle Petros and Goldbach's Conjecture.*
Science, December 22, 2000, David Foster Wallace, review of *Uncle Petros and Goldbach's Conjecture,* p. 2263.
Times Educational Supplement, March 31, 2000, Geraldine Brennan, review of *Uncle Petros and Goldbach's Conjecture,* p. B22.
Times Literary Supplement, April 14, 2000, Jessica Smerin, review of *Uncle Petros and Goldbach's Conjecture,* p. 26.
World Literature Today, summer, 2000, Minas Savvas, review of *Uncle Petros and Goldbach's Conjecture,* p. 684.*

DRAPER, Ellen Dooling   1944-

PERSONAL: Born January 27, 1944, in Santa Fe, NM; daughter of John and Dorothea (Matthews) Dooling; divorced; children: Frederick, Matthew, Linda. *Education:* San Francisco Conservatory of Music, B.Mus. *Politics:* Democrat. *Religion:* Protestant.

ADDRESSES: Home—Monsey, NY. *Office*—c/o Author Mail, Larson Publications, 4936 NYS Rte. 414, Burdett, NY 14818. *E-mail*—edraper@fcc.net.

CAREER: Parabola: Magazine of Myth and Tradition, New York, NY, editor, 1988-95; *Living Treasures, Inc.,* Monsey, NY, cofounder and president, 1996—.

WRITINGS:

(Editor) D. M. Dooling, *The Spirit of Quest,* Parabola Books (New York, NY), 1994.
(Editor with Jenny Koralek) *A Lively Oracle: A Centennial Celebration of P. L. Travers, Creator of Mary Poppins,* Larson (Burdett, NY), 1999.

Contributor to periodicals.

WORK IN PROGRESS: A novel based on the journal of the author's mother, a Montana rancher's wife in the 1930s and 1940s; a collection of essays on the subject of "home."

SIDELIGHTS: Ellen Dooling Draper once commented in *CA:* "My interest in writing began when I was the editor of *Parabola: Magazine of Myth and Tradition.* In addition to developing the theme of each issue, contacting and working with contributors, and editing their submissions, I wrote and translated (from French into English) for certain issues. I was fascinated with the exploration of such themes as healing, time and presence, or the stranger, all from the perspectives of myth, story, and tradition. During those years I worked with D. M. Dooling, my mother and the founder of *Parabola,* and P. L. Travers, author of the Mary Poppins books and cofounder of *Parabola.* The unique ways of thinking and writing of these two remarkable women continue to be a strong influence on me to this day.

"After both their deaths, I left *Parabola* and, along with Virginia Baron, founded *Living Treasures.* This not-for-profit venture is dedicated to the investigation of themes and questions as they are expressed in the oral traditions within American culture. Since 1996 we have presented programs on the hidden inner dimensions of New York City and on the traditions and stories of Na-

tive American cultures. Our workshops have explored the individual stories of our own lives—our names and origins, and the idea of home.

"At the same time, I have continued editing and writing, first of all focusing on the work of D. M. Dooling and P. L. Travers. *The Spirit of Quest* is a collection of Dooling's essays and poems. *A Lively Oracle* was a three-year project I undertook with Jenny Koralek to celebrate the work of P. L. Travers on the centennial of her birth. I am currently working on a fictionalization of the journals of D. M. Dooling, which describe her early years as a Montana cattle rancher's wife. I am also collecting material for a book about home, based on the programs of *Living Treasures.*

"The process of editing, translating, and essay writing are, for me, primarily disciplines of thinking: identifying the questions, then sorting, separating, and reconnecting different aspects of the question until a new understanding is reached. It is a process that requires vigilance, so as not to be satisfied with easy answers or led astray by random associations. The challenge is to persevere until the deepest possible relationship between thoughts can be discovered. I find that the crafting of words to express these relationships requires an equal vigilance, and that language itself is a source of meaning. I usually write and rewrite many times before I am able to reach the level of clarity that I am willing to share with others.

"The small excursions I have made into the field of fiction writing have indicated to me that it is, in some ways, a very different process. It is not so much a discipline of the mind as an opening toward the wealth of story that lies within, a kind of listening. The crafting of words and the use of language are as important as in essay writing, but the demand is, again, to listen and to recognize their music.

"Writing, for me, is a demanding and rewarding task, one in which I often lose track of time."

BIOGRAPHICAL/CRITICAL SOURCES:

PERIODICALS

Publishers Weekly, November 22, 1999, review of *A Lively Oracle.*

DROZ, Vanessa 1952-

PERSONAL: Born 1952, in Puerto Rico. *Education:* Universidad de Puerto Rico (comparative literature).

ADDRESSES: Office—c/o Vanessa Droz & Asociados, San Sebastian 270, San Juan, Puerto Rico.

CAREER: Writer. Vanessa Droz & Asociados, San Juan, Puerto Rico, owner, public relations firm. Teacher; journalist; graphic designer; member of editorial board of various periodicals including *Penélope o el otro mundo;* cofounder, journal *Reintegro;* weekly columnist, 1982-current.

WRITINGS:

La cicatriz a medias (title means "The forest of Scars"), Cultural (Rio Pedras, Puerto Rico), 1982.
Vicios de ángeles y otras pasiones privadas: poesia, self-published (San Juan, Puerto Rico), 1996.

Droz is also a contributor to *Gráfica y poesia,* an anthology of Puerto Rican poetry. Her work has appeared in a wide variety of literary journals and periodicals.

SIDELIGHTS: Vanessa Droz is a Puerto Rican writer. She studied comparative literature at the University of Puerto Rico and has been a teacher, journalist, and graphic designer. In addition, she was a member of the editorial board of several important literary journals in the 1970s, and was a cofounder of the journal, *Reintegro,* in 1980. Her poetry has appeared in a variety of journals and anthologies, and she writes a weekly newspaper column.

La cicatriz a medias is a collection of poems written between 1974 and 1979, in chronological order. The first section, "Poemas," contains various poems not related by any theme; the second section, "Vasos," uses the image of the vase, which can hold various things, including love, death, or a woman's body; "Payosos" includes poems about masks; and "Inicio del mapa" emphasizes the image of a scar, mark, or special sign, similar to the markings made when writing poetry. These marks can be added together to form a map or "forest of scars," the meaning of the title of the book.*

E

EDWARDS, Sean J(ames) A(lexander) 1964-

PERSONAL: Born September 6, 1964, in London, England; son of James Edwards (a journalist); married Robin Jennifer Leiter (a lawyer), September 6, 1998. *Education:* University of Virginia, B.A., 1990; Georgetown University, M.A. (with distinction), 1996; RAND Graduate School of Policy Studies, M.Phil., 1998.

ADDRESSES: Home—230 North Kenwood St., Apt. #245, Burbank, CA 91505. *E-mail*—Sean-Edwards@ RAND.org.

CAREER: Infodata Systems Inc., Falls Church, VA, programmer analyst, 1990-92; American Management Systems, Arlington, VA, software consultant, 1992-95; Pacific-Sierra Research Corporation, Arlington, VA, independent consultant intern, 1996; RAND, Santa Monica, CA, doctoral fellow, 1996—. *Military service:* U.S. Army, 1981-84; served as airborne ranger, machine gunner, armorer, team and team leader in the 2/ 75th Ranger Battalion and 2/47th Infantry Battalion; became sergeant; received airborne wings, expert infantry badge, good conduct medal, army achievement medal, honor graduate of infantry basic training, and honor graduate of non-commissioned officer school.

WRITINGS:

(With Russell W. Glenn, Randall Steeb, John Matsumura, Robert Everson, Scott Gerwehr, and John Gordon) *Denying the Widow-Maker: Summary of Proceedings: RAND-DBBL Conference on Military Operations on Urbanized Terrain,* RAND (Santa Monica, CA), 1998.
(With James Dewar, Steven C. Bankes, and James C. Wendt) *Expandability of the Twenty-first Century Army,* RAND (Santa Monica, CA), 2000.

(With Glenn, David Johnson, Jay Bruder, Michael Scheiern, Elwyn D. Harris, Jody A. Jacobs, Iris Kameny and John Pinder) *Getting the Musicians of Mars on the Same Sheet of Music: Army-Joint, Multinational, and Interagency C4ISR Interoperability,* RAND (Santa Monica, CA), 2000.
Mars Unmasked: The Changing Face of Urban Operations, RAND (Santa Monica, CA), 2000.
Swarming on the Battlefield: Past, Present and Future, RAND (Santa Monica, CA), 2000.

Contributor to *National Security Studies Quarterly.*

WORK IN PROGRESS: Research on "the potential of swarming as a future operational concept."

*　　*　　*

ELLIS, Bill 1950-

PERSONAL: Born January 3, 1950, in Roanoke, VA; son of William Robert (a railway claims agent) and Mae Downs (a social worker) Ellis; married Carol Ann Ellis (a writer/editor), September 20, 1980; children: Elizabeth May. *Education:* University of Virginia, B.A. (with high honors), 1972; Ohio State University, M.A., 1973, Ph.D. (with distinction), 1978. *Politics:* "Democrat." *Religion:* "Lutheran (ELCA)." *Avocational interests:* "Music, hiking, heirloom gardening, cooking, Japanese manga/anime."

ADDRESSES: Office—The Hazleton Campus, Pennsylvania State University, Highacres, Hazleton, PA 18201-1291; fax: 570-450-3182. *E-mail*—wce2@ psu.edu.

CAREER: Ohio State University, Columbus, OH, lecturer in English Department, 1978-82, supervisor, Center for Textual Studies, 1982-83; Pennsylvania State University, Hazleton, PA, assistant professor, 1984-90, associate professor of English and American studies, 1990—. Indiana University, Folklore Institute, visiting assistant professor, 1982; media expert for television shows, including features by the Fox Family Network and Arts & Entertainment Network; participant in numerous scholarly meetings and conferences.

MEMBER: International Society for Contemporary Legend Research (president, 1994-99), American Folklore Society (president, Folk Narrative Section, 1989-98; president, Children's Folklore Section, 1987-89 and 1998-2000), Modern Language Association of America, Pennsylvania Folklore Society, Nathaniel Hawthorne Society.

AWARDS, HONORS: Fellows' Prize, American Folklore Society, 1978, for best student publication in folklore; Centennial Award, American Folklore Society, 1989, for service to Folk Narrative Section.

WRITINGS:

(Editor, with Thomas Woodson, L. Neal Smith, and Norman Holmes Pearson) *The Letters, 1813-1843* and *The Letters, 1843-1853. The Centenary Edition of the Works of Nathaniel Hawthorne,* Volumes 15-16, Ohio State University Press (Columbus, OH), 1985.

(Editor) *The Consular Letters, 1853-1855* and *The Consular Letters, 1856-1857. The Centenary Edition of the Works of Nathaniel Hawthorne,* Volumes 19-20, Ohio State University Press (Columbus, OH), 1988.

(Editor, with Thomas Woodson) *The English Notebooks, 1853-1856* and *The English Notebooks, 1856-1861. The Centenary Edition of the Works of Nathaniel Hawthorne,* Volumes 21-22, Ohio State University Press (Columbus, OH), 1997.

Raising the Devil: Satanism, New Religions, and the Media, University Press of Kentucky (Lexington, KY), 2000.

Aliens, Ghosts, and Cults: Legends We Live, University of Mississippi Press, 2001.

Editor, *Contemporary Legends in Emergence* (monograph), California Folklore Society, 1990. Editor, *FOAFtale News* (newsletter of the International Society for Contemporary Legend Research), 1989-94. Contributor to books, including *Halloween and Other Festivals of Death and Life,* edited by Jack Santino, University of Tennessee Press (Knoxville, TN), 1994; *Jack in Two Worlds: Contemporary North American Tale-tellers,* edited by William Barnard McCarthy, University of North Carolina Press (Chapel Hill, NC), 1994; and *Folklore: An Encyclopedia of Beliefs, Customs, Tales, Music, and Art,* edited by Thomas A. Green, ABC-CLIO (Santa Barbara, CA), 1997. Contributor to various periodicals, including *Journal of American Folklore, Studies in the American Renaissance, Psychology Today, Skeptical Inquirer,* and *Fortean Times.*

WORK IN PROGRESS: In League with the Devil: Masons, Spiritualists, and Devil-Worshipers, for University Press of Kentucky; research on Hawthorne and contemporary legend, and on semiotics of Japanese anime.

SIDELIGHTS: Bill Ellis told *CA:* "The impetus for my writing and research stems from the heady days of the 1970s, when a generation of bright scholars sought to transform the discipline of folkloristics from a bookish investigation of dying cultural materials into a radical critique of contemporary traditions. I began studying a storytelling tradition at a summer camp serving a multiethnic community of young people from inner-city Cleveland. Needing to expand existing folkloristic concepts to describe the functions of these stories, I, like many other young scholars, freely adapted ideas from sociolinguistics and semiotics. This work then drew me to look more globally at the roles of other traditions of adolescence, such as 'legend-tripping,' the custom of visiting allegedly haunted sites by car and ritually invoking the supernatural. Like my colleagues, I felt confident that folkloristics could be a key player in the study of contemporary youth culture.

"The euphoria of these days was broken by the academic retrenchment of the 1980s. I saw many colleagues silenced—many by leaving the field, some (like the brilliant Sue Samuelson) through premature death. A position with Ohio State's edition of Nathaniel Hawthorne allowed me first to continue academic research, though I came to identify with Hawthorne's search for desk work that would let him support his family and continue to think and write creatively. In the 1990s I found the discipline of folkloristics decimated and my research agenda marginalized. The elements of youth culture I had studied before now were being cited as evidence for omnipresent 'satanic cults.' This led to *Raising the Devil,* a cultural history of the origins of the 1980s 'Satanism Scare.' Researching this panic's roots, through grassroots traditions of exorcism, anti-Semitism, Ouija board use, and graveyard desecration, was like consuming a steaming bowl of maggot soup.

But the job needed doing, and too few academics were willing to do it.

"*Raising the Devil* will be followed by two additional books. The first, *Aliens, Ghosts, and Cults: Legends We Live* revisits much of my earlier work on the narratives in youth culture and on 'ostension,' the way in which oral narratives model real-life actions, even deadly ones. The second, *In League with the Devil,* will look at the Satanism Scare in a broader historical context, showing how it enveloped out of much older occult traditions.

"Seeing my folkloristic work appear now brings mixed emotions: I can't help feeling that a more conventional field of study would have helped me protect my family from economic and social hardship. Still, I feel a duty to my silenced colleagues of the 1970s to carry on some of their intellectual excitement. While I am reconciled to the marginal status of my discipline at present, and of my work within this discipline, I still believe that the study of folklore remains essential to an understanding of human culture at large. Information communicated orally and through computer networks is often as influential (or more so) than that disseminated through the media and official channels. And folklorists have a civic responsibility to address social problems directly rather than to veil their work in a hermetic, self-referential jargon."

BIOGRAPHICAL/CRITICAL SOURCES:

PERIODICALS

Lexington Herald-Leader, November 19, 2000, Dwight A. Moody, " 'The Devil' Is in the Details."

*   *   *

ENGDAHL, Sylvia Louise 1933-

PERSONAL: Born November 24, 1933, in Los Angeles, CA; daughter of Amandus J. and Mildred Allen (a writer under her maiden name of Butler) Engdahl. *Education:* University of California, Santa Barbara, B.A., 1955; Portland State University, graduate study, 1978-80. *Religion:* Episcopalian.

ADDRESSES: Home—Eugene, OR. *Office*—c/o Walker and Company, 435 Hudson St., New York, NY 10014. *E-mail*—sle@sylviaengdahl.com.

CAREER: Writer. Elementary teacher in Portland, OR, 1955-56; System Development Corp. (computer pro-

Sylvia Louise Engdahl

gramming for SAGE Air Defense System), 1957-67, began as programmer, became computer systems specialist, working in Lexington, MA, Madison, WI, Tacoma, WA, and Santa Monica, CA; freelance writer, 1968-80; developer and vendor of software for home computers, 1981-84; Connected Education Inc., White Plains, NY, member of online faculty, 1985-97.

AWARDS, HONORS: Newbery Honor Book Award, 1971, Notable Book citation, American Library Association, Honor List citation, *Horn Book,* Phoenix Award, 1990, and Junior Literary Guild selection, all for *Enchantress from the Stars;* Christopher Award, 1973, for *This Star Shall Abide.*

WRITINGS:

Children of the Star (adult fiction omnibus edition; contains *This Star Shall Abide, Beyond the Tomorrow Mountains,* and *The Doors of the Universe*), Meisha Merlin (Atlanta, GA), 2000.

FICTION; FOR YOUNG ADULTS

Enchantress from the Stars, illustrated by Rodney Shackell, Atheneum (New York, NY), 1970, new edition with jacket and vignettes by Leo and Diane Dillon, Walker (New York, NY), 2001.

Journey between Worlds, illustrated by James and Ruth McCrea, Atheneum (New York, NY), 1970.

The Far Side of Evil, illustrated by Richard Cuffari, Atheneum (New York, NY), 1971, revised edition, Walker (New York, NY), 2002.

This Star Shall Abide (first novel in a trilogy), illustrated by Richard Cuffari, Atheneum (New York, NY), 1972, published as *Heritage of the Star,* Gollancz (London, England), 1973.

Beyond the Tomorrow Mountains (second novel in trilogy), illustrated by Richard Cuffari, Atheneum (New York, NY), 1973.

The Doors of the Universe (third novel in trilogy), Atheneum (New York, NY), 1981.

NONFICTION; FOR YOUNG ADULTS

The Planet-girded Suns: Man's View of Other Solar Systems, illustrated by Richard Cuffari, Atheneum (New York, NY), 1974.

(With Rick Roberson) *The Subnuclear Zoo: New Discoveries in High-Energy Physics,* Atheneum (New York, NY), 1977.

(With Rick Roberson) *Tool for Tomorrow: New Knowledge about Genes,* Atheneum (New York, NY), 1979.

OTHER

(Editor, with Rick Roberson) *Universe Ahead: Stories of the Future* (anthology), illustrated by Richard Cuffari, Atheneum (New York, NY), 1975.

(Editor) *Anywhere, Anywhen: Stories of Tomorrow* (anthology), Atheneum (New York, NY), 1976.

Our World Is Earth (picture book), illustrated by Don Sibley, Atheneum (New York, NY), 1979.

SIDELIGHTS: Sylvia Louise Engdahl told *CA* that as a writer she aims to "bring present-day issues into perspective through speculation about the future as related to the past, with particular emphasis on space exploration, which I believe to be the most significant challenge facing the human race and the only long-range goal that will unite mankind in peace. . . . It is also my belief that today's tendency to equate realism with pessimism is invalid. My science fiction is not intended primarily for fans of that genre; rather, it is directed to readers without an SF background, and deals not so much with technological progress as with the human values I consider important."

"Because of the awards won by *Enchantress of the Stars,* I became known as an author for children; how-

ever, that is the only one of my novels intended for an audience below high school age. Unfortunately, the original editions of the others were generally placed next to it in the children's rooms of libraries, and thus often failed to reach the mature readers most apt to enjoy them. This was particularly true in the case of the second and third volumes of my trilogy, which has now been reissued as adult science fiction and is finally available in paperback.

"Although I have for some time been working on an adult nonfiction book about the emerging mythology of the Space Age, much of my present activity is centered on the Internet. I have done some Web design work, and in addition I maintain a site of my own, www.sylviaengdahl.com, through which I enjoy interacting with readers. The discovery that people on the Net remember my novels, and still want to read them, has led directly to their republication after being out of print for many years. One of the advantages of writing about future or hypothetical worlds is that the stories do not become outdated. It is my hope that my trilogy will find a new audience of older teens and adults, and that the 2001 hardcover edition of *Enchantress from the Stars* will reach a new generation of children."

Engdahl's first novel, *Enchantress from the Stars,* was a 1971 Newbery Honor Book. It tells the story of Elana, an anthropology student from an interstellar civilization who becomes embroiled in a struggle to save a world with a feudal culture from being overtaken by technology-driven interplanetary invaders. The novel uses the device of shared narration to highlight its theme of mutual respect. The author makes clear that the fact that Elana's culture is the most advanced of those portrayed does not make her "better" than the other characters, who also receive an opportunity to speak to readers. Claudia Nelson wrote in *Twentieth-Century Young Adult Writers:* "In *Enchantress from the Stars,* Engdahl foregrounds concerns that extend throughout her works: the importance of empathy, intelligence, and moral courage; the individual's role in effecting change; and the need to approach problems on a symbolic as well as a literal level and to combine the mundane with the spiritual."

This Star Shall Abide, Beyond the Tomorrow Mountains, and *The Doors of the Universe* comprise a trilogy, published in an omnibus edition as adult science fiction under the title *Children of the Star.* It is the story of Noren, who as an adolescent rebels against his planet's restrictive society, and who as an adult devotes his life to the hope of restoring his people's rightful heritage. "The trilogy is an extended meditation on the need for total commitment to an ideal, for willingness to challenge assumptions, and for change," Nelson explained. "Again the individual is paramount." Assessing Engdahl's body of work, Nelson concluded: "The consistently high quality of her prose and the unity of her moral vision make Engdahl's works exciting and deserving of addition to the canon of young-adult science fiction."

AUTOBIOGRAPHICAL ESSAY:

Sylvia Engdahl contributed the following autobiographical essay to *CA:*

As far back as I can remember I felt different from people around me. Perhaps that was one reason I chose to write about other worlds. It was not the main one—mainly I write about them because I believe the humanization of space is vitally important to the future of our species. But before talking about my books, I should tell something about my life.

I was born and grew up in Los Angeles, California, which is a place I never have liked and do not recall with nostalgia. My father, born in 1881, came to America from Sweden as a small child, but he had forgotten his Swedish heritage at the time I knew him and had no living relatives except a grown son and granddaughter from a previous marriage. He was a real estate salesman, only occasionally successful. My mother came from New England, and my grandmother, her mother, lived with us during most of my youth. I had no brothers or sisters other than my half brother, whom I seldom saw and thought of as an uncle. A second cousin, ten years older than I, was the one relative outside my immediate family that I knew well.

I never had anything in common with other children and didn't enjoy playing with them. My mother tells me I was a happy child so I must have seemed outwardly content, but I don't remember being happy often. On the other hand, I was rarely especially unhappy, either. I simply waited, in a sort of resigned way, to grow up, assuming that in the adult world life would really begin. It didn't turn out like that, of course, but I have done quite a few interesting things as an adult, whereas not much of interest happened during my school years.

I was bored by school. What I learned, I learned at home from my mother and from reading; school was mainly hours to live through, punctuated by moments of fierce anger at teachers who wanted me to participate in active games not only during Phys Ed periods, which I despised, but during recess. This I considered (and

Sylvia Engdahl at age ten

still consider, despite today's faddish idolization of "fitness") an intolerable injustice—I can remember hiding in the girls' room to get out of it. At that time it was thought very important to keep children who were poor readers and yet manually skilled from feeling inferior. The reverse, alas, was not true. I got no recognition for superior reading and writing ability, but all too much for my deficiency of physical coordination (I was the only child in kindergarten who couldn't skip) and my total lack of interest in physical activities, which arose in part from an inborn lack of energy that made all such activities exhausting for me. I did not feel inferior on this account, but I was given the impression that I ought to, and perhaps as a result learned very early to ignore the opinions of so-called authorities in other areas, too. I was never openly rebellious except in refusing to play ball games and to socialize with my peers; certainly I never told teachers or classmates that my views on most subjects didn't match those of society. But my inner convictions were always my own.

Outside school I had little companionship apart from that of my mother, who was, and remains, the chief personal influence on my life. Our tastes were similar, though as I grew up my specific interests became very different from hers. Mother, who had been an English teacher and a little theater director, fostered my innate enthusiasm for reading, writing, and the world of ideas. Her marriage was an unhappy one, for my father liked none of these things (I cannot remember his ever opening a book or magazine) and she thus turned to me, much as I turned to her because I found no friends of my own age with compatible interests. Neither of us had any domestic inclinations; Mother kept house only because at the time she had no alternative. Had she told me when I was small that she disliked it, I would have helped more with the housework, but she made the mistake of trying to persuade me to learn such skills for my own future good, and I reacted against that right from the beginning. I had no desire to marry, raise children, or be a homemaker, though in those days it was assumed that a girl "naturally" would—and unlike my mother, I didn't believe one should do things merely because they were expected. When I was older I envisioned someday marrying for love, but the sad example of my parents' marriage had put me on guard against falling in love with anyone who did not share my intellectual interests and who had none of his own that I could admire. This, I believe, was fortunate, since I might otherwise have plunged rashly into a conventional life for which I was not at all suited.

The highlights of my younger years were our short summer vacations at Bass Lake, north of Los Angeles in the Sierra Nevada. We went there for the first time when I was ten, and ever since I've dated the beginning of my life from that trip; no earlier memory has any meaning for me. When I saw Bass Lake, I realized what was missing in Southern California, which I'd hitherto taken for granted. At Bass Lake trees cloaked the mountains and shoreline—forest trees, in this case Ponderosa pines, very unlike the cultivated trees found in Los Angeles. There was green forest undergrowth and clear, fresh air. And of course, there was the water. We rented a boat that first year; later on my father bought one, the only thing he ever did that I found enjoyable. I counted the days between our trips to Bass Lake, and during my teen years I was convinced that nothing could make me happier than to live there permanently. I even hoped I might someday get a job teaching the one-room school there.

I planned from earliest childhood to be a teacher. Even when I was so young as to enjoy dolls, I always imagined myself as "teacher" rather than "mother," and by the time I was eleven I was running a Saturday morning "nursery school" for neighborhood children. During my early teens I organized summer arts and craft classes through which I earned some spending money. What I really enjoyed was planning and being in charge, not the actual contact with children; but I was too young to realize that. Anyway, I preferred it to social contact with my agemates, of which I had little because I could not share the interests of other teens.

If I were a teenager today, it would be different. Today many teenagers are interested in computers, and I often think of what a social life I'd have had if I had grown up in such an era. When I phone electronic bulletin boards used largely by teens, I am reminded that had these existed during my own youth I would not have been isolated and lonely. In addition to having a natural bent for programming, I communicate better via a keyboard than in person, and would have done so even in adolescence. At that time it was assumed, even by me, that I could not talk because I was shy; but now I know that it was the other way around. I was shy because I could not talk easily, and I could not do so because I need visual feedback rather than audible feedback when expressing my ideas. I am a natural writer, and today natural writers are coming into their own socially via electronic mail and interactive computer conferencing. But of course, when I was in my teens, no one had heard of computers at all, let alone home computers.

So high school, like the earlier period, was merely a time of waiting for me. I kept busy with my own pursuits but had as little to do with school as possible. I didn't get particularly high grades because the classes didn't seem worth bothering with, and also because teachers often marked down students who didn't talk effectively, however well they did on written work. Still I met the requirements for graduation easily enough, and in fact met them in time to graduate a semester ahead of schedule—but the counselor wouldn't let me do it because I was "too young" and not "socially mature," by which she meant she thought I ought to participate in class activities. As usual, I was silently resentful, and not as assertive in fighting that decision as I now feel I should have been. I was indeed young, barely sixteen, but ironically my few friends happened to be in the class ahead. They graduated, while I was forced to remain without any classes of substance left to take (I hadn't been permitted to enroll in physics because I didn't plan a science major in college). I repeated Library Practice, which I enjoyed, and signed up for the class that produced the yearbook, ending up as Assistant Editor; I suppose this looked good on my record but it did not really involve much editing work.

The one school incident with lasting influence on my life happened when I was twelve, in a ninth-grade science class. It was there that I first heard about space. We were studying astronomy, which for a while captured my imagination; but more significantly, one day the teacher read aloud a short description of what it might be like to travel in space, and for some reason it excited me in a way nothing else ever had. I had not read any science fiction, and had never talked to anyone who knew of it; and of course this was in 1946, before space travel was widely discussed. Yet I went home that day and began drawing pictures of rockets on the way to Mars. A friend happened to be with me; I said to her—on the basis of no information or reading whatsoever—that I was willing to bet a spaceship would reach the moon within twenty-five years. As it turned out, I was just two years off, on the conservative side, in my wild estimate. I will never know what prompted it.

From then on I read whatever I could find about space, though I did not care for much of the science fiction I encountered. I was interested in what space travel and colonization of other planets might actually be like, not in wild adventure tales or stories designed to be as exotic and far-removed from real life as possible—and for this reason, I still don't consider myself a "science fiction fan." I honestly don't know why space fascinated me in those early years. It was before I had developed the convictions about its importance that have been so central to me since, and though it may seem as if, being a social misfit, I might understandably have daydreamed about some better world, that was not what happened. I didn't imagine alien societies. I simply thought about man's coming exploration of nearby planets. It never occurred to me to doubt that space travel would come.

*

The year I was sixteen, my life changed radically. My parents finally separated, and after I graduated from high school our house was sold; I moved with my mother and grandmother into an apartment while waiting for college to start in the fall. All these events were welcome. I had everything I thought I wanted—I had been accepted by Pomona College in Claremont, California, which I'd long planned to attend, deliberately avoiding the large universities to which other members of my class applied. I hated big cities, and Pomona seemed ideal. When I got there, however, I met exactly the same problems I'd had in high school: classes that were uninspiring and no social life of a kind that appealed to me. Furthermore, I found the company of dorm residents less congenial than that of my mother and the lack of privacy burdensome. I don't know what would have happened if I'd stayed. A further change, however, drove any thought of staying from my mind.

With her parents and cousin at Bass Lake, 1946

My mother decided to get a master's degree in drama at the University of Oregon in Eugene. We went for a preliminary visit there during Christmas vacation, and after one look at Oregon I knew that under no circumstances would I be willing to be left behind in Southern California.

It seems strange to me now that I did not immediately enroll in the University of Oregon myself; but we still felt—probably because Mother was a Wellesley graduate—that a small private college would have advantages, and though we didn't have much money, my grandmother had planned to pay my tuition. So I transferred to Reed College in Portland for the spring semester of my freshman year. When I didn't fit in there, either, we belatedly realized that for both financial and personal reasons I would be better off in Eugene. My sophomore year, I did attend the U of O. We lived in a small old-fashioned rented house on a tree-lined street near the campus; I still think of it with longing, though we have had many nicer homes since. It was different from anything I'd known in California, and in my eyes much to be preferred. I loved Oregon; I loved the tall firs and the greenness and the change of seasons, and even the steady soft rain. Then too, I was seventeen, and had left childhood and its scenes behind without yet having met any disillusionments of maturity.

This interlude couldn't last. Mother's degree program took only a year and a half, and there was nothing for her to do in Eugene afterwards. I didn't want to live in a dormitory despite my liking for the campus—which had turned out to be the best thing about the U of O from my standpoint. Then too, at that time no elementary teaching certificate was offered there, and I still believed I wanted to teach; so it was necessary to transfer again for my junior and senior years in any case. Mother planned to return to Los Angeles with my grandmother (who remained with us through all our moves until she died in 1965 at the age of 101). I was unwilling to go there, so I chose the nearby University of California at Santa Barbara, in part because it was the only place I could get a B.A. without foreign language courses, and whereas I'd been good at reading and writing languages in high school, my strongly visual mode of expression made me incapable of learning to speak them.

When at the beginning of my junior year we got back from a summer in the East, my father having died in the meantime, Mother decided to come to Santa Barbara too and start a theater group for children. We lived there two years. But after all my transfers I needed longer than that to get the required credits for a degree and teaching certificate. Mother was offered a directing job at the Portland Civic Theater—which, incidentally, she had directed long before in 1927-29—and I could not escape staying behind to finish up. I roomed off-campus, counting the days till I'd be in Oregon again. Fortunately I was able to visit during the winter to interview for teaching jobs, and managed to obtain one in the Portland area for the following fall.

All this time, I had remained firm in my conviction that teaching was the career I wanted, perhaps because I could think of no other, and also because I wanted the summers free for camp work. Summers had been the high spot of my college years, just as Bass Lake had highlighted the earlier era; I had worked as a camp counselor my first year in Oregon, and later in New York State, California, and best of all at Camp Sweyolakan on Coeur d'Alene Lake in Idaho, where I was a Unit Director during the summers of 1954 and 1955. Aside from its beauty, Sweyolakan was particularly enjoyable because I had opportunity to go on canoe trips—though my lack of physical energy kept me from doing much hiking at any of the camps and I spent my time teaching handcrafts and planning campfire programs, I found that paddling was far less tiring for me than walking. I will always cherish the memory of those trips on the water. Also, I liked organizing camp life, and dreamed of someday directing a camp of my own. The fact that being with children was becoming more and more nerve-wearing somehow escaped my attention.

When I found myself at last a fourth-grade teacher in a Portland suburb, however, my temperamental unfitness for the job became all too apparent. It was a disaster. I could tutor the children effectively on an individual basis, but I could not cope with them as a group, nor could I handle classroom discipline. As a matter of fact, I was asked to resign after the first year; but nothing could have induced me to continue in any case. I discovered that I really didn't like young children, even apart from the fact that I violently disagreed with the theories of education and psychology then in vogue: a fact that had made my college training merely something to be endured for the sake of the required certificate.

So I didn't know what to do. We had acquired a lovely old house on a hilltop in Portland where I was determined to remain, yet I had to earn a living, and I was not qualified for any job outside the field of education. I knew I could never teach at the high school or college level because I could not express ideas effectively aloud, and anyway I didn't want to specialize in a particular subject. I would have liked to be a librarian, but that would have meant two more years of expensive college training outside the state of Oregon, which did not offer a librarianship program. I couldn't do clerical work since my poor physical coordination made it impossible for me to type by the touch system (I still, after many years as a writer, use only two fingers on each hand in typing, which does not bother me but means I can't attain a typist's speed). By default, therefore—after a summer as Resident Camp Director at a Camp Fire Girls camp nearby—I began to work toward a Master of Education degree through night courses available in Portland, thinking this would enable me to become a school counselor.

Strangely, the year I spent on that graduate work proved one of the most fruitful of my life. The courses, which demanded little study, were even less inspiring than undergraduate Education courses; but they left me with a great many free hours at home, and for the first time I devoted deep thought to my ideas about space. Furthermore, I began to write them down. Unlike most authors, I had never written stories during my youth, other than a few unpublishable pieces of children's fiction about such things as Bass Lake and camp life. My creative ideas were abstract intellectual ones, not incidents for stories. It had never occurred to me to become a writer because I knew people didn't want to read philosophical tracts. But that one year, for reasons I still haven't been able to decipher, I did get ideas for stories, albeit stories of a quite offbeat sort that were not then marketable. Partial drafts of those that ultimately became my novels were all written then—and I haven't had an idea for a real story since! I only hope it will someday happen again.

Also during that year, I developed my beliefs about the importance of space to human survival; and that, of course, is something I've had a great many more ideas about since. I am by nature more of an analytical person than a storyteller. I can write endlessly about speculations concerning not only space but other subjects; but to express these in story form requires more than writing skill. It demands ideas not just about truths but about happenings. It demands not merely portrayal of characters, but the ability to visualize action in which those characters are involved—and that type of creativeness is not something that can be learned. Most writers have plenty of it; it's a faculty they start out with and must learn to channel. I, as in so many areas of life, am the opposite of most others; the analytical skills, those taught in writing courses, came naturally to me, but the story-creation faculty has arisen in me rarely.

I did try to put some of my ideas into short-story form that year of 1956-57, but they were not suitable for short stories and were of course rejected by the magazines to which I sent them. I never thought of making novels of them then. At that time such novels would not have been publishable; space was not yet a topic of general interest.

Among these stories was the one that later became *The Far Side of Evil,* based on the concept of the Critical Stage about which I was (and still am) entirely serious. Young people today may believe that worry about nuclear war is new, but it isn't—in 1956 it was a major concern. I thought to myself then, and attempted to say in the story, that planet Earth was indeed in a Critical Stage, that if we didn't turn our attention to space soon we would very likely be wiped out by a nuclear war. I saw no signs, unfortunately, that we were making any attempt to get into space. One of the most encouraging experiences I've ever had was hearing the very next year that Sputnik had been launched into orbit, making it impossible, I believed, for the setting of my story to be Earth. I still believed this when the novel was published in 1971; I assumed after the Apollo moon landing that Earth was fully committed and thus safely past the crisis. Now I am not so sure. Now I am nervous again when I see cutbacks in the space program, since evidently a planet can stay in the Critical Stage much longer than I first thought.

*

In the spring of 1957, nearing the end of my graduate work and without hope of earning money through writing, I came to another turning point. I did not really want to be a school counselor, but I'd been putting off thinking about that problem. I had to go to summer school in Eugene in order to qualify for the degree. One day in May—the most fateful day of my life—I drove down to Eugene from Portland to make the arrangements. I talked to one of the professors there. And some casual remark I made suddenly opened my eyes to the futility of the whole plan. I was, I saw, a hypocrite! I was pretending to believe the officially-approved theories of Educational Psychology when I privately thought they were rubbish, and sooner or later I would be found out. Even if I went on pretending long enough to receive a degree in the field, I would despise working in it. To continue would be intolerable.

I barely managed to conclude the conversation with the professor, then, without registering for summer school, I numbly drove the 125 miles back to Portland. At home, not knowing what to do next, I picked up the nearest magazine and glanced through it; it was Mother's Wellesley alumnae magazine, something I never read. In it was an article about a young woman who was learning to program computers, which I skimmed with some interest, but did not connect in any way with everyday life—I'd heard of computers, I suppose, in science fiction, but didn't imagine that people not trained as scientists could experiment with them. Next, I picked up the want-ad section of the newspaper. I'd never looked at that before either, since jobs in the education field aren't listed in classified ads. To my amazement, there was a box ad there for people to join the same computer programming project mentioned in the magazine article.

The project was the SAGE Air Defense System, then a new and unique concept, which was being developed by the Rand Corporation. Its recruiter was touring the country, stopping in Portland just that one day. The ad appeared in the paper that day only; I will never stop marveling at the uncanny series of coincidences that caused me to see it.

The qualifications mentioned in the ad were not too far from mine; more math courses than I'd taken were specified, but I had done well in math and thought it might be possible to catch up on my own. The listing appeared under "Help Wanted—Men" (in those days newspapers separated jobs by sex) but the magazine article had told me women were included. So I called the recruiter. They did hire women, he said, but his interview schedule was filled; I would have to go to see him

College senior portrait, 1954

late that night at his hotel. Dubious as this might otherwise have sounded, having read about the work in the Wellesley magazine convinced me that it was legitimate, and so I went. When I got there, he gave me a written aptitude test, then asked me to return for a second interview the next morning. And that morning I was hired on the spot. He told me he'd have accepted me the night before except that it was so obviously a sudden move on my part that he wanted me to think it over.

I didn't have to think long; I was twenty-three years old with no other prospect of employment, and though I had little idea what computer programming was, it sounded interesting. To be sure, it meant leaving Oregon, but my sorrow over that was overshadowed by the excitement of doing something entirely new. Also the salary offered me was astonishing—$400 a month, which in that era, by my standards, seemed like a fortune; it was far more than I had earned as a teacher. I later learned that many of the people hired for the project were former teachers. Now, computer programmers are trained in college; but there was no such thing as a college Computer Science department then. There were

no programmers at all except a few mathematicians doing developmental work. SAGE was a large project and its staff had to be found among men and women with degrees in other fields. Our training was provided on the job.

At the end of June, 1957, I reported for work at Rand's SAGE headquarters in Lexington, Massachusetts. Since this was to be a temporary location and I had no idea where I'd be sent next—we were to be moved around the country to install the system at different Air Force bases—I rented a room in a private home; the most convenient location proved to be in Wellesley Hills, where Mother had lived many years before. The initial phase of training, to my surprise, was a formal course given by IBM on the MIT campus in Cambridge. I was nervous the first day, since I didn't have all the math prerequisites I'd been told would be expected, but it turned out that no math at all was needed. (Most kinds of programming do not involve mathematics; they'd specified math background only because people with math aptitude are likely to also have programming aptitude.) I found programming easy and loved it right from the start. How strange it seemed to be paid a salary for attending a class much more interesting than any I'd had in college! My free time was filled with more activities than in the past, too, since I had a car, a whole new region of the country to explore, and classmates to take trips with on weekends. That summer was one of the happiest of my life.

I'll never forget my first look at the computer. Computers in those days were not at all like what they are today—the one used for SAGE, the IBM ANFS-Q7 (called simply the Q7 for short) filled several rooms. In Lexington we had access only to an experimental prototype located at MIT's Lincoln Laboratory. Since a great many people had to share it besides trainees, our brief computer time during the course was scheduled at three o'clock in the morning. Our government security clearances hadn't come through yet, so we had to wait in a locked classroom while pairs of students were escorted to the computer room to try out short programs. These programs were of course written in assembly language, the only computer language that yet existed for non-mathematical applications (besides binary machine language, which we also learned). The Q7 didn't have a keyboard as personal computers now do; to communicate with it, you had to put a deck of punched cards into the card reader. Then, after the program was assembled, you got a deck of binary cards out of the automatic punch machine and put them into the card reader in turn. In later years these operations became very familiar to me, though later, we used magnetic tape rather than cards for most program assemblies. But that first night it all seemed mysterious and exciting.

To modern computer users it might seem mysterious still, for the Q7 had a room-wide "front panel" of flashing lights. If you knew machine language, you could read the contents of CPU and memory registers in these lights; that's how debugging was done. The computer room was dimly lit so the lights could be easily seen; the adjacent room containing consoles with air defense displays was called the Blue Room because its dim light was blue. There were still more rooms filled with frames of vacuum tubes. Yet despite its immense array of hardware, the Q7 had only an 8K memory! It seemed ample to us, and several years later, when it was expanded to 64K, we thought that was phenomenal. Now [1987] the computer on my own desk, on which I'm writing this article, has a memory ten times that large (though it's not quite a fair comparison because it stores less information per address than the Q7 did). There has been a lot of progress in the past thirty years. Yet I still feel affection for the old Q7 and in some ways I rather miss it. It did its job well; the reason it could handle air defense surveillance with so little memory was that in those days we used programming techniques more efficient, from the machine language standpoint, than those now commonly employed.

When my training was finished, I was sent, somewhat ironically, to Santa Monica, California, a part of greater Los Angeles near where I'd grown up; but since that too was to be temporary, I didn't object. In the summer of 1958 I was transferred to Madison, Wisconsin, and in 1959 to Tacoma, Washington. I had my own apartment in each of these places and enjoyed the variety of moving to different areas, but my life centered on my job.

Most of my work was not with the air defense program itself, but with programs of the type now called systems software. SAGE was a real-time system, the most advanced of its era. At the field locations, I had a lot of time to operate the computer personally, since there were only a few programmers at each Air Force base and the computers (which we weren't allowed to touch except for their front panel switches) needed to be kept busy continuously to break them in. So I became an expert on systems software of the sort—primitive by today's standards—that existed then, and had a chance to develop some of what was used. In 1960 I was transferred back to Santa Monica on a permanent basis; that was the home office of SDC, for which I had worked since it separated from its parent company Rand. It was the place where I would have the most opportunity to do developmental programming, so I wanted to be

there; moreover, Mother had left Portland and was living in Santa Barbara again. It did not seem that I would ever have an opportunity to return to Oregon.

I sometimes see it said, even today, that there is prejudice against women in technical fields like computer science. That strikes me as strange, since I never encountered any, and if it is now true, then SDC must have been an exception. There were relatively few women among the SAGE programmers, but I certainly received raises and promotions as fast as the men did, and I never went out of my way to seek them. I was the first female Unit Head in my group, but nobody seemed to think that was any big deal. By 1965 I ranked as a Computer Systems Specialist. I didn't want to get away from programming into a wholly supervisory job, for which I wasn't temperamentally fitted; so in lieu of line promotion I became a Technical Assistant to the Group Head and was Project Head for design and development of a major experimental change in the program organization of SAGE. Also, I did more and more technical writing—I liked it and was good at it, which is the exception rather than the rule among programmers. Though the normal procedure was to use a secretary, I convinced my boss that I could neither write drafts by hand nor dictate, and was thus entitled to have a typewriter in my own office. How much more I could have produced with a word processor, something then not even dreamed of!

There were problems with this situation, though. In the first place, writing began to take me away from programming. Furthermore, what I wrote was either classified (secret) or proprietary, so that I couldn't show it to anybody outside the company. And I began to feel that if I was going to write most of the time I would like to do it in a form that would appear publicly under my name. I did not have energy to do writing of my own in my off-hours, as many authors do; one full-time job was all I could manage without collapsing from fatigue. In the evenings I could do no more than read. Strangely, I didn't even think much about space during those years, pleased though I was by the manned missions of the early sixties. I suppose underneath I avoided it because I wasn't personally involved in the space effort. Many programmers worked on Gemini and Apollo, but I was neither energetic nor assertive enough to seek a new job and in any case, neither Florida nor Houston was a place we wanted to live.

By this time, Mother and I were sharing a home; for a while we'd had a very pleasant one with a swimming pool in the San Fernando Valley, but after my grandmother's death we moved closer to Santa Monica because we preferred its climate and because commuting in rush hour traffic, which took longer and longer, tired me too much. Despite our new home's high-priced locale and ocean view, I wasn't happy there. I didn't mind my lack of social life, since that of my office acquaintances appeared to revolve around sports and/or drinking, neither of which was my idea of fun; still my days seemed increasingly monotonous. My salary had enabled us to take wonderful vacations, including two to Europe—but these were somewhat shadowed by the fact that I was no better able to stay on my feet in Europe than anywhere else. I wanted freedom to travel at a more leisurely pace. Mother, for her part, was nearing seventy and found she didn't want to be home alone all day while I worked, whereas I didn't want to share our home with a housekeeper as had been necessary during the many years when my grandmother couldn't be left alone.

Above all, I was homesick for Oregon; yet I had too much seniority to switch to the type of programming job then available in Portland. For the first time I seriously considered trying to write professionally. Mother's income, we thought, had become more than ample for us to live on indefinitely (we didn't foresee what inflation would do to it). Although once I'd have been unwilling to give up programming, my job didn't involve much actual programming any more. Among the other difficulties I was being sent on business trips—for example, to talk with some Air Force officers at an underground installation in North Bay, Canada—and I found such assignments physically exhausting; yet I felt that to refuse them would mean the loss of my program design responsibilities. All in all, it seemed the time for another change was at hand.

*

I had worked as a programmer for almost exactly ten years when, in May of 1967, I came back to Oregon to stay. We bought another house in Portland—the first of several homes we've since had here—and I began to write novels. I didn't look on writing as a career in the income-production sense, for I knew that very few authors earn a living from their books (and as it turned out, even the most successful of mine never brought in enough money for me to do that). It's important to make this plain, because I wouldn't want aspiring writers to assume that one can quit a job thinking that publication of books like mine will provide support. I had no such illusions; I simply wanted to share some of my ideas. One reason I'd begun to feel I could publish in the young adult field was that Mother had recently begun to write for young people herself. Her second

Sylvia with her grandmother Sarah Louise Butler, 1958

and best-known book, *Twice Queen of France,* was published that same spring (under her maiden name, Mildred Allen Butler). I thought that if she could do it, then, maybe, so could I.

I wrote *Journey Between Worlds* first. I felt it would appeal to readers of romances for girls, and I wanted very much to make teenage girls aware of how important the colonization of space is to mankind's future. I deliberately did *not* direct the book to science fiction fans. One such person wrote to me once, saying rather indignantly that I should have known no science fiction enthusiast could sympathize with a young woman who *did not want* to go to Mars—and of course I did know that! The idea was to reach girls who don't ordinarily like science fiction. Unfortunately, in many places the book never did reach them because librarians put it on the "science fiction" shelf instead of the "romance" shelf. (I'd be happy if any librarians reading this would please go and move it right now.) Where it got into the hands of its intended audience, however, it was well liked. One of my happiest experiences as a writer was having a librarian tell me my book had convinced her that the space program really is worthwhile.

All this was quite a bit later, though. I submitted *Journey Between Worlds* to several publishers, all of which rejected it, and in the meantime I wrote *Enchantress from the Stars*. I didn't feel *Enchantress* would ever be publishable—it wasn't the sort of book that could appear as an adult novel (though I felt some adults would like it) yet it was over the heads of most readers below teenage and seemed far too long and complex to be called a children's book, at least by the standards of the fifties and sixties. But the story took hold of me and I simply couldn't leave it alone. I would forget all the rules, I decided, and amuse myself with something that didn't fit any market while I waited for *Journey Between Worlds* to find a publisher; I couldn't submit a new manuscript while that was unsettled in any case.

When *Enchantress from the Stars* was finished, though, I found I couldn't bear not to have it read by anyone. I put *Journey* away and submitted *Enchantress* instead, after learning that at least a few publishers of junior books would consider manuscripts of its length. I sent it to Atheneum because they had published the longest children's book I could find in the library, and also because the editor's taste appeared compatible with mine. This proved to be a good guess; the book was accepted, after some revision, and went on to be a Junior Literary Guild selection and a Newbery Honor Book. I was fortunate in having written it just at a time when a trend toward issuing more mature fiction as "young adult" was beginning. For of course, *Enchantress* was never intended for preadolescent children, and its Newbery Honor status was therefore somewhat misleading.

I have never written a novel for children—unless one considers teenagers "children," which personally I don't—and it bothers me somewhat to be known as a writer of children's books. This doesn't mean I don't admire the gift of people who are able to work in that field; I'd be much better off professionally if I possessed it. But I, after all, didn't identify with children even while I was a child myself, and have never understood them or their activities well enough to write about them. The characters in my novels are all in late adolescence or older.

The reason I mind being classed with children's authors is that it tends to prevent my books from being found by the majority of readers most apt to like them. Teenagers do not consider *themselves* children, after all. Comparatively few of them visit the children's rooms of libraries. The larger libraries shelve extra copies of my novels in their young adult or adult collections; that's where teenagers are most likely to come across them. There are, to be sure, a few teen library users who know not all books in the children's room are beneath them, and a few advanced readers below teenage for whom my books aren't too mature. By and large, however, the "junior" label limits my audience, especially by keeping my books out of high school libraries, where I feel they'd reach more young people.

This labeling of books by age group does a great deal of damage, I think, except in the case of those meant for preadolescent readers. The reason for it is solely commercial; it arises from the structure of the publishing business. The "children's book" departments of publishers issue young adult novels because of the way books are marketed, not because there's any good reason for fiction directed toward older teens to be branded as different from adult fiction. This is not to say that editors of children's books, such as my own editor, Jean Karl, have not done a fine job with novels appropriate for high school age or that they shouldn't be the ones to edit them—but they should be allowed, I feel, to do so without having such novels categorized as being on the "juvenile" side of a firm dividing line in literature. Even Library of Congress catalog numbering marks this division! Worse yet, because children's libraries are patronized mainly by children, books for younger readers usually sell better than those that demand more maturity; and consequently publishers' sales departments often list a novel as being for a lower age group than the author had in mind. This can backfire. Some of my novels were criticized by reviewers for being "too difficult for ages 10-14," a judgment with which I wholeheartedly agreed.

With *Enchantress from the Stars* this problem was not as serious as with my later novels, since it could indeed be enjoyed by many readers of junior-high age. But *Enchantress* was given by teachers even to fifth and sixth graders; I was often asked to talk to those grades, and got letters from children who'd evidently read the book as a school assignment without having the slightest notion of what it was all about. I found this very frustrating. To me, a story's plot incidents are not what matter; they were what I always found hardest to think of, and such action scenes as I managed to put in (usually long after the first draft of the rest) were a real struggle to write. The ideas in the story, plus the thoughts and feelings of the characters, were what inspired me, and in most cases these could be absorbed only by introspective older teens.

Adult readers, on the other hand—having less of a Space Age outlook than teenagers—didn't all grasp what *Enchantress* was about either. To my dismay, some of them didn't realize it dealt literally with relationships between peoples of different worlds. They assumed it was an allegory about our own world not merely in its portrayal of human feelings, but in a specific political sense; they thought that in saying an advanced interstellar civilization shouldn't try to help less advanced ones, I was saying Americans shouldn't give technological aid to undeveloped nations. I never meant that at all; people of different nations on this planet are all members of the same human race, the same species. Whether highly evolved species can help those younger than themselves is another issue entirely. *Enchantress from the Stars* was intended to counter the "Gods from Outer Space" concept, the growing idea, especially prevalent among young people, that UFOs may come here and solve all Earth's problems for us. I simply don't believe that's how advanced interstellar civilizations act; I feel, as my novels explain, that it would be harmful to young species and that they know that. As I recall, I got tired of seeing Captain Kirk violate his Federation's nominal noninterference policy in *Star Trek,* and that was what prompted me to create a Federation that lived up to its own code.

It's tempting, of course, to hope that one will be contacted by people from the stars, especially if one doesn't quite fit into society on this planet—and I suspect that dream is more common among the young than adults suppose. In my own late teens I indulged in it at times, very secretly, because there was no *Star Trek* or *Close Encounters* then and no one I knew was interested in space and I thought the wish for contact must be unique to my special form of imagination. A few years ago I heard a rock singer express the same wish in lyrics about a girl in a bar who longed to be taken aboard the "silvery ship" she was sure must be overhead. Evidently it is a universal longing. But I don't think we should let it shape our view of the universe, because it's a lot more constructive to assume we of Earth are going to have to solve our own world's problems.

Do I really believe interstellar civilizations exist? I've often been asked that, and the answer is that I do, though I don't believe we are going to have any proof of it before we build starships of our own to explore with. But of course I don't think inhabitants of other solar systems are as much like our species as they are shown to be in my fiction. Actually I rarely describe what they look like—partly because I'm not good at physical descriptions, but partly, too, because I want to leave readers free to imagine the characters as being like themselves. (In *Enchantress from the Stars,* for instance, I hoped black readers would picture Elana as black, and I've often wondered if any of them did.) This, I think, is just as accurate as making up weird descriptions for them would be; we haven't the faintest idea what alien races look like, so why not portray them in a way that makes them easy to identify with? To me it's the same form of literary license as writing the dialogue in English when we know that alien beings don't speak English: it's necessary for the sake of the audience. Few science fiction fans agree with me about this, but many people who don't like other science fiction say they like mine, and I feel this is one reason why.

Alien cultures aren't as much like ours as those in my books, either. And in fact, all the cultures in *Enchantress from the Stars* were purposely portrayed in an unrealistic, stylized way. This was something else a lot of adult readers didn't understand. They saw that part of the book was told in fairy-tale style, and though they knew medieval cultures were not just like those in fairy tales, they recognized this as a literary device—which, if they were folklore enthusiasts, they enjoyed. Surprisingly, a lot of the same people said the culture of the invaders in the book was "stereotyped!" Indeed it was, deliberately so; real interstellar invaders would no more behave like comic-book villains with ray guns than real medieval heroes went around looking for dragons to slay. (This might have been clearer if my original Foreword had been printed intact, but that, like a number of other passages in *Enchantress* and a good deal of the punctuation, was altered by Atheneum without my knowledge, and it wasn't possible to fix everything after the book was in galleys—something I've always regretted. Though I'm glad to revise my work repeatedly, I do not believe any author's wording should be changed without his or her approval.)

Even the very advanced culture in *Enchantress from the Stars,* the Federation, was not shown realistically. How could it have been? I don't know what the day-to-day life of people belonging to interstellar civilizations is like, but I'm fairly sure it's not like Elana's—in particular, a society composed of people possessing spectacular psychic powers would have to be very different and, from our standpoint, incomprehensible. Yet I believe that species more advanced than our own do possess such powers, and perhaps could awaken them in exceptional individuals of younger worlds. That, in fact, was the portion of the story I started with, the part conceived in 1957. Though its premise is classed with "magic" by today's science, the book wasn't meant to be fantasy in the sense that tales of magical worlds are fantasy.

Rather, it was based on mythology (which is something quite different from fantasy)—not just traditional mythology, but that of our own age. At the time I wrote it, I didn't fully appreciate the extent to which interstellar travelers with telepathic and psychokinetic powers are a contemporary myth; I was inclined to believe in their literal existence. Now I recognize that our current conceptions of advanced civilizations are much further from reality than fairy tales are from history. Nevertheless, I think the underlying ideas of the book, and of my subsequent ones, are valid.

When I finished writing *Enchantress from the Stars* (and had revised *Journey Between Worlds,* by then also accepted by Atheneum) I went ahead with *The Far Side of Evil.* It fit naturally into the same Federation setting as *Enchantress,* though my original story about the Critical Stage, which involved only Randil's role, was set on Earth. I've sometimes been asked why the book's conclusion didn't reveal the key to the Critical Stage for which the Federation was searching: the reason why some worlds conquer space while others fail to, and blow themselves up in a nuclear war. My reply has always been that if I *knew* the key, I'd tell the President of the United States instead of putting it in a novel! For some reason this seems to surprise people; they don't realize that I believe the Critical Stage is real. More disturbingly, some, again, thought the book was about politics instead of about space; they assumed I used a space story as a vehicle for political statements when in fact, it was the other way around: I used political melodrama as a vehicle for ideas about the importance of space exploration. I would like to think that readers of the book have found these ideas convincing, because they become more and more relevant to our world's situation with each passing year. It frightens me when I hear people say we should solve the problems on Earth before we devote money and effort to leaving it. I do not believe they *can* be solved as long as our species is confined to a single planet. The natural course of evolution is for all successful species to expand to new ecological niches, and space is the one awaiting us. Attempts to postpone that destiny can lead only to disaster, for us and for all other life here on our home world.

*

My last remaining story draft was the one that became the foundation for *This Star Shall Abide,* which eventually turned into a trilogy. My previous novels had been written mainly from young women's viewpoints, and had been praised for that reason by people who'd noticed the lack of space stories for girls. (Though there are quite a few of these now, *Enchantress from the*

Stars was the first science fiction novel with a female protagonist to be issued as young adult.) But I wanted to try something different, and in any case, the society in which the new novel was to be set was not one in which an adolescent girl would act as the plot required. It was a society that had regressed from its former state; the very sexism of its people was typical of their backward attitudes about a lot of other things—a point that somehow escaped feminists who later criticized the book and its sequel for portraying a sexist culture. So my main character was necessarily a boy, and he became very real to me, which was not surprising since Noren, more than any of my other characters, had a personality like mine. He viewed life as I had always viewed it: as a loner and a heretic. In my own case this had never been a very dramatic stance, but our society is not as bad as Noren's, and I had not been forced to choose, as he was, between unjustifiable conformity and persecution. I can't be sure that I would have acted as Noren did if I'd been born into his world, but I know I would have wanted to.

At the time *This Star Shall Abide* was written, the issue of youthful heresy was a major one in America, so I believed teenage readers would sympathize with him. Young people seemed a great deal more serious-minded than they had been during my own youth. To be sure, I felt that many of the causes to which they were devoting themselves were misguided, and that their methods of protest were often neither justified nor effective—I would not have felt at home in the counterculture of the sixties. Still, the young had begun to *care* about the world, and that in itself was progress. It's better to care and make mistakes than not to care; both *The Far Side of Evil* and *This Star Shall Abide* dealt with that theme. In both there was real evil to fight, and in both, a young man's sincere effort to oppose it turned out to be based on false premises: the point being that it's right to defy authority for the sake of one's conscience, yet necessary to take responsibility if one's view of the situation proves inaccurate. But in Noren's case deeper issues were involved. The original theme of the story concerned heresy not in the political but in the religious sense, and this facet of it became more and more central to me as the books developed.

I had never been an overtly religious person; my parents were not churchgoers, and though I'd taught Sunday School for a while during my high school years, I'd given it up because it made me feel hypocritical. I didn't believe the teachings of any church literally, and at that time I knew of no other way to view them. That myth *is* true—that the underlying idea is more significant than the words and imagery through which it's expressed—was something I came to understand slowly over a long period of years. I didn't connect it specifically with religion at first. Even when I based *Enchantress from the Stars* on that theme, I wasn't conscious of the fact that I was saying something about religious symbolism. Then, later, when I read *Enchantress* over after publication, it dawned on me that I had unknowingly written a strong defense of religious views I'd long rejected. To this day I don't know if anybody else interpreted the book that way.

At that time, I had been ill for some months and was very depressed. Though my condition was not medically serious, I was not only too lacking in physical energy to do even what little had previously been possible for me, but had lost all desire and enthusiasm for such things as travel. I could write—and often did write ten hours a day—but leaving the house for more than brief errands brought on nervous exhaustion. Intellectually I was thrilled by the publication of my books, but emotionally I could feel no joy in that or anything else; my optimistic view of the universe did not extend to my private life. In desperation, I began to attend church, looking for some anchor in the dark sea that was engulfing me. For the first time I found the ritual meaningful—not because my beliefs had changed, but because I now recognized it as an expression of what I'd believed all along.

This was the period from which *This Star Shall Abide* and its sequel *Beyond the Tomorrow Mountains* emerged. Originally, I tried to tell the story in just one volume, but its structure was all wrong. When my editor didn't find it convincing, I soon realized why: a lot of important things were still in my mind instead of on paper. So I expanded it to two and received a contract for both before the second was even partially written. Revising the first volume was merely a matter of removing an anticlimactic chapter from the end and adding a lot more detail in the portrayal of the planet's society; that completed the novel as I'd first conceived it, the part I already had a plot for. But it didn't finish Noren's story, not even the love story to which readers would naturally want a conclusion, and my editor felt that it didn't make the reasons for the inescapably bad situation on the planet clear enough. I agreed; moreover, by this time some of Noren's later conflicts had become more crucial to me than his initial rebellion.

Presenting these conflicts in a way meaningful to young readers—or for that matter, to any readers at all—proved tremendously difficult. I didn't yet have a plot, at least not in the sense of the action. I knew how Noren's outlook would change but I hadn't any idea what events would bring this about; thinking of them was a year-long struggle. Furthermore, *Beyond the Tomorrow Mountains* dealt more explicitly with religion than was customary in the young adult field. The old taboos concerning sex and politics had fallen, but judging from the books I saw, I feared religion might still be off-limits, if not to my publisher, then perhaps to reviewers and book-buyers. I thought I might offend some readers by suggesting that a religion unlike any on this planet could be valid to its adherents, and went out of my way in an Author's Note to make plain that the colonists in the story were not descendants of Earth people. To my surprise, I later encountered adults who did not realize that the novel was really about religion! It didn't mention God by name, so they apparently went on thinking of the faith depicted in the way Noren did initially, as no more than a feat of social engineering. But in my eyes, his ultimate commitment to a priest's role was genuine.

This Star Shall Abide was well received, and won a Christopher Award for "affirmation of the highest values of the human spirit." Despite good reviews *Beyond the Tomorrow Mountains* was less successful; the majority of those who evaluated it by young-adult criteria considered it too heavy and slow-moving, and my British publisher refused to accept it. (They had not liked the religious aspect of even the first volume and had insisted on changing its title to remove any suggestion of religious content—not because of a taboo, but because they felt, probably with justification, that religion doesn't appeal to average science fiction fans.) Then too, some reviewers objected to the plot climax, calling it *deus ex machina* as if I'd been unable to think of any better way to save Noren than to drag in an improbable coincidence. There was much irony in this, since though I do indeed have trouble thinking up plot incidents, in this case the unforeseeable nature of Noren's rescue was entirely deliberate. That was the *point*—sometimes one must have faith in an improbable outcome. That was what awakened Noren's faith in the still more improbable salvation of his endangered people. But the book was not an action-adventure story, and those looking for excitement didn't like its departures from action-adventure story rules.

Beyond the Tomorrow Mountains was primarily a psychological story. The younger readers had no comprehension of Noren's emotions, especially during his period of what one reviewer aptly called "existential anxiety"—still I remained firm in my conviction that older adolescents would identify with them. I got confirmation that some did when one day a teenage girl approached me in a library and remarked appreciatively,

With mother reading galley proofs, 1969

"Noren really tripped out, didn't he?" So much for the prevalent theory that action-adventure is what science fiction for young people has to focus on.

After publication of the second volume, some people felt the story still wasn't complete; they told me I should write another sequel in which Noren succeeded in saving his people. I resisted this idea, since only in action-adventure fiction is it credible for a hero to single-handedly save the world. The book was about faith in the face of impossible odds, and that theme would be overridden if I altered the odds to the extent of saying that even during Noren's lifetime, they hadn't been so impossible after all. Besides, I'd done such a thorough job of making them impossible that I couldn't think of a way out myself—and knew that even if I could, that would weaken the justification for the planet's social system, which was an evil defensible only on the basis of its offering the sole means of temporary survival.

Years later, however, something happened that changed my mind. I got interested in the new field of genetic engineering, and learned to my dismay that the system on Noren's world really *wasn't* the sole means of survival! I'd honestly believed it was, since I'd been ignorant of genetics, but I was ignorant no longer and had just published a nonfiction book on the subject;

what if people thought I'd known all along? I couldn't let them assume I had let Noren endorse a morally objectionable system on false grounds. And so I wrote *The Doors of the Universe,* and once I got into it, I could scarcely believe that I hadn't envisioned Noren's story as a trilogy in the first place.

It was truly uncanny the way things fit together. Details that just happened to have been mentioned in the earlier volumes looked like "plants" for essential premises of the new book. Moreover, in the new volume I had a chance to emphasize the theme, implicit in the earlier ones, of the tragedy that can result if a civilization turns its back on a promising technology—something I feel very strongly about. And I brought in connections with the themes of my books about the Federation. All this came easily (though as usual, I had trouble thinking of events through which Noren actually *could* reach his goal and was stalled in the middle for over a year without any more notion of the solution than he had). So now, the conclusion of *Beyond the Tomorrow Mountains* does indeed seem incomplete to me, which for a middle volume of a trilogy is entirely proper. I hope that young people who grew up during the interval between publication of the second and third volumes have found that the third exists, though in most cases this is unlikely; the story really is much better when read as a whole. *The Doors of the Universe* got excellent reviews but was not widely distributed because by then the library market was diminishing, and, dealing as it did with Noren as an adult, it was much too heavy for average readers of young people's fiction. Genetic engineering being a timely topic, I hoped it would go into paperback even if the whole trilogy did not, but Atheneum did not succeed in selling the reprint rights.

My greatest disappointment as a writer has been the lack of mass-market paperback editions of my novels. This is a matter not so much of money (though by now I surely need the money) but of the fact that many teenagers prefer paperbacks. Science fiction readers in particular don't all have access to, or opportunity to use, public libraries; I've talked to some on electronic bulletin boards who'd like to read my books, yet cannot get copies. I would have a far larger audience, particularly for the trilogy—which unlike some of my books, did not appear even in children's paperback form—if it were available on racks where science fiction is sold. Yet according to Atheneum, my novels were repeatedly offered to reprint houses and turned down. It was not because they were originally issued as young adult novels—I think I'm the only author of teenage science fiction whose books had success in hardcover and yet were not picked up for mass-market reprint. I was told it was because they hadn't enough action, that they were considered "too difficult" even for average adults. Possibly so; but I think a larger factor was the restrictive categorization of the paperback field.

Under the current marketing system, a mass-market paperback line must be labeled either "general audience" or "science fiction"—there is no common ground between the two. Books about other worlds are not issued in "general audience" lines. Yet my novels don't appeal to typical SF fans; I don't slant them that way. A science fiction writer once told me that in order to do so I would have to direct them to people who have read at least 500 other science fiction novels previously! Such readers are looking for far-out material that I wouldn't be able to imagine even if I wanted to, and I don't want to. I write for those, adults as well as teens, who care about the real world and its relation to the rest of the universe.

*

Once *Beyond the Tomorrow Mountains* had gone to the typesetter, I had no other story idea. But I did have something else in mind. I wanted to try nonfiction. Especially, I wanted to write about what people have thought in the past about other worlds: not science fiction authors, but scientists, philosophers, and average citizens. Radio astronomers were then implying, and in some cases saying, that their belief in the existence of other inhabited solar systems was something new; but I was aware that this view of history was a limited one. The philosopher Giordano Bruno was burned at the stake in the year 1600 for holding to such ideas. And if a conviction that we're not alone in the universe goes back that far—if it's not an invention of science fiction at all—then surely that is an important fact. Perhaps it reveals something of what people instinctively sense to be true.

Ordinary history books don't tell the facts about things like views of extrasolar worlds; only a few specialized scholars know them. None of these scholars had written about the subject in detail—the information was to be found only in actual writings of the past. I had never done scholarly research before, but I soon became fascinated with it. I ended up spending an entire year searching the writings of well-known people who lived in the seventeenth, eighteenth and nineteenth centuries, plus a lot of magazines printed in those centuries. Portland's libraries didn't have all I wanted to see, and I thought with regret of the lost years in Southern California, where I'd lived near many great libraries without ever using them for research purposes. I sent for a

few crucial books via interlibrary loan, obtaining them from cities in the East as well as California, often finding them so frail from disuse that they fell apart in my hands. And what I learned was that the educated people of those centuries almost *all* believed that other inhabited solar systems exist. Benjamin Franklin and Thomas Jefferson did. The majority of clergymen did. In the nineteenth century, the few writers who argued against the idea were considered dissenters.

These facts are still not generally known. My collection of Xeroxed sources on the subject provided material not merely for a young people's book, but for a long scholarly one—which I still intend to write when I have opportunity. I have found that both my writing style and my approach to ideas are far better suited to scholarly writing than to anything else, and that that's the type of work I normally find most fulfilling. I've since gathered material for a number of other scholarly books on different subjects, and have enough ideas to last for the rest of my life. Scholarly writing, however, is not usually publishable unless it's the work of a college professor or other recognized authority. It remains to be seen whether any of the projects I'm working on will ever appear in print.

During 1973, I wrote *The Planet-Girded Suns: Man's View of Other Solar Systems,* which was publishable when a scholarly book would not have been. I did my best to make it understandable to young readers; it was revised many times at the request of Atheneum, and was eventually accepted and well reviewed. However, it was actually neither one thing nor the other—not scholarly, though it presented material that popular-level adult books don't include, and yet much too difficult reading for average teens. It was interesting to some because the subject of other worlds is interesting, but on the whole I am unable to explain complicated ideas in a way that appeals to large audiences. I hoped, because adult books about extraterrestrial intelligence were then popular, that *The Planet-Girded Suns* would have a better chance than the novels at paperback publication, but paperback houses showed no interest in it. Perhaps this was because, in the section about modern scientific beliefs, I didn't endorse the existence of UFOs.

There followed a period of years during which I tried desperately to write yet could not produce any fiction. Several times I thought I had the basis for a new novel, but despite interesting themes and settings I proved unable to think of events. Unlike the situation of authors who experience "writer's block," this was not a matter of having trouble putting words on paper, or of producing things that weren't good. I couldn't write narrative at all because I had no incidents or images in mind to describe, but I wrote thousands of words, constantly, about abstract ideas, often in long letters to friends. At the time I felt I *should* write more novels because I'd assumed I would keep on doing so, and Atheneum was waiting for one; it seemed terrible not to take advantage of that opportunity. Apart from liking to publish I was beginning to need income; Mother's no longer went so far because of inflation, yet I couldn't work outside my home because her health was poor and she needed me. So for a long time I kept struggling. But I've since come to realize that the mystery is not why I could no longer write fiction, but why I'd ever been able to do it in the first place. Most people with analytical minds (the kind now called "left-brain dominant") never can.

One of the friends I wrote long letters to was a young man named Rick Roberson, who lived in Tennessee. He'd first written to me when he was sixteen, and just the type of teen reader toward whom I'd directed my books—he grasped what was in them and identified with the characters more than anyone else I knew. Rick and I went on corresponding because we were both seriously interested in space and the future, and neither of us had other friends who were. Also, he had writing talent. The year he entered college and I had no book ready to publish, science fiction anthologies for young people were needed, and it occurred to me that between us we could produce one. I had little background even as a reader in the SF short-story field, but Rick did, and he knew what young people liked. We mailed stories we found back and forth to each other and enjoyed discussing them; then Rick wrote the introductions and I handled the business of obtaining permission to reprint them. This became the anthology *Universe Ahead.* Rick wrote a story for the book, and when we became desperate to fill a remaining "slot" I produced one myself, which I was able to write only because I based it on his ideas and which therefore appeared under both our names.

I found I liked editing. The next year Rick wrote another story and I asked some of my other friends, all published authors, to do so also for a new anthology, *Anywhere, Anywhen,* which contained only fiction that hadn't been printed before. Again, I co-authored a story, this time with my mother. Sadly, Mother's career in writing for young people had come to an abrupt end when book markets changed so that her special interest—history—was no longer an acceptable topic; it was felt that teenagers weren't interested in history. (After four books for Funk & Wagnalls she had had a new one accepted by Harcourt Brace, only to have the new man-

Mother, Mildred Butler Engdahl, 1965

agement there decide not to issue it despite their loss of the advance already paid.) Finding it hard to believe young people couldn't see the relevance in history, I adapted one of Mother's historical narratives into a time-travel story that we felt made that relevance plain. I don't know if readers of *Anywhere, Anywhen* agreed or not. In any case the book was not successful, largely because it was usually passed to science fiction specialists for review. Naturally, such specialists didn't like it; everything in it was "old hat" to them, since it had been deliberately designed to appeal to people in the children's literature field who don't care for typical science fiction anthologies. Hardly anyone, though, recognizes the wide gap in taste that exists between genre-oriented SF fans and other readers, or that efforts to bridge that gap are not welcomed by the specialists.

*

In the summer of 1976 Rick Roberson came to Portland and stayed with us while attending summer school at Portland State University. His college major was physics, and I felt that there would be interest in a children's book about the exciting new discoveries being made in high-energy physics. I wouldn't have ventured to write nonfiction on such a subject alone, since I knew nothing whatsoever about it; but together we produced *The Subnuclear Zoo.* Then the next year, Rick started to write a similar book about genetic engineering, a subject in which he was also knowledgeable—but as it turned out, he didn't have time to finish it, so we co-authored that one also: *Tool for Tomorrow.* Atheneum wanted these books to be for younger readers than my previous ones, and I tried very hard to comply. Nevertheless, I wasn't able to achieve a style appropriate for sixth graders. That being where the major market was, neither book did well, though they both got some good reviews.

I tried a picture book. While working as a science consultant for a textbook literature series, I discovered that there weren't any picture books about space, and I felt that even very young children were aware of space from television and movies. So I wrote *Our World Is Earth.* Ironically, that book was assumed by reviewers to be for *older* readers than I intended! (Some of them said it was too elementary to appeal to the first and second grades, which of course it was; I'd meant it to be read aloud to preschoolers.) I tried other nonfiction that I never submitted; though my major interest had come to be in the promise of orbiting colonies, which I now feel are the solution to Earth's long-term problems, I was unable to express my thoughts about them in words concrete enough for children. This is an insurmountable problem for me—once I wrote a controlled-vocabulary piece about Skylab for a reading series, and was told that the editor had to rewrite it because despite my accurate vocabulary/sentence structure calculations, my approach was "too abstract" for the intended audience. This is the underlying difference between my view and other people's, and it bars me not only from writing children's nonfiction, but from the popular-level adult science field.

But working on *The Subnuclear Zoo* and *Tool for Tomorrow* had opened new doors for me. Though originally, I had assumed Rick would provide all the technical information, I found myself inwardly compelled to absorb it myself before I could express any ideas on paper. Furthermore, I found it wasn't as obscure as I'd been expecting. One day, coming back from a summer school class to find me reading a technical article about physics in *Scientific American,* Rick said, "Oh, Sylvia, you can't understand that!" And I reacted indignantly—I felt challenged, and became aware that there really was no subject I couldn't comprehend if I made the effort. To be sure, I couldn't understand the mathematical equations, not having nearly as much math background as Rick did; but contrary to what's often asserted, math is not necessary to the understanding of

concepts, indispensable though it is for practical or experimental work. My lack of college training in science did not limit the subjects I could deal with as a writer.

So while I was working on the genetic engineering book, I got very deeply involved in the source material. That was when I saw its application to Noren's situation, and started *The Doors of the Universe* (an exception to my inability to think of stories because it was a continuation of the original story). But besides that, I wanted to learn more about the relation of genetics to human evolution. I visited Rick's home in Tennessee to put the finishing touches on *Tool for Tomorrow;* he was then making plans to enter graduate school. I realized that soon he would have a master's degree, while I had none. My mother and most of my friends had master's degrees in one subject or another, though they knew far less about scholarly research than I. Also I felt that perhaps a master's degree would enable me to publish adult nonfiction about other worlds without its getting classed with the sensational variety—I'd gotten tired of hearing "Oh, you mean like *Chariots of the Gods?*" when trying to tell people about my research for *The Planet-Girded Suns.*

In 1978 I had a contract with Atheneum for a book about future human evolution. I knew little about past evolution, but instead of learning from books alone I decided to try taking a class. I had never been fond of the Academic Establishment or in agreement with its accepted theories, but the appeal of a master's degree was at that time motivating me; I found out that it would be possible for me to get one in anthropology at Portland State University. The professor for the evolution class in which I enrolled turned out to be excellent, and, by coincidence, interested both in genetics and in philosophy of science—both fields in which I'd developed background. He encouraged me to apply for admission to the graduate program, and I was accepted. For the next two years I attended part-time and met all the M.A. requirements, receiving almost straight A's because I found researching and writing term papers easy. The book for young people on future evolution, however, was never written. My views on that subject proved to be at odds with those of anthropologists, and I could scarcely express them in print while a candidate for a degree; moreover, to do so wouldn't have been fair to Atheneum. Nonfiction published for young people (as opposed to fiction) is supposed to reflect the current views of authorities, not the heretical ones of its author. I transferred the contract to *The Doors of the Universe* and abandoned children's nonfiction with little regret.

I never did get the master's degree. I had to stop work on my thesis temporarily for personal reasons, and then wasn't able to go back; it had become too expensive to have someone stay with Mother during my hours on campus. I wasn't too disappointed, for by then, I realized that the degree would not really enable me to publish nonfiction for adults. The scholarly book field was in a depressed state and it was unlikely that I could get the thesis accepted by a university press, as I'd first hoped. Without that prospect, I didn't want to write it under Academic Establishment guidance—term papers are one thing, but an original book-length manuscript containing controversial ideas is something else! I would rather use my material for something wholly my own, far longer than a master's thesis is allowed to be. I do plan to finish that book whether or not it proves publishable; it's about the significance of space colonization to human evolution.

*

Going to graduate school was largely a matter of pride with me, and though I gained confidence from it, with hindsight it appears to have been the most expensive mistake I ever made. Those two years were when personal computers first came on the market. I avoided looking at the ads because I longed to program again and yet saw no way I could ever afford such an expensive luxury; but if I had put the money I spent on graduate courses into a computer, I undoubtedly could have sold software profitably. Although my programming experience was by then too outdated to be applicable to large business computers, I had just the kind of systems software knowledge that was needed for programming early microcomputers in assembly language. But I didn't realize people were selling programs by mail from their homes. I assumed one would have to work in an office, which I wasn't free to do.

When in 1981 my electric typewriter gave out, and I'd developed a vision problem that made it difficult for me to use a typewriter anyway, I did get a computer for word processing. I couldn't afford to buy software but I enjoyed writing my own. By that time I'd become aware of what was going on and tried to market what I wrote, but it was already too late. Advertising rates were by then geared to the price of products for business customers rather than home users. Though my software was bugfree and my few customers were pleased with it, there wasn't any way to publicize it—and furthermore, my computer soon became too obsolete to use for commercial software development. It was a cassette-based TRS-80, which like the old Q7 did its job well, but was scorned by people interested in having

the latest and most efficient equipment. Personally, I liked it, and did all sorts of things with it that are supposedly impractical with cassette text storage.

The attempt to market my software, like so many other things I've done, had serendipitous results. That was what got me into telecommunications and computer conferencing, a fascinating new field in which I'm now active. I hope that ultimately it, or the contacts I make through it, will offer me ways to earn money at home, for I no longer foresee any writing income; my talents don't fit present markets. I will write in the future as I did at the first, for the satisfaction it brings to me and to prospective readers. But even if I were to get an idea for a novel like my others, it's unlikely that it would be published. Libraries are low on funds these days and books for advanced readers, long and costly to print yet without appeal for typical younger teens, are no longer salable. The seventies were really the only time during which they were; I was very lucky to go through my story-creation period in the right decade.

Mother is over ninety now. Though her mind is sharp and she does a lot of reading, she's very weak physically due to medical problems; I can't leave her alone at any time. During my grandmother's lifetime we could get someone to live with us for little more than room and board, but that's no longer possible, so except for taking her to the doctor I'm virtually homebound. We live very quietly with two beloved cats, Hesper and Phoebus (called Sunny), who are the center of our household. Recently we sold the house we'd owned for thirteen years—far longer than either of us had lived in one place before—and moved into a mobile home west of Portland. It's in a beautiful park surrounded by tall firs, with a view of tree-rimmed fields and a red barn from my bedroom window.

I don't mind this lifestyle, except for its financial drawbacks—after all, I stayed home by choice before it became necessary. I have always been an observer of this planet more than a participant in its affairs. All writers are good observers; the difference between me and most others is that I tend to observe in terms of long-range things, like the evolution of space-faring species, rather than nearby specific ones.

It has been ten years since I've traveled anywhere and I see few people, yet I am not isolated. My computer is my link to the world, not only because I write with it, but because of computer conferencing. At present I am on the staff of Connected Education, an organization headed by Dr. Paul Levinson that offers graduate courses for credit from the New School for Social Research in New York City. Every night I connect my computer by phone to a central computer in New Jersey, where Connect Ed's "electronic campus" is located. Though I haven't met Dr. Levinson in person and I have never seen the New School itself, I've team-taught a class there, and will be teaching more courses as the program grows. Connect Ed has students and faculty all over the world—Japan, South America and England, among other places. These people are as easy to "talk" to as they would be if they lived in my own city. In my case, because writing's easier for me than speaking, it's far better than attending face-to-face conferences. Long ago I assumed that because I couldn't lecture I would never be able to teach in college, yet now technology has found a way to break down barriers not only of distance, but of individual differences in skills. In computer conferencing, people's minds and personalities are all that matter. Irrelevant things like foreign accents or physical handicaps aren't even visible; we all meet on equal ground. This is truly the medium of the future, I believe.

Of course computer conferencing isn't just for people who can't meet otherwise; most Connect Ed students live ordinary lives and choose online courses for scheduling convenience. Because it's an expensive medium at present, the majority of them are business people, though other adults such as teachers are certainly welcome. But I foresee a day when young people will be involved, as they now are with free electronic conferencing on local BBS systems. National recreational computer conferencing has great appeal for teens. In 1985 I was a helper and volunteer writer for the Participate conferencing system on The Source, which I learned about while participating in Paul Levinson's public "electure" conference about Space Humanization there. We had enthusiastic teen users as well as adults, though there too, the expense barred all but those from affluent families. I'm hoping for a time when all young people will have access to such systems. There may even be a time when young readers can exchange ideas with their favorite authors via a computer conference.

In any case, computer conferencing is an exciting field to pioneer in. It's something I'll be doing for many years to come. I have a brand new computer now (this article is the first thing I've written with it) and many hundreds of thousands of words will scroll across its screen. Some won't ever be printed on paper; I send words to readers nowadays merely by pressing a few keys. But there's still an important place for books—unlike some of my fellow electronic text enthusiasts, I

don't believe books will ever become obsolete. I hope to write more of them someday.

POSTSCRIPT

Sylvia Engdahl contributed the following update to *CA* in 2000:

What a difference a few more years made in computer technology! The desktop PC that was new in 1987 when I wrote my original essay, primitive by today's standards, is long gone; I've just acquired my third successive improved model. I said then that online communication was expensive (which it was, in the days when we paid by the minute for connections to host conferencing systems) but that I hoped someday all teenagers would have access to it. Now they can contact people all over the world, from schools and libraries if they lack computers at home, via the Internet—a development I then hadn't imagined.

There might even be a time, I said, when readers could exchange ideas with authors online; but I pictured that as a quite futuristic possibility. Only ten years later I opened my own Web site and began corresponding by e-mail with fans of my books in many regions of the United States, as well in other nations. As a direct result of this, I've at last been able to get most of my novels back into print.

But before that, there were other major changes in my life.

In the fall of 1987, shortly after my autobiographical essay went to press, my mother died. This loss was crushing for a while, although it was scarcely unexpected, since she was ninety years old and had serious medical problems. We had lived together all my life, except for a few years during the 1950s, and for most of that time she'd been more like a sister to me than a parent. I will never stop missing her company.

And there was another problem. I had chosen to share a home with my mother not only because of our closeness, but because she wanted a full-time companion and, ultimately, caregiver. Had I not been present she would have hired someone; thus I didn't object to the arrangement whereby her modest income—inherited from my grandmother, for whom she had cared in turn—supported both of us. After all, I had never craved a high-powered career or upscale lifestyle. Our assumption was that after she was gone I could live comfortably on my own inheritance. We didn't antici-

Sylvia Engdahl at Children's Literature Association conference, San Diego, 1990, after accepting the Phoenix Award, with Alethea Helbig

pate the extent to which it would be depleted by inflation.

It's just as well that we didn't, I suppose, because there was nothing different I could have done. After I stopped publishing I tried—and have since tried—to earn money at home; but the amounts have been small, and though I would have been free to take a job in the years immediately following Mother's death, there was no position for which I was qualified. My programming knowledge was by that time far too outdated to have value in the marketplace, and because of my lifelong typing-speed limitation I could not do office work. Moreover, I didn't have the physical stamina for a regular job; I'd always found commuting exhausting, and by this time there were often days when I hadn't the energy to go out—though I am always able to work at home at my desk.

So the immediate question was where I was going to spend the rest of my life. I owned the mobile home we'd been living in, but it was sited in a park where there was rent to pay; I knew that I must own my land, too, in order to make ends meet in the future. I couldn't afford property in the Portland area—and found that I didn't want to stay there in any case. For years I'd been virtually homebound, and had few local contacts; now I discovered that the distances I had to drive through traffic in order to get anywhere, even the main public library, were too great to make the effort seem worth-

while. Portland had changed. It wasn't the same place I'd so eagerly moved to, twenty years before. I felt I must make a new beginning.

At this point came another of the astonishing coincidences that have shaped my life, and which, along with several other instances of fortunate timing, have made me wonder whether such synchronicities may be more than mere chance. Strangely, a trip from Portland to Eugene triggered both of them. Since the spring day in 1957 when I went to Eugene and made a sudden decision resulting in my coincidental entry into the computer programming field, I had been there only three times. But in April of 1988, I decided to drive down to Eugene again. I wasn't really sure it was where I wanted to live, although I had loved it during my brief stay in the early 1950s—and when I arrived, mobile home lots proved scarce and costly. I was about to give up the search. Then, through a casual inquiry, I discovered a subdivision of such lots involved in a bank foreclosure, the prices of which had been drastically reduced the day before. Realizing I must act fast, I bought one of them. By the next weekend they were all gone; if I had not picked that particular time to visit, I would never have found land within my means.

So all my early contacts with Eugene proved fateful—not to mention the fact that I've settled permanently here, and thus may, in due course, come to the end of my life in the hospital less than a block from where I lived that magical year when I was seventeen. How surprised I'd have been then to know that Eugene is where I'll grow old! Going through boxes of papers not long ago, I came across a houseplan I drew in a high school homemaking class. We were required to design our dream homes. I labeled mine "Engdahl Home, Eugene, Oregon" although at that time I had never been to Oregon and had no reason to expect that I'd ever have occasion to see this particular city. I just picked it from a map. Prescience? Who can say?

Having my mobile home moved from Portland to Eugene proved to be quite an adventure. Actually it was easier (for me, anyway) than a regular move, since all the furniture moved with the house; I didn't have to pack anything that wasn't fragile. The double-wide home was split in two; though I moved the books from shelves to the floor, I have such a lot of them that their weight caused one half 's hitch to break, and it got stuck overnight on the highway. I was already in Eugene by that time, wondering why only the bedroom side of my house had arrived. Eventually it was all put together, the only other snag being the requirement of Eugene's building inspectors that my sloping carport be built with strong enough timbers to support four feet of snow, although it rarely snows more than a few inches here and some years get none at all. The expense of this proved so great that I'd have been better off building a garage, which, if I'd realized I would be keeping my 1978 Chevrolet—now approaching "classic" status—for the rest of my life, I would have done. There were a few other lot-development choices I now regret, but on the whole, the move was a big success.

My cats, Hesper and Sunny, moved with me, of course. Hesper lived to be nearly nineteen, which for a cat is very old indeed. Sunny died much earlier, and I got Marigold, an orange tabby who now rules the house. Cats have always been important to me; I could never be happy without feline companionship.

I love this place, although the site isn't as pleasant as when I first came. Then, wild geese flew low overhead, and over the back fence I saw trees between here and the river; I often sat in my screen porch and watched the sunset. Now those trees are gone and they have built a rock quarry bordered by huge berms of dirt that block the western view, and fill the porch with dust every time the wind blows. They are planning to widen the highway in back, which I don't welcome since it's only a short distance from my bedroom and is bound to create more dust and noise. But the trees in my yard have grown tall, and I can still see forested hills from my living room windows.

Eugene is just the right size city for me. It has everything, including a major university, yet it takes me only ten minutes to get downtown from the outskirts where I live—even less time to reach the main shopping mall. It has retained the natural beauty of its setting. And I'm active in community organizations in which, in a large metropolitan area, I could never have become involved. I've been on the board of the Friends of the Eugene Public Library since a few months after I arrived, and as a volunteer, I desktop-publish the Library's newsletter at home on my computer. I also produce a newsletter for the Alzheimer's Association, and I'm on the advisory council of the local RSVP (Retired Senior Volunteer Program), for which I've done various computer tasks.

Nevertheless, I live quietly, and am home most of the time, usually with the computer on (my latest enthusiasm is for selling things I no longer need on eBay and Half.com). It's the way of life that best suits me. I no longer drive to the nearby mountains or coast as I sometimes used to, partly because of my car's aging condition and partly because of my own. I have no specific

medical problems, just ongoing depletion of my already-low energy level and, in recent years, chronic muscle pain. I lack both the funds and the stamina for travel, and were I to be miraculously provided with one, I would still be held back by the absence of the other. It's been nearly a decade since I even visited Portland.

Yet sitting at my computer, I come alive! I will never tire of the various pursuits it makes possible for me.

In 1989, to my great surprise, I was informed that I would receive the 1990 Phoenix Award for *Enchantress from the Stars*. This award is given annually by the Children's Literature Association, a national organization of scholars in the field, "from the perspective of time" to a book published twenty years prior to the award date. I received an expense-paid trip to San Diego to accept the award and speak at the organization's 1990 conference. Also in 1989, rack-size trade paperback editions of *Enchantress* and *The Far Side of Evil* were issued, which stayed in print for a while; but their covers didn't attract the right audience and they weren't widely distributed where teens would find them. It seemed that although my novels were still valued by critics, they were destined to remain inaccessible outside of children's rooms of public libraries.

In the late eighties and early nineties I was still doing the part-time online work for Connected Education that I described in my original essay; but the cost of that program—the same as on-campus tuition at New York's New School for Social Research—put it out of the reach of all but the most affluent students, and enrollment was never large. I did teach an online graduate course titled "Science Fiction and Space Age Mythology" in 1989, 1994, and 1995, which I greatly enjoyed; I wish there had been enough students for it to run every year that it was offered. The course dealt with popular culture science fiction, not the literary kind, and was focused largely on films. (An idea of its content is given in my Phoenix Award acceptance speech, "The Mythic Role of Space Fiction," a slightly revised version of which is now at my Web site.) In my opinion this new mythology is an extremely significant reflection of our culture's outlook on the universe. I have worked, off and on, on a nonfiction book on the subject, the scope of which keeps growing; but because it's not suitable for publication in today's commercial market, and I would not have the academic credentials to publish scholarly books even if there were a bigger demand for them, I have not given it high priority.

Connected Education was conducted via private text-based online conferencing systems rather than on the

Internet, which in those days was just getting started. In 1996, when the public was becoming aware of the Web, I was asked to develop a site publicizing Connect Ed's offerings, and was provided with access to the Net. This was all new to me. I had been online for more than a decade but had never seen a Web page; I didn't even have Windows on my computer, and didn't have memory enough to run it—they also paid for me to install more memory and get a faster modem. But when I started to learn HTML, I found it fascinating. This is a wonderful new career! I thought. It's something I'm naturally fitted for!

Alas, it has not turned out that way. Web design is a highly competitive field in which a freelancer cannot find work without contacts or money for advertising. I haven't been able to get much, though I did create, and continue to maintain, one site for another author. By now, of course, there are thousands of Web designers looking for freelance jobs and plenty of high school and college students with as much capability as I have—and besides, today's software enables people to produce their own Web pages.

So as in the case of all my ventures, the financial return was not large. But the rewards of developing my personal Web site were another matter.

*

Early in 1997, Connect Ed's program came to an end, and I was faced with having to pay for my own Internet account, an ongoing expense I could not justify unless it brought me income. I had some extra copies of my novels left, and since I saw that a few people had been searching for them through Usenet groups, it occurred to me that it might be possible to sell them. I didn't think many Internet users would have heard of them; still, I placed a notice saying they were available, and also opened a Web site where they were offered. As their original prices were out of line with current ones, I thought it would be legitimate to charge what a new book of equivalent format would cost—even a few dollars more, in the case of those that were scarce and had never been issued in paperback.

The response was overwhelming. It seemed I was better known than I thought, although often viewed as a bygone author (comments appeared in a couple of places expressing surprise that I was not dead!) I sold all the hardcovers—of which I had only a few—within a week or so, and the paperbacks in about three months. I could have charged much more; I later found that used book dealers were getting well over $100 apiece for some of

Engdahl in 1992 with her cat Marigold

the hardcover titles. If only I had bought more while they were still in print! I hadn't dreamed then, of course, that there might someday be a way to contact potential buyers.

My Internet presence was paying off, but more than that, I began to wonder if it might not lead to new hope of attracting reprint publishers. For much more gratifying than the sale of copies was the e-mail I received. I'd had no idea that my novels were so widely remembered.

Nothing in my experience, at any time in my life, has pleased (or astonished) me more than the discovery of how many adults had read my books during their childhood or teen years and felt that they had been influenced by them. Not only did people send e-mail, but in searching the Web for ways to publicize my site I came across comments made previously in public forums. In former years, I had received praise from reviewers and librarians, and had sometimes gotten letters from children assigned to write to authors in school, but only on rare occasions had I heard from readers who reacted personally to the novels. I was, and still am, deeply touched to know they've had lasting impact.

After I suggested at my site that Guest Book comments might help to get the books back in print, many were made. Then in 1998, Meisha Merlin—at that time a brand new press—stated at their own Web site that they would welcome e-mail about books people would like to see reprinted. I asked the people who had written to me to respond, and a lot of them did. Subsequently Meisha Merlin offered me a contract, and in 2000 my trilogy—*This Star Shall Abide, Beyond the Tomorrow Mountains,* and *The Doors of the Universe*—was published, with minor updating and a new Afterword, in an omnibus edition under the title *Children of the Star.* It was issued as adult science fiction. The Web has created a whole new way of reaching people who like books of a kind not interesting to large mass-market audiences.

All that I said in 1987 about publishing categories is still true, and furthermore, large publishers have become increasingly oriented toward commercial success. Meisha Merlin specializes in reprinting science fiction and fantasy with good reviews and an established following, but not enough mass appeal to be wanted by those publishers. It has issued the work of many authors whose books had gone out of print. Without the Web and its new outlets, such as online bookseller, publisher and author sites, the marketing of such novels would not be possible; small presses cannot get books into many local stores, and there would be no way to publicize them sufficiently for conventional distribution. The wide reach of the Web is now changing the rules of the game.

Unlike some traditional publishers, small presses don't object to authors selling copies of their own books, and—since I get a bookseller's share of the cover price—I have earned far more per copy from offering *Children of the Star* at my Web site than I earn in royalties. The book, which has stunning cover art by noted fantasy artist Tom Kidd, had a limited print-to-order hardcover edition for which both the publisher and I took advance orders, followed by a high-quality trade softcover edition that's available through normal book trade channels. The only problem is that few people discover it unless they're already familiar either with my books or with Meisha Merlin's. Catch-22: science fiction media didn't review the original editions because they were YA books, and now that it has been issued as adult, they won't review it because it's a reprint. There have been some enthusiastic reader reviews at Amazon.com, though (which unfortunately are seen only by people who search for me there). And I do what I can to publicize it myself via the Internet, something many authors are now doing; the days of expecting even a major publisher to handle all publicity are past. I hope that in time it will reach new readers, both older teens and adults besides those who've read it previously.

An even more exciting development is the publication of a new hardcover edition of *Enchantress from the Stars* this spring by Walker and Company, with an introduction by Lois Lowry and a striking new jacket plus interior vignettes by artists Leo and Diane Dillon, who have won top awards in both the children's and the science fiction fields. Walker, which has a large and successful children's book department, contacted me last year about obtaining the rights to it for their Newbery Honor Roll series. Whether this resulted from the revival of interest in my work brought about by my Web presence, I don't know. But I'm delighted that *Enchantress* is available to a new generation, and furthermore, I am glad it's been issued by a different publisher than the trilogy. They will both benefit from separate marketing; having my books side by side in the same catalog often misled people as to their intended readership.

This limited not only the trilogy's original audience, but that of *The Far Side of Evil,* which in some ways I regret having made a sequel to *Enchantress from the Stars.* I wish I had used a different protagonist, for the two books, despite being set in the same SF "universe," are quite different from each other and don't always appeal to the same people. The younger fans of *Enchantress* are often disappointed or even depressed by *Far Side,* which is a darker story demanding greater maturity on the part of both heroine and reader. Of course, when I wrote *Far Side,* I had no idea that *Enchantress* would become a Newbery Honor Book and be given to as many pre-teen readers as it was, so I didn't foresee that problem. Nor did I realize under the marketing conditions prevailing at the time of its original publication, few of the older teen readers for whom *Far Side* was intended would discover a sequel to a children's book. There have been recent changes in those conditions, however, and I am delighted that it, too, is to be published by Walker (in 2002) as a book for teens rather than children.

I still feel strongly about the theme of *Far Side.* I still believe that expansion into space is essential to our species' survival, and have a page at my Web site discussing my ideas about this in detail (which, I'm happy to see, gets even more visitors than my home page; there are links to it from many other space sites). The original edition of *Far Side* is somewhat dated: not by the political situation it portrays, as some people assume—the setting was never current, since the planet in the story resembles Earth of the fifties rather than the seventies—but by the fact that it's now obvious that merely developing space travel capability does not necessarily cause a world to use that capability. And it's also obvious that nuclear war is not the only peril that exists during the Critical Stage. Thus in addition to the oversimplification of the book due to its having been written as young adult, some of its statements turned out to be oversimplified in terms of what we now know after thirty years of neglecting the space program. I've therefore done some minor revision in the new edition. All it says about the need to colonize space is, in my opinion, true—although there is a good deal more that needs saying about why a species able to expand beyond its home world fails to do so, and what its fate is likely to be if it continues to cling solely to that world. I suspect that an advanced interstellar civilization would know these things, and that Elana too would know them later in her life.

Unfortunately, I myself do not know the solution to such a species' apathy. I would like to write a sequel in which Elana visits a world where it's almost too late; but I haven't yet come up with an idea of how her people could save its inhabitants—any more than I know what will ultimately save our own world. Will Mars be a sufficient impetus for us? I thought so when I wrote *Journey Between Worlds,* and I hope that book, which I've revised to fix portions that today seem sexist, will eventually be reprinted. It has new relevance now that there's public interest in Mars missions and active Mars enthusiasts are on the Web. For a while in the eighties I believed orbiting colonies would come sooner than the colonization of Mars; but despite their practicality, the concept has failed to win wide support. Mars inspires more emotion . . . if traces of life were found there, might that not prove the crucial factor in getting us back on track? I pray that it will, and that it will happen soon.

Space is not the only topic of interest to me. More and more, in recent years, I've turned to ideas about human potential, especially in the area of "paranormal" capacities such as those portrayed in *Enchantress from the Stars.* Unlike most people as strongly science-oriented as I am, I have always believed that ESP is real, and that it's been a much larger factor in human history than is recognized. I have never had psychic experiences myself; I'm much too "left-brained" for that—but I don't doubt that other people do, and that in the future we'll learn to control such powers. (Some of what I "made up" about them for *Enchantress* has been validated by recent nonfiction.) And we'll also learn more about the relationship between mind and body. Human beings are far more than biological machines.

In this connection, and in accord with my usual tendency toward heretical views, I deplore the attitude fostered by our society's medical philosophy, which I believe is based on false premises. I've devoted a good deal of thought and research to this issue; I once taught a Connect Ed media studies course on "Technology and 21st Century Medicine," dealing with assumptions I feel will be abandoned. Not that I favor "natural" or "alternative" healing methods, with which I don't agree either—unlike some today, I have no doubts about the benefits of high technology. Twice since moving to Eugene I have had major surgery for life-threatening conditions (which were quickly and completely cured) and I am thankful that this was available; modern medicine is very good at essential surgical repairs. But in most other respects, it's apt to cause more problems than it solves, and worse, its conception of health has become a virtual religion to many, overshadowing all other scales of value. Some years ago I began an adult novel about a planet where the Medical Establishment had acquired dictatorial political power, which I still believe is a valid theme; but it lacked the key incidents needed to make a story.

It was the same old stumbling block—I'm no more action-oriented in my imagination than in real life. I can write about thoughts and feelings of characters, but I don't visualize scenes in my mind as do most authors. Though I may know a desired plot outcome, I can't think of events to bring it about. And I can no more *force* such material into consciousness than I could when I stopped producing fiction for Atheneum, despite my longing to do so and my enjoyment of the actual writing process. This is my greatest regret, and it is intensified by the frequent e-mails I receive that urge me to write another novel. People naturally believe that if I wanted to, I could. As if all I needed was encouragement! As if I hadn't been frustrated for the past twenty years and more, wishing that it would again become possible for me!

To be sure, novels like mine, with the possible exception of more about Elana, would probably not be publishable today even if I could write them. Meisha Merlin publishes reprints and continuations of series; traditional publishers of adult fiction want books with bestseller potential, a situation affecting many authors with far greater past success than I. And "young adult" in recent years has meant books suitable for average middle school kids, not advanced readers or older teens (although there are signs that the pendulum is swinging back again). But if I had an idea for a *story* rather than a mere philosophical treatise—for readers of any age—I would not let lack of a publisher for it hold me back. I might even investigate electronic publishing, as I may in time for nonfiction; that's a growing technology that may transform the way writers' work is disseminated.

It's not my lack of energy that has kept me from writing more books. And it certainly isn't lack of motivation. In the past, I resigned myself to the fact that except during one mysteriously atypical long-ago period, the creation of fiction was just not among my talents. But now, I feel I'm letting down the fans I've so recently discovered I have—and there's no way to explain in a short e-mail reply that it isn't by choice. People assume that proven writing ability is all it takes to produce a novel. If only that were true!

Lately, I've begun to be aware that I have less time ahead than I used to have for future work. Since I never had much youthful vigor at any age—at least not in the physical sense—growing older hasn't changed my lifestyle; so it's a bit startling to realize that now, I really am well along in years. Perhaps this will produce the urgency needed to bring my nonfiction projects to fruition. But it can't change anything as far as new fiction is concerned. For that, I can only hope that someday the door to imaginative realms may once more open for me. It surprised me (and everyone who knew me) when it happened before . . . might I not, without warning, be surprised again?

Meanwhile, most of my past novels are back in print, in beautiful new editions. I know from the many e-mails I treasure that they've affected readers' lives. And that's much more enduring success than I ever anticipated.

BIOGRAPHICAL/CRITICAL SOURCES:

BOOKS

Authors and Artists for Young Adults, Volume 36, Gale (Detroit, MI), 2001.
Children's Literature Review, Volume 2, Gale (Detroit, MI), 1976.
The Phoenix Award of the Children's Literature Association 1990-1994, Scarecrow Press, 1996.
St. James Guide to Young Adult Writers, St. James Press (Detroit, MI), 1999.
Twentieth-Century Young Adult Writers, St. James Press (Detroit, MI), 1994.

PERIODICALS

Booklist, May 15, 1971, p. 798.
Bulletin of the Center for Children's Books, January, 1971, p. 72; February, 1973, p. 89; June, 1973, p. 153.
Horn Book, April, 1970, pp. 165-166, 481; October, 1970; June, 1972, p. 274; June, 1973, p. 276.
Kirkus Reviews, February 15, 1973.

Library Journal, October 15, 1970, p. 3636; April, 1971, p. 1514.
New York Times Book Review, March 5, 1970, p. 22; May 3, 1970, p. 22; February 17, 1980, p. 24.
Publishers Weekly, May 31, 1971, p. 135.
San Jose Mercury News, June 4, 2000.
School Library Journal, March, 1975, p. 105; November, 1975, p. 88; October, 1976, p. 116; October, 1977, p. 123; September, 1979, p. 135; February, 1980, p. 44; April, 1981, p. 138.
Times Literary Supplement, September 20, 1974, p. 1006; September 19, 1975, p. 1052.
Voice of Youth Advocates, June, 1981, p. 37.

OTHER

Sylvia Louise Engdahl Web site, http://www.sylviaeng dahl.com (October 2, 2001).

*   *   *

ENNIS, Charles A(lbert) 1954-
(Kerr Cuhulain)

PERSONAL: Born March 6, 1954, in Vancouver, British Columbia, Canada; son of Ronald Alfred (a printer and lithographer) and Beatrice Agnes (Young) Ennis; married Laurel Jean Jackson (a writer), 1991. *Ethnicity:* "Caucasian." *Education:* Attended Royal Roads Military College. *Religion:* Wiccan. *Avocational interests:* "Anti-defamation work."

ADDRESSES: Home—Surrey, British Columbia, Canada. *Office*—Vancouver Police Department, 312 Main St., Vancouver, British Columbia, Canada V6A 2T2. *E-mail*—kcuhulain@aol.com.

CAREER: Vancouver Police Department, Vancouver, British Columbia, Canada, detective, 1977—, member of emergency response team, 1980-85, member of gang crime unit, 1989-93, also assigned to child abuse and neglect investigation. Witches League for Public Awareness, Canadian coordinator, 1986; Wiccan Information Network, founder, 1989, director and publisher of a quarterly journal, 1989-94; speaker at Wiccan gatherings; public speaker on Wicca and related topics, including lectures at University of Victoria, University of Memphis, and University of British Columbia; guest on media programs; consultant to California Office of Criminal Justice Planning, Canada Immigration Enforcement Section, and Cult Awareness Network. Society for the Prevention of Cruelty to Animals, volunteer inspector, 1985-87; Orphaned Wildlife Rehabilitation Society, volunteer rescue worker, 1987-90. *Military service:* Canadian Armed Forces, pilot, 1973-76.

MEMBER: American Society of Law Enforcement Trainers.

AWARDS, HONORS: Governor General's Exemplary Service Medal, 1998.

WRITINGS:

UNDER PSEUDONYM KERR CUHULAIN

Law Enforcement Guide to Wicca, Horned Owl Publishing, 1989, 3rd edition, 1997.
Wiccan Warrior: Walking a Spiritual Path in a Sometimes Hostile World (nonfiction), Llewellyn (St. Paul, MN), 2000.
Full Contact Magick: A Warrior's Book of Shadows, Llewellyn (St. Paul, MN), 2000.

Author of safety training manuals; contributor to periodicals, including *Law and Order* and Wiccan periodicals.

WORK IN PROGRESS: "Attempted Exculpations," to be included in a collection of police stories, for Odd Squad Productions; a biographical work, under pseudonym Kerr Cuhulain.

SIDELIGHTS: Charles A. Ennis told *CA:* "I've always had a passion for writing. I'm a trainer and a storyteller, so I write to get a message across to others. I'm a police officer, which means that I do a lot of investigative writing. . . . My favorite authors are Charles Dickens, Ellis Peters, Diana Gabaldon, and Tanith Lee. . . . My inspiration to write on the subjects I have chosen are my Wiccan beliefs and my experiences as a police officer."

BIOGRAPHICAL/CRITICAL SOURCES:

BOOKS

Marron, Kevin, *Witches, Pagans, and Magic in the New Age,* Seal Books, 1989.
Streiker, Lowell, *New Age Comes to Main Street,* Abingdon (Nashville, TN), 1989.

PERIODICALS

Publishers Weekly, February 14, 2000, review of *Wiccan Warrior: Walking a Spiritual Path in a Sometimes Hostile World.*
Seattle Times, September 1, 1990, Carol M. Ostrom, "Pagans: Live and Let Live?" and "A Gathering of

Pagans: There Are a Whole Lot More of Us Than You Think."
Sun (Vancouver, Canada), May 9, 1991, Douglas Todd, "Satanism: The Other Side of the Story," "Broad Cult Definitions Fuel Fears of Satanism," and "Troubled Teens Adopt Satanic Symbols;" January 22, 1994, Mia Stainsby, "Constable from the Coven," "Which Is Witch?," and "Music, Dance, and Spirituality Are the Wiccan's Way."
Westworld, September 12-18, 1990.

* * *

ERIKSSON, Ulf (Nils Erik) 1958-

PERSONAL: Born February 8, 1958, in Stockholm, Sweden; son of Nils and Mildred (Gustavsson) Eriksson; married Anna-Karin Palm, June 30, 1989. *Education:* Degree from University of Stockholm, 1982.

ADDRESSES: Home—Grindsgatan 33 V, 11657 Stockholm, Sweden.

CAREER: Poet, author, and critic.

MEMBER: Swedish PEN, Swedish Writers Association.

AWARDS, HONORS: Stig Carlsson award for poetry, 1986; Denzos pris award for poetry, 1990; Obstfelder Prize.

WRITINGS:

Varelser av gräs: dikter, Bonniers (Stockholm, Sweden), 1982.
I förut lugna rum: dikter, Bonniers (Stockholm, Sweden), 1983.
Det gjorda återstår (novel), Bonniers (Stockholm, Sweden), 1984.
Brevet: en dikt, Bonniers (Stockholm, Sweden), 1985.
Färjefärd: dikter, Bonniers (Stockholm, Sweden), 1986.
Ulrike ler (novel), Bonniers (Stockholm, Sweden), 1986.
Äppelaffärer (novel), Bonniers (Stockholm, Sweden), 1987.
Liv i överflöd: prolegomena till Emilia Fogelklou, Bokförlaget Åsak (Delsbo, Sweden), 1988.
Byte (novel), Bonniers (Stockholm, Sweden), 1988.
Rum för läsande: kulturkritik (essays), Bonniers (Stockholm, Sweden), 1990.
Fria andar: essäer om det antända livet (essays), Symposion (Stockholm, Sweden), 1990.

Byggnad med kreatur: dikter, Bonniers (Stockholm, Sweden), 1990.

Mörkret bland färgerna (poetry), Bonniers (Stockholm, Sweden), 1992.

Xaviers hemlighet (novel), Bonniers (Stockholm, Sweden), 1993.

I det uppenbara: dikter, Bonniers (Stockholm, Sweden), 1994.

Paradis (novella), Bonniers (Stockholm, Sweden), 1996.

Min vän Mr Ho (novel), Bonniers (Stockholm, Sweden), 1997.

Flamma livsstund kalla eld, Bonniers (Stockholm, Sweden), 1998.

Is (novella), Bonniers (Stockholm, Sweden), 1999.

SIDELIGHTS: Beginning with his debut at age twenty-five, Ulf Eriksson has published more than a dozen works of poetry and prose, establishing himself both as a creative voice and as an emerging literary critic in his native Sweden. *World Literature Today* contributor Rose-Marie Oster, who noted traces of Heidegger and Wittgenstein in the author's style, added that in such works as *Mörkret bland färgerna* it "becomes clear how firmly grounded he is in Swedish lyric tradition, with his emphasis on landscape and nature."

Assessing Erikkson's poetry, Oster pointed to a sense of "restlessness" in its continual use of "metaphors, states of being and modes of perception." Turning to fiction, Eriksson characters "exist in a world where existential despair has become trivialized, where the search for individuality and freedom becomes a lonely walk through a hall of mirrors . . . [and where language itself] implodes under the constant pressure, to reveal unexpected and disconcerting patterns," as Oster wrote in a *World Literature Today* review of the short-story collection *Paradis.*

In 1997 Eriksson published *Min vän Mr Ho,* a novel that can be read "as a parable about the future of Sweden," according to Adma d'Heurle of *World Literature Today.* Central character Mia engages in a lustful liaison with an ex-terrorist while experiencing "a continuous stream of consciousness" with "her frequent dreams . . . barely distinct from her waking state." Meanwhile, a conspiracy is underway via the mysterious Mr. Ho, to steal energy from major European cities. While acknowledging that the novel has "not much of a coherent plot," d'Heurle still recommended *Min vän Mr Ho* as a book "written in a vigorous and sensuous prose."

BIOGRAPHICAL/CRITICAL SOURCES:

PERIODICALS

World Literature Today, spring, 1993, Rose-Marie Oster, review of *Mörkret bland färgerna,* p. 401; autumn, 1997, Adma d'Heurle, review of *Min vän Mr Ho,* p. 81; winter, 1997, Oster, review of *Paradis,* p. 171.*

*　*　*

ERSKINE, Carl 1926-

PERSONAL: Born December 13, 1926, in Anderson, IN; son of Matthew and Bertha Erskine; married Betty L. Erskine, October 5, 1947; children: Carl Dan, Gary W., Susan D., James L. *Ethnicity:* "Scotch." *Education:* Attended Anderson University and Marian College, holds Dr. of Letters and Dr. of Laws degrees. *Religion:* Baptist. *Avocational interests:* "Music, golf, woodworking."

ADDRESSES: Home—6214 South Madison Ave., Anderson, IN 46013. *Office*—Star Financial Bank, 735 Main St., Anderson, IN 46016.

CAREER: Brooklyn Dodgers, major league baseball pitcher, 1946-57; Los Angeles Dodgers, major league baseball pitcher, 1958-59; affiliated with Midwestern United Life Insurance Co., 1960-75; Star Financial Bank, president, 1982-93. Johns Health Systems, trustee, 1970; Anderson University, trustee, beginning 1973; YMCA, trustee emeritus; state and national Special Olympics, chair. *Military service:* U.S. Navy, 1945-46.

MEMBER: Indiana Bankers Association (chair, 1991-92), Fellowship of Christian Retirees (trustee).

AWARDS, HONORS: Named one of Jaycee's ten outstanding young Americans, 1956; named Indiana Living Legend, 1998; Family of the Year, Indiana Association of Retarded Citizens.

WRITINGS:

Tales from the Dodger Dugout, Sports Publishing, 2000.

SIDELIGHTS: Carl Erskine told *CA:* "The book *Tales from the Dodger Dugout* evolved from a group of short articles I was writing for a baseball newsletter called *Baseball Assistance Team* (B.A.T.)—a foundation for assisting former major league players and their families. I found and researched a number of appropriate pictures, and Sports Publishing published the book in June 2000. These stories are from my fourteen years with the Dodgers—and many all time great players, as teammates and friends—that's enough inspiration. I wrote in doctors' offices, on airplanes, and late at night when I would recall another story."

F

FAIN, Gordon L. 1946-

PERSONAL: Born November 24, 1946, in Washington, DC; son of Robert Forbes and Margaret (maiden name, Smith; present surname, Zwickert) Fain; married Margery Jones, June 22, 1968; children: Timothy P., Nicholas H. *Education:* Stanford University, B.A., 1968; Johns Hopkins University, Ph.D., 1973. *Avocational interests:* Poetry, ancient Greek and Latin literature.

ADDRESSES: Office—University of California, Box 951527, Los Angeles, CA 90095.

CAREER: University of California, Los Angeles, CA, professor, 1975—.

AWARDS, HONORS: Guggenheim fellow, 1998.

WRITINGS:

Molecular and Cellular Physiology of Neurons, Harvard University Press (Cambridge, MA), 1999.*

*   *   *

FANGEN, Ronald (August) 1895-1946

PERSONAL: Born April 29, 1895, in Kragerø, Norway; died in an airplane crash, May 22, 1946, in Fornebu, Norway; son of a mining engineer.

CAREER: Writer and translator.

WRITINGS:

De svake: En fortælling, Erichsen (Oslo, Norway), 1915.

Slægt føder slægt, Erichsen (Oslo, Norway), 1916.

En roman, Erichsen (Oslo, Norway), 1918.

Streiftog i digtning og tænkning (essays), [Oslo, Norway], 1919.

Krise, 1919.

Syndefald (three-act play; title means "The Fall"), Gyldendal (Oslo, Norway), 1920.

Fienden (three-act play; title means "The Enemy"), [Oslo, Norway], 1922.

Den forjættede dag (three-act play; title means "The Promised Day"), Gyldendal (Oslo, Norway), 1926.

Tegn og gjærninger (essays), Gyldendal (Oslo, Norway), 1927.

Nogen unge mennesker (novel), Gyldendal (Oslo, Norway), 1929.

(Editor) *De 16 beste noveller fra den nordiske konkurranse,* Gyldendal (Oslo, Norway), 1930.

Erik (novel; sequel to *Nogen unge mennesker*), Gyldendal (Oslo, Norway), 1931.

Duel (novel), Gyldendal, 1932, translation by Paula Wiking, Viking (New York, NY), 1932.

En kvinnes vei (novel; title means "A Woman's Way"), Gyldendal (Oslo, Norway), 1933.

Mannen som elsket rettferdigheten (novel; title means "The Man Who Loved Justice"), Gyldendal (Oslo, Norway), 1934.

Dagen og veien, Gyldendal (Oslo, Norway), 1934.

Det nye liv, Gyldendal (Oslo, Norway), 1934.

En kristen verdensrevolusjon: Mitt møre med Oxford-gruppe-bevegelsen, Gyldendal (Oslo, Norway), 1935.

Som det kunde ha gått (play), Gyldendal (Oslo, Norway), 1935.

Paulus og vår egen tid, Gyldendal (Oslo, Norway), 1936.

På bar bunn (novel; title means "On Rock Bottom"), Gyldendal (Oslo, Norway), 1936.

Allerede nu (novel; title means "Already Now"; sequel to *På bar bunn*), Gyldendal (Oslo, Norway), 1937.

Kristen enhet, 1937.

Kristendommen og vår tid, Gyldendal (Oslo, Norway), 1938.

Kristent budskap til vår tid: Nordiske prekener, Gyldendal (Oslo, Norway), 1939.

Kvernen som maler langsomt (novel), Gyldendal (Oslo, Norway), Volume I: *Borgerfesten* (title means "Civic Festival"), 1939, Volume II: *Presten,* 1946.

Krig og kristen tro, 1940.

Norsk litteraturs historie: Tre breve, Folkfung, 1940.

En lysets engel: Beretningen om to norske gutter som falt i krigen (novel), Gyldendal (Oslo, Norway), 1945, translation by Dermot McKay published as *Both Are My Cousins,* Blandford (London, England), 1945.

Om troskap: Oktober 1940, Land og kirke (Oslo, Norway), 1946.

Nåderiket: Prekener, Gyldendal (Oslo, Norway), 1947.

Om frihet, og andre essays, Gyldendal (Oslo, Norway), 1947.

Samlede verker, nine volumes, Gyldendal (Oslo, Norway), 1948-49.

Essays, edited by Carl F. Engelstad, Gyldendal (Oslo, Norway), 1965.

I nazistenes fengsel (1940-1941), Gyldendal (Oslo, Norway), 1975.

Contributor of reviews to newspapers and magazines, including *Bonniers literrära magasin.* Founder and editor, *Vor verden,* 1923-30; editor of other literary magazines.

BIOGRAPHICAL/CRITICAL SOURCES:

BOOKS

Elseth, Egil Yngvar, *Ronald Fangen: Fra humanist til kristen,* [Oslo], 1953.

Encyclopedia of World Literature in the Twentieth Century, 3rd edition, St. James Press (Detroit, MI), 1999.

Engelstad, Carl F., *Ronald Fangen: En mann og hans samtid,* [Oslo], 1946.

PERIODICALS

American-Scandinavian Review, Volume 49, number 2, 1961, S. D. Govig, "Ronald Fangen: A Christian Humanist."

Books Abroad, Volume 20, 1946, Lawrence Thompson, "Ronald Fangen: 1895-1946."

New York Times Book Review, June 17, 1934, H. Strauss, review of *Duel.*

Spectator, June 22, 1945, W. Plomer, review of *Duel.*

Times Literary Supplement, June 28, 1934, P. Quennell, review of *Duel.**

*   *   *

FARRELL, Fiona 1947-
(Fiona Farrell Poole)

PERSONAL: Born 1947, in Oamaru, New Zealand; divorced. *Education:* Otago University, B.A., 1968; University of Toronto, M.A., M.Phil, 1976.

ADDRESSES: Home—Otanerito, Akaroa 3, New Zealand. *Agent*—c/o Auckland University Press, University of Auckland, 1-11 Short St., Auckland, New Zealand.

CAREER: Writer. Lecturer in drama at Palmerston North Teachers' College, 1977-82; teacher at secondary schools, 1983-90. Writer-in-residence, Canterbury University, 1992; Katherine Mansfield Memorial Fellow, Menton, New Zealand, 1995.

AWARDS, HONORS: Bruce Mason Playwrights' Award, 1983; BNZ Katherine Mansfield Memorial Award for short fiction, 1984; American Express Award for short fiction, 1987; Mobil-*Dominion Sunday Times* Award for short fiction, 1988; Mobil Award for Best Radio Drama, 1990, for *The Perils of Pauline Smith;* New Zealand Book Award for fiction, 1993, for *The Skinny Louie Book.*

WRITINGS:

Passengers (play), 1984.

Images of Women (radio play), 1984.

In Confidence: Dialogues with Amy Bock (play), 1986.

Bonds (play), 1986.

(Under name Fiona Farrell Poole) *Cutting Out* (poetry), Auckland University Press (Auckland, New Zealand), 1988.

(Under name Fiona Farrell Poole) *The Rock Garden* (short stories), Auckland University Press (Auckland, New Zealand), 1989.

Thatcher, Vitelli, and Small (play), 1990.

Vitelli and Small (play), 1990.

The Perils of Pauline Smith (radio play), 1990.

The Skinny Louie Book (novel), Penguin (Auckland, New Zealand), 1992.

(With others) *Song of the Shirt: Three One-Act Plays for Young Actors,* McIndoe (Dunedin, New Zealand), 1993.

(With Angio Farrow) *Looking Forward* (radio play),
    1993.
Airwaves (radio play), 1993.
Chook Chook (play), 1994.
Six Clever Girls Who Became Famous Women (novel),
    Penguin (Auckland, New Zealand), 1996.
The Inhabited Initial (poetry), Auckland University
    Press (Auckland, New Zealand), 1999.
Light Readings (short stories), Random Vintage, 2001.

Work included in anthologies, including *Best Short Stories 1990*, edited by Gordon and Hughes, Heinemann;
and *Best Short Stories 1995*, edited by Gordon and
Huges, Heinemann. Contributor to periodicals, including *NZ Listener*.

SIDELIGHTS: Fiona Farrell is an award-winning
writer of plays, prose fiction, and poetry. Her work is
unified by themes such as isolation and the intolerance
society has for people who look or behave differently
from others. In 1990, writing as Fiona Farrell Poole, she
published the short-story collection *The Rock Garden.*
Fleur Adcock, reviewing *The Rock Garden* in the *Times
Literary Supplement,* declared that Farrell proved herself "very good at dialogue" with this debut volume.

Farrell's ensuing publications include the poetry collection *The Inhabited Initial,* which *Landfall* contributor
Elizabeth Smither called "both a discourse on language,
including punctuation, alphabet and capital letters, but
also . . . an orthodox collection of poems."

Farrell's novels *The Skinny Louie Book* and *Six Clever
Girls Who Became Famous Women* each span several
decades of time as they observe changes in New Zealand society. The former looks at the years following
World War II into the future, and the latter follows six
women from the 1960s through thirty-five years of
change.

BIOGRAPHICAL/CRITICAL SOURCES:

PERIODICALS

Landfall, March, 2000, Elizabeth Smither, review of
    The Inhabited Initial, pp. 138-142.
Times Literary Supplement, February 2, 1990, Fleur
    Adcock, "Vigorous Designs," p. 123.

FINNEY, Paul Corby 1939-

PERSONAL: Born July 29, 1939, in Springfield, MA;
son of R. Regan (in the newspaper industry) and
Kathryn B. (a retailer) Finney; married Kathleen E.
McVey, 1966; children: Nathaniel, Siobhan. *Ethnicity:*
"Anglo/Celtic." *Education:* Yale University, A.B.,
1962; attended Ludwig Maximilians University (Germany), 1962-63, and University of Aix en Provence,
1963; Harvard University, M.A. and Ph.D., 1973. *Politics:* Democrat. *Religion:* "No affiliation." *Avocational
interests:* "Art, music, photography, literature."

ADDRESSES: Home—11 Alexander St, Princeton, NJ
08540. *Office*—Department of History, University of
Missouri, 421 LH, 8001 Natural Bridge Rd., St. Louis,
MO 63121; fax: 314-516-5415. *E-mail*—corbyfinney@
aol.com; and finney@msx.umsl.edu.

CAREER: Boston University, Chestnut Hill, MA, assistant professor, 1964-65; University of Missouri, St.
Louis, 1973-2000, began as assistant professor, became
professor, professor emeritus, 2000—. Hebrew University, (Israel), visiting professor, 1979-80; Institute for
Advanced Study, visiting fellow, 1980; Princeton
Theological Seminary, visiting lecturer, 1983; American School of Classical Studies (Greece), senior associate, 1987; Greek Ministry of Antiquities, associate archaeologist, 1987; Princeton University, visiting fellow, 1992-95.

MEMBER: American Society of Church History, Archaeological Institute of America, Association of Ancient Historians, North American Patristic Society, Society for the Promotion of Hellenic Studies (London),
Society for the Promotion of Roman Studies (London).

AWARDS, HONORS: A. Congar Goodyear Award,
Yale University, 1962; Fulbright fellowship, 1962;
awards from American Council of Learned Societies,
1977 and 1987, American Philosophical Society, 1979,
and National Endowment for the Humanities.

WRITINGS:

(Editor) *Art, Archaeology and Architecture of Early
    Christianity,* Garland (New York, NY), 1993.
Invisible God, Oxford University Press (New York,
    NY), 1994.
(Editor) *Seeing beyond the Word,* Eerdmans (Grand
    Rapids, MI), 1999.

Contributor to periodicals, including *Journal of Jewish
Art, Art Bulletin, Church History, American Journal of*

Archeology, Journal of Biblical Literature, Journal of Theological Studies, Journal of Early Christian Studies, Second Century, and *Harvard Theological Review,* and books, including *The Image and the Word,* edited by J. Gutmann, 1977; *Encyclopedia of Early Christianity,* edited by E. Ferguson, M. P. McHugh, F. W. Norris, and D. M. Scholar, 1990; and *Oxford Encyclopedia of Archaeology in the New East,* Oxford University Press, 1997.

WORK IN PROGRESS: Editor-in-chief, *Encyclopedia of Early Christian Art and Archaeology,* for Eerdmans; *Visual Intelligence in Late Antiquity,* for Oxford University Press; *Engraved Gemstones in Late Antiquity;* with wife, K. E. McVey, *Early Christianity: A New History,* for Oxford University Press.

*   *   *

FLANAGAN, Richard   1961-

PERSONAL: Born 1961, in Tasmania, Australia.

ADDRESSES: Home—Tasmania, Australia. *Agent*—c/o Grove Atlantic, 841 Broadway, New York, NY 10003-4793.

CAREER: Author, editor, and director.

AWARDS, HONORS: Australian National Fiction Award, 1996, for *Death of a River Guide.*

WRITINGS:

A Terrible Beauty: History of the Gordon River Country, Greenhouse (Richmond, Victoria, Australia), 1985.
(Editor, with Cassandra Pybus) *The Rest of the World is Watching,* Sun (Sydney, New South Wales, Australia), 1990.
(With John Friedrich) *Codename Iago: The Story of John Friedrich,* Heinemann Australia (Melbourne, Victoria, Australia), 1991.
"Parish-Fed Bastards": A History of the Politics of the Unemployed in Britain, 1884-1939, Greenwood (New York, NY), 1991.
Death of a River Guide (novel), McPhee Gribble (Ringwood, Victoria, Australia), 1994, Grove (New York, NY), 2001.
The Sound of One Hand Clapping (play), Macmillan (Sydney, New South Wales, Australia), 1997, re-

printed, Atlantic Monthly Press (New York, NY), 2000.

Contributor to *The Penguin Book of Death.*

ADAPTATIONS: The Sound of One Hand Clapping was adapted for film by Palace Films and directed by Flanagan.

SIDELIGHTS: Tasmanian-born Richard Flanagan is the author of novels and nonfiction books, including *"Parish-Fed Bastards": A History of the Politics of the Unemployed in Britain, 1884-1939.* The title was taken from an abusive term used by police for an activist workers' movement in 1932. Flanagan seeks to disprove the belief that the unemployed were politically passive, as well as the assumption that they were victims unable to change their situation.

In the book Flanagan studies unemployment and the political activism of the unemployed from the Tudor period to the passage of the New Poor Law, up to the time of the Social Democratic Federation. He emphasizes that the National Unemployed Workers Movement (NUWM) was the primary agency used for protest by the unemployed. *Choice* reviewer J. H. Wiener wrote that "unfortunately, his efforts at scholarship are drowned in a sea of anticapitalist rhetoric." *American Journal of Sociology* contributor Richard Lewis called Flanagan's study "interesting" and "useful," but felt that he does not disprove the accepted idea that the unemployed were not a potential threat to public order or that their collective action could change their destiny. Lewis noted two ways in which he found the book particularly useful. "It helps to kill the once widely held but erroneous idea that the NUWM was simply a front for the Communist Party of Great Britain. Second, it has a valuable chapter on the role of state-supported voluntary social service for the unemployed."

Flanagan's first novel, *Death of a River Guide,* is narrated by Aljaz Cosini, a guide who at the beginning of the story is drowning, trapped in the rocks of Tasmania's Franklin River. Aljaz's father is Tasmanian and his mother Italian, and he is married to Couta Ho, an Australian-Chinese woman. The death of their daughter Jemma, at two months of age, marks the beginning of the events which lead up to Aljaz's death. Aljaz's flashbacks are of his own life and the lives of his ancestors. Vivian Smith wrote in the *Times Literary Supplement* that "stories of old convict Tasmania—of cannibalism and the rape and pillage of Aboriginal women—are woven into the text of Cosini's discovery of his own Aboriginal forebears. More recent events—the depredation of forests and rivers, the slow destruction of native fauna and flora by the mining and timber industries and the hydro-electric development schemes, the attempts to save the remaining wilderness—are presented, matter-of-factly, as they impinge on the family. It is a grim picture of what has happened to Tasmania. Flanagan's novel is above all an elegy for a lost world."

World Literature Today contributor John Scheckter commented that "without losing a shred of postmodern irony, the narrative allows Cosini's drowning to seem psychologically appropriate and emotionally fulfilling; thus, *Death of a River Guide* powerfully extends the tradition of Australian representations of character in the animate, transcendent landscape of the spirit." Liam Davison added in *Australian Book Review* that "tempering the sense of loss and regret is Flanagan's awareness of the comfort to be drawn from others and the almost religiously redemptive qualities to be gained from seeing one's self as part of some vast interconnected scheme. Aljaz Cosini operates largely as a representative character, a loner who feels he doesn't belong but whose genealogy branches out like an extensive river system to embrace Aboriginal stories, Celtic stories, stories from Italy, England, Yugoslavia, and China. He is none of us and all of us, and we are all part of each other." Davison concluded that *Death of a River Guide* is "an uplifting and immensely rewarding book." The novel earned the Australian National Fiction Award in 1996.

Flanagan's *The Sound of One Hand Clapping* was originally a play and was also adapted for film. The story begins in Tasmania in 1954, at a construction site where Eastern Europeans who had come seeking new lives are living an isolated existence and paid laborers' wages. One of these men is Bojan Buloh, a Slovenian whose experiences as a child in a war-torn land are also traced. While Bojan is away drinking, his wife, Maria, walks off in the snow to commit suicide. At the time, their daughter Sonja is three. Sonja flees to Sydney while in her teens to escape her father's abuse. At thirty-eight she returns to reconcile with her father and, with the support of families who had known her mother, bear the child she had planned to abort.

"The contrast with the self-confident storytelling of the earlier novel is disheartening," opined Stephen Henighan in the *Times Literary Supplement.* "The narrative unease betrays Flanagan's uncomfortable relationship to his subject; his familiarity with his assimilated material . . . seems to prevent him from assessing it with the tough-mindedness he brought to bear on the broader Tasmanian society in his first novel." Henighan

concluded that "in the final analysis, Flanagan denies his immigrant characters their hybrid experience. The novel's closing assertion that 'only those who lived it can ever know' a particular history cuts both ways, separating Sonja and her daughter from the Slovenian past while shutting the gates of Tasmanian society against the 'wogs' the novel set out to include." *Booklist* reviewer Nancy Pearl, however, allowed that Flanagan's "strong writing and ability to express the points of view of both father and daughter enrich the reading experience." "There are some stunning set pieces," clarified Judith Kicinski in *Library Journal.* "Flanagan's telling of Sonja's childhood offers some of the novel's best prose," lauded Lucy Frost in *Australian Book Review.* "One of the novel's unforgettable moments tracks Bojan Buloh in 1990 'to the one place he had vowed never to return,' the dam at Butlers Gorge 'whose concrete felt entwined with his very flesh.' " Frost called *The Sound of One Hand Clapping* "haunting." A *Publishers Weekly* reviewer concluded that Flanagan "brilliantly illuminates the lives of those who are 'forgotten by history, irrelevant to history, yet shaped entirely by it.' His characters here transform tragedy as they discover their individual worth."

Variety contributor David Stratton reviewed the film version of *The Sound of One Hand Clapping*, which Flanagan directed. Stratton noted that the film is limited to Sonja's childhood and her return to Tasmania. Flanagan "sensitively creates a world where old traditions, good as well as bad, are reduced to memories, where such a basic asset as your own language is no longer useful, where the bitterness of the past must be forgotten if there's to be a future." Though noting that "there's little variation in the generally gloomy tone of the drama," Stratton stated, "Given pretty much a free hand to bring his vision to the screen as few novelists are, writer-director Flanagan has done a generally solid job."

BIOGRAPHICAL/CRITICAL SOURCES:

PERIODICALS

American Journal of Sociology, November, 1992, Richard Lewis, review of *"Parish-Fed Bastards,"* pp. 692-694.

Australian Book Review, December, 1994, Liam Davison, review of *Death of a River Guide,* pp. 7-8; November, 1997, Lucy Frost, "Difference," p. 41.

Booklist, December 15, 1999, Nancy Pearl, review of *The Sound of One Hand Clapping,* p. 757; November 15, 2000, Donna Seaman, review of *Death of a River Guide,* p. 615.

Choice, June, 1992, J. H. Wiener, review of *"Parish-Fed Bastards,"* p. 1595.

Economist, July 11, 1998, review of *The Sound of One Hand Clapping,* p. 17.

Library Journal, January, 2000, Judith Kicinski, review of *The Sound of One Hand Clapping,* p. 158; January 1, 2001, Marc Kloszewski, review of *Death of a River Guide,* p. 153.

Publishers Weekly, January 3, 2000, review of *The Sound of One Hand Clapping,* p. 55; January 15, 2001, review of *Death of a River Guide,* p. 51.

Times Literary Supplement, October 3, 1997, Vivian Smith, "Down the Franklin," p. 21; March 13, 1998, Stephen Henighan, "European past, Tasmanian present," p. 22.

Variety, March 2, 1998, David Stratton, review of *The Sound of One Hand Clapping* (film), p. 93.

World Literature Today, spring, 1998, John Scheckter, "Asia and the Pacific," pp. 453-454.

OTHER

CNN.com Reviews, http://cgi.cnn.com/ (April 13, 2000), Stephanie Bowen, review of *The Sound of One Hand Clapping.*

The Write Stuff, http://www.the-write-stuff.com.au/ (March 26, 2001), interview with Flanagan.*

*　*　*

FOGARTY, Michael P(atrick)   1916-2001

OBITUARY NOTICE—See index for *CA* sketch: Born October 3, 1916, in Maymyo, Burma; died January 20, 2001. Political analyst, educator, and author. Fogarty was a professor of industrial relations at the University of Wales from 1951 to 1966 who went on to conduct research on such societal injustices as unequal wages and opportunities for women in the work field. Founder of the British Christian Democratic movement, he later stood in several elections, though unsuccessfully. Fogarty wrote a number of works including his 1944 *Prospects of the Industrial Areas of Great Britain* and his 1947 *Further Studies in Economic Organisation.* Some of his later works include the 1961 *Just Wage,* his 1967 *Women and Top Jobs,* which he wrote with Rhona and Robert Rapoport, and his 1982 *Families in Britain.*

OBITUARIES AND OTHER SOURCES:

PERIODICALS

Times (London, England), March 5, 2001, p. 21.

FOREMAN-PECK, James S.   1948-

PERSONAL: Born June 9, 1948, in London, England. *Education:* University of Essex, B.A., 1970; London School of Economics, M.Sc., 1971, Ph.D., 1977.

ADDRESSES: Home—53 Portland Rd., Oxford OX2 7EZ, England. *Office*—H. M. Treasury, Parliament St., London SW1P 3AG, England; fax: 44 171 270 5807. *E-mail*—james.foreman-peck@hm-treasury.gov.uk.

CAREER: Electricity Council, London, England, economist, 1971-72; University of Greenwich, London, England, lecturer in economics, 1972-79; University of Newcastle upon Tyne, lecturer in economics, 1979-88; University of Hull, professor of economic history, 1988-90; University of Oxford, fellow of St. Antony's College and university lecturer in economic history, 1991-98; H. M. Treasury, London, England, economic adviser, 1999—. University of Reading, visiting lecturer in economics, 1974-75; University of California, Davis, visiting associate professor of economics, 1981-82; University of Warwick, visiting fellow in Department of Economics, 1989; University of Manchester, Hallsworth Fellow in Political Economy, 1990-91; European Historical Economics Society, secretary/treasurer, 1992-99, president, 1999; Middlesex University Business School, associate professor; consultant, including work with British Telecom, Alcatel NV, Oxford Analytica, and Rank Hovis.

WRITINGS:

A History of the World Economy: International Economic Relations Since 1859, Barnes and Noble (New York, NY), 1983.

(Editor, with J. Mueller, coauthor of introduction, and contributor) *European Telecommunications Organisation,* Nomos, 1998.

(Editor, author of introduction, and contributor) *New Perspectives on the Late Victorian Economy: Essays in Quantitative Economic History,* Cambridge University Press (New York, NY), 1991.

(With R. Millward) *Private and Public Ownership of British Industry in Britain 1820-1990,* Clarendon, 1994.

Smith & Nephew in the Health Care Industry 1856-1993, Edward Elgar, 1995.

(With S. Bowden and A. McKinlay) *The British Motor Industry,* Manchester University Press, 1995.

(Editor) *Historical Foundations of Globalization,* Edward Elgar, 1998.

(Editor, with G. Federico) *European Industrial Policy: The Twentieth Century Experience,* Oxford University Press (New York, NY), 1999.

Contributor to various publications, including *Business History, European Review of History, Oxford International Review, Journal of Law and Society, fiscal Studies, National Westminster Bank Review, Economic History Review, Economic History Review,* and *Applied Economics.* Editorial board member, *Explorations in Economic History,* 1993-97, and *European Review of Economic History,* 1997—.

* * *

FREEMAN, Douglas Southall 1886-1953

PERSONAL: Born May 16, 1886, in Lynchburg, VA; died June 13, 1953, in Richmond, VA; son of Walker Burford Freeman (a Confederate soldier, later an insurance agent) and Bettie Allen Hamner; married Inez Virginia Goddin, 1914; children: three. *Education:* Richmond College (later the University of Richmond), A.B., 1904; Johns Hopkins University, Ph.D.,1908. *Religion:* Baptist.

CAREER: Historian, biographer, journalist, editor, teacher, radio broadcaster. *Richmond News Leader,* editor, 1915-49; Columbia University, New York, NY, visiting professor of journalism, 1934-35 (also held title 1936-41 but was not in residence).

AWARDS, HONORS: Pulitzer Prize, 1935, for *R. E. Lee,* and again in 1958, for *George Washington;* Franklin Medal of American Philosophical Society, 1947; twenty-five honorary degrees.

WRITINGS:

(Editor) *A Calendar of Confederate Papers,* The Confederate Museum (Richmond, VA), 1908.
Tax Reform in Virginia, State Tax Commission (Richmond, VA), 1911.
(Editor) *Lee's Dispatches to Jefferson Davis, 1862-1865,* Putnam's (New York, NY), 1915.
The Last Parade, Whittet & Shepperson (Richmond, VA), 1932.
R. E. Lee, four volumes, Scribners (New York, NY), 1934-1935, abridged edition, Southern Living Gallery, 1982.
The Lengthening Shadow of Lee, Division of Purchase and Printing (Richmond, NY), 1936.
The South to Posterity: An Introduction to the Writing of Confederate History, Scribners (New York, NY), 1939.
Lee's Lieutenants: A Study in Command, Scribners (New York, NY), Volume 1: *Manassas to Malvern Hill,* 1942, Volume 2: *Cedar Mountain to Chancellorsville,* 1943, Volume 3: *Gettysburg to Appomattox,* 1944.
Virginia, 1864-1865, Scribners (New York, NY), 1947.
George Washington, Scribners (New York, NY), Volumes 1 and 2: *Young Washington,* 1948, Volume 3: *Planter and Patriot,* 1951, Volume 4: *Leader of the Revolution,* 1951, Volume 5: *Victory with the Help of France,* 1952, Volume 6: *Patriot and President,* 1954, Volume 7: (based on Freeman's research) *First in Peace,* by John Alexander Carroll and Mary Wells Ashworth, 1957, abridged edition, Collier Books (New York, NY), 1992.
Lee of Virginia, Scribners (New York, NY), 1958.
Douglas Southall Freeman on Leadership, edited with commentary by Stuart W. Smith, Naval War College Press (Newport, RI), 1990.

Freeman's papers are housed at the Library of Congress.

SIDELIGHTS: Douglas Southall Freeman is recognized as one of the leading biographers and military historians of the twentieth century. His many volumes on Robert E. Lee and the Confederate officers who served under him are considered definitive books on the American Civil War.

Growing up, Freeman became interested in the war because his father was a Confederate veteran who had served in Lee's Army of Northern Virginia. After graduation from Richmond College, the young Freeman studied at Johns Hopkins. At the age of twenty-two, he received a doctorate in history. Before he graduated, Freeman edited *A Calendar of Confederate Papers* (1908), which describes the books, documents, and pamphlets collected by the Confederate Memorial Literary Society. A man who read the book asked Freeman to look at some letters he had bought. They turned out to be confidential correspondence from Robert E. Lee to Jefferson Davis, which had been presumed lost. *Lee's Dispatches to Jefferson Davis, 1862-1865* was published in 1915.

The same year, Freeman became editor of the *Richmond News Leader,* where he worked for the next thirty-four years. Because *Lee's Dispatches* was reviewed on the front page of the Sunday book section of *The New York Times,* Freeman also received an offer in 1915 from the publishing company Charles Scribner's Sons to write a biography of Robert E. Lee. Scribners wanted only a short book on the general, but Freeman was determined to produce a definitive biography, and he spent nearly two decades on the project. He once told his father that "twenty years is but a trifle for so great a work."

R. E. Lee was published as a four-volume series during 1934 and 1935, and indeed it was considered a great work. It not only received widespread critical acclaim but also won the 1935 Pulitzer Prize and established Freeman's reputation as a preeminent biographer and historian. In a review of *R. E. Lee* in the *New York Herald Tribune Books,* the poet Stephen Vincent Benet notes that Freeman "shows us from the very first lines of his foreword the thoroughness, the patience, the honesty, and the true gift for research which are the rare marks of the real biographer. He has winnowed, and winnowed away an enormous mass of legend. . . . He has woven together a thousand strands of testimony from the words of forgotten reports to the words on the lips of old men remembering their great youth."

In evaluating Lee's military performance, Freeman strove for objectivity. According to John L. Gignilliat, writing in the *Dictionary of Literary Biography,* "Freeman brought dispassion to his analysis. . . . He acknowledged some flaws in the commander—only peripheral flaws in the case of Gettysburg, but more serious ones in his strategy during the Seven Days, in his occasional overestimation of his men's endurance or of an individual officer's potential for leadership, and especially in his general courteous deference to his subordinates. On balance, though, Freeman declared the credit to Lee's military performance 'clear and absolute.' " Gignilliat also noted that "in Freeman's judgment, the population of the South was sustained in its will to fight during the final year of the war primarily by its perception of Lee's character. In *R. E. Lee* the military hero blends inextricably with the moral hero."

Although the text of *R. E. Lee* contained over a million words, Freeman still had many notes left over. He used them to begin a separate work focusing on the officers who had reported to Lee. Before he finished the first volume, however, he wrote *The South to Posterity: An Introduction to the Writing of Confederate History* (1939), which was an informal examination of Confederate memoirs. According to another review by Benet, this one in the *Saturday Review of Literature,* Freeman's *The South to Posterity* "is not, nor does it pretend to be, a complete history of Confederate literature—but, for either layman or scholar who is interested in the subject, it offers a remarkably engaging and readable introduction to the field."

The first volume of *Lee's Lieutenants: A Study in Command,* was published in 1942. Two other volumes were published during the next two years. Gignilliat noted that "*Lee's Lieutenants* is not a technical study of command or strategy. Rather, its genre is highly personal military biography. The focus remains consistently on the individual officers, and the unifying theme is the procurement of able commanders as the principals are winnowed by failure or casualty." As with his previous multi-volume work, *Lee's Lieutenants* received widespread critical praise. Writing about the first volume for the *Saturday Review of Literature,* Bernard DeVoto said, "As both a history and a critique of war, the book is a new and independent study, usually based on wider investigation than anything that has preceded it, dispassionate in judgement, obviously authoritative, alive and enthusiastic."

In sales of individual volumes, *Lee's Lieutenants* was even more popular than *R. E. Lee,* and Freeman became a national celebrity. His work habits and time-management skills were publicized and became legendary. He held to a strict schedule for each daily task (e.g., twelve minutes for shaving and dressing, seventeen minutes for driving to work). He arrived at the *Richmond News Leader* every day at 3:30 a.m., completed his editorial tasks, and then spent afternoons working on history.

Benet had ended his review of *R. E. Lee* with the wish to chain Freeman to a desk and "make him spend his next twenty years writing a life of Washington." After the publication of *Lee's Lieutenants,* Freeman undertook just such a project. The first two volumes of *George Washington* were published in 1948. A year later, Freeman relinquished his editorship at the newspaper to devote himself to the biography full time. He wrote four more volumes before his death in 1953. His assistants used his to research to finish a seventh book. Reviewing the first two volumes in the *New England Quarterly,* Perry Miller wrote, "the only question that existed in anticipation of Mr. Freeman's *George Washington* was whether it would or could match his *[R. E.] Lee.* The first two volumes, subtitled *Young Washington,* prove that it can and does. Here is the same broad canvas, the meticulous piecing together of detail, the full documentation, the leisurely pace, the relish for drama and for human personality, and especially the elevated, even Jovian, tone." However, the series did not achieve the popular success of his earlier works, and as Gignilliat noted, it also did not receive a universally positive response from critics: "The critical consensus admired Freeman's battle descriptions and military judgment but found *George Washington* lacking in social, intellectual, and political context." In spite of this criticism, *George Washington* was awarded the Pulitzer

Prize in 1958, and Freeman's overall contributions to the fields of Civil War history and biography are unquestionably monumental.

BIOGRAPHICAL/CRITICAL SOURCES:

BOOKS

Cyclopedia of World Authors, Harper (New York, NY), 1958.

Dictionary of Literary Biography, Volume 17: *Twentieth-Century American Historians,* Gale (Detroit, MI), 1983.

Encyclopedia of World Biography, 2nd edition, Gale (Detroit, MI), 1998.

The McGraw-Hill Encyclopedia of World Biography, McGraw (New York, NY), 1973.

The Oxford Companion to American Literature, 4th edition, Oxford University Press (New York, NY), 1965.

The Reader's Encyclopedia of American Literature, Crowell, 1962.

Twentieth-Century Literary Criticism, Volume 11, Gale (Detroit, MI), 1983.

PERIODICALS

Journal of Southern History, February, 1955, pp. 91-100; May, 1977, pp. 217-236.

New England Quarterly, June 1949, pp. 253-257.

New Republic, May 10, 1943, p. 644.

New York Herald Tribune Books, October 14, 1934, p. 1.

Richmond Literature and History Quarterly, spring 1979, pp. 33-41.

Saturday Review of Literature, November 25, 1939, p. 6; October 24, 1942, p. 15.*

*   *   *

FRIEDMAN, Meyer   1910-2001

OBITUARY NOTICE—See index for *CA* sketch: Born July 13, 1910, in Kansas City, KS; died April 27, 2001, in San Francisco, CA. Cardiologist and author. Friedman is best known for helping identify the connection between lifestyle and heart attacks in men, and coined the phrase "Type A" behavior to describe people who were instantly impatient and furious with traffic jams or anything they viewed as a waste of time. His most famous book, written with Ray H. Rosenman, is *Type A Behavior and Your Heart.* Friedman and Rosenman began studying the link between heart problems and behavior in the 1950s, publishing their findings in their 1974 best-selling book. Soon the term "Type A" became a catchphrase throughout the country, with people associating it with a personality type rather than learned behavior that could be changed. Friedman was himself—after two heart attacks—a recovering Type A. Friedman believed Type As could modify their behavior—and therefore their chances of heart attacks—with practice and learning to slow down. His study on that subject led to the 1984 book *Treating Type A Behavior And Your Heart.* Friedman worked until shortly before his death as director of the institute he founded that was part of the University of California at San Francisco's Mount Zion Medical Center. He had always wanted to be a doctor, deciding before finishing junior high school that he would attend Yale University and Johns Hopkins Medical School, which he did. After receiving his medical degree in 1935, Friedman worked at hospitals in Missouri and Illinois before moving to Mount Zion in 1939. In addition to his groundbreaking research on heart attacks, Friedman also helped develop the angiogram, and added important research in the study of gout and cholesterol. He wrote more than five hundred articles and two additional books: *Functional Cardiovascular Disease* and *Pathogenesis of Coronary Artery Disease.*

OBITUARIES AND OTHER SOURCES:

PERIODICALS

Chicago Tribune, May 2, 2001, sec. 2, p. 11.

Los Angeles Times, May 6, 2001, p. B12.

New York Times, May 1, 2001, p. C14.

Washington Post, May 2, 2001, p. B6.

*   *   *

FRITZ, Marianne   1948-

PERSONAL: Born December 14, 1948, in Weiz, Austria.

ADDRESSES: Office—c/o Suhrkamp Verlag, Postfach 101945, 60019 Frankfurt am Main, Germany.

CAREER: Novelist.

AWARDS, HONORS: Nachwuchsstipendium für Literatur des Bundesministeriums für Unterricht und Kunst, 1977; Robert Walser Prize, 1978; Jahresstipendium des Bundesministeriums für Unterricht und Kunst für dramatische Autoren, 1978; Fördergungspreis der Stadt Wien für Literatur, 1979; Staatstipendium des Bundesministeriums für Unterricht und Kunst für Literatur, 1980; City of Vienna, Elias-Canetti-Stipendium, January 1983 to December 1985; Rauriser Literaturpreis der Österreichischen Länderbank, 1986; Literaturpreis des Landes Steiermark, 1988; Förderunspreis des Bundesministeriums für Unterricht und Kunst für Literatur, 1989; Förderungsgabe für Kunst und Wissenschaft des Landes Vorarlberg für Literatur; Robert-Musil-Stipendium, 1990-93; Würdigungspreis der Stadt Wien für Literatur, 1994.

WRITINGS:

Die Schwerkraft der Verhältnisse, S. Fischer (Frankfurt, Germany), 1978.

Das Kind der Gewalt und die Sterne der Romani, S. Fischer (Frankfurt, Germany), 1980.

Dessen Sprache du nicht verstehst, Suhrkamp (Frankfurt, Germany), 1985.

Was soll man da machen: eine Einführung zu dem Roman Dessen Sprache du nicht verstehst, Suhrkamp (Frankfurt, Germany), 1985.

Naturgemäss I: entweder Angstschweiss ohnend oder pluralhaft: Roman, Suhrkamp (Frankfurt, Germany), 1996.

Naturgemäss II: es ist ein Ros entsprungen; Wedernoch heisst sie: Roman, Suhrkamp (Frankfurt, Germany), 1998.

SIDELIGHTS: Austrian novelist Marianne Fritz has written several books that are noted for their exploration of human suffering and innovative, if often difficult, use of language. Her first novel, *Die Schwerkraft der Verhältnisse,* earned the first Robert Walser Prize before it was published. The story's central character is Bertha, a woman who is so desperate to keep her children from enduring the hardships of her life that she kills them and then tries to kill herself. Fritz does not seek to create a realistic description of these events, but rather uses a restrained narrator to passively recount Bertha's experiences and inability to deal with her situation.

Writing for *World Literature Today,* Thomas H. Falk stated that Fritz's second novel, *Das Kind der Gewalt und die Sterne der Romani* "was hesitantly received because of its highly complex linguistic structure." Fritz went on to write a third novel that was even more unconventional in its language and its length. *Dessen Sprache du nicht verstehst* was created with the aid of an Elias-Canetti-Stipendium given to Fritz by the city of Vienna, and its first 100 pages were published as *Was soll man da machen.* This proved to be a small fraction of the entire novel. Falk wrote enthusiastically about *Dessen Sprache du nicht verstehst,* considering it no less than "a most wonderful and extraordinary novel." Falk explained, however, that the author was not likely to receive proper recognition for her achievement in the near future, because of the simple fact that the novel fills twelve volumes and runs over 3,300 pages. Yet he felt that ultimately it would "certainly rank among the half-dozen most important novels of this century."

The critic described *Dessen Sprache du nicht verstehst* as "an epic poem in the grandest style." Fritz's modern twist to the epic form is to place at its center a protagonist who will be totally forgotten after his death. As Falk explained, "the hero is a member of the Null family, who live in the town of Nirgendwo on the Nullweg number Null in the summer of 1914. It is essential that the reader take these names literally, because these Null family members are the real zeros, the total nobodies in our society." The youngest son of the Null family, Johannes, is the tragic hero. Required to join the military, he becomes a deserter and hides in the country. Ultimately, a priest who has earlier helped Johannes reveals his hiding place. Johannes is shot for his crime and, in order to keep his story secret from those who might consider him a hero, his home is demolished and the Null family history is effectively erased. These actions are facilitated by the fact that the rest of the family members have disappeared in other ways. For example, the widowed mother is committed to an insane asylum; the eldest son has committed suicide; and another son was killed in a workers' demonstration.

The novel's greatest strength, according to Falk, is Fritz's use of language. He called it "so magnificent and different" that she "has certainly matched, if not surpassed, the great masters James Joyce and Marcel Proust." While he noted that it was likely to put the reader in "total shock," Falk was enraptured with the novelist's linguistic virtuosity: "Our traditional conventions of rules of grammar and punctuation have been dissolved and re-created into a new system which is used throughout this modern epic. The language is so wonderful that one wants to quote the entire novel."

BIOGRAPHICAL/CRITICAL SOURCES:

PERIODICALS

World Literature Today, Winter, 1989, Thomas H. Falk, "Marianne Fritz's *Dessen Sprache dunicht verstehst:* A Contemporary Epic," pp. 61-62.*

G

GAYE, Marvin (Pentz, Jr.) 1939-1984

PERSONAL: Born on April 2, 1939, in Washington, DC; died of two gunshot wounds inflicted by his father on April 1, 1984 in Los Angeles, CA; son of Marvin Pentz Gay (minister, House of God) and Alberta Gay; married Anna Gordy 1962 (divorced 1976); married Janis Hunter in 1977; children: (first marriage) Marvin III; (second marriage) Nona, Frankie.

CAREER: Singer, songwriter, guitar player, piano player from 1956; member of The Marquees, 1957-58, The Moonglows, 1958-61; solo, duet performing artist, 1961-84. *Military service:* Served in Air Force.

AWARDS, HONORS: Two Grammy Awards for "Sexual Healing," 1983; gold and platinum album citations.

WRITINGS:

SOUND RECORDINGS

Soulful Mood, Motown (Detroit, MI), 1961.
That Stubborn Kinda Fellow, Motown (Detroit, MI), 1963, re-released, 1989.
Marvin Gaye Live on Stage, Motown (Detroit, MI), 1963.
When I'm Alone I Cry, Motown (Detroit, MI), 1964.
Marvin Gaye's Greatest Hits, Motown (Detroit, MI), 1964.
How Sweet It Is to Be Loved by You, Motown (Detroit, MI), 1964, re-released, 1989.
Hello Broadway, Motown (Detroit, MI), 1964.
(With Mary Wells) *Together,* Motown (Detroit, MI), 1964.
Tribute to Nat King Cole, Motown (Detroit, MI), 1965.
The Moods of Marvin Gaye, Motown (Detroit, MI), 1966, re-released, 1989.

Take Two, Motown (Detroit, MI), 1966.
(With Tammi Terrell) *United,* Motown (Detroit, MI), 1966.
(With Tammi Terrell) *You're All I Need to Get By,* Motown (Detroit, MI), 1968.
In the Groove, Motown (Detroit, MI), 1968.
MPG, Motown (Detroit, MI), 1969, re-released, 1989.
Marvin Gaye & His Girls, Motown (Detroit, MI), 1969.
Easy, Motown (Detroit, MI), 1969.
That's the Way Love Is, Motown (Detroit, MI), 1969, re-released, 1989.
Marvin Gaye's Greatest Hits, Motown (Detroit, MI), 1970.
What's Going On, Motown (Detroit, MI), 1971.
Troubled Man, Motown (Detroit, MI), 1972.
Let's Get It On, Motown (Detroit, MI), 1973.
(With Diana Ross) *Marvin & Diana,* Motown (Detroit, MI), 1974.
Marvin Gaye Live, Motown (Detroit, MI), 1974.
Marvin Gaye Anthology, Motown (Detroit, MI), 1974.
I Want You, Motown (Detroit, MI), 1976, re-released, 1989.
The Best of Marvin Gaye, Motown (Detroit, MI), 1976.
Marvin Gaye Live at the London Palladium, Motown (Detroit, MI), 1977.
Here My Dear, Motown (Detroit, MI), 1978.
In Our Lifetime, Motown (Detroit, MI), 1981.
Midnight Love, Columbia (New York, NY), 1982.
Dream of a Lifetime, Columbia (New York, NY), 1986.
Romantically Yours, Columbia (New York, NY), 1986.
Motown Remembers Marvin Gaye, Motown (Detroit, MI), 1986.
Compact Command Performance, Volumes 1 and 2, Motown (Detroit, MI), 1986.
I Heard It Through the Grapevine, Motown (Detroit, MI), 1989.

SIDELIGHTS: Marvin Gaye's vocals swayed a generation of listeners. Through such hits as "Sexual Healing," "Let's Get It On," "Mercy, Mercy Me," and "Inner City Blues (Make Me Wanna Holler)," Gaye revolutionized the Motown sound; he was the first solo artist to produce his own album of socially conscious recordings, and in so doing he influenced the music business's treatment of African American artists. Steve Bloom, eulogizing Gaye in *Down Beat,* described his work as "a body of brilliant . . . music that will endure and continue to serve as inspiration to us all." And he added: "Risk-taking, rule-breaking, and love-making were what Marvin Gaye was all about."

Marvin Pentz Gay, Jr. was born in Washington, DC on April 2, 1939. His parents, Marvin Pentz and Alberta Gay, were conservative Christians; Gaye's father was a minister in the House of God church. Jeff Pike explained in *The Death of Rock 'n' Roll: Untimely Demises, Morbid Preoccupations, and Premature Forecasts of Doom in Pop Music:* "From the evidence, it's likely that his father was a repressed homosexual, and certainly he was alcoholic. He beat Marvin daily throughout Marvin's childhood." Whether or not Pike's suspicions are accurate, Gaye's upbringing seems to have been a difficult one, and he maintained a painful relationship with his father until the last day of his life. Nevertheless, Gaye began his singing career in his father's church, and in many ways his later song-writing career seems to have been influenced by his father's work. Bloom praised Gaye's 1971 *What's Going On* as "a blistering indictment of America's misguided priorities combined with God-is-the-answer proselytizing—clearly the work of a preacher's son."

Gaye served briefly in the Air Force before beginning a music career. In 1957, after singing on street corners for a time, Gaye formed The Marquees, a group backed by Bo Diddley. (At this time, Gaye added the final "e" to his surname, following in the tradition of Sam Cooke.) Gaye's group had some modest successes—their song "Wyatt Earp" was recorded on the Okeh label—and by 1958 they were picked up by Harvey Fuqua to be his new back-up group, The Moonglows. Pike wrote, "Harvey Fuqua taught Gaye much about singing and performance techniques, and moved him to Chicago." In 1961, Gaye met the music producer Berry Gordy, who induced him to sing on the new Motown Records label. Gaye worked for a time as a studio drummer, providing rhythm for Smokey Robinson's albums before signing on as a solo artist. Stanley Crouch suggested that this early training may have influenced much of Gaye's later work: "His is a talent for which the studio must have been invented. Through overdub-

bing, Gaye imparted lyric, rhythmic, and emotional counterpoint to his material. The result was a swirling stream-of-consciousness that enabled him to protest, show allegiance, love, hate, dismiss, and desire in one proverbial fell swoop. In his way, what Gaye did was reiterate electronically the polyrhythmic African underpinnings of black American music and reassess the domestic polyphony which is its linear extension. Much of this probably has to do with his early experience as a Motown drummer, for the arrangements he wrote or supervised staggered off percussion voices and instruments with almost peerless precision."

Soon after joining Motown, Gaye married Gordy's sister Anna. He soon after became a top-selling crooner, with a great career in front of him. Pike remarked, "Gaye was one of those who clearly benefitted from Berry Gordy's fairness and patience. Gordy never let Gaye's marriage to his sister, nor his later divorce from her, interfere with their own relationship, even if Gaye did." Gaye's singing created hit after hit, including "Can I Get a Witness," "How Sweet It Is to Be Loved By You," and "I Heard It through the Grapevine." He was particularly successful in duet recordings, such as those he recorded with Tammi Terrell: "Your Precious Love," "Ain't Nothing Like the Real Thing," "You're All I Need to Get By," and "Ain't No Mountain High Enough."

But Gaye's partnership with Terrell ultimately forced him to express himself in a new way. In 1967, Terrell collapsed into Gaye's arms during a concert; three years later she died of a brain tumor. Gaye hid for a full year. A contributor to *Contemporary Black Biography* commented: "Although Gaye claimed that he was not romantically involved with Terrell, her illness and death affected him profoundly. He took a hiatus from the business, and when he returned he insisted on retaining creative control of his work." The result was the ground-breaking *What's Going On,* in which he developed a social conscience for soul. Pike remarked: "He embarked on the most radical departure from form ever seen at Motown, before or since. Easily Gaye's finest hour, his self-produced *What's Going On* from 1971 had enormous impact on soul music and was rewarding on an astonishing number of levels. Its overarching sadness captured perfectly the bewildering sense of the time, calling down its concerns one by one: Vietnam, the environment, urban troubles, a general plea for sanity, and more. Overdubbing afforded the rich tapestry of sound that would remain Gaye's hallmark for the rest of his career—it's not pretentious bluster to compare it to painting, painstakingly assembled as it was track by track as if applying brushstrokes."

The album caused a sensation. A *Time* reviewer described Gaye as "part mystic, part pentecostal fundamentalist, part socially aware ghetto graduate." Vince Aletti, writing for *Rolling Stone,* marveled, "There are very few performers who could carry a project like this off. I've always admired Marvin Gaye, but I didn't expect that he would be one of them. Guess I seriously underestimated him. It won't happen again." Other critics viewed Gaye's message-music a little more cynically; Alan Lewis wrote in *Melody Maker,* "Is [*What's Going On*] a heartfelt personal statement by a brilliant singer who has at last been given the chance to express his true self? Or is it that Motown are determined not to be caught with their social consciences down when people like Curtis Mayfield have done so well out of displaying theirs." Nonetheless, Lewis admitted, "It has to be said that his is an impressive album, and that Gaye does emerge as a man of integrity with a deep love of life and God. Politically, the lyrics aren't going to scare anybody, but coming from a man who has spent the past ten years singing other people's song, they are surprisingly sharp."

Despite the huge outpouring of support for the album, Gaye followed the work with a few albums of love songs. A contributor to *Contemporary Black Biography* commented, "Ironically, having established himself as more than a dance-stepping, crooning Motown star, Gaye returned to romantic music almost immediately. Here too he blazed a new trail, however, offering frankly sexual songs that heaped praises on unseen lovers." Aletti found the album something of a disappointment. He wrote, "With Barry White on the wane, Marvin Gaye seems determined to take over as soul's master philosopher in the bedroom, a position that requires little but an affectation of constant, rather jaded horniness . . . . All of this might have been more acceptable—or less disappointing—from a lesser performer than Gaye, but after a landmark album like *What's Going On* one expects a little more substance and spirit. But there's no fire here, only a well-concealed pilot light."

During this period, moreover, Gaye was experiencing difficulties both personal and financial. His fourteen-year marriage to Anna Gordy dissolved in 1976, and he was married one year later to Janis Hunter. A contributor for *Contemporary Black Biography* explained, "Gaye began a long downward spiral in the mid-1970s, largely because he became seriously involved in cocaine use . . . [His second] marriage too collapsed, with allegations of beating and mental harassment. At one point Gaye even arranged for his son by his second marriage to be kidnaped and brought to him in

Hawaii . . . During this period Gaye also attempted suicide by ingesting an ounce of cocaine in an hour." In 1982, Gaye made a comeback with *Midnight Love,* which included the great hit "Sexual Healing." Gaye won two Grammies for this single, but his difficulties continued to dog him. He hunkered down in his parents' house, but there he was forced to re-enter his toxic relationship with his father. On the day before his forty-fifth birthday, Gaye and his father fought, apparently over the elder Gay's treatment of Gaye's mother. Gaye struck his father; his father got a gun and shot him twice in the chest, point blank. Gaye died almost immediately.

Gaye's legacy is considered one of both lush harmony and jarring dissonance. His troubled family life, his social concerns, and his struggles to become an independent artist all influenced his music. Richard Mortifoglio wrote in *The Village Voice,* "Marvin Gaye is a man of contradictions—the best kind, usually. And he has carried these contradictions to the heart of his great music. While *What's Going On* gave slick class to social realism, *Let's Get It On,* the modern make-out manual, can be rough going for the casual listener. From the grating 'ugly' opening to the sweet, string quartet severity of 'Just to Keep You Satisfied,' Gaye demonstrated uncompromising good taste along with the occasional bad as an independent composer and producer."

BIOGRAPHICAL/CRITICAL SOURCES:

BOOKS

Contemporary Black Biography, Gale (Detroit, MI), 1992.
Contemporary Musicians, Gale (Detroit, MI), 1991.
Dictionary of Twentieth-Century Culture, vol. 5, Gale (Detroit, MI), 1996.
Ritz, David, *Divided Soul* (biography), 1986.

PERIODICALS

Down Beat, January 1986.
High Fidelity, April 1979.
News Week, April 16, 1984.
New York Times, April 2, 1984.
People, January 24, 1983; April 16, 1984.
Rolling Stone, May 10, 1984; May 24, 1984; October 9, 1986.
Time, October 11, 1971; April 16, 1984.*

GEVIRTZ, Don L(ee) 1928-2001

OBITUARY NOTICE—See index for *CA* sketch: Born March 1, 1928, in Chicago, IL; died of a heart attack, April 22, 2001, in Montecito, CA. Fundraiser, ambassador and author. Gevirtz studied business at the University of Southern California, where he had a basketball scholarship. He had already co-founded Pee Cee Tape and Label Co. by the time he graduated in 1950 and from there he worked for a variety of companies in successively important roles. He co-founded the Foothill Group in Los Angeles in 1969 and was chairman of the board and chief executive officer there. His asset-lender business did well lending money to small firms that some banks considered too much of a risk. Gevirtz advised several Democrat politicians on economic matters, among them President Jimmy Carter, Vice President Walter Mondale, California Governor Jerry Brown, and Senator Dianne Feinstein. He was successful as a fundraiser and pulled together hundreds of thousands of dollars for the Democratic party. In 1995 President Bill Clinton named Gevirtz the ambassador to Fiji, Nauru, Tuvalu and Tonga. Gevirtz wrote one book, *Business Plan for America: An Entrepreneur's Manifesto,* in 1984.

OBITUARIES AND OTHER SOURCES:

PERIODICALS

Los Angeles Times, April 24, 2001, p. B6.
Washington Post, April 25, 2001, p. B6.

*   *   *

GILBERT, Virginia 1946-

PERSONAL: Born December 19, 1946, in Elgin, IL; daughter of Blair Edward and Florence Amelia Swalles Gilbert. *Ethnicity:* "Caucasian." *Education:* Iowa Wesleyan College, B.A., 1969; University of Iowa, M.F.A., 1971; studied creative writing at University of Utah, 1974-75; University of Nebraska-Lincoln, Ph.D., 1991. *Politics:* "Democrat or Independent." *Religion:* Methodist. *Avocational interests:* "Guitar, travel, archeology, reading."

ADDRESSES: Home—136 Stone Meadow Ln., Madison, AL 35758. *Office*—Department of English, Alabama A & M University, Box 453, Normal, AL 35762; fax: 256-464-9130. *E-mail*—vgilb36005@aol.com.

CAREER: Alabama A & M University, Normal, AL, assistant professor, 1980-84, 1987-92, associate professor of English, 1992—, director, Program in Creative Writing and Reading. Peace Corps, Korean Middle School Program English instructor, 1971-73; The Academy of American Poets and the Writers Community, administrator, 1976; Department of Defense Sub-Contracts, instructor of English as a second language and test writer, 1976-79; College of Lake County, instructor of English as a second language, 1979; Share Our Strength Writers' Harvest, coordinator, 1996—; has performed numerous readings in various venues, including festivals, conferences, universities, libraries, and public television.

MEMBER: Modern Language Association, Associated Writing Programs, Poets & Writers, Poetry Society of America, National League of American Pen Women (president, Huntsville Chapter, 1990-94), North Alabama Returned Peace Corps Volunteers Group (founder and vice president), Huntsville Photographic Society (former vice president; president, 1997).

AWARDS, HONORS: Harlan Award, Iowa Wesleyan College, 1966-69; fellowship in poetry, National Endowment for the Arts, 1976-77; first place, Sakura Festival Haiku Contest, 1992; Fulbright fellow, 1993; fellow, Alabama Humanities Foundation Speakers Bureau, 1997-98; first place, Alabama State Poetry Society's Poetry Slam, 1998; Poet of the Year, Alabama State Poetry Society, 2001.

WRITINGS:

Keep at Bay the Hounds (chapbook), Nebraska Poets' Association, 1985.
The Earth Above (chapbook), Catamount, 1993.
That Other Brightness (poetry), Black Star (Lincoln, NE), 1995.

Contributor of poems to magazines, including *Beloit Poetry Journal, Seneca Review, Prairie Schooner, Poetry Now, Sumac, North American Review, Southern Poetry Review, New York Quarterly,* and *Poetry Society of America's Poetry Review;* and anthologies, including *Ordinary and Sacred as Blood, Alabama Women Speak; Claiming the Spirit Within: A Source Book of Women's Poetry; Cameos: Twelve Small Press Women Poets; I Hear My Sisters Saying; New Voices in American Poetry;* and *I Love You All Day.* Also contributor of articles to various publications, including *Crazy Horse, Bulletin of the Poetry Society of America,* and *New Voices in American Poetry,* Winthrop, 1973. Former editor, *Muse Messenger* (newsletter for the Alabama State Poetry Society).

WORK IN PROGRESS: Editor, *An Anthology of Peace Corps Poetry and Photography; A History of Alabama Poets,* an anthology; a second book of poems; a novel; short stories.

BIOGRAPHICAL/CRITICAL SOURCES:

PERIODICALS

Huntsville Times, May 9, 1993, Ann Marie Martin, "Traveling a Path to Poetry," pp. H1, H6; October 4, 1995, Laura Arce, "Former Volunteer Brings Peace Corps Experience to City"; October 6, 1999, Rebecca Salleee, "A & M Professor Gets Treat on England Trip," p. M6.

*   *   *

GILMORE, J(on) Barnard   1937-

PERSONAL: Born May 31, 1937, in Oakland, CA; citizenship, Canadian. *Education:* Stanford University, B.A., 1959; Yale University, M.Sc., Ph.D., 1964. *Politics:* "Reluctantly." *Religion:* "Yes."

ADDRESSES: Home—R.R.2, Site 1, Comp. 2, Kaslo, British Columbia V0G 1M0, Canada. *E-mail*—ccold@netidea.com.

CAREER: University of Toronto, Toronto, Ontario, Canada, faculty member, 1968-93, professor emeritus, 1993.

AWARDS, HONORS: CASE Canadian Professor of the Year, 1987.

WRITINGS:

In Cold Pursuit: Medical Intelligence Investigates the Common Cold, Stoddart (North York, Ontario, Canada), 1998.

WORK IN PROGRESS: Reflections on Retirement, completion expected in 2008; *Collected Haiku,* 2009.*

*   *   *

GISE, Joanne
   See MATTERN, Joanne

GLENN, Russell W(illiam)   1953-

PERSONAL: Born March 2, 1953, in Fort Belvoir, VA; son of Russell A(lger) and Priscilla B(eardsley) Glenn; married Deirdre B(urns) Glenn, June 27, 1976; children: Russell Andrew, Andrew Thayer. *Ethnicity:* "Caucasian." *Education:* United States Military Academy, B.S., 1975; University of Southern California—Los Angeles, M.S. (systems management), 1979; Stanford University, M.S. (operations research) and M.S. (civil engineering), 1982; School of Advanced Military Studies, Master of Military Art and Science, 1988; University of Kansas—Lawrence, Ph.D., 1997.

ADDRESSES: Office—RAND, 1700 Main St., P.O. Box 2138, Santa Monica, CA 90407-2138; fax: 310-451-7067. *E-mail*—rglenn@rand.org.

CAREER: U.S. Army, 1975-97, became lieutenant colonel, work included roles as platoon leader, 1976-79, operations officer, 1980, U.S. Military Academy instructor and assistant professor, 1983-86, assistant division engineer, 1988-90, and G3 Plans and Exercises chief, 1990-91. Royal School of Military Engineering, U.S. Army exchange officer, 1991-93; RAND, Santa Monica, CA, senior army fellow, 1993-94, senior defense and political analyst, 1997—; School of Advanced Military Studies, instructor and course development manager, 1994-96.

MEMBER: Society for Military History, Institution of Royal Engineers.

AWARDS, HONORS: Received Bronze Star Medal, Meritorious Service Medal, and other medals and commendations, U.S. Army.

WRITINGS:

(Co-author) *Lightning over Water: Sharpening America's Light Forces for Rapid-Reaction Missions,* RAND (Santa Monica, CA), 2000.
(Author of introduction) S. L. A. Marshall, *Men Against Fire: The Problem of Battle Command in Future War,* University of Oklahoma Press (Norton, OK), 2000.
Reading Athena's Dance Card: Men Against Fire in Vietnam, Naval Institute Press (Annapolis, MD), 2000.

Also author of ten RAND reports/publications, 1996-2001, and coauthor of *Operations,* the U.S. Army's Field Manual 100-5 (the Army's keystone operational doctrine publication). Contributor to *Historical Dictio-*

nary of the U.S. Army, edited by Jerold E. Brown, Greenwood (Westport, CT), 2000. Contributor to various publications, including *Armed Forces Journal International, Parameters, Proceedings of the United States Naval Institute, Royal Engineer Journal,* and *Military Review.*

WORK IN PROGRESS: American Civil War novel.

*   *   *

GOETZ, Rainald 1954-

PERSONAL: Born 1954. *Education:* studied medicine and history.

ADDRESSES: Office—c/o Suhrkamp Verlag, Postfach 101945, 60019 Frankfurt am Main, Germany.

CAREER: Writer, thinker, popular culture theorist, c. 1983—.

WRITINGS:

Irre, Suhrkamp (Frankfurt am Main, Germany), 1983.
Hirn, Suhrkamp (Frankfurt am Main, Germany), 1986.
Krieg, Suhrkamp (Frankfurt am Main, Germany), 1986.
Kontrolliert, Suhrkamp (Frankfurt am Main, Germany), 1988.
Spectaculum 54: sechs moderne Theaterstücke, Suhrkamp Verlag (Frankfurt am Main, Germany), 1992.
Festung 3, Kronos, Suhrkamp (Frankfurt am Main, Germany), 1993.
Festung 2, 3, 1989, Material 3, Suhrkamp (Frankfurt am Main, Germany), 1993.
Festung 2,2, 1989, Material 2, Suhrkamp (Frankfurt am Main, Germany), 1993.
Festung 2,1, 1989, Material 1, Suhrkamp (Frankfurt am Main, Germany), 1993.
Festung 1, Suhrkamp (Frankfurt am Main, Germany), 1993.
Festung, Suhrkamp (Frankfurt am Main, Germany), 1993.
1989: Material, Suhrkamp (Frankfurt am Main, Germany), 1993.
Festung: Stücke, Suhrkamp (Frankfurt am Main, Germany), 1993.
Kronos: Berichte, Suhrkamp (Frankfurt am Main, Germany), 1993.
Spectaculum 59: sechs moderne Theaterstücke, Suhrkamp Verlag (Frankfurt am Main, Germany), 1995.

Mix Cuts & Scratches, Merve (Berlin, Germany), 1997.
Rave, Suhrkamp (Frankfurt am Main, Germany), 1998.
Jeff Koons, Suhrkamp (Frankfurt am Main, Germany), 1998.
Abfall für alles, Suhrkamp (Frankfurt am Main, Germany), 1999.
Celebration, Suhrkamp (Frankfurt am Main, Germany), 1999.
Dekonspiratione, Shurkamp (Frankfurt am Main, Germany), 2000.
Jahrzehnt der schönen Frauen, Krank und Kaputt / 1990 und 2000 / Taggedichte und Interviews, Merve (Berlin, Germany), 2001.

RECORDINGS

Heiner Goebbels, ECM Records (Munich, Germany), 1993.
Word. Kronos, Eye Records/WEA Music (Offenbach, Germany), 1994.

SIDELIGHTS: Always fascinated with new technologies and their embodiment in popular culture, Rainald Goetz is a literary and media jack-of-all-trades who likes to experiment with trends. His work is experimental and unconventional; he has been a pioneer of Internet publishing and a critic of the media. He buys and sells newspapers by the dozen, he reads intellectual and literary theories of all kinds, listens to talk on television, and lets music take its effect on him. His writing is not characterized by theory but by observation.

Goetz's writing style is like a literary analogy of contemporary trends in pop music, film, and music video. His work is also a continuation of the literary polemics of Thomas Bernhard and Gottfried Benn; he frequently draws his content from the phenomena of pop culture, whose relevance for contemporary literature he seems to increase in value and importance. Goetz concerns himself with the exterior forms of pop culture. At the literary level, Goetz is an advocate of "art polemic." In his first novel *Irre* and in the short story "Subito" he pursues a hate-filled statement of the culture "establishment." Both of these texts are set in the area of pop culture themselves.

The author is quite interested in psychological themes. In his novel *Kontrolliert,* Goetz offers a psychic motive for people's readiness to experience terror. He explores psychological aspects of family relationships and dysfunctions. In *Irre,* he discourses on the absurdity of psychiatry, which he encountered in his studies of medicine.

A pioneer in publishing forms, Goetz was at the forefront of Internet publishing in the late 1990s with his Internet diary *Abfall für Alle*. In this book, the author provides insights into his daily business, letting the reader participate in his desires and reflections as he goes about his life. During the year he was compiling the diary, which he began in February 1998 and finished in January 1999, he posted this "trash," as he called it, on the Internet every day. He called it his "novel in progress." The material included lecture notes, accounts of his experiences, observations on pop culture, reflections on the previous evening's Harald Schmidt talk show, successful and not-so-successful attempts at rhetorical devices, and tidbits of poetry. Entries on the Web were organized by day and week, and each day had its own internal organization. The site contained no links, pictures, or animation, but nevertheless was relentlessly exciting to read. It generated a great deal of critical notice and comment.

Goetz has also turned his hand to playwriting and recording, producing the play *Jeff Koons* in 1998 and the recording *Word* in 1994, as well as a recorded conversation with disk jockey Westbam, called *Mix, Cuts & Scratches* in 1997. *Jeff Koons* is about the artist Jeff Koons, whose art for Goetz serves as a model for the connection of kitsch and junk and lifestyle thus at the same time a model for artist Rainald Goetz. Goetz's 1998 techno-story *Rave* also attracted a great deal of critical attention; in this work, the author addresses the question of why the literary establishment is reluctant to discuss popular music, such as "techno." He employs the first-person narrator that has been a characteristic of much of his recent writing. Part of the work is a "composition" of dance music compiled from clubs in Munich, Berlin, and Cologne.

Goetz has been fascinated by morning talk shows, and explored this topic in his 2000 novel *Dekonspiratione,* which completed his "Heute-Morgen-Zyklus." The main character in the novel is a young female student, Katharina, who has lost respect for her boyfriend and wants to make a clean, sharp break with him. Her boyfriend, Benjamin, works for a firm that creates new formulae for talk shows; his actual mission is the reform of the Harald Schmidt Show. At the end of the book, the talk show has a new format, Katharina and Benjamin get back together, and everything has worked out happily. The first-person narrator has reformed his story-telling project and completed his story making *Dekonspiratione* the counterpart of *Rave.* One of the main subjects of *Dekonspiratione* is our media world; few other authors set themselves so apart from the world of media as Goetz. The title "Deconspiatione"

means the opposite of "conspiracy"; Goetz works to expose and determine the mechanisms and principles that form the basis of media politics. He helps orient his reader by referring to actual events in television programming in the late 1990s. The narrator of the story appears to be Goetz himself, the real dates helping to create this impression. This poses the question, if the story is real, how can it be fiction?

At the end of the twentieth century, Goetz was still energetically publishing his controversial and original works, and still raising questions about the nature of literature, the media, and popular culture.

BIOGRAPHICAL/CRITICAL SOURCES:

PERIODICALS

Merkur, February, 1987, Jürgen Oberschelp, "Raserei," pp. 170-174.
Neue Rundschau, issue 3, 1990, Uwe Wittstock, "Der Terror und seine Dicther," pp. 65-78.

OTHER

Context: Redaktionsburo Hannover, http://www.contextredaktion.de/ (April 16, 2001), Julia Förster, "Rainald Goetz im Internet."
OCLC FirstSearch, http://newfirstsearch.OCLC.org/ (June 22, 2000).
Rainald Goetz, http://www.kat.ch/bm/goetz.htm (April 13, 2001), "Rainald Goetz, 'Heute Morgen.'"
Schauspielhaus, http://www.schauspielhaus.de/ (July 7, 2000), "Hamburger Fassung von Rainald Goetz."
University of Marburg, http://www.uni-marburg.de/ literaturekritik/ (July 7, 2000), Ekkehard Knöver, "Rainald Goetz in seinem neuen Theaterstück 'Jeff Koons.'"
University of Marburg, http://www.uni-marburg.de/ literaturekritik/ (July 7, 2000), Lutz Hagestedt, "Rainald Goetz vollendet seinen Heute-Morgen-Zyklus mit der Erzählung 'Dekonspiratione.'"
University of Marburg, http://www.uni-marburg.de/ literaturekritik/ (July 7, 2000), Lutz Hagestedt, "Neue Schreibformen in Internet."
University of Marburg, http://www.uni-marburg.de/ literaturekritik/ (July 7, 2000), Günther Fischer, "Rainald Goetz' Internet-Tabebuch ist bei Suhrkamp erschienen."*

GOFFIN, Robert 1898-1984

PERSONAL: Born 1898, in Ohain, Belgium; died 1984. *Education:* University of Brussels, J.D.

CAREER: Poet, music critic, lawyer. Lectured on jazz, New York, NY, 1942; lawyer, Brussels Court of Appeals.

MEMBER: Royal Academy of French Language and Literature of Belgium, PEN (national president and international vice-president).

AWARDS, HONORS: Honorary citizen of New Orleans; honorary lawyer of Pittsburgh.

WRITINGS:

Rosaire des soirs (title means "Evening Rosary"), 1918.

Jazzband (poems), 1922.

Cide élémentaire des agents de change, P. van Fleteren (Brussels, Belgium), 1927.

Aux frontieres du jazz, Éditions du Sagittaire (Paris, France), 1932.

Sur les traces d'Arthur Rimbaud, Éditions du Sagittaire (Paris, France), 1934.

La Proie pour l'ombre (title means "The Prey for A Shadow"), G. Chambelland (Paris, France), 1935.

Coleur d'absence: poème, Les cahiers du Journal des Poètes (Brussels, Belgium), 1936.

Le roman des anguilles, Gollimard (Paris, France), 1936.

Routes de la gourmandaise, Les Édutuibs de Belgique (Brussels, Belgium), 1936.

Charlotte, l'impératrice fantome, Les Éditions de France (Paris, France), 1937.

Le roman des rats, Gallimard (Paris, France), 1937.

Rimbaud vivant: documents et témoignages inédits, Corréa (Paris, France), 1937.

Élisabeth, limperatrice passionnée, Les Éditions de France (Paris, France), 1939.

Sang bleu (title means "Blue Blood"), Gallinard (Paris, France), 1939.

Le roi des Belges a-t-il trahi, Éditions de la Maison française (Paris, France), 1940.

Le chat sans tête, roman, Éditions de la Maison française (New York, NY), 1941.

Le fusillé de Dunkerque, roman, Éditions de la Maison française (New York, NY), 1941.

Le nouveau sphinx roman, Éditions de la Maison française (New York, NY), 1941.

Les cavaliers de la déroute, roman, Éditions de la Maison française (New York, NY), 1941.

Was Leopold a Traitor? The True Story of Belgium's Eighteen Tragic Days, H. Hamilton (London, England), 1941.

Sabotages dans le ciel, roman, Éditions de la Maison française (New York, NY), 1942.

De Pierre Minuit aux Roosevelt l'épopée Belge aux États-Unis, Brentano's (New York, NY), 1943.

La colombe de la Gestgapo: roman, Éditions de la Maison française (New York, NY), 1943.

Oeuvres, Brentano (New York, NY), 1943.

Jazz: From the Congo to the Metropolitan, Doubleday, (Garden City, NY) 1944.

Louis Armstrong, le roi du jazz (title means "Louis Armstrong, the King of Jazz"), P. Seghers (Paris, France), 1944, English translation published as *Horn of Plenty,* Allen, Towne, & Heath (New York, NY), 1947.

Passeports pour l'Audelà; recit de l'underground Belge, Éditions de la Maison française (New York, NY), English translation published as *The White Brigade,* Doubleday, (New York, NY), 1944.

Histoire du jazz, L. Parizeau (Montréal, Canada), 1945.

Patrie de la poésie, L'Arbre (Montréal, Canada), 1945.

Jazz: From Congo to Swing, Musicians Press (London, England), 1946.

La Nouvelle-Orleans, capitale du jazz, Éditions de la Maison française (New York, NY), 1946.

(With Pierre Seghers and Charles Delaunay) *America et le Hot-club de France vous offrent Jazz 47,* (Paris, France), 1947.

Autour de "Crimen amoris" de Paul Verlaine, Éditions L'Écran du monde (Brussels, Belgium), 1947.

Le temps de noires épines, roman, Éditions de la paix (Brussels, Belgium), 1947.

(With Herman van den Driessche) *Stéphane Mallarmé,* (Brussels, Belgium), 1948.

Entrer en poésie (title means "To Take Up Poetry"), Poésie (Paris, France), 1948.

Nouvelle histoire du jazz du Congo au bebop, L'Écran du monde (Brussels, Belgium), 1948.

Rimbaud et Verlaine vivants (title means "Living Rimbaud and Verlaine"), Éditions L'Écran du monde (Brussels, Belgium), 1948.

Jean Cocteau, Éditions L'Écran du Monde (Brussels, Belgium), 1950.

Le voleur de feu (title means "The Fire Thief"), Éditions L'Ecran du monde (Brussels, Belgium), 1950.

Filles de l'onde, Seghers (Paris, France), 1954.

Foudre natale (title means "Native Bolt"), Dutilleul (Paris, France), 1955.

Mallarmé vivant (title means "Living Mallarmé"), Nizet (Paris, France), 1956.

Le roi du Colorado (title means "The King of Colorado"), 1958.

Le temps sans rives (title means "Time Without Edges"), Éditions de Paris (Paris, France), 1958.

Oeuvres poetiques, 1918-1954, Éditions universitaires (Paris, France), 1958.

Archipels de la sève (title means "Lymph Archipelagos"), Nizet (Paris, France), 1959.

Poèmes choisis, L'Audiothèque (Paris, France), 1960.

Sources du ciel (title means "Heavenly Springs"), Nizet (Paris, France), 1962.

Le guerre de Corée (title means "Conflict"), R. Laffont (Paris, France), 1963.

Corps combustible (title means "Combustible Matter"), Nizet (Paris, France), 1964.

Fil d'Ariane pour la poésie (title means "Ariane's Thread for Poetry"), Nizet (Paris, France), 1964.

Sablier pour une cosmogonie (title means "Hourglass for a Cosmogony"), A. de Rache (Brussels, Belgium), 1965.

(With Alain Bosquet) *Robert Goffin. Présentation,* P. Seghers (Paris, France), 1966.

Le versant noir (title means "The Black Slope"), Flammarion (Paris, France), 1967.

Faits divers (title means "Press News"), Flammarion (Paris, France), 1969.

Solyane, un chef d'oeuvre oublié, Seghers (Paris, France), 1969.

Les wallons, fondateurs de New York, Institut Jules Destrée (Gilly, Belgium), 1970.

Ouvre poétique, A. De Rache (Brussels, Belgium), 1970.

Phosphores chanteurs (title means "Singing Phosphorus"), A. De Rache (Brussels, Belgium), 1970.

L'envers du feu (title means "The Reverse of the Fire"), G. Chambelland (Paris, France), 1971.

Choix de poèmes, G. Chambelland (Paris, France), 1973.

Chroniques d'outre-chair (title means "Chronicles beyond the Flesh"), G. Chambelland (Bagnois-sur-Cèze), 1975.

La Hulpe: de la préhistoire à nos jours, P. Pandor, 1979.

Souvenirs à bout portant, Édition institut Jules Destrée (Charleroi, France), 1979.

Souvenirs avant l'adieu: par le monde, avec le P.E.N. Club, Institut Jules Destrée (Charleroi, France), 1980.

SIDELIGHTS: Robert Goffin was a Belgian poet, music critic, and lawyer in Brussels. He is known for his deep interest in jazz, and was one of the first people to write seriously about this musical form. He wrote poems inspired by jazz, which appeared in his collection, *Jazzband,* and also wrote several critical studies of jazz and jazz musicians, including *Aux Frontieres du Jazz* and *Jazz: From the Congo to the Metropolitan.*

Goffin studied law at the University of Brussels and became a well-known lawyer in Brussels. Despite the success of his legal career, however, he was far more interested in music, literature, and gastronomy, and while he was still a student, published *Rosaire des soirs* and *Jazzband,* collections of poetry.

After working as a lawyer for a few years, he published essays on a wide variety of topics, including Arthur Rimbaud, jazz, gastronomy, historical biographies, novels, and verse.

In 1940, when World War II began, Goffin left Belgium and moved to the United States, where he made a living giving lectures and writing articles and books, including novels such as *Passeports pour l'Audelà,* which takes place during the wartime German occupation of Belgium, and essays such as *Jazz: from the Congo to the Metropolitan.*

In 1942 Goffin and Englishman Leonard Feather collaborated to teach a class on jazz history and musical analysis. They gave fifteen lectures on jazz, and presented recordings by jazz greats such as Louis Armstrong and Benny Goodman. Close to 100 students enrolled the class, which was held at the New School for Social Research in New York City. The class was so successful that it was held again later that same year.

For his work on jazz, Goffin was made an honorary citizen of New Orleans, as well as an honorary lawyer of Pittsburgh.

When World War II ended and Belgium was liberated from the Nazi occupation, he returned to Brussels and resumed his former seat on the Court of Appeals. He wrote several volumes of poetry, *Le Voleur de feu, Foudre natale, Le Temps sans rives, Archipels de la sève, Sources du ciel, Corps combustible, Sablier pour une cosmogonie, Le Versant noir, Faits divers, Phosphores chanteurs, L'Envers du feu,* and *Chroniques d'outrechair.* According to a writer in the *Columbia Dictionary of Modern European Literature,* all of these poems "espouse neoclassicism in the manner of Stéphane Mallarmé and Paul Valéry."

During the same period, he wrote several critical works, including *Louis Armstrong, le roi du jazz, Entrer en poésie, Rimbaud et Verlaine vivants, Mallarmé vivant,* and *Fil d'Ariane pour la poésie.* He also wrote a novel, *Le Roi du Colorado.*

Goffin saw jazz as a gift that African-Americans had given to the world, and believed that its universal appeal would further good relations among races. In his essay, "The Best Negro Orchestra," reprinted in the *Evergreen Review,* he wrote that jazz "has done more to further friendly relations between blacks and whites than all the laws and edicts ever issued," and added, "Jazz is abundantly and gloriously alive. All honour to those who . . . gave America this music of which she will one day be proud."

BIOGRAPHICAL/CRITICAL SOURCES:

BOOKS

Bede, Jean-Albert, and William Edgerton, editors, *Columbia Dictionary of Modern European Literature,* 2nd edition, Columbia University Press, 1980.

OTHER

Evergreen Review, http://www.evergreenreview.com/ (July 7, 2000).*

*   *   *

GOMRINGER, Eugen 1925-

PERSONAL: Born January 20, 1925, in Chachuela Esperanza, Bolivia; married Klara Stöckli, 1950; divorced; married Norturd Ottenhausen; children: five sons, one daughter. *Education:* Studied art history and economics in Berlin and Rome, 1946-50. *Avocational interests:* Mountaineering, art collecting, farming, dogs.

ADDRESSES: Office—c/o Edition Splitter, Edition Fragment, Salvatorgasse 10, A-1010 Vienna, Austria.

CAREER: Swiss poet. Graphic designer; secretary to artist Max Bill, 1954-58; founded his own publishing house, 1959; business manager of Schweizer Workbund, Zurich, Switzerland, 1962-67; artistic advisor to Rosenthal; professor of aesthetic theory, Art Academy, Dusseldorf, Germany.

WRITINGS:

Konstellationene, Spiral Press (Berne, Switzerland), 1953.

Max Bill, A. Niggli (Teufen, Switzerland), 1958.

33 Konstellationen, Tschudy-Verlag (St. Gallen, Switzerland), 1960.

Die Konstellationen, 1953-1962, Eugen Gomringer Press, 1962.

Das Stundenbuch, M. Hueber (Munich, Germany), 1965.

Concrete poetry sheets, 1965.

Manifeste und Darstellungen der konkreten Poesie, 1954-1966, Galerie Press (St. Gallen, Switzerland), 1966.

Six Concrete Poems, Brighton Festival, 1967, Chelsea School of Art, 1967.

Erwin Rehmann, Éditions du Griffon (Neuchâtel, France), 1967.

The Book of Hours, and Constellations. Being Poems of Eugen Gomringer, Something Else Press (New York, NY), 1968.

Josef Albers: das Werk des Maiers und Bauliausmeisters als Beitrag zur visuellen Gestaltung im 20. Jahrhundert, J. Keller (Starnberg, Germany), 1968.

Poesie als Mittel der Umweltgestaltung, Hansen & Hansen, 1969.

Worte sind Schatten: die Konstellationen 1951-1968, Rowohlt (Reinbeck bei Hamburg, Germany), 1969.

Konkrete Poesie: deutschsprachige Autoren: Anthologie, Reclam (Stuttgart, Germany), 1972.

Der Pfeil: Spiel-Gleichnis Kommunikation, J. Keller (Starnberg, Germany), 1972.

Visuelle Poesie: Ideogramme, Konstellationen, Dialektggedichte, Palindrome, Typogramme, Pictogramme, [Hamburg, Germany], 1972.

Modulare und serielle Ordnungen, M. DuMont Schaumburg (Cologne, Germany), 1973.

Richard Paul Lohse: Modulare u. serielle Ordnungen, DuMont Schaumburg (Cologne, Germany), 1973.

Eugen Gomringer: 1970-1972, Edition UND, (Munich, Germany), 1973.

Konkrete texte, S Press Tombard, 1973.

Konkretes von A. Stankowski: Malerei und visuelle information, G. Hatje (Stuttgart, Germany), 1974.

Stundenbuch für 12 Stimmen un 12 Bläser, C.F. Peters (New York, NY), 1974.

Norbert Kricke, Wilhelm-Lehmbruck-Museum (Duisberg, Germany), 1975.

Wie weiss ist wissen die Weisen, Edition für moderne Kunst im Belser Verlag (Stuttgart, Germany), 1975.

Otto Müller, Zürcher Kunstgesellschaft (Zurich, Switzerland), 1975.

Farbstadt, Bruckmann (Munich, Germany), 1977.

Konstellationen, Ideogramme, Stundenbuch, Reclam (Stuttgart, Germany), 1977.

Zeile für Zeile = line by line, Edition Neue Texte (Linz, Austria), 1977.

Fruhtrunk, J. Keller (Starnberg, Germany), 1978.

Kein Fehler im System, Verlag 3 (Zurich, Switzerland), 1978.

Bilder un bildnerisches Gestalten, Edition 7&70, 1979.

Zum Schweigen der Schrift oder Die Sprachlosigkeit, Erker-Verlag (St. Gallen, Switzerland), 1979.

Das Stundenbuch, Josef Keller (Starnberg, Germany), 1980.

Gewebte Bilder, Aroca Verlag (Landsberg, Germany), 1984.

Zur Sache der Konkreten, Erker (St. Gallen, Switzerland), 1988.

Inversion und öffnung: zwei sprachspiele, Ottenhausen Verlag (Piesport, Germany), 1988.

(with Cornelius Schnauber) *Deine Träume, mein Gedicht,* Greno (Nördlingen, Germany), 1989.

(With Otto Herbert Hajek) *O. H. Hajek: Farbwege in Moskau,* Belser (Stuttgart, Germany), 1989.

Museum für Konkrete Kunst Ingolstadt, Westermann (Braunschweig, Germany), 1991.

(With Raoul Hausman) *Briefwechsel mit Eugen Gomringer,* Universität-Gesamthochschule Siegen (Siegen, Germany), 1992.

Kunst stiftet Gemeinschaft: O. H. Hajek, das Werk und seine Wirkung, Kohlhammer (Stuttgart, Germany), 1993.

Pfleghar: Arbeiten, 1983-1993, Neue Presse (Passau, Germany), 1993.

Würth. 2: eine Sammlung: Abstrakte Tendenzen, J. Thorbecke (Sigmaringen, Germany), 1993.

Ich habe mein Schirm vergessen, Edition Wandelweiser (Berlin, Germany), 1993.

Andreas Brandt, Waser (Weiningen, Germany), 1994.

Fred Thieler Preis für Malerei 1995, Berlinische Galerie (Berlin, Germany), 1995.

Vom Rand nach innen: die Konstellationen, 1951-1995, Edition Splitter (Vienna, Austria), 1995.

Gesamtwerk, Edition Splitter (Vienna, Austria), 1995.

Visuelle Poesie: Anthologie, Reclam (Stuttgart, Germany), 1996.

Theorie der konkreten Poesie: Texte und Manifeste 1954-1997, Edition Splitter (Vienna, Austria), 1997.

O. H. Hajek: eine Welt der Zeichen, Wienand (Cologne, Germany), 2000.

Zur Sache der Konkreten: eine Auswahl von Texten und Reden über Künstler und Gestaltungsfragen 1958-2000, Edition Splitter (Vienna, Austria), 2000.

Also author of *Josef Albers: His Work as Contribution to Visual Articulation in the Twentieth Century,* George Wittenborn (New York, NY), and *Konkrete Poesie,*

Verlag Herausgeber Eugen Gomringer (Frauenfeld, Switzerland).

SIDELIGHTS: Eugen Gomringer "is considered to be the father of concrete poetry," according to Robert Acker in the *Encyclopedia of World Literature.* Gomringer was born in Bolivia in 1925 but grew up in Switzerland, raised by his grandparents. He studied art history and economics in Berlin and Rome from 1946 to 1950. In 1952 he cofounded the magazine *Spirale,* which featured concrete art. He was secretary to the artist Max Bill from 1954 to 1958, and in 1959 he briefly ran his own publishing company. From 1962 to 1967 he was the business manager for the Rosenthal company. He was also a professor of aesthetic theory at the Art Academy in Dusseldorf, Germany.

In 1953, he published his first poems in *Spirale,* and received enough attention to become known as the founder of the concrete art movement, which influenced writers and artists in Europe and the United States. He was particularly influential in Germany and Austria.

Concrete poetry does not rely on traditional grammar, metaphor, or description, but instead arranges the words on the page in a visual arrangement that usually represents what the poem is about. Thus, a poem about a tree might be shaped like a tree, with words instead of branches. Or, for example, consider his poem "Schweigen," which means silence. The word "schweigen" appears fourteen times and forms a rectangle on the page, inside of which is white space. The white space is a visual representation of the "silence" of the poem.

Gomringer's poems fall into four categories, according to Acker: "Purely visual constellations, visual-audio constellations that can also be read aloud, constellations in languages other than German, and constellations in book form, which develop a series of images over several pages, much like the individual frames of a film."

According to Acker, Gomringer had a great deal of influence on poets and artists, but it was not lasting; interest in this form of poetry waned after the early 1970s, and he turned to writing about art.

BIOGRAPHICAL/CRITICAL SOURCES:

BOOKS

Johnson, Eric, editor, *ICEBOL 85 Proceedings,* Dakota State College, 1985.

Klein, Leonard, *Encyclopedia of World Literature in the 20th Century,* rev. ed., St. James Press (Detroit, MI), 1999.

Kopeczi, Bela and Gyorgy Vajda, editors, *Proceedings of the 8th Congress of the International Comparative Literature Association, II,* Bieber, 1980.

Morrison, Jeff, and Florian Krobb, editors, *Text into Image: Image into Text,* Rodopi, 1997.

Wellman, Donald, Cola Franzen, and Irene Turner, editors, *Translation: Experiments in Reading,* O. ARS, 1986.

PERIODICALS

Poetics Today, summer, 1982, pp. 197-209.*

* * *

GOODFELLOW, Samuel Huston 1957-

PERSONAL: Born October 19, 1957, in Washington, DC; son of Guy Fair (a history professor) and Jane Huston (a biologist) Goodfellow; married Judith Claire Goodman (a psychology professor), 1982; children: Elizabeth Miller, Benjamin Charles. *Education:* Tufts University, B.A., 1979; Indiana University, M.A., 1984, Ph.D., 1991. *Politics:* Democrat.

ADDRESSES: Home—211 Westwood Ave., Columbia, MO 65203. *Office*—Westminster College, Fulton, MO 65251-1299; fax: 573-592-5191. *E-mail*—Goodfels@ jaynet.wcmo.edu.

CAREER: Westminster College, Fulton, MO, assistant and associate professor, 1993—. Churchill Memorial and Library, inter director, 1998, curator, 1998-99, guest curator and Churchill Fellow, 1999; consultant, including work for television and Children's Museum of San Diego; presenter at professional meetings and conferences, including the Churchill Memorial and Library and various colleges.

MEMBER: American Historical Association, American Association of University Professors, Society for French Historical Studies, German Studies, Western Society for French History.

AWARDS, HONORS: Fellowships, Indiana University, 1981-83, 1987 and 1989-90.

WRITINGS:

Between the Swastika and the Cross of Lorraine: Fascisms in Interwar Alsace, Northern Illinois University Press (DeKalb, IL), 1999.

Also author, with Kirt W. Jefferson, of brochures, including *From Solidarity to Liberation: Poland and Lech Walesa* (for Lech Walesa's 1998 Green Lecture). Contributor to books, including Peter Novick's *The Holocaust in American Life,* Houghton (Boston, MA), 1999, and Norman Finkelstein's *The Holocaust Industry: Reflections on the Exploitation of Jewish Suffering,* Verso (New York, NY), 2000. Contributor to *Fulton Sun, French History, Journal of Contemporary History, Journal of Interdisciplinary History, German Studies Review,* and *American Historical Review.*

WORK IN PROGRESS: "Reappraisals of Fascism; a social history of Leipzig, 1939-1949."

SIDELIGHTS: Samuel Huston Goodfellow told *CA:* "As an undergraduate, I had the opportunity to live in Germany for a year. While there, I became interested in Nazism, fascism, and the question of how ordinary people experienced such political turmoil. An extended trip to the former East Germany sparked an interest in communist Europe during the Cold War. Writing history is different from other types of writing, involving years of research in which you build in your head a broad and detailed picture that you can only partially represent in a book. Then you sit down and try to bring coherence to this world that you have recreated. Although writing is frequently aggravating, it is also rewarding because it forces me to be precise and clear—in short to think better."

* * *

GOODMAN, Jon 1969-

PERSONAL: Born April 20, 1969, in New York, NY; son of Dickie (a record producer) and Esther (a singer) Goodman. *Ethnicity:* "Jewish." *Education:* Pacific Western University, B.S.; also holds M.B.A. *Politics:* Democrat. *Religion:* Catholic. *Avocational interests:* "Comedy radio writer and novelty record producer."

ADDRESSES: Office—c/o Author Mail, Xlibris Press, 436 Walnut St., 11th Fl., Philadelphia, PA 19106. *E-mail*—Luniverse@aol.com.

CAREER: Luniverse Records, producer, 1989—; Estate of Dickie Goodman, administrator, 1989—; City of

Lumberton, police officer, 1990-95; retail and insurance editor for America Online search engine; WSNJ radio broadcaster, program producer, writer, news correspondent and copy editor. *Military service:* Army R.O.T.C.; became corporal.

MEMBER: North Carolina Police Benevolent Association (founding president of Robeson/Scotland County chapter).

WRITINGS:

The King of Novelty: Dickie Goodman, Xlibris (Philadelphia, PA), 2000.

Contributor to magazines.

WORK IN PROGRESS: "Screenplay placement for *The King of Novelty;* quest for gold record certification for Dickie Goodman and other artists not recognized effectively by the R.I.A.A."

SIDELIGHTS: Jon Goodman told *CA:* "I am on a crusade to perpetuate my father's pop culture legacy. Books such as *Celestine Prophecy* and *The Souls Code* have influenced my sense of purpose for what I am doing. My father was famous, but his fame is fleeting due to the same principals that drive our popular culture; a lack of publicity. It is my goal to rejuvenate my father's intellectual property and carry it into the new millenium for future generations to enjoy. I am doing this by following my plan which has three stages (of which I am currently in the third): 1) Audio; 2) literary, and; 3) video. I put out CD's, then a book, and now I seek to have the book immortalized in film."

*   *   *

GRACE, Theresa
  See MATTERN, Joanne

*   *   *

GRAY, Ginna   1938-

PERSONAL: Born February 2, 1938, in Houston, TX; daughter of Roy (a fire chief) and Ruby Minze (a homemaker) Conn; married; second husband's name, Brad; children: (first marriage) Beth Ann Daugherty, (second marriage) Meghan Kathleen Emmons. *Avocational interests:* "Oil painting."

ADDRESSES: Home and Office—61 Fawn Lake Rd., Durango, CO 81301. *Agent*—Denice Marcil, Denise Marcil Literary Agency, 685 West End Ave. #9C, New York, NY. *E-mail*—ginnagray@compuserve.com.

CAREER: Author. Wanda Petroleum, secretary, 1959-62; Ada Oil Co., secretary, 1962-66; Dow B. Hickam Pharmaceuticals, accounting clerk, 1970-71; Hollan, Inc., office manager, 1971-73.

MEMBER: Romance Writers of America.

AWARDS, HONORS: Golden Heart Award, Romance Writers of America, 1983; Reviewers Choice, *Romance Times* magazine, 1984; Career Achievement Award, *Romance Times* magazine, 1992.

WRITINGS:

NOVELS

The Gentling, Silhouette (New York, NY), 1984.
Golden Illusion, Silhouette (New York, NY), 1984.
The Perfect Match, Silhouette (New York, NY), 1984.
Heart of the Hurricane, Silhouette (New York, NY), 1985.
Images, Silhouette (New York, NY), 1985.
First Love, Last Love, Silhouette (New York, NY), 1985.
The Heart's Yearning, Silhouette (New York, NY), 1985.
The Courtship of Dani, Silhouette (New York, NY), 1986.
Sweet Promise, Silhouette (New York, NY), 1986.
Cristin's Choice, Silhouette (New York, NY), 1987.
Season of Miracle (Christmas novella), Silhouette (New York, NY), 1987.
Fools Rush In (Book #1 of "The Blaines and McCalls of Crockett, Texas" Series), Silhouette (New York, NY), 1987.
Where Angels Fear (Book #2 of "Texas" Series), Silhouette (New York, NY), 1988.
If There Be Love, Silhouette (New York, NY), 1989.
Once in a Lifetime, (Book #3 of "Texas" Series), Silhouette (New York, NY), 1991.
Quiet Fires, HarperCollins (New York, NY), 1991.
Sting of the Scorpion, Silhouette (New York, NY), 1991.
A Good Man Walks in (Book #4 of "Texas" Series), Silhouette (New York, NY), 1992.
Building Dreams (Book #5 of the "Texas" Series), Silhouette (New York, NY), 1993.

Forever (Book #6 of "Texas" Series), Silhouette (New York, NY), 1993.

Always (Book #7 of "Texas" Series), Silhouette (New York, NY), 1994.

Coming Home, Pinnacle (New York, NY), 1994.

The Bride Price, Silhouette (New York, NY), 1995.

For the Love of Grace, Pinnacle (New York, NY), 1995.

Soul Mates (Mother's Day novella), Silhouette (New York, NY), 1996.

No Truer Love, Pinnacle (New York, NY), 1996.

Alissa's Miracle, Silhouette (New York, NY), 1997.

Meant for Each Other (Book #8 of "Texas" Series), Silhouette (New York, NY), 1999.

A Man Apart (Book #1 of "A Family Bond" Series), Silhouette (New York, NY), 2000.

In Search of Dreams (Book #2 of "A Family Bond" Series), Silhouette (New York, NY), 2000.

The Prodigal Daughter, MIRA (New York, NY), 2000.

The Ties that Bind, Silhouette (New York, NY), 2001.

The Witness, MIRA (New York, NY), in press.

SIDELIGHTS: Ginna Gray told *CA:* "A native Texan, I lived in Houston all of my life until 1993, when my husband Brad and I built our 'dream home' and moved to the mountains of Colorado. Coming from a large, Irish/American family, in which spinning colorful yarns was commonplace, made writing a natural career choice for me. I grew up hearing so many fascinating tales; I was eleven or twelve before I realized that not everyone made up stories.

"Throughout my school years, whenever I turned in essay papers my teachers would say, 'Ginna, you should be a writer,' and I would always reply, 'That's what I'm going to be.' However, life has a way of getting in the way.

"I married young, had a daughter and divorced. As a single mom and the sole breadwinner, raising a child alone became my top priority. I also managed to attend college part-time in the evenings, which left precious little time to pursue my dream of becoming a writer. However, during those years I continued to keep a journal and occasionally write short stories for my own gratification."

"Finally, after putting my youngest child [who is seventeen years younger than my first child] on the bus for her first day of kindergarten, for the first time in my life I had no job to rush off to, no classes to take, and the house all to myself. I realized that it was now or never. I marched home from that school bus stop and plopped myself down in front of my fifteen-year-old typewriter and started my first novel. (At that point, I hadn't even heard of a personal computer. Since then, I've gone through five of them.)

"There followed three years of rejections. And rightly so. The first novel I wrote was awful. The next one was better, and the one after that, better still, but not quite good enough. I knew that because the rejection letters were getting more encouraging and much more personal. I still have those first three efforts in a drawer, and every now and then I take them out and skim a few pages and laugh. Still, I consider those first attempts a valuable learning experience.

"I sold my first novel in 1983, after winning the Golden Heart Award, given by Romance Writers of America for the best unpublished novel in a category. I have been working as a full-time writer ever since. When I finish my current contracts, I will have written forty-three books. I have also given many lectures and writing workshops, and judged in writing contests.

"Now that both of my daughters are grown and have 'flown the nest,' I also enjoy other creative activities, such as oil painting, sewing, sketching, knitting and needlepoint. But my first love will always be writing. It is simply part of who I am."

*   *   *

GREGORY, J. Dennis
  See WILLIAMS, John A(lfred)

*   *   *

GRIFFITH-JONES, Robin   1956-

PERSONAL: Born May 29, 1956, in London, England; son of Mervyn (a judge) and Joan Baker Griffith-Jones. *Education:* Attended Oxford University, New College, 1974-78, and Cambridge University, Christ's College and Westcott House, 1986-89. *Religion:* "Christian (Episcopalian)."

ADDRESSES: Home and Office—Masters House, Temple, London EC4Y 7BB, England; fax: 44 020 7353 1736. *E-mail*—master@templechurch.com. *Agent*—Bryan Feharty, 2A North Parade, Banbury Rd., Oxford OX2 6LX, England.

CAREER: Christies Fine Art Auctioneers, London, Department of English Drawing and Watercolours,

1978-84; The Church of England, Liverpool, curate (assistant minister), 1989-92; Lincoln College, Oxford University, Oxford, Chaplain, 1992-99; The Temple Church, London, master of the temple, 1999—.

WRITINGS:

The Four Witnesses (theology/history), HarperSanFrancisco, 2000.

WORK IN PROGRESS: "Scripts for the TV-series on the Four Witnesses, under development by South Carolina Educational TV (SCETV) for PBS nationwide; research on St. Paul and his churches."

*   *   *

GRØNDAHL, Jens Christian 1959-

PERSONAL: Born November 9, 1959, in Lyngby, Denmark; married Charlotte Louise Truelsen, July 19, 1989; children: two sons. *Education:* Danish Cinema School.

ADDRESSES: Office—c/o Forlaget Vindrose, Valbygardsvij 33, DK 2500 Valby, Denmark.

CAREER: Writer. Coeditor of *Fredag,* a literary quarterly, 1990—.

MEMBER: Danish PEN, Danish Writers' Society.

AWARDS, HONORS: Otto Monsted award, 1988.

WRITINGS:

Kvinden i midten (title means "The woman in the middle"), Vindrose (Copenhagen, Denmark), 1985.
Syd for floden (title means "South of the river"), Vindrose (Copenhagen, Denmark), 1986.
Rejsens bevaegelser (title means "Movements of the journey"), Vindrose (Copenhagen, Denmark), 1988.
Det indre blik (title means "The inward eye"), 1990.
Overflodighedshorn: Den selvmodsigende kulturkritik hos Kundera og Flogstad, Vinduet (Oslo, Norway), 1991.
Mens den ene hvisker og den annen lytter, Vinduet (Oslo, Norway), 1992.
Tavshed i oktober, Munksgaard/Rosinante (Copenhagen, Denmark), 1996.
Lucca, Munksgaard/Rosinante (Copenhagen, Denmark), 1998.

Night Mail: Essays, Munksgaard/Rosinante (Copenhagen, Denmark), 1998.
Hjertelyd, Rosinante (Copenhagen, Denmark), 1999.
Schweigen im Oktober, Zsolnay, 1999, translation by Anne Born published as *Silence in October,* Harcourt (New York, NY), 2001.
Indian Summer, DTV, 2001.

SIDELIGHTS: Jens Christian Grøndahl was born in Lyngby, Denmark, in 1959, and was educated at the Danish Cinema School. After graduating, he worked at a newspaper. He has written more than ten novels since 1985, and has received the Herman Bang Prize, the Otto Monsted award, and a grant from the Danish Artistic Fund.

Grøndahl's *Rejsens bevaegelser* explores themes already touched upon in his earlier works, *Kvinden i midten* and *Syd for floden,* most notably the image of a man who is searching for his true love. The "journey" of the title is the male protagonist's seeking, and movement toward, a woman he can love.

The story is told with an experimental narrative style that interweaves different times and angles of vision with an almost cinematic quality. As Svend Birke Espegård wrote in *World Literature Today,* "His education as a director at the Danish School of Film has certainly not been wasted!"

In a review in *World Literature Today,* Svend Birke Espegård wrote that *Det indre blick* is not a traditionally plotted novel, but a "mosaic of detailed descriptions and accounts." The book presents the "mind's eye" of a man and a woman, known only as "She" and "He" as they conceive a child, in a stream-of-consciousness style. The setting is a large, domed room, similar to the Roman Pantheon, and the dome itself is depicted as a large eye taking in the events and "recording the transformations of the world, the decomposition toward death, the regeneration of new life," according to Espegård. Espegård also noted that because of its experimental style, the book is "certainly not for a large circle of readers, but it does blaze a trail," similar to that taken by other postmodern Scandinavian writers.

Silence in October is Grøndahl's first book translated into English. The story is told from the point of view of a man whose wife has just left him after eighteen years of marriage. The man, an art historian, reflects upon his years of marriage and the possible causes of its demise. Emily Melton, in a review for *Booklist,* wrote that "The journey he takes is both painful and illuminating." She found *Silence in October* "A lucid and lyrical book from a gifted writer." Philip Hensher of the *Spectator* wrote, "*Silence in October* is a most beautifully poised novel of Danish domestic life," while a reviewer in *Publishers Weekly* felt that the book has "a poetic depth that never ceases to surprise."

BIOGRAPHICAL/CRITICAL SOURCES:

PERIODICALS

Booklist, July, 2001, Emily Melton, review of *Silence in October,* p. 1979.
Publishers Weekly, August 27, 2001, review of *Silence in October,* p. 47.
Spectator, August 4, 2001, Philip Hensher, review of *Silence in October,* p. 29.
World Literature Today, winter, 1990, Svend Birke Espegård, review of *Rejsens bevægelser,* p. 124; winter, 1992, p. 141.*

*   *   *

GROVE, Vicki

PERSONAL: Born in IL.

ADDRESSES: Home—P.O. Box 36, Ionia, MO 65335-9327.

CAREER: Writer.

AWARDS, HONORS: Silver Angel Award, for *He Gave Her Roses.*

WRITINGS:

Goodbye, My Wishing Star, Putnam, 1988.
Circles of Love, Thomas Bouregy, 1988.
Junglerama, Putnam, 1989.
The Fastest Friend in the West, Putnam, 1990.
He Gave Her Roses, Group Publishing, 1990.
A Time to Belong, Group Publishing, 1990.
Rimwalkers, Putnam, 1993.
The Crystal Garden, Putnam, 1995.
Reaching Dustin, Putnam, 1998.
The Starplace, Putnam, 1999.
Destiny, Putnam, 2000.

SIDELIGHTS: Vicki Grove has written a number of novels for young readers that revolve around life in the American Midwest, often inside rural farming communities, but the themes and conflicts her protagonists en-

counter strike a resonant note with adolescent readers everywhere. Grove's teens struggle with sibling rivalry, peer pressure and, most often, economic hardship. As their stories progress, they realize that family, school, and the larger community have provided them with a good moral framework to help them through their particular crises. As Grove once commented, "I picture my reader as being a young person with an open heart, trying to find the way to live as a decent and compassionate human being in a complicated yet beautiful world."

Grove is a product of the same Midwestern communities in which her novels are set. "My childhood was idyllic," she once said. "I grew up on the Illinois prairie, in a little one-room schoolhouse near the big white houses of my grandparents and great-grandparents. They were all storytellers from the word go, and I heard all about ancestors who took the Oregon Trail, who fought in the Civil War or went to the front to nurse their fallen sons there, uncles who had jumped off the roof with umbrellas, lightning that hit horses in the corral and left four hoof-prints branded in the ground, ghosts in the attics, etc, etc. I imagine they had more respect for the inner truth of a story than for the absolute facts, as I think all first-class storytellers do.

"My family has farmed until our present generation, and from them I also learned a deep respect for the land and the weather. I probably have the most fun writing when I'm using a farm setting. I have a younger sister and a much younger brother. Kathy and I were Peter Pan and Tinkerbell, or Dorothy and the Scarecrow. She's the pretty one, so I was always the boy in our games. Reed was always our baby. We nursed him with nightgowns over our heads to look like "nurses' hats" or we forced him into one of our doll buggies and wheeled him around until he yelled bloody murder. (I think he may still hold that against us a teeny bit—ha!) My mother read to us, usually from the Bible, but also from big, fat books. She never 'read down' to us, always expected us to pick up the meaning of challenging stories. I especially remember Ralph Moody's *Little Britches.*

"I had wonderful elementary teachers," Grove continued, "and from them I learned the excitement of reading. Last summer I saw my second grade teacher again—after over 40 years, she remembered me! 'You were my best reader,' she said. I still glow when I think of that. As a child, once in a while I would think of how wonderful it would be to be a writer, so that your teachers would be proud of you. So seeing Mrs. Peters, having a chance to send her copies of my books, was literally one of my longest-held and deepest-held dreams, come true.

"I have always been self-conscious," Grove once stated. "Not exactly quiet, but very easily flustered and not very sure of myself. I get embarrassed easily, and always have. For instance, I knew I couldn't catch balls as a child, so I couldn't. It doesn't take long for that kind of thinking to translate into being chosen last every time for the team. I often write characters who are self-conscious, and whose self-consciousness turns out to be a self-fulfilling prophecy. I can relate to that. Confidence breeds confidence. I see that, but can't really emulate it, and never have been able to. As you can probably guess, I loved school, but hated physical-education class. I think my most impressive achievement, maybe ever, is to have started going regularly to a gym four years ago. In middle age, I've become something of a weight lifter! Finally, I'm a jock (kind of). I can do push-ups now, but couldn't in school, and hated not being able to. Also, I often spent time crying in the rest room because of some real or, more usually, imagined slight from one of the other kids. I was far too easily bruised. Probably I still am. Yikes!

"When I was twelve we moved from Illinois to Oklahoma, and I lived there until I was 18, going through both junior high and high school there. Teens in Oklahoma do the car thing, drag Main, build bonfires on the beaches of the lakes, live a frontier life that is very fun and outdoorsy and cool. I set one of my books, *The Starplace,* in Oklahoma and used a lot of those teen memories. Unfortunately, I also remember blatant small-town racism from those years, and that book concerns those not-so-great memories, too. I would never have said I wanted to be a writer when I was a teen, or even in college. I've never had the self-confidence to make that kind of pronouncement. But from about third grade on I always journaled my feelings, and wrote, wrote, wrote to try and understand the world. I wanted to be an English teacher, and went through graduate school thinking I'd eventually do that.

"I fell into writing in my early thirties, much by accident. I sent a few magazine pieces out, and when they began to be accepted I was totally shocked, but I kept with it, and it grew into a career that I love with all my heart. When I'd been writing for magazines for about eight years, I wrote a short book about a farm foreclosure, told from the viewpoint of a twelve-year-old girl. I entered that book in a contest G.P. Putnam's Sons was having for a first novel for young people, and to my vast surprise, it won and was published."

That novel was *Goodbye, My Wishing Star,* published in 1988. The premise was a timely one, for during the 1980s many American farmers had fallen into financial quagmires and were forced to give up their land. The story is told from the point of view of twelve-year-old Jens Tucker, whose mother's family has farmed their property for generations. Jens knows the end is near, however; other farms in the area have been sold off, and her parents discuss following suit and moving to the city to find work instead. The title of the book comes from a knothole in the barn where Jens milks cows before sun-up. Through it, she can see a special star, and wishes upon it that her family's finances might improve. Her father works hard to keep the farm viable, but Jens's mother believes that life in the city will be far easier for Jens and her little brother, Roger.

Jens's story is recounted in diary form, and when it appears that their farm will indeed be sold, she is angry at having to give up the acreage, the animals, and the sense of heritage that the farm gives her. Feeling powerless at first, she plans to hide her journal in the barn, so the new owners might find it and learn how her family agonized over their decision to leave their land, and how heartbroken a twelve-year-old was that she would never be part of its future. But Jens also becomes aware that injustice and hardship are not her own to claim. The father of one of her friends has also lost their farm and then dies of a heart attack. The mother of another classmate drinks and forces the younger brother to beg to support them. In contrast, Jens's best friend, Marla, has had a relatively easy life, but helps Jens come to terms with the change with some astute observations.

Jens must say goodbye to her beloved animals before a public auction in which the Tuckers' farm tools and livestock are sold. When she meets Jack Shire, an eccentric who collects old cars and stores them in an old bank building in town, he reminds her that even if the Tucker farm is sold, it will always remain in her heart. As the diary comes to a close, Jens realizes she is looking forward to the adventure of starting over anew—that after so many farewells "something inside me is about ready for some hellos," she admits. *Goodbye, My Wishing Star* earned enthusiastic reviews for Grove. "The country setting is very appealing as are Jens' family relationships and her friendship with Marla," declared Eleanor Klopp in a *Voice of Youth Advocates* review. "Though the story is sad, there is also a strength as Jens recognizes that she must get on with her life," observed *Booklist*'s Denise M. Wilms.

Grove's next novel for middle-school readers, *Junglerama,* appeared in 1989. In it, a trio of twelve-year-old boys in a small town find an abandoned carnival trailer one summer and creates a traveling exhibition of animals. The boys' particular hardships are the real focus of the story, however. The work is narrated by T. J., whose parents quarrel constantly, and whose mother neglects them. Jack, an orphan, must care for his alcoholic uncle. Mike's father has lost the family farm and now works as a stablehand. Over the course of the summer, a series of incidents incites gossip and then panic through the town, and some come to believe that their community has fallen under a witch's spell. Blame falls upon an eccentric woman, Cora Beeson, and the boys help rescue her from a dangerous situation in a gripping finale. Again, the work won positive reviews for Grove. T. J's narrative, noted *School Library Journal* reviewer Gerry Larson, "conveys both innocence and discovery . . . . Plot twists, well-paced action, and T. J.'s gradual maturing make this summer unforgettable."

In her next novel, *The Fastest Friend in the West,* Grove again presents an adolescent heroine who must deal with personal trauma. When Lori's best friend finds a new crowd and rejects her, she suffers as any twelve-year-old might; her situation is made all the more difficult by her weight problem. In response, she becomes obsessed with all things marine, painting her bedroom dark blue and decorating it with shells. She even renames herself Lorelei, after the legendary mermaid. At school, a girl who is somewhat of an outcast strikes up a friendship with her. Other kids shun Vern Hittlinger because of her odd clothes and disheveled appearance, but Lori worries when Vern stops coming to school. A teacher tells her that the Hittlingers live in their car on the outskirts of town.

In the second half of the book, Lori goes to see Vern, and learns about the hardships the Hittlingers have encountered over the past few years. Vern's strategy, when finding herself in a new school, has been to make one friend as quickly as possible. They depart again, and Lori later receives a postcard from Vern, saying that her family has found a real home. Toward the novel's close, Lori comes to terms with her weight problem, and resolves to make some changes in her life. "The specter of homelessness," remarked *Horn Book* writer Nancy Vasilakis, "the strain it puts on a proud family with little in the way of resources and more than its share of bad luck—will be a revelation to young readers."

Grove also won laudatory reviews for her 1993 book, *Rimwalkers.* Told in flashback form from twenty years ahead, the work revolves around the summer that fourteen-year-old Victoria, or "Tory," spent on her grandparents' Illinois farm. Both she and her younger sister, Sara, have been relegated here because their parents have decided to take a second honeymoon overseas. Tory is quiet and studious, and looks forward to the science and nature experiments she will be able to carry out in the country. The more vivacious Sara, however, is resentful at being removed from her familiar world of friends, cheerleading, and the usual summer exploits. Also visiting the grandparents that summer are the girls' cousins, Elijah and Rennie. Elijah, the product of a farm family himself, is there to help the grandfather with the chores and summer crop. Rennie, at sixteen, is the oldest of them all and is a high-school dropout from California. At first, the others are put off by his free-spirited, rebellious attitude and daring pranks.

Tory, Elijah, and Rennie soon begin to bond, however, when they believe they see the ghost of a small child at the boarded-up old homestead that sits at the edge of the family property. It had been built by their great-great-grandparents, and when Tory asks her grandmother about the family history, she learns that a four-year-old boy died one summer in the 1840s when four cousins were visiting. Meanwhile, Sara begins to feel left out, especially when Rennie shows Tory and Elijah how to "rimwalk," or traverse a narrow ledge or attic beam. They try it successfully over a river bridge; jealous, Sara tries it as well, but falls and is badly hurt. "The true magic" in Grove's tale, noted Margaret Cole in a *School Library Journal* review, revolves around the alliance between the other three, by which "the teens teach one another to believe in themselves and in life's delicate balance between risk and security." Writing for *Booklist,* Jeanne Triner also offered words of praise for *Rimwalkers.* "The setting is richly drawn, making the farm and its magic real to even the most urban reader," she noted.

A death in the family brings changes to her heroine's life in Grove's 1995 novel, *The Crystal Garden.* Eliza's father has been killed in an accident, and she and her mother struggle to make ends meet. In time, they decide to move to a small Missouri town with Burl, her mother's friend, who is also a country-music hopeful. There, Eliza tries to fit in at school, and keeps her distance from a neighbor girl around her own age, Dierdre, whose difficult home life has made her somewhat of an outcast at school. A science-fair project brings them together, and Eliza discovers that one of Dierdre's parents has an alcohol problem, and their household is very nearly destitute. Yet Dierdre manages her situation so well that Eliza realizes that her peer is far more balanced than she is. Other revelations help Eliza come to terms with the loss of her father. "A satisfying ending and epilogue leave room for hope, thought, and discussion," observed *School Library Journal* reviewer Susan Oliver.

Grove won unstinting praise for her 1998 book, *Reaching Dustin*. The tale involves Carly, a sixth-grade aspiring writer who comes from a pleasant, supportive family. But Carly is dismayed by a new school assignment to interview a classmate when she is paired with her grade's most reviled member. Dustin is sullen and withdrawn, and rumors abound around Carly's Missouri farm community involving his family, their isolated compound, and their possible ties to white supremacist militia groups. As Carly recounts, Dustin's behavioral problems began in the third grade, not long after his mother committed suicide, and she and her friends have snubbed him ever since.

Dustin's family is suspected of harboring a cache of weapons and running an illegal drug enterprise as well. As Carly begins to learn more about Dustin's situation, she is surprised by some of the revelations. He loves animals, for example, and carries a pet frog with him; he also "plays the recorder allotted to each sixth grader with a grace that belies his dirty and hard exterior," wrote *Horn Book*'s Susan P. Bloom. When the frog creates an incident and the situation escalates into a town uproar, Dustin is removed from school. Carly, worried and feeling guilty about her own role in one incident back in the third grade, tries to help him. "Carly's inner development is convincingly painful as she realizes the part she played in creating Dustin's problems," noted Steven Engelfried in a *School Library Journal* review. The "heartfelt story," noted a *Publishers Weekly* review, "unmasks the vulnerabilities of two preadolescents from very different walks of life." Bloom's *Horn Book* review found that "the emotional tone rings true," and *Kirkus Reviews* also praised Grove's talents. "Among a cast of memorable characters, Dustin is obviously pitiable but also noble," its assessment noted, and described *Reaching Dustin* as "written with grace" and "brimming with compassion."

As she noted, Grove drew upon some of her own experiences growing up in Oklahoma for her 1999 novel *The Starplace*. Its story is told through the voice of Frannie, who is thirteen years old in 1961 when an African American family moves into their small town of Quiver. Frannie makes friends with the daughter, Celeste, but soon learns that others in the town, and even at her school, are far less accepting. Celeste is greeted with taunts, and racist incidents occur, but she maintains her poise amidst the ugliness. Her father is a historian writing a book about white-supremacist groups in

this part of Oklahoma, and her grandfather was the victim of a lynching in the area. Celeste shows Frannie some old Ku Klux Klan books she found in the attic of their home, which others believe may be haunted, and "Quiver's sunny image is gradually shattered for Frannie," noted a *Publishers Weekly* assessment.

At school, Celeste finds her niche in the school choir because of her talents, but is ejected from the group just before a competition. In a *Kirkus Reviews* critique, the newcomer is described as "beautiful, mature, worldly, and a great singer . . . close to being a type," but asserted that the other adolescents presented in the novel offered a more balanced portrait. Writing in *School Library Journal*, Connie Tyrell Burns commended *The Starplace* as a "powerful coming-of-age tale, written with grace and poignancy," and found Grove's "characterizations, particularly of Frannie and Celeste, . . . strong and memorable."

The title character of Grove's eighth novel for Putnam, *Destiny*, is another young woman who emerges from hardship to find her own strength. As the work begins, Destiny recounts a home life in which her unskilled mother is addicted to playing the lottery in the hopes of becoming rich. Jack, her mother's deceitful boyfriend, forces Destiny to help him at his job—selling shoddy fruits and vegetables door-to-door in their town, which humiliates her. When a sympathetic adult helps Destiny find better work as a reader to a homebound elderly woman, Mrs. Peck, Destiny starts to see some parallels in her life with the travails of the beleaguered heroes of the Greek myths she reads aloud. When Jack auctions a beloved pet rabbit belonging to Destiny's younger brother, she saves it in her own act of heroism. Mrs. Peck reveals to her some enlightening truths about Destiny's family, and after Jack winds up in jail, Destiny's mother decides to go back to school. The critic Burns, writing for *School Library Journal*, praised "Grove's lyrical writing style" and the "narration, which rings true with Destiny's memorable and poignant voice."

Though some of Grove's characters come from supportive family environments, others are forced to find other role models in their immediate community, as Destiny, Dierdre, Vern, and the boys from *Junglerama* must do. Recognizing that her own encouraging home life was not a universal one spurred Grove to write for adolescents. "My parents always gave me the most amazing encouragement and support of all kinds, and still do," she once stated. "They are my models for compassionate thinking, and I hope I do them honor in my characterizations of people trying to be compassionate in complicated situations. They are always my models for the striving, sacrificing parents in my books—I've been told by readers and teachers that I use a lot of those. They have always put other people before themselves, especially their children.

"I'm very disciplined in my work," Grove once said. "My father built me a wonderful, tiny office in the hayfield behind our house, and I spend most of every day out there (out here!), writing. Writing is really rewriting, and it takes me most of a year to do a book—slow! I begin a book with a character that intrigues me. Sometimes he or she will be from memory, sometimes from observation, or even, occasionally, purely imaginary. This person could be a girl whose father has just died, or a boy in a white supremacist compound, or someone experiencing prejudice at school. At the moment I'm writing about a girl in a family that experiences tragedy and, as a way of escaping from themselves (ultimately impossible, as they will find out), goes on the migrant circuit. I've done lots of research into the lifestyles and challenges of migrant farmworker families, have talked to kids involved in that life, etc.

"Still, it's a huge responsibility trying to put someone else's life on paper, especially a life so much unlike your own, and probably much harder. I take that responsibility very, very seriously. And, as I mentioned, I'm always thankful my parents taught me to view other people with compassion, first and foremost. I hope I learned that lesson well. I hope I learned how to empathize well enough to actually slip into other hearts. I have to have lots of quiet around me when I work, and lots of peace in my life when I'm in the middle of a book. It's a weird sensation, living your own life and also the life of your main character, simultaneously! My family says I zombie out when I'm immersed in a book, and that's true. I burn dinner, have car wrecks (seriously), the whole ball of wax.

"I didn't decide to write for young adults—I wrote for 'regular old adults' like myself when I started magazine writing. But when I wrote the book I entered in the Putnam contest, *Goodbye, My Wishing Star,* I felt like I'd died and gone to heaven. Once I tried it, I realized I absolutely love to write in the voice of a 13-or 14-or 16-year-old. Maybe because I honestly believe young teens are the most interesting and important of people, balanced with one foot in childhood and a heavier foot in adulthood, making the most important decisions they'll ever make, forming the most intense of friendships, having the most bitter of feuds and misunderstandings. I tapped into something deep inside myself when I first wrote in a teen voice, and I've become ad-

dicted to going back to that well of memory, sensation . . . whatever it is."

Grove hopes her readers will take away a lesson from her books through the difficulties that her characters rise above. She realizes that all teens face their own personal challenges. "I want to tell that person that I admire the quest they're on, and think it's worthy of their immense effort," she once commented. "As for the goals and concerns I bring to my work, I guess one more time I'll have to use that word 'compassion.' As the world gets more various and challenging, I think it's got to be a big goal for everyone, to truly empathize with other people. My characters are flawed and vulnerable, but you've got to say for them that in their stumbling ways, they all attain compassion for others. Two of my recent books, *Reaching Dustin* and *The Starplace,* deal with white supremacy and the KKK. These are things that make me livid, so angry I can hardly breathe. For that reason, those books weren't easy to write, but I almost had to write them.

"It still staggers me to think that my books might possibly have some effect—what an idea, and what an obligation. It's thrilling to get a letter from a young reader telling me that one of my books influenced how they thought about someone at their school, or how they acted toward someone, or how they felt about themselves. Mind-boggling, and humbling. I just want my readers to realize what good hearts they have, what amazing creatures they are, how small and intricate the world is, how much love matters. If I had to describe my work to someone, I'd say I hope it's about people who are learning those things."

BIOGRAPHICAL/CRITICAL SOURCES:

BOOKS

Authors and Artists for Young Adults, Volume 38, Gale (Detroit, MI), 2001.

PERIODICALS

ALAN Review, fall, 2000, Anne Sherill, review of *Destiny,* p. 35.
Booklist, April 15, 1988, Denise M. Wilms, review of *Goodbye, My Wishing Star,* p. 1431; July, 1990, Deborah Abbott, review of *The Fastest Friend in the West,* p. 2089; October 15, 1993, Jeanne Triner, review of *Rimwalkers,* pp. 430-431; May 1, 1998, Michael Cart, review of *Reaching Dustin,* p. 1518; June 1, 1999, Hazel Rochman, review of *The Starplace,* p. 1813.

Horn Book, July-August, 1990, Nancy Vasilakis, review of *The Fastest Friend in the West,* p. 455; March-April, 1998, Susan P. Bloom, review of *Reaching Dustin,* p. 220.

Kirkus Reviews, May 1, 1988, review of *Goodbye, My Wishing Star,* p. 692; March 1, 1998, review of *Reaching Dustin,* p. 339; May 15, 1999, review of *The Starplace,* p. 800.

Kliatt, January, 1997, Dean E. Lyons, review of *Rimwalkers,* p. 8.

Publishers Weekly, September 29, 1993, review of *Rimwalkers,* p. 64; May 11, 1998, review of *Reaching Dustin,* p. 68; July 5, 1999, review of *The Starplace,* p. 72; July 31, 2000, review of *Destiny,* p 96.

School Library Journal, July, 1989, Gerry Larson, review of *Junglerama,* p. 82; October, 1993, Margaret Cole, review of *Rimwalkers,* p. 151; May, 1995, Susan Oliver, review of *The Crystal Garden,* p. 106; May, 1998, Stephen Engelfried, review of *Reaching Dustin,* p. 142; June, 1999, Connie Tyrell Burns, review of *The Starplace,* p. 129; April, 2000, Connie Tyrell Burns, review of *Destiny,* p. 134.

Voice of Youth Advocates, October, 1988, Eleanor Klopp, review of *Goodbye, My Wishing Star,* p. 181; December, 1993, Deborah A. Feulner, review of *Rimwalkers,* p. 291; June, 2000, Roxy Ekstrom, review of *Destiny,* p. 114.

* * *

GRUNBERG, Arnon 1971-

PERSONAL: Born February 22, 1971, in Amsterdam, Netherlands.

ADDRESSES: Home—New York, NY. *Office*—c/o St. Martin's Press, 175 Fifth Ave., New York, NY 10010.

CAREER: Writer. Former waiter and actor.

WRITINGS:

Blauwe maandagen (novel), Nijgh and Van Ditmar (Amsterdam, Netherlands) 1994, English translation by Arnold and Erica Pomerans published as *Blue Mondays,* Farrar, Straus (New York, NY), 1997.

Figuranten (novel), Nijgh and Van Ditmar (Amsterdam, Netherlands), 1997, English translation by Sam Garrett published as *Silent Extras,* St. Martin's Press (New York, NY), 2001.

De helige Antonio, Nijgh and Van Ditmar (Amsterdam, Netherlands), 1998.

De troost van de slapstick (essays), Nijgh and Van Ditmar (Amsterdam, Netherlands), 1998.

Het 14e kippetje (film script), Nijgh and Van Ditmar (Amsterdam, Netherlands), 1998.

Liefde is business, Nijgh and Van Ditmar (Amsterdam, Netherlands), 1999.

Fantoompijn, Nijgh and Van Ditmar (Amsterdam, Netherlands), 2000.

SIDELIGHTS: Hailed as a Dutch literary *wunderkind,* Arnon Grunberg dropped out of school at age seventeen and by twenty-two had published his first novel, the Netherlands' bestseller translated as *Blue Mondays.* In setting the autobiographical story of a disaffected Jewish teen who indulges in postmodern middle-class behavior—"hanging out and thinking of ways to kill time," as a *Booklist* review put it—Grunberg presents a portrait of contemporary society in Amsterdam.

Some critics compare Grunberg to a Jewish *wunderkind* of years past, Philip Roth. The dysfunctional family, the depressing school system and the general feeling of emotional disconnect are throwbacks to Roth's classic novel *Portnoy's Complaint.* In *Blue Mondays,* the young Arnon (the author named the character after himself, a la Roth), numb to emotion and lacking in ambition, watches his life plunge downward. Because Arnon is detached from everything he experiences, some critics have seen this as limiting the reader's ability to identify. But reviewers have also noted that Grunberg's prose indicates talent which will continue to be evident in future novels.

In an online *Toespraak* article, contributor F. van der Ploeg noted that Grunberg's quirky writing style is so popular in his homeland that his name has coined a verb: to "Grunberg" is to repeat an expression over and over "until people fall about laughing." An English translation of *Figuranten* illustrates this: "Then she suddenly got hold of my head as if it were a football and kissed me. I had no objection to her treating my head as if it were a football. If only she would hold my head as if it were a football more often."

BIOGRAPHICAL/CRITICAL SOURCES:

PERIODICALS

Booklist, January 1, 1997, Brad Hooper, review of *Blue Mondays,* pp. 818-819.

Economist, February 24, 2001, "Below the Skin; Novels from the Netherlands," p. 8.

Library Journal, January, 1997, Joshua Cohen, review of *Blue Mondays,* p. 146.

Publishers Weekly, December 9, 1996, review of *Blue Mondays,* p. 61; February 26, 2001, review of *Silent Extras,* p. 55.

World Literature Today, spring, 1998, Martinus A. Bakker, review of *Figuranten,* p. 390.

OTHER

Toespraak, http://www.minocw.nl/toespr99/(July 10, 2000), "Literature from the Low Countries".*

* * *

GUERIN, Daniel   1904-1988

PERSONAL: Born May 19, 1904, in Paris, France; died 1988.

CAREER: Writer, theorist, activist, gay-rights advocate, anticolonialist and historian.

MEMBER: The Bellville group of the Socialist Party (SFIO), Confederation General du Travail, Confederation Generale du Travail Unife, Syndicat des Correcteurs, Centre Laique des Auberges de la Jeunesse (cofounder), Comite d'Amnistie aux Indochinois, Gauche Revolutionnaire, Parti Socialist Ouvrier et Paysan, Comite France-Maghreb, Nouvelle Gauche, 1955-57, Mouvement de Liberation du Peuple (later Parti Socialiste Unifie), 1957-69, Mouvement Communiste Libertaire (later the Organisation Communiste Libertaire), 1969-73, Organisation Revolutionnaire Anarchiste, 1973-1980, Union des Travailleurs Communistes Libertaires, 1980.

WRITINGS:

La Peste brune, 1945, revised edition, 1963, translation published as *The Brown Plague: Travels in Late Weimar & Early Nazi Germany,* with an introduction by Robert Schwarzwald, Duke University Press (Durham, NC), 1994.

Les Antilles Decolonisees, Presence Africaine (Paris, France), c1956.

Negroes on the March: A Frenchman's Report on the American Negro Struggle, G.L. Weissman (New York, NY), 1956.

Jeunesse du socialisme libertaire, M. Riviere (Paris, France), 1959.

l'Anarchisme, 1965, translation published as *Anarchism; from Theory to Practice,* with an introduction by Noam Chompsky, 1970.

Sur le fasime (contains *La Peste brune* and *fascisme et grand capital*), F. Maspero (Paris, France), 1969.

Autobiographie de Jeunesse, 1972.

L'armee en France, Filipacchi (Paris, France), 1974.

Les Assassins de Ben Barka: Dix ans D'enquete, G. Authier (Paris, France), 1975.

Vers la Liberte en Amour, Gallimard (Paris, France), 1975.

L'Anarchisme: De la Doctrine a L'action . . . , Gallimard (Paris, France), 1976.

La Revolution Francaise et Nous, F. Maspero (Paris, France), 1976.

Class Struggle in the First French Republic: Bourgeos and Bras Nus 1793-1795, Pluto (London, England), 1977.

Le Mouvement Ouvrier aux Etats-Unis: De 1866 a Nos Jours, F. Maspero (Paris, England), 1977.

Le feu du sang: autobiographie politique et charnelle, B. Grasset (Paris, France), c1977.

Proudhon, Oui et Non, Gallimard (Paris, France), c1978.

100 Years of Labor in the USA, translated by Alan Adler, Pathfinder Press (New York, NY), 1979.

Quand L'Algerie S'insurgeait, 1954-1962: Un Anticolonialiste Temoigne, Pensee Sauvage (Claix, France), 1979.

Ben Barka, Ses Assassins: Seize Ans D'enquete, Plon (Paris, France), c1982.

Homosexualite et Revolution, Vent du Ch'min (Saint-Denis, France), c1983.

A le Rechezche d'un communism Libertaire, 1984.

Les Antilles decolonisees, 1986.

(Editor) Paul Gauguin, *The Writings of a Savage,* with an introduction by Wayne Andersen, translated by Elenor Levieux, Da Caop Press (New York, NY), 1996.

Also author of *Fascisme et grand capital.*

SIDELIGHTS: As a writer, theorist, activist, gay-rights advocate, anticolonialist and historian, Daniel Guerin made national and international politics his life. His was a continual struggle to reconcile Marxism with anarchy, and the personal and the political. Born May 19, 1904, in Paris, France, Guerin came from a liberal, wealthy, but restrictive family. He described himself in his autobiography, *Autobiographie de Jeunesse,* as a "son of the bourgeoisie" who "sought to merge with the people in order ultimately to put himself at the service of the revolution." Through his career he joined a series of political organizations, moving further toward the left. As a result of his involvement in so many different occupations and political organizations, he was misunderstood by colleagues as well as critics; but these people failed to see the many facets of this man.

In 1927, Guerin escaped his controlling family and traveled to Syria, Lebanon, and Indochina. While working in the Middle East as a bookseller he became aware of the injustices of French colonialism. Upon his return to France in 1930 he wrote a number of articles about his impressions of colonialism for *Monde.* An active member of the revolutionary syndicalist headed by Pierre Monatte, he contributed articles to *La Revolution Proletarienne* and to *Le Cri du peuple.* Later he became involved in the Comite d'Amnistie aux Indochinois. Guerin's interest in communism grew, and he helped campaign for the reunification of the Confederation General du Travail and the Communist-controlled Confederation Generale du Travail Unife. For some time he was a member of the Bellville group of the Socialist Party (SFIO) until he encountered its anti-communist municipal councillors.

Guerin made trips to Germany in 1932 and 1933, where he studied Nazism and fascism. He reported his findings in French newspapers and periodicals, and eventually collected these writings into two books, *La Peste brune* (*The Brown Plague: Travels in Late Weimar & early Nazi Germany*) and *Fascisme et grand capital* (re-published together by Maspero in Paris in 1969 as *Sur le fasime*). *La Peste brune* is primarily a memoir of Guerin's stays in Weimar youth hostels, and describes German youth and labor movements. The book criticizes the German Social Democrats and Communists for failing to unite against the Nazis, and the leaders in particular for not taking stronger action. But he is heartened to find that many of Germany's youth and working-class are still resisting. A critic for *Publishers Weekly* pointed out that though Guerin's homosexuality was closeted, his descriptions of the young men "had an unmistakable erotic allure ('Sculptured knees emerged from [Lederhosen]. Legs were deeply tanned muscles taut and hard. Thick socks tumbled down to strong, monumental shoes.')" Guerin draws a connection between the far right and the far left of this period, suggesting that the revolutionary temper created by the Communists set the stage for the Nazis' anti-Semitism and chauvinism.

Fascisme et grand capital is a survey of fascism in Germany and Italy. At the time of its original publication, it was one of the most influential works for France's young, left-wing intellectuals. Guerin's main thesis, as explained by a reviewer for the London *Times Literary Supplement,* was that "both in Italy and Germany heavy industry showed more eagerness to subsidize fascism and to crush the proletariat by force than did light industry—*Fertigindustrie.*" Guerin credits this idea to Andres Nin, a Spanish political leader. Both books are

heavily influenced by Trotsky's ideas, and Guerin acknowledges his debt.

In 1932 Guerin joined the Syndicat des Correcteurs, and remained a lifetime member. He cofounded the Centre Laique des Auberges de la Jeunesse and rejoined the SFIO in 1935. As a member of the new Gauche Revolutionnaire (revolutionary left) party he held several posts, but frequently quarreled with other members. In January 1938, when the Gauche Revolutionnaire gained control of the SFIO's Seine Federation, Guerin became one of the assistant secretaries. He joined the Parti Socialist Ouvrier et Paysan after the Gauche Revolutionnaire was expelled from the SFIO. An attendee of the International Congresses of the Front Ouvrier International in 1938 and 1939, he was delegated to establish a secretariat in Oslo in the event of war. After publishing a monthly bulletin from October 1939 to April 1940, he was arrested by the German army and imprisoned in Germany. He found his way back to France in 1942, and joined the underground Trotskyist organization. Following the war he lived in the United States from 1946 to 1949. Upon his return he wrote a two-volume study, *Ou va le peuple americain.* This volume focuses on the American labor movement, and the conditions of black Americans.

Through the 1950s, Guerin involved himself in anticolonial activism. He traveled to Maghreb in 1952 to establish contact with the syndicalist and nationalist militants there, and became a member of the Comite France-Maghreb. In 1960 he became one of the first signatories of the "Appeal of the 121" opposing compulsory fighting in the Algerian war. Three yeas later he presented President Ben Bella a report on Algerian self-management. Following the coup of 1965, he cofounded a committee in support of Ben Bella and opposing repression in Algeria. He founded another committee to expose the disappearance of Moroccan leader Ben Barka in 1965. Through the 1950s to the 1970s, Guerin joined several different political organizations, leaning further to the left with each new group. In 1955 he joined the Nouvelle Gauche; in 1957 the Mouvement de Liberation du Peuple (later Parti Socialiste Unifie); in 1969 the Mouvement Communiste Libertaire (later the Organisation Communiste Libertaire); in 1973 the Organisation Revolutionnaire Anarchiste; and in 1980 the Union des Travailleurs Communistes Libertaires.

One of Guerin's most important works from this period is *L'Anarchisme,* a concise description of the concepts and revolutionary practice of European anarchism. He emphasizes the tensions between social and individualistic anarchism and authoritarian and libertarian social- ism, concluding that "Socialism is still alive in the hearts of the young but, if it is to attract them, it must break with the tragic terrors of Stalinism, it must appear in a libertarian guise." The English translation, *Anarchism; from theory to practice,* features an introduction by Noam Chompsky. During the 1970s Guerin wrote two autobiographies, *Autobiographie de Jeunesse,* and *Le feu du sang: autobiographie politique et charnelle.* He also confronted his homosexuality and began to campaign for gay rights as a member of the *Front Homosexuel d'Action Revolutionnaire.* He published a book on sexuality and politics, *Homosexualite et Revolution,* in 1983. Guerin continued writing into his last years, completing *A le Rechezche d'un communism Libertaire* in 1984 and *Les Antilles decolonisees* in 1986. He died in 1988.

BIOGRAPHICAL/CRITICAL SOURCES:

BOOKS

Biographical Dictionary of French Political Leaders since 1870, Simon & Schuster (New York, NY), 1990.

PERIODICALS

Choice, March, 1995.
Publishers Weekly, May 9, 1994.
Times Literary Supplement (London, England), August 12, 1965.*

H-I

HABERMAS, Ronald Thomas 1951-

PERSONAL: Born September 20, 1951, in Detroit, MI; son of Robert (a professor) and Roberta Habermas; married Mary Vrazo (a librarian and proof-reader), August 25, 1973; children: Elizabeth Anne, Melissa Marie, Susan Rebecca. *Education:* William Tyndale College, B.R.E., 1973; North American Baptist Seminary, M.Div., 1976; Wheaton Graduate School, M.A. (with highest honors), 1981; Michigan State University, Ph.D., 1985; post-doctoral studies, Union Theological Seminary, 1987.

ADDRESSES: Office—John Brown University, 2000 W. University St., Siloam Springs, AR 72761; fax: 501-524-9548. *E-mail*—rhabermas@jbu.edu.

CAREER: Ordained minister, 1997. Trinity Baptist Church, Kelowna, BC, Canada, associate pastor/director of Christian education, 1976-80; Bloomingdale Baptist Church, Bloomingdale, IL, assistant/interim pastor, 1980-82; First Baptist Church, Stockbridge, MI, pastor, 1982-83; Liberty Baptist Theological Seminary, Lynchburg, VA, associate professor of educational ministries, 1983-88; Columbia International University (formerly Columbia Biblical Seminary), Columbia, SC, associate professor of Christian education and department chair, 1988-93; John Brown University, Siloam Springs, AR, J. Vernon McGee Chair of Biblical Studies, 1991, McGee Professor of Biblical Studies, 1993—. Student pastor, Northside Baptist Church, 1973-74, Komstad Covenant Church, 1974-75, and Lake Norden Baptist Church, 1975; Okanagan Bible Institute, Kelowna, BC, Canada, instructor, 1978-80; North American Professors of Christian Education, member, Board of Directors, 1986-88 and 1990-94; Grace University (formerly Grace College of the

Bible), Staley Distinguished Christian Scholar Lectureship, 1991; Pioneer Clubs, member, Christian Education Advisory Council, 1992—; Fellowship Bible Church, elder, 1994—, associate pastor, 1997—; presenter at numerous professional meetings.

MEMBER: North American Professors of Christian Education, Professional Association of Christian Educators.

AWARDS, HONORS: Christian Education Merit Award, North American Baptist Seminary, 1976; doctoral fellowship, Michigan State University, 1982; Larry Richards Award in Christian Ministries, Wheaton Graduate School, 1982.

WRITINGS:

(With Klaus Issler) *Teaching for Reconciliation: Foundations and Practice of Christian Educational Ministry,* Baker (Grand Rapids, MI), 1992.

(With Klaus Issler) *How We Learn: A Teacher's Guide to Educational Psychology,* Baker (Grand Rapids, MI), 1994.

(With David Olshine) *Down But Not Out Parenting: 50 Ways to Win with Your Teen,* Standard (Cincinnati, OH), 1995.

(With David Olshine) *Tag-Team Youth Ministry: 50 Practical Ways to Involve Parents and Other Caring Adults,* Standard (Cincinnati, OH), 1995.

(With Joyce Armstrong Carroll) *Jesus Didn't Use Worksheets: A 2000 Year Old Model for Good Teaching,* Absey (Houston, TX), 1996.

(With David Olshine) *How to Have REAL Conversation with Your Teen,* Standard (Cincinnati, OH), 1998.

Raising Teens while They're Still in Preschool: What Experts Advise for Successful Parenting, College (Joplin, MO), 1998.

Contributor to books, including *With an Eye on the Future: Development and Mission in the 21st Century,* edited by Duane H. Elmer and Lois McKinney, MARC (Monrovia, CA), 1996; and *Reaching a Generation for Christ: A Comprehensive Guide to Youth Ministry,* edited by Rick Dunn and Mark Senter, Moody (Chicago, IL), 1997. Contributor to various periodicals, including *Threefold Advocate, Vision, Christian Parenting Today, Christian Camp and Conference Journal, Light and Life, R & E Journal, Children's Ministry Magazine, Youthworker, Door, Christian Education Journal, Religious Education, Fundamentalist Journal,* and *Christian Century.* Contributor of book reviews to *Youthworker, Religious Education, Fundamentalist Journal,* and *Grace Theological Journal.*

WORK IN PROGRESS: "A book based on a holistic approach of well-being from an evangelical perspective."

SIDELIGHTS: Ronald Thomas Habermas told *CA:* "My primary motive for writing comes from an ever-growing passion to convey insights from three integrated disciplines: spirituality, human development, and education. I share my thoughts from a Christian evangelical perspective. I tend to primarily think more globally and divergently, focusing upon human quest issues like immortality, intimacy, identity, and legacy. Then I attempt to connect those four universal questions with 'daily newspaper' topics like religion, relationships, character, and vocation. To aid in this process I create several files with various types of resources, each of which link with these basic quests; resources include any pertinent data from Web sites to the comic page. I also try to write in some interactive format to encourage reader engagement and response. My first article was published in a professional journal of Christian education, following the prompting of my friend and mentor Ted Ward, as he directed my doctoral studies at Michigan State University. I still retain the notes I took of our discussion which critiqued that article."

*   *   *

HADLEIGH, Boze 1954-
(George Hadley-Garcia)

PERSONAL: Born May 15, 1954, in Syria; son of a professor; married, October 5, 1975. *Education:* University of California at Santa Barbara, B.A. (Spanish literature), 1975; San Jose State University, M.S. (journalism), 1976. *Politics:* Liberal. *Religion:* Buddhist. *Avocational interests:* "The world's diversity, including travel—about four dozen countries—and communication—I speak five languages."

ADDRESSES: Home—Beverly Hills, CA, and Sydney, New South Wales, Australia. *Office*—c/o Author Mail, Kensington Publishing Group, 850 3rd Ave., New York, NY 10022.

CAREER: Author and freelance journalist.

WRITINGS:

(As George Hadley-Garcia) *The Films of Jane Fonda,* Citadel Press (Secaucus, NJ), 1981.

Conversations with My Elders, St. Martin's Press (New York, NY), 1986, reprinted with new foreword as *Celluloid Gaze,* Limelight Editions (New York, NY), 2002.

(As George Hadley-Garcia) *Hispanic Hollywood: The Latins in Motion Pictures,* Citadel Press (Secaucus, NJ), 1990, translation to Spanish by Hadleigh published as *Hollywood Hispano: Los Latinos en las Películas,* 1991.

The Vinyl Closet: Gays in the Music World, Los Hombres Press (San Diego, CA), 1991, updated edition published as *Sing Out! Gays and Lesbians in the Music World,* Barricade Books (New York, NY), 1997.

Leading Ladies, Robson Books (London, England), 1992.

The Lavender Screen: Gay and Lesbian Films, Citadel Press/Carol Publishing Group (Secaucus, NJ), 1993, updated edition, Kensington Publishing (New York, NY), 2001.

(Compiler) *Hollywood Babble On,* Birch Lane Press/Carol Publishing Group (Secaucus, NJ), 1994.

Hollywood Lesbians: Conversations with Barbara Stanwyck, Agnes Moorehead, Marjorie Main, Nancy Kulp, Patsy Kelly, Edith Head, Sandy Dennis, Capucine, Dorothy Arzner, Dame Judith Anderson, Barricade Books (New York, NY), 1994.

Bette Davis Speaks, Barricade Books (New York, NY), 1996.

Hollywood Gays: Conversations with Cary Grant, Liberace, Tony Perkins, Paul Lynde, Cesar Romero, Brad Davis, Randolph Scott, James Coco, William Haines, David Lewis, Barricade Books (New York, NY), 1996.

(Compiler) *Hollywood and Whine,* Birch Lane Press/Carol Publishing Group (Secaucus, NJ), 1998, revised edition, Kensington Publishing (New York, NY), 2001.

Celebrity Feuds!, Taylor Publishing (Dallas, TX), 1999.

(Compiler) *In Or Out: Gay & Straight Celebrities Talk About Themselves & Each Other,* Barricade Books (New York, NY), 2000.

Hadleigh's books have been translated into fourteen languages.

SIDELIGHTS: Author Boze Hadleigh began his career as a freelance journalist, eventually publishing in hundreds of periodicals in the United States and abroad on a wide variety of topics, from health and travel to history, pop culture, and Hollywood. His books, however, have all focused on the entertainment world, its impact and its behind-the-scenes workings. Several of Hadleigh's books have been firsts in their subject matter, and six of his works have examined the homosexual and bi-sexual presence in and contributions to show business, particularly motion pictures.

Hadleigh, a "smart, resourceful, and daring conversationalist," to quote E. C. of *Film Quarterly,* has written four question-and-answer interview books, commencing with the 1986 title *Conversations with My Elders.* The subjects were gay men of cinema: designer Sir Cecil Beaton, actors Rock Hudson and Sal Mineo, and directors George Cukor, Luchino Visconti, and Rainer Werner Fassbinder. *Hollywood Gays* and *Hollywood Lesbians* each featured interviews with ten gay, lesbian, or bisexual luminaries, mostly actors. Columnist Liz Smith of *Newsday* called Hadleigh's interviews in *Hollywood Lesbians* "fascinating." A reviewer for *Publishers Weekly* noted, "An enlightening picture emerges of Tinseltown, different from that presented by the Fanzines."

Bette Davis Speaks was based on numerous interviews taped over the years with the screen legend, as well as briefer interviews with Davis' associates and intimates. *Booklist* critic Charles Harmon predicted that the actress' fans would "purr with delight" while reading this book by a "world-class interviewer." *Leading Ladies* was a non-question-and-answer collection of profiles of British stage and screen stars, from Dames Edith Evans and Sybil Thorndike to Elsa Lanchester, Joan Greenwood, and Estelle Winwood. "The main pleasure comes from the leading ladies' own words," remarked *Sight and Sound* reviewer Geoffrey Macnab, who found "Hadleigh's enthusiasm" to be "infectious, if wearing."

Two of Hadleigh's books, *The Films of Jane Fonda* and *Hispanic Hollywood* (as well as its Spanish-language translation) were written via a familial pseudonym. *The Lavender Screen*—an illustrated genre overview, like *Hispanic Hollywood*—was called a "clever, entertaining, and shameless compendium" by *Films in Review's* John Nangle. In *The Lavender Screen,* Hadleigh showcased around fifty films featuring major gay, lesbian, or bi-sexual characters, also describing the behind-the-scenes conflicts, closetings, and censorship involved in their production. *Sing Out,* first published as *The Vinyl Closet,* was, according to Hadleigh, the first overview of gay men in music, from Tchaikovsky to Cole Porter, to Johnny Mathis, Boy George, George Michael, and Leonard Bernstein, who penned the foreword. One of the chapters spotlights the many lesbian and bi-sexual women singers who pre-dated k.d. lang and Melissa Etheridge.

Hadleigh, who once won $16,400 on the game show "Jeopardy" and donated a portion of it to a library in Australia damaged by fire, is also the compiler of three celebrity quotations books, including the lesbian, bi-sexual, and gay collection *In or Out.* His first such book, *Hollywood Babble On,* comprised only star vs. star quotes and led *People's* Alex Tresnowski to conclude that Hollywood celebrities are "major-league trash talkers." In the same combative vein, the non-quotes book *Celebrity Feuds!* chronicles over two dozen feuds, from David Letterman vs. Jay Leno to Sonny vs. Cher. *Celebrity Feuds!* also contains a section on family feuds, including siblings Eric and Julia Roberts. Ilene Cooper of *Booklist* described the work as a "quick, funny read," and a *Publishers Weekly* reviewer called it a "sassy compendium of fights, feuds, and flying fur." Hadleigh noted that the book is as much about relationships—"why they sometimes sour and stay soured, even within families"—as about celebrities. "Hopefully, my books enlighten as well as entertain," Hadleigh told *CA.* He added, "You can't always judge a book by its title!"

BIOGRAPHICAL/CRITICAL SOURCES:

PERIODICALS

Booklist, October 15, 1992, Charles Harmon, review of *The Lavender Screen,* p. 391; November 1, 1994, Ilene Cooper, review of *Hollywood Lesbians,* p. 470; April 15, 1996, Charles Harmon, review of *Bette Davis Speaks,* p. 1406; October 15, 1999, Ilene Cooper, review of *Celebrity Feuds!,* p. 407.

Film Quarterly, fall, 1988, E. C., review of *Conversations with My Elders,* p. 64.

Films in Review, December, 1993, John Nangle, review of *The Lavender Screen,* p. 425; March-April, 1995, John Nangle, review of *Hollywood Lesbians,* p. 69.

Library Journal, October 1, 1996, Ed Halter, review of *Hollywood Gays,* p. 79.

Newsday, November 8, 1994, Liz Smith, column.

Observer (London, England), June 21, 1992, Peter Matthews, review of *Leading Ladies,* p. 59.

People, August 1, 1994, Alex Tresnowski, review of *Hollywood Babble On,* p. 26.

Publishers Weekly, October 17, 1994, review of *Hollywood Lesbians,* p. 73; September 9, 1996, review of *Hollywood Gays,* p. 73; October 4, 1999, review of *Celebrity Feuds,* p. 56.

Sight and Sound, October, 1992, Geoffrey Macnab, "Preserved for Posterity," p. 41.

*   *   *

HAHN, Ulla 1946-

PERSONAL: Born April 30, 1946, in Brachthausen, Germany. *Education:* Ph.D., University of Hamburg. *Avocational interests:* Walking, reading, music, theatre.

ADDRESSES: Office—c/o Deutsche Verlags-Anstalt, Neckarstr 121, Postfach 106012, 7000 Stuttgart 1, Germany.

CAREER: Lecturer at Universities of Hamburg, Bremen and Oldenburg, 1975-80; radio editor, Bremen, 1979-91; freelance writer, beginning 1992.

AWARDS, HONORS: Leonce und Lena Award, 1981; Hölderlin Award, 1985; Roswitha von Sandersheim Medal, 1986; Medal of the Federal Republic of Germany.

WRITINGS:

Literatur in der Aktion: zur Entwicklung operativer Literaturformen in der Bundesrepublik (history and criticism), Akademische Verlagsgesellschaft Athenaion (Weisbaden, Germany), 1978.

(With Michael Töteberg) *Günter Wallraff,* Beck (Munich, Germany), 1979.

(With Gerhard Wimberger) *Wir hören zu atmen nicht auf: Liedzyklus nach Gedichten von Ulla Hahn: für mittelhohe Frauenstimme und Lavier 1988* (songs for mezzo-soprano and piano), Bärenreiter (New York, NY), 1989.

Ein Mann im Haus (novel), Deutsche Verlags-Anstalt (Stuttgart, Germany), 1991.

Stechäpfel: Gedichte von Frauen aus drei Jahrtausenden, Philipp Reclam (Stuttgart, Germany), 1992.

Poesie und Vergnügen, Poesie und Verantwortung, C. F. Muller Juristischer Verlag (Heidelberg, Germany), 1994.

(With Klaus von Dohnanyi) *Gedichte furs Gedachtnis: zum Inwendig-Lernen und Auswendig-Sagen,* Deutsche Verlags-Anstalt (Stuttgart, Germany), 1999.

Das verborgene Wort, Deutsche Verlags-Anstalt (Stuttgart, Germany), 2001.

POETRY

Herz über Kopf, Deutsche Verlags-Anstalt (Stuttgart, Germany), 1981.

Spielende, Deutsche Verlags-Anstalt (Stuttgart, Germany), 1983.

Freudenfeuer, Deutsche Verlags-Anstalt (Stuttgart, Germany), 1985.

Unerhörte Nähe: Gedichte, mit einem Anhang für den, der fragt, Deutsche Verlags-Anstalt (Stuttgart, Germany), 1988.

Liebesgedichte (love poems), Deutsche Verlags-Anstalt (Stuttgart, Germany), 1993.

Klima für Engel, Deutscher Tasenbuch Verlag (Munich, Germany), 1993.

Epikurs Garten, Deutsche Verlags-Anstalt (Stuttgart, Germany), 1995.

Schloss umschlungen, T. Pongratz (Hauzenberg, Germany), 1996.

Galileo und zwei Frauen, Deutsche Verlags-Anstalt (Stuttgart, Germany), 1997.

SIDELIGHTS: Poet Ulla Hahn "first came to attention in 1981 with *Herz über Kopf,*" which, according to Michael Hulse in *Antigonish Review,* was lauded by "the pope of German feuilletonism," Marcel Reich-Ranicki. To Reich-Ranicki, Hahn's collection "represented a return to lyric for the common reader," noted Hulse. "Light of touch, merry and sardonic, speaking of familiar feelings in a clear language, with an intelligent use of the lyric tradition behind it and a sensitive deployment of emotional emblematics."

Trained to work in industrial sales, Hahn, a native of Brachthausen, Germany, completed her secondary education in night school, studying literature, history and sociology. In a *Literary Review* piece, Reich-Ranicki suggested that Hahn's poetry "is two things at once and in one—a quiet but by no means bashful affirmation of the self, and a response to our time that is defiant but conceals none of its disorientation." Also characteristic of the poet, said Reich-Ranicki, is a distance from traditional connections with readers. "Those standing in need of answers will hardly get their money's worth from Ulla Hahn," he stated. "Her poems do not wish to console or encourage anyone. . . . The didactic is foreign to this poet, and in agitation she is apparently and fortunately—and this has to do with her past—no longer interested."

Further, wrote Reich-Ranicki, Hahn's poems "possess absolutely no interlocutor; they always get by without addressee. Irrespective of their form, their tone of voice, their motifs and themes, they are rigorous conversations with the self. But precisely this introspective and monologic poetry, which never appears to concern itself with the audience, is what we urgently need and what in our contemporary literature still has rarity value: poetry for readers."

A Hahn collection of love poems, *Liebesgedichte,* was reviewed by Rita Terras in *World Literature Today;* the volume, Terras stated, "breaks with the now common practice of furtively presenting the ostracized love poem among the also-rans." Rather, Hahn "dissects the intricate web of emotions and actions that constitute human love."

BIOGRAPHICAL/CRITICAL SOURCES:

PERIODICALS

Antigonish Review, spring, 1986, Michael Hulse, "Three German Poets of the Eighties," pp. 171-182.
Literary Review, fall, 1989, Marcel Reich-Ranicki, "Enthusiasm for Poetry Is the Other Side of Horror: The Poetry of Ulla Hahn," pp. 80-86.
Studies in Twentieth Century Literature, winter, 1997, Charlotte Melin, "Improved Versions: Feminist Poetics and Recent Work by Ulla Hahn and Ursula Krechel, pp. 219-243.
World Literature Today, winter, 1998, review of *Galile und zwei Frauen,* p. 126; summer, 1994, Rita Terras, review of *Liebesgedichte,* p. 560.*

HAMMOND, N(icholas) G(eoffrey) L(empriere) 1907-2001

OBITUARY NOTICE—See index for *CA* sketch: Born November 15, 1907, in Ayr, Scotland; died March 24, 2001. Educator, scholar, and author. Hammond was a lifelong scholar of Greek language, history, and classics who taught at various institutions, including Clare College in Cambridge, England. During World War II, he was sent to Greece as part of the Allied Military Mission. He wrote about this wartime experience in his book, *Allied Military Mission and the Resistance in West Macedonia.* He wrote several other books on Greece, such as *Venture into Greece with the Guerillas, The Classical Age of Greece,* and *A History of Greece,* which has seen three editions. Hammond was elected to the British Academy in 1968. He was named Commander of the Order of the British Empire in 1974.

OBITUARIES AND OTHER SOURCES:

PERIODICALS

Guardian (London, England), April 5, 2001, p. 20.
Independent (London, England), March 28, 2001, p. 6.
Times (London, England), April 2, 2001, p. 17.

*   *   *

HANDLER, Daniel
See SNICKET, Lemony

*   *   *

HARTWELL, (William) Michael Berry 1911-2001

OBITUARY NOTICE—See index for *CA* sketch: Born May 18, 1911; died April 3, 2001, in London, England. Newspaper executive. Hartwell's father was editor in chief and owner of the *Daily Telegraph,* so the youngster grew up with journalism as the family trade. He attended Eton and Christ Church College at Oxford University before heading to Scotland and working in newsrooms there. Hartwell served in the army during World War II and worked for the organization that planned the invasion of Europe. Upon returning to England after the war, Hartwell married Lady Pamela Smith and returned to journalism, taking over the family's chain of papers in 1954 when his father died. He had already served as editor of the *Glasgow Sunday Mail,* managing editor of the *Financial Times* and chaired the *Amalgamated Press* by the time he took over the *Telegraph.* In 1960 Hartwell created *The Sunday Telegraph* in London to compete with *The Sunday Times* and the *Telegraph* overtook the *Times* in circulation, eventually selling 1.25 million copies a day. In 1968 he was elevated to the peerage as Lord Hartwell. Hartwell was always more concerned with editorial content than the business side of journalism, and that proved to be his downfall when finances at the company hit a rocky point and he was behind the times in turning the newsrooms electronic. In 1985, after more than three decades in the business, he was forced to sell a majority of the company shares he owned to a newspaper publisher from Canada. He retired in 1987. Hartwell wrote two books during his career: *Party Choice,* published in 1948 and focusing on the British political system; and *William Camrose: Giant of Fleet Street,* a biography of his father that was published in 1992.

OBITUARIES AND OTHER SOURCES:

PERIODICALS

Daily Telegraph (London, England), April 4, 2001, p. 33.
Financial Times (London, England), April 5, 2001, p. 6.
Independent (London, England), April 4, 2001, p. 6.
New York Times, April 5, 2001, p. A18.
Times (London, England), April 4, 2001, p. 23.

* * *

HAUSER, Gerard A. 1943-

PERSONAL: Born May 20, 1943, in Buffalo, NY; son of Albert Clement (a police officer) and Ann John (Michalaxes) Hauser; married Jean Marie Brown, August 14, 1965; children: Gerard A., Kirsten Suzanne Hauser Hofmoekel. *Ethnicity:* "American." *Education:* Canisius College, B.A., 1965; University of Wisconsin—Madison, M.A., 1966, Ph.D., 1970. *Religion:* Roman Catholic. *Avocational interests:* Sailing, cooking, ballroom dancing.

ADDRESSES: Home—Boulder, CO. *Office*—Department of Communication, CB 270, University of Colorado at Boulder, Boulder, CO 80309-0270; fax: 303-492-8411. *E-mail*—hauserg@spot.colorado.edu.

CAREER: Pennsylvania State University, University Park, professor of speech communication, 1969-93, di-

rector of University Scholars Program, 1987-93; University of Colorado at Boulder, professor of communication and chairperson of department, 1993—.

MEMBER: International Society for the History of Rhetoric, National Communication Association, Rhetoric Society of America (president-elect, 2000-02).

WRITINGS:

Introduction to Rhetorical Theory, Waveland (Prospect Heights, IL), 1986.
Vernacular Voices, University of South Carolina Press (Columbia, SC), 1999.

WORK IN PROGRESS: Research on the rhetoric of prisoners of conscience.

SIDELIGHTS: Gerard A. Hauser told *CA:* "I write in order to better understand my world and what I think about it. I find that, as I write, I come face to face with my own lack of clarity, my need to gather more information or to think more deeply. It is a selfish motive, but also a necessary one if I am to teach college students in ways that provoke them to get past the obvious or to challenge their own presuppositions. If I am not clear on what I know and where I am ignorant, how can I expect more of them?

"My work has been influenced first by caring teachers. Robert Chambers, my high school English teacher in freshman and sophomore years, made reading and experiencing texts come alive. Father Louis Gansel, who was the faculty moderator of our high school civics club, inspired me to believe that ideas have consequences worth caring about. Donald Cushman, my undergraduate rhetoric teacher, taught me to think on my own and to love intellectual work. Lloyd Bitzer, my doctoral mentor, taught me the intellectual practice of scholarship. All of them shared passion for ideas and instilled the same in me. I also have been influenced by my students, whose boundless curiosity and creative extensions of course content have opened my mind to non-canonical understandings of rhetoric. Finally, my family, a blue-collar family, engaged me in spirited conversation from childhood onward. They taught me that you don't need a college education to think critically or to be a good citizen, and that exploring disagreements is an important part of learning and growing.

"I try to read until I think I am no longer learning new ideas or acquiring relevant new information. I write my introductions first in fits and starts. I list ideas, try to organize them, write a few paragraphs, rethink what I thought I was arguing, and so forth. I find that once I have written the introduction, the rest of the essay or chapter is structured in my mind, and I have an easier time getting it on paper. I try to write five solid pages a day. I write at the same place and same time of day, usually in the morning. I try to block out time to complete a project in a sustained way from beginning to end.

"I write on rhetoric because I find the symbolic process by which we constitute the human world fascinating. I write about publics, public opinion, and public spheres because they are central to our social and political life, are fundamentally based in how we communicate to each other, and are under assault as discourse-based concepts. The specific case studies I undertake usually grow from inspiration by or outrage at the specific practices that define political relations."

*   *   *

HAYES, Roger S(tanley) 1947-

PERSONAL: Born February 22, 1947, in Freeport, IL, son of Stanley Hayes; married Lonnie Ferarri, December 22, 1972; children: Casey, Chad. *Ethnicity:* "Caucasian." *Education:* Southern Illinois University, B.S., 1975.

ADDRESSES: Home—1771 Washington, Carlyle, IL 62231. *E-mail*—RHAYES17@accessus.net.

CAREER: U.S. Army Corps of Illinois, park ranger and recreation specialist, 1976—. *Military service:* U.S. Army, 1967-69; served as infantryman in Vietnam; became sergeant; received bronze star and two purple hearts.

WRITINGS:

On Point (memoir/military history), Presidio, 2000.

WORK IN PROGRESS: "Military memoir of my company commander in Vietnam."

SIDELIGHTS: Roger S. Hayes told *CA:* "Writing is one of the best ways of expressing one's self. Spoken sentences are structured while they are being delivered. On the contrary, writing offers the time to organize thoughts and to edit the text to deliver a precise message. Moreover, many of our best writers and authors

have said that they write not for an audience, but for themselves. So it is with me. I was compelled to get my thoughts down on paper and wasn't all that concern whether my work would be published.

"The largest influence on my writing skill is the large amount of writing I perform in my work. I believe that if one wishes to write well, little tips are learned along the way. I would also recommend that those who wish to improve their craft delve into some of the literature. Two of my favorite books, also recommended by my publisher's executive editor, are: Patricia T. O'Conner's *Woe Is I,* and *On Writing Well* by William Zinsser.

"One of my college teachers, in grading writing assignments, deducted points if we used the same word more than one in a paragraph. The technique, I believe, was not to limit the use of words, but to stimulate us to search for alternate ways of delivering our message. It helped make me a more creative writer.

"I have quite a bit of experience writing technical documents in which personality should not appear—management plans, policies, correspondence, etc. While writing my book, I wondered if I would have a voice or writing style of my own. I was surprised to find that I had no reason to be concerned. When writing something of book length, it is almost impossible not to show one's personality. Writing style comes naturally. In addition, I believe that effective writing does not need to be fancy or filled with big words; it simply must be understandable. A technique I use is to place myself mentally in the scene then describe what I see, experience, or fell.

"My first and only book to date is a military memoir of the time I spend as an infantryman in Vietnam. I was filled with more thoughts and emotions than one might believe. My story was straining to get out; I was compelled to write about the experience. I plan to write more on the subject. I have told my story but I have more subtle messages that I wish to convey. Perhaps writing for me is driven by a certain amount of passion."

*   *   *

HAYWARD, Douglas J. J. 1940-

PERSONAL: Born June 24, 1940, in Midland, Ontario, Canada; son of David Penzer (a maintenance mechanic) and Georgina Ellen Mae (an assembler; maiden name, Bourne) Hayward; married Joanne LaDorna Rummel (a teacher), September 9, 1961; children: James Nathan, John Scott, Holly Rae. *Ethnicity:* "White." *Education:* Westmont College, B.A., 1963; Fuller Theological Seminary, M.A., 1977; University of California, Santa Barbara, Ph.D., 1987. *Religion:* Baptist.

ADDRESSES: Home—404 West Summerfield Cir., Anaheim, CA 92802. *Office*—Biola University, 13800 Biola Ave., La Mirada, CA 90639. *E-mail*—doug—hayward@peter.biola.edu.

CAREER: UFM International, Bala-Cynwyd, PA, missionary, 1967-87; Biola University, La Mirada, CA, professor, 1989—. Speaker at seminars.

MEMBER: American Society of Missiology, Evangelical Missiological Society, Association of Social Anthropologists in Oceania.

WRITINGS:

The Dani of Irian Jaya, Regions Press, 1980.
Missionaries in Bare Feet, Regions Press, 1980.
Vernacular Christianity among the Mulia Dani, University Press of America (Lanham, MD), 1997.
"Saturday Night in Pasadena" in the Religion of Generation X, Routledge (New York, NY), 2000.

Author of four books in the Dani language. Contributor to periodicals.

WORK IN PROGRESS: Editing *Christian Reflections on Anthropological Theory;* research on missiological reflections on the letters of the apostle Paul, on missiological insights from the work of missionaries among the western Dani, and on demon possession as a theological, psychological, and anthropological phenomenon.

*　　*　　*

HEFLIN, Ruth J. 1963-

PERSONAL: Born June 19, 1963, in Pratt, KS; daughter of Charles A. and Mary Rosella (Mallonee) Heflin; married James P. Cooper (a professor of English), October 27, 1989; children: Harland James Paul Charles Cooper. *Ethnicity:* "European American." *Education:* Kansas State University, B.A., 1985, M.A., 1988; Okla-

homa State University, Ph.D., 1997. *Politics:* Green Party. *Religion:* "Pantheist."

ADDRESSES: Home—Leavenworth, KS. *Office*—Kansas City Kansas Community College, 7250 State Ave., Kansas City, KS 66112. *E-mail*—hefruth@ hotmail.com.

CAREER: University of Missouri—Kansas City, adjunct professor of English, 1990-92; Oklahoma State University, Stillwater, adjunct professor of English, 1992-98; Kansas City Kansas Community College, Kansas City, KS, assistant professor of English, 1998—, and member of Intercultural Council. American Indian Heritage Month, committee chairperson; member of local Women's Community.

MEMBER: Modern Language Association of America, Western American Literature Association.

WRITINGS:

I Remain Alive: The Sioux Literary Renaissance, Syracuse University Press (Syracuse, NY), 2000.
(Contributor) Clyde Holler, editor, *The Black Elk Reader,* Syracuse University Press (Syracuse, NY), 2000.

WORK IN PROGRESS: Editing *American Indian Literary Traditions Anthology;* research on symbolism of the Lakota star quilt, the literary traditions of specific American Indian nations, and rebellion in the poetry of Phillis Wheatley.

SIDELIGHTS: Ruth J. Heflin told *CA:* "I write to explore. Writing not only helps me to sort through ideas, but it also helps me to discover what it is I really know or really believe. I want to capture the essence of my ideas and offer them up for discussion in what I see as an ongoing conversation with other scholars and writers.

"When I started writing about Charles Eastman and Gertrude Bonnin, I was working from an obvious angle—they were Indians writing for a Euro-American audience. Or were they? As I went, I routinely questioned long-held beliefs about these writers, only to discover that many ideas some people seem to believe firmly are really up for interpretation. In my search for a new way to see the writers' works and their lives, I discovered much prejudice on my part and on the parts of other scholars before me.

"I read thoroughly, then write some, and read some more. I write as much as I can, then try to pull ideas together—looking for that moment when logic falls into the abyss in an attempt to rediscover ways of thinking and writing.

"I wanted to write about American Indian literature because I firmly believe that all literature relies heavily on the stories that came before it. More scholars ignore this idea when it comes to Indians, even though they embrace it wholeheartedly for other cultures. Why? What I love about literary analysis is breaking through molds and stereotypes and seeing things freshly, even if I'm just using an old polished lens."

* * *

HELLER, Janet Ruth 1949-

PERSONAL: Born July 8, 1949, in Milwaukee, WI; daughter of William C., Jr. (an investor and manager) and Joan Ruth (a homemaker and community volunteer; maiden name, Pereles) Heller; married Michael A. Krischer (a college professor), June 13, 1982. *Ethnicity:* "Jewish." *Education:* Attended Oberlin College, 1967-70; University of Wisconsin—Madison, B.A. (with honors), 1970, 1973, M.A., 1973; University of Chicago, Ph.D., 1987. *Politics:* Democrat. *Religion:* Jewish. *Avocational interests:* Hiking, birdwatching, singing.

ADDRESSES: Home—Portage, MI. *Office*— Department of English, Western Michigan University, Kalamazoo, MI 49008. *E-mail*—janet.heller@wmich. edu.

CAREER: University of Chicago, Chicago, IL, coordinator of Writing Program, 1976-81; Northern Illinois University, DeKalb, instructor in English, 1982-88; Nazareth College, Kalamazoo, MI, assistant professor of English, 1989-90; Grand Valley State University, Allendale, MI, assistant professor of English, 1990-97; Albion College, Albion, MI, assistant professor of English, 1998; Western Michigan University, Kalamazoo, assistant professor of English and women's studies, 1998—. Rape Crisis Center, Madison, WI, founding mother, 1972-73.

MEMBER: Modern Language Association of America, Society for the Study of Midwestern Literature (member of board of directors, 1999—), Michigan College English Association (member of board of directors, 1990—).

AWARDS, HONORS: Contest winner, Friends of Poetry of Kalamazoo, 1989.

WRITINGS:

Coleridge, Lamb, Hazlitt, and the Reader of Drama, University of Missouri Press (Columbia, MO), 1990.

Work represented in anthologies, including *Mothers' Daughters,* Shameless Hussy Press, 1979; *New Poet's Anthology,* 1987; *Red Flower,* 1988; *Women's Spirituality, Women's Lives,* Haworth, 1995; and *Moon Days,* Summerhouse Press, 1999. Contributor of articles, poems, and reviews to periodicals, including *Minnesota Review, Cottonwood, Organic Gardening, Modern Maturity, MidAmerica, Nineteenth-Century Prose,* and *George Eliot—George Henry Lewes Studies.* Editor, *Primavera,* 1974-83.

WORK IN PROGRESS: A book of poems, *Folk Concert;* research on the comedies of Oscar Wilde, the fiction of Toni Cade Bambara, poetic techniques in the essays of Charles Lamb and William Hazlitt, and David Mamet's play *Oleanna.*

SIDELIGHTS: Janet Ruth Heller told *CA:* "My primary subjects for poetry include my family, nature, characters in the Bible, and psychological exploration. I am strongly influenced by the women's movement, music, my Jewish heritage, and my interest in both humanities and the social sciences.

"Unlike most scholars, my research interests are broad. I enjoy large topics that involve interdisciplinary research. For example, literature draws on linguistics, psychology, anthropology, women's studies, music, art, history, et cetera, and these connections fascinate me."

* * *

HENSHER, Philip 1965-

PERSONAL: Born February 20, 1965, in London, England; son of R. J. (a banker) and M. (a librarian; maiden name Foster) Hensher. *Education:* Oxford University, B.A., 1986; Cambridge University, Ph.D., 1992.

ADDRESSES: Home—83a Tennyson St., London SW8 3TH, England. *Agent*—The Wylie Agency, 36 Parkside, 52 Knightsbridge, London SW1P, England. *E-mail*—hensherp@dircon.co.uk.

CAREER: Writer. Journalist, *Independent* (London, England); columnist, *Spectator* and *Times Literary Supplement*; clerk, House of Commons, 1990-96.

MEMBER: Royal Society of Literature.

AWARDS, HONORS: Somerset Maugham Award, 1997, for *Kitchen Venom,*; Fellow of the Royal Society of Literature, 1998.

WRITINGS:

Other Lulus, Hamish Hamilton, 1994.
Kitchen Venom, Hamish Hamilton, 1996.
Pleasured, Chatto and Windus, 1998.
The Bedroom of the Mister's Wife, Chatto and Windus, 1999.

SIDELIGHTS: In *Other Lulus,* Philip Hensher presents the story of an heiress, Friederika, whose grandfather studied with a famous composer, and her pursuit of an operatic career. In the *Observer,* Jennifer Selway wrote that the novel was "cold, remote and affected . . . a very stuffy comedy of manners." Nick Kimberly commented in *New Statesman and Society* that Hensher "manages the difficult job of writing about self-centred people without annoying the reader." In the *Spectator,* Amanda Craig wrote, "He can write dialogue and keep a plot whirring; this is more than many and produces an enjoyable debut that will not disgrace the author."

Kitchen Venom, set in Parliament during Margaret Thatcher's administration, depicts the disintegrating family of a Commons clerk. Hensher, who was a clerk in the Commons, was forced to quit his job after the publication of this book, perhaps showing that it was more than fiction, according to a reviewer in the *Observer;* Jason Cowley in the *Times Literary Supplement* noted that he was dismissed after he gave an interview about the book to the gay magazine *Attitude.* Cowley wrote that although the book is "mannered and sometimes cruel," it also "has a fierce originality" and his dialogue has a "fluent virtuosity." In the *Spectator,* Matthew Paris wrote, "I found *Kitchen Venom* a hateful work: a brilliant, hateful work. I really did throw it at the wall."

Pleasured is set in 1989 in West Berlin, before the Berlin Wall came down. The book stars Peter Picker, an Englishman, and Friedrich and Daphne, two Germans he gives a ride to; by the end of the novel, Picker's young son dies of meningitis, Friedrich tries to cheat Picker out of his money, and Daphne finds that her boyfriend is an East German spy. Michael Hulse wrote in the *Spectator* that Hensher "is not a Tolstoy," but that its strength is in its "core sense of the unknowability of our fellows," that people may think they truly know each other, but never do. A reviewer in the *Observer*

praised Hensher's wit and concise prose, and wrote that the book "is the definitive novel" of one of the most significant events of the twentieth century—the fall of the Berlin Wall. In the *New Statesman,* Phil Whitaker noted, "There is much to admire in *Pleasured,* even though the pace is uneven and the narrative too often static." He also wrote that the challenge for Hensher as a writer is to combine his "large ambition with the tight narrative control we glimpsed in *Kitchen Venom*" and that when Hensher does this, he may be seen as an "important new voice" in British writing.

In *The Bedroom of the Mister's Wife,* Hensher presents a collection of fourteen short stories, many of which "exert a compelling attraction," according to Sean O'Brien in the *Times Literary Supplement.* Tamsin Todd remarked in the *New Statesman* that there was "a cold cleverness to much of Hensher's writing, and some of the stories can read like the work of a callous teenager." In the *Observer,* however, Jonathan Keates commented that "Some of [the stories] strain for effect but the writing has the authority of an artist with no need to be looking over his shoulder." And Anne Chisholm, in the *Spectator,* described the stories as "clever, cool" and "unsettling."

Hensher told *CA:* "My novels are all concerned with the history of Europe and the idea of history itself. For me, the huge historical shifts which enter into the action of *Kitchen Venom* and *Pleasured* do not have any inevitability, but can only be read through the half-understood motivation of individual men and women. I am a European writer in outlook and a more narrowly English one in stylistic temperament; my heroes are I. Compton-Burnett and Henry Green. I have no interest in America. I have been described as a stylist, which is fair enough. I hope my style always reflects the sometimes odd turns of phrase of ordinary speech rather than the conventions of the literary sentence."

BIOGRAPHICAL/CRITICAL SOURCES:

PERIODICALS

New Statesman, August 14, 1998, p. 45; September 20, 1999, p. 58.
New Statesman & Society, April 1, 1994, p. 48.
New Yorker, August 18, 1997, p. 76.
Observer, March 20, 1994, p. 22; June 18, 1995, p. 17; April 28, 1996, p. 15; March 23, 1997, p. 18; August 22, 1999, p. 12.
Spectator, April 16, 1994, p. 38; July 25, 1995, p. 35; April 20, 1996, p. 9; April 27, 1996, p. 30; August 15, 1998, p. 33; August 21, 1999, p. 34.
Time, December 28, 1998, p. 186.

Times Literary Supplement, March 25, 1994, p. 19; April 19, 1996, p. 22; July 31, 1998, p. 20; July 30, 1999, p. 14.

*   *   *

HIMELBLAU, Jack J. 1935-

PERSONAL: Born February 6, 1935, in Chicago, IL; son of Jonas David (self-employed) and Sarah Grika (a housekeeper) Himelblau; married Ana Isabel Anderson Lambert, 1964 (divorced); children: Robert E., Vanessa Ann. *Ethnicity:* "Caucasian." *Education:* University of Chicago, B.A., 1958, M.A., 1959; University of Michigan, Ph.D., 1965. *Politics:* "Democrat/Liberal." *Avocational interests:* "Hiking."

ADDRESSES: Home—9834 John Rolfe Dr., San Antonio, TX 78230-3212. *Office*—Division of Foreign Languages, University of Texas at San Antonio, 6900 North Loop 1604 W., San Antonio, TX 78249-0644. *E-mail*—jhimelbl@utsa.edu.

CAREER: Mills College, associate professor, 1972-76; University of Texas, San Antonio, professor of Spanish, 1976—. Consultant for National Public Radio's Series "Latin-American Fiction," 1983.

MEMBER: American Association of Teachers of Spanish and Portuguese.

WRITINGS:

Alejandro O. Deustua: Philosophy in Defense of Man, University Presses of Florida (Gainesville, FL), 1979.

Quiche Worlds in Creation: The Popol Vuh as a Narrative Work of Art, Labyrinthos (Culver City, CA), 1989.

The Indian in Spanish America: Tow Centuries of Removal, Survival, and Integration, Labyrinthos (Culver City, CA), 1993.

(Editor and contributor) *The Indian in Spanish America: Centuries of Removal, Survival, and Integration* (two volumes), Labyrinthos (Culver City, CA), 1994-95.

Contributor of articles to books, including *Visión de la Narrativa Hispánica: Ensayos,* edited by Juan Cruz Mendizábal and Juan Fernández Jiménez, Indiana University of Pennsylvania, 1999; and *Studies in Honor of Myron Lichtblau,* edited by Fernando Burgos, Juan de

la Cuesta (Newark, DE), 2000. Contributor of reviews and articles to various publications, including *Hispania, Romance Notes, Hispanic Review, Kentucky Romance Quarterly Hispanic Journal,* and *Inter-American Review of Bibliography.* Associate editor, *Latin-American Indian,* 1985-86; member of advisory board, *Hispanic Journal,* 1992—.

WORK IN PROGRESS: The Spanish-American Chronicle of the Sixteenth and Seventeenth Centuries: The Transformation of Reality into Fiction; Bartolomé de las Casas's Historia de las Indias: The Rhetorical Transformation of Facts into Fiction, a monograph; *Miguel Angel Asturias' El Señor Presidente: A Morphological Analysis,* a monograph.

*   *   *

HODGE, Deborah 1954-

PERSONAL: Born November 6, 1954, in Moose Jaw, Saskatchewan, Canada; daughter of John Lyndon (a writer, editor, and broadcaster) and Marion Joyce (a nursing instructor; maiden name, Baker) Grove; married David Ian Hodge (a businessman), April 24, 1977; children: Emily, Michael, Helen. *Education:* Simon Fraser University, B.A. (psychology), 1977; graduated from the Professional Development Program, Simon Fraser University, 1978.

ADDRESSES: Office—c/o Kids Can Press, 29 Birch Ave., Toronto, Ontario, Canada M4V 1E2. *E-mail*—dhodge@istar.ca.

CAREER: Elementary school teacher in Armstrong and Golden school districts, British Columbia, Canada, 1978-91; British Columbia Ministry of Education, writer, editor, and instructional designer of elementary school curriculum, 1991-99; children's author, 1994—.

MEMBER: Canadian Children's Book Center, Association of Children's Writers and Illustrators (British Columbia), Children's Literature Roundtable, Writer's Union of Canada, Canadian Society of Children's Authors, Illustrators, and Performers (CANSCAIP).

AWARDS, HONORS: Parents' Choice Approval, Parents' Choice Foundation, and Pick of the Lists, fall selection, *American Bookseller,* both 1997, both for *Bears, Wild Cats, Wild Dogs,* and *Whales;* Parents' Choice Approval, Parents' Choice Foundation, 1997, and Parents' Guide to Children's Media award, 1997 and 1999, both for *Starting with Science: Simple Machines;* Best Books for Children designation, *Science Books and Films,* 1998, for *Bears,* and 1999, for *Deer, Moose, Elk and Caribou;* shortlist, Red Cedar Book Award, 2000, for *Beavers;* shortlist, Silver Birch Award, 2000, *The Kids Book of Canada's Railway and How the CPR Was Built.*

WRITINGS:

NONFICTION

Bears: Polar Bears, Black Bears, and Grizzly Bears, illustrated by Pat Stephens, Kids Can Press (New York, NY), 1996.

Wild Cats: Cougars, Bobcats, and Lynx, illustrated by Nancy Gray Ogle, Kids Can Press (New York, NY), 1996.

Wild Dogs: Foxes, Wolves, and Coyotes, illustrated by Pat Stephens, Kids Can Press (New York, NY), 1996.

Whales: Killer Whales, Blue Whales, and More, illustrated by Pat Stephens, Kids Can Press (New York, NY), 1996.

Starting with Science: Simple Machines ("Starting with Science" series), photographs by Ray Bourdeau, Kids Can Press (New York, NY), 1996.

Deer, Moose, Elk, and Caribou, illustrated by Pat Stephens, Kids Can Press, 1998.

Beavers, illustrated by Pat Stephens, Kids Can Press (New York, NY), 1998.

The Kids Book of Canada's Railway and How the CPR Was Built, illustrated by John Mantha, Kids Can Press (Toronto, Canada), 2000.

Eagles, illustrated by Nancy Gray Ogle, Kids Can Press (New York, NY), 2000.

WORK IN PROGRESS: Salmon, for Kids Can Press, publication expected in 2002.

SIDELIGHTS: "A child's thinking level is usually above his or her reading level, so the children's nonfiction writer must operate on two different planes— providing interesting, thought-provoking information that is accessible through words the child won't stumble over," Hodge commented. According to Hodge, books have fascinated her ever since she was a young child, "I loved the bedtime stories my parents read to me. Some, like the Brothers Grimm fairy tales, I have never forgotten."

Hodge was born in Moose Jaw, Saskatchewan, and grew up in Burnaby, British Columbia, Canada. She studied psychology at Simon Fraser University (SFU),

intending to become a psychologist, but instead ended up as an elementary school teacher in British Columbia after completing a professional development program at SFU in 1978. Her teaching career spanned more than twelve years before she took a temporary leave of absence to work on the curriculum for the British Columbia Ministry of Education. While working on the assignment, Hodge happened to mention to a coworker the lack of stimulating books available to young readers. As a teacher she had often observed young children looking for books that were easy enough to read, yet still contained useful information.

This chance remark to Linda Bailey, creator of the popular "Stevie Diamond" mystery series, paved the way to a new and exciting career for Hodge. On Bailey's suggestion Hodge submitted a proposal for a children's book to Kids Can Press and then immediately followed it up with a completed manuscript. The book was published as *Bears: Polar Bears, Black Bears, and Grizzly Bears* in 1996.

The choice of subject was not very difficult for Hodge as her years as an elementary school teacher had given her an insight into the mind of young readers. She explained, "They're fascinated by very big, very fast, or very fierce animals. They want answers to such questions as how long are a grizzly bear's claws, or how much does a Blue Whale eat?" Hodge has since published seven different titles dealing with various animals. All the books in her series are about animals that children are drawn to. Both *Bears* and its follow-up, *Wild Cats: Cougars, Bobcats, and Lynx,* were praised by Carolyn Phelan of *Booklist* for not crowding the pages with pictures and sundry facts as most books with a two-page layout do. Each set of pages covers a different topic, such as food, habitat, or birth, and "maintains a sense of visual calm and verbal continuity from one spread to the next." Jonathan Webb claimed in *Quill & Quire* that Hodge's books "fulfill, reliably and attractively, the modest objective they set themselves."

Other titles in Hodge's wildlife series include *Wild Dogs: Foxes, Wolves, and Coyotes* and *Whales: Killer Whales, Blue Whales, and More,* both which were published in 1996, and *Eagles,* published in 2000. These volumes follow the same basic, easy-to-read format of Hodge's earlier books, featuring large print, naturalistic drawings, and cut-away diagrams. They also contain interesting trivia boxes on each page. Fred Boer, reviewing both *Wild Dogs* and *Whales* for *Quill & Quire,* commented, "Both books are well organized, with a glossary and an index." Judy Diamond, reviewing the books for *Science Books and Film,* deemed them effective for an early elementary school readership and praised the material as clearly presented. Diamond concluded that, "Overall the information presented is accurate and complete. The volume will serve as a useful tool for school reports on its topics."

Other books in the series are *Deer, Moose, Elk, and Caribou* and *Beavers,* both of which were published in 1998. *Beavers* was praised by a contributor to *Kirkus Reviews* as having "concise, clearly organized facts corralled into brief, dual-page chapters." Dave Jenkinson, a contributor to *CM: Canadian Materials,* described *Beavers* as "a superb example of a well-written information book for pre-readers which will also appeal to students in the early elementary grades." *Deer, Moose, Elk, and Caribou* was reviewed by Robert G. Hoehn of *Science Activities,* who wrote, "The potpourri of information in this beautifully illustrated book is guaranteed to pique the interest of readers. . . . Adult readers will also enjoy the tidbits they learn about members of the deer family."

Hodge explores the world of science in the "Starting with Science" series published by Kids Can Press. Her book *Starting with Science: Simple Machines* contains a presentation of thirteen attractive and interactive experiments, accompanied by clear and detailed directions in an easy-to-follow format which encourages children's participation. According to critics, the book has much visual appeal and lists all the materials needed along with their methodology and an explanation of the principles engaged. Safety precautions are also addressed in the text or illustrated in sidebars, and further details about each activity are listed in the appendix. Maureen Garvie, reviewing *Starting with Science: Simple Machines* for *Quill & Quire,* noted that "The book reflects energy, esthetics, community, and curiosity. . . . With the aid of kitchen equipment and minimal supervision, science is no longer a fusty world of stained test-tubes, wire coils, and rotten-egg smells."

In 2000, the author turned her hand to the story of the Canadian Pacific Railway (CPR), Canada's first transcontinental railway, in *The Kids Book of Canada's Railway and How the CPR Was Built.* The granddaughter of CPR employees, Hodge details the quest to stretch a single track of rail across Canada and includes information about William van Horne's planning of the railway, the laborers who blasted through mountains and tackled difficult terrain, the types of trains eventually used on the railway, and the impact the CPR had on aboriginal peoples. Writing in *Quill & Quire,* reviewer Gweneth Evans suggested that "The building of the Canadian Pacific Railway is an incredible story, and

this informative new book . . . does quite a good job of presenting it."

Although Hodge has not returned to teaching, she admits that the feedback she receives from children motivates her to continue writing and shapes her work as an instructional designer of elementary school curricula. She commented: "Every day when I wake up I have more ideas for books I want to write."

BIOGRAPHICAL/CRITICAL SOURCES:

PERIODICALS

Booklist, September 15, 1997, Carolyn Phelan, review of *Bears* and *Wild Cats,* p. 238; April 15, 1998, Carolyn Phelan, review of *Starting with Science: Simple Machines,* p. 448; January 1, 1999, April Judge, review of *Deer, Moose, Elk, and Caribou* and *Beavers,* p. 865; November 1, 2000, Gillian Endberg, review of *Eagles.*

CM: Canadian Materials, August 11, 2000, Dave Jenkinson, review of *Beavers.*

Kirkus Reviews, October 1, 1998, review of *Beavers,* p. 1459.

Quill & Quire, March, 1996, Jonathan Webb, "Charismatic Cats and Winsome Bears," p. 73; December, 1996, Maureen Garvie, review of *Starting with Science: Simple Machines,* p. 39; January, 1997, Fred Boer, review of *Wild Dogs, Whales,* and *Living Things,* p. 38; September 1, 2000, Gwyneth Evans, review of *The Kids Book of Canada's Railway and How the CPR Was Built.*

School Library Journal, November, 1997, Lisa Wu Stowe, review of *Wild Dogs* and *Whales,* pp. 108-109; July, 1998, Kathryn Kosiorek, review of *Starting with Science: Simple Machines,* p. 88.

Science Activities, spring, 1999, Robert G. Hoehn, review of *Deer, Moose, Elk, and Caribou,* p. 39.

Science Books and Films, December, 1997, Judy Diamond, review of *Wild Dogs* and *Whales,* p. 275.

*   *   *

HOEM, Edvard 1949-

PERSONAL: Born March 10, 1949, in Fræna, Norway. *Education:* Attended university.

ADDRESSES: Agent—c/o Genesis Förlag, P.O. Box 1180, 0107 Oslo, Norway.

CAREER: Writer.

AWARDS, HONORS: Awards include Kritikerprisen, 1975; Aschehougprisen, 1985; Melsomprisen, 1988; and Doblougprisen, 1988.

WRITINGS:

Som grønne musikantar (poems), Noregs boklag (Oslo, Norway), 1969.

Landet av honning og aske: Frå dei bleike myrer medden våte ving, Noregs boklag (Oslo, Norway), 1970.

Anna Lena (novel), Samlaget (Oslo, Norway), 1971.

Kvinnene langs fjorden, Samlaget (Oslo, Norway), 1973.

Kjærleikens ferjereiser (novel), Samlaget (Oslo, Norway), 1974, translation by Frankie Denton Shackelford published as *The Ferry Crossing,* Garland Publishing (New York, NY), 1989.

Musikken gjennom Gleng og Tuden fjordar, tusen fjell (play; title means "The Music through Gleng"), Samlaget (Oslo, Norway), 1977.

Gi meg de brennende hjerter (two novels; title means "Give Me the Burning Hearts;" contains *Melding frå Petrograd* and *Fjerne Berlin*), Samlaget (Oslo, Norway), 1978-80.

Der storbåra bryt (play), Samlaget (Oslo, Norway), 1979.

God natt, Europa: Skodespel (play; title means "Goodnight, Europe"), Oktober (Oslo, Norway), 1982.

Du er blitt glad i dette landet: Dikt og songar, 1972-1982, Samlaget (Oslo, Norway), 1982.

Lenins madam (play), Samlaget (Oslo, Norway), 1983.

Prøvetid (novel; title means "Rehearsal Time"), Oktober (Oslo, Norway), 1984.

Heimlandet Barndom (novel), Oktober (Oslo, Norway), 1985.

Ave Eva (novel), Oktober (Oslo, Norway), 1987, translation by Schackelford published as *Ave Eva: A Norwegian Tragedy,* Xenos Books, 2000.

Sankt Olavs skrin: Dramatisk forteljing (play), Oktober (Oslo, Norway), 1989.

Til ungdommen: Nordahl Griegs liv (title means "The Death of Nordahl Grieg"), Gyldendal, 1989.

I Tom Bergmanns tid (novel), Oktober (Oslo, Norway), 1991.

Engelen din, Robinson (novel), Oktober (Oslo, Norway), 1993.

(Editor and author of afterword) Halldis Moren Vesaas, *Dikt i omsetjing,* Samlaget (Oslo, Norway), 1993.

I kampens hete: Europeiske refleksjonar, Aschehoug (Oslo, Norway), 1994.

Bibel-historier (title means "Bible Stories"), Aschehoug (Oslo, Norway), 1995.

Meisteren og Mirjam: Pasjonsdrama, Oktober (Oslo, Norway), 1995.

Tid for klage, tid for dans (novel), Oktober (Oslo, Norway), 1996.

Mitt tapre språk (nonfiction), Samlaget (Oslo, Norway), 1996.

Den fyrste song, eller, Evas pilegrimsferd: Eit mysteriespel (verse play), Genesis (Oslo, Norway), 1999.

ADAPTATIONS: Work by Hoem has been included in the recording *Den fattige Gud,* released by Aschehoug, 1993.

BIOGRAPHICAL/CRITICAL SOURCES:

PERIODICALS

Malcolm Lowry Review, fall-spring, 1991-92, Gordon Bowker, editor, "The Death of Nordahl Grieg," pp. 29-30, 122-25.

Scandinavian Studies, summer, 1991, Jan I. Sjåvik, review of *The Ferry Crossing,* p. 395.

OTHER

Edvard Hoem, http://www.aftenposten.no/ (July 17, 2000).*

*   *   *

HOFFHEIMER, Michael H. 1954-

PERSONAL: Born December 21, 1954, in Cincinnati, OH; son of Harry M. (a lawyer) and Charlotte (O'Brien) Hoffheimer; married Luanne Buchanan (an educator), June 15, 1985; children: Joseph Allen, Jean Sarah. *Education:* Johns Hopkins University, B.A. (with honors), 1977; University of Chicago, M.A., 1978, Ph.D., 1981; University of Michigan, J.D. (cum laude), 1984.

ADDRESSES: Home—306 Phillip Rd., Oxford, MS 38655. *Office*—School of Law, University of Mississippi, University, MS 38677; fax 662-915-6842.

CAREER: Frost & Jacobs (law firm), Cincinnati, OH, associate, 1984-87; University of Mississippi, University, assistant professor, 1987-90, associate professor, 1990-97, professor of law, 1997—, Mitchell, McNutt, Threadgill, Smith & Sams Lecturer in Law, 1991-97. University of Cincinnati, adjunct faculty member, 1985-87; Mississippi Defense Lawyers Association, lecturer, 1998—; guest lecturer at institutions including University of Southern California, 1994, York University, 1996, University of Kansas, 1997, and Georgetown University and University of Georgia, both 1998; public speaker. Public Defender Panel of Hamilton County, OH, member, 1985-87; American Inns of Court, bencher emeritus of William C. Keady Inn of Court. Licensed private detective in the state of Mississippi.

MEMBER: American Bar Association, Association of Trial Lawyers of America, American Society for Legal History, Hegel Society of America.

WRITINGS:

Justice Holmes and the Natural Law: Studies in the Origins of Holmes Legal Philosophy, Garland Publishing (New York, NY), 1992.
Directory of Law Reviews, Anderson Publishing (Cincinnati, OH), 1994, 4th edition, 1999.
Eduard Gans and the Hegelian Philosophy of Law, Kluwer Academic (Dordrecht, Netherlands), 1995.
(Contributor) Jon Stewart, editor, G. W. F. Hegel, *Miscellaneous Writings,* Northwestern University Press (Evanston, IL), 1999.
Fiddling Viola: Irish and American Fiddle Tunes Transcribed for Viola, Mel Bay Publications (Pacific, MO), 2000.

Contributor of articles and reviews to law journals and other periodicals, including *Idealistic Studies, Clio, Law and Psychology Review, History of Political Theory,* and *Hegel-Studien.*

* * *

HOFFMAN, Frank B. 1888-1958

PERSONAL: Born August 28, 1888, in Chicago, IL; died March 11, 1958; married Hazel Nelson, May, 1925. *Education:* Art Institute of Chicago. *Avocational interests:* Boxing, horse training, racing.

CAREER: Horse trainer, racer, and boxer; Great Northern Railroad, illustrator of promotional ads; advertisement illustrator for Cream of Wheat, General Electric, and Montgomery Ward; illustrator for *American Weekly, Redbook, Ladies' Home Journal, Saturday Evening Post, Country Gentleman, Liberty, Shrine Magazine, Cosmopolitan,* and *Woman's Home Companion;* Brown and Bigelow Calendar Company, Saint Paul, MN, calendar illustrator, 1940-53.

WRITINGS:

Contributor to several periodical publications, including *Redbook, Country Gentleman, Liberty, Cosmopolitan, Ladies' Home Journal, Shrine Magazine, Scribner's Magazine, Woman's Home Companion, McCall's, American Magazine, Collier's,* and *Saturday Evening Post.*

SIDELIGHTS: A prolific artist, Frank B. Hoffman portrayed Western themes and outdoor sports in his sketches and paintings. He illustrated for periodicals such as *Redbook, Ladies' Home Journal,* and the *Saturday Evening Post,* and worked on advertising campaigns for Cream of Wheat, General Electric, and Montgomery Ward, among others. He is best known for the paintings he produced for the Brown and Bigelow Calendar Company, from 1940 until he stopped painting in 1953.

Hoffman was born on August 28, 1888, in Chicago, Illinois. As a young boy, he had little interest in school, preferring to spend time drawing than listening to his teachers or completing his homework. Hoffman took two years to complete the fourth grade, and his father, having noticed his son's lack of interest, withdrew Hoffman from elementary school and sent him to racing stables the family owned in Ohio. There, Hoffman acquired an education more suited to his interests. He exercised the horses and rode in races throughout the South, Midwest, and Canada, and sketched the horses that he was around. At nineteen, Hoffman was too heavy to continue riding horses in competitions, and he returned to Chicago, where he found a job in a steel mill in Gary, Indiana swinging a sledgehammer. The work was strenuous and he developed physically, so much so that he decided to pursue boxing, a sport in which he had also participated while racing and caring for the horses. To support himself while training to become a professional fighter, he ran a dice box in a Chicago saloon. He continued in this work until his mother introduced him to Joseph E. J. Ryan, a family friend and editor of the *American Weekly* in Chicago. Once he saw Hoffman's horse drawings, Ryan suggested he apply for a position in the *Weekly's* art department.

Hoffman accepted the job at the paper even though he would have to prove himself as an illustrator before he would get a paycheck. Once he convinced the staff that he could draw, he was assigned to accompany reporters and make on-the-scene sketches of newspaper stories. He would then ink over the sketches with an ink brush instead of a pen. Though his work was respected by his employers, Hoffman did not have the formal training in painting with oils that magazine art editors required for features illustrations. To advance in his career, he studied drawing and portrait painting for the next five years, while still working for the newspaper, with J. Wellington Reynolds, an instructor at the Art Institute of Chicago.

Hoffman began to branch out professionally in 1913 when he accepted an offer from Ray Long, the editor of *Redbook,* to illustrate a dog story by James Oliver Curwood. In 1916, after being deemed unfit to serve in World War I due to poor eyesight, Hoffman was hired by the Great Northern Railroad to paint wildlife scenes for the promotion of Glacier National Park. The position required he move to Montana, where for the next year he painted elk, deer, buffalo, and moose in addition to Native Americans, cowboys, and miners, all of which he would continue to use in his work throughout his career. While in Montana, he met John Singer Sargent, a painter from whom Hoffman learned much and who inspired him to focus on his own work.

After experiencing a severe case of pneumonia, Hoffman, on his doctor's suggestion, moved to the drier climate of Santa Fe. There, he hired Leon Gaspard, whom he had met at Gaspard's one-man show at the Art Institute of Chicago, to critique his work at $25 per piece. They each had an interest in outdoor subjects and worked from the same models. In *Dictionary of Literary Biography,* Stephen Zimmer noted: "Thereafter Hoffman's work reflected Gaspard's influence, particularly in his use of heavy pigment in an impressionistic manner."

Hoffman continued to spend summers in Taos for the next several years, and met many other artists there and became increasingly enamored with the landscape, and the cowboys, Native Americans, and Mexicans who populated the region and whom he frequently used as subjects of his paintings. He continued to spend winters in Chicago, where he earned money working on advertising commissions to finance his summers in Taos. His opportunities snowballed and he took on more advertising commissions and also began illustrating short stories.

In 1923, Hoffman hired Hazel Nelson to pose for him for a Cream of Wheat advertisement. She sat for him for other projects and they eventually became romantically involved. They married in May, two years after they had met.

In February of 1926, Hoffman illustrated Zane Grey's serialized Western "Forlorn River," which appeared in

Ladies' Home Journal. Hoffman's career had taken off, and that year he illustrated stories for Peter B. Kyne, Mary Heaton Vorse, Lucia Zora, Florence Dorsey Welch, Guy Fletcher, and Zack Cartwright, and five of his paintings appeared in full-page magazine ads. Most of his work centered on subjects that he knew about, such as horse racing, boxing, and Western-themes, but as Zimmer pointed out, "his popularity with editors and writers stemmed from his ability to embellish a story rather than simply illustrating scenes described within."

The Hoffmans moved to Taos in the fall of 1928, into an adobe ranch house on two hundred acres of land. Hoffman named it Hobby Horse Ranch. His first work-related project while in Taos was illustrations for "Desert Bloom," a story by Vingie Roe that appeared in the August 1929 issue of *McCall's.*

At this point in his career, Hoffman's workload was overwhelming, and he took a break from it in late 1931. He and Hazel had been training thoroughbreds, and he decided to make them the focus of his work. Over the next year, he finished three paintings of his own horses, which were later hung in a Chicago gallery. He also again began sketching and inking horse races, rodeos, and other sporting events, which he submitted to the *Chicago Tribune.* Hoffman had hoped to receive commissions from horse owners to paint their horses, but had little luck and was forced to return to illustrating commercially.

In December of 1939, Hoffman submitted sketches for paintings to the Bigelow Calendar Company in Saint Paul, Minnesota. A month later, Hoffman received word that one of his sketches had been accepted. He was offered $750 for the completed painting of *Trouble on the Trail,* and encouraged to send more work. *Trouble on the Trail* appeared in 1942, the first of more than 150 of Hoffman's paintings that Bigelow would publish.

The art editors at Brown and Bigelow were so enamored by Hoffman's first painting that they asked him to submit sketches for a twelve-part mailing-card outdoor series. Hoffman accepted and was paid $200 per finished picture. Brown and Bigelow's vice president, Harry Huse, wrote Hoffman to inform him that the company wanted to use three of Hoffman's paintings from the outdoor series in a series of calendars, and asked him if he would provide three additional works. Huse also expressed that Brown and Bigelow was interested in exclusive rights to Hoffman's work, and Hoffman continued to provide paintings for the company until 1953.

Due to failing eyesight, Hoffman quit painting in the fall of 1953. He died at Hobby Horse Ranch on March 11, 1958. Though he was quite popular during his lifetime, his work has received little recognition since his death.

BIOGRAPHICAL/CRITICAL SOURCES:

BOOKS

Ainsworth, Ed, *The Cowboy in Art,* World (New York, NY), 1968.
Dictionary of Literary Biography, Volume 188: *American Book and Magazine Illustrators to 1920,* Gale (Detroit, MI), 1998.*

*   *   *

HOLT, Kimberly Willis   1960-

PERSONAL: Born September 9, 1960, in Pensacola, FL; daughter of Julian Ray (a data processing manager) and Brenda (a teacher; maiden name, Mitchell) Willis; married Jerry William Holt (director of Amarillo CVC), February 23, 1985; children: Shannon. *Education:* Attended University of New Orleans, 1978-79, and Louisiana State University, 1979-81.

ADDRESSES: Home—Amarillo, TX. *Office*—P.O. Box 20135, Amarillo, TX 79114. *Agent*—Flannery Literary Agency, 114 Wickfield Ct., Naperville, IL 60563.

CAREER: Radio news director, 1980-82; worked in advertising and marketing, 1982-87; interior decorator, 1987-93; writer, 1994—.

AWARDS, HONORS: Boston Globe/Horn Book Award for Fiction, 1998, Notable Book selection, American Library Association (ALA), 1999, and Top Ten Best Books for Young Adults selection, ALA, 1999, all for *My Louisiana Sky;* National Book Award for Young People's Literature, 1999, for *When Zachary Beaver Came to Town.*

WRITINGS:

My Louisiana Sky, Holt, 1998.
Mister and Me, Putnam, 1998.
When Zachary Beaver Came to Town, Holt, 1999.
Dancing in Cadillac Light, Putnam, 2001.

SIDELIGHTS: Kimberly Willis Holt writes poignant coming-of-age fiction for young readers, books that hum with the sleepy rhythms of small-town life in her native South and the cadences of its vernacular. Since her 1998 debut novel, *My Louisiana Sky,* Holt has won a number of awards, including two American Library Association citations for that particular work, and a prestigious National Book Award for Young People's Literature for her third, 1999's *When Zachary Beaver Came to Town.* But all of her titles have garnered enthusiastic praise from critics of young adult fiction for their realistic portrayals of life in the rural South, and for the iconoclastic, but sympathetic characters she creates to lead her stories.

Holt was born in 1960, in Pensacola, Florida, the site of a large U.S. Navy base. Her father worked for many years as a chef for the U.S. Navy, and her mother was a teacher. Julian Willis's job took the family to several far-flung places during Holt's young life, including France and the Pacific Ocean territory of Guam. They also lived in a number of American states, but always made Forest Hill, Louisiana, their spiritual home. Holt's grandmother lived there, and the future author loved spending time in a place where her roots ran so deep. She began to consider writing as a career at the age of twelve, when she read Carson McCullers's *The Heart Is a Lonely Hunter.* This 1940 work, like others by the Georgia native, explored human isolation and life in the South through the vantage point of an eloquent outsider, and the style of fiction moved the young Holt. "It was just life-changing because of the characters," she told *School Library Journal* writer Kathleen T. Horning. "That was the first time I read a book where the characters seemed like real people to me."

Holt studied broadcast journalism at the University of New Orleans in the late 1970s and Louisiana State University until 1981, but left school to work as a news director for a radio station. The work was far from challenging, however, and so she took another job at the station selling advertising time. She also worked as an interior decorator for six years before thinking about writing for publication. As a teen and young adult, she had always envisioned a life as an author, but never pursued it in earnest. Part of the reason she abandoned her calling was due to a tough writing teacher she once had, who refused to provide her with any encouraging feedback. "In all fairness to her, she was a great teacher, but she would praise other people's writing but not mine," Holt told Horning in the *School Library Journal* interview. "I was very shy and insecure and I took it as though I really wasn't meant to be a writer."

Around 1994, Holt—by then married and with a young child—moved to Amarillo, Texas, for her husband's job. She was bereft, as she recalled, but recognized the sudden isolation as a surprise opportunity to begin writing for children. "I didn't know a soul there and I thought, 'If I'm ever going to do it, this is the time,'" she told Horning. The result was *My Louisiana Sky,* published by Holt in 1998. Set in a small town in central Louisiana, the story was inspired by a memorable incident that occurred when Holt was just nine. She had been traveling through rural Louisiana with her parents, and saw a woman carrying groceries walking on the side of the road. "This lady looked strange to me," Holt recalled in the interview with Horning. "She just had a different look about her on her face and I mentioned her to my mom and my mom said, 'That lady's mentally retarded and her husband is mentally retarded and they have a lot of kids.' It haunted me for the rest of my life."

Tiger Ann Parker is the unlikely heroine of *My Louisiana Sky,* which takes place in a town called Saitter in 1957. Tiger is twelve years old. She does well in both school and athletics, but she feels a certain degree of social ostracism because of her parents. Her father, who works in a local plant nursery, cannot even do simple math, but Tiger's mother is even more developmentally challenged. As a young child, it used to delight Tiger that her mother played games with her so enthusiastically, but entering adolescence and yearning for a more "normal" life, Tiger begins to feel embarrassed by her parents' limitations. She knows that some townspeople view the family as odd and are of the opinion that the Parkers should have never been allowed to marry and start a family.

Fortunately, Tiger also lives with her astute, practical grandmother, who helps her face the teasing of others. Her beloved grandmother points out in *My Louisiana Sky* that "people are afraid of what's different. That don't mean different is bad. Just means different is different." But things begin to change in sleepy Saitter: Tiger's baseball-playing pal surprises her with a kiss one day, and then her grandmother dies suddenly. Tiger's sophisticated aunt comes to Saitter in the midst of the crisis, and offers to take Tiger home with her to the big city of Baton Rouge. Tiger is torn between her parents, who love her dearly, and the glamorous Dorie Kay and a world of new opportunities far from the small-mindedness of Saitter.

When a natural disaster nearly wrecks her father's workplace and another crisis arises, Tiger begins to realize the more positive aspects of life in Saitter. "With the help of Hurricane Audrey, Tiger learns how strong she is and where she truly belongs," remarked Lynn Evarts in a *Voice of Youth Advocates* critique of *My Loui-*

siana Sky. The debut work won a slew of awards for Holt, and sincere words of praise from reviewers. Betsy Hearne, writing in the *Bulletin of the Center for Children's Books,* found that in Tiger, the writer had created a character "with a distinctive voice" as well as "a credible resolution showing Tiger's values to be as strong as her family ties." *School Library Journal* writer Cindy Darling Codell asserted that "Holt has nicely portrayed the rhythms, relationships, and sometimes harsh realities of small-town life." Marilyn Bousquin, writing in *Horn Book,* found that Holt "eases the action along with a low-key, unpretentious plot, never resorting to over-dramatization or sentimentality in developing her uncannily credible characters." *Booklist*'s Hazel Rochman commented that "all the characters, including Tiger's parents, are drawn with warmth but no patronizing reverence," while a *Publishers Weekly* assessment asserted that Holt "presents and handles a sticky dilemma with remarkable grace."

Holt followed the success of her debut with another work published that same year, *Mister and Me.* Just eighty pages in length, the work is aimed at younger readers, aged seven to eleven, but still won praise for its depiction of a time and place that had long passed. Young Jolene Johnson, however, knows no other world except the sometimes tough realm of life in the segregated South as an African American child in the 1940s. Jolene lives in a logging town in Louisiana—two of Holt's great-grandfathers had worked in the industry—and is the daughter of a widowed seamstress mother, and also lives with her grandfather. Life begins to change a bit too quickly for Jolene when a Mister Leroy Redfield, a logger new to the town, begins wooing her mother. The presence of this rival for her mother's affection makes Jolene miss her deceased father, whom she never knew, even more.

During the course of *Mister and Me,* Jolene tries in vain to rid "Mister," as she calls him, from their lives, but her strategies only backfire. On one occasion, Leroy buys her mother some expensive fabric, and Jolene cuts it to small, unusable pieces. Then her mother and grandfather must suddenly travel to New Orleans for a brief time, and Jolene is left with Leroy for caretaking. They come to a truce, and then a new beginning. Lynda Short, writing in *School Library Journal,* called it a "touching short novel" that depicts Jolene's coming to terms with the presence of a "man whose love and patience allow her to expand her notion of family." A *Publishers Weekly* review declared that "the warmth and love in the Johnson household envelops the novel," and Kay Weisman, critiquing it for *Booklist,* noted that "this heartfelt story is filled with richly developed characters who deal with all-too-real problems."

Holt's third novel, *When Zachary Beaver Came to Town,* won the National Book Award for Young People's Literature after its 1999 publication, and it made her a sought-after speaker in schools. On her visits and in her interviews, Holt makes it a point to remind aspiring writers—and all other aspirants—not to become discouraged by perceived negativity from a teacher, as she had once done.

The plot of *Zachary Beaver* originated with another memorable event in Holt's life; when she was thirteen, she went to the Louisiana state fair and paid two dollars to see a youth billed as "the fattest boy in the world." He sat in a small trailer and, in a manner somewhat out of character for the shy Holt, she asked him several questions about himself. He answered them, but he was understandably a bit surly about it.

Later in life, Holt met someone who had met the boy as well when the trailer made a stop near an office. The woman in question paid two dollars every day to see him, but ate her lunch with him. "And I just remember thinking, 'I didn't do that. I didn't come across in a kind way,' " she told Horning in the *School Library Journal* interview. Holt sets her story in Antler, Texas—a composite of two towns she knows in the Texas Panhandle—in the summer of 1971. This time, her protagonist is a boy, Toby Wilson, who is thirteen that summer. Antler is so small that the arrival of a trailer bearing "the world's fattest teenaged boy" is an interesting event, and Toby and his best friend Cal are fascinated by the tragic figure of Zachary.

Toby's life is somewhat difficult for him that summer. His mother has left the family in order to pursue a career in the music industry in Nashville. His father, Otto, is Antler's postmaster, but also runs a worm business for bait-supply shops on the side. Toby and Cal dream of life and its possibilities outside of Antler and, like others, have made Cal's popular older brother, Wayne, a role model. Toby is also suffering from a crush on a girl named Scarlett. When Zachary Beaver arrives in his trailer, Toby and Cal visit the 643-pound boy and ask him innumerable questions. Zachary seems to possess an oddly encyclopedic knowledge of the world, but relies on his legal guardian—who disappears shortly after Zachary's trailer arrives in the parking lot of the local Dairy Maid. Toby and Cal do a bit of sleuthing and wonder why Zachary, who says he's been baptized, possesses a Bible that doesn't register that date in it, as was customary in the rural United States. Zachary fi-

nally confesses the truth, and the boys help him fulfill this dream of his. "This rebirth twists the small-town perspective in a way that serves the novel well," noted Bousquin in a *Horn Book* review. "To Zachary, Antler becomes the place on the map that has opened his heart and his life to barely-hoped-for possibilities."

Meanwhile, military officials arrive at Cal's house to tell the family that his brother Wayne has been killed in Vietnam. Toby realizes that his parents' marriage is irreparably damaged, but his quiet, kind father helps him through these difficult times. "Holt tenderly captures small-town life and deftly fills it with decent characters who ring true," wrote Linnea Lannon in the *New York Times Book Review.* Other reviewers gave it equally solid praise. "Picturesque images . . . drive home the point that everyday life is studded with memorable moments," stated *Publishers Weekly.*

Holt lives with her husband and daughter in Amarillo still, and published her fourth book, *Dancing in Cadillac Light,* in 2001. Set in Texas, the novel follows the story of Jaynell, an eleven-year-old girl who must change her perception of poverty after her grandfather's death. When Horning asked Holt, in the *School Library Journal* interview, about the eccentricity of her characters and whether she would concur with this assessment, the author agreed wholeheartedly. "I think I am too," she laughed. "I'm attracted to people like that. I like the flaws in people. . . . And I also love the people that seem normal on the surface and then they're really not. I find that a high compliment when people say that they think my characters are eccentric or quirky, because I guess that's what I love about life."

BIOGRAPHICAL/CRITICAL SOURCES:

PERIODICALS

Booklist, April 15, 1998, Hazel Rochman, review of *My Louisiana Sky,* p. 1438; November 15, 1998, Kay Weisman, review of *Mister and Me,* p. 590; January 1, 2000, review of *When Zachary Beaver Came to Town,* p. 820.

Bulletin of the Center for Children's Books, June, 1998, Betsy Hearne, review of *My Louisiana Sky,* p. 364.

Horn Book, July-August, 1998, Marilyn Bousquin, review of *My Louisiana Sky,* p. 489; November, 1999, Marilyn Bousquin, review of *When Zachary Beaver Came to Town,* p. 741.

New York Times Book Review, December 19, 1999, Linnea Lannon, review of *When Zachary Beaver Came to Town.*

Publishers Weekly, May 4, 1998, review of *My Louisiana Sky,* p. 213; August 31, 1998, review of *Mister and Me,* p. 76; November 1, 1999, review of *When Zachary Beaver Came to Town,* p. 85.

School Library Journal, July, 1998, Cindy Darling Codell, review of *My Louisiana Sky,* pp. 95-96; November, 1998, Lynda Short, review of *Mister and Me,* p. 122; February, 2000, Kathleen T. Horning, "Small Town Girl," pp. 43-45; March, 2001, William McLoughlin, review of *Dancing in the Cadillac Light,* p. 250.

Texas Monthly, December, 1999, Mike Shea, review of *When Zachary Beaver Came to Town,* p. 34.

Voice of Youth Advocates, August, 1998, Lynn Evarts, review of *My Louisiana Sky,* p. 202; February, 1999, review of *My Louisiana Sky,* p. 411; April, 2001, Diane Tuccillo, review of *Dancing in the Cadillac Light,* p. 42.*

*   *   *

HÖSLE, Vittorio   1960-

PERSONAL: Born June 25, 1960, in Milan, Italy; son of Johannes (a professor) and Carla (Gronda) Hösle; married Jieon Kim, December 11, 1997; children: Johannes, Paul. *Ethnicity:* "Italian/German." *Education:* Attended University of Regensburg, 1977-78, University of Tübingen, 1978-79, Ruhr Universität Bochum, 1980, and Albert Ludwigs Universität Freiburg, 1981; University of Tübingen, Ph.D. (summa cum laude), 1982. *Religion:* Catholic. *Avocational interests:* Film.

ADDRESSES: Home—712 Forest Ave., South Bend, IN 46616. *Office*—Department of German and Russian, University of Notre Dame, Notre Dame, IN 46616. *E-mail*—vhosie@nd.edu.

CAREER: New School for Social Research, New York, NY, visiting assistant professor, 1986, associate professor, 1988-89; Deutsche Forschungsgemeinschaft, Heisenberg fellow, 1987-93; University of Essen, professor, 1993-97; Research Institute of Philosophy, Hanover, Germany, director, 1997-2000; University of Notre Dame, South Bend, IN, Paul Kimball Professor of Arts and Letters, professor of philosophy, and professor of government and international studies, 1999—. Technische Hogeschool Twente in Enschede, visiting lecturer, 1985; Istituto Italiano per gli Studi Filosofici, fellow, 1985-86; University of Porto Alegre (Brazil), visiting professor, 1989; University of Ulm, visiting professor, 1989-90, Humboldt Professor, 1995; Academy of Sciences and the Lomonossov University, Moscow, Russia, visiting professor, 1990; affiliated with German

Department of Ohio State University, 1990-91, the Philosophy Department of the University of Trondheim, 1991, and the Sociology Department of the University of Delhi, 1992; DAAD-Kommission for Southern Europe, member, 1991-98; Eidgenössische Technische Hochschule Zurich, visiting professor, 1992-93; Kulturwissenschaftliches Institut Essen, fellow, 1995-96; South Korean universities, visiting professor, 1995; Ohio State University, Max Kade Distinguished Visiting Professor, 1996; European College of Liberal Arts, Berlin, Germany, member, Board of Trustees, 1999—; University of Regensburg, chair position, 2000; Nanovic Institute for European Studies, fellow; presenter at numerous conferences.

AWARDS, HONORS: Fellowships, Bavarian Begabtenförderung, 1977-82, Studienstiftung des deutschen Volks, 1978-82, and Deutsche Forschungsgemeinschaft, 1982-84; Fritz Winter Award, Bavarian Academy of Sciences, 1994, for outstanding achievements in the humanities.

WRITINGS:

Wahrheit Undgeschichte, Frommann, 1984.
Hegel's System, Meiner, 1987.
Moral und Politik, Bech, 1997.
The Dead Philosophers Café, Notre Dame Press, 1999.

Contributor of numerous works, including prefaces, articles, essays, reviews, and other works, to various books and periodicals. Editor of monograph series "Ethik im technischen Zeitalter," C. H. Beck (Munich), 1990—; and editor, with C. C. Buchner, of the series "Faszination Philosophie," 2000—.

WORK IN PROGRESS: Research on hermeneutics.

SIDELIGHTS: Vittorio Hösle told *CA:* "I want to communicate philosophical ideas. I am interested in an application of the tradition of objective idealism, founded by Plato, to pressing issues of our time, as the ecological problem or the question of development of third world countries. The subjects I chose are inspired by the feeling that they are not yet reflected enough by our society."

*   *   *

HU, Hua-linh   1938-

PERSONAL: Born December 5, 1938, in China; naturalized U.S. citizen; daughter of Kai-ting (a military officer) and Shu-yen (a homemaker; maiden name, Fan) Wang; married Chia-Lun Hu (a professor), 1965; children: Carl. *Ethnicity:* "Chinese." *Education:* Tunghai University, B.A., 1959; University of Colorado at Boulder, M.A., 1962, Ph.D., 1971. *Avocational interests:* Reading, walking, gardening, travel.

ADDRESSES: Home—Carbondale, IL. *Office*—c/o Southern Illinois University Press, P.O. Box 3697, Carbondale, IL 62902-3697.

CAREER: University of Colorado, Boulder, CO, instructor, 1963-70; National Chiao Tung University, Taiwan, associate professor, 1972-74; National Chung Hsin University, Taiwan, associate professor, 1973; Tunghai University, Taiwan, associate professor, 1973; University of Denver, Denver, CO, assistant professor, 1977-78; writer and editor.

MEMBER: Association of Asian Studies.

AWARDS, HONORS: Chinese Literary and Arts Medal of Honor, biography category, Chinese Association of Literature and Arts, 1998, for *Ginling Forever;* nonfiction award, Southern Illinois Regional Writers Contest, 1985.

WRITINGS:

Fate of Destiny, Chiu Ko Publishing (Taipei, Taiwan), 1992.
Ginling Forever: A Biographical Account of Miss Minnie Vautrin (in Chinese), Chiu Ko Publishing (Taipei, Taiwan), 1997, revised edition, People's Literature Publishing House, (Beijing, China), 2000, revised and expanded English translation published as *American Goddess at the Rape of Nanking,* Southern Illinois University Press (Carbondale, IL), 2000.
Ten Thousand Days of Laughter and Tears, Chiu Ko Publishing (Taipei, Taiwan), 1999.

Editor, *Journal of Studies of Japanese Aggression against China,* 1990-95. Contributor to anthologies, including *Collection of Selected Articles of the Central Daily News' Literary Section,* edited by Sun Ju Ling, Central Daily News (Taipei, Taiwan), 1971, and *A Floating Milky Way,* edited by Ya Hsun, Lian Chin Publishing (Taipei, Taiwan), 1990. Also contributor to journals and periodicals, including *World, Weekly, World Journal, China Times Weekly, United Daily, Central Daily News, China Daily, China Weekly, Ramble, American Chinese Forum, Nineties, Journal of Studies of Japanese Aggression against China,* and *Journal of Oriental Studies.*

WORK IN PROGRESS: Research on the Nanking Safety Zone during the Rape of Nanking, 1937-38; *The Journey of Winter Plum and Her Sisters* (tentative title), "a novel based on the turbulent life of my mother and her peers through China's social, cultural, and economic upheaval and endless wars."

SIDELIGHTS: Hua-linh Hu told *CA:* "Ever since I was a little girl, I dreamed of being a novelist someday. Because of my parents' staunch opposition to permitting their eldest daughter to be a 'starving writer' and the grueling schedule of the Chinese education system, I had no courage or chance to test the water (turn my childhood dream into reality), even on a small scale. It was not until 1971, after I completed my doctorate in history at the University of Colorado and stayed home to nurture my toddler son that I began to write short stories. I wrote mostly about the bittersweet experiences of the Chinese students who came to the States to pursue their dreams; their sufferings, paradoxes, loves, and successes became my favorite subjects. Although I only wrote off and on, I found self-fulfillment and satisfaction in writing, and I often cried and laughed with the characters I created in my stories.

"In 1991, one day, as I was doing research for a paper on the Rape of Nanking and reading the proceedings of the International Military Tribunal for the Far East after World War II, I found an eye-catching written statement submitted to the tribunal by Mrs. Tsen Shui-fang, the director of dormitories of Ginling (Women's) College in Nanking during the Rape. In the statement, it claimed the Ginling campus was fortunate to have a 'foreign lady in charge,' Miss Vautrin, to protect the women refugees on the campus. Shortly thereafter, I read that Ko Chi, in his eyewitness account *Blood and Tears: Records of the Fallen Capital,* commented on how courageous an American professor at Ginling, Miss Huang, was to keep the Japanese soldiers from raping women refugees. It was not until I finished reading a four-page section on 'Miss Hua' in Hsu Chi-ken's book *The Great Nanking Massacre: Testimonies of the Eyewitnesses* that I realized Miss Vautrin, Miss Huang, and Miss Hua were the same person.

"I became interested in Miss Vautrin's life and developed respect for the unsung heroine. I wanted to tell the world about her heroic story and her eyewitness account of Chinese women's suffering during the Rape of Nanking. Subsequently I began my long quest for materials on Vautrin's life. I searched through eyewitness accounts or memories, documents, and writings by the authorities on the Rape. All I could find was a limited amount of material about Vautrin's protection of the Chinese women during that period, far from adequate to write an article. Then in 1994, on a most unexpected occasion, I learned that Vautrin's diary was deposited at Yale University and her niece, Mrs. Emma Lyon, was still alive. Finally I was able to acquire Vautrin's diary and correspondence, interview Mrs. Lyon, and visit Vautrin's birthplace, alma mater, and grave-site. In April of 1997, the Chinese edition of my book was published by the reputable Chiu Ko Publishing Company in Taiwan and excerpted by the leading newspaper on the island, the *United Daily*. Response to the biography was overwhelming.

"After publication of the Chinese version of my book, many Americans and Chinese—from scholars to college students and housewives—told me that Miss Vautrin's story should be told to a large audience and encouraged me to translate it into English. Some of these were people I had not even met, but their encouragement moved me. So I translated the book into English and rewrote many sections. I studied additional sources published after the book appeared in Chinese, such as the Chinese translation of *Rabe's Diary* (originally penned in German), *American Missionary Eyewitnesses to the Nanking Massacre*, edited by Martha Smalley, and *The Rape of Nanking: The Forgotten Holocaust of World War II* by Iris Chang. I also added extensive materials on historical background and missionary activities in China. Further, Mrs. Lyon provided me with more valuable pictures of her aunt, Minnie Vautrin, for use in the English version.

"In April, 2000, the English version of my book was published. I hope my book will encourage more scholars to do further research on Miss Vautrin and other righteous foreigners who protected Chinese refugees during the Rape of Nanking. I wish the courage of Miss Vautrin will be remembered in the hearts of our generation and the hearts of our children and their children. I wish the Nanking holocaust will never repeat itself in any place on this earth."

BIOGRAPHICAL/CRITICAL SOURCES:

PERIODICALS

Booklist, March 15, 2000, p. 1295.
Central Daily News (Taipei, Taiwan), December 8, 1981; March 26-April 1, 1982; April 8, 1997.
China Daily, July 7, 1997.
China News, May 11, 1997.

China Times, February 27, 1997; April 8, 1997; July 17, 1997.
Chinese American Forum, April, 2000, pp. 15-18.
Chiu Ko Magazine, April 7, 1997.
Li Pao, April 8, 1997.
Library Journal, March 1, 2000, p. 108.
People's Daily (overseas edition), December 4, 2000.
People's Livelihood News, April 8, 1997; May 3, 1998.
Japan Time, July 25, 2000.
Journal Star, April 10, 2000.
Pantagraph, April 10, 2000.
United Daily, February 18, 1997; April 1-2, 1997; April 8, 1997.
World Journal, March 2, 1997.
World Weekly, December 4, 1994.

*   *   *

HULTBERG, Peer 1935-

PERSONAL: Born November 8 (one source says November 18), 1935, in Vangede, Denmark. *Education:* Attended Viborg Cathedral School, 1953, and Copenhagen University, 1959; received Ph.D. from University of London, 1969; further study at C. G. Jung Institute (Zurich), 1978. *Avocational interests:* Polish language and literature.

ADDRESSES: Home—Isestrasse. 45, Hamburg 20144 Germany. *Agent*—Leonhardt & Høier Literary Agency, Studiestræde 35, 1455 Copenhagen K, Denmark.

CAREER: Dramatist, novelist, author of short stories, and translator, c. 1964—. Lecturer in Polish at University of London, 1967-68, and at Copenhagen University, 1968-73. Certified Jungian psychologist.

AWARDS, HONORS: Critics' Award, 1992; Nordic Council Prize for Literature, 1993; Danish Fund for the Endowment of the Arts lifelong subsidy, 1993.

WRITINGS:

(Translator from Polish to Danish, and author of foreword) *From Chopin's Correspondence,* Hasselbalchs Culture Library, 1964.
Mytologisk landskab med Daphnes forvandling (title means "Mythological Landscape with the Transformation of Daphne"), Arena (Copenhagen, Denmark), 1966, 2nd edition, Lindhardt og Ringhof, (Copenhagen, Denmark), 1993.
(Translator from Polish to Danish) Witold Gombrowicz, *Ferdydurke,* Fredensborg (Copenhagen, Denmark), 1967.

Desmond!, Arena, 1968.

The High Prose Style of Storyteller Waclawa Berenta, Zaklad Narodny Press, (Wroclaw) 1969.

Requiem, Arena, 1985, 3rd edition, Gyldendal, 1993.

Slagne vej : fortællinger (title means "Beaten Tracks: Stories"), Gyldendal, 1988.

Præludier, Gyldendal, 1989, 3rd edition, 1993.

(Translator into Polish and adapter) Søren Kierkegaard, *Dnevnik obol'stitelja: instsenirovka* (title means "The Seducer's Diary") Slavic Booksellers, 1990.

Fjernt fra Viborg (title means "Far From Viborg"), illustrated by Alfreed Wäspi, Nørhaven (Copenhagen, Denmark), 1991.

Byen og verden : roman i hundrede tekster (title means "The City and the World"), Lindhardt og Ringhof, 1992, 3rd edition, 1994.

Kronologi : prosa 1964-1994, Lindhardt og Ringhof, 1995.

Contributor to books, including *Texts from the End of the '60s: A Prose Anthology,* edited by Vagn Lundbye, Borgens Billigbogs Bibliotek (Copenhagen, Denmark), 1969; *Narcissism and the Text: Studies in Literature and the Psychology of Self,* edited by Layton and Shapiro, New York University Press, 1986; *Viborg's Brick Cathedral School: Texts From and About a Time in Viborg,* by Johannes Jensen, Viborg Cathedral School, 1993; and *Historier med humor: fra Ewald til Møllehave* (title means "Stories with Humor: from Ewald to Møllehave"), edited by Ejgil Søholm, Sesam, 1994. Also contributor to various journals, including *Polish Literary History and Criticism.*

DRAMA

De Skrøbelige (title means "The Weak and the Frail"), Lindhardt og Ringhof, 1998.

Fædra, Lindhardt og Ringhof, 2000.

Kunstgreb, (title means "Artifice"), Lindhardt og Ringhof, 2000.

SIDELIGHTS: In his acceptance speech after receiving the Nordic Council's prize for literature in 1992, Peer Hultberg said, "It seems to me that the author's task in our day, both as an artist and as a human being, is to turn his attention to the area where he is the true expert—the nature of Man." Hultberg, who is a Jungian psychoanalyst as well as an author, has made the study of human nature a central theme in his life. According to some critics, Hultberg is able to examine the people he writes about from a distance and, at the same time, in close-ups.

As critic Poul Borum, wrote in *Ekstra Bladet* in 1985, in reference to Hultberg's book, *Requiem,* "Imagine a snapshot of a huge crowd of people. Hultberg provides each individual in this picture with a voice." *Requiem* is a compilation of 537 monologues, or as Borum calls them, "537 pain spots." The motifs are fear, murder, humiliation, ridicule, sadomasochistic pain, and also an ever-present love. In the long run, the impression is one of a shimmering, painful, crazy-talking world and one is bound to meet oneself somewhere in the text.

Critic Erik Skyum-Nielsen, writing in *Information,* pointed out in his review of Hultberg's 1992 book, *Byen og verden,* "the reader meets them all: man and woman, old and young, rich and poor, spread like a fan—right from the fanatically normal to the power-hungry and rabidly perverse." The scrutiny takes place with non-judgmental detachment, the critic points out: "It is often difficult to distinguish between them, for irrespective of the kind of human fate dealt with, Hultberg's omniscient narrator retains the same elegance and coolness."

Hultberg's books are very different in form and tone, but they all deal with the human condition. Hultberg the analyst/author splinters and fragments the individual. In doing so, according to Werner Lewrenz in *Die Horen: Journal of Literature, Art and Critique,* he is quite atypical of Danish literature, but instead places himself in the ranks of European modernism along with Samuel Beckett, James Joyce and T. S. Eliot.

In his 1989 novel, *Preludier,* Hultberg uses a combination of memories, dreams, legends and anecdotes to tell the story of the French-Polish musical prodigy Frederic Chopin. The book is both the story of Chopin's childhood and a tale of childhood in general. Hultberg weaves together Chopin's view of his world with that world's view of Chopin. What Hultberg shows is a very ordinary little boy, with all the concerns of a little boy, and the awakening of a great artist with an artist's view of music and the life around him.

Critic Thorkild Nyholm in *Litteraturmagasinet Standart* described Hultberg as "one of the greatest linguistic virtuosi in Danish." Speaking of Hultberg's book *Slagne vej,* Nyholm said that the author, "Entirely without affectation, but stubbornly insisting that the words must be used as artistic raw material, he modulates his Danish language into long, rhythmical, melodious passages which can really most fittingly be compared with the best in modern poetry." However, Nyholm pointed out, Hultberg is not a poet and "his texts are not prose poems." Instead, the critic observed that behind the harmony of the language, "lies the story of life's own, existential progression as it unfolds before the personal, interior mirror of the individual consciousness."

Slagne vej is a collection of stories and vignettes of individuals, settings and events in America. The obscure characters are made even more anonymous and obscure by being referred to as "she" or "he" and being placed in ambiguous situations in unmemorable settings. The works are all very different in their form and unique in their tone, but they all deal with, or have as their driving force, guilt and shame, in a universe where only death can resolve that pain.

Does that mean Hultberg is the novelist of death and pessimism? Speaking at the Nordic Council Award ceremony, he said no. For him, it is rather a question of seeing the world around him exactly as it is. "I am often, if not accused of being a pessimist, nevertheless seen as having a somber view of life. I have always found it difficult to accept this view. I am much more inclined to the belief that my task, the task of literature and of an author, is as far as possible to reach a view of humanity and produce a human portrait without illusion."

BIOGRAPHICAL/CRITICAL SOURCES:

BOOKS

Encyclopedia of World Literature in the Twentieth Century, St. James Press (Detroit, MI), 1999.
Jensen, Johannes, *Viborg's Brick Cathedral School: Texts From and About a Time in Viborg,* Viborg Cathedral School, 1993.

PERIODICALS

Die Horen: Journal for Literature, Art and Critique, Volume 38, 1993, pp. 163-169.
Ekstra Bladet, October 18, 1985.
Information, February 3, 1993.
Litteraturmagasinet Standart, number 2, 1998.
Scandinavian Studies, summer, 1999, pp. 207-219.
World Literature Today, spring, 1989, pp. 314-315; autumn, 1990, p. 647.

OTHER

Danish Literature Information Center, http://www.literaturnet.dk/ (October 28, 2000).
Det Kongelige Bibliotek (The Royal Library), http://www.kb.dk/ (October 28, 2000).
Litteraturmagasinet Standart, http://www.statsbib lioteket.dk/ (October 28, 2000).*

HUMPHREYS, Richard Stephen   1942-

PERSONAL: Born August 11, 1942, in Hutchinson, KS; married in 1964. *Education:* Amherst College, B.A., 1964; University of Michigan—Ann Arbor, M.A., 1966, Ph.D., 1969.

ADDRESSES: Office—Department of History, University of California Santa Barbara, Santa Barbara, CA 93106; fax: 805-893-8795. *E-mail*—humphreys@ history.uscb.edu.

CAREER: Medieval Islamic historian; assistant professor, Arabic history, State University of New York—Buffalo, 1969-75; associate historian, American University of Beirut, 1972-73; National Endowment for Humanities younger humanist fellow, 1972-73; Social Sciences Resource Counsel Fellow, 1971, 1972-73, and 1977-78; assistant professor, 1981-82; visiting assistant professor of history, 1975-77; visiting associate professor, Newar Eastern language and civilization, University of Chicago, Chicago, IL, 1978-80; Institute for Advanced Study, Princeton, NJ, 1980-81; associate professor of history, University of Wisconsin, Madison, WI, from 1982; visiting fellow, Princeton University, 1982; American Council of Learned Societies fellow, 1982; professor of history and Islamic Studies at the University of California—Santa Barbara.

MEMBER: American Oriental Society; Middle Eastern Studies Association of North America; Middle Eastern Institute.

WRITINGS:

From Saladin to the Mongols: The Ayyubids of Damascus, 1193-1260, State University of New York Press (Albany, NY), 1977.
Islamic History: A Framework for Inquiry, Bibliotheca Islamica (Minneapolis, MN), 1988.
Tradition and Innovation in Late Antiquity, University of Wisconsin Press (Madison, WI), 1989.
Between Memory and Desire: The Middle East in a Troubled Age, Princeton University Press (Princeton, NJ), 1991.

SIDELIGHTS: Medieval Islamic historian Richard Stephen Humphreys has focused his studies on Islamic political institutions, Islamic architecture, and Arabic historiography. He was born August 11, 1942, in Hutchinson, Kansas, and married in 1964. After graduating from Amherst College with a B.A. in 1964 he earned an M.A. (1966) and Ph.D. (1969) at the University of Michigan, Ann Arbor. He began his professional career as an assistant professor of Arabic history at the State University of New York, Buffalo in 1969. He has since taught at the Newar Eastern language and civilization at the University of Chicago, the University of Wisconsin, Madison, and currently teaches history and Islamic studies at the University of California, Santa Barbara. He has been a Social Sciences Resource Counsel Fellow, a National Endowment for Humanities younger humanist fellow, an American Council of Learned Societies fellow, a visiting fellow at Princeton University, and an associate historian at the American University of Beirut. Humphreys is a member of the American Oriental Society, the Middle Eastern Studies Association of North America, and the Middle Eastern Institute.

Humphreys continued his mentor Andrew Ehrenkreutz's work with the history *From Saladin to the Mongols: The Ayyubids of Damascus, 1193-1260* (1977). Ehrenkreutz had written a biography of Saladin, and Humphreys begins his history of the medieval Ayyubid dynasty with the same leader. The Ayyubids controlled the Fertile Crescent for almost 100 years. Humphreys's history focuses on the dynasty's military history, and the intellectual and moral context of Ayyubid politics. He asserts that the principled dynasty Saladin founded deteriorated through familial power struggles and fractions within the military; it was this infighting, more than the invasion of the Mongols, which brought about the dynasty's downfall. Humphreys relied on Arabic narrative sources, diplomatic, numismatic and epigraphic evidence, and current research for his monograph. A reviewer for *Choice* wrote, "Humphreys sticks close to his sources and, where they fail him, ventures interpretative hypotheses that are plausible and convincing. Because the book is well written, the confusing panorama of events never totally overwhelms the reader." But Michael W. Dols, in *The American Historical Review,* disagreed with Humphreys's thesis that "a profound transformation of the structure of political life occurred in Egypt and Syria in the first half of the thirteenth century," and that "a decisive change took place both in the territorial relations between Egypt and Syria and in the political goals of the Ayyubid elite."

From Saladin to the Mongols was written for scholars; the same is true of Humphreys's second book, *Islamic History: A Framework for Inquiry* (1988). This advanced Islamic history, ranging from c.600 to c.1500, begins with a detailed summary of the currently available bibliographic resources. The ten essays focus on significant difficulties in interpreting and analyzing medieval Islamic history. As Humphreys writes in the introduction, "these chapters try to show how this field can be developed and even transformed, as it must be if the study of the Islamic past is ever to take its rightful place in the study of human societies and cultures." A critic for the London *Times Literary Supplement* concurred, adding, "the chapter on the origins of the Islamic community demonstrates just how resistant this crucial field of study is to efforts to make more of it than the historiographical impasse it has become. As to Humphrey's wider message, it is not only timely but expressed with great subtlety and clarity." And Bernard Lewis wrote in the *New York Review of Books,* "Professor Humphreys's book, as it stands, will henceforth be indispensable to teachers of Middle Eastern history, invaluable to serious students in the field, and extremely useful to scholars whose fields of study abut on medieval Middle Eastern Islam."

Humphreys's third book is accessible to scholars and non-scholars alike. The ten "interlocking essays" in *Between Memory and Desire: The Middle East in a Troubled Age* (1991) describe Middle Eastern political and social discourse and provide analysis of Islamic polity. Humphreys covers topics such as Islamic human rights, the concept of *jihad,* Economic growth, the role of women in Islam, national movements, Islamic human rights philosophy, and the diversity within the religion. The purpose of the book is to provide readers interested in world current events with a better understanding of the Middle East in all its vast complexity. "People know a lot of things that aren't so," Humphreys writes, and he has undertaken the task of correcting misconceptions. Max Rodenbeck praised the book in the *New York Times Book Review* writing, "A wealth of observations . . . place Humphreys's work in the best tradition of writing of foreign cultures. Objective yet sympathetic, scholarly yet accessible, his book ends up revealing as much about our own society as about those is describes."

BIOGRAPHICAL/CRITICAL SOURCES:

PERIODICALS

American Historical Review, December, 1978.
Choice, June, 1978.
New York Review of Books, December 5, 1991; June 13, 1999.
Times Literary Supplement, February 7, 1992.*

HUNTER, Marjorie 1922-2001

OBITUARY NOTICE—See index for *CA* sketch: Born June 2, 1922, in Bethany, WV; died of leukemia, April 10, 2001, in Washington, DC. Journalist. Hunter, a journalism pioneer, was the first woman from the *New York Times* Washington bureau to cover more than the schedule of the first lady. Hunter graduated in 1942 from Elon College where he father was a professor, and promptly took a job at the *Raleigh News and Observer,* where she was a member of the editorial staff until 1949. She worked briefly in Texas before joining the *Winston-Salem Journal* and was hired by the *Times* in 1961. Hunter did cover the first lady, but grew bored with that beat and her editor eventually assigned her to cover Congress and other political news. She was elected president of the Women's National Press Club in 1969 and at the time was ineligible for membership in The National Press Club, which didn't admit women until two years later. Hunter retired in 1986 and was elected to the North Carolina Journalism, Advertising and Public Relations Hall of Fame in 1992.

OBITUARIES AND OTHER SOURCES:

PERIODICALS

New York Times, April 11, 2001, p. A25.
Washington Post, April 14, 2001, p. B7.

*   *   *

HUSS, Sally 1940-

PERSONAL: Born June 8, 1940, in Long Beach, CA; daughter of Laurren (an oil refinery manager) and Marie (a homemaker) Moore; married Marv Huss (CEO of Sally Huss, Inc.), December 31, 1976; children: Mike. *Ethnicity:* "Caucasian." *Education:* Attended Occidental College, 1958-61; University of California, degree in fine arts. *Avocational interests:* Tennis, golf.

ADDRESSES: Office—1025 Prospect, La Jolla, CA 92037. *E-mail*—mike@sallyhuss.com.

CAREER: Professional tennis player, including member of U.S. Wightman Cup Team, 1959; performed research and production work on several films for Samuel Goldwyn, Jr., beginning in 1963; Paul Simon's music publishing company, Beverly Hills, operator, beginning in 1967; played competitive senior tennis, beginning in 1981; motivational speaker, beginning in 1981; as painter, affiliated with local art shows and street fairs, beginning in 1985; Sally Huss Gallery, Laguna Beach, CA (and later other locations), founder, 1987—.

AWARDS, HONORS: National and Wimbledon Junior Tennis Champion, 1958; winner, U.S. National Clay Court Championship (tennis), 1959.

WRITINGS:

How to Play Power Tennis with Ease, Harcourt (New York, NY), 1976.
(Illustrator) Bob Carlisle, *Butterfly Kisses* (children's book), Tommy Nelson, 1997.
(Author and illustrator) *I Love You with All My Hearts* (children's book), Tommy Nelson, 1998.
The Happy Book (inspirational), Ten Speed/Celestial Arts, 1999.
The Happy Day Book, Celestial Arts, in press.
The Happy Kids Book (children's book), Tricycle, in press.

WORK IN PROGRESS: Thirty children's books.

SIDELIGHTS: Sally Huss told *CA* that by 1999 the businesses affiliated with herself had sold more than ten million pieces of gift art; and the sales volume of Sally Huss designed products exceeded five million dollars. Huss indicated that by the year 2000 the twenty-seventh Sally Huss Gallery opened, and the third wallpaper collection under her name was released as "Sally Huss' Happy Home." Huss informed *CA* that, in 1997, she was commissioned to create a special work of art—titled "Happy Child"—as a fiftieth birthday present for Hilary Clinton.

*   *   *

HUTCHINSON, Gloria 1939-

PERSONAL: Born February 8, 1939, in Plattsburgh, NY; daughter of Frank I. (a cook) and Pearl I. (a seamstress) Capone; married David I. Hutchinson, May 4, 1963; children: David L. *Education:* State University of New York College at Plattsburgh, B.A. (magna cum laude), 1967, M.A. (with honors), 1989. *Politics:* Independent. *Religion:* Roman Catholic. *Avocational interests:* Travel, snowshoeing, photography.

ADDRESSES: Home and Office—H.C. 67, Box 525, Dixfield, ME 04224.

CAREER: Writer and editor, 1979—. Director of retreats and workshops; participant in media programs and videotape productions.

MEMBER: Greenpeace, Pax Christi USA, Defenders of Wildlife, Network.

WRITINGS:

Mary and Inner Healing, St. Anthony Messenger Press (Cincinnati, OH), 1980.

Six Ways to Pray from Six Great Saints, St. Anthony Messenger Press (Cincinnati, OH), 1981.

Jesus' Saving Questions, St. Anthony Messenger Press (Cincinnati, OH), 1983.

Jesus and John: A Book about Friends—for Friends, St. Anthony Messenger Press (Cincinnati, OH), 1986.

Christ Encounters: A Journal Retreat, Ave Maria Press (Notre Dame, IN), 1988.

Praying the Rosary: New Reflections on the Mysteries, St. Anthony Messenger Press (Cincinnati, OH), 1991.

Praying the Way: Reflections on the Stations of the Cross, St. Anthony Messenger Press (Cincinnati, OH), 1994.

The Heart's Healing Journey: Seeking Desert Wisdom, St. Anthony Messenger Press (Cincinnati, OH), 1995.

A Retreat with Gerard Manley Hopkins and Hildegard of Bingen: Turning Pain into Power, St. Anthony Messenger Press (Cincinnati, OH), 1995.

A Retreat with Teresa of Avila: Living by Holy Wit, St. Anthony Messenger Press (Cincinnati, OH), 1999.

Author of textbooks and teachers' materials. Creator and editor of a series of retreat books. Contributor to periodicals.

WORK IN PROGRESS: Reel Spirit Guides: 25 Popular Videos to Light Your Spiritual Path.

SIDELIGHTS: Gloria Hutchinson told *CA:* "I zigzagged my way into religion and spirituality via various side roads in the secular press (as a family page editor, investigative reporter, feature story writer), but after a brief experience of living a monastic life, I was lured into writing as contemplation. The bait was a best-seller by a Trappist monk named Thomas Merton, and I was one of a few zillion young writers whose lives were radically changed by *The Seven Storey Mountain.* Merton's unexpected success revealed a spiritual hunger which has yet to be sated in the soul of America. His discovery that writing was not a distraction from prayer but the stuff of prayer itself intoxicated me with its possibilities for unifying my life: writing equals prayer equals witness to those who seek it. My gut-level need for silence and solitude had led me into the monastery, but Merton made it clear that contemplatives ply their trade wherever the Spirit plants them. Writers, like monks and hermits, survive by staying in touch with the God who lodges within. Once when Merton was asked what he did all day, he responded, 'What I do is live. How I pray is breathe.' God knows I may never reach that degree of contemplative union. I do know that if I were not free to write of the Word I find in scripture and creation and the profoundly inexplicable lives of those around me, getting out of bed in the morning would be too much to ask of me."

*   *   *

INBAR, Efraim   1947-

PERSONAL: Born January 22, 1947, in Romania; son of Shlomo (an accountant) and Clara Inbar; married, 1980; wife's name Rivka (a teacher); children: five. *Education:* Hebrew University, B.A., 1973; University of Chicago, M.A., 1976, Ph.D., 1981. *Religion:* Jewish.

ADDRESSES: Office—Barilan University, Ramat-Gan, Israel 52900; fax: 972-2-5359195.

CAREER: Barilan University, Israel, university professor. *Military service:* "Private paratrooper."

WRITINGS:

Outcast Countries in the World Community (Monograph Series in World Affairs), University of Denver Press (Denver, CO), 1985.

War and Peace in Israeli Politics: Labor Party Positions on National Security, The Leonard Davis Institute Studies in International Politics, Lynne Rienner (Boulder, CO), 1991.

Yitzhak Rabin and Israel's National Security, Wilson Center and Johns Hopkins University Press (Baltimore, MD), 1999.

(Editor) *The Politics and Economics of Defense Industries,* Frank Cass (London, England), 1998.

WORK IN PROGRESS: Research on Turkish-Israeli relations.

ISAAC, Megan (Lynn) 1966-

PERSONAL: Born July 17, 1966, in IL; daughter of Walter James and Barbara Jo Isaac; married William Dale Harrison, 1998. *Ethnicity:* "White"; *Education:* Lawrence University, B.A., 1988; University of California-Los Angeles, M.A. and Ph.D., 1994.

ADDRESSES: Office—1 University Plaza, Youngstown State University, Youngstown, OH 44555. *E-mail*—mlisaac@cc.ysu.edu.

CAREER: Educator and author. Youngstown State University, Youngstown, OH, associate professor of English, 1994—.

MEMBER: Modern Language Association, Shakespeare Association of America, NCTE, Society of Children's Book Writers and Illustrators, Phi Beta Kappa.

WRITINGS:

Heirs to Shakespeare (nonfiction), Heinemann, 2000.

Contributor to journals, including *Lion & Unicorn, Studies in the Novel, Voice of Youth Advocates,* and *ALAN Review.*

WORK IN PROGRESS: Research on young adult literature, Shakespeare studies.

SIDELIGHTS: "I wrote about Shakespeare's plays and young adult literature because I believed both genres were under-appreciated," Megan Isaac told *CA.* "Shakespeare is too often viewed as difficult and elitist literature. Young adult novels are too often viewed as simplistic and undemanding. I wanted to show how canonical and contemporary literature both participate in a long tradition of artistic dialogue. I wanted to show how Shakespeare's characters and themes influence young adult literature and how many young adult authors use their novels to respond to Shakespeare's plays."

*   *   *

ISAACS, Jeremy (Israel) 1932-

PERSONAL: Born September 28, 1932; son of Isidore Isaacs and Sara Jacobs; married Tamara Weinreich, 1958 (died 1986); married Gillian Widdicombe, 1988; children: (first marriage) two. *Education:* Studied at Glasgow Academy, Merton College, Oxford. *Avocational interests:* Reading, walking.

ADDRESSES: Office—Jeremy Isaacs Productions, 11 Bowling Green Lane, London EC1R 0BG, England.

CAREER: Performing company executive and writer. Granada TV, producer, *What the Papers Say, All Our Yesterdays,* 1958; Associate Rediffusion, producer, *This Week,* 1963; BBC-TV, producer, *Panorama,* 1965; Associated Rediffusion, features contributor, 1967; Thames TV, 1968-78 (director of programs, 1974-78); Channel 4 TV Co., CEO, 1981-88; Royal Opera House, general director, 1988-95 (director 1985-97); Jeremy Isaacs Productions, director. Producer: *The World at War,* 1974, *A Sense of Freedom,* ITV, *Ireland,* a television documentary, BBC, *Battle for Crete,* N.Z. TV; co-executive producer, *Cold War* (epic documentary), CNN; British Film Institute, governor, 1979—, chair of the Production Board, 1979-81; Edinburgh TV Festival, James MacTaggart Memorial Lecturer, 1979.

MEMBER: British Academy of Film and TV Arts; British Film Institute; Garrick Club.

AWARDS, HONORS: Desmond Davis award for outstanding creative contribution on TV, 1972; George Polk Memorial Award, 1973; Cyril Bennett Award, 1982; Lord Willis award for distinguished service to TV, 1985; Dr. h.c. Council for National Academy Awards, 1987; Fellow, Royal TV Society; honorary degrees from the University of Strathclyde, 1983 and the University of Bristol, 1988; knighted by Queen Elizabeth II "for services to broadcasting and the arts;" has won Emmy Awards; received France's Commander of Arts and Letters and L'Ordre National du Merit awards.

WRITINGS:

Storm Over 4: A Personal Account, Weidenfeld and Nicolson, 1989.
(Author of introduction) John Lazarus, *The Opera Handbook,* G. K. Hall, 1990.
(With Taylor Downing) *Cold War: An Illustrated History, 1945-1991,* Little, Brown (Boston, MA), 1998.
Never Mind the Moon, Bantam (New York, NY), 1999.

SIDELIGHTS: As the CEO of England's innovative Channel 4 for nearly a decade, Jeremy Isaacs is familiar with controversy. He has worked as a television news producer, a features contributor, and a documentary filmmaker. Isaacs chronicles his years at the head of

Channel 4 in his memoir, *Storm Over 4: A Personal Account.* An advocate of free expression, Isaacs worked to air challenging programs, often in defiance of conservative opponents who sought to censor him. The book title comes from the ruckus journalists raised every time an especially controversial program appeared on Channel 4. Headlines such as "Storm over IRA film" or "Party for gays starts new row" would appear in the papers. Isaacs was nominated for director-general of the British Broadcasting Corporation, but was rejected because of his controversies. Isaacs, nevertheless, is known for his influence on British television. Phillip Whitehead wrote in the *Times Literary Supplement* that "Channel 4 found new ways to entertain, as well as inform. It did more for the British film industry than all of British television had done in the previous quarter-century. It made new sports popular, and turned some serious minority viewing into an intellectual spectator sport."

After leaving Channel 4, Isaacs was hired as general director of the Royal Opera House. There, he made a six-part documentary film titled *The House,* hoping viewers would see how hard the artists worked and help fund the renovation of the Covent Garden theater. His plan, however, backfired. Audiences became more fascinated with the artists' and administrators' boorish behavior. Isaacs left, and a planned seventh part of the documentary was canceled; the new chairman, Sir Colin Southgate, banned cameras from the building and would not let his staff participate.

Shortly after this disappointment, Isaacs collaborated with Taylor Downing to produce a CNN documentary series, *Cold War,* and to co-write a companion book, *Cold War: An Illustrated History, 1945-1991.* Isaacs and Downing describe how the Cold War evolved after World War II. They also examine the effects of the Cold War on literature, art, film, and pop culture. Critics mostly praised the documentary, though some said it was biased toward the Soviet Union. Harvey Wasserman wrote in *Nation,* "With more than 500 interviews, 8,500 archival and newsreel films from nearly three dozen countries . . . and several current and former heads of state putting it in perspective for us, it is a neat but weighty capsule of recent history." Many writers, however, dismissed the companion book as little more than a coffee-table book. Michael Harrington wrote in his review for the *Times Literary Supplement* that with its "undistinguished text" and "predictably banal opinions," *Cold War* "very much belongs in the category of something commissioned by a publisher to accompany a television production, with its dutiful, broadly reliable narrative and its absence of passion or engagement." A *Kirkus Reviews* critic who said the book illuminates little in diplomacy and national strategy, defended it for casual readers: "Those requiring an accessible survey of the causes and effects of the Cold War need search no further."

BIOGRAPHICAL/CRITICAL SOURCES:

PERIODICALS

Kirkus Reviews, August 1, 1998.
Nation, October 19, 1998.
Times Literary Supplement, December 8-14, 1989; January 22, 1999.

OTHER

CNN—Cold War: About the Series, http://asia.cnn.com/SPECIALS/ (September 28, 2001).*

J

JACK, Belinda E(lizabeth)

PERSONAL: Female; children: three. *Education:* Oxford University, Ph.D. in French and Francophone literatures.

ADDRESSES: Office—Modern Languages, Oxford University, 37 & 47 Wellington Square, Oxford OX1 2JF, England.

CAREER: Researcher, writer, and teacher of French at Christ Church, Oxford.

WRITINGS:

Negritude and Literary Criticism: The History and Theory of "Negro-African" Literature in French, Greenwood Press (Westport, CT), 1996.
Francophone Literatures: An Introductory Survey, Oxford University Press (New York, NY), 1996.
George Sand: A Woman's Life Writ Large, Knopf (New York, NY), 2000.

SIDELIGHTS: Belinda E. Jack received her doctorate from Oxford University, and published her doctoral dissertation soon after, through the academic Greenwood Press in Westport, Connecticut. In her book, *Negritude and Literary Criticism,* Jack advanced the premise that the "typological terms of secondary discourses are not simply descriptive terms; they also operate explicitly or implicitly as criteria of evaluation." In other words, the categories in which critics include (or from which they exclude) writers can have a powerful impact on how (or even whether) those writers will be later viewed. The main subjects of her study are Lilyan Kesteloot's *Black Writers in French: The Birth of a Literature* (1961), and its 1974 translation by Ellen

Conroy Kennedy called *Black Writers in French: A Literary History of Negritude.* These books have had an extremely powerful influence on how Francophone writing by authors of African descent is thought about today. As A. James Arnold of the University of Virginia wrote for the *African American Review,* Jack's "analytical method seeks to point up the ideological investment that scholars have made in their construction and dissemination of this relatively new field of inquiry."

As a case in point, Arnold observed, Jack reevaluates the work of the Martinican poet Gilbert Gratiant, whom Kesteloot "excluded . . . from the emerging canon she was the first to describe on the grounds that Gratiant failed to meet her test as a protest writer." Arnold went on to write that Jack uses later appreciations of Gratiant to show just "how wrong-headed this appreciation of Gratiant was." She demonstrates the intrinsic instability of the category of "Negritude" (a term that contains the concepts of black consciousness and black pride developed in the early and mid-twentieth centuries). According to Arnold, it "was the child of the last decades of French imperialism and its assimilationist doctrine . . . [but which was only adopted by the] English-speaking world in the 1960s, at the time of the Black Power Movement, when African independence was well underway." That instability is an outgrowth of the ways that different groups have used and understood the term in different racial and political contexts. Arnold added that Jack brings in little known documentation from obscure doctoral theses that help to clarify the "multiple inaccuracies disseminated by Kesteloot twenty years earlier and, alas, still frequently repeated today."

Jack's first book received a lengthy and admiring treatment from Arnold in the *African American Review,* although Arnold did feel obligated to point out errors in its bibliography that he felt might impede the work of future scholars. Still, Arnold concluded by stating that "Belinda Jack's book belongs in every college library." Its *Choice* review, while briefer, was similarly complimentary, stating that the book "offers a balanced view and raises legitimate questions about the validity of a homogenous interpretation of Francophone black culture and nationalism."

Jack also published *Francophone Literatures: An Introductory Survey* in 1996, which itself was subject to some of the same sorts of criticisms Jack leveled at Kesteloot and Kennedy. While *Choice* thoroughly approved of the new survey, calling it a "treasure of information about Francophone literatures around the globe, . . . [and a] stimulating and satisfying introductory survey," Adele King of Ball State University, who reviewed the book for *World Literature Today,* was more judicious in her praise. King praised the book's organization into four parts: Europe and North America, the Creole Islands, North Africa and the Near East, and sub-Saharan Africa and Madagascar. She especially praised Jack's demarcation of Francophonie as "descriptive of a subversive linguistic usage and one which denationalizes French," and her discussion of French as a "language of liberation" in North African countries where Arabic is the " 'language of tradition and a new oppressive conformism.' " King also termed Jack's "[d]iscussions of Quebec nationalism, of early colonial writing in sub-Saharan Africa, and the forms of Malagasy poetry . . . particularly valuable." But from there her review was devoted to what she saw as problems in the book, from lack of inclusiveness of certain areas, such as Southeast Asia, to her observation that "[t]oo often authors are praised mainly for winning literary prizes in France."

Jack's *George Sand: A Woman's Life Writ Large,* covers new territory for the author: the nineteenth century, and a famous French (rather than Francophone) writer. George Sand was a woman writer who took a man's name. Born Aurore Dupin in 1804, Sand was the daughter of an ex-prostitute who had been raised in poverty, Sophie-Victoire Delaborde, whom her father, a member of an aristocratic family, met while on military service in Milan. Dupin brought his wife home to live with his family after he and Delaborde married. Michele Roberts of the *Times Literary Supplement* wrote that "Sand's mother was highly emotional and difficult, though charming and beautiful, and was deemed unstable and unsuitable by the aristocratic family into which she had married." Matters became much worse when Sand's father died in a riding accident

when she was five years old. The tensions between her mother and paternal grandmother, Madame Dupin, were severe, and eventually led to Sand being removed from her mother's household. Roberts wrote that Jack's biography makes clear that "[a] sense of injustice, of being dominated, formed part of the traumas and losses of her childhood, which seem to have inflicted deep wounds. As an adult, Sand tried to heal these" through her devotion to revolutionary ideals, her romantic affairs, and "her exploration of the power struggles between men and women."

Sand became an extremely well known, and even a notorious, figure in Paris in the mid-nineteenth century. Besides many best-selling novels, she left a detailed historical record in the form of a lengthy autobiography and twenty-five volumes of letters. Her first marriage to Casimiar Dudevant broke apart when her children were still young, after Sand took up with Jules Sandeau. The end of her first marriage marked a turning point in her life—when she began to publish. In her review, Roberts remarked that this was the beginning of the "Sand legend: the only woman journalist on *Le Figaro,* cross-dressing in order to see rather than be seen, . . . falling in love with the actress Marie Dorval, becoming involved in politics, collecting a large group of friends ranging from distinguished men of letters to her beloved proletarian minor poets, an indulging in numerous love affairs." Among her contemporaries, Sand inspired mixed reactions. As Jack's biography recounts, the famous poet Baudelaire wrote of Sand that "The fact that some men have been able to become infatuated with that latrine is proof of the degradation of man this century." The novelist Flaubert was a close friend of Sand and said, "You had to know her as I knew her to realize how much of the feminine there was in this great man, the immensity of tenderness to be found in this genius." Her reputation as a cross-dresser and sexual profligate was countered by another—as the "good lady of Nohant" (her country estate) who would bring herbal remedies to the poor.

Jack's biography works through these contradictions. Michele Roberts, who reviewed the book for *Times Literary Supplement,* praised it highly: Jack's "biography works like a novel; it is structured as a narrative rich in metaphor, . . . its chapters carefully crafted to end like those in a classic serial with moments of cliff-hanging suspense." Roberts particularly notes Jack's talent in bringing readers' attention to Sand's novels, which have lost much of the critical success which first greeted them: "Jack's sympathetic rereading and spirited defense of George Sand's fiction sends one straight back to those ignored novels."

BIOGRAPHICAL/CRITICAL SOURCES:

BOOKS

Jack, Belinda E., *Negritude and Literary Criticism: The History and Theory of "Negro-African" Literature in French,* Greenwood Press (Westport, CT), 1996.

PERIODICALS

African American Review, summer, 1998, A. James Arnold, review of *Negritude and Literary Criticism: The History and Theory of "Negro-African" Literature in French,* pp. 336-337.
Choice, September, 1996, A. J. Guillaume, review of *Negritude and Literary Criticism: The History and Theory of "Negro-African" Literature in French,* p. 133; October, 1997, A. J. Guillaume, review of *Francophone Literatures: An Introductory Survey,* p. 303.
Times Literary Supplement, October 15, 1999, Michele Roberts, "Large-brained Chatelaine."
World Literature Today, spring, 1998, Adele King, review of *Francophone Literatures: An Introductory Survey.**

*   *   *

JACKSON, Joe   1954-

PERSONAL: Born August 11, 1954, in Burton-on-Trent, Staffordshire, England; son of Ron (a navy plasterer) and Vera (a homemaker; maiden name, Collins) Jackson; married and divorced twice. *Education:* Royal Academy of Music, London, earned Licentiate degree.

ADDRESSES: Agent—c/o Big Hassle Management, 150 Fifth Ave., Suite 1102, New York, NY 10011.

CAREER: Singer, songwriter, musician, composer, and author. Began as a piano player in the (British) National Youth Jazz Orchestra; vocalist for several bands, including Edward Bear, and Arms and Legs; piano player in clubs and bars, including the Portsmouth Playboy Club; musical director for Koffee 'n' Kreme (cabaret act). Under contract with A & M Records, 1978-90; Virgin Records, c. 1990-96.

AWARDS, HONORS: Nominee, Grammy Awards, for record of the year and best male pop vocal performance, and gold record, all for *Night and Day;* nominee, Grammy Awards, for *Steppin' Out: The Very Best*

of Joe Jackson and film music for *Mike's Murder* and *Tucker;* Grammy Award for Best Pop Instrumental Album, 2001, for *Symphony No. 1.*

WRITINGS:

Troubadours and Troublemakers: Ireland Now: A Culture Reclaimed, Blackwater Press (Tallaght, Dublin, Ireland), 1996.
(With Nanci Griffith) *Nanci Griffith's Other Voices: A Personal History of Folk Music,* Three Rivers Press (New York, NY), 1998.
A Cure for Gravity: A Musical Pilgrimage (memoir), Perseus/Public, 1999.

A Cure for Gravity was published in German.

MUSICAL RECORDINGS

Look Sharp, A & M, 1979.
I'm the Man, A & M, 1979.
Beat Crazy, A & M, 1980.
Joe Jackson's Jumpin' Jive, A & M, 1981.
Night and Day, A & M, 1982.
Mike's Murder (soundtrack to the film), A & M, 1983.
Body and Soul, A & M, 1984.
Shijin No Ie (title means "The House of the Poet"), IMAX, 1985.
Big World, A & M, 1986.
Will Power, A & M, 1987.
Tucker: The Man and His Dream (soundtrack to the film), A & M, 1988.
Live, 1980-86, A & M, 1988.
Blaze of Glory, A & M, 1989.
Queens Logic (soundtrack to the film), A & M, 1991.
Steppin' Out: The Very Best of Joe Jackson, A & M, 1991.
Laughter and Lust, Virgin Records, 1991.
Night Music, Virgin Records, 1994.
Greatest Hits, A & M, 1996.
This Is It! The A & M Years, A & M, 1997.
Heaven and Hell, Sony Classical, 1997.
Symphony No. 1, Sony Classical, 1999.
Summer In the City (live), Manticore, 1999.
Night and Day II, Manticore, 2000.

Also released *Tilt,* a three-song extended play recording in England, 1980, and *I'm the Man: The Classic Tracks, 1979-89,* 1995. Soundtracks include *Private Eye* (1987), *Interfilm - I'm Your Man* (1992), *Three of Hearts* (1993), *The White Cat* (1994), *Ironbound* (1995), and *Party of Five* (1996). Contributed tracks to *No Wave: An Album of a Lot of Different Groups,* A &

M, 1978, and *Propaganda,* 1979; contributed synthesizer playing to a track on *Escenas,* Elektra, 1985.

SIDELIGHTS: Joe Jackson is known as an eclectic musician, composer, singer, and songwriter. Educated in jazz and classical music at the Royal Academy of Music in London, Jackson's first solo recording, 1979's *Look Sharp,* was one of the first "New Wave" recordings to enjoy widespread popular success. This was quickly followed by *I'm the Man* later in 1979, and *Beat Crazy* in 1980, the first a top-40 hit in both the United States and Jackson's native England, and the second, with a reggae-influenced sound, nearly as successful. Jackson was commonly compared to Elvis Costello during this era of his career, for his edgy lyrics and smart, driven music. Then Jackson took a turn, the first of many, in his career, and began experimenting with swing-era jazz on *Jumpin' Jive* (1981), salsa and Latin-inflected percussion on *Night and Day* (1982), and the jazz and Latin inspired 1984 release *Body and Soul.* Ira Robbins, editor of the *Trouser Press Record Guide,* is quoted in *Entertainment Weekly* as saying: "What Jackson did after his early success was indulge what turned out to be an extremely superior musical intellect."

With the 1987 release *Will Power* Jackson began experimenting with ways to incorporate his knowledge of and love for classical music, a trend that became more obvious after he left A & M Records. In 1991 Jackson signed with Virgin Records and produced two theme-based recordings, *Laughter and Lust* in 1991, and *Night Music* in 1994, both of which feature significant contributions by other artists, such as Suzanne Vega and Maire Brennan. *Heaven and Hell,* released in 1997 by the Sony Classical label, was described as a blend of pop and classical styles, while his 1999 release *Symphony No. 1* is considered pure classical music.

In 1994, Jackson told Jim Bessman of *Billboard* magazine, "My roots are in classical music more than anything else. . . . But I make eclectic music because I'm an eclectic person, which most of us are these days. To me, it's the more natural and honest way to go, rather than to consciously make music in a specific genre. Anyway, I can't help it." But for some music critics, "it's easier to admire Jackson's adventurous, eclectic spirit than some of the fruit it bears," as Eric Levin put it in *People Weekly.* Throughout his musical career, Jackson has received mixed reviews for his risk-taking approach to making music which, especially in the 1990s, yielded creations that demanded a kind of careful listening unknown in the world of "Top 40" pop music. Similarly, Jackson's autobiography, *A Cure for*

Gravity: A Musical Pilgrimage, which focuses on the musician's early career, was deemed rewarding for those most likely to be willing to go on the ride Jackson wants to take them on. "Jackson presents a portrait of the artist as a young geek," wrote a reviewer in *Publishers Weekly.* The reviewer stated that the author spends much of the book detailing his experiences as a student of classical music, first at the Portsmouth Technical High School, then at the Royal Academy of Music in London. Jackson's success as a musician, starting with the 1979 release *Look Sharp,* is relegated to a few chapters at the end of the book. Reviewers singled out Jackson's prose, as well as the focus of his subject, for praise. Rosellen Brewer, writing for *Library Journal,* called *A Cure for Gravity* "an honest, gritty look inside the music business and the mind of a musician." *Booklist* contributor Mike Tribby called Jackson's autobiography "literate," noting, "how many other pop stars would bring up the second Shostakovich string quartet?"

BIOGRAPHICAL/CRITICAL SOURCES:

BOOKS

Almanac of Famous People, sixth edition, Gale (Detroit, MI), 1998.

PERIODICALS

Action Now, April, 1981, "Jamming," p. 42; January, 1982, Darin Hallstrom, review of *Jumpin' Jive,* p. 36.

Audio, December, 1981, Jon Tiven, Sally Tiven, review of *Jumpin' Jive,* p. 74; November, 1982, Michael Tearson, review of *Night and Day,* p. 26; January, 1984, Michael Tearson, review of *Mike's Murder* soundtrack, p. 38; July, 1984, Paulette Weiss, review of *Night and Day,* p. 76; July, 1986, Michael Tearson, review of *Big World,* p. 104; November, 1988, Michael Tearson, review of *Live, 1980-86,* p. 159.

Billboard, July 7, 1984, Len Epand, "Music Videos: Another View," p. 10; February 15, 1986, Steven Dupler, "Joe Jackson Cuts *'Big World'* Direct to Two-Track Digital," p. 42A; October 1, 1994, Jim Bessman, "Jackson Veers Toward Classical on Virgin Set," p. 10; August 2, 1997, p. 12.

Booklist, October 1, 1999, Mike Tribby, review of *A Cure for Gravity,* p. 333.

Consumers' Research Magazine, December, 1981, Robert Henschen, review of *Jumpin' Jive,* p. 37.

Down Beat, January, 1982, Steve Bloom, review of *Jumpin' Jive,* p. 31; August, 1985, "Auditions," p.

61; May, 1986, Bill Milkowski, "Joe Jackson's So-phisticated Pop," p. 20; May, 1986, Bill Milkowski and David Kershenbaum, "Joe Jackson: Live and in the Studio," p. 54.

Entertainment Weekly, October 7, 1994, Josef Woo-dard, review of *Night Music,* p. 79; August 2, 1996, Steven Mirkin, review of *Greatest Hits,* p. 59; September 12, 1997, Don Gordon, review of *Heaven and Hell,* p. 139; October 23, 1998, p. 92.

Esquire, December, 1982, Billy Altman, review of *Night and Day,* p. 134.

High Fidelity, October, 1981, Crispin Cioe, review of *Jumpin' Jive,* p. 98; March, 1984, Sam Sutherland, review of *Night and Day,* p. 58; July, 1986, Mark Moses, review of *Big World,* p. 74; September, 1988, Ken Richardson, "Joe Jackson: Live in Tokyo," and review of *Live, 1980-86,* p. 86.

Library Journal, August, 1999, Rosellen Brewer, review of *A Cure for Gravity,* p. 92.

Interview, May, 1991, Dimitri Ehrlich, "Joe Cool," p. 40.

Jet, August 28, 1980, "'Foolproof' Joe Jackson Gets Big Birthday Surprise," p. 24.

Los Angeles Magazine, March, 1982, "Joe Jackson's *Jumpin' Jive,*" p. 211.

Newsweek, March 14, 1983, "Joe Jackson's Sizzling Salsa," p. 68; May 26, 1986, Bill Barol, review of *Big World,* p. 72.

New York, December 14, 1981, Tom Bentkowski, review of *Jumpin' Jive,* p. 74.

People Weekly, October 25, 1982, p. 26; February 14, 1983, David Fricke, "How Different Is Joe Jackson's New Sound?," p. 53; April 30, 1984, Eric Levin, review of *Body and Soul,* p. 26; May 26, 1986, Eric Levin, review of *Big World,* p. 18; June 15, 1987, Eric Levin, review of *Will Power,* p. 24; September 14, 1987, Jeff Jarvis, review of *Private Eye,* p. 13; June 12, 1989, Andrew Abrahams, review of *Blaze of Glory,* p. 25; May 20, 1991, David Hiltbrand, review of *Laughter and Lust,* p. 23; September 29, 1997, Amy Waldman, review of *Heaven and Hell,* p. 28.

Playboy, November, 1981, review of *Jumpin' Jive,* p. 33; July, 1984, review of *Body and Soul,* p. 22.

Publishers Weekly, October 4, 1999, review of *A Cure for Gravity,* p. 57.

Rolling Stone, September 18, 1980, Kurt Loder, "Joe Jackson's Latest Disc Reggae-Influenced," p. 12; October 14, 1982, Parke Puterbaugh, "Joe Jackson's Classy Act," p. 62; November 24, 1983, Errol Somay, review of *Mike's Murder* soundtrack, p. 70; May 10, 1984, Don Shewey, review of *Body and Soul,* p. 54; August 30, 1984, Christopher Connelly, "Why Joe Jackson Said No to Rock Video,"

p. 32; January 30, 1986, Anthony DeCurtis, review of *Escenas,* p. 47; March 27, 1986, Steve Bloom, "The Stage as Studio," p. 22; September 11, 1986, Tony Seideman, "Joe Jackson: *The Big World* Sessions," p. 86; July 16, 1987, David Wild, "Joe Jackson Orchestrates a New Wave," p. 27; May 18, 1989, Parke Puterbaugh, review of *Blaze of Glory,* p. 167; November 29, 1990, Alan Light, "Joe Jackson (In the Studio)," p. 35; May 30, 1991, Elysa Gardner, review of *Laughter and Lust,* p. 73.

Seventeen, August, 1984, review of *Body and Soul,* p. 285.

Stereo Review, January, 1980, Steve Simels, review of *I'm the Man,* p. 89; October, 1981, Steve Simels, review of *Jumpin' Jive,* p. 108; November, 1982, review of *Night and Day,* p. 108; January, 1984, Mike Peel, review of *Mike's Murder* soundtrack, p. 65; July, 1984, Mark Peel, review of *Body and Soul,* p. 63; August, 1986, Mark Peel, review of *Big World,* p. 107; August, 1987, Louis Meredith, "The Big World Sessions," p. 93; October, 1987, Mark Peel, review of *Will Power,* p. 106; September, 1989, Steve Simels, review of *Blaze of Glory,* p. 130; October, 1991, Ron Givens, review of *Laughter and Lust,* p. 95; December, 1994, Peter Puterbaugh, review of *Night Music,* p. 129.

Variety, July 15, 1981, "Joe Jackson, 20-20," p. 62; August 19, 1981, review of *Jumpin' Jive,* p. 65; September 8, 1982, "Joe Jackson and Marshall Crenshaw," p. 110; May 9, 1984, review of *Body and Soul,* p. 545; June 13, 1984, "Joe Jackson Puts Down Video," p. 71; February 19, 1986, "Jackson's Digital Transfer Method Breaks New Ground in Pop Field," p. 429; February 26, 1986, p. 98; May 28, 1986, review of *Big World,* p. 79; August 6, 1986, p. 80; September 10, 1986, "The *Big World* Sessions," p. 90; October 25, 1989, p. 69.

Wilson Library Bulletin, September, 1986, Bruce Pollock, review of *Big World,* p. 71; December, 1988, Bruce Pollock, review of *Live, 1980-86,* p. 103.

OTHER

Joe Jackson, http://www.joejackson.com/joe/ (October 3, 2001).*

*   *   *

JAMES, Siân 1932-

PERSONAL: Born 1932, in Llandysul, Wales. *Education:* University College of Wales, Abersystwyth.

ADDRESSES: Agent—c/o St. Martin's Press, 175 Fifth Ave., New York, NY 10010.

CAREER: Formerly a teacher, now a novelist.

WRITINGS:

One Afternoon, P. Davies (London, England), 1975.
Yesterday, Collins (London, England), 1978.
A Small Country, Collins (London, England), 1979.
Another Beginning, Collins (London, England), 1980, Houghton Mifflin (Boston, MA), 1980.
Dragons and Roses, Duckworth (London, England), 1983.
A Dangerous Time, Century Publishers (London, England), 1984.
Not Into Temptation, St. Martin's Press (New York, NY), 1984.
(Editor, with Tony Curtis) *With Love from Wales: An Anthology,* Dufour Editions, 1991.
Storm at Arberth, Seren (Bridgend, Wales), 1994.
Not Singing Exactly: The Collected Stories of Sian James, Honno (Dinas Posys, South Glamorgan, Wales), 1996.
Two Loves, St. Martin's Press (New York, NY), 1999.
Second Chance, St. Martin's Press (New York, NY), 2001.

SIDELIGHTS: Siân James is a Welsh writer who began publishing novels in the 1970s, after a successful career as a schoolteacher. One of her earliest and most critically acclaimed works was *A Small Country,* which described life in a farming community in west Wales during the period of the First World War. While some of her novels look back to earlier times, others are set in contemporary Britain, and all focus at some level on women's lives and loves in challenging times.

Her 1980 novel, *Another Beginning,* reflects many of the issues of its time, including divorce, extramarital sex, and feminism. The novel follows Meg, a wife and mother whose contented if not ecstatic life is upended when her husband leaves her to live with a younger, more glamorous woman. Meg takes in lodgers to help pay her bills, and Ben, a young university student, becomes not just a boarder but a lover. These new experiences change Meg's view of life's possibilities. Through the course of the novel, Meg moves beyond her affair with Ben and develops richer and deeper relationships with her two daughters and with her own mother.

The British journal *New Statesman* found *Another Beginning* a "scented-soap operetta for those who prefer a superior piece of magazine-type fiction to the real article." However, *Publishers Weekly* called it a "sensitive portrayal of the breakup of a marriage and the emotional fallout that changes several lives," and concluded that the book was "a satisfying treatment of a modern life-crisis."

With *Not Into Temptation,* James revisited the setting of life during wartime, but this time in Britain just before and during World War II. Its protagonist is Laura Brown, a young woman who wants to assert control over her destiny by becoming a career woman rather than following the more conventional route of early marriage and babies. Motherless Laura is assisted through her difficult teenage years by the intervention of her long-lost aunt. But in her personal life, Laura runs into trouble, falling in love with married men and, according to a *Publishers Weekly* review, "struggl[ing] in silence to find her way in a storm of conflicting passions." The novel also recounts Laura's relationship with her best friend Susan, who takes the more conventional route and marries Peter. The marriage is not a happy one, and Peter later becomes one of Laura's lovers. *Publishers Weekly* opined the fact that the book relied on Laura's stream of consciousness to work out most of its major issues made it "sometimes less than engrossing," but noted that the book covered many women's issues, including abortion and out-of-wedlock birth.

James's *Two Loves* creates an intricate plot that intertwines the lives of three women who have all been married to or in love with the same man. The main character is 35-year-old Rosamund, the third wife and recent widow of Anthony Gilchrist, a famous poet. Laura's painting allows her to support herself and her nine-year-old son, and makes her the subject of a reporter's interview. During the interview she is informed that Erica Underhill, an eighty-year-old woman who was once her husband's greatest love, is seeking to advance herself out of penury by publishing the erotic poems that Gilchrist wrote to her during their affair. Rosamund is intrigued, and goes to visit Erica, whom she befriends. Meanwhile, Molly, Gilchrist's second wife, tries to enlist Rosamund's aid to block the publication. Back home, an affair that Rosamund has been carrying on with her neighbor ends, and soon after she runs into a man she loved in college, an artist who has become addicted to heroin.

Reviewers had no trouble working through the book's complicated plot lines. *Publishers Weekly* appreciated its "memorable secondary characters [and] clever dialogue," while *Booklist* pointed to the character of Josh,

Rosamund's son, as a "spot-on portrayal of a smart, sassy, and recognizable boy." *Publishers Weekly* noted that the novel's "community of ex-spouses and estranged lovers giv[es] James ample opportunity to cast her incisive eye on the vagaries of love." And *Booklist* concluded that the novel was "[r]ecognizably British but universally candid."

BIOGRAPHICAL/CRITICAL SOURCES:

PERIODICALS

Booklist, November 15, 1999, review of *Two Loves,* p. 604.
New Statesman, May 2, 1980, review of *Another Beginning,* p. 682.
Publishers Weekly, June 26, 1981, review of *Another Beginning,* p. 52; June 22, 1984, review of *Not Into Temptation,* p. 86; October 11, 1999, review of *Two Loves,* p. 52.*

* * *

JARDINE, Lisa A(nne)   1944-

PERSONAL: Born April 12, 1944; daughter of Jacob Bronowski (a scientist and historian) and Rita Coblenz; married Nicholas Jardine, 1969 (marriage ended); married John Robert Hare, 1982; children: (first marriage) one son, one daughter, (second marriage) one son. *Education:* Cheltenham Ladies' College, B.A., 1966; University of Essex, M.A., 1967; Newnham College, M.A., 1973; Associate, 1992. *Avocational interests:* Conversation, cookery, and contemporary art.

ADDRESSES: Home—51 Bedford Court Mansions, Bedford Avenue, London WC1B 3AA, England. *Office*—Queen Mary, University of London, Mile End Rd., London E1 4NS, England. *E-mail*—L.A.Jardine@ qmw.ac.uk.

CAREER: Historian, author, and educator. Queen Mary and Westfield College, University of London, professor of English and dean of the Faculty of Arts.

AWARDS, HONORS: Cornell University, resident fellow, 1974-75; Girton College, University of Cambridge, resident fellow, 1974-75; King's College, fellow, 1975-76, honorary fellow, 1995; Orange Prize for Fiction, Chair of Judges, 1997.

WRITINGS:

Francis Bacon: Discovery and the Art of Discourse, Cambridge University Press (New York, NY), 1974.
Still Harping on Daughters: Women and Drama in the Age of Shakespeare, Barnes and Noble (Totowa, NJ), 1983.
(With Anthony Grafton) *From Humanism to Humanities: Education and the Liberal Arts in Fifteenth- and Sixteenth-Century Europe,* Harvard University Press (Cambridge, MA), 1986.
(With Julia Swindells) *What's Left? Women in Culture and the Labour Movement,* Routledge (New York, NY), 1990.
Erasmus, Man of Letters: The Construction of Charisma in Print, Princeton University Press (Princeton, NJ), 1993.
Reading Shakespeare Historically, Routledge (New York, NY), 1996.
Worldly Goods: A New History of the Renaissance, Nan A. Talese (New York, NY), 1996.
(Editor) *Erasmus, The Education of a Christian Prince,* translation by Neil M. Cheshire, Cambridge University Press (New York, NY), 1997.
(With Alan Stewart) *Hostage to Fortune: The Troubled Life of Francis Bacon,* Hill and Wang (New York, NY), 1999.
Ingenious Pursuits: Building the Scientific Revolution, Nan A. Talese (New York, NY), 1999.
(Editor, with Michael Silverthorne) *The New Organon: Francis Bacon,* Cambridge University Press (New York, NY), 2000.
(With Jerry Brotton) *Global Interests: Renaissance Art between East and West,* Cornell University Press (Ithaca, NY), 2000.

Also contributor to numerous newspapers and magazines.

SIDELIGHTS: Professor of English and dean of the Faculty of Arts at Queen Mary and Westfield College, University of London, Lisa A. Jardine has illustrated through her published works an intense interest in history, culture, and social movement. Jardine's first published work was titled *Francis Bacon: Discovery and the Art of Discourse.* Francis Bacon will remain an historical figure of interest to Jardine in her later work.

Another figure of interest for Jardine is William Shakespeare. In *Still Harping on Daughters: Women and Drama in the Age of Shakespeare,* Jardine argues that the portrayal of women on stage does not prove that Shakespeare desired social change for women. Frank

Kermode, a reviewer in *New York Review of Books,* commented that Jardine "doesn't think Shakespeare was holding up a mirror to the condition of women, or that he had strong views about the need to change it." Kermode further commented that during the Elizabethan Age "the need to keep women down engendered the myth of their dangerous sexuality," and Kermode stated that Jardine "makes the interesting and possibly controversial point that social change had the effect of constricting women not, as the books more usually say, of liberating them." Tinsley Helton, a reviewer in *Seventeenth-Century News,* concurred when he stated that Jardine "alerts readers to material they may not have encountered before." Jardine herself states in the introductory chapter, "interest in women shown by Elizabethan and Jacobean drama . . . is related to the patriarchy's . . . worry about the great social changes which characterize the period." Helton emphasized that the "wealth of material drawn from contemporary documents and records and the references . . . to secondary works on social and intellectual history constitute the major value of Jardine's work."

Jardine's collaboration with Anthony Grafton titled *From Humanism to Humanities: Education and the Liberal Arts in Fifteenth- and Sixteenth-Century Europe,* questions the enduring impact of a classical education on students. George Huppert, a reviewer in *American Historical Review,* stated that Jardine and Grafton "contend [that] classical education . . . produced docile subjects in Renaissance." Francis Oakley, a reviewer in *America,* concurred, stating that Jardine and Grafton identify "an enormous gap between the theoretical ideals trumpeted by . . . distinguished humanist educators" and those "so often taken at face value." Lawrence W. Hyman, a reviewer in *Humanist,* commented that Jardine and Grafton "believe that literary training in the fifteenth and sixteenth centuries had little effect on the character of its practitioners as it does today." Huppert called the book a "handy introduction to humanist classroom practices."

Jardine collaborated with Julia Swindells in *What's Left? Women in Culture and the Labour Movement.* Skipping several centuries, Jardine and Swindells' focus concentrates on twentieth-century labour party members' regard for women. Maria Marmo Mullaney, a reviewer in *American Historical Review,* insisted that Jardine and Swindells' "woman question" is the "major forgotten issue of contemporary socialist policies." Mullaney insisted that Jardine and Swindells "show how women have not only been ignored but . . . humiliated in the political discourse of the Left." Mullaney emphasized that "as active members of the Labour

party" Jardine and Swindells "aim to challenge the party's male dominated ideology." Angela McRobbie, a reviewer in *New Statesmen and Society,* agreed that "the question of the place occupied by women in the huge literature which has sought to document working class life this century . . . is an important and long overdue area of study." Patricia Simpson, a reviewer in *Labor Studies Journal,* claimed the book has "an exceptionally broad sweep" and that Jardine and Swindells "support their argument by textual analysis of the works of George Orwell, other socialist intellectuals, and early union leaders."

Returning to the Elizabethan Age, Jardine again visits the texts of William Shakespeare. "All essays in [*Reading Shakespeare Historically*] discuss agency, especially female, both staged and recorded in domestic, social, legal, and political history of early modern England," observed Goran Stanivukovic, a reviewer in *Sixteenth Century Journal.* Stanivukovic called the work "a densely written book . . . written in a style devoid of theoretical jargon," and one that "brims with critical insights."

Jardine was drawn into a controversial light with her book *Worldly Goods: A New History of the Renaissance.* Although the book has had its share of criticism, Gilbert Taylor, a reviewer in *Booklist,* called the book a "provocative work," which is "explicitly revisionist." Taylor commented on Jardine's "connection between money and art," which "give general readers a challengingly insightful view of the relationship." A reviewer in *Publishers Weekly* claimed Jardine writes with "critical intelligence and authority." The same reviewer asserted that Jardine's "examination of exploration and commerce provides a window onto the times."

Jardine collaborated with Alan Stewart in *Hostage to Fortune: The Troubled Life of Francies Bacon.* Diarmaid MacCulloch, a reviewer in *New Statesman and Society,* called the book a "curiously old-fashioned biography" of Francis Bacon. Jonathan Sumption, a reviewer in *Spectator,* considered *Hostage to Fortune* an "excellent new biography" that "demonstrates [that] the rest of Bacon's life was every bit as unattractive as the circumstances of his departure from high office." Sumption contended that the book is "well-written" and "superbly researched." Bryce Christensen, a reviewer in *Booklist,* affirmed that the "author's aim is not to brand Bacon as a hypocrite but . . . to investigate . . . unresolved tensions in Bacon's brilliant yet deeply divided mind." Susan A. Stussy, a reviewer in *Library Journal,* called the book an "unvarnished biography . . . with a new understanding of this complex character." A reviewer in *Publishers Weekly* commented that Jardine and Stewart "give readers a rollicking portrait" of "England's Renaissance man par excellence" and "founder of [the] scientific method" as well as the Elizabethan world.

Using a broader point of view, Jardine wrote *Ingenious Pursuits: Building the Scientific Method.* Michael Hunter, a reviewer in *History Today,* called the book "ambitious in scope" with the aim of "introduc[ing] the general reader to seventeenth century science." Hunter insisted Jardine has "an enviable eye for telling detail, and the book is full of entertaining stories and effective characterizations of individuals and episodes." A reviewer in *Publishers Weekly* called the book "a memorable account of cultural ferment and individual genius during the scientific revolution." Wade Lee, a reviewer in *Library Journal,* recommended the book "for both academic and large public libraries."

BIOGRAPHICAL/CRITICAL SOURCES:

BOOKS

Jardine, Lisa A., *Still Harping on Daughters: Women and Drama in the Age of Shakespeare,* Barnes and Noble (Totowa, NJ), 1983.

PERIODICALS

America, November 18, 1989, Francis Oakley, review of *From Humanism to Humanities: Education and the Liberal Arts in Fifteenth- and Sixteenth-Century Europe,* p. 357.
American Historical Review, April, 1988, George Huppert, review of *From Humanism to Humanities: Education and the Liberal Arts in Fifteenth -and Sixteenth-Century Europe,* p. 405; April, 1991, Marie Marmo Mullaney, review of *What's Left? Women in Culture and the Labour Movement,* p. 524.
Booklist, November 1, 1996, Gilbert Taylor, review of *Worldly Goods, A New History of the Renaissance,* p. 478; May 15, 1999, Bryce Christensen, review of *Hostage to Freedom: The Troubled Life of Francis Bacon,* p. 1664.
Economist, October 15, 1996, review of *Worldly Goods, A New History of the Renaissance,* p. 56; September 30, 2000, review of *Global Interests: Renaissance Art between East and West,* p. 90.
English Historical Review, June, 2001, George Holmes, review of *Global Interests: Renaissance Art between East and West,* p. 714.

History Today, November, 1999, Michael Hunter, review of *Ingenious Pursuits: Building the Scientific Revolution,* p. 52.
Humanist, July-August, 1987, Lawrence W. Hyman, review of *From Humanism to Humanities: Education and the Liberal Arts in Fifteenth- and Sixteenth-Century Europe,* pp. 41-42.
Labor Studies Journal, fall, 1992, Patricia Simpson, review of *What's Left? Women in Culture and the Labour Movement,* pp. 84-85.
Library Journal, May 15, 1999, Susan A. Stussy, review of *Hostage to Fortune: The Troubled Life of Francis Bacon,* p. 102; November 1, 1999, Wade Lee, review of *Ingenious Pursuits: Building the Scientific Revolution,* p. 121.
New Statesman and Society, February 16, 1990, Angela McRobbie, "The Body Brigade," p. 32; March 27, 1998, Diarmaid MacCulloch, "Money Troubles," p. 49.
New York Review of Books, April 28, 1983, Frank Kermode, "Shakespeare For the Eighties," pp. 30-32; November 6, 1997, Ingrid D. Rowland, "The Renaissance Revealed," pp. 30-33; November 4, 1999, Quentin Skinner, "The Advancement of Francis Bacon," pp. 53-57.
Publishers Weekly, October 14, 1996, review of *Worldly Goods: A New History of the Renaissance,* p. 69; April 26, 1999, review of *Hostage to Fortune: The Troubled Life of Francis Bacon,* p. 66; October 25, 1999, review of *Ingenious Pursuits: Building the Scientific Revolution,* p. 62.
Renaissance Quarterly, spring, 1988, Lauro Martines, "The Renaissance and the Birth of the Consumer Society," pp. 193-203.
Science, March 3, 2000, Steven Shapin, review of *Ingenious Pursuits: Building the Scientific Revolution,* p. 1598.
Seventeenth-Century News, fall, 1984, Tinsley Helton, review of *Still Harping on Daughters: Women and Drama in the Age of Shakespeare,* pp. 40-41.
Sixteenth Century Journal, fall, 1997, Goran Stanivukovic, review *of Reading Shakespeare Historically,* pp. 1008-1010.
Spectator, April 18, 1998, Jonathan Sumption, "The Special Charm of Failure," p.36
Times Literary Supplement, October 15, 1999, John D. North, "Surface Tensions," p. 35.

OTHER

W.W. Norton, http://www.wwnorton.com/ (February 10, 2000.)*

JOENPELTO, Eeva (Elisabeth) 1921-

PERSONAL: Born June 17, 1921, in Sammatti, Finland; married Jarl Helemann, 1945 (marriage ended, 1975). *Avocational interests:* History and shooting.

ADDRESSES: Home—Werlanderintie 231, 09220 Sammatti, Finland.

CAREER: Novelist and artist.

AWARDS, HONORS: Finlandia Prize, 1994.

WRITINGS:

Kaakerholman kaupunla (title means "The Town of Kaakerholman"), W. Söderström (Porvoo, Finland), 1950.

Veljen varjo, W. Söderström (Porvoo, Finland), 1951.

Johannes vain, Suuri Suomalalainen Kirjakerno (Helsinki, Finland), 1952.

Kivi palaa, W. Söderström (Porvoo, Finland), 1953.

Neito kulkee vetten päällä, W. Söderström (Porvoo, Finland), 1955, translation by Therese Allen Nelson published as *The Maiden Walks Upon the Water,* Söderström (Porvoo, Finland), 1991.

Missä lintuset laulaa, W. Söderström (Porvoo, Finland), 1957.

Ralli, W. Söderström (Porvoo, Finland), 1959.

Syyskesä, W. Söderström (Porvoo, Finland), 1960.

Kipinöivät vuodet (sequel to *Neito kulkee vetten päällä;* title means "The Sparkling Years"), W. Söderström (Porvoo, Finland), 1961.

Naisten kesken, W. Söderström (Porvoo, Finland), 1962.

Viisaat istuvat varjossa, W. Söderström (Porvoo, Finland), 1964.

Ritari metsien pimennosta, W. Söderström (Porvoo, Finland), 1966.

Liian suuria asioita, W. Söderström (Porvoo, Finland), 1968.

Halusit tai et, W. Söderström (Porvoo, Finland), 1969.

Vesissä toinen silmä, W. Söderström (Porvoo, Finland), 1971.

Rikas ja Junniallinen, W. Söderström (Porvoo, Finland), 1984, translation by Irma Margareta Martin published as *Rich and Respected,* FATA (New Paltz, NY), 1997.

Jottei varjos haalistur, W. Söderström (Porvoo, Finland), 1986.

Ei ryppyä, ei tahraa (title means "Not a Wrinkle, Not a Stain"), W. Söderström (Porvoo, Finland), 1989.

Avoin, hellä ja katumaton (title means "Open, Tender, Unrepentant"), W. Söderström (Porvoo, Finland), 1991.

Tuomari Müller, hieno mies (title means "Judge Muller, a Fine Man"), W. Söderström (Porvoo, Finland), 1994.

"LOHJA" SERIES

Vetää kaikista ovista (title means "A Draft from Every Door"), W. Söderström (Porvoo, Finland), 1974.

Kuin kekäle kädessä (title means "Like Holding a Red Hot Coal in Your Hand"), W. Söderström (Porvoo, Finland), 1976.

Sataa suloaista vettä (title means "Salty Rain"), Suuri Suomalalainen Kirjakerho (Helsinki, Finland), 1978.

Eteisiin ja kynnyksville (title means "Into the Hallways and Onto the Thresholds"), W. Söderström (Porvoo, Finland), 1980.

Elämän rouva Glad, W. Söderström (Porvoo, Finland), 1982, translation by Ritva Koivu published as *The Bride of Life,* Braun-Brumfield (Ann Arbor, MI), 1995.

Joenpelto's works have been translated into several languages, including English, Czech, Estonian, Danish, Polish, and Russian.

ADAPTATIONS: The "Lohja" series has been adapted for stage and television. *Rikas ja kunniallinen* has also been produced for television.

SIDELIGHTS: Finnish novelist Eeva Joenpelto published her first book, *Kaakerholman Kaupunla,* when she was nearly thirty. Twenty-six novels later she was awarded the Finlandia Prize for her novel *Tuomari Müller, heino mies.* Many critics, however, considered her fifth book, *Neito kulkee vetten päällä,* and its sequel, *Kipinöivät vuodet,* to be her breakthrough novels. Margareta I. Martin, a reviewer in *World Literature Today,* commented that the translated version of *Neito kulkee vetten päällä* titled *The Maiden Walks Upon the Water* lost much of Joenpelto's "wonderful style" but was pleased to see an attempt to bring Joenpelto's work to an English audience.

Joenpelto was born and raised in the southern Finnish community of Lohja, the namesake for her acclaimed "Lohja" series. The series included *Vetää kaikista ovista, Kuin kekäle kädessä, Sataa suolaista vettä,* and *Eteisin ja kynnyksille.* Kai Laitinen, a reviewer for *World Literature Today,* considered that the novels contained "vividly drawn characters who may appear often though they are not central to the story" and that "all of them give special color to the novel(s)." Laitenen praised Joenpelto for her "natural and forceful characterization, a plot marked with dramatic climaxes," and "a historically exact picture of the times." Erkka Lehtola, an interviewer in *Books from Finland,* stated that Eeva Joenpelto's work "often brings together a timeless narrative skill and a worldly concern with current events." Of the worldly concerns, Joenpelto told Lehtola, "Life's beauty is in its bitterness and harshness. You don't get anything that's worth anything in this world cheap, let alone for free."

According to Margareta I. Martin, writing in *Encyclopedia of World Literature in the Twentieth Century,* another theme in Joenpelto's works is that of the "irreparable harm caused to children by depravation of love." Among these works were *Ei ryppyä, ei tahraa* and *Tuomari Müller, heino mies.* Anne Fried, a reviewer in *World Literature Today,* called *Ei ryppyä, ei tahraa* "a wise, sad, and bitter" book with its "atmosphere . . . of aging and decline, of disappointment and longing." Fried considered the novel "a book for readers who like to delve into long narratives that are . . . accessible by way of compassion and that transmit the insights of many years' experience."

Critics considered Joenpelto's 1991 title, *Avoin, hellä ja katumaton,* one of her most clever works. In a review for *World Literature Today,* Margareta I. Martin commented that Joenpelto brought "together representatives of different social strata" and showed that "each contains honest people and crooks." Martin concurred that Joenpelto is "one of Finland's best-loved and most prolific writers."

BIOGRAPHICAL/CRITICAL SOURCES:

BOOKS

Encyclopedia of World Literature in the Twentieth Century, St. James Press (Detroit, MI), 1999, pp. 557-558.

PERIODICALS

Books from Finland, 1987, Erkka Lehtola, "Eeva Joenpelto: Portraits of Change," pp. 25-28.
World Literature Today, 1980, Kai Laitinen, "Life at the Turning Point: Eeva Joenpelto and Her Lohja Trilogy," pp. 33-37; summer, 1990, Anne Fried, review of *Ei ryppyä, ei tahraa,* pp. 496-497; autumn, 1992, Margareta I. Martin, review of *The Maiden Walks Upon the Water,* p. 749; winter, 1993, Margareta I. Martin, review of *Avoin, hellä ja katumaton,* pp. 213-214; winter, 1999, Seija Paddon, review of *Rich and Respected,* p. 183.*

JOHNSON, Pamela
(Pamela Dalton)

PERSONAL: Born in Pipeston, MN; daughter of Donald and Eleanor Mather (a teacher) Gewecke; married Mark Johnson, June 8, 1974. *Ethnicity:* "English and German." *Education:* Augustana College, B.A., 1975.

ADDRESSES: Office—c/o Author Mail, Silhouette Romance, 300 East 42 St., 6th Fl., New York, NY 10017. *Agent*—Irene Goodman Literary Agency, New York, NY. *E-mail*—pamela@pameladalton.com.

CAREER: Modern Press, Inc., Sioux Falls, SD, accountant, 1975-77. Rocking Horse Academy, finance chair, 1984; MG Choral Booster Club, president, 1997-98.

MEMBER: American Association of University Women (treasurer, 1984; president elect, 1985), Romance Writers of America (board of directors, 1993-95), Authors Guild, Novelists Inc.

WRITINGS:

The Prodigal Husband, Silhouette Romance, 1993.
Second Chance at Marriage, Silhouette Romance, 1995.
And Baby Makes Six, Silhouette Romance, 1997.
Who's Been Sleeping in Her Bed, Silhouette Romance, 2000.

WORK IN PROGRESS: Suspense projects.

*   *   *

JOHNSTON, Terry C(onrad)   1947-2001

OBITUARY NOTICE—See index for *CA* sketch: Born January 1, 1947, in Arkansas City, KS; died March 25, 2001, in Billings, MT. Author. Johnston was the prolific, award-winning author of Western historical novels. An individual dedicated to the preservation of Western history, he was an active member with the Save the Battlefield Association, a group dedicated to setting aside land surrounding Little Bighorn Battlefield National Monument. His first book, *Carry the Wind,* earned him the Medicine Pipe Bearers Award for best first Western novel from the Western Writers of America. Some of his best-selling works include *Cry of the Hawk, Long Winter Gone,* and *Lay the Mountains Low.*

OBITUARIES AND OTHER SOURCES:

PERIODICALS

Dallas Morning News (TX), March 27, 2001, p. 23A.
Los Angeles Times, March 29, 2001, p. B8.
Washington Post, March 28, 2001, p. B7.

* * *

JONES, Richard Wyn 1966-

PERSONAL: Born May 26, 1966, in Los Angeles, CA.

ADDRESSES: Office—c/o Lynne Reinner, 1800 30th St., Ste. 314, Boulder, CO 80301.

CAREER: University of Wales, Aberystwyth, 1991—, began as lecturer, became senior lecturer in international politics.

WRITINGS:

Security, Strategy and Critical Theory, Lynne Rienner, 1999.
(Editor) *Critical Theory and World Politics,* Lynne Rienner, 2000.

WORK IN PROGRESS: Book on Welsh nationalism.

* * *

JORDAN, Judy 1961-

PERSONAL: Born December 24, 1961, in Marshville, NC; daughter of William Heath and Cynthia Nell (farmers and factory workers) Jordan. *Education:* University of Virginia, B.A., 1990, M.F.A. (poetry), 1995; University of Utah, M.F.A. (fiction), 2001.

ADDRESSES: Home—323 Whippoorwill Glen, Escondido, CA 92026. *Agent*—Wales Literary Agency, Inc., 108 Hayes St., Seattle, WA 98109. *E-mail*—jjordan@csusm.edu.

CAREER: Author. Worked variously as an equipment salesperson, constructor of houses and poultry houses, at an ice cream factory, as manager of Domino's Pizza and Little Caesar's Pizza, pizza deliverer, landscaper, and organic farmer. Has taught at University of Virginia and Piedmont Virginia Community College. California State University at San Marcos, San Marcos, assistant professor of creative writing and literature, 2001—.

AWARDS, HONORS: Virginia Commission for the Arts fellowship, 1996; Walt Whitman Award, Academy of American Poets, 1999, National Book Critics Circle Award, 2000, Utah Book of the Year for Poetry, 2000, and Oscar Arnold Young Book of the Year, 2000, all for *Carolina Ghost Woods;* Wesleyan Writers' Conference Poetry fellow, 2000; Utah Commission for the Arts fellow, 2000; Steffenson Cannon Scholarship, Henry Hoyns fellowship; first place, *Western Humanities Review* Utah Writers Competition.

WRITINGS:

Carolina Ghost Woods: Poems, Louisiana State University Press (Baton Rouge, LA), 2000.

Contributor of poetry to numerous periodicals, including *Poetry, Western Humanities Review, Third Coast, Crossroads, Ellipses, Poet Lore,* and *Writer's Eye.* Work represented in anthologies, including *American Poetry: Next Generation.*

Also author of two unpublished novels.

WORK IN PROGRESS: A play, a memoir, and a book-length poem.

SIDELIGHTS: Judy Jordan is an American poet and educator. She grew up in North Carolina, the daughter of sharecroppers, and was the first in her family to attend college. She holds B.A. and M.F.A. degrees in poetry from the University of Virginia and an additional M.F.A. in fiction from the University of Utah.

Jordan's collection, *Carolina Ghost Woods: Poems,* received the 2000 National Book Critics Circle Award and the 1999 Walt Whitman Award, selected by James Tate. In his citation for the award, Tate wrote: "*Carolina Ghost Woods . . .* is a startling first collection of poems—startling because of the bone-crushing violence and poverty, and startling also because of the beautiful and precise language the poet brings to bear on these scenes." Anne-Marie Oomen, in *Fore Word,* added, "The poems in this text contain equal doses of beautifully figurative and rhythmic language to balance the disturbing behavior of the inhabitants of these woods." She also noted that Jordan's "is the kind of subject matter that could put a reader off if the imagistic word-play and gripping narratives weren't so skillful."

Poetry reviewer F. D. Reeve reflected that the poems in *Carolina Ghost Woods* "report the violence, but they aren't about it. . . . The violence is part of the background. Art itself has taken over; . . . the view to the horizon is painterly, and the figures in it, surreal."

Other critics were also impressed with the work. A *Publishers Weekly* critic found that alliteration and rhyme were on "impressive display" in the work, though finding that the "whole can't quite lift grief out of the specific grievings." Oomen, in *Fore Word,* suggested that in the collection of poems, Jordan "seems to have set out to upset the myth that silence offers serenity or peace. In these poems, silence and its cousin, sorrow, never leave, but the world does continue to evolve." Reeve felt that "like Blue Mountain aspen, the poems quake with life." The *Poetry* reviewer also remarked, "What could be more apt, in the post-Vietnam/Gulf War culture of Oklahoma City and Columbine, of the LAPD and the NYPD, than an autobiography in poetry created out of violence?"

Louis McKee in *Library Journal* argued that Jordan's level of skill and maturity were uncommon in even the most established and respected of poets. McKee commended that *Carolina Ghost Woods* was "solid, memorable poetry from a talented young voice." David Roderick commented in *Boston Review* that Jordan "renders the landscape of her childhood with a stylistic and thematic unity that is rare for a first book of poems." *National Book Critics Circle* reviewer Rochelle Ratner praised Jordan, noting that the poet "does not wallow in pity, nor does she permit readers to feel sorry for her. As soon as we begin to recoil from the pain, she's on to the next image, the next horrific incident. . . . The pacing never becomes heavy and the action never slows." Oomen concluded that the poems in *Carolina Ghost Woods* "examine closely a less than admirable humanity, but do so with such sensitivity to the tenderness interrupting hard existence that the poems ring with honest vision and human truth, fallible as that may be."

BIOGRAPHICAL/CRITICAL SOURCES:

PERIODICALS

Boston Review, February-March, 2001, David Roderick, review of *Carolina Ghost Woods: Poems.*
Fore Word, March, 2000, Anne-Marie Oomen, review of *Carolina Ghost Woods,* p. 42.
Library Journal, February 15, 2000, Louis McKee, review of *Carolina Ghost Woods,* p. 168.
Poetry, June, 2001, F. D. Reeve, review of *Carolina Ghost Woods,* pp. 159-162.

Publishers Weekly, April 17, 2000, review of *Carolina Ghost Woods,* p. 73.
Washington Times, July 9, 2000, Matt Getty, "Poetry that Captures Land from Carolinas to Alaska."

OTHER

Academy of American Poets, http://www.poets.org/ (February 12, 2000), James Tate, citation for 1999 Walt Whitman Award.
National Book Critics Circle, http://www.bookcritics. org/ (August 25, 2001), Rochelle Ratner, review of *Carolina Ghost Woods.*
Poetic Voices, http://www.poeticvoices.com/ (July, 2000), Robin Travis-Murphree, feature on Judy Jordan.

*   *   *

JORDAN, Sherryl 1949-

PERSONAL: Born June 8, 1949, in Hawera, New Zealand; daughter of Alan Vivian and Patricia (Eta) Brogden; married Lee Jordan, 1970; children: Kym. *Education:* Attended Tauranga Girls' College, 1962-64; two years of nursing training, 1967-68. *Religion:* Christian. *Avocational interests:* "Music, friends, conversation, and solitude to write."

ADDRESSES: Home—165 Kings Ave., Matua, Tauranga, New Zealand. *Agent*—Tracy Adams, McIntosh and Otis, Inc., 310 Madison Ave., New York, NY 10017.

CAREER: Illustrator, 1980-85; full-time writer, 1988—. Part-time teacher's aide in primary schools, working with profoundly deaf children, 1979-87. Writer-in-residence, University of Iowa, 1993. Frequent speaker at schools and conferences in New Zealand, Australia, Denmark, and the United States.

MEMBER: Children's Literature Association (Bay of Plenty branch, committee member), Society of Children's Book Writers and Illustrators, New Zealand Children's Book Foundation, New Zealand Society of Authors.

AWARDS, HONORS: National illustrating competition winner, 1980; Choysa Bursary, 1988, for *Rocco;* AIM Story Book of the Year Award, New Zealand, 1991, for *Rocco;* AIM Story book of the year award runner-up, and Esther Glen Award shortlist, New Zealand Library

Association, both 1992, both for *The Juniper Game;* Esther Glen Award shortlist, New Zealand Library Association, and AIM Junior Story Book of the Year Award, both 1992, both for *The Wednesday Wizard;* AIM Story Book of the Year Award shortlist, 1993, for *Denzil's Dilemma;* selected by *American Bookseller* magazine as a "Pick of the List," 1993, American Library Association (ALA) Best Book for Young Adults, ALA Recommended Book for the Reluctant Young Adult Reader, Children's Book of the Year, Bank Street School of Education, New Zealand AIM Book of the Year Award shortlist, all 1994, and listed in Whitcoull's New Zealand Top 100 books, 1997, all for *Winter of Fire;* short-listed for the New Zealand AIM Book of the Year Awards, short-listed for the New Zealand Library Association Esther Glen Award, and ALA Best Book for Young Adults, all 1995, all for *Tanith (Wolf-Woman); New Zealand Post* Children's Book Awards shortlist (formerly the New Zealand AIM Awards), 1997, for *Secret Sacrament;* best book in translation award (Belgium), 1999, and Junior Library Guild selection, 2000, both for *Secret Sacrament;* Junior Library Guild selection, Best Children's Book of the Year, Bank Street College of Education, Best Book, *School Library Journal,* all 1999, Ten Best Books for Young Adults, ALA, Books for the Teen Age, New York Public Library, NASEN Special Needs Award, and Notable New Zealand Children's and Young Adult Books citation, New Zealand Children's Book Foundation, all 2000, all for *The Raging Quiet;* Margaret Mahy Medal and Lecture Award, Children's Literature Foundation of New Zealand, 2001, for contributions to children's literature, publishing, and literacy.

WRITINGS:

FICTION

(Self-illustrated) *The Firewind and the Song* (juvenile), Kagyusha Publishers, 1984.
Matthew's Monsters (juvenile), illustrated by Dierdre Gardiner, Ashton Scholastic, 1986.
No Problem Pomperoy (juvenile), illustrated by Jan van der Voo, Century Hutchinson, 1988.
Kittens (juvenile), Shortlands, 1989.
The Wobbly Tooth (juvenile), Shortlands, 1989.
Babysitter Bear (juvenile), illustrated by Trevor Pye, Century Hutchinson, 1990.
Rocco (young adult fantasy), Ashton Scholastic, 1990, published as *A Time of Darkness,* Scholastic, 1990.
The Juniper Game (young adult), Scholastic, 1991.
The Wednesday Wizard (juvenile), Scholastic, 1991.
Denzil's Dilemma (juvenile; sequel to *The Wednesday Wizard*), Scholastic, 1992.

Winter of Fire (young adult), Scholastic, 1993.
The Other Side of Midnight, illustrated by Brian Pollard, Scholastic, 1993.
Tanith (young adult), Omnibus, 1994, published as *Wolf-Woman,* Houghton, 1994.
Sign of the Lion, Penguin, 1995.
Secret Sacrament (young adult), Penguin, 1996, HarperCollins, 2001.
Denzil's Great Bear Burglary (juvenile; sequel to *Denzil's Dilemma*), Mallinson Rendel, 1997.
The Raging Quiet (young adult), Simon & Schuster, 1999.

ILLUSTRATOR; WRITTEN BY JOY COWLEY

Mouse, Shortland, 1983.
Tell-tale, Shortland, 1983.
The Silent One, Whitcoull's, 1984.
Mouse Monster, Shortland, 1985.

OTHER

Also contributor to journals, including New Zealand Author, Southern Scribe, and Signal.

SIDELIGHTS: Award-winning New Zealand author Sherryl Jordan began her writing career with books for children, but soon moved on to novels for older readers. Her breakthrough came with *Rocco,* published in the United States as *A Time of Darkness,* and since that time she has gone on to pen many more titles for young adult and juvenile readers which have been published both in her native New Zealand and throughout the world. The recipient of a 1993 fellowship to the prestigious Writing Program at the University of Iowa, Jordan used her time in the United States to speak widely at schools and conferences about her books, which blend fantasy with bits of science fiction and romantic realism. "All my young adult novels have been gifts," she noted in the *St. James Guide to Children's Writers.* "I don't think them up. They hit me over the head when I least expect them; overwhelm me with impressions, sights, and sounds of their new worlds; enchant me with their characters; and dare me to write them."

The road to success, however, was a long one for Jordan. Born in Hawera, New Zealand, in 1949, she started writing stories and even novels when she was only ten years old, works which her hopeful teachers sent out to publishers, but none of them sold. Though she attended a nurse's training school, Jordan was always headed for a career in writing or illustration. "From my earliest days I was also good at art," Jordan once commented. "I began to seriously work on children's books in 1980, when I won a national competition for illustrations for my work on Joy Crowley's book *The Silent One.*" Jordan continued illustrating for several more years, but she finally decided writing was the one thing she loved more than anything else.

Throughout her long apprenticeship, Jordan wrote twenty-seven books for children as well as twelve novels. Three of her books for younger readers were published and none of the novels. With novel number thirteen, however, she decided she would make or break her career: if the book was rejected, she would give up writing. Fortunately for readers, she hit it big with number thirteen, *Rocco,* which was published in the United States as *A Time of Darkness.* A fantasy for young adults, the book explores themes ranging from the nature of time to parallel worlds through the journey of a contemporary teenager in search of himself. Rocco, the teenager in question, has recurring dreams of a wolf leaping toward him. Each time, he awakes from these dreams scared and smelling of wood smoke. Finally, he awakes to find that he has slipped in time; he is in a valley called Anshur where the people dress in animal skins and live in caves; Rocco quickly adapts to their lifestyle. At first, Rocco believes he is living in the past, but slowly, as the clues accumulate, he realizes he is actually in a post-holocaust future. Suddenly returned to his own time, Rocco feels he must stop the chain of events that will lead to his dreams of Anshur.

Submitted for the 1988 Choysa Bursary prize in New Zealand, *Rocco* won and publication of the novel was assured. Critics around the world were impressed with this debut novel. Writing in *Magpies,* Jo Goodman called the book "an impressive first novel," while a reviewer for *Junior Bookshelf* noted, "So coherently, continuous and convincing is the narration that the reader will be forgiven for taking it as reality." This same reviewer went on to note that the story "plucks cleverly at the hidden hopes and fears of humanity." Reviewing the United States edition of the novel under the title *A Time of Darkness,* Gene Lafaille commented in *Wilson Library Bulletin* that the book "is a strong, dramatic adventure novel that explores interesting family relationships with their inevitable tensions and moments of humor." Lafaille further noted that *A Time of Darkness* is "suspenseful" and "rapid-paced . . . with a wide range of emotions." Writing in *Voice of Youth Advocates,* Catherine M. Dwyer observed that *A Time of Darkness* has all the right elements: "characters that the reader cares about, a story line that captures the imagination, and an ending that does not disappoint."

With her next novel, *The Juniper Game,* Jordan further explored the world of telepathy, a sub-theme in her first novel. Juniper is a contemporary girl fascinated by the medieval world and by the possibilities of telepathy. She persuades her classmate Dylan to help her with an experiment in sending each other messages. They soon become quite successful at the game, but when Juniper sends him pictures of medieval England, they are transported to a far- distant time and become involved with a young woman, Joanna, who is accused of witchcraft and burned at the stake. "With vividly depicted, believable characters, this is superior fantasy," declared a writer for *Kirkus Reviews. Booklist* contributor Chris Sherman observed, "Fantasy lovers will enjoy Jordan's story," while Dwyer asserted in *Voice of Youth Advocates,* "Jordan has again demonstrated her skill as a storyteller."

Next up for Jordan was a novel for younger readers, *The Wednesday Wizard,* about a medieval sorcerer's apprentice, Denzil, who discovers a spell to send him through time. Reversing the time slip of *The Juniper Game,* Jordan sends this young apprentice catapulting forward through time to 1990s New Zealand, where he takes up lodgings with the MacAllister family with humorous results. "Whoever it is that suffers the most displacement, plenty of humour arises from the inevitable confusions that occur," noted Ann Darnton in a *School Librarian* review. Two more Denzil novels followed: *Denzil's Dilemma,* in which a friend from the future comes back to Denzil's world to visit him, and *Denzil's Great Bear Burglary.* In the latter title, the young apprentice gets into trouble for stealing a dancing bear from a passing circus and rushes forward in time to escape the problems this has created for him in his own time. The MacAllister household is once again his refuge, but this time the future holds as much chaos as the past. In the end, however, all turns out well, as in all the "Denzil" books. But the three books of this trilogy are more than just lighthearted reading, as Frances Hoffman pointed out in a *Magpies* review of the third book in the series. "Some serious issues, in particular the ethics of animal experimentation, are also touched on in the book," observed Hoffman, "giving depth to this well-written and thoroughly recommended novel." Another book for younger readers is the picture book *The Other Side of Midnight,* which is also set in a medieval age. In this story, a young girl who has been orphaned by the plague goes in search of her brother and ends up finding out some hard truths about herself.

Following the writing of the first "Denzil" book, Jordan was diagnosed with Repetition Strain Injury, a result of her many years of typing manuscripts. Her physician told her she might never be able to type again, but she has managed to continue writing, though she concentrates only on novels. In a way, she commented, the writing of the young adult novel *Winter of Fire* was something of a salvation for her. This novel about a young slave woman called Elsha helped Jordan work through her own affliction. "Elsha . . . was unstoppable, charismatic, and a warrior at soul," Jordan said. "It was only because of her that I refused to accept that my writing days were over—only because of her that I picked myself up out of despair and wrote another book. We were warriors together in our battles against the impossible."

In Elsha's future world, the sun has been blocked by a meteorite shower which has caused the natural equivalent of a nuclear winter. Society has been divided into the haves, the Chosen, and the have-nots, the Quelled, who work the coal mines. One of the Quelled, Elsha, longs for freedom for herself and her people. "*Winter of Fire* chronicles Elsha's quest to achieve her desires," noted *Magpies* reviewer Stephanie Owen Reeder, "and does it brilliantly." Reeder further commented, "This is strong, compelling and moving reading of the fantasy/ quest genre," with "strongly delineated" characters and a "carefully crafted" plot. Cathi Dunn MacRae, writing in *Wilson Library Bulletin,* felt that young adult fantasy fans "will certainly appreciate Elsha's courageous pursuit of her revolutionary vision amid persecution and disbelief." MacRae called special attention to the "atmosphere of spirituality" that "pervades the whole tale." A writer for *Publishers Weekly* also observed that "as a whole, the stalwart heroine's visionary struggles are nothing short of inspiring."

In *Tanith,* published in the United States as *Wolf-Woman,* a young girl from the distant past is raised by wolves until the age of three. Then, removed from her den, she lives for many years as the daughter of the chief of a warrior-like clan who delight in slaughtering other tribes as well as the wolves who were once Tanith's protectors. She becomes a companion to the chief's wife, but Tanith never feels really accepted in her human society, and finally she must choose between wolves and men. Reviewing the title in *Booklist,* Candace Smith commented on the "prehistoric imagery and legend" in which Jordan's tale is steeped, and called the story "a compelling search for identity and self-worth within a richly drawn setting." Roger Sutton, writing in *Bulletin of the Center for Children's Books,* concluded, "Tanith's ultimate rejection of human society . . . closes the novel on a note of splendid defiance, and most readers will hope for a sequel."

In *Secret Sacrament* Jordan once again employs an imaginary world, Navora, where young Gabriel must come to terms with individual choices. Instead of following in his father's footsteps as a merchant, he opts to become a Healer in the Citadel. Falling afoul of palace intrigues, however, he flees to the Shinali people, who are subjugated by the Navoran Empire, and there falls in love and begins to fight for the rights of the dispossessed. A writer for the *St. James Guide to Children's Writers* called the novel Jordan's "most ambitious tale to date." Originally published in New Zealand in 1995, a revised edition appeared in the United States in 2001.

Jordan returned to her familiar grounds of the Middle Ages for her 1999 novel, *The Raging Quiet.* In this book the author creates a historical romance rather than a fantasy. Marnie is a young widow who is trying to make the best of her life in a small village by the sea. She befriends a local wild boy whom the villagers think is mad and possessed by the devil, but whom Marnie discovers is simply deaf. When she begins communicating with him with hand gestures, the villagers are sure she is a witch, but the resourceful Marnie refuses to become a victim of ignorance. "This well-written novel is an irresistible historical romance that also offers important messages about love, acceptance, respect, and the tragic repercussions of closed minds," wrote Shelle Rosenfeld in a *Booklist* review. A reviewer for *Publishers Weekly* noted that "Jordan blends a zealous supporting cast with the flavor of Hawthorne with the societal forces of Hardy as she plays out Marnie's tortuous fate." A writer for *Kirkus Reviews* called the book "a passionate and sensuous tale," and concluded, "Fire and sweetness, the pulse of daily existence, how to cope with differences, and the several kinds of love are all present, wrapped in a page-turner to keep readers enthralled." Claire Rosser declared in *Kliatt,* "This novel is quite an achievement, and one that will surely appear on best books lists as more and more people discover it."

Jordan combines a compelling narrative line with rich imagination. According to critics, her fantasy and historical worlds are well thought out and filled with the details of the quotidian, whether actual or fantastical. And lightly sprinkled throughout are lessons to be learned, insights to be gained. "In all of my books there is that lesson that life itself has taught me," Jordan commented. "I hope all my books will inspire readers to explore these astounding fields themselves—to realize that all is not what it seems and that there are no boundaries between fact and fiction, the tangible and the mystical, the real and the truth we imagine."

BIOGRAPHICAL/CRITICAL SOURCES:

BOOKS

St. James Guide to Children's Writers, 5th edition, St. James (Detroit, MI), 1999.

PERIODICALS

Booklist, November 15, 1991, Chris Sherman, review of *The Juniper Game,* p. 617; November 15, 1994, Candace Smith, review of *Wolf-Woman,* p. 590; August, 1997, p. 1892; May 1, 1999, Shelle Rosenfeld, review of *The Raging Quiet,* p. 1587.

Bulletin of the Center for Children's Books, March, 1993, p. 214; December, 1994, Roger Sutton, review of *Wolf-Woman,* pp. 131-132; June, 1999, p. 356.

Junior Bookshelf, August, 1992, review of *Rocco,* pp. 153-154.

Kirkus Reviews, August 1, 1991, review of *The Juniper Game,* p. 1011; March 15, 1999, review of *The Raging Quiet,* p. 451.

Kliatt, November, 1992, p. 16; September, 1995, p. 22; September, 1996, p. 11; March, 1999, Claire Rosser, review of *The Raging Quiet,* p. 8.

Magpies, November, 1991, Jo Goodman, review of *Rocco,* p. 32; November, 1993, Stephanie Owen Reeder, review of *Winter of Fire,* p. 34; March, 1997, p. 1; March, 1998, Frances Hoffman, review of *Denzil's Great Bear Burglary,* p. 7.

Publishers Weekly, January 4, 1993, review of *Winter of Fire,* p. 73; March 22, 1999, review of *The Raging Quiet,* p. 93.

School Librarian, February 4, 1994, Ann Darnton, review of *The Wednesday Wizard,* p. 21.

School Library Journal, January, 1991, p. 110; October, 1991, p. 145; March, 1993, p. 221; August, 1995, p. 38; May, 1999, p. 125; December, 1999, p. 42.

Voice of Youth Advocates, December, 1990, Catherine M. Dwyer, review of *A Time of Darkness,* p. 298; December, 1991, Catherine M. Dwyer, review of *The Juniper Game,* p. 313; December, 1994, p. 275; August, 1999, p. 184.

Wilson Library Bulletin, April, 1991, Gene Lafaille, review of *A Time of Darkness,* p. 107; April, 1993, Cathi Dunn MacRae, review of *Winter of Fire,* p. 100.

*   *   *

JULIÁ, Edgardo Rodriguez
  See RODRIGUEZ JULIÁ, Edgardo

*   *   *

JULIA, Edgardo Rodriguez
  See RODRIGUEZ JULIÁ, Edgardo

K

KAMALI, Masoud 1956-

PERSONAL: Born April 22, 1956, in Shiraz, Iran; son of Alinaz Kamali and Govhar Sabzloun; married Narmin Khoubehi; children: Nima, Sam, Sara. *Education:* University of Tabiz, B.S. (social science), 1981; University of Linköping, B.S. (sociology), 1990; Stockholm's School of Social Work, M.S. (social science), 1991; University of Uppsala, M.S. (sociology), 1993, Ph.D., 1995.

ADDRESSES: Home—Botvidsgatan 3B, S-75329 Uppsala, Sweden. *Office*—Department of Sociology, University of Uppsala, Box 821, S-75108, Uppsala, Sweden; fax: 4618-4711170. *E-mail*—Masoud.Kamali@ soc.uu.se.

CAREER: Social worker, Linköping, Motala, and Uppsala municipalities, 1989-92; Uppsala Municipality, project leader, 1992-95; University of Uppsala, Sweden, research fellow, 1994-98, associate professor (docent) and research fellow, 2000; Center for Evaluation of Social Work, research fellow, 1998-99; Mid-Sweden University, lecturer, 1999—.

WRITINGS:

Distorted Integration: Clientization of Immigrants in Sweden, Center for Multiethnic Research, Uppsala University (Uppsala, Sweden), 1997.

Revolutionary Iran: Civil Society and State in the Modernization Process, Ashgate (Aldershot, UK), 1998.

Varken familjen eller samhället: en studie om invandrarungdomarnas attityder till det svenska samhället, Carlssons (Stockholm, Sweden), 1999.

Iranian Revolution in a Global Perspective: Theoretical and Empirical Challenges, Nashr-E-mail—digar, 2001.

Contributor of articles to books, including *Civil Society and Islam,* Fredrich Nauman Stiftung (Berlin, Germany), 2000; journals, including *European Journal of Social Theory, European Journal of Intercultural Education, European Journal of Social Sciences,* and *Citizenship Studies;* and various Swedish and Persian newspapers and weekly reviews. Also contributor of a book review to *Multiethnica.*

WORK IN PROGRESS: Selective Modernization and Islamic Resurgence: A Comparative Study of Modern Iran and Turkey.

* * *

KARABAN, Roslyn A. 1953-

PERSONAL: Born June 27, 1953, in Waterbury, CT; daughter of William J. and Regina R. (McGinn) Karaban; married D. N. Premnath (a professor and academic dean), May 15, 1982; children: Deepa L., Micah R. *Education:* Stonehill College, B.A. (summa cum laude), 1975; Harvard University, M.Div., 1978; Graduate Theological Union, Ph.D., 1984. *Politics:* Democrat. *Religion:* Roman Catholic. *Avocational interests:* Kung fu (black belt), step aerobics.

ADDRESSES: Home—30 Gregory Hill Rd., Rochester, NY 14620. *Office*—St. Bernard's Institute, 1100 South Goodman St., Rochester, NY 14620; fax 716-271-2045. *E-mail*—rkaraban@sbi.edu.

CAREER: Stonehill College, North Easton, MA, instructor in archaeology, 1974; Pacific School of Religion, Berkeley, CA, instructor in cross-cultural counseling, 1981; United Theological College, Bangalore, India, instructor in pastoral counseling, 1985-87; St. Bernard's Institute, Rochester, NY, instructor, 1987-88, assistant professor, 1988-91, associate professor of ministry studies, 1991—, professor, 2001—. Certified death educator and grief therapist; Samaritan Pastoral Counseling Center, associate counselor, 1990—, member of teaching faculty and primary supervisor, 1996—; Genesee Region Home Care, member of teaching faculty and primary supervisor of pastoral training in hospice program, 1996—; Lloyd Counseling Center, San Anselmo, CA, worked as counseling intern; Halfway Home, Bangalore, India, worked as counseling supervisor. Roman Catholic Diocese of Rochester, NY, member of Theological Commission, 1988-90; member of Corpus Christi Adult Religious Education Committee, 1998—; also worked as student chaplain and student minister. Member of Tel Dan Archaeological Dig in Israel.

MEMBER: Society for Pastoral Theology, American Association of Pastoral Counselors (chairperson of ethics committee, 1999-2001), Association for Death Education and Counseling, Phi Alpha Theta, Delta Epsilon Sigma.

AWARDS, HONORS: Claretian social justice grant for Mexican American Cultural Center, San Antonio, TX, 1980.

WRITINGS:

(Editor and contributor) *Extraordinary Preaching: Twenty Homilies by Roman Catholic Women,* Resource Publications (San Jose, CA), 1996.
Responding to God's Call: A Survival Guide, Resource Publications (San Jose, California), 1998.
Complicated Losses, Difficult Deaths: A Practical Guide for Ministering to the Grieving, Resource Publications (San Jose, CA), 2000.

Contributor to *Feminist and Womanist Pastoral Theology: Implications for Care, Faith, and Reflection,* edited by Brita Gill-Austern and Bonnie Miller-McLemore, Abington (Nashville, TN), 1999.

Contributor of articles and reviews to periodicals, including *Journal of Pastoral Theology, New Women/New Church, Pastoral Psychology,* and *Journal of Pastoral Care.*

SIDELIGHTS: Roslyn A. Karaban once commented in *CA:* "Much of what I write comes directly out of my teaching. I write in areas in which I am interested, and in which I believe there are 'holes' in the field. The books I have written are used in my teaching, and I hope others will also use them to teach. My writing often begins as a talk for a church or school. It expands into an article or book. I write to reach a wider audience. My experience and the experiences of my students greatly influence and motivate me.

"I write best in the morning, alone in my office with no interruptions. I can only write for four or five hours a day, then I need to talk, exercise, do other things. First drafts are very hard for me. Once a first draft is written, I am able to revise and edit, particularly after my editor has given me specific feedback."

*   *   *

KASSY, Karen Grace 1964-

PERSONAL: Born December 6, 1964, in Denver, CO; daughter of Stanley (head of estimating, Martin-Marietta Astronautics) and Dorothy Starcevich (a homemaker) Kassy; married, July 27, 1995. *Ethnicity:* "Caucasian-American (Ukrainian/Croatian descent)." *Education:* Front Range Community College, associate degree in business, 1994; Greenwich University, B.S., 1997, M.S., 1999. *Avocational interests:* Volunteer for Newfoundland dog rescue.

ADDRESSES: Home and Office—P.O. Box 8043, Bend, OR 97708-8043. *E-mail*—info@healthintuition.com. *Agent*—Anthony Gardner, 2 Cornelia St., New York, NY 10014.

CAREER: Self-employed health intuitive, lecturer, and consultant, 1997—. Worked in jewelry sales, 1980-85, and data entry/proofreading in insurance industry, 1986-87; Brock Publishing, office manager, publisher's assistant, and section editor, 1987-90; CareerTrack, administrative assistant, production coordinator, graphic artist, international customer service and collections, 1990-93; Body Dynamics/FitBall, business manager, graphic artist, workshop organizer, 1993-94; Sounds True, conference director and consultant, 1994-97.

WRITINGS:

Health Intuition, Hazelden-Transitions, 2000.

SIDELIGHTS: Karen Grace Kassy told *CA:* "I never thought, or aspired to be, a professional author. I was perfectly happy as a business person and felt more than apprehensive when my life changed in 1996 and I began working as a 'Health Intuitive' (one who 'sees' intuitively inside the body). As a health intuitive, I consult with clients long-distance and my ability is physician-verified at 80-90% average accuracy. One of the physicians I worked with asked me to start teaching, again, a case of 'last on my list' of career choices. However, it turned out I loved it, and have been giving health intuition workshops to sold-out audiences since. Many who attended my workshops asked me to write a book. Long story short, in 1999 I started and finished the book, and out-of-the-blue a friend who owned a bookstore called about another matter. When I told him about the book, he excitedly said his company had just merged with a publisher and if he didn't get first crack at my book, he'd be upset. So, I sent it to him in December of 1999. In February of 2000, that company (Hazelden-Transitions Publishing) agreed to publish my book and bring it out in September of 2000. They did.

"I now know that I am the 'Cinderella Story' poster girl for publishing. I recently heard that the frontier explorer John Wesley Powell was blessed with a mix of vision, optimism and ignorance. That works for me. I knew relatively little about book publishing so was not limited by naysayers or standard publishing practice. As a result, whoosh, out came a book and fast. And, successfully: a third printing within five weeks of its release.

"I'm often asked, 'How did you write your book?' Again, the answer seems to be, 'not in the standard way.' I got it all out on paper, writing from me. My primary influence of writing style would be anyone who sounds like themself. And, I love it when people meet me and say my book sounds just like I do. Once the book was 'finished' (note the foreshadowing quotation marks), I sent it to a friend who does a lot of editing for government-related publications. She nicely sent it back, and told me to 'organize it.' Her suggestion was great: make an outline. It worked well, and I later used the outline for my 'book proposal'—another thing I never knew about, and that an author is supposed to write first (then sell the book, get an advance, write the book). Well, it didn't quite work out in the order, but it did work. I think the lesson for anyone aspiring to be a writer is if you don't let other people's ideas and policies limit you, you might just become an author. And in my case, a happy one."

KEARNEY, Milo 1938-

PERSONAL: Born January 10, 1938, in Kansas City, MO; son of Milo, Sr. (a professor) and LaNelle (a teacher) Kearney; married Vivian Zgodzinski Kundorf, June 11, 1970; children: Kathleen Kearney Anzak, Sean. *Ethnicity:* "Caucasian." *Education:* University of Texas at Austin, B.S., 1962; University of California, Berkeley, M.A., 1966, Ph.D., 1970. *Politics:* Democrat. *Religion:* Christian. *Avocational interests:* Piano, art.

ADDRESSES: Home—19 Acacia Dr., Brownsville, TX 78520. *Office*—Department of History, University of Texas at Brownsville, Brownsville, TX 78520.

CAREER: University of Texas at Brownsville, professor of history, 1970—. *Military service:* U.S. Army Reserve, 1963-69.

AWARDS, HONORS: Woodrow Wilson fellow, 1965-66; Minnie Stevens Piper Teaching Award, 1982; Chancellor's Teaching Award, University of Texas, 1992; Fulbright scholar in Mexico, 1992-93.

WRITINGS:

(With Anthony Knopp) *Boom and Bust: The Historical Cycles of Matamoros and Brownsville,* Eakin Publications (Austin, TX), 1991.
The Role of Swine Symbolism in Medieval Culture: Blanc Sanglier, Edwin Mellen (Lewiston, NY), 1991.
The Historical Roots of Medieval Literature: Battle and Ballad, Edwin Mellen, 1992.
(With Knopp) *Border Cuates: A History of the U.S.-Mexican Twin Cities,* Eakin Publications, 1995.

WORK IN PROGRESS: Who We Are Is Who We Were: The Medieval Roots of Mexican-American Border Culture, for Texas A&M University Press (College Station).

* * *

KELLER, Lynn 1952-

PERSONAL: Born April 29, 1952. *Education:* Stanford University, B.A., 1973; University of Chicago, Ph.D., 1981.

ADDRESSES: Office—Department of English, University of Wisconsin—Madison, Helen C. White Hall, 600

North Park St., Madison, WI 53706. *E-mail—* rlkeller@facstaff.wisc.edu.

CAREER: Professor of English, University of Wisconsin—Madison.

WRITINGS:

Re-making It New: Contemporary American Poetry and the Modernist Tradition, Cambridge University Press (New York, NY), 1987.
(Editor, with Cristanne Miller) *Feminist Measures: Soundings in Poetry and Theory,* University of Michigan Press (Ann Arbor, MI), 1994.
Forms of Expansion, University of Chicago Press (Chicago, IL), 1997.

SIDELIGHTS: Lynn Keller is best known for her feminist studies of contemporary American poetry. As a professor at the University Madison—Wisconsin and an editor, with Cristanne Miller, of *Feminist Measures,* Keller has worked to make postmodern poetry and theory accessible to a wide audience.

Keller's first study, *Re-making It New: Contemporary American Poetry and the Modernist Tradition,* offers a look at postmodernist poets—including Ashbery, Bishop, Creeley, and Merrill—and considers how each of them has received the tradition of modernist poetry. David Porter, in a review for *American Literature,* called the book "A vigorously discerning study of contemporary poetry and its modernist background." W. J. Martz, in an article for *Choice,* commented, "The study is exceptionally ambitious—wide-ranging and scholarly—and takes care to keep the reader historically oriented; moreover, the author generalizes with commanding skill. Nevertheless, it is stylistically marred, jargon-ridden." Paul Miller, however, remarked in *Modern Language Review,* "Those who approve criticism written in a supple, lucid style, with an eye to cogent fact rather than polemic, will delight in this work, which makes a lasting contribution to our understanding and appreciation of the work of Elizabeth Bishop, John Ashbery, Robert Creeley, and James Merrill."

Keller next coedited a collection of essays, entitled *Feminist Measures: Soundings in Poetry and Theory.* In it, fourteen famous literary critics explain the relevance of postmodern theory to poetry of various periods, including discussions of Chicana poetry, African-American poetry, and ethics. Wanda A. Kelley, in the pages of *Canadian Literature,* explained, "The collection attempts to rescue poetry from its relative critical obscurity while allowing women to 'experiment with the soundings of their own clear, personalized voices.' " Kelley applauded the effort: "What emerges from *Feminist Measures* is a woman's literary history . . . women have been writing poetry which explores what it means to be a woman, and to be a woman writing. The various authors represented in this collection help us to lay claim to this heritage by providing us with reading strategies which, while they are by no means tentative, manage to escape being prescriptive: to break the critical silence around women's poetry is only the beginning." Camille Roman, in *American Studies International,* echoed this sentiment, writing, "One feels the need to respond to, to argue with, and to add to the conversations in *Feminist Measures.* For this reason, it is essential reading for exploring the intersections between feminist criticism and theory and women's poetry."

Keller continues to explore these intersections; in 1997, she published *Forms of Expansion: Recent Long Poems by Women,* in which she argues that many sequences and verse novels may be considered long poems, though they are not epic poetry. Jeanne Heuving, a critic for *Signs,* wrote, "In *Forms of Expansion,* Lynn Keller establishes an important new field for feminist poetry criticism, women's long poems. Keller suggests that women poets empowered by feminism have turned increasingly to the primarily masculine genre of the long poem." Heuving continued, "Keller's capacities to describe complex critical debates succinctly and to empathize with each writer's poetic struggles afford a nuanced account of gendered subjectivity." *Contemporary Literature* contributor Karen Crown explained, "Keller cuts across conventional boundaries and definitions of the 'long poem' to redefine the genre and to expand its cannon in ways that can account for the richness and diversity of women's contemporary writing in extended poetic forms. . . . Her generic definition has the immediate effect of bringing into view a dazzling array of works by women." Noting the difficulty in the type of "critical eclecticism" Keller employs, Crown praised, "Keller . . . negotiates this critical minefield with tremendous success," concluding, "*Forms of Expansion* feels weighty densely compressed, and richly woven."

BIOGRAPHICAL/CRITICAL SOURCES:

PERIODICALS

American Literature, March, 1989, David porter, review of *Re-making It New,* p. 146; September, 1995, review of *Feminist Measures,* p. 631.

American Studies International, April, 1996, Camille Roman, review of *Feminist Measures,* p. 93.

Canadian Literature/Litterature canadienne, winter, 1996, Wanda A. Kelley, review of *Feminist Measures,* p. 173.

Choice, September, 1988, W. J. Martz, review of *Re-making It New,* p. 116; H. Susskind, December 1997, p. 637.

Contemporary Literature, summer, 1996, Jeanne Heuving, review of *Feminist Measures,* p. 315; winter, 1998, Kathleen Crown, review of *Forms of Expansion,* p. 644.

Modern Language Review, January, 1990, Paul Miller, review of *Re-making It New,* p. 172.

Signs, winter, 1999, Jeanne Heuving, review of *Forms of Expansion,* p. 514.

University of Michigan Press Catalogue, 1994.

*   *   *

KERR, LaRae Free   1944-

PERSONAL: Born November 28, 1944, in Caliente, Lincoln, NV; daughter of Lory M. and Myrtle Joy (Wadsworth) Free; married Ronald VanderBeek (divorced); married Walter J. Kerr, November 20, 1993; children: (first marriage) Simone A. VanderBeek Hentish, Margo J. VanderBeek Gunnarsson, David L. *Education:* Brigham Young University, B.A. (clothing and textiles), 1966, B.A. (English), 1970; Idaho State University, M.Ed., 1993. *Religion:* Church of Jesus Christ of Latter-day Saints (Mormons).

ADDRESSES: Home—New Harmony, UT 84757. *Office*—c/o Author Mail, Gateway Press, 1001 N. Calvert St., Baltimore, MD 21202. *E-mail*—KerrWorks@ bigfoot.com.

CAREER: College English teacher.

WRITINGS:

George Wadsworth, Gateway Press (Baltimore, MD), 1986.

Author of technical books on writing. Columnist. Contributor to history and genealogy journals.

WORK IN PROGRESS: Who Are You? A Workbook for Finding Your Ancestors; research for a novel about the mining era of Pioche, NV.

KIRKBY, Bruce   1968-

PERSONAL: Born January 8, 1968, in Toronto, Ontario, Canada; son of Peter and Joan Kirkby. *Education:* Queen's University, Kingston, Ontario, degree in engineering physics.

ADDRESSES: Office—1312 Edmonton Trail N.E., Calgary, Alberta, Canada T2E 3K7. *Agent*—Joanne Kellock. *E-mail*—bruce@brucekirkby.com.

CAREER: Organizer and leader of adventure expeditions, 1991—. Active with online children's education programs in Canada.

AWARDS, HONORS: Finalist, Banff International Mountain Book Festival, for *Sand Dance.*

WRITINGS:

Sand Dance: By Camel across Arabia's Great Southern Desert, McClelland & Stewart, 2000.

WORK IN PROGRESS: A book of guides' stories.

SIDELIGHTS: Bruce Kirkby told *CA:* "As an engineer who never did well in English, writing a book was one of the last things I ever envisaged doing. But I enjoyed every aspect of the book creation process so much, from writing to image selection and layout, that I knew I would write again.

"As a longtime guide and adventurer, my natural bent is storytelling, and my writing is centered around that—taking the audience away to an exotic faraway place and conveying the excitement I felt at the time. My second book contains campfire tales from ten years of guiding, some funny, some scary, some touching—many that your mother would not want to believe."

*   *   *

KLEIN, Jonas   1932-

PERSONAL: Born September 3, 1932, in Boston, MA; son of David G. (a dentist) and Mary Cohen Klein; married Lois Kanter (a librarian), May 27, 1956; children: Betsy K. Couture, Leslie J. *Education:* Bates College, B.A., 1954; Syracuse University, M.S.Sc., 1985. *Avocational interests:* Family, visual and performing arts, sports, collecting.

ADDRESSES: Office—P.O. Box 456, Georgetown, ME 04548. *E-mail*—lojo@gwi.net.

CAREER: IBM Corporation, Armonk, NY, communications manager, 1957-87; Town Planning Board, chair, 1988-94; Comprehensive Plan, editor, 1989-93. *Military service:* U.S. Army, 1955-57; noncommissioned officer.

MEMBER: Maine Historical Society, Georgetown Historical Society, Bates College Alumni Association (officer, 1994—).

AWARDS, HONORS: Outstanding contribution, IBM, 1965, for elections processing programs; Bates College Key, 1997, for service to college.

WRITINGS:

Corporate Design, GE House Organ, 1988.

Also author of *Beloved Director,* Paul S. Eriksson. Contributor to *Clients and Designers,* Watson Guptill, 1989.

*   *   *

KNEESE, Allen V(ictor)   1930-2001

*OBITUARY NOTICE—See index for *CA* sketch:* Born April 5, 1930, in Fredricksburg, TX; died March 14, 2001, in Alexandria, VA. Economist, educator, and author. Kneese was an environmental economist who led the development of the policies used today to encourage environmentally sound practices, especially in business and industry. A strong advocate of using economic incentives to bring about responsible pollution control, he researched for several years with an environmental research organization known as Resources for the Future, developed theories, and in 1978 was named a senior fellow there. Kneese authored dozens of works on environmental issues; some of these books include *Water Pollution: Economic Aspects and Research Needs, Quality of the Environment,* and *Economic Theory of Natural Resources.* Kneese was a professor of economics on and off during his career at the University of New Mexico.

OBITUARIES AND OTHER SOURCES:

PERIODICALS

Washington Post, March 17, 2001, p. B7.

KOCHHAR-LINDGREN, Gray   1955-

PERSONAL: Born January 15, 1955, in Memphis, TN; son of Gray (a businessman) and June (Thomason) Lindgren; married Kanta Kochhar (a professor and performer), May 24, 1980; children: Duncan. *Ethnicity:* "Caucasian." *Education:* University of Colorado, B.A., 1977; Yale Divinity School, M.A.R., 1982; University of North Carolina-Greensboro, M.S., 1987; Emory University, Ph.D., 1990.

ADDRESSES: Home—3156 North Concourse Dr., Mt. Pleasant, MI 48858. *Office*—Department of English, 219 Anspach, Central Michigan University, Mt. Pleasant, MI 48859. *E-mail*—GKochhar@aol.com.

CAREER: Univsersitat Regensburg, Regensburg, Germany, Lektor, 1991-93; Temple University, Philadelphia, PA, assistant professor of intellectual heritage, 1994-98; Central Michigan University, Mt. Pleasant, MI, assistant professor of English, 1998—.

MEMBER: Modern Language Association, International Association.

AWARDS, HONORS: First prize for short stories, *Colonnades Magazine,* 1985; first prize for essays, "Mind and Nature," 1987, for "Reading Archetypally: The Text as a Locus for Soul-Making"; ROCAD Teacher of the Year, 1997.

WRITINGS:

Narcissus Transformed: The Textual Subject in Psychoanalysis and Literature, Pennsylvania State University Press, 1993.
Starting Time: A True Account of the Origins of Creation, Sex, Death, and Golf, White Cloude, 1995.

Contributor of articles, essays, poems, and reviews to periodicals.

WORK IN PROGRESS: TechnoLogics: The Figure of Reason and the Suspension of Animation, scholarly work; *Q: A Novel;* research on humanities and technology, and literature, philosophy, psychoanalysis.

*   *   *

KOFAS, Jon V.   1953-

PERSONAL: Born September 29, 1953, in Greece; naturalized U.S. citizen; son of Vasilis (in the military) and

Matina (a homemaker; maiden name, Pappas) Kofas; married, October 13, 1994; wife's name Helen (a bank manager); children: Lena. *Ethnicity:* "Greek." *Education:* Loyola University of Chicago, Ph.D., 1979. *Politics:* Independent. *Religion:* None.

ADDRESSES: Home—14391 George Ct., Carmel, IN 46032. *Office*—Department of History, Indiana University at Kokomo, P.O. Box 9003, Kokomo, IN 46904-9003. *E-mail*—jkofas@iu.edu.

CAREER: Indiana University at Kokomo, professor of history, 1992—.

WRITINGS:

Greece and the Great Powers, 1832-1862, Columbia University Press (New York, NY), 1981.
Authoritarianism in Greece, Columbia University Press (New York, NY), 1983.

Dependence and Underdevelopment in Colombia, University of Arizona (Tucson, AZ), 1986.
Foreign Intervention and Underdevelopment, Pennsylvania State University Press (University Park, PA), 1989.
The Struggle for Legitimacy, Arizona State University (Tempe, AZ), 1992.
Foreign Debt and Underdevelopment: U.S.-Peru Economic Relations, 1930-1970, University Press of America (Lanham, MD), 1996.

Contributor to periodicals, including *International History Review, Journal of Developing Areas,* and *Journal of Third World Studies.*

WORK IN PROGRESS: Research for the book *The Sword of Damocles: The International Monetary Fund, the World Bank, and U.S. Foreign Policy in Chile and Colombia, 1950-1970.*

L

LACY, Dan (Mabry) 1914-2001

OBITUARY NOTICE—See index for *CA* sketch: Born February 28, 1914, in Newport News, VA; died April 17, 2001, in Durham, NC. Professor, copyright expert and author. Lacy was a nationally known copyright law expert and appointed by several presidents to serve organizations that handled copyright legislation. Lacy graduated with honors from the University of North Carolina in 1933 and again with a master's in 1935. His 1968 doctorate also came from that school and he was a member of Phi Beta Kappa. Lacy taught at his alma mater briefly after receiving his master's, but left for a job as assistant state director of the Historical Records Survey, which was part of the Works Progress Administration project. He stayed there for five years and then moved to the National Archives and later the U.S. Library of Congress, where he was deputy chief assistant librarian. After a stint as director of Information Center Services for the U.S. State Department, Lacy was hired at the American Book Publishers Council and then as a senior vice president of McGraw-Hill, where he stayed until retirement. In 1967 Lacy was appointed to the National Advisory Commission on Libraries and Information by President Lyndon B. Johnson. President Gerald R. Ford also recognized Lacy by selecting him for the National Commission on New Technological Uses of Copyrighted Works. He wrote several books during his career including *Books and the Future: A Speculation, The Meaning of the American Revolution, The Abolitionists* and 1996's *From Grunts to Gigabytes: Communications and Society.*

OBITUARIES AND OTHER SOURCES:

PERIODICALS

New York Times, April 29, 2001, p. A27.

LAI, Him Mark 1925-

PERSONAL: Born November 1, 1925, in San Francisco, CA; son of Mark Bing and Hing Mui (Dong) Lee; married Laura Jung, June 12, 1953; *Education:* San Francisco Junior College, A.A., 1945; University of California—Berkeley, B.S., 1947.

ADDRESSES: Home—357 Union St., San Francisco, CA 94133-3519.

CAREER: Utilities Engineering Bureau, San Francisco, CA, mechanical engineer, 1948-51; Bechtel Corporation, San Francisco, CA, mechanical engineer, 1953-84; San Francisco State University, San Francisco, CA, lecturer in Chinese American history, 1969, 1972-75; University of California, Berkeley, CA, lecturer in Chinese American history, 1978-79, 1984; University of California, Berkeley, CA, Asian American Studies Program, Chinese materials research collection, 1986-88; San Francisco State University, San Francisco, CA, professor of Asian American studies, 1990—; Chinese Culture Foundation, San Francisco, CA, *Chinese of America 1785-1980* (exhibition), director, Chinese in America in Search of Roots program, coordinator, 1991—; worked for Americans All, 1992-96. Coordinator for radio program "Hon Sing" (title means "Voice/Sounds"), 1971-84.

MEMBER: Chinese Historical Society (board of directors; president, 1971, 1976, 1977), Chinese Culture Foundation (board of directors; president 1982).

AWARDS, HONORS: American Book Award, 1982, for *Island: Poetry and History of Chinese Immigrants on Angel Island 1910-1940.*

Him Mark Lai

WRITINGS:

(With Thomas W. Chinn and Philip P. Choy) *A History of the Chinese in California: A Syllabus,* Chinese Historical Society of America (San Francisco, CA), 1969.

(Compiler, with Karl Lo) *Chinese Newspapers Published in North America, 1854-1975,* Center for Chinese Research Materials, Association of Research Libraries (Washington, DC), 1977.

(Translator, and editor with Genny Lim and Judy Yung) *Island: Poetry and History of Chinese Immigrants on Angel Island 1910-1940,* HOC DOI (San Francisco, CA), 1980.

The Chinese of America, 1785-1980: An Illustrated History and Catalog of the Exhibition, Chinese Culture Foundation (San Francisco, CA), 1980.

(Compiler) Russell Leong and Jean Pang Yip, editors, *A History Reclaimed: An Annotated Bibliography of Chinese Language Materials on the Chinese of America,* University of California Asian American Studies Center (Los Angeles, CA), 1986.

(Coeditor) *Collected Works of Gilbert Woo,* 1991.

Cong Hua qiao dao Hua ren: er shi shi ji Meiguo Hua ren she hui fa zhan shi (title means "From Overseas Chinese to Chinese American: History of Development of Chinese American Society During the Twentieth Century"), San lian shu dian (Hong Kong, China), 1992.

Contributor to journals, including *East-West* and *Chinese America: History and Perspectives,* and to the *Harvard Encyclopedia of American Ethnic Groups* (Cambridge, MA), 1980; *Asian American Encyclopedia* (New York, NY), 1995; and *The Encyclopedia of Chinese Overseas* (Singapore), 1998. Member of editorial boards for *Amerasia Journal,* 1979—, and *Chinese America: History and Perspectives,* 1986—.

SIDELIGHTS: Him Mark Lai is a leading historian whose writings, in both English and Chinese, are read by international audiences. He has accumulated a vast amount of information about his passion, Chinese-American history, much of it during his long career as an engineer. Decades before Asian-American studies programs became available on campuses, Lai was offering access to his huge collection to students, researchers, and writers who sought to understand and record the details of the lives of Chinese immigrants who had settled in America.

Lai began his life-long celebration of Chinese-American history in 1965, when he joined the Chinese Historical Society of America and studied under historian Stanford Lyman at the University of California Extension. He spent weekends visiting university libraries and other sites, as well as Chinese-Americans in their homes, collecting fragments of data on all aspects of the lives of Chinese immigrants and their ancestors. Eventually the field expanded, and Lai wrote a series of newspaper columns that became *A History of the Chinese in California: A Syllabus,* which he compiled with Thomas W. Chinn and Philip P. Choy in 1969, the same year Asian-American and other minority students staged a strike in support of establishing courses on ethnic studies at San Francisco State University. Both Choy, an architect, and Lai were invited by the school to teach their first courses in Chinese-American history. Lai taught there and at the University of California, Berkeley, during the 1970s and 1980s. Lai and Karl Lo, a librarian at the University of California, San Diego, compiled *Chinese Newspapers Published in North America, 1854-1975,* in which they noted that Chinese-language newspapers were published in the United States before they existed in China.

Lai's father came to the United States in 1910, his mother in 1923. They arrived at the Angel Island Immigration Station, located in a state park not far from Alcatraz off San Francisco Bay and that was modeled after Ellis Island in New York City. They were both detained during the Chinese Exclusion period that ran from 1882 until the 1940s, during which time Chinese immigrants were questioned before a decision was made as to whether they would be accepted into this country. During the holding period, some carved poems into the walls where they were housed, many of which reveal their frustrations. The Chinese were required to undergo more medical and legal tests than were required of other Asian immigrants, including the Japanese. Lai translated 135 of these poems and edited them with Judy Yung, associate professor of American Studies at the University of California, Santa Cruz, and playwright Genny Lim. They include historic photographs and oral histories of detainees and workers at the immigration station interviewed for this collection.

The poems are grouped into sections titled "The Voyage," "The Detainment," "The Weak Shall Conquer," "About Westerners," and "Deportees, Transients." The first edition of *Island: Poetry and History of Chinese Immigrants on Angel Island 1910-1940* was reviewed by David Meltzer in *American Book Review.* Meltzer said that the book "exists simultaneously on many levels: history, poetry, the pathology of racism. . . . *Island* is a moving and significant work." Lorraine Dong wrote in *Journal of American Ethnic History* that "translating from one language medium to another is not an easy task. This is especially the case with regard to poetry or any form of creative writing because translation itself is another creative activity. The process is complicated when it is not enough merely to know standard Chinese. One must also have a Chinese American sensibility to comprehend any Chinese work written about the American experience. Lai, Lim, and Yung have taken great pains to ensure accuracy." Charles Solomon reviewed the later edition for the *Los Angeles Times Book Review,* saying that "this moving volume documents a neglected chapter of American history."

Lai's *A History Reclaimed: An Annotated Bibliography of Chinese Language Materials on the Chinese of America* contains 1,600 items selected from the libraries of the University of California—Berkeley, the East Asian collection of the Hoover Institute, and the Chinese Historical Society of America. Topics covered include literature, journalism, emigration, business, Chinese-American organizations, and politics. Fluent in both Cantonese and Mandarin, Lai coordinated a long-running Chinese-language radio show that featured news, interviews, and music. Lai's articles have been published in many journals, including *Chinese America: History and Perspectives,* which he also edits for the Chinese Historical Society. His topics have included the history of Chinese benevolent societies and the Chinese-American left.

"The Chinese-American left, although it strongly supported nationalist movements in China, did work closely with the U.S. Communist Party and anti-imperialist causes, until the McCarthy era put an end to the movement," wrote Peter Monaghan in *Chronicle of Higher Education.* "Mr. Lai had his own McCarthyite experience. In the 1950s, he helped run Mun Ching, a community organization that held English classes, published a newsletter, and presented drama and music—until the Federal Bureau of Investigation agents pressured it to shut down, judging its activities too leftist."

In order to preserve his life's work. Lai is working with University of California, Berkeley on the indexing and housing of his collection. Through the San Francisco program, In Search of Roots, Lai continues to help young Chinese-Americans trace their ancestry through genealogical research.

BIOGRAPHICAL/CRITICAL SOURCES:

PERIODICALS

Amerasia Journal, Volume 26, number 1, 2000.
American Book Review, July, 1983, David Meltzer, "Snaps; or, Blips," p. 11.
Chronicle of Higher Education, January 14, 2000, Peter Monaghan, "The Scholar Who Legitimized the Study of Chinese in America," p. A21.
Journal of American Ethnic History, summer, 1995, Lorraine Dong, review of *Island,* p. 80.
Journal of the West, October, 1993, Jeffrey G. Barlow, review of *Island,* p. 103.
Los Angeles Times Book Review, July 19, 1992, Charles Solomon, "Paperbacks," p. 14.
MELUS, summer, 1991, Stan Yogi, review of *Island,* p. 77.
Pacific Affairs, fall, 1992, David Chuenyan Lai, review of *Island,* p. 448.*

*   *   *

LAKE, Inez Hollander 1965-

PERSONAL: Born 1965. *Education:* Earned advanced degrees in English, with emphasis on American and Southern literature, from Leiden University and the University of Nijmegen in the Netherlands, and from Leicester University in England.

ADDRESSES: Home—2050 Leyden Street, Denver, CO 80207-3937.

CAREER: Freelance writer.

WRITINGS:

The Road from Pompey's Head: The Life and Work of Hamilton Basso, Louisiana State University Press (Baton Rouge, LA), 1999.

SIDELIGHTS: In *The Road from Pompey's Head: The Life and Work of Hamilton Basso,* Inez Hollander Lake provides a biography of Basso (1904-64), who was a well-known writer from the South during the 1930s to the 1950s, but whose work has fallen into obscurity. He wrote eleven novels; the best known of these was *The View from Pompey's Head,* published in 1954.

According to Lake, Basso's work was an important part of Southern literature. He was friends with writers Thomas Wolfe, William Faulkner, Sherwood Anderson, Van Wyck Brooks, Malcolm Cowley, Edmund Wilson, and F. Scott Fitzgerald, and was edited by Maxwell Perkins. His work appeared in the *New Republic* and the *New Yorker,* and he was an editor of the *New Yorker.* After his death, however, his work was no longer published, and he was largely forgotten, despite the fact that *The View from Pompey's Head* spent over forty weeks on the *New York Times* bestseller list and was translated into seven languages. Lake discusses the importance of this book, and also contends that his less well-known books, such as *Cinnamon Seed* and *Courthouse Square,* need to be reexamined.

Lake examined archives and previously unavailable and unpublished material, such as letters, diaries, and manuscripts, and interviewed Basso's family and friends, to provide a balanced biography of Basso and an assessment of his work.

BIOGRAPHICAL/CRITICAL SOURCES:

PERIODICALS

Library Journal, April 1, 1999, p. 98.*

*   *   *

LANG, Robert (Peregrine) 1912-2001

OBITUARY NOTICE—See index for *CA* sketch: Born March 25, 1912, in Hope, ND; died of complications from surgery, March 11, 2001, in Long Beach, CA. Librarian and author. Lang helped increase the size of the of the University of California at Riverside's library collection from 200,000 to 900,000 volumes in the fifteen years he worked there as a librarian. Lang received bachelor's and master's degrees from the University of California and his library degree from Columbia University. He was a librarian and instructor at several schools before moving to the University of California at Riverside, among them Oberlin, Cornell and the State University of New York College at New Paltz. Lang had a Fulbright scholarship in 1960 and taught at the University of the Punjab in Lahore, Pakistan, while his wife, an English professor, taught at Foreman Christian College, which was close by. The Langs returned to the United States and both accepted jobs at Riverside—he in the libraries and she in the English department. They wrote the book *In a Valley Fair: A History of the State University of New York College at New Paltz* in 1961. And in 1968 Lang wrote *The Land and People of Pakistan.* Lang retired in 1978 but continued to work on special library projects until he died, including a timeline of sixteenth and seventeenth century English history for the university's English Short Title Catalogue project.

OBITUARIES AND OTHER SOURCES:

PERIODICALS

American Libraries, May 21, 2001, p. 84.
Press-Enterprise (Riverside, CA), March 18, 2001, p. B4; April 21, 2001, p. B4.

*   *   *

LANGLEY, Jonathan 1952-

PERSONAL: Born October 31, 1952, in Lancaster, Lancashire, England; son of Raymond (a civil engineer) and Margaret (a homemaker; maiden name, Bickerstaff) Langley; married Karen Arnold (a teacher), February 10, 1978; children: Toby, Holly, Rosita. *Education:* Attended Lancaster College of Art, 1970-71; Liverpool Polytechnic College of Art and Design, B.A. (with honors; graphic design/illustration), 1974; Central School of Art and Design, postgraduate studies; Camberwell School of Art, postgraduate studies in bookbinding, M.A. (with honors; graphic design),1978. *Politics:* Socialist. *Religion:* "Non-specific." *Avocational interests:* Cinema, music (particularly modern jazz), walking, travel, photography, food and drink.

ADDRESSES: Office—c/o Collins, 77-85 Fulham Palace Rd., Hammersmith, London W6 8JB, England. *Agent*—John Hodgson, 38 Westminster Palace Gardens, Artillery Row, London SW1P 1RR, England. *E-mail*—j@zzer.globalnet.co.uk.

CAREER: Author and freelance illustrator/designer. Worked in the fields of publishing, editorial, design, advertising, film, gift marketing, and packaging, 1974—.

AWARDS, HONORS: Best Illustrated Book Award, *Parents* magazine, and Play and Learn Awards, both 1998, both for *SNORE!;* Highly Commended Award in picture book category, Sheffield Children's Book Award, 2000, for *The Biggest Bed in the World.*

WRITINGS:

SELF-ILLUSTRATED

(Reteller) *The Three Billy Goats Gruff,* Collins (London, England), 1992, HarperCollins (New York, NY), 1998.
(Reteller) *The Three Bears and Goldilocks,* Collins (London, England), 1991, HarperCollins (New York, NY), 1993.
(Reteller) *The Story of Rumpelstiltskin,* Collins (London, England), 1991, HarperCollins (New York, NY), 1993.
(Reteller) *Little Red Riding Hood,* Collins (London, England), 1992, HarperCollins (New York, NY), 1994.
The Collins Book of Nursery Tales, Collins (London, England), 1993.
Nursery Pop-up Book: Goldilocks and the Three Bears, HarperCollins (New York, NY), 1993.
(Reteller) *The Princess and the Frog,* Collins (London, England), 1993, HarperCollins (New York, NY), 1995.
(Reteller) *The Ugly Duckling,* Collins (London, England), 1993, HarperCollins (New York, NY), 1995.
Nursery Pop-up Book: Little Red Riding Hood, Collins (London, England), 1995, Barron's Educational (Hauppauge, NY), 1996.
Nursery Pop-up Book: Three Little Pigs, Collins (London, England), 1995, Barron's Educational (Hauppauge, NY), 1996.
Nursery Pop-up Book: Hansel and Gretel, Collins (London, England), 1996, Barron's Educational (Hauppauge, NY), 1997.
Collins Bedtime Treasury of Nursery Rhymes and Tales, Collins (London, England), 1997.
Babies Bedtime Lullabies and Verse, Collins (London, England), 1997.
Favourite Nursery Rhymes, Collins (London, England), 1999.

MISSING!, Francis Lincoln (London, England), 2000, Marshall Cavendish (New York, NY), 2000.

ILLUSTRATOR

Fay Maschler, *Cooking is a Way round the World,* Penguin Books (London, England), 1978.

Kenneth Grahame, *The Wind in the Willows,* Octopus, 1984.

L. Frank Baum, *The Wizard of Oz,* Octopus, 1985.

Carolyn Sloan, *The Friendly Robot,* Derrydale Books (New York, NY), 1987.

Anne Civardi, *Potty Time,* Simon & Schuster (New York, NY), 1988.

Lizzy Pearl, *What Have I Lost?,* Dial (New York, NY), 1988.

Lizzy Pearl, *What Time Is It?,* Dial (New York, NY), 1988.

Martin Waddell, *Alice the Artist,* Dutton (New York, NY), 1988.

Rudyard Kipling, *How the Whale Got His Throat,* Philomel (New York, NY) 1988.

Rudyard Kipling, *How the Camel Got His Hump,* Philomel (New York, NY) 1988.

Rudyard Kipling, *How the Rhinoceros Got His Skin,* Philomel (New York, NY), 1988.

Martin Waddell, *Daisy's Christmas,* Ideals (Nashville, TN), 1990.

Martin Waddell, *Daisy the Dreamer,* Methuen (London, England), 1990.

The Collins Book of Nursery Rhymes, Collins (London, England), 1990.

Lisa Taylor, *A Pig Called Shrimp,* Collins (London, England), 1990.

Rain, Rain, Go Away!: A Book of Nursery Rhymes, Dial (New York, NY), 1991.

Miss Read, *The Little Red Bus and Other Rhyming Stories,* Penguin Books (London, England), 1991.

Betty Root, *My First Dictionary,* Dorling Kindersley (New York, NY), 1993.

Nursery Pop-up Book: Animal Rhymes, Collins (London, England), 1994.

Nursery Pop-up Book: Favourite Rhymes, Collins (London, England), 1994.

The Giant Sandwich, Ginn (London, England), 1994.

Hilary Aaron, *Three Little Kittens in the Enchanted Forest: A Pop-up Adventure,* Collins (London, England), 1995.

Collins Nursery Treasury, Collins (London, England), 1996.

Michael Rosen, *SNORE!* Collins (London, England), 1998.

Hiawyn Oram, *Where Are You Hiding Little Lamb?,* Collins (London, England), 1999.

Lindsay Camp, *The Biggest Bed in the Whole World,* Collins (London, England), 1999, HarperCollins (New York, NY), 2000.

OTHER

Author of *Doris and the Mice from Mars,* illustrated by Hilary Hayton, 1981.

WORK IN PROGRESS: Children's picture books for HarperCollins and Frances Lincoln.

SIDELIGHTS: Jonathan Langley has been a freelance writer and illustrator of children's books for more than twenty-five years. During these years he has worked in various associated areas such as publishing, editing, design, advertising, film, gift marketing, and packaging. He has also written several books of his own, as well as illustrating them. Many of these are original stories whereas others are refreshing retellings of classic tales for children.

Langley was born on October 31, 1952, in Lancaster, Lancashire. His father was a civil engineer and his mother was a homemaker. Langley attended the Lancaster College of Art and completed his foundation studies in 1971. He went on to attend Liverpool College of Art and Design, where he earned his bachelor's degree in graphic design in the area of illustration in 1974. He followed that up with a master's degree in graphic design from the Camberwell School of Art located at the Central School of Art and Design (London), in 1978. While at Camberwell, he also studied bookbinding as part of his postgraduate course. Langley has a variety of interests like cinema, music (particularly modern jazz), walking, travel, photography, food, and drink which give him breadth of focus and help him in his work.

Rain, Rain, Go Away!: A Book of Nursery Rhymes is a combination of popular nursery rhymes interspersed with less familiar verses, sayings, and poems. Dorothy F. Houlihan notes in *School Library Journal* that Langley's text is accompanied by lively illustrations that are pleasing in their rhythm and imagery. She further states that Langley maintains the tempo throughout the book, loosely grouping his rhymes according to subject. According to Houlihan, Langley's black-pen outline and bright watercolor illustrations are extremely attractive, lending personality and charm to the book. In a tribute to his dexterity in handling the subject, the critic comments that, "Multiracial characters are depicted with disarming ease, ignoring stereotypical assumptions about the nature of traditional nursery rhymes."

The same lively spirit permeates Langley's retelling of the classic *The Story of Rumpelstiltskin.* "Iconoclastic additions [are] freely incorporated into the spritely retelling," according to a *Kirkus Reviews* contributor. The critic further notes that the illustrations are executed with the same vivacious energy, the characters are drawn like cheerful children, and even Rumpelstiltskin is less than menacing with hardly an unkind gleam in his eye. Langley's treatment is contemporary and quite naturally leads to a " 'fractured' ending that has the king falling victim to (and *into*) his own Crocodile Pool," according to Linda Boyles in *School Library Journal.*

The Three Bears and Goldilocks is subject to the same contemporary treatment, with an extension of traditional gender roles. The father bear helps in cleaning the house by vacuuming it and takes his turn making breakfast while the mother bear uses an electric drill to fix the baby bear's chair. According to reviewers, Langley's lively text is full of good humor and the artwork, and the illustrations are detailed with numerous bear motifs for young readers to discover along their journey.

The Princess and the Frog and *The Ugly Duckling* were both praised by critics for their invitingly large format and attractive presentation. Langley's attention to detail in the illustrations, ranging from two-page spreads to depictions of minute insects in the margins, was appreciated. Critic Trevor Dickinson of *School Librarian* similarly admired *The Collins Book of Nursery Tales* for its "briskly energetic" language and its "lively, joyful brashness." Though Langley's *Nursery Pop-up Book: Little Red Riding Hood* follows the traditional pattern of the tale, critics say it nevertheless contains numerous details that give it a modern feel. As with *The Story of Rumpelstiltskin,* Langley adds his unique touch to the end of the classic tale.

In her review of several of Langley's books for *School Librarian,* Cathy Sutton noted that the author/illustrator "rounds off and enhances the tales by attaching a humorous conclusion which tells of later events." It is perhaps such refreshing viewpoints and novel postscripts that make Langley's books widely appreciated and make them stand out from the numerous already available on the subjects.

BIOGRAPHICAL/CRITICAL SOURCES:

PERIODICALS

Booklist, May 15, 1991, Carolyn Phelan, review of *Rain, Rain, Go Away!,* p. 1801; February 1, 1992, review of *The Story of Rumpelstiltskin,* p. 1034; May 1, 2000, Carolyn Phelan, review of *The Biggest Bed in the World,* p. 1675.

Books for Keeps, November, 1994, Jill Bennett, review of *The Princess and the Frog,* p. 11.

Junior Bookshelf, February, 1994, review of *The Ugly Duckling,* p. 16.

Kirkus Reviews, December 15, 1991, review of *The Story of Rumpelstiltskin,* p. 1593; February 15, 1993, review of *The Three Bears and Goldilocks,* p. 229.

Magpies, July, 1992, Jo Goodman, review of *The Story of Rumpelstiltskin* and *The Three Bears and Goldilocks,* p. 25.

Publishers Weekly, September 4, 1995, review of *Three Little Kittens in the Enchanted Forest,* p. 68; January 24, 2000, review of *The Biggest Bed in the World,* p. 310.

School Librarian, February, 1993, Cathy Sutton, review of *The Three Billy Goats Gruff, Nursery Pop-up Book: Little Red Riding Hood,* and *The Story of Rumpelstiltskin,* p. 16; May, 1994, Trevor Dickinson, review of *The Collins Book of Nursery Tales,* p. 56.

School Library Journal, August, 1991, Dorothy F. Houlihan, review of *Rain, Rain, Go Away!,* p. 162; February, 1992, Linda Boyles, review of *The Story of Rumpelstiltskin,* p. 82; March, 1993, Kate McClelland, review of *The Three Bears and Goldilocks,* pp. 191-192; January, 1994, Dorcas Hand, review of *My First Dictionary,* p. 110.

*   *   *

LaPLANTE, Royal   1929-

PERSONAL: Born September 1, 1929, in Oakland, CA; son of Royal (a logger and grocery store owner) and Margaret Shannon (a grocery store owner) LaPlante; married Joanne I. Corfman; children: Royal III, Marc, Joseph. *Ethnicity:* "Caucasian." *Education:* University of Puget Sound—Tacoma, B.A., 1954, M.Ed., 1959; Washington State University—Pullman, D.Ed., 1968. *Politics:* "Fiscal conservatism." *Religion:* "Christian (not active in church)." *Avocational interests:* Writing.

ADDRESSES: Home—826 Browns Point Blvd. N.E., Tacoma, WA 98422. *Agent*—Sherwood Broome, Inc., Box 778, Absarokee, MT, 59001.

CAREER: Bethel High School, Spanaway, WA, math and science teacher, 1954-56 and 1958-59; Vicenza

High School (Army), Vicenza, Italy, math and science teacher, 1956-58; Baumholder High School, Baumholder, Germany, teacher, assistant principal, and principal, 1959-62 and 1964-66; Livorno High School, Livorno, Italy, principal, 1962-63; Bad Krevznach High School, Germany, principal, 1963-64; Longview Schools, Longview, WA, administrative assistant, 1968-72; Lake Chelan Schools, Chelan, WA, superintendent, 1972-76; Concrete Schools, Concrete, WA, superintendent, 1976-81; Liberty Schools, Spangle, WA, superintendent, 1981-83; Mannheim Middle School, Mannheim, Germany, math and science teacher, 1983-84; Zaragoza High School, Zaragoza, Spain, principal, 1984-88; Wuerzburg Elementary School, Wuerzburg, Germany, principal, 1988-91. Cowlitz County Drug Council, 1968-72; Lake Chelan Chamber of Commerce, president, 1975-76; Lake Chelan Rotary, vice president, 1975-76; Concrete Chamber of Commerce, executive board, 1976-81; Concrete Lions, president, 1978-79; Washington Association of School Administrators, executive board, 1974-76, regional president, 1981. *Military service:* U.S. Marine Corps, 1947-50; became corporeal; received good conduct medal and sharpshooter badge.

WRITINGS:

The Myrtlewood Grove (western/historical fiction), Northwest, 1994.
Penalomah, The Eagle Soars (western/historical fiction), Blackforest, 1997.

WORK IN PROGRESS: Uncle Jack's Creek; Cottage Cove, a Chechako in Alaska, for Blackforest; "genealogical research on LaPlantes (Quebec 1656-1876)."

SIDELIGHTS: Royal LaPlante told *CA* that his primary motivation for writing is "creative expression during my retirement years." "Places I have lived and experiences I have had (Northwest USA), plus my wife" are influences on LaPlante's work. His writing process includes "research of the site and in the library for history, and writing three hours per day." "Personal knowledge and interest, plus stories old friends told me over the years" are what inspired LaPlante to write on the subjects he has chosen.

*   *   *

LAUX, Dorianne (Louise) 1952-

PERSONAL: Born January 10, 1952, in Augusta, ME; daughter of Alton (a mill worker) and Frances Comeau (a nurse; maiden name, Turner; present surname, Laux) Green; married Ron Salisbury, 1991 (marriage ended, 1994); married Joseph Millar, December 12, 1997; children: Tristem Laux. *Education:* Mills College, B.A. (with honors), 1988. *Politics:* Democrat.

ADDRESSES: Home—1755 West 17th Ave., Eugene, OR 97402. *Office*—Program in Creative Writing, University of Oregon, Eugene, OR 97403; fax 541-346-0538. *E-mail*—dlaux@darkwing.uoregon.edu.

CAREER: California College of Arts and Crafts, Oakland, adjunct teacher of poetry and independent studies, 1992-93; University of Oregon, Eugene, assistant professor, 1994-97, associate professor of writing, 1997—, director of Program in Creative Writing, 1998-99. University of Arkansas, visiting writer, 1998; University of Minnesota, visiting teacher, 1998; University of Memphis, visiting writer, 1999; University of Idaho, distinguished visiting writer in poetry, 1999; Hamline University, writer in residence, 2000; guest lecturer at other institutions, including Antioch University, California State University, Fresno, Lewis and Clark College, Swarthmore College, and Sarah Lawrence College. Frequent judge of poetry contests; participant in conferences and workshops; gives readings from her works.

AWARDS, HONORS: Pushcart Prize, 1986; award from Ina Coolbrith Statewide Poetry Competition, 1988; Isabella Gardner fellow, MacDowell Colony, 1988; resident at Djerassi Foundation, 1988, and Yaddo, 1989; Bread Loaf fellow and Margaret Bridgeman fellow in poetry, 1990; fellow of National Endowment for the Arts, 1990 and 2001; Editor's Choice III Award, 1991; resident at Villa Montalvo, 1994; finalist for National Book Critics Circle Award, poetry category, 1995, for *What We Carry.*

WRITINGS:

(With Laurie Duesing and Kim Addonizio) *Three West Coast Women* (poems), Five Fingers Poetry (San Francisco, CA), 1983.
Awake (poems), BOA Editions (Rochester, NY), 1990.
What We Carry (poems), BOA Editions (Rochester, NY), 1994.
(With Addonizio) *The Poet's Companion: A Guide to the Pleasures of Writing Poetry,* Norton (New York, NY), 1997.
Smoke (poems), BOA Editions (Rochester, NY), 2000.

Work represented in more than a dozen anthologies, including *The Best American Poetry, 1999,* Scribner (New York, NY), 1999; *Catholic Girls,* Harper (New

York, NY); *Gender Issues,* McGraw-Hill Ryerson; *Pushcart Press: Best of the Small Presses;* and *Touching Fire,* Carroll & Graf (New York, NY). Contributor of poems, essays, and reviews to periodicals, including *American Poetry Review, Five Fingers Review, Kenyon Review, Ploughshares, Poet Lore,* and *Shenandoah.* Coeditor, *Americas Review,* 1990-94; guest editor, *Alaska Quarterly,* 1998; contributing editor, *Poetry Flash,* 1990—, and *Editor's Choice IV.*

WORK IN PROGRESS: A poetry collection, *Music in the Morning;* research on "camera oscura," the poetry of work, and women's issues.

BIOGRAPHICAL/CRITICAL SOURCES:

PERIODICALS

American Poetry Review, July-August, 1992, Sam Hamill, "A Poetry of Daily Practice: Adrienne Rich, S. J. Marks, Dorianne Laux," pp. 35-38.
Poet Lore, Volume 90, number 1, 1994, Judith Vollmer, "The Body's Devotion and Astonishment."

*   *   *

LAYTON, Neal (Andrew) 1971-

PERSONAL: Born December 19, 1971, in Chichester, England; son of Harry (a taxi driver) and Joyce (Davidson) Layton. *Education:* University of Northumbria at Newcastle, B.A. (with honors), 1994; Central St. Martin's College of Art and Design, M.A. (with distinction), 1998.

ADDRESSES: Home—31 High St., Flat 1, Eton, Berkshire SL4 6AX, England; fax 01-75-367-1360. *Agent*—Arena, 11 King's Ridge Rd., Long Valley, NJ 07853. *E-mail*—neal.layton@virgin.net.

CAREER: Freelance writer and illustrator, 1997—. Epsom Art College, tutor, 2000. Work has been included in exhibitions in London and other British cities, and at the Society of Illustrators Museum of American Illustration, New York City.

WRITINGS:

SELF-ILLUSTRATED CHILDREN'S BOOKS

The Photo, Bloomsbury, 1998, published as *Smile If You're Human,* Dial Books for Young Readers (New York, NY), 1999.

Oscar and Arabella, Hodder & Stoughton (London, England), in press.

Also author of *Emily's Animals.*

ILLUSTRATOR

Susan McPadden, *Baked Beans, Bananas, and Tomato Sauce,* Tango, 1998.
Michael Rosen, *Rover,* Bloomsbury, 1999.
Lucy Coates, *Neil's Numberless World,* Dorling Kindersley, 2000.
Francesca Simon, *Three Cheers for Ostrich,* David & Charles, 2000.
Frieda Wishinsky, *Nothing Scares Us,* Bloomsbury, 2000.
Herbie Brennan, *Zartog's Remote,* Bloomsbury, 2000.
Alphapets, Ladybird, 2001.

Contributor of illustrations to other books. Contributor to periodicals, including *Nickelodeon, Sunday Express, Human Resources,* and *20/20 Vision.*

WORK IN PROGRESS: Steve's Sunday Blues, a picture book, for Hodder & Stoughton.

SIDELIGHTS: Neal Layton told *CA:* "*Smile If You're Human* was the first picture storybook I both wrote and illustrated. It began life as a project on my degree at the University of Northumbria, and after further development it was published in England, the United States, Germany, and Japan. I have always been interested in animals and space travel. The idea of combining the two came about after discovering an essay I had written as a child, 'What I Did at the Weekend.' One of the key points in the story was to make an alien family actually look alien. After experimenting with various green, bug-eyed creatures, and other clichés, I eventually found the inspiration I sought in a cubist painting by Picasso.

"I like my work to be funny and stupid and nonsensical and meaningful and sensical all at the same time. Humor is a very powerful and multifaceted thing—and it's fun, too!

"I don't specifically think of myself as drawing or writing exclusively for children. I think that a good book can appeal, amuse, and have meaning for people of all ages."

BIOGRAPHICAL/CRITICAL SOURCES:

PERIODICALS

Publishers Weekly, February 8, 1999, "Spring 1999 Children's Books," p. 111.
Sunday Telegraph, July 19, 1998, review of *The Photo.*

* * *

LEVINE, Terri 1957-

PERSONAL: Born December 29, 1957, in Yonkers, NY; daughter of Seymour Walter (a sales/marketing vice-president) and Helen (Morgenbesser) Levine; married Mark Elliot Levine (a financial planner), June 3, 1979. *Education:* University of Pittsburgh, B.A., 1978; Ithaca College, M.S., 1979; Coach C, C.T.P., 2000. *Religion:* Jewish. *Avocational interests:* Career coaching.

ADDRESSES: Home and Office—727 Mallard Pl., N. Wales, PA 19454; fax: 215-699-3153. *E-mail*—terri@ workyourselfhappy.com.

CAREER: Prism Rehab Systems, Boston, MA, director of operations, 1993-96; RehabWorks, Longhorne, PA, regional president, 1996-98; Comprehensive Coaching U, Inc., N. Wales, PA, president, 1998—; business coach for healthcare organizations.

MEMBER: International Coach Federation, Business Network International, National Association of Women Business Owners, American Society of Training and Development, American Speech-Language Hearing Association, Philadelphia Area Coaches Alliance.

WRITINGS:

Work Yourself Happy, Lahaska, 2000.

WORK IN PROGRESS: Work Yourself Happy Workbook; Work Yourself Happy for Entrepreneurs.

SIDELIGHTS: Terri Levine told *CA:* "I write because I have a powerful message to share with many people and want to share it. Writing is natural and effortless for me. My writing is inspired by my passion for the career coaching work I do and the real experiences and stories are shared through my work. When I write I typically do brain-dumps with all my thought and then chunk this into sections and then create chapters from there. I limit myself to two drafts per chapter. *Work Yourself Happy* is my message for life, my legacy and is my coaching. I am totally inspired to help people find joy and delight in their work and their lives. *Work Yourself Happy* IS my message."

* * *

LIDZ, Theodore 1910-2001

OBITUARY NOTICE—See index for *CA* sketch: Born April 1, 1910, in New York, NY; died February 16, 2001, in Hamden, CT. Psychiatrist, educator, and author. Lidz was a psychiatrist who taught at Yale University from 1951 to 1978, when he retired as Sterling Professor Emeritus there. A doctor with a passion for seeking the external and internal causes of mental illness, he spent several years observing and researching the backgrounds of patients in hopes of finding the etiology of their illnesses. Lidz wrote several books on the subject. His first work, *The Family and Human Adaptation,* was published in 1963. *Schizophrenia and the Family,* written with Fleck and Cornelison, followed in 1965. Some of his other works include *Hamlet's Enemy* and *Relevance of the Family to Psychoanalytic Theory.* Lidz was the 1967 recipient of the Salmon Lecturer Medal for his outstanding lectures in psychiatry.

OBITUARIES AND OTHER SOURCES:

PERIODICALS

New York Times, February 28, 2001, p. A23.

* * *

LIMÓN, Graciela 1938-

PERSONAL: Born August 2, 1938, in, Los Angeles, CA; daughter of Jesús (a truck driver) and Altagracia (a laundress; maiden name, Gómez) Limón. *Education:* Marymount College, B.A., 1965; University of the Americas, Mexico City, M.A., (Spanish literature), 1969; University of California, Los Angeles, Ph.D. (Latin American literature), 1975.

ADDRESSES: Home—740 North Bradshawe St., Montebello, CA 90640. *Office*—Loyola Marymount University, Dept. of Modern Languages, 7101 West 80th St., Los Angeles, CA 90045-2659.

CAREER: Novelist and educator. Loyola Marymount University, Los Angeles, CA, assistant professor,

1969-75, associate professor, 1975-80, professor and chair of the Department of Chicana and Chicano Studies, 1980—.

AWARDS, HONORS: Chicano Literature award, University of California, Irvine, Before Columbus Foundation Book Award, and critics's choice award, *New York Times Book Review,* all 1993, all for *In Search of Bernabé.*

WRITINGS:

María de Belén: The Autobiography of an Indian Woman, Vantage (New York, NY), 1990.
In Search of Bernabé, Arte Público Press (Houston, TX), 1993.
The Memories of Ana Calderón, Arte Público Press (Houston, TX), 1994.
Song of the Hummingbird, Arte Público Press (Houston, TX), 1996.
The Day of the Moon, Arte Público Press (Houston, TX), 1999.
Erased Facts, Arte Público Press (Houston, TX), 2001.

Contributor to periodicals and anthologies.

SIDELIGHTS: Graciela Limón is an educator and author whose novels address the issues of multiculturalism, national identity, feminism, and social justice. Limón was born in Los Angeles to parents who had emigrated from Mexico. As a student she was a voracious reader, particularly of historical works, and she aspired to becoming a writer at an early age. Her schooling followed the track traditional for women during the mid-twentieth century, but while she worked as a stenographer Limón saved for her education, which culminated with a Ph.D. from the University of California in 1975. She began her teaching career at Loyola Marymount University in 1969 and became a full professor of U.S. Hispanic literature and chair of the Department of Chicana and Chicano Studies in 1980. Into the twenty-first century she remains a prominent voice in the genre of Latina literature, novels such as *Song of the Hummingbird* and *Erased Facts* gaining her the respect of critics.

Limón began writing fiction in the late 1980s. She researched the conquest of Mexico and its colonial period for her first work, *María de Belén: The Autobiography of an Indian Woman,* in which she combines fiction, history, autobiography, *testimonio, crónica,* transcription, and translation. The prologue is narrated by the translator of the sixteenth-century autobiography of an indigenous woman who witnessed the takeover of her country and its aftermath. Ellen McCracken wrote in

Dictionary of Literary Biography that "the multiple frames around the indigenous woman's narrative self-consciously question the validity of historiography. The fictitious translation reminds readers to question other material outside the main narrative, such as the scholarly endnotes that annotate the main text and other historical narratives that claim to present a truthful account of the events of the conquest. María de Belén's account is intended by the author to call into question the accepted master narratives of the conquest without itself becoming another master narrative."

The inspiration for her next novel came from Limón's interaction, from 1986 to 1991, with Salvadoran refugees who were given asylum at the church at La Placita in Los Angeles, declared a sanctuary by Father Luis Olivares, and from a 1990 trip to El Salvador as part of a delegation investigating the murders of Jesuit priests the previous year. Limón demonstrated at the church and at the federal building against the involvement of the United States in the civil war waging in El Salvador. She wrote *In Search of Bernabé,* a novel critical of U.S. involvement that questions the decisions of characters in the story. "Neither the Left nor the Right can be classified as entirely good or entirely evil," explained McCracken. "Limón rereads the Bible and religious motifs in terms of the political upheaval in Central America but also brings ethical and moral values to bear on the social turmoil."

In Search of Bernabé covers the period from the 1980 bombing of the funeral procession of assassinated Archbishop Oscar Romero to the signing of the peace treaty in 1992. The central character is Luz Delcano, the mother of two sons who are moral opposites. Luz, herself the result of her servant mother's union with an aristocrat, bore Lucio after being raped, at age thirteen, by her employer and grandfather. Forced to surrender Lucio to her rapist and his aristocratic family, Luz took a position with another family and conceived a second son, Bernabè, while in a relationship with her new employer.

As the story opens, Bernabè, a seminarian marching in the funeral procession of the murdered archbishop, loses sight of his mother in the crowd. He abandons his path to the priesthood and joins guerrillas hiding in the Chalatenango Mountains while Lucio, who now leads the death squads of the Salvadorian army, is determined to kill the brother he has never met. Luz travels from El Salvador to Mexico and Los Angeles, then home again in search of her youngest son.

"As she lays out this plot, Ms. Limón also paints a detailed portrait of Salvadoran society, concentrating on the war that threatened to destroy the Salvadoran nation," noted Ilan Stavans in a *New York Times Book Review* appraisal of *In Search of Bernabé*. "At the end, having revisited what Graham Greene called 'the lawless roads' south of the Rio Grande, the reader is left with a sense of both sadness and redemption." *Booklist* reviewer Martha Schoolman called the novel "tightly woven," while "Luz's search for her son and her deteriorating mental state as a result of war are compelling and chilling," according to a *Publishers Weekly* critic.

Limón's *The Memories of Ana Calderón,* told in both the first and third person, is the story of a woman born in a southern Mexico fishing village. Ana is blamed for poisoning her mother's womb, because none of the three sons she bore following Ana's birth survived. When her mother dies, Ana's father, Rodolfo, takes the family, including an adopted son, Octavio, north to harvest tomatoes. Sandra Scofield wrote in *Washington Post Book World* that "the difficulties of that journey and the exigencies of the migrants' lives are developed with the scene-by-scene simplicity of a heartfelt young adult novel. . . . The life of the barrio is also rendered ably, as is Ana's yearning for education." The family crosses the border and settles in Los Angeles, where Rodolfo forces Ana to quit high school and work in a factory. She becomes pregnant by Octavio and is beaten by Rodolfo, who doesn't know the identity of the baby's father. Octavio agrees to marry Ana but doesn't fulfill his promise, and Ana is taken in by a kindly Anglo couple who own a chicken ranch. Octavio marries Ana's sister, Alejandra, and tries to steal the baby, Ismael, whereupon Ana shoots him and is sent to jail and the baby given up for adoption. When Ana is released, she completes her education and eventually becomes rich and successful. In response to the novel's plotline, a *Publishers Weekly* contributor felt that what began "as a sensitive exploration of one woman's attempt to come to terms with two cultures now becomes an increasingly chaotic portrait of a dysfunctional family."

Booklist reviewer Greg Burkman called *The Memories of Ana Calderón* "a story of the hard realities that command a contemporary choice between personal freedom and familial, cultural tradition." A *Kirkus Reviews* contributor praised Limón's fiction, dubbing it an "artfully written novel." Greg Sanchez commented in *World Literature Today* that the novelist's account of Ana's life "is informed by an array of traditional themes and archetypal patterns, from the story of Oedipus to the American Dream. In fact, the extraordinary quality of Ana's life is due less to her development as a character than to her position at the hub of the text's thematic wheel and the narrative sequence which sets the wheels spinning."

Attempting to rewrite her first book, *María de Belén,* for Arte Público, Limón found it impossible. Instead she rewrote the novel as *Song of the Hummingbird,* which according to *Library Journal* reviewer Mary Margaret Benson "explores the endurance of the human spirit in a world of political, social, and emotional violence." Hummingbird is Huitzitzilin, who, nearing the end of her life, calls for a priest to hear her last confession. She tells her sins to Franciscan friar Benito Lara, a Spaniard, in the context of the history during which they occurred. Huitzitzilin had been an Aztec princess in the court of Montezuma before the conquest of Mexico by Cortes. She tells the young priest how conditions deteriorated when greed and religious zeal forced her people to become slaves of the Spaniards. She describes how she cut her own face after the deaths of her husband and child and of other pagan rituals practiced by her people. The priest is horrified by these descriptions and attempts to refocus Huitzitzilin to focus on her confession without the associated details.

Delia A. Culberson wrote in *Voice of Youth Advocates* that Huitzitzilin's "passionate recounting of her tormented past is so detailed, so graphic, that despite his initial disbelief, the priest knows in his heart that the old woman is telling the truth. He now sees her not as a heathen savage but as a fellow suffering human being; he comes to admire her endurance in the face of disaster, and experiences a profound sorrow over the loss of her precious heritage." *Washington Post Book World* contributor Elizabeth Hanley called the story "downright hypnotic" and said that "what makes Hummingbird so compelling has of course a great deal to do with what she's incorporated from a culture long destroyed."

Another deathbed confession serves as the framework for Limón's 1999 novel. In *The Day of the Moon,* patriarch Don Flavio recounts his life from his deathbed in Los Angeles. The son of a Spanish father and an Amerindian mother, Flavio won his wealth in a single card game, thus enabling him to live as an upper-class gringo. With his power came cruelty and a denial of his native American heritage. McCracken wrote that "the narrative frame of *The Day of the Moon* begins in Los Angeles in 1965, before the advent of the Chicano Movement, and certain problematic issues of the movement leave their mark on the text, as the novel considers *mestizaje,* or mixed Spanish and Indian heritage, an issue of significance to many Chicanos during the late

1960s and 1970s. . . . Focusing on the painful rather than the celebratory aspects of *mestizaje* for Chicanos and Latinos across the Americas, Limón notes in the preface that the dual heritage is 'a condition of anguish, because to be Mestiza or Mestizo is to dangle between being Spanish and indigenous . . . existing between gratitude and rage. It means choosing white or brown. It means acceptance or denial of color.' "

Flavio's wife, Velia Carmelita, a victim of his patriarchal and racial authoritarianism, finds solace in the arms of Brigida, Flavio's sister, and his daughter, Isadora, who marries Flavio's choice of husbands, returns to the arms of Santiago, a native Amerindian she has loved since childhood, and who like all indios, is of the servant class. Flavio has Santiago killed and puts Isadora in a mental hospital. After Flavio's death, Alondra, the dark-skinned daughter born to Isadora and Santiago, explores her heritage and searches for her mother, ultimately finding peace in the village of her father. A *Publishers Weekly* reviewer wrote that Limón "contextualizes her saga with crucially placed details of Mexican political and social history, providing a sharp critique of the Mexican class system while embedding several passionate and eloquently rendered love stories."

BIOGRAPHICAL/CRITICAL SOURCES:

BOOKS

Castillo-Speed, Lillian, editor, *Latina: Women's Voices from the Borderlands,* Touchstone (New York, NY), 1995.

McCracken, Ellen, *New Latina Narrative: The Feminine Space of Postmodern Ethnicity,* University of Arizona Press (Tucson, AZ), 1999.

Dictionary of Literary Biography, Volume 209: *Chicano Writers, Third Series,* Gale (Detroit, MI), 1999.

Notable Hispanic American Women, Gale (Detroit, MI), 1998.

PERIODICALS

Booklist, September 15, 1993, Martha Schoolman, review of *In Search of Bernabé,* p. 127; September 1, 1994, Greg Burkman, review of *The Memories of Ana Calderón,* p. 23.

Choice, October, 1996, review of *Song of the Hummingbird,* pp. 278-279.

Kirkus Reviews, June 15, 1994, review of *The Memories of Ana Calderón,* p. 797.

Library Journal, August, 1993, David A. Berona, review of *In Search of Bernabé,* p. 153; August,

1994, Janet Ingraham, review of *The Memories of Ana Calderón,* p. 130; March 15, 1996, Mary Margaret Benson, review of *Song of the Hummingbird,* p. 96.

New York Times Book Review, November 14, 1993, Ilan Stavans, "Children's Books; Questions of Legitimacy," p. 66.

Publishers Weekly, July 26, 1993, review of *In Search of Bernabé,* p. 63; July 11, 1994, review of *The Memories of Ana Calderón,* p. 64; April 19, 1999, review of *The Day of the Moon,* p. 61; September 10, 2001, review of *Erased Facts,* p. 63.

Voice of Youth Advocates, August, 1997, Delia A. Culberson, review of *Song of the Hummingbird,* pp. 186-187.

Washington Post Book World, October 30, 1994, Sandra Scofield, review of *Memories of Ana Calderón,* p. 6; April 28, 1996, Elizabeth Hanly, review of *Song of the Hummingbird,* p. 9.

World Literature Today, summer, 1995, Greg Sanchez, review of *The Memories of Ana Calderón,* p. 582.*

*   *   *

LITTLESUGAR, Amy   1953-

PERSONAL: Born March 8, 1953, in Bermuda; daughter of Kevin (in sales) and Rosalind (a homemaker) Alme; married David Zuccarini (an artist), 1974; children: Christie, Ethan, Will. *Education:* University of Maryland, B.A. *Politics:* Democrat.

ADDRESSES: Home—7402 Mellenbrook Rd., Columbia, MD 21045. *Office*—c/o Putnam Berkley Group, 200 Madison Ave., New York, NY 10016. *Agent*—Pesha Rubinstein Literary Agency, Inc., 1392 Rugby Rd., Teaneck, NY 01666. *E-mail*—Littlesugar@ mindspring.com.

CAREER: Author, 1990—. Howard Community College, Columbia, MD, writing instructor.

MEMBER: Society of Children's Book Writers and Illustrators.

WRITINGS:

The Spinner's Daughter, illustrated by Robert Quackenbush, Pippin Press (New York, NY), 1994.

Josiah True and the Art Maker, illustrated by Barbara Garrison, Simon & Schuster (New York, NY), 1995.

Marie in Fourth Position: The Story of Degas's "The Little Dancer," illustrated by Ian Schoenherr, Philomel (New York, NY), 1996.

Jonkonnu: A Story from the Sketchbook of Winslow Homer, illustrated by Ian Schoenherr, Penguin (New York, NY), 1997.

A Portrait of Spotted Deer's Grandfather, illustrated by Marlowe DeChristopher, Albert Whitman, 1997.

Shake Rag: From the Life of Elvis Presley, illustrated by Floyd Cooper, Philomel (New York, NY), 1998.

Tree of Hope, illustrated by Floyd Cooper, Philomel (New York, NY), 1999.

The Rag Baby, Simon & Schuster (New York, NY), 2000.

Lisette's Angel, illustrated by Max Ginsburg, Dial (New York, NY), 2001.

Freedom School, Yes!, illustrated by Floyd Cooper, Philomel (New York, NY), 2001.

Also author of *Clown Child,* Penguin (New York, NY).

SIDELIGHTS: Children's book author Amy Littlesugar once commented: "When I write, the idea for a story usually comes first. But it is the main character in the story who must make you care about that idea." All of Littlesugar's books feature strong, captivating characters. *Marie in Fourth Position: The Story of Degas's "The Little Dancer"* is an imaginative and realistic story about a chorus girl immortalized by artist Edgar Degas in his sculpture *The Little Dancer.* Littlesugar's book is a fictionalized account of the tale and depicts a shy chorus girl's transformation whose dancing improves dramatically through her modeling work for Degas. Not much is known about the girl and the author clarifies the fact through a footnote at the end of the book. In a tribute to Littlesugar's expert handling of the story, Melissa Hudak commented in a review for *School Library Journal* that "This gives an added drama to a beautifully written story that focuses not only on Degas's work, but also the suffering Marie endured for both the sculptor and her ballet."

Jonkonnu: A Story from the Sketchbook of Winslow Homer "provides backgrounds for multi-cultural history, stories in paintings and American history," noted Annette C. Blank in *Children's Book Review Service.* Littlesugar's book reconstructs an event from the late 1800s, when painter Winslow Homer visited Petersburg, Virginia, to sketch freed slaves who were celebrating "Jonkonnu," an old slave holiday. Elizabeth Bush, reviewing the book for *Bulletin of the Center for Children's Books,* found Littlesugar's treatment of an incident involving Homer and a staring match with a town bigot of particular mention. *Jonkonnu* is a fiction-

alized portrayal of a part of Homer's career; the book is based at times on history, even though the War between the States had been over for more than a decade, and former slaves had still not been accepted into the mainstream of Southern life. Shirley Wilton of *School Library Journal* described Littlesugar's narrative as evocative of "the heat and lush green growth of Southern summer, and with vocabulary and pronunciation suggestive of soft Southern speech."

A Portrait of Spotted Deer's Grandfather draws its inspiration from a journey made in 1836 by the U.S. artist George Catlin. It is a fictionalized account of an old Native American's realization that an artist's impressions are an essential method of preservation and a means to communicate one's culture to future generations. The book, which contains an outline of Catlin's life, was recommended by Karen Hunt in *Booklist* as "Useful for introducing Catlin's life or a unit on American Indians."

Shake Rag: From the Life of Elvis Presley is a picture-book presentation of Presley's childhood and his introduction to music by gospel singers of the South. It records the influences of people, both black and white, on Elvis and their contribution in shaping his music. Ronald Jobe of *School Library Journal* commented, "The quality of storytelling is remarkable," and Barbara Baker agreed in *Children's Book Review Service,* commenting that *Shake Rag* is "helpful in the study of American racial history." *Tree of Hope* explores the rebirth of African-American theatre in Harlem during the Great Depression. A *Publishers Weekly* review noted that "Littlesugar unobtrusively uses history to anchor the experiences of a particular fictional family."

Littlesugar's next book, *Freedom School, Yes!,* focuses on the civil rights movement of the 1960s. Explaining the motivation behind the book, Littlesugar once commented, "In *Freedom School,* inspiration came out of a photograph of three African-American children and their eighteen-year-old white schoolteacher smiling for the camera in the window of a one-room schoolhouse back in the tense and dangerous Civil Rights summer of 1963. The hand-lettered sign above said *FREEDOM SCHOOL,* and I soon learned that Freedom Schools were makeshift classrooms built and taught by black and white college students from the North. They mushroomed all across the South, where black children were still denied the opportunity of education. It took courage then, not only to teach, but to experience learning, so I knew I'd need to create the voices of two very brave characters. However, only after tracking down and interviewing some of the teacher volunteers and listening to their experiences, would Annie, an eighteen-year-old, first-time teacher, and Jolie, the Mississippi girl who comes to love learning in spite of her fears, be born."

"For me, the writing of *Freedom School* was an exciting challenge, yet I knew it would happen, thanks to the support of the real people who participated in it, an agent and editor who believed in it, and characters I felt young readers would care about." The book resulting from Littlesugar's research succeeds, in the opinion of a *Publishers Weekly* critic, in "personaliz[ing] the events of an era by colorfully detailing one girl's experience." *School Library Journal*'s Barbara Buckley wrote that "Littlesugar has created a slice-of-life story with a potent message." While the *Publishers Weekly* reviewer felt that at points "the story stumbles a bit," Buckley described Floyd Cooper's illustrations as "masterful and lush," and said the narrative is "a unique and poignant look at a moment in history."

BIOGRAPHICAL/CRITICAL SOURCES:

PERIODICALS

Booklist, January 1, 1998, Karen Hunt, review of *A Portrait of Spotted Deer's Grandfather,* p. 813; December 15, 1999, Hazel Rochman, review of *Tree of Hope,* p. 790; February 15, 2000, review of *Tree of Hope,* pp. 1, 109; February 15, 2001, Hazel Rochman, review of *Freedom School, Yes!,* p. 1155.

Bulletin of the Center for Children's Books, January, 1998, Elizabeth Bush, review of *Jonkonnu,* p. 165.

Children's Book Review Service, April, 1998, Annette C. Blank, review of *Jonkonnu,* p. 102; December, 1998, Barbara Baker, review of *Shake Rag,* p. 43.

Kirkus Reviews, September 1, 1996, review of *Marie in Fourth Position,* p. 324; August 15, 1997, review of *A Portrait of Spotted Deer's Grandfather,* p. 308; December 15, 1997, review of *Jonkonnu,* p. 836; October 15, 1998, review of *Shake Rag,* p. 533; October 15, 1999, review of review of *Tree of Hope,* p. 1646.

New York Times Book Review, February 14, 1999, Peter Keepnews, review of *Shake Rag,* p. 27.

Publishers Weekly, May 31, 1999, review of *Marie in Fourth Position,* p. 86; November 29, 1999, review of review of *Tree of Hope,* p. 70; January 8, 2001, review of *Freedom School, Yes!,* p. 65.

School Library Journal, October, 1996, Melissa Hudak, review of *Marie in Fourth Position,* p. 101; September, 1997, Pam Grosner, review of *A Portrait of Spotted Deer's Grandfather,* p. 186; Febru-

ary, 1998, Shirley Wilton, review of *Jonkonnu,* p. 86; October, 1998, Ronald Jobe, review of *Shake Rag,* p. 106; November, 1999, Miriam Lang Budin, review of *Tree of Hope,* p. 123; January, 2001, Barbara Buckley, review of *Freedom School, Yes!,* p. 104.*

* * *

LIU, Shaozhong 1963-
(Zhong Rong)

PERSONAL: Born June 8, 1963, in Guilin, China; son of Manzhu and Tiansao (Jiang) Liu; married Fengrong Liao (a teacher), February 28, 1984; children: Zhipeng. *Ethnicity:* "Han." *Education:* Guangxi Normal University, B.A., 1983, postgraduate diploma, 1987; Guangzhou Teachers College, interactive activities teaching diploma, 1990; Guangdong University of Foreign Studies, diploma in linguistics, 1996, Ph.D., 1997; also earned intermediate level certificate of Esperanto, 1989.

ADDRESSES: Office—c/o Department of East Asian Languages and Literatures, Wake Forest University, Winston-Salem, NC 27106. *E-mail*—liusx@wfu.edu and szliu@mailbox.gxnu.edu.cn.

CAREER: Guangxi Normal University, Guilin, China, assistant professor, then professor of linguistics and languages, 1983-98, 2001—; Wake Forest University, Winston-Salem, NC, visiting professor of East Asian languages, 1998-2000. Guangxi Esperanto Institute, general secretary, 1991—.

MEMBER: International League of Esperantist Teachers (member, board of directors, 1990-94), Guilin Esperanto Association (general secretary and deputy director, 1984-98).

WRITINGS:

IN CHINESE

(With Chungun Yang and Yanhua Yang) *A Handbook of TOEFL Glossaries,* Guangxi Normal University Press (Guilin, China), 1988.

(With Tongshu Wu, Han Wei, and Zhi Liang) *Learning English at High School: How,* Guangxi Normal University Press (Guilin, China), 1993.

(Editor) *Junior English: One Hundred Days,* Guangxi Teachers University Press (Guilin, China), 1993.

(Translator) Guoshi Zhong, Fengrong Liao, and others, *An Introduction to Western Philosophy,* Guangxi Normal University Press (Guilin, China), 1993.

(Associate editor-in-chief and contributor) *A Grand Dictionary of English Usage,* Beijing Science and Technology Press (Beijing, China), 1995.

Editor of several books on teaching the English language in China. Contributor to Chinese periodicals. Translator, under pseudonym Zhong Rong.

WORK IN PROGRESS: Pragmatism and Pragmatics; A Dictionary of Pragmatics; Interlanguage Pragmatics; research on pragmatic relevance, pragmatic failure, and pragmatic transfer; research on competence theories and the development of pragmatic competence in the acquisition of a second language; research on Chinese culture and linguistics behaviors.

SIDELIGHTS: Shaozhong Liu told *CA:* "I am extremely interested in the study of negative pragmatic transfer. I have started looking at this phenomenon of second language use, beginning in 1995, and initial findings were reflected in my doctoral dissertation in 1997. What I have been trying to argue is that there are problems in Kasper's dichotomies of negative pragmatic transfer, and I have been considering the occurrence, the types, the distribution, and the cross-cultural communication effects of the phenomenon. Another interest I have developed since the end of the 1970s is Esperanto. I am inclined to consider Esperanto as a second language and am looking at the culture unique to Esperanto-speakers."

* * *

LOCHRIE, Karma

PERSONAL: Female. *Education:* DePauw University, B.A., 1977; Princeton University, M.A., 1978, Ph.D., 1981.

ADDRESSES: Office—Department of English, Loyola University, 6525 North Sheridan Rd., Chicago, IL 60626. *E-mail*—klochri@wpo.it.luc.edu.

CAREER: Writer, 1991—. Loyola University, Chicago, IL, associate professor of English.

WRITINGS:

Margery Kempe and Translations of the Flesh, University of Pennsylvania Press (Philadelphia, PA), 1991.

Constructing Medieval Sexuality, University of Minnesota Press (Minneapolis, MN), 1997.

Covert Operations: The Medieval Use of Secrecy, University of Pennsylvania Press (Philadelphia, PA), 1999.

SIDELIGHTS: Karma Lochrie's works feature in-depth examinations of particular aspects of medieval times. Regarding *Margery Kempe and Translations of the Flesh,* Sue Ellen Holbrook, writing in *Modern Philology,* noted: "By examining the *Book of Margery Kempe* within the ideology of medieval culture, Lochrie offers modern readers a serious, sophisticated, and useful analysis of Kempe's mystical text." In a review for *Choice,* M. A. Dalbey claimed: "Lochrie presents both a reevaluation of Margery Kempe's work in the light of current feminist literary theory and a call for a reassessment of the ways in which scholars have constructed the medieval mystical tradition." Dalbey commended the book not only for its argument but also for the manner in which the argument is presented. "With its extensive notes and excellent bibliography of both primary and secondary materials, Lochrie's work is a valuable contribution both to feminist theory and to medieval studies."

In *Covert Operations: The Medieval Uses of Secrecy,* which Henrietta Leyser in *English Historical Review* called "a tantalizing work," Lochrie explores both the methods and reasons of secret-keeping during the Middle Ages and how they were used by each gender. In addition, she discusses how such behavior may compare to that of modern-day people. Throughout the book, Lochrie uses several kinds of texts to offer examples, including *Sir Gawain and the Green Knight.* Though Leyser said that *Covert Operations* was "fragmentary" in nature and that Lochrie's "attempts to provide historical grounding for her chapters are not always helpful," she noted that "hidden away in this book are treasures well worth the hunt."

BIOGRAPHICAL/CRITICAL SOURCES:

PERIODICALS

Choice, July, 1992, M. A. Dalbey, review of *Margery Kempe and Translations of the Flesh,* p. 1678.

English Historical Review, September, 2000, Henrietta Leyser, review of *Covert Operations: The Medieval Uses of Secrecy,* p. 936.

Modern Philology, November, 1994, Sue Ellen Holbrook, review of *Margery Kempe and Translations of the Flesh,* pp. 224-227.*

LONGENECKER, Dwight

PERSONAL: Born in PA; married; wife's name, Alison; children: four. *Education:* Attended Bob Jones University; attended Wycliffe Hall, Oxford. *Religion:* Catholic.

ADDRESSES: Home—Chippenham, Wiltshire, England. *Office*—c/o Editorial Office, Morehouse Publishing Co., 4775 Linglestown Rd., Harrisburg, PA 17112. *E-mail*—dwight@longenecker.fsnet.co.uk.

CAREER: St. Barnabas Society, district organizer; freelance writer and broadcaster. Worked previously in the Anglican ministry as a curate, a chaplain, and a country parson.

WRITINGS:

(Editor) *The Path to Rome,* Gracewing (Leominster, England), 1999.
Listen, My Son: St. Benedict for Men Who Seek to Be Better Parents, Morehouse (Harrisburg, PA), 2000.

BIOGRAPHICAL/CRITICAL SOURCES:

PERIODICALS

Times Literary Supplement, December 17, 1999, J. Leslie Houlden, "Place of Safety," p. 30.

OTHER

Christendom-Awake, http://www.christendom-awake. org/ (March 20, 2001), "Dwight Longenecker."*

*   *   *

LOTT, Tim 1956-

PERSONAL: Born 1956; son of Frank (a grocer) and Jean (a homemaker) Lott; married; children: Ruby, Cissy. *Education:* Attended London School of Economics.

ADDRESSES: Home—Notting Hill, England. *Office*—c/o Author Mail, Viking, 27 Wright's Lane, London W8 5TZ, England.

CAREER: Writer. Worked variously as a businessman, publisher, broadcaster, editor, and television producer.

AWARDS, HONORS: J. R. Ackerly Prize for autobiography, 1996, for *The Scent of Dried Roses;* Whitbread Prize for first novel, 1999, for *White City Blue.*

WRITINGS:

The Scent of Dried Roses (autobiography), Viking (London, England), 1996.
White City Blue (novel), Viking (London, England), 1999.

SIDELIGHTS: Tim Lott is a British author who has achieved success in many arenas but whose personal life has been diminished by bouts of depression, an illness he shared with his mother, Jean, who committed suicide by hanging. In his autobiographical *The Scent of Dried Roses,* Lott details his life, including the harelip with which he was born, his drug abuse as a teen, romances, his success as a businessman, his studies as an adult student at the London School of Economics, and the editor's job he gave up as soon as he got it. "These took some writing," commented Frank Kermode in *London Review of Books,* "and Lott can write." Lott also relates the history of his family and explores the underlying causes of his and his mother's depression, an affliction once believed curable with the scent of dried roses.

Jean and Lott's father, Jack, raised their three sons in middle-class Southall. Jean was an old-fashioned homemaker who was there for her children when they experienced their own difficulties, including Lott's depression, but who saw their problems as her failures. Lott writes that his mother, like himself, was affected by England's decay and the decline of their suburban environment. Andrew O'Hagan wrote for *Mail & Guardian* online that "the Southall Lott describes is a place where immigrants were to find a forbidding home, where fire was to engulf the splendour of the Crystal Palace, and where hairstyles and social ambitions and madness were heightened in the family just as community life and health diminished with the size of skirts. Lott's parents created a family that was in most respects like any other; they tried their best to improve things, and they wanted to be happy. . . . They wanted life to be soft and fair: it didn't turn out that way. It was harsher than the English weather." Lott and his brothers left Southall, which they hated, a sentiment Jean expressed in her suicide note. "Revisiting, Lott sees how much his mother wanted to belong to another England, innocent, decent, quiet, faintly eccentric—and long since dead," wrote Blake Morrison in the *Times Literary Supplement.*

Lott tries to understand why his mother took her life at the age of fifty-seven. Morrison wrote that "his fear is that he is somehow responsible; that there were warning signs and cries for help which he ignored; that having enjoyed his mother's support through a long period of depression of his own, he did not reciprocate; worse, that his gloom and maundering sadness were somehow unloaded on and transferred to her." Lott's "is a story told with courage, candour, and astonishing command of detail," concluded Morrison. "Though not intended as therapy, there is no doubt it, too, will help others cope with depression and bereavement." Jay Rayner wrote in the London *Observer* that "when Lott writes about his illness and the way he clambered out of it, there is a vividness to the prose which anybody who has ever found themselves reaching for the antidepressants will recognise. The passages where he describes his love for the mother he knows was never destined to be the centre of attention are genuinely touching."

Books reviewer Roger Tagholm called Lott's novel *White City Blue* "a very well-observed story about childhood, schooldays, summer holidays, the onset of adulthood, and the changing nature of friendship." The narrator is Frankie Blue, a.k.a. "Frankie the fib." Frankie has asked his girlfriend, Veronica, to marry him, a fact he must now reveal to his single friends, flashy Tony, Colin the nerd, and trendy Nodge. The friends have been mates since childhood, and Frankie realizes that their relationship, like that of many men, centers around sports, drinking, and easygoing fun. The story climaxes when the friends celebrate an annual ritual with a game of golf that ends with a great deal of uncomfortable truth telling.

Veronica is a pathologist, which *Times Literary Supplement* contributor David Horspool said "allows for some fairly specious comparisons between her view of the living and the dead as subjects for dissection. . . . More successful is the description of Frankie's slow realization of where he stands, and who his friends are. . . . By presenting their situation honestly . . . Lott gives an affecting and rounded picture of a world without either sentimentalizing or condemning it."

BIOGRAPHICAL/CRITICAL SOURCES:

PERIODICALS

Books, summer, 1999, Roger Tagholm, "Bonding Patterns," p. 10.
London Review of Books, October 17, 1996, Frank Kermode, "England's Troubles," p. 30.
Observer (London, England), October 13, 1996, Jay Rayner, "Tomb with a View," p. 16.

Sewanee Review, fall, 2000, Merritt Moseley, review of *White City Blue,* p. 648.
Times Literary Supplement, October 11, 1996, Blake Morrison, "England Unmade Me," p. 35; May 7, 1999, David Horspool, "Singular Men," p. 24.

OTHER

Mail & Guardian, http://www.mg.co/za/mg/books/ (March 24, 1997), Andrew O'Hagan, "Tim Lott's Scream of Roses."*

*   *   *

LOVISI, Gary   1952-

PERSONAL: Born April 28, 1952, in New Hyde Park, NY; son of Aldo Mario and Vivian Maria (DeGaetano) Lovisi; married Pat Mastronardi, 1975 (divorced, 1981); married Lucille Cail, November 7, 1999. *Ethnicity:* "Sicilian." *Education:* Kingsborough Community College, A.A.S., 1984. *Avocational interests:* writing, book publishing and collecting.

ADDRESSES: Home—P.O. Box 209, Brooklyn, NY 11228.

CAREER: Writer, 1986—. Gryphon Publications, founder, 1984; New York Collectible Book Expo, founder and sponsor, 1989.

WRITINGS:

Science Fiction Detective Tales, Gryphon Books (Brooklyn, NY), 1986.
Sherlock Holmes: The Great Detective in Paperback, Gryphon Books (Brooklyn, NY), 1990.
Sherlock Holmes in the Loss of the British Bark Sophy Anderson, Gryphon Books (Brooklyn, NY), 1992.
(With Terry Arnone) *The Woman in the Dugout: The Story of the Brooklyn Kings,* Gryphon Books (Brooklyn, NY), 1992.
Doc Atlas in Arctic Terror, Gryphon Books (Brooklyn, NY), 1994.
(Compiler) *Dashiell Hammett and Raymond Chandler: A Checklist and Bibliography of Their Paperback Appearances,* Gryphon Books (Brooklyn, NY), 1994.
Minesweeper, Gryphon Books (Brooklyn, NY), 1995.
Hellbent on Homicide, Bloodlines (Chester Springs, PA), 1997.
Sarasha: A Novel of the Future, Gryphon Books (Brooklyn, NY), 1997.

Collecting Science Fiction and Fantasy, Alliance Books, 1997.

Blood in Brooklyn, Do-Not Press (London, England), 1999.

The Sexy Digests, Gryphon Books (Brooklyn, NY), 2001.

Contributor to professional journals. Editor and publisher, *Hardboiled* and *Paperback Parade* magazines.

SIDELIGHTS: Gary Lovisi is recognized for his contributions to the science fiction and detective genres as well as the furthering of a new genre that combines elements of both science fiction and detective fiction. Of *Hellbent on Homicide,* Marvin Lachman, writing for *The Armchair Detective* asserted that "Lieutenant Bill Griffin and Sgt. Herman 'Fats' Stubbs are a pair of tough honest detectives, with Griffin the jarringly ungrammatical narrator." Wes Lukowsky of *Booklist* offered simple praise for the novel, saying that "this short novel is first-rate hard-boiled fiction." He called the book "unusual and very satisfying reading." Regarding *Blood in Brooklyn,* Lukowsky observed that "Lovisi's world is unremittingly dark; love exists ephemerally if at all, and revenge is the dominant theme. Fans of Andrew Vachss will clutch Vic Powers to their black little hearts and regale in the vigilante street justice that is so satisfying in print and so frightening in the real world."

Lovisi's compilation, *Science Fiction Detective Tales,* earned praise for highlighting the congruencies between the two different genres. Lachman noted that in the anthology, Lovisi "blends his knowledge of the two popular genres and shows how they make quite comfortable bedfellows," and concluded that "I have seen articles about science-fiction mysteries, even attended Bouchercon panels on the subject, but this is the first book I have come across which combines the fields, and it is a welcome addition to critical writing."

BIOGRAPHICAL/CRITICAL SOURCES:

PERIODICALS

Armchair Detective, summer 1988, Marvin Lachman, review of *Science Fiction Detective Tales,* pp. 286-287; summer 1996, Marvin Lachman, review of *Hellbent on Homicide,* p. 310.

Booklist, October 1, 1997, Wes Lukowsky, review of *Hellbent on Homicide,* p. 310; October 1, 1999, Wes Lukowsky, review of *Blood in Brooklyn,* p. 346.

Fantasy Review, June, 1986, Walter Albert, review of *Science Fiction Detective Tales,* pp. 27-28.

Kirkus Reviews, September 1, 1997, review of *Hellbent on Homicide,* p. 1341.

Publishers Weekly, October 4, 1999, review of *Blood in Brooklyn,* p. 69.

OTHER

Gary Lovisi Information Sheet, http://www.cyber boiled.com/, (December 14, 1999).

*   *   *

LUCIER, Charles B(rooks) 1956-

PERSONAL: Born October 17, 1956, in New Britain, CT; son of F. P. and Nancy Ann (Maier) Lucier; married first wife, Constance A. F., December 31, 1991 (divorced, August, 1998); married, wife's name Anneliese; children: Charles Brooks, Jr. *Education:* Attended Roanoke College, University of Southern California, and Art Center College of Design. *Politics:* "Independent (moderate)." *Avocational interests:* "Compassion, peace."

ADDRESSES: Home and Office—R.R. 2, Box 716, New Freedom, PA 17349. *E-mail*—Lucieux@ gateway.net.

CAREER: Forge and Farrier Services, New Freedom, PA, proprietor, 1987—. Licensed farrier. Also worked as production manager, art director, copywriter, and graphic designer.

MEMBER: International Union of Journeymen Horseshoers.

WRITINGS:

Of My Flesh and This Wicked World (fiction), Noble House (Baltimore, MD), 1999.

Coauthor of a screenplay, *Nomads.*

WORK IN PROGRESS: Horses, Jockeys, Crooks, and Kings.

SIDELIGHTS: Charles B. Lucier once commented in *CA:* "Writing has been a lifelong pursuit. I have written reams of work, with plenty of rejections. I have 'journalized' much of my life, and I create fiction from it, publishing only *Of My Flesh and This Wicked World* last year. I attempt to incorporate contemporary issues into my fiction. Cinema greatly inspires me. I studied filmmaking at Art Center in the early eighties, and screenwriting with author and screenwriter Syd Field. My favorite novelists are Ken Kesey, Daniel Quinn, Norman Mailer, Kurt Vonnegut, and Oliver Stone. I am highly enthusiastic about my current project. I strongly believe in the unique work ethic and the approach I have to my topic."

*   *   *

LUDLUM, Robert 1927-2001
(Jonathan Ryder, Michael Shepherd)

OBITUARY NOTICE—See index for CA sketch: Born May 25, 1927, in New York, NY; died March 12, 2001, in Naples, FL. Actor, producer, and author. Ludlum was a successful novelist who wrote a number of best-selling suspense books. An actor on Broadway and on television, he turned to producing stage works first at the North Jersey Playhouse, then in New York City, and finally, after receiving grants from the American National Theatre and Academy, at his own Playhouse-on-the-Mall. His first book, The Scarlatti Inheritance, which was adapted for film and originally published in 1971, initiated Ludlum into devoting his energies entirely to writing. Some of his later works include The Apocalypse Watch, The Bourne Supremacy, and The Rhinemann Exchange, which was adapted for television during the 1970s. Ludlum received the Scroll of Achievement from the American National Theatre and Academy in 1960.

OBITUARIES AND OTHER SOURCES:

BOOKS

Contemporary Popular Writers, Gale (Detroit, MI), 1997.
St. James Guide to Crime and Mystery Writers, 4th Edition, St. James Press (Detroit, MI), 1996.

PERIODICALS

Chicago Tribune, March 13, 2001, section 2, p. 8.
Los Angeles Times, March 13, 2001, p. B7.
New York Times, March 14, 2001, p. A23.
Times (London, England), March 14, 2001.

LUDWIG, Ken 1950-

PERSONAL: Born March 15, 1950, in York, PA; married Adrienne George, 1976; children: one daughter. Education: Haverford College, B.A. (magna cum laude), 1972; Trinity College, Cambridge, L.L.M., 1975; Harvard Law School, J.D., 1976.

ADDRESSES: Home—Washington, D.C. Agent—Peter Franklin, William Morris Agency, 1325 Avenue of the Americas, New York, NY 10019.

CAREER: Attorney and playwright. Steptoe & Johnson, Washington, DC, attorney, 1976-89. Director stage performances, including Who's Afraid of Virginia Woolf, 1972.

AWARDS, HONORS: Helen Hayes Award, 1991-92; Tony Award, 1992.

WRITINGS:

Class Night (sketches), 1970.
Divine Fire, 1979.
Sullivan and Gilbert: A Play with Music (produced 1983), S. French (New York, NY), 1989.
Postmortem (produced 1984), S. French (New York, NY), 1989.
Dramatic License, produced, 1985.
Lend Me a Tenor (produced in London, England and New York, NY, 1986), S. French (New York, NY), 1986.
Crazy for You (adaptation of Girl Crazy by George and Ira Gershwin), produced in Washington, DC, 1991.
Moon over Buffalo (produced on Broadway, 1996), S. French (New York, NY), 1996.
The Adventures of Tom Sawyer, produced in New York, NY, 2001.

WORK IN PROGRESS: An adaptation of the 1932 comedy Twentieth Century, by Ben Hecht and Charles MacArthur.

SIDELIGHTS: Playwright Ken Ludwig is best known for his play Crazy for You, an adaptation of the musical Girl Crazy by George and Ira Gershwin. Also notable is Ludwig's farcical play Lend Me a Tenor, which illustrates the exploits of an ingenious opera house manager in 1930s Cleveland. Ludwig shines in this convoluted, sometimes confusing, and often deceptive stage comedy reminiscent of Shakespeare's Much Ado about Nothing. Ludwig himself has said "This is the form of drama, which, when it has greatness about it, touches me most deeply. My goal as a writer is to reinvent this tradition for our own times."

Ludwig first received critical attention for his 1986 hit *Lend Me a Tenor,* which opened in London and later moved to New York. The story revolves around a scheming 1930s opera theater manager in Cleveland. In the classic farce style, the plot is full of ever increasing complexities, some more transparent and predictable than others. The theater manager runs up against the first of several touchy predicaments when the Italian tenor hired to sing Otello is found on opening night unconscious, a presumed suicide, leaving only an ambiguous note behind. As the show must go on, the manager scrambles for a replacement, only to come up empty-handed. Pressured by a theater rapidly filling with paid ticket-holders, the manager decides to pull a simple ruse by replacing the apparently expired tenor with his assistant, who happens to be an aspiring tenor. Comical situations erupt following the performance when the Italian tenor awakes from his stupor and the young stand in is still in disguise. The play proved a great success, largely due to the synergy of cast, plot, and exquisite sets. *New York Post* reviewer Clive Barnes noted of the playwright, "Ludwig is a writer who will descend to any depths for a good laugh . . . but his real skill is a gift for farcical situations."

Ludwig's 1989 follow-up play, *Sullivan and Gilbert,* explores the trials and tribulations of collaboration between two massive musical egos: British light opera greats Sir Arthur Sullivan and Sir William Gilbert. The piece elaborates on the overtly argumentative nature of the pair's relationship, focusing on the escalation of small squabbles into explosive situations which often resulted in nearly a year's time off from each other. John Bemrose, writing in *Maclean's,* commented, "The dramatic parts by American playwright Ken Ludwig are capable of provoking everything from loud guffaws to sentimental tears."

The Gershwin musical *Girl Crazy* inspired Ludwig's 1992's update *Crazy for You,* which centers around Bobby Childs, an aspiring young dancer forced to work in the family business rather than pursue his dreams. The family business is forced to foreclose on a small township in Nevada where, as luck would have it, stands an unused theater. To make matters even more farcical, Bobby impersonates a famous New York impresario in an attempt to gain the property and open the theater, only to be confronted by the very person he is impersonating. While *Crazy for You* reinvents some of the elements of *Lend Me a Tenor,* critics found it fell short of the ingenious hilarity of Ludwig's earlier play.

Ludwig continues to mine the past for inspiration. An original work, *Moon over Buffalo,* which hit the New York stage in 1996, takes place in 1953, as members of a second-rate acting company try to attract the attention of film director Frank Capra, who is in town scouting for talent. While full of the pratfalls, mistaken identities, and zany characters one has come to expect from a nostalgic comedy, the play met with an indifferent reaction from critics, as did 2001's *The Adventures of Tom Sawyer* made its appearance as a musical version, Ludwig's book complemented by Don Schlitz's musical score. In a review for *Back Stage,* Victor Gluck called the Mark Twain update "pleasant and inoffensive," but added that it was also "bland and uninspired," and unfocused with relation to its audience. However, *Variety* contributor Markland Taylor was more upbeat about the show, calling Ludwig's book "deft" and noting that "the show pleasingly evokes a simpler time, establishes a rollicking, youthful energy and honors rather than belittles Mark Twain's Tom."

Ludwig's ambition to bring the farcical comedy style of Shakespeare into the modern day has brought him several critical successes in his career as a playwright. His delight in the convoluted, borderline confusing twists of plot have enamored theatergoers around the world.

BIOGRAPHICAL/CRITICAL SOURCES:

BOOKS

Contemporary American Dramatists, St. James Press (Detroit, MI), 1994.
Contemporary Literary Criticism, Volume 60, Gale (Detroit, MI), 1990.

PERIODICALS

Back Stage, May 11, 2001, Victor Gluck, review of *The Adventures of Tom Sawyer,* p. 45.
Dance, January, 1996, Robert Sandla, review of *Moon over Buffalo,* p. 98.
Maclean's, July 18, 1988, John Bemrose, "Operetta's Odd Couple," p. 55.
New York Daily News, March 3, 1989, Howard Kissel, " 'Tenor' Opens with a Bang."
New York Magazine, March 13, 1989, John Simon, "Who's Broadway Is It, Anyway?," pp. 72, 74-75.
New York Post, March 3, 1989, Clive Barnes, "It's Something to Sing About."
New York Times, March 3, 1989, Frank Rich, "When One Tenor Is Much Like Another," p. C3.
Variety, March 12, 2001, Markland Taylor, review of *The Adventures of Tom Sawyer,* p. 45.

Wall Street Journal, March 8, 1989, Edwin Wilson, "Farce and Tour de Force."*

*　　*　　*

LUTZ, Norma Jean 1943-

PERSONAL: Born January 31, 1943, in Bay City, TX; daughter of Norman Hilbert and Helen Louise Sherry-Bronson; stepdaughter of Tom Wayne Sherry; married Clifford N. Lutz (divorced, 1986); children: Kerry Lee, Rhonda Jean Huber. *Education:* Attended college. *Religion:* Christian.

ADDRESSES: Office—4308 South Peoria, Suite 701, Tulsa, OK 74105.

CAREER: Writer and professional speaker. Notations un-Limited (writing business), Tulsa, OK, founder and owner, 1986—. Founder of Professionalism in Writing School (annual Christian writer's conference), 1983-96; worked for the Institute of Children's Literature, 1988-97. Speaker at seminars, writers conferences, and schools throughout the United States, c. 1983—.

MEMBER: Toastmasters International, Tulsa Christian Writers Club (founder and former president).

AWARDS, HONORS: First place awards, Tulsa City-County Library Writing Contest, 1989, 1991, 1993; first place awards, *Tulsa Woman News* Fiction Contest, 1997, 1998.

WRITINGS:

JUVENILE FICTION

Blossom into Love, Silhouette, 1985.
Good-bye Beedee, Chariot (Elgin, IL), 1986.
Once over Lightly, Chariot (Elgin, IL), 1986.
Oklahoma Summer, Chariot (Elgin, IL), 1987.
Rock & Romance, Weekly Reader Book Club, 1988.

Contributor to anthology *God Is Everywhere,* Standard Publishing, 1986.

"AMERICAN ADVENTURE" SERIES; JUVENILE; ILLUSTRATED BY ADAM WALLENTAJ

Smallpox Strikes! Cotton Mather's Bold Experiment, Barbour (Ulrichsville, OH), 1997.
Maggie's Choice: Jonathan Edwards and the Great Awakening, Barbour (Ulrichsville, OH), 1997.

Trouble on the Ohio River: Drought Shuts Down a City, Barbour (Ulrichsville, OH), 1997.
Escape from Slavery: A Family's Fight for Freedom, Barbour (Ulrichsville, OH), 1997.
Enemy or Friend, Barbour (Ulrichsville, OH), 1997.
Fight for Freedom, Barbour (Ulrichsville, OH), 1997.
The Rebel Spy, Barbour (Ulrichsville, OH), 1998.
The War's End, Barbour (Ulrichsville, OH), 1998.
A Better Bicycle, Barbour (Ulrichsville, OH), 1998.
Marching with Sousa, Barbour (Ulrichsville, OH), 1998.
Clash with the Newsboys, Barbour (Ulrichsville, OH), 1998.
Prelude to War, Barbour (Ulrichsville, OH), 1998.
The Great War, Barbour (Ulrichsville, OH), 1998.
Battling the Clan, Barbour (Ulrichsville, OH), 1998.
Rumblings of War, Barbour (Ulrichsville, OH), 1998.
War Strikes, Barbour (Ulrichsville, OH), 1998.

JUVENILE NONFICTION

Females First in Their Field: Business and Industry, Chelsea House (Philadelphia, PA), 1999.
(Editor) Jean Holmes, *Do Dogs Go to Heaven? Eternal Answers for Animal Lovers,* JoiPax, 1999.
Cotton Mather ("Colonial Leaders" series), Chelsea House (Philadelphia, PA), 2000.
William Penn: Founder of Democracy ("Colonial Leaders" series), Chelsea House (Philadelphia, PA), 2000.
Increase Mather ("Colonial Leaders" series), Chelsea House (Philadelphia, PA), 2000.
Jonathan Edwards ("Colonial Leaders" series), Chelsea House (Philadelphia, PA), 2000.
John Paul Jones: Father of the U.S. Navy ("Revolutionary War Leaders" series), Chelsea House (Philadelphia, PA), 2000.
Benedict Arnold: Traitor to the Cause ("Revolutionary War Leaders" series), Chelsea House (Philadelphia, PA), 2000.
J. C. Watts, Chelsea House (Philadelphia, PA), 2000.
Britney Spears, Chelsea House (Philadelphia, PA), 2000.
Celine Dion, Chelsea House (Philadelphia, PA), 2000.
History of the Republican Party ("Your Government: How It Works" series), Chelsea House (Philadelphia, PA), 2000.
History of Third Parties ("Your Government: How It Works" series), Chelsea House (Philadelphia, PA), 2000.
History of the Black Church ("Black Achievement" series), Chelsea House (Philadelphia, PA), 2000.
Frederick Douglass ("Civil War Leaders" series), Chelsea House (Philadelphia, PA), 2001.

Harriet Tubman ("Civil War Leaders" series), Chelsea House (Philadelphia, PA), 2001.

Sojourner Truth ("Civil War Leaders" series), Chelsea House (Philadelphia, PA), 2001.

Nunavut ("Canada" series), Chelsea House (Philadelphia, PA), 2001.

Jane Austen ("Bloom's BioCritiques" series), Chelsea House (Philadelphia, PA), 2001.

The Brontë Sisters ("Bloom's BioCritiques" series), Chelsea House (Philadelphia, PA), 2001.

F. Scott Fitzgerald ("Bloom's BioCritiques" series), Chelsea House (Philadelphia, PA), 2001.

Tennessee Williams ("Bloom's BioCritiques" series), Chelsea House (Philadelphia, PA), 2001.

"HEARTSONG" FICTION SERIES; FOR ADULTS

Fields of Sweet Content, Barbour (Ulrichsville, OH), 1993.

Love's Silken Melody, Barbour (Ulrichsville, OH), 1993.

Cater to a Whim, Barbour (Ulrichsville, OH), 1994.

The Winning Heart, Barbour (Ulrichsville, OH), 1995.

Tulsa Tempest, Barbour (Ulrichsville, OH), 1995.

Tulsa Turning, Barbour (Ulrichsville, OH), 1996.

Tulsa Trespass, Barbour (Ulrichsville, OH), 1997.

Return to Tulsa, Barbour (Ulrichsville, OH), 1997.

OTHER

(With P. Harold Purvis) *A Matter of Conscience: Court Martialed for His Faith* (nonfiction), Review & Herald Publishing, 1998.

Contributor to *Inspirational Romance Readers,* Barbour (Ulrichsville, OH), 1999. Contributor of articles and short stories to periodicals, including *Christian Herald, Home Life, Sunday Digest, Power for Living, Sunday Visitor, Living with Teenagers, Young Ambassador, Teen Talk, Venture, Ohio Writer, Canadian Writer, Writers Connection, Design for Profit, Single Life, Single Parent, Mahoning Valley Parent, Atlanta Single, Atlanta Parent, South Florida Parenting, Christian Single, Tulsa Woman News, Christian Retailing, Merly's Pen, Mature Lifestyles, Grit,* and *Rotarian.*

SIDELIGHTS: Norma Jean Lutz is a professional writer and lecturer who has built a career writing series fiction and nonfiction for young readers. Contributing many installments to Chelsea House's "Colonial Leaders," "Revolutionary War Leaders," and "Civil War Leaders" series, Lutz has also written many tales of historical fiction involving young protagonists through her

work for the "American Adventure," a book series published in the late 1990s.

Born in 1943 in Bay City, Texas, Lutz and her family relocated to Kansas when she was still young. "As a young girl growing up in a small Kansas town, we had few books in our home," the author once recalled. "There was no public library in the town, only small libraries at both the grade school and the high school. Fortunately for me, at the grade school where I attended each of my elementary teachers read to us every morning before we began our studies. From first grade through sixth, I was introduced to exciting worlds through such stories as *Boxcar Children, Little House in the Big Woods, Betsy-Tacy, Mary Poppins, The Secret Garden,* and scores of others. I believe it was through these precious teachers that I acquired the 'love of story' that I possess today."

Within such a small school system, Lutz's interest in writing was given little in the way of encouragement. "Nevertheless, I constantly dreamed of writing and becoming a writer. In my mind, I pretended to be Laura Ingalls Wilder (she had actually lived in Kansas like I did, which seemed to mean a great deal to me at the time). I kept journals during my junior and senior years, both of which I still have in my possession." Finally, a high school English teacher boosted her confidence when he suggested "that I might have a measure of talent in this area. He even went so far as to say he would help me submit my work," Lutz added. But his encouragement went no further. "When nothing else was said or done, I assumed he had changed his mind and decided I wasn't so talented after all."

After graduating from high school, Lutz attended college for a brief time, but left to marry and raise a family. While "writing remained on the back burner," the author added, "the flame never went out. When my children were in grade school, I enrolled in a correspondence course with the Christian Writers Institute. When I completed that, I enrolled with the Institute of Children's Literature and graduated from there. But before finishing, I was selling magazine articles and short stories, plunking them out on my old black manual Royal typewriter. The check from my very first sale was dated on my birthday—January 31, 1979—a momentous day in my life!" Lutz still has a copy of that check hanging on a wall in her office.

From magazine publications Lutz moved gradually into writing book-length manuscripts and had several teen romance novels published between 1985 and 1988. Among these is *Oklahoma Summer,* which combines a budding summer romance with a thirteen-year-old girl's love of horses in a story that *Booklist* critic Barbara Elleman praised as "perceptive," featuring "warm, likeable characters."

Around 1990 Lutz changed her focus and worked for a few years writing adult romance novels, among them *Love's Silken Melody, The Winning Heart,* and *Return to Tulsa.* In the mid-1990s she began a professional relationship with Barbour Publishing, and her first novel in the "American Adventures" series arrived on bookstore shelves in 1997. *Smallpox Strikes!: Cotton Mather's Bold Experiment* is a fictional tale about an eleven-year-old boy named Robert Allerton who lived in Boston in the early 1720s, the height of a smallpox epidemic in that city. When both his stepfather and his younger stepbrother are stricken by the illness, Rob must take on an adult's responsibility in caring for his family. While *School Library Journal* contributor Connie Tyrrell Burns bemoaned Lutz's use of exclamation points and a "predictable" outcome, she noted the novel's inclusion of "life lessons" as well as its "Christian emphasis." *Smallpox Strikes!* would be followed by such novels as *The Rebel Spy, Clash with the Newsboys,* and *Trouble on the Ohio River.*

In addition to fiction, Lutz has penned several nonfiction titles, among them biographies of such diverse figures as Cotton Mather, John Paul Jones, Harriet Tubman, and Britney Spears. She also contributed one installment to the "Female Firsts in Their Fields" series: *Business and Industry.* In this sixty-five-page book, she profiles six figures, among them media star Oprah Winfrey, reigning home decorating queen Martha Stewart, cosmetics company founder Mary Kay, and Madam C. J. Walker, the country's first black millionaire. *Voice of Youth Advocates* critic Beth E. Anderson praised the series as "the perfect tool for introducing students to a broad field of noteworthy champions," while *School Library Journal* contributor Rebecca O'Connell commented that the somewhat brief treatment given to each

woman will still "spark students' interest in seeking out" more detailed biographical information.

From the sale of her first article through the publication of her first book, a romance novel about a young man ready to abort a promising college career to care for his retarded sister titled *Blossom into Love,* Lutz has devoted herself to her writing. "I have nearly fifty books to my credit," she once commented, "and hundreds of magazine articles and short stories. I have ghosted scores of books for clients, as well as assisting many writers through my professional critique service." In 1988 she joined the staff of the Institute of Children's Literature and remained there until 1997, when she left to devote more time to her own work.

"Being a Christian, I give credit to God for my talents and abilities," Lutz added. "I'm thankful to be in a business that allows me to do what I love each and every day. While some may look at what I have accomplished and measure it as a tidy little sum, I feel I've barely begun. I plan to be busy writing books right up until the very moment when God calls me Home. And if He has a computer waiting for me in heaven, I won't miss a beat!"

BIOGRAPHICAL/CRITICAL SOURCES:

PERIODICALS

Booklist, June 15, 1987, Barbara Elleman, review of *Oklahoma Summer,* p. 1608.
School Library Journal, January, 1986, Kathy Fritts, review of *Blossom into Love,* p. 81; September, 1987, Patricia G. Harrington, review of *Oklahoma Summer,* pp. 197-198; January, 1999, Connie Tyrrell Burns, review of *Smallpox Strikes!,* p. 128; September, 1999, Rebecca O'Connell, review of *Female Firsts in Their Field,* p. 232.
Voice of Youth Advocates, August, 1999, Beth E. Anderson, review of *Female Firsts in Their Field,* p. 201.*

M

MABIE, Grace
See MATTERN, Joanne

* * *

MABIE, Hamilton Wright   1845-1916

PERSONAL: Born December 13, 1845, in Coldspring, NY; died December 31, 1916; son of Levi Jeremiah and Sarah (Colwell) Mabie; married Jeanette Trivett, 1876. *Education:* Williams College, B.A., 1867; Columbia, LL.B., 1869.

CAREER: Lawyer, 1869-79; *Christian Union* (renamed *Outlook,* 1893), literary editor, 1879-83, promoted to associate editor, 1884; Carnegie Endowment for International Peace, exchange professor in Japan, 1912; literary critic, author, lecturer.

MEMBER: National Institute of Arts and Letters, first secretary, 1898; American Academy of Arts and Letters, 1908.

WRITINGS:

Norse Stories Retold from the Eddas, Roberts (Boston, MA), 1882.
My Study Fire, Dodd, Mead (New York, NY), 1890.
Under the Trees and Elsewhere, Dodd, Mead (New York, NY), 1890.
Our New England, Roberts (Boston, MA), 1890.
Short Studies in Literature, Dodd, Mead (New York, NY), 1891.
Essays in Literary Interpretation, Dodd, Mead (New York, NY), 1892.
An Undiscovered Island, Dodd, Mead (New York, NY), 1893.

My Study Fire: Second Series, Dodd, Mead (New York, NY), 1895.
Books and Culture, Dodd, Mead (New York, NY), 1896.
Essays on Nature and Culture, Dodd, Mead (New York, NY), 1896.
Essays on Work and Culture, Dodd, Mead (New York, NY), 1898.
In the Forest of Arden, Dodd, Mead (New York, NY), 1898.
The Life of the Spirit, Dodd, Mead (New York, NY), 1899.
William Shakespeare: Poet, Dramatist, and Man, Macmillan (New York, NY), 1900.
A Child of Nature, Dodd, Mead (New York, NY), 1901.
Parables of Life, Outlook (New York, NY), 1902, revised and enlarged edition, Macmillan, 1904.
Works and Days, Dodd, Mead (New York, NY), 1902.
Backgrounds of Literature, Outlook (New York, NY), 1903, enlarged edition, Macmillan (New York, NY), 1904.
In Arcady, Dodd, Mead (New York, NY), 1903.
The Great Word, Dodd, Mead (New York, NY), 1905.
Christmas To-Day, Dodd, Mead (New York, NY), 1908.
The Writers of Knickerbocker New York, Grolier Club (New York, NY), 1912, reprinted with illustrated engraving by Walworth Stilson, Kraus Reprint (New York, NY), 1980.
American Ideals, Character and Life, Macmillan (New York, NY), 1913.
Japan To-Day and To-Morrow, Macmillan (New York, NY), 1914.
Fruits of the Spirit, Dodd, Mead (New York, NY), 1917.
Essays in Lent, Dutton (New York, NY), 1919.

When All the World is Kin, Ludlow Typograph Co. (Chicago, IL), 1925.

EDITOR

The Portrait Gallery of Eminent Lawyers, Shea & Jenner (New York, NY), 1880.

(And contributor) Joseph Francois Michand, *The History of the Crusades,* Armstrong (New York, NY), 1882.

(With Marshal Bright) *The Memorial Story of America,* Winston (Philadelphia, PA), 1893.

Fairy Tales That Every Child Should Know, Doubleday, Page (New York, NY), 1905.

Myths That Every Child Should Know, Doubleday, Page (New York, NY), 1905.

(And contributor) *Legends That Every Child Should Know,* Doubleday, Page (New York, NY), 1906.

(And contributor) *Heroes Every Child Should Know,* Doubleday, Page (New York, NY), 1906.

(And contributor) *Famous Stories Every Child Should Know,* Doubleday, Page (New York, NY), 1907.

(And contributor) *Essays That Every Child Should Know,* Doubleday, Page (New York, NY), 1908.

(And contributor) *Fairy Tales From Grimm,* Stern (Philadelphia, PA), 1909.

(And contributor) *Folk Tales Every Child Should Know,* Doubleday, Page (New York, NY), 1910.

The Blue Book of Fiction: A List of Novels Worth Reading Chosen From Many Literatures, Globe-Wernicke (Cincinnati, OH), 1911.

(Author of introduction) *Fashions in Literature, and Other Literary and Social Essays and Addresses,* Books for Libraries Press (New York, NY), 1970.

Author of introduction for *A Book of Old English Love Songs,* drawings by George Wharton Edwards, Books for Libraries Press, 1970; *In the Days of Chaucer,* by Tutor Jenks, Folcroft Library Editions (Folcroft, PA), 1974; and *Rabindranath Tagore, The Man and His Poetry,* by Basanta Koomar Roy, Norwood Editions (Norwood, PA), 1978.

Contributor to periodicals, including *Andover Review, Christian Union, Forum, Chautauquan, International Monthly, Harper's Monthly, North American Review,* and *Munsey's.*

SIDELIGHTS: Hamilton Wright Mabie was extremely productive during his adult life as an author, essayist and editor of many books and of *Outlook* magazine. His writings ranged from books on spirituality to literary criticism, children's books to current affairs. David J. Rife asserted in *Dictionary of Literary Biography,* that

Mabie "qualifies for a place in the cultural history of the United States by virtue of his representativeness. He . . . [at times] demonstrated an ability to go beyond the stringent patterns of conservative, genteel thought to display the intellectual independence of a first-rate critic."

Mabie was born December 13, 1845 in Cold Spring, New York to Levi Jeremiah Mabie, a businessman, and Sarah (Colwell) Mabie. The family moved several times before settling in Tarrytown, New York in 1864. Hamilton attended the local public schools and was also taught by private tutors. In 1863 he enrolled in Williams College where he studied literature and worked on the school newspaper, the *Williams Quarterly,* as contributor and editor. He graduated with a B. A. degree in 1867 and then enrolled in Columbia University to study law, earning an LL.B. degree in 1869. The same year, Mabie was admitted to the New York bar. He begrudgingly practiced law for the next eight years, spending much of his time in the office reading literature instead of working on cases. During this time he met Jeanette Trivett and they married in 1876.

Mabie disliked practicing law so much that he left it entirely in 1879, on an invitation by Lyman Abbott, to work as literary editor for the *Christian Union,* a reputable magazine of the time that changed its name to the *Outlook* in 1893. During his first year with the magazine, Mabie edited *The Portrait Gallery of Eminent Lawyers.* He also wrote stories for children that were published in the magazine and then republished the stories in the collection, *Norse Stories Retold from the Eddas.* In 1884, Abbott promoted him to associate editor and Mabie was elected to the Author's Club. Having adjusted to his new career and discovered a new sense of self-confidence, Mabie entered the world of the men of letters and began writing for other publications. In 1885, he published a critically acclaimed review of William Dean Howells's *The Rise of Silas Lapham* in the *Andover Review,* a very respected journal of the time. Mabie went on to publish *My Study Fire,* a collection of previously published essays that discussed the seasonal effects experienced by a man of letters in his relationship with his books. The outdoor companion piece to *My Study Fire, Under the Trees and Elsewhere,* followed the same year. Both books were extremely popular, as was his *My Study Fire: Second Series.* Rife commented that today's readers might be put off by their "bookish sentimentality and cloying gentility" but acknowledged their popularity as they "demonstrat[ed] once again the often inverse relationship between the intrinsic value of a work and its reception by the public."

Departing from the sentimental tones of his previous books and turning to literary topics, Mabie published *Short Studies in Literature* and *Essays in Literary Interpretation.* The former volume contained thirty short essays, and the latter eight long articles. Mabie dove into literary theory in three of his pieces in *Essays in Literary Interpretation.* The remaining essays, except for the last, which dealt with humor, focused on individual authors: Robert Browning, Dante, John Keats, and Dante Gabriel Rossetti. Over the next twelve years, three additional critical works followed. *Books and Culture,* aimed at younger readers, provided a general introduction to the classics. Here, Mabie explored the Bible, and discussed several great authors, among them Homer, Dante, Shakespeare, and Goethe. Mabie published a more in-depth look at Shakespeare in *William Shakespeare: Poet, Dramatist, and Man.* The biographical qualities of Shakespeare overshadowed any critical aspects in the writing, which most likely accounted for the favorable reception of the book by reviewers and the public in general.

Mabie's last literary criticism book, *Backgrounds of Literature,* delved into the work of Emerson, Goethe, Washington Irving, Walt Whitman, William Wordsworth, R. D, Blackmore, and Sir Walter Scott. Mabie continued to write critical essays, but published them only in periodicals and journals. Beginning in 1899 with *The Life of the Spirit,* Mabie began publishing books on spirituality and ethics based on editorials he had written for *Outlook.* He continued with these themes until his death, publishing *A Child of Nature, Works and Days, In Arcady, The Great Word, Christmas To-day,*

Fruits of the Spirit, and *Essays in Lent.* A reviewer from *Outlook,* where Mabie worked, commented on *Fruits of the Spirit,* saying, "The essays will be found spiritually valuable," while a reviewer form the *Nation* criticized the work: "Ethical in content, hortatory in spirit, they are unexceptional in matter and form and are also quite undistinguished." Mabie's self-improvement books were popular because of the easy-to-read, light writing, but the overarching sympathetic tones drew much criticism.

Mabie also edited a series of children's books, which he intended to serve as moral guides for the younger readers. The series included famous stories and essays, and popular authors of Mabie's time retold legends, myths, and folk tales, and described the lives of historical heroes and heroines. Beginning with *Fairy Tales Every Child Should Know,* Mabie went on to edit nine more titles in the series over the next five years. In 1912, Mabie was selected by the Carnegie Endowment for International Peace to work in Japan as an exchange professor. Upon his return to the United States, he gathered selections from the addresses he delivered in Japan, Korea, and Manchuria, and published *American Ideals, Character, and Life. Japan To-day and To-morrow* followed in 1914, and drew on his experiences abroad as well. Both books were considered insightful, but faced a few less-than-pleasant reviews; as a critic from the *Nation* commented on *Japan To-day and To-morrow,* "the pages bristle with inaccuracies and 'non sequiturs' and his style is so slipshod as to be a constant irritation." Mabie fell ill while lecturing at the University of Pennsylvania. He died on December 31, 1916 at the age of seventy-one.

BIOGRAPHICAL/CRITICAL SOURCES:

BOOKS

Dictionary of Literary Biography, Volume 71: American Literary Critics and Scholars 1880-1900, Gale (Detroit, MI), 1988.
Morse, Edwin, *The Life and Letters of Hamilton W. Mabie,* Dodd, Mead, (New York, NY), 1920.

PERIODICALS

American Literary Realism, Winter, 1987, pp. 30-47.
American Transcendental Quarterly, Fall, 1978.
Nation, January 21, 1915; September 27, 1917.
Outlook, May 23, 1917.*

*   *   *

MACCABEE, Bruce S. 1942-

PERSONAL: Born May 6, 1942, in Rutland, VT. *Education:* Worcester Polytechnic Institute, B.S., 1964; American University, Washington, DC, Ph.D. (physics), 1970. *Avocational interests:* UFO investigation, music.

ADDRESSES: Home—Maryland. *Agent*—Robin James, Llewellyn Publications, P.O. Box 64383, St. Paul, MN 55164-0383. *E-mail*—brumac@compuserve. com.

CAREER: U.S. Navy, Naval Surface Warfare Center, White Oak, MD, then Dahlgren, VA, research physicist, 1972—. Fund for UFO Research, cofounder and chairman.

MEMBER: American Physical Society, Optical Society of America, Society for Scientific Exploration, Mutual UFO Network (Maryland State director, 1975—), Center for UFO Studies, Sigma Xi, Tau Kappa Epsilon.

WRITINGS:

(With Edward Walters) *UFOs Are Real, Here's the Proof,* Avon (New York, NY), 1997.
The UFO-FBI Connection: The Secret History of the Government's Cover-up, Llewellyn (St. Paul, MN), 2000.
Abduction in My Life: A Novel of Alien Encounters, Wildflower Press (Columbus, NC), 2001.

Contributor of UFO articles to numerous magazines.

WORK IN PROGRESS: The Lightning Master, a film script about Nicola Tesla.

SIDELIGHTS: Called "one of the leading lights of UFOlogy" of the late twentieth-century, Dr. Bruce Maccabee is a U.S. Navy physicist who has published several books focusing on the presence of unidentified flying objects (UFOs) in the United States during the past century. In *The UFO-FBI Connection: The Secret History of the Government Cover-up,* he releases formerly classified FBI and U.S. Air Force files involving what was termed "Flying Discs: Security Matter X" from the late 1940s through 1954. Maccabee points out numerous inconsistencies in government reportage in an effort to lay the groundwork for his contention that the U.S. government orchestrated a cover-up of UFO-related observations during the mid-twentieth century.

In addition to his books, Maccabee is a cofounder of the Fund for UFO Research, and is active in the Mutual UFO Network, of which he has been Maryland state director since 1975.

BIOGRAPHICAL/CRITICAL SOURCES:

PERIODICALS

Omni, August, 1994, Patrick Huyghe, "Secret Agent Man: Has a Leading Light of the UFO Community Been Briefing the CIA?," p. 71.

OTHER

Additional information obtained from Llewellyn Publications press release.*

MacCURDY, Marian (Mesrobian)

PERSONAL: Born in Syracuse, NY; daughter of William J. (a cost accountant) and Arpena (a university press director) Mesrobian; married Bruce MacCurdy (deceased); children: Robert, Meline. *Ethnicity:* "Armenian." *Education:* Syracuse University, Ph.D., 1980.

ADDRESSES: Home—172 Brooktondale Rd., Brooktondale, NY 14817. *Office*—Department of Writing, Park Hall, Ithaca College, Danby Rd., Ithaca, NY 14850. *E-mail*—maccurdy@ithaca.edu.

CAREER: Onondaga Community College, Syracuse, NY, instructor in English, 1976-77; Syracuse University, Syracuse, NY, instructor in English, 1975-85; Ithaca College, Ithaca, NY, assistant professor, 1985-96, associate professor of writing and head of department, 1996—. Professional singer, 1971—; Cayuga Vocal Ensemble, past president of board of directors. Cornell University, visiting lecturer, summers, 1995-96; guest lecturer at colleges and universities, including Kearney State College, Pennsylvania State University, Susquehanna University; speaker at women's studies and writing conferences.

MEMBER: Associated Writing Programs, National Council of Teachers of English, Conference on College Composition and Communication, Modern Language Association of America, Society for Utopian Studies, Association for the Fantastic in the Arts, Association for the Interdisciplinary Study of the Arts, National Association for Poetry Therapy, Phi Kappa Phi.

AWARDS, HONORS: Muse National Poetry Competition, Pearl Muse Award, 1989, for the poem "Healing," and certificate of merit, 1989, for the poem "Apparition."

WRITINGS:

(Editor with Charles Anderson) *Writing and Healing: Toward an Informed Practice,* National Council of Teachers of English (Urbana, IL), 2000.

Contributor to *Utopia and Gender in Advertising: A Critical Reader,* edited by Luigi Manca and Alessandra Manca, Procopian Press (Lisle, IL), 1994.

Composer and performer of the music for the films *Collage* and *Willow,* produced at Syracuse University. Contributor of articles, poems, and reviews to periodicals, including *Literature and Medicine, Ararat, Jour-*

nal of Teaching Writing, Journal of Poetry Therapy, and *Platte Valley Review.*

WORK IN PROGRESS: The Mind's Eye: Image and Memory in Writing about Trauma; and a collection of personal essays.

SIDELIGHTS: Marian MacCurdy once commented in *CA:* "My interest in the subject of writing and healing arose out of my experiences teaching writing and reading students' narratives, which have become increasingly centered around experiences of personal loss and trauma such as sexual abuse, rape, street crime, divorce, and the death of family members. My work in writing and healing has a personal as well as a professional motivation. I am, on both sides of my family, a product of genocide survival. Both sets of grandparents survived the attempted massacres of the Armenians by the Turks during the late nineteenth and early twentieth centuries, and I have written about my family's experiences in personal essays and poetry. As it is true for many marginalized groups—and one of the effects of trauma is to marginalize—personal writing for survivors can provide a way within, a journey which can ultimately take them out of the past and into the present which can establish our common humanity."

*   *   *

MALIK, Iftikhar H(aider) 1949-

PERSONAL: Born 1949. *Education:* Michigan State University, Ph.D.

ADDRESSES: Office—Bath Spa University College, Newton Park, Newton St. Loe, Bath BA29BN, England. *E-mail*—i.malik@bathspa.ac.uk.

CAREER: Academic, radio commentator, and writer. Bath Spa University College, senior lecturer in international history. St. Anthony's College, Oxford University, Quaid-e-Azam, fellow, 1989-94; postdoctoral appointments held at Columbia University and University of California—Berkeley; has given seminars at various universities and institutions.

MEMBER: Fellow, Royal Historical Society.

WRITINGS:

Pakistan: People and Places, Reflections on Living and Travelling, Margalla Publications (Islamabad, Pakistan), 1985.

Sikandar Hayat Khan (1892-1942): A Political Biography, National Institute of Historical and Cultural Research (Islamabad, Pakistan), 1985.

U.S.-South Asia Relations, 1784-1940: A Historical Perspective, Quaid-i-Azam University (Islamabad, Pakistan), 1988.

Africa in Our Time, Quaid-i-Azam University (Islamabad, Pakistan), 1989.

Pakistanis in Michigan: A Study of Third Culture and Acculturation, AMS Press (New York, NY), 1989.

U.S.-South Asia Relations, 1940-47: American Attitudes Toward the Pakistan Movement, St. Martin's Press (New York, NY), 1991.

State and Civil Society in Pakistan: Politics of Authority, Ideology, and Ethnicity, St. Martin's Press (New York, NY), 1997.

Islam, Nationalism, and the West: Issues of Identity in Pakistan, St. Martin's Press (New York, NY), 1999.

Contributor to various international journals.

SIDELIGHTS: Iftikhar H. Malik is an experienced commentator on Pakistani political life and society as well as U.S. relations with Pakistan. He is a commentator on current Muslim politics and Asian history for the BBC and the Voice of America. He has written several books about Pakistan and its relations with western countries.

In *U.S.-South Asia Relations, 1940-47: American Attitudes toward the Pakistan Movement,* Malik discusses recent policies and attitudes toward South Asian countries, including Pakistan. In 1991, when the book was published, the U.S. interest in the region concentrated on preventing conflict between Pakistan and India and on preventing the spread of nuclear weapons. American trade and aid to the region was also dwindling. As Sumit Ganguly noted in the *Journal of Asian Studies,* Malik's thesis is that American interest in the region has been shaped by two factors: American ignorance and apathy toward the region, and the necessity during World War II for Americans to cooperate with the British. Although President Roosevelt supported the prospect of India becoming independent of British rule, naturally, the British were not in favor of this idea. Roosevelt and British prime minister Winston Churchill both signed the Atlantic Charter in 1941, a document that specified that nations should be governed by themselves and promoted "the right of all peoples to choose the form of Government under which they live." However, Churchill specified that this did not apply to India. Although Roosevelt tried to change Churchill's mind, he was not successful and in the end, the Americans had to go along with British interests in the region. Ganguly praised Malik's deep study of historical detail, and wrote, "He has examined a large corpus of primary sources, including recently declassified U.S. foreign policy documents, the *British Transfer of Power* (TOP) sources, as well as published accounts of many of the principals of the period."

In *State and Civil Society in Pakistan: Politics of Authority, Ideology and Ethnicity,* Malik discusses the uneasy and unequal relationship in Pakistan between the national government and local civic governments. In addition, he examines how various government regimes have used Islamic symbols and beliefs to manipulate the people, foster divisions between different ethnic groups in Pakistan, and how these governments' attempts to solve the problems arising from these divisions between groups have been only administrative, not political or economic.

BIOGRAPHICAL/CRITICAL SOURCES:

PERIODICALS

Journal of Asian Studies, May, 1992, p. 431.
New Statesman, December 5, 1997, p. 45.
Research and Reference Book News, August, 1991, p. 7.
Times Literary Supplement, October 15, 1999, p. 36.

OTHER

The Institute of Ismaili Studies: Iftikhar Malik, http://www.iis.ac.uk/ (September 28, 2001).*

*   *   *

MANNING, Brennan

PERSONAL: Born Richard Francis Xavier Manning, in New York, NY; son of Emmett and Amy Manning; married, 1982. *Education:* Attended St. Johns University, Queens, NY, and University of Missouri; St. Francis College, B.A. (philosophy), 1955, advanced degree in theology, 1963; attended Columbia University and Catholic University of America.

ADDRESSES: Home—New Orleans, LA. *Office*—Willie June Ministries, P.O. Box 6911, New Orleans, LA 70114.

CAREER: Author and inspirational speaker. Ordained Franciscan priest, 1963; St. Francis Seminary, Loretto,

PA, instructor in liturgy; joined Little Brothers of Jesus of Charles de Foucauld, c. 1969; cofounded ministry in Bayou La Bastre, AL, early 1970s; Broward Community College, Broward, FL, member of campus ministry, c. 1975; left Franciscan Order, 1980; preacher and lecturer, 1982—. *Military service:* U.S. Marine Corps; fought in Korean War.

WRITINGS:

Lion and Lamb, Revell (Old Tappan, NJ), 1986.
The Signature of Jesus, Chosen Books (Old Tappan, NJ), 1988, revised edition, Multnomah (Sisters, OR), 1996.
The Ragamuffin Gospel: Good News for the Bedraggled, Beat-up, and Burnt Out, Multnomah (Portland, OR), 1990, published as *The Ragamuffin Gospel: Embracing the Unconditional Love of God,* 1996, revised edition, foreword by Michael W. Smith, 2001.
Abba's Child: The Cry of the Heart for Intimate Belonging, NavPress (Colorado Springs, CO), 1994.
The Boy Who Cried Abba: A Parable of Trust and Acceptance, HarperSanFrancisco (San Francisco, CA), 1997.
Reflections for Ragamuffins: Daily Devotions from the Writings of Brennan Manning, edited by Ann McMath Weinheimer, HarperSanFrancisco (San Francisco, CA), 1998.
Ruthless Trust: The Ragamuffin's Path to God, edited by Ann McMath Weinheimer, HarperSanFrancisco (San Francisco, CA), 2000.
(Author of introduction) James Bryan Smith, *Rich Mullins: An Arrow Pointing to Heaven,* 2000.

SIDELIGHTS: Brennan Manning is a former Franciscan priest, a popular preacher and lecturer, and the author of a number of books with Christian themes. Among his most well-known books are his "Ragamuffin" books, which include 1990's *The Ragamuffin Gospel: Good News for the Bedraggled, Beat-up, and Burnt Out.* Manning's second published book, 1988's *The Signature of Jesus,* is about discipleship in the 1980s and 1990s. Reviewing the book for *Publishers Weekly,* William Griffin noted that Manning's first sentence "irresistibly draws the reader" into the book.

Manning's first "Ragamuffin" book, which has since gone through several editions, was followed by *Reflections for Ragamuffins: Daily Devotions from the Writings of Brennan Manning,* in which he discusses the definition of "ragamuffin" given by Noah Webster: "a 'street urchin.' The biblical definition of ragamuffin is much more profound. . . . Ambling down the corridors of salvation-history, we notice that God has ever shown a special affection for the poor and lowly, the humble of heart. . . . The ragamuffins were the homeless, the landless, the street urchins, the dispossessed, whom God would one day restore to prosperity."

A *Publishers Weekly* contributor who reviewed Manning's *Ruthless Trust: The Ragamuffin's Path to God,* called the book "highly readable" and noted that Manning draws on the writings of such authors as Dallas Willard, Philip Yancey, Frederick Buechner, and Richard Foster. Foster wrote the foreword for the book. "Fans of those authors should also appreciate Manning's work, finding his call to ruthless trust both commanding and challenging," remarked the reviewer.

BIOGRAPHICAL/CRITICAL SOURCES:

BOOKS

Manning, Brennan, *Reflections for Ragamuffins: Daily Devotions from the Writings of Brennan Manning,* edited by Ann McMath Weinheimer, HarperSanFrancisco (San Francisco, CA), 1998.

PERIODICALS

Publishers Weekly, July 8, 1988, William Griffin, review of *The Signature of Jesus,* p. 34; September 25, 2000, review of *Ruthless Trust,* p. 112.

OTHER

Brennan Manning Web site, http://www.brennan manning.com/ (March 6, 2001).*

*   *   *

MANTHORPE, Helen   1958-

PERSONAL: Born January 9, 1958, in Adelaide, Australia; daughter of John Ross and Doreen June (Valentin) Manthorpe; married William Gregory Duddy (a lawyer), May 25, 1991; children: William, Nicholas, Alice. *Education:* University of South Australia, BAP-PSC (occupational therapy), 1980. *Avocational interests:* Animal care, horticulture, silk painting, and music (singing).

ADDRESSES: Home—244 Longwood Rd., Heathfield, South Australia 5153, Australia. *Office*—P.O. Box 616, Stirling, South Australia 5152, Australia. *Agent*—

Carole Carroll, 2 Second Ave., Glenelg East, South Australia 5045, Australia. *E-mail*—helen@iweb.net.au.

CAREER: University of South Australia, Adelaide, tutor in occupational therapy, beginning 1985—. Koala handler, Cleland Wildlife Park. Also serves as speaker.

MEMBER: Fauna Care and Release.

AWARDS, HONORS: Rotary Foundation (Pittsburgh, PA) scholar, 1982-83.

WRITINGS:

"SOLO BUSH BABIES" SERIES

Possum, illustrated by Yvonne Ashby, Omnibus (Norwood, South Australia), 2000.
Kangaroo, illustrated by Yvonne Ashby, Omnibus (Norwood, South Australia), 2000.

WORK IN PROGRESS: Koala ("Solo Bush Babies" series) for Omnibus.

SIDELIGHTS: A trained occupational therapist, author Helen Manthorpe also shares a lifelong love of animals and nature. Her interest in fauna care has led to work as a koala handler at Australia's Cleland Wildlife Park and the adoption of two orphaned kangaroos, now fourteen years old. In 2000 Manthorpe turned her experience and knowledge about animals into the books *Solo Bush Babies: Possum* and *Solo Bush Babies: Kangaroo.*

To help educate her young audiences about animals during author visits to Australian schools, Manthorpe often brings a baby kangaroo or possum with her as she conducts her presentations. In addition to writing and working with animals, Manthorpe teaches at the University of Southern Australia.*

*   *   *

MARGOLIS, Julius   1920-

PERSONAL: Born September 26, 1920, in New York, NY; son of Sam and Fannie (Weiner) Margolis; married Doris Lubetsky, October 30, 1942; children: Jane S., Carl W. *Education:* City College (now of the City University of New York), B.S.S., 1941; University of Wisconsin—Madison, Ph.M., 1943; Harvard University, M.P.A., 1947, Ph.D., 1949.

ADDRESSES: Home—45 Whitman Ct., Irvine, CA 92612-4059. *Office*—Department of Social Sciences, University of California, Irvine, CA 92697. *E-mail*—jmargoli@uci.edu.

CAREER: Economist, educator, and author. Tufts College (now University), Medford, MA, instructor in economics, 1947-48; University of Chicago, Chicago, IL, assistant professor of economics and planning, 1948-51; Stanford University, Stanford, CA, assistant professor of economics, 1951-54; University of California, Berkeley, professor of business administration, 1954-64; University of Pennsylvania, Philadelphia, professor and director of Fels Center of Government, 1969-76; University of California, Irvine, professor of economics, 1976—, director of Center on Global Peace and Conflict Studies, 1985—. Consultant to government and industry. *Military service:* U.S. Army, 1943-46.

MEMBER: American Economic Association, Royal Economic Society.

WRITINGS:

(With M. Hufschmidt and J. Krutilla) *Standards and Criteria for Formulating and Evaluating Federal Water Resources Development,* U.S. Bureau of the Budget (Washington, DC), 1961.
(Editor and author of introduction) *The Public Economy of Urban Communities,* Johns Hopkins Press (Baltimore, MD), 1965.
(With Joe Staten Bain and Richard E. Caves) *Northern California's Water Industry: The Comparative Efficiency of Public Enterprise in Developing a Scarce Natural Resource,* Johns Hopkins Press (Baltimore, MD), 1966.
(Editor and author of introduction) *Public Economics: An Analysis of Public Production and Consumption and Their Relations to the Private Sector,* St. Martin's Press (New York, NY), 1969.
(Editor) *The Analysis of Public Output,* Columbia University Press (New York, NY), 1970.
(Editor with Robert H. Haveman, and contributor) *Public Expenditures and Policy Analysis,* Markham (Chicago, IL), 1970, 3rd edition, Houghton (Boston, MA), 1983.

Contributor to books, including *Problems in Public Expenditure Analysis,* edited by Samuel Chase, Brookings Institution (Washington, DC), 1968; *Issues in Urban Economics,* edited by H. S. Perloff and L. Wingo, Johns Hopkins Press (Baltimore, MD), 1968; *The Governance of Metropolitan Areas,* Volume IV: *Reform as Reorganization,* edited by L. Wingo, Johns Hopkins Press (Baltimore, MD), 1974; *Internal Migration,* edited by A. Brown and E. Neuberger, Academic Press, 1977; *Tax and Expenditure Limitations,* edited by H. Ladd and N. Tideman, Urban Institute (Washington, DC), 1982; *American Domestic Priorities,* edited by J. M. Quigley and D. L. Rubinfeld, University of California Press (Berkeley, CA), 1985.

Contributor to scholarly journals, including *Science and Public Policy, Quarterly Journal of Economics, American Economic Review, Wharton Quarterly, Journal of Business,* and *Journal of Law and Economics.*

BIOGRAPHICAL/CRITICAL SOURCES:

PERIODICALS

Times Literary Supplement, June 2, 1972.

OTHER

University of California—Irvine Web site, http://aris.ss.uci.edu/econ/personnel/ (February 3, 2000), "Julius Margolis."*

*   *   *

MARTIN, Calvin
  See MARTIN, Calvin Luther

*   *   *

MARTIN, Calvin Luther   1948-
  (Calvin Martin)

PERSONAL: Born February 13, 1948; married; children: two. *Education:* Westmont College, B.A., 1969; University of California—Santa Barbara, M.A., 1971, Ph.D., 1974.

ADDRESSES: Office—c/o Author Mail, Yale University Press, 302 Temple St., New Haven, CT 06511.

CAREER: Educator and historian. Hartwick College, Oneonta, NY, assistant professor of history, 1974-75; Rutgers University, New Brunswick, NJ, assistant professor, 1975-78, associate professor of history, beginning 1978. Canadian Faculty Enrichment Program, research fellow, 1978-79.

MEMBER: American Historical Association, Organization of American Historians, American Anthropological Association.

AWARDS, HONORS: Albert J. Beveridge Award, American Historical Association, 1979.

WRITINGS:

(As Calvin Martin) *Keepers of the Game: Indian-Animal Relationships and the Fur Trade,* University of California Press (Berkeley, CA), 1978.

(Editor, as Calvin Martin) *The American Indian and the Problem of History,* Oxford University Press (New York, NY), 1987.

In the Spirit of the Earth: Rethinking History and Time, Johns Hopkins University Press (Baltimore, MD), 1992.

The Way of the Human Being, Yale University Press (New Haven, CT), 1999.

SIDELIGHTS: Calvin Luther Martin is an historian who focuses on the role of Native Americans in U.S. history in such works as *The Way of the Human Being* and *Keepers of the Game: Indian-Animal Relationships and the Fur Trade.* His 1992 work, *In the Spirit of the Earth: Rethinking History and Time,* lays a foundation draw from myth, literature, and other writings on which Martin shows the interconnection between the events of history and the cycles of the natural world. This connection was broken when civilizations advanced beyond the "primitive" notion that the earth is a benign force that sustains all living creatures; Western society instead developed along the notion that the natural world is something to be feared and held back. While praising Martin for his research, Michael Harkin noted in the *Journal of American History* that the author's limited definition of history as "an ideology of history of the teleological sort" flaws his analysis. Richard C. Bruce disagreed in his review of *In the Spirit of the Earth* for *Society,* commenting that Martin's book "can guide and inspire us toward reestablishing the old, half-forgotten connections with nature upon which the survival of life on earth depends."

BIOGRAPHICAL/CRITICAL SOURCES:

PERIODICALS

American Historical Review, April, 1979.

Booklist, May 15, 1999, Patricia Monaghan, review of *The Way of the Human Being.*

Journal of American History, June, 1993, Michael Harkin, review of *In the Spirit of the Earth,* p. 231.

New Republic, December 9, 1978.

Society, January-February, 1993, Richard C. Bruce, review of *In the Spirit of the Earth,* p. 87.*

*   *   *

MASKIN, Eric S.   1950-

PERSONAL: Born December 12, 1950, in New York, NY; married; children: two. *Education:* Harvard University, A.B., 1972, A.M., 1974, Ph.D., 1976.

ADDRESSES: Office—School of Social Science, Institute for Advanced Study, Princeton, NJ 08540; fax: 609-951-4457. *E-mail*—maskin@ias.edu.

CAREER: Cambridge University, Jesus College, research fellow, 1976-77; Massachusetts Institute of Technology (MIT), Boston, MA, assistant professor, 1977-80, associate professor, 1980-81, professor of economics, 1981-84, visiting professor, 1999-2000; Harvard University, professor of economics, 1985-86, Louis Berkman Professor of Economics, 1997-2000; Princeton University, Institute for Advanced Study, Albert O. Hirschman Professor of Social Science, 2000—.

MEMBER: American Economic Association, Econometric Society (fellow, 1981—; member of council, 1989-95 and 1999-2002; member of executive committee, 1993-94 and 2000-02), Society for Social Choice and Welfare.

AWARDS, HONORS: Graduate fellowship, National Science foundation, 1972-75; Master of Arts degree, Cambridge University, 1977; overseas fellow, Cambridge University, Churchill College, 1980-82; Guggenhein fellow, 1980-81; Sloan Research fellow, 1983-85; visiting overseas fellow, Cambridge University, St. John's College, 1987-88; Galbraith Teaching Prize, 1990 and 1992; fellow, American Academy of Arts and Sciences, 1994.

WRITINGS:

(Editor, with P. Dasgupta, D. Gale, and O. Hart) *Economic Analysis of Markets and Games,* MIT Press (Boston, MA), 1992.

(Editor) *Recent Developments in Game Theory,* Edward Elgar, 1999.

(Editor, with A. Simonovits), *Planning, Shortage, and Transformation,* MIT Press (Boston, MA), 2000.

American editor, *Review of Economic Studies,* 1977-82; associate editor, *Social Choice and Welfare,*

1983—, *Games and Economic Behavior,* 1988—, *Review of Economic Design,* 1993—, and *QR Journal of Theoretical Economics,* 2000—; advisory editor, *Journal of Risk and Uncertainty,* 1987-94; editor, *Quarterly Journal of Economics,* 1984-90, and *Economics Letters,* 1992—. Contributor of more than eighty journal articles and book chapters to various publications, including *Review of Economic Studies, National Tax Journal, Journal of Mathematical Economics, Journal of Public Economics, American Economic Review, Journal of Political Economy, European Economic Review,* and *Quarterly Journal of Economics.* Contributor of book reviews to *Economic Journal* and *Journal of Economic Literature.*

* * *

MASS, Jeffrey P(aul) 1940-2001

OBITUARY NOTICE—See index for *CA* sketch: Born June 29, 1940, in New York, NY; died March 30, 2001, in Palo Alto, CA. Historian, educator, editor, and author. Mass was an historian who taught medieval Japanese history at Stanford University from 1973 until his death. A scholar whose writings challenged conventional thought about early Japanese history, Mass was awarded a number of fellowships, including a Guggenheim in 1978. His published works include *Warrior Government in Medieval Japan, Antiquity and Anachronism in Japanese History,* and *Yoritomo and the Founding of the First Bakufu.* Mass also served as editor of his *Origins of Japan's Medieval World.* He was an avid collector of ancient English coins.

OBITUARIES AND OTHER SOURCES:

PERIODICALS

San Francisco Chronicle, April 10, 2001, p. A22.
Times (London, England), April 30, 2001, p. 17.

* * *

MASTERS, William H(owell) 1915-2001

OBITUARY NOTICE—See index for *CA* sketch: Born December 27, 1915, in Cleveland, OH; died February 16, 2001, in Tucson, AZ. Doctor, educator, and author. Masters was an obstetrician and gynecologist who, with co-researcher and wife Virginia Johnson, wrote several books on the human sexual experience and ways to overcome sexual dysfunction. A professor of obstetrics and gynecology at the Washington University School of Medicine from 1947 to 1973, he went on to co-found with Johnson, the Masters and Johnson Institute. He and Johnson served as the organization's co-directors from 1973 to 1980. Masters authored a host of books with others, and his first published work, written with Johnson, was the 1966 *Human Sexual Response.* Some of Masters' later works, written also with Johnson and Kolodny, include *Textbook of Sexual Medicine, Masters and Johnson on Sex and Human Loving,* and *Crisis: Heterosexual Behavior in the Age of AIDS.* Masters was the 1979 recipient of the World Association for Sexology Biomedical Research Award.

OBITUARIES AND OTHER SOURCES:

PERIODICALS

Chicago Tribune, February 25, 2001, section 4, p. 6.
Los Angeles Times, February 19, 2001, p. B4.
New York Times, February 19, 2001, p. A1, A18.
Times (London, England), February 19, 2001.
Washington Post, February 19, 2001, p. B6.

* * *

MATHES, Valerie Sherer 1941-

PERSONAL: Born 1941, in Toledo, OH; daughter of Robert W. (a lithographer) and Bonnie Lee (a homemaker; maiden name, Bollenbacher) Sherer. *Education:* University of New Mexico, B.A., 1963, M.A., 1965; Arizona State University, Ph.D., 1988. *Avocational interests:* horsewoman.

ADDRESSES: Home—505 Michael Dr., Sonoma, CA, 95476. *Office*—City College of San Francisco, 50 Phelan Avenue, San Francisco, CA 94112.

CAREER: Writer and college professor.

MEMBER: Western History Association, Western Writers of America.

AWARDS, HONORS: Two Spurs Award from Western Writers of America, 1989 and 1990; American Philosophical Grant, 1999.

WRITINGS:

Helen Hunt Jackson and Her Indian Reform Legacy,
    University of Texas Press (Austin, TX), 1990.

(Editor) *The Indian Reform Letters of Helen Hunt Jackson 1879-1885,* University of Oklahoma Press (Norman, OK), 1998.

WORK IN PROGRESS: History of Ponca Chief Standing Bear as a Catalyst for Indian Reform with Dr. Richard Lowitt; article on the Boston Indian Citizenship Committee.

SIDELIGHTS: Valerie Sherer Mathes, a member of the Social Sciences Department of the City College of San Francisco, has written over 30 scholarly articles as well as over 30 book reviews. Her book *Helen Hunt Jackson and Her Indian Reform Legacy* is intended to restore Helen Hunt Jackson "to her rightful position as a prominent nineteenth century author and reformer," as Mathes writes in the introduction. Helen Hunt Jackson was a white woman who was an activist for Indian reform, mostly on behalf of the Ponca, Cheyenne, Ute, and California Mission tribes. Jackson, who was orphaned at age seventeen and widowed in 1863 at age 33, became a writer to support herself and later married William Sharpless Jackson, a banker whose wealth allowed her to write and follow her interests without worrying about supporting herself. At a time when many white people were becoming active in Native American culture and causes, Jackson had never displayed any interest—even though a controversial situation involving the eviction of Ute people had occurred near her home in Colorado. However, at the age of 49, she suddenly became very interested and active. She wrote numerous letters to the editors of several newspapers, and attracted considerable attention to her cause. Jackson also wrote *Ramona,* a romantic novel about a Native American woman in Spanish California. She hoped that this novel would arouse sympathy for Native Americans in the same way that Harriet Beecher Stowe's book *Uncle Tom's Cabin* aroused public anger against the slavery of African Americans, but this did not happen.

In *The Indian Reform Letters of Helen Hunt Jackson 1879-1885,* Mathes reprints Jackson's letters to several editors, along with personal letters Jackson wrote at the same time. Jackson also wrote *A Century of Dishonor,* a history of broken treaties with the Delawares, Cheyennes, Nez Perces, Sioux, Poncas, Winnebagos, and Cherokees. Also included were several historical massacres of Native Americans by whites. Jackson sent a copy of this work to every member of Congress, with few results. H. Kassia Fleisher wrote in the *American Book Review* that Mathes's "University of Oklahoma version of *A Century of Dishonor* is a real find, as it restores the original appendix (one-third of the original text [of this work])," as well as Jackson's correspon-

dence with the Secretary of the Interior, Carl Schurz. Fleisher also commented that the book "makes for an elucidating tour of the complex relationship between race and gender . . . particularly as they apply when white women . . . advocate on behalf of people of color."

The University of Oklahoma Press quoted Glenda Riley, professor of history at Ball State University, as saying the *Indian Reform Letters* provides "an insightful—even critical—look into the Indian reform movement. This will be an important resource for scholars for decades to come." In *The American Historical Review,* Sherry L. Smith wrote, "This book is long overdue and an important contribution to the history of Indian reform, women, and the West." Smith also noted that the strengths of the book include Mathes' assessment of the importance of women in Indian reform; her analysis of the complex land issues of the Mission Indians; her assessment of Jackson's personality; and her discussion of Indian reformers, their motives and the positive as well as negative results of their actions.

Mathes once commented in *CA:* " My main research interest is the role of 19th Century white women in the Indian reform arena; including Helen Hunt Jackson, Annie Bidwell and Amelia Stone Quenton and the Women's National Indian Association. But I am also interested in 19th Century Indian women and their importance, such as Susan La Hesche Picotte and her sister Suzette La Hesche Tibbles."

BIOGRAPHICAL/CRITICAL SOURCES:

PERIODICALS

American Historical Review, April, 1991, Sherry L. Smith, review of *Helen Hunt Jackson and Her Indian Reform Legacy,* p. 615.

American Literature, March, 1991, H. Kassia Fleisher, review of *The Indian Reform Letters of Helen Hunt Jackson 1879-1885,* p. 175.

Choice, March, 1991, G. Thompson, review of *Helen Hunt Jackson and Her Indian Reform Legacy,* p. 1210.

Journal of American History, September, 1991, Lisa E. Emmerich, review of *Helen Hunt Jackson and Her Indian Reform Legacy,* p. 688.

Pacific Historical Review, August, 1991, p. 412.

Roundup, winter 1990, p. 46.

Western Historical Quarterly, August, 1991, p. 346.

MATTERN, Joanne 1963-
(Joanne Gise, Theresa Grace, Grace Mabie,
M. L. Roberts, Mary Scott)

PERSONAL: Born March 5, 1963, in Nyack, NY; daughter of Robert F. (a banker) and Genevieve (a homemaker; maiden name, Porri) Gise; married James J. Mattern (a chef), June 16, 1990; children: Christina Xinwei. *Education:* Hartwick College, B.A. (English), 1985. *Religion:* Roman Catholic. *Avocational interests:* Music, animal welfare, international adoption, baseball, needlework.

CAREER: Morrow Junior Books, New York, NY, assistant editor; Troll Publications, Mahwah, NJ, editor of children's books until 1995; freelance writer of children's books, 1990—; Institute of Children's Literature, West Redding, CT, instructor, 1997—.

MEMBER: Society of Children's Book Writers and Illustrators.

WRITINGS:

Young Martin Luther King Jr.: I Have a Dream, illustrated by Allan Eitzen, Troll, 1992.
Brer Rabbit in the Briar Patch, Macmillan/McGraw-Hill, 1997.
I Can't Believe My Eyes! Extraordinary Photos of Ordinary Things, Macmillan/McGraw-Hill, 1997.
Telling Time with Goofy, Advance Publisher, 1997.
Smart Thinking! Clever Ways Animals Make Their Lives Easier, Macmillan/McGraw-Hill, 1997.
Tiger Woods: Young Champion, illustrated by Robert F. Goetzl, Troll, 1998.
(Contributor) *Encyclopedia of American Immigration,* 10 volumes, Grolier, 1998.
The Bighorn Sheep (part of "Wildlife of North America" series), Capstone (Mankato, MN), 1998.
The Coyote (part of "Wildlife of North America" series), Capstone (Mankato, MN), 1998.
Structures of Life, Delta Education, 1999.
Solar Energy, Delta Education, 1999.
Variables, Delta Education, 1999.
The Story of Molly Pitcher, McGraw-Hill, 1999.
The Trojan Horse, McGraw-Hill, 1999.
Big and Small, Homes for All: The Story of Bird Nests, Scott Foresman-Addison Wesley, 2000.
A Visit to the Past, Scott Foresman-Addison Wesley, 2000.
From Flowers to Honey: The Story of Beekeeping, Scott Foresman-Addison Wesley, 2000.
Mountain Climb, Scott Foresman-Addison Wesley, 2000.

Tower of Stone: The Story of a Castle, Scott Foresman-Addison Wesley, 2000.
Claws and Wings and Other Neat Things, McGraw-Hill, 2000.
Recycling with Mickey and Friends, Landoll, 2000.
Mickey's Home and Neighborhood Safety, Landoll, 2000.
Curse of Gold, Lyrick, 2000.
The Shoshone People, Capstone (Mankato, MN), 2001.
The Shawnee Indians, Capstone (Mankato, MN), 2001.
Coming to America: The Story of Immigration, Perfection Learning, 2001.
The Outrageous Animal Record Book, Perfection Learning, 2001.
Crazy Creatures of the World, Perfection Learning, 2001.
Crazy Creatures of Australia, Perfection Learning, 2001.
Going, Going . . . Gone? Saving Endangered Animals, Perfection Learning, 2001.
Tom Cruise, Lucent (San Diego, CA), 2001.
Hi-Tech Communications, Enslow, 2001.
Telephones, Enslow, 2001.
100 American Heroes, Kids Books, 2001.
Lizards, Marshall Cavendish, 2001.
Sharks, Marshall Cavendish, 2001.

"ILLUSTRATED CLASSICS" SERIES; ADAPTOR

Mark Twain, *Adventures of Tom Sawyer,* illustrated by Ray Burns, Troll, 1990.
Twain, *Adventures of Huckleberry Finn,* illustrated by Ray Burns, Troll, 1990.
Robert Louis Stevenson, *Kidnapped,* illustrated by Steven Parton, Troll, 1992.
L. M. Montgomery, *Anne of Green Gables,* illustrated by Renee Graef, Troll, 1992.
The Merry Adventures of Robin Hood, illustrated by Susi Kilgore, Troll, 1992.
L. Frank Baum, *The Wonderful Wizard of Oz,* illustrated by Tom Newsom, Troll, 1993.

"A PICTURE BOOK OF" SERIES

A Picture Book of Birds, Troll, 1990.
A Picture Book of Dogs, Troll, 1990.
A Picture Book of Forest Animals, Troll, 1990.
A Picture Book of Underwater Life, Troll, 1990.
A Picture Book of Wild Animals, Troll, 1990.
A Picture Book of Cats, illustrated by Roseanna Pistolesi, Troll, 1991.
A Picture Book of Desert Animals, Troll, 1991.
A Picture Book of Farm Animals, Troll, 1991.
A Picture Book of Horses, Troll, 1991.

A Picture Book of Insects, illustrated by Janice Kinnealy, Troll, 1991.

A Picture Book of Animal Opposites, Troll, 1992.

A Picture Book of Night-Time Animals, Troll, 1992.

A Picture Book of Swamp and Marsh Animals, Troll, 1992.

A Picture Book of Water Birds, Troll, 1992.

A Picture Book of Wild Cats, Troll, 1992.

A Picture Book of Baby Animals (also see below), Troll, 1993.

A Picture Book of Flowers (also see below), Troll, 1993.

A Picture Book of Reptiles and Amphibians (also see below), illustrated by Janice Kinnealy, Troll, 1993.

A Picture Book of Butterflies and Moths (also see below), illustrated by Roseanna Pistolesi, Troll, 1993.

A Picture Book of Baby Animals, A Picture Book of Butterflies and Moths, A Picture Book of Flowers, and *A Picture Book of Reptiles and Amphibians* have also been published, each with audiocassette, in the "A Picture Book of . . . Read Alongs" series by Troll in 1993.

ACTIVITY BOOKS

Home Alone 2 Activity Book, Troll, 1992.

Last Action Hero Activity Book, Troll, 1993.

Inspector Gadget Coloring/Activity Book, Troll, 1993.

Thanksgiving Coloring and Activity Book, Troll, 1994.

Summer Fun Fill-in Book, Troll, 1996.

School Days Memory Book, Troll, 1997.

Back to School Puzzle Fun, Troll, 1998.

Teletubbies Giant Coloring Activity Book, Modern, 2000.

"ANIMAL MINI-BOOKS" SERIES

Reptiles and Amphibians, illustrated by Lynn M. Stone, Troll, 1993.

Bears, illustrated by Tom Leeson and Pat Leeson, Troll, 1993.

Lions and Tigers, illustrated by Lynn M. Stone, Troll, 1993.

Monkeys and Apes, Troll, 1993.

Australian Animals, Troll, 1993.

Baby Animals, illustrated by Lynn M. Stone, Troll, 1993.

"WORLD'S WEIRDEST ANIMALS" SERIES

World's Weirdest Reptiles, Troll, 1995.

World's Weirdest Sea Creatures, Troll, 1995.

World's Weirdest Bugs, Troll, 1995.

World's Weirdest Birds, Troll, 1995.

World's Weirdest Dinosaurs, Troll, 1996.

World's Weirdest Bats, Troll, 1996.

"GREAT BEGINNINGS FIRST LEARNING BOOKS" SERIES

Alphabet Party, Troll, 1995.

Amazing Animals, Troll, 1995.

Happy Surprises, Troll, 1995.

Holiday Fun, Troll, 1995.

Rainy Day Fun, Troll, 1995.

"WISHBONE CLASSICS" SERIES; ADAPTOR

Homer, *The Odyssey,* HarperCollins (New York, NY), 1996.

Howard Pyle, *The Merry Adventures of Robin Hood,* HarperCollins (New York, NY), 1996.

Charles Dickins, *Oliver Twist,* illustrated by Ed Parker and Kathryn Yingling, HarperCollins (New York, NY), 1996.

Robert Louis Stevenson, *The Strange Case of Dr. Jekyll and Mr. Hyde,* HarperCollins (New York, NY), 1996.

Sir Walter Scott, *Ivanhoe,* illustrated by Ed Parker and Kathryn Yingling, HarperCollins (New York, NY), 1997.

"FIRST START EASY READERS" SERIES

Good Night, Bear!, illustrated by Susan T. Hall, Troll, 1998.

Candytown, Troll, 1998.

A Special Letter, Troll, 1998.

Halloween Parade, Troll, 1999.

Inchworm Helps Out, Troll, 1999.

Come Back, Class Pet!, Troll, 2000.

Head, Shoulders, Knees, and Toes, Troll, 2000.

"COMPETE LIKE A CHAMPION" SERIES

Gymnastics: The Vault, Rourke, 1999.

Gymnastics: The Balance Beam and Floor Exercises, Rourke, 1999.

Gymnastics: The Pommel Horse and Rings, Rourke, 1999.

Gymnastics: The Uneven Parallel Bars, Rourke, 1999.

Gymnastics: The Parallel Bars and Horizontal Bar, Rourke, 1999.

Gymnastics: Training and Fitness, Rourke, 1999.

"BARBIE FIRST-GRADE WORKBOOKS" SERIES

Hands-on English, Modern, 1999.

Hands-on Math, Modern, 1999.

Hands-on Phonics, Modern, 1999.

Hands-on Reading and Writing, Modern, 1999.

"SAFETY FIRST" SERIES

Safety on the Go, Abdo & Daughters, 2000.
Safety in Public Places, Abdo & Daughters, 2000.
Safety at School, Abdo & Daughters, 2000.
Safety in the Water, Abdo & Daughters, 2000.
Safety on Your Bicycle, Abdo & Daughters, 2000.

"ANIMAL GEOGRAPHY" SERIES

Africa, Perfection Learning, 2000.
Asia, Perfection Learning, 2000.
Australia, Perfection Learning, 2001.
Europe, Perfection Learning, 2001.
North America, Perfection Learning, 2001.
South America, Perfection Learning, 2001.

"LEARNING ABOUT CATS" SERIES

The Abyssinian Cat, Capstone, 2000.
The Main Coon Cat, Capstone, 2000.
The Persian Cat, Capstone, 2000.
The Siamese Cat, Capstone, 2000.
The Birman, Capstone, 2001.
The Exotic, Capstone, 2001.
The Ragdoll, Capstone, 2001.
The Sphinx, Capstone, 2001.

FISHER-PRICE LITTLE PEOPLE STICKER WORKBOOKS

Fisher-Price Little People Sticker Workbooks: Alphabet Zoo, Modern, 2000.
Fisher-Price Little People Sticker Workbooks: Numbers Train, Modern, 2000.
Fisher-Price Little People Sticker Workbooks: Opposite Park, Modern, 2000.

"EXPLORERS" SERIES

John and Sebastian Cabot, Raintree/Steck-Vaughn, 2000.
Samuel De Champlain, Raintree/Steck-Vaughn, 2000.
Vasco Da Gama, Raintree/Steck-Vaughn, 2000.
Henry Hudson, Raintree/Steck-Vaughn, 2000.
Ferdinand Magellan, Raintree/Steck-Vaughn, 2000.

"BEATING THE ODDS" SERIES

Breaking Barriers: Athletes Who Led the Way, Perfection Learning, 2001.
Courageous Comebacks: Athletes Who Defied the Odds, Perfection Learning, 2001.

Record Breakers: Incredible Sports Achievements, Perfection Learning, 2001.
Teamwork: Working Together to Win, Perfection Learning, 2001.

OTHER

Author of books under various pseudonyms, including Joanne Gise, Theresa Grace, Grace Mabie, M. L. Roberts, and Mary Scott.

SIDELIGHTS: Joanne Mattern once commented: "I always knew my future lay in books. As a child I wrote stories about anything I could think of, while becoming a voracious reader. During high school and college I worked in the local library and planned to pursue a career in library science. But fate stepped in during my senior year of college when I was offered an internship at Morrow Junior Books. After just a few days in the office, I knew the world of children's books was for me. I was lucky enough to land a job at Morrow after I graduated. Working under the guidance of other editors and editing books by such authors as Beverly Cleary and Norma Fox Mazer taught me invaluable lessons about working with authors to make their books the best they could be.

"But it wasn't until I moved on to an editorial position at Troll that my writing career took shape. Troll was a very hands-on publishing house, and editors were expected and encouraged to be writers as well. When my boss found out I love animals, I was immediately assigned the 'Picture Book of ' series. Things just took off from there!

"I left Troll in 1995 to pursue a career as a freelance writer and editor. Working for myself has allowed me to pursue many different projects. Being a full-time writer isn't easy, but the rewards are terrific. You're touching the lives of children and helping them learn about the world. If I can get a child excited about science, about reading, I feel like I've made a difference in the world."

BIOGRAPHICAL/CRITICAL SOURCES:

PERIODICALS

Appraisal, autumn, 1991, review of *A Picture Book of Cats* and *A Picture Books of Insects,* p. 95; spring, 1993, review of *A Picture Book of Butterflies and Moths,* p. 106.
Horn Book, fall, 1991, review of *A Picture Book of Cats* and *A Picture Books of Insects,* pp. 305, 302.

Library Talk, May, 1993, review of *A Picture Book of Butterflies and Moths,* p. 42.

School Library Journal, January, 1994, Fay L. Matsunaga, review of *A Picture Book of . . . Read Alongs,* p. 74; January, 2000, Susan Knell, review of *Safety at School* and *Safety in Public Places,* p. 124, and Lucinda Snyder Whitehurst, review of *Safety in the Water, Safety on the Go,* and *Safety on Your Bicycle,* p. 124.

*   *   *

MAYNARD, Bill

PERSONAL: Born in Highland, NY; married; wife's name Marilyn; children: four. *Education:* Union College, B.A. *Avocational interests:* Watercolors, golf, tennis, sailing.

ADDRESSES: Home—Westchester County, NY; Martha's Vineyard, MA. *Agent*—c/o G. P. Putnam's Sons, 200 Madison Ave., New York, NY 10016.

CAREER: Advertising executive and children's book author. Worked as mailroom clerk; Ted Bates Worldwide (advertising agency), former managing director of creative services; Colgate Palmolive, former vice president of advertising; B.S.B., Canada, former president and chief creative officer; writer. Juror (advertising) at Cannes Film Festival. *Military service:* U.S. Army; served in 936th Field Artillery Battalion.

WRITINGS:

Incredible Ned, illustrated by Frank Remkiewicz, Putnam (New York, NY), 1997.
Santa's Time Off (poetry), illustrated by Tom Browning, Putnam (New York, NY), 1997.
Rock River, Putnam (New York, NY), 1998.
Quiet, Wyatt!, illustrated by Remkiewicz, Putnam (New York, NY), 1999.
Pondfire, Putnam (New York, NY), 2000.

Contributor of essays to periodicals, including *New York Times.* Contributing editor of *International Business.*

SIDELIGHTS: Bill Maynard is a successful advertising executive and a writer of children's books. *Incredible Ned,* his first book for youngsters, concerns a boy who has the ability to make objects appear simply by saying their names. Ned's extraordinary—and extraordinarily problematic—power renders him a difficult student, one who is, ultimately, informed by an imperious principal to remain silence rather than promote classroom chaos. An art teacher, however, believes that Ned's feats are simply the consequence of overwhelming artistic urges. With the help of this understanding teacher, Ned manages to harness his powers towards artistic ends. Deborah Stevenson, writing in the *Bulletin of the Center for Children's Books,* proclaimed *Incredible Ned* a book that will "keep the audience entertained and sympathetic." A *Publishers Weekly* reviewer, meanwhile, acknowledged the book's "uplifting, pro-creativity, be yourself message."

Maynard followed *Incredible Ned* with *Santa's Time Off,* a collection of poems attributed to the legendary Christmas figure. In these poems, Santa Claus reveals that he enjoys bicycling, sunning at the beach, and driving his automobile. A *School Library Journal* critic concluded that the book is "a winner for families to share," while a writer for the *Children's Book Review Service* deemed the poems a "delight."

Maynard's *Rock River* is the story of a timid schoolboy who has feared water since his brother's accidental drowning. When a friend's life is endangered during a fishing contest, the hero manages to overcome his fear and rescue his friend. Shawn Brommer concluded in *School Library Journal* that *Rock River* demonstrates "how children cope and continue after the death of a loved one," and a *Publishers Weekly* critic found the book suitable for readers "who crave excitement and expect happy endings."

Pondfire, published in 2000, finds sixth-grader Jed Webster getting a reputation as a firebug after he almost burns down the family garage while trying to master the techniques of his fireman father. When he and his friends stumble into a swamp fire at the edge of town, Jed's reputation makes him a prime suspect. Soon more fires break out, one injuring Jed's dad, and it becomes clear that an arsonist is at work. Jed realizes that the only way to remove suspicion from him is to find the culprit himself. While noting that the novel's pace is uneven, *Booklist* contributor Todd Morning called Maynard's prose "at its best in descriptions of the fires and the teamwork needed to put them out."

BIOGRAPHICAL/CRITICAL SOURCES:

PERIODICALS

Booklist, February 15, 2000, Todd Morning, review of *Pondfire,* p. 1113.

Bulletin of the Center for Children's Books, November, 1997, Deborah Stevenson, review of *Incredible Ned,* p. 93.

Children's Book Review Service, October, 1997, review of *Incredible Ned,* p. 16; November, 1997, review of *Santa's Time Off,* p. 32.

Publishers Weekly, August 11, 1997, review of *Incredible Ned,* p. 401; August 24, 1998, p. 57.

School Library Journal, October, 1997, p. 46; October, 1998, review of *Santa's Time Off,* p. 140; May, 2000, Alison Follos, review of *Pondfire,* p. 174.

OTHER

Penguin Books Web site, http://www.penguinputnam. com/ (January 8, 1999).*

*   *   *

McCOMBS, Davis 1969-

PERSONAL: Born 1969, in Louisville, KY; married Carolyn Guinzio (a writer); children: Warren James. *Education:* Harvard University, B.A., 1993; University of Virginia, M.F.A., 1995.

ADDRESSES: Home—Munfordville, KY. *Agent*—c/o Yale University Press, P.O. Box 209040, New Haven, CT 06520-9040.

CAREER: Author. Park ranger at Mammoth Cave in Kentucky.

AWARDS, HONORS: Wallace Stegner fellow, Stanford University, 1996-98; Tom McAfee Discovery Feature Poet, *Missouri Review,* 1998; Yale Younger Poets Prize, 1999, for *Ultima Thule;* National Book Critics Circle award nomination, 2000, for *Ultima Thule;* Jim Wayne Miller Prize in Poetry, Kentucky Writers' Coalition, 2000.

WRITINGS:

Ultima Thule, foreward by W. S. Merwin, Yale University Press (New Haven, CT), 2000.

Work featured in *The Best American Poetry 1996.* Contributor to periodicals, including *Missouri Review, no roses review,* and *Columbia Poetry Review.*

SIDELIGHTS: Davis McCombs is an American poet. He earned a B.A. degree from Harvard University in 1993 and an M.F.A. degree from the University of Virginia in 1995. His first collection, *Ultima Thule,* was selected by acclaimed poet W. S. Merwin for the Yale Younger Poets Prize in 1999. He lives in Munfordville, Kentucky, where he works as a park ranger at Mammoth Cave.

Ultima Thule is a collection of poems set in cave country in Kentucky. Mammoth Cave, consisting of some 350 miles of tunnels, has not been charted in its entirety. The name "Ultima Thule" refers to the location where the cave was once thought to end. "This understanding reflects McCombs' drive to explore the cave not only as a physical entity but as something rich yet mysterious in its spiritual aspects," noted Art Jester in *Knight-Ridder/Tribune News Service.*

Critics were largely enthusiastic in their response to the collection. Megan Harlan in the *New York Times Book Review* found that the ragged geology of Mammoth Cave became "urgent images that strikingly illuminate darkened interior spaces." Jester called *Ultima Thule* "certainly the most notable literary work about Mammoth Cave since Robert Penn Warren's *The Cave.*" A critic for *Publishers Weekly* concluded that the work was "the finest Yale Poets selection in years."

BIOGRAPHICAL/CRITICAL SOURCES:

PERIODICALS

Knight-Ridder/Tribune News Service, June 15, 2000, Art Jester, "Davis McCombs Is 'Poet Laureate' of Mammoth Cave," p. K453.

Library Journal, April 15, 2001, Barbara Hoffert, review of *Ultima Thule,* p. 102.

New York Times Book Review, June 11, 2000, Megan Harlan, review of *Ultima Thule.*

Poetry, June, 2001, F. D. Reeve, review of *Ultima Thule,* p. 159.

Publishers Weekly, April 24, 2000, review of *Ultima Thule,* p. 84.*

*   *   *

McELHENY, Victor K(ing) 1935-

PERSONAL: Born September 8, 1935, in Boston, MA; son of Hugh King and Katharine Randolph (Royce) McElheny; married Ruth G. Sullivan, May 12, 1973; *Education:* Harvard University, A.B., 1957.

ADDRESSES: Office—c/o Science Tech & Society, Bldg. E51-185, Massachusetts Institute of Technology, Cambridge, MA 02139-4307.

CAREER: Journalist and author. *Observer,* Charlotte, NC, science reporter, 1957-63; A.A.A.S., London, England, overseas *Science* magazine correspondent, 1964-66; *Boston Globe,* science editor, 1966-72; *New York Times,* science reporter, 1973-98. Director, Knight Science Journalism Fellowships, Massachusetts Institute of Technology; member of the board of directors of *Technology Review.*

MEMBER: National Association of Science Writers.

AWARDS, HONORS: Nieman fellow, Harvard University, 1962-63.

WRITINGS:

(Editor with Seymour Abrahamson) *Assessing Chemical Mutagens: The Risk to Humans,* Cold Spring Harbor Laboratory (Cold Spring Harbor, NY), 1979.
(Editor with Abraham W. Hsie and J. Patrick O'Neill) *Mammalian Cell Mutagenesis: The Maturation of Test Systems,* Cold Spring Harbor Laboratory (Cold Spring Harbor, NY), 1979.
Insisting on the Impossible: The Life of Edwin Land, Perseus Books (Reading, MA), 1998.

Also contributed an essay to *SX-70 Art,* edited by Ralph Gibson, Lustrum Press, 1979.

SIDELIGHTS: Science and technology journalist Victor K. McElheny has written for several publications, including the *New York Times, Science,* and *Technology Review.* His first book, *Assessing Chemical Mutagens: The Risk to Humans,* edited with Seymour Abrahamson, explores the effects of environmental exposure (through food or workplace, for instance) to potentially hazardous chemicals on humans and, in particular, on their DNA. Published in 1979 by the Cold Spring Harbor Laboratory on Long Island, New York, it was based on a conference there on chemical mutagens a year earlier involving twenty-six scientists. As E.H.Y Chu and T. Featherstone wrote in *BioScience,* "This volume records the extensive deliberations of a very timely and urgent topic of both scientific importance and social concern. . . . The volume will continue to be useful for some time as a resource book for the specialists in the field, policy makers, and the concerned public."

Insisting on the Impossible: The Life of Edwin Land, is the first comprehensive biography of the Polaroid camera inventor, Edwin Land. The reclusive Land rarely granted interviews and had his papers destroyed after his death in 1991. McElheny, however, portrays Land as a brilliant inventor and businessman, creative and driven since youth. McElheny's research into Land's life reveals the extent of his technological skills. He held 535 U.S. patents at the time of his death, second only to Thomas Edison, and in addition to instant photography, worked on developments in military reconnaissance and color vision biology. In the 1950s and 1960s, for example, he worked with the military on spy planes and satellites, such as the U-2 aircraft that carried thousands of feet of film and helped document the extent of the Soviet Union's bomber force during the Cold War. He was even a consultant to filmmaker Alfred Hitchcock on a 3-D film. McElheny's biography concentrates on these kinds of details of Land's work more than his personality. Reviewing the book for the *New York Times,* Nancy Mull wrote, "The biography McElheny constructs from available written records and some interviews is both detailed and overfull, painstaking and underanalyzed. This is partly because of the record Land left—scientific and business papers, the text of speeches, but no diaries or memoir and few letters. The biographical consequence is an elaborate account of Land's achievements, ups and downs in business, and patent fights."

McElheny was also a coeditor of *Mammalian Cell Mutagenesis: The Maturation of Test Systems,* and contributed an essay to *SX-70 Art,* a book about artworks made with Polaroid cameras published the same year.

BIOGRAPHICAL/CRITICAL SOURCES:

PERIODICALS

Art in America, January 1981, p. 25, 27.
BioScience, December 1981, pp. 843-844.
Business Week, November 16, 1998, Otis Port, review of *Insisting On the Impossible: The Life of Edwin Land,* p. 38A.
Library Journal, October 15, 1998, Dale F. Farris, review of *Insisting On the Impossible: The Life of Edwin Land,* p. 76.
New York Times, March 21, 1999, p. 28.
Publishers Weekly, September 28, 1998, review of *Insisting On the Impossible: The Life of Edwin Land,* p. 80.
Technology Review, September-October 1998, p. 82.*

McHARG, Ian L(ennox) 1920-2001

OBITUARY NOTICE—See index for CA sketch: Born November 20, 1920, in Clydebank, Scotland; naturalized United States citizen, 1946; died March 5, 2001, in Chester, PA. Landscape architect, planner, educator, and author. McHarg was professor of landscape architecture at the University of Pennsylvania from 1954 to 1986. A landscape architect, he gained notoriety as a planner and designer who incorporated the ecological aspects of an area within the plan for its development. McHarg authored a number of books in which he expounded upon his methodology; some of his works include Design With Nature, a best-selling book published in 1969 and reissued in 1992, Man: Planetary Disease, and A Quest for Life: An Autobiography. He also contributed writings to several works including a collection entitled The Future Environments of North America. In 1992 McHarg received an outstanding achievement award from Harvard University; he was also the 1972 recipient of the American Institute of Architects' Allied Professions medal.

OBITUARIES AND OTHER SOURCES:

PERIODICALS

Architectural Record, April 1, 2001.
Grand Rapids Press, March 31, 2001, p. A22.
Milwaukee Journal Sentinel, March 13, 2001, p. 5.
New York Times, March 12, 2001, p. A17.
Pittsburgh Post-Gazette, March 8, 2001, p. D7.
Scotsman, March 8, 2001, p. D7.
Star-Ledger (Newark, NJ), March 7, 2001, p. 28.

*   *   *

McNULTY, John K. 1934-

PERSONAL: Born October 13, 1934, in Buffalo, NY; son of Robert W. (an attorney) and Margaret D. (a homemaker) McNulty; married Linda Conner (died, 1996); children: Martha J., Jennifer, John K. Jr. Ethnicity: "Caucasian." Education: Swarthmore College, A.B., 1956; Yale Law School, LL.B., 1959. Politics: "Middle of the road liberal." Religion: "Not active." Avocational interests: Classical music, opera, travel, photography.

ADDRESSES: Home—1176 Corrily Peak Blvd., Berkeley, CA 94708. Office—335 Bvalt Hall, University of California, Berkeley, CA 94720; fax: 510-643-2672. E-mail—mcnultyj@law.berkeley.edu.

CAREER: U.S. Supreme Court, Washington, DC, law clerk to Mr. Justice Hugo L. Black, 1959-60; Jones, Day, Reavis & Pogue, Cleveland, OH, attorney, 1960-64; University of California, Berkeley, professor of law, 1964—. California Continuing Education of the American Bar, governing board; affiliated with IRS Practitioners Panel.

MEMBER: International Fiscal Association and U.S. Council, International Tax Association, American Bar Association, American Law Institute, San Francisco Tax Club, East Bay Tax Club, Order of the Coif, Phi Beta Kappa.

AWARDS, HONORS: Guggenheim fellowship, 1977.

WRITINGS:

(With A. Kragen) Cases and Materials on Federal Income Taxation, West, 4th edition, 1985.
Federal Income Taxation of S Corporations, Foundation, 1992.
Federal Estate and Coift Taxation, West, 5th edition, 1994.
Federal "Income Taxation of Individuals, West, 6th edition, 1999.

Contributor to periodicals, including California Law Review.

WORK IN PROGRESS: Research on "international taxation of e-commerce; consumption verses income taxation; estate and gift taxation reforms."

*   *   *

MEDINA, Jane 1953-

PERSONAL: Born June 13, 1953, in Alhambra, CA; daughter of Harry R. (a civil engineer) and Anna M. (a secretary) Peirce; married Pablo Medina (a carpenter), June 14, 1980; children: Annie, Joey. Education: Azusa Pacific University, B.A., 1975; California State University—Fullerton, M.S., 1999. Religion: Christian. Avocational interests: "Walking by the ocean, in the mountains, or just down the street—especially with my family."

ADDRESSES: Home—773 South Breezy Way, Orange, CA 92869. Office—California Elementary School,

1080 North California St., Orange, CA 92869. *E-mail—*
Demedina@cs.com.

CAREER: Orange Unified School District, Orange, CA, elementary music teacher, 1977-82, bilingual education teacher, 1982-96, parent educator, 1995-97, English-as-a-second-language skills center teacher, 1996-97, elementary education teacher, 1997-99, reading specialist, 1999—. California State University, Fullerton, CA, guest instructor, 1997, model lesson teacher, 1998, instructor, 1999—. *The Reading Teacher,* member of review team, 1999, member of executive review board, 1999—. Presenter at elementary schools.

MEMBER: International Reading Association, California Reading Association, Orange County Reading Association, National Council of Teachers of English, National Association of Bilingual Educators, Teachers of English to Speakers of Other Languages, California Teachers of English to Speakers of Other Languages, National Education Association, Orange Unified Education Association, Society of Children's Book Writers and Illustrators, Southern California Council on Literature for Children and Young People.

AWARDS, HONORS: Edwin Carr Fellowship, California State University, Fullerton, 1999; finalist, Tomas Rivera Mexican-American Children's Book of the Year, and Notable Book Award, National Council of Teachers of English, both 2000, both for *My Name Is Jorge on Both Sides of the River.*

WRITINGS:

My Name Is Jorge on Both Sides of the River, illustrated by Fabricio Vanden Broeck, Boyds Mills Press (Honesdale, PA), 1999.

Contributor of articles to educational journals, including *Language Arts* and *NEA Today,* and books, including *Portfolios in the Classrooms.*

WORK IN PROGRESS: The Dream on Blanca's Wall, a poetry anthology in English and Spanish; *A Box of Squiggles,* a poetry anthology for young children.

SIDELIGHTS: Growing up in Garden Grove, California, poet Jane Medina recalled in a Boyds Mills Press release that she began writing letters and poems while still a teenager. Being sensitive to criticism from others, the budding poet refused to share her work with anyone but her closest friends. However, when writing a letter to thank the "editor of a book for teachers . . . for the

instruction and inspiration," Medina decided to enclose a short poem as well. "To my surprise," Medina explained, "the editor wrote back—not to thank me for the letter, but to ask if I had any more poetry." Soon after, Medina realized that she had a talent for capturing the emotions of children through her poetry and began work on a collection of children's poems, *My Name Is Jorge on Both Sides of the River.*

In *My Name Is Jorge on Both Sides of the River,* a book of poems written in both Spanish and English, Medina describes the thoughts and feelings of Jorge, a young boy trying to adjust to life in the United States. After his family crosses the river from Mexico, Jorge finds himself in a different world. While his parents keep their Mexican traditions and ways of life alive in the new country, Jorge is torn between fitting in with U.S. society and preserving his Mexican heritage. Throughout the collection of poems, Medina illustrates the challenges Jorge faces as he learns the language and customs of America. Describing the poems as "insightful," *School Library Journal* reviewer Ann Welton claimed the book "depicts the sometimes painful experience of adjusting to a new language and a new culture." A reviewer for *Horn Book* praised the seriousness of Medina's collection, concluding: "Finally—bilingual poems that aren't overflowing with happy colors and tortilla chips."

BIOGRAPHICAL/CRITICAL SOURCES:

PERIODICALS

Horn Book, July-December, 1999, review of *My Name Is Jorge on Both Sides of the River,* p. 153.
School Library Journal, February, 2000, Ann Welton, review of *My Name Is Jorge on Both Sides of the River,* p. 136.

OTHER

Press release from Boyds Mills Press, 1999.

*   *   *

MEEKS, Kenneth   1963-

PERSONAL: Born October 26, 1963, in Louisville, KY; son of Florian and Eloise Kline Meeks; married Glenna Batiste Meeks, February 6, 1996; children: Giovanni, Cingve, Seneca. *Ethnicity:* "African American."

ADDRESSES: Home—220 Manhattan Ave. #1H, New York, NY 10025. *Office*—Black Enterprise Magazine,

New York, NY 10011; fax: 212-932-1874. *Agent*—Marie Brown, Marie Brown Associates, 412 West 154th St., New York, NY 10032. *E-mail*—meeksmedia@aol.com.

CAREER: Guideposts Magazine, New York City, features editor assistant, 1986-90; Enlightenment Press, New York City, copy editor, 1992-94; *Black Elegance* and *Belle* Magazines, New York City, managing editor, 1994-98; *New York Amsterdam News* Newspaper, New York City, assistant managing editor, 1998-99; *Black Enterprise* Magazine, New York City, managing editor, 1999—. Has worked in editorial departments at Macmillan Publishing Company and *Columbia Journal of World Business.*

MEMBER: National Association of Black Journalist.

WRITINGS:

Driving While Black: Highways, Shopping Malls, Taxicabs, Sidewalks: What to Do If You Are a Victim of Racial Profiling, Broadway (New York, NY), 2000.

Contributor of a short story to *Brotherman: The Odyssey of Black Men in America: An Anthology,* edited by Herb Boyd and Robert E. Allen, One World/Ballantine, 1995. Contributor, under a pseudonym, to *Essence.*

SIDELIGHTS: Kenneth Meeks told *CA:* "When my children are asleep, I operate a private news and literary organization. I am known for helping aspiring writers and struggling journalists find their niche in this changing world of publishing. I think one of the greatest fundamental principles of this country is our unique freedom of speech. Anyone who has something to say has the right to make it last forever, and the print media is the only way to go. I always say in this vast world of technology, print media may be old-fashion, but it still works."

*   *   *

MEISTER, Maureen   1953-

PERSONAL: Born August 25, 1953, in Spokane, WA; daughter of Robert (a newspaper editor) and Amy June (an editor; maiden name, Rosenberg) Meister; married David Louis Feigenbaum (an attorney), April 28, 1979; children: Peter J., Stephen M. *Education:* Attended Columbia University Advanced Institute in Paris, 1974;

Mount Holyoke College, A.B. (English), 1975; University of Pittsburgh, B.A. (art history), 1980; Brown University, A.M., 1983, Ph.D., 2000.

ADDRESSES: Home—38 Rangeley Rd., Winchester, MA 01890. *E-mail*—mmeister@ix.netcom.com.

CAREER: Pittsburgh Press, Pittsburgh, PA, copy editor, 1975-79, worked at news desk, 1975-77, feature writer and art critic, 1977-79, dance critic, 1978-79; *Pittsburgh Post-Gazette,* Pittsburgh, PA, copy editor of daily magazine, 1979; Art Institute of Boston, Boston, MA, instructor, 1982-86, adjunct assistant professor, 1986-91, associate professor of art history, 1991-2001. School of the Museum of Fine Arts, Boston, MA, visiting lecturer, 1985; Northeastern University, lecturer, 1989; Tufts University, visiting lecturer, 1998-2001. Gibson House Museum, member of board of directors, 1992—, vice-president, 1993-96, president, 1996-99. Winchester Historical Commission, member, 1983-86, chairperson, 1985-86; Winchester Design Review Committee, member, 1986-95; Winchester Planning Board, member, 2000—.

MEMBER: Winchester Historical Society (member of board of directors, 1992-2001).

AWARDS, HONORS: Grant from Graham Foundation, 1997.

WRITINGS:

(Editor) *H. H. Richardson: The Architect, His Peers, and Their Era,* MIT Press (Cambridge, MA), 1999.

Author of exhibition catalogs. Contributor to periodicals, including *Art News, Winchester, Antiques, Visual Resources: International Journal of Documentation* and *Nineteenth Century.*

*   *   *

MELOEN, Josien
See van KEULEN, Mensje

*   *   *

MILLER, Kenneth R(aymond)   1948-

PERSONAL: Born 1948. *Education:* University of Colorado, Ph.D., 1974. *Religion:* Christian.

ADDRESSES: Office—Department of Molecular Biology, Cell Biology, and Biochemistry, Brown University, Providence, RI 02912; fax: 401-863-1971. *E-mail*—Kenneth—Miller@brown.edu.

CAREER: Biologist and educator. Brown University, Providence, RI, professor of biology.

WRITINGS:

(With Joseph S. Levine) *Biology: Discovering Life,* Volume I: *Core Concepts,* Volume II: *The Diversity of Life,* Volume III: *Plant Systems,* Volume IV: *Animal Systems,* Heath (Lexington, MA), 1992, 2nd edition, with instructor's edition, 1994.

Finding Darwin's God: A Scientist's Search for Common Ground between God and Evolution, Cliff Street Books (New York, NY), 1999.

SIDELIGHTS: Kenneth R. Miller is a biologist who attempts to reconcile evolutionary theory with Christianity in *Finding Darwin's God: A Scientist's Search for Common Ground between God and Evolution.* Published in 1999, the book draws on biology, astronomy, physics, and geology to oppose the ill-founded scientific arguments and illogic of some creationists "with persuasive reasons based on the known physical properties of the universe and the demonstrable effects of time on the radioactivity of various elements," according to a *Publishers Weekly* reviewer. Arguing also against an atheistic theory of creation, Miller discusses the reason why the scientific community is dismissive of any discussion involving religious belief as they relate to the creation of the universe. Calling Miller's book "an act of intellectual daring and spiritual integrity," *Booklist* contributor Bryce Christensen noted that "with scrupulous evenhandedness," the author "challenges both sides to reexamine their premises and subdue their rhetoric."

BIOGRAPHICAL/CRITICAL SOURCES:

PERIODICALS

Booklist, September 15, 1999, Bryce Christensen, review of *Finding Darwin's God,* p. 200.
Publishers Weekly, September 27, 1999, review of *Finding Darwin's God,* p. 83.

OTHER

Brown University Web site, http://biomed.brown.edu/ (December 14, 1999).*

MOONEY, Bill 1936(?)-

PERSONAL: Born c. 1936, in MO.

ADDRESSES: Office—P.O. Box 17493, Boulder, CO 80303. *E-mail*—BMooney303@aol.com.

CAREER: Storyteller and actor. Participant in storytelling festivals, including National Storytelling Festival, New Jersey Folk Festival, Jackson Storyfest, Alabama Tale-tellin' Festival, and Cave Run Festival. Storytelling performer for Holland America cruise line. Played role of Paul Martin on the American Broadcasting Company (ABC) soap opera *All My Children.* Guest on television shows, including the *Today Show, As the World Turns, One Life to Live, Loving,* and *The Guiding Light.* Appeared on and off-Broadway, including *A Man for All Seasons, Lolita, We,* and *The Brownsville Raid.* Appeared in motion pictures, including *Network, Beer,* and *A Flash of Green.*

AWARDS, HONORS: Two-time Emmy nominee for role of Paul Martin on the ABC soap opera *All My Children;* Grammy nominee, 1995, Gold Award, Parents Choice, and Notable Children's Recording, American Library Association, all for *Why the Dog Chases the Cat;* Grammy nominee, 1998, for *Spiders in the Hairdo: Modern Urban Legends.*

WRITINGS:

(With Donald J. Noone) *ASAP: The Fastest Way to Create a Memorable Speech,* Barron's (Hauppauge, NJ), 1992.
(Editor, with David Holt) *Ready-to-Tell Tales: Surefire Stories from America's Favorite Storytellers,* August House (Little Rock, AK), 1994.
(And editor, with David Holt) *The Storyteller's Guide: Storytellers Share Advice for the Classroom, Boardroom, Showroom, Podium, Pulpit, and Center Stage,* August House (Little Rock, AK), 1996.
(Reteller, with David Holt) *Spiders in the Hairdo: Modern Urban Legends* (also see below), August House (Little Rock, AK), 1999.
(Editor, with David Holt) *More Ready-to-Tell Tales from around the World,* August House (Little Rock, AK), 2000.

Coauthor, with David Holt, of produced play *Banjo Reb and the Blue Ghost.* Recorded storytelling performances with Holt include *Why the Dog Chases the Cat,* High Windy Audio, 1995; *Half Horse, Half Alligator,* August House Audio, 1997; and *Spiders in the Hairdo: Modern Urban Legends,* High Windy Audio, 1999.

BIOGRAPHICAL/CRITICAL SOURCES:

OTHER

Bill Mooney, Storyteller, http://www.billmooney.com (April 23, 2001).

*　　*　　*

MOORE, John Norton 1937-

PERSONAL: Born June 12, 1937, in New York, NY; married Barbara Schneider, December 12, 1981; children: Victoria Norton, Elizabeth Norton. *Education:* Drew University, B.A., 1959; Duke University, LL.B. (with distinction), 1962; University of Illinois at Urbana-Champaign, LL.M., 1965. *Religion:* Episcopal.

ADDRESSES: Home—824 Flordon Dr., Charlottesville, VA 22901. *Office*—Center for National Security Law, School of Law, University of Virginia, 580 Massie Rd., Charlottesville, VA 22903. *E-mail*—colp@virginia.edu and cnsl@virginia.edu.

CAREER: University of Virginia, Charlottesville, professor of law, 1965-72, director of graduate program in law, 1968-72, codirector of Council on Legal Education Opportunity Program, 1969, sesquicentennial associate of Center for Advanced Studies, 1971-72; U.S. Department of State, Washington, DC, counselor on international law, 1972-73; National Security Council, Washington, DC, chairperson of Interagency Task Force on the Law of the Sea and deputy special representative of the president (rank of ambassador), 1973-76; University of Virginia, director of Center for Oceans Law & Policy and Center for National Security Law, director of graduate program in law, 1972-93, and Walter L. Brown Professor of Law, 1976—. U.S. Institute of Peace, chair of board of directors, 1985-91; Oceans and International (consulting firm), president. Licensed real estate agent in state of Virginia, 1991—.

Member, U.S. delegation to U.N. General Assembly, 1972-75; Conference on Security and Cooperation in Europe, 1984; presidential delegation to observe elections in El Salvador, 1984; National Advisory Committee on Oceans and Atmosphere, 1984-85; Forum for U.S.-Soviet Dialogue advisory board, 1987—; International Security Council board of governors, 1988—; (and co-chairperson) U.S. delegation of U.S.-USSR talks on the rule of law (Moscow and Leningrad Seminars), 1990; Center for Strategic and International Studies international research council, 1991; Ocean Policy Institute advisory council, 1991—; World Strategy Network legislative task group; and National Strategy Information Center board of directors.

U.S. special counsel to International Court of Justice, 1981-84; Hamilton Shirley Amerasinghe Memorial Fellowship on the Law of the Sea, chairperson of U.N. advisory panel, 1991—; legal adviser to Kuwaiti ambassador to the United States during Persian Gulf crisis, 1991-94; witness before congressional committees; consultant to President's Intelligence Oversight Board, U.S. Information Agency, and Arms Control and Disarmament Agency. Republican National Committee, chairperson of advisory committee on oceans policy, 1978-79; Conflict Analysis Center, president, 1983—; Ethics and Public Policy Center, associated scholar, 1986—; Washington Legal Foundation, member of academic board of advisers, 1986—.

University of California fellow of International Legal Studies, 1963; Yale University fellow in law, 1965-66; Wilson Center fellow, 1976; Myres McDougal Lecturer in International Law, University of Denver, 1981; Brendon Brown Lecturer, Catholic University of America, 1982; Waldemar Solf Lecturer in International Law, Judge Advocate General's School of the Army, 1983; People's University of Beijing lecturer, 1986; Corliss Lamont Lecturer, University of Wisconsin—Madison, 1987; Andrew R. Cecil Lecturer on Moral Values in a Free Society, University of Texas at Austin, 1991; adjunct professor at Georgetown University and American University; Tufts University Institute for Foreign Policy Analysis, member of board of research consultants; consultant or lecturer at National War College, Naval War College, Army War College, and Foreign Service Institute.

MEMBER: International Law Association (American branch), International Council of Environmental Law, World Technology Foundation, American Bar Association (vice-chairperson of Section of International Law and Practice, 1980-83, member of section council, 1986-92; chairperson of Standing Committee on Law and National Security, 1982-86), American Law Institute, U.S. Maritime Law Association, Marine Technology Society (fellow), American Oceanic Organization (member of board of directors, 1979-85), Consortium for the Study of Intelligence, Council on Foreign Relations, American Arbitration Association (member of panel of arbitrators, 1993—), National Forum Foundation, Washington Institute of Foreign Affairs, Freedom House (member, board of trustees), Phi Beta Kappa, Omicron Delta Kappa, Phi Delta Phi, Coif, MENSA,

Cosmos Club (Washington, DC), New York Yacht Club.

AWARDS, HONORS: Phi Beta Kappa Award, c. 1972, for *Law and the Indo-China War;* Hardy Dillard Award in International Law, Virginia Bar Association, 1984; George Washington Honor Medal, Freedoms Foundation, 1985.

WRITINGS:

Law and the Indo-China War, Princeton University Press (Princeton, NJ), 1972.

(Editor) *The Arab-Israeli Conflict,* Volumes I-III, Princeton University Press (Princeton, NJ), 1974, abridged edition, 1977, Volume IV, 1991.

(Editor) *Law and Civil War in the Modern World,* Johns Hopkins University Press (Baltimore, MD), 1974.

(With others) *Deep Seabed Mining in the Law of the Sea Negotiations: Toward a Balanced Development System,* Center for Oceans Law and Policy, University of Virginia (Charlottesville, VA), 1979.

(Editor with Richard B. Lillich) *Readings on International Law from the Naval War College Review, 1947-1977,* 2 volumes, Naval War College Press (Newport, RI), 1980.

Law and the Grenada Mission, Center for Law and National Security and Center for Strategic and International Studies, 1984.

(Editor) *International and United States Documents on Oceans Law and Policy,* five volumes, William S. Hein, 1986.

The Secret War in Central America, University Publications of America, 1986.

(With Robert F. Turner) *International Law and the Brezhnev Doctrine,* University Press of America (Lanham, MD), 1987.

The Secret War in Central America: Sandinista Assault on World Order, University Publications of America, 1987.

(Editor with Frederick S. Tipson and Robert F. Turner) *National Security Law,* Carolina Academic Press (Durham, NC), 1990.

(Editor) *The Vietnam Debate: A Fresh Look at the Arguments,* University Press of America (Lanham, MD), 1990.

Crisis in the Gulf: Enforcing the Rule of Law, Oceana (Dobbs Ferry, NY), 1992.

(Editor with Robert B. Turner) *Readings on International Law from the Naval War College Review, 1978-1994,* Naval War College Press (Newport, RI), 1995.

(Editor, with Myron H. Nordquist) *Entry into Force of the Law of the Sea Convention,* foreword by Sir Robert Y. Jennings, M. Nijhoff (Boston, MA), 1995.

(Editor, with others) *National Security Law Documents,* Carolina Academic Press (Durham, NC), 1995.

(Editor) *Deception and Deterrence in "Wars of National Liberation," State-sponsored Terrorism, and Other Forms of Secret Warfare,* Carolina Academic Press (Durham, NC), 1997.

(Editor with Myron H. Nordquist) *Security Flashpoints: Oil, Islands, Sea Access, and Military Confrontation,* M. Nijhoff (Boston, MA), 1998.

(Editor, with Myron H. Nordquist) *Current Maritime Issues and the International Maritime Organization,* M. Nijhoff (Boston, MA), 1999.

(Editor, with Myron H. Nordquist) *Oceans Policy: New Institutions, Challenges, and Opportunities,* M. Nijhoff (Boston, MA), 1999.

(Editor, with Myron H. Nordquist) *Current Fisheries Issues and the Food and Agriculture Organization of the United Nations,* M. Nijhoff (Boston, MA), 2000.

(Editor, with Alex Morrison) *Strengthening the United Nations and Enhancing War Prevention,* Carolina Academic Press (Durham, NC), 2000.

(Editor, with Myron H. Nordquist) *Current Marine Environmental Issues and the International Tribunal for the Law of the Sea,* M. Nijhoff (Boston, MA), 2001.

The National Law of Treaty Implementation, Carolina Academic Press (Durham, NC), 2001.

Contributor of numerous articles to periodicals, including *Foreign Affairs, Virginia Law Review, New York Times,* and *Wall Street Journal.* Member of board of editors, *American Journal of International Law,* 1972-87, *Marine Technology Society Journal,* 1976-91, *Comparative Strategy, Terrorism: International Journal,* and *Journal of Political Communication and Persuasion;* member of international editorial board, *Annual on Terrorism,* 1986; member of advisory boards, *Terrorism: International Resource File, American University Journal of International Law and Policy, Journal of Law and Politics,* and *Denver Journal of International Law and Policy.**

*   *   *

MORAN, Michael   1946-

PERSONAL: Born 1946. *Education:* University of Lancaster, B.A.; University of Essex, M.A., Ph.D.

ADDRESSES: Office—Department of Government, University of Manchester, Dover Street Building, Dover Street, Manchester M13 9PL, England. *E-mail*—Michael.Moran@man.ac.uk.

CAREER: Writer. Department of Government, University of Manchester, Manchester, England, professor.

WRITINGS:

The Union of Post Office Workers: A Study in Political Sociology, Macmillan (London, England), 1974.

The Politics of Industrial Relations: The Origins, Life, and Death of the 1971 Industrial Relations Act, Macmillan (London, England), 1977.

Trade Unions and Politics: Past Patterns, Future Problems, University of Hull (Hull, England), 1978.

The Politics of Banking: The Strange Case of Competition and Credit Control, St. Martin's (New York, NY), 1984.

Politics and Society in Britain: An Introduction, St. Martin's (New York, NY), 1985.

The Politics of the Financial Services Revolution: The U.S.A., U.K., and Japan, St. Martin's (New York, NY), 1991.

(With Bill Jones, Andrew Gray, Dennis Kavanagh, Philip Norton, and Anthony Seldon) *Politics U.K.,* Philip Allan, 1991.

(With Bruce Wood) *States, Regulation, and the Medical Profession,* Open University Press (Philadelphia, PA), 1993.

Sovereignty Divided: Essays on the International Dimensions of the Cyprus Problems, CYREO (Mersin, Turkey), 1998.

Governing the Health Care State: A Comparative Study of the United Kingdom, the United States, and Germany, Manchester University Press (Manchester, England), 1999.

EDITOR

(With Martin Burch) *British Politics: A Reader,* Manchester University Press (Manchester, England), 1987.

(With Leigh Hancher) *Capitalism, Culture, and Economic Regulation,* Oxford University Press (New York, NY), 1989.

(With Ursula Vogel) *The Frontiers of Citizenship,* St. Martin's (New York, NY), 1991.

(With Maurice Wright) *The Market and the State: Studies in Interdependence,* St. Martin's (New York, NY), 1991.

(With Tony Prosser) *Privatization and Regulatory Change in Europe,* Open University Press (Philadelphia, PA), 1994.

(With Geraint Parry) *Democracy and Democratization,* Routledge (New York, NY), 1994.

(And author of introduction) *Rauf Denktash at the United Nations: Speeches on Cyprus,* Eothen Press (Huntington, England), 1997.

SIDELIGHTS: Michael Moran is an educator and writer who has produced numerous works in the fields of sociology, economics, and politics. His first book, *The Union of Post Office Workers: A Study in Political Sociology,* is a 1974 publication that exposed the apathy at the time within England's postal workers' union. A *Times Literary Supplement* reviewer noted that Moran's book derived from "a detailed study," while an *Economist* critic affirmed that "the heart of the book is a survey of attitudes of ordinary union members in Colchester." The *Economist* reviewer added that *The Union of Post Office Workers* demonstrates "how a modern British union can follow policies which are opposed by the majority of its members."

Moran's second book, *The Politics of Industrial Relations: The Origins, Life, and Death of the 1971 Industrial Relations Act,* concerns what Anthony Giddens, writing in the *Times Literary Supplement,* described as a "phase in the fraught history of industrial relations in Britain: the decade or so from the middle 1960s to the middle 1970s." Giddens observed that Moran's book "treats the Industrial Relations Act of 1971 as something of a watershed, an attempt on the part of the Conservatives to provide, or rather to impose, a comprehensive framework in law for the organization of industrial interests and the conduct of industrial disputes."

Moran also examines England's changing society in *The Politics of Banking: The Strange Case of Competition and Credit Control,* which analyzes the Conservative government's endeavor to shift the nation's monetary system towards public regulation and a greater dependence on competition. *Perspective* reviewer Michael D. Reagan acknowledged that Moran's work "tells a fascinating dual story of competition and increased regulation," and he found it "of considerable value to students of financial politics and theories of public policy making." Another reviewer, Richard C. Schiming, wrote in the *Wall Street Review of Books* that *The Politics of Banking* constitutes "a thoughtful essay about the unintended results of a major policy decision on the structure and regulation of British banking."

In *Politics and Society in Britain: An Introduction,* Moran provides what *British Book News* contributor John Dearlove called "a good bread-and-butter account" of British politics. In addition, he described the book's individual chapters as "alive to contemporary debates." Robert Cole, meanwhile, contended in *Perspective* that *Politics and Society in Britain* serves as "a useful introduction to the problem of socio-political analysis for beginning students of the discipline." Cole added that the book "contains both hard and rational analysis . . . and is well written." A more urgent recommendation came from Frances Cairncross, who praised the book in a *Times Literary Supplement* review as "a riveting read for anyone who wants to understand what has been happening to the British electorate."

Moran's next publication, *The Politics of the Financial Services Revolution: The U.S.A., U.K., and Japan,* traces the evolution of economic regulations as they developed in the three countries. Philip G. Cerny, writing in *West European Politics,* found *The Politics of the Financial Services Revolution* "clearly written and wide-ranging," and he called it "an excellent introduction to the subject for use in courses on comparative and international political economy." W. S. Curran, meanwhile, wrote in *Choice* that Moran's work "will interest economists and political scientists interested in regulation of financial markets."

After publishing *The Politics of the Financial Services Revolution,* Moran teamed with Bill Jones, Andrew Gray, Dennis Kavanagh, Philip Norton, and Anthony Seldon to produce *Politics U.K.,* which Peter Caterall praised in the *Times Educational Supplement* as a work of "considerable value to students." Catterall also acknowledged the volume's "wealth of illustrative material."

Moran collaborated with Bruce Wood in writing *States, Regulation, and the Medical Profession,* a 1993 publication that Rudolf Klein introduced in *Journal of Social Policy* as an examination of "the relationship between the state and the medical profession in Britain, the United States and Germany." He called it "a useful addition to the literature on comparative health policy." Another reviewer, Joe Jacob, wrote in the *British Journal of Sociology* that *States, Regulation, and the Medical Profession* "is a brave little book," and he deemed it "a worthy contribution to a developing discourse."

In addition to his writings, Moran has served as editor of various publications. In *Capitalism, Culture, and Economic Regulation,* for example, he joined with Leigh Hancher to produce what Wyn Grant described in *Political Studies* as an "important collection of essays" and *Business History Review* critic Jim Tomlinson called "a significant contribution to our understanding of regulation." Another volume, *The Frontiers of*

Citizenship, notes what J. M. Barbalet described in *American Political Science Review* as "the liveliness of citizenship in current politics and scholarship." Barbalet attested that Moran and co-editor Ursula Vogel, in their introductory essay, write of the likelihood that "citizenship has . . . overtaken class, market, and even democracy as the 'strategic concept of political science.' "

Moran's other publications as editor include *The Market and the State: Studies in Interdependence,* a 1991 volume on the relationship between economics and politics. A *Journal of Economic Literature* reviewer noted that the book—on which Moran collaborated with Maurice Wright—includes essays on economists, markets, and even "the collapse of the power monopoly in Eastern Europe."

In the 1994 publication *Privatization and Regulatory Change in Europe,* Moran and Tony Prosser present essays on what a *Harvard International Review* critic called "the recent economic developments in post-Cold War Europe." Peter Curwen protested in *Public Administration* that the book's "overall structure . . . leaves room for only eight fairly brief case studies." But Leonard Geron, in his *International Affairs* review, praised the work as "a timely collection of essays written by experienced lawyers and economists."

A later volume, *Democracy and Democratization,* comprises what Alan Ware praised in *Political Studies* as "a well-structured book." Another reviewer, *Government and Opposition* writer Andrew Gamble, acknowledged the book—on which Moran collaborated with Geraint Parry—as "a rich feast," and he noticed "much that is useful for both the specialist and the general reader." Gamble was particularly impressed with the work's various analyses and methodologies. "A considerable strength of the book," he wrote, "is that it combines theoretical analysis of concepts and methods of analysis, reflections on the present condition of the global political system, and a wide range of empirical studies of democratization of authoritarian regimes as well as of democratization within established democracies."

BIOGRAPHICAL/CRITICAL SOURCES:

PERIODICALS

American Political Science Review, June, 1993, J. M. Barbalet, review of *The Frontiers of Citizenship,* pp. 509-511, Peter Evans, review of *The Market and the State: Studies in Interdependence,* pp. 518-519.

British Book News, January, 1986, John Dearlove, review of *Politics and Society in Britain: An Introduction,* p. 23.

British Journal of Sociology, December, 1994, Joe Jacob, review of *States, Regulation, and the Medical Profession,* pp. 705-707.

Business History Review, autumn, 1990, Jim Tomlinson, review of *Capitalism, Culture, and Economic Regulation.*

Choice, January, 1992, W. S. Curran, review of *The Politics of the Financial Services Revolution,* pp. 789-790.

Economist, August 31, 1974, review of *The Union of Post Office Workers,* pp. 79-80.

Government and Opposition, spring, 1994, Andrew Gamble, "The Age of Democracy," pp. 283-287.

Harvard International Review, winter, 1994, review of *Privatization and Regulatory Change in Europe,* p. 96.

International Affairs, January, 1995, Leonard Geron, review of *Privatization and Regulatory Change in Europe,* pp. 171-172.

Journal of Economic Literature, June, 1992, review of *The Politics of the Financial Services Revolution,* p. 983; December, 1992, review of *The Market and the State,* p. 2276.

Journal of Social Policy, October, 1993, Rudolf Klein, review of *States, Regulation, and the Medical Profession,* p. 588.

Perspective, November-December, 1984, Michael D. Reagan, review of *The Politics of Banking,* pp. 174-175; April-May, 1987, Robert Cole, review of *Politics and Society in Britain,* p. 49.

Political Studies, June, 1990, Wyn Grant, review of *Capitalism, Culture, and Economic Regulation,* p. 388; December, 1994, Alan Ware, review of *Democracy and Democratization,* p. 773.

Public Administration, winter, 1992, Philip G. Cerny, review *The Market and the State,* p. 617-618; summer, 1996, Peter Curwen, review of *Privatization and Regulatory Change in Europe,* pp. 333-335.

Times Educational Supplement, December 27, 1991, Peter Caterall, review of *Politics U.K.,* p. 17.

Times Literary Supplement, July 19, 1974, review of *The Union of Post Office Workers,* p. 772; March 17, 1978, Anthony Giddens, "Travails with Labour," pp. 324-325; October 4, 1985, Frances Cairncross, "Revolution or Watershed?," p. 1084.

Wall Street Review of Books, winter, 1986, Richard C. Schiming, review of *The Politics of the Financial Services Revolution,* pp. 5-9.

West European Politics, April, 1992, Philip G. Cerny, review of *The Politics of the Financial Services Revolution,* pp. 176-177; October, 1995, Wyn Grant, review of *Privatization and Regulatory Change in Europe.**

*   *   *

MORGANSTERN, Anne McGee 1936-

PERSONAL: Born February 5, 1936, in Morgan, GA; daughter of Jefferson DeWitt (a farmer and lobbyist) and Sarah Thornton (a homemaker) McGee; married James Morganstern (a professor), 1966. *Ethnicity:* "Scots/Irish & English." *Education:* Wesleyan College, B.F.A., 1958; New York University, M.A., 1961, Ph.D., 1970. *Politics:* Democrat. *Religion:* Protestant. *Avocational interests:* Gardening, painting, cinema, classical music.

ADDRESSES: Office—Department of the History of Art, Ohio State University, 100 Hayes, Columbus, OH 43210-1318.

CAREER: Manhattenville College, Purchase, NY, instructor, 1961; Vassar College, Poughkeepsie, NY, instructor, 1965-66; University of Wisconsin, Milwaukee, WI, lecturer, 1970-73; Ohio State University, Columbus, OH, 1973—, began as assistant professor, currently associate professor. First Congregational Church, Art Committee member and occasional lecturer.

MEMBER: Medieval Academy of America.

AWARDS, HONORS: Fulbright Fellow to France, 1961-63; American Council of Learned Societies Grant-in-Aid, 1973; CASVA Kress Senior Fellow, 1982-83; Distinguished Achievement in a Profession Award, Wesleyan College Alumnae Association, 1983.

WRITINGS:

Gothic Tombs of Kinship in France, the Low Countries and England, Penn State Press (University Park, PA), 2000.

Contributor to *Memory and the Medieval Tomb,* edited by Elizabeth Valdez del Alamo with Carol Stamatis Pendergast, Ashgate/Scolar (Aldershot), 2000; *Dictionary of the Middle Ages,* edited by Joseph S. Strayer, 1982; and catalogs and periodicals, including *Bulletin*

Monumental, Speculum, Art Bulletin, National Gallery of Art Studies in the history of Art, and *In the Arts.*

WORK IN PROGRESS: Research on the "relation of Gothic tomb sculpture to cathedral sculpture."

SIDELIGHTS: Anne McGee Morganstern told *CA*: "Aside from being a mandatory professional activity, writing provides the occasion for collecting my thoughts, directing my research, and clarifying my position on various historical problems. *What* I write about is largely dictated by what I find beautiful, or rich in human interest, and what I judge to have been neglected or misunderstood. In every scholar there probably lurks a sleuth, and certainly curiosity keeps me going when the path is rough, and has seldom been trodden. What has always fascinated me about the particular period and region that I write about—Northern Europe in the High and Late Middle Ages primarily—is its chaotic history and the potential for evidence in obscure or forgotten corners to illuminate the 'mainstream' of historical writing. I am interested in the human side of the History of Art, which is one of the reasons I write about tombs.

"The historians from whom I have learned the most, Richard Krautheimer and Willibald Sauerländer, with whom I studied in graduate school; and François Baron and Karl Schmid, whose work I have greatly admired, have certainly all influenced my work."

*   *   *

MORRIS, Brian (Robert) 1930-2001

OBITUARY NOTICE—See index for *CA* sketch: Born December 4, 1930, in Cardiff, Wales; died of leukemia, April 30, 2001, in Derby, England. Scholar and writer. Morris was an editor of plays from the Elizabethan, Jacobean and Caroline periods but also a published poet and member of the House of Lords. He graduated from Cardiff High School and then Worcester College at Oxford University, from which he received bachelor's, master's and then a doctoral degree. After graduation he stayed at Oxford as a tutor in Old and Middle English and then completed a fellowship at the Shakespeare Institute. From there he had teaching posts at Reading and York universities. Beginning in 1964 and continuing for more than twenty years, Morris edited the *New Mermaid Dramatists* series and in 1974 began editing the *New Arden Shakespeare* series. By then he was already teaching English at Sheffield University,

where he was hired in 1971 and stayed almost a decade. During those years his first book of verse, *Tide Race,* was published. Three others followed: *Dear Tokens, Stones in the Brook* and *The Waters of Comfort.* In 1980 he edited and contributed to *Ritual Murder: Essays on Liturgical Reform,* a series of essays that defended the historic liturgy of the Anglican church. That year he also became principal of St. David's University College at the University of Wales in Lampeter, where he remained for more than ten years. In 1990 Morris was made a life peer and two years later was named the Opposition's Deputy Chief Whip and was its main spokesman for education. Days before he died Morris' last work, *Collected Poems,* was published.

OBITUARIES AND OTHER SOURCES:

PERIODICALS

Guardian (London, England), May 3, 2001, p. 22.
Independent (London, England), May 2, 2001, p. 6.
Times (London, England), May 3, 2001, p. 21.

*   *   *

MORRIS, Monica B. 1928-

PERSONAL: Born 1928, in London, England. *Education:* Sonoma State College (now University), B.A., 1968; University of Southern California, M.A., 1970, Ph.D., 1972.

ADDRESSES: *Office*—c/o Author Mail, Avery Publishing Group, 89 Baldwin Terrace, Wayne, NJ 07470. *E-mail*—MBMWrite@aol.com.

CAREER: Educator and author. California State Polytechnic University, Pomona, assistant professor of sociology, 1971-73; Pomona College, Claremont, CA, assistant professor of sociology, beginning 1973. Also taught at California State University, Los Angeles.

MEMBER: American Sociological Association.

WRITINGS:

The Demystification of Ethno-Methodology, General Learning Co., 1973.
An Excursion into Creative Sociology, Columbia University Press (New York, NY), 1977.
Last-Chance Children: Growing up with Older Parents, Columbia University Press (New York, NY), 1988.

Looking for Love in Later Life: A Woman's Guide to Finding Joy and Romantic Fulfillment, Avery (Garden City Park, NY), 1997.

Contributor to periodicals, including *Journalism Quarterly* and *Sociology and Social Research.*

BIOGRAPHICAL/CRITICAL SOURCES:

PERIODICALS

Contemporary Sociology, March, 1989, Leland J. Axelson, review of *Last-Chance Children.*
Readings, September, 1988, Charlotte Ellinwood, review of *Last-Chance Children.**

* * *

MOSATCHE, Harriet (S.) 1949-

PERSONAL: Born April 10, 1949, in New York, NY; married Ivan Lawner (an attorney), February 19, 1983; children: Robert Lawner, Elizabeth Kim Lawner. *Education:* Brooklyn College, B.A., 1970; Hunter College, M.A., 1972; Graduate Center, City University of New York, Ph.D., 1977. *Avocational interests:* Reading, dancing, playing piano.

ADDRESSES: Office—Girl Scouts of the USA, 420 Fifth Ave., New York, NY 10018. *E-mail*—hmosatche@aol.com.

CAREER: Psychologist. Department of Psychology, College of Mt. St. Vincent, Riverdale, NY, professor and chair of department, 1977-84; Girl Scouts of USA, New York City, director of program development, 1984-86, 1992—.

MEMBER: American Psychological Association, Eastern Psychological Association, Society for Research in Child Development.

AWARDS, HONORS: National Institutes of Health grant, 1982-84; National Science Foundation grant, 1996-2000; Gold Award, National Parenting Publications, 2000, for *Too Old for This, Too Young for That! Your Survival Guide for the Middle-School Years.*

WRITINGS:

Searching: Practices and Beliefs of Religious Cults and Human Potential Movements, Stravon Educational, 1984.

(With Karen Unger) *Too Old for This, Too Young for That! Your Survival Guide for the Middle-School Years,* Free Spirit, 2000.
Girls: What's So Bad about Being Good?, Prima, 2001.

Contributor to updated editions of the *Girl Scout Handbook* and *Leaders' Guide,* Girl Scouts of the USA, 1986-2000. Author of advice column, "Ask Dr. M.," on Girl Scouts Web site, 1997-2000. Contributor to periodicals, including *Girl Scout Leader, Science and Children,* and *New Moon Network,* and to scholarly journals such as *Child Development* and *Journal of Psychology.*

SIDELIGHTS: Psychologist Harriet Mosatche once commented: "My children played an enormous role in every stage of writing *Too Old for This, Too Young for That! Your Survival Guide for the Middle School Years.* They found kids for me to interview, they shared their own ideas and insights, and they were incredibly honest and helpful critics. If some bit of advice didn't ring true or the language wasn't quite right, they let me know. They have always been my inspiration."

BIOGRAPHICAL/CRITICAL SOURCES:

PERIODICALS

Booklist, July, 2000, Lauren Peterson, review of *Too Old for This, Too Young for That! Your Survival Guide for the Middle School Years,* p. 2022.
School Library Journal, September, 2000, Leslie Ann Lacika, review of *Too Old for This, Too Young for That! Your Survival Guide for the Middle School Years.*

* * *

MOTAVALLI, Jim 1952-

PERSONAL: Born August 4, 1952, in Norwalk, CT; son of Hossein (a civil engineer) and Margaret (an artist) Motavalli; married Mary Ann Masarech, May 6, 1989; children: Maya, Delia. *Ethnicity:* "White, Iranian/English heritage." *Education:* Attended Syracuse University, 1970; University of Connecticut, B.A., 1974; Fairfield University, graduate study, 1975-76. *Politics:* Independent. *Avocational interests:* Radio broadcasting.

ADDRESSES: Home—261 Brooklawn Terr., Fairfield, CT 06432. *Office*—E Magazine, 28 Knight St., Norwalk, CT 06851; fax 203-866-0602. *Agent*—Sabine

Hrechdakian, Susan Golomb Agency, 288 Norfolk St., Cambridge, MA 02129. *E-mail*—jimm@emagazine. com.

CAREER: Save the Children, Westport, CT, producer, 1979-80; *Fairfield County Advocate,* Stamford, CT, editor, 1980-94; *E: The Environmental Magazine,* Norwalk, CT, editor, 1995—. Fairfield University, professor, 2000—. WPKN-FM Radio, press and publicity director, 1999-2000, and host of a music, news, and public affairs program.

MEMBER: International Motor Press Association, Society of Environmental Journalists.

AWARDS, HONORS: Global Population Award, Population Institute, 1999.

WRITINGS:

Forward Drive: The Race to Build "Clean" Cars for the Future, Sierra Club Books (San Francisco, CA), 2000.
Breaking Gridlock: Moving Toward Transportation That Works, Sierra Club Books (San Francisco, CA), 2001.

Author of "Wheels," a column distributed by Los Angeles Times Syndicate; columnist for *AMC Outdoors* and *Environmental Defense Newsletter.*

WORK IN PROGRESS: Research for an anthology on global warming, demonstrating that warming has already begun.

SIDELIGHTS: Jim Motavalli is an editor and environmentalist whose two works of nonfiction focus on the future of the automobile in the United States. In *Forward Drive: The Race to Build "Clean" Cars for the Future,* after presenting a history of alternative-fueled personal transportation, he contends that, through development of hydrogen fuel-cell technology, the free market system is making progress toward a zero-emission standard, thus making government regulations unnecessary. Calling his book "cogently written" and "well-researched," a *Publishers Weekly* contributor added that Motavalli, while "firmly in favor of . . . less-polluting autos, . . . is pragmatic enough to realize that such a change is not going to occur at the snap of some environmentalist's fingers." While noting that Motavalli's environmentalist stance causes him to place excessive blame on the U.S. auto industry, Eric C. Shoaf praised the author's thoroughness, noting in his *Library Journal* appraisal of *Forward Drive* that

Motavalli "interviewed energy researchers, early adopters of alternative-fuel vehicles, and key auto industry figures to produce this uniquely insightful look at the future."

Motavalli told *CA:* "My primary motivation in writing is to inform people about environmental crises that we face. I want to bring sometimes-difficult scientific subjects alive for the average reader.

"I'm influenced by the best literary fiction, especially American writers like Richard Ford, Geoffrey Wolff, Richard Yates, Robert Stone, and Ethan Canin, and also by reporters who used fiction techniques to enliven their work, from Truman Capote onward.

"I do all my work on computers, including most of my interviews, which I transcribe as I talk on the telephone. I put all of those interviews together in a single file, which becomes a searchable database—much easier than note cards! I also do considerable Internet research.

"I decided to write about 'clean cars' because the subject is of huge importance. Since more than ninety-five percent of all our trips are by car, just cleaning up the exhaust a tiny bit makes an immeasurable difference, and it has a greater impact than adding mass transit lines."

BIOGRAPHICAL/CRITICAL SOURCES:

PERIODICALS

Booklist, February 15, 2000, David Rouse, review of *Forward Drive,* p. 1064.
Economist, January 15, 2000, "Cleaner Cars—As Pure as Driven Snow?," p. 86.
Library Journal, Eric C. Shoaf, review of *Forward Drive,* p. 114.
Publishers Weekly, February 21, 2000, review of *Forward Drive,* p. 77.

*   *   *

MUNGER, Robert Boyd   1910-2001

OBITUARY NOTICE—See index for *CA* sketch: Born July 28, 1910, in Santa Cruz, CA; died February 16, 2001, in Pasadena, CA. Clergyman, educator, and author. Munger was a minister who led various churches on the west coast of the United States between 1936 and

1969. A professor at Fuller Theological Seminary in the latter portion of his life and career, Munger received his theological education at the Princeton Theological Seminary. In 1954 he authored a sermon, *My Heart, Christ's Home,* which has been quoted by clergy around the world and has sold some ten million copies. Munger also authored several books, including *What Jesus Says, New Life to Live* and *Jesus, Man of His Word.*

OBITUARIES AND OTHER SOURCES:

PERIODICALS

Los Angeles Times, February 22, 2001, p. B9.

N

NADEAU, Robert (L.) 1944-

PERSONAL: Born November 5, 1944, in Montreal, Quebec, Canada; married 1967; children: one. *Education:* University of Montreal, B.Ph., 1966, M.A.Ph., 1967; University of Paris, Ph.D., 1973.

ADDRESSES: Office—Department of Philosophy, University of Quebec, C.P. 8888, Downtown Area Branch, Montreal, Quebec H3C 3P8, Canada.

CAREER: Educator. University of Quebec, Montreal, Quebec, Canada, professor of epistemology, beginning 1971, then director, Department of Philosophy; professor, George Mason University. Consultant, Social Science and Humanities Research Council of Canada, 1976; referee for three philosophical conferences.

MEMBER: Canadian Philosophy Association, Philosophical Science Association.

WRITINGS:

(Coeditor) *Genese de la pensee linguistique,* Librarie Armand Colin, 1973.
Bibliographie des textes sur Ernst Cassirer, International Philosophy Review, 1974.
(Coeditor) *La philosophie et les savoirs,* Bellarmin, 1975.
Readings from the New Book on Nature: Physics and Metaphysics in the Modern Novel, University of Massachusetts Press (Amherst, MA), 1981.
Nature Talks Back: Pathways to Survival in the Nuclear Age, Orchises (Washington, DC), 1984.
(With Menas Kafatos) *The Conscious Universe: Parts and Wholes in Modern Physical Theory,* Springer (New York, NY), 1990.

Mind, Machines, and Human Consciousness, Contemporary Books (Chicago, IL), 1991.
S/he Brain: Science, Sexual Politics, and the Myths of Feminism, Praeger (Westport, CT), 1996.
(With Menas Kafatos) *The Non-local Universe: The New Physics and Matters of the Mind,* Oxford University Press (New York, NY), 1999.
(With Menas Kafatos) *The Conscious Universe: Parts and Wholes in Physical Reality,* Springer (New York, NY), 2000.

Also editor of *Philosophy et Psychology,* Volume 4, 1977, Volume 5, 1978. Contributor to *Actes du Congres d'Ottawa sur Kant,* University of Ottawa Press (Ottawa, Ontario, Canada), 1976.

BIOGRAPHICAL/CRITICAL SOURCES:

PERIODICALS

Library Journal, May 15, 1991, Hilary D. Burton, review of *Mind, Machines, and Human Consciousness,* p. 105.
Publishers Weekly, December 20, 1999, review of *The Non-local Universe,* p. 74.*

*   *   *

NAKAGAMI, Kenji 1946-1992

PERSONAL: Born August 2, 1946, in Shingu, Wakayama Prefecture, Japan; died of cancer, August 12, 1992; son of a man named Suzuki and Kinoshita Chisato (an itinerant merchant); married in 1970.

CAREER: Novelist. Worked at Haneda Airport after 1970. Columbia University, New York, NY, writer-in-residence, 1986.

AWARDS, HONORS: Akutagawa Prize, Society for the Promotion of Japanese Literature, 1976, for *Misaki.*

WRITINGS:

Jukyu-sai no chizu (short stories; title means "Map of a Nineteen-Year-Old"), Kawade Shobo (Tokyo, Japan), 1974.

Hatodomo no ie (title means "House of Pigeons"), Shueisha (Tokyo, Japan), 1975.

Misaki, Bungei Shunjosha (Tokyo, Japan), 1976, translated by Eve Zimmerman and published as *The Cape and Other Stories from the Japanese Ghetto,* Stone Bridge Press (Berkeley, CA), 1999.

Jain, Kawade Shobo (Tokyo, Japan), 1976.

Tori no yoni, kemono no yoni, Hokuysha (Tokyo, Japan), 1976, revised edition, Shueisha (Tokyo, Japan), 1981.

Karekinada (title means "Witherwood Bay"), Kawade Shobo (Tokyo, Japan), 1977.

Nakagami Kenji vs. Murakami Ryo: Oretachi no funewa, ugokanu kiri no naka o, tomozuna o toite, Kadokawa (Tokyo, Japan), 1977.

Juhassai, umi e, (title means "Eighteen and To the Sea"), Shueisha (Tokyo, Japan), 1977.

Kesho (title means "Makeup"), Kodansha (Tokyo, Japan), 1978.

Kisho: kinokuni nenokuni monogatari (title means "Kisho: Tales of the Land of Trees, the Land of Roots"), Asahi Shinbunsha (Tokyo, Japan), 1978.

Nakagami zenhatsugen 1970-1978, Shueisha (Tokyo, Japan), 1978.

Mizu no onna, Sakuhinsha (Tokyo, Japan), 1979.

Yume no chikara, Hokuyosha (Tokyo, Japan), 1979.

Hakkaiseyo to Aira wa itta, Shueisha (Tokyo, Japan), 1979.

Kobayashi Hideo o koete (title means "Surpassing Kobayashi Hideo"), Kawade Shobo (Tokyo, Japan), 1979.

Hosenka (title means "Balsam"), Sakuhinsha (Tokyo, Japan), 1980.

Nakagami zenhatsugen II 1978-1980 (title means "The Complete Utterances of Nakagami Kenji"), Shueisha (Tokyo, Japan), 1980.

Toyo ni ichisuru (title means "Positioning in the Orient"), Sakuhinsha (Tokyo, Japan), 1981.

Sennen no yuraku (title means "The Joy of a Thousand Years"), Kawade Shobo (Tokyo, Japan), 1982.

Akutagawasho zenshu 10, Bungei Shunju (Tokyo, Japan), 1982.

Chinohate shijonotoki (title means "The Ends of Earth, the Supreme Time"), Shinchosha (Tokyo, Japan), 1983.

Fokei no muko e (title means "Beyond the Landscape"), Tojusha (Tokyo, Japan), 1983.

Nakagami Kenji zen tanpen shosetsu, Kawade Shobo (Tokyo, Japan), 1984.

Monogatari soru, PARCO (Tokyo, Japan), 1984.

Nichirin no tsubasa (title means "The Wings of the Sun"), Shinchosha (Tokyo, Japan), 1984.

Kumanosho (title means "Kumano Collection"), Kodansha (Tokyo, Japan), 1984.

Kii monogatari, Shueisha (Tokyo, Japan), 1984.

Kimi wa yayoijin ka jomonjin ka: Umehara Nippongaku kogi, Asahi Shuppansha (Tokyo, Japan), 1984.

Genjitsu ni totte chi wa nani o nashiuru ka, Hobesuto Henshoshitsu (Tokyo, Japan), 1984.

Gekiron zenkyto oretachi no genten, Kodansha (Tokyo, Japan), 1984.

Shokanbon 16 Miyako Harumi ni sasageru: geino genron, Asahi Shuppansha (Tokyo, Japan), 1985.

Amerika, Amerika: aoza no Mongoroido to shite (title means "America, America: As a Blue-Spotted Mongoloid"), Kadokawa (Tokyo, Japan), 1985.

Hino bungaku, Bungei Shunju (Tokyo, Japan), 1985.

Rinmaisuru, soru, Kadokawa (Tokyo, Japan), 1985.

Haikuno jidai: Tono Kumano Yoshino seichi junrei, Kadokawa (Tokyo, Japan), 1985.

Himatsuri (screenplay), Cine Saison/Production Gunro, 1985.

Yasei no kaenju, Magajin Hausu (Tokyo, Japan), 1986.

Jokyo-sai no jeikobu, Kadokawa (Tokyo, Japan), 1986.

Supanisshu kyaraban o sagashite, Shinchosha (Tokyo, Japan), 1986.

On the Border, Torebiiru (Tokyo, Japan), 1986.

Himatsuri, Bungei Shunju (Tokyo, Japan), 1987.

Ten no uta: shosetsu Miyako Harumi, Mainichi Shinbunsha (Tokyo, Japan), 1987.

Amerika to gasshokoku no aida, Jijitsoshinsha (Tokyo, Japan), 1987.

Joryoku no miyako, Shinchosha (Tokyo, Japan), 1988.

Nakagami Kenji, Showa Bungaku Zensho Series 29, Shogakkan (Tokyo, Japan), 1988.

Jidai ga owari, jidai ga hajimaru, Fukutake Shoten (Tokyo, Japan), 1988.

Baffaro sorujo, Fukutake Shoten (Tokyo, Japan), 1988.

Kiseki (title means "The Miracle"), Asahi Shinbunsha (Tokyo, Japan), 1989.

Sanka (title means "The Paean"), Bungei Shunju (Tokyo, Japan), 1990.

Misaki, in Nihon no Meizuihitsu Series 92, Sakuhinsha (Tokyo, Japan), 1990.

20-jikan kanzen toron: kaitaisareru basho, Shueisha
  (Tokyo, Japan), 1990.
Keibetsu (title means "Contempt"), Asahi Shinbunsha
  (Tokyo, Japan), 1992.
Wani no seiiki (title means "The Sacred Realm of the
  Alligator"), Shueisha (Tokyo, Japan), 1992.
Monto muyo, Kodansha (Tokyo, Japan), 1992.

SIDELIGHTS: Kenji Nakagami's death in 1992 at the
age of forty-six brought an end to the career of one of
postwar Japan's most important writers. Best known
for the trilogy of novels referred to as the *Akiyuki-
mono,* or "Akiyuki Tales," Nakagami was literary celebrity in his native country, and often used his position
to speak frankly about inter-Asian racism. His career
was all the more remarkable for the barriers he had tran-
scended: his family were *burakumin,* a small minority
in the homogenous Japanese population who were cen-
turies-long victims of social and economic discrimination. Nakagami was the first in his family to attend
school, and he made the plight of the burakumin the
focus of much of his fiction. "For a writer still at the
peak of his creative ability, it was an untimely and premature death, and the Japanese literary world lost a
genuine voice of dissent," asserted *Dictionary of Literary Biography* writer Faye Yuan Kleeman.

Nakagami was born in 1946. He was the fifth child born
to his mother, Chisato Kinoshita, and because she was
unmarried at the time, he took her surname, Kinoshita.
His four elder half-siblings were later joined by a younger half-brother; his biological father, a man named
Suzuki, also fathered other children. "This complex
network of human relations is delineated in great detail
in many of Nakagami's fictional and nonfictional writings," noted Kleeman.

Growing up in a burakumin village on banks of the Kumano River, in Shingu, Wakayama Prefecture, Nakagami was close to his mother, an itinerant merchant,
and the family struggled to survive economically.
When he was around nine years old, she began a relationship with man named Nakaue, and only the Nakagami went to live with them; his four elder half-siblings
were left on their own, which caused a certain degree
of resentment among them. But at the new household,
Nakagami learned to read and write, which was unusual
among the burakumin at time. He also became the first
in his family to attend the local school.

Burakumin make up only one to two percent of the Japanese population. Beginning in the ninth century, however, this small group began to suffer ostracism on the
spurious charge of having "tainted" blood; it is thought

that a clan may have done something to offend the emperor. They became associated with certain professions, like butcher and executioner; when the classes
were officially stratified in the seventeenth century, the
burakumin were at the bottom. Other terms for them included *Eta,* which means "extreme filth," and even
Hinin, or nonhuman. In more modern times, all forms
of discrimination have been eliminated by decree, but
prejudices persisted in Japanese society well into the
twentieth century. Agencies sold secret lists of people
with burakumin heritage, which were purchased by potential employers and in-laws.

When Nakagami was twelve, his older half-brother
Ikuhei hung himself. Prone to bouts of drinking and violent behavior, Ikuhei had suffered greatly over their
mother's abandonment, and sometimes appeared at
their home to threaten them physically. "For the twelve-
year-old Nakagami, this event was traumatic and led to
a sense of guilt over the death, jealousy for his mother's
love, and a gradual identification with his late brother,"
explained Kleeman in the *Dictionary of Literary Biography* essay. The event became a recurring incident in
much of his later fiction through a suicidal or otherwise
self-destructive hero.

When his mother married Nakaue, which occurred
when Nakagami was around sixteen years of age, he
took this surname; a few years later, when he had
moved to Tokyo, others began calling him Nakagami.
He left Shingu after graduating from high school in
1965 with money to pay for preparatory classes for the
university entrance examinations, but never continued
his education. Instead he frequented jazz clubs and
drifted into drug abuse. For several years during the late
1960s he wrote for *Bungei Shuto* ("Literary Capital"),
and was also involved in left-wing political activities
and experimental theater. When *Bungei Shuto* folded in
1970, he married and found work at Haneda Airport. He
also began to concentrate more seriously on writing for
publication around this time.

Nakagami's first volume was a collection of short stories, *Jukyu-sai no chizu* ("Map of a Nineteen-Year-
Old"), which appeared in 1974. Many of the tales involve young adults who move from the countryside to
Tokyo, and soon find themselves mired in the pitfalls
of urban life. In the title story, a teenager arrives in
Tokyo to attend a cram school, finds a newspaper delivery job, and grows increasingly disillusioned with his
lowly status in an educated, affluent society. In his misery he begins to make a map of his route, marking each
dwelling according to the treatment he receives from its
inhabitants, perceived or actual. He sometimes destroys

a flower bed or kicks a dog to alleviate his frustration, and the story concludes after he makes a bomb threat to the local commuter railroad. "The feeling of vulnerability and isolation of a lonely young boy trapped in a desperate situation is one of the characteristics shared by all of Nakagami's early works," remarked Kleeman in the *Dictionary of Literary Biography*.

Early in his career, Nakagami was termed a *shinsedai no sakka,* or "New Generation" writer, but his style differed considerably from the others of this movement. After 1975's *Hatodomo no ie,* another collection of short stories, Nakagami turned to his own impoverished life in a buraku ghetto as the basis for his fiction. His first novel and the start of his *Akiyuki-mono* was *Misaki,* which appeared in 1976. It won him the Akutagawa Prize from the Society for the Promotion of Japanese Literature that same year, making him the first Japanese writer born after World War II to receive it. It marked a positive turning point in his career.

When he began writing about burakumin life, Nakagami's style changed considerably, becoming more aggressive; incidents of violence also appeared more frequently. Akiyuki, the hero of *Misaki*—translated for English publication as *The Cape* in 1999—is twenty-four when the work begins, and a construction worker in the Kishu area. He has half-siblings, but his mother was abandoned by his father; when she moved in with another man, she left the first three children to fend for themselves. One of them commits suicide, and the story begins just after this incident. Akiyuki has long been obsessed with his biological father, and despises his imagined likeness to him. The work takes its name from the family burial ground, a small inlet. The oppressiveness of the cramped and dark burakumin ghetto—called the *roji,* or "alley"—also plays a strong role in the work.

When one man on Akiyuki's work crew kills another, the discordant burakumin community erupts in conflict. Akiyuki meets a prostitute rumored to be the daughter of his own father, and sleeps with her. "The rushing blood inside him is like a wave surrounding the cape, foreshadowing the continuing saga of Akiyuki, his clan, and their fate," wrote *Dictionary of Literary Biography* essayist Kleeman. An English translation, *The Cape and Other Stories from the Japanese Ghetto* included "House on Fire" and "Red Hair," an erotic short story. "Nakagami's tough, ruthless prose is often abstruse, with a taut psychological subtext, while elsewhere the clarity is unassailable," declared a *Publishers Weekly* reviewer.

The next *Akiyuki-mono* was published in 1977, *Karekinada.* Here Akiyuki forges a strained relationship with his biological father, Hamamura Ryozo, but the work concludes when Akiyuki accidentally kills one of his half-brothers during a violent melee at a community festival. "The narrative reveals how difficult it is for Akiyuki to distinguish his paternal identity, represented by Ryozo and the outside world, from his maternal identity, symbolized by 'Alley,' " Kleeman noted.

The Akiyuki tales concluded in 1983 with the publication of *Chinohate shijnotoki.* Its narrative begins after Akiyuki's release from prison, where he served time for the death of half-brother, and he returns to his rural burakumin village to find the area suddenly booming. Economics and overcrowding have made the region attractive to developers, and things begin to change; the burakumin community, however, suffers from this modernization. Akiyuki finds work with Ryozo, his biological father, and the two become close, but Ryozo inexplicably kills himself. The Alley burns, and Akiyuki is suspected of arson and must flee. It is a symbolic end to the burakumin ghetto.

Nakagami wrote several other acclaimed works during the two decades of his career. Many of them are set in Kumano, the southern part of Kii Peninsula that lies between Wakayama and Mie Prefectures. It is mountainous area, and a sacred site to both the Buddhist and Shinto religions. It features prominently in a pair of short-story collections, *Kesho,* published in 1978, and *Kumanosho,* which appeared in 1984. Some of the tales are set during Japan's medieval era, and nearly all feature an *otoko* ("the man") or *hijiri* (an itinerant ascetic priest), but they are not always sympathetic characters. Nakagami places his heroes at odds with themselves and prone to violence, and are usually outcasts or outlaws in some way. "Often this generic 'man' roams the mountain of Kumano, encountering a mysterious realm occupied by unquiet spirits of fallen noble warriors and half-human, half-demonic creatures," wrote Kleeman in the *Dictionary of Literary Biography*.

Another of Nakagami's well-received works was the 1982 collection *Sennen no yuraku.* Its six tales feature a sextet of heroes whom the author based on a traditional Japanese literary type, the *kishu ryri,* or wandering noble hero. All six men are from the Nakamoto clan, and, as *Dictionary of Literary Biography* writer Kleeman stated, "all exceptionally good-looking men who possess otherworldly beauty—their bodies 'radiate and emanate sweet fragrance'—and they are audacious Casanovas who attract the opposite sex effortlessly."

The stories are linked by the narrative voice of Oryo, whose husband is the priest Reinyo. All the protagonists, as she recounts, die young, either through self-destructive habits or suicide. "Even though their deaths are brutal and untimely, they are the chosen ones who possess special qualities that can redeem the guilt and impurity of the whole community," observed Kleeman. "The style of these tales is a unique combination of a highly ornate, semiclassical diction and vulgar colloquialisms." *Kiseki,* published in 1989, is a sequel of sorts to *Joy of a Thousand Years.* Its protagonist is Taichi, also of the Nakamoto clan, who has been involved in criminal behavior since his childhood. After he finds himself embroiled in some vicious gang warfare, he is kidnapped, tied up in a bamboo mat, and tossed in the river to drown.

In *Nichirin no tsubasa,* Nakagami's 1984 novel, the symbolic Alley ghetto of the burakumin has vanished, but in this work it exists metaphorically still, for its former denizens carry it with them. The narrative revolves around two young men, Tsuyoshi and Tanaka, who take a truck full of elderly women on a pilgrimage to important shrines in Kumano; they also travel to Tokyo for a visit to Japan's Imperial Palace. Along the way, one of the women dies, and another vanishes. At the Imperial Palace, the remaining five women show their respect by sweeping the grounds, but are swept away themselves in a religious rapture.

Sanka, Nakagami's 1990 novel, continues the story of the drivers from *Wings of the Sun.* Tsuyoshi is now a hustler who goes by the name "Eve," and Tanaka is also a male prostitute whose clients are women from the American Embassy. They find the elderly ladies who disappeared at the close of *Wings of the Sun,* and decide to drive them home, but the women once again vanish. *Keibetsu,* published in 1992, is Nakagami's last finished work. Its plot revolves around a romance between an exotic dancer, Machiko, and a seductive gangster type named Kazu. After Kazu is murdered over a gambling debt, Machiko believes she sees him, but it is another man. "The cycle of death and rebirth, manifest in this reincarnation of the prototypical hero first depicted in the death of the author's own brother in his earliest works, resonates in this last novel," Kleeman wrote in the *Dictionary of Literary Biography.*

Diagnosed with liver cancer, Nakagami died in August of 1992. He left a trio of unfinished novels, only one of which, *Wani no seiiki,* appeared in print.

BIOGRAPHICAL/CRITICAL SOURCES:

BOOKS

Dictionary of Literary Biography, Volume 182: *Japanese Fiction Writers Since World War II,* Gale (Detroit, MI).

PERIODICALS

Booklist, May 1, 1999, review of *The Cape,* James Klise, p. 1577.
New York Times Book Review, October 24, 1999, Mark Morris, "The Untouchables," p. 23.
Publishers Weekly, February 27, 1995, "Chasing Nakagami," p. 28; April 12, 1999, review of *The Cape,* p. 55.
Washington Post Book World, May 16, 1999, Jennifer Howard, "Out of the Gutter," p. 10.

OBITUARIES:

PERIODICALS

New York Times, August 13, 1992.*

*   *   *

NATSUME, Soseki   1867-1916

PERSONAL: Born Kinnosuke Natsume, January 5, 1867, in Tokyo, Japan; died December 9, 1916, from stomach ulcers; son of Shoubei Naokatsu (a landlord) and Chie Natsume; married Kyoko Nakane, June, 1896. *Education:* Tokyo University, B.A., 1893; attended University College, London University, 1900-02.

CAREER: Novelist, professor of English. Teacher, Tokyo Normal School, 1893-1895; teacher at high school in Matsuyama, Shikoku, c. 1895-96; teacher at Fifth National College in Kumamoto, Kyushu, 1896-1900; teacher of English at First National College and English Literature at Tokyo Imperial University, 1903-06; full-time writer and freelance journalist, 1907-16.

AWARDS, HONORS: Honorary doctorate, Ministry of Education (refused).

WRITINGS:

Wagahai wa neko de aru (novel; title means "I Am a Cat"), three volumes, Kura Shoten & Hattori Shoten (Tokyo, Japan), 1905-06, translation by Katsue Shibota, Motonari Kai, and Harold W. Price published as *I Am a Cat: A Novel,* Kenkyusha (Tokyo, Japan), 1961, translation by Aiko It and Graeme Wilson published as *I Am a Cat,* Tuttle (Rutland, VT), 1972.

Ykyosh, Kura Shoten (Tokyo, Japan), 1906.

Nihyakutka, 1906.

Bungakuron (title means "Theory of Literature"), Kura Shoten (Tokyo, Japan), 1907.

Uzurakago (short stories; includes "Botchan" and "Kusamakura"), Shun'yd (Tokyo, Japan), 1907, translation by Yasotaro Mori published as *Master Darling,* Ogawa Seibundo (Tokyo, Japan), 1918, translation by Alan Turney published as *The Three-Cornered World,* Regnery (Chicago, IL), 1965, translation by Alan Turney published as *Botchan,* Kodansha International (Tokyo, Japan), 1972.

Kof, Shun'yd (Tokyo, Japan), 1908, translation by Jay Rubin published as *The Miner,* Stanford University Press (Palo Alto, CA), 1988.

Gubijinso (title means "The Poppies"), Shun'yd (Tokyo, Japan), 1908.

Kusa awase, Shun'yd (Tokyo, Japan), 1908.

Sanshir, Shun'yd (Tokyo, Japan), 1908, translation by Jay Rubin published as *Sanshiro: A Novel,* University of Washington Press (Seattle, WA), 1977.

Bungaku hyron, Shun'yd (Tokyo, Japan), 1909.

Sorekara, Shun'yd (Tokyo, Japan), 1910, translation by Norma Moore Field published as *And Then,* Louisiana State University Press (Baton Rouge, LA), 1978.

Mon (title means "The Gate"), 1910, translation by Francis Mathy published as *Mon,* Tuttle (Tokyo, Japan), 1972, Putman (New York, NY), 1982.

Shihen, Shun'yd (Tokyo, Japan), 1910.

Kirinukich yori, Shun'yd (Tokyo, Japan), 1911.

Asahi ken sh, Asahi Shinbunsha (Tokyo, Japan), 1911.

Higan sugi made, Shun'yd (Tokyo, Japan), 1912, translation by Kingo Ochiai and Sanford Goldstein published as *To the Spring Equinox and Beyond,* Tuttle (Tokyo, Japan), 1985.

Koujin (title means "The Wayfarer"), Kura Shoten (Tokyo, Japan), 1912, translation by Beongcheon Yu published as *The Wayfarer,* Wayne State University Press, 1967.

Shakai to jibun, Jitsugy no Nihonsha (Tokyo, Japan), 1913.

Kokoro (title means "The Heart"), Iwanami Shoten (Tokyo, Japan), 1914, translation by Ineko Sato published as *Kokoro,* Japan Writers' Society (Tokyo, Japan), 1941, translation by Edwin McClellan published as *Kokoro: a Novel,* Regnery (Chicago, IL), 1957.

Garasudo no naka, Iwanami Shoten (Tokyo, Japan), 1915, translation by Iwao Matsuhara and E. T. Iglehart published as *Within My Glass Doors,* Shinseido (Tokyo, Japan), 1928.

Shikich, Shinchsha (Tokyo, Japan), 1915.

Mishikusa, Iwanami Shoten (Tokyo, Japan), 1915, translation by Edwin McClellan published as *Grass on the Wayside,* University of Chicago Press (Chicago, IL), 1969.

Kongso, Shiseid (Tokyo, Japan), 1915.

Meian, Iwanami Shoten (Tokyo, Japan), 1917, translated by V. H. Viglielmo as *Light and Darkness,* University of Hawaii Press (Honolulu, HI), 1971.

Soseki haiku sh, Iwanami Shoten (Tokyo, Japan), 1917.

Soseki shish, Iwanami Shoten (Tokyo, Japan), 1919.

Eibungaku keishiki ron, Iwanami Shoten (Tokyo, Japan), 1924.

Soseki no Osero, Tett Shoin (Tokyo, Japan), 1930.

Mokuseiroku, Iwanami Shoten (Tokyo, Japan), 1932.

COLLECTIONS

Soseki zensh, Iwanami Shoten (Tokyo, Japan), 1917.

Natsume Soseki zensh, Meiji Bungaku Kankkai (Tokyo, Japan), 1948-49.

Natsume Soseki zensh, seven volumes, Sgeisha (Tokyo, Japan), 1953.

Soseki bungaku zensh, ten volumes, edited by Ara Masat, Shueisha (Tokyo, Japan), 1970-74.

Natsume Soseki zensh, sixteen volumes, edited by Yoshida Selichi, Chikuma Shob (Tokyo, Japan), 1973.

Natsume Soseki zensh, eleven volumes, edited by Et Jun and Yoshida Seiichi, Kadokawa Shoten (Tokyo, Japan), 1975.

Meicho fukkoku Soseki bungakukan, twenty-five volumes, Nihon Kindai Bungakuken (Tokyo, Japan), 1975.

Soseki zensh, thirty-five volumes, edited by Komiya Toyotaka, Iwanami Shoten (Tokyo, Japan), 1978-80.

Natsume Soseki iboku sh, six volumes, Kyuryud (Tokyo, Japan), 1979-80.

Soseki zensh, Iwanami Shoten (Tokyo, Japan), 1993.

SIDELIGHTS: One of the most widely read novelists in Japan (his portrait graces the thousand-yen bill), Soseki Natsume produced a variety of novels at the end of the Meiji period, from 1868-1912. His writing ranges from the lighthearted to the profoundly alienated; his later works are beset with themes of loneliness that predate the existentialist movement in the West. The debilitating effects of Western influences on Japanese culture was one of his favorite topics.

Natsume was born Kinnosuke Natsume in 1867, the youngest of eight children born to a wealthy landlord and his wife. His father was fifty-three at the time of his birth and his mother was forty. Ashamed of having produced a child so late in life, they sent their infant son to a foster home rather than welcome him into the family. The couple who raised the boy were unhappily married and tried to buy his love with material possessions. They divorced when he was nine years old, and he returned to his biological parents' home, where he learned the truth of his origin not from his relatives but from a maid. His family's fortunes were on the wane, and Natsume's mother died when he was thirteen, adding to his sense of being unloved.

Growing up in the Meiji era, young Natsume soon became convinced that Japan was extremely backward compared to the West, a sentiment shared by most Japanese intellectuals of the time. Though he studied Chinese classics as a teenager, he began to question their worth in the modern age and refocused his attention on English. During preparatory school, he worked diligently on improving his English and also began writing haiku under the influence of the famous writer Shiki Masaoka. It was around this time (1889) that he began using the pen name Soseki, which comes from a Chinese word meaning "being stubborn."

In 1890 Natsume entered Tokyo Imperial University's department of English, where he began publishing articles and translations of English writers such as Walt Whitman. He graduated in 1893, the second person ever to finish an English major there. He was, however, unsatisfied with his training; he felt that he had wasted a good deal of time memorizing useless facts and still knew little about English literature. He sought solace in Zen meditation while he continued graduate studies in English and taught at the Tokyo Normal School for two years. Still depressed, he moved on to a teaching job at a high school in Matsuyama on the island of Shikoku. After a year, he moved again, this time to the Fifth National College in Kumamoto, Kyushu. He stayed there for four years, composing a number of haiku and going on long walks on mountain paths. During this time, he married Kyoko Nakane, the daughter of Jichi Nakane, chief secretary of the House of Peers.

In 1900 Natsume sailed to England with a government stipend. He found the social life of Cambridge too expensive for his budget, so he instead studied at the University College of London University and with the Shakespeare scholar William J. Craig. He set himself the goal of determining scientifically what literature is and sacrificed his health and mental stability in his sin-

gle-minded pursuit of this goal. After returning to Japan in January of 1903, he went to work teaching English at the First National College and at Tokyo Imperial University, where he replaced Lafcadio Hearn, a hard act to follow. Natsume was not as popular as his famous predecessor, the students finding his lectures too difficult.

Natsume published his first work of fiction in 1905, the famous *Wagahai wa neko de aru.* He had not originally planned to write a novel, but the reception to the first chapter, published in the magazine *Hototogisu,* was so positive that he eventually wrote ten more chapters. This novel is a satire of the everyday life of the weak Mr. Kushami, a high school English teacher, as told by the family tomcat. The cat muses on the illogical actions of humans and contrasts them with the superior way of life of cats. The novel made Natsume famous and continues to be one of his most widely read works.

In 1907 Natsume published a collection of short stories titled *Uzurakago,* which contains the famous stories "Botchan" and "Kusamakura." "Botchan" tells the story of a young man who leaves Tokyo to teach in a provincial high school in the south of Japan; it is partly based on Natsume's own experience teaching in Matsuyama. The young man learns about life and then returns to Tokyo, where he finds a good job as an engineer. This story remains the most popular of Natsume's works among Japanese readers, who enjoy its brisk style and the protagonist's disregard for convention. "Kusamakura" is written in the style of a haiku; it is an impressionistic account of a painter from the city wandering in a mountain village. Natsume grew to hate this story as he got older, feeling ambivalent about its endorsement of aestheticism at the expense of really living life.

Also in 1907, Natsume produced *Nowake,* which addresses social problems due to class differences between the rich and the poor. Though the novel has been seen as awkwardly constructed, it foreshadows the tragic style that characterizes his later works. He also wrote up his findings on the nature of literature in *Bunkaguron.* Although his theories were not well received by his compatriots, his studies in England had allowed him to construct his own view of Japanese literature and its merits relative to works from the West. Through studying writing from many European countries, he came to the conclusion that he could create something new by combining Western ideas with traditional Japanese thought. That same year, Natsume was offered a position with the Asahi Newspaper publishing company, and he resigned his teaching posts to become a full-time writer. This was shocking to his peers, who considered writing for a newspaper far beneath the dignity of a university professor.

Natsume continued to produce novels at a rapid rate. *Sanshiro,* published in 1908, describes a young man's disillusionment with life and love; *Sorekara* tells of a bored and hypochondriac youth; *Mon* describes a middle-aged couple's quest for happiness. Assessing the title in the *New Yorker,* John Updike thought that *Mon* was full of blank areas in the plot that a Western novelist would have filled in, but he still commented that "as a portrait of domestic life and daily discontents, Japanese style, *Mon* is pleasant to read, and its very diffidence serves to pique our interest." These three novels form a trilogy.

Themes of loneliness continued to pervade Natsume's later work. In *Kojin* the hero, a hypersensitive, middle-aged professor, almost goes mad from loneliness. In *Comparative Literature Studies* Shihoko Hamada noted the similarities between the characters in this story and those in Shakespeare's *Hamlet,* which Natsume first read in his youth. *Kokoro* is Natsume's most pessimistic novel. The teacher protagonist, having suffered throughout his life, finally finds the courage to master his own destiny by committing suicide. Critics have said that in this novel Natsume was writing confessional prose, using the traditional diary and epistolary styles but charging them with new awareness. The language is stark and simple, influenced by the austere beauty of medieval Japanese prose. *Kokoro* is one of Natsume's later novels that was more widely appreciated in the West.

By 1915 Natsume was suffering from stomach ulcers that made his health deteriorate rapidly, and this illness figures as a metaphor in much of his later writing. In the autobiographical *Michikusa,* Natsume details his own resentment toward life and his unhappy childhood with his foster parents. He was still working on his last novel, *Meian,* at the time of his death in 1916. This book is a complex analysis of personalities in the modern world, describing the torments of selfish desires that isolate people from the rest of humanity. Western commentators have found *Meian* less than exciting, criticizing the characters' petty self-centeredness. The Japanese critic Reiko Abe Auestad, however, pointed out in the *Journal of the Association of Teachers of Japanese* that *Meian*'s characters have experienced a gap between themselves and the social positions into which they have been born and that the work must be read while keeping in mind the social constraints to which the Japanese are subject.

Some critics have called Natsume a novelist of victims, especially self-victimizers, such as those Japanese who were traumatized by long exposure to the West during the Meiji period, a time when many Japanese came to despise their own culture. Paul Anderer said in *Masterworks of Asian Literature in Comparative Perspective* that Natsume's work "reveals a scrutiny and an intelligence lacerating enough to expose both the inner turmoil and the dislocations this transformative age produced." The critic William N. Ridgeway suggested in *Japan Quarterly* that Natsume was addressing the psychological disorder now known as "male identity crisis;" as Japan modernized at a breakneck speed, the astonishingly fast social change threatened the identity of Japanese men who had one foot in the traditional age and the other in the modern. Though some Western readers have difficulty appreciating Natsume's work, Japanese critics have no such trouble, and they continue to read his writings as those of a major Meiji period intellectual.

BIOGRAPHICAL/CRITICAL SOURCES:

BOOKS

Miller, Barbara Stoler, editor, *Masterworks of Asian Literature in Comparative Perspective,* M. E. Sharpe (Armonk, NY), 1994.

Miyoshi, Masao, *Accomplices of Silence: The Modern Japanese Novel,* University of California Press, 1974.

Rimer, J. Thomas, *Modern Japanese Fiction and Its Traditions: An Introduction,* Princeton University Press, 1978.

Twentieth Century Literary Criticism, Volume 2, Gale (Detroit, MI), 1979.

Ueda, Makoto, *Modern Japanese Writers and the Nature of Literature,* Stanford University Press, 1976.

Yamanouchi, Hisaaki, *The Search for Authenticity in Modern Japanese Literature,* Cambridge University Press, 1978.

Yoshie, Okazaki, editor, *Japanese Literature in the Meiji Era,* Obunsha, 1955.

PERIODICALS

American Scholar, autumn 1965, Jun Eto, "Natsume Soseki: A Japanese Meiji Intellectual," pp. 603-619.

Choice, June, 1999, p. 1780.

Comparative Literature Studies, fall, 1993, Mihoko Higawa, "Soseki and Swinburne: A Source Study of the Pre-Raphaelite Features in *Kairo-ko,*" pp. 377-387; winter, 1996, Shihoko Hamada, "*Kôjin* and

Hamlet: The Madness of Hamlet, Ophelia,and Ichirô," pp. 59-68; summer 1998, Inger Sigrun Brodey, "Natsume Soseki and Laurence Sterne: Cross-Cultural Discourse on Literary Linearity," pp. 193-219.

Harvard Journal of Asiatic Studies, Volume 22, 1959, Edwin McClellan, "An Introduction to Soseki," pp. 150-208; June, 1982, Kathryn Sparling, "Meian: Another Reading," pp. 139-176; December, 1986, Jay Rubin, "The Evil and the Ordinary in Soseki's Fiction," pp. 333-352; December, 1989, James A. Fujii, "Contesting the Meiji Subject: Soseki's *Neko* Reconsidered," pp. 553-574.

Japan Quarterly, October-December, 1990, Leslie Pincus, "Transgressing the Frames of Fiction," pp. 433-449; April-June, 1998, William N. Ridgeway, "Natsume Soseki and Male Identity Crisis," pp. 82-90.

Journal of Japanese Studies, winter 1990, Paul Anderer, review of *The Miner,* pp. 140-142; winter 2000, pp. 200-203.

Journal of the Association of Teachers of Japanese, November, 1988, Reiko Abe Auestad, "The Critical Reception of Soseki's *Kojin* and *Meian* in Japan and the West," pp. 169-188; November, 1993, Kin'ya Tsuruta, "Soseki's *Kusamakura:* A Journey to 'The Other Side,'" pp. 229-257.

Library Journal, June 15, 1982, p. 1243.

Monumenta Nipponica, October, 1958 and January, 1959, Edwin McClellan, "Implications of Soseki's 'Kokoro,'" pp. 110-124.

New Yorker, January 3, 1983, John Updike, "Spent Arrows and First Buddings," pp. 66-67.

Publishers Weekly, June 4, 1982, Barbara A. Bannon, review of *I Am a Cat,* p. 59.

Times Literary Supplement, April 28, 1989, p. 466.

UNESCO Courier, October, 1966, pp. 25-27.

World Literature Today, autumn 1999, Erik R. Lofgren, "Chaos and Order in the Works of Natsume Soseki," p. 826.*

*   *   *

NELSON, Eric 1952-

PERSONAL: Born December 10, 1952, in San Angelo, TX; son of David (an educator) and Emma (Hutcheson) Nelson; married Stephanie Tames, October 17, 1980; children: Benjamin Tames, Claire Tames. *Ethnicity:* "Caucasian." *Education:* Virginia Polytechnic Institute and State University, B.A., 1975; Johns Hopkins University, M.A., 1977.

ADDRESSES: Home—109 College Blvd., Statesboro, GA 30458. *Office*—Department of Writing and Linguistics, Georgia Southern University, Statesboro, GA 30460. *E-mail*—enelson@gasou.edu.

CAREER: Virginia Polytechnic Institute and State University, Blacksburg, VA, instructor in English, 1984-89; Georgia Southern University, Statesboro, GA, assistant professor, 1989-95, associate professor of creative writing, 1995—. Also taught at Rutgers University. Georgia Poetry Circuit, institutional representative, 1999—; judge of poetry contests.

MEMBER: Associated Writing Programs.

AWARDS, HONORS: Irene Leache Award in Poetry, Chrysler Museum (Norfolk, VA), 1977 and 1978; Doris Kellog Neale Award in Poetry, *Mickle Street Review,* 1982; fellow, Virginia Center for Creative Arts, 1987 and 1988; Pushcart Prize nominations, 1990, 1994, 1996, 1998-2000; Arkansas Poetry Award, 1990; winner of Georgia Poetry Circuit Competition, 1992; Readers' Choice Award, *Blue Moon Review,* 1997; fellow, Hambidge Center for the Arts, 1997 and 1998; Featured Poet, *poetrymagazine.org,* June, 2001.

WRITINGS:

On Call (poems), Moonsquilt Press (Miami, FL), 1983.
The Light Bringers (poems), Washington Writers Publishing House (Washington, DC), 1984.
The Interpretation of Waking Life (poems), University of Arkansas Press (Fayetteville, AR), 1991.

Work represented in anthologies, including *The Unitarian Univeralist Poets: A Contemporary American Survey,* Pudding House Publications (Johnstown, OH), 1996; *I Feel a Little Jumpy around You,* Simon & Schuster (New York, NY), 1996; and *Georgia Voices: Poetry,* University of Georgia Press (Athens, GA), 2000. Contributor of more than seventy poems, articles, and reviews to journals, including *Yankee, Poetry, Texas Review, Mid-American Review, The Southern Review,* and *Laurel Review.* Coeditor, *Ogeechee Poetry Journal,* 1990-98.

*   *   *

NIJHOFF, Martinus 1894-1953

PERSONAL: Born April 20, 1894, in The Hague, Netherlands; died January 26, 1953, in The Hague, Netherlands; married A. H. Nijhoff-Wind, 1916 (marriage ended); married G. Hagedoorn, 1952. *Education:* Attended University of Amsterdam; University of Utrecht, degree in language and literature, 1937.

CAREER: Poet, translator, and journalist, c. 1916-53; *De Guids,* editor and contributor, 1926-33 and 1945-53; *Nieuwe Rotterdamsche Courant,* critic; served as literary adviser to Ministry of Education and Science after 1945; also worked in family business. *Military service:* Served two years as a draftee.

WRITINGS:

POETRY

De wandelaar (title means "The Wayfarer"), Versluys (Amsterdam, Netherlands), 1916.
Pierrot aan de lantaarn (title means "Pierrot by a Lantern"), [The Hague, Netherlands], 1919.
Vormen (title means "Forms"), Van Dishoeck, 1924.
Gedachten op dinsdag (title means "Thoughts on Tuesday"), A. A. M. Stols (Brussels, Belgium), 1931.
Nieuwe gedichten (title means "New Poems"), Querido (Amsterdam, Netherlands), 1934.
Het uur u, A. A. M. Stols (Brussels, Belgium), 1936, translation by Adriaan Barnouw published as "Zero Hour," and by Peter K. King as "Your Zero Hour," both in *Dit meldt her uur u, teksten omtrent Het uur u van Martinjus Nojhoff* by Dirk Kroon, 1986.
Wij zijn vrij; gedicht, Vrij Nederland (Amsterdam, Netherlands), 1945.
Tot de gevallenen; gedicht, Vrij Nederland (Amsterdam, Netherlands), 1945.
Der Ster van Bethlehem (title means "The Star of Bethlehem"), Vrijzinnig Christelijke Jeugd Centrale (Utrecht, Netherlands), 1947.
Het heilige hout (title means "Holy Wood"), D. A. Daamen (The Hague, Netherlands), 1950.

Other volumes of poetry include *De vliegende Hollander* (title means "The Flying Dutchman"), 1930; *Halewijn,* 1933; *Awater,* 1934, translation published as *Awater,* 1954; *In Holland staat een huis* (title means "In Holland Stands a House"), 1937; and *Het uur u gevolgd door een idylle* (title means "Zero Hour Followed by an Idyll"), 1942.

TRANSLATIONS

André Gide, *Moer,* A. A. M. Stols, 1929.

Also translated Ramuz, *De Geschiedenis van de soldaat,* 1930; Ramuz, *Het verhaal va de vos,* 1930; Wil-

liam Shakespeare, *De Storm,* 1930; Euripides, *Iphigenia in Tauris,* 1951; and T. S. Eliot, *De Cocktail partij,* 1951.

PROSE

Den pen op papier, gevolgd door een vertaling van Lafontaine's Fabel van de twee duiven, Joh. Enschede en Zonen (Haarlem, Netherlands), 1927, translation by W. C. Niewenhous published as "Pen on Paper," in *Harvest of the Lowlands,* 1945.
Kritisch, berhalend en negelaten proza, B. Bakker (The Hague, Netherlands), 1961.
Brieven aan mihn vrouw (correspondence), B. Bakker (The Hague, Netherlands), 1996.

COLLECTIONS

Lees maar, er staat neit wat er staat (title means "Read for Yourself: It Does Not Say What It Says," anthology), B. Bakker (The Haague, Netherlands), 1959.
Verzamelde gedichten (title means "Collected Poems"), Bakker/Daaman, 1978.
Verzamelde werk (title means "Collected Works"), three volumes, edited by G. Borgers and G. Kamphuis, Daamen, 1982.

Work also collected in *Martinus Nijhoff, een guer van hoger honing* (title means "Martinus Nijhoff: A Scent of Purer Honey"), edited by W. J. van den Akker and G. J. Dorelijn, 1990; and in *The Sacred Wood* (contains three plays: "De ster van Bethlehem" [title means "The Star of Bethlehem"], "De Dag des Heren" [title means, "The Lord's Day"], and "Des heilands tuin" [title means, "The Savior's Garden."])

SIDELIGHTS: Martinus Nijhoff is regarded as one of the most important Dutch poets of the twentieth century. Born in The Hague in 1894, he studied law at the University of Amsterdam and later earned a degree in literature from the University of Utrecht. His first two collections of poems, *The Wayfarer* and *Pierrot by a Lantern,* coincided with the beginning and end of World War I; they reflect the themes of alienation, hopelessness, and passivity that were to become hallmarks of the age. Deeply influenced by the French symbolist poets, especially Verlaine, Nijhoff 's early poems are distinguished by their startling, almost surrealistic, imagery. References to death recur frequently, and suicide is suggested as the only escape from a meaningless existence. As Fred J. Nichols observed in *Encyclopedia of World Literature,* these early poems are "informed by a sense of disquiet, at times of anguish, and a recurring thematic action is breaking, both in the sense of giving way and of breaking through."

Known for the skill with which he handled matters of form and technique, Nijhoff employed the sonnet frequently in his early work. As Kendall Dunkelberg explained in a *Dutch Crossing* article, Nijhoff distrusted or even disdained free verse, which had become increasingly popular in Dutch poetry. But he used traditional forms in experimental ways. "This amount of experimentation," wrote Dunkelberg, "implies a thorough knowledge or intuitive sense of the sonnet's intrinsic structure." Later in his career, Nijhoff moved toward looser forms and verse dramas, developing, in Nichols's words, "a flowing verse line closer to the conversational."

In 1926, Nijhoff became editor of the journal *De gids.* His criticism also began to appear in various periodicals, including *Nieuwe Rotterdamsche Courant.* By the 1930s, he had shifted from the brevity of sonnets to longer poems, and had begun his move toward more traditional Dutch symbolism. According to Martin Bakker in a *Canadian Journal of Netherlandic Studies* article, Nijhoff began to use "modern, realistic and in most cases typically Dutch symbols like dunes and dykes and lighthouses, boats and ferries, kitchen utensils, and cars and bicycles . . . which, together with the style that went with the modern symbols, caused critics to call [him] the first modern poet in The Netherlands." Other critics, though—as Bakker pointed out—associated Nijhoff with classicism, romanticism, realism, the baroque, impressionism, existentialism, cubism, and even magic realism.

Of Nijhoff's work during the 1930s, his *New Poems,* which includes the celebrated "Awater," a poetic narrative with mythic and biblical overtones, is considered his best. As Peter King observed in *Reference Guide to World Literature,* "the theme of escape and return, self-deception and confrontation, is more broadly applied to reality and ideal, to the now and the hereafter, and in a number of poems there is the reassurance that across the divide there is a bridge, ferry, or ship, to unite the here-and-now with the ideal." *New Poems* presents poems that are, as the collection's title suggests, a significant departure from earlier trends in Dutch literature. In fact, Nijhoff declares as much in the book's opening poem, announcing his intention to break from romanticism and create a new poetics: modern and decidedly urban. As the poet remarked in a lecture given a year after *New Poems* appeared, and quoted by Wiljan van den Akker in *Dutch Crossing:* "The motor is for our century the only invention we can set against the

Parthenon as its equal. . . . I have had modernistic moods: sitting in a cinema and seeing the skyscrapers of New York on the news reel, I have felt the same emotion as when I saw for the first time the cathedral looming in the narrow streets of Chartres."

Among the important works in *New Poems* are "Het veer" (title means "The Ferry"), a long poem in blank verse in which the martyred St. Sebastian comes back to life in the twentieth-century Dutch landscape. A difficult poem that has elicited varying interpretations from critics, it can be considered, in the view of A. L. Soetemann in *Nijhoff, Van Ostaijen, De Stijl: Modernism in the Netherlands and Belgium in the First Quarter of the Twentieth Century,* "the first demonstration of Nijhoff's new, though ostensibly effortless modernism." The poet's other great poem from this book, "Awater," is thematically similar though much longer and more technically complex. Also in blank verse, it is structured in long assonating stanzas called *laisses monorimes,* from the French epic *Chanson de Roland.* The poem describes the quest of Awater, an accountant, for a traveling companion through hell of the modern city. "Nijhoff has banished all overt emotion from his poem," observed Soetemann, "referring to the method of surrealist paintings 'with their stillness, their unemotional lucidity, their clear objects, as banal as they are mysterious,' and to what he considered to be their literary equivalent: 'new objective' prose."

Nijhoff returned to the quest motif once more in "Het uur U" (title means "Zero Hour" or "H-Hour"), his last long poem and one regarded as a masterpiece. Like "Awater," it describes a man's journey through a city landscape and contains mythic and religious elements. As the man, who lacks any distinguishing characteristics, passes along the street, he exerts a strange effect on those who see him. As Soetemann explained, "The surprising effect of this passing is that the adults who live there are confronted with their human deficiency. Yet, the children in the street are not affected and normal life resumes its course after the man [has] disappeared." The fact that the individual and the those he encounters fail to make any real contact is related, according to Nichols, to Nijhoff's recurrent theme of "leaving others and of being left." Though the poem is enigmatic, it constitutes, in Soetemann's opinion, "an ultimate, precarious but successful result of Nijhoff's individual solution to the problem of modernism." After "Zero Hour," Nijhoff's poems turned away from the concerns of modernism, as if the poet believed he had exhausted its possibilities.

Later in his career, Nijhoff turned his attention to verse drama. During World War II, which he reportedly spent in hiding, he wrote three plays for the Christian liturgical year: *De ster van Bethlehem, De Dag des Heren,* and *Des heilands tuin,* later published together as *The Sacred Wood.*

Widely admired for his own poems, Nijhoff also achieved recognition for his translations of Gide, Ramuz, Shakespeare, Euripides, and T. S. Eliot, who was one of Nijhoff's major influences. In addition, he outlined and developed the principles of his poetics in a large body of critical writing.

BIOGRAPHICAL/CRITICAL SOURCES:

BOOKS

Bulhof, Francis, editor, *Nijhoff, Van Ostaijen, De Stijl: Modernism in the Netherlands and Belgium in the First Quarter of the Twentieth Century: Six Essays,* Martinus Nijhoff (The Hague, Netherlands), 1976.

Demetz, Peter, Thomas Greene, and Lowry Nelson, Jr., editors, *The Disciplines of Criticism: Essays in Literary Theory, Interpretation, and History,* Yale University Press (New Haven, CT), 1968.

Encyclopedia of World Literature in the Twentieth Century, 3rd edition, St. James Press (Detroit, MI), 1999.

Reference Guide to World Literature, 2nd edition, St. James Press (Detroit, MI), 1995.

Snapper, Johan P., and Thomas F. Shannon, editors, *The Berkeley Conference on Dutch Literature 1987,* University Press of America (Lanham, MD), 1989.

Wintle, Michael, editor, *Modern Dutch Studies: Essays in Honour of Peter King,* Athlone Press (Atlantic Highlands, NJ), 1988.

PERIODICALS

Canadian Journal of Netherlandic Studies, spring, 1990, pp. 23-29.

Dutch Crossing, spring, 1990, pp. 109-124; summer, 1990, pp. 23-34.

Dutch Quarterly Review of Anglo American Letters, Volume 2, 1972, pp. 65-72.*

*   *   *

NOWRA, Louis   1950-

PERSONAL: Born December 12, 1950, in Melbourne, Victoria, Australia; married Sarah de Jong, 1974. *Edu-* *cation:* Studied at La Trobe University, Bundoora, Victoria, Australia. *Avocational interests:* Cricket, mycology.

ADDRESSES: Office—Level 18, Plaza 11, 500 Oxford St., Bondi Junction, New South Wales 2011, Australia.

CAREER: Writer-in-residence, University of Queensland, Brisbane, 1979, Lighthouse Company, Adelaide, Australia, 1982, Playbox Theatre, Melbourne, Australia, 1985, and Capricornia Institute, 1987; Associate Artistic Director, Sydney Theatre Company, 1980, and Lighthouse Company, 1983.

AWARDS, HONORS: Australian Literature Board fellowship, 1975, 1977-79, 1981, 1983; Prix Italia, 1990; Australia/Canada Award, 1993.

WRITINGS:

PLAYS

Kiss the One-eyed Priest, produced in Melbourne, Australia, 1973.

Albert Names Edward (broadcast in 1975), published in *Five Plays for Radio,* Currency Press (Sydney, Australia), 1976.

Inner Voices (produced in Sydney, Australia, 1977; produced in London, England, 1982) Currency Press (Sydney, Australia), 1977.

Visions (produced in Sydney, Australia, 1978), Currency Press (Sydney, Australia), 1979.

Cyrano de Bergerac (adaptation of the play by Edmund Rostand), produced in Sydney, Australia, 1980.

Beauty and the Beast, produced in Sydney, Australia, 1980.

Death of Joe Orion, produced in Adelaide, Australia, 1980.

Inside the Island (produced in Sydney, Australia, 1980), published with *The Precious Woman,* Currency Press (Sydney, Australia), 1981.

The Song Room (broadcast in 1980), published in *Seven One-Act Plays,* Currency Press (Sydney, Australia), 1983.

Lulu (adaptation of a play by Frank Wedekind), produced in Adelaide, Australia, 1981.

(And director) *The Prince of Homburg* (adaptation of the play by Heinrich von Kleist), produced in Adelaide, Australia, 1982.

Royal Show, produced in Adelaide, Australia, 1982.

Spellbound, produced in Adelaide, Australia, 1982, produced in London, 1986.

Sunrise (produced in Adelaide, Australia, 1983), Currency Press (Sydney, Australia), 1983.

The Golden Age (produced in Melbourne, Australia, 1985; produced in Bristol, 1992), Dramatic (Woodstock, IL), 1985.

Capricornia (adapted from the novel by Xavier Herbert; produced in Sydney, Australia, 1988), Currency Press (Sydney, Australia), 1988.

Whitsunday (opera), music by Brian Howard, produced in Sydney, Australia, 1988.

Byzantine Flowers, produced in Sydney, Australia, 1989.

Summer of the Aliens (broadcast as *The Summer of the Aliens,* 1989; produced in Melbourne, Australia, 1992), Currency Press (Sydney, Australia), 1992.

Cosi (produced in Sydney, Australia, 1992), Currency Press (Sydney, Australia), 1992.

Radiance, Currency Press (Sydney, Australia), 1993.

The Temple, Currency Press (Sydney, Australia), 1993.

Crow, Currency Press (Sydney, Australia), 1994.

The Incorruptible, Currency Press (Sydney, Australia), 1995.

The Language of the Gods, Currency Press (Sydney, Australia), 1999.

NOVELS

The Misery of Beauty: The Loves of Frogman, Angus & Robertson (London), 1976.

Palu, St. Martin's Press (New York City), 1987.

Red Nights, Picador (Sydney, Australia), 1997.

SCREENPLAYS

(With others) *Cosi: The Screenplay* (based on Nowra's play), Currency Press (Sydney, Australia), 1996.

(With Karen Janszen and Graham Linehan) *The Matchmaker,* PolyGram, 1997.

OTHER

(Editor) *The Cheated,* Angus & Robertson (Sydney, Australia), 1979.

The Twelfth of Never, Picador, 1999.

(Editor, with Mandy Sayer) *In the Gutter—Looking at the Stars: A Literary Adventure through Kings Cross,* Random House (Australia), 2000.

Also author of *Displaced Persons* (television play), 1985; *Hunger* (television play), 1986; *The Widows* (radio play), 1986; *The Lizard King* (television play), 1987; *Map of the Human Heart,* 1991; *The Watchtower,* 1992; and *Heaven's Burning,* 1997.

SIDELIGHTS: Since the mid-1970s, Australian writer Louis Nowra has created dozens of stage plays, as well

as authored novels and film scripts. Most often his plays have been performed in Australia, where several of his scripts have been produced for radio and television. His work is often controversial and has repeatedly mixed traditional styles or genres. His plot elements have included the fate of Aboriginal peoples and the political history of Australia. In the 1990s, his work became noticeably more autobiographical and has since met with increased commercial success. In 1996 Nowra wrote the screenplay for the internationally released film *Cosi,* based on his stage play of the same name.

Nowra perplexed audiences with his first plays, which used remote settings but featured characters that used Australian ways of thinking and speaking. *Inner Voices* is set in eighteenth-century Russia and *Visions* takes place in Paraguay in the 1870s; both are anti-imperialist war stories. Stylistically, Nowra was working outside of the nationalist and naturalistic trends that were current in Australia. When Nowra's early writing was compared to that of German dramatist Bertolt Brecht, he distanced himself from that stylistic school as well, urging psychological readings of his work rather than the use of a political or historical focus.

However, Nowra's plays are filled with events and issues from Australian and post-colonial history. For example, in *Inside the Island,* his subject was the behavior of young soldiers on a remote Australian wheat farm a few years prior to the World War I battle of Gallipoli. The dispossession of Aboriginal people is an important context for this and later plays. Helen Gilbert considered *Inside the Island* in a *Southern Review* article that explored the relationship of character and landscape. She judged the work to be "a direct and sustained challenge to romanticized narratives of settlement (read invasion)." *Sunrise* deals with a wealthy, land-owning white family's involvement in British nuclear tests at Maralinga. *The Precious Woman* shows the changing relationships between a woman and her husband and son during a revolution.

A writer in *Contemporary Dramatists* characterized Nowra's plays as "comic and savage theatrical parables." Regarding the repeated comparison of Nowra to Brecht, the writer said, "[Nowra's] theater owes more to expressionistic, mythical, and musical modes, which produce an expansive, highly visual, and tonally mixed dramaturgy. Through this dramaturgy the contradictions and decentered consciousness of a multicultural and multiracial society are explored with complexity unequalled in contemporary Australian writing." The writer identified *The Golden Age* as Nowra's "most resonant play." This drama centers on the 1939 discovery of a fictional "lost" tribe of whites who are locked up in an asylum, echoing the real fate of Tazmanian Aboriginals in the 1800s.

In a 1984 article in *Meanjin,* John McCallum explored the work of Nowra, along with a handful of "cosmopolitan" or "internationalist" playwrights, and found a "basic paradox" in Nowra's work to that date. "He has managed to take styles and dramatic devices originally forged for political analysis and render them so 'interestingly ambiguous' as to strip them of much of their political content," explained McCallum. "A dominant theme in all Nowra's work is the confrontation between the characters' personal vision and the reality of the world outside. . . . It is this interaction between inner and outer worlds which explains some of the political indirectness in these plays."

Nowra's later writings took on a semi-autobiographical slant beginning with *Summer of the Aliens.* In this play the central character is a boy who shares Nowra's given name, Lewis, and who begins to wonder if the strange behavior of his family and neighbors is the result of their being inhabited by aliens. Lewis appears again in *Cosi* as a young man who is trying to direct a performance of the Mozart opera *Cosi fan tutti* with a cast of mental patients. Kelly called *Cosi* "a witty example of the in-joke rehearsal play genre. It presents humanity as pitifully fragile, sometimes appalling, but always spiritually resilient."

In 1996 *Cosi* was turned into a motion picture with a screenplay written by Nowra. In his review for *New Republic,* Stanley Kauffmann considered it "daringly cynical" that the film tread ground covered so successfully by two famous earlier films: "*Cosi* has nothing like the implicit commentary of *King of Hearts* [1966], and any comparison in gravity with *Marat/Sade* [1966] would be ridiculous. Besides, the directing and most of the acting don't give us the chance to like the film (if this were possible) on its own." However, *American Spectator* critic James Bowman was more pleased by the film's evocation of the "gap between what we continue to hope and expect of love and what it actually is." As Bowman's Film of the Month, *Cosi* was chosen for its "artistic . . . maturity." Nowra worked with *Cosi*'s director, Mark Joffe (a fellow Australian), soon thereafter when he helped co-author the screenplay for the more mainstream British-U.S. film *The Matchmaker.*

As a novelist, Nowra's themes and experimentation with genre have resembled his work in the theater. His first novel, *The Misery of Beauty,* is the story of a deformed magician's assistant who is called Frogman, appearing or being part frog, part man. In an article for *Westerly,* Gerry Turcotte called the work both a "straightforward account" of an individual who is rejected by society for being different and an analogy for those who are "marginalized as a result of race, class, skin colour, and physical or other deformities."

Palu was Nowra's first novel to be published in the United States. It is an account narrated by a young woman who awaits execution. She tells of having left her native tribe and meeting her husband, who has become a corrupt dictator in his attempt to lead their newly independent island country in the Pacific. A *Publishers Weekly* critic described how in *Palu* "Nowra develops parallel themes of black/white relationships in the clash of ancient and modern worlds."

In a larger discussion of Gothic elements in these first two novels, Turcotte said, "[Nowra's] active interest in blurring genres and borrowing from conflicting traditions may explain some of the critical dissatisfaction which has been expressed over his use of such conventions as the epic. Nowra's inconsistency, however, signals not so much a failure in technical terms as a refusal to conform; it represents concretely the theme of so many of his works—that it is necessary to retrieve the past and rewrite it in new terms and according to different rules."

Nowra has since written a third novel, *Red Nights,* which was reviewed in *Overland* by Foong Ling Kong. The story is set in inner-city Sydney, where Nelson Taylor has enjoyed his new-found wealth as the host of outlandish "Red Night" parties, the hottest invitation in Sydney. But when Taylor's money starts to run out, he does not change his lavish habits. According to Kong, "on the last day of his life" an unhappy Taylor learns that he has made more enemies than friends. Kong complimented the book, saying, "Nowra displays a sure and deft hand in this morality tale of class mobility. . . . He has a marvellous ear for scandalously funny conversation and the characters are confident, arch, *de trop.*"

BIOGRAPHICAL/CRITICAL SOURCES:

BOOKS

Contemporary Dramatists, sixth edition, St. James Press, 1999.

PERIODICALS

American Spectator, April, 1997, James Bowman, "Polyester Slackers," pp. 68-69.

Meanjin, June, 1984, John McCallum, "The World Outside: Cosmopolitanism in the Plays of Nowra and Sewell," pp. 286-296.

New Republic, March 3, 1997, Stanley Kauffmann, review of *Cosi,* p. 30.

New York Times Book Review, July 9, 1989, Ken Kalfus, review of *Palu,* p. 18.

Overland, winter, 1998, Foong Ling Kong, "Interest in the Amoral," pp. 106-107.

Publishers Weekly, December 2, 1988, review of *Palu,* p. 46.

Southern Review, December, 1994, Helen Gilbert, "Ghosts in a Landscape: Louis Nowra's *Inside the Island* and Janis Balodis' *Too Young for Ghosts,*" pp. 432-447.

Variety, January 21, 1981, review of *The Precious Woman,* p. 114.

Westerly: A Quarterly Review, September, 1991, Gerry Turcotte, " 'Speaking the Formula of Abjection': Hybrids and Gothic Discourses in Louis Nowra's Novels," pp. 61-72.*

O

OAKES, John Bertram 1913-2001

OBITUARY NOTICE—See index for *CA* sketch: Born April 23, 1913, in Elkins Park, PA; died of complications from a stroke, April 5, 2001, in New York, NY. Journalist and editor. Oakes, born into a family of journalists, was editor of the *New York Times'* editorial page for fifteen years during some of the country's most turbulent times. His father, George Washington Ochs (who changed the spelling of his sons' names to Oakes in protestation of German aggression), edited *The Philadelphia Public Ledger* and *Current History* magazine and was director of The New York Times Company. His uncle, Adolph Ochs, owned *The Times* and his cousin, Arthur Ochs Sulzberger, eventually was publisher of the paper. Oakes graduated from Princeton University in 1934 where he was valedictorian, voted "most brilliant" by his classmates and elected to Phi Beta Kappa. The next year he studied at the University of Dijon in France and in 1936 received two degrees from Oxford University where he was a Rhodes scholar. Shortly after he joined the staff of *The Trenton Times* in New Jersey and then moved to *The Washington Post*, where he covered politics until 1941. He joined the Army as a private and, after a series of promotions, ended his career as a major. During his five years in the service he was in the infantry and then the Office of Strategic Services, a precursor to the Central Intelligence Agency. His efforts resulted in his receiving the Bronze Star and the Croix de Guerre. After he was discharged, Oakes rejoined newspapers, this time at *The Times*. He was an editor and then a member of the editorial board, writing columns on a variety of environmental and liberal issues as well as editorials. Under his leadership the editorial page started taking a stronger stance on issues, usually liberal, and was an early opponent of the Vietnam War and President Nixon. Oakes is credited with retooling the editorial section into the current "op-ed" format in which one page features the paper's editorials and the opposing page includes columns from various experts and leaders, a format that has been copied by papers around the country. Oakes wrote *The Edge of Freedom* in 1961, a book about American policies toward emerging countries in Eastern Europe and the sub-Sahara, and contributed to the books *Foundations of Freedom* and *Tomorrow's American*. He led the editorial page from 1961 to 1976, when Sulzberger replaced him after a series of disputes over political endorsements and what management viewed as an anti-business leaning on the editorial page. Oakes was then senior editor and senior vice president, retiring in 1978. He continued writing for the Op-Ed page until 1993. Twice he was honored with the George Polk Award for his journalistic skills: first in 1965 and posthumously, in 2001.

OBITUARIES AND OTHER SOURCES:

PERIODICALS

Chicago Tribune, April 6, 2001, sec. 2, p. 6.
Los Angeles Times, April 6, 2001, p. B6.
New York Times, April 6, 2001, p. C10.
Washington Post, April 6, 2001, p. B6.

*   *   *

OBERT, Genevieve 1959-

PERSONAL: Born July 20, 1959, in Los Angeles, CA; daughter of John M. (in computer security) and Ann Furlong (an artist) Williams; married Chris Obert (a business owner), 1982; children: Jesse, Molly. *Ethnicity:* "White." *Education:* University of California—Santa Cruz, B.A., 1980; Monterey Institute of International Studies, M.B.A., 1988.

ADDRESSES: Home—301 Encinal Street, Santa Cruz, CA 95060. *E-mail*—genobert@aol.com

CAREER: Journalist, author.

MEMBER: Motor Press Guild, Western Auto Journalists, Sisters-in-Crime, Society of Automotive Historians.

AWARDS, HONORS: Dean Batchelor Award for excellence in automotive journalism, Motor Press Guild, for *Prince Borghese's Trail: 10,000 Miles over Two Continents, Four Deserts, and the Roof of the World in the Peking to Paris Motor Challenge.*

WRITINGS:

Prince Borghese's Trail: 10,000 Miles over Two Continents, Four Deserts, and the Roof of the World in the Peking to Paris Motor Challenge, Council Oak Books (San Francisco, CA), 1999.

Articles published in *Auto Week, Auto Italia, BIMMER: The Magazine about BMW, British Car Magazine, Car Collector, European Car, FORZA: The Magazine about Ferrari, Robb Report, Special Interest Autos, Sports Car International, Vintage Motor Sports,* and *Ciao! NEWS.*

WORK IN PROGRESS: Fast Women: 100 Years of Women Racers, nonfiction, expected publication date 2003. Also, a historical mystery.

SIDELIGHTS: Genevieve Obert is a journalist who specializes in news about classic cars and road rallies. Her book, *Prince Borghese's Trail: 10,000 Miles over Two Continents, Four Deserts, and the Roof of the World in the Peking to Paris Motor Challenge,* recounts Obert's six-week journey over half the world in a classic car race held in 1997. Obert's title cites the first winner of the Peking to Paris race, who along with the other participants, set out to prove that the automobile could provide a reliable means of transportation for long journeys in 1907. The British Classic Car Rally Association staged the ninetieth anniversary reenactment of the earlier race, stipulating that the 1997 participants must drive cars at least twenty-five years old. Nearly one hundred teams participated in the 1997 race across eleven countries in six weeks driving cars dated from

1907 to 1972. Obert's book focuses on the personalities of the other drivers and their various cars, and the trials and tribulations suffered in trying to coerce antique cars over rough and narrow mountain roads. Eric C. Shoaf, who reviewed *Prince Borghese's Trail* for *Library Journal,* commented that "Obert's detailed descriptions of the countries, cultures, and car nuts involved in the race are compelling." Gary Anderson, editor of *British Car Magazine,* wrote, "I read the book in three evenings, not able to put it down. [Obert] has mingled a detailed history . . . a travelogue . . . a gripping real-life automotive adventure and her own personal mental journey."

BIOGRAPHICAL/CRITICAL SOURCES:

PERIODICALS

British Car Magazine, October-November, 1999, Gary Anderson, review of *Prince Borghese's Trail,* p. 54.
Library Journal, September 1, 1999, Eric C. Shoaf, review of *Prince Borghese's Trail,* p. 222.

*   *   *

O'DONOGHUE, David   1952-

PERSONAL: Born 1952, in Cork, Ireland. *Education:* Attended Dublin City University.

ADDRESSES: Office—c/o Author Mail, Beyond the Pale, Unit 2.1.2., Conway Mill, 5-7 Conway St., Belfast BT13 2DE, Northern Ireland.

CAREER: Journalist and author. Worked as a journalist for RTE, the Irish broadcasting service, Agence France-Presse in Paris, and in Singapore and Great Britain.

WRITINGS:

Hitler's Irish Voices: The Story of German Radio's Wartime Service, Beyond the Pale (Belfast, Northern Ireland), 1998.

SIDELIGHTS: David O'Donoghue is a journalist who has worked for press services in Ireland and France. When he returned to Northern Ireland in 1989, he began working on *Hitler's Irish Voices: The Story of German Radio's Wartime Service.* O'Donoghue drew on research from Germany, Ireland, and Great Britain in writing of the German radio broadcast from Berlin that ran from December 1939 to May 1945, first as a talk show in Irish, later as a bilingual service in Irish and English. Although Ireland was divided in preparation for later bifurcation, with James Dillon favoring the democratic powers and the Irish Republican Army (IRA) wishing to advance the cause of Germany as a means of hurting Britain, the two sides agreed they did not want to enter World War II.

The German radio service, Irland-Redaktion, attempted to sway the Irish but was not successful. Broadcasters were, for the most part, civil servants and academics who were unable to change public opinion or politics through their addresses. Describing the Dublin Nazi community before and during the war, O'Donoghue explains that the creator of the Irish service was Austrian-born Dr. Adolf Mahr, a member of the Nazi party and director of the National Museum in Dublin. He returned to Berlin at the beginning of the war where he was put in charge of the Irish desk of the German Foreign Office, and where he began the German Radio's Irish service. Other party members involved were Heinz Meicking of the Turf Board; Frederick Weckler, accountant of the ESB; and Colonel Fritz Brase, director of the Army School of Music. Maurice Manning wrote in *World of Hibernia* that *Hitler's Irish Voices* "whets the reader's appetite for more." Manning posed the question of what would have happened if Germany had invaded Ireland and concluded that "The experience of other countries shows that the firing squads would have been busy." Manning called *Hitler's Irish Voices* "well-written, accurate . . . very readable" and "eminently worthwhile." Voicing a similar conclusion, Ben Novick stated in his *Irish Literary Supplement* review that O'Donoghue "should be applauded for the formidable research and scholarship" upon which he based *Hitler's Irish Voices.* Describing the writing as "clear and concise," Novick further praised the author for his ability to "bring to life an amazing cast of characters and a fascinating and disturbing story."

BIOGRAPHICAL/CRITICAL SOURCES:

PERIODICALS

Irish Literary Supplement, spring, 1999, Ben Novick, review of *Hitler's Irish Voices,* p. 9.
World of Hibernia, autumn, 1998, Maurice Manning, review of *Hitler's Irish Voices,* p. 138.*

OKUIZUMI, Hikaru
See OKUIZUMI, Yasuhiro

*   *   *

OKUIZUMI, Yasuhiro   1956-
  (Hikaru Okuizumi)

PERSONAL: Born 1956. *Education:* International Christian University (Tokyo, Japan), B.A., 1980, M.A., 1982.

ADDRESSES: Agent—c/o Shueisha Inc., 5-10 Hitotsu-bashi 2 chome, Chiyoda-ku, Tokyo 112-0002, Japan.

CAREER: Novelist, 1985—.

AWARDS, HONORS: Akutagawa Prize, Japan, for *Ishi no raireki.*

WRITINGS:

Taki (title means "The Waterfall"), Shueisha (Tokyo, Japan), 1990.
Ashi to yuri, Shueisha (Tokyo, Japan), 1991.
Hebi o korosu yoru, Shueisha (Tokyo, Japan), 1992.
Novarisu no in'yo, Shinchosha (Tokyo, Japan), 1993.
Banaru na gensho, Shueisha (Tokyo, Japan), 1994.
Ishi no raireki, Bungei Shunju (Tokyo, Japan), 1994, translation by James Westerhoven published as *The Stones Cry Out,* Harcourt (New York, NY), 1998.
Wagahai wa neko de aru: satsujin jiken: junbungaku kakioroshi tokubetsu sakuhin, Shinchosha (Tokyo, Japan), 1996.
Puraton gakuen, Kodansha (Tokyo, Japan), 1997.
Gurando misuteri (title means "Grand Mystery"), Kadokawa Shoten (Tokyo, Japan), 1998.

Ishi no raireki has been translated into French.

SIDELIGHTS: Japanese author Yasuhiro Okuizumi, who writes under the name Hikaru Okuizumi, received Japan's prestigious Akutagawa Prize for his novel *Ishi no raireki.* The title, which was translated by James Westerhoven and published as *The Stones Cry Out,* was Okuizumi's English-language debut. It is the story of a man's war experiences and their effect on him and his family. A *Publishers Weekly* reviewer said it is "a lyrical, riveting study of obsession, family disintegration, and war's dehumanizing effects," and called Okuizumi "a natural storyteller, his deceptively simple, low-key style magnetizing."

The protagonist is Tsuyoshi Manase, a Japanese man who served in World War II as a private and who is haunted by the events that took place in a cave on the Philippine island of Leyte, where he took refuge with his fellow soldiers. Many of the men were sick with malaria, and all were starving because of the small food supply. Manase stood by when his captain ordered that the able-bodied among them kill those who were dying and could not care for themselves. Among those massacred was a lance corporal and geologist who held up a stone and told Manase that "even the most ordinary pebble has the history of this heavenly body we call earth written on it."

Manase carries the shame of this event with him. Following the war he reopens the bookstore that had belonged to his father. He becomes an amateur geologist, collecting rocks and fossils, obsessively categorizing and cleaning them in an effort to ease his pain. When Manase's eldest son, Hiroaki, who also has an interest in geology, is murdered in a cave, Manase is linked to the death and accused by his grieving alcoholic wife. But it is not made clear whether he is connected through his own actions or whether he is morally responsible. A serial killer is also suspected, as is Manase's younger son, Takaaki, who has been emotionally neglected by his father.

In the second half of the novel the relationship between Manase and Takaaki is explored. Takaaki becomes a student protestor during the riots of 1968 and joins a revolutionary group. A writer said in a *Kirkus Reviews* article that the younger son's "climactic confrontation with his father dovetails beautifully with Manase's realization that the 'hallucinations' he suffers have a disturbing basis in reality . . . it precipitates the story's bone-chilling visionary ending." David B. Livingstone of the *Detroit Free Press* wrote, "The horror of Manase's story is only magnified by the quietness of its telling."

Booklist reviewer Bonnie Johnston called it "a monstrous tale," and said the book "is written with a lyrical beauty that only underscores the horror Manase's life becomes." Shirley N. Quan wrote in *Library Journal* that Okuizumi's "well-drawn characters reveal the depth of the human psyche." William Ferguson wrote in the *New York Times Book Review* that the recurring image of the cave "in dreams and in waking life, suggests that this ostensibly realistic novel is in fact an allegory of expiation, a symbolic protest against the passivity that so often accompanies gratuitous cruelty." In a *Los Angeles Times Book Review* article, the writer

called *The Stones Cry Out* an "expansive work, delving into frightening territory."

BIOGRAPHICAL/CRITICAL SOURCES:

PERIODICALS

Booklist, November 15, 1998, Bonnie Johnston, review of *The Stones Cry Out,* p. 568.
Detroit Free Press, March 14, 1998, David B. Livingstone, "A Life Comes Unraveled in Postwar Japan."
Kirkus Reviews, December 15, 1998, review of *The Stones Cry Out,* p. 1754.
Library Journal, October 15, 1998, Shirley N. Quan, review of *The Stones Cry Out,* p. 100.
Los Angeles Times Book Review, February 1, 1999, review of *The Stones Cry Out,* p. 8.
New York Times Book Review, July 4, 1999, William Ferguson, review of *The Stones Cry Out,* p. 15.
Publishers Weekly, December 7, 1998, review of *The Stones Cry Out,* p. 50.
World & I, November, 1994, p. 346.
World Literature Today, autumn, 1999, review of *The Stones Cry Out,* p. 825.

OTHER

Alumni Open Lecture Series, http://subsite.icu.ac.jp/prc/bird/birdsong—e/v.41/63.html (March 26, 2001), Hikaru Okuizumi, "Resisting the Age of the Senses."
ICU Gazette, http://www.icu.ac.jp/NEWS/E-org/ (March 26, 2001), *Birdsong,* Hikaru Okuizumi and Koichi Namiki, "Reality is Multifaceted.*"

*   *   *

OOKA, Shohei 1909-1988

PERSONAL: Born March 6, 1909, in Tokyo, Japan; died of cerebral infarction, December 25, 1988, in Tokyo, Japan; married; children: one daughter, one son. *Education:* Kyoto University, received degree in French literature, 1932.

CAREER: Writer. Translator for Teikoku Sanso Corp., 1938-c. 44; lecturer in French literature at Meiji University, 1952-57. *Military service:* Japanese Army, 1944-45.

AWARDS, HONORS: Grant, Rockefeller Foundation, 1953; Shincho Prize and Mainichi Prize, both 1961, both for *Kaei;* Yokomitsu Prize, for *Furiyoki.*

WRITINGS:

IN ENGLISH TRANSLATION

Furyoki (novel), Sogensha (Tokyo, Japan), 1948, translated by Wayne P. Lammers as *Taken Captive: A Japanese P.O.W.'s Story,* Wiley (New York, NY), 1996.

Nobi (novel), Chikuma Shobo (Tokyo, Japan), 1952, translated by Ivan Morris as *Fires on the Plain,* Knopf (New York, NY), 1957.

Kaei, Shinchosha (Tokyo, Japan), 1961, translated by Dennis Washburn as *The Shade of Blossoms,* Center of Japanese Studies, University of Michigan (Ann Arbor, MI), 1998.

OTHER

Tominaga taro shishu, Sogensha (Tokyo, Japan), 1949.

Sanhose no seibo, Sakuhinsha (Tokyo, Japan), 1950.

Musashino Fujin (novel; title means "A Woman of the Musashino Plain"), Kodansha (Tokyo, Japan), 1950.

Kinomiya shinju, Shinchosha (Tokyo, Japan), 1951.

Chichi (novel; title means "Father"), 1951.

Sanso (novel; title means "Oxygen"), 1952.

Ooka Shohei shu, Kawade Shobo (Tokyo, Japan), 1952.

Shi to shosetsu no aida, Sogensha (Tokyo, Japan), 1952.

Haha, Bungeishunjushinsha (Tokyo, Japan), 1952.

Waga shi waga tomo, Sogensha (Tokyo, Japan), 1953.

Kesho, Shinchosha (Tokyo, Japan), 1954.

Zarutsuburuku no koeda, Shinchosha (Tokyo, Japan), 1956.

Akage no reddomen, Tokyosogensha (Tokyo, Japan), 1956.

Mebana (fiction), Shinchosha (Tokyo, Japan), 1957.

Asa no Uta (biography; title means "A Morning Song"), Kadokawa Shoten (Tokyo, Japan), 1958.

Hanakage (fiction), Chuo Koronsha (Tokyo, Japan), 1961.

Wakakusa Monogatari (novel; title means "A Story of Tender Shoots"; first serialized in the evening edition of *Asahi shimbun*), 1961-1962.

Joshikiteki bungakuron (literary criticism), Kodansha (Tokyo, Japan), 1962.

Bundan ronsojutsu (literary criticism), Sekkasha (Tokyo, Japan), 1962.

Gendai shosetsu sakuho, Daisanbunmeisha (Tokyo, Japan), 1962.

Uta to shi to sora, Kobunsha (Tokyo, Japan), 1962.

Bungakuteki sovieto kiko, Kodansha (Tokyo, Japan), 1963.

Masakadoki (fiction), Chuo Koronsha (Tokyo, Japan), 1966.

Shomonki, Chuo Koronsha (Tokyo, Japan), 1966.

Horyoki, Chikuma Shobo (Tokyo, Japan), 1966.

Sonzoi no tankyu, Gakugei Shorin (Tokyo, Japan), 1967.

Haruka naru danchi: Gendai kigeki, Kodansha (Tokyo, Japan), 1967.

Arishi hi no uta: Nakahara Chuya no shi, Kadokawa Shoten (Tokyo, Japan), 1967.

(With others) *Nikki shokan,* Kadokawashoten (Tokyo, Japan), 1968.

Saisho no shogeki, Gakugei Shorin (Tokyo, Japan), 1968.

Showa bungaku eno shogen, Bungei Shunju (Tokyo, Japan), 1969.

Mindoro to hutatabi, Chuo Koronsha (Tokyo, Japan), 1969.

Ai ni tsuite, Shinchosha (Tokyo, Japan), 1970.

Senso, Taikosha (Tokyo, Japan), 1970.

Ooka Shohei shu, Shinchosha (Tokyo, Japan), 1971.

Haha rokuya, Shinchosha (Tokyo, Japan), 1971.

Reite senki, Chuo Koronsha (Tokyo, Japan), 1971.

Leyte senki, Chuo Koronsha (Tokyo, Japan), 1971.

Senso to bungaku to: Ooka Shohei taidan shu, Chuo Koronsha (Tokyo, Japan), 1972.

Gendai shosetsu sakuho, Daisan Bunmeisha (Tokyo, Japan), 1972.

Corsica kiko, Chuo Koronsha (Tokyo, Japan), 1972.

Watakushi jishin eno shogen, Chuo Koronsha (Tokyo, Japan), 1972.

Nakahara Chuya zenshishu, Kadokawashoten (Tokyo, Japan), 1972.

Kootta honoo, Kodansha (Tokyo, Japan), 1972.

Korushika kiko, Chuo Koronsha (Tokyo, Japan), 1972.

Ooka Shohei zenshu, Chuo Koronsha (Tokyo, Japan), 1973.

Sakka to sakuhin no aida, Daisan Bunmeisha (Tokyo, Japan), 1973.

Higashi to Nishi no hazama de, kindai Nihon bunka o kataru, Asahi Shuppansha (Tokyo, Japan), 1973.

Yonen (autobiography), Ushio Shuppansha (Tokyo, Japan), 1973.

Moya (travel), Kodansha (Tokyo, Japan), 1973.

Tenchugumi, Kodansha (Tokyo, Japan), 1974.

Rekishi shosetsu no mondai, Bungei Shunju (Tokyo, Japan), 1974.

Shomonki, Chuo Koronsha (Tokyo, Japan), 1975.

Shonen: Aru jiden no kokoromi, Chikuma Shobo (Tokyo, Japan), 1975.

Waga bungaku seikatsu, Chuo Koronsha (Tokyo, Japan), 1975.

Bungaku ni okeru kyo to jitsu, Kodansha (Tokyo, Japan), 1976.

Sakura to ginnan, Mainichi Shinbunsha (Tokyo, Japan), 1976.

Mindoro-to futatabi, Chuo Koronsha (Tokyo, Japan), 1976.

Waga biteki senno: Geijutsu esse, Bancho Shobo (Tokyo, Japan), 1976.

Jiken, Shinchosha (Tokyo, Japan), 1977.

Aru hojuhei no tatakai, Gendaishi Shuppankai (Tokyo, Japan), 1977.

Me to bungaku: Gendai no zuiso (essays), Nihon Shoseki (Tokyo, Japan), 1978.

Zarutsuburuku no koeda: Amerika. Europpa kiko, Chuo Koronsha (Tokyo, Japan), 1978.

Waga fukuin waga sengo, Gendaishi Suppankai (Tokyo, Japan), 1978.

Raigu shinju, Shueisha (Tokyo, Japan), 1978.

San so, Shinchosha (Tokyo, Japan), 1979.

Bungaku no kanosei, Sakuhinsha (Tokyo, Japan), 1980.

Hamletto nikki, Shinchosha (Tokyo, Japan), 1980.

Hamuretto nikki, Shinchosha (Tokyo, Japan), 1980.

Seijo dayori, Bungei Shunju (Tokyo, Japan), 1981.

Aoi hikari, Shinchosha (Tokyo, Japan), 1981.

Sei to uta: Nakahara Chuya sonogo, Kadokawa Shoten (Tokyo, Japan), 1982.

Nagai tabi, Shinchosha (Tokyo, Japan), 1982.

Muzai, Shinchosha (Tokyo, Japan), 1982.

Kantsu no kigogaku, Bungei Shunju (Tokyo, Japan), 1984.

Kumo no shozo, Shinchosha (Tokyo, Japan), 1984.

Yamai, Sakuhinsha (Tokyo, Japan), 1985.

Sakai-ko joi shimatsu, Chuo Koronsha (Tokyo, Japan), 1989.

Translator of works by such writers as Stendhal and Balzac.

ADAPTATIONS: Nobi was adapted for film by writer Natto Wada and director Kon Ichikawa in 1959.

SIDELIGHTS: Ooka Shohei was a prolific Japanese writer who produced more than eighty publications during a career that spanned six decades. After graduating from Kyoto University, he began producing criticism for various periodicals. He then worked as a translator for a Japanese corporation. He served in the Japanese army during World War II, and he was captured by American forces before the war ended in 1945.

Ooka derived his first well-known work, *Furyoki* (published in translation as *Taken Captive: A Japanese P.O.W.'s Story*), from his wartime experiences as a prisoner of war. In this autobiographical novel, he addresses the Japanese notion of honor, which is compromised by captivity. As John Glenn reported in the *New York Times Book Review,* "Captivity was bewildering because Japanese military indoctrination prevented the prisoners from accepting the Americans' warmheartedness with simple gratitude." Keiko McDonald, writing in the *Journal of the Association of Teachers of Japanese,* acknowledged that *Furyoki* was the work that managed to "establish [Ooka] as one of Japan's most promising and innovative postwar writers." McDonald noted that "Ooka uses an ingenious technique of combining retrospection and analysis in order to achieve his insight." In addition, McDonald described *Furyoki* as "both a compelling story and an influential development in autobiographical writing." Janet Goff, meanwhile, wrote in *Japan Quarterly* that Ooka is "a shrewd observer of human behavior" and that his book provides "a vivid picture of the society that formed inside the abnormal confines of the prison camp." Another reviewer, Roland Green, wrote in *Booklist* that *Taken Captive* "makes a major addition to English reader's knowledge of how World War II looked from the Japanese perspective"; Erick R. Lofgren, in his *World Literature Today* assessment, hailed the book as "a welcome addition to the corpus of Japanese literature accessible in English."

Among Ooka's next publications of note is *Nobi,* a 1952 novel about a desperate Japanese soldier's horrifying return home at the end of World War II. The novel's events are recalled by the hero as he writes from a mental institution. Neil H. Donahue described the hero's recollections in a *Comparative Literature Studies* essay as "a personal account of his war experiences with the political intention of unveiling the atrocities of war to a population he views as susceptible to militant, nationalist excesses." Another essayist, Dennis Washburn, acknowledged in *Journal of Japanese Studies* that *Fires on the Plain* "has been widely acclaimed as one of the finest Japanese novels on the subject of war." Washburn declared that the novel serves as "much more than a merely sensational account of the horrors of war," and he observed that it "raises important issues about guilt and responsibility."

Among Ooka's other works in English translation is *Kaei,* a 1961 book that appeared in the late 1990s as *The Shade of Blossoms.* A *Publishers Weekly* reviewer described the work as "the haunting story of an aging nightclub courtesan." The novel's heroine is Yoko Adachi, a thirty-eight-year-old woman who suddenly calls a halt to her affair with a married man, then resumes her job as a bar hostess in which capacity she observes younger women scheming to exploit sexual partners for financial gain. The *Publishers Weekly* critic concluded that "there is great pathos in this story." Another reviewer, Davide Galef, wrote in the *New York Times Book Review* that Yoko possesses "a definite sense of self-esteem, which makes her romantic entanglements and spiritual descent all the more affecting."

BIOGRAPHICAL/CRITICAL SOURCES:

PERIODICALS

Booklist, May 15, 1996, Roland Green, review of *Taken Captive: A Japanese P.O.W.'s Story,* p. 567.

Comparative Literature Studies, Volume 1, number 1, 1987, Neil H. Donahue, "An East-West Comparison of Two War Novels: Alfred Andersch's *Die Kirschen der Freiheit* and Shohei Ooka's *Fires on the Plain,*" pp. 58-82.

Japan Quarterly, October-December, 1997, Janet Goff, review of *Taken Captive: A Japanese P.O.W.'s Story,* pp. 107-108.

Journal of Japanese Studies, winter, 1997, Dennis Washburn, "Toward a View from Nowhere: Perspective and Ethical Judgment in *Fires on the Plain,*" 105-131.

Journal of the Association of Japanese Teachers, April, 1987, Keiko McDonald, "Ooka's Examination of the Self in *A POW's Memoirs,*" pp. 15-36.

New York Times Book Review, September 1, 1996, John Glenn, review of *Taken Captive: A Japanese P.O.W.'s Story;* October 25, 1998, David Galef, review of *The Shade of Blossoms.*

Publishers Weekly, April 1, 1996, review of *Taken Captive: A Japanese P.O.W.'s Story,* p. 65; July 27, 1998, review of *The Shade of Blossoms,* p. 52.

World Literature Today, spring, 1997, Erick R. Lofgren, review of *Taken Captive: A Japanese P.O.W.'s Story,* p. 462.*

*   *   *

OTERO, Gerardo 1952-

PERSONAL: Born August 4, 1952, in Torreón, Coahuila, Mexico; son of Napoleón Otero-San-Vicente (a field geologist) and Yolanda Rodríguez-González; married C. Patricia Ordóñez-de-la-Peña (a teacher), December 21, 1974; children: G. Alejandro Otero-Ordóñez, Rodrigo Otero-Ordóñez. *Ethnicity:* "Hispanic." *Education:* Instituto Tecnológico y de Estudios Superiores de Monterrey, B.A., 1975; University of Texas, M.A., 1977; University of Wisconsin, Ph.D., 1986. *Politics:* "Social democrat." *Religion:* Christian.

ADDRESSES: Office—Department of Sociology, 220 Newcomb Hall, Tulane University, New Orleans, LA; fax: 504-865-5544. *E-mail*—otero@tulane.edu.

CAREER: Universidad Autonoma de Puebla, Mexico, assistant professor, 1980-83, acting chair, Department of Social Anthropology, 1982; University of California—San Diego, La Jolla, CA, visiting postdoctoral fellow, 1986-87; University of Guadalajara, Guadalajara, Mexico, research professor, 1987-90; Simon Fraser University, Vancouver, BC, Canada, assistant professor, 1990-93, associate professor, 1993-2000; affiliated with Tulane University, New Orleans, LA, 2001—. Research consultant to various organizations, including the Presidency of Mexico, 1981, International Labour Organization (Geneva, Switzerland), 1988 and 1990, Interamerican Institute for Cooperation in Agriculture (Costa Rica), 1989, and United Nations Convention on Biological Diversity (Montreal), 1999; University of Wisconsin—Madison, visiting senior lecturer, 1989-90; presenter of more than forty papers at professional and scholarly meetings.

MEMBER: International Sociological Association, American Sociological Association, Rural Sociological Society, Latin American Studies Association, Canadian Association for Mexican Studies (president, 1996-98).

AWARDS, HONORS: Fellowships, University of Texas, 1975-77, Consejo Nacional de Ciencia y Tecnologia, 1978-80, and Organization of American States, 1984-85; research grants, Social Sciences and Humanities Research Council of Canada, 1994-97 and 1997-2000.

WRITINGS:

(Editor and contributor) *Neoliberalism Revisited: Economic Restructuring and Mexico's Political Future,* Westview (Boulder, CO), 1996.

Farewell to the Peasantry?: Political Class Formation in Rural Mexico, Westview (Boulder, CO), 1999.

Contributor of chapters to books, including *Searching for Agrarian Reform in Latin America,* edited by William Thiesenhusen, Unwin Hyman (Boston, MA), 1989; *America and the Americas,* edited by Jacques Zylberberg and Francois Demers, Les Presses de L'Université Laval (Sainte-Foy), 1992; and *The Transformation of Rural Mexico: Reforming the Ejido Sector,* edited by Wayne Cornelius and David Myhre, Center for U.S.-Mexican Studies, University of California—San Diego (La Jolla, CA), 1998. Contributor of articles to periodicals, including *Latin American Per-*

spectives, Latin American Research Review, Rural Sociology, Canadian Review of Sociology and Anthropology, Sociological Forum, Indian Food Industry, and *Journal of Peasant Studies.* Contributor of book reviews to periodicals, including *Contemporary Sociology, Journal of World Systems Research, Rural Sociology, Journal of Developing Societies,* and *Society and Natural Resources.*

WORK IN PROGRESS: *Sweetness and NAFTA: State Policy and Employment in the Sugar Industries of Canada, Mexico and the United States.*

* * *

OWEN, David Lanyon Lloyd   1917-2001

OBITUARY NOTICE—See index for *CA* sketch: Born October 10, 1917, in Hampton, England; died April 5, 2001. Soldier and author. Owen was a career soldier who commanded the Long Range Desert Group (LRDG) for two years during World War II. Owen graduated from the Royal Military Academy Sandhurst and in 1938 received a commission in the Queen's Royal Regiment. He served in the Middle East and then had an administrative post, but heard about the secret LRDG and was immediately interested. He was offered a position with the special-forces group and took part in a number of operations in enemy territory in Libya, Egypt, Lebanon and Sudan. Although severely wounded in 1942, Owen was later able to rejoin his unit and after the commanding officer was killed, Owen was put in command. After the war Owen continued in a variety of posts around the world including military assistant to High Commissioner in Malaya, commander of 1st Queen's Royal Regiment, commander of 24th Infantry Brigade Group and commander of Cyprus District. He retired as a major general in 1972. He wrote two memoirs about his time with the LRDG: *The Desert My Dwelling Place,* published in 1957, and *Providence Their Guide,* in 1980.

OBITUARIES AND OTHER SOURCES:

PERIODICALS

Daily Telegraph (London, England), April 7, 2001, p. 32.
Guardian (London, England), April 16, 2001, p. 18; April 21, 2001, p. 17.
Times (London, England), April 7, 2001, p. 27.

OWEN, Henry D.   1920-

PERSONAL: Born August 26, 1920, in New York, NY. *Education:* Harvard University, A.B., 1941.

ADDRESSES: Office—1616 H St. N.W., Washington, DC 20006-4903.

CAREER: U.S. Department of State, Washington, DC, economist, 1946-55, member of policy planning staff, 1955-62, deputy counselor and vice-chairperson, 1962-66, then chairperson of policy planning council, 1966-69; Brookings Institution, Washington, DC, director of foreign policy studies, 1969-77; U.S. Department of State, personal representative of the president (with rank of ambassador), 1977-81; Salomon Brothers, Washington, DC, senior adviser, 1981—. *Military service:* U.S. Navy, 1942-46; became lieutenant.

WRITINGS:

(Editor) *The Next Phase in U.S. Foreign Policy,* Brookings Institution (Washington, DC), 1973.
(With François Duchene and Kinhide Mushakoji) *The Crisis of International Cooperation: A Report of the Trilateral Political Task Force to the Executive Committee of the Trilateral Commission,* Trilateral Commission, Trilateral Task Force on Constructive Trilateral- Communist Cooperation on Global Problems (New York, NY), 1974.
(With Charles Schultze) *Setting National Priorities: The Next Ten Years,* Brookings Institution (Washington, DC), 1976.
(With Chihiro Hosoya and Andrew Shonfield) *Collaboration with Communist Countries in Managing Global Problems: An Examination of the Options,* Trilateral Commission, Trilateral Task Force on Constructive Trilateral-Communist Cooperation on Global Problems (New York, NY), 1977.
(Editor with Edward R. Fried) Robert S. McNamara and others, *The Future Role of the World Bank: Addresses,* Brookings Institution (Washington, DC), 1982.

BIOGRAPHICAL/CRITICAL SOURCES:

PERIODICALS

America, September 29, 1973, P. J. Weber, review of *The Next Phase in Foreign Policy.*
Choice, December, 1973, review of *The Next Phase in Foreign Policy.*
Commonweal, January 21, 1977.
Library Journal, August, 1973, R. F. Delaney, review of *The Next Phase in Foreign Policy.*

New Republic, June 30, 1973, C. G. Bolte, review of
   The Next Phase in Foreign Policy.
Times Literary Supplement, September 21, 1973.
Virginia Quarterly Review, autumn, 1973.*

* * *

OZIEBLO, Barbara 1948-

PERSONAL: Born March 10, 1948, in London, En-
gland. *Ethnicity:* "European." *Education:* University of
London, B.A. (honors), 1970; University of Salamanca,
Ph.D., 1984.

ADDRESSES: Office—Departamento de Filologia In-
glesa, Facultad de Filosofia y Letras, Universidad de
Málaga, 29071, Málaga, Spain; fax: 34-52-131843. *E-
mail*—ozieblo@uma.es.

CAREER: Various full-time English teaching posts,
Madrid, 1971-78; National High School (INB. Torre-
molinos), Málaga, head of Department of English,
1978-82; University of Málaga, Department of English,
part-time lecturer, 1978-82, full-time lecturer, 1982-86,
Professor Titular of American Literature, 1986—, director, Department of English and French, 1987-89,
dean, Facultad de Filosofia y Letras, 1995-97. Presenter
at conferences; speaker in various venues, including
universities.

MEMBER: Asociación de Estudios Históricos sobre la
Mujer (president, 1993-95; vice-president, 1995—).

WRITINGS:

El protagonista de Jerzy Kosinski: personaje único,
   Universidades de Málaga y Salamanca (Málaga y
   Salamanca, Spain), 1986.
(Editor) *Conceptos y metodologia in los estudios sobre
   la mujer,* Universidad de Málaga, Colección
   Atenea (Málaga), 1993.
(Editor and author of introduction) *The Provincetown
   Players: A Choice of the Shorter Plays,* Sheffield
   Academic Press (Sheffield), 1994.
*Cien años de lucha: la consecución del voto in los Esta-
   dos Unidos,* Diputación de Málaga, Colección
   Biblioteca de Estudios sobre la Mujer (Málaga),
   1996.
(Editor and author of introduction) *El Vinculo
   poderoso: madres e hijas in la literatura
   norteamericana,* Universidad de Granada (Gra-
   nada), 1998.
Susan Glaspell: A Critical Biography, University of
   North Carolina Press, 2000.

Contributor of more than fifteen chapters and articles
to books, and articles to various other publications, including *Alalba, Atlantis,* and *Revista Alicantina de Estudios Ingleses.* Editorial board, *Analecta Malacitana,*
1986-89, *Atlantis,* 1986-90, *Hojas de Warmi,* 1998—.

WORK IN PROGRESS: A critical biography of Gamel
Woolsey and Alyse Gregory; research on "American
women dramatists."

P-Q

PAGE, Philip 1942-

PERSONAL: Born August 11, 1942, in Fayette, MO; son of Eugene R. and Helen F. Page; children: Katherine, Elliot. *Ethnicity:* "Caucasian." *Education:* Oberlin College, B.A., 1964; Washington University, M.A., 1966; Johns Hopkins University, Ph.D., 1973.

ADDRESSES: Home—4710 Somerset Dr., Riverside, CA 92507. *E-mail*—ppage@csusb.edu.

CAREER: Monmouth College, IL, instructor, 1966-69; University of Wisconsin, Madison, lecturer, 1973-74; University of Wisconsin Center System, half-time lecturer, 1983-85; California State Polytechnic University, Pomona, and Riverside Community College, lecturer, 1987-88; California State University, San Bernardino, lecturer, 1989-92, assistant professor, 1992-95, associate professor, 1995-98, professor of English, 1998—, department chair, 1999—. Presenter at conferences.

AWARDS, HONORS: Summer research grant, California State University, 1993; summer study grant, National Endowment for the Humanities, 1994; Eudora Welty Prize and Toni Morrison Society Book Prize, both 1996, both for *Dangerous Freedom; Reclaiming Community in Contemporary African-American Fiction* named by *Choice* as one of the best academic books of 1999.

WRITINGS:

Dangerous Freedom: Fusion and Fragmentation in Toni Morrison's Novels, Mississippi University Press (Jackson, MS), 1996.
Reclaiming Community in Contemporary African-American Fiction, Mississippi University Press (Jackson, MS), 1999.

Contributor to *The Critical Response to Gloria Naylor,* edited by Sharon Felton and Michele C. Loris, Greenwood (Westport, CT), 1997; *Toni Morrison's Sula,* edited by Harold Bloom, Chelsea House (Philadelphia, PA), 1999; and *Gloria Naylor's Early Novels,* edited by Margot Anne Kelley, University Press of Florida, in press. Contributor of articles and reviews to journals, including *African American Review, Mosaic, University of Mississippi Studies in English, Studies in Short Fiction, Tennessee Studies in Literature* and *American Literature.*

SIDELIGHTS: Philip Page told *CA:* "I guess my impulse to write derives from a couple of compulsions. When I am fascinated by a literary work—-for me, almost always prose fiction—I feel compelled to reread it, to chew on it, to develop my interpretation of it, and then to express my views to my students, to colleagues at conferences, and in print. Fortunately, that inner drive dovetails with external pressures to teach well and to maintain a record of scholarly achievement. For example, my first book happened to be accepted for publication just in time to push over the top my request for promotion to associate professor, and, strangely enough, my second book was similarly timed for my promotion to professor.

"Both books—and my work on contemporary African-American fiction—began during Christmas vacation of 1988 when my daughter came home from college reading Toni Morrison's *Beloved.* She couldn't put it down; she wouldn't talk to us. When she finished, my wife and I read it as fast as possible, as totally absorbed in it as my daughter had been. I knew instantly that I had to reread it, teach it, write about it, and read more of Morrison's novels. I did teach it many times, starting the following spring. Students react differently to Morrison than to any other writer I've taught: they say things like, 'I'm so glad you had us read Morrison' and '*Beloved* changed my life.' In some ways my first book, *Dangerous Freedom,* was an attempt to explain why my students, and Americans in general, are so intrigued by Morrison's fiction.

"My second book grew out of my work on Morrison. After reading and writing about her fiction, it seemed natural to read more contemporary—and earlier—African-American fiction. With the help of a summer reading grant from the National Endowment for the Humanities, I read as much as I could, and the result was my look at the work of five contemporary African-American fiction writers."

*   *   *

PAKSOY, H. B. 1948-
(Hasan B. Paksoy, H. Bulent Paksoy)

PERSONAL: Born 1948. *Education:* Trinity University, Texas, B.S., 1970; University of Texas, M.A., 1976; Oxford University, England, D.Phil., 1987.

ADDRESSES: Home—P.O. Box 2321, Amherst, MA 01004-2321. *Office*—Franklin University, 201 South Grant Ave., Columbus, OH 43215. *E-mail*—Paksoy@babbage.franklin.edu.; Paksoy@franklin.edu.

CAREER: Harvard University, Center for Middle Eastern Studies, faculty associate, 1986-94; Central Connecticut State University, New Britain, CT, Department of History, instructor, 1987-90; University of Massachusetts, Amherst, MA, instructor, 1990-91; consulting editor/writer, NBC News, Moscow, Radio Free Europe-Radio Liberty, Paris, Munich, *Economist,* London, Voice of America, Washington, DC, Woodrow Wilson Center for International Scholars, Smithsonian Institution, Washington, DC, 1994-96; Franklin University, Department of Intercultural Studies, 1996—; Ohio State University, Department of History, sabbatical replacement, 1999-2000.

Cofounder, telecommunications project, Texas Scottish Rite Crippled Children's Hospital, Dallas, TX, 1980; chairman, youth services committee, 1980-81, chairman, world community services committee, 1981-82, Park Cities Rotary Club, Dallas.

AWARDS, HONORS: Received grants from NSF, 1976-77, Committee of Vice Chancellors and Principles of Universities of the United Kingdom, 1983-86, Society for Central Asian Studies, Oxford, 1984, Japanese Ministry of Education, 1991, and Fondation Nationale des Sciences Politiques, Centre D'Etudes et de Recherches Internationales, Paris, 1991; travel grantee, International Research and Exchanges Board, 1992.

MEMBER: Association for Advancement of Central Asian Research, Inc. (founding editor of AACAR bulletin, founding president, 1988-90, member executive council, 1990—), American Association for the Advancement of Slavic Studies, American Historical Association, Association for Asian Studies, Association for Study of Nationalities of U.S.S.R., Middle Eastern Studies Association, Permanent International Altaistic Conference, Oxford Society (founder Conn. br., 1987, honorary secretary, 1987-90).

WRITINGS:

Alpamysh: Central Asian Identity under Russian Rule, Association for the Advancement of Central Asian Research (Hartford, CT), 1989.
(Editor, under name Hasan B. Paksoy) *Central Asian Monuments,* Isis Press (Beylerbeyi, Istanbul), 1992.
(Editor and translator) *Central Asia Reader: The Rediscovery of History,* M. E. Sharpe (Armonk, NY), 1994.
(Under name H. Bulent Paksoy) *Turk Tarihi, Toplumlarin Mayasi ve Uygarlik,* Mazhar Zorlu Holding, Kultur Sanat Yayini (Ismir, Turkey), 1997.
(Editor, with David Sconyers) *Intercultural Studies,* 1998.
Essays on Central Asia, Carrie (Lawrence, KS), 1999.

SIDELIGHTS: H. B. Paksoy is a scholar in the field of Middle Eastern studies, focusing on the fate of the Asian cultures under the rule of the Soviets. His book *Central Asia Reader: The Rediscovery of History* collects nineteen essays or excerpts from larger documents written by Central Asians attempting to rediscover or reinvent political, historical, or cultural identities since the demise of the Soviet Union. In *Central Asian Monuments,* editor Paksoy collects essays and fiction that reference some of the most important literature written by Central Asians, as evidenced by their influence on contemporary political, literary, and historical writings by Central Asians.

BIOGRAPHICAL/CRITICAL SOURCES:

PERIODICALS

Harvard Middle Eastern and Islamic Review, February, 1994, review of *Central Asian Monuments.**

* * *

PAKSOY, H. Bulent
See PAKSOY, H. B.

* * *

PAKSOY, Hasan B.
See PAKSOY, H. B.

* * *

PALMER, Tony 1941-

PERSONAL: Born 1941, in London, England; raised by godparents Bert (a railway engineer) and Elsie Spencer. *Avocational interests:* Walking.

ADDRESSES: Office—Nanjizal House, St. Levan, Cornwall TR19 6JH, England.

CAREER: Writer, director, and film and theatre producer. Worked for the British Broadcasting Corporation (BBC) during the late 1960s. Director of films, including *All My Loving* and *Farewell, Cream,* both 1968; *200 Motels,* 1971; *A Time There Was,* 1979; *At the Haunted End of the Day,* 1980; *Once at a Border,* 1981; *Wagner,* 1982; *God Rot Tunbridge Wells,* 1985; *Maria,* 1986; *Testimony,* 1987; *The Children,* 1989; *Menuhin,* 1990; *The Symphony of Sorrowful Songs,* 1993; *England, My England,* 1995; *Parsifal,* 1998; *The Kindness of Strangers,* 1999; and *The Harvest of Sorrow,* 1999. Director of stage performances, including *John Osborne's Deja Vu,* 1992, and numerous operas.

MEMBER: Garrick Club.

AWARDS, HONORS: Italia prizes, 1979, for *A Time There Was,* 1980, for *At teh Haunted End of the Day;* Special Jury Prize, San Francisco Film Festival, 1981, for *Once at a Border;* Best Drama citations, New York

Film and Television Festival, 1982, for *Wagner,* 1983, for *God Rot Tunbridge Wells,* 1986, for *Maria;* Fellini Prize, 1987, for *Testimony;* Gold Mask prize and first prize, Casta Diva, both 1998, both for *Parsifal;* Sony Award, 1996; numerous Emmy awards and awards from British Association of Film and Television Artists.

WRITINGS:

NONFICTION

Born under a Bad Sign (history and criticism), illustrated by Ralph Steadman, Kimber (London, England), 1970.
The Trials of Oz, Blond & Briggs (London, England), 1971.
Electric Revolution, 1972.
Biography of Liberace, 1976.
All You Need Is Love: The Story of Popular Music, edited by Paul Medlicott, Grossman (New York, NY), 1976.
Charles II: Portrait of an Age (biography), Cassell (London, England), 1979.
Julian Bream: A Life on the Road, MacDonald (London), 1982, F. Watts (New York, NY), 1983.
Menuhin: A Family Portrait (screenplay), WETA-TV, 1991.

WORK IN PROGRESS: A film about Fryderyk Chopin titled *The Strange Case of Delfina Potocka.*

SIDELIGHTS: Director and producer Tony Palmer has worked both in theatre and film during his long career which began in the 1970s. While his work for theatre has included operas produced throughout Europe as well as in his native England, Palmer's works for film focus on the lives of great musical composers. *Menuhin: A Family Portrait,* produced for public television in 1991, focuses on noted violinist Sir Yehudi Menuhin, while 1999's *The Kindness of Strangers* showcases the talents of composer, pianist, and conductor André Previn as Previn directs a stage production of Tennessee Williams's *A Streetcar Named Desire. The Harvest of Sorrow,* which Palmer also produced and directed in 1999, profiles the life of Russian composer Sergey Rachmaninoff, narrated by Sir John Gielgud through a series of letters the elderly composer wrote to his daughter in the early twentieth century. Palmer wanted to film *Harvest of Sorrow* because, as he explained to Shirley Ratcliffe in *Music and Vision,* the works the Russian composer wrote during the late nineteenth century are even more relevant a century later. "The world [Rachmaninoff] grew up in which had a social security and a religious belief [has been] disintegrating. Artists sense it in a way we ordinary mortals don't. The family and family values are vanishing. . . . The sands are shifting and a lot of us are sinking straight into them. We are slithering toward the end of a totally miserable, appalling, blood-thirsty century *but* am I talking about the end of the 19th century or the 20th century? That's why Rachmaninoff's music . . . is going to take its place among the very great." His film premiered at the Rachmaninoff festival in London in May of 1999.

BIOGRAPHICAL/CRITICAL SOURCES:

PERIODICALS

Economist (London, England), December 18, 1976, review of *All You Need Is Love.*
Guardian, September 10, 1999, Jessica Duchen, "Sex and Chopin," p. S18.
Library Journal, December 1, 1976, S. M. Fry, review of *All You Need Is Love.*
New Statesman & Society, May 10, 1999, Dermot Clinch, "Sergey Rachmaninoff: Memories," p. 36.
New York Review of Books, February 3, 1977, M. C. Miller, review of *All You Need Is Love.*
New York Times Book Review, December 12, 1976, Michael Lydon, review of *All You Need Is Love.*
Opera News, August, 1997, George W. Loomis, review of Russian production of *Parsifal,* p. 47.

OTHER

Music and Vision Daily, http://www.mvdaily.com/ (March 21, 1999), Shirley Ratcliffe, "Tony Palmer in Conversation with Shirley Ratcliffe: In Search of a Title."*

*　　*　　*

PARRISH, (Frederick) Maxfield 1870-1966

PERSONAL: Born July 25, 1870 in Philadelphia, PA; died March 30, 1966; son of Stephen (an artist) and Elizabeth (Bancroft) Parrish; married Lydia Austin (a painter), June 1, 1895; children: John Dillwyn, Maxfield, Jr., Stephen, Jean. *Education:* Haverford College, B.A., 1892; attended Pennsylvania Academy of Fine Arts and Drexel Institute. *Religion:* Quaker.

CAREER: Painter, 1890-1966; magazine illustrator, 1895-1966; book illustrator, 1897-1966.

MEMBER: Phi Kappa Sigma.

WRITINGS:

Thirty Favorite Paintings, Collier (New York, NY), 1908.

ILLUSTRATOR

L. Frank Baum, *Mother Goose in Prose,* Way & Williams (Chicago, IL), 1897.
Opie Read, *Bolanyo: A Novel,* Way & Williams (Chicago, IL), 1897.
Emma Rayner, *Free to Serve,* Copeland & Day (Boston, MA), 1897.
Albert Lee, *The Knave of Hearts: A Fourth of July Comedietta,* Russell (New York, NY), 1897.
William Mill Butler, *Whist Reference Book,* Yorkston (Philadelphia, PA), 1898.
Kenneth Grahame, *The Golden Age,* Bodley Head (London, England), 1899.
Washington Irving, *A History of New York from the Beginning of the World to the End of the Dutch Dynasty . . .,* Russell (New York, NY), 1900.
Kenneth Grahame, *Dream Days,* Bodley Head (London, England), 1902.
Arthur Cosslett Smith, *The Turquoise Cup and The Desert,* Scribner (New York, NY), 1903.
Eugene Field, *Poems of Childhood,* Scribner (New York, NY), 1904.
Edith Wharton, *Italian Villas and Their Gardens,* Century (New York, NY), 1904.
Guy Wetmore Carryl, *The Garden of Years and Other Poems,* Putnam (New York, NY), 1904.
The Arabian Nights, Their Best-Known Tales, edited by Kate Douglas Wiggin and Nora A. Smith, Scribner (New York, NY), 1909.
The Children's Book, edited by Horace Elisha Scudder, Houghton Mifflin (Boston, MA), 1910.
Nathaniel Hawthorne, *A Wonder Book and Tanglewood Tales for Girls and Boys,* Duffield (New York, NY), 1910.
Hildegarde Hawthorne, *Lure of the Garden,* Century (New York, NY), 1911.
The Golden Treasury of Songs and Lyrics, edited by Francis Turner Palgrave, Duffield (New York, NY), 1911.
King Alberts Book, edited by Thomas H. H. Caine, Daily Telegraph (London, England), 1914.
Louise Saunders, *The Knave of Hearts,* Scribner (New York, NY), 1925.
Ealeen Stein, *Troubador Tales.* Bobbs-Merrill (Indianapolis, IN), 1929.
Maxfield Parrish: A Treasury of Art and Children's Literature, compiled by Alma Gilbert, Atheneum (New York, NY), 1995.

A Treasury of Poems, compiled and edited by Laurence S. Cutler and Judy Goffman Cutler, Pomegranate (San Francisco, CA), 1998.

OTHER

The Maxfield Parrish Poster Book, introduction by Maurice Sendak, Harmony Books (New York, NY), 1974.

Maxfield Parrish, Master of Make Believe (exhibition catalog), Brandywine River Museum (Chadds Ford, PA), 1974.

"In the Beginning": Twenty-five Maxfield Parrish Drawings from the Men's Day Life Class at the Pennsylvania Academy of Fine Arts, 1892-1894, compiled by Virginia Hunt Reed, Imperial Printers (Hartford, VT), 1976.

John Goodspeed Stuart, *Young Maxfield Parrish: His Early Illustrated Letters and Sketches,* J.G. Stuart (Aurora, CO), 1992.

Maxfield Parrish: The Poster Book, introduction by Alma Gilbert, Tenn Speed Press (Berkeley, CA), 1994.

Contributor to periodical publications, including *Harper's Weekly, Ladies' Home Journal, Scribner's Magazine, Century, Life,* and *Collier's.*

SIDELIGHTS: Maxfield Parrish's rich, witty illustrations lit advertising posters, magazine covers, and art prints throughout the golden age of illustration. In that period, Parrish won high fame for his glowing visions of pretty girls and fantastic landscapes—what art critic Clement Greenberg called his "hallucinatory high-octane realism"—but he gradually left those subjects for a less commercial style. As Michael Scott Joseph summarized in *Dictionary of Literary Biography,* "Parrish was a popular artist in the best sense of the word. Supremely capable of meeting the demands of art for mass consumption, he never sacrificed his personal standards." Parrish's career was marked by loud public acclaim, great wads of cash, and an artistic sensibility that surpassed both.

Parrish was born on July 25, 1870 in Philadelphia, Pennsylvania. His parents, Stephen and Elizabeth Bancroft Parrish, were wealthy Quakers with artistic leanings; Stephen Parrish was an accomplished painter and etcher in his own right. Parrish's parents encouraged his artistic ambitions, teaching him at home and also taking him to Europe for a prolonged tour. In 1888, Parrish began college at Haverford, where he continued to draw and even began to sell some of his early work. After graduation in 1892, he continued his studies at the

Pennsylvania Academy of Fine Arts, where he was mentored by Robert W. Vonnoh and Thomas P. Anschultz. By 1893 he was already exhibiting his artwork. He accepted several commissions for the design and painting of the University of Pennsylvania's Mask and Wig Club, in which Parrish's architectural, boy's-dream aesthetic began to emerge.

During the 1890s, Parrish also studied briefly with Howard Pyle at the Drexel Institute. There he met Lydia Austin, a painter and instructor at Drexel—like Parrish, Austin was a Quaker from the northeast. The two were married on June 1, 1895, just as Parrish's first magazine covers were published. During the last years of the nineteenth century, Parrish would produce many more magazine covers, winning a reputation as one of the most desirable cover artists in the country. "Parrish employed a variety of techniques in this early magazine work," according to Joseph. "He sometimes drew with a lithographic crayon on Steinbach paper and sometimes used wash, ink, and lithographic crayon. Afterward, he photographed his illustrations and colored the prints. He then varnished them and finished them in oil glazes when they were dry." The fine-tuned process generated luminous, fairy-tale like artwork that seemed ideally suited to children's books.

Parrish began illustrating children's books in 1897, with L. Frank Baum's *Mother Goose in Prose.* Parrish's drawings show to advantage his humor and fancy, but also display his sense of architectural design. Joseph explained that "the landscape of *Mother Goose in Prose* evokes a bygone era that actually never was. Like the imaginary worlds of the late-Victorian illustrators such as Edmund Dulac and Arthur Rackham, the world of Parrish's *Mother Goose in Prose* fancifully conflates elements of divergent periods and milieus: its castled towns synthesize Gothic and Dutch architectural motifs that invite a mood of nostalgic longing for a moment in history when, one imagines, medieval grandeur might have been wedded to bourgeois civility."

Parrish's strong sense of architectural form also led him, in 1898, to construct his famous, eccentrically designed home, The Oaks of Cornish, New Hampshire. There, he and his wife raised their four children while Parrish created his world-famous illustrations in a gargantuan art studio just over the lawn. The Oaks, as Joseph explained, was central both to Parrish's reputation and to his creativity, as the house "commanded public attention through articles written about it in many architectural journals. Parrish himself often borrowed some of the architectural features from The Oaks for his book and magazine illustrations; its latches and intricate hinges, for example, appear in the castle setting of his illustrations for *The Knave of Hearts,* written by Parrish's neighbor Louise Sanders."

Parrish's sense of architectural design runs throughout his artwork; his children's books, for example, often utilize a geometric sense of form in order to evoke emotional states. Joseph emphasized that "geometric designs recur throughout Parrish's work and reflect the artist's adherence to Jay Hambidge's neoclassical theory of Dynamic Symmetry, which involves laying out designs and compositions as a series of divisions based upon the rectangle" The three-dimensional quality of his drawings were heightened, moreover, by Parrish's innovation of working in colored glazes. The glazes offered a sort of translucent quality, enabling viewers to look through his work, not just at it.

During the early years of the twentieth century, Parrish continued to be the most highly demanded and highly paid of magazine illustrators. He worked for *Century, Ladies' Home Journal* and others while also producing luminous pictures for Eugene Field's *Poems of Childhood* and Edith Wharton's *Italian Villas and Their Gardens,* both published in 1904. He also began painting children's illustrations on a grander scale, including a thirty-by-eight foot mural of *Old King Cole,* a mural of *The Pied Piper,* and another of *Sing a Song of Sixpence.* He also created an eighteen-panel mural for the Curtis Publishing Company Building that dazzled the critics. A contributor to the *Ladies' Home Journal,* for example, marveled at Parrish's depiction of "a land where nobody is old," and further noted that "the whole will be a wonderfully successful result of the artist's idea to present a series of paintings that will refresh and 'you-then' the spirit and yet will not tire the eye."

In this period, youth seems to have charmed Parrish in other ways; he began to live with his very young model, Sue Lewin, in his large studio. They lived together from 1911 to 1953, during which time Parrish painted Lewin in such notable works as *The Lantern Bearers, Rubaiyat, Djer Kiss, Garden of Allah,* and the enormously popular *Daybreak,* which was completed in 1922. This last painting—which Hilarie M. Sheets called "a subtly erotic vision of youth set in an Arcadian landscape"—was his first painting commissioned as a mass-produced print. Joseph describes its extraordinary appeal: "The painting became the decorating sensation of the decade as hotels exhibited it in their lobbies; housewives used it to brighten their kitchens or dining rooms; and collegians accorded it a place of pride among their pennants, crew oars, fencing foils, and moose heads."

The original, moreover, sold for a whopping $10,000 at the Scott and Fowles gallery in New York.

After this dizzying level of success, however, Parrish backed out of commercial art. He had always considered illustration a congenial means of showing his work, but after the 1930s, the sixty-year-old Parrish began to focus on figureless landscapes and fantasy lands. Though he created work for General Electric and for Edison Mazda lamps, Parrish's work became less prominent in the illustration world. In 1925, Parrish completed his last illustrated book, Louise Sanders's *The Knave of Hearts,* which Joseph calls "his unquestionable masterpiece," adding that the illustrations' "printed in rich colors on heavy, coated stock, the bold, rectangular compositions; deep and luminous landscapes; elaborate costumes; droll improvisations; tender Pre-Raphaelite youths; and the vigorous old monarch coalesce to give *The Knave of Hearts* a singular visual opulence."

Parrish continued to create art until his death in 1966; though he turned away from the enormous money-making and fame-generating artwork of his middle period, Parrish found a thematic freedom that illustration couldn't offer him. He seemed to find his own tremendous monetary success untrustworthy as a marker of his artistic value; he once remarked ruefully that "there are countless artists whose shoes I am not worthy to polish whose prints would not pay the printer." His enormous success as an illustrator provided him with tremendous rewards, including his final period of creativity, in which he used his wealth and reputation to create only what he thought beautiful.

BIOGRAPHICAL/CRITICAL SOURCES:

BOOKS

Cutler, Laurence, C., and Judy Goffman Cutler, *Maxfield Parrish: A Retrospective,* Pomegranate (San Francisco, CA), 1995.

Dictionary of Literary Biography, Volume 188: *American Book and Magazine Illustrators to 1920,* Gale (Detroit, MI), 1998.

Gilbert, Alma M., *The Make Believe World of Maxfield Parrish and Sue Lewin,* Pomegranate (San Francsico, CA), 1990.

Gilbert, Alma M., *Maxfield Parrish: The Masterworks,* Ten Speed Press (Berkeley, CA), 1992.

Gilbert, Alma M., *Maxfield Parrish: The Landscapes,* Ten Speed Press (Berkeley, CA), 1998.

Gomes, Rosalie, *Buried Treasures: The Black-and-White Work of Maxfield Parrish,* edited by Fershid

Bharucha, Pomegranate (San Francisco, CA), 1992.

Ludwig, Coy, *Maxfield Parrish,* Schiffer (Atglen, PA), 1973.

Sendak, Maurice, *Caldecott & Co.: Notes on Books and Pictures,* Noonday (New York, NY), 1990.

Wagner, Margaret E., *Maxfield Parrish and the Illustrators of the Golden Age,* Pomegranate (San Francisco, CA), 2000.

Yount, Sylvia, *Maxfield Parrish, 1970-1966,* Abrams, 1999.

PERIODICALS

American Artist, November, 1985, Hilton Brown, "Unfamiliar Views and Distant Lands: How Ten Artists Composed Design Elements to Make Interesting Paintings," p. S30; September, 1999, "Daydream Believer," p. 78.

Antiques, November, 1995, "Romance and Fantasy," p. 592; July, 1999, Allison Eckhardt Ledes, "Maxfield Parrish: A Man for His Age," p. 22.

Antiques & Collecting, June, 1999, Ester Raye Dean, "The Magic of Maxfield," p. 32.

Architectural Digest, December, 1999, Ann E. Berman, "New Port News: An Illustration Museum Debuts in Rhode Island," p. 76.

Art in America, March, 1996, Ken Johnson, "Kitsch Meets the Sublime," p. 80.

ARTnews, October, 1998, Miriam Seidel, "They'll Always Have Parrish," p. 49.

Booklist, February 1, 1996, Carolyn Phelan, review of *Maxfield Parrish: A Treasury of Art and Children's Literature,* p. 929.

Christian Science Monitor, March 3, 1989, Theodore F. Wolff, "Parrish, Al Illustrator Deserving More Respect," p. 11.

Horn Book, January, 2000, Michael Patrick Hearn, "Those Maxfield Parrish Blues," p. 110.

New York, June 12, 2000, Mark Stevens, "Past Perfect?", p. 61.

New York Times Book Review, October 10, 1999, p. 22.

Saturday Evening Post, March, 2000, "The Timeless Art of Maxfield Parrish, p. 58.

School Arts, April, 1997, Blake D. Bradford, "Maxfield Parrish," p. 33.

School Library Journal, November, 1995, Virginia Golodetz, review of *Maxfield Parrish: A Treasury of Art and Children's Literature,* p. 89.

Smithsonian, July, 1999, Bruce Watson, "Beyond the Blue: The Art of Maxfield Parrish," p. 52.

Yankee, October, 1985, "To Be Sorted Later," p. 142.*

PARSONS, Malcolm B(arningham) 1919-1993

PERSONAL: Born October 29, 1919, in Greenville, MI; died in Florida, July 4, 1993; son of St. Clare and Mary (Barningham) Parsons; married Jeanne Elizabeth Cram, December 3, 1950; children: John Malcolm. *Education:* University of Arizona, B.A. (magna cum laude), 1946, M.A., 1947; University of Illinois at Urbana-Champaign, Ph.D., 1950.

CAREER: Educator. University of Oklahoma, instructor, 1949-50, assistant professor of government, 1950-51; Florida State University, Tallahassee, assistant professor, 1951-53, associate professor, 1953-57, professor of government and public administration, 1957-90, university service professor, 1985-90, professor emeritus, 1990-93, department head, 1963-69, chairperson of Division of Instruction in Public Administration, 1954-55, 1956-58, visiting scholar at university study center in Florence, Italy, 1973. University of Michigan, visiting professor assigned to University of the Philippines, 1955-56; University of California, Berkeley, visiting scholar, 1969; University of London, visiting scholar, 1978. *Military service:* U.S. Army, 1942-43. Michigan National Guard, 1943-45; became first sergeant.

MEMBER: Southern Political Science Association (vice president, 1971), Phi Beta Kappa, Omicron Delta Kappa, Phi Kappa Phi, Pi Sigma Alpha, Pi Alpha Alpha.

WRITINGS:

Use of the Licensing Power by the City of Chicago, University of Illinois Press (Urbana, IL), 1952.
(Editor and contributor) *Perspectives in the Study of Politics,* Rand McNally (Chicago, IL), 1968.

Contributor to books, including *Political Behavior in America,* 1966, and *The Future of the American Presidency,* 1975. Contributor to professional journals, including *American Political Science Review, Public Administration Review,* and *American Journal of Political Science.*

BIOGRAPHICAL/CRITICAL SOURCES:

PERIODICALS

American Political Science Review, June, 1969, A. R. Wilcox, review of *Perspectives in the Study of Politics.*

Choice, November, 1968, review of *Perspectives in the Study of Politics.**

PATERSON, Kent 1956-

PERSONAL: Born November 7, 1956, in San Jose, CA. *Education:* University of New Mexico, B.U.S., 1983, M.A., 1990.

ADDRESSES: Office—P.O. Box 30482, Albuquerque, NM 87190. *E-mail*—kentnews@unm.edu.

AWARDS, HONORS: First, second, and third place radio awards, Associated Press Broadcasters Association (New Mexico), 1992-99.

WRITINGS:

Hot Empire of Chile (nonfiction), Bilingual Review Press, 2000.

WORK IN PROGRESS: Research on "U.S.-Mexico relations; environment; Southwest history."

SIDELIGHTS: Kent Paterson told *CA:* "My work is based on investigative journalism. I try to combine oral history with thorough research. Creative nonfiction and poetry are other influences. My goal is to keep alive serious, provocative journalism, a dying profession." [PATTERSON

*   *   *

PATTERSON, Raymond R. 1929-2001

OBITUARY NOTICE—See index for *CA* sketch: Born December 14, 1929, in New York, NY; died of heart failure, April 5, 2001. Poet, professor and author. Patterson, English professor emeritus at City College of the City University of New York, was best known for his 1969 book *26 Ways of Looking at a Black Man and Other Poems.* Other titles include *Elemental Blues* and *Three Patterson Lyrics for Soprano and Piano.* Much of the work explored black life and the political and cultural changes that erupted in the 1960s. After receiving his bachelor's degree in 1951 from Lincoln University, Patterson was in the Army for two years and then joined the staff of the Youth House for Boys in New York. In 1956 he received a master's from New York University and later joined the faculty at Benedict College as an English instructor. He taught in public schools during the early 1960s and in 1968 returned to higher education with a post at City College. Patterson received several awards during his career, including the Borestone Mountain Award, City College Langston Hughes

award, James Madison University Furious Flower Lifetime Achievement award in literature, and two grants, one from the National Endowment for the Arts.

OBITUARIES AND OTHER SOURCES:

PERIODICALS

New York Times, April 12, 2001, p. C17.]

*   *   *

PAXTON, Nancy L. 1949-

PERSONAL: Born July 19, 1949, in Boston, MA; daughter of R. Robert (a chemical engineer) and Mary Louise Espy Paxton; married Richard Stockinger (a builder), August 11, 1996. *Ethnicity:* "Anglo." *Education:* Cornell University, B.A.; Rutgers University, M.A., Ph.D. *Politics:* Liberal. *Religion:* Unitarian. *Avocational interests:* Music, hiking, ballet/dance, Native American art and culture.

ADDRESSES: Home—1320 West University Heights Drive, South, Flagstaff, AZ 86001. *Office*—Northern Arizona University, Department of English, Box 6032, Flagstaff, AZ 86011. *E-mail*—Nancy.Paxton@nau.edu.

CAREER: Northern Arizona University, Flagstaff, AZ, professor of English; Andrew W. Mellon faculty fellow, 1988-89; Radcliffe College, Mary Ingraham Bunting fellow, 1990; University of California, Davis, Davis Humanities Institute fellow, 1991. Writer.

AWARDS, HONORS: Choice Outstanding Academic Book award, 1999, for *Writing Under the Raj.*

WRITINGS:

George Eliot and Herbert Spencer: Feminism, Evolutionism, and the Reconstruction of Gender, Princeton University Press (Princeton, NJ), 1991.
Writing Under the Raj: Gender, Race, and Rape in the British Colonial Imagination, 1830-1947, Rutgers University Press (New Brunswick, NJ), 1999.
(Contributor and editor, with Lynne Hapgood) *Outside Modernism: In Pursuit of the English Novel, 1900-1930,* St. Martin's Press (New York, NY), 2000.

Paxton has also published numerous essays on Victorian fiction and on British modernist writers in scholarly journals and edited collections. Contributor to books, including *Decolonizing the Subject: Gender and the Politics of Women's Autobiography,* edited by Sidonie Smith and Julia Watson, University of Minnesota Press (Minneapolis, MN), 1992; *Writing India, 1757-1900,* edited by B. J. Moore-Gilbert, University of Manchester Press (Manchester, England), 1996; and *The New Nineteenth Century: Readings in Underread Victorian Fiction,* edited by Barbara Leah Harman and Susan L. Meyer, Garland (New York, NY), 1996. Contributor of articles to numerous journals, including *Victorian Studies, Women's Studies International Forum,* and *Texas Studies in Literature and Language.*

SIDELIGHTS: As a professor of English at Northern Arizona University, Nancy L. Paxton not only researches and writes books and articles of literary criticism, but also teaches courses on British literature, women's writings, feminist theory, and on autobiography. Her books have brought all of these elements together within the context of nineteenth-and twentieth-century British writing, especially for writers such as George Eliot and E. M. Forster.

Paxton's book on George Eliot and Herbert Spencer considered Eliot's novels within the context of their historical moment—in dialogue with some of the prevalent ideas about gender of the time. Mark Ridley wrote, in a review in the *Times Literary Supplement,* that Herbert Spencer was a friend of Eliot's and a philosopher who, influenced by Darwin's ideas about survival of the species, came to the opinion that "women [must] devote themselves to reproduction, and that men should pick wives on grounds of physical beauty, because . . . beautiful women make the best mothers." In novels like *Silas Marner* and *Adam Bede,* Eliot shows characters who choose beautiful wives based more on lust than concerns about good mothering, with sad results: the beautiful Hetty Sorrel of *Adam Bede* murders her illegitimate baby at birth, and dies soon after in a penal colony in Australia. Ridley writes that, in *Silas Marner,* Godfrey Cass chooses a beautiful wife, Nancy Lameteer, who "ends up childless. Meanwhile, the character with the most strongly developed maternal instincts is old Silas, who is a man."

Paxton posits a more personal side to Eliot's exchanges with Spencer—that the novelist (Marian Evans, who chose to publish under the name George Eliot to avoid prejudiced responses to her work) was in love with Herbert Spencer. Carol Gallagher, in *Educational Studies,* wrote that "George Eliot's contemporaries considered her physically unattractive. In fact, Henry James called her 'hideous'; Eliot was sensitive about her looks. She

fell passionately in love with Spencer, but he could not reciprocate because of feelings about her appearance."

Paxton concludes that, through novels like *The Mill on the Floss,* whose smart and independent protagonist Maggie Tulliver has much in common with Eliot's own childhood, Eliot develops a new paradigm of the maternal: "The most 'maternal' heroines in Eliot's novels are not those who conceive and bring forth children . . . but those . . . who give birth to a self . . . responsive to the demands of mutual and passionate love."

Reviewers responded variously to *George Eliot and Herbert Spencer.* Mark Ridley, who reviewed the book for *Times Literary Supplement,* felt that Paxton placed Eliot and Spencer "in relative isolation from the rest of Victorian culture . . . and the reader may occasionally wonder, at least when some general human issue is at stake, whether Eliot could not have been reacting to someone other than Spencer." Carol T. Gallagher of Owensboro Community College, who wrote a lengthy treatment of the book in *Educational Studies,* concluded that the book "is a tour de force, combining both new insight and exhaustive knowledge of Spencer's work and letters as well as Eliot's." In contrast to Ridley, Gallagher felt that Paxton had an especially strong "socio-historic sense." And *Choice* concurred with Gallagher, noting that "Paxton's brilliant study offers a fascinating approach to a misunderstood chapter in Victorian intellectual history."

Paxton told *CA:* "I am currently working on a project on literary censorship which will consider the response to novels by D. H. Lawrence and other famous examples from the 1920s in a larger global context."

BIOGRAPHICAL/CRITICAL SOURCES:

PERIODICALS

Albion, winter, 2001, Mrinalini Sinha, review of *Writing Under the Raj,* pp. 381-382.

Choice, November, 1991, S. A. Parker, review of *George Eliot and Herbert Spencer,* p. 448.

Educational Studies, spring, 1993, Carol Gallagher, review of *George Eliot and Herbert Spencer,* pp. 62-68.

Times Literary Supplement, August 2, 1991, Mark Ridley, review of *George Eliot and Herbert Spencer,* pp. 3-4.

Victorian Studies, spring, 1992, pp. 332-333; winter, 2001, Philippa Levine, review of *Writing Under the Raj,* pp. 293-294.

OTHER

Northern Arizona University Web site, http://
jan.ucc.nau.edu/üpaxton/ (October 2, 2001).

*   *   *

PAYNE, C. D. 1949-

PERSONAL: Born July 5, 1949, in Akron, OH; son of
Herman (a construction worker) and Arlene (a homemaker) Payne; married Joy Stocksdale (an artist), April
28, 1989. *Ethnicity:* "Mixed European." *Education:*
Harvard College, B.A., 1971. *Politics:* "None: I'm a
democrat." *Religion:* "Very little." *Avocational interests:* Woodworking, metal working.

ADDRESSES: Home and Office—P.O. Box 1922, Se-
bastopol, CA 95472; fax: 707-829-3285. *E-mail*—
paynecd@sonic.net. *Agent*—Winifred Golden, Cas-
tiglia Literary Agency, 1155 Camino del Mar #510, Del
Mar, CA 92104.

CAREER: Writer.

WRITINGS:

Youth in Revolt: The Journals of Nick Twisp (fiction),
     Aivia, 1993.
Civic Beauties: A Musical Novel, Aivia, 1999.
Frisco Pigeon Mambo (fiction), Aivia, 2000.
Revolting Youth: The Further Journals of Nick Twisp
     (fiction), Aivia, 2000.
Queen of America (drama), Aivia, 2001.

ADAPTATIONS: Youth in Revolt was filmed by Brill-
stein-Grey for a FOX television pilot, 1996; optioned
by MTV for development as a mini-series; broadcast on
Germany's SWR2 radio as a ten-part dramatization,
December, 2000; and staged as a play in San Francisco,
Denver, and Rohnert Park, CA. *Frisco Pigeon Mambo*
is being adapted as an animated film for Twentieth-
Century Fox, produced by the Farrelly Brothers.

SIDELIGHTS: C. D. Payne told *CA:* "Having arrived
on the scene during the twilight of the comic novel, I've
been doing my part to hasten its demise. My first novel,
Youth in Revolt: The Journal of Nick Twisp, has been
published in the U.S., UK, Germany, Czech Republic,
Hungary, and Croatia [and has been adapted into various media formats]. Foreign rights to [*Frisco Pigeon
Mambo*] have been sold in Germany and Czech Republic."

BIOGRAPHICAL/CRITICAL SOURCES:

PERIODICALS

Berkeley Express, July, 1995, Glen David Gold,
     "Twisp's Twists: The Last Adolescent Novel?."
Los Angeles Times Book Review, May 15, 1995, Christ
     Goodrich, "Being 14 and Coming of Age Were
     Never This Hilarious," p. E5.
Publishers Weekly, September 25, 2000, review of
     Frisco Pigeon Mambo.
San Francisco, October, 1999, Josh Emmons, "The
     Bird Is the Word," p. 51.

*   *   *

PEARLMAN, Bill 1943-

PERSONAL: Born August 19, 1943, in Los Angeles,
CA; son of Jack and Mary Jane (Vandervort) Pearlman;
married Meredith Rice, September, 1967 (divorced,
October, 1970); married Lynn Williams, June, 1973
(divorced, September, 1976); children: (second marriage) Wave Adrienne. *Education:* University of California—Los Angeles, B.A., 1967; University of New
Mexico, M.A., 1977; also studied with Inter-Regional
Jung Society. *Politics:* Democrat. *Avocational interests:* Tennis, volleyball (past member of an All-
American team).

ADDRESSES: Home—P.O. Box 613, Placitas, NM
87043. *Office*—Department of English, Technical Vocational Institute, 525 Buena Vista S.E., Albuquerque,
NM 87106. *E-mail*—B2pearl@juno.com.

CAREER: University of New Mexico, Albuquerque,
NM, instructor in English, 1968-69, 1976-77, and
1998-99; Technical Vocational Institute, Albuquerque,
NM, instructor in English, 1998—. Institute for Archetypal Drama, private practice of drama therapy.
Worked as a clinical counselor and drama therapist at
mental health centers, including Charter Hospital,
Santa Fe Guidance Center, and a center at University
of New Mexico, between 1979 and 1996. Also professional actor, 1988—.

MEMBER: Actors' Equity Association, Screen Actors
Guild, American Academy of Poets, National Association for Drama Therapy.

WRITINGS:

Surfing off the Ark (poems), Grasshopper Press, 1970.

Inzorbital (novel), Duende Press (Oakland, CA), 1975.
Elegy for Prefontaine (poems), Living Batch Press, 1977.
Characters of the Sacred: The World of Archetypal Drama, Duende Press, 1995.
Flareup of Twosomes (poems), illustrated by Jim Jacob, La Alameda Press, 1996.

Author of the plays *Thanks Be to Gomez* and *Two Sides of a Net,* both produced in Los Angeles, CA, 1965; *The Scout,* produced in Albuquerque, NM, 1976; *Voices in the Wind;* and *Hitting the Wall.* Contributor to the book *Applying Adult Development Strategies,* Jossey-Bass (San Francisco, CA). Contributor to literary magazines, including *Truck, Io, Isthmus,* and *Road Apple Review.* Coeditor, *Fervent Valley,* 1972-76.

WORK IN PROGRESS: A Brazilian Incarnation, poems; *Otherworld,* a play about Hart Crane; research on "archetypal psychology."

SIDELIGHTS: Bill Pearlman told *CA:* "Writing has always been primarily a way to center, to go deeper into the possibilities of language and soul. Early influences were Jack Hirschman and Robert Creeley, as well as an older generation of masters, including William Carlos Williams, Yeats, Eliot, Lawrence, Rilke, and Crane. My poetry has always had an ascending tendency, and there was the influence of those heady days of the sixties when the world was alive with energy and driving rhythm. *Inzorbital,* my first novel, was a wild tour of sixties dreams and the fallout from warfare and turbulence.

"A later book, *Elegy for Prefontaine,* was a celebration of Steve Prefontaine, an athlete and town hero in Eugene, Oregon, with whom I spent time and exchanged letters. The collection of poems, *Flareup of Twosomes,* is a look at the braveries and foolishness of passionate love, with some of the ups and downs of this recurring obsession. A recent year in Brazil has produced the groundwork for a new collection, *A Brazilian Incarnation,* and is a further inquiry into the nature of romantic love and its powers and disappointments.

"Along the way, I have written a creative nonfiction book, *Characters of the Sacred,* about archetypal psychology and its influence on my creation, archetypal drama therapy. This practice is a confluence of ideas from Jung, Moreno, and Hillman, and modern theater traditions by way of Grotowski, Artaud, and Peter Brook. It's an exciting and delightful form of active inquiry into the ancient realm of the archetype and its potential in dialogue and dramatic enactment. I conduct

workshops all around the world, with great interest recently in Brazil and Mexico."

*   *   *

PEARSON, M. N.
    See PEARSON, Michael N(aylor)

*   *   *

PEARSON, Michael N(aylor)   1941-
    (M. N. Pearson)

PERSONAL: Born May 30, 1941, in Morrinsville, New Zealand. *Education:* University of Auckland, B.A., 1963, M.A., 1965; University of Michigan, Ph.D., 1971.

ADDRESSES: Home—36 Pacific Parade, Lennox Head, New South Wales 2478, Australia.

CAREER: Historian and educator. University of Pennsylvania, Philadelphia, PA, instructor, 1970-71, assistant professor of history and South Asian studies; University of New South Wales, School of History, lecturer, senior lecturer, associate professor, professor, 1992-2001 (retired); Southern Cross University, Linsmore, New South Wales, Australia, adjunct professor of history, 1996-97.

MEMBER: Asian Studies Association of Australia, Australian Academy of Humanities (fellow), Oriental Society of Australia (fellow).

AWARDS, HONORS: Wattamull Prize for best book on South Asian history, 1977, for *Merchants and Rulers in Gujarat: The Response to the Portuguese in the Sixteenth Century; Port Cities and Intruders* designated an Outstanding Academic Book, *Choice,* 1998.

WRITINGS:

AS M. N. PEARSON

Merchant and Rulers in Gujarat: The Response to the Portuguese in the Sixteenth Century (based on thesis), University of California Press (Berkeley, CA), 1976.
(Editor, with Blair B. King) *The Age of Partnership: Europeans in Asia before Dominion,* University Press of Hawaii (Honolulu, HI), 1979.

Coastal Western India: Studies from the Portuguese Records, Concept (New Delhi, India), 1981.

(Editor) *Legitimacy and Symbols: The South Asian Writings of F. W. Buckler,* Center for South and Southeast Asian Studies, University of Michigan (Ann Arbor, MI), 1985.

(Editor, with Ashin Das Gupta) *India and the Indian Ocean, 1500-1800,* Oxford University Press (New York, NY), 1987.

The Portuguese in India ("New Cambridge History of India" series), Cambridge University Press (New York, NY), 1987.

Before Colonialism: Theories on Asian-European Relations, 1500-1750, Oxford University Press (New York, NY), 1988.

(With Ian Bickerton and others) *Forty-three Days: The Gulf War,* Text Publishing (East Melbourne, Australia), 1991.

(With Ian Bickerton) *The Arab-Israeli Conflict: A History,* 2nd edition, Longman Cheshire (Melbourne, Australia), 1991.

Pious Passengers: The Hajj in Earlier Times, Sterling (New Delhi, India), 1994.

Pilgrimage to Mecca: The Indian Experience, 1500-1800, Markus Wiener (Princeton, NJ), 1996.

(Editor) *Spices in the Indian Ocean World,* Variorum (Brookfield, VT), 1996.

Port Cities and Intruders: The Swahili Coast, India, and Portugal in the Early Modern Era, Johns Hopkins University Press (Baltimore, MD), 1998.

Contributor of nearly fifty articles to periodicals, including *Indian Economic and Social History Review, Journal of the Economic and Social History of the Orient, Journal of Asian Studies,* and *Modern Asian Studies.*

WORK IN PROGRESS: The Indian Ocean, part of the "Seas in History" series, edited by Geoffrey Scammell, for Routledge (London, England), expected 2002.

SIDELIGHTS: Michael N. Pearson is a noted scholar in the field of South Asian and Portuguese history during the age of colonial expansion. Among his books, the 1998 work *Port Cities and Intruders: The Swahili Coast, India, and Portugal in the Early Modern Era* received positive critical attention. Noting that the subject is a challenging one, Edward A. Alpers praised the work in *Historian,* citing Pearson's ability to "boldly take . . . on the complex history of coastal East Africa during and especially dramatic period that witnessed the coming together of two major pre-modern world systems." Noting that the work is more useful for an academic readership, Ivana Elbl nonetheless commended

the volume, writing in her *Canadian Journal of History* review that the author's "command of theory and historiography, and his capacity for empirical research are both inspiring and generate respect." Pearson's "intrepid contribution deserves recognition in the growing literature on world history," Alpers concluded.

BIOGRAPHICAL/CRITICAL SOURCES:

PERIODICALS

American Historical Review, December, 1998, Richard M. Eaton, review of *Pilgrimage to Mecca,* p. 1675; October, 1990, Robert Eric Frykenberg, review of *The Portuguese in India,* p. 1270; June, 1999, Randall L. Pouwels, review of *Port Cities and Intruders,* p. 870.
Canadian Journal of History, August, 2000, Ivana Elbl, review of *Port Cities and Intruders,* p. 392.
Historian, spring, 2000, Edward A. Alpers, review of *Port Cities and Intruders,* p. 678.
History Today, December, 1988, Francis Robinson, review of *The Portuguese in India,* p. 58.
Pacific Affairs, winter, 1999, Balkrishna Govind Gohkale, review of *The Portuguese in India,* p. 587.

OTHER

Johns Hopkins University Press Web site, http://www.press.jhu.edu/press (September 26, 2001), review of *Port Cities and Intruders.*
Markus Weiner Publishers Web site, http://www.markuswiener.com/ (September 26, 2001), review of *Pilgrimage to Mecca.*

* * *

PICCARD, Bertrand   1958-

PERSONAL: Born 1958, in Switzerland; son of Jacques (a marine scientist) Piccard; married; children: three daughters.

ADDRESSES: Office—c/o Author Mail, John Wiley & Sons, 605 Third Ave., New York, NY 19158.

CAREER: Psychiatrist and balloonist. Operates a hypnosis clinic in Switzerland.

AWARDS, HONORS: European aerobatics champion; holder of world altitude record; winner (with Wim Versträten) Chrysler Transatlantic Challenge, 1992; with Brian Jones, first to circumnavigate the world nonstop in hot-air balloon, 1999.

WRITINGS:

(With Brian Jones) *Around the World in Twenty Days: The Story of Our History-making Balloon Flight,* Wiley (New York, NY), 1999.

SIDELIGHTS: Swiss psychiatrist Bertrand Piccard, along with British balloon instructor Brian Jones, became the first men to circumnavigate the globe in a hot-air balloon in March, 1999. They chronicle their historic journey in *Around the World in Twenty Days: The Story of Our History-making Balloon Flight.* Reminiscent of Jules Verne's nineteenth-century novel *Around the World in Eighty Days,* the story is told alternately from Piccard's and Jones's points of view.

Piccard has always experimented with free flight, from hang-gliding as a teenager to becoming an aerobatics champion and devising his own aerobatic figures. He was a crew member during two earlier balloon circumnavigation attempts. Piccard comes from a line of adventurers: he is the grandson of Auguste Piccard, who invented the Bathyscaphe for deep-sea exploration and was the first man to reach the stratosphere in a balloon. Piccard's father, Jacques Piccard, continued the work by taking the Bathyscaphe to the deepest point of the ocean.

Piccard and Jones were competing for a $1 million prize offered by Anheuser-Busch. Launching their balloon, the *Breitling Orbiter 3,* from Châteaud'Oex, Switzerland, they landed successfully twenty days later in the Egyptian desert. Expertly riding wind currents, the two had a relatively smooth flight, though not without some difficulties. They encountered mind-numbingly long hours over the ocean, loss of heat in their cabin, problems with air-traffic controllers, and the government of China let them use Chinese air space only after a great deal of negotiation.

The two balloonists achieved what many others had tried and failed to do. About twenty others since 1981 have attempted to cross the world by balloon, among them Steve Fossett, who tried five times and endured a hair-raising rescue at sea with a partner in December, 1998. In close competition with Piccard and Jones in March, 1999, were Brits Andy Elson and Colin Prescot, who ditched in the Pacific after seventeen days aloft. Nadya Labi wrote in *Time* just after Piccard and Jones's successful landing that the two "have won the last world-spanning contest of our era. And now they are history."

Reviewers of *Around the World in Twenty Days* were generally complimentary, if a bit disappointed that the book was not more exciting. Louise Jarvis in the *New York Times* called the narrative structure a "tag team dialogue" which revealed the differing sensibilities of the authors. Piccard, Jarvis noted, is something of a "Frasier Crane" character who packed gourmet foods and wrote about French writer Antoine de Saint-Exupery in his journal. Jones, a jokester, wrote scatological limericks and slept in the nude. Yet they were an effective team who rose above a number of difficulties. Unfortunately, Jarvis said, "their style resembles the balloon itself: drifting, often deft and swift, but slightly detached from the moment." A critic for *Publishers Weekly* commented that the book shows "the thoroughness of [the] team's planning" but "makes for some surprising dull reading."

BIOGRAPHICAL/CRITICAL SOURCES:

PERIODICALS

Library Journal, November 1, 1999, Larry Little, review of *Around the World in Twenty Days,* p. 92.
New York Times Book Review, November 14, 1999, Louise Jarvis, "Are We There Yet?," p. 8.
Popular Science, June, 1999, Gunjan Sinhan, "Floating to Victory," p. 33.
Publishers Weekly, October 25, 1999, review of *Around the World in Twenty Days,* p. 66.
Time, March 29, 1999, Nadya Labi, review of *Around the World in Twenty Days.*

OTHER

Breitling-Orbiter 3-Tour du Monde en Ballon, http://www.breitling-orbiter.ch/ (February 7, 2000), "Bertrand Piccard."
Celebrity Speakers International, http://www.speakers.co.uk/ (February 7, 2000).*

*   *   *

PICCO, Giandomenico 1948-

PERSONAL: Born October 8, 1948, in Udine, Italy; married; wife's name, Elena (an Italian national). *Education:* Attended University of Prague, 1970; University of Padua, Italy, B.A., 1971; University of California, M.A., 1972; University of Amsterdam, postgraduate degree in European International Studies, 1973. *Avocational interests:* Jogging, drawing.

ADDRESSES: Home—531 Main St., No. 1503, Roosevelt Island, NY 10044.

CAREER: Office of the Under-Secretary-General for Special Political Affairs, United Nations (U.N.), New York, NY, Political Affairs Officer, beginning 1981, then Director and Assistant to the Secretary-General for Special Assignments in the Executive Office of the Secretary General. Currently leading a private international consulting firm in New York.

MEMBER: U.N. International School (Board of Trustees); Association of Italian International Civil Servants in New York (President).

WRITINGS:

Man Without a Gun: One Diplomat's Secret Struggle to Free the Hostages, Fight Terrorism, and End a War, Times Books (New York, NY), 1999.

SIDELIGHTS: As an attache to U.N. Secretary General Javier Perez de Cuellar in the 1980s and early 1990s, Giandomenico Picco was involved in high-stakes diplomacy that led to the Soviet withdrawal from Afghanistan and the 1988 ending of the Iran-Iraq war. But, although he was a behind-the-scenes player in the resolution of the Lebanese hostage crisis, since his publication of *Man Without a Gun: One Diplomat's Secret Struggle to Free the Hostages, Fight Terrorism, and End a War,* his role as the chief negotiator with the Lebanese captor groups has become better known.

A 1991 *Time* magazine article by David Ellis offered contemporary details of the negotiations that Picco later dramatized in his memoir. "Once pragmatists in Iran's government concluded that the hostage crisis had to be resolved, the first man they turned to was Picco [whom] they trusted . . . because of his evenhanded role as head of the task force behind the 1988 U.N.-sponsored cease-fire that ended the Iran-Iraq war." The article continues by saying that Picco brought this news to Perez de Cuellar, who "mounted a high-profile diplomatic campaign, repeatedly visiting Iran, Syria and Israel to obtain official backing for Picco's veiled bargaining." While Perez de Cuellar attended high-level meetings, Picco worked at ground level in Lebanon, negotiating with different captor groups for the hostages' release.

Picco's negotiations were intensive and wide-ranging, and were accomplished at great personal risk. One of the hostages, Terry Waite, had himself been the envoy of the Church of England before he was taken hostage in 1987. At one point, under a death threat, Picco slept in a different residence every night. The *Time* article reported that his trips to meet the captor groups were harrowing as well: "On several occasions he traveled with Syrian secret police to the border of Lebanon, where he was met by intermediaries waiting in a black Mercedes. Then he was driven—alone, with his head covered by a cloth bag—into the Bekaa alley, in the eastern portion of Lebanon . . . At times he disappeared from sight for days on end." According to the *New York Times Biographical Service,* Picco managed his fear by "jogging nearly every morning to keep his energy level up and his blood pressure down during months of grueling negotiations."

The *Time* article stated that Picco had a special relationship with his commander, U.N. Secretary-General Perez de Cuellar. "Picco is more of a soldier than an international civil servant," Perez de Cuellar said, "and I have a fatherly love for him. . . . He is always where I need him." In his memoir, according to a *Library Journal* review, Picco extols Perez de Cuellar's leadership style of "forc[ing] the U.N. to operate independently of its member states (and their narrow interests);" his book makes clear that he does not feel that this method of leadership has been followed by the Secretary-General's successors.

Man Without a Gun emphasizes the human element in international negotiations, writing that "the human factor is at the basis of crises and the individual at the source of solutions." He makes it clear that the hostage negotiations hinged not only on what the U.N. could offer the captors, but on the captors' perceptions of the negotiators as human beings. The *Time* article revealed that at one point, when he "feared that the process might unravel in the atmosphere of mutual suspicion, Picco instructed the Beirut U.N. Information office to announce than an American would be released within 24 hours." This power move put extreme pressure on the captor groups to begin releasing hostages, and by early December, only two Western hostages (Germans who were being held ransom by a group with no connections to Iran) and an Israeli pilot remained captive.

Reviewers found Picco's memoir compelling. The *Library Journal* called *Man Without a Gun* "exciting." The *New York Times Book Review* found Picco's account sometimes callous and sometimes confusing, but always "engrossing." And *Publishers Weekly* deemed it a "memoir of an extraordinary career [that] reads like a combination of a thriller and a textbook on the delicate and dangerous art of diplomacy in an often explosive region."

BIOGRAPHICAL/CRITICAL SOURCES:

PERIODICALS

Library Journal, April 15, 1999, Daniel K. Blewett, review of *Man Without a Gun: One Diplomat's Secret Struggle to Free the Hostages, Fight Terrorism, and End a War,* p. 125.
New York Times Biographical Service, December, 1991, p. 1315.
New York Times Book Review, July 11, 1999, Gary J. Bass, review of *Man Without a Gun: One Diplomat's Secret Struggle to Free the Hostages, Fight Terrorism, and End a War,* p. 35.
Publishers Weekly, April 19, 1999, review of *Man Without a Gun: One Diplomat's Secret Struggle to Free the Hostages, Fight Terrorism, and End a War,* p. 50.
Time, December 16, 1991, David Ellis, review of *Man Without a Gun: One Diplomat's Secret Struggle to Free the Hostages, Fight Terrorism, and End a War,* p. 23.*

*   *   *

POLAK, Ada Buch   1914-

PERSONAL: Born September 19, 1914, in Oslo, Norway.

CAREER: Art historian and writer. Worked as deputy curator of arts and crafts museums in Norway and England, beginning 1948.

ADDRESSES: Office—c/o Author Mail, Huitfeldt Forlag, Box 148, Kalbakken, 0902 Oslo, Norway.

WRITINGS:

Gammelt norsk glass, with English summary, Gyldendal (Oslo, Norway), 1953, reprinted, Bjørn Ringstrøms antikvariat, 1983.
Glassboken, Aschehoug (Oslo, Norway), 1958.
Venetiansk glass på ny, with English summary, [Trondheim, Norway], 1958.
Modern Glass, T. Yoseloff (New York, NY), 1962.
Norwegian Silver, Dreyer (Oslo, Norway), 1972.
Glass: Its Tradition and Its Makers, Putnam (New York, NY), 1975, published as *Glass: Its Makers and Its Public,* Weidenfeld & Nicolson (London, England), 1975.
Gammelt Porsgrund porselen, C. Huitfeldt (Oslo, Norway), 1980.

Gamle glass fra Hurdal og Gjövik, C. Huitfeldt (Oslo, Norway), 1992.

BIOGRAPHICAL/CRITICAL SOURCES:

PERIODICALS

Times Literary Supplement, September 25, 1969.*

*   *   *

POOLE, Fiona Farrell
See FARRELL, Fiona

*   *   *

POWELL, Lawrence Clark   1906-2001

OBITUARY NOTICE—See index for *CA* sketch: Born September 3, 1906, in Washington, DC; died March 14, 2001, in Tucson, AZ. Librarian and author. Powell was the founder and founding dean of the University of California at Los Angeles' School of Library Service, as well as the institution's head librarian from 1944 to 1961. An avid reader and collector of books, Powell's passion was building a foundation upon which the UCLA library could grow; the institution was so enamored with his extensive work that upon his retirement, the library was named the Powell Library Building. Powell was also a skilled writer who penned several works on literature. Some of his books include *The Alchemy of Books, and Other Essays and Addresses on Books and Writers* and *Books Are Basic.* He also penned such novels as *The Blue Train* and *The River Between.* In 1971 the University of Arizona named Powell a Doctor of Humanities.

OBITUARIES AND OTHER SOURCES:

PERIODICALS

Arizona Daily Star, March 20, 2001, p. B1.
Independent (London, England), April 3, 2001, p. 6.
Los Angeles Times, March 20, 2001, p. B6.
Tucson Citizen, March 21, 2001, p. 1C.

PRIESTLY, Doug(las Michael) 1954-

PERSONAL: Born January 9, 1954, in Melbourne, Victoria, Australia. *Avocational interests:* Wildlife photography, keeping tropical fish, reading, gardening, films.

ADDRESSES: Home and Office—3 Downer Place, Kambah, 2902, Australian Capital Territory.

CAREER: Wildlife artist, 1976—; author and illustrator of books for children, 1988—. Fairhill Native Nursery, South East Queensland, Australia, native aquatic plant/watergarden consultant, 1995-97; Noosa Park Association member, 1994—.

MEMBER: Australian and New Guinea Fishes Association.

WRITINGS:

SELF-ILLUSTRATED

Australia's Wonderful Water Creatures, Puffin, 1995.
Curious Creatures of Australia, Puffin, 1995.
All about Whales, Dolphins, and Porpoises of the Southern Ocean, Puffin, 1998.

ILLUSTRATOR

Harry Breidahl, *Bush Secrets,* Macmillan, 1989.
Harry Breidahl, *Fantastic Facts and Figures,* Macmillan, 1989.
Reptiles, Penguin, 1989.
Dinosaurs, Penguin, 1989.
Space, Penguin, 1989.

Contributed illustrations to *Macmillan's Children's Encyclopedia,* 1991.

SIDELIGHTS: Doug Priestly once commented: "Ever since I was a child, the main driving force in my life, the 'core of my being,' has been a deep and abiding love of the natural world. Writing children's books about nature is my way of attempting to share and encourage that love in others, especially younger readers. I would like to awaken in them a sense of awe and wonder. A real appreciation of the beauty and endless variety of life on Earth. Something that they can nurture and take with them into adulthood. Enriching and sustaining them over the years as it has me. Even when not much else is working in your life, you can usually go for a walk and watch the birds, touch the trees, savour the sky.

"It's been said many times that we can't care about things we don't know about. I hope that by reading my books, children will become aware of just how precious our wild plants and animals are. How one thing depends on another and why we need to preserve as much of nature as possible, not only for future generations, but indeed, for our own as well. Reading picture books and browsing through encyclopedias was a great influence during my childhood so now I've come full circle. With luck, some of those children who enjoy my books may be led to play an active part in conservation, possibly of their local environment or maybe even on a wider scale. A lofty aim perhaps, but I can only try.

"In writing and illustrating *Curious Creatures,* I was looking to show people, and kids in particular, some of the more unusual and unfamiliar forms of Australian wildlife. To go beyond the highly popularized 'kangaroos, kookaburras, and koalas' view and present the lives of plants and animals most of us would consider quite extraordinary. Focusing on survival strategies such as camouflage allows me to give readers some idea of the great number of fascinating creatures that also inhabit our land, while explaining the reasons for their often bizarre appearance and habits. Many are unique to Australia and give me a great opportunity to charm and intrigue my audience to the extent that they are eager to find out more. Weird is wonderful!

"Despite many claims to the contrary, I don't think the rise of CD-ROMs and other forms of electronic publishing spell the end of the conventional book. Far from it. You can take a book with you virtually anywhere and read it almost anywhere as well. No batteries or power point needed! Books are tactile *and* visual. The best ones (especially picture books) can enthrall you with their lushness and the sense of holding something to be treasured. The act of turning the pages to reveal each new discovery is a pleasure that I hope will never be replaced by a flickering screen. Imagine cuddling up with your children to read from a computer. It's not the same, is it?

"As we venture into the twenty-first century and face all the challenges that it brings, with technological, environmental, and social change, to name a few, it's getting harder to be heard. People are inundated with information. With the book market swamped with titles and growing each year and the sheer volume of material on the Internet, authors need not only talent but also luck to be noticed. If in some small way I can influence a few children and get them to see that nature really is magical and worthwhile, my purpose in writing will have been achieved."

Priestly has written and illustrated several books for children focusing on Australian flora, fauna, and marine life. Focusing on those plants and creatures that have evolved in highly unusual ways in order to adapt to the Australian climate, Priestly offers brief descriptions of his subjects, often lightened by humorous asides, and accompanied by a watercolor illustration. A smaller, more detailed close-up of some aspect of the plant or animal or its environment may also appear. The author "lays out a surprisingly huge amount of information . . . in just thirty-two highly illustrated pages," asserted Kevin Steinberger in a *Magpies* review of *All about Whales, Dolphins, and Porpoises of the Southern Ocean.* Other reviewers made similar observations about Priestly's *Australia's Wonderful Water Creatures* and *Curious Creatures of Australia.* While some felt that the information presented might have been organized in a more clearly logical fashion, and bemoaned the lack of an index, these books also garnered praise for introducing students to the more unusual members of the Australian wildlife community. Though not overly detailed, "the range which is covered here is brief and comprehensive enough to serve as an introduction to each species," remarked Russ Merrin in *Magpies.* "Doug Priestly is a full-time wildlife painter and illustrator whose love of Australian flora and fauna is obvious," proclaimed Lynne Babbage in *Magpies.*

BIOGRAPHICAL/CRITICAL SOURCES:

PERIODICALS

Magpies, September, 1995, Russ Merrin, review of *Australia's Wonderful Water Creatures* and *Curious Creatures of Australia,* p. 36; November, 1998, Kevin Steinberger, review of *All about Whales, Dolphins, and Porpoises of the Southern Ocean,* p. 42; November, 1999, Lynne Babbage, review of *Curious Creatures of Australia,* p. 43.

* * *

PROBERT, Richard Ezra

PERSONAL: Married; children. *Education:* Wilkes University, B.S. (music); Indiana University, M.S.; studied conducting under Helmut Rilling, John Nelson, and Gregg Smith.

ADDRESSES: Home—Rochester, NY. *Office*—c/o Author Mail, Lyons Press, 123 West 18th St., New York, NY 10011.

CAREER: Conductor, musician, educator, and author. Hazleton Oratorio Society, PA, founding director; Wilkes University, PA, instructor in music; Mount Senario College, Ladysmith, WI, department chairman and associate professor of music. Rochester Philharmonic Orchestra, vice president for planning and advancement; Eastman School of Music, Summer Music Festival, conductor; Newark Community School of the Arts, Newark, NJ, executive director; Bergen Choral, music director; guest conductor at Trenton Symphony and Wyoming Valley Oratorio Society, Wilkes-Barre, PA.

WRITINGS:

Archie's Way: A Memoir of Craftsmanship and Friendship, Lyons Press (New York, NY), 1998.

WORK IN PROGRESS: Since Singing Is So Good a Thing.

SIDELIGHTS: Richard Ezra Probert is a conductor, soloist, teacher, and administrator living in Rochester, New York. In addition to his musical talents Probert is a woodworker. After losing his Pennsylvania home and the workshop that had been in his family for generations to Hurricane Agnes in 1972, Probert and his family moved to Ladysmith, Wisconsin, where he taught and advanced his musical career from 1972 to 1979. He also spent considerable time with Archie Raasch, a machinist and the owner of two Model-A Fords whom Probert met while on a drive in the northern Wisconsin countryside. Raasch, then in his seventies, was a master craftsman who worked with metal and wood, and he served as a father figure to Probert as they worked in Raasch's shop and developed a deep friendship. In *Archie's Way: A Memoir of Craftsmanship and Friendship* Probert offers reflections and meditations on craftsmanship and life.

A *Publishers Weekly* reviewer opined that *Archie's Way* has potential, but said that "it's undermined by stilted, unnatural dialogue and particularly Probert's unfortunate self-absorption." *Booklist* reviewer John Rowan felt the book would be enjoyed by the readers of Thomas Glynn's similar *Hammer, Nail, Wood.* Rowan called Probert's writing "accessible . . . well-wrought, the literary equivalent of a plane sliding a long, smooth shaving from a beautiful piece of wood."

BIOGRAPHICAL/CRITICAL SOURCES:

PERIODICALS

Booklist, August, 1998, p. 1944.

Publishers Weekly, August 27, 1998, p. 61.*

*   *   *

QUINT, David   1950-

PERSONAL: Born 1950. *Education:* Yale University, Ph.D.

ADDRESSES: Office—Yale University, Comparative Literature, P.O. Box 208299, New Haven, CT 06520-8299. *E-mail*—david.quint@yale.edu.

CAREER: Professor of English and comparative literature, Yale University; formerly associate professor of comparative literature at Princeton University. Member of the advisory board of *Modern Language Quarterly.*

WRITINGS:

Origin and Originality in Renaissance Literature: Versions of the Source, Yale University Press (New Haven, CT), 1983.
(Editor, with Patricia Parker) *Literary Theory/ Renaissance Texts,* Johns Hopkins University Press (Baltimore, MD), 1986.
(Editor, with others, and contributor) *Creative Imitation: New Essays on Renaissance Literature in Honor of Thomas M. Greene,* Medieval and Renaissance Texts and Studies (Binghamton, NY), 1992.
Epic and Empire: Politics and Generic Form from Virgil to Milton, Princeton University Press (Princeton, NJ), 1993.
(Translator, with Alexander Sheers, and author of introduction) Lodovico Ariosto, *Cinque canti/Five Cantos* (English and Italian), University of California Press (Berkeley, CA), 1996.
Montaigne and the Quality of Mercy: Ethical and Political Themes in the "Essais," Princeton University Press (Princeton, NJ), 1998.

SIDELIGHTS: David Quint is a professor of comparative literature at Yale University and the author of several scholarly studies of Renaissance and Reformation writers in France as well as classical writers of antiquity. Quint's project, which highlights the political context out of which literary texts arise, and which they comment upon in a variety of ways, has been compared to that of Thomas M. Greene. Quint is one of the editors and a contributor to the festschrift volume *Creative Imitation: New Essays on Renaissance Literature in Honor*

of Thomas M. Greene. In his book *The Light in Troy,* Greene argued for the intertextuality of Renaissance texts, and the contributors to *Creative Imitation* explore the self-consciousness of Renaissance writers invoking other texts through parody, imitation, or allusion. The range of writers discussed is broad, Mary Villeponteaux concluded in her review in *Seventeenth-Century News,* and the approach yields interesting insights. In his contributing essay, Quint puts braggart figures in Shakespeare and Spenser in context with their counterparts on the Elizabethan political scene. Villeponteaux remarked: "*Creative Imitation* is an impressive collection of essays, any one of which is valuable in its own right."

In his first book, *Origin and Originality in Renaissance Literature: Versions of the Source,* based on Quint's doctoral thesis at Yale, the author examines the pull between two powerful Renaissance notions: "The view of literature and literary art as divinely inspired and thus having an a-historical kind of allegorical authenticity, and the view that literature was the 'original' product of the particular human creativity of its author," as a reviewer put it in *AB Bookman's Weekly.* According to Quint, the resolution of the struggle between these two ideas yielded the first recognition of literature as a separate system of knowledge. For Donald Stone, Jr., who reviewed *Origin and Originality in Renaissance Literature* for the *French Review,* "this volume is as provoking as it is provocative," not least because Quint's argument relies upon a set of assumptions Stone wishes the author seemed more aware of or was more willing to discuss the parameters of. James Kaufmann, on the other hand, writing for the *Los Angeles Times Book Review,* merely characterized *Origin and Originality in Renaissance Literature* as "a difficult and quite specialized book on a very interesting subject."

In *Epic and Empire: Politics and Generic Form from Virgil to Milton,* Quint examines epics from the classical era to the Augustan with the idea that an individual epic often arises within a political context, as celebration of a military victory or lament of a defeat, but often takes on a larger life when it is read as emblematic of a later political period. Furthermore, Quint emphasizes the allusiveness of the epic genre, partly due to the epic tradition of characterizing the present in terms of the past. "Quint has an exceptionally keen eye for the detail of this aspect of epic continuity," said Philip Hardie in the *Times Literary Supplement,* "and triumphantly vindicates his opening claim for the validity of this older kind of intertextual study, alongside the contextual homologies or analogies dear to New Historicists." Quint also notes that winners' epics, such as the *Aeneid,* are able to tell a coherent story in recounting the tale of how the world came to be as it is, while losers' epics, such as the *Pharsalia,* more closely resemble the ramblings of the plots of the romance genre, as they perforce do not conclude with the defeat of the loser. Alastair Fowler contended in his review in the *Modern Language Review* that Quint's thesis only works when significant authors and texts are omitted from the discussion.

Thomas R. Hart in *Comparative Literature* took a different view of the author's accomplishment: "Quint's book is the most important survey of the epic tradition since Thomas M. Green's *The Descent from Heaven* (1963), providing new insights into some of the central texts of Western literature. His conception of an important, if secondary, tradition of losers' epic is a major contribution to our understanding of epic continuity, as is the contrast he establishes between the coherent teleological narrative that characterizes epic and the episodic and endlessly expandable structure of romance."

In *Montaigne and the Quality of Mercy: Ethical and Political Themes in the "Essais,"* Quint makes a case for the political import of Montaigne's famous essays, emphasizing the French aristocrat's stress on extending mercy to one's enemies and its relevance to the bloody civil war that was tearing apart France at the time. In this reading of the *Essais,* Montaigne's discussion of the reign of Alexander the Great, or his famous description of Brazilian cannibals, was intended to be read allegorically by Montaigne's contemporaries in order to teach them the superior moral value of pardoning one's enemies rather than exacting endless retribution. "Readers will be impressed by the lucidity of Quint's exposition, bolstered through and through by the elegant clarity of his prose style," remarked Marc-Andre Wiesmann in *Sixteenth-Century Journal.* Similarly, John J. Conley, writing in *Theological Studies,* commended Quint's scholarship in preparing his argument. Unlike Wiesmann, however, Conley concluded that "the portrait of Montaigne, the patron of tolerance, does not completely convince," noting that Montaigne offset statements about the political value of clemency with others touting the efficacy of vengeance.

BIOGRAPHICAL/CRITICAL SOURCES:

PERIODICALS

AB Bookman's Weekly, December 19, 1983, review of *Origin and Originality in Renaissance Literature: Versions of the Source,* p. 4354.

Classical Review, number 2, 1994, review of *Epic and Empire: Politics and Generic Form from Virgil to Milton,* p. 408.

College Literature, June, 1994, review of *Epic and Empire,* p. 190.

Comparative Literature, fall, 1986, review of *Origin and Originality in Renaissance Literature,* p. 384; summer, 1994, review of *Epic and Empire,* p. 304.

Comparative Literature Studies, number 3, 1996, Thomas R. Hart, review of *Epic and Empire,* pp. 304-306.

French Review, May, 1984, Donald Stone, Jr., review of *Origin and Originality in Renaissance Literature,* p. 870.

Journal of English and Germanic Philology, April, 1985, review of *Origin and Originality in Renaissance Literature,* p. 253.

Los Angeles Times Book Review, April 22, 1984, James Kaufmann, review of *Origin and Originality in Renaissance Literature,* p. 8.

Modern Language Review, January, 1995, Alastair Fowler, review of *Epic and Empire,* pp. 126-128.

Modern Philology, November, 1985, review of *Origin and Originality in Renaissance Literature,* p. 189; November, 1995, review of *Epic and Empire,* p. 225.

Renaissance and Reformation, November, 1985, review of *Origin and Originality in Renaissance Literature,* p. 278; fall, 1994, review of *Epic and Empire,* p. 72.

Renaissance Quarterly, spring, 1985, review of *Origin and Originality in Renaissance Literature,* p. 153; autumn, 1995, review of *Epic and Empire,* p. 632.

Seventeenth-Century News, fall-winter, 1997, Mary Villeponteaux, review of *Creative Imitation: New Essays on Renaissance Literature in Honor of Thomas M. Greene,* pp. 63-64.

Sixteenth-Century Journal, spring, 1999, Marc-Andre Weismann, review of *Montaigne and the Quality of Mercy: Ethical and Political Themes in the "Essais,"* p. 252.

Theological Studies, March, 1999, John J. Conley, review of *Montaigne and the Quality of Mercy,* p. 192.

Times Literary Supplement, August 19, 1994, Philip Hardie, review of *Epic and Empire,* p. 24.

Yale Review, July, 1993, Maureen Quilligan, review of *Epic and Empire,* p. 93.*

R

RABIKOVITZ, Dalia   1936-
(Dalyah Rabikowitz, Dahlia Ravikovitch, Dalia Ravikovitz)

PERSONAL: Born November 17, 1936, in Ramat Gan, Palestine (now Israel). *Religion:* Jewish.

ADDRESSES: Office—Institute for the Translation of Hebrew Literature, 66 Shlomo Melech St., Tel Aviv, Israel.

CAREER: Poet. Worked as a high school teacher in Israel, 1959-63.

WRITINGS:

(Editor) *The New Israeli Writers: Short Stories of the First Generation,* Funk (New York, NY), 1969.
A Dress of Fire, Menard Press, 1976.

Author of several books in Hebrew.

BIOGRAPHICAL/CRITICAL SOURCES:

PERIODICALS

Choice, November, 1970, review of *The New Israeli Writers.*
Library Journal, November 1, 1969, E. M. Oboler, review of *The New Israeli Writers.*
New Republic, February 10, 1979.
New York Times Book Review, December 14, 1969, Alan Hislop, review of *The New Israeli Writers,* p. 44; April 15, 1979.
Saturday Review, December 6, 1969, Curt Leviant, review of *The New Israeli Writers.*
World Literature Today, winter, 1978.*

RABIKOWITZ, Dalyah
See RABIKOVITZ, Dalia

*   *   *

RAIMOND, C. E.
(See ROBINS, Elizabeth)

*   *   *

RANSOM, Harry Huntt   1908-1976

PERSONAL: Born November 22, 1908, in Galveston, TX; died April 19, 1976; son of Harry Huntt (a high school Latin teacher) and Marion (Goodwin) Ransom; married Hazel Louise Harrod, 1951. *Education:* Attended University of the South, 1924-28; Yale University, M.A., 1930, Ph.D., 1938.

CAREER: State Teacher's College, Valley City, ND, professor of English and journalism, 1930-34; Colorado State College, professor of English and history, 1934-35. University of Texas, assistant professor, 1935-38, associate professor, 1938-47, full professor, 1947, associate dean of the graduate school, 1953, dean of the College of Arts and Sciences, 1954, appointed president of the Austin campus in 1960; chancellor of University of Texas System. Founded the *Texas Quarterly,* 1958. *Military service:* Intelligence officer in the Air Corps, 1942-46.

WRITINGS:

The First Copyright Statute: An Essay on an Act for the Encouragement of Learning, 1710, University of Texas Press (Austin, TX), 1956.

The Collection of Knowledge in Texas, Carl Hertzog (El Paso, TX), 1957.

The Conscience of the University, edited by Hazel H. Ransom, University of Texas Press (Austin, TX), 1982, republished and enlarged as *Chronicles of Opinion on Higher Education, 1955-1975,* edited by Hazel H. Ransom, University of Texas Press (Austin, TX), 1990.

The Other Texas Frontier, edited by Hazel H. Ransom, University of Texas Press (Austin, TX), 1984.

(With Hazel H. Ransom) *Snow in Austin: A Collection of Photographs from 1895 to 1985,* Clearstream Press (Austin, TX), 1986.

The Song of Things Begun: A Selection of Verse, compiled by Hazel H. Ransom, University of Texas Press (Austin, TX), 1988.

OTHER

(Editor, with J. Frank Dobie and Mody C. Boatright) *Coyote Wisdom,* Texas Folk-lore Society (Austin, TX), 1938.

(Editor, with J. Frank Dobie and Mody C. Boatright) *In the Shadow of History,* Texas Folk-lore Society (Austin, TX), 1939.

(Editor, with J. Frank Dobie, Mody C. Boatright, and others) *Mustangs and Cow Horses,* Texas Folk-lore Society (Austin, TX), 1940.

(Editor, with J. Frank Dobie and Mody C. Boatright) *Texian Stomping Grounds,* Texas Folk-lore Society (Austin, TX), 1941.

SIDELIGHTS: Harry Huntt Ransom founded the Humanities Research Center at the University of Texas at Austin and through his stewardship of the Center, the University of Texas was able to acquire one of the earliest institutional collections of twentieth century literature.

Ransom was born November 22, 1908 in Galveston, Texas. His father, Harry Huntt, taught high school Latin; his mother was Marion Goodwin Ransom. The family moved to Sewanee, Tennessee upon the death of his father, and lived in the hospital where his mother worked. Ransom attended private school at an academy connected to the University of the South, and entered the University in 1924. He graduated as valedictorian in 1928, taking honors in Greek, Latin, French and Speech. That same year, he entered the master's program in English at Yale, taking the degree in 1930. He continued on for a Ph.D. at Yale, and in the meantime taught English and journalism at State Teacher's College in Valley City, North Dakota, and English and History at Colorado State College.

In 1935, he was appointed as a part-time instructor at the University of Texas at Austin, where he would remain for the next forty-one years. He received his doctoral degree in 1938 from Yale, and began to advance through the ranks at the University of Texas, making assistant professor in 1938 and full professor in 1947, with a break from 1942 to 1946 for Ransom's service as an intelligence officer in the Air Corps. In 1947, Ransom became assistant dean of the graduate school, beginning an administrative career that, though it would detract from his scholarly output—which had focused mainly on copyrights and Texas folklore—enabled him to make his mark on the institution in a more material way.

In 1948, he served on a committee to address the library holdings. The library owned several important collections at the time, but none had been acquired in three decades. Ransom and the committee recommended expansion of the paltry $1,000 acquisitions budget for rare books and manuscripts and an aggressive program of buying.

Ransom married Hazel Louise Harrod in 1951. He continued advancing, becoming associate dean of the graduate school in 1953 and dean of the College of Arts and Sciences in 1954. Throughout, he continued to focus on his grand scheme for the library, buying numerous rare books of modern literature, such as first editions of works by T. S. Eliot and William Butler Yeats from Margie Cohn, a prominent New York dealer.

In 1956, Ransom gave a speech to the Philosophical Society of Texas that outlined his plan for the library. He noted the anti-intellectual heritage of Texas as an obstacle to the development of a major collection, but he also spoke of Texas's striving for progress and greatness. A library development program for the University would help Texas come into its own on the national stage.

In 1957, Ransom replaced Fannie Ratchford as head of the rare books program, and was appointed vice president and provost of the University. He asked for and received a commitment of one million dollars to build the library's holdings, having won the battle of public relations that would allow him to implement his program. His plan had four elements: the university would purchase collections rather than focusing on one book at a time; the library would have its own specialty, modern English and American literature since 1870, so as not to compete with the larger and more established eastern libraries; the library would collect works by both known and minor literary personages; and the library would focus on manuscripts rather than rare books.

Ransom was prescient. Very few libraries focused on this area, and as a result, the library was able to acquire a wealth of material at modest prices. Ransom also sought to acquire authors' papers as a whole, in order to be able to show a complete picture of the writer. The program was successful; the University acquired major collections from several collectors, and a core collection in theater arts. In 1958, Ransom was able to buy a large portion of the collection of T. Edward Hanley, a wealthy industrialist for just over one million dollars. The collection included the largest D. H. Lawrence and George Bernard Shaw collections in private hands, as well as volumes by Dylan Thomas, Walt Whitman, Samuel Beckett and James Joyce. The Joyce material included the final page proofs for *Ulysses.*

In 1958, Ransom also founded the *Texas Quarterly,* modeled after the *Sewanee Review* and focusing special issues on individual counties. Ransom was appointed president of the Austin campus in 1960, and was quickly elevated to chancellor of the entire University of Texas System. As chancellor, Ransom focused on, in addition to building the library, expansion of student services and hiring young faculty.

Ransom's book purchasing brought him close to many of the book dealers, whose relationship with collectors and libraries was critical in the process of building a collection. His most trusted confidant was Lew David Feldman, who headed the House of El Dieff in New York. Ransom and Feldman corresponded frequently, and Feldman was responsible for Ransom's acquisition of such items as letters by Robert Southey and Oscar Wilde, architectural drawings by Thomas Hardy, the autograph copy of E. M. Forster's *A Passage to India,* and a fair copy of T. S. Eliot's *The Wasteland.* Feldman was a terror in the auction room, and while his alliance with Ransom was good for Texas, it was a source of chagrin to many of the other prospective buyers.

The Humanities Research Center mounted an exhibition in 1964. Called "A Creative Century," such items as Sinclair Lewis's typescript for *Main Street,* the first draft of D. H. Lawrence's *Sons and Lovers,* and Shaw's handwritten *Pygmalion* were put on display. In 1970, the library was treated in Anthony Hobson's book, *Great Libraries,* and Hobson gave Ransom great praise for his role in building it. Another exhibit in 1971 further cemented the library's reputation. Richard W. Oram, writing in *Dictionary of Literary Biography,* stated that Ransom "intended the center to be much

more than a storehouse for rare materials; its holdings were meant to promote research, discussion, and understanding of the humanities." Over the years, it is estimated that Ransom spent approximately twenty million dollars on increasing the special holdings, inevitably incurring criticism that he had neglected the research portion of the library.

Ransom resigned that year, amid a changing attitude toward acquisitions. While Ransom had been free-spending in pursuing his goal of creating a world-class collection, the trend was now toward fiscal conservatism and research libraries. Ransom was named chancellor emeritus, and he remained involved with special collections. The University's president relieved him of those responsibilities in 1974, and set him to work on a history of the university. He died on April 19, 1976. The Humanities Research Center—now named the Harry Ransom Humanities Research Center, "put Texas on the map" according to Albert A. Knopf. Oram said of him: "Ransom was at heart a nineteenth century man, a bookman in the old-fashioned sense, though his reputation paradoxically rests on his visionary insight into the research values of manuscript materials relating to the modern movement in British and American literature."

BIOGRAPHICAL/CRITICAL SOURCES:

BOOKS

Dictionary of Literary Biography, Volume 187: *American Book Collectors and Biographers,* Second Series, Gale (Detroit, MI), 1998.
Hirth, Mary, *Cyril Connolly's One Hundred Modern Books from England, France, and America, 1880-1950,* Humanities Research Center (Austin, TX), 1971.

PERIODICALS

Library Chronicle of the University of Texas at Austin, new series 10, 1978, Albert A. Knopf, "Harry Huntt Ransom."
Times Literary Supplement, June 9, 1961.*

*   *   *

RAPHAEL, Marc Lee   1942(?)-

PERSONAL: Born October 11, 1942 (some sources cite 1944), in Los Angeles, CA.

ADDRESSES: Office—Department of Religion, College of William & Mary, Williamsburg, VA 23185. *E-mail*—mlraph@wm.edu.

CAREER: Educator and ordained Jewish rabbi. Hebrew Union College-Jewish Institute of Religion, Cincinnati, OH, teacher of history and literature, 1968-71; Ohio State University, Columbus, teacher of Jewish history, beginning 1971; College of William & Mary, Williamsburg, VA, currently Gumenick Professor and chairperson of Department of Religion.

AWARDS, HONORS: Woodrow Wilson fellow, 1971; fellow, Western Jewish Historical Center, 1972-74.

WRITINGS:

(Editor with Robert Chazan) *Modern Jewish History: A Source Reader,* Schocken (New York, NY), 1975.

Jews and Judaism in a Midwestern Community: Columbus, Ohio, 1840-1975, Ohio Historical Society (Columbus, OH), 1979.

(Editor) *Understanding American Jewish Philanthropy,* Ktav (New York, NY), 1979.

A History of the United Jewish Appeal, 1939-1982, Scholars Press (Chico, CA), 1982.

(Editor and author of introduction and notes) *Jews and Judaism in the United States: A Documentary History,* Behrman (New York, NY), 1983. (Editor) *Approaches to Modern Judaism,* Scholars Press (Chico, CA), 1983.

Profiles in American Judaism: The Reform, Conservative, Orthodox, and Reconstructionist Traditions in Historical Perspective, Harper (San Francisco, CA), 1984.

Abba Hillel Silver: A Profile in American Judaism, Holmes & Meier (New York, NY), 1989.

(Editor) *What Is American about the American Jewish Experience?,* Department of Religion, College of William & Mary (Williamsburg, VA), 1993.

(Editor with Jeffrey S. Gurock) *An Inventory of Promises: Essays on American Jewish History in Honor of Moses Rischin,* Carlson (Brooklyn, NY), 1995.

(Editor) *What Is Modern about the Modern Jewish Experience?,* Department of Religion, College of William & Mary (Williamsburg, VA), 1997.

(Editor with Linda Schermer Raphael) *When Night Fell: An Anthology of Holocaust Short Stories,* Rutgers University Press (New Brunswick, NJ), 1999.

(Editor) *The Margins of Jewish History,* Department of Religion, College of William & Mary (Williamsburg, VA), 2000.

Advisory editor to *An Encyclopedia of American Synagogue Ritual,* Greenwood Press (Westport, CT), 2000.

BIOGRAPHICAL/CRITICAL SOURCES:

PERIODICALS

American Historical Review, February, 1991, Jerold S. Auerbach, review of *Abba Hillel Silver.*

American Jewish History, March, 1998, Rafael Medoff, review of *Abba Hillel Silver,* p. 117.

Commentary, January, 1990, David G. Dalin, review of *Abba Hillel Silver.*

Journal of American History, September, 1990, Henry L. Feingold, review of *Abba Hillel Silver.**

*   *   *

RAVIKOVITCH, Dahlia
    See RABIKOVITZ, Dalia

*   *   *

RAVIKOVITZ, Dalia
    See RABIKOVITZ, Dalia

*   *   *

RECHY, John (Francisco)   1934-

PERSONAL: Born 1934, in El Paso, TX; son of Roberto Sixto and Guadalupe (Flores) Rechy; companion, Michael. *Education:* Texas Western College (now University of Texas at El Paso), B.A.; attended New School for Social Research.

ADDRESSES: Home—Los Angeles, CA; and New York, NY. *Agent*—c/o Georges Borchardt Inc., 136 East 57th St., New York, NY 10022.

CAREER: Writer. Guest writer in creative writing, Occidental College, Los Angeles, CA, 1973-74, University of California, Riverside, 1978, University of California, Los Angeles, 1976-77; University of Southern California, graduate school, adjunct professor in creative writing, 1983-99. *Military service:* U.S. Army; served in Germany.

MEMBER: National Writers Union, Authors Guild, Authors League of America, PEN, Texas Institute of Letters.

John Rechy

AWARDS, HONORS: Longview Foundation fiction prize, 1961, for short story "The Fabulous Wedding of Miss Destiny"; International Prix Formentor nominee, for *City of Night;* National Endowment for the Arts grant, 1976; *Los Angeles Times* Book Award nomination, 1984, for body of work; PEN-USA-West Lifetime Achievement Award, 1997; William Whitehead Award for Lifetime Achievement, the Publishing Triangle, 1999; Lifetime Achievement Award, University of Southern California, Masters in Professional Writing Program, 2001; Tribute to John Rechy, Association of Writing Programs Convention, Palm Springs, CA, 2001; first Best Body of Work award, National Gay Archives; nomination for Texas Institute of Arts & Letters Best Novel Award, for *The Fourth Angel;* Teaching Excellence Citation, Masters in Professional Writing Program, University of Southern California; elected to El Paso Hall of Fame in writing. *The Sexual Outlaw: A Documentary* was included among the one hundred best nonfiction books of the century by the *San Francisco Chronicle Book Review,* 2000; *City of Night* was

named one of the twenty-five all time best novels by the Publishing Triangle, 2000.

WRITINGS:

FICTION

City of Night, Grove (New York, NY), 1963.
Numbers, Grove (New York, NY), 1967.
This Day's Death, Grove (New York, NY), 1969.
The Vampires, Grove (New York, NY), 1971.
The Fourth Angel, W. H. Allen (London, England), 1972, Viking (New York, NY), 1973.
Rushes, Grove (New York, NY), 1979.
Bodies and Souls, Carroll & Graf (New York, NY), 1983, with an introduction by Rechy, Grove (New York, NY), 2001.
Marilyn's Daughter, Carroll & Graf (New York, NY), 1988.
The Miraculous Day of Amalia Gomez, Arcade (New York, NY), 1991, with an introduction by Rechy, Grove (New York, NY), 2001.
Our Lady of Babylon, Arcade (New York, NY), 1996.
The Coming of the Night: A Novel, Grove (New York, NY), 1999.

OTHER

The Sexual Outlaw: A Documentary (nonfiction), Grove (New York, NY), 1977.
Momma as She Became—Not as She Was (play), produced in New York, NY, 1978.
Tigers Wild (play), produced at Playhouse 91 in New York, NY, 1986.

Also author of a screenplay based on his novel *City of Night* and a play based on *Rushes.* Contributor to *The Moderns,* edited by LeRoi Jones, Corinth, 1963; *Voices,* edited by Robert Rubens, M. Joseph, 1963; *Black Humor,* edited by Bruce Jay Friedman, Bantam, 1965; *New American Story,* edited by Donald M. Allen and Robert Creeley, Grove, 1965; *Collision Course,* Random House, 1968; *Scripts,* edited by Floren Harper, Houghton, 1973; *Passing Through,* edited by W. Burns Taylor, Richard Santelli, and Kathleen McGary, Santay Publishers, 1974; *Chicano Voices,* edited by Carlota Cardeneste Dwyer, 1975; *Urban Reader,* edited by Susan Cahill and Michele F. Couper, Prentice-Hall, 1979; *Rediscoveries II,* edited by David Madden and Peggy Bach, Carroll & Graf, 1988; and *Literatura Chicana,* edited by Edmundo Garcia Giron, Prentice-Hall. Interviewed in *Gay Fiction Speaks: Conversations with Gay Novelists,* by Richard Canning, Columbia University Press, 2001.

Contributor of short stories, articles, and reviews to periodicals, including *Evergreen Review, Nugget, Big Table, Mother Jones, London Magazine, Los Angeles Times Book Review, New York Times Book Review, Saturday Review, Washington Post Book World, Village Voice,* and *Nation;* contributor of translations from Spanish to periodicals. Rechy's works have been translated into more than a dozen languages and published in over twenty countries.

WORK IN PROGRESS: Three novels: *The Naked Cowboy, In the Blue Hour,* and *Autobiography: A Novel.*

SIDELIGHTS: John Rechy's importance to American literature has been recognized three times with lifetime achievement awards. PEN-USA-West awarded him such an honor in 1997, making Rechy the first novelist to receive such an honor. In 1999, the Publishing Triangle awarded him their William Whitehead Lifetime Achievement Award. The University of Southern California added a third such award in 2001. In the *New York Blade News,* Jameson Currier wrote, "Perhaps more than any other American author in the twentieth century, [Rechy's] writings have helped shape the sexual consciousness of several generations of gay men." Gerald Fraser, writing for the *New York Times,* called Rechy "the country's most important author on homosexual life." Rechy's life and works were explored in the CD Rom *Mysteries and Desire: Searching the Worlds of John Rechy.*

Rechy's first book, *City of Night,* was "hailed as the advent of a unique voice by critics and writers as diverse as Larry McMurtry, James Baldwin, Herbert Gold, and Christopher Isherwood," declared Gregg Barrios in *Newsday.* It became a best seller in 1963, a rare accomplishment for a first novel, and it is now regarded as a modern classic and is taught in modern literature courses. However, the book's controversial subject matter—tracing the journey of a sexual adventurer through the night life of urban America—has drawn attention away from what Rechy considers a more important aspect of his work: the structure of the novel and the craftsmanship of Rechy's art, aspects the author continues to emphasize in his more recent fiction. Rechy told Richard Canning, interviewing him for *The Gay and Lesbian Review,* "I've always been attentive toward literary form. The misconception occurred early on that I was an accidental writer. . . . Because the subject was sexual, the form and structure of the books weren't viewed."

Rechy draws on many aspects of his Mexican-American heritage, as well as his past, to create his own vision of art. His novels, commented Julio A. Martinez and Francisco A. Lomeli in *Chicano Literature: A Reference Guide,* "reveal the underlying power that Chicano culture can exert even on those Mexican-American writers generally considered outside the mainstream of Chicano literature." One recurring symbol Rechy uses in his novel *Rushes* is drawn from the Catholic faith he practiced in childhood; as the protagonist advances further into despair, his trip reflects the stations of the cross, the route that Jesus took through Jerusalem on his way to Calvary. "Whether Chicano literature is defined as literary work produced about Mexican-Americans or by them," stated Martinez and Lomeli, "his works can be included in that category, especially since their plots usually contain some Mexican details and their themes frequently derive, at least in part, from Chicano culture." "Still, beyond these restrictive labels," Rechy once explained, "I am and always have been a LITERARY WRITER, a novelist, a creative writer who has experimented with various forms."

Much of Rechy's work concerns finding patterns in life, and reflecting those patterns in his fiction. His first novel, he told John Farrell in the University of Southern California's faculty newsletter *Transcript,* grew out of his "desperate need to try to give order to the anarchy I had experienced." In later books, such as *Numbers, The Vampires, The Fourth Angel, The Sexual Outlaw,* and *Bodies and Souls,* Rechy has experimented not only with content, but also with the form of storytelling itself.

Bodies and Souls relates the story of three runaways who have come to Los Angeles looking for answers and the realization of their dreams. However, Rechy intersperses their tale with vignettes of Los Angeles residents whose lives are as empty as those of the three young people. "The all-pervading isolation and loneliness that Mr. Rechy dramatized so effectively in his novels about homosexual night life," wrote Alan Cheuse in the *New York Times Book Review,* "becomes in this . . . book a commonplace about daily life in California." Rechy told interviewer Jean Ross, "I think of it as an epic novel of Los Angeles today—an 'apocalyptic' novel. In it, through the many lives I depict, I explore what I call 'the perfection of what is called accident'—the seemingly random components that come together perfectly to create what in retrospect we name 'fate.' " *Bodies and Souls* was called "a memorable feast . . . powerful, chilling, moving . . . extraordinary" by a reviewer for the *Los Angeles Times.* A reviewer for *Publishers Weekly* noted that Rechy "is very good at evoking the seamier side of the streets, and he is masterful in funny, graphic sex scenes." In the *New York Times Book Review,* a contributor asserted, "There's so much energy, ambition and humor . . . that the phrase 'scarred beauty' might well describe the novel."

Marilyn's Daughter tells the story of Normalyn Morgan, who may or may not be Marilyn Monroe's daughter by Robert Kennedy. Richard Hall, writing in the *San Francisco Chronicle,* called the novel "a marvel of literary engineering," praising its "complex plot . . . which loops and doubles back in time." Normalyn travels to Los Angeles after her foster mother's suicide to find out if Monroe was, in fact, her mother. This journey of discovery leads Normalyn through a many-layered maze of deception and ambiguity—some of it laid down by Monroe herself, other parts hidden or forgotten by people whose lives intersected at one time with hers. "In her search for Monroe," explained Hall, "Normalyn comes up against one of the great, overarching symbols of American confusion." Farrell commented, "Rechy notes that, whether [the book] succeeds on its own terms or not, what the novelist intended was a truly innovative approach to narrative and a serious exploration into the origin of legends and their power over truth."

Marilyn's Daughter, Rechy told a writer for *Newsday,* is "an extravagant literary creation. It deals with how one finally cannot run away from one's self." Rechy explained to Farrell, "Marilyn Monroe was a monument to self-creation, to self-consciousness. She was artifice as art."

In *The Miraculous Day of Amalia Gomez,* Rechy relates the plight of a beautiful, twice-divorced Mexican-American woman in Los Angeles who recalls traumatic events of her life after seeing what she believes is a divine apparition in the form of a silver cross in the sky. While Amalia attempts to rationalize the religious vision, through a series of flashbacks the reader learns of her abusive childhood in El Paso, Texas, with an alcoholic father, her first marriage to a man who raped her, the death of her son in prison, and a procession of related misfortunes. Judith Freeman described the novel in the *Los Angeles Times Book Review* as "a disturbing portrayal of one day in the life of a middle-aged Mexican-American woman who is struggling to raise her children amid the decaying and drug-ridden neighborhoods of East Los Angeles and Hollywood." Though critical of the novel's denouement, Karen Brailsford wrote in the *New York Times Book Review* that Rechy is "most successful in his graphic descriptions of the hellish underbelly of East Los Angeles." A *Publishers*

Weekly reviewer wrote, "Rechy probes the dark underside of the American dream in this powerful portrait. . . . [He] scorchingly evokes the prejudice faced by Mexican Americans . . . the poverty, gang warfare, illegal border crossings and visions of salvation."

Our Lady of Babylon, set in eighteenth-century Europe, describes the flight and redemption of a woman wrongly accused of killing her husband. Pursued by papal authorities, the unnamed lady finds refuge at a countryside estate with Madame Bernice, to whom she recounts her numerous incarnations as Eve, Delilah, Helen of Troy, Mary Magdalene, and Medea. Though finding fault in the novel's frequent narrative disjunctions, *Washington Post Book World* contributor Elizabeth Hand wrote, "Rechy writes gracefully, and sometimes poignantly, of the fate of fallen women over the centuries." Marsha Kinder of the *Los Angeles Times* called *Our Lady of Babylon* a "brilliant work of comic satire," continuing, "Rechy's Lady delivers not a 'true' account of history but an intricate structure of language that exposes the destructive power of mythic babble."

Rechy's eleventh novel, *The Coming of Night,* takes place in Los Angeles in 1981, at the beginning of the AIDS epidemic, still unnamed. All of the action happens in the span of one day, the day on which Jesse celebrates his first year of being gay. The celebration, which takes place in West Hollywood Park and consists of Jesse having as much sex as possible, occurs at the same moments when others are having conversations of disbelief about the rumors of the invasion of AIDS. "I wanted to convey the franticness that had been reached in gay men's lives, where we were now in danger of surrendering everything to our sexuality and entering a new time of danger," Rechy told Canning. R. Hunter Garcia, writing for the *Advocate,* quoted Rechy as saying, with *The Coming of Night,* he broaches a new territory, with "the central question that it asks rhetorically, 'Would you die for sex?'" Thom Nickels, writing for *Lambda Book Report,* called *The Coming of Night* a "lyric ocean of storytelling. . . . The dynamic prose quality of the novel upholds Rechy's reputation as the father of the gay world. The writing is good, and the dialog is even better." Roger Durbin of the *Library Journal* wrote, "It's pretty raw stuff but a good read."

In her presentation of the PEN-USA-West Lifetime Achievement Award, Carolyn See said, "John Rechy doesn't fit into categories. He transcends them. His individual vision is unique, perfect, loving, and strong." Canning, in his interview, asked if Rechy's goal was to leave his mark. Rechy responded, "More than a mark. A big splash! I don't like small goals."

AUTOBIOGRAPHICAL ESSAY:

John Rechy contributed the following autobiographical essay to *CA:*

My beautiful mother fled the City of Chihuahua during the revolution when word reached her family that Pancho Villa was sending one of his lieutenants to kidnap her after having seen her at a ball which he had invaded, and my Scottish father fled his wealthy home in Mexico City as his mother fired a gun at his heels to emphasize her act of banishment. Or so I was to learn throughout accounts of my family history as I inherited ghosts that roamed the memories of others and floated into mine.

My mother bore the grand name of Guadalupe Flores de Rechy, and my father bore the equally grand name of Roberto Sixto Rechy. The "Sixto," or sixth, was attributable not to any sequence of birth—he was an only child—but to a remote lord, the sixth, exhumed in versions of his aristocratic lineage, originating in Scotland but transferring to Mexico City, where my father's father, a respected doctor, was a frequent guest, with his family, of President Porfirio Díaz, the Mexican dictator with European loyalties.

While the revolution raged across the Rio Grande, both my father and mother—still unknown to each other—simultaneously fled their respective threats miles apart and crossed the border into El Paso, Texas, at exactly the same time. In the new city my mother's youngest brother, playing, thrust a ball through the window of my father's house. Chasing the young destroyer, my father encountered my mother—and married her.

In the deep of the Depression, when Texas was swept by poverty, and winds gathered to grind the crops of nearby Oklahoma into dust, I was born into a sea of clashing memories, the youngest of five children, two brothers, two sisters.

Another sister, Valeska, died at age twelve before I was born. I inherited my mother's haunted memory through her daily tears. I had a half-brother named John, too, my father's son, a beautiful boy with curls who died before I was born. When on the somber Day of the Dead we went to decorate with dark flowers the graves of my father's mother and father—who also fled to Texas—I would stare in fascination at the grave which bore my own name.

Now of course my father and mother did not flee at the exact time. Of course they did not cross the border at

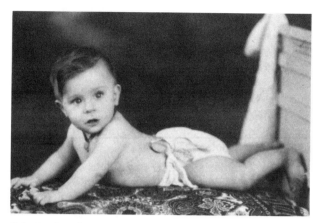

John Rechy, about one year old

the same moment. Autobiography creates its own time in rearranged memories. It orders random accidents into inevitability. I am able to reconstruct my life from birth, even before birth through inherited memories, and so to provide structure to what is shapeless, reason to anarchy—and the only meaning possible, a retrospective meaning, imposed—and the only truth, one's own. That is, autobiography as novel.

Oh, my mother was a conquering beauty, her dance card instantly filled during the balls she reigned over in Chihuahua. Her aunt, my great-aunt, *Tia* Ana (who practiced white magic and converted, through efficacious prayers and holy incantations, my first novel—I believe this—into a top best-seller) loaned me her recollections of my mother as a girl, of her beautiful green eyes, flawless fair skin and hair. My mother denied it all, but in tones which asserted happily, "Yes, it's all true, tell him more." And *Tia* Ana did, gave me such careful memories that in them I become my mother's chosen escort—she draws a line cancelling out all dances with others. And, years later, she did teach me how to waltz! Her skin remained flawless, her hair bright, her eyes truly green—until death attempted to close them; they remain in my mind clear-green.

Death exists only for the living. It is a presence, not an absence, a new presence born at the moment of death. People gone, places left behind continue to grow and change, are resurrected, rediscovered. And die daily.

My father willed me deep memories, too. His were of fortune and fame, then withering fortune, withering fame, finally assaulting loss. There was a tenuous reconciliation between him and his mother. She left me two paintings: One was of their family home in Mexico City, the horse-drawn carriage before it emphasizing their former station in life; for me, years later, that carriage looked like a surrendered relic. The other was a portrait of herself, painted on glass: a handsome haughty woman with stark-black hair and a white lace-ruffled blouse rising to her chin, deliberately isolating the face of the powerful woman who had banished my father with gunshots. Why?

My life-as-novel allows me to supply motives that satisfy me, adhering to autobiography by basing them on subsequent evidence, always allowing for mystery. Re-ordered memory at times discovers only the shape of mystery.

At dinnertime while oppressed servants silently attended, my father announced, "I oppose the tyranny of the Dictator Díaz!"

"I forbid you to continue," says my grandmother.

My grandfather does not take sides, but quietly champions my father—as do the servants. My father goes on to assert sympathy for agrarian reforms. "And the revolutionaries!" exclaims one of the maids. (She was a pretty Indian woman, and she had introduced my father to sex and the ways of social justice.)

"Yes, and them!" my father asserts. My grandmother grabs her jeweled gun. Yes! That is exactly how it happened; now it is lodged in my memory. I remember it! Reordered time, inherited memories, and imagination allow me to applaud my father's act while my grandmother glares at me, too, and my mother smiles approvingly at it all in adjusted time. The Indian maid's name was—. . .

Maria.

I have based that reconstruction on what happened subsequently: My father was run out of a small Southwest town for opposing municipal corruption by exposing it in a "radical" newspaper he printed by himself. A daring pioneer against injustice, especially in bigoted giant Texas, he was defiant, courageous—and cruel, with the cruelty he inherited from the woman in the glass portrait.

Autobiography changes from moment to moment. It is not what happened but what is remembered, when it is remembered. Its only sequence is that of memory. Alter the order of events and you change meaning.

In my memories I discover this: My father's eyes were always filled with tears!—perhaps unseen tears.

Before that new discovery, I knew only this: He was my father and he hated me. Now that I remember real and invisible tears, I find a new man bearing the same life. Early he became a notable figure in the world of music. He had been a child prodigy, learning to play "every instrument." The music faded. Aging memories were replaced by those of decline. He is no longer the conductor of his own celebrated orchestra, composer of musical scores, no longer the director of his own touring theater, no longer writes music for the films that occupied him briefly, no longer even tutors untalented Texas children. Now he spends dark hours reorchestrating music no one wants, music filed in an old wooden cabinet, eventually lost. Soon he will no longer be even the caretaker of a public park. Now he is an old gray man, mocked by ghosts. He gets up at dawn to clean the night's debris at a hospital, fragments of accidents and death. When he returns home, he lashes out with threats of fire and violence. Then he screams for recognition: "I am respected, known!" My mother soothes him, agreeing. When he died, telegrams came from important figures all over the country and Mexico, who had ignored his slow dying.

Remembered—or inserted—unseen tears reveal this now. He hated only the reflection of himself in me.

Truth changes with new memories. We do not move into the past, we bring it forward with new life. My mother and father speak words I heard long ago (or heard about) but hear now anew, spoken only to me, spoken through me. Tomorrow, if I find my father's anger in me, I may forget his tears, insist that *I* inserted them, revise today's truth.

Before that happens, I will remember this, which will now color all subsequent recollections: After the rampages of anger, my father would bring me presents. He lavished armsful of fresh flowers on my mother, the flowers splashed the drab house of poverty with astonishing colors. He loved her! Shall I allow myself to believe that she loved him, too?

On her Saint's Day, December 12—the day of Our Lady of Guadalupe—he would serenade her at the tint of dawn, turning up with dashing mariachis to sing *"Las Mañanitas"* outside her window. She, pretending surprise but having gone to bed carefully arranged for her appearance at the window, would then invite everyone grandly to an already prepared breakfast of coffee, chocolate, *pan de dulce*. She reigned with her smile. He continued the yearly serenades even when he was old, turning up at the window with a band of increasingly ragged musicians.

*

Facts—what someone continues to remember, a live memory—are reshaped by the growing past. Only the past changes.

But for me this is constant: On the steps of a bandaged Texas house that has a tattered screened porch, four-years-old I lie on my mother's lap. The Texas sky multiplies a million stars. I begin to doze as my mother curls with her saliva-moistened finger my eyelashes, which were long and thick.

We had moved from a pretty house we could no longer afford. Poverty invaded our lives. Over fire made from wood and propped on bricks, my mother heats tin tubs of water to wash our clothes. I remember white sheets. They hang on a line. Memory washes them again. My mother empties the tub, water carves mysterious shapes on the dry soil. I see her against the blue sky under a white sun.

A sharp memory asserts: In kindergarten Miss Stowe was showing us how to make butter in an old-fashioned churn. But the butter remained curdled liquid. Angered, longing for a vanished frontier, its props (I find this for her in my recollection), she kept us after school while she churned. I stand by the window, knowing my mother is waiting for me. Will she think I've been stolen, go through her life looking for me while Miss Stowe churns? Did the teacher succeed in making butter? I don't know. Right now I'm rushing out of the room, down corridors, out the schoolyard. Now I walk home holding my reward for defiance—my mother's hand.

There was another teacher. Miss Oliver. A Texas Cassandra. In El Paso Junior High she was a dreaded teacher because she was smart and demanded attention in class. Black, black hair, a pale, pale face, she seemed always on the brink of unendurable pain. Someone said that in her clenched fists she clutched secret pins. She walks into the classroom. She looks more pained and angered than ever. I hear her now. She says to me—no, to us, all the children there: "You will always be as unhappy as you are now. Always!" A curse? A projection? A prophecy? A challenge? Her truth?

Years later when I denied God melodramatically, I was certain he was listening and caring. Did he hear Miss Oliver? Still later I cherished the splendid indifference of beautiful cold stars in limitless unseeing darkness and hoped that she did, too.

The Greeks had Gods that intervened on tragedy. Euripides was not sure and so did not win first prizes. Newer Gods were seducible by prayer and offerings and sacrifice. Then there was One, then there was none, and there was no substitute for salvation. Miss Oliver just taught me that.

The despised Texas windstorms begin in February, howling across the desert, thrusting gray dust against hints of spring, budding trees confused into resurrection by brief hours of sun, and the wind hurls tangled masses of tumbleweeds into the city.

We lived near railroad tracks. Hundreds of men and women fleeing the Depression from one state to another would ride through, hidden in freight trains. Police raid the cars, bludgeoning flesh. Tramps sweep across the tracks in search of shelter and, for me, they sweep into ambiguous memories.

Mystery, too, grows in memory, deepens, reveals clues, only clues, and mystery, sharper mystery providing only more precise questions, not answers.

Lean men and women often handsome but dirtied, the tattered wanderers would appear at our back door. My mother would seat them at a wooden table kept for that purpose in the back porch. She serves them each a plate of rice and beans, a container of hot coffee.

Slides flash on the scrim of memory, at times unwind images like strips of film. Autobiography contains photographs, faded or sharp. And silhouettes—shadows that exist only when exact light is at the exact angle.

A face. A man among the tramps. He was kind to me, a gentle figure like a dirtied angel. I was six years old. Memory jerks into a dark freight car of twisting shadows where—Is this real? Imagined? Memory invents what it requires for today's truth, or to conceal it, memory's subterfuge—disguising one memory with another. Then why, years later as a youngman roaming America, will I wander into skid rows, filled with rage and terror, and then I will flee, away, anger and terror flowing into sorrow. And, then, sometimes, a brief, warm peace.

When I was nine, I acted with a famous theater company, headed by Virginia Fabrigas (the Ethel Barrymore of Mexican theater). In an allegorical Spanish drama titled *El Monje Blanco,* I played the Christ-child. As my carpenter-father begins to walk away from me and my mother, I lean against an arrangement of boards on stage, converting two into a cross, and I say:

"Why are you abandoning me, father?"

When others were taking curtain calls, I rushed into the audience, to be embraced by weeping women and men—who loved me! Or merely the child in the role?

I will splice two memories, containing others, for a growing meaning: I was poor with borrowed memories of gentility; of "mixed blood"—a *guerro*—Mexican but not looking it, by Texas standards. In Texas discrimination saturates the soil. "Oh," they would say, "you must never claim to be Mexican, you're too fair." As a *guerro,* I was doubly exiled—by other Mexicans, when they knew, and by other "Anglos" when *they* knew. Asserting my unique identity, without overt "allegiance" then to either of the banishing camps, I managed to become "popular" in high school, president of all the clubs I belonged to. But my "popularity" ended when school was over and I fled to secret poverty. Now jump across many years, when two "Anglos" are proposing me for membership in a popular fraternity. We went to visit the ranch of one of their families, in Balmorhea, darkest gothic Texas—where *all* Texas Rangers are bred. A single theater, playing only on weekends, separated Mexicans from Anglos and never allowed Negroes. At dinner, a relative of my would-be "fraternity brother" expressed her dismay at eating while the Mexican maid "is still in the room." It was Maria's daughter! I didn't know it then but I know it now. Yes! And that is in strong part why I walked out of that house and began my ethnic rebellion—furthering my isolation. Now—as I leave that Texan dinner of hatred—I say *"buenas noches"* to Maria's daughter. Her name was—. . . Maria, like her mother. *But why was she still in servitude?*

What is strongly imagined is finally remembered. Maria has become a living ghost, the first Maria—and an influence on my whole life! Yes, and when my father told my mother—and told her with some hesitation—about Maria, my beautiful mother—of course—approved. "Was she pretty?" she asks him. "Yes—but not as beautiful as you," he answers; he had to be truthful. "But why didn't you go back later to say goodbye to her?" my mother chides him. "I did," he tells her, "but she had run away, too; to join the *Zapatistas."*

I edited the college magazine and then was removed because I had turned it into a "radical" literary periodical. Like my father before me! A welcome ambush of memory.

Teaching me independence, my father allowed me to miss school whenever I wanted. A truant officer coura-geous enough to object was confronted by his enormous wrath and never did it again. My father therefore allowed me—on windy afternoons, when Texas clouds shut the rest of the world out—to go to the Texas Grand Theater for magical hours, splendor of delights, especially during recurrent "revival week"—"old" movies. Hedy Lamarr! Tyrone Power, Bette Davis! My father made that possible.

Memories of him tangle. Oh, did my mother love him? She stayed with him until he died—and, after, remembered him only as the dashing Scotsman who married her, serenaded her.

A film clip unwinds beautifully on the screen of memory. I'll keep it in slow motion. After my first novel was published, I bought my mother a house; and soon after, we drove to Los Angeles to visit my sister. Halfway there, so she will not grow tired, I rent for overnight a suite in the gaudiest and most expensive motel in Phoenix, Arizona. We collect stares as we enter the pretentious lobby, because I am wearing torn jeans, no shirt; my mother wears a lovely summer hat, white gloves, a faintly violet lace dress. I ask for the best accommodations.

Closeup. Tight focus. The motel pool sprawls across a green lawn under pastel-haloed palm trees, the water is colored silver in the desert night. My mother has taken her sleeping pill. She wears a summer robe, so light it sighs in a breezeless night. We sit by the pool. She tells me she would like a cool soft drink. I order it, and it comes on a platter. She sips it. She smiles her magical smile. "Thank you, my son. Now I'll have a restful sleep. Goodnight, my son." I see her small form moving in and out of tinted shadows. I want that mysterious moment to stay, to halt. If it is true that when you die, images of your life flash by, I hope this one will linger.

Dual Catholicisms, Scottish and Mexican, but more Mexican, because I was raised in El Paso: Splattered colors, ritual, confession, Mass, sin, guilt, and no substitute allowed for salvation. Painted saints with painted tears writhe in gorgeous agony. Christ poses on his cross. Excessive, that religion burrows into roots of superstition, at best white magic.

A memory rustles, stirs, calls, speaks:

"Treasure is buried under the house!"

Tia Ana said that. A spirit has told her that treasure is buried under the crawl space of our house. My mother says nonsense, my father says it's worth a try to find

The Rechy family, about 1953: (standing, from left) sister Olga, John, brothers Yvan and Robert, sister Blanca; (seated) mother Guadalupe and father Roberto

out—his background in opera allowed acceptance of the unseen. *Don* Ben, pope of El Paso's good witches, a tiny root of an old man, is summoned. The late sun waits in suspense on the purple horizon. My brothers, my sisters, my mother, my father, myself, *Tia* Ana, and *don* Ben gather in the yard.

Don Ben becomes rigid. Something *is* buried nearby. "Treasure," my aunt interprets. Only *don* Ben and I—I think I was five years old then—are small enough to crawl into the dank darkness. No treasure, no sign. Coughing from the dampness, and cramped in that prostrate position, *don* Ben is about to crawl out. I will help *Tia* Ana and God. I move ahead, twist two sticks into a hurried cross, and I put it atop a mound of dirt. "Look! *Don* Ben, the sign!" *Don* Ben groans. From beyond, *Tia* Ana issues a relieved "Amen." But in the dusking evening, a weary *don* Ben testily says we must pray twelve novenas before he can proceed. He rubs his back to emphasize the need for a long, long devotional period. My mother loses patience, my aunt has a lapse

of faith, and only the Texas dust remains under our house.

But perhaps I didn't make that cross. Perhaps it was there and I found it. Perhaps there *was* treasure. No. Yes. No. Memory and autobiography are affected by the time of day, the month, the season. Winter memories in summer, summer memories of winter. Of spring. Day. Night—light and angles of shadows alter form. When at another time I remember *Tia* Ana's prophecy of treasure, I may imbue it with the sense of sad loss that followed for days: There was, after all, no treasure. The poverty continued—and new waves of tramps swept across the tracks.

This remembrance asserts: When I was finishing *City of Night* in my mother's home after years of desultory wandering about the country, in the evenings I would translate into Spanish passages I thought appropriate, and I would read them to her. "You're writing a beautiful book, my son," she said.

The longer a distance in time it survives, the more "real" the assertive memory; it has survived the onslaught of new ones. With new power, it may even be borrowed.

My brother Robert. Smart, sensitive, brooding. When he was a child and before I was born, my grandmother, the woman in the glass portrait, asked him as he stared outside the window, "Robertito, Robertito, what are you staring at so hard?" He answered, "I am occupied with life." But in my mind I give myself that fact, link myself even more closely to my brother. I look out the window, and it is my mother who asks me the question.

I answer: "I am occupied with life."

Given another series of accidents, my brother might have become the writer. But being the oldest, he had to sacrifice his education because we could not otherwise survive on what my father was able to earn. My loving brother-father, handsome enough to be Robert Taylor's double, got the only job he could then, in a pool hall. Sometimes he would wake me up when he came home on a hot summer night, and he would take me out to the Spinning Wheel to get a hamburger and a malted milk—magic potions which I never was able to finish.

With his help—and a journalism scholarship—I went to a small college in El Paso. It nestles in the desert; we climbed rocks to get to class. In an English literature class—majoring in English, minoring in French—I wrote a paper "proving" that John Milton was on the side of the rebel angels, and had succeeded in justifying the ways of *man* to God. Emboldened, I wrote a private poem in which at judgment day all humanity, led by Jesus, turns the final trial about and sentences God to hell. If I were writing it now, Miss Oliver would lead the prosecution.

I read a lot, eclectically; Greek tragedies, Margaret Mitchell, Dostoevsky, Garcia Lorca, Ben Ames Williams, Rimbaud, Emily Brontë, Nietzsche, Henry Bellamann, Joyce, Proust, Frank Yerby, Donne, Kathleen Winsor, Swift, Faulkner. And I saw many, many movies.

After classes in college, I often climbed the nearby Mount Cristo Rey, a barren rocky mountain bordered by the Rio Grande, usually waterless—the passageway by which *braceros* make their way into the farms and ranches of Texas. At the top of the mountain is a giant Christ, an Indian Christ, looking down as the Border Patrol rounds up the "illegals." Vast empty desert marked with cactuses. I climbed for hours, sweating.

Once I climbed with a beautiful girl I was in love with. Was I? People said we resembled each other. A doomed girl whose beauty never ages in my mind; a strange wounded girl as joined by hatred to her mother as I was by love to mine. Years later she taught my mother—who by then had recurrent fainting spells—how to do a graceful oriental "dance." I see them in my mother's bedroom as they make floating ghost movements.

No, it isn't true that that girl did not age in my memories. I tried to avoid this: She returned to El Paso when I had returned, too. Then only for a few moments was I able to see in that new stark presence the vague resemblance of the girl I had loved. A specter, it glided over her and then was gone. She had returned for her mother's death.

I grasp an earlier memory of her. On Times Square, hustling, I ran into her—beautiful then. But we did not speak, not that night. She understood why I was there as she left a movie theater with another youngman.

*

I finished college at an early age. An English teacher offered to recommend me for a scholarship to Harvard, his school; but rather than extending the wait, I allowed myself to be drafted into the army. I didn't tell anyone—except my immediate family—that I was going away.

I get up early. My mother is already up. She has been crying. I hug her. My father is up, too! Is he crying? Yes! I remember it. He has just started to cry. We hadn't spoken to each other for months, locked silence replaced rage and curses—rage I had begun to vent back at him—yes, cruelly, I can't escape that—thrusting his collapse from musical grace back at him as "failure," yes, I see that I did that, but then I knew I was only trying to escape from drowning in his rages.

That morning: He gives me a ring he wore—a ruby mounted in gold, he told us. I take it, put it on my finger and look at him both for the last time and the first time: The man standing before me is a defeated old man, crushed by conflicting memories of what was and what became; his sorrow, hidden before by rampaging anger, is clear now as he looks at me through his tears of loss and regret. In a few weeks he will be dead. I will return to his funeral. I will go on forever finding him within the present of alleviated memories. Memory interprets.

I went into the army a private and came out a private, never staying in one place enough to be promoted, maneuvering to be transferred, feeling a restlessness that will soon take me over. Stationed in Germany, I traveled over Europe. Accepted by Columbia University, I applied for, and got, an early release. I returned briefly to my mother in Texas, telling her that I had to leave now on my own, beginning another pattern—leaving, returning, leaving, returning, always dreading the moment of separation.

I arrived in New York with only twenty dollars and on an electrified late afternoon when a hurricane threatened the island. A cop told me I could find a room at the nearby YMCA. There I met a merchant marine. He buys me hamburgers and tells me I can make quick money on Times Square—"hustling." A new word has opened a new world to me.

Instead of Columbia, I went to Times Square.

Autobiography as novel allows revealing juxtapositions. Out of chronological sequence, events that occurred later in "real time" illuminate what came before.

This happened a year before: In Paris one late night near the Café de Flor the area suddenly assumed a strange clarity for me. I knew why I had remained late on that street. There are only men idling about. And I *know.* No, I may not have known then, exactly. Yes! Memory comes forth. An attractive man talks to me, in French, and then English. I say yes, feeling that I am in a lucid trance. I go to his nearby apartment. He touches me intimately. I pull away, but I wait. Then I turn away and rush out.

As a child I had crushes on the pretty actresses in my father's theatrical company, and on girls in my classes, especially one, who was chosen to be a "couple" with me, and model grown-up clothes for the PTA! We were both eight. There was a girl named Barbara. I was infatuated with the Wicked Queen in *Snow White,* never insipid Snow White. Later I would hear the queen described as looking like a man in drag. I fell in love with Hedy Lamarr, Veronica Lake, Dorothy Lamour, and I think—I'm not sure now—Lauren Bacall. I wanted to be like Erroll Flynn, Tyrone Power, Alan Ladd—that superb. The demarcation between admiration and desire is thin. Did they intersect even then?

On Times Square, which the merchant marine has told me about—arousing a cacophony of terrified excitement, strange magic—I study other idling young men selling their bodies. From them I learn quickly how to stand, look—as if I had *always* known. A middle-aged man approaches me and says, "I'll give you ten dollars

and I don't give a damn for you." Two needs of my time then: to be desired powerfully, and not to be expected to care.

This memory comes forward: As a little boy in Texas, I stood in the back yard of our house and looked up at a million stars. God was there. That's where I said nightly prayers, each night adding new ones as the miseries I was increasingly aware of in the world became clearer. (There was so much poverty and hunger in El Paso and Juárez that we did not consider ourselves poor because we ate and had a home.) Finally, the list of violations I thought my prayers would alleviate grew so long, so complex, that I made a unilateral agreement with God: In the future I would merely say, in my thoughts: "You already know why I'm praying."

I hustled in New York, Los Angeles, San Francisco, St. Louis, Chicago, New Orleans—and once—no, twice—in El Paso. If it had been only once, I would have said I did so to banish pursuing ghosts. My journey begun on Times Square led me—"inevitably"—to the epiphany of Mardi Gras, my own Ash Wednesday.

I fled the shrouded city during Lent. New Orleans is always black and white, never in color, in my mind—and I returned to the gentle sanctuary of my mother's house and love. There I wrote a letter to a friend in Evanston, Illinois, about the frantic events in New Orleans—crowded with sex and pills, and casual dope, feeling myself out of control, falling. Unsent, crumpled, found later, reshaped, that letter became my first published "story"—"Mardi Gras" in *Evergreen Review;* it was also the beginning (although it would be incorporated into its last chapter) of my first novel, *City of Night.* As sections of that book continued to appear in literary quarterlies, I had offers from several publishers for a contract. I chose Grove Press, the company I admired most for its quality and courage, and because its senior editor, Don Allen, had been the first to assert belief in the book.

Despite a contract and an advance, I did not write that book for years. I returned to the "nightcities" and to the private, beautiful, and ugly magic of hustling, playing there the then-required role of "paid tourist."

Autobiography as novel allows for a "flashforward" for extended meaning: Soon—not yet—I will start going with certain men because of desire, not for money. The same night will find me hustling once, and then cruising many times in the territory of unpaid sex, mutual desire—finding a refuge for mystery in numbers, countless anonymous encounters.

Rechy, New York, about 1964

Hitchhiking in Los Angeles, I met a man who made it possible for me to return to El Paso to finish in a year the novel I had started three years earlier.

*

From childhood I had wanted to write—and paint. I wrote and illustrated stories always titled "Long Ago"—perhaps I was revising my life to a time when I would become my mother's escort at her triumphant dance affairs. Influenced by the film *Marie Antoinette,* I wrote about 500 pages of a novel about the French Revolution, researched diligently. I abandoned it to write about 200 pages of a novel about a boy of "mixed blood" in Texas. By age sixteen or seventeen, I had written many stories, many poems, including two epics—about war in heaven. Most of my writings were started in pencil and continued on a portable Royal typewriter my father gave me. My father! I discover him anew constantly with new evidence.

I destroyed all those manuscripts when I went into the army, with the exception of a finished novel, *Pablo!*—a "realistic fantasy" framed about the Mayan legend of doomed love between the moon and the sun, separated at the dawn of time. In it, a narcissistic young man tells the story of a "beautiful woman who died."

City of Night became a best-seller before official publication; and it was bought by about a dozen foreign countries for translation. The initial critical reaction was vitriolic, cruel. My very existence—literally—was questioned in the *New York Review of Books* and *New Republic.* Even restrained critics concentrated on the book's subject. With precious exceptions, its careful structure was virtually ignored. (I believe that self-appointed "important" critics should be licensed to practice—like doctors, so that an artist may sue them for malpractice—the recklessness with which they often assault work they know to be good but which disturbs them for private reasons.) It pleases me that today—when I speak to new readers in college courses where it is required reading—they assume that the book was always highly admired. And it continues to be read widely; new foreign editions appear; it is frequently referred to as "a modern classic." (Autobiography allows sensitive journalism.)

I chose not to promote the book, to retain my private life. I did not want my life to change radically while the lives of the people I had written about remained the same; that seemed betrayal. When I had bought my mother her new house but we had not yet moved in, a letter and some telephone calls from a man who admired my novel extended into an invitation to go to Tanglewood to hear the American premiere of Benjamin Britten's *War Requiem.* During the following weeks, perhaps two months, I stayed with this extraordinary caring man—in Riverdale outside New York. (Focus: An eagle appears on the balcony of his fourteenth-storey apartment and peers in through a glass wall.) We went to Puerto Rico, the Virgin Islands. Through newspaper and magazine items placing me in cities I have never been to, the guest of people I have never known, I learned of several imposters.

I returned to El Paso. I will hold this memory, too, in slow motion: My mother shows me through the house I have bought for her. She points out the new furniture. She holds my arm, and I link mine through hers, and she takes me outside to see the magnificent late roses.

Strangers appeared at my house, inventing ruses to be let in. I answered hundreds of letters—good letters—from readers. Increasingly reclusive, I had only two or three friends. I took frequent drives into the Texas desert, or the banks of the Rio Grande. I climbed bluish mountains. I began the transition from "youngman" to "man." I created my own gym in my mother's house and I began body-building fiercely with weights—an activity that continues to be central to my life.

With my mother I took a trip to Los Angeles. Because it belongs by itself, a part of nothing else, I have pulled out for special attention the cherished moments with her by that Arizona motel pool. Autobiography allows separation of memories.

In Los Angeles, my mother stayed with my sister, and I rented a motel room—and I crammed my life with sex again—as if to make up for lost years—in an area of a vast park, a sexual paradise that could become a sexual hell when the hunt became frantic, without surcease.

As I drove out of the city of daily apocalypse—my mother holding a writing pad firmly on the console of my cherished black-and-tan 1965 Mustang as I steered with my left hand—I began my second novel, *Numbers.*

Written in exactly three months, this book, as much about sex as about dying, was strongly influenced by Poe. It has some of my best writing, including a first chapter that introduces all the themes and symbols that illuminate the protagonist's—Johnny Rio's—descent into the dark heart of the sexual park I had discovered. In this novel my attention to structure increased, shaping chaos.

Again, the critical reaction was largely hysterical. Even the photograph of me on the front of the book's jacket aroused anger. Again, only the sexual content was glared at.

Then love enclosed—locked—me and my mother in that new house, the love that occurs, when it does, only between mother and son. Freud was wrong, so wrong. It has nothing to do with sex, incest; only a special love that defines itself. With the money from my books, I would try to make up for all her years of poverty and sacrifice, the demands I and the rest of my family had placed on her love. In wanting to give her everything I thought she needed, did I deprive her of everything she really needed? Her rose garden—I gave to a man to tend for her. Her kitchen—I gave it to a woman to take it over for her. I insisted on giving her a superb vacation to Mexico City, with my sister; I know now she did not want to go back. I insisted she visit distant friends, insisted we go out to lunch, dinner. I did not know she wanted, increasingly, to rest now, just rest; that she was tired; that the unscreamed protests of her life were being screamed at last—but inside, burrowed inward, wearing. What I did was all out of love—and all destroying. And so I raged at her. (The way my father had done when I despised him most! His unwelcome presence asserts that now. No, I refuse to accept that. It was not like that, no.) "What do you want me

Guadalupe Flores de Rechy, about sixty-two years old

to do—become young!" she pled once to me. Yes! But she was seventy then. In defense, she retreated to her bedroom, decorated like a doll's room, with delicate filigree, in shades of pastel, white golden-gilded drapes drawn so that the room glowed faintly.

I understand only now. What remains constant from that time is this: Her eyes grew even more beautiful, more luminous than ever. Yes, I remember that. And I know this: I did not realize that my beloved mother, who had waltzed with me in imagination and then in reality—had grown old. I never saw her aging.

This Day's Death—a novel that does not understand the situations it attempts to explore, because I did not understand them—came out of that time. I will return to the subject in another book, the subject of a mother and son trapped by love—only love—so powerful it begins killing both.

During that same period I wrote *The Vampires,* a book that sometimes baffles me. It came out of a central reality—a time I had spent on a private island with a man, his mistress, his ex-wives. Beyond that, it is a strange, exotic creation, a splashy luxurious novel about opulent decay and corruption as beautiful wealthy guests gather on an island mansion to play out a pageant of confessions and judgment. It is written in "Technicolor," employing filmic techniques in prose. It is influenced by the exaggerations of classic comic strips like "Terry and the Pirates"—and, too, again, much influenced by Poe.

It was virtually ignored, in major part because its publisher was in a financial crisis at the time, publication constantly postponed. There was no promotion, no galleys sent out for review.

On October 9, 1970, my mother died.

In the hospital, she had come out of a coma to say: "I understand—we love each other so much, my son, that we hurt because of it." I clasped her hand and she clasped mine. I told her she had to live. And although I would not face that she would—could—die, I had her transferred to a room where a wide window faced the giant Indian Christ atop the Cristo Rey Mountains. There was a brilliant Texas sunset before it all became night.

The ungraspable horror of her death sent me to drugs. But I suppose I chose to live. I stopped the drugs. I return more and more to that time by the swimming pool in Arizona when she asked for a cool soft drink and said she would have a restful night.

Like memory, art falsifies, altering experience, bringing the added artifice of words, symbols. In *The Fourth Angel,* I converted myself into a teenager who cannot cope with his mother's death; I turned other "real" characters into the same age. I added invented situations. I was still keeping away the reality of my mother's death and my involvement with drugs. The teenagers in the book are so wounded that they embark on playing "games" that will teach them to stop feeling, stop hurting. In the process, they almost destroy themselves and each other. For me it is a moving, frightening, powerful book. But it, too, was ignored.

I was broke. Ten years after the huge success of *City of Night* had made me rich and "famous" (I had managed to remain private), I was back in Los Angeles hustling the same streets that first book had described; anonymous again. At first I was terrified that after

many years away, that world, relying on physical desirability, would spit me out. Had I unconsciously prepared for this return by my physical conversion through body-building, now that I was no longer a "young-man"? I was able to survive again on those streets.

Then I was invited to be a guest writer at Occidental College. Since then, I have taught at UCLA and USC—and I've lectured at many universities, including Yale and Duke. I am considered to be an excellent "teacher" of writing; that is, I recognize and encourage creativity.

The Sexual Outlaw, which came in part out of my return to the streets, both hustling and cruising, is the literary equivalent of a film documentary—influenced by Robbe-Grillet's theories on the new novel. Plotless, "black-and-white," it is a minute-by-minute accounting of three days and nights of anonymous sex as "Jim" roams the sexual underground of Los Angeles. Many characters appear, only briefly, as their lives intersect with Jim's. All are "pastless." I wanted all the characters, including Jim, to be "defined" only through their sexual journeys. Interspersed throughout the account of this night odyssey are voice-over essays, multi-media splices of commentary. It is a brooding exploration of a misunderstood world.

It was knocked quickly off best-seller lists when bookstores refused to carry it; major television stations would not advertise it. In England news of its publication drew threatened lawsuits.

While receiving "mixed reviews," it was—again—discussed almost solely on the basis of its content. Its adventurous form was not considered.

Rushes is a "realistic" account of one night in a sado-masochistic leather bar and orgy room. It is also a Catholic Mass. The sleazy bar finds careful parallels in the structure of a church, the pornographic drawings on the walls evoke the stations of the cross. The contemporary dialogue at times paraphrases sections from the Mass. Realistic incidents involving people that would frequent such a bar, find equivalents in the rituals of baptism, initiation, sacrifice, even possible purgation. There are two crucifixions, one symbolic in the orgy room, one real—a brutal murder occurring outside perpetrated by "gay-bashers." It is a dark novel, and the structure is central to its meanings.

Again, sexual content was emphasized in even favorable reviews—with a few notable exceptions, and these exceptions encouraged me to believe that my *writing*

In Los Angeles, 1971

was now receiving careful attention at least from a few critics.

Bodies and Souls is an apocalyptic view of Los Angeles today as a modern paradise for still-rebelling "angels." Its gallery of characters ranges from a pornographic actress to a Mr. Universe; a bagwoman, a Chicano teenager, a gothic female evangelist, a black maid from Watts, a male stripper, a TV anchorwoman. A youngwoman and two youngmen—"lost angels"—bring about the apocalyptic ending.

The peculiar aspects surrounding the novel's publication created almost insurmountable barriers to its reception, through nobody's deliberation. My talented editor on two earlier books had formed his own publishing house. He made a good bid for *Bodies and Souls*. I withdrew the book from other publishers, feeling that a new company's first original book would bring major attention to it; and I did not want to break an excellent editorial relationship. Too, the book would be brought out in a few months as opposed to the usual almost-year. I was dubious about the book being issued simul-

taneously in hardback and trade editions; but I became convinced that was, indeed, a trend of the future, with notable antecedents among respected books. Because of pressures endemic to new publishing enterprises, the hardcover edition of the book was makeshift, ugly; it and the trade edition contained dozens of typographical errors, pages askew. I would have demanded publication be stopped until a new edition was printed, but the book was already advertised, galley proofs sent to reviewers. I knew that the shoddy appearance of the book would arouse incorrect suspicions that the book had been widely rejected. That, of course, was not so. Far from so.

Written from advance galleys before the shoddy edition was seen, two fine reviews appeared, one in the *New York Times Book Review,* which borrowed my description of Los Angeles to call the book "a scarred beauty"; and one in the *Los Angeles Times Book Review,* which lauded it as a "memorable feast."

Reviews stopped. Just as I had known, the book's condition had done inestimable damage to the book. I wrote individual letters to book-review editors I respected, calling attention to my novel, letting them know that a new respectable edition was being prepared. In some instances, I knew, my letters would arouse further antagonism, and they did—but excellent reviews eventually appeared in the book sections of the *San Francisco Chronicle,* two Dallas newspapers, the *Los Angeles Herald,* and a few others.

Eventually the publishers did release a good looking limited hardback and a handsome trade edition. There is also a handsome paperback. My relationship with my publishers and my editor is restored to the point that they will publish my next novel. It was a nightmarish situation that had entrapped everyone concerned.

Despite all these obstacles, *Bodies and Souls* continues to draw attention, and praise. It is, I believe, a daring novel in content and form; a grand and lasting artistic achievement.

Now that autobiography has slipped into passionate journalism, I will remain there for a while longer: Today, I find myself a "Texas" writer left out of discussions of Texas writers, a Chicano writer omitted from anthologies of Chicano writers, a "California writer" ignored in books about California. Even though I am excluded from several anthologies of homosexual writers, I am still known as "the homosexual writer." Yet several of my books do not deal centrally with the subject of homosexuality; and for the *Nation, Saturday Re-*

view, the *Texas Observer, Evergreen Review,* and many other publications, I have written essays on poverty among Mexican-Americans, injustice against juveniles in detention homes, discrimination against black athletes, the persecution of dissenting soldiers during the Vietnam War. I have translated the writing of notable Mexican authors, and have written essay-reviews of books by William Golding, William Burroughs, Jean Rhys, Jonathan Swift, André Gide, Elizabeth Bowen. My one-act play *Momma As She Became—But Not As She Was* is widely performed, anthologized.

My books continue in print, gaining readers and attention. *City of Night, Numbers,* and *The Sexual Outlaw* were just reissued in new format, with Forewords by me. New translations appear. My play *Tigers Wild*—which ranks with my best writing—is moving toward Off-Broadway production in 1986. My next novel, *Marilyn's Daughter,* about the legend of Marilyn Monroe, will appear the same year. I want to write two more books: *In the Beginning,* about war in Heaven, and *Autobiography: A Novel.*

If I died tomorrow, I would know that I have written as formidable a body of work as that of any other writer of my generation.

*

Collision of memories!

One emerges, seizes completely—is followed by a question. I sort through other memories.

This cherished one! A beloved friend and I have been let into the Museum of Modern Art before the doors open to the public. My friend and I and rooms and rooms of the magnificence of Picasso!

This! Miss Stowe changed my name from Juan Francisco Rechy to John, no, Johnny (when she counted to ten and I heard "one," I thought, knowing only Spanish, that she was calling me, "Juan").

And this: Reflecting the grisly determined optimism of that vast State of Texas, Miss Stowe made us change a word in one of the songs we had to sing for her daily: "Home on the Range." "Where seldom is heard a discouraging word" became "where *never* is heard a discouraging word." In the text, she made us draw a dark line through "seldom" and substitute, with blue ink, "never."

What would Miss Oliver have done?

Now the avoided memory flows into the present: I am five years old. I have been told that I must start school. I refuse to go. I do not want to leave my mother unprotected. "What will happen if the robbers come or the house burns? Who will save you?" I ask her. "You will," she tells me. "You will know if anything threatens me and you will save me."

But did I? Years later—after the wandering from city to city—I did return to El Paso, and stayed until her death. In that new house I bought her, she retained this: An old glass case from years back which contained delicate figurines, crystal angels, hand-painted cups and saucers, miniature white statues of the Madonna. Why, in my memories, do those objects seem imprisoned in a beautiful glass cage?

This is an outline of my "autobiography" today. Only today. Even it contains contradictory "truths." Tomorrow it may all change.

With one exception. Perhaps two. And another—

POSTSCRIPT

John Rechy contributed the following update to *CA* in 2001:

As the years of living extend into a vista of recollections and the future shrinks, one begins to collect memories before they end. Then, autobiography becomes a series of recalled highlights that shift constantly and rearrange themselves out of sequence, reshaping different versions of the same life. On the scrim of memory, images flash, and in the film of one's life, there are long shots, closeups, freeze-frames—and persistent voice overs that attempt to explain it all, most often encountering only mystery, more mystery.

EXPOSITORY VOICE OVER: Since 1986, I have published four more novels, a total of eleven, and I have completed another, *The Naked Cowboy,* to appear in 2002. *Marilyn's Daughter,* perhaps the most difficult book I ever wrote, is ostensibly about Normalyn Morgan, who may or may not be the daughter of great star Marilyn Monroe and Robert Kennedy; it is actually an exploration of artifice raised to the level of art—and Monroe is its quintessence. It explores the power of legend over truth.

In it, I extended my experimentation with form to illustrate content. In one instance I'm particularly proud of, I used the most artificial of all filmic devices, the flashback, seven times back, to the origin of one memory:

A group of malicious teenagers called the Dead Movie Stars perform scenes from scandals involving the great stars. The pullback begins during such a performance of a suicidal attempt by Marilyn Monroe. It moves back through various steps preceding it (the information carried like the baton in a relay match), finally locating Marilyn Monroe speaking to her psychiatrist about the attempt—and then I pull into the scene she's narrating, dramatizing it as it occurred. I pull away then, layer by layer until we're back at the performance that began the sequence.

I invented the character of Troja, a beautiful Marilyn impersonator, a black transsexual involved with an aging bodybuilder; both are variations on the theme of artifice as beauty.

In *The Miraculous Day of Amalia Gómez,* I dealt for the first time centrally in my novels with the Mexican-American people of my roots through Amalia and her family (although, a point often missed, there is in every one of my books at least one Mexican-American character, usually the protagonist, and I have written many articles, several in the *Nation* about prejudice against Mexican Americans). Her life in disarray—a son dead in prison, a daughter running wild, another son hustling the streets—Amalia has reached a dead-end, and only a miracle can save her. I spent more than a week on one single passage in the novel, when Amalia has confronts the Holy Mother, woman to woman. I wanted the confrontation to be like an aria of lament and defiance.

The novel received glowing reviews, and is required reading in several college courses. The only negative review was in the *New York Times,* where the reviewer did not read even the first paragraph, which sets the novel, for necessary irony, in Hollywood; she placed it in East Los Angeles. That review drew a scathing rebuttal from José David Saldívar in his book on Chicano literature, *Border Matters,* citing the reviewer's ignorance of and indifference to Hispanics, viewing them from her perch as an editor at *Elle* magazine.

The most misunderstood of my novels appeared in 1996, an epic titled *Our Lady of Babylon.* It is told in the first person by a woman who claims to have been all the fallen women of history, blamed unfairly for terrible catastrophes. She is on a mission to redeem all those falsely accused, and to locate their persistent accuser, finally revealed, throughout history. The novel is also an exploration about the impossibility of locating "truth" once a distortion is entrenched, corrected only by transformation into art, bearing its own truth.

In it, I retell the stories, among others, of Adam and Eve, Salome and St. John, Medea and Jason, Jesus, Judas, and Magdalene (a love affair among the three). Some of it takes place in Heaven, during the war of angels. Again, I experimented with form. The novel contains a novel within a novel, a scandalous "pornographic" story modeled after the genre classics of the eighteenth century. But that novel within the novel contains essential clues to the riddle of Our Lady.

AN INTRUSIVE VOICE: An author should not explain his work.

VOICE OVER: Why shouldn't an author explain his work? Why should he leave it in the hands of reviewers and critics who often do not even bother to read what they write about?—and so distort, create barriers between writer and reader.

VOICE OVER (CONTINUING OVER INTERRUPTION): In 1999, I returned to the territory of my first novel, the homosexual world of cursory encounters. *The Coming of the Night,* an immediate bestseller, was set in 1982, the year that AIDS was about to invade. I trace its course, virtually minute by minute, following a varied cast of characters until the end of one hot windy summer day in Los Angeles. It is a stark book that I chose to write in "black and white"—few adjectives that evoke other than basic colors. Throughout, there are silhouettes, shadows, darkening imagery, the imagery of contagion. The ending of the novel edges toward surrealism as the night finally comes down in all its blackness.

I based that novel on an incident I saw in a park in West Hollywood in 1982, an incident that continued to haunt me for years: A youngman surrendered his body in a park late at night over and over to different men while even in that park, that night, there were bruitings about a deadly illness emerging. For years I kept from writing about that in my novels (although I wrote several articles for magazines). As the death toll from AIDS rose, I felt that it was a time to listen to those who were stricken.

GO TO BLACK, HOLD BLACK OVER VOICE OVER: They died daily, people we loved, young, older. Our holocaust, which continues. Greeted with indifference. We all lived daily in terror. But out of that time, those who were dying and those who stood by them revealed an untapped source of courage and strength among gay men and their non-gay allies. Lesbians came nobly to our aid. AIDS exposed this unwelcome truth: For many, we were still pariahs; an illness that struck us—as randomly as legionnaire's disease had struck legionnaires and polio had struck pool-swimmers—was blamed on us as punishment.

PANNING SHOT: With my partner Michael I roam the Los Angeles Design Center, where a portion of the huge remembrance quilt has been laid out. Patches commemorate those dead from AIDS; some patches are highly decorated, with messages of love and remembrance, others are stark and just as moving in their simplicity. We roam from quilt to quilt, and stop, frequently, to learn of the death of someone we knew, a death discovered only then.

VOICE OVER (CONT'D): Somehow, somehow, my partner and I survived it. Like everyone else of the time, we possess a graveyard of memories, of all those people, many anonymous, dead now, that entered our lives, quite often only briefly but intimately.

FADE OUT OVER VOICE OVER: I have just finished writing *The Naked Cowboy,* a picaresque novel loosely inspired by Fielding's Tom Jones. It is set, today, in Texas, Los Angeles, Las Vegas. I borrow the form of the eighteenth century picaresques, using brief chapter headings that guide the reader in. This novel has already become one of my favorites.

INSISTENT, TRIUMPHANT VOICE-OVER: My novel *Bodies and Soul*s, ambushed by a shoddy initial publication by another publisher, was reissued in 2001 in a new, fine edition by Grove Press; it includes an introduction by me. *The Miraculous Day of Amalia Gómez* also appeared in a new edition from Grove Press, also with an introduction by me.

My reputation as a writer—and I have fought to uphold it—gains, deservedly. *City of Night,* so excoriated by some critics when it first appeared, is now often referred to as a modern classic. Several of my novels are required reading in college literature courses. Many of my books—eight presently in print—have never gone out of print. New translations of my work continue, into approximately twenty languages now.

In 1997, I was the first novelist to receive PEN-USA West's Lifetime Achievement Award, previously given only to Billy Wilder, Neil Simon, and Betty Friedan.

FLASHBACK: It's 1950-something. I'm hustling Pershing Square. I'm picked up by a man who is staying at the fancy Biltmore Hotel across the street. To avoid floor detectives constantly spying, the man instructs me to go in a back way and meet him in the elevator on a

Michael Snyder, Rechy's "long-time life partner"

second floor. It works. On the third floor, the door opens and a detective appears, demanding I leave; and I do.

FLASHFORWARD: Thirty-some years later. I am in the same hotel, in the grand ballroom. I am accepting the grand PEN Lifetime Achievement Award.

SOUND UP: The applause of two standing ovations. . . .

Where is the house detective?

CLOSEUP: Those I love most are there: Michael, my partner of many years, is with me, and I am flanked by my sister Blanche, my brother Roberto. When author Carolyn See, presenting the award, calls me up to receive it, I kiss my sister Blanche, express my love, and then I lean over my brother Roberto, and say, "I owe you so much" (and I do; he sacrificed his own education, working in a pool room to allow our family to survive financially; he made it possible for me to go to college). I kiss his tears of joy.

QUICK CUT: The next year, Michael and I are in New York. I am receiving the William Whitehead Publishing Triangle Award for lifetime achievement.

SOUND UP: The applause of another standing ovation.

VOICE OVER: In a Los Angeles Times Book Review roundup, I was named by many fellow writers as among the most important authors writing about California. Several of those fluky best-books of the millennium lists—which I nevertheless disdain—include writing by me.

An elaborate CD Rom of my life and works, *Mysteries and Desire: the Worlds of John Rechy,* produced by Marsha Kinder through the USC Annenberg Center for Communication, was released, receiving several awards, shown at Sundance, shown at the Museum of Contemporary Art in Los Angeles.

This CD Rom introduced a new form that has not yet received the attention it deserves. In it, a viewer can go to confession with me, roam through cruising areas, listen to passages of my novels. In 2000, a large drawing of me appeared on the cover of the Los Angeles Times Book Review in connection with the publication of *The Coming of the Night.* When I attend in book signings, I am moved by the many people who come to tell me that one or another of my novels has affected their lives deeply.

STEADY MYSTERIES: What tortured my father so profoundly that he extended that torture to me, so cruelly? He remains an angry, sad dark shadow in my life. My memories of his brutality can still rack me violently; I see him constantly preparing to menace me in some new hideous way. I will not remember him listening to operas on the radio and futilely pretending he is conducting them. I must edit his tears, out of my mind, when compassion for his decline tends to compromise my anger. I will not be sad for him . . . despite those tears, those haunting, haunted tears.

LONG SHOT IN FLASHBACK: In 1977, I met a Michael. For years I had avoided any relationship; I would literally flee—leave a city to get away from anyone who came too close. That ended with Michael. Lovers, partners, companions—we became all that and more and have been together since we met.

CLOSEUP: 1999, April. London.

We are dazzled by palaces, cathedrals, the mystery of Stonehenge.

TIGHT CLOSEUP: Riskily, our driver has managed to take us to the top of the moors in Emily Brontë country. A reclusive man appears, points out where the ruins of what was Wuthering Heights are. The sky darkens, sleet slashes—in tribute to the moody writer and the turbulence she captured, physical and emotional. I gather a bouquet of heather.

QUICK CUT: While Michael stands beside me, I place the bouquet on Emily Brontë's grave in the beautiful church where she's buried.

FLASHBACK: It's 1983. Michael and I are alone—only guards and us—in the Museum of Modern Art with roomful of Picasso's paintings. We have been let in early by the Museum Director. A memory that astounds each time it recurs.

LONG PANNING SHOT: In 2001, in Italy.

Snapshots that need no camera to record: Venice. A room that faces the Grand Canal and a glistening Cathedral. Rome—Nero's palace buried in darkness, under the earth. The Coliseum (where, our private guide, Flamieta, tells us, Christians were *not* fed to the lions—that occurred only in Cecil B. DeMille's movies). The constant miracle of the Sistine paintings. The awesome splendor of that city spills before us as we stand looking down from the top of a hill on a vista of ruins that have achieved their own beautiful form, a vista carved out by history, a vista within which art seems grandly, recklessly squandered—so ubiquitous is it.

CLOSEUP: Florence. We stare at Michelangelo's "unfinished blocks" of statuary. The figures are struggling to come out. He left them like that, to create that impression—and it does, extending to all art that struggles out of a metaphoric stone.

LINGERING SHOT: At opulent Villa d'Estee, from our suite, we stand admiring the pristine water of Lake Como.

QUICK CUT: Mass at Maria Maggiore chapel in Rome. Michael is not a Catholic, I lapse every day. He suggests we take communion. We march up to the railing, and we take the host together.

VOICE OVER FLASHBACK: In 1986, my play *The Fourth Angel* opened to a wonderful reception in Los Angeles, beautifully directed by my Michael, who had, in its first reading, played the lead. Brashly, we took it directly to New York—by then the play was titled *Tigers Wild,* with Russell Barnard as producer. We took it there without previewing it in the traditional way, not allowing intrusive "critics" and so-called dramaturges to interfere. It was a superb production at Playhouse 91.

But we were considered upstarts, invaders. Astonishingly, negative notices appeared, including in the *New York Times,* weeks before the play opened.

PROUD PROGRAM NOTE: The first biography of me will appear in 2002, titled *Midnight's Child* by Charles Casillo, published by Allyson House.

MONTAGE OF MEMORIES:

FREEZE FRAME: My mother dies every day in my mind. I try to stop her death. I resurrect her. In a flood of memories, she returns, her green eyes are as brilliant as ever, and they banish death.

QUICK CUT WITH VOICE OVER: I'm reading a *Los Angeles Times Magazine* article about a Tijuana healer brought back to the United States to stand trial for fraud. I see my sister's name. I read that she was there to testify on behalf of the healer. Only then do I learn that she is dying from cancer. Weeks away from death, she testifies that the healer gave her and other women what doctors wouldn't—hope, special kindness, warmth.

CLOSEUP: She's on the stand, she bares her bloodied breast and says to the judge: "He gave us hope that we could recover from this."

FLASHBACK: On a street in El Paso. I'm nine years old, my sister Olga is twelve, almost thirteen. A roaming photographer shoots a snapshot of us as we walk along to the movies. He gives us a ticket with which we may claim the photograph.

TIGHT CLOSEUP: The photograph. My sister is wearing a yellow dress my mother sewed for her—"the butterfly dress." She's not yet the great beauty she will become, but the traces are there. We're walking along and clearly speaking spiritedly. . . . She was already walking toward her destiny on the courtroom stand, preparing to bare her mutilated breast.

My beloved brother Yvan died soon after.

FLASHBACK: He has returned from the Army, World War II, the front-line. He smokes constantly; he's still very young. My father is shouting vile insults at me, I'm thirteen. My brother intercedes. "Call him another name and I'll shut your mouth!" he menaces my father. I love him for that time, a short time because, soon after, my brothers and sisters were all married, and my mother and I were left with my father and the daily terrors of his wrath.

John Rechy, about 1995

VOICE OVER: In 1998, my brother Roberto was in a terrible car accident that left him with a fractured memory. I hope that among those memories there are recurring ones of him and me, he being more of a father to me than that strange old man who tormented me.

MONTAGE: MY BROTHER'S POINT OF VIEW: He remembers only the past. His injured mind is reordering time, not unlike the way I am doing here. I hope he remembers that, every Friday, his pay day—I was a kid—he would bring me a box of pastries, and I would hug him in gratitude. I hope he remembers teaching me, patiently, to drive, remembers buying me my first car—a bullet-like Studebaker. I hope he remembers only happy times.

VOICE OVER: Only my sister Blanche, alone now, a proud, beautiful, elegant old lady, and I are alive from among our immediate family.

FLASHBACK: She's eighteen, she's getting married to her handsome husband, Gus. Still in her glorious white bride's dress, at her reception she removes her shoes and dances, her black hair courting the light as she swirls.

FADE OUT OVER RECURRING VOICE OVER: I have continued to breach the exhortation that writers must never protest mistreatment by reviewers or editors because it will only get them ignored, or treated even worse. Nonsense. I believe in protesting. Silence brings only more abuse. After thirty years of protest, I was finally given space to rebut the *New York Review of Books'* 1963 personal assault on me when *City of Night* appeared. When I received the PEN Award, PEN Director Sherrill Britton wrote to the paper: "The writer whose identity your reviewer questioned in 1963 is being honored with a PEN Lifetime Achievement Award for his highly original and exceptionally honest work [and] literary distinction." The letter was published in that journal's correspondence columns under the exclamatory headline, "CONGRATULATIONS!"—perhaps the first time that journal has employed an exclamation mark!

PANNING SHOT WITH CLOSEUPS: In several letters I complained to Victor Navasky, editor of the *Nation,* that, although for years I had written lead articles for that magazine under the editorship of the great Carey McWilliams, I had apparently been banished even from publicity roster of writers who have written for the magazine. No answer from him, until my friend, Molly Shapiro, a financial donor to the *Nation,* queried Mr. N. He wrote that he had no knowledge of the matter, but he would look into it, since he was an admirer of mine. I did not hear from him. So I sent him copies of the many letters I had written about the matter he claimed no knowledge of. He could, he wrote me, "explain or apologize." "I apologize," he wrote.

CUT TO: A book party in Los Angeles. Mr. N. and I have a friendly encounter. Whatever accounted for my being ignored, he promised me, was over and I would be receiving a call from the magazine with an assignment. No word, nothing. I remain banished from the liberal magazine that upholds standards of social decency.

I have succeeded in having vituperative reviews deleted from Amazon and Barnes & Noble websites. I had an apology from Gore Vidal—my agent Georges Borchardt's wife claims that must be the only one—after, in a book of his essays, he praised a negative review of my first novel and I reminded him that he was often the object, himself, of similar vituperation.

I have had telephonic and mail exchanges with two editors of the *New York Times Book Review,* in response to my inquiries about why books of mine had not been reviewed. I ended my latest exchange with Charles ("Chuck") McGrath with a letter in which I wrote him words I would advise other writers to heed:

"But, finally, Mr. McGrath, reviews and reviewers do not matter. They are remembered, if at all, in derisive footnotes about their mistakes."

ASSERTIVE VOICE OVER: I grow more and more confident of my place in literature. When the emphasis on my supposedly "outrageous life" as a gay man, but, more, as a hustler, settles, my work will be acknowledged as among the best of its time. There are already indications, in the awards—a class on my work was taught in Germany last year; new anniversary editions of my novels are appearing in France, Italy, Spain, Holland. Am I arrogant to state so boldly that I know my place in literature?

A VOICE INTRUDING: How arrogant to say that about himself!

VOICE OVER (CONT'D): There is nothing humble about the act of creation; and in my work I have roamed from the hustling streets of New York and Los Angeles to the plains of Heaven, the war of angels.

I am as vain as ever, I continue to work out with weights and to look terrific, and I make that statement knowing that to praise one's appearance is considered a punishable sin by many. But I find posturing humility offensive, hypocritical.

At times it infuriates me, at other times it puzzles me, but mostly it amuses me that, even now that I am in my seventh decade, I arouse many of the passions and angers that I aroused with my first novel in 1963. Today, my writing is at its best.

This person—myself—who wanted romantically, and like so many other young people, to die at twenty-nine—now has amassed seventy years. That person cherishes life.

Given all the horrors that one has to live with in the world—daily cruelties and brutalities and ignorance exposed—I am happy. I want to continue to live, workout, experience everything with my partner, and to create more, much more, adding to a body of work that will endure and triumph.

BIOGRAPHICAL/CRITICAL SOURCES:

BOOKS

Canning, Richard, *Gay Fiction Speaks: Conversations with Gay Novelists,* Columbia University Press (New York, NY), 2001.

Casillo, Charles, *Midnight's Child: The Lives and Careers of John Rechy,* Allyson, 2001.

Contemporary Literary Criticism, Gale (Detroit, MI), Volume 1, 1973; Volume 7, 1977; Volume 14, 1980; Volume 18, 1981.

Dictionary of Literary Biography, Volume 122: *Chicano Writers, Second Series,* Gale (Detroit, MI), 1992.

Dictionary of Literary Biography Yearbook: 1982, Gale (Detroit, MI), 1983.

Gilman, Richard, *The Confusion of Realms,* Random House (New York, NY), 1963, 5th edition, 1969.

Hispanic Literature Criticism, Gale (Detroit, MI), 1994.

Martinez, Julio A., and Francisco A. Lomeli, editors, *Chicano Literature: A Reference Guide,* Greenwood Press (New York, NY), 1985.

PERIODICALS

Advocate, September 14, 1999, R. Hunter Garcia, review of *The Coming of Night,* p. 86.

Booklist, June 1 & 15, 1996, p. 1677.

Chicago Review, 1973.

Gay and Lesbian Review, spring, 2000, Richard Canning, "Transformations and Continuitites," p. 9.

Lambda Book Report, October, 1999, Thom Nickels, "Nitty-Gritty Nights," p. 13.

Library Journal, February 1, 1963; June 15, 1996, p. 92; August, 1999, Roger Durbin, review of *The Coming of Night,* p. 142.

London Magazine, June, 1968.

Los Angeles Times, September 7, 1988; September 15, 1996, Pamela Warrick, "Best-selling Author John Rechy Says He Has Been Long Misread," p. 5; September 29, 1996, Marsha Kinder, "Failing to See the Humor," p. 5; October 26, 1997, Pamela Warrick, "His Writing Began with Controversy. Now John Rechy's Life Work Is Saluted," p. 5.

Los Angeles Times Book Review, July 17, 1982; January 27, 1985; October 2, 1988; September 22, 1991, p. 3.

Nation, January 5, 1974.

Newsday, September 10, 1988.

New York Blade News, April 2, 1999, Jameson Currier, article on John Rechy.

New York Times, December 27, 1967.

New York Times Book Review, June 30, 1963; January 14, 1968; April 3, 1977; July 17, 1977; February 17, "John Rechy's Bodies," 1980; July 10, review of *Bodies and Souls,* 1983; May 10, 1992, Karen Brailsford, review of *The Miraculous Day of Amalia Gomez,* p. 16.

People, May 22, 1978.

Prairie Schooner, Fall, 1971.

Publishers Weekly, May 13, 1983, review of *Bodies and Souls,* p. 47; June 28, 1991, review of *The Miraculous Day of Amalia Gomez,* p. 87; May 13, 1996, p. 58.

Religion and American Culture, summer, 1999, Luis Leon, "The Poetic Uses of Religion in *The Miraculous Day of Amalia Gomez,*" p. 205.

San Francisco Chronicle, August 7, 1988.

Saturday Review, June 8, 1963.

Times Literary Supplement, September 11, 1970.

Transcript, November 28, 1988.

Village Voice, August 22, 1977; October 3, 1977; March 3, 1980.

Washington Post Book World, August 12, 1973; July 21, 1996, p. 8.

OTHER

Advocate, http://www.advocate.com/ (September 12, 2001).

John Rechy's Official Web site, http://www.johnrechy.com/ (October 8, 2001).

Mysteries and Desire: Searching the Worlds of John Rechy, produced by Marsha Kinder, USC Annenberg Center for Communication, 2000.

*   *   *

REED, John (Silas)   1887-1920

PERSONAL: Born October 22, 1887 near Portland, Oregon; died of typhus, October 19, 1920, in Moscow, Russia; son of Charles Jerome and Margaret (Green) Reed; married Louise Bryant, 1917. *Education:* Graduated from Harvard, 1910. *Politics:* Communist Labor Party.

CAREER: Journalist, historian, poet, short story writer, and dramatist.

WRITINGS:

Sangar, privately printed, 1912.

The Day in Bohemia; Or Life among the Artists (also see below), privately printed, 1913.

Insurgent Mexico (also see below), Greenwood (New York, NY), 1914, edited and with an introduction and notes by Albert L. Michaels and James W. Wilkie, Simon and Schuster (New York, NY), 1969.

The War in Eastern Europe (also see below), 1916.

Tamburlaine and Other Verse, 1917.

Ten Days that Shook the World (also see below), Boni and Liveright (New York, NY), 1919, with a foreword by V. I. Lenin and an introduction by Granville Hicks, Modern Library (New York, NY), 1935, with an introduction by Harold Shukman, St. Martin's Press (New York, NY), 1997.

Daughter of the Revolution and Other Stories, edited and with an introduction by Floyd Dell, Vanguard (New York, NY), 1927.

The Education of John Reed (selected writings), with an introduction by John Stuart, International Publishers (New York, NY), 1955.

An Anthology, Progress Publishers (Moscow, Russia), 1966.

Adventures of a Young Man: Short Stories from Life, Seven Seas (Berlin, Germany), 1966, City Light Books (San Francisco, CA), 1975.

The Complete Poetry of John Reed, edited by Jack Alan Robbins, introduction by Granville Hicks, memoir and sonnet by Max Eastman, Pine Hill Press (Freeman, SD), 1973.

The Provincetown Plays: Second Series, Core Collection Books (Great Neck, NY), 1976.

Labor's Grand Old Man, Slienger (London, England), 1976.

Collected Poems, edited and with a foreword by Corliss Lamont, Lawrence Hill (Westport, CT), 1985.

John Reed of the Masses, edited by James C. Wilson, McFarland (Jefferson, NC), 1987.

John Reed: The Early Years in Greenwich Village (includes *The Day in Bohemia; Or Life among the Artists*), Archives of Social History, 1990.

John Reed and the Russian Revolution: Uncollected Articles, Letters and Speeches on Russia, 1917-1920, edited by Eric Homberger and John Biggart, St. Martin's Press (New York, NY), 1992.

The Collected Works of John Reed (includes *Insurgent Mexico, The War in Eastern Europe,* and *Ten Days that Shook the World*), Modern Library (New York, NY), 1995.

Contributor to *American Magazine, The Masses, Metropolitan,* and *New Republic.* Editor of *Voice of Labour;* served on editorial boards of *Harvard Monthly* and *Lampoon.* Reed's works have been translated into Russian, Italian, and Spanish.

ADAPTATIONS: Ten Days that Shook the World has been adapted for film as *Octobre,* by Sergei Eisenstein, Seuil (Paris, France), 1971; and as *Oktiabr'skaia buria,* Molodaia gvardiia, 1987.

SIDELIGHTS: A journalist, historian, and poet, John Reed is best known for his *Ten Days that Shook the World,* an eyewitness account of the Russian Revolution. Though he thought of himself as a poet and fiction writer, he had little success in these genres; it was as a journalist that Reed gained acclaim. Known for crossing over the line from objective reporting into advocacy for a cause, Reed's work as both a war correspondent and an activist led Walter Lippmann, a contemporary reporter, to say that "with Jack Reed reporting begins." As critic Elmer Bendiner of the *Nation* explained, "The name of John Reed is breathed nowadays like a sigh for lost innocence. He was a journalist of a sort that has gone out of style . . . a reporter on horseback seeking his story in the faces and gestures of the living warriors, not in word games of press handouts or news conferences." The leader of the Communist Labor Party in the United States, Reed is the only American and one of the few foreigners to have ever been buried at the foot of the Kremlin wall.

Born and raised in a wealthy family in Oregon, Reed was educated at Harvard and began his writing career there, writing poetry and plays and serving on the editorial boards of the *Lampoon* and *Harvard Monthly.* After his graduation in 1910, he moved to Greenwich Village and joined the staff of the *American Magazine* as both a contributor and editor. It was during this time that Reed first became interested in social problems, and quickly became a radical. "John Reed was so active in radical politics as to have too little time left for poetry," wrote Harriet Monroe in *Poetry* magazine, explaining why Reed's poetry career had never reached its full potential. "Knowing himself for a poet, he hoped to prove his vocation by many poems worthy to endure; but life was so exciting, and the social struggle in these States and Mexico, in Finland, Russia—everywhere—so tempting to a fighting radical, that poetry had to wait for the leisure which—alas!—never came." In 1913, Reed joined the staff of *The Masses,* a periodical that reflected his political views. For *The Masses,* he wrote an account of the silk workers's strike in Paterson, New Jersey; during the writing of the article, he was arrested for his attempts to speak on behalf of the strikers. He went on to write a play about the strike, which he produced in Madison Square Garden, performed by the strikers themselves.

In 1914, Reed was hired as a war correspondent by *Metropolitan* magazine to cover the Mexican revolution. Reed followed Pancho Villa's army and lived among his soldiers for four months, traveling with them across the desert, sleeping on the ground, celebrating in looted *haciendas,* and being with them in battle. The resulting series of articles, republished in book form as *Insurgent Mexico,* attracted more critical attention and earned Reed the reputation "the American Kipling." *Insurgent Mexico,* divided into six sections, provides descriptions of the Desert War, the attack on Torreón, rebel leader Pancho Villa, and an interview with Carranza, another leader of the rebellion. "The articles he sent back from the border were as hot as the Mexican desert," reported Walter Lippman, writing for the *New Republic,* "and Villa's revolution, till then reported only as a nuisance, began to unfold itself into throngs of moving people in a gorgeous panorama of earth and sky."

Robert Rosenstone, in his biography of Reed, *Romantic Revolutionary,* noted that the book's "artistically arranged scenes have a balance, coherence and integrity that daily experience lacks. Skies often turn blood-red after battles, simple peons speak with uncanny folk wisdom, the narrator has sudden flashing insights into the symbolic meanings of complex events—such things occur too often to be taken as a literal transcription of what Reed saw, heard and did." Granville Hicks, in his biography *John Reed: The Making of a Revolutionary,* said of this quality in the work, Reed "was indifferent to the accuracy of the historian, but he had the integrity of a poet."

Not all critics were won over by Reed's narrative style. A reviewer for the *Nation* commented, "The book is a lurid exaggeration of some few aspects, and the frenzied manner of the whole composition aims not so much at depicting sober truths as at shocking the reader by disgusting naturalism in describing an irregular assortment of horrors such as were to be found nowhere else in the world at the time that Reed wrote." Critics in the late twentieth century, however, recognized the merits of *Insurgent Mexico;* a writer in *History Today* called it "a classic indeed," and Richard Elman of the *Nation* claimed that the book was "Reed's finest writing, a book of such vividness, empathy and daring that much of what passes for personal journalism today does seem callow by comparison."

Reed himself described his travel to Mexico in his essay "Almost Thirty," printed in the *New Republic.* "A terrible curiosity urged me on," he described. "I felt I *had to know* how I would act under fire, how I would get along with these primitive folks at war. And I discovered that bullets are not very terrifying, that the fear of death is not such a great thing, and that the Mexicans are wonderfully congenial. . . . I loved them and I loved the life. I found myself again. I wrote better than I have ever written."

Reed returned from Mexico a popular figure, but his acclaim soon faded due to his opposition to World War I and his participation in the Socialist Party. Many magazines would no longer print his work, and his next book, *The War in Eastern Europe,* was called by Harry Henderson in the *Massachusetts Review* a "dismal failure." The articles for this book were again commissioned by *Metropolitan,* and Reed traveled to Europe, behind both Allied and German lines. Because of Reed's socialist views, he was not granted the same insider's view as he had been in Mexico. Though he used the same form as he had for *Insurgent Mexico,* without his being able to identify with a specific cause, according to Henderson, "Reed becomes entirely disoriented as a narrator." Unable to recreate his earlier successes, Reed began co-writing and producing short plays for the Provincetown Players with Louise Bryant and Eugene O'Neill. Bryant became his wife in 1917.

In August of 1917, Reed and Bryant sailed to Russia to cover the coming revolution. As a supporter of communism, Reed quickly sided with V. I. Lenin and his supporters, and was an enthusiastic witness to the Bolshevik revolution in Petrograd. Reed alone among the foreign correspondents was given an insider's view and treated as a fellow to the cause. He kept a diary of his conversations with educated leaders and peasants alike. The book that recorded the events of the revolution, *Ten Days that Shook the World,* is, according to Henderson, "most often regarded as a journalistic fluke, as the great case in the history of eye-witness accounts of the right reporter being in the right place at the right time." *Ten Days that Shook the World* was "the first major account in America of the revolution's universal impact," according to John Stuart in his introduction to *The Education of John Reed,* and is often considered by critics the finest first-hand account of the Russian revolution.

Bertram D. Wolfe, in his book *Strange Communists I Have Known,* explained that Reed "tried to see it all and put it all on paper. The dream of the Bolsheviks, the realities of their deeds, and the tension between the dream and reality are in his pages." Stuart praised Reed, declaring, "What he wrote about the Russian Revolution in *Ten Days that Shook the World,* with its extraordinary weaving of significant detail into a triumphal theme, was a measure of the great leap forward he had made." But the reception of the book in America at the time was not positive. Even before its publication, Reed had not been allowed to return to the United States due to a sedition charge against him for articles he had written for *The Masses.* When he was finally allowed entrance into the country, he turned from journalism to politics, and organized the Communist Labor Party, one of the two rival communist parties in the United States. When *Ten Days that Shook the World* was published in 1919, Reed was indicted as a communist leader during the "Red Scare" after World War I, due to his radical stance and obvious support of communism. He fled the country, eventually returning to Russia where he died of typhus. Reed was buried, honored as a Soviet hero, under the Kremlin wall facing the Red Square, the only American and one of the few foreigners to receive such an honor.

BIOGRAPHICAL/CRITICAL SOURCES:

BOOKS

Aaron, Daniel, *Writers on the Left,* Harcourt (New York, NY), 1961.

Eastman, Max, *Heroes I Have Known: Twelve Who Lived Great Lives,* Simon and Schuster (New York, NY), 1942.

Gelb, Barbara, *So Short a Time: A Biography of John Reed and Louise Bryant,* Norton (New York, NY), 1973.

Hicks, Granville, *John Reed: The Making of a Revolutionary,* Macmillan (New York, NY), 1936.

Lerner, Max, *Ideas Are Weapons: The History and Uses of Ideas,* Viking (New York, NY), 1940.

Madison, Charles A., *Critics and Crusaders: A Century of American Protest,* Henry Holt (New York, NY), 1974.

Malone, Duman, editor, *Dictionary of American Biography,* Volume 8, Scribners (New York, NY), 1935.

Reed, John, *The Education of John Reed: Selected Writings,* International (New York, NY), 1955, John Stuart, introduction.

Rosenstone, Robert A., *Romantic Revolutionary: A Biography of John Reed,* Knopf (New York, NY), 1975.

The McGraw-Hill Encyclopedia of World Biography, McGraw (New York, NY), 1973.

Twentieth-Century Literary Criticism, Volume 9, Gale (Detroit, MI), 1983.

Wolfe, Bertram D., *Strange Communists I Have Known,* Stein and Day (New York, NY), 1965.

PERIODICALS

Dial, March 22, 1919, Harold Stearns, "The Unending Revolution," pp. 301-303.

History Today, April, 1984, review of *Insurgent Mexico,* p. 60.

Massachusetts Review, spring, 1973, Harry Henderson, III, "John Reed's Urban Comedy of Revolution," pp. 421-435.

Nation, January 21, 1915, "A Gory Volume," pp. 82-83; June 30, 1969, Elmer Bendiner, "Troubadour of Revolution," pp. 32-33; February 21, 1976, David H. Rosenthal, "The Other United States," pp. 217-218; April, 17, 1982, Richard Elman, "Partisan Journalist," pp. 469-470.

New Masses, October, 1930, John Dos Passos, "Jack Reed," pp. 6-7.

New Republic, December 26, 1914, Walter Lippmann, "Legendary John Reed," pp. 15-16; April 29, 1936, John Reed, "Almost Thirty," pp. 332-336; November 4, 1967, Stanley Kauffman, "Ya Americanski Sotsialist," pp. 18, 30; July 3, 1976, Robert A. Rosenstone, review of *Adventures of a Young Man: Short Stories from Life,* pp. 31-32.

New York Evening Post, November 12, 1927, Thomas Boyd, "John Reed As an Ironic Realist before His Time," p. 12.

Poetry, January, 1921, Harriet Monroe, "Two Poets Have Died," pp. 208-212.

Soviet Literature, 1977, Able Startsey, "Writer and Revolutionary," pp. 165-168.

Village Voice, February 3-9, 1982, Paul Berman, "To Russia with Love," pp. 6-9.

OTHER

American Decades CD ROM, Gale (Detroit, MI), 1998.
Pegasos, http://www.kirjasto.sci.fi/ (April 5, 2001).
Reds, Paramount Pictures, 1981.*

*   *   *

REIF, Stefan C. 1944-

PERSONAL: Born January 21, 1944; son of Peter and Annie (Rapstoff) Reif; married Shulamit Stekel (a publications subeditor), September 19, 1967; children: Tanya, Aryeh (son). *Education:* Attended University of London; Jews College, certificate, 1961; University College, B.A. (first class honors), 1964, Ph.D., 1969; University of Cambridge, M.A., 1976. *Religion:* Jewish. *Avocational interests:* Squash, cricket and football.

ADDRESSES: Home—23 Parsonage St., Cambridge CB5 8DN, England. *Office*—Cambridge University Library, West Rd., Cambridge CB3 9DR, England; fax 01223 333160. *E-mail*—scr@cam.ac.uk.

CAREER: University of Glasgow, lecturer in the Department of Hebrew & Semitic Languages, 1968-72; Dropsie College, Philadelphia, academic dean and assistant professor of Hebrew language and literature, 1972-73; University of Cambridge, director, Taylor-Schechter Genizah Research Unit, 1973—, head, Cambridge University Library's Division of Oriental and Other Languages, 1983—, professor of medieval Hebrew studies, 1998—, St John's College fellow. Hebrew University and the Oxford Centre for Postgraduate Hebrew Studies, visiting scholar, 1979; Hebrew University, Lady Davis Visiting Professor, 1989; Institute for Advanced Studies, visiting fellow, 1996-97; external examiner for various universities, including Glasgow University, 1979-82, and Jews' College, 1976-78 and 1987-88.

MEMBER: World Union of Jewish Studies, American and European Associations for Jewish Studies, Royal Asiatic Society (fellow), Jewish Historical Society of England (president, 1991-92), Society for Old Testament Study, Society of Biblical Literature, Hebraica Libraries' Group (founder convener, 1981-84), British Association for Jewish Studies (president, 1992), Society of Jewish Study.

AWARDS, HONORS: William Lincoln Shelley Studentship, University of London, 1967-68; various research awards, British Academy, 1978-94; honorary fellow, Mekize Nirdamim Society for the Publication of Ancient Hebrew Manuscripts, Jerusalem.

WRITINGS:

Shabbethai Sofer and His Prayer-Book, Cambridge University Press (New York, NY), 1979.
(Editor, with J. A. Emerton) *Interpreting the Hebrew Bible: Essays in Honour of E. I. J. Rosenthal,* Cambridge University Press (New York, NY), 1982.
Published Material from the Cambridge Genizah Collections: A Bibliography 1896-1980, Cambridge University Press (New York, NY), 1989.
(Editor, with Joshua Blau) *Genizah Research after Ninety Years,* Cambridge University Press (New York, NY), 1992.
Judaism and Hebrew Prayer: New Perspectives on Jewish Liturgical History, Cambridge University Press (New York, NY), 1993.

Hebrew Manuscripts at Cambridge University Library: A Description and Introduction, Cambridge University Press (New York, NY), 1997.
A Jewish Archive from Old Cairo: The History of Cambridge University's Genizah Collection, Curzon, 2000.

Initiator and general editor, *Genizah Series,* fourteen volumes, Cambridge University Press (New York, NY), 1978-2002.

WORK IN PROGRESS: Editor, *Fragments Found and Fathomed: An Introduction to the Cambridge Genizah Collections,* for Cambridge University Press; research on "Hebrew liturgy; Genizah research; mediaeval Hebrew Bible commentary; historical development of Hebrew; Hebrew studies at Cambridge."

* * *

REYNOLDS, Oliver   1957-

PERSONAL: Born 1957, in Wales. *Education:* Studied drama at University of Hull, 1977-80.

ADDRESSES: Office—c/o Faber & Faber, Author Mail, 3 Queen Square, London WC1N 3AU, England.

CAREER: Writer, 1983—. Cambridge University, Judith E. Wilson Junior Fellow in creative writing; University of Glasgow, writer-in-residence; University of Strathclyde, writer-in-residence.

WRITINGS:

POETRY

Skevington's Daughter, Faber & Faber (London, England), 1985.
The Player Queen's Wife, Faber & Faber (London, England), 1987.
The Oslo Tram, Faber & Faber (London, England), 1991.
Almost, Faber & Faber (London, England), 1999.

SIDELIGHTS: Oliver Reynolds's debut collection of poetry, *Skevington's Daughter,* contains three sections each concerning a different subject. The first section features poetry on language, the second, on photography, and the third, on Wales, though, according to Dick Davis in *Listener,* "in its obsession with the Welsh language Section 3 is closely linked to Section 1." This cyclical association is a device Reynolds employs in his later work, *Almost*. The continuity of the poems is debated by Blake Morrison in his review for *London Review of Books*. "Reynolds is learned and laconic and his mind leaps about a bit, a combination which makes some of his poems difficult: the links aren't explained, the endings can seem inconclusive." Claude Rawson, a *Times Literary Supplement* critic, offered similar praise for Reynolds's poetry: "Oliver Reynolds is an original. He has mastered an odd, unpredictable flatness, the source of haunting effects of violence and bizarrerie."

In his assessment of Reynolds's *The Player Queen's Wife, Times Literary Supplement* critic Lachlan Mackinnon posited that Reynolds's penchant for humor and manipulation might have caught up with him in his second collection. "Like Reynolds's first collection, *Skevington's Daughter,* this is a book of quite unusual unevenness. The danger for Reynolds is cleverness, an ability to make neat verse-shapes with little in them and to avoid any but the lightest implication of feeling." Mackinnon pointed out, however, that "there are enough good poems here to make this a distinguished volume." Brad Leithauser, writing for the *London Review of Books,* noted Reynolds's innovative condensing of the sonnet form. "On the face of it, the arguments for a limerick-sized sonnet may not appear compelling. But in Reynolds's hands, there is a jocose pleasure in the form's extreme concision. One delights, too, in the way that Reynolds's triad and couplet roughly preserves the pleasing disproportion of the traditional octave and sestet."

Times Literary Supplement critic Mark Wormald observed a distinction between *The Oslo Tram,* Reynolds's third collection, and his two previous efforts. "Oliver Reynolds's third collection consists almost entirely of departures. These begin with its title. Where *Skevington's Daughter* and *The Player Queen's Wife* suggested a penchant for narratives surrounding quirky relationships, this seems to have been left behind." "What Reynolds is about now," Wormald continued, "seems rather to be an attack on the sort of 'eventuality' that an imaginative but land-locked literary figure can now expect to confront, and an exploration of those aspects of the self these encounters reveal."

Reynolds's fourth collection, *Almost,* featured poems that *Times Literary Supplement* critic Robert Potts, saw as linked, loosely or otherwise, by their association with a woman named Helen, represented in the collection as Reynolds's elusive lover. "With wit and style, Reynolds sculpts his visions of Helen, rendering pain

or paean; but this is also a creative triumph over hard facts, which are at least as 'refractory' as the structures and games he insists on working with." "Every detail of this thoroughly crafted collection," Potts concluded, "offers a chime or link to another piece; this review can only begin to suggest the pleasures of reading, rereading and freshly recognizing."

BIOGRAPHICAL/CRITICAL SOURCES:

PERIODICALS

Listener, December 5, 1985, Dick Davis, "Obliquities," pp. 33-34.
London Review of Books, December 5, 1985, Blake Morrison, "Dialect Does It," pp. 14-15; October 15, 1987, Brad Leithauser, "Narrow Places," pp. 22-23.
New Statesman, May 13, 1988, Robert Sheppard, "Time's the Whole Sentence," pp. 31-32.
Times Literary Supplement, February 7, 1986, Claude Rawson, "Knowing the Throne," pp. 137-138; January 15-21, Lachlan Mackinnon, "Two Kinds of Cleverness," 1988, p. 56; May 10, 1991, Mark Wormald, "Rocking the Boat of Language," p. 23; September 17, 1999, Robert Potts, "Meaningless as an O," p. 11.*

*   *   *

RHODES, James A(llen)   1909-2001

OBITUARY NOTICE—See index for *CA* sketch: Born September 13, 1909, in Coalton, OH; died March 4, 2001, in Columbus, OH. American politician and author. Rhodes was Ohio's longest-serving governor who, in addition to bringing drastic improvement to infrastructure statewide, was responsible for ordering National Guard troops to quell anti-Vietnam War demonstrators on the campus of Ohio's Kent State University in 1970. After four unarmed students were killed by soldiers, Rhodes' political reputation was tarnished enough for him to lose the Senate primary a few days later; however he was later re-elected as governor for a fourth term during the late 1970s. Rhodes authored a number of books including *The Court-Martial of Commodore Perry, Alternative to a Decadent Society,* and *Vocational Education and Guidance.*

OBITUARIES AND OTHER SOURCES:

PERIODICALS

Chicago Tribune, March 5, 2001, section 2, p. 5.

Los Angeles Times, March 5, 2001, p. B4.
New York Times, March 6, 2001, p. A19.
Times (London, England), March 6, 2001.
Washington Post, March 5, 2001, p. B6.

*   *   *

RICHTER, Stacey 1965-

PERSONAL: Born 1965; daughter of Herschel and Valerie Richter.

*ADDRESSES: Home—*Tucson, AZ. *Office—*c/o Author Mail, Scribners, c/o Simon & Schuster, 1230 Avenue of the Americas, New York, NY 10020.

CAREER: Fiction writer.

AWARDS, HONORS: Pushcart Prize, 1998, for "The Beauty Treatment".

WRITINGS:

My Date with Satan (short stories), Scribner (New York, NY), 1999.

SIDELIGHTS: Stacey Richter's *My Date with Satan* is a collection of thirteen tales narrated by what *Newsday* reviewer Susan Salter Reynolds described as "blustery teens and twenty-year-olds who act like they know everything just to survive but carry some earnest kindness or need inside of them." *Booklist* reviewer Kathleen Hughes called Richter's stories "imaginative, unusual, and somewhat creepy" and her characters "voyeuristic and somewhat sordid." One story, "Goal 666," is narrated by a member of a Swedish goth band called Lords of Sludge. In spite of their powerful performances of the dark songs he writes for them, the narrator/songwriter notices that the bandmembers have scrupulous hygiene habits, perfect manners, and that he is becoming as sensitive as they. The band changes its tune when all involved fall for a new female member, switching to Karen Carpenter and Rodgers & Hammerstein melodies. In "The Beauty Treatment," a rich high school student looks for her inner beauty when her face is forever scarred by a razor-wielding girl. This story, which a *Publishers Weekly* reviewer called "the collection's strongest story . . . a convincing look into the minds of overindulged kids," was awarded a 1998 Pushcart Prize.

A young woman who goes on a cruise finds herself shipwrecked on an island of men in "An Island of Boy-

friends." When she tires of the hunks, the narrator withdraws to become the island recluse. In "Rats Eat Cats," a young woman submits a grant application to become a "cat lady," her plan being to become old amidst dozens of cats in a small apartment where she will collect public assistance, most of which she will spend on cat food. The title story is about Satan and PipiLngstck, the online names of a couple who link up in an S & M chat room and plan to meet to indulge their fantasies. *Library Journal* reviewer Kimberly G. Allen found Richter's writing to contain "an irony that is familiar yet fresh," while Elizabeth Gleick wrote in the *New York Times Book Review* that Richter's stories "are sometimes funny, sometimes too bizarre for their own good, and most definitely eccentric. But despite their superficial differences . . . all are linked by a delicate understanding of the fundamental humanity that underlies our put-on personas, however frail, freakish or off-putting they may seem."

BIOGRAPHICAL/CRITICAL SOURCES:

PERIODICALS

Booklist, July, 1999, Kathleen Hughes, review of *My Date with Satan,* p. 1924.
Library Journal, July, 1999, Kimberly G. Allen, review of *My Date with Satan,* p. 139.
Newsday, July 18, 1999, p. B12.
New York Times Book Review, August 15, 1999, Elizabeth Gleick, "Stranger than Most Fiction," p. 9.
Publishers Weekly, June 7, 1999, review of *My Date with Satan,* p. 73.*

*   *   *

RITTER, John H. 1951-

PERSONAL: Born October 31, 1951, in CA; son of Carl W. (a journalist) and Clara Mae Ritter; married Cheryl B. Ritter (a teacher and curriculum developer), 1972; children: Jolie. *Education:* Attended University of California—San Diego. *Avocational interests:* "Speaking to teachers, students, and writers at conferences and universities about creativity and the writing process; playing baseball in an amateur league; playing guitar and writing songs; walking the streets, observing people, and walking in the country under the stars at night."

*ADDRESSES: Home—*San Diego, CA. *Office—*c/o Children's Marketing, 345 Hudson Street, 15th Floor,

New York, NY 10014. *Agent*—Ginger Knowlton, Curtis Brown, Ltd., Ten Astor Place, New York, NY 10003.

CAREER: Writer. Speaker in schools and conferences. Custom painting contractor, 1973-98.

MEMBER: Society of Children's Book Writers and Illustrators, International Reading Association, National Council of Teachers of English (member, Assembly of Literature for Adolescents), Native Cultures Institute of Baja California.

AWARDS, HONORS: Judy Blume Award, Society of Children's Book Writers and Illustrators, 1994; Children's Book Award, International Reading Association (IRA), Best Book for Young Adults, American Library Association (ALA), and Blue Ribbon Book, *Bulletin of the Center for Children's Books,* all 1999, and Young Adult Readers Choice, IRA, 2000, all for *Choosing up Sides;* Books for the Teen Age list, New York Public Library, Parents' Guide to Children's Media Award, Shenandoah University, and Texas State Lone Star Book designation, all 2001, all for *Over the Wall.*

WRITINGS:

Choosing up Sides, Philomel (New York, NY), 1998.
Over the Wall, Philomel (New York, NY), 2000.

Ritter's work has also appeared in various periodicals, including *Spitball: The Literary Baseball Magazine* and the *Christian Science Monitor.*

WORK IN PROGRESS: "A novel about a strange boy who shows up to join a ragged baseball team in order to help them win a crucial game to save their small town."

SIDELIGHTS: "I grew up with my left hand tied behind my back. Well, actually, it was only tied up till I was six or seven." Thus begins John H. Ritter's *Choosing up Sides,* a "debut tale of epiphany and apocalypse," according to Elizabeth Bush in a review for *Bulletin of the Center for Children's Books.* Ritter's 1998 novel introduces readers to the world of fervent baseball, Bible-thumping religion, and a life-altering choice imposed on a young boy with an incredible talent. Ritter's novel is at once morality tale and sports book, but not your ordinary play-by-play sports book. Winner of the prestigious International Reading Association's Children's Book Award as well as an American Library Association Best Book for Young Adults citation, *Choosing up Sides* augured a fine career for the new author. With his

second novel, *Over the Wall,* such a promise was fulfilled. As Chris Crowe colorfully put it in *ALAN Review,* "With his baseball novel *Choosing up Sides* . . . rookie YA author John H. Ritter landed a spot on the All Star team. . . . Ritter's second at bat, *Over the Wall,* will secure him a regular spot in the line up of notable authors writing about sports for young adults."

"I never intended [my books] to be play-by-play sports novels," Ritter told Crowe in an *ALAN Review* interview. "I'm more interested in using baseball scenes as metaphor, or for challenges of character, or to advance the story. I could as easily set the stories in the world of ballet, were I as knowledgeable in that arena. But the thrust would be the same. Kids dealing with hard choices. To me, that's the definition of YA lit." Success with his first two books meant Ritter could quit his day job and go at writing full time. Working for twenty-five years as a painting contractor, he was ready to give painting with words a larger place in his life.

"I grew up in a baseball family," Ritter noted on his Web site. He and his brothers played one-on-one hardball in the dry hills of rural San Diego County, near the Mexican border. His father, sports editor of the *San Diego Union,* was a large influence in his love for the game. But there was more than simply sports in the family background. "We were also a family of musicians and mathematicians, house painters and poets," Ritter explained. Originally from Ohio, the family moved to California just before Ritter's birth; at age four he lost his mother to breast cancer. "One thing I can remember about my mom is that she sang to us constantly, making up a song for each of her four children that fit our personalities perfectly. So from her, I got a sense of how to capture a person's spirit in a lyrical phrase."

Another early influence on Ritter was his rural upbringing, the solitude and independence of depending on yourself and your siblings for entertainment and friendship. "Out in that country," Ritter explained on his Web site, "the neighbor kids lived so far away, my brothers and I developed a half-real, half-imaginary game where we pitched and hit the ball, then dreamed up the rest, keeping the score, game situations, and full, major league line-ups in our heads." Such games were an early training for Ritter in the art of storyline and plot development.

At school Ritter was, as he described himself to Crowe, a "wild student. . . . A rabble rouser and a contrarian." Ritter was always looking for the exception to the rule, and in spite or perhaps because of this questioning nature, he was also a high achiever. But he had something of a dual personality in school. "I could be extremely focused one day, then get tossed out of class the next," he admitted to Crowe. "As proof, in high school I was voted both the Senior Class President and the Senior Class Clown." Teachers along the way also discovered that Ritter had a way with words, and would read his work out to the class as an example of good writing.

Meanwhile, Ritter's father had remarried and two more sisters were added to the Ritter family mix. Baseball continued to dominate his free-time activities; some even thought he might have a chance at playing pro ball. By the time he was in high school, however, Ritter discovered the joys of song writing, heavily influenced by Bob Dylan and Dylan's working-class perspectives. Graduating from high school, Ritter went to college at the University of California—San Diego, carrying around a little notebook in which he would write lyrics for songs, noting riffs and phrases. At school he met his future wife, but by his second year, Ritter knew that he needed to get on with life, that college was not the place he needed to be at that time. "I knew I had to walk the streets, touch life, embrace life, gain experience," he told Crowe. "I wanted to learn from life. To hit the road like Kerouac, Dylan, and Twain. To have something real to write about." So one spring day he filled out a withdrawal card and left the university behind, taking a job as a painter's apprentice with a commercial contractor he had already worked for during the summers. Working for three or four months per year, he could save enough to travel and write the rest of the year. After several years, he married and had a baby daughter; that upped the work year to nine months. However, Ritter always scheduled time for writing.

Ritter struggled with his writing part-time until the late 1980s when he joined a local fiction group led by YA novelist Joan Oppenheimer. Working in this environment of feedback and comment, Ritter soon grew in his abilities. He took extension writing classes, joined another writing group, and in 1994 won the Judy Blume Award for a novel in progress. Though the novel remained unpublished, it did build confidence in the young writer and opened doors with editors. When he settled down to writing another coming-of-age novel, Ritter opted for a baseball setting. He chose such a background for two reasons: not only is this a topic close to his heart, but also baseball carries a heavy and resonant metaphorical value in American culture. Further influences for his first novel came from the author's personal juvenile experiences with prejudice and bias. Growing up in the 1960s, he watched nightly news reports of the civil rights movement, graphic film clips

of marchers set upon by snarling dogs, pummeled by police batons, and crushed by sprays of water from fire hoses. Then came the kidnapings and murders in Mississippi. As a ten-year-old country boy, the world seemed to make no sense. About that same time, a teacher put the word "sinister" on the board and asked Ritter and his fellow students the meaning of the word. When the same teacher revealed that, instead of "diabolical" or "evil", it was simply the Latin root for "left" or "left-sided," Ritter learned another lesson in bias. For him and other baseball players, lefties were highly valued—there was nothing sinister about them. But later in life, these feelings and experiences coalesced in the writing of the novel that became *Choosing up Sides.*

Ritter sets his first novel in Southern Ohio in the 1920s, and to research the book he read widely on religious movements, the characteristics of left-handedness, and the Appalachian dialect. He visited relatives in the region who helped with interviewing local people to get to know more intimately customs and culture. Also blended into the stew is a story Ritter's father liked to tell, about a buddy who was so fond of tossing crab apples at a telephone pole that ultimately he became a great pitcher.

The novel's protagonist is thirteen-year-old Luke Bledsoe, the oldest son of a preacher. Born left-handed, Luke is, in the eyes of his Fundamentalist father, a throwback, a potential follower of Satan, for that is the hand of the devil. The authoritarian father, Ezekiel, tries to "cure" Luke of his left-handedness by tying that hand behind his back, but with little luck. Luke's father is the new minister at the Baptist Church in Crown Falls, Ohio, and Luke is the new boy in a town that is baseball crazy. The local team won the county championship the previous year and hopes to do so again this year. But for Luke's father, baseball is, like dancing, a temptation that needs to be resisted. Then one day, while Luke is watching a forbidden game, a ball lands at his feet. Throwing it back with his left hand, he amazes the crowd with his distance and placement. He looks to be the natural the team desperately needs to clinch the championship, and everyone sets about trying to recruit the boy, who has quite accidentally built up his pitching arm by tossing apples. Classmate and slugger Skinny Lappman counters Ezekiel's religious objections by saying that the wasting of talent such as Luke's is the bigger sin. Also enlisted in the campaign is baseball fanatic Annabeth Quinn, for whom Luke has a strong attraction. Uncle Micah, a sports reporter on his mother's side, also plays a part in this conversion, whisking the talented youngster off to see Babe Ruth, another southpaw, play. Finally Luke gives in and decides to pitch for the team, becoming the local hero until a confrontation with his father leads to a violent beating. His father breaks Luke's pitching arm in the altercation, and the boy vows to run away. Tragically and ironically, Luke's father falls into the Ohio River and Luke is unable to throw a lifeline to him because of his broken arm.

The bare outline of the plot does little to describe a book rich in characterization, nuance, metaphor, and dialogue. Ritter did not commit the first-time writer's mistake of flat characterization. Even Luke's father Ezekiel is shown to have his human side; he is not simply a tyrant. Jealous of Luke's bond with Uncle Micah, Ezekiel overcomes his fear of water and takes his son fishing. At one point, he gently touches his son's shoulder with his left hand, indicating to Luke that he too was born left-handed and has had to repress it all these years. The irony of Ezekiel's death is all the stronger not only because he dies because he has broken his son's throwing arm, but also because his favorite hymn for sinners is "Throw out the Lifeline."

Critics and reviewers responded strongly to *Choosing up Sides,* Bush describing it as a novel that "pits fire and brimstone Fundamentalism against a rival religion—Baseball—and treats both with cathartic understanding." Ritter uses an even hand not only in treatment of theme, but in style. Bush further commented, "leavening the sober elements of this morality tale . . . is the pure joy of baseball and, at least in Luke's case, its redemptive power." Patricia K. Ladd, writing in *ALAN Review,* felt that Ritter "addresses themes of autonomy and independence common to young adult readers and portrays plot through authentic dialect and well-developed characters." Ladd went on to note that though the tale was, at first glance, "a simple story of realistic fiction, perhaps even a parable," Ritter's use of dialogue, similes, metaphors and imagery all "add dimensions to the plot that leave readers pondering the book's messages long after turning the final page." Kate Clarke, reviewing the title in *Book Report,* called it an "entertaining and thought-provoking coming-of-age story" about "being true to one's self and choosing how to live." A reviewer for *Publishers Weekly* noted that, "Despite its somewhat didactic tone, this story offers enough curve balls to keep readers engaged." "Unlike many sports novels, *Choosing up Sides* does more than offer a mere glimpse of the grand old game of baseball—it takes a deeper look at faith, truth, and individuality," maintained Stefani Koorey in her *Voice of Youth Advocates* review, going on to dub the tale a "well-designed study of personal choice" and concluding: "With its wide appeal, this first-person story is a

recommended purchase for all public and school libraries." Joel Shoemaker, reviewing *Choosing up Sides* for *School Library Journal,* also praised the writing and theme of Ritter's publishing debut. "Cleverly told in a colloquial first-person twang, this thoughtful tale of authority questioned and dreams denied will be real enough to many readers," Shoemaker averred. And in announcing the Children's Book Award in *Reading Today,* the IRA committee felt that Ritter's tale was "laced with humor," and presented a "realistic and inspirational picture of a young man torn between two worlds."

News of the IRA award literally brought tears to Ritter's eyes; it was a vindication of his many years of hard work and perseverance. The author, who writes his first drafts longhand and subsequent drafts on the computer, was quick to follow up this initial success with another hard-hitting novel using baseball as a further metaphor for life.

"Writing a book is a lot like growing a plant," Ritter noted in a letter to a young reader posted on the author's Web site. "It starts with a seed, which is only an idea. But like all seeds, it does have the potential to grow into something interesting if you nurture it and are patient. The seed of the idea for *Over the Wall* came from my discovery of two facts. One is that twice as many Vietnam vets died by suicide after the war ended than actually died in the war. The other is that fifty times as many Vietnamese died fighting to save their country as did Americans, but there is no 'wall' for them that lists all of their names. When I realized how unfair and how self-centered that was for Americans to only care about their own people, I realized that the Vietnam War was not really over for many Americans."

In his second novel, Ritter once again takes an historical setting, though one closer to the present, in a story about a boy's journey attempting to reconnect with his father and discover who he is in the process. There are many "walls" in thirteen-year-old Tyler's life: the literal wall of the baseball field he wants to clear with a mighty slam; the Vietnam memorial wall bearing his grandfather's name; and the invisible wall Tyler's dad has built around himself ever since the death of his daughter—Tyler's sister—nine years earlier. When he is invited to spend the summer in New York City with his cousin, Tyler is determined to make it onto the roster of an all-star baseball team. However, Tyler's explosive temper gets in the way of his obvious talent. With the help of his pretty cousin and with the sage advice of his coach, a Vietnam vet, Tyler manages to navigate the risky waters of this passage. The coach helps the boy reconnect with himself and his guilt-ravaged dad. "By the end," noted Todd Morning in a review of *Over the Wall* for *School Library Journal*, "Tyler has gained a level of self-awareness by unraveling some of the tangled stories in his family's past and understanding the intricacies lying beneath the surface of life." Morning concluded, "Sports are just a part of this ambitious work that presents a compelling, multilayered story." A *Publishers Weekly* reviewer found Ritter's second novel to be a "powerful lesson in compassion," and Roger Leslie agreed in *Booklist,* commented that *Over the Wall* is a "fully fleshed-out story about compassion and absolution." Connie Russell, reviewing the title for *ALAN Review,* called the book a "poignant and accessible coming-of-age story," while Ladd described the novel as a "profound story of realistic fiction for young and mature adults."

"The driving force behind all my stories comes primarily from finding something that really bugs me," Ritter explained to Crowe. "And so far, it tends to be some sort of injustice. But I refuse to write revenge stories. I hate them. I won't even watch a revenge movie. To me, it's the easy response to injustice, and it lacks integrity. . . . So I try to look for an alternative solution. That's what spawns my ideas." In an interview with Teri Lesesne in *Teacher Librarian,* Ritter also added insight into the type of novel he enjoys writing: "I don't believe in choosing between character-and plot-driven novels. To me, the greatest stories are a finely woven blend of both. That's what I shoot for. Of the two, character comes easier for me, so I fret more about my plots. That becomes the sand in the oyster—or the ointment—for me. What if a left-handed boy is forced to be right-handed? What's the best thing that could happen? What's the worst? Or what steps, what events would lead an angry and bitter kid to learn to embrace his enemies as a way of freeing himself from the prison of his emotions? How does one get over that wall? These kind of questions nag at me until I can answer them. That's how my books begin."

Fans of Ritter's first two novels—young readers, critics, and award committees alike—await what other thing might "bug" or "nag" at the author, and result in his next work of fiction. Meanwhile, Ritter carries on with his craft, putting in ten-hour days at the writing desk in hopes of getting just the right word, the right phrase. "I love using that voice to say something I need to say," he concluded on his Web site. "I love the rhythms and the musicality of language. I love discovering a good story, building it, and telling it. And when they all come together between the covers of the book, it's like magic."

BIOGRAPHICAL/CRITICAL SOURCES:

BOOKS

Ritter, John H., *Choosing up Sides,* Philomel (New York, NY), 1998.

PERIODICALS

ALAN Review, spring-summer, 2000, Chris Crowe, "An Interview with John H. Ritter," pp. 5-9; spring-summer, 2000, Patricia K. Ladd, "Covering the Bases with Young Adult Literature," pp. 10-17; fall, 2000, Connie Russell, review of *Over the Wall,* p. 33.
Booklist, March 1, 1998, p. 1513; March 15, 1999, p. 1302; April 1, 2000, Roger Leslie, review of *Over the Wall,* p. 1451.
Book Report, March-April, 1999, Kate Clarke, review of *Choosing up Sides,* p. 63.
Bulletin of the Center for Children's Books, June, 1998, Elizabeth Bush, "The Big Picture."
Childhood Education, spring, 1999, p. 174.
Publishers Weekly, April 13, 1998, review of *Choosing up Sides,* p. 76, May 29, 2000, review of *Over the Wall,* p. 83.
Reading Today, June-July, 1999, "IRA Names Award-winning Children's Books," p. 21.
School Library Journal, June, 1998, Joel Shoemaker, review of *Choosing up Sides,* p. 152; June, 2000, Todd Morning, review of *Over the Wall,* p. 152.
Teacher Librarian, March, 2001, Teri Lesesne, "Complexities, Choices, and Challenges," pp. 44-47.
Voice of Youth Advocates, December, 1998, Stefani Koorey, review of *Choosing up Sides.*

OTHER

John H. Ritter Web site, http://www.johnhritter.com/ (May 12, 2001).*

*   *   *

RIVERA, Beatriz 1957-

PERSONAL: Born September 27, 1957, in Havana, Cuba; daughter of Mario Rivera and Aida Ruffin; married Denis Beneich (marriage ended); married Charles Barnes, June 21, 1988; children: Nigel Barnes, Rebecca Barnes. *Ethnicity:* "Hispanic." *Education:* Paris IV—Sorbonne, D.E.U.G., licence, Maîtrise; Paris III—

Sorbonne, D.E.A.; doctoral studies in Spanish literature, City University of New York.

ADDRESSES: Home—105 Upper Whitfield Rd., Accord, NY 12404. *E-mail*—riverabarnesaol.com.

CAREER: Jersey Journal, Jersey City, NJ, reporter.

WRITINGS:

African Passions and Other Stories, Arte Público, 1995.
Midnight Sandwicher (novel), Arte Público, 1997.
Playing with Light (novel), Arte Público, 2000.

WORK IN PROGRESS: The Iron Monkey, novel; *Latina Poetry and the Canon: A Study of the Anthologies.*

*   *   *

ROBERTS, M. L.
    See, MATTERN, Joanne

*   *   *

ROBINS, Elizabeth   1862(?)-1952
    (C. E. Raimond)

PERSONAL: Born August 6, 1862 (some sources say 1865) in Louisville, KY; died May 8, 1952, in Brighton, England; daughter of Hannah Maria (an opera singer; maiden name, Crow) and Charles Ephraim (a banker) Robins; married George Richmond Parks (an actor), in 1885 (died 1887).

CAREER: Actress, 1878-1902; writer, 1893-1952.

MEMBER: Women's Social and Political Campaign, Actresses's Franchise League, Association of Social and Moral Hygiene, Women's Institute, Six Point Group.

WRITINGS:

(As C. E. Raimond) *George Mandeville's Husband,* Appleton (New York, NY), 1894.
(As C. E. Raimond) *The New Moon,* Appleton (New York, NY), 1895.
(As C. E. Raimond) *Below the Salt,* Heinemann, 1896, revised as *The Fatal Gift of Beauty and Other Stories,* Stone (Chicago, IL), 1896.

(As C. E. Raimond) *The Open Question: A Tale of Two Temperaments,* Heinemann, 1898, reprinted under the name Elizabeth Robins, Harper (New York, NY), 1899.
The Magnetic North, Stokes (New York, NY), 1904.
A Dark Lantern: A Story with a Prologue, Macmillan (New York, NY), 1905.
The Convert, Methuen (London, England), 1905, Macmillan (New York, NY), reprinted with introduction by Jane Marcus, Women's Press (London, England), 1907, reprinted 1980, Feminist Press (Old Westbury, NY), 1980.
Under the Southern Cross, Stokes (New York, NY), 1907.
Come and Find Me!, Century (New York, NY), 1908.
The Mills of the Gods, Moffat, Yard (New York, NY), 1908, expanded edition published as *The Mills of the Gods, and Other Stories,* Butterworth (London, England), 1920.
The Florentine Frame, Moffat, Yard (New York, NY), 1909.
Why? Women Writers' Suffrage League (London, England), 1910.
Under His Roof, Woods (London, England), 1912.
"Where Are You Going To . . .?", Heinemann, 1913, reprinted as *My Little Sister,* Dodd, Mead (New York, NY), 1913.
Way Stations, Dodd, Mead (New York, NY), 1913.
Camilla, Dodd, Mead (New York, NY), 1918.
The Messenger, Century (New York, NY), 1919.
Time Is Whispering, Harper (New York, NY), 1923.
(As Anonymous) *Ancilla's Share: An Indictment of Sex Antagonism,* Hutchinson, 1924, reprinted under name Elizabeth Robins, Hyperion (Westport, CT), 1976.
The Secret That Was Kept: A Study in Fear, Harper (New York, NY), 1926.
(With Octavia Wilberforce) *Prudence and Peter, a Story for Children about Cooking Out-of-doors and Indoors,* Benn (London, England), 1928, reprinted as *Prudence and Peter and Their Adventures with Pots and Pans,* Morrow (New York, NY), 1928.
Ibsen and the Actress, Hogarth (London, England), 1928, Haskell House (New York, NY), 1973.
Both Sides of the Curtain, Heinemann, 1940.
Raymond and I, Hogarth (London, England), 1956, Macmillan (New York, NY), 1956.
The Alaska-Klondike Diary of Elizabeth Robins, 1900, edited by Victoria Joan Moessner and Joanne E. Gates, University of Alaska Press, 1998.

OTHER

(Translator; as Anonymous) Bjoernsterne Bjoernsen, *Magnhild and Dust,* in *The Novels of Bjoernsterne Bjoernsen,* edited by Edmund Gosse, Heinemann, 1897.

(Author of introduction) Evelyn Sharp, *Rebel Women,* United Suffragists (London, England), 1915.

(Editor) Henry James, *Theatre and Friendship: Some Henry James Letters, with a Commentary by Elizabeth Robins,* Putnam (New York, NY), 1932.

PLAYS

(With Florence Bell) *Alan's Wife,* produced in London at Terry's Theatre, April, 1893, published as *Alan's Wife: A Dramatic Study in Three Acts,* Henry (London, England), 1893.

Votes for Women, produced in London at Court Theatre, May, 1907, published as *Votes for Women: A Play in Three Acts,* Dramatic Publishing (Chicago, IL), 1907, Mills & Boon (London, England), 1909.

SIDELIGHTS: Elizabeth Robins is best known for her rich characterizations of women; as both a novelist and as an actress, Robins found insightful ways of delineating female motivations. Though Robins's work was criticized for its lack of literary expertise and for its somewhat old-fashioned tone, her books were also beloved for their passion and their unique characters. Because Robins was able to delineate women's characters with warmth and understanding, moreover, she pioneered the idea of the twentieth-century woman. Sue Thomas wrote in *Dictionary of Literary Biography* that "Robins's fiction and its reception played key roles in the development, contestation and historical fortunes of New Woman and first-wave British feminist fictional aesthetics."

Robins was born on August 6, 1862 in Louisville, Kentucky. Her parents, Charles Ephraim Robins and Hannah Maria Crow Robins, were both wealthy and artistic; Hannah Robins was a former opera singer, and Charles Robins (who was also Hannah's first cousin) was a banker. The family was also prone to depression, however, and by 1885 Robins's mother was institutionalized. Robins was educated away from home, at the Putnam Female Seminary, but she maintained a close relationship with her family, particularly with her youngest brother, Raymond. The two would remain correspondents throughout their lives; in 1956, their letters were published as *Raymond and I,* delineating a trail of devotion leading from 1894 to 1926.

Against the wishes of her family, Robins became an actress. She debuted in 1878, and eventually became renowned for her portrayals of Ibsen's women: Hedda Gabler, Hilda Wangel, and others. These characters offered her a way of thinking about women's selves that she would return to again and again; she wrote in 1928: "Ibsen not only transformed dramatic art, he was an instrument used by the zeitgeist to enfranchise the spirit of women." In 1885 (the year her mother was institutionalized), Robins married a fellow actor, George Richmond Parks. Two years later, he committed suicide. Robins never married again. She did develop some intense friendships with various literary figures, however; in particular, she became closely linked to Henry James and William Archer, who encouraged her to write. In 1894, Robins heeded Archer's advice by publishing *George Mandeville's Husband* under the pseudonym "C. E. Raimond," a pen name she would use throughout her career.

The novel was not a huge hit with the critics, but it was popular enough to lead to other books. Robins's fiction was praised for its insightful treatment of character—particularly its treatment of women's and servants's characters. For example, a critic in *Academy* explained the allure of Robins's 1896 *Below the Salt:* "There is no trace of that satisfaction with superficial observation—the meaningless record of daily tasks and uneducated speech—which commonly condemns stories of servant-life. They are matter-of-fact, it is true, altogether without the triumphant exaggeration with which [William Makepeace] Thackeray wrote of servants, or the triumphant idealisation of [Benjamin] Disraeli. But if they are not triumphant, they are sure: they go far into character."

In part, Robins seems to have managed her insightful treatment of character by drawing heavily on her own experiences; many of her novels contain traces of autobiography, and she almost published *A Dark Lantern* anonymously. According to Thomas, Robins feared "that it would be read as an autobiography with her doctor Sir Vaughn Harley being seen as Garth Vincent, the 'black magic' man, who inspires Katherine Dereham's sexual and poetic awakening." The novel tells the story of a beautiful young woman who has fallen hopelessly in love with a prince. But as she becomes ill from this unrequited love, she becomes sexually involved with her monstrous doctor—the "man with the dark-lantern face." Gradually, their relationship is domesticated, and in the end the doctor is able to rise in the world. Critics found the story bizarre, but they praised its passion and its fine characterizations. A critic for the *New York Times* commented that "it must be called, plainly, a distorted picture. But it is full of sincerity, and has much fine detail. In strength, in originality, in emotional force it is far out of the common." William Payne, writing for the *Dial,* concurred that Robins's "characters certainly have vitality, and an extraordinary power to interest us."

During this period, Robins was also in the midst of her correspondence with Raymond, who had been engaged in the Klondike Rush; her 1908 novel, *Come and Find Me!,* uses his experiences as the setting for a romance. In the novel, a group of characters make their way toward the hidden gold fields of Alaska, while family mysteries are sorted through. Critics found the work flawed in its structure, but winning in its characterizations. A contributor to *Review of Reviews* complained that "there is an evident lack of homogeneity, an unsatisfying absence of balance, too many untied ends that mar its completeness and leave it roughly unfinished." A critic for the *New York Times,* however, suggested that "Miss Robins is not so well endowed with the story teller's instinct as she is with the faculty for the dramatic portrayal of character." F. T. Cooper, reviewing Robins's 1908 publication *Under the Southern Cross* for *Bookman,* praised her ability to construct a genial protagonist, and commented that "it is seldom that one comes across a new type of hero in the lighter sort of hammock fiction who is so sympathetic, so genuine, so altogether attractive as the Baron de Bach." Again, critics of 1909's *Florentine Frame* questioned Robins's structures but lauded her characters. A reviewer for *Atheneum* noted that "the minor characters are admirable, and, despite the subject, the whole book is interesting."

As Robins grew increasingly well known for limning character ably, she also grew increasingly involved with the women's movement. She aided the Women's Social and Political Campaign, the Actresses's Franchise League, the Association of Social and Moral Hygiene, the Women's Institute, and the Six Point Group, and agitated for women's rights in a variety of other settings as well. Eventually, Robins's political activities began to show in her literary efforts—most notably in her splashy 1912 novel *My Little Sister.* The novel tells the story of two sisters raised by a protective mother in the country. The two go to visit a wealthy relative in London, but wind up being smuggled into a bordello instead. Though the narrator-sister escapes, her sister Bettina is sold into white slavery. Thomas explains: "The implicit criticism of the mother's overprotectiveness and conservatism in the early part of the novel is overwhelmed by the outrage at the abduction and the seeming complacency of the police."

Critics were both outraged and delighted by the book; in general, reviewers seemed to be confused by an unstructured story that packed an emotional wallop. F. T. Cooper, writing for *Bookman,* found the story to be "a curious combination of an exceptionally tragic situation and a faulty technique, inexcusable from an author of her repute." Hildegarde Hawthorne, writing for the *New York Times,* commented that the "characters are alive and the sister love story pleasing. But there is too much of it. It seems what is padding is padding of the best, but not inevitably required." Nevertheless, many readers found the book breathtaking. H. B. Laidlaw, writing in *Survey* called it "an exquisite work of art. . . . From a literary point of view it is a great book. One is reminded of the Aeschylean definition of tragedy: 'That which purifies the heart through pity and terror.' "

Robins approached feminist issues once more in her non-fiction study of feminism, *Way Stations,* published in 1913. In it, she collects speeches and magazine articles along with connecting narrative, so that the book provides both Robins's unpublished writings along with a history of the suffrage movement. Fola La Follette, writing for *Bookman,* remarked that "*Way Stations* will prove, to the majority of us, the most illuminating and comprehensive presentation that has yet been given of the militant activities. In this book, as in all her work, Miss Robins shows a broad philosophical understanding." Hildegarde Hawthorne, writing for the *New York Times,* noted that "the book has, of course, that added vigor found in work done with enthusiasm and by conviction; and it is, in a measure, the inner history of Miss Robins's own conversion to and progress in the faith whose story she tells."

Though Thomas suggests that "Robins's subsequent fiction marks a creative decline," critics tended to find Robins's work much as it ever was: defective in plot and story-telling, but surprisingly lively in character and feeling. In reviewing Robins's 1923 *Time Is Whispering,* the *Times Literary Supplement* commented that her "insight into the feminine character does not falter even in the extremely delicate situation she has chosen to present." But Isabel Paterson, writing for the *New York Tribune,* found that "the book is too long for the story, and Miss Robins's fervor in making her point creates a curiously wrong atmosphere."

Robins's reputation, though it has not bloomed over time, has not exactly withered either. She was endeared to her readership for describing women's characters in a way that was new, but critics long complained that her books did not seem to stand up very well. No wonder that, as her ability to see into women's minds became more common, the failures of her writing became more apparent. Nonetheless, Robins deserves note as one of the novelists who helped to construct a modern notion of female identity, just as women became politically and culturally enfranchised.

BIOGRAPHICAL/CRITICAL SOURCES:

BOOKS

Courtney, W. L., *The Feminine Note in Fiction,* Chapman & Hall (London, England), 1904.
Dictionary of Literary Biography, Volume 197: *Late-Victorian and Edwardian British Novelists,* Gale (Detroit, MI), 1999.

PERIODICALS

Atheneum, November 27, 1909.
Bookman, October 19, 1907; January 1913; April 1913, Fola La Follette, review of *Way Stations.*
Dial, September 1, 1905.
Nation and Atheneum, June 19, 1926.
New Statesman & Nation, September 15, 1956.
New York Tribune, May 27, 1923, p. 21.
New York Times, June 3, 1905; April 11, 1908; February 23, 1913, Hildegarde Hawthorne, review of *Way Stations;* April 27, 1913.
Outlook, December 18, 1909.
Review of Reviews, June 1908.
San Francisco Chronicle, October 15, 1956, p. 25.
Survey, May 3, 1913.
Times Literary Supplement, April 26, 1923, p. 286; May 27, 1926, p. 354.*

* * *

ROBSON, Justina   1968-

PERSONAL: Born June 11, 1968, in Leeds, England; daughter of Alec (a textile chemistry professor) and Ruth Bones (a doctor of textile physics) Robson; married Richard Fennell, February 18, 1999. *Ethnicity:* "Caucasian." *Education:* University of York, B.A. (honors), 1991. *Religion:* "Atheist." *Avocational interests:* Yoga, fitness, mathematics, art, science.

ADDRESSES: Home—Westroyding, Low Moor Side Ln., Leeds LS12 SHY, England. *Agent*—John R. Parker, MBA literary Agents Ltd., 62 Grafton Way, London W1P 5LD, England. *E-mail*—justina@lulu.co.uk.

CAREER: Leeds Leisure Services, Leeds, England, yoga teacher, 1999—.

MEMBER: British Science Fiction Association, British Fantasy Society.

WRITINGS:

Silver Screen (science fiction), Macmillan (London, England), 1999.
Mappa Mundi (science fiction), Macmillan (London, England), 2001.

Contributor of stories to magazines.

WORK IN PROGRESS: Research on "maths, genetic and bio-engineering."

SIDELIGHTS: Justina Robson told *CA:* "I write because it's the most fun you can have on your own. I get to study all kinds of subjects, read all the books I want and get paid for what I enjoy. I've written stories as long as I've been able to write. Everything in my life and research goes into my work, nothing in particular, unless it's a fact I need.

"I write one or two drafts as exploratory work, then mine-out the story and write a final draft after a lot of thinking about what's interesting in the work and how to best present it. The first two drafts are thrown out— they barely resemble the end product.

"I write about whatever interests me at the time. A recurring theme is my attempt to understand what makes individuals who they are and how the way we see ourselves determines what we perceive of the world around us."

* * *

RODRIGUEZ, Aleida   1953-

PERSONAL: Born 1953, in Cuba; immigrated to United States, c. 1962.

ADDRESSES: Home—1811 Baxter St., Los Angeles, CA 90026-1935. *Office*—c/o Author Mail, Sarabande Books, 2234 Dundee Rd., Suite 200, Louisville, KY 40205. *E-mail*—arodedit@aol.com.

CAREER: Poet.

WRITINGS:

Garden of Exile (poems), Sarabande Books (Louisville, KY), 1999.

Work represented in anthologies, including *Grand Passion,* Red Wind Books, 1995; and *In Short,* Norton (New York, NY), 1996. Contributor to periodicals, including *Kenyon Review, Phoebe, Ploughshares, Prairie Schooner, Progressive,* and *Rattle.*

BIOGRAPHICAL/CRITICAL SOURCES:

PERIODICALS

Publishers Weekly, September 27, 1999, review of *Garden of Exile,* p. 101.*

* * *

RODRIGUEZ JULIA, Edgardo
  See RODRIGUEZ JULIÁ, Edgardo

* * *

RODRIGUEZ JULIÁ, Edgardo 1946-

PERSONAL: Born October 9, 1946, in Rio Piedras, Puerto Rico. *Education:* Attended University of Puerto Rico and New York University.

ADDRESSES: Agent—c/o Editorial Cultural, Inc., Calle Robles No. 51, Rio Piedras 00925, Puerto Rico.

CAREER: Novelist, short story writer, educator, and lecturer.

AWARDS, HONORS: Premio del Instituto de Literatura Puertorriqueno Bolivar Pagan, 1981, for *Las tribulaciones de Jonás,* 1983, for *El entierro de Cortijo;* PEN award for Best Novel, 1985, for *La noche oscura del niño Avilés;* Guggenheim grant, 1986.

WRITINGS:

La renuncia del héroe Baltasar (novel), Antillana (San Juan, Puerto Rico), 1974, translated by Andrew Hurley as *The Renunciation,* Four Walls Eight Windows (New York, NY), 1997.
Las tribulaciones de Jonás, Huracan (Rio Piedras, Puerto Rico), 1981.
El entierro de Cortijo, Huracan (Rio Piedras, Puerto Rico), 1983.
La noche oscura del niño Avilés, Huracan (Rio Piedras, Puerto Rico), 1984.
Campeche; o, Los diablejos de la melancolía, Instituto de Cultura Puertorriqueña (San Juan, Puerto Rico), 1986.

Una noche con Iris Chacón, Antillana (San Juan, Puerto Rico), 1986.
Maldonado, Adál Alberto: Galería Luigi Marrozzini presenta Mango mambo, Ilustres Estudios (San Juan, Puerto Rico), 1987.
Puertorriqueños: álbum de la sagrada familia puertorriqueña a partir de 1898, Editorial Plaza Mayor (Rio Piedras, Puerto Rico), 1988, fourth edition, 1998.
El cruce de la bahía de Guánica, Cultural (Rio Piedras, Puerto Rico), 1989.
El camino de Yyaloide, Grijalbo (Caracas, Venezuela), 1994.
Cámara secreta: ensayos apócrifos y relatos versimiles de la fotografía erótica, Monte Avila (Rio Piedras, Puerto Rico), 1994.
Sol de medianoche, Grijalbo (Rio Piedras, Puerto Rico), 1995.
Armando Reverón: luz y cálida sombra del Caribe: exposición itinerante 1996-1997, Consejo Nacional de la Cultura (Rio Piedras, Puerto Rico), 1996.
Peloteros, Editorial de la Universidad de Puerto Rico (San Juan, Puerto Rico), 1997.
Cartegena, Editorial Plaza Mayor (Rio Piedras, Puerto Rico), 1997.
Cortejos fúnebres: Relatos, Editorial Cultural (Rio Piedras, Puerto Rico), 1997.

SIDELIGHTS: A contemporary of Puerto Rican novelist Magali Garcia Ramis, Edgardo Rodriguez Juliá is part of the body of writers that emerged in Puerto Rico during the 1970s. Acclaimed by *Dictionary of Literary Biography* contributor Ruben Rios Avila as "one of the most important narrative writers in contemporary Puerto Rican literature." Rios Avila also noted that Rodriquez Julia's writing "tends toward openness but remains nostalgic for a center that would give it a finished texture and allow it to stand for that sort of traditional work referring to a perceiving subject creating that work." The critic continued, "Rodriguez Juliá is a postmodern author possessed by a premodern nostalgia."

Modern Language Review contributor John D. Perivolaris commended Rodriguez Juliá's "re-examination of his island's passing, in 1898, from Spanish to United States dominance" as "a clear example of how Spanish Caribbean intellectuals have increasingly used popular culture as a prism through which to refract privileged narratives of historical identity." Perivolaris noted this to be particularly applicable to *Las tribulaciones de Jonas* in which the central character is an "everyman" whose voyage to Guanica is a "debt of loyalty to a friend" and a "nationalist imperative." In Rodriguez Juliá's work, Perivolaris noted, " 'manhood' is defined not by boundaries and frontiers but by the connections afforded by friendships, family, and memories: personal ritual rather than political allegiance."

An English translation of *La renuncia del heroe Baltasar* titled *The Renunciation* was published in 1997. Ted Leventhal, a reviewer for *Booklist,* called the work "an excellent novel . . . an accurate portrayal of history." A *Publishers Weekly* critic called the book an "ironic morality tale." And *Library Journal* reviewer Lawrence Olszewski proclaimed the book a "literary tour de force" and recommended it for public and academic libraries.

BIOGRAPHICAL/CRITICAL SOURCES:

BOOKS

Dictionary of Literary Biography, Volume 145: *Modern Latin-American Fiction Writers,* Gale (Detroit, MI), 1994.
Spanish-American Authors, H. W. Wilson (New York, NY), 1992.

PERIODICALS

Booklist, September 1, 1997, Ted Leventhal, review of *The Renunciation,* p. 58.
Library Journal, August, 1997, Lawrence Olszewski, review of *The Renunciation,* p. 135.
Modern Language Review, July, 1999, John D. Perivolaris, "Heroes, Survivors, and History," pp. 691-699.
Publishers Weekly, August 25, 1997, review of *The Renunciation,* pp. 43-44.*

*   *   *

ROGOVIN, Sheila Anne 1931-

PERSONAL: Born February 28, 1931, in New York, NY; daughter of Irving Benjamin and Eva (Klein) Ender; married Mitchell Rogovin, January 31, 1954; children: Lisa Shea, Wendy Meryl, John Andrew. *Education:* Queens College, B.S., 1952; American University, Ph.D., 1979.

ADDRESSES: Office—c/o Perigee Books, 375 Hudson St., New York, NY 10014.

CAREER: Montgomery County Health Department, Silver Spring, MD, 1973-77; general practice psychology in Silver Spring, 1977—.

MEMBER: American Psychological Association, American Group Psychotherapy Association, American Personnel and Guidance Association, Maryland Psychological Association, D.C. Psychological Association.

WRITINGS:

(With Evelyn S. Cohen and Andrea Thompson) *Couple Fits: How to Live with the Person You Love,* Perigee Books (New York, NY), 2000.

BIOGRAPHICAL/CRITICAL SOURCES:

PERIODICALS

Publishers Weekly, December 20, 1999, review of *Couple Fits: How to Life with the Person You Love,* p. 75.*

*   *   *

RONG, Zhong
See LIU, Shaozhong

*   *   *

ROSEN, Jay 1956-

PERSONAL: Born 1956. *Education:* State University of New York, B.A., 1979; New York University, M.A., 1981, Ph.D., 1981.

ADDRESSES: Office—Department Of Journalism and Mass Communications, New York University, 10 Washington Place, New York, NY 10003; fax: 212-995-4576. *E-mail*—jr3@is2.nyu.edu.

CAREER: New York University, professor of journalism and mass communications, 1986—. Gannett Center for Media Studies (now the Freedom Forum Media Studies Center), Columbia University, fellowship, 1990-91; Shorenstein Center on the Press, Politics, and Public Policy, Harvard University, fellow, 1994.

Project on Public Life and the Press, New York University, director, 1993-97; member of the Penn National Commission on Society, Culture, and Community, University of Pennsylvania; associate of the Kettering Foundation, Dayton, OH.

WRITINGS:

(With Paul Taylor) *The New News v. the Old News: The Press and Politics in the 1990s,* Twentieth Century Fund Press (New York, NY), 1992.

Getting the Connections Right: Public Journalism and the Troubles in the Press, Twentieth Century Fund (New York, NY), 1996.

(Compiler, with Joseph Harris) *Media Journal: Reading and Writing about Popular Culture,* Allyn and Bacon (Boston, MA), 1995, second edition, with Gary Calpas, 1999.

What Are Journalists For?, Yale University Press (New Haven, CT), 1999.

Also author of *Community Connectedness Passwords for Public Journalism: How to Create Journalism that Listens to Citizens and Reinvigorates Public Life,* Poynter Institute for Media Studies (St. Petersburg, FL), 1993, and (with Davis "Buzz" Merritt and Lisa Austin) *Public Journalism Theory and Practice: Lessons from Experience,* Kettering Foundation (Dayton, OH), 1997.

Articles and essays have appeared in the *Columbia Journalism Review, Harpers, Nation, New York Times,* and *Salon* online magazine; media editor of *Tikkun* magazine, 1993-97.

SIDELIGHTS: A professor of journalism and mass communications, Jay Rosen has been at the forefront of a movement variously known as public journalism or civic journalism, which attempts to improve civic life by changing the role of the media from objective purveyor of news to advocate for public involvement in civil affairs. Rosen has written several books on the subject. An early effort, *Getting the Connections Right: Public Journalism and the Troubles in the Press,* published in 1996, advocates that journalists leave behind their traditional stance as bystanders to the events they report and take up their role as citizens in order to heal the growing disenchantment between the news media and its audiences. Critics of public journalism fear that wholesale adoption of its ethos would turn newspapers into marketing tools for whomever owned them, that journalists would be controlled by polls and the like in deciding what should be reported, or that the press would lose its objectivity and become partisan. According to Hanno Hardt, a contributor to the *Journal of Communication,* "[Rosen] concedes the potential dangers of this approach to traditional notions of journalism and its place in society, but expresses an overriding need for change that is supported by the actual work of practitioners." Hardt remained unconvinced, however,

stating that though the goals of civic journalism as Rosen outlines them in *Getting the Connections Right* are "impressive," "there is little to suggest that the bias of journalists as community workers will help revive civic life or produce professionalism."

In *What Are Journalists For?,* Rosen traces his own interest in the ideals behind civic journalism beginning with his disillusionment with the 1988 presidential election and its coverage by the media, which seemed controlled by the candidates' handlers, a subject he briefly takes up in his 1992 book *The New News v. the Old News: The Press and Politics in the 1990s,* co-written with Paul Taylor. In *What Are Journalists For?* Rosen recounts that he retreated to the writings of John Dewey and Jurgen Habermas, both of whom espouse the notion that ordinary citizens are capable of making responsible decisions on matters of import in civil affairs if given the opportunity and pertinent information. Rosen then moves on to discuss his advocacy work in convincing news organizations to adopt this ideal in their dealings with the public, and offers examples of their successes. Chief among these successes may be counted convincing several newspapers to take the information gleaned from polling their readers about their concerns and redirecting their questioning of political candidates along those lines, instead of passively reporting on the issues as candidates presented them in press conferences. In another example, an Ohio newspaper went beyond reporting on local racial tensions to actively challenging their readership to devise solutions to the problem.

"What Rosen offers may not be the ultimate cure for journalism and public life," conceded *New York Times Book Review* contributor Tom Goldstein. "But his book is a valuable addition to a meager list of books that take journalism seriously." Elaine Machleder, writing for *Library Journal,* faulted Rosen's presentation of his ideas in *What Are Journalists For?* as overwritten and repetitious, implying the author had padded an article in order to make a book-length publication. A reviewer for *Publishers Weekly* was also disappointed, but for a different reason: Rosen responds to the attacks of his critics in a way that is "mostly thoughtful," but fails to resolve the issue of how public journalism would approach the problem of "subjects readers should care about but don't, like foreign news." Nevertheless, this critic called Rosen's book a "partisan but fair-minded history" of this controversial topic in the field of journalism.

BIOGRAPHICAL/CRITICAL SOURCES:

PERIODICALS

Editor and Publisher, October 15, 1994, M. L. Stein, "A Catalyst for Public Awareness?," p. 11.
Journal of Communication, summer, 1997, review of *Getting the Connections Right,* pp. 102-107.
Library Journal, November 1, 1999, Elaine Machleder, review of *What Are Journalists For?,* p. 96.
National Civil Review, winter, 1996, review of *Public Journalism,* p. 19, review of *Getting the Connections Right,* p. 20.
New York Times Book Review, November 14, 1999, Tom Goldstein, "Good Question: 'Public Journalism,' the Author Has Learned, Is Easier to Say Than to Do," p. 27.
Presidential Studies Quarterly, fall, 1993, review of *The New news v. the Old News,* p. 845.
Publishers Weekly, November 1, 1999, review of *What Are Journalists For?,* p. 67.

OTHER

New York University Web site, http://www.nyu.edu/ (October 2, 2001).*

*   *   *

ROSS, Janice L(ynn) 1950-

PERSONAL: Born December 11, 1950, in Los Angeles, CA; married Keith Bartel, May 6, 1979; children: Joshua Z. Bartel, Mimi Jenny Bartel. *Education:* University of California—Berkeley, B.A. (honors), 1972; Stanford University, M.A., 1975, Ph.D., 1997; studied dance technique with David Wood, Marnie Wood, Margaret Jenkins, Merce Cunningham, Inga Weiss, Gus Solomons, and Ronn Guidi. *Religion:* Jewish.

ADDRESSES: Home—148 Greenoaks Dr., Atherton, CA 94025. *Office*—Stanford University, Roble Gym, 375 Santa Teresa St., Stanford, CA 94305. *E-mail*—jross@leland.stanford.edu.

CAREER: De Anza College, Cupertino, CA, instructor, 1976-80; Stanford University, Stanford, CA, lecturer in Dance/Drama Department, 1988—. California Arts Council, founding member, dance panel, 1977-79; National Endowment for the Arts, member, dance panel, 1987-96; Dance Critics Association, member, board of directors, vice president, 1988-89, president, 1989-90, advisory, 1990-92; lecturer, San Francisco Performing Arts Library & Museum, 1994, Stanford Alumni Association, 1990, University of California Berkeley Extension, 1980 and 1981, and New Performance Gallery, 1983; San Jose State University, instructor, 1990; Cottages at Hedgebrook Writers Colony, fellow, 1992-93; consultant, Educational Testing Service, 1994, Dance Heritage Coalition, 1999-2001; George Balanchine Foundation, principal researcher, 2000-01; presenter and speaker in various venues, including festivals and colleges.

MEMBER: Society of Dance History Scholars (member of board of directors, 1999-2002).

AWARDS, HONORS: Dance Critics Fellowship, National Endowment for the Arts, 1976; eight Publishers Awards for Excellence in Arts Writing, Oakland Tribune, 1985-90; Isadora Duncan Award, 1989, for special project, co-directing "Why a Swan?" conference, 1994, for special achievement, curating the symposium "Mark Morris & the Body Eclectic".

WRITINGS:

Moving Lessons: Margaret H'Doubler and the Beginning of Dance in American Education, University of Wisconsin Press (Madison, WI), 2000.

Editor, with Stephen Steinberg of *Why a Swan?,* San Francisco Performing Arts Library and Museum Journals, 1989; and *On the Edge: Challenges to American Dance,* Dance Critics Association (San Francisco, CA), 1990. Contributor to *American National Biography,* Oxford University Press (New York, NY), 1995; *International Dictionary of Ballet,* Volume 2, St. James Press (London, England), 1995; *Moving Towards Life: Five Decades of Transformational Dance—Collected Writings of Anna Halprin,* edited by Kaplan Rachel, Wesleyan University Press (Middleton, CT), 1995; *Jewish Women in America: An Historical Encyclopedia,* edited by Paula Hyman and Deborah Moore, Routledge, 1997; *Passion and Pedagogy,* edited by Debra Sherman and Elijah Mirochnik, Peter Lang, 2000; and *Notable American Women,* Harvard University Press, 2001. Contributor to periodicals, including *Dance Teacher, Arts Education Policy, Jewish Folklore and Ethnology Review, Dancemagazine, Dance Research Journal, Los Angeles Times, San Francisco Examiner, New York Times Dance Theatre Journal, Liberal Education, Drama Review (TDR), Diversion Magazine, Stanford Magazine, Dance Teacher Now, Confetti Magazine,* and *Horizon Magazine.* Dance critic and columnist, *Berkeley Gazette,* 1975-77, *S.F. Bay Guard-*

ian, 1977-80; performance art critic and editor, *Artweek,* 1976-80; staff critic, Oakland Tribune, 1980-90; contributing editor, *Dancemagazine,* 1977—; editorial board, *Journal of Dance Education,* 2000.

WORK IN PROGRESS: *Anna Halprin: Revolution for the Art of It,* a critical biography of choreographer Anna Halprin, for University of California Press (Berkeley, CA); editor, *Leonid Jacobson: Unhonored Prophet of Russian Ballet,* a collection of essays about the Russian choreographer Leonid Jacobson; research on "artists as social activist."

* * *

ROSS, Robert 1949-

PERSONAL: Born July 26, 1949.

ADDRESSES: *Agent*—c/o Cambridge University Press, 40 West 20th St., New York, NY 10011-4221.

CAREER: Historian and writer.

WRITINGS:

Adam Kok's Griquas: A Study in the Development of Stratification in South Africa, Cambridge University Press (New York, NY), 1976.

(Editor) *Racism and Colonialism: Essays on Ideology and Social Structure,* M. Nijhoff Publishers (Hingham, MA), 1982.

Cape of Torments: Slavery and Resistance in South Africa, Routledge and Kegan Paul (Boston, MA), 1983.

(Editor, with Raymond F. Betts and Gerard J. Telkamp) *Colonial Cities: Essays on Urbanism in a Colonial Context,* M. Nijhoff (Boston, MA), 1985.

(With Peter van Duin) *The Economy of the Cape Colony in the Eighteenth Century,* Centre for the History of European Expansion (Leiden, Netherlands), 1987.

(Editor, with J. Thomas Lindblad and Marion Johnson) *Anglo-African trade in the Eighteenth Century: English Statistics on African Trade, 1699-1808,* Centre for the History of European Expansion (Leiden, Netherlands), 1990.

Beyond the Pale: Essays on the History of Colonial South Africa, Wesleyan University Press (Hanover, NH), 1993.

(Editor, with Henry Bredekamp) *Missions and Christianity in South African History,* Witwatersrand

University Press (Johannesburg, South Africa), 1995.

A Concise History of South Africa, Cambridge University Press (New York, NY), 1999.

SIDELIGHTS: According to Dunbar Moodie in the *American Historical Review,* Robert Ross is "a leading member of a group of scholars who have transformed our understanding of the early history of the Cape Colony." In *Beyond the Pale: Essays on the History of Colonial South Africa,* Ross presents a collection of his own essays on white society in South Africa in the eighteenth and nineteenth centuries, written during the 1980s and 1990s. The essays discuss the presence of racism in colonial African society, and examine issues of demographics, economy, and social class. Moodie described the essays as "accessible and useful" and praised Ross's discussion of the South African economy and its reliance on wine and wheat production.

In *Adam Kok's Griquas: A Study in the Development of Stratification in South Africa,* based on his doctoral dissertation, Ross describes nineteenth-century life in South Africa, particularly the relationships among people of the Xhosa, San, and KhoiKhoi tribes, and Boer farmers, Griqua farmers, and British settlers. Ross describes the northward push of settlement, and the campaign of Adam Kok and his people to keep their land, freedom, and self-respect. Like Native Americans, the local people were deeply affected by racism, greed, and the militarism of those who settled in their territories. In the *Journal of the American Anthropological Association,* Brian du Toit praised the book as "solidly researched and documented" and noted that it would be of particular interest to scholars specializing in the history of South Africa.

In *Cape of Torments: Slavery and Resistance in South Africa,* Ross asks why slave revolts in that country were so rare, and answers by noting that slaves there did not have a cohesive identity and culture that would provide strength for revolts. In addition, he notes, the white masters were well-armed and always suspicious, and so were the local tribes that were not enslaved. Using slave traders' records and records from the Court of Justice in Cape Town during the time when the colony was controlled by the Dutch East India Company, Ross examines the largest revolts and provides anecdotes of resistance. The book is largely devoted to the eighteenth century, but Ross does discuss the period of British rule in South Africa, and also discusses the effects of slavery on their current-day descendants in South Africa. In the *British Book News,* E. Halladay wrote, "This is an important book on a neglected topic," and noted that

Ross' account of groups of escaped slaves in the eighteenth century is deeply moving.

A Concise History of South Africa covers the economic, cultural, environmental, and political history of this turbulent country, from prehistory to the present, although Ross devotes more than two-thirds of the book to the twentieth century. In the *Times Literary Supplement,* James Barber commented that because the book is relatively short, Ross often skips over events and topics that should have been given more attention, but also wrote that Ross "writes clearly and vigorously and covers a remarkable range of topics." He praised Ross' analysis of social changes, such as the development of apartheid, the changing role of women in rural African society, and changes in traditional values with the development of a new economy.

BIOGRAPHICAL/CRITICAL SOURCES:

PERIODICALS

American Historical Review, December, 1994, p. 1734.
British Book News, August, 1983, p. 482.
Economist, July 19, 1997, p. S12.
Historian, winter, 2001, Sean Redding, review of *A Concise History of South Africa,* p. 397.
Journal of the American Anthropological Association, March, 1978, p. 189.
New York Times Book Review, April 2, 1977, p. 50.
Publishers Weekly, February 7, 1977, p. 92; June 1, 1998, p. 48; December 13, 1999, p. 45.*

*   *   *

ROSSI, Agnes   1959-

PERSONAL: Born August 11, 1959, in Paterson, NJ; daughter of Frank and Maura (Devlin) Rossi; married Dan Conaway (an editor), May 9, 1992; children: Mary, Grace, Alina. *Ethnicity:* "Italian-Irish." *Education:* Rutgers, B.A.; NGU, M.A.

ADDRESSES: Home—208 Saint James Place, Brooklyn, NY 11238-2302.

AWARDS, HONORS: New York University Creative Writers Competition winner, 1986, for *Athletes and Artists;* Granta Best American Novelist Under 40 finalist, 1996; Paterson Prize for Fiction winner, 1996, for *The Quick.*

WRITINGS:

Athletes and Artists: Stories, New York University Press (New York, NY), 1987.
The Quick: A Novella and Stories, Norton (New York, NY), 1992.
Split Skirt, Random House (New York, NY), 1994.
The Houseguest: A Novel, Dutton (New York, NY), 2000.

WORK IN PROGRESS: A Brief History of Weights and Measures: A Novel.

SIDELIGHTS: Agnes Rossi's short story collection *Athletes and Artists* won the 1986 New York University Creative Writers Competition. These ten stories show a variety of characters wandering through their lives, with expectations that are never matched by reality. A *Publishers Weekly* reviewer wrote, "Her clear, restrained prose and spare . . . dialogue infuse the slim episodes with the quality of contemporary life."

The Quick is a collection of stories and a novella. In the novella, also titled "The Quick," Marie Russo deals with her father's death and her own loneliness. In the other stories, a teacher leaves her abusive husband and finds a new lover; a girl in a relationship with a man believes it will make her grown up; and a widower realizes that he doesn't love his new wife, but he does love the child she gave him. In the *New York Times,* Michiko Kakutani wrote that Rossi is "a gifted writer, a dazzling ventriloquist . . . she convinces you that her characters are real." Stuart Dybek wrote in the *New York Times Book Review* that in *The Quick,* "a story of a death is told with uncompromising honesty." A *Publishers Weekly* reviewer noted, "Rossi uses unadorned and forceful prose to bare the uneasy relationships between children and parents, husbands and wives."

In *Split Skirt,* two women spend three days and nights together in a jail cell. Mrs. Tyler, a rich woman with a wealthy husband who cannot stop herself from shoplifting, meets Rita, a young, tough girl who has become addicted to drugs and alcohol. Rita is in jail because her boss has banned split skirts in her office; angered, she went out to a bar and was soon arrested for driving drunk and possessing cocaine. The two women, seemingly so different, find out that they have a lot in common as they discuss their lives and their marriages through alternating chapters. A *Publishers Weekly* reviewer called the book "uneven," noting that a scene in which the two women make friends with two Puerto Rican prostitutes is cliched, and that Rossi's decision not to give reader's Rita's last name or Mrs. Tyler's first name is "artificial."

In the *New York Times Book Review,* however, Elizabeth Benedict wrote that Rossi is "an elegant, perceptive writer, partial to the lives of women who repeatedly find themselves in very tight spots brought on by a husband's untimely death, a boyfriend's or spouse's bullying, a father's drunken cruelty or by the women's own dark, unknowable impulses."

Rossi's *The Houseguest* is based on the facts of her own mother's life. In the book, Edward Devlin returns to Ireland with his young wife, who has tuberculosis and is about to die. He leaves his young daughter in Ireland with his sister Sadie, then returns alone to America with the help of his friend John Fitzgibbon. Fitzgibbon is well established in New Jersey as a successful businessman, and he invites Devlin to dinner, gets him a job, and allows him to stay in his own house. Their relationship is strained when Devlin becomes involved with Fitzgibbon's wife, and Devlin is also upset by the news that his daughter has been sent to a convent boarding school. A *Los Angeles Times Book Review* writer remarked, "It's a rare writer who can treat big subjects without falling into sentimentality, oversimplification, or showy theatrics, but Rossi is such a one."

A *New Yorker* writer called *The Houseguest* "an artfully told story." A contributor in the *Wall Street Journal* wrote: "readers will marvel at Rossi's gift for capturing the lilting speech of the Irish."

BIOGRAPHICAL/CRITICAL SOURCES:

PERIODICALS

Atlantic Monthly, March, 1993, p. 130; August, 1993, p. 44.
Belles Lettres, summer, 1992, p. 56.
Bloomsbury Review, June, 1992, p. 12.
Booklist, February 1, 1992, Marie Kuda, review of *The Quick: A Novella and Stories,* p. 1010; March 15, 1994, Alice Joyce, review of *Split Skirt,* p. 1328; November 15, 1999, Michele Leber, review of *The Houseguest: A Novel,* p. 605.
Christian Science Monitor, June 14, 1994, p. 13.
Library Journal, January, 1992, Lenore Hart, review of The Quick, p. 180; March 15, 1994, Nancy Pearl, review of *Split Skirt,* p. 102.
Los Angeles Times Book Review, February 16, 1992, Chris Goodrich, review of *The Quick,* p. 6; May 8, 1994, p. 17; November 20, 1994, p. 6.
New Statesman & Society, January 8, 1993, Elizabeth Young, review of *The Quick,* p. 42.

New York Times (late edition), February 18, 1992, p. C17; May 10, 1994, p. C20.
New York Times Book Review, June 14, 1992, Stuart Dybeck, review of *The Quick,* p. 14; May 8, 1994, Elizabeth Benedict, review of *Split Skirt,* p. 17; October 13, 1996, p. 32.
Observer, December 13, 1992, p. 53.
Publishers Weekly, May 22, 1987, review of *Athletes and Artists,* p. 66; November 29, review of *The Quick,* 1991, p. 43; March 7, 1994, review of *Split Skirt,* p. 51; April 1, 1996, p. 69; October 18, 1999, review of *The Houseguest,* p. 67.

OTHER

W.W. Norton Web site, http://www.norton.com (October 10, 2001).

*   *   *

RUBIN, Rhea Joyce   1950-

PERSONAL: First name pronounced "Ree-uh"; born June 14, 1950, in Chicago, IL; married Lawrence Berman, June 7, 1975. *Education:* Attended University of Vienna, 1970-71; University of Wisconsin, B.A., 1972, M.A., 1973.

ADDRESSES: Office—Rubin Consulting, 5860 Heron Dr., Oakland, CA 94618-2628; fax: 510-339-1274. *E-mail*—rjrubin@mindspring.com.

CAREER: Independent library services consultant, project manager, and trainer, 1980—.

MEMBER: American Library Association, American Society for Training and Development, California Library Association, Sigma Epsilon Sigma.

AWARDS, HONORS: Ralph R. Shaw Award for Outstanding Contribution to the Literature of Librarianship, American Library Association, 1980, for *Using Bibliotherapy* and *Bibliotherapy Sourcebook;* Outstanding Reference Source, American Library Association, 1984, for *Challenge of Aging;* Monroe Library Adult Services Award, American Library Association, 1992; Exceptional Service Award, ASCLA/American Library Association, 1993.

WRITINGS:

Bibliotherapy Sourcebook, Oryx (Phoenix, AZ), 1978.
Using Bibliotherapy: A Guide to Theory and Practice, Oryx (Phoenix, AZ), 1978.

(With Margaret E. Monroe) *The Challenge of Aging: A Bibliography,* Libraries Unlimited (Littleton, CO), 1983.

(With Alan Moores) *Let's Talk About It: A Planner's Manual,* American Library Association (Chicago, IL), 1984.

Working with Older Adults: A Handbook for Libraries, third edition, California State Library Foundations (Sacramento, CA), 1990.

Of a Certain Age: A Guide to Contemporary Fiction Featuring Older Adults, ABC-CLIO (Denver, CO), 1990.

Intergenerational Library Programs: A How-To-Do-It Manual for Librarians, Neal-Schuman (New York, NY), 1993.

(With Daniel Suvak) *Libraries Inside: A Practical Guide for Prison Librarians,* McFarland (Jefferson, NC), 1995.

Humanities Programming: A How-To-Do-It Manual for Librarians, Neal-Schuman (New York, NY), 1997.

Defusing the Angry Patron: A How-To-Do-It Manual for Librarians and Paraprofessionals, Neal-Schuman (New York, NY), 2000.

Planning for Library Services for People with Disabilities: A Process for Libraries, ASCLA (Chicago, IL), 2001.

Author of reports, including *An Evaluation of System-Provided Library Services to State Correctional Centers in Illinois,* Illinois State Library (Springfield, IL), 1983; *Future Directions in Library Services for the Print Handicapped in Washington,* Washington State Library (Olympia, WA), 1990; and *Planning for Library Services for People with Disabilities: A Process for Libraries in Massachusetts,* Massachusetts Board of Library Commissioners, 1999. Associated with the videos *From the Front of the Room: Trainers Discuss Diversity Training,* ALA Video/Library Video Network, 1995; and *Beyond the Ramp: Disability Awareness and ADA Compliance,* California State Library, 1996. Contributor to books, including *What Else You Can Do With a Library Degree,* second edition, edited by Betty-Carol Sellen, Neal-Schuman, 1997; and periodicals, including *Library Mosaics, Aging Today, Reference Librarian, Library Journal, Public Library Quarterly,* and *Perspectives on Aging.* Contributor of book reviews to *American Reference Books Annual, RQ, Interface,* and *Inside/Outside.* Guest editor, *Health and Rehabilitative Libraries,* October, 1975, and *Wilson Library Bulletin,* February, 1977; contributing editor, *Collection Building,* winter, 1986.

RUIZ, Don Miguel
See RUIZ, Miguel Angel

*   *   *

RUIZ, Miguel Angel   1952-
(Don Miguel Ruiz)

PERSONAL: Born August 27, 1952, in Mexico. *Ethnicity:* "Hispanic."

ADDRESSES: Office—Sixth Sun Foundation and don Miguel Ruiz, 4015 Park Blvd., Suite 203, San Diego, CA 92103; fax 619-291-9002. *Agent*—Janet Mills, P.O. Box 6657, San Rafael, CA 94903. *E-mail*—sixthsun@pacball.net.

CAREER: Affiliated with Sixth Sun Journeys, San Diego, CA.

WRITINGS:

UNDER NAME DON MIGUEL RUIZ

The Four Agreements, Amber-Allen Publishing (San Rafael, CA), 1997.

The Mastery of Love, Amber-Allen Publishing (San Rafael, CA), 1999.

The Four Agreements Daily Companion Guide, Amber-Allen Publishing (San Rafael, CA), 2000.

ADAPTATIONS: The Four Agreements was released in an audio version in 1999, and has also been published in Spanish.

WORK IN PROGRESS: The Voice of Knowledge, for Amber-Allen Publishing, completion expected in 2001.

*   *   *

RUSHDOONY, Rousas J(ohn)   1916-2001

OBITUARY NOTICE—See index for *CA* sketch: Born April 25, 1916, in New York, NY; died February 8, 2001, in Vallecito, CA. Minister, educator, and author. Rushdoony was a Christian Reconstructionist who advocated the use of biblical law, rather than civil law, to maintain order in societies around the world. Ordained a Presbyterian minister in 1944, he went on to serve as a missionary abroad and later a pastor at various California churches. Rushdoony was a prolific writer, and some of his works include *Politics of Guilt and Pity, God's Plan for Victory,* and *The Institutes of Biblical Law,* a collection of five years' worth of his sermons. He spent a period of time guest lecturing at educational institutions, and also served as president of the educational Chalcedon Foundation. During the 1960s Rushdoony was awarded grants from the William Volker Fund.

OBITUARIES AND OTHER SOURCES:

PERIODICALS

Los Angeles Times, March 3, 2001, p. B7.

*   *   *

RUSSELL, David L. 1946-

PERSONAL: Born May 25, 1946, in Wauseon, OH; son of William W. (a farmer) and Berdae (Gee) Russell; married Patricia Hajek (a college professor), November 11, 1978; children: Jennifer Burns, Megan Gifford, Elizabeth. *Ethnicity:* "Caucasian." *Education:* Bowling Green State University, B.A., 1968, M.A., 1971, Ph.D., 1979.

ADDRESSES: Home—729 Marion Ave., Big Rapids, MI 49307. *Office*—Department of Languages and Literature, Ferris State University, Big Rapids, MI 49307. *E-mail*—russelld@ferris.edu.

CAREER: High school English teacher in Pioneer, OH, 1968-71; Bowling Green State University, Bowling Green, OH, instructor, 1971-77, lecturer in English, 1979-80; Ferris State University, Big Rapids, MI, assistant professor, 1980-85, associate professor, 1985-90, professor of English, 1990—, president of academic senate, 1990-92. Mecosta County Council for the Humanities, charter member, president, 1985-88; Michigan Council for the Humanities, scholar for Humanities Resource Center, 1986-98; Humanities Council of West Central Michigan, vice-president, 1989-90; Me-

costa County Council for the Arts, member; workshop presenter. City of Big Rapids, member of City Plan Board, 1990-95, chair, 1993-95; city commissioner and mayor pro-tempore, 1995—.

MEMBER: Children's Literature Association (member of executive board, 1993-96, chairperson of publications, 1993-2000, treasurer, 2000), Society for Theater Arts Growth and Advancement in Mecosta County, Ferris Faculty Association (member of executive board), Omicron Delta Kappa.

AWARDS, HONORS: Distinguished Faculty Award, Michigan Association of Governing Boards, 1997; Ferris State University Award for Excellence, 1998.

WRITINGS:

Stuart Academic Drama: An Edition of Three University Plays, Garland Publishing (New York, NY), 1987.
Children's Literature: A Short Introduction, Longman (White Plains, NY), 1991, 4th edition, 2001.
Patricia MacLachlan, Twayne (New York, NY), 1997.
Scott O'Dell, Twayne (New York, NY), 1999.

Contributor to *The Dictionary of Literary Biography,* Gale (Detroit, MI), Volume 42, 1985, Volumes 160 and 161, 1996; *The Cambridge Guide to Children's Literature,* Cambridge University Press (New York, NY); and *Continuum Encyclopedia of Children's Literature.* Contributor of articles and reviews to periodicals, including *Lion and the Unicorn, Children's Literature Association Quarterly, Para*doxa: Studies in World Literary Genres,* and *Children's Literature in Education.*

WORK IN PROGRESS: Research on folk tales and mythology and on topics in children's literature.

*   *   *

RYDER, Jonathan
    See LUDLUM, Robert

S

SALMON, Wesley C(harles) 1925-2001

OBITUARY NOTICE—See index for *CA* sketch: Born August. 9, 1925, in Detroit, MI; died in a car accident, April 22, 2001, in Madison County, OH. Professor of philosophy and author. Salmon posited the theory that events with a low predictability of occurring could still be scientifically explained. His theory flew in the face of the popular view at that time, which was that to explain a scientific occurrence there had to be at least a 50 percent chance it actually would happen. Salmon wrote several books on that topic, including *Logic, Scientific Explanation and the Causal Structure of the World,* and *Causality and Explanation.* He also contributed to numerous books by other scientific philosophers. Salmon received a master's from the University of Chicago in 1947 and a doctorate from the University of California at Los Angeles in 1950, where he was an instructor. From there he was hired at Washington State College and stayed until 1954. Salmon taught at many universities around the country and settled at the University of Pittsburgh in 1981, where he stayed until retirement in 1999.

OBITUARIES AND OTHER SOURCES:

PERIODICALS

New York Times, May 4, 2001, p. A24.

*   *   *

SANDIFORD, Keith A(rlington) P(atrick) 1936-

PERSONAL: Born March 2, 1936, in Barbados, West Indies; son of Goulburn McDonald and Myra Elizabeth Sandiford; married Lorraine Small, 1963; children: Gary, Shelley. *Education:* University of the West Indies, B.A. (Honors), 1960; University of Toronto, M.A., 1961, Ph.D., 1966.

ADDRESSES: Office—Department of History, 403 Fletcher Argue Bldg., University of Manitoba, Winnipeg, MB, R3T 2N2, Canada. *E-mail*—sandifo@ cc.umanitoba.ca

CAREER: York University, Toronto, Canada, lecturer in history, 1964-65; University of Toronto, Toronto, Canada, lecturer in history, 1965-66; University of Manitoba, assistant professor, 1966-70, associate professor, 1970-82, professor of history, 1982-98, senior scholar, 1998-2001, now retired.

WRITINGS:

Great Britain and the Schleswig-Holstein Question, 1848-64: A Study in Diplomacy, Politics, and Public Opinion, University of Toronto Press (Toronto, Canada), 1975.

(Editor, with Ronald G. Hughes and Sir Carlisle Burton) *100 Years of Organised Cricket in Barbados, 1892-1992,* Barbados Cricket Association (Bridgetown, Barbados), 1992.

Cricket and the Victorians, Ashgate Publishing (Brookfield, VT), 1994.

(With Earle H. Newton) *Combermere School and the Barbadian Society,* The Press, University of the West Indies (Kingston, Jamaica), 1995.

Everton DeCourcey Weekes: His Record Innings-by-Innings, Association of Cricket Statisticians and Historians (Nottingham, England), 1995.

Clyde Leopold Walcott: His Record Innings-by-Innings, Association of Cricket Statisticians and Historians (Nottingham, England), 1996.

Frank Worrell: His Record Innings-by-Innings, Association of Cricket Statisticians and Historians (Nottingham, England), 1997.

Gary Sobers: His Record Innings-by-Innings, Association of Cricket Statisticians and Historians (Nottingham, England), 1998.

Cricket Nurseries of Colonial Barbados: The Elite Schools, 1865-1966, The Press, University of the West Indies (Kingston, Jamaica), 1998.

(Editor, with Brian Stoddart) *The Imperial Game: Cricket, Culture, and Society,* St. Martin's Press (New York, NY), 1998.

Wes Hall: His Record Innings-by-Innings, Association of Cricket Statisticians and Historians (Nottingham, England), 2001.

Contributor of over one hundred articles, essays, and reviews to numerous journals, including *Albion, Canadian Journal of History, Culture, Sport, Society: An Interdisciplinary Journal, History, International Journal of the History of Sport, Journal of the Barbados Museum and Historical Society, Journal of Caribbean Studies, Journal of Social History, Journal of Sport History,* and *Sports Historian.*

WORK IN PROGRESS: The West Indies at Lord's, 1928-2000: A Study in Sociology and Statistics; John Douglas Claude Goddard: His Record Innings-by-Innings; At the Crease with Gary Sobers: A Study of His Partnerships in Test Cricket; Batting with Bradman: A Study of His Partnerships in Test Cricket.

SIDELIGHTS: An historian by profession and a cricket-buff by inclination, Keith A. P. Sandiford successfully combined these interests in his *Cricket and the Victorians.* Greeted by *Sports Historian*'s Richard Cashman as an "authoritative, impressive and broad-ranging study," Sandiford's book makes the point that cricket, perhaps the most important Victorian sport, is a mirror of Victorian England's social and religious conservatism. The book captures "the massive nature of the topic," as Mark D. Noe pointed out in *Aethlon: The Journal of Sport Literature,* but Sandiford also focuses on individual players and their struggles to succeed in the sport, like W. G. Grace, the Babe Ruth of cricket in the late nineteenth century. Noe further observed that Sandiford "illustrates conservative cricket—and England—through glimpses of the sport, thereby creating an historical reference work of value for its look at the period as well as the sport." John Lowerson summed up his *Canadian Journal of History* review: "This book deserves to be read widely: by cricket enthusiasts who need a dose of a more critical perspective than mere performance lists and saintly myths can offer, by many

'sports historians' who need to locate their enthusiasms in a more rigorous framework, and by many 'social historians' who will find some current emphases well complemented here. Sandiford has given us a useful piece." In his extensive examination of race and sport literature for the *Journal of Sport History,* Jeffrey T. Sammons noted, "Keith A. P. Sandiford deserves recognition as one of the leading scholars of African ancestry writing on the subject of cricket."

Sandiford told *CA:* "Having given up all pretence about being a serious academic in the field of Victorian Studies, I am now free to write copious nonsense about international cricket—which it has always been my great desire to do. Having visited several parts of the Commonwealth in the twentieth century, I remain convinced that Bradman, Grace, and Sobers are immeasurably more important in the overall scheme of things than Disraeli, Gladstone, and Palmerston."

BIOGRAPHICAL/CRITICAL SOURCES:

PERIODICALS

Aethlon: The Journal of Sport Literature, fall, 1998, Mark D. Noe, review of *Cricket and the Victorians,* pp. 210-211.

Canadian Journal of History, August, 1995, John Lowerson, review of *Cricket and the Victorians,* pp. 362-363.

Journal of Sport History, fall, 1994, Jeffrey T. Sammons, " 'Race' and Sport: A Critical, Historical Examination," pp. 203-278 (commentary on Sandiford, p. 232).

Sports Historian, May, 1997, Richard Cashman, review of *Cricket and the Victorians.*

*   *   *

SARAC, Roger
See CARAS, Roger A(ndrew)

*   *   *

SAUNDERS, Margaret Marshall   1861-1947

PERSONAL: Born April 13, 1861, in Milton, Nova Scotia, Canada; died February 15, 1947; daughter of Edward Manning (a Baptist clergyman) and Maria

(Freeman) Saunders. *Education:* Attended Dalhousie University and Boston University.

CAREER: Children's writer, novelist, feminist, activist, lecturer, and teacher.

MEMBER: Child Labour Committee.

AWARDS, HONORS: First prize, contest to find a sequel to Anna Sewell's *Black Beauty,* and American Humane Society Award, both 1893, both for *Beautiful Joe;* M.A., Acadia University, 1911; Commander of the Order of the British Empire, 1935.

WRITINGS:

My Spanish Sailor, Ward & Downey (London, England), 1889, expanded edition published as *Her Sailor: A Love Story,* Page (Boston, MA), 1900.

Beautiful Joe: The Autobiography of a Dog, Bane (Philadelphia, PA), 1893, reprinted as *Beautiful Joe: An Autobiography,* Baptist Book Room (Toronto, Canada), 1894.

Charles and His Lamb, Banes (Philadelphia, PA), 1895.

For the Other Boy's Sake, and Other Stories, Banes (Philadelphia, PA), 1896.

The House of Armour, Rowland (Philadelphia, PA), 1897.

The King of the Park, Crowell (New York, NY), 1897.

Rose a Charlitte: An Acadian Romance, Page (Boston, MA), 1898.

Deficient Saints: A Tale of Maine, Page (Boston, MA), 1899.

For His Country and Grandmother and the Crow, Page (Boston, MA), 1900.

'Tilda Jane: An Orphan in Search of a Home, Page (Boston, MA), 1901.

Beautiful Joe's Paradise; or, The Island of Brotherly Love, Page (Boston, MA), 1902.

The Story of the Graveleys, Briggs (Toronto, Canada), 1903, Page (Boston, MA), 1904.

Nita, the Story of an Irish Setter; Containing Also Uncle Jim's Burglar and Mehitable's Chicken, Page (Boston, MA), 1904.

Princess Sukey: The Story of a Pigeon and Her Human Friends, Eaton & Mains (New York, NY), 1905.

Alpatak: The Story of an Eskimo Dog, Page (Boston, MA), 1906.

My Pets: Real Happenings in My Aviary, Griffith & Rowland (Philadelphia, PA), 1908.

'Tilda Jane's Orphans, Page (Boston, MA), 1909.

The Girl From Vermont: The Story of a Vacation School Teacher, Griffith & Rowland (Philadelphia, PA), 1910.

Pussy Black-Face; or, The Story of a Kitten and Her Friends, Page (Boston, MA), 1913.

The Wandering Dog: Adventures of a Fox Terrier, Doran (New York, NY), 1916.

Golden Dicky: The Story of a Canary and His Friends, Stokes (New York, NY), 1919.

Bonnie Prince Fetlar: The Story of a Pony and His Friends, Doran (New York, NY), 1920.

Jimmy Gold-coast; or, The Story of a Monkey and His Friends, Hodder & Stoughton (Toronto, Canada), 1923, McKay (Philadelphia, PA), 1924.

Esther de Warren: The Story of a Mid-Victorian Maiden, Doran (New York, MA), 1927.

Contributor to periodicals, including *Frank Leslie's Popular Monthly, Our Home, Union Signal, Baptist Visitor, Ontario Library Review* and *Godey's Lady's Book.*

SIDELIGHTS: Canadian children's writer and novelist Margaret Marshall Saunders fell into her career in an unusual way. After composing a letter for her father, a Baptist preacher, a friend of the family read it and was so impressed that she encouraged Saunders to try her hand at descriptive writing. Saunders responded by writing a story about a burglar that *Frank Leslie's Popular Monthly* in New York published, paying the author forty dollars. She then began publishing in other magazines, such as *Our Home,* the *Union Signal,* the *Baptist Visitor,* and *Godey's Lady's Book.* Saunders's first novel, *My Spanish Sailor,* was published in 1889 when she was twenty-eight years old. It was a romance that received positive reviews. Her second novel, *Beautiful Joe: The Autobiography of a Dog,* which was published in 1893, won a contest to find a sequel to Anna Sewell's *Black Beauty* as well as an American Humane Society award, thereby establishing her reputation as a writer. The story is told from the perspective of a dog, the pet of a New England family loosely based on the author's own. The pet, which had been abused by a previous owner, teaches the readers lessons of kindness. *Beautiful Joe* remains Saunders's most well-known work. A bestseller that was translated into seventeen languages, it was the first Canadian novel reputed to sell over a million copies. In 1895 Saunders moved to Boston and attended classes at Boston University. The same year she published the book *Charles and His Lamb* followed the next year by a short story collection entitled *For the Other Boy's Sake, and Other Stories.* After two years in Boston, she moved on to California in 1898.

Throughout her life Saunders traveled in the United States, Canada, and Europe. Later, Saunders explained her own nomadic impulses in "The Story of My Life" published in the *Ontario Library Review* in 1927, writing, "It was absolutely necessary that I should be on the scene where my story was laid." The adult novel, *Rose a Charlitte: An Acadian Romance,* was published in 1898. Set in the territory of Nova Scotia where the author spend her early childhood, it is a love story that is among the most successful of her adult fiction. Another work in this category is *Deficient Saints: A Tale of Maine* published in 1899. The New England setting of this novel serves as a backdrop for the author's critique of the hypocrisies she finds in the Puritan religion. *A Girl From Vermont: The Story of a Vacation School Teacher,* published in 1910, also received fairly favorable reviews for its fervent interest in the cause of exploited children. In the children's novel *'Tilda Jane: An Orphan in Search of a Home,* published in 1901, Saunders created an unattractive but endearing young heroine who was a precursor to Little Orphan Annie. 'Tilda Jane appeared again in 1909 in *'Tilda Jane's Orphans.* But it was as a writer of animal stories that Saunders found her niche. *Princess Sukey: The Story of a Pigeon and Her Human Friends* was published in 1905. The title character, Princess Sukey, is a pigeon that is saved by a little boy. The boy's retired grandfather takes in the bird along with his grandson and the bird brings life into the home. In a statement that might be applied to the whole of Saunders's work, a critic for the *New York Times* reviewed this work, writing, "It might be a tract promulgated jointly by the societies for the prevention of cruelty to animals and children."

Most of Saunders's writing has a moral tone. Drawing on the values taught to her as a child by her father, a populist Baptist preacher, and her mother, Saunders's stories advocate the protection of children and animals. Carole Gerson considered Saunders's body of work in the *Dictionary of Literary Biography,* writing that "more noteworthy for the nobility of their sentiments than the quality of their expression, most of her more than twenty books proclaim the ills of urban, industrialized society can be cured by banning child labor, providing constructive recreation programs, and inculcating compassion by promoting kindness to animals." The numerous pets Saunders had as a child, her early work as a teacher, and her association with the national Child Labour Committee and other socially conscious groups were experiences that influenced her choices of subject matter.

Back in Halifax where she had lived as a child, Saunders filled her home with animals and birds. She described her eccentric lifestyle in her only work of nonfiction, *My Pets: Real Happenings in My Aviary,* published in 1908. In it she relates tales about rabbits, rats, guinea pigs, owls, robins, pigeons, canaries, and other beasts. Saunders's obsession with animals only grew throughout her life and especially after the death of her mother in 1913. A canine was once again the narrator of a Saunders novel in *The Wandering Dog: Adventures of a Fox Terrier,* published in 1916. The hero of this story is a transient in New York City who knows how to take care of himself. But his life changes for the better when a Riverside Drive family adopts him and the terrier gets to spend some time in the country.

The tensions and contrasts between urban and rural environments are issues that appear in others of Saunders's writing and also figured prominently in her own life. Living her first six years in the countryside of Berwick in the Annapolis Valley of Canada, Saunders and her family moved to the densely populated Halifax in 1867 after her father got a job there as pastor of the First Baptist Church. Saunders didn't like her new home and always in her writings depicts the country as a more favorable place to be than the city.

Other of Saunders's children's stories written from the perspective of an animal include 1919's *Golden Dicky: The Story of a Canary and His Friends* and *Bonnie Prince Fetlar: The Story of a Pony and His Friends,* published the following year. Saunders's last published work is notable for its autobiographical elements. In *Esther de Warren: The Story of a Mid-Victorian Maiden,* published in 1927, the heroine of the novel leaves home to visit Scotland as a young woman, much as Saunders herself did when she attended finishing school in Edinburgh at the age of fifteen. The character in the novel makes a new friend on the ship taking her across the Atlantic, a boy with a pet squirrel. Esther reveals the details of her journey in letters to her mother back home in Halifax. A reviewer for the *Boston Transcript* wrote, "In a singularly imaginative manner this author has contrived to write the diary of a little girl of only fifteen, and yet to fill it with the vague feeling of impending womanhood." In the 1920s Saunders began to have money troubles because of the mismanagement of the royalties she earned from her books. Although she retired from writing around this time, she began to work as a lecturer to earn some income. She traveled the country giving talks and slide shows on topics titled "Marshall Saunders and Her Pets" and "Marshall Saunders: Her Life and Literary Adventures." She continued to lecture until 1940, seven years before her death in 1947.

BIOGRAPHICAL/CRITICAL SOURCES:

BOOKS

Blain, Virginia, Patricia Clements, and Isobel Grundy, *The Feminist Companion to Literature in English,* Yale University Press, 1990.

Buck, Claire, *The Bloomsbury Guide to Women's Literature,* Prentice Hall General Reference, 1992.

Dictionary of Literary Biography, Volume 92: *Canadian Writers, 1890-1920,* Gale (Detroit, MI), 1990.

PERIODICALS

Boston Transcript, November 11, 1916, p. 8; December 24, 1919, p. 6; November 26, 1927, p. 3.

Canadian Bookman, November 1930, pp. 223-228.

Dial, November 30, 1916.

Nation, October 1, 1908.

New York Evening Post, November 8, 1919, p. 16; October 23, 1920, p. 25.

New York Times, July 1, 1905; March 26, 1910; January 4, 1920; December 12, 1920, p. 23; November 6, 1927, p. 7.

Nova Scotia Historical Quarterly, 1, 1971, pp. 225-238.

Springfield Republican, December 17, 1916, p. 14; December 21, 1919, p. 15.*

*   *   *

SCHAPER, Edzard (Hellmuth)   1908-1984

PERSONAL: Born September 30, 1908 in Ostrowo, Poland; died January 29, 1984 of chronic heart disease; son of a military official; married Alice Pergelbaum in 1932; children: Katharina, Elin Christiane. *Politics:* Opponent of the National Socialist Party. *Religion:* Christian. *Avocational interests:* Church, religion.

CAREER: Author of historical/religious novels, short stories, essays, dramatic pieces, and radio plays; worked various odd jobs, including assistant stage manager in theaters and an opera house, gardener, trawler hand, woodcutter, translator, social worker, lecturer, freelance writer for Insel publishers, and correspondent for United Press.

AWARDS, HONORS: Berlin Fontane Prize, 1958; Ph.D., University of Freiburg.

WRITINGS:

Der letzte Gast: Roman (title means "The Last Guest"), Bonz (Stuttgart. Germany), 1927.

Die Bekenntnisse des Föersters Patrik Doyle, Roman (title means "The Confessions of Forest Ranger Patrick Doyle"), Bonz (Stuttgart. Germany), 1928.

Die Insel Tüetarsaar: Roman (title means "The Island Tüetarsaar"), Insel (Leipzig, Germany), 1933.

Erde über dem Meer: Roman (title means "Earth over the Sea"), Die Buchgemeinde (Berlin, Germany), 1934.

Die Arche, die Schiffbruch erlitt, Insel (Leipzig, Germany), 1935.

Die sterbende Kirche: Roman (title means "The Dying Church"), Insel (Leipzig, Germany), 1935.

Das Leben Jesu, Insel (Leipzig, Germany), 1936, parts reprinted as *Die Weihnachtsgeschichte,* Arche (Zurich, Switzerland), 1950, and *Nikodemus: Eine Erzählung,* Arche (Zurich, Switzerland), 1952.

Das Lied der Väter, Insel (Leipzig, Germany), 1937.

Der Henker: Roman (title means "The Executioner"), Insel (Leipzig, Germany), 1940, revised edition, Atlantis (Zurich, Switzerland), 1949, reprinted as *Sie mähten gewappnet die Saaten: Roman,* Hegner (Cologne, Germany), 1956.

Semjon, der ausging, das Licht zu holen: Eine Weihnachtserzählung aus dem alten Estland, Reinhardt (Basel), 1947, reprinted as *Stern über der Grenze,* Hegner (Cologne, Germany), 1950, translation by Isabel and Florence McHugh published as *Star over the Frontier,* Helicon Press (Baltimore, MD), 1960.

Der letzte Advent: Roman (title means "The Last Advent"), Atlantis (Zurich, Switzerland), 1949.

Der große, offenbare Tag: Die Erzählung eines Freundes, Hegner (Cologne, Germany), 1949.

Die Freiheit des Gefangenen: Roman (title means "The Freedom of the Prisoner"), Hegner (Cologne, Germany), 1950, reprinted with *Die Macht der Ohnmächtigen* as *Macht und Freiheit* (title means "Power and Freedom"), 1961.

Der Mensch in der Zelle: Dichtung und Deutung des gefangenen Menschen, Hegner (Cologne, Germany), 1951.

Die Macht der Ohnmächtigen: Roman (title means "The Power of the Powerless"), Hegner (Cologne, Germany), 1951, reprinted with *Die Freiheit des Gefangenen* as *Macht und Freiheit* (title means "Power and Freedom"), 1961.

C. G. Mannerheim, Marschall von Finnland: Eine Rede zu seinem Gedächtnis, Arche (Zurich, Switzerland), 1951.

Norwegische Reise, Arche (Zurich, Switzerland), 1951.

Finnisches Tagebuch, Arche (Zurich, Switzerland), 1951.

Hinter den Linien, Hegner (Cologne, Germany), 1951.

Vom Sinn des Alters: Eine Betrachtung, Arche (Zurich, Switzerland), 1952.

Untergang und Verwandlung: Betrachtungen und Reden, Arche (Zurich, Switzerland), 1952, revised edition, Ullstein (Berlin, Germany), 1956.

Um die neunte Stunde oder Nikodemus und Simon, Hegner (Cologne, Germany), 1953.

Der Mantel der Barmherzigkeit: Erzählung, Hegner (Cologne, Germany), 1953.

Die heiligen drei Könige, Arche (Zurich, Switzerland), 1953.

Der Gouverneur oder Der glückselige Schuldner: Roman, Hegner (Cologne, Germany), 1954.

Die letzte Welt: Ein Roman, Fischer (Frankfurt, Germany), 1956.

Erkundungen in Gestern und Morgen, Arche (Zurich, Switzerland), 1956.

Bürger in Zeit und Ewigkeit: Antworten, edited by Lutz Besch, von Schroeder (Hamburg, Germany), 1956.

Unschuld der Sünde, Fischer (Frankfurt, Germany), 1957.

Attentat auf den Mächtigen: Roman, Fischer (Frankfurt, Germany), 1957.

Das Wiedersehen und Der gekreuzigte Diakon, Hegner (Cologne, Germany), 1957.

Der Held: Weg und Wahn Karls XII, Fischer (Frankfurt, Germany), 1958.

Das Tier oder Die Geschichte eines Bären, der Oskar hieß: Roman, Fischer (Frankfurt, Germany), 1958, translation by Norman Denny published as *The Dancing Bear (A Novel),* Bodley Head (London, England), 1960, Day (New York, NY), 1961.

Die Eidgenossen des Sommers, 1958.

Die Geisterbahn: Eine Erzählung, Hegner (Cologne, Germany), 1959.

Der Abfall vom Menschen: Du bist nicht allein; Das Martyrium der Lüge, Walter, 1961.

Der vierte König: Roman, Hegner (Cologne, Germany), 1961, parts reprinted as *Die Legende vom vierten König,* 1964.

Die Söhne Hiobs, Hegner (Cologne, Germany), 1962.

Verhüllte Altäre: Ansprachen, Hegner (Cologne, Germany), 1962.

Unser Vater Malchus, Vereinigung Oltner Buecherfreunde (Olten, Germany), 1962.

Heiligung der Opfer: Eine Rede zur Woche der Brüderlichkeit, Hegner (Cologne, Germany), 1963.

Der Aufruhr des Gerechten: Eine Chronik, Hegner (Cologne, Germany), 1963.

Dragonergeschichte: Novelle, Hegner (Cologne, Germany), 1963.

Strenger Abschied: Ein Hörspiel, Hegner (Cologne, Germany), 1964.

Der Gefangene der Bötschaft: Drei Stücke, Hegner (Cologne, Germany), 1964.

Flucht und Bleibe: Ein Wort an die geflüchteten und vertriebenen Deutschen, Hegner (Cologne, Germany), 1965.

Das Feuer Christ: Leben und Sterben des Johannes Hus in siebzehn dramatischen Szenen, Kreuz (Stuttgart, Germany), 1965.

Einer trage des andern Last: Eine Elegie auf den letzten Gepäckträger, Arche (Zurich, Switzerland), 1965.

Wagnis der Gegenwart: An Kreuzwegen christlicher Geschichte, Kreuz (Stuttgart, Germany), 1965.

Die baltischen Länder im geistigen Spektrum Europas, Baltische Gesellschaft in Deutschland (Munich, Germany), 1965.

Gesammelte Erzählungen, Hegner (Cologne, Germany), 1965.

Über die Redlichkeit, Hegner (Cologne, Germany), 1967.

Schattengericht: Vier neue Erzählungen, Hegner (Cologne, Germany), 1967.

Schicksale und Abenteuer: Geschichten aus vielen Leben, Hegner (Cologne, Germany), 1968.

Die Heimat der Verbannten: Erzählung, Hegner (Cologne, Germany), 1968.

Dank an Edzard Schaper: Zu seinem 60. Geburtstag, Hegner (Cologne, Germany), 1968.

Gespräche mit Edzard Schaper, edited by Lutz Besch, Arche (Zurich, Switzerland), 1968.

Der letzte Advent, Hegner (Cologne, Germany), 1968.

Auf der Brücke der Hoffnung: Betrachtungen zur Weihnacht, Arche (Zurich, Switzerland), 1968.

Am Abend der Zeit: Ein Roman, Hegner (Cologne, Germany), 1970.

Taurische Spiele: Ein Roman, Hegner (Cologne, Germany), 1971.

Sperlingschlacht: Ein Roman, Hegner (Cologne, Germany), 1972.

Aufstand und Ergebung: Drei Romane, Hegner (Cologne, Germany), 1973.

Degenhall: Ein Roman, Artemis (Zurich, Switzerland), 1975.

Die Reise unter dem Abendstern: Ein Roman, Artemis (Zurich, Switzerland), 1976.

Geschichten aus vielen Leben: Sämtliche Erzählungen, Artemis (Zurich, Switzerland), 1977.

Grenzlinien: Ein Lesebuch, edited by Matthias Wörther, Artemis (Zurich, Switzerland), 1987.

OTHER

(Editor) *Nachfolge Christi,* by Thomas à Kempis, Fischer (Frankfurt, Germany), 1957.

(Author of introduction) *Kein Landsmann sang mir gleich: Zwanzig seiner Gedichte,* by Paul Fleming, Hegner (Cologne, Germany), 1959.

(Author of epilogue) *Abendstunde,* by R. A. Schröder, edited by Lutz Besch, Arche (Zurich, Switzerland), 1960.

(Editor, with Otto Karrer) *Altchristliche Erzählungen,* Ars sacra (Munich, Germany), 1967.

TRANSLATIONS

Gudmundur Kamban, *Die Jungfrau auf Skalholt,* Insel (Leipzig, Germany), 1934.

Gabriel Scott, *Fant: Roman,* Insel (Leipzig, Germany), 1934.

Gunnar Gunnarsson, *Das Haus der Blinden,* Insel (Leipzig, Germany), 1935.

Gudmundur Kamban, *Ich seh ein große, schönes Land: Roman,* Insel (Leipzig, Germany), 1937.

Sally Salminen, *Katrina: Roman,* Insel (Leipzig, Germany), 1937.

Gudmundur Kamban, *Der Herrscher auf Skalholt: Roman,* Insel (Leipzig, Germany), 1938.

Kaj Munk, *Dänische Predigten,* Neuer Verlag (Stockholm, Sweden), 1945.

Harry Blomberg, *Eva: Der Roman einer tapferen Frau,* Reinhardt, 1947.

Efraim Briem, *Kommunismus und Religion in der Sowjetunion: Ein Ideenkampf,* Reinhardt, 1948.

Frans Eemil Sillanpää, *Das fromme Elend: Ein überstandenes Menschenschicksal in Finnland: Roman,* Claassen (Zurich, Switzerland), 1948.

Carl Herman Tillhagen, *Taikon erzählt: Zigeunermärchen und-geschichten, aufgezeichnet,* Artemis (Zurich, Switzerland), 1948.

Erik Hesselberg, *Kon-Tiki und ich,* Arche (Zurich, Switzerland), 1950.

Aleksis Kivi, *Die sieben Brüder: Roman,* Manesse (Zurich, Switzerland), 1950.

Pär Lagerkvist, *Barabbas: Roman,* Nymphenberger Verlagshandlung (Munich, Germany), 1950.

Ernst Manker, *Menschen und Götter in Lappland,* Morgarten (Zurich, Switzerland), 1950.

Petter Moen, *Der einsame Mensch: Petter Moens Tagebuch. Geschrieben im Gefängnis der Gestapo,* Arche (Zurich, Switzerland), 1950.

Nils-Eric Ringbom, *Jean Sibelius: Ein Meister und sein Werk,* Walter (Olten, Germany), 1950.

Thorfinn Solberg, *Die Wanderer im Norden: Roman aus dem Leben der norwegischen Lappen,* Reinhardt, 1950.

Lagerkvist, *Gast bei der Wirklichkeit: Roman,* Arche (Zurich, Switzerland), 1952.

Stanislaw Mackiewicz, *Der Spieler seines Lebens: F.M. Dostojewskij,* Thomas (Zurich, Switzerland), 1952.

Frans Eemil Sillanpää, *Sonne des Lebens: Roman,* Arche (Zurich, Switzerland), 1952.

Harry Martinson, *Der Weg nach Glockenreich: Roman,* Nymphenburger Verlagshandlung (Munich, Germany), 1953.

Frans Eemil Sillanpää, *Sterben und Auferstehen,* Fischer (Frankfurt, Germany), 1956.

Charly Clerc, *Der Herbergswirt verteidigt sich,* Fischer (Frankfurt, Germany), 1958.

Contributed "Des Vaters Mühle: Erinnerungen" to *Mein Elternhaus,* Warneck (Berlin, Germany), 1937.

Contributor to periodical publications including *Velhagen & Klasings Monatshefte, Insel-Schiff, Die Neue Rundschau,* and *Schweizer Monatshefte fuer Politik und Kultur.*

SIDELIGHTS: Edzard Schaper's writings received most attention just after World War II. He was a major German Christian novelist at a time when the German Christian novelists had a far-reaching audience. He was a historical as well as religious writer who in addition to novels also wrote short stories, essays, and a few dramatic pieces and radio plays. He also lectured, could often be heard on the radio, and made several television appearances.

Schaper was born September 30, 1908 in Ostrowo (now Ostrowo Wielkopolski), Poland, the son of a military official and the youngest of eleven children. After armistice had been declared in World War I, the family moved to Glogau in Silesia, and then to Hannover, Germany, in 1920, where Schaper began secondary school. He also began studying music, but had to abandon his dreams of becoming a musician to help support the family financially. He became an assistant stage manager and worked in theaters in Herford and Minden before landing a position with an opera in Stuttgart. While working in the performing arts, he began writing, and in 1927, left Stuttgart to spend three years on Christianso, a Danish island in the Baltic sea, to focus on his new interest. He then found work as a gardener in Pottsdam and afterwards went to sea as a trawler hand. The same evening he met Alice Pergelbaum in Berlin, in 1931, he proposed to her. Pergelbaum was from Estonia and together they returned to her native country, where Schaper resumed writing, as a freelance writer for Insel publishers in Leipzig, a correspondent for the United Press, and on his own fiction.

By 1934, he had published four novels and had begun a novel about Handel that he never completed. He repudiated three of his first four novels: *Der Letzte Gast; Die Bekenntnisse des Foersters Patrick Doyle; Erde ueber dem Meer*r; and eventually came to consider his with his third, *Die Insel Tuetarsaar,* published in 1933, to be his first novel. In public opinion, *Die Insel Tüetarsaar* was considered his most important work at that point in his career.

The alienated individual trying to come to terms with his position in society is a recurring theme in Schaper's works and is the most prevailing theme in *Die Insel Tüetarsaar.* The narrator of this novel abandons his wife and the malaise of day-to-day existence to spend the summer on an island that is inhabited only by two shepherd boys, who believe there is a hidden treasure somewhere on the island. The treasure is a metaphor for the narrator's loss of a sense of self, of the naïve inner strength of childhood. Once the "treasure" is discovered, the narrator is content to return to his wife and the responsibilities of career, family, and future.

Schaper also explores the individual's responsibility in relation to power, God, and freedom, all issues that affected his own life and the lives of his family in their frequent moves around Europe to escape political persecution. As Virginia M. Anderson elaborated in *Dictionary of Literary Biography,* Schaper's "characters live not only on a geographical border, but on the border between earth and heaven, and good and evil. They are not just refugees with no earthly home but spiritual refugees alienated from themselves and from God."

Religion and belief and faith in God are also themes Schaper incorporated into most of works. While the protagonists are often members of the clergy or parishioners, his writings are not morally pedantic. As Mary Garland stated in *The Oxford Companion to German Literature,* Schaper's "ubiquitous religious standpoint is unobtrusive."

His next major novel, 1935's *Die sterbende Kirche,* is set in Estonia and depicts the struggles of Father Seraphim, a priest in a small Russian Orthodox church, as his religious faith is tested by a series of family tragedies. The priest's struggles end when the dome of the church crumbles onto him and ten parishioners, killing all of them. The novel ends with a shift in focus to the survivors of the catastrophe, a young boy and a girl who had recently abandoned communist ideology to join the church. The ceremonies for the priest and parishioners are held in a Lutheran church, a twist Schaper incorporated into the plot to demonstrate the necessity of unity among Protestants and Catholics at a time when both were under attack from the National Socialists, and to suggest that the oneness found in faith in Christ transcends any apparent loss.

Der Henker, released in 1940, was Schaper's next major novel and in it, he again concentrated on marginalized groups. *Der Henker* chronicles the struggles of Estonians fighting against Germans in the early 1900s. The protagonist, a Russian officer of German lineage, inherits land when his relatives are killed in Estonia's uprising against the German landowners. The officer answers to a higher calling, that of his faith in God, and the novel ends in reconciliation.

In 1940, the Russians annexed Estonia, placing Schaper, his wife and two daughters in immediate danger. Since the Soviets and Nazis considered him to be involved in espionage, an in-absence death sentence had been placed on him by both sides. He and his family fled to Finland, were granted citizenship, and remained there until, in danger of being turned over to the Soviets, the family fled once again, to Sweden. In Sweden, Schaper worked as a woodcutter, translator, and as the secretary to an organization that focused on the welfare of war prisoners. In 1947 he moved the family to Brigue, Switzerland, and again resumed a writing career.

Over the next four years, Schaper published three novels. *Der letzte Advent,* a sequel to *Die sterbende Kirche,* tells of the deacon Sabbas, a survivor of the church incident, who is condemned to death for preaching Christianity in the Soviet Union. During the next two years Schaper published *Die Freiheit des Gefangenen* and its sequel, *Die Macht der Ohnmächtigen.* Both novels were reprinted together as a set titled *Macht und Freiheit* in 1961. The novels were set during the time of Napoleon I and tell the story of an imprisoned officer who, in conversations with a priest, finds renewed faith in God.

Schaper was extremely prolific and continued to write until his death. He also translated works from Finnish and Scandinavian languages, and received five literary awards and an honorary doctorate from the University of Freiburg. Interest in Schaper's writings waned in the 1970s, and they have yet to regain the popularity they once had. In 1984, Schaper died of chronic heart disease.

BIOGRAPHICAL/CRITICAL SOURCES:

BOOKS

Dictionary of Literary Biography, Volume 69: *Contemporary German Fiction Writers,* Gale (Detroit, MI), 1988.
The Oxford Companion to German Literature, Oxford University Press (Oxford, England), 1997.
Science Fiction & Fantasy Literature, 1975-1991, Gale (Detroit, MI) 1992.*

* * *

SCHOENBERGER, Karl 1954-

PERSONAL: Born February 6, 1954, in IL; son of James A. (a cardiologist) and Sally Schoenberger; married Susan K. Moffat, March 1, 1991; children: Sonya, Hannah. *Education:* Stanford University, B.A., 1976, graduate work in communication, 1981-82. *Politics:* "Independent." *Religion:* "Fallen Buddhist." *Avocational interests:* Carpentry, maps, childcare, poetry.

ADDRESSES: Home—1612 Sonoma Ave., Albany, CA, 94707. *E-mail*—kschoenb@pacbell.net. *Agent*—Kim Witherspoon, 235 East 31st St., New York, NY 10016.

CAREER: Associated Press, Tokyo and Philadelphia, reporter/news wire editor, 1982-84; *Hartford Courant,* Hartford, CT, state reporter, 1984-85, investigative reporter, 1985-86; *Asian Wall Street Journal,* Tokyo correspondent, 1986-87, Tokyo bureau chief, 1987-88; *Los Angeles Times,* Los Angeles, CA, Tokyo correspondent, 1988-91, Asia Pacific correspondent, 1991-94, general assignment reporter, 1995; *Fortune* Magazine, New York, NY, senior writer/Hong Kong bureau chief, 1995-97; University of California, Berkeley, CA, Koret Teaching Fellow and visiting scholar in Graduate School of Journalism and also in Human Rights Center, 1997-99; *San Jose Mercury News,* San Jose, CA, assistant business editor for technology, 1999-2000; freelance writer, 2000—.

MEMBER: International House of Japan, Japan Society of Northern California.

AWARDS, HONORS: Monbusho Research Fellow, Kyoto University, 1977-79; Nieman Fellow, Harvard University, 1994-95.

WRITINGS:

Levi's Children: Coming to Terms with Human Rights in the Global Marketplace, Atlantic Monthly Press, 2000.

Contributor to periodicals, including *Industry Standard* (San Francisco, CA) and *New York Times.*

WORK IN PROGRESS: Corporate Social Responsibility in the High Tech Industry; research on "Okinawan society, religion and politics; U.S.-Japan security policy."

* * *

SCOTT, Mary
See MATTERN, Joanne

* * *

SCZESNOCZKAWASM, Jun
See SMITH, Warren Allen

* * *

SEDLEY, David Neil 1947-

PERSONAL: Born May 30, 1947; son of William and Rachel (Seifert) Sedley; married Beverley Anne Dobbs, 1973; children: Jonathan, William, Rachel. *Education:* Trinity College, Oxford, B.A., 1969, M.A., 1973; University of London, Ph.D., 1974. *Avocational interests:* Vegetable gardening, cinema.

ADDRESSES: Home—97 Hills Rd., Cambridge CB2 1PG, England. *Office*—Christ's College, Cambridge University, Cambridge CB2 3BU, England.

CAREER: Oxford University, Oxford, England, Dyson junior research fellow in Greek culture at Balliol College, 1973-75; Cambridge University, Cambridge, England, assistant lecturer, 1975-78, lecturer in classics, 1978-89, reader, 1989-96, professor of ancient philosophy, 1996—, fellow of Christ's College, 1976—.

WRITINGS:

(With A. A. Long) *The Hellenistic Philosophers,* two volumes, Cambridge University Press (New York, NY), 1987.

Lucretius and the Transformation of Greek Wisdom, Cambridge University Press (New York, NY), 1998.

Contributor to books. Also contributor to classical and philosophical journals. Editor, *Classical Quarterly,* 1986-92, and *Oxford Studies in Ancient Philosophy,* 1998—.

WORK IN PROGRESS: Plato's Cratylus, the Townsend lectures, for Cornell University, 2001, publication of the book version expected in 2003.

BIOGRAPHICAL/CRITICAL SOURCES:

PERIODICALS

Times Literary Supplement, April 16, 1999, p. 32.

*   *   *

SHAW, Donald Leslie   1930-

PERSONAL: Born February 11, 1930, in Manchester, England; son of Stephen Leslie (a cashier) and Lily (Hughes) Shaw; married Mariella Cristini, 1958; children: Andrew, Silvia. *Ethnicity:* "Caucasian." *Education:* Victoria University of Manchester, B.A. (with first class honors), 1952, M.A., 1954; Trinity College, Dublin, Ph.D., 1961. *Politics:* Labour. *Religion:* None.

ADDRESSES: Home—1800 Jefferson Park Ave., Apt. 207, Charlottesville, VA 22903. *Office*—Department of Spanish, Italian, and Portuguese, University of Virginia, Charlottesville, VA 22903; fax: 804-924-7160. *E-mail*—dls6h@virginia.edu.

CAREER: University of Dublin, Dublin, Ireland, assistant lecturer, 1955-57; University of Glasgow, Glasgow, Scotland, lecturer, 1957-64; University of Edinburgh, Edinburgh, Scotland, lecturer, 1964-69, senior lecturer, 1969-72, reader, 1972-79, professor of Latin American studies, 1979-86, chairperson of department, between 1969 and 1985; University of Virginia, Charlottesville, VA, Brown Forman Professor, 1986—, chairperson of department, 1989-92. Brown University, visiting professor, 1967p; University of Stirling, visiting professor, 1976-78; University of Virginia, visiting professor, 1983. *Military service:* Royal Air Force, flying officer, 1953-55.

WRITINGS:

A Literary History of Spain: The Nineteenth Century, Barnes & Noble (Totowa, NJ), 1972.
Gallegos, Dona Barbara: A Critical Study, Grant & Cutler (London, England), 1972.
The Generation of 1898 in Spain, Barnes & Noble (Totowa, NJ), 1975.
Borges, Ficciones: A Critical Study, Grant & Cutler, 1976, revised edition, 1992.
Nueva Narrativa Hispanoamericana, Catedra (Madrid, Spain), 1981, 6th edition published as *Nueva narrative Hispanoamericana: Boom, Posboom, Posmodernismo,* 1999.
Alejo Carpentier, G. K. Hall (Boston, MA), 1985.
Borges' Narrative Strategy, Liverpool Monographs in Hispanic Studies (Liverpool, England), 1992.
Antonio Skarmeta and the Post-Boom, Ediciones del Norte (Hanover, NH), 1994.
The Post-Boom in Spanish American Fiction, State University of New York Press (Albany, NY), 1998.
Companion to Spanish American Fiction, Boydell and Brewer (Woodbridge, Suffolk, England), 2001.

Editor of books by Virgilio Malvezzi, Eduardo Mallea, Pio Baroja, Agustin Duran, and Angel de Saavedra. Contributor of more than a hundred articles to scholarly journals, including *Anthropos, Foro Hispanico,* and *Latin American Literary Review.* Guest editor, *Studies in Twentieth Century Fiction,* 1995; member or past member of editorial board, *Bulletin of Hispanic Studies, Hispanic Review, Chasqui, Insula, Antipodas, Revista Contemporanea/Contemporary Spain, Journal of Hispanic Research, Indiana Journal of Hispanic Literature, Romance Quarterly, Studies in Twentieth Century Literature, New Novel Review,* and *North Colina Studies in Romance Languages and Literatures.* Several of Shaw's works have been published in Spanish translation.

Contributor to publications, including *The European History of a Word,* edited by H. Eichner, University of Toronto Press (Toronto, Ontario), 1972; *Literature and Western Civilization,* edited by A. Thorlby, Aldus Books (London, England), 1976; *Five Essays on M. L. Guzman,* edited by W. W. Megenney, University of California, 1978; *Nine Essays on Romulo Gallegos,* edited by H. Rodrigiez-Alcala, University of California, 1979; *Contemporary Latin American Fiction,* edited by S. Bacarisse, Academic Press (Edinburgh, Scotland), 1980; *Eight Essays on Manuel Galvez,* edited by W. W. Megenney, University of California, 1982;, *Borges the Poet,* edited by Carlos Cortinez, University of Arkansas Press (Fayetteville, AR), 1986; *Critical Perspectives on*

Gabriel Garcia Marquez, edited by D. A. Shaw and N. Vera, Society of Spanish and Spanish American Studies (Lincoln, NE), 1986; *Landmarks in Modern Latin American Fiction,* edited by Phillip Swanson, Routledge (New York, NY), 1990; *Love, Sex, and Eroticism in Contemporary Latin American Literature,* edited by Alun Kenwood, Voz Hispanica (Melbourne, Australia), 1992; *Carnal Knowledge,* edited by P. Bacarisse, Tres Rios (Pittsburgh, PA), 1993; *Negotiating Past and Present,* edited by D. T. Gies, Rookwood (Charlottesville, VA), 1996; *Spain and Its Literature: Essays in Memory of E. Allison Peers,* edited by A. L. Mackenzie, Liverpool University Press (Liverpool, England), 1997; *Onetti and Others,* edited by Gustavo San Roman, State University of New York Press (Albany, NY), 1999. Contributor to books published in Spanish.

SIDELIGHTS: Donald Leslie Shaw commented in *CA:* "My primary motivation is vanity; that is, attachment to professional prestige. My work is chiefly influenced by a desire to offer students and other researchers in the field either a springboard to further research or something to disagree with. When writing, I try to produce two pages a day, usually in the morning, proceeding incrementally. As a schoolboy I fell in love with things Hispanic, and I have spent my life happily working in the field."

*   *   *

SHEA, Christina   1963-

PERSONAL: Born in 1963 in West Hartford, CT; married; children: one son. *Education:* Kenyon College, B.A.; University of Michigan, M.F.A., 1989.

ADDRESSES: Home—Boston, MA. *Office*—c/o St. Martin's Press, 175 Fifth Ave., New York, NY 10010.

CAREER: Novelist.

WRITINGS:

Moira's Crossing, St. Martin's Press (New York, NY), 2000.

SIDELIGHTS: American novelist Christina Shea's debut work, *Moira's Crossing,* which is about two sisters who migrate from Ireland to Boston in the early 1900s, earned mostly praise from literary critics. Shea, who lives in Boston with her husband and son, is originally from West Hartford, Connecticut.

Moira's Crossing is the tale of sisters Moira and Julia O'Leary who, as teenagers, are sent to America by their father after tragedy strikes their sheep farm in Ireland. The story begins in 1921 in Ireland, as the girls' mother dies during childbirth. As a result, their father turns to alcohol, leaving the two girls to care for their new infant sister, Ann. Seven years later, Ann also dies, and the grief-stricken father sends the girls to Boston, where they find work as servants and eventually grow into maturity. As Shea develops the two characters, it becomes apparent that Moira and Julia are in many ways opposites. Moira is pretty, energetic and outspoken, while Julia is physically deformed, subdued and very proper. In addition, Moira has abandoned the church because of the tragedies the family has endured, while Julia remains pious. Despite their differences, the two girls remain together. Julia uses her talents as a seamstress, while Moira falls in love with an artist and fellow Irish immigrant named Michael Sheehan, who painted her portrait on the voyage from Ireland. Michael and Moira marry, and Julia develops a secret love for Michael.

The story follows Michael and Moira to Maine, where he finds work as a fisherman. The move crushes Julia, who stays behind. The couple have two daughters before Michael is shipped off to serve in World War II. After Michael dies, Julia moves to Maine to once again be near Moira. She gains employment as a columnist for a local newspaper and helps raise Moira's two daughters. The story is ultimately about the close relationship, and subtle friction, between the two sisters, who both harbor a common secret about Ann's death.

Several critics lauded the debut novel, including a contributor for *Publishers Weekly,* who called it "a fluid, meditative family saga." The same contributor went on to comment on the author's ability to shed light on the immigration experience: "Drawn in broad strokes, the sisters and their families are plausible characters typifying the Irish immigrant experience." GraceAnne A. DeCandido of *Booklist* stated that it was "hard to put down this first novel, even though its elements will seem familiar." Nancy Linn Pearl of *Library Journal* was less impressed with the novel, however. Pearl felt the plot moved along "monotonously," where "even the most dramatic parts fall flat." Furthermore, Pearl believed Shea's writing made it difficult to "differentiate among the characters." Phoebe-Lou Adams, who reviewed the novel for the *Atlantic Monthly,* called it "quietly appealing." Adams also thought Shea's writing style blended "a briskly practical surface with a lyrical undertone."

BIOGRAPHICAL/CRITICAL SOURCES:

PERIODICALS

Atlantic Monthly, February, 2000, Phoebe-Lou Adams, review of *Moira's Crossing,* p. 105.
Booklist, December 15, 1999, GraceAnne A. De-Candido, review of *Moira's Crossing,* p. 758.
Library Journal, January, 2000, Nancy Lin Pearl, review of *Moira's Crossing,* p. 163.
Publishers Weekly, November 22, 1999, review of *Moira's Crossing,* p. 42.*

*   *   *

SHEPHERD, Michael
    See LUDLUM, Robert

*   *   *

SHLAPENTOKH, Dmitry (V.)   1950-

PERSONAL: Born May 31, 1950, in Kiev, U.S.S.R. (now Ukraine); naturalized U.S. citizen; son of Vladimir (a sociologist) and Liubov' (Alievskaia) Shlapentokh; married Angela Burlako, 1982 (divorced, 1988); married Nataliia Mogileva, 1994; children: Leon, Anna-Vera. *Ethnicity:* "Caucasian." *Education:* Attended Novosibirsk State University, 1967-69; Moscow State University, B.A., 1973; Michigan State University, M.A., 1980; University of Chicago, Ph.D., 1988.

ADDRESSES: Home—1534 Hoover Ave., South Bend, IN 46615-1311. *Office*—Department of History, Indiana University at South Bend, P.O. Box 7111, South Bend, IN 46634. *E-mail*—dshlapentokh@iusb.edu.

CAREER: State University of New York College, Oswego, NY, visiting assistant professor, 1987-88; Harvard University, Cambridge, MA, fellow of Russian Research Center, 1990-91; Indiana University, South Bend, IN, associate professor of history, 1991—. Hoover Institute on War, Revolution, and Peace, fellow, 1992; Columbia University, visiting scholar, 1997; also taught at Michigan State University, Marygrove College, and Queens College of the City University of New York; guest lecturer at educational institutions, including London School of Slavonic and East European Studies, London, University of Canterbury, Anglia Polytechnic University, Ohio State University.

MEMBER: International Napoleonic Society (fellow).

AWARDS, HONORS: Grant from President's Council on International Programs, 1993; REX grant, 2000; travel grant, American Council of Learned Societies, 1995; fellow of National Endowment for the Humanities, 1997; Lady Davis fellow, Hebrew University of Jerusalem.

WRITINGS:

(Coauthor) *Ideologies in the Period of Glasnost: Response to Brezhnev's Stagnation,* Praeger (Westport, CT), 1988.
(Coauthor) *Soviet Cinematography, 1918-1991: Ideological Conflict and Social Reality,* de Gruyter (Hawthorne, NY), 1993.
Mark Aldanov and the French Revolution: The Case of the Writers as Historian, Hoover Institution on War, Revolution, and Peace (Stanford, CA), 1993.
The French Revolution in Russian Intellectual Life, 1865-1905, Praeger (Westport, CT), 1996.
The French Revolution and the Anti-Democratic Tradition in Russia, Transaction Books (New Brunswick, NJ), 1997.
The Counterrevolution in Revolution, Macmillan (London, England), 1999.

Contributor to publications, including *Research on the Soviet Union and Eastern Europe,* Volume I, edited by Anthony Jones, JAI Press (Greenwich, CT), 1990; *Christianity in Russian Culture and Soviet Society,* Westview (Boulder, CO), 1990; *State Organized Terror: The Case of Violent Internal Repression,* Westview, 1991; *Ramifications of the French Revolution,* Woodrow Wilson Press (Washington, DC), 1994; *The Bolsheviks in Russian Society,* Yale University Press (New Haven, CT), 1997.

Contributor of more than eighty articles and reviews to academic journals and other magazines and newspapers, including *Contemporary Review, Russian History, Journal of Philosophical Research, Washington Quarterly, World and I,* and *East European Quarterly.* Advising editor, *International Journal of Sociology and Social Policy,* 1999.

*   *   *

SHORE, Arabella   1820(?)-1901

PERSONAL: Born c. 1820; died January 9, 1901; daughter Thomas (a clergyman and tutor) and Margaret

Anne (Twopeny) Shore. *Education:* Home schooled by her father.

CAREER: Poet, essayist, translator, and editor.

WRITINGS:

(With Louisa Shore) *War Lyrics: Dedicated to the Friends of the Dead. By A. and L.,* Saunders & Otely (London, England), 1855, enlarged edition, 1855.

(With Louisa Shore) *Gemma of the Isles, a Lyrical Drama, and Other Poems: By A. and L.,* Saunders & Otley (London, England), 1859.

(Author of introduction) *Hannibal: A Drama,* by Louisa Shore (first published anonymously), Smith & Elder (London, England), 1861, Richards (London, England), 1898.

(With Louisa Shore) *Fra Dolcino, and Other Poems: By A. and L., Authors of War Lyrics,* Smith, Elder (London, England), 1870.

An Answer to John Bright's Speech on the Women's Suffrage, [London, England], 1877.

(Translator) Henriette Etiennette Fanny Reybaud, *A Daughter of the Malepeires: A Tale of the Ancien Regime,* Remington (London, England), 1885.

Dante for Beginners: A Sketch of the Divina Commedia. With Translations, Biographical and Critical Notices, and Illustrations, Chapman & Hall (London, England), 1886.

(With Louisa Shore) *Elegies and Memorials. By A. and L.,* Kegan Paul, Trench, Truebner (London, England), 1890.

(Editor with Louisa Shore) *Journal of Emily Shore,* Kegan Paul, Trench, Truebner (London, England), 1891, revised edition, 1898, edited by Barbara Timm Gates, University Press of Virginia (Charlottesville, VA), 1991.

(With Louisa Shore) *Poems by A. and L.,* Richards (London, England), 1897.

First and Last Poems, Richards (London, England), 1900.

Work included in anthologies, including *Before the Vote Was Won: Arguments for and against Women's Suffrage,* edited by Jane Lewis, Routledge & Kegan Paul (New York, NY), 1987. Contributor to periodicals, including *British Quarterly Review, Gentleman's Magazine,* and *Westminster Review.*

SIDELIGHTS: The literature of Arabella Shore is intimately tied to that to her two sisters, Margaret Emily and Louisa Catherine. All three were educated at home, along with their two brothers, by their father, Thomas

Shore. Thomas was a private tutor by profession, as well as a clergyman, and he taught his children languages, literature, science, philosophy, and politics.

All three Shore girls began writing at a young age essays about birds in *Penny Magazine* in 1838, though none would reveal their writing talents until the 1850s, when they were in their thirties. Margaret Emily, who suffered from tuberculosis, died in 1838 before she had a chance to see much of her own work or that of her sisters in print. However, Arabella and Louisa faithfully edited the journal their older sister kept during the last eight years of her life. *The Journal of Emily Shore* was released in 1891 with Arabella and Louisa's annotations. A second edition that included Margaret Emily's drawings appeared in 1898.

The two remaining Shore sisters started publishing their poetry together. Beginning by contributing poems about the Crimean War to *The Spectator,* Arabella and Louisa gathered these pieces to make a single book titled *War Lyrics: Dedicated to the Friends of the Dead. By A. and L.,* which was published in January of 1855. The collection of these six pieces by Arabella and nine by Louisa sold out in two weeks. The volume's success may be due to the unique take that the sisters had on the war. The Crimean War, which was a popular topic for writers of the time because of the unprecedented media coverage that it received, was most often reacted to by poets and authors of the time with a sense of patriotism. This sense was revealed through representations of specific battles that came from descriptions of the war's events in the newspapers. Arabella and Louisa, on the other hand, focused their poetry on the people who were left behind as their family members and friends went off to fight. They particularly concentrated on the emotional responses of women at home—mothers, daughters, sisters, wives, and girlfriends.

In the *Dictionary of Literary Biography,* Natalie M. Houston explained the literary partnership between the two sisters, writing, "Although Louisa was the more skilled poet and received more critical attention, without Arabella's encouragement she would probably never have published any of her poems, which she wrote for her own enjoyment and self-expression." The youngest of the sisters, Louisa was shy, retiring, and often sickly. Arabella, on the other hand, was the assertive one who first sent one of Louisa's poems to *The Spectator* for publication without her sister's knowledge.

The differential of talent between the two can be seen in their second jointly published collection of poetry.

For *Gemma of the Isles, a Lyrical Drama, and Other Poems: By A. and L.,* published in 1859, Louisa wrote the title work, a long narrative poem, while Arabella contributed only a few short poems, including one entitled "The Ungifted." The same year that this second poetry collection was published, the Shore sisters lost their mother. The following year, their younger brother, Mackworth Charles, with whom both Arabella and Louisa had a close relationship until he immigrated to Australia in 1841, also died. At this time, Louisa broke out on her own and published her first solo work, a verse drama entitled *Hannibal: A Drama,* released in 1861. Two years later, however, their father, who had supported Louisa's solo endeavor, also died. The two sisters grew closer together after the loss of most of their family (their older brother Richard was still alive but lived in India) and lived together for the next eight years.

In 1870, Arabella and Louisa again published their work together. The title poem of *Fra Dolcino, and Other Poems: By A. and L., Authors of "War Lyrics"* was, this time, by Arabella. Louisa, however, lost her belief that there was an audience out there for her work after the release of this collection. For the next twenty years, she stopped publishing her poetry despite Arabella's urging.

The sisters then turned their attentions to another subject that they found particularly important, the rights of women, and especially women's suffrage. In 1874 Louisa published a title on women's suffrage, and three years later, Arabella published *An Answer to Mr. John Bright's Speech on the Women's Suffrage.* Arabella also published essays of literary criticism that appeared in journals. Her guide for readers of Dante that included her own English translations of his work, *Dante for Beginners: A Sketch of the "Divina Commedia." With Translations, Biographical and Critical Notices, and Illustrations,* was published in 1886.

Despite Louisa's feelings about publishing her literary work, Arabella continued to put together volumes of her poetry as well as her sister's. Arabella had Louisa's lyric poem, *Elegies,* published privately in 1883. It includes tributes to their sister, Margaret Emily, and brother Mackworth. In 1890, another joint volume of poetry was published. *Elegies and Memorials. By A. and L.* includes Louisa's "A Requiem," about the forgotten dead, and Arabella's "In Memoriam," which describes her reaction to a poem by Alfred Lloyd Tennyson.

Arabella and Louisa lived together until Louisa's death in 1895. Two years later Arabella published a selection of Louisa's work from her early Crimean War poems to those written just before her death. *Poems: With a Memoir by Her Sister, Arabella Shore, and an Appreciation by Frederic Harrison* also included an essay by Arabella describing her close relationship with her sister. The same year Arabella also published a retrospective of both their work entitled *Poems by A. and L.* In 1900, Arabella published her first and only volume that consists exclusively of her own poetry. *First and Last Poems* includes works from her collections with Louisa, as well as some previously unpublished works. Arabella died only a year after this book was published.

BIOGRAPHICAL/CRITICAL SOURCES:

BOOKS

Dictionary of Literary Biography, Volume 199: *Victorian Women Poets,* Gale (Detroit, MI), 1999.
Feminist Companion to Literature in English: Women Writers From the Middle Ages to the Present, Yale University Press (New Haven, CT), 1990

PERIODICALS

Englishwoman's Review, October 15, 1895, pp. 269-271.*

*   *   *

SHULTS, Sylvia   1968-

PERSONAL: Born August 30, 1968, in Chicago, IL; daughter of David (a computer programmer) and Ellen (a piano teacher; maiden name, Mishur) Zethmayr; married Robert D. Shults (a photographer), December 31, 1999. *Ethnicity:* "White (mostly Scots and Swedish)." *Education:* Monmouth College, B.A., 1990; Illinois State University, M.S., 1992. *Politics:* "Try to avoid." *Religion:* "Egyptian pagan." *Avocational interests:* "Wine and cordial making, cooking, embroidery, camping, hiking, horseback riding, gardening, reading, baking . . . the list is endless!"

ADDRESSES: Office—c/o Author Mail, Xlibris Publishing, 436 Walnut St., 11th Fl., Philadelphia, PA 19106. *E-mail*—pompeii@MTCO.com.

CAREER: Bloomington Public Library, Bloomington, IL, bookmobile driver, 1990-95; Fondulac District Library, East Peoria, IL, desk assistant, 1997—.

MEMBER: Society for Creative Anachronism.

WRITINGS:

The Golden Apples, Volumes 1 and 2 (Greek mythology), Lion Roe, 1991.
The Midsummer Knight (young adult time travel), Fatbrain, 2000.
Games of Venus (historical romance), Xlibris (Philadelphia, PA), 2000.
Golden Horus (time-travel romance), Xlibris (Philadelphia, PA), 2000.

Also contributor of erotica to *Anachronists Own Erotica,* Folump Enterprises, Volume IV, 1989, and Volume VII, 1991.

WORK IN PROGRESS: Voices in an Empty Room, horror short stories; *Price of Admission,* a time-travel supernatural; *"Price of Admission* is set in 1927, so I'm doing a lot of research on the Jazz Age and gangsters. The final story in *Voices* is an alternate history of the Titanic sinking, so a lot of research is going into that too."

SIDELIGHTS: Sylvia Shults told *CA:* "I started out my writing career by penning erotic stories for my boyfriend at the time. We're no longer together, but the writing has gone on and flourished.

"Along with the erotica, I found that I enjoyed writing horror short stories. Actually, that's an understatement: I am the world's biggest sucker for a good horror short story. I love to read them, I love to write them.

"If I had to restrict myself to writing in one genre, I would choose horror fiction. My literary idols are guys with names like Stephen King, Dean Koontz, Bentley Little, Richard Laymon, etc. When I was in college, during finals I would gorge on King whenever I had a study break. The pressure of academics would pale next to the hell of what these characters were going through. That's the real escape of horror fiction—maybe even of all fiction. Whatever problems you're dealing with in your own life, you can be pretty sure that the hero of a horror novel has got it worse than you do!

"I've got plans for horror novels in the future, but the novels I've felt compelled to write so far have had barely a breath of the supernatural in them. (So far, I've confined the other world to my short stories.) I have such a deep respect for the giants of that field—I feel as if I have to work my way into writing horror by starting off with the short stories, then 'graduating' to nov-

els. In the meantime, I've been writing the other novels that come into my head, books that aren't horror fiction at all.

"How very lucky writers are when we first start out! Our readers don't expect us to fit into a certain genre slot yet—we can tell any story we want to, at least for a while.

"I think that writers are among the most fortunate people on earth in any case. We have an idea, we set it up in our minds, looking at it from every angle, we put flesh on the bones of the story. We create something entirely new out of thin air, and by doing so, we can entertain ourselves and everyone else who reads our work. What better job could there possibly be?

"I learned to read when I was two years old. Since then, I've spent countless hours immersed in whatever new universes I find within the pages of a book. I want to be a part of that. I want to take people away from the boredom of waiting in the doctor's office or in an airport somewhere. I want other people to see the world through my eyes for 300 pages. I want to say, 'Welcome to my universe. Have a good time while you're here, and come again soon.' "

*　　*　　*

SHYAMALAN, M. Night   1970-

PERSONAL: Born Manoj Shyamalan, August 3 (some sources say August 6), 1970, in Pondicherry, India; citizen of India and the United States; son of Jaya (a physician) and Nelliate (a physician) Shyamalan; married Bhavna Vaswani; two children. *Education:* Received degree from New York University, 1992.

ADDRESSES: Home—Philadelphia, PA. *Agent*—c/o United Talent Agency, Inc., 9560 Wilshire Blvd., 5th Floor, Beverly Hills, CA 90212.

CAREER: Screenwriter and film director. Made feature-film debut with *Praying with Anger* as director, screenwriter, and actor.

AWARDS, HONORS: Film debut of the year award, American Film Institute, 1993, for *Praying with Anger;* Bram Stoker Award for best screenplay, 1999, Nebula Award for best script, Science Fiction and Fantasy Writers of America, and Golden Satellite Award for best original screenplay, all 1999, and Visionary

M. Night Shyamalan

Award, Palm Springs International Film Festival, and nominations for Best Director and Best Original Screenplay, Academy of Motion Picture Arts and Sciences, all 2000, all for *The Sixth Sense.*

WRITINGS:

SCREENPLAYS

(And director) *Praying with Anger,* 1992.
(And director) *Wide Awake,* Miramax, 1998.
(And director) *The Sixth Sense,* Buena Vista, 1999.
Stuart Little, Columbia, 1999.
(And director) *Unbreakable,* Buena Vista, 2000.

WORK IN PROGRESS: Signs, a supernatural thriller.

SIDELIGHTS: M. Night Shyamalan is a Hollywood phenomenon who steers clear of the city and its heavy mix of entertainment and corporate politicking. He both wrote and directed *The Sixth Sense,* a 1999 thriller starring Bruce Willis as a doctor treating a little boy with troubling psychic abilities. With that picture and his next work, *Unbreakable,* Shyamalan brought in over $1 billion in box-office receipts for producer Disney Studios; in turn the studio granted him the creative license to continue shooting his own scripts free from executive interference. He signed a reported eight-figure deal

with Disney to make his fifth film, which, like the others, would also be set and shot near his hometown of Philadelphia. "I started out trying to do more personal films," Shyamalan told a writer for *Newsweek.* "But I wasn't fitting in doing that. My instincts are: How do I make the most intelligent commercial movie for a mass audience? How do I make a superintelligent decision for both the seventy-year-old woman and the thirteen-year-old boy? It sounds silly, but I get satisfaction from making stories that way."

Shyamalan was born in India in 1970. Both of his parents were doctors, scions of affluent families that owned large plantations near Madras. Immigrating to the United States, they traveled back to India for their son's birth so that he could enjoy dual citizenship. Shyamalan grew up outside Philadelphia, in Conshohocken, and as the only son in the family was admittedly indulged as a child. "My parents were loose, very relaxed," he told *Esquire* contributor Michael D'Antonio. "Their attitude was, 'You don't want to go to bed? Okay, go when you're tired.' " Nevertheless, he was expected to excel academically, and though his religious heritage was Hindu, his parents sent him to Catholic school for the academic challenge. There, however, Shyamalan sometimes felt ostracized because he was not a practicing Roman Catholic. He once earned the top grade in his religion class—but his teacher publicized it to make other students feel bad for not trying harder.

Shyamalan was fascinated by film at an early age, and directed his first project when he was just twelve years old, using his father's eight-millimeter movie camera. He was especially entranced by horror films, and cites the 1973 classic *The Exorcist* as one of his perennial favorites. He penned his first film script at the ripe old age of fifteen, around the same time his Catholic school experiences led him to become interested in a more nondenominational spirituality. Born Manoj, he added the middle name "Night" after reading a work about Native American beliefs. He wrote four more scripts while a student at New York University, graduating in 1992. "Even in film school, everybody else was into [French director Jean Luc] Godard and I was the one with the [Steven Spielberg-directed] *Raiders of the Lost Ark* cap on," Shyamalan recalled in *Newsweek.*

Determined to direct only his own scripts—not sell them to studios, nor hire himself out as an assistant to a big-name director—Shyamalan refused to relocate to Hollywood and instead asked his family for help in funding his first film project. His ambition-oriented family, full of cousins who are investment bankers on

Wall Street or physicians, lent him the $750,000 to finance his first feature, *Praying with Anger.* The film centers on a student, born in the United States but of East Indian heritage, who visits India as an exchange student at the insistence of his parents. The work won Shyamalan the film debut of the year award from the American Film Institute, and though it was not very successful as an independent film, *Praying with Anger* did attract notice from industry insiders. An entertainment lawyer who liked it helped Shyamalan find an agent, and that agent in turn arranged a deal with Miramax to make another screenplay by Shyamalan into a feature film.

Released in 1998, *Wide Awake* starred Joseph Cross as Joshua Beal, a Philadelphia fifth-grader, with parents played by Dana Delaney and Denis Leary. Though loved, Joshua feels his parents don't understand him, and he finds a great friend in his enigmatic grandfather, played by Robert Loggia. Their relationship is shown in flashbacks, for the grandfather dies, despite his reassurances to Joshua, and the boy is overwhelmed by grief. Joshua insists that the grandfather's room at their house remain the same, and begins asking questions about the afterlife and one's purpose on earth; even the nuns at Joshua's Catholic school cannot provide satisfactory answers. He sets about finding the answers himself, and in the process saves the life of a classmate. Despite the fact that it failed to make an impact with the public, *Variety* critic Emanuel Levy called *Wide Awake* "an earnest coming-of-age tale with explicitly moral and spiritual overtones." Levy also noted the film possesses "some funny sequences that capture the absurd distance between the audacity with which kids typically approach the world, and the disenchanted, sarcastic manner with which adults tend to avoid dealing with unpleasant issues."

Although Shyamalan said little about his first Hollywood project, *Esquire* contributor D'Antonio reported that some people involved in *Wide Awake* admitted that the film's producer had "bullied" Shyamalan, "demanding one change after another, overriding the director by threatening to pull the plug on the project. The result was a muddy mess of a film that audiences avoided in droves." But Shyamalan told *Time* journalist Christopher John Farley that the project was, in the end, a learning experience for him, an experience that forced his writing into a different direction—one with "darker and deeper" elements. "Had that not happened and had I not failed so absolutely, I wouldn't have been able to grow as fast as I did." The writer-director expounded further about his first setback in filmmaking to D'Antonio. "I know it sounds weird, but I decided I was

going to write the greatest script and everything was going to change. It was going to be mine, and they would have to let me direct it because they wouldn't get it any other way."

The result of that determination was Shyamalan's screenplay for *The Sixth Sense,* which he took to Disney Studios. Disney bought the project for $3 million, and agreed to let him direct as well. Some of the inspiration for the story came from Shyamalan's wife, who was studying child psychology at the graduate level. Set in Philadelphia, the film centers upon child psychologist Malcolm Crowe, played by Bruce Willis. One evening, a former patient confronts Crowe in his home, shoots him, and then turns the gun on himself. Crowe survives, and feels remorse over his inability to help the former patient years ago when he was under his care. He turns his energies to saving a current patient, eight-year-old Cole Sear, played by Haley Joel Osment. Cole is troubled, and reveals to his doctor that the dead speak to him. The boy is understandably terrified, afraid to tell even his mother. "Some of these are newly dead, others are historic revenants, like the hanged family of three dangling in a doorway," noted *National Review* critic John Simon. "Just why they single out Cole is left open, but this seems to be a quasi-autobiographical fantasy, and it figures that the dead would seek out a man who is Night to his friends."

Crowe sets out to save Cole, with several references to Roman Catholicism along his path, and the shocker of a surprise ending gave *The Sixth Sense* tremendous word-of-mouth appeal. The film grossed $650 million at the box office worldwide and became the ninth-highest-grossing film in history. It also brought Shyamalan some major industry accolades, including Oscar nominations for best director and best original screenplay. *Entertainment Weekly* critic Lisa Schwarzbaum called *The Sixth Sense* "a psychological thriller that actually thrills," and compared it to a popular television series for presenting " 'believable' fears and coincidences [and] *X-Files*-ish moments of pleasurable anxiety."

Unlike other directors of thriller films, Shyamalan took a less cinematic approach to creating a sense of dread in *The Sixth Sense,* as he told Farley in *Time.* He refused to use blue lights, for instance, because he wanted it to "look like your hallway when the lights go down. Now put someone walking through it when they're not supposed to be there. Now it'll bother you when you go home." He discussed his own spirituality and belief in the afterlife with *Esquire* interviewer D'Antonio: "I do think it's possible there are things like ghosts that we don't see, but that's not what I feed off of. I believe you won't become a really successful person by being treacherous. I believe the more you act in an appropriate way, the more honest you are, the more you will be treated that way in return."

Some critics compared Shyamalan's astounding success as a relative novice filmmaker to that of George Lucas and Steven Spielberg. People recognized his name, and some came forth to confess that they had psychic abilities themselves, or saw dead people. Based on such growing renown, Disney bought his next screenplay for $5 million, a record sum, then paid him another $5 million to direct *Unbreakable*. Released in 2000, the film is an homage to the comic-book heroes of Shyamalan's youth. "I was trying to show how powers could affect an ordinary person, but in a way that my parents, who aren't into comic books, wouldn't be embarrassed by," he told *U.S. News & World Report* contributor James M. Pethokoukis.

Shyamalan wrote *Unbreakable*'s script after fracturing his leg playing basketball, which gave him some of the kernel of the story. He admitted to D'Antonio, however, that he found it increasingly difficult to write with experience. "Early in your development as a writer, you get better exponentially with each new script," he revealed to the *Esquire* interviewer. "But as you learn the basics, the improvement starts getting more and more difficult. Now I know what's wrong with a scene right away, and I believe I can solve almost any problem on the page. But it takes much more time and effort to find answers that I am satisfied with."

Unbreakable opens with a train accident in which David Dunn, played by Willis, is the sole survivor among 124 dead. He does not even have a scratch on him, which astonishes the emergency-room doctors as well as Dunn. An average Philadelphian who works as a security guard, "Dunn was once a football star, but his spirit is now broken," explained Shanda Deziel in *Maclean's*. "He works security at the stadium, cowering inside his rain slicker—a postmodern superhero's cape." But Dunn soon learns the answers to some nagging questions about himself. "Shyamalan takes a topic that might be the focus of the first 20 minutes of a film about superheroes—the process of coming to understand the extent of their powers—and devotes the entire film to it," remarked *Christian Century* writer Matthew Prins in a favorable review.

The train wreck and its aftermath serve as a catalyst for changing Dunn's moribund life: his wife, played by Robin Wright Penn, was about to leave him, but changes her mind. He realizes that he has never been sick a day in his life, and can touch people and have a psychic vision of their criminal past. He meets Elijah, played by Samuel L. Jackson, who suffers from a rare bone condition that makes fractures a constant threat. Elijah owns an art gallery specializing in comic-book art. Dunn's battle with himself over his "powers" involve him in increasingly dangerous situations as the film moves to a close. Shyamalan himself appears in the work as a suspected drug dealer, and like *The Sixth Sense*, *Unbreakable* was shot in Shyamalan's hometown. *Newsweek* critic David Ansen found other similarities between the two films: "There's the same tone of hushed gravity," Ansen noted, "the same gray skies and dark Philadelphia interiors; the same measured pace, the camera sitting still and staring while an atmosphere of dread settles upon the audience like a damp fog."

Though *Unbreakable* failed to achieve the success of its predecessor, it earned its director positive reviews. "As a director, Shyamalan unfolds his story with stately assurance, slowly upping the ante of creepiness like an anesthesiologist toying with his patient," stated Ansen, a sentiment echoed by Deziel, who noted in *Maclean's* that Shyamalan "skillfully draws out the film's suspense." *People* reviewer Leah Rozen also commended the gripping story. "The highs come from the movie's taut script, deliberate visual style and willingness to grapple with the big question of why any of us are put here on earth," Rozen declared.

By early 2000, Shyamalan had written the screenplay for the big-screen adaptation of the classic E. B. White children's novel *Stuart Little*, about a mouse and the human family with whom he lives. He wrote it for his young daughter but was forced to shift his attention to *The Sixth Sense*—"and they added the fart jokes. They ended up making a much more generic, formulaic movie," Shyamalan explained to Ansen. Still, he expressed satisfaction that his works have been able to find such a wide audience. "When I went to the airport the other day, and I tried to check my bags in—they saw my name, and all the baggage people started going nuts. 'I saw "Sixth Sense" four times!' 'That was the best film of the year!' I'll take that, you know? Those decisions that I made that were so restricting in the storytelling process became so rewarding."

Despite his growing stature as a director and screenwriter, Shyamalan prefers to distance himself from the Hollywood lifestyle, finding Philadelphia an ideal place to raise a family. "I'm there to take the kids to school and put them to bed 330 days out of the year," he told

Farley in *Time.* "This life can get so overwhelming. You have to protect your family as much as you can. Nobody else is going to do it for you." Next on deck, *Signs,* is again set in Philly and its surrounding environs, and centers upon the phenomenon of crop circles, which some believe to be a clever hoax but others consider unexplained phenomena. Disney Studios again bought Shyamalan's script and right to direct, this time for a sum that reportedly hit eight figures. "The money isn't important on its own," Shyamalan told *Esquire* interviewer D'Antonio. "It's important for what it says. It says you are the highest, the best at what you do. That's what I want. That's what I am hungry for."

BIOGRAPHICAL/CRITICAL SOURCES:

PERIODICALS

Christian Century, January 17, 2001, Matthew Prins, "Unusual Powers," p. 25.
Entertainment Weekly, August 13, 1999, Lisa Schwarzbaum, "Phantom Menace," p. 50.
Esquire, August, 2000, Michael D'Antonio, "I See Blockbusters," p. 98.
Maclean's, November 27, 2000, Shanda Deziel, "In Search of a Superhero," p. 89.
National Review, August 30, 1999, John Simon, review of *The Sixth Sense,* p. 53.
Newsweek, February 7, 2000, David Ansen and Jeff Giles, "The Envelope, Please," p. 58; November 27, 2000, David Ansen, "If It Ain't Broke, Don't Fix It," p. 80.
People, December 4, 2000, Leah Rozen, review of *Unbreakable,* p. 43.
Time, November 27, 2000, Christopher John Farley, "A New Day Dawns for Night," p. 80.
U.S. News & World Report, December 18, 2000, James M. Pethokoukis, "Breaking the Comic-Book Mold," p. 69.
Variety, March 16, 1998, Emanuel Levy, review of *Wide Awake,* p. 64; April 30, 2001, "Disney Makes Quick Work of Shyamalan," p. 77.*

*   *   *

SICHEL, Deborah (Anne)

PERSONAL: Born in Durban, South Africa; married Harold Schiff (a doctor), January, 1976; children: Megan, Lauren. *Education:* University of the Witwatersrand, Johannesburg, South Africa, completed medical school training.

ADDRESSES: Home—446 Brookline Street, Newton Center, MA 02459. *Office*—Hestia Institute, Center for Women and Families, 12 Mica Lane, Wellesley, MA 02481. *E-mail*—dsichel@womensmoods.com.

CAREER: Cofounder of Hestia Institute, Wellesley, MA; Harvard Medical School, Cambridge, MA, associate professor of psychiatry; Massachusetts General Hospital, Outpatient Psychiatry Division, Boston, MA, psychiatrist. Lectures at medical schools across the United States.

WRITINGS:

(With Jeanne Watson Driscoll) *Women's Moods: What Every Woman Must Know about Hormones, the Brain, and Emotional Health,* William Morrow (New York, NY), 1999.

SIDELIGHTS: Deborah Sichel is a practicing psychiatrist whose work focuses on the treatment of female mood disorders. After meeting Jeanne Watson Driscoll at the Brigham and Women's Hospital, the two teamed up to co-found the Hestia Institute in Wellesley, Massachusetts, dedicated to the treatment of mood disorders in women.

In 1999, Sichel and Driscoll published *Women's Moods: What Every Woman Must Know about Hormones, the Brain, and Emotional Health.* The work explores the factors, primarily hormonal, which the authors believe contribute to mood and anxiety disorders in women. In addition, the authors offer a prescription for alleviating and preventing these problems, involving medication, nutrition, exercise, and spirituality.

Critics were largely positive in their assessment of *Women's Moods.* William Beatty in *Booklist* commented that the work should be an eye-opener for both patients and health care providers. Beatty found that the authors "write clearly and support their arguments with solid, pertinent references." Mary J. Jarvis, writing in *Library Journal,* called the book "well researched and well written" and praised the "extensive selected bibliography." A *Publishers Weekly* critic was also positive, concluding that the book "offers a wealth of detailed information on how to maintain proper hormonal balance and thus a happy and productive life" for women.

Sichel and Driscoll also established a Web site to provide more information on women's mood disorders. They are online at www.womensmoods.com.

BIOGRAPHICAL/CRITICAL SOURCES:

PERIODICALS

Booklist, November 1, 1999, William Beatty, review of
Women's Moods, p. 496.
Library Journal, November 1, 1999, Mary J. Jarvis, re-
view of *Women's Moods,* p. 116.
Publishers Weekly, November 8, 1999, review of
Women's Moods, p. 58.

OTHER

Women's Moods, http://www.womensmoods.com/
(November 22, 2000).*

* * *

SIGLER, Hollis 1948-2001

PERSONAL: Born March 2, 1948, in Gary, IN; died of
cancer, March 29, 2001, in Prairie View, IL; partner of
Patricia Locke. *Education:* Studied in Florence, Italy,
1968-69, Moore College of Art, B.F.A., 1970, School
of Art Institute of Chicago, M.F.A., 1973.

CAREER: Painter. *Exhibitions:* Whitney Museum of
American Art, New York, NY, 1981, Museum of Mod-
ern Art, New York, NY, 1985, National Museum of
Women in the Arts, Washington, DC, 1991; David
Adler Cultural Center, Libertyville, IL, 1992; and Elve-
hjem Museum of Art, University of Wisconsin, Madison, WI, 1997; also participated in numerous group exhibitions; represented in permanent collections, including the Museum of Contemporary Art, Chicago, IL,
National Museum of Women in the Arts, Washington,
DC, and the American Academy and Institute of Arts
& Letters, New York, NY. Columbia College, Chicago,
IL, teacher of drawing and painting, became professor
of art, 1978-2001. Founding member of Artemisia, a
women's cooperative gallery, Chicago, IL.

AWARDS, HONORS: Emilie L. Wild prize for painting,
Art Institute of Chicago, 1980; chairman's grant and individual artists grant, Illinois Council on the Arts, 1986;
National Endowment for the Arts fellowship, 1987;
honorary D.F.A., Moore College of Art, 1994; Distinguished Artist Award for Lifetime Achievement, College Art Association, 2001.

WRITINGS:

Hollis Sigler's Breast Cancer Journal, Hudson Hills
Press (New York, NY), 1999.

SIDELIGHTS: Hollis Sigler was an American artist and
educator. Her paintings have been exhibited in solo and
group exhibitions since the 1980s. She also taught
drawing and painting at Columbia College in Chicago
where she had been a member of the faculty since 1978.

In her early career, Sigler painted in an abstract expressionist and photo-realist style. In the late 1970s she
began to create folk-influenced narrative paintings, set
in domestic or suburban settings, that drew on her personal experiences and feminist views. Her paintings focused on themes of love, family, and dealing with loss,
disease, and death.

Sigler was diagnosed with breast cancer in 1985. After
undergoing a mastectomy as well as chemotherapy and
radiation treatments but still experiencing a third recurrence of the disease in 1992, Sigler decided to thereafter
devote her work to informing others about breast cancer. In her work Sigler combined references to cancer
in images of fragmented bodies and text, resulting in a
series of oil pastel paintings. The series, *Breast Cancer
Journal: Walking With the Ghosts of My Grandmoth-
ers,* explores Sigler's fifteen-year struggle with cancer,
a disease from which her grandmother and her mother
died. In 1993 the series was exhibited at the National
Museum of Women in the Arts in Washington, DC.
The Museum of Contemporary Art in Chicago also exhibited the work. Part of the resulting ongoing work is
published in *Hollis Sigler's Breast Cancer Journal.*

Critics were enthusiastic about Sigler's collection,
which is supplemented by a foreword from breast cancer advocate Susan M. Love and an introduction by art
critic James Yood. A *Publishers Weekly* critic compared Sigler's works to those of Jim Nutt and Frida
Kahlo, calling the work "powerful." Bette-Lee Fox in
Library Journal wrote that "the book will move those
affected by breast cancer as well as those attracted by
the art." Patricia Monaghan in *Booklist* noted that Sigler
combines the pains and passions of art and her cancer
experiences in her "unforgettable paintings. . . . May
this book bring them to countless others who will be
moved and invigorated by them."

Sigler succumbed to cancer on March 29, 2001 at the
age of fifty-three.

BIOGRAPHICAL/CRITICAL SOURCES:

PERIODICALS

Advocate, February 3, 1998, B. Ruby Rich, "In Sick-
ness and in Health," p. 43.

Booklist, December 15, 1999, Patricia Monaghan, review of *Hollis Sigler's Breast Cancer Journal,* p. 745.

Library Journal, November 15, 1999, Bette-Lee Fox, review of *Hollis Sigler's Breast Cancer Journal,* p. 66.

Publishers Weekly, November 8, 1999, review of *Hollis Sigler's Breast Cancer Journal,* p. 58.

OTHER

Columbia Chronicle, http://www.ccchronicle.com (April 9, 2001), Ryan Adair, "College loses noted artist, instructor."

Dialogue, http://www.dialoguearts.com/ (September 5, 2001), Jeanette Wenig Drake, "Hollis Sigler."

OBITUARIES:

PERIODICALS

Art in America, May, 2001, p. 190.
College Art Association Newsletter, May, 2001.
New York Times, April 3, 2001, p. B10.*

* * *

SILVERMAN, Franklin H(arold) 1933-

PERSONAL: Born August 16, 1933, in Providence, RI; son of Meyer (in business) and Reba (a homemaker) Silverman; married, wife's name Ellen-Marie, February, 1967 (divorced, February, 1981); married Evelyn Behling, November, 1983; children: Catherine Bette Silverman Thomas. *Education:* Emerson College, B.S., 1960; Northwestern University, M.A., 1961; University of Iowa, Ph.D., 1966. *Politics:* Independent. *Religion:* Jewish. *Avocational interests:* Photography, cooking.

ADDRESSES: Home—5918 Currant Lane, Greendale, WI 53129. *Office*—Marquette University, P.O. Box 1881, Milwaukee, WI 53201-1991; fax 414-288-3980. *Agent*—Elisabet McHugh TechServices, Inc., 1420 South Blaine, Suite 150, Moscow, ID 83843. *E-mail*—franklin.silverman@marquette.edu.

CAREER: University of Iowa, Iowa City, IA, research associate, 1965-67; University of Illinois—Urbana-Champaign, assistant professor of speech pathology, 1967-71; Marquette University, Milwaukee, WI, professor of speech pathology, 1971—. Medical College of Wisconsin, clinical professor of rehabilitation medi-

cine, 1979—. Wisconsin Telecommunication Relay Service, member of governor's advisory committee, 1991—.

MEMBER: American Speech-Language-Hearing Association (fellow), Text and Academic Authors Association (fellow; president, 1997-98).

AWARDS, HONORS: Alumni Achievement Award, Emerson College, 1997; DCA Prize, Disabled Children's Association of Saudi Arabia, 1998; Keedy Service Award, Text and Academic Authors Association, 1999.

WRITINGS:

La comunicazione per il privo de parola, Edizoni Omega (Turin, Italy), 1987.

Legal/Ethical Considerations, Restrictions, and Obligations for Clinicians Who Treat Communicative Disorders, C.C. Thomas (Springfield, IL), 1992.

Speech, Language, and Hearing Disorders, Allyn & Bacon (Needham, MA), 1995.

Communication for the Speechless, 3rd edition, Allyn & Bacon (Needham, MA), 1995.

Stuttering and Other Fluency Disorders, 2nd edition, Allyn & Bacon (Needham, MA), 1996.

Computer Applications for Augmenting the Management of Speech, Language, and Hearing Disorders, Allyn & Bacon (Needham, MA), 1997.

Communication for the Speechless in Arab Countries, Joint Centre for Research in Prosthetics and Orthotics and Rehabilitation Programmes (Riyadh, Saudi Arabia), 1997.

Research Design and Evaluation in Speech-Language Pathology and Audiology, 4th edition, Allyn & Bacon (Needham, MA), 1998.

Authoring Books and Materials for Students, Academics, and Professionals, Praeger (Westport, CT), 1998.

Fundamentals of Electronics for Speech-Language Pathologists and Audiologists, Allyn & Bacon (Needham, MA), 1999.

Professional Issues in Speech-Language Pathology and Audiology, Allyn & Bacon (Needham, MA), 1999.

The Telecommunication Relay Service (TRS) Handbook, Aegis Publishing (Middletown, RI), 1999.

Publishing for Tenure and Beyond, Praeger (Westport, CT), 1999.

Self-Publishing Books and Materials for Students, Academics, and Professionals, CODI Publications (Greendale, WI), 2000.

Second Thoughts about Stuttering, CODI Publications (Greendale, WI), 2000.

WORK IN PROGRESS: Teaching for Tenure and Beyond, for Bergin and Garvey (Westport, CT), completion expected in 2001; *A Unique Cooperative American University USAID Funded B.S. Degree Speech Pathologist, Audiologist, and Deaf Educator Training Program for the Gaza Strip* (with R. Moulton), for the Edward Mellen Press, completion expected in 2001; research on stuttering and other speech disorders. Other books in process: *Coping with Stuttering and Other Fluency Disorders as Impairments, Disabilities, and Handicaps* for Allyn & Bacon, completion expected in 2002; *Introduction to Speech, Language, and Hearing Disorders* for Atomic Dog Publisher (Cincinnati, OH), completion expected in 2002; *Introduction to Augmentative Communication* for Merrill-Prentice Hall (Columbus, OH), completion expected in 2003.

SIDELIGHTS: Franklin H. Silverman once commented in *CA:* "I've been authoring books for speech-language pathologists, academics, and the general public for more than twenty-five years. My primary motivation for doing so has been to provide helpful information in a manner that can be easily understood by my readers, including those in the general public.

"I'm an early riser and write every morning for a half-hour or so. By writing in this manner, I'm usually able to complete a manuscript for a 300-to 400-page book in eighteen months or less. When I began drafting book manuscripts this way during the early 1970s, I thought that I had discovered a unique approach for doing so; that is, one that doesn't require large blocks of time. Since then, however, I've discovered that many prolific academic and trade book authors use a similar approach."

*   *   *

SIMES, Dimitri (Konstantin) 1947-

PERSONAL: Born October 17, 1947, in Moscow, USSR (now Russia); emigrated to United States, 1973; son of Konstantin M. and Dina (Kaminsky) Simes; married Anastasia Ryurikov, May 27, 1993; children: Dimitri Alexander. *Education:* Moscow State University, M.A., 1969.

ADDRESSES: Office—The Nixon Center, 1615 L St. NW, Ste. 1250, Washington DC, 20036.

CAREER: Center for Strategic and International Studies, senior research fellow, 1973-76; Director of Soviet Studies, 1976-80; Executive Director of Soviet and East European Research Program, School for Advanced International Studies; Johns Hopkins University, Washington, professor of Soviet studies, 1980-83, lecturer, 1983-90; Carnegie Endowment for International Peace, Washington, senior associate, 1983-94; The Nixon Center, president, 1994—. Columnist for the *Christian Science Monitor,* 1983-87, the *Los Angeles Times Syndicate,* 1987-89, and *Newsday,* 1991—.

Visiting professor of political science, University of California, Berkeley, 1982; adjunct professor of government, Columbia University, New York City, 1985, 1992; Consultant, CBS News, New York City, 1985-87, NBC News, 1987-94.

MEMBER: Council on Foreign Relations, Nixon Administration.

WRITINGS:

(With associates) *Soviet Succession: Leadership in Transition,* Sage Publications (Beverly Hills, CA), 1978.
Soviet Strategy in Syria and the Persian Gulf, Middle East Institute (Washington, DC), 1984.
After the Collapse: Russia Seeks Its Place as a Great Power, Simon & Schuster (New York, NY), 1999.

Simes has contributed numerous articles to newspapers and journals.

SIDELIGHTS: Born Jewish in Moscow in 1947, Dimitri Simes managed to gain a position as an analyst of international affairs at the IMEMO institute in the Soviet Union, but emigrated to the United States in 1973. According to the *National Review,* "In the Brezhnev era, Jews were allowed to leave the Soviet Union simply because they did not like it there, and Simes was among them. . . . Once in the United States, Simes was able to write with authority about the political system that he knew at firsthand . . . A think-tank maestro, he became a foreign policy advisor to President Nixon and today is president of the Nixon Center in Washington."

Simes's insider knowledge of Soviet foreign-policy making and its makers allowed him to be a valuable asset to Nixon as well as to the journalists wanting to know how America was viewed by the Soviet Union. He has brought similar insight, seasoned by nearly thirty years of life in the United States and work in Soviet studies, to his book *After the Collapse: Russia Seeks Its Place as a Great Power.* During the period of

Prime Minister Gorbachev, and around the time of the collapse of the Berlin Wall (1991) and the ensuing dismemberment of the Soviet Union, Simes traveled to Moscow with Nixon as the former-President's advisor. From those visits, along with Simes's analysis of the former-Soviet Union in the years since its break-up, came *After the Collapse. Foreign Affairs* called it a "blend of memoir and essay."

In a 1985 interview with *U.S. News and World Report,* Simes predicted that, with Mikael Gorbachev as Soviet Prime Minister, "the real point to remember is that nothing is going to change radically." The events that ensued in the early 1990s obviously proved him wrong. According to the *National Review,* in *After the Collapse,* Simes tries to explain that "Gorbachev actively dynamited central control and Party authority—the foundations of the system—in the wondrously mistaken belief that he was perfecting Communism . . . Thanks to that improbable psychological disposition in a Party leader, Communism was able to have a quick and painless death."

In Simes's analysis of Boris Yeltsin's tenure as Prime Minister, a major component of the book, a more disturbing picture appears. The *National Review* posited that Yeltsin is shown to have openly fixed his re-election through the help of government insiders and wealthy oligarchs, to rule "by decree, signing thousands of them every year, put before him by fortune-hunting cronies to whom he turns a blind eye." And that Yeltsin's inability to grasp economic privatization led to his establishment of a "clique of officials, bankers, and businessmen, privileged to steal the state's assets for themselves." But Simes's portrait of Yeltsin, while negative, contains nuances as well. Ian Bremmer, in the *New York Times,* stated that "It would have been easy for someone so openly, and justifiably, critical of Yeltsin to concentrate on his failures. But Simes makes a case for nothing in Russia being simple. Yeltsin is at once fiercely loyal yet hopelessly arbitrary, supremely self-confident yet dreadfully insecure."

Reviewers appreciated Simes's insights into Russia since 1991, but had different reactions to elements in the book. *Economist* appreciated the inclusion of Nixon's thoughts and statements in the book, describing him as having "a keen eye for hidden motives and unacknowledged agendas" and the ability to "read body language well." The *New York Times,* however, found Nixon's presence in the book irrelevant, concluding that "Nixon may have been a central character in Simes's personal history, but he wasn't one in post-Soviet Russia." *Booklist* gave a synopsis of Simes's ar-

guments about past and current U.S. policy towards Russia (which he criticizes as sentimental in its hopefulness that Russia can instantly transform itself into a democracy, as well as overbearing in its insistence on the forms Russia takes in adopting free market economic policies), and concluded that the book "provides readers with a capable view of the cast of reformers, oligarchs, and criminals ruling Russia today." And *Foreign Affairs* called "the book's most impressive portions [its] insights into Russia's plight and the challenges ahead—insights of one raised in Russia and well connected to its elite but no less well attuned to the United States, his adopted country."

BIOGRAPHICAL/CRITICAL SOURCES:

PERIODICALS

Booklist, January 1, 1999, Gilbert Taylor, review of *After the Collapse: Russia Seeks Its Place as a Great Power,* p. 826.
Economist (U.S.), April 10, 1999, review of *After the Collapse: Russia Seeks Its Place as a Great Power,* p. 9.
Foreign Affairs, March, 1999, Robert Legvold, review of *After the Collapse: Russia Seeks Its Place as a Great Power,* p. 152.
National Review, April 19, 1999, review of *After the Collapse: Russia Seeks Its Place as a Great Power,* p. 62.
New York Times, June 20, 1999, Ian Bremmer, review of *After the Collapse: Russia Seeks Its Place as a Great Power,* p. 23.
U.S. News and World Report, March 25, 1985, "Nothing is Going to Change Radically," pp. 29-30.*

* * *

SIMON, Anne Elizabeth 1956-

PERSONAL: Born June 8, 1956, in Manhasset, NY; daughter of Mayo and Sandra (Fingerman) Simon; married Clifford D. Carpenter, June 29, 1980. *Education:* University of California, B.A., 1978; Indiana University, Ph.D., 1982. *Politics:* Democrat. *Religion:* Jewish.

ADDRESSES: Office—Department of Cell Biology and Molecular Genetics, University of Maryland, 1109 Microbiology Bldg., College Park, MD 20742; fax: 301-314-9489. *E-mail*—Anne—Simon@umail.umd.edu.

CAREER: Virologist and writer. "The X-Files," scientific consultant; Indiana University, Bloomington, IN, research associate, 1982-84; University of California—San Diego, research associate, 1984-87; University of Massachusetts at Amherst, Department of Biochemistry and Molecular Biology, assistant professor, beginning 1987; University of Maryland, Department of Cell Biology and Molecular Genetics, professor. Panel member, National Science Foundation, 1991.

AWARDS, HONORS: National Science Foundation research grants, 1987, 1988, 1990, 1991; University of Massachusetts, Distinguished Teaching Award, 1997.

WRITINGS:

The Real Science Behind the X-Files: Microbes, Meteorites and Mutations, Simon & Schuster (New York, NY), 1999.

SIDELIGHTS: Scientific correspondent for television's "The X-Files," Anne Simon has written a book, *The Real Science Behind the X-Files: Microbes, Meteorites and Mutations,* which may prove that the truth is not as elusive as the program's FBI agents think. Simon is currently a professor at the University of Maryland's Department of Cell Biology and Molecular Genetics.

Gilbert Taylor, in a review for *Booklist,* pronounced that *The Real Science Behind the X-Files'* main objective is to explain "the underlying biological plausibility of various plot devices in the series." Taylor indicated that, in his estimation, Simon's most reliable audiences are those people fascinated by the series. "Interspersed by her fanzine-style commentary about the series, Simon's science should snare viewers of the extremely creepy program." Simon's book is multidimensional, taking information from a variety of sources. A reviewer in *Publishers Weekly* contended: "Her informative book cuts back and forth between the X-Files script excerpts, behind-the-scenes anecdotes of her work on the series and accounts of the real-life counterparts and inspirations for the show's many biological plot devices." Like Taylor, the *Publishers Weekly* reviewer believed that the audiences Simon can count on are the avid X-Files fans. " 'X-philes' who enjoy these and similar stories will learn plenty of biology in the bargain; among the other hot fields and ideas Simon explains are extraterrestrial bacteria, cloning, genetic mutations, likelihood of extending the human life span."

For *New York Times Book Review* critic Jerry A. Coyne, the book is not blunder-free. "Although the scientific lessons are usually models of clarity, they sometimes bog down in detail, and her breeziness is sometimes irritating. More serious are the scientific mistakes

and confusing discussions that pepper the book. The former include erroneous descriptions of the theory of punctuated equilibrium and the methods used to produce a forensic DNA profile, while the latter include some misleading speculations about evolutions and mischaracterization of the 'nature versus nurture' debate. To be sure, these are minor glitches that will not bother most readers but are surprising in a book by a professional fact checker." However, Coyne commented on the success of the book's volleying from an episode to real scientific information. "Although each question involves forays into several fields of science, Simon manages to deliver a palatable and surprisingly large dose of information with each episode."

BIOGRAPHICAL/CRITICAL SOURCES:

PERIODICALS

Booklist, September 15, 1999, p. 207.
New York Times Book Review, October 10, 1999, p. 32.
Publishers Weekly, August 23, 1999, p. 32.*

*   *   *

**SIMONS, Michelle Blake
(Michelle Blake)**

PERSONAL: Female; married Dennis McFarland (a writer); children: Katharine, Sam. *Education:* Goddard College; Harvard Divinity School, Master of Theological Studies, 1993.

ADDRESSES: Home—Cambridge, MA. *Office*—Tufts University, School of Arts and Sciences, Dept. of English, East Hall-6, The Green, Medford, MA 02155. *E-mail*—meeshblake@aol.com.

CAREER: Poet and author. Tufts University, Medford, MA, lecturer in English, 1998—. Has also worked at Stanford University, Warren Wilson College, and Goddard College.

WRITINGS:

(As Michelle Blake) *The Tentmaker* (mystery), Putnam (New York, NY), 1999.
(As Michelle Blake) *Earth Has No Sorrow* (mystery), Putnam (New York, NY), 2001.

Contributor of poetry to publications, including *Ploughshares, Southern Review, Seneca Review,* and *Anthology of Magazine Verse.*

SIDELIGHTS: Michelle Blake Simons, who writes as Michelle Blake, is a lecturer in English with Tufts University, as well as a poet and author. Her mystery, *The Tentmaker,* was called "a sensitive, deliberate debut," by a *Kirkus Reviews* contributor. The protagonist, Lily Connor, is an Episcopalian priest, a path Simons had considered while studying at Harvard Divinity School. The liberal Lily is a "tentmaker," or interim priest, serving while the wealthy Boston St. Mary of the Garden parish seeks a replacement for Father Frederick Barnes, who has died from an insulin overdose. Lily comes to St. Mary's grieving over the death of her father and dealing with her own alcoholism. Her problems are compounded when she is not embraced by either the parish or the church wardens.

Lily soon learns that Father Barnes had recently shifted from his conservative position to one supporting the ordination of homosexual spiritual leaders. There is a suspicion that the priest may have had a homosexual relationship with a young teen from the parish, now missing, and it is possible that Barnes may have been helped to his death. Lily digs for the truth with her friend Charlie, an Anglican brother, and her mentor, Bishop Lamont Spencer. A *Publishers Weekly* reviewer wrote that "although the novel frequently sags under the weight of its intricate plot, Blake's writing is graceful, often elegiac, and her characters hum with humanity." *Library Journal* contributor Rex E. Klett called *The Tentmaker* "deftly written and firmly anchored in both subject and surroundings." "Sure to appeal to crime-fiction fans with an interest in religion," was the assessment of Jenny McLarin in *Booklist.*

Earth Has No Sorrow features main character Lily Connor as an Episcopalian priest officiating at a Holocaust memorial service marred by a Nazi flag draped over the altar and other acts of vandalism. Anna Banieka, the main speaker at the service and Lily's friend, disappears after confiding to Lily that she thinks she knows who committed the vandalism. Lily's investigation uncovers Anna's link to a conservative religious group responsible for violent acts. Harriet Klausner, a *BookBrowser* reviewer, called the novel "a powerful work that does not preach, but questions some of the basic tenets of organized religion through Lily's crisis of faith." *Library Journal*'s Rex Klett praised the book as "taut and thought-provoking." Connie Fletcher, writing in *Booklist,* found the plot "a bit wobbly" but felt the book was "strong on issues of faith and social justice." A reviewer for *Publishers Weekly* wrote that Blake "exposes the very souls of her unforgettable characters with honesty, poignancy and wit. Rich set-

tings and eloquent prose further enhance this most satisfying story."

BIOGRAPHICAL/CRITICAL SOURCES:

PERIODICALS

Booklist, September 1, 1999, Jenny McLarin, review of *The Tentmaker,* p. 70; May 15, 2001, Connie Fletcher, review of *Earth Has No Sorrow,* p. 1735.

Kirkus Reviews, August 15, 1999, review of *The Tentmaker,* pp. 1260-1261; May 1, 2001, review of *Earth Has No Sorrow.*

Library Journal, September 1, 1999, Rex E. Klett, review of *The Tentmaker,* p. 236; June 1, 2001, Rex Klett, review of *Earth Has No Sorrow,* p. 224.

Publishers Weekly, August 23, 1999, review of *The Tentmaker,* p. 51.

OTHER

BookBrowser, http://www.bookbrowser.com/ (April 24, 2001), Harriet Klausner, review of *Earth Has No Sorrow.**

* * *

SLATE, Joseph (Frank) 1928-

PERSONAL: Born January 19, 1928, in Hollidays Cove, WV; son of Frank Edward (a building contractor) and Angela (Palumbo) Slate; married Patricia Griffin (a research director), September 11, 1954. *Education:* University of Washington, B.A., 1951; studied printmaking, Tokyo, Japan, 1955-56; Yale University School of Art, B.F.A., 1960; independent study, Kyoto, Japan, 1975.

ADDRESSES: Home—15107 Interlachen Dr., Apt. 701, Silver Spring, MD 20906-5032. *Office*—Department of Art, Kenyon College, Gambier, OH 43022.

CAREER: Children's book author and illustrator. *Seattle Times,* Seattle, WA, member of editorial staff, 1950-53; Foreign Broadcast Information Service, editor, 1953-57. Yale University, New Haven, CT, consultant on aesthetics, 1960-66; Kenyon College, Gambier, OH, instructor, 1962-64, art professor, 1969-88, professor emeritus, 1988—, department chairman, 1963-75, 1981-82. National Endowment for the Arts, consultant and organizer of media literature program, 1977-78. *Exhibitions:* Twelfth National Print Show, Brooklyn

Museum, 1960; Kenyon College, biennial group show, 1960-87, and retrospective show, 1988; Pioneer Gallery, Cooperstown, NY, 1961; Milton College and University of Wisconsin, 1963; Mt. Union College, OH, 1965; Whitney Museum, NY, 1974; Schumacher Gallery, Columbus, OH, 1975; Waiting Gallery, Mt. Vernon, OH, 1976; Hopkins Gallery, Ohio State University, 1976; Mansfield Art Gallery, OH, 1978; and Ohio Expositions, Columbus, 1979. *Military service:* U.S. Marine Air Corps, 1946-48.

MEMBER: Society of Children's Book Writers and Illustrators, Authors' Guild.

AWARDS, HONORS: Top-Flight Award for journalism, and Fir Tree and Oval Club Awards for service, University of Washington, both 1951; Yale University Alumni fellowship, 1960; painting award, Ohio Expositions, 1962; Kenyon College Outstanding Educators Award, 1973; Doctor of Fine Arts, Kenyon College, 1988; award for distinguished service in the field of children's literature, Ohioana Library Association, 1988; Notable Children's Books selection, American Library Association, 2000, and Sugarman Award, both for *The Secret Stars.* Several of the author's works have been included on state reading lists and have received awards from state library associations.

WRITINGS:

The Star Rocker, illustrated by Dirk Zimmer, Harper-Collins (New York, NY), 1982.

How Little Porcupine Played Christmas, illustrated by Felicia Bond, Crowell, 1982, revised edition published as *Little Porcupine's Christmas,* Laura Geringer, 2001.

The Mean, Clean, Giant Canoe Machine, illustrated by Lynn Munsinger, Crowell, 1983.

Lonely Lula Cat, illustrated by Bruce Degan, Harper-Collins (New York, NY), 1985.

Who Is Coming to Our House?, illustrated by Ashley Wolff, Putnam (New York, NY), 1988.

Miss Bindergarten Gets Ready for Kindergarten, illustrated by Ashley Wolff, Dutton (New York, NY), 1996.

Miss Bindergarten Celebrates the 100th Day of Kindergarten, illustrated by Ashley Wolff, Dutton (New York, NY), 1998.

The Secret Stars, illustrated by Felipe Davalos, Marshall Cavendish (New York, NY), 1998.

Crossing the Trestle, Marshall Cavendish (New York, NY), 1999.

Miss Bindergarten's Stays Home from Kindergarten, illustrated by Ashley Wolff, Dutton (New York, NY), 2000.

Story Time for Little Porcupine, illustrated by Jacqueline Rogers, Marshall Cavendish (New York, NY), 2000.

Miss Bindergarten Takes a Field Trip with Kindergarten, illustrated by Ashley Wolff, Dutton (New York, NY), 2001.

The Great Big Wagon That Rang, illustrated by Craig Spearing, Marshall Cavendish (New York, NY), 2002.

OTHER

(With Martin Garhart) *Poetry and Prints,* Pothanger Press, 1974.

Contributor of short stories and articles to periodicals, including the *New Yorker, Saturday Review, Art Journal, Kenyon Review,* and *Contempora.*

SIDELIGHTS: Artist and educator Joseph Slate has parlayed his creative talents into a successful second career as a children's book author. With books such as *The Secret Stars* and *Who Is Coming to Our House?* to his credit, Slate is also the creator of the popular Miss Bindergarten, a teacher of the pre-elementary set that has captured the hearts of readers and critics alike in such volumes as *Miss Bindergarten Gets Ready for Kindergarten, Miss Bindergarten Celebrates the 100th Day of Kindergarten,* and *Miss Bindergarten Stays Home from Kindergarten.*

Slate was born on January 19, 1928, in West Virginia. "I was born in Hollidays Cove, one of five children," he once recalled. "I suppose my greatest influence was an invalid sister. She was a wonderfully talented and witty person, and I'm sure my dual interest in art and writing was fostered by her. Rose entertained us by drawing and painting picture books on the back of discarded floral wallpaper. Then she carefully bound them with pink yarn. They were finished products—highly colored adventure stories in the style of 'Flash Gordon.'"

Slate joined the U.S. Navy in 1946, as a way to take advantage of the G.I. Bill and go on to college. The Navy transferred him to the Marine Corps. After leaving the service he majored in journalism at the University of Washington. The *Seattle Times* initially hired him as its stringer while Slate was still in college and later as a full-time reporter upon his graduation. A few years later, while on a posting to Tokyo from the Foreign

Broadcast Information Service, Slate's interest turned to painting after Japanese artist Saito showed him how to cut a woodblock. "I sent a pretty shaky portfolio of [my] work to Josef Albers at Yale," Slate recalled. "I don't know why, but he admitted me to the B.F.A. program. After three years at Yale, and one year trying to make it as a painter, I came to Kenyon College and set up the art program they have now."

The death of Slate's sister Rose at age sixteen was devastating. "The first national attention my writing received was for stories inspired by her," he explained. "They were written from a child's perspective for the *New Yorker*. That child's perspective should have told me something about the future. But I had no idea I would ever write for children. The actual writing of picture books didn't come for me until the eighties. The photographer Gregory Spaid, a former student, urged me to tackle what seemed to many of my students a natural leaning."

Slate first picture book effort, 1982's *The Star Rocker*, illustrated by Dirk Zimmer, pursued a theme that was to reappear in his later books. Drawing on the myth of Cassiopeia, the author transforms her into a kindly old black woman whose tethered raft rocks the animal world to sleep. Slate once commented: "I've always been fascinated at how myth functions in the human mind from cradle to grave." That same year, one of his most enduring books, *How Little Porcupine Played Christmas*, also appeared. The book reappeared with a new title, *Little Porcupine's Christmas*, and new cover art by Felicia Bond in the 2001. Nearly twenty years after the publication of *How Little Porcupine Played Christmas*, Slate wrote a sequel, *Story Time for Porcupine*, featuring illustrations by Jacqueline Rogers. In a *Booklist* review, Shelley Townsend-Hudson described the work as a "terrific story-within-a-story book [that] revels in the joys of family love. From start to finish, this enchanting book is a delight."

1988's *Who Is Coming to Our House?* recounts the Nativity in quiet and simple rhymed couplets. Calling the book "A lovely addition to the Christmas canon," a contributor to *Kirkus Reviews* went on to praise the "gently cadenced couplets [which] finally reveal the arrival of Mary and Joseph." A decade later, Slate's *The Secret Stars* revisits the celebration of Jesus' birth but also continues a theme he introduced in *The Star Rocker*. Focusing on the Hispanic tradition of the Night of the Three Kings, Slate's story was given substantial praise by *School Library Journal* reviewer Mary M. Hopf, who commended the work for a text that reads like a poem and makes use of a number of poetic devices.

Miss Bindergarten Gets Ready for Kindergarten is a lively and energetic book about the first day of school. The book alternates between the teacher, Miss Bindergarten, and her pupils as they prepare for school. The characters, all young animals, are cleverly named in alphabetical sequence, the first letter of each name corresponding to the appropriate animal type—Adam is an alligator; Jessie is a jaguar. Martha V. Parravano, reviewing the book for *Horn Book*, noted that "The internal rhymes in short sentences and the recurring refrain make the book a natural for reading aloud." *Miss Bindergarten Celebrates the 100th Day of Kindergarten*, the second book in the series, concentrates on counting with Miss Bindergarten asking her pupils to collect one hundred objects to commemorate the hundredth day of school. John Peters noted in his *Booklist* review that "the short, rhymed text both comments on what's going on and provides a unifying backbeat."

Miss Bindergarten's adventures continue in *Miss Bindergarten Stays Home from Kindergarten*, the third book in the series. Like the earlier books, this one follows the days of the week and hides the alphabet as well. Writing in *School Library Journal*, Sheliah Kosco predicted "This book will alleviate the concerns of children who worry what will happen if their teacher is absent or sick." According to Slate, the next entry in the series, *Miss Bindergarten Takes a Field Trip with Kindergarten* also has some hidden lessons, but, as the author once commented, "We want the books to be fun. The hidden lessons are secondary. Children want to be entertained, not preached to."

While working on the "Miss Bindergarten" series, Slate also wrote his first young adult novel, *Crossing the Trestle*. Set in a fictional West Virginia town that is, according to Slate, "based somewhat on my home territory," the novel features a young boy who must overcome his fears and help his family begin a new life. Describing the book "as a warm period piece," *Bulletin of the Center for Children's Books* reviewer Elizabeth Bush claimed that the story's "happy ending is merited rather than contrived, and readers will watch them head off for new prospects westward with the utmost satisfaction." Writing in *Booklist*, Chris Sherman praised Slate's "cast of thoroughly likable, believable characters," going on to say that "it's a pleasure to see how the gentle story unfolds."

Discussing his approach to children's books, Slate once explained: "You can't be self-indulgent when you write for children. But they do give you far more freedom than do adult readers, editors, or critics. I guess the artist in me loves the picture-book form because of that freedom."

BIOGRAPHICAL/CRITICAL SOURCES:

PERIODICALS

Booklist, August, 1996, Carolyn Phelan, review of *Miss Bindergarten Gets Ready for Kindergarten,* p. 1906; September 15, 1998, Hazel Rochman, review of *The Secret Stars,* p. 240; October 15, 1998, John Peters, review of *Miss Bindergarten Celebrates the 100th Day of Kindergarten,* p. 430; January 1, 2000, Chris Sherman, review of *Crossing the Trestle,* p. 927; October 15, 2000, Shelley Townsend-Hudson, review of *Story Time for Porcupine,* p. 466.

Bulletin of the Center for Children's Books, September, 1996, Elizabeth Bush, review of *Miss Bindergarten Gets Ready for Kindergarten,* p. 31; December, 1999, Elizabeth Bush, review of *Crossing the Trestle,* p. 150.

Children's Book Review Service, March, 1985, review of *Lonely Lula Cat,* p. 80; January, 1999, Annette C. Blank, review of *The Secret Stars,* pp. 52-53; November, 1999, John E. Boyd, review of *Crossing the Trestle,* pp. 35-36.

Horn Book, September-October, 1996, Martha V. Parravano, review of *Miss Bindergarten Gets Ready for Kindergarten,* p. 587.

Kirkus Reviews, November 1, 1988, review of *Who Is Coming to Our House?,* p. 1610; June 1, 1996, review of *Miss Bindergarten Gets Ready for Kindergarten,* p. 829; October 15, 1999, review of *Crossing the Trestle,* p. 1652.

New York Times Book Review, January 5, 1997, Marigny Dupuy, review of *Miss Bindergarten Gets Ready for Kindergarten,* p. 22.

Publishers Weekly, June 28, 1985, review of *Lonely Lula Cat,* p. 74; October 28, 1988, review of *Who Is Coming to Our House?,* p. 77; July 27, 1998, review of *Miss Bindergarten Celebrates the 100th Day of Kindergarten,* p. 75.

School Library Journal, August, 1985, Joan McGrath, review of *Lonely Lula Cat,* p. 82; November, 1988, Heide Piehler, review of *Who Is Coming to Our House?,* p. 96; August, 1996, Virginia Opocensky, review of *Miss Bindergarten Gets Ready for Kindergarten,* p. 129; September, 1998, Marlene Gawron, review of *Miss Bindergarten Celebrates the 100th Day of Kindergarten,* p. 182; October, 1998, Mary M. Hopf, review of *The Secret Stars,* p. 45;

October, 2000, Kate McLean, review of *Story Time for Porcupine,* p. 137; November, 2000, Sheilah Kosco, review of *Miss Bindergarten Stays Home from Kindergarten,* p. 134.

Tribune Books (Chicago), December 4, 1988, Mary Harris Veeder, review of *Who Is Coming to Our House?,* p. 13.

*   *   *

SMITH, Francis   1949-

PERSONAL: Born 1949. *Education:* Georgetown University; Boston College Law School.

ADDRESSES: Office—Institute for Civil Society, One Bridge Street, Suite 101, Newton, MA, 02458-1101. *E-mail*—icsthree@erols.com.

CAREER: Attorney, consumer advocate, and author. Future Strategies, Cambridge, MA, president.

MEMBER: Institute for Civil Society.

WRITINGS:

(With Jamie Court) *Making a Killing: HMOs and the Threat to Your Health,* Common Courage Press (Monroe, ME), 1999.

SIDELIGHTS: Francis Smith, a lawyer and consumer advocate, authored a 1999 book that criticized the state of managed health care in America. Smith is president of a Massachusetts-based public policy consulting firm called Future Strategies, as well as a senior fellow at the Institute for Civil Society, a non-profit organization which has the goal of strengthening American democracy.

His book, *Making a Killing: HMOs and the Threat to Your Health,* was co-written with Jamie Court, another consumer advocate and director of the non-profit Foundation for Taxpayer and Consumer Rights, which is based in California. The book is an indictment of health maintenance organizations, or HMOs, which are corporations that provide health care to millions of Americans. The authors explain that profitability is the most important issue for HMOs, and almost always takes priority over the medical needs of member patients. Citing numerous case histories, the authors show how HMO accountants and clerks often disregard the medical advice of doctors even when patients, who are treated as numbers, face critical situations. Smith and Court believe HMOs cut back on the whole spectrum of patient care, from the actual surgeries, to the length of inpatient stays, to prescription drug coverage, in an effort to save money. They claim the system is corrupt and is costing U.S. taxpayers billions of dollars. The authors also devote a section of the book to how they believe the system can be radically reformed, so patients can get better care. Included in the book is an appendix, entitled "HMO Patient Self-Defense Kit," which provides readers with advice about dealing with HMOs, including how to manipulate them to get the best available medical care.

Several literary critics praised *Making a Killing*, because of its ability to educate the public about such an important issue. A reviewer for the *Los Angeles Times* said that the authors "make a compelling case for the absurdity of a health-care system based on the concept of minimizing care to increase profits and please shareholders." Ralph Nader, writing in the *San Francisco Bay Guardian*, called *Making a Killing* "a well-written book, on an important topic" that "paints a troubling tale of what has become of our health system." Nader concluded, "this highly motivating book should help band together a critical mass of citizens who are aroused and determined to forge a health care system in which patients and health care matter." A contributor for *Publishers Weekly* called the book "powerful" and "a scathing expose" of the HMO system. "This lively probe is must reading for anyone concerned with the health of the U.S. medical system," the same reviewer wrote.

BIOGRAPHICAL/CRITICAL SOURCES:

PERIODICALS

Los Angeles Times, February 28, 2000, *Making a Killing: HMOs and the Threat to Your Health. Progressive,* May, 2000, Kellia Ramares, *Making a Killing: HMOs and the Threat to Your Health,* p. 44.

Publishers Weekly, November 22, 1999, review of *Making a Killing: HMOs and the Threat to Your Health,* p. 53.

San Francisco Bay Guardian, June 26, 2000, Ralph Nader, "Health Matters."

OTHER

Making a Killing: HMOs and the Threat to Your Health, http://www.makingakilling.org/ (September 5, 2001).*

SMITH, Harold F. 1923-

PERSONAL: Born July 9, 1923, in Kansas City, MO; son of Lee L. (in railway mail service) and Georgia Irene Hamptmann Smith; married Carolyn Jo Douglas, August 9, 1947; children: Douglas Lee, Gregory Lynn, Alan Wren. *Ethnicity:* "Caucasian." *Education:* Park College, A.B., 1944; University of Kansas, A.M., 1946; University of Denver, A.M.L.S., 1950; Southern Illinois University, Ph.D., 1963. *Politics:* Democrat. *Religion:* Presbyterian.

ADDRESSES: Home—206 Summer St., Parkville, MO 64152. *Office*—Park College, 8700 N.W. River Park Dr., Parkville, MO 64152; fax: 816-741-4911.

CAREER: University of Denver, circulation librarian, 1950-51; University of Nebraska-Lincoln, senior assistant librarian, Public Services, 1951-52; University of Northern Colorado, Greeley, CO, acquisitions librarian, 1952-57; Southern Illinois University, Carbondale, IL, general services librarian, 1957-64; Park College, Parkville, MO, library director, 1964-90, archivist, 1990—, also currently librarian emeritus. Kansas City Regional Council for Higher Education, joint periodicals bank founder and Library Project director, 1967-74; Northwest Missouri Library Network, co-founder, 1975-77; Kansas City Metropolitan Library Network, co-founder and founding president, 1977-79; University of Missouri School of Library and Informational Science, Advisory Council member, 1978-98; affiliated with Association of Colleges & Research Libraries mentoring program for small private colleges, 1993—; Presbyterian Historical Society in Philadelphia, board member, 1997-99; has taught summers and extension for the Library Schools at Emporia State University and the University of Missouri; presenter at history and library conferences.

MEMBER: American Library Association, Oral History Association, American Association for Higher Education, Western History Association, Midwest Archives Conference.

AWARDS, HONORS: Archivist of the Year Award, Kansas City Area Archivists, 1995.

WRITINGS:

American Travellers Abroad: A Bibliography of Accounts Published before 1900, Southern Illinois University (Carbondale, IL), 1969, second edition, Scarecrow Press (Lanham, MD), 1999.

Contributor to periodicals, including *Colorado Library Association Bulletin, College and Research Libraries, Wilson Library Bulletin, Civil War History, Journal of the Illinois State Historical Society, American History Illustrated, Minnesota History, Show-Me Libraries,* and *Park Allumniad.* Book review editor, *Overland Journal,* 1990-2000.

WORK IN PROGRESS: "I continue to search for fugitive title of American travellers abroad."

SIDELIGHTS: Harold F. Smith told *CA:* "I have loved history from my childhood. My majors at Park College in the 1940s and at the University of Kansas in 1946 were in history. I entered Librarianship because it allowed me to be paid for living with books. And that led me to express some of those interesting but often untold stories that I would come across.

"This I have shared through publications in journals, but in later years I have also presented papers at history and library conferences. My process for writing is to think about a subject of interest I wish to share, gather and study and mull over the subject. I will usually do a complete draft for an article at one time, and then wait until I have thought some more about its focus and organization, and then refine it and polish it before I offer it for presentation or publication.

"As to the book *American Travellers Abroad,* the best description is probably found in the Introduction and Acknowledgments. This topic has become a lifelong search, and I continue to look for fugitive titles that I know were published before 1900 but which I had not included without examining them. I still darken the doors of libraries as I move around the country to see if it may be there so that I may examine, verify and annotate."

*   *   *

SMITH, Taylor 1952-

PERSONAL: Born April 2, 1952, in Winnipeg, Canada; married May 11, 1979; husband's name, Richard; children: Kate, Anna. *Education:* University of Manitoba, B.A., 1975; L'Institut D'Etudes Politiques (Paris), C.E.P., 1976; Carleton University, M.A., 1979.

ADDRESSES: Office—P.O. Box 4818, Mission Viejo, CA 92690; fax: 949-855-8579. *E-mail*—taylrsmith@ aol.com. *Agent*—Philip Spitzer, 50 Talmage Farm Ln., East Hampton, NY 11937.

CAREER: Government of Canada, diplomat, Foreign Affairs Department, 1978-84, analyst, Treasury Board, 1984-86, privy council officer, 1986-90; author, 1990—.

MEMBER: Sisters in Crime, Fictionaires (former president).

WRITINGS:

SUSPENSE NOVELS

Guilt by Silence, Mira, 1995.
Common Passions, Mira, 1996.
The Best of Enemies, Mira, 1997.
Random Acts, Mira, 1998.
The Innocents Club, Mira, 2000.
Deadly Grace, in press.

SIDELIGHTS: Taylor Smith told *CA:* "[F]rom the time I was a child, I deliberately set out *not* to become a novelist, since my older sister had literary aspirations. As a headstrong second child, I wanted to blaze my own trail. But when I moved to California a few years back, talking a leave of absence to spend more time with my kids, I turned to writing fiction for intellectual stimulation—never planning to make a career of it."

"[I have used my diplomatic and intelligence career as a starting point], but not without some trepidation. I retired from public service just as my first novel, *Guilt by Silence,* was about to be published. In writing it, I worried about the detail I'd put into the political intrigue, and spent a lot of time back-researching the facts to be sure that there were public sources available so I wouldn't be arrested for violating the Official Secrets Act."

"[My involvement in the Canadian government's international affairs was really top secret.] After several years as a diplomat, I moved on to become an intelligence analyst for the head of Canadian Security and Intelligence, who liaises with the director of the CIA as well as Britain's MI6. In my work, I was indoctrinated into beyond-top secret files and visited those sister agencies. Obviously, in retrospect, this provided great grist for the writing mill."

"For me, character is everything. If I can't believe or relate to the characters in a work of fiction, then the plot, no matter how clever or action-packed, won't hold my attention. I'm a student of human nature and I'm fascinated with the notion of how fairly ordinary people react when faced with extraordinary circumstances. At the same time, even the best of people have flaws and weaknesses, and even villains have vulnerabilities and likable traits. It's what makes telling the good guys from the bad so hard to do. I love to play with those ambiguities."

"Both [mapping out plot intricacies and creating a heroine true to my vision] are challenging. I start out with a rough idea of my characters and the general dilemma in which they find themselves (the novel's core conflict), and I always know how that conflict will resolve itself and what the final scene will be. How I'm going to get to that final resolution is the voodoo part of the process—difficult, mysterious, and almost as much a surprise to me as to the reader.

"I find that my voice really comes through my protagonists. When I began *The Best of Enemies,* I had intended Leya Nash, my lead character, to be a fairly weak person until she uncovers her father for what he really is. But I found I couldn't write her that way. Leya's her father's daughter, after all, raised to be strong. Creating her became much easier with that realization."

"[I do a great deal of extensive research for my novels.] I've been on police ride-alongs, served as both hostage and go-between in SWAT exercises, taken courses in forensics, interviewed everyone form journalists to talk show producers to FBI agents. I try to convince my kids not to tell their teachers when mom's off at the morgue, watching autopsies. Makes home life sound very strange."

"Watch for *Deadly Grace* to appear late this year (2001). . . . *Deadly Grace* is set in 1979, and opens in a small prairie town with the murder of an elderly woman. English war bride Grace Meade has served with the French Resistance during the Nazi occupation, and has helped rescue, then married, a shot-down American flyer. Joe Meade died in the waning days of the war, but Grace brought their infant daughter to America to be raised in his home town. When Grace is killed thirty-five years later, however, it's that same daughter who stands accused of her murder—with a motive, FBI agent Alex Cruz discovers, buried deep in their war-torn past.

"This novel grew out of a family visit to England and France in September of 1999, on the occasion of the sixtieth anniversary of the outbreak of World War II. I found myself visiting wartime sites and becoming im-

bued with the spirit of that battle against one of the greatest evils of the last millennium. The story of *Deadly Grace* just seemed to evolve from that."

*   *   *

SMITH, Warren Allen   1921-
(Jun Sczesnoczkawasm, Allen Windsor)

PERSONAL: Born October 27, 1921, in Minburn, IA; son of Harry Clark (a minor league baseball player and Iowa grain dealer) and Ruth Marion (maiden name, Miles; a homemaker) Smith; companion of Fernando (Fred) Rodolfo Vargas Zamora, from 1948 (died, 1989); companion of Gilbert Price (died). *Ethnicity:* "Caucasian white." *Education:* Attended University of Chicago, 1946; University of Northern Iowa, B.A., 1948; Columbia University, M.A., 1949. *Politics:* "Independent (Liberal Party)." *Religion:* "Unitarian (Humanistic Naturalist/Non-Theist)." *Avocational interest:* Music composition; teratology.

ADDRESSES: Home—31 Jane St., Apt. #10-D, New York, NY 10014. *Agent*—Carole and Lyle Stuart, 185 Bridge Plaza N. (308-A), Fort Lee, NJ 07024. *E-mail*—wasm@idt.net.

CAREER: Bentley School, New York, NY, chair, English Department, 1949-54; New Canaan High School, New Canaan, CT, instructor and chair, English Department, 1954-86. Humanist Book Club, president, 1957-62; Columbia University Teachers College, New York, NY, instructor of English, 1961-62; Variety Sound Corporation and Variety Recording Studio, New York, NY, founder and president, 1961-90; Taursa (Mutual) Fund, Philadelphia, PA, president and co-founder, 1971-73; Afro-Carib Records, New York, NY, president, 1971-90; Talent Management, president, 1982-90; AAA Recording Studio, founder and president, 1985-90. *Military service:* U.S. Army, 1942-46, served in France as Adjutant General's Office chief clerk; received Battle of the North Atlantic and Battle of the Bulge decorations.

MEMBER: ASCAP, British Humanist Association, Bertrand Russell Society (vice president, 1977-80; board of directors, 1973—), Hume Society, Mensa, Rationalist Press Association, Thomas Paine Foundation, Voltaire Society.

AWARDS, HONORS: Leavey Award, Freedoms Foundation at Valley Forge, 1985.

WRITINGS:

Who's Who in Hell: A Handbook and International Directory for Freethinkers, Humanists, Naturalists, Rationalists, and Non-Theists, Barricade (New York, NY), 2000.

Editor, *Humanist Newsletter,* 1953-54, *Taking Stock,* 1967-93, *Pique,* 1990-93, *Van Rijn's Pad,* 1991; book review editor, *Humanist,* 1953-58; associate editor, *Free Inquiry,* 1992—; columnist, "Manhattan Scene" (syndicated in 22 English-speaking West Indian states), 1960s and 1970s, "Gossip from across the Pond," *Gay and Lesbian Humanist,* 1989—. Contributor of articles to various periodicals, including *Humanist, Free Inquiry, Vice, Bertrand Russell Society Quarterly, Skeptical Inquirer, New Humanist, Freethinker, Freethought Today, American Rationalist, Humanist in Canada, Sinfonian, Gay & Lesbian Humanist,* and *American Rationalist.* Contributor of book reviews to *Brooklyn Eagle* and *Library Journal.*

WORK IN PROGRESS: Manuel Salazar: Costa Rica's Forgotten Tenor, a compact disk made from early 78rpm records of Caruso's competitor.

SIDELIGHTS: Warren Allen Smith told *CA:* "If I had my life to live all over again, I would . . . [partial list]

"* choose to be born in Central Iowa (near the birthplaces of Mamie Eisenhower, George Gallup, and John Wayne);

"* have as my father a baseball player from the Portland farm team of the Chicago Cubs; and as my mother an equestrienne from the South Dakota plains;

"* work on the University of Northern Iowa literary publication with poet Mona Van Duyn;

"* as an active 1st sergeant on my way to Europe, get a free Broadway ticket to see Mae West in 'Catherine was Great,' then get her autograph while riding in her taxi from the Shubert Theatre to Eighth Avenue;

"* be in the biggest battle of all history, lead my company onto Omaha Beach, and survive as an Adjutant General's chief clerk in the Little Red Schoolhouse in Reims;

"* work on cues for Broadway plays with Paddy Chayevsky; Arthur Miller; Harold Prince; Robert Whitehead; and Jerry Bock who, when asked how to

file one particular song, suggested 'Tevye,' later changing it to 'Fiddler on the Roof ';

"* record Steve Allen, Tiny Tim, Paul Simon (when he was Jerry Landis), Barry Manilow, Tito Puente, David Amram, [Liza Minnelli (first demo)], and others;

"* be entirely alone with Tennessee Williams . . . finding him difficult to recognize because he was shaved; also be entirely alone with Langston Hughes at the Harlem funeral parlor before others arrived;

"* take 50 years to write *Who's Who in Hell,* which was inspired by a letter Thomas Mann sent me when Lionel Trilling was my department chairman at Columbia University in 1948; get interviewed on CNN and National Public Radio, and receive favorable comments about my 7-pound 'baby' from [numerous sources].

"In short, if I had my life to live all over again, I'd not change a thing, . . . for, luckily and with plenty of perspiration and red wine, it all has transpired!"

*   *   *

SNICKET, Lemony 1970-
(Daniel Handler)

PERSONAL: Born Daniel Handler, 1970, in San Francisco, CA; married Lisa Brown. *Education:* Wesleyan University.

ADDRESSES: Home—San Francisco, CA. *Office*—c/o Author Mail, HarperCollins, 10 East 53rd St., New York, NY 10022. *E-mail*—lsnicket@harpercollins.com.

CAREER: Author, poet, and self-styled "studied expert in rhetorical analysis." Comedy writer, "The House of Blues Radio Hour," San Francisco, CA; freelance book and movie reviewer.

AWARDS, HONORS: Academy of American Poets Prize, 1990; Olin Fellowship, 1992.

WRITINGS:

ADULT FICTION; AS DANIEL HANDLER

The Basic Eight, St. Martin's Press (New York, NY), 1999.
Watch Your Mouth, St. Martin's Press (New York, NY), 2000.

JUVENILE FICTION; AS LEMONY SNICKET; "A SERIES OF UNFORTUNATE EVENTS" SERIES

The Bad Beginning, illustrated by Bret Helquist, HarperTrophy (New York, NY), 1999.

The Reptile Room, illustrated by Bret Helquist, HarperTrophy (New York, NY), 1999.

The Wide Window, illustrated by Bret Helquist, HarperTrophy (New York, NY), 2000.

The Miserable Mill, illustrated by Bret Helquist, HarperTrophy (New York, NY), 2000.

The Austere Academy, illustrated by Bret Helquist, HarperTrophy (New York, NY), 2000.

The Ersatz Elevator, illustrated by Bret Helquist, HarperTrophy (New York, NY), 2001.

The Vile Village, illustrated by Bret Helquist, HarperTrophy (New York, NY), 2001.

The Hostile Hospital, illustrated by Bret Helquist, HarperTrophy (New York, NY), 2001.

A Series of Unfortunate Events (omnibus; contains *The Bad Beginning, The Reptile Room,* and *The Wide Window*), HarperTrophy (New York, NY), 2001.

Lemony Snicket: The Unauthorized Autobiography, HarperTrophy (New York, NY), 2002.

Handler has also written for the *Voice Literary Supplement, Newsday, Salon,* and the *New York Times.* "A Series of Unfortunate Events" has been published in England, Canada, Germany, Italy, Norway, Israel, Japan, and Denmark.

ADAPTATIONS: The Basic Eight was optioned for a film by New Regency, a division of Warner Brothers; "A Series of Unfortunate Events" was optioned for film and television by Nickelodeon.

WORK IN PROGRESS: Writing as Daniel Handler, a third novel, about pirates. Writing as Lemony Snicket, more volumes in the projected thirteen-part "A Series of Unfortunate Events." Adaptation of a movie for the Independent Film Channel from Joel Rose's novel, *Kill the Poor,* and a movie script with songwriter Stephin Merritt of the band The Magnetic Fields.

SIDELIGHTS: Daniel Handler has a fine sense of timing. As a writer for adults, he has produced two popular novels which have had an eerie prescience to them: his 1999 *The Basic Eight* deals, partly in a tongue-in-cheek manner, with a teenage murder, and hit the shelves just a month before the tragic events at Colorado's Columbine High School focused the nation's attention on teen violence; his second novel, a "mock-operatic incest comedy" as Amy Benfer of *Salon* described *Watch*

Your Mouth, came out in time to benefit from a similar theme broached at the Oscar awards ceremony of 2000.

However, it is his juvenile writings, penned under the pseudonym of Lemony Snicket, that have most benefitted from chronological serendipity: "A Series of Unfortunate Events" has ridden the tsunami created by J. K. Rowling's "Harry Potter" books, tapping into a youthful readership eager to deal with irony, intelligent silliness, and Goth-like depressing situations in their fiction. When the *New York Times Book Review,* influenced by the huge sales of the "Harry Potter" books, initiated a children's bestseller list, Mr. Snicket weighed in at number fifteen; within a year, all five of the books written by the illusive and mysterious Mr. Snicket had made the top twenty-five, and the series had been optioned by Nickelodeon for a film treatment.

Handler was born and raised in San Francisco, the son of an accountant and a college dean. Growing up, Handler was "a bright and obvious person," as he characterized himself for Sally Lodge in *Publishers Weekly.* However, the incipient novelist "always wanted to be a dark, mysterious person." In books, he preferred stories "in which mysterious and creepy things happen," he told Lodge, hating books "where everyone joined the softball team and had a grand time or found true love on a picnic." The youthful Handler sought out stories à la Roald Dahl or Edward Gorey, and indeed his fiction for juveniles has often been compared to that duo. Snicket enjoyed reading the sort of things "set in an eerie castle that was invaded by a snake that strangled the residents." The first book Handler bought with his own money was Gorey's *The Blue Aspic.*

A student of San Francisco's prestigious and demanding Lowell High School, Handler graduated in 1988, tying for Best Personality of his graduating class. Eleven years later, Handler set his first novel at a barely concealed stand-in for this school, Roewer High with students "pushed to the limit academically, socially and athletically," as Handler wrote. After high school graduation, Handler attended Wesleyan University, winning a Poets Prize from the Academy of American Poets in 1990. His love for poetry soon developed into a passion for novels. "My poems were getting longer and longer, and more proselike," Handler commented to Greg Toppo in an Associated Press story carried on *CNN-fyi.com.* Upon graduation, he received an Olin Fellowship which provided him with the financial support to work on his first novel. Publication of that book, however, would come several years later. Meanwhile, there was a living to be earned. Handler spent a couple of years in the mid-1990s writing comedy sketches for a nationally syndicated radio show based in San Francisco, "The House of Blues Radio Hour."

Things began looking up for Handler when he moved to New York City and began his literary career as a free-lance movie and book critic. By 1999, his first novel, *The Basic Eight,* was finally published and earned respectful if not praiseworthy reviews in major media. *The Basic Eight,* though written for adults, caused some reviewers and booksellers to label it YA as it focused on a cast of high school students in a clique called The Basic Eight. The school in question, Roewer High, was plainly a thinly disguised Lowell High in San Francisco. As Handler told Philana Woo in his alma mater's paper, *The Lowell,* "When I was at Lowell, it was called Roewer. . . . Lowell then was predominantly Asian, . . . and Roewer was the name people of all races referred to it. It was sort of the kids' joke about the fact that most of the school was Asian. I guess Roewer could be an offensive way of making a pun on an Asian accent."

Essentially beginning at the end of the action, *The Basic Eight* is narrated by Flannery Culp, who depicts the events of her senior year at Roewer High from her journal written in prison where she is serving time for the murder of a teacher and fellow student. Flan is, as a reviewer for *Publishers Weekly* observed, "precocious" and "pretentious," and now means to set the record straight. Reviled in the press as a leader of a Satanic cult, Flan has kept her journal to tell the real truth of the tragicomic events that have landed her in prison instead of in some Ivy League school.

At school, Flan, editor of the student paper but having trouble in calculus, relies on her seven friends—the "Queen Bee" Kate, lovely Natasha whom Flan admires, Gabriel, a black student and chef in the making who has a crush on Flan, Douglas, who has access to absinthe, V, whose name has been changed to provide anonymity to her wealthy family, Lily, and Jennifer Rose Milton. These eight form the elitist clique in question. Childhood games turn serious when the group begins experimenting with absinthe; Natasha comes to Flan's rescue by poisoning a biology teacher who has been plaguing her. There is also Adam State, love interest of Flan's, and it is her jealousy that ultimately leads to his murder—by croquet mallet—as well. The talk show circuit quickly picks up on the story, calling these privileged kids a Satanic cult.

Handler's characters are all coming of age and aping the adult world of their parents by throwing dinner parties and toting around hip flasks. "The links between teen social life, tabloid culture and serious violence have been explored below and exploited before," noted the reviewer for *Publishers Weekly,* "but Handler, and Flannery, know that. If they're not the first to use such material, they may well be the coolest." This same reviewer concluded, "Handler's confident satire is not only cheeky but packed with downright lovable characters whose youthful misadventures keep the novel neatly balanced between absurdity and poignancy." *Booklist*'s Stephanie Zvirin called the book "Part horror story, part black comedy," noting that *The Basic Eight* shows what can happen to "smart, privileged, cynical teens with too few rules, too much to drink, too little supervision, and boundless imagination." Zvirin felt that *The Basic Eight* "will leave readers on the brink of both laughter and despair." *Library Journal*'s Rebecca Kelm found Handler's writing to be "witty and perceptive, especially as schools and society are parodied," and the reviewer also noted his "clever use of vocabulary and study questions" that poke fun at the conventions of literary criticism in high schools. Kelm's admiration for the book, however, was tempered with the brutal murder at its center.

Other reviewers also had mixed praise. A writer for *The New Yorker* commented, "Handler is a charming writer with a lovely mastery of voice, but the book is weakened by his attempt to turn a clever idea into a social satire." Brian Howard, writing in *Citypaper.net,* felt that Handler "beautifully captures the ennui and distorted perspectives of a suburban upbringing, where dinner parties are the biggest concern." Howard also pointed to "a lot of excellent suspense writing" in the book, but concluded that "the oh-my-gosh plot twist, which ultimately ruins Culp's credibility, also does much to undo Handler's otherwise fine debut."

Handler told Woo in *The Lowell* that his theme with his first novel "is that young people are oftentimes full of great ideas and creativity and that those things are often stifled." For his second novel, *Watch Your Mouth,* Handler chose another coming of age crucible, the college years. Joseph is just finishing his junior year at prestigious Mather College. There he has met luscious and lascivious Cynthia Glass, whom he delights in calling Cyn with its intended double meaning. A surfeit of sex has caused Joseph to fall behind in his studies and earn an incomplete in one class. When Cyn recommends that Joseph spend the summer with her and her family in Pittsburgh, he leaps at the chance to stay close to his lover. There the two will work days as Jewish day-camp counselors, Joseph will finish his incomplete, and their nights will be their own.

Once settled in the Glass's home, however, Joseph is filled with a sort of foreboding. "Perhaps it's the summer heat in his attic room," noted Ted Leventhal in a *Booklist* review of *Watch Your Mouth,* "or the overly erotic environment, but Joseph begins to imagine that there is something unhealthy about the family's intimacy." It seems father Ben pines for his daughter, Cyn; that mother Mimi yearns for her son, Stephen, and that Stephen may return the favor. Is this a product of Joseph's warped imagination, or is there any truth in it?

Joseph soon discovers or uncovers a triad of fascinations for the family: science, Kabbalah, and, well, incest. And in the basement, is that a golem Mrs. Glass is constructing? Written in the form of an opera, the novel employs realism and surrealism side by side, references to Judaism and modern literature share the same page. Billed as an "incest comedy," the novel steps perilously close to the bounds of good taste. "Did I hear you right, Mr. Reviewer, did you say 'incest comedy'?" wrote Jonathan Shipley in a *BookBrowser* review. "That's 'comedy'? It can be if you write it right. And who writes it right. Daniel Handler. Handler, the author of the critically-acclaimed *The Basic Eight,* comes back with a very odd, quirky, unusual story." A *Publishers Weekly* reviewer felt that Handler's second novel is so "twisted that even its protagonist can't keep up with the perverse turns of plot," and further observed that "this melodramatic satire of family life trembles between virtuosity and utter collapse." *Library Journal*'s Kelm called the book "quirky" and "offbeat," while *Salon*'s Edward Neuert noted that Handler "is more than ready to pick up the torch [of Kurt Vonnegut] and write the kind of deftly funny absurdist story that both horrifies with its subject matter and hooks you with its humor." Leventhal concluded his review noting that there are "plays within plays and puns within puns. . . . *Mouth* is clever, witty, and unpredictable."

If Handler has a way of getting away with the quirky novel or two, his alter ego, Lemony Snicket has perfected the gambit. "Try pitching this as a series of children's novels," wrote Toppo. "Three young siblings—handsome, clever and rich—lose their loving parents in a fire that destroys their mansion. Too gloomy? It gets worse." And indeed it does, in the ongoing adventures of "A Series of Unfortunate Events," siblings Violet, Klaus, and Sunny Baudelaire not only lose their parents, but are then set upon by the vile Count Olaf, whose one goal in life, it seems, is to bilk the children out of their fortune. After a close encounter with this dastardly villain in the opening novel of the series, *The Bad Beginning,* the children make their painful way from one relative to the next, each more hideous than

the last. The Count, of course, makes reprise appearances in each successive volume, much to the delight of the legion of young readers these books have attracted. The trio of kids is led by inventive fourteen-year-old Violet, her rather bookish brother, twelve-year-old Klaus, and baby Sunny who has incredibly sharp teeth for an infant and employs a baby argot that speaks volumes. Eschewing the magic of Harry Potter, Snicket/Handler has imbued these children with survival skills of a more practical nature, enabling them to defend themselves from a cornucopia of hurled knives, falling lamps, storms, snakes, leeches, and just plain rotten folks. And all of this is related in a deadpan, sophisticated text that has its tongue firmly planted in cheek.

The birth of Lemony Snicket was actually influenced by Handler's debut novel, *The Basic Eight.* Susan Rich, editor at HarperTrophy and a fan of Handler's first novel, decided to try and woo him over to children's books. "I knew we shared a similar sensibility about children's books," Rich told Lodge in *Publishers Weekly,* "which I'd define as a resistance to fall into overly trodden paths of traditional stories, and a resistance to anything that is too sweet or patronizing or moralistic." Handler was at first resistant, but offered the chance to pen books he might have enjoyed reading himself when he was ten, he set to reworking the hundred or so pages of a mock-Gothic novel for adults that he had long ago abandoned. Handler, writing as Snicket—a name he had once devised to avoid getting on unwanted mail lists—was delighted to revamp the entire notion of what constitutes an appropriate novel for juveniles, repealing the old sports or fantasy categories that were available to him as a youth. The result was *The Bad Beginning,* the first of what Handler/Snicket see as a thirteen-volume set chronicling the adventures of the Baudelaire orphans. "If you are interested in stories with happy endings," the author wrote on the first page of that novel, "you would be better off reading some other book. In this book, not only is there no happy ending, there is no happy beginning and very few happy things in the middle. . . . I'm sorry to tell you this, but that's how the story goes."

When the three Baudelaire children lose their parents in a fire, they become—through the oversight of the ineffectual banker, Mr. Poe—wards of Count Olaf, a distant cousin. He sets them to labor in his house, meanwhile devising schemes with his theatrical troupe to deprive the orphans of their inheritance. The three survive the Count's attacks with spunk, initiative, and, in the case of Sunny, a set of sharp teeth. "The author uses formal, Latinate language and intrusive commentary to hilarious effect," noted a review for *Publishers Weekly* of this first title in the series. The same reviewer felt that the author "paints the satire with such broad strokes that most readers will view it from a safe distance." In the second book of the series, *The Reptile Room,* it seems the orphans will have a chance for happiness when they go to live with Dr. Montgomery Montgomery, a "very fun, but fatally naïve herpetologist," according to Ron Charles in the *Christian Science Monitor.* Unfortunately, their safe haven is short-lived, spoiled once again by the arrival of the oafish Count Olaf. Susan Dove Lempke, reviewing the first two titles in *Booklist,* thought that the "droll humor, reminiscent of Edward Gorey's, will be lost on some children; others may not enjoy the old-fashioned storytelling style that frequently addresses the reader directly and includes definitions of terms." Lempke went on, however, to conclude: "But plenty of children will laugh at the over-the-top satire; hiss at the creepy nefarious villains; and root for the intelligent, courageous, unfortunate Baudelaire orphans." Linda Bindner, writing in *School Library Journal,* noted that "While the misfortunes hover on the edge of being ridiculous, Snicket's energetic blend of humor, dramatic irony, and literary flair makes it all perfectly believable." Bindner also found that the use of sophisticated vocabulary and inclusion of author definitions make "these books challenging to older readers and excellent for reading aloud."

The third book in the series, *The Wide Window,* finds the orphans with elderly Aunt Josephine who lives on a house on stilts which overlooks Lake Lachrymose. Josephine is a widow as well as a frightful grammarian, and when Olaf finally tracks down the Baudelaires, he fools the aunt for a while into believing he is a sailboat captain. When she finally stumbles onto his true identity, he gets rid of her by pushing the good woman into leech-infested waters and the peripatetic children must find a new protector. *Booklist*'s Lempke noted that Snicket writes in "an old-fashioned tone," offering "plenty advice to readers in asides." "The effect is often hilarious as well as edifying," Lempke observed. Most importantly, as Lempke concluded, "readers never truly worry that [the Baudelaire orphans] will be defeated in this or their next adventure."

The fourth in the series, *The Miserable Mill,* begins with the three children on their way to Paltryville and yet another guardian, this time the owner of the Lucky Smells Lumbermill. Here they must work in the mill, survive on gum for lunch and casserole for dinner. Count Olaf, is of course, just off-stage ready to pounce. "The story is deliciously mock-Victorian and self-

mockingly melodramatic," noted *Booklist*'s Carolyn Phelan, who also commented on the artwork and "the author's many asides to the reader" which both "underscore the droll humor. . . ." Phelan concluded, "Another plum for the orphans' fans." "This is for readers who appreciate this particular type of humor," observed Sharon R. Pearce in *School Library Journal.* Pearce noted that such humor "exaggerates the sour and makes anyone's real life seem sweet in comparison." The adventures continue in *The Austere Academy* and *The Ersatz Elevator.* In the former title, the Baudelaire children are consigned to a shack at the Prufrock Preparatory School where they will face snapping crabs, strict punishments, dripping fungus and the evils of the metric system. In the latter book, they must contend with new guardians Jerome and Esme Squalor, while trying to save two friends from the clutches of Count Olaf.

"The Snicket novels are morality tales, albeit twisted ones," observed Benfer in *Salon.* "Among other things, Snicket tells children that one should never stay up late on a school night, except to finish a very good book; he insists that there is nothing worse than someone who can't play the violin but insists upon doing so anyway." He employs continual authorial intrusions, providing definitions, giving stage directions. "I was mostly just knocking the heavy-handedness that I remembered from kid's books that I didn't like as a child," Handler reported to Benfer. "That sort of mockery seems to really appeal to kids." Another Handler trademark is the use of names in the Snicket books which come from literature: the Baudelaire orphans themselves are but the most obvious example of a long list including Mr. Poe and Prufrock Prep. "There's plenty of literary names and the like," Handler told Benfer, "but there's not so many outright jokes. And the literary names are there mostly because I look forward to kids growing up and finding Baudelaire in the poetry anthology and having that be something else to be excited about."

The formula has worked quite well, sending the Handler/Snicket books onto the best-seller charts and establishing a devoted fan base. More than 125,000 of the books in "A Series of Unfortunate Events" are in print, the Snicket Web site is a popular venue in cyberspace, and the elusive Mr. Snicket himself has become a popular speaker at schools. Correction. Mr. Snicket's representative, Mr. Handler, performs stand-ins for his friend, who has variously been injured or delayed or unaccountably held hostage somewhere while Mr. Handler entertains the youthful audience with his accordion and tales of the Snicket family tree. According to the official Snicket web site, "Lemony Snicket was born before you were and is likely to die before you as well."

Lodge wrote in *Publishers Weekly* that obviously "the author's knack for combining the dark with the droll has hit a nerve just about everywhere," and word-of-mouth has greatly contributed to the success of the series. With Nickelodeon working on the film and Handler/Snicket collaborating on an expected thirteen volumes, the future looks surprisingly bright for the Baudelaire orphans.

BIOGRAPHICAL/CRITICAL SOURCES:

PERIODICALS

ALAN Review, winter, 2001, Linda Broughton, review of *The Miserable Mill,* p. 35.
Book, July, 2001, *Kathleen Odean,* review of The Ersatz Elevator, p. 81.
Booklist, March 15, 1999, Stephanie Zvirin, review of *The Basic Eight,* p. 1289; December 1, 1999, Susan Dove Lempke, review of *The Bad Beginning,* p. 707; February 1, 2000, Susan Dove Lempke, review of *The Wide Window,* p. 1024; May 1, 2000, Carolyn Phelan, review of *The Miserable Mill,* p. 1670; June 1, 2000, Ted Leventhal, review of *Watch Your Mouth,* p. 1857; October 15, 2000, Susan Dove Lempke, review of *The Austere Academy,* p. 439.
Boys' Life, December, 2000, Stephen G. Michaud, review of "A Series of Unfortunate Events" titles, p. 61.
Christian Science Monitor, August 12, 1999, Ron Charles, review of *The Bad Beginning* and *The Reptile Room,* p. 21.
Horn Book, March, 2001, Christine Heppermann, "Angel Wings and Hard Knocks," p. 239.
Library Journal, March 15, 1999, Rebecca Kelm, review of *The Basic Eight,* p. 108; June 1, 2000, Rebecca Kelm, review of *Watch Your Mouth,* p. 196.
New Yorker, June 21, 1999, review of *The Basic Eight.*
New York Times Magazine, April 29, 2001, Daphne Merkin, "Lemony Snicket Says, 'Don't Read My Books!' ".
Publishers Weekly, March 1, 1999, review of *The Basic Eight,* p. 59; September 6, 1999, review of *The Bad Beginning,* p. 104; January 17, 2000, p. 58; May 29, 2000, Sally Lodge, "Oh, Sweet Misery," p. 42; June 19, 2000, review of *Watch Your Mouth,* p. 60.
School Library Journal, November, 1999, Linda Bindner, review of *The Bad Beginning,* p. 165; January, 2000, p. 136; July, 2000, Sharon R. Pearce, review of *The Miserable Mill,* p. 110; October, 2000, Ann Cook, review of *The Austere Academy,* p. 171; August, 2001, Farida S. Dowler, reviews of *The Ersatz Elevator* and *The Vile Village,* pp. 188-189.
Time for Kids, April 27, 2001, "He Tells Terrible Tales," p. 7.

OTHER

A Series of Unfortunate Events Web site, http://www.lemonysnicket.com/ (March 26, 2001).
BookBrowser Review, http://www.bookbroswer.com/ (July 15, 2000), Jonathan Shipley, review of *Watch Your Mouth.*
Citypaper.net, http://www.cpcn.com/ (June 17-24, 1999), Brian Howard, review of *The Basic Eight.*
CNNfyi.com, http://www.cnn.cm/200/fyi/news/ (May 12, 2000), Greg Toppo, "Wry 'Series of Unfortunate Events' Books Earn Fans, Praise."
Lowell, http://www.thelowell.org/ (February 15, 1999), Philana Woo, "Author Reflects on High School Life."
Nancy Matson's Web site, http://www.nancymatson.com/ (March, 2000).
Salon, http://www.salonmag.com/ (July 24, 2000), Edward Neuert, "What to Read: July Fiction;" (August 17, 2000) Amy Benfer, "The Mysterious Mr. Snicket."*

* * *

SNYDER, Robert W. 1955-

PERSONAL: Born 1955. *Education:* New York University, Ph.D.

ADDRESSES: Office—Rutgers University, Fine Arts, 110 Warren St., Newark, NJ 07102; fax: 973-353-1392. *E-mail*—rwsnyder@andromeda.rutgers.edu.

CAREER: Writer; teacher at Princeton University and New York University; Rutgers University, Newark, NJ, associate professor, director of journalism program; managing editor, *Media Studies Journal.*

WRITINGS:

The Voice of the City, Oxford University Press (New York, NY), 1989.
(With Rebecca Zurier) *Metropolitan Lives: The Ashcan Artists and Their New York,* Norton (New York, NY), 1996.
(Editor with Everette E. Dennis) *Media and Public Life,* Transaction (New Brunswick, NJ), 1997.
(Editor with Everette E. Dennis) *Covering Congress,* Transaction (New Brunswick, NJ), 1998.

(Editor with Nancy J. Woodhull) *Defining Moments in Journalism,* Transaction (New Brunswick, NJ), 1998.

(Editor with Nancy J. Woodhull) *Journalists in Peril,* Transaction (New Brunswick, NJ), 1998.

(Editor with Everette E. Dennis) *Media and Democracy,* Transaction (New Brunswick, NJ), 1998.

(Editor with Nancy J. Woodhull) *Media Mergers,* Transaction (New Brunswick, NJ), 1998.

(With Pete Hamill) *Transit Talk: New York's Bus and Subway Workers Tell Their Stories,* Rutgers University Press, 1998.

(Editor) *Covering China,* Transaction (New Brunswick, NJ), 1999.

(Editor with Robert H. Giles) *Covering the Courts: Free Press, Fair Trials and Journalistic Performance,* Transaction (New Brunswick, NJ), 1999.

(Editor with Robert H. Giles) *What's Fair?: The Problem of Equity in Journalism,* Transaction (New Brunswick, NJ), 1999.

(Editor with Robert H. Giles) *What's Next: Problems & Prospects of Journalism,* Transaction (New Brunswick, NJ), 2000.

(Editor with Robert H. Giles) *Reporting the Post-Communist Revolution,* Transaction (New Brunswick, NJ), 2001.

SIDELIGHTS: Robert W. Snyder's grandfather was a New York City transit worker for forty-eight years, and before writing *Transit Talk: New York's Bus and Subway Workers Tell Their Stories,* Snyder interviewed over a hundred men and women who work for the New York City transit system. The book presents a behind-the-scenes look at what really goes on in the working lives of New York's 44,000 transit workers, who transport over five million people each day and whose jobs often expose them to dangers such as high-voltage train lines, holdups and gang fights. In addition, workers see the real underside of the city and its people. Most New Yorkers never even notice transit workers, who are an almost invisible part of any ride. A *Publishers Weekly* reviewer wrote, "Some [stories] are sweet, like when a baby is born in the last car of a train and named after the nervous worker who helped in the delivery. Others are more grim, as when a jumper lands under a train and miraculously lives."

The Voice of the City: Vaudeville and Popular Culture in New York shows what social, economic, and cultural factors led to the growth of vaudeville in New York City. The book follows the history of vaudeville from the late 19th century through the early 20th century to the 1930s, and shows how many aspects of our current culture had their beginnings in vaudeville. Mary C.

Curtis wrote in *The New York Times* that "this book is well researched . . . and tells some interesting stories about vaudeville's evolution." Curtis stated that "these stories (and) quirky profiles . . . reflect the vitality of the performers." Mark Woodhouse, a reviewer in *Library Journal,* called *The Voice of the City* a "scholarly but highly readable discussion" of Vaudeville.

Hundreds of journalists have been killed while covering wars or other dangerous situations, or they have been killed because of what they wrote, broadcast, or photographed. In *Journalists in Peril,* Snyder and co-editor Nancy J. Woodhull present a collection of articles by journalists telling the story of their work in war zones and dictatorships, and telling the stories of immigrant reporters who have been killed in the United States because of what they reported about their home countries. A reviewer in *Library Journal* called *Journalists in Peril* "a book that will be of interest to academic journalism collections . . . and to public libraries."

Covering China is a collection of essays analyzing American reporting in China, from the time of the Chinese Civil War in the 1930s and 1940s until the present. Chapters examine Chinese political movements and how they influenced journalism, as well as trends now emerging in China and how they will affect both journalists and Chinese people, including new roles for Chinese women, unrest among ethnic minorities in China, and economic and environmental issues.

What's Fair?: The Problem of Equity in Journalism is a collection of essays by journalists exploring issues of privacy, truth, fairness, and appropriateness in reporting. The book is not merely a series of abstract ethical discussions, however; the debate is grounded in stories of journalists' experiences with difficult issues.

With Rebecca Zurier, Snyder wrote *Metropolitan Lives: the Ashcan Artists and their New York.* Adam Mazmanian, a reviewer in *Library Journal* called the book "a fine effort to recognize the movement that blurs critical distinctions between high and popular art."

BIOGRAPHICAL/CRITICAL SOURCES:

PERIODICALS

Choice, February, 1990, J. Sochen, review of *The Voice of the City,* p.957.

Library Journal, November 1, 1989, Mark Woodhouse, review of *The Voice of the City,* p. 102; March 1, 1996, Adam Mazmanian, review of *Metropolitan*

Lives, p. 78; July, 1998, Judy Solberg, review of *Journalists in Peril,* p. 104.

Publishers Weekly, November 2, 1998, review of *Transit Talk,* p. 58.

New York Times, March 4, 1990, Mary C. Curtis, "In Short: Nonfiction," p.25.*

*   *   *

SOLOW, Ruth
See COMBS, Maxine

*   *   *

SOVA, Dawn B(everly) 1949-
(Aurora Street)

PERSONAL: Born October 6, 1949, in Passaic, NJ; daughter of Emil J. (a skilled machinist) and Violet Tomczyk (a hair stylist) Sova; married Robert W. Gregor, January 4, 1975 (died, November 20, 1995); children: Robert Gregor. *Ethnicity:* "Polish/Czech." *Education:* Montclair State University, B.S., 1971; Ball State University, M.A., 1972; Drew University, Ph.D., 1990. *Politics:* "Liberal." *Religion:* Roman Catholic. *Avocational interests:* Computer gaming, travel.

ADDRESSES: Office—Department of English, Montclair State University, Upper Montclair, NJ. *Agent*—Bert Holtje, James Peter Associates, P.O. Box 670, Tenafly, NJ 07670. *E-mail*—dawndr@aol.com.

CAREER: Montclair State University, Upper Montclair, NJ, adjunct professor of English, 1993—.

MEMBER: Modern Language Association, Authors' Guild.

AWARDS, HONORS: Nominated for Edgar Award, Mystery Writers of America, 1999, for *Agatha Christie A to Z.*

WRITINGS:

The Woman's Guide to Zero Stress, Zebra (New York, NY), 1984.

Eddie Murphy, Zebra (New York, NY), 1985.

Sex and the Single Mother, Dodd, Mead (New York, NY), 1987.

The Encyclopedia of Mistresses, Longmeadow, 1993.

Agatha Christie A to Z, Facts on File (New York, NY), 1996.

How to Write Articles for Newspapers and Magazines, Macmillan (New York, NY), 1998.

Banned Books: Literature Suppressed for Sexual Content, Facts on File (New York, NY), 1998.

Banned Books: Literature Suppressed for Social Content, Facts on File (New York, NY), 1998.

Women in Hollywood: From Vamp to Studio Head, Fromm International, 1998.

(Coauthor) *100 Banned Books,* Checkmark, 1999.

Word Problems in Geometry: The Solved Problem Approach, McGraw-Hill (New York, NY), 1999.

Quick Guide to the Verbal SAT, McGraw-Hill (New York, NY), 2000.

Censored Stage, Facts on File (New York, NY), 2001.

Edgar Allan Poe A to Z, Facts on File (New York, NY), 2001.

Forbidden Films, Facts on File (New York, NY), 2001.

Contributor of chapters to *The New Immigrant Literatures,* Greenwood, 1996; and of articles to various periodicals, including *Woman's Day, Computer Decisions, Reader's Digest, Army Times Magazine, Redbook,* and *Cosmopolitan.*

SIDELIGHTS: Dawn B. Sova told *CA:* "The topics about which I choose to write are those that interest me, so I guess my motivation to write is selfish. I very much enjoy doing research, and when I come across a subject that intrigues me I often begin to dig deeply into it and seek to learn everything that I can about it. Sometimes, the subject is one in which other people are also interested, and then a book is born. The topic that has obsessed me in recent years is censorship—examining what types of literature, film, artwork, or music have been challenged, censored or banned—and who attempts to suppress such material. Even after writing four books on the issue—*Banned Books: Literature Suppressed for Sexual Content, Banned Books: Literature Suppressed for Social Content, Forbidden Films,* and *Censored Stage*—and co-authoring another (*100 Banned Books*), I feel as if a lot more remains to be revealed.

"My books take me in many directions, all of which are interesting. *Agatha Christie A to Z* and *Edgar Allan Poe A to Z* allowed me to explore the lives and works of two writers of relatively modest critical reception who have great popular appeal. What made their writing popular? Who were they? What influenced them? *The Encyclopedia of Mistresses* led me to research the fascinating stories of women who wielded great power over men during periods of history in which women were seemingly powerless.

"In sum, I suppose that I write to learn—and to teach."

*   *   *

SPALDING, David A(lan) E(dwin)   1937-

PERSONAL: Born June 23, 1937, in Sheffield, England; son of Charles William (an engineer) and Elsa Maud (a nurse) Spalding; married Andrea Judith Clarke, July 30, 1966; children: Jane Melanie Spalding-Jamieson, Penelope Alice Libby, Lucy Miranda Mardres. *Ethnicity:* "White." *Education:* University of Sheffield, B.S., 1959. *Avocational interests:* Music.

ADDRESSES: Home and Office—1105 Ogden Rd., R.R. #1, Pender Island, British Columbia, Canada V0N 2M1. *Agent*—Melanie Colbert, 17 West St., Holland Landing, Ontario, Canada L9N 1L4. *E-mail*—brandywine@gulfislands.com.

CAREER: Sheffield City Museum, deputy director, 1959-67; Provincial Museum of Alberta, Alberta, Canada, head curator of natural history, 1967-81; freelance musician and writer, 1981—. Royal Tyrrell Museum of Paleontology, acting director and interpretive planner, c. 1980; Kanta Heritage Corporation, heritage planning consultant, 1981-95; British Columbia Museums Association, executive director, c. 1990-92; Red Deer College, instructor of writing and publishing courses.

MEMBER: Canadian Museums Association, Canadian Society for Traditional Music, Writers' Union of Canada, Pender Islands Conservancy Association (chair).

AWARDS, HONORS: Minister of Education Award (Japan), for educational radio program *The Prairie Rattlesnake;* Queen's Jubilee Medal; grants from Alberta Literary Arts Foundation, Alberta Culture, and University of Tennessee; *The Lost Sketch* was selected as a millennium book by the British Columbia government and was short-listed for the Silver Birch Award in Ontario.

WRITINGS:

(Senior editor) *A Nature Guide to Alberta,* Provincial Museum of Alberta and Hurtig Publishers, 1980.
(Editor and author of introduction) C. H. Sternberg, *Hunting Dinosaurs on the Red Deer River,* third edition, NeWest, 1985.
Dinosaur Hunters, Prima, 1993.
(With Andrea Spalding) *The Flavours of Victoria,* photographs by Kevin Oke, Orca, 1994.

(With Andrea Spalding, Georgina Montgomery and Lawrence Pitt) *Southern Gulf Islands of British Columbia,* Altitude (Canada), 1995.
(With Andrea Spalding and Lawrence Pitt) *BC Ferries and the Canadian West Coast,* Altitude (Canada), 1996.
(With Andrea Spalding) *Adventure*Net the Lost Sketch* (juvenile fiction), Whitecap, 1999.
Into the Dinosaurs' Graveyard: Canadian Digs and Discoveries, Doubleday Canada, 1999.
Whales of the West Coast, Harbour, 1999.
(With Andrea Spalding) *Adventure*Net the Silver Boulder* (juvenile fiction), Whitecap, 2000.

Author, with Andrea Spalding, of *The Whistlers, Jasper National Park,* Environment Canada Parks, 1986; also author of many radio and television scripts, including works for ACCESS CKUA, Indian Affairs, Jasper National Park, Tyrrell Museum of Paleontology, the ACCESS TV series *Discovery Digest,* and many local, provincial and national programs. Contributor of nonfiction to books, including *Vertebrate Fossils and the Evolution of Scientific Concepts,* edited by W. A. S. Sarjeant, Gordon & Breach, 1995; and *Life in Stone, A Natural History of British Columbia's Fossils,* edited by Rolf Ludvigsen, University of British Columbia Press, 1996. Contributor of many articles to magazines, journals, encyclopedias, and other publications, including *Canadian Encyclopedia, Encyclopedia Britannica, Biblio, Canadian Collector, Cottage Magazine, Nature Canada, NeWest Review, Brigham Young University Geology Studies, Gazette, Museums Journal, Journal of Biological Education, Mercian Geologist, Alberta Naturalists, Canadian Folk Music Bulletin, Discovery,* and *Museum Round-Up.* Editor of various publications, including *Alberta Naturalist, Edmonton Naturalist, Sorby Record,* and books by Peggy Holmes.

WORK IN PROGRESS: Two juvenile novels, for Whitecap; research on the "world history of dinosaur collecting."

SIDELIGHTS: David A. E. Spalding told *CA:* "I began writing as a child, and have done so through my years working in museums, interpretive planning and performance, contributing to many exhibits and radio and television programs as well as magazines, journal, encyclopedias and symposia. Recognition came in mid-life through educational radio, where I won a major award for the second program I wrote. Since then writing has played an increasing part in my life, and now I write full-time, for a living and for the pleasure it brings me. I now write at home, in a house in the forest on a small island. Here I am daily reminded of the natural environment which as so well concealed during years of city living.

"My attention is focused primarily on non-fiction books for adults. I am inspired firstly by my own experiences in Europe and North America, through which I have come into contact with many areas of the natural sciences and their history. These have in turn given me insight into the work of the great naturalists of past and present, whose unending struggle for the truth presents as rich as human drama as can be found in any area of society.

"In presenting this material I seek inspiration where I find it, not only in my library of scientific biographies, histories and classics, but in fiction, poetry, and in folklore—that constant reminder of the spoken work. Nonfiction writing is continuously challenging as radio and television move us back to an oral society, and the Internet becomes a popular source of information. Linear text can now be supplemented by multiple approaches, the use of different voices to bring diverse perspectives, and links to other media such as audio, film, fiction and the web. Science is not often seen as part of our culture, yet it brings to public attention icons such as whales, and dinosaurs which have a fictional and symbolic life beyond their factual reality, becoming part of our rich relationship with nature, which in turn helps us to define ourselves.

"A constant inspiration comes through ongoing collaboration with my wife Andrea Spalding in her writing for children, to who stories are always new. A current challenge is our joint creation of series of novels for children (Adventure*Net), in which we are endeavoring to explore Canadian culture, environment and history through a hypertext blending fiction, fact, and Internet sources."

*   *   *

SPEART, Jessica

PERSONAL: Born in Washington, DC.

ADDRESSES: Agent—Dominick Abel, 146 West 82nd St., New York, NY 10024. *E-mail*—speartj@aol.com.

CAREER: Former actress in off-Broadway productions, repertory theatres, commercials and soap operas, including a recurring role on *One Life to Live;* investigative journalist focused on wildlife law enforcement, en-

dangered species issues, and the environment. Former photo editor at a New York City photography stock house.

MEMBER: Mystery Writers of America, Sisters in Crime, Outdoor Writers of America, Society of Environmental Journalists.

WRITINGS:

"RACHEL PORTER" MYSTERY SERIES

Gator Aide, Avon (New York, NY), 1997.
Tortoise Soup, Avon (New York, NY), 1998.
Bird Brained, Avon (New York, NY), 1999.
Border Prey, Avon (New York, NY), 2000.
Black Delta Night, Avon (New York, NY), 2001.

OTHER

Contributor to *The Animal Dealers,* Animal Welfare Institute, 1997; and contributor of articles to various periodicals, including *New York Times Sunday Magazine, Onmi, Travel & Leisure, Audubon, National Wildlife, Mother Jones,* and *Wildlife Conservation.*

WORK IN PROGRESS: Bare Bones, a mystery, for Avon.

SIDELIGHTS: Jessica Speart told *CA:* "My primary motivation for writing is to convey my passion for wildlife and the environment—especially concerning the plight of endangered species. We are on the brink of a new Dark Ages, one in which species and plants are beginning to disappear at an increasingly alarming rate. The illegal trade in wildlife is estimated at $5 billion a year, placing it right behind the ranks of drug smuggling and gun running, and often involving many of the same people. It is due to this fact that my heroine, U.S. Fish and Wildlife special agent Rachel Porter, always stumbles upon deeper and darker misdeeds than she originally suspects.

"I spent a number of years writing magazine articles on different cases involving special agents with the U.S. Fish and Wildlife Service. It was this work which opened my eyes to the battle taking place to protect native species within our own country. Our wildlife is considered an extremely valuable commodity by much of the rest of the world and is being poached to the point where it is a dwindling resource. U.S. Fish and Wildlife agents compose the thin green line who are battling to save it. These are the people who inspire and influence my work.

"My writing process can be broken down into two definite parts. Half of the year is spent doing research. The other six months are spent writing the book, itself."

*   *   *

STAGAMAN, David 1935-

PERSONAL: Born July 29, 1935, in Cincinnati, OH; son of Harry (a laundry plant manager) and Elinor Willen Brink (a homemaker) Stagaman. *Ethnicity:* "German-American." *Education:* Loyola University of Chicago, A.B., 1958. M.A., 1967; West Baden College, Ph.L., 1960; Bellarmine School of Theology, S.T.L., 1967; Institut Catholique de Paris, docteur en theologie, 1975; attended Warren H. Deem Institute for Theological Education Management, 1998. *Politics:* Democrat. *Religion:* Roman Catholic. *Avocational interests:* NFL Football, walking.

ADDRESSES: Home—2517 Virginia #8, Berkeley, CA 94709. *Office*—Jesuit School of Theology at Berkeley, 1735 LeRoy Ave., Berkeley, CA 94709; fax: 510-841-8536. *E-mail*—dstagama@jstb.edu AND dstagaman@ yahoo.com.

CAREER: Entered Society of Jesus, 1953; St. Xavier High School, Cincinnati, OH, math teacher, 1960-63; Ordained Roman Catholic Priest, Aurora, IL, 1966—; Jesuit School of Theology at Berkeley, associate professor of theology, 1972—, acting rector, Jesuit Community, 1974-75; chair, Department of Historical/ Systematic Theology, 1974-78, dean and senior vice president, 1987-96, acting president, 1995. Presenter at conferences.

MEMBER: American Academy of Religions, American Association for Higher Education, National Association of Church Personnel Administrators, Catholic Theological Society of America, Pacific Coast Theological Society, Society of Jesus Chicago Province, Alpha Sigma Nu.

AWARDS, HONORS: Fellow, American Theological Schools, 1978-79.

WRITINGS:

Authority in the Church, Michael Glazier/Liturgical (Collegeville, MN), 1999.

Contributor to books, including *Speaking of God: Essays on Belief and Unbelief,* edited by Denis Dirscherl,

Bruce (Milwaukee, WI), 1967; and *The Thought of Pope John Paul II,* edited by John McDermott, Gregorian University (Rome, Italy), 1993. Contributor of articles to various periodicals, including *Occasional Papers of Center for Hermeneutics, Proceedings of Catholic Theological Society of America, Tripod, Christian Century,* and *Budhi;* and book reviews to *America, Theological Studies,* and *Christian Century.*

WORK IN PROGRESS: Empowering the Urban Poor in Metro Manila; What Cultural Anthropology Can Teach the Church.

*   *   *

STARER, Robert 1924-2001

OBITUARY NOTICE—See index for *CA* sketch: Born January 8, 1924, in Vienna, Austria; emigrated to the United States, 1947; naturalized citizen, 1957; died of congestive heart failure, April 22, 2001, in Kingston, NY. Composer and author. Starer grew up in Austria but his family left for Jerusalem in 1938 when Hitler's forces took over his homeland. He attended the Palestine Conservatory and served in the Royal British Air Force from 1943 to 1946. After being discharged, Starer came to the United States to attend the Juilliard School of Music, from which he received a postgraduate diploma in 1949. He joined Juilliard's faculty that same year and stayed there until 1974. During those years Starer also served on the faculties of Brooklyn College and the Graduate Center of the City University of New York; he finally retired from teaching in 1991. He received many honors during his career including two Guggenheim fellowships, the Austrian Medal of Honor for Science and Art, and an honorary doctorate from the State University of New York. Among Starer's works are four operas, including *The Last Lover* and *Apollonia;* seven ballets including three with choreographer Martha Graham: *Samson Agonistes, Phaedra* and *The Lady of the House of Sleep.* Other compositions include symphonies, chamber music, vocal and choral music. Starer wrote four books: the autobiographical *Continuo: A Life in Music,* the textbooks *Basic Rhythmic Training* and *Rhythmic Training,* and the fictional *The Music Teacher.*

OBITUARIES AND OTHER SOURCES:

PERIODICALS

Guardian (London, England), May 5, 2001, p. 22.
Independent (London, England), May 31, 2001, p. 6.

Milwaukee Journal Sentinel, April 26, 2001, p. 5.
New York Times, April 24, 2001, p. C19.

*   *   *

STILL, James   1906-2001

OBITUARY NOTICE—See index for *CA* sketch: Born July 16, 1906, in LaFayette, AL; died April 28, 2001, in Hindman, KY. Librarian, poet and author. Still was one of the strongest voices to emerge in Appalachian literature and he received numerous awards during his lifelong career. Still was born in Alabama, but moved to Tennessee to attend Lincoln Memorial University where a student could work for tuition. He graduated in 1929 with a bachelor's and followed with a master's from Vanderbilt University the following year. In 1931 he received a bachelor's in library science from the University of Illinois. He left Illinois for the Hindman Settlement School in Kentucky and was librarian there until 1939. That year he received the O. Henry Memorial Prize for his short story "Bat Flight." The next year he was honored with the Southern Authors Award from Southern Women's National Democratic Organization for his novel *River of Earth.* His next post was a four-year stint in the Air Force during World War II, taking part in campaigns in Africa and the Middle East. When he returned to the United States he was a freelance writer for several years and contributed stories and poems to anthologies, but in 1952 went back to the Hindman Settlement School, again as the librarian. He stayed for ten years, but left to be an associate professor of English at Morehead State University. From 1971 on he was a freelance writer. Among his books are the poetry collections *Hounds on the Mountain* and *The Wolfpen Poems,* and the novels On Troublesome Creek and *Sporty Creek.* He also wrote several children's books and short stories. His last work, *From the Mountain, From the Valley: New and Collected Poems,* was published in 2001.

OBITUARIES AND OTHER SOURCES:

BOOKS

Contemporary Southern Writers, St. James Press (Detroit, MI), 1999.

PERIODICALS

Milwaukee Journal Sentinel, April 30, 2001, p. 4.
Washington Post, April 30, 2001, p. B6.

STRAMM, August   1874-1915

PERSONAL: Born July 29, 1874, in Münster, Westphalia, Prussia (now Germany); killed in action, September 1, 1915, in Gorodenka, Russia; father, a railway official; married. *Education:* Attended University of Berlin, 1905-08; University of Halle, Ph.D., 1909. *Avocational interests:* Painting, cello.

CAREER: Dramatist and poet; German Postal Administration, administrator, 1893-1914. *Military service:* Prussian Army, 1913-15; became captain.

WRITINGS:

Rudimentär (drama), Verlag der Sturm (Berlin, Germany), 1914, translation by Henry Marx, 1970.

Die Haidebraut (drama), Verlag der Sturm (Berlin, Germany), 1914, translation published as *The Bride of the Moor,* [Boston, MA], 1914.

Sancta Susanna (drama), Verlag der Sturm (Berlin, Germany), 1914, translation by Edward J. O'Brien published as *Sancta Susanna: The Song of a May Night,* 1914.

Du: Liebesgedichte (title means "Thou: Love Poems"), Verlag der Sturm (Berlin, Germany), 1915.

Erwachen (drama; title means "Awakening"), Verlag der Sturm (Berlin, Germany), 1915, translation by James MacPherson published in *Seven Expressionist Plays,* edited by J. M. Ritchie, Calder & Boyars (London, England), 1968.

Kräfte (drama; title means "Forces"), Verlag der Sturm (Berlin, Germany), 1915.

Geschehen (drama; title means "Happening"), Verlag der Sturm (Berlin, Germany), 1916.

Die Unfruchtbaren (drama; title means "The Sterile Ones"), Verlag der Sturm (Berlin, Germany), 1916.

Die Menschheit, Verlag der Sturm (Berlin, Germany), 1916.

Dichtungen in drei Bänden, Verlag der Sturm (Berlin, Germany), 1918-19.

Tropfblut (poetry; title means "Drip-Blood"), Verlag der Sturm (Berlin, Germany), 1919.

Dein Lächeln weint, 1956.

Das Werk (collected works), edited by René Radrizzani, Verlag der Sturm (Berlin, Germany), 1963.

Twenty-two Poems, translated by Patrick Bridgwater, Brewhouse (Wymandham, England), 1969.

Die Dichtungen: Sämtliche Gedichte, Dramen, Prosa, edited by Jeremy D. Adler, Piper (Munich, Germany), 1990.

Gedichte, Dramen, Prosa, Briefe, edited by Jörg Drews, P. Reclam (Stuttgart, Germany), 1997.

Other plays include "The Peasants," 1905 (produced, 1929); "The Sacrifice," 1908 (produced, 1928); and "The Husband." Works are contained in anthologies, including *Sturm-Bücher: Nummern 1-10, 1914-1919,* Nendeln/Liechtenstein, 1974; *Sturm-Abende ausgewählte Gedichte,* Verlag der Sturm (Berlin, Germany), 1983; correspondence with Herwarth Walden included in *Briefe an Nell und Herwarth Walden,* Edition Sirene (Berlin, Germany), 1988 and *Alles is Gedicht: Briefe, Gedichte, Bilder, Documente,* edited by Jeremy D. Adler, Arche (Zurich, Switzerland), 1990.

ADAPTATIONS: Poems from *Du: Liebesgedichte* have been set to music in *Du: Song Cycle for Voice and Piano,* by Milton Babbitt, Boelke-Bomart (Hillsdale, NY), 1951, and in *Music of Mel Powell and Milton Babbitt,* Son-Nova Records, 1962; other poems have been set to music in *Kreigslieder (Tears of Battle) for Solo Tenor, Mixed Chorus, Trumpet and Percussion* by Gerard Victory, Fairfield Music, 1972 and *Epitaffio per Alban Berg: Varianten für Klavier; drei Sprechleider nach August Stramm; Sonances; Mondräume; Versoinverso,* Communauté de travail pour la diffusion de la musique suisse (Lausanne, Switzerland), 1983; *Sancta Susanna* was used as the libretto for the Hindemith opera of the same name, 1921, produced 1922.

SIDELIGHTS: Though he struggled for literary recognition for most of his career and did not live to see most of his work published or performed, German dramatist August Stramm is now considered one of the leading avant-garde writers of his era. According to Henry Marx in *Drama Review,* Stramm was not only the most experimental German writer of his time but also "a precursor, if not already a true culmination point of Expressionism." Little in Stramm's early life, however, indicated that he would achieve literary renown. He had a middle-class childhood as the son of a petty official who pushed the boy toward a career in the German postal service—against the wishes of the child's Catholic mother, who fervently desired that her son enter the priesthood. Stramm attended gymnasiums in Dueren, Eupen, and Aix-la-Chappelle and then received a position in the German Postal Administration in 1893. Continuing his training while apprenticed there, he studied administrative law, economics, finance, and communications technology at the Post and Telegraphy School in Berlin and qualified for an advanced position in 1902. From 1905 to 1908, he studied at the University of Berlin, and in 1909 earned a Ph.D. from the University of Halle. His dissertation topic was "historical, critical, and cameralistic investigation of the letter postage rates of the Universal Postal Union and their foundations."

Between 1897 and 1902, Stramm often traveled to New York City as a member of the German Postal Administration's Overseas Department. It is possible that he became acquainted, while there, with experimental American writings. Marx wrote that Stramm's letters indicate that he was familiar with the work of Ralph Waldo Trine and Prentice Mulford. Other literary influences included Arno Holz and Maurice Maeterlinck.

Stramm did not begin writing seriously until 1902, when he began work on his first play, *The Peasants;* it was completed in 1905, but was not produced until 1929. A second play, *The Sacrifice,* was written in 1908. It had one production in 1928, but has not survived; its manuscript was destroyed during World War II. Stramm followed these two plays with *The Husband* and *Die Unfruchtbaren,* also unproduced during his lifetime. Despite consistent rejection by publishers, Stramm continued writing plays as well as poems; he was on the verge of giving up, however, when he met Herwarth Walden in 1913. Stramm was nearly forty and still an unknown. Walden, editor of the expressionist magazine *Der Sturm* and leader of the Storm Circle, a group of writers and artists interested in modernist theories and techniques, promoted Stramm's work and introduced him to the literary mainstream in Europe, after which Stramm quickly rose to prominence among the avant-garde. Indeed, according to Malcolm M. Jones in an article published in *Seminar,* during the eighteen months of Stramm's association with *Der Sturm,* his work appeared in the journal more often than that of any other writer in its history. This role as a literary radical, critics have pointed out, seemed a contradictory one for a man who lived a bourgeois life as a bureaucrat, devoted husband and father, and talented amateur painter and cellist.

Around the same time that he met Walden, Stramm discovered the revolutionary literary theories of Italian futurist Filippo Tommaso Marinetti. Inspired by Marinetti's radical ideas about language and dramatic technique, Stramm moved away from the Naturalist and Symbolist influences that had marked such earlier works as *Sancta Susanna, Rudimentär,* and *Die Haidebraut.* He rejected conventions such as dialogue, monologue, and even, in his later works, character, focusing instead on action, gesture, and pantomime. Indeed, as Marx pointed out, German critic Julius Bab considered Stramm's plays to be "mystical pantomime texts with spoken interjections." Abandoning syntax, Stramm used only the present tense and rejected almost all words except verbs. Marx wrote that Stramm created "a word synthesis [that] often became more than the sum of the individual parts. Thus, one scene in *Happening*

[*Geschehen*] ended with these words: 'Screams (Flicker, swish, pile up, heap, press, choke, tremble, stretch, die, flicker). Sweep Rush Thunder Quake Abyss Rage Night.' "

Critic Jeremy Adler, in a piece in *Publications of the English Goethe Society,* explained that Stramm was able to convey complex and subtle meanings in his work with a bare minimum of speech and action. Showing how Stramm used only six words and twelve gestures in the first scene of his last—and in Adler's view, best—play, *Geschehen,* the critic remarked that the playwright "presents a familiar pattern of relationships in its entirety, with all its complexities and ambiguities," adding that, for Stramm, "one word has the weight of a whole speech in a traditional drama, for . . . it is not a reduction in meaning which Stramm seeks, but a reduction in means and a proportional increase in meaning." This interest in compression can also be seen in Stramm's earlier plays. *Sancta Susanna,* in which a nun experiences sensual and religious ecstasy and is stoned for it by the other members of her convent, takes up only ten pages in the collected edition of Stramm's works and fewer than 650 words are spoken in the whole play. But, Adler argued, the stage directions "integrate word, gesture, action and environment into one symbolic whole," adding that "it is not simply as a one-act play, but as the compression of a classical drama that *Sancta Susanna* can best be understood." Paul Hindemith used the play as the libretto for his third opera in 1921; when it was performed the following year, it provoked intense controversy from both the literary world and the Church. Hindemith later repudiated this work.

Stramm's poems, too—many of which were written from the military front, where the writer was posted as an officer after the outbreak of World War I—are distinguished by their experimental use of language. Jones explained that Stramm developed a style that, increasingly, focused on the individual word, personified abstract concepts, and rejected normal syntax in favor of word associations. One of the most distinctive features of Stramm's work, according to Jones, is the single-word line. Adler, too, noted the "frequently staccato" effect of Stramm's later poems, which the critic saw not as a rejection of poetry but "a return to the fundamentals of poetry, to the single stress and to the root of the word, at the very moment when the whole culture was threatened." He pointed out that the poem "Abend," written at the front and the second-shortest among all Stramm's poems, comes very close to T. S. Eliot's ideal that, in rare instances, " 'a word can be made to insinuate the whole history of a language and a civilization.' "

Though many critics emphasize the radical aspects of Stramm's use of language, Richard Sheppard, in a *Journal of European Studies* article, suggested that more importance must be given to Stramm's experience of war and how its traumas affected his writing. "Despite its surface realism," Sheppard wrote, "Stramm's poetry is, to an extent which has not always been appreciated, the product of an imagination which was informed by a highly conservative, classical set of beliefs" such as a faith in a metaphysically ordered universe and a respect for poetry as, in Sheppard's words, "a means of mirroring and celebrating what is pure and enduring." What is crucial in Stramm's work, Sheppard argued, is the "immense gap between [his] ideal beliefs and the implications of his experience, especially after the outbreak of war." The critic quoted from Stramm's letters home from the front to convey the extent of his shock and horror; in a letter to his wife in 1915, Stramm described the "howling of the heavy shells" as the noises of wild beasts, and declared, "It was not world, but underworld." He expressed a similar sense of unreality in a 1914 letter to Walden: "Wretched, cowardly, treacherous terror, and the very air sniggers sneeringly as well and gurgles and thunders down from the mountains. . . . It's none of it true and all of it a lie."

Stramm, Sheppard explained, had been excited about his awareness that reality was composed not of static objects but of dynamic energies, but "whereas, in the days of peace, Stramm had . . . been able to reconcile [that dynamic] theoretically with a sense of inherent providential order, his experience of war opened up an ever-widening gap between those two concepts." This erosion of faith led Stramm to further experiments with syntax; these new linguistic patterns, Sheppard suggested, "diminish[ed] the elements that make for synthesis and connectedness" in language. Indeed, the critic went on to claim: "As the War went on, Stramm increasingly lost his faith in the necessary, and, in the strict sense, essential connection between language and reality, and, concomitantly, in the ability of language to pin things down." Aware that the very tradition of literature as a reflection of reality was under threat in his era, Stramm "was increasingly compelled to forgo that ease of expression which betokens an imagination at one with its own assumptions, and to resort to a tortured mode of writing in which the poet seeks to grasp and stabilize those forces." Reading Stramm's poetry as "a conflict between two simultaneously present but fundamentally irreconcilable belief systems," Sheppard pointed out that Stramm "experienced those dilemmas . . . as acutely painful problems which involved his whole personality, not just his abstracting intellect, and it is for this reason that his strange, challenging poetry will continue to intrigue long after so much of the autistic inflation which currently passes for 'theory' has been consigned to the waste-paper baskets of intellectual history."

In 1913, Stramm was made a captain in the Prussian Army. During World War I, he saw action on both the eastern and western fronts. He survived more than seventy battles, and became perversely fascinated, according to Sheppard, with the "primal violence of battle." In a 1914 letter to Walden, quoted by the critic, Stramm wrote: "We ourselves are demons and laugh at all the others. That's how the soldier in the field feels. . . . He kicks the earth and shoots the sky / Heaven to death. And horror is within him and around him, he himself is horror." Stramm was killed during an attack in the Rokitno Swamps, Gorodenka, Russia, on September 1, 1915.

After Stramm's death, Walden continued the task of publishing his work. Walden published *Du: Liebesgedichte,* the first collection of Stramm's poems, in 1915. These early poems, according to Christoph Herin in the *Encyclopedia of World Literature,* explored "love as a cosmic experience" and eroticism in all its manifestations, "from the sacred to the profane." Stramm's wartime poems, included with his earliest poems in the 1919 collection *Tropfblut,* are "impressionistic sketches of war and death or abstract word groupings." Stramm's later plays, including *Erwachen, Kräfte,* and *Geschehen,* were also published posthumously. Herin also observed that his work influenced the Dada movement and "foreshadowed the techniques of modern concrete poetry."

BIOGRAPHICAL/CRITICAL SOURCES:

BOOKS

Adler, Jeremy, and John J. White, editors, *August Stram: Kritische Essays und unveröffentlichtes Quellenmaterial aus dem Nachlaß des Dichters,* Erich Schmidt Verlag (Berlin, Germany), 1979, pp. 158-164.

Encyclopedia of World Literature in the Twentieth Century, St. James Press (Detroit, MI), 1999, pp. 230-231.

PERIODICALS

Drama Review, Volume 19, 1975, Henry Marx, "August Stramm," pp. 13-17.

Forum for Modern Language Studies, October, 1982, Karin von Abrams, "The *Du* of August Stramm's *Liebesgedichte,*" pp. 299-312.

German Life and Letters, January, 1980, Jeremy Adler, "The Arrangement of the Poems in Stramm's *Du:/ Liebesgedichte,*" pp. 124-134.

Journal of European Studies, December, 1985, Richard Sheppard, "The Poetry of August Stramm: A Suitable Case for Deconstruction," pp. 261-294; September, 1996, Sheppard, "August Stramm: Beitrage zu Leben, Werk, und Wirkung," p. 351.

Publications of the English Goethe Society, Volume 44, 1974, Jeremy Adler, "On the Centenary of August Stramm: An Appreciation of *Geschehen, Rudimentär, Sancta Susanna,* and 'Abend,' " pp. 1-40.

Seminar, November, 1977, Malcolm Jones, "The Cult of August Stramm in *Der Sturm,*" pp. 257-269.*

*   *   *

STRAUSS, Darin

PERSONAL: Male. *Education:* New York University, graduate of creative writing program.

ADDRESSES: Office—c/o Sara Golier, Senior Publicist, Penguin/Putnam/Dutton, 375 Hudson St., New York, NY 10014. *E-mail*—darinstrauss@hotmail.com.

CAREER: Author of novels and short fiction.

WRITINGS:

Chang and Eng (novel), Dutton (New York, NY), 2000.

Contributor to periodicals, including *Gentleman's Quarterly* and *Time Out.*

WORK IN PROGRESS: A novel.

SIDELIGHTS: Darin Strauss's first novel, *Chang and Eng,* is a fictional account of the lives of the brothers for whom the term "Siamese twins" was coined. Born to a fisherman and his wife in 1811 in Siam, the twins, conjoined at the chest by a seven-inch ligament, led fairly normal lives until they were six years old. King Rama, who considered them a sign of bad luck, had them seized with the intention of killing them but then decided to display them at court. In 1825 a promoter brought the twins to the United States where they were incorporated into the sideshow of P. T. Barnum. They later married sisters, moved to North Carolina, and fathered a total of twenty-one children. *Time* contributor Paul Gray felt that "the most winning—and moving—

chapters . . . involve the love that blooms, recipro-cally, between the brothers and Adelaide and Sarah Yates."

The novel is narrated by Eng, the quiet brother who reads the Bible and Shakespeare. Eng longs to be free of his brother, whose drinking is affecting Eng. The more outgoing Chang does not want to be separated, and enjoys being a performer. *Library Journal* reviewer Douglas McClemont reflected that "the 'distance' be-tween the twins is at first intriguing, but one comes to crave more details about the relationship." McClemont noted that little is written about P. T. Barnum, who made the brothers rich and famous. Michiko Kakutani wrote in the *New York Times Book Review* that Strauss's debut novel is "spirited and promising," and added that he "does not dwell on the humiliations Chang and Eng are forced to undergo as performers; he gives us just enough glimpses of their experience to make us understand their plight as double outsiders—foreigners mocked as both 'Chinamen' and 'mon-sters.' "

A *Publishers Weekly* reviewer judged that "Strauss's vivid imagination, assiduous research, and instinctive empathy find expression in a vigorous, witty prose style that seduces the reader and delivers gold in a provoca-tive story of two extraordinary men." In a *Booklist* re-view Brian Kenney called *Chang and Eng* "a wonderful piece of storytelling" and felt "the real magic lies in the emotional closeness Strauss achieves."

BIOGRAPHICAL/CRITICAL SOURCES:

PERIODICALS

Booklist, May 1, 2000, Brian Kenney, review of *Chang and Eng,* p. 1654.
Library Journal, April 15, 2000, Douglas McClemont, review of *Chang and Eng,* p. 125.
New York Times Book Review, July 28, 2000, Michiko Kakutani, "Inseparable Brothers in Life and Love."
Publishers Weekly, April 10, 2000, review of *Chang and Eng,* p. 73; July 17, 2000, Bridget Kinsella, "A Hard Sell, but a Handsell," p. 87.
Time, June 12, 2000, Paul Gray, "Doubly Good: A Winning First Novel about Siamese Twins," p. 86.
Wall Street Journal, June 2, 2000, Kate Flatley, review of *Chang and Eng,* p. W10.*

STREET, Aurora
  See SOVA, Dawn B(everly)

                              *   *   *

STRINGER, Lee   1952?-

PERSONAL: Born c. 1952, in New York, NY.

ADDRESSES: Home—Mamaroneck, NY. *Office*—c/o Seven Stories Press, 140 Watts St., New York, NY 10013-1738.

CAREER: Writer. Co-owner of graphic design com-pany, New York City, c. 1970s.

WRITINGS:

Grand Central Winter: Stories From the Street, fore-word by Kurt Vonnegut, Seven Stories Press (New York, NY), 1998.
(With Kurt Vonnegut) *Like Shaking Hands with God: A Conversation about Writing,* Seven Stories Press (New York, NY), 1999.

Editor and contributor of column "Ask Homey" to *Street News.* Contributor to periodicals, including *Na-tion, New York Times,* and *Newsday.*

SIDELIGHTS: A former homeless drug addict, Lee Stringer rose above his troubles in large part through a natural talent for writing. A native of New York City, he describes the unseen side of 1980s Manhattan in his 1998 volume, *Grand Central Winter: Stories from the Street.* In this autobiographical work, Stringer provides an unflinching, unsentimental account of himself and his street comrades and describes the hardship many of the city's homeless must endure to stay alive. Intro-duced to the author as he sits in his "hole"—"this long, narrow crawl space in Grand Central's lover regions" where he makes his home atop a pile of cast-off blan-kets surrounded by a wall of cardboard positioned to keep "any rats at bay"—readers follow Stringer on a tour of his old haunts, including Central Park, Central Booking, and Grand Central Station.

John Jiler, in a review of *Grand Central Winter* for the *New York Times Book Review,* characterized the work as "born of pain but delivered with style and heart." "Love, pride, pity, compassion, dignity, hatred, long-ing," declared a reviewer for the *San Francisco Chroni-cle;* "It is the confrontation of these contradictory human elements that makes *Grand Central Winter . . .* such a provocative and haunting memoir." Despite such high praise, Stringer remains modest about his work, telling *CNN Interactive* interviewer Peg Tyre, "I didn't know what I was doing. I just kind of fumbled my way through it."

Stringer, who once co-owned a graphic design business, suffered greatly when his brother and business partner died. Shortly thereafter, he went into a tailspin of drinking and drugs, was evicted from his apartment, and landed on the street, where he languished. After several years on the street, Stringer discovered he had a talent for writing, composing his first story with the pencil he used to clean his crack pipe. for twelve years until he completed his novel. He began writing for a homeless newspaper called *Street News,* and his writing became so popular that he was eventually appointed editor of the newspaper. His confidence boosted, Stringer began to work on compiling his columns into *Grand Central Winter,* a work Kurt Vonnegut dubbed "beguiling and seductive" in his foreword to the work. Stringer's book, noted Vonnegut, proves "that writers are born, not made."

BIOGRAPHICAL/CRITICAL SOURCES:

PERIODICALS

Independent, September 3, 1998, Damian Fowler, "The Pen Is Mightier than the Rock," p. S8.
New York Times Book Review, June 28, 1998.

OTHER

CNN Interactive, http://europe.cnn.com/ (July 1, 1998), Peg Tyre, "Homeless Author Finds Home in the Pages of His Book."
Salon, http://www.salonmagazine.com (July 1, 1998), Matthew Flamm, "From Crackhead to Literary Star."
USA Today, http://www.usatoday.com/ (June 22, 1999), Bob Minzesheimer, "Writer Goes from Homeless to Homage.*

*   *   *

SUTPHEN, Joyce   1949-

PERSONAL: Born August 10, 1949, in St. Cloud, MN; daughter of Robert B. and Rita Marie Rassier; married Jeffrey Carlyle Sutphen, 1971 (divorced, 1996); chil-

dren: Sarah, Alicia, Marna. *Education:* University of Minnesota, B.A., M.A., Ph.D.

ADDRESSES: Home—110928 Van Hertzen Cir., Chaska, MN 55318. *Office*—Gustavus Adolphus College, 800 College Ave., St. Peter, MN 56082. *E-mail*—jsutphen@gac.edu.

CAREER: Gustavus Adolphus College, St. Peter, MN, visiting lecturer, 1993-97, assistant professor, 1997—.

MEMBER: Shakespeare Association of America.

AWARDS, HONORS: Barnard New Women's Poets Prize, 1994; Eunice Tutjean's Memorial Prize for poetry, 1996.

WRITINGS:

Straight out of View (poetry), Beacon Press (Boston, MA), 1995.
Coming Back to the Body (poetry), Holy Cow! (Minneapolis, MN), 2000.

WORK IN PROGRESS: A memoir of the author's farm childhood in the 1950s; research on Shakespeare's sonnets and on memory and Shakespeare.

SIDELIGHTS: Joyce Sutphen told *CA:* "Here's what happens when I sit down to write a poem. I think that I will say something about this, but I end up writing about that. I have a catch in my heart (lump in my throat? whatever it is that Robert Frost says gets the poem going), and I am thinking about my brothers and sisters and all of the musical instruments they can play. My mind is filled with trombones, saxophones, trumpets, and drums. The brass glints, the black and white piano keys appear, and I begin caressing words: embouchure, vibrato, andante, and resin. I think of fingerings and positions, of tonguing and sustaining the last sweet note. I never realized how much music is like sex—how the technical aspects of music and sex share a vocabulary. I have a different poem in mind now from the one I was going to write, but to be honest I probably wouldn't have gotten this far.

"I don't always come away with a poem. Sometimes all I have is a notebook filled with starts, a few lines here, lots of crossed out lines there, a space and another couple of lines. In the last year or so my pages are filled with the funny marks I use to keep track of the poem's meter. Sometimes—but only rarely—there are columns of rhyming or slant rhyming words down the side of a page. Other times there are phone numbers, names of

songs I heard on the radio, directions to a party in dou-
ble-lined boxes. 'This is not a poem!' the boxes say,
'this is a reminder,' but sometimes when I go back to
read them, they have become more like poems.

"Sometimes I go back to thinking that it's all nothing
but what the preacher called it: vanity, vanity. These
thoughts dissolve quickly when I remember what life
was like without poetry, when all I had was the holy
hush of ancient sacrifice. Poetry makes the world real
for me.

"Two reasons keep me coming to the empty page: the
desire to make a place for the glinting shard, the divine
detail, and the hope that this caressing, this pressing
against the visible will reveal the invisible. In the end,
it isn't hard: when I sit down to write a poem, one thing
just leads to another."

T

TADIE, Jean-Yves 1936-

PERSONAL: Born September 7, 1936, in Paris, France; son of Henri and Marie (Ferester) Tadie; married Arlette Khoury; children: Alexis, Benoit, Jerome. *Education:* Ecole Normale Superieure, Lic. es Lettres, 1956; University of Paris, Sorbonne, D. es Lettres, 1971; Oxford University, M.A., 1988. *Avocational interests:* Opera, antique books, tennis.

ADDRESSES: Office—University of Paris, Sorbonne, 1 Rue Victor Cousin, 75005 Paris, France.

CAREER: University of Paris III, professor, 1970-88; Cairo University, head of French Department, 1972-76; French Institute, London, England, director, 1976-81; All Souls College, Oxford, England, fellow, 1988-91; Oxford University, Marshal Foch professor, 1988-91; University of Paris, Sorbonne, Paris, France, professor of French literature, 1988—. Editor, Gallimard Press, Paris, France, 1991—.

MEMBER: Anglo-Belgian Club, British Academy (fellow).

AWARDS, HONORS: National Book Critics Circle Award nomination, 2000, for *Marcel Proust: A Life.*

WRITINGS:

Introduction à la vie littéraire du XIXe siècle, Bordas (Paris, France), 1970.
Lectures de Proust, A. Colin (Paris, France), 1971.
Proust et le roman: essai sur les formes et techniques du roman dans "À la recherche du temps perdu," Gallimard (Paris, France), 1971.
Le récit poétique, PUF (Paris, France), 1978.
Le roman d'adventures, PUF (Paris, France), 1982.

Proust, P. Belfond (Paris, France), 1983.
La critique littéraire au XXe siècle, P. Belfond (Paris, France), 1987.
(Editor) Marcel Proust, *À la recherche du temps perdu,* (title means "In Search of Lost Time"; previously translated as "Remembrance of Things Past"), 4 volumes, Gallimard (Paris, France), 1987-88.
Le roman au XXe siècle, P. Belfond (Paris, France), 1990.
(Editor) Nathalie Sarraute, *Oeuvres complètes,* Gallimard (Paris, France), 1996.
Marcel Proust: biographie, Gallimard (Paris, France), 1996, translation by Euan Cameron published as *Marcel Proust: A Life,* Viking (New York, NY), 2000.
Marcel Proust: la cathédrale du temps, Gallimard (Paris, France), 1999.
Marcel Proust: l'écriture et les arts, Gallimard (Paris, France), 1999.
(With Mark Tadié) *Le sens de la mémoire,* Gallimard (Paris, France), 1999.

Also contributor of essays to periodicals.

SIDELIGHTS: Jean-Yves Tadie is a French nonfiction author, editor, and educator. He is widely considered to be among the world's foremost scholars of Marcel Proust. He teaches at the Sorbonne in Paris, where he has been a professor of French literature since 1988.

Marcel Proust: biographie, published in the United States as *Marcel Proust: A Life,* is a comprehensive biography of the great twentieth-century French writer. The work focuses on Proust's written works, following his own dictum that writers should be judged by their works as opposed to the facts of their individual lives. The work was a bestseller in France and received a National Book Critics Circle Award nomination in 2000. Tadie is "completely at home in the complex culture that spawned the genius" of Proust, commented Daniel Mark Epstein in *New Criterion.* "It is not hard to imagine M. Tadie himself, witty, proud, and a trifle long-winded, as a character in *The Guermantes Way.*"

The work was published to critical acclaim in France, and its English-language counterpart also received accolades by many critics. "Tadie's new biography is itself a model of the genre," wrote Barbara Hoffert in *Library Journal,* "richly informed and as engrossing as the novel [*In Search of Lost Time*] itself. Like Proust, Tadie has delivered a masterpiece."

Other critics, however, found fault with *Marcel Proust: A Life.* Michiko Kakutani in the *New York Times* felt that Tadie's biography shed no new light, either into Proust the man or on his mammoth work. Kakutani described the work as "an exercise designed not for the reader's edification or pleasure but to showcase the author's own erudition and prodigious capacity for research." Jean Charbonneau in the *Denver Post,* along similar lines, felt that the "wealth of details is indigestible at times." It takes an immense amount of effort, noted Charbonneau, to read Proust's entire *Remembrance of Things Past,* and "the same could be said for his [Tadie's] biography." The majority of critics, however, were positive in their reviews. Henry L. Carrigan, Jr., in the *Holland Sentinel,* argued that Tadie's biography of Proust was "a majestic accomplishment well worth every moment spent reading it." Ron Ratliff in *Library Journal* noted that in the work, Tadie explores not only Proust's novels, but also the books, paintings, music and other influences on the great novelist that led to the publication of his masterwork. Ratliff lauded *Marcel Proust: A Life* as a "magnificent biography, certain to be a standard for years to come."

BIOGRAPHICAL/CRITICAL SOURCES:

PERIODICALS

Booklist, June 1, 2000, Bryce Christensen, review of *Marcel Proust: A Life,* p. 1838.
French Studies, April, 1992, John Cruickshank, review of *Le roman au XXe siècle,* p. 234.
New Criterion, October, 2000, Daniel Mark Epstein, review of *Marcel Proust,* p. 13.
Library Journal, August, 2000, Ron Ratliff, review of *Marcel Proust,* p. 104; September 1, 2000, Barbara Hoffert, review of *Marcel Proust,* p. 207.
New York Review of Books, March 18, 1999, Roger Shattuck, review of Marcel Proust, *A la recherche du temps perdu,* p. 10.

New York Times, September 5, 2000, Michiko Kakutani, review of *Marcel Proust,* p. B8.
New York Times Book Review, September 17, 2000, Roger Pearson, review of *Marcel Proust,* p. 16.
Times Literary Supplement, October 4, 1996, review of *Marcel Proust,* p. 3.

OTHER

Denver Post, http://www.denverpost.com/ (August 20, 2000), Jean Charbonneau, review of *Marcel Proust.*
Holland Sentinel, http://www.thehollandsentinel.com/ (December 10, 2000), Henry L. Carrigan, Jr., review of *Marcel Proust.*
Spike Magazine, http://www.spikemagazine,com/ (February, 2000), Stephen Mitchelmore, review of *Marcel Proust.**

* * *

TAYLOR, Judith M. 1934-

PERSONAL: Born July 26, 1934, in London, England; daughter of Max (an optometrist and writer) and Fanny (an office manager) Mundlak; married Irvin S. Taylor (a medical doctor), November 23, 1961; children: David Henry, Hugh Benjamin. *Education:* University of Oxford, Somerville College, B.A., 1956, M.A., 1959; Oxford University Medical School, B.M., B.Ch., 1959. *Avocational interests:* Reading, music, cooking.

ADDRESSES: Home—2121 Broadway, Apt. #5, San Francisco, CA 94115; fax: 415-563-3741. *E-mail*—jtaylor196@aol.com.

CAREER: Resident in Neurology, Kings County Hospital Centre, 1960-61, and Bronx Municipal Hospital Centre, 1961-65; attending physician, Burke Rehabilitation Centre (White Plains, NY), 1965-75, and Bronx Municipal Hospital Centre (Bronx, NY), The Hospital of the Albert Einstein College of Medicine (Bronx, NY), White Plains Hospital (White Plains, NY), Lawrence Hospital (Bronxville, NY), and Philps Memorial Hospital (North Tarrytown, NY), 1965-78; Albert Einstein College of Medicine, Bronx, NY, clinical instructor in neurology, 1967-76, associate clinical professor of neurology, 1976-82, appointment in History of Medicine Department, 1976; Woodhull Medical and Mental Health Center, Brooklyn NY, medical director, and president of Medical Associates of Woodhull, PC, 1982-83; Mobile Health Services, Pelham Manor, NY, medical director, 1983-86; Travelers Health Network of New York and New Jersey (The Travelers Insurance Company), director of medical administration, 1986-92; Tristate Health Care Management: New York, New Jersey and Southern Connecticut (Prudential Insurance Company), director of medical services, 1992-94. Professional appointments with various organizations, including Institute for Health Care, United Hospital Fund, 1977-78, and Division of Health Sciences, Rockefeller Foundation, 1979; consultant, including work for Rockefeller Foundation, 1980-81, Woodhull Task Force, 1981-82, New York State Department of Health, Bureau of Medical Management Systems, 1981-83, and New York City Health and Hospitals Corporation, 1981-83; presenter in academic venues. Medical licenses in New York, New Jersey, Connecticut, North Carolina, all currently in senior status; board certificates include American Board of Psychiatry and Neurology (Neurology), 1966, American Board of Qualification in Electroencephalography, 1976, and American Board of Quality Assurance and Utilization Review, 1991.

MEMBER: New York Academy of Medicine (fellow), American College of Physician Executives, Medical Administrators' Conference.

AWARDS, HONORS: Jane Willis Kirkaldy Prize in Science, Somerville College, University of Oxford, 1955; Physicians' Recognition Award, American Medical Association (CME), 1976.

WRITINGS:

The Olive in California: History of an Immigrant Tree, Ten Speed (Berkeley, CA), 2000.

Contributor of scientific works to various books and periodicals, including *Nature, Neurology, AMA Archives of Neurology, Journal of Neurosurgery, Neurology,* and *Ophthalmology.* Author of column, "Doctor at Play," *Bulletin of the Westchester County Medical Society,* 1971-74.

WORK IN PROGRESS: California's Gardens—Past and Present, for Ten Speed.

SIDELIGHTS: Judith M. Taylor told *CA:* "One does what comes easily. As a child, I was able to write school essays without too much difficulty, and received high grades. This reinforcement was valuable. My father was an amateur writer who had had several books published. Both my sons had books published. Pride

demanded that I too join this family endeavor. After all, had I not always been told I was good at writing.

"While I was engaged in the practice of neurology, I wrote a number of cameo pieces for the local medical journals in New York, as well as academic articles. A book eluded me. I certainly had no gift for fiction. It was not until we retired to California and planted a truly California garden that the inspiration and key idea arose.

"Northern California has a Mediterranean climate, and I decided to plant two dozen olive trees. They are ineffably lovely and I wanted to find out more about them. No book existed. It dawned on me that in this situation I should be the one to write the book. Never mind that I knew no more than the average well-educated person about these trees, the notion kept going around and around in my head, giving me no peace. The result was *The Olive in California: History of an Immigrant Tree.*

"It was as if a flood gate then opened. Doing the research, and traveling all over the state to learn about its history and the stories of people who had grown olive trees all their lives, was so enriching that the book was almost just a bonus.

"The principal influence on my writing style was the English teacher at my school in London, back in the dark ages when things were still very strict. Seven years at Oxford honed those skills. When you have to write an essay every week during term for four years about a wide range of scientific topics and defend them to your tutor, your writing develops a lot of polish.

"Among modern writers, John McPhee is one of my icons. He combines encyclopaedic knowledge with a riveting narrative, a narrative which yet has a slight crisp edge to it. Kevin Starr is another model. His ability to see unique aspects of even quite ordinary events and clothe them in golden prose continues to amaze me."

*   *   *

**ter BALKT, H(erman) H(endrik)   1938-
(Foel Aos, Habakuk II de Balker)**

PERSONAL: Born September 17, 1938, in Enschede, Netherlands.

ADDRESSES: Office—c/o De Bezige Bij, P.O. Box 75184, 1070 AD, Amsterdam, Netherlands.

CAREER: Teacher.

MEMBER: Vereniging van Letter kundigen.

AWARDS, HONORS: Poetry Prize, Municipality of Amsterdam, 1973; Triennial Gnome of the East Prize, 1975.

WRITINGS:

Hemellichten, Harmonie (Amsterdam, Netherlands), 1983.
How to Start a Wine Cellar: Selected Poems, 1969-1984, translated by Wanda Boeke and others, introduction by Johanna H. Prins, S. Rollins (Amsterdam, Netherlands), 1984.
Aardes deuren, Harmonie (Amsterdam, Netherlands), 1987.
Het strand van Amsterdam, Ravenberg Pers (Oosterbeek, Netherlands), 1990.
In de kalkbranderij van het absolute (poems), Bezige Bij (Amsterdam, Netherlands), 1990.
Ode aan de Grote Kiezelwal en andere gedichten (poems), Bezige Bij (Amsterdam, Netherlands), 1992.
Laaglandse hymnen, Bezige Bij (Amsterdam, Netherlands), 1993.
Tegen de biljen: Oden en anti-oden, Bezige Bij (Amsterdam, Netherlands), 1998.

Other writings include *Ulier van t Ooston,* 1970; *De Gloeilampen/De Varkens,* 1972; *Groenboek,* 1973; *Zwijg,* 1973; *Ikonen,* 1974; *Oud Gereedschap Mensheid Moe,* 1975; *Hegeel Landjuweel,* 1977; *Gilleleje,* 1993; *Gebad aan de razernij,* 1995; *Op de rotonden,* 1996; and (under pseudonym Habakuk II de Balker) *Boerengedichten,* 1969; also uses the pseudonym Foel Aos. Work represented in anthologies, including *Nieuw verschenen: Een bloemlezing met nooit eerder in boekvorm verschenen werk,* Herfstschrift (Groningen, Netherlands), 1984; *Het Overijssels landschap,* photographs by Ger Dekkers, Waanders (Zwolle, Netherlands), 1992; and *Eine Jacke aus Sand: Poesie aus den Niederlanden* (poems in Dutch, with German translations and commentary), edited by Gregor Laschen, Wirtschaftsverlag NW Verlag für neue Wissenchaft (Bremerhaven, Germany), 1993. Contributor to periodicals, including *De Revisor.**

THIBODEAU, David 1969(?)-

PERSONAL: Born c. 1969, in ME; married, wife's name, Michele (deceased); children: Serenity (deceased).

ADDRESSES: Agent—c/o PublicAffairs, 250 West 57th St., Ste. 1321, New York, NY 10107.

CAREER: Author, 1999—. Employee at marketing firm in Austin, TX. "Groovius Maximus" (funk rock band), drummer.

WRITINGS:

(With Leon Whiteson) *A Place Called Waco: A Survivor's Story,* PublicAffairs (New York, NY), 1999.

SIDELIGHTS: David Thibodeau, a former Branch Davidian who survived the raid at Waco in 1993, without imprisonment, has written a book encapsulating his experiences at Mount Carmel and with the sect's leader, David Koresh, who, he told *CNN.com* in an interview, "was more rational than people want to give him credit for. David Koresh was human in every sense of the word, but he had a teaching or, . . . he was given a wisdom that I believe was out of this world." A critic for *Kirkus Reviews* called Thibodeau's autobiographical account, *A Place Called Waco: A Survivor's Story,* "a surprisingly balanced and honest account of his time as a Branch Davidian."

Thibodeau himself comments on the motivation for the book, which involved dispelling the media-hyped stereotypes surrounding the tragedy. According to *Amazon.com* Thibodeau declares: "I wrote this book both to move on in my life and to set the record straight. It's for anyone who wonders what life was like at Mt. Carmel." Of the other members at Mount Carmel, Thibodeau wrote in *Salon,* "I met folks who hadn't finished high school, and others with degrees from places like Harvard law school. I spent time with African-Americans, Australians, black Britons, Mexican-Americans and more. One irony of the Waco disaster is that right-wing extremists and racists look to Mount Carmel as a beacon; if they realized that so many of us were black, Asian and Latino, and that we despised their hateful politics and anger, they would probably feel bitterly betrayed."

Booklist reviewer Eric Robbins described the book as "sometimes self-serving, largely revealing (perhaps not always intentionally)." A *Publishers Weekly* reviewer perceived a larger lesson in Thibodeau's book, one that goes beyond the actual events at Waco. "Admirably, Thibodeau never lapses into overstatement, and his book is far from an extremist apologia. Instead, it is an insider's account of an event that tested and found wanting the nation's tolerance for people who . . . were, apparently, for the most part, innocent of the charges leveled against them."

BIOGRAPHICAL/CRITICAL SOURCES:

PERIODICALS

Booklist, September 15, 1999, Eric Robbins, review of *A Place Called Waco: A Survivor's Story,* p. 228.
Kirkus Reviews, August, 1999, review of *A Place Called Waco.*
Library Journal, October 15, 1999, Michael Sawyer, review of *A Place Called Waco,* p. 85.
Publishers Weekly, August 30, 1999, review of *A Place Called Waco,* p. 63; September 13, 1999, Steven M. Zeitchik, "A Well-Timed Waco Book," p. 21.

OTHER

Charlotte Gusay Literary Agency, http://www.mediastudio.com/gusay/ (October 2, 2001), *A Place Called Waco.*
CNN.com, http://www3.cnn.com/2000/law/05/10/ (May 5, 2000), "Waco Survivor Says the Government is to Blame."
CNN.com, http://www9.cnn.com/community/transcripts/2000/8/2/ (August 2, 2000), interview with David Thibodeau.
Reason Online: Exclusive Interview with David Thibodeau, http://www.reason.com/ (October 4, 1999).
Salon, http://www.salon.com/news/feature/1999/09/09/waco/ (September 9, 1999), "The Truth About Waco."*

*   *   *

THOMAS, Robert L.   1928-

PERSONAL: Born June 4, 1928, in Atlanta, GA; married Joan D. Thomas, July 16, 1953; children: Barbara Erselivs, Robert Thomas, Jr., Jonathan Thomas, Mark Thomas, Michael Thomas. *Ethnicity:* "White." *Education:* Georgia Tech, B.M.E.; Dallas Theological Seminary, Th.D. *Religion:* Protestant.

ADDRESSES: Home—11582 Santa Cruz St., Stanton, CA 90680. *Office*—The Master's Seminary, 13248

Roscoe Blvd., Sun Valley, CA 91352; fax: 818-909-5725. *E-mail*—rthomas@thms.edu.

CAREER: Talbot Theological Seminary, La Mirada, CA, professor of New Testament, 1959-87; The Master's Seminary, Sun Valley, CA, professor of New Testament, 1987—. Former affiliations with Moody Bible Institute and Faith Theological Seminary. *Military service:* U.S. Army; became first lieutenant.

MEMBER: Evangelical Theological Society (president, 1989-90), IFCA International, Anaheim Community Church.

AWARDS, HONORS: Gold Medallion Book Award for the outstanding reference work of 1981-82, Evangelical Christian Publishers Association, for *New American Standard Exhaustive Concordance.*

WRITINGS:

A Harmony of the Gospels, Harper (New York, NY), 1978.
(General editor) *New American Standard Exhaustive Concordance,* Holman, 1981.
Revelations 1-7, an Exegetical Commentary, Moody, 1992.
Revelations 8-22, an Exegetical Commentary, Moody, 1992.
The Jesus Crisis, Kregel (Grand Rapids, MI), 1998.
Understanding Spiritual Gifts, a Verse-by-Verse Study of 1 Corinthians 12-14, revised edition, Kregel (Grand Rapids, MI), 1999.
How to Choose a Bible Version: An Introductory Guide to English Translations, Christian Focus, 2000.
Charts on the Gospels and the Life of Christ, Zondervan (Grand Rapids, MI), 2000.

Contributor to *Expositor's Bible Commentary,* Zondervan, 1978. Executive editor, *Master's Seminary Journal.* Translator of *New American Standard Bible* during the 1960s.

WORK IN PROGRESS: "Who Am I?" *The Christina View of Self,* for Christian Focus; *Hermeneutics; The New Vs. the Old,* for Kregel; research on "commentary on 2 Corinthians."

*   *   *

THOMPSON, Eugene Allen   1924-2001

OBITUARY NOTICE—See index for *CA* sketch: Born June 28, 1924, in San Francisco, CA; died of cancer,

April 14, 2001, in Los Angeles, CA. Novelist and scriptwriter. Thompson holds the record for writing the most scripts for the television series *Love, American Style,* and also wrote scripts for shows as varied as *Gilligan's Island, The Lucy Show, Marcus Welby, M.D.,* and *Columbo.* Thompson grew up in California and graduated from high school when he was sixteen. Leaving San Francisco for Los Angeles, Thompson connected with Groucho Marx and became the comedian's protégé. Marx insisted Thompson go to college, so Thompson enrolled and received a bachelor's in Greek, English and philosophy from the University of California at Berkeley. He worked in Germany in the early 1950s and returned to the United States to write copy for several advertising agencies. He returned to Hollywood in 1964 and began writing for television, where he stayed for ten years. After tiring of TV, Thompson began writing novels. His first novel, *Lupe,* was published in 1977 and dealt with a Chicano boy involved in the occult. Other titles include *Murder Mystery, Nobody Cared for Kate,* and *A Cup of Death.*

OBITUARIES AND OTHER SOURCES:

PERIODICALS

Los Angeles Times, April 18, 2001, p. B6.
New York Times, April 25, 2001, p. A21.

*　　*　　*

THORNE, Matt Lewis

PERSONAL: Female. Married John Thorne (a cook and writer).

ADDRESSES: Home—P.O. Box 778, Northampton, MA 01061.

CAREER: Writer.

AWARDS, HONORS: International Association of Culinary Professionals (IACP)/Julia Child Award for *Outlaw Cook;* IACP/Julia Child Award nomination for *Serious Pig: An American Cook in Search of his Roots; Simple Cooking* was named one of the *Saveur* One Hundred by *Saveur,* 1999; James Beard Culinary Award, James Beard Foundation/Kitchen Aid Book Awards, 2001, for *Pot on the Fire: Further Exploits of a Renegade Cook.*

WRITINGS:

(With husband, John Thorne) *Simple Cooking,* 1987.

(With John Thorne) *Outlaw Cook,* Farrar Straus Giroux (New York, NY), 1992.
(With John Thorne) *Serious Pig: An American Cook in Search of his Roots,* North Point Press, Farrar, Straus and Giroux (New York, NY), 1996.
(With John Thorne) *Pot on the Fire: Further Exploits of a Renegade Cook,* North Point Press (New York, NY), 2000.

Also publisher and writer of *Simple Cooking,* a bimonthly food newsletter, with husband John Thorne.

SIDELIGHTS: Matt Lewis Thorne, with her husband John Thorne, edits the bimonthly food newsletter *Simple Cooking.* The Thornes have also published four books on food and cooking. Many of their newsletter essays have appeared in their books. After titling their first book after their newsletter, they produced *Outlaw Cook.* According to Michael A. Lutes in *Library Journal,* the title is derived from "Thorne's insistence that people use recipes only as a guideline and experiment heavily according to individual tastes." Their book is for amateur cooks who just want to enjoy themselves, as they explain: "I think you don't have to be a good cook . . . to be an interested cook." The essays explore foods the Thornes love for their simple perfection, such as avocados; foods to which a people bond, such as *boeuf aux carottes* for the French during World War II; and food with personal meaning. The Thornes cover other aspects of cooking, from Martha Stewart's need to be loved, to a culinary epiphany evoked by Günter Grass's *The Tin Drum.* And they write about food and human life: "The genuinely interesting question about the food we eat is not where it comes from or who grows it or even which of it tastes the best, but why it wants to kill its father and sleep with its mother." The Thornes conclude their book urging a return to simpler culinary roots.

A *New Yorker* reviewer wrote of *Outlaw Cook,* "In its psychological penetrations, this is more a novel than a cookbook, but you get recipes, too." A *Publishers Weekly* critic added, "As in other collections of short, previously published works, the voice and pace of the essays may wane on repetition. . . . But in moderate spells, the essays delight with passion and originality." And, according to Barbara Jacobs in *Booklist,* "The 33 essays in this collection incite laughter, head nodding, argument, and admiration . . . peppered with quotes, salted with a dry, wry humor, and baked with enough miscellanea to satisfy any gourmand."

The Thornes' third book, *Serious Pig: An American Cook in Search of his Roots,* combines autobiography, culinary and regional history, and part cookbook. The book consists of three sections. "Here" is about the regional foods of Maine, the Thornes' home for more than a decade before they relocated to Northampton, Massachusetts. "There" is about Cajun and Creole food, and "Everywhere" is about the Thornes' trip to Texas in search of barbecue and chili. They convey not only the best way to make a dish, and its origins and development, but also its relationship to regional history. For example, they introduce Cajun roux by declaring "gumbo contains within itself the entire history of the Cajun diaspora." A *Publishers Weekly* reviewer wrote, "If these essays were recipes, they'd yield a rich and utterly unbalanced table of dishes likely to start readers thinking seriously about their own gustatory identities. The bibliography is better than dessert."

A reviewer in *January Magazine* called *Pot on the Fire: Further Exploits of a Renegade Cook* "a culinary expedition." Not unlike their previous three books, *Pot on the Fire* includes not just recipes, but also detailed literary discussions on food, the background behind each fare, and each dish's preparation.

BIOGRAPHICAL/CRITICAL SOURCES:

PERIODICALS

Booklist, October 1, 1992, Barbara Jacobs, review of *Outlaw Cook,* p. 226; November 15, 1996, Bill Ott, review of *Serious Pig: An American Cook in Search of his Roots,* p. 561.
Library Journal, November 15, 1992, Michael A. Lutes, review of *Outlaw Cook,* p. 94; November 15, 1996, John Charles, review of *Serious Pig,* p. 83.
New Yorker, March 22, 1993, review of *Outlaw Cook,* p. 111.
Publishers Weekly, October 26, 1992, review of *Outlaw Cook,* p. 65; October 21, 1996, review of *Serious Pig,* p. 66.

OTHER

Food Fun and Facts, http://www.foodfunandfacts.com/ (October 3, 2001), review of *Pot on the Fire: Further Exploits of a Renegade Cook.*
FSB Associates, http://www.fsbassociates.com/ (October 3, 2001), reviews of *Pot on the Fire* and *Serious Pig: An American Cook in Search of his Roots.*
January Magazine, http://www.januarymagazine.com/ features/ (October 3, 2001), review of *Pot on the Fire.*
Simple Cooking, http://www.outlawcook.com/ (October 3, 2001).*

THORP, Lillian 1914-

PERSONAL: Born January 16, 1914, in Guin, AL; daughter of Willis Manual (a farmer) and Martha Mariah (maiden name, Bowlan; a homemaker) Homer; married Lonnie Doyle Thorp, Sr. (a production control manager), December 24, 1931; children: Lonnie Doyle, Jr., Patricia Ann Hook, Donna Susanne Duhon, Tamara Jane Hines. *Ethnicity:* "English-Irish." *Education:* Attended Hills Business College and Draughan Business College. *Politics:* Democrat. *Religion:* Southern Baptist. *Avocational interests:* "Writing, music, camping, cake decorating, church activities, trips, family get-togethers, group and family cards, domino, etc., games, conversations, neighborhood association."

ADDRESSES: Agent—Chelsey Publishing, 1145 S.W. 23rd St., Suite 2, Oklahoma City, OK 73109-1603.

CAREER: Worked as secretary and administrative assistant, 1961-78.

MEMBER: American Association of Retired Persons (registrar), Poetry Society of Oklahoma, Oklahoma Writers and Federation of Writers, Roadrunner Camping Club, Airpark Neighborhood Watch Association (trustee).

AWARDS, HONORS: Golden Poet Award, *Who's Who in Poetry,* 1989, for poem "Be Yourself"; first place in humorous category, Vivian McCullough Memorial Award, 1994, for poem "Autopsy"; Editors' Preference Award for Excellence, Creative Arts and Science Enterprise, for poem "In Mother's Steps" (published in *Visions and Beyond*).

WRITINGS:

Edge of a Ledge (poems), 1993, revised edition, Chelsey (Oklahoma City, OK), 1996.
Patchwork Poetry (poems), 1995, revised edition, Chelsey (Oklahoma City, OK), 1996.
Poetic Delight (poems), 1996, revised edition, Chelsey (Oklahoma City, OK), 1997.
In Whose Shadow Do We Walk?: For My Children (autobiography), Chelsey (Oklahoma City, OK), 1997.

Also author of *Mom's Recipe Collection,* 1989; *Wiggle Willie* (children's chapbook), 1993; and *Poetry Fundamentals Simplified,* 1993. Contributor of poetry to *Visions and Beyond, A View from the Edge, Capitol Hill Beacon,* and *Writer's World.*

WORK IN PROGRESS: Another poetry book, for Chelsey.

SIDELIGHTS: Lillian Thorp told *CA:* "I love [writing]. It's fulfilling!. The inner urge, relatives, [and] friends [influence my work]. The magic of how I come to write poetry is still a mystery to me. So how can I tell you something I cannot understand myself. Little did I know one Easter Sunday morning that I would feel the urge to write my first verse of poetry, which was to change my entire goal in life.

"Thus, suddenly began my interest in poetry writing and have been writing ever since—influenced by experiences—others and mine, TV, etc.

"After writing 2,600 poems, three poetry books, a children's book, a cookbook and fundamentals of poetry, here I have in the last year, at eighty-two to eighty-three years of age, written the story of my life.

"My autobiography—curiosity about why my grandfather disappeared, leaving my grandmother with five children, expecting another when my mother was eight. I wanted my children and readers to know about my wonderful grandmother, my parents and the children's heritage. I needed to solve the mystery about where he went, if he remarried and had other children. Research into the matter for the book helped me solve the question in my mind.

"My grandmother and parents left a great heritage-shadow to follow. Before the book was finished, I learned my grandfather was a cheat—so *In Whose Shadow Do We Walk?* was born."

*   *   *

TIERNEY, Nathan (L.)   1953-

PERSONAL: Born March 16, 1953, in Wales; son of Leonard Tierney (a professor); married, August 25, 1985; wife's name, Helen; children: Lachlann, Kathleen. *Education:* University of Melbourne, B.A. (honors), 1975; Columbia University, Ph.D., 1989. *Politics:* "Constructive." *Religion:* Episcopalian.

ADDRESSES: Home—1634 Glenbrock Ln., Newbury Park, CA 91320. *Office*—Department of Philosophy, California Lutheran University, 60 West Olsea Rd., Thousand Oaks, CA 91360. *E-mail*—tierney@clunet.edu.

CAREER: California Lutheran University, Thousand Oaks, CA, professor of philosophy, 1990—. Philosophy in the Real World (ethics consultants), partner.

MEMBER: American Philosophical Association, National Association of Scholars.

WRITINGS:

Imagination and Ethical Ideals, State University of New York Press (Albany, NY), 1994.

WORK IN PROGRESS: Ethics for the Evolving Self.

SIDELIGHTS: Nathan Tierney told *CA:* "My work focuses on the juncture between theory and practice, especially in ethics. My goal is to contribute to new and constructive forms of philosophical understanding, and to counteract current trends toward decay and fragmentation in our society."

*   *   *

TIKKANEN, Märta   1935-

PERSONAL: Born April 3, 1935 in Helsinki, Finland; daughter of a prominent educator; married Henrik Tikkanen (a writer and artist), 1963 (died, 1984); children: five.

ADDRESSES: Office—c/o Soederstroem et Co., PB 97, 00210 Helsingfors, Finland.

CAREER: Novelist and poet. Worked as upper school teacher and director of an adult education institution.

AWARDS, HONORS: Suomi Prize, State Literature Committee, 1996, for *Personliga angelägenheter.*

WRITINGS:

Nu imorron (novel; title means "Now Tomorrow"), Söderström (Helsinki, Finland), 1970, Trevi (Stockholm, Sweden), 1970.
Ingenmansland (novel; title means "No-man's Land"), Söderström (Helsinki, Finland), 1972.
Vem bryr sej om Dori Mihailov? (novel; title means "Who Cares About Doris Mihailov?"), Söderström (Helsinki, Finland), 1974.
Män kan inte väldtas (novel), Trevi (Stockholm, Sweden), 1975, translation by Alison Weir published as *Manrape,* Virago (London, England), 1978.
Våldsam kärlek (play; title means "Violent Love"), 1979.

Århundradets Kärlekssaga (poems), Trevi (Stockholm, Sweden), 1978, Söderström, (Helsinki, Finland), 1978, translation by Stina Katchadourian published as *Love Story of the Century,* Borgo Press (San Bernadino, CA), 1984.

Mörkret som ger glädjen djup (poems; title means "The Darkness That Gives Depth to Joy"), Trevi (Stockholm, Sweden), 1981.

Sofias egen bok (nonfiction; title means "Sofia's Own Book"), Söderström (Helsinki, Finland), 1982.

Rödluvan (title means "Little Red Ridinghood"), Trevi (Stockholm, Sweden), 1986.

Storfångaren (title means "The Great Huntsmen"), Söderström (Helsinki, Finland), 1989.

Arnaía kastad i havet (poems), Söderström (Helsinki, Finland), 1992.

Personliga angelägenheter (title means "Personal Affairs," novel), Söderström (Helsinki, Finland).

Sofia vuxen med sitt MBD (title means "Sofia Grown-up With Her ADHD"), Trevi (Stockholm, Sweden), 1998.

Tikkanen's work has also appeared in the anthology *Du tror du kuvar mig liv?*

ADAPTATIONS: *Manrape* was made into a film by Jörn Donner in 1978.

SIDELIGHTS: One of Finland's most popular authors, Märta Tikkanen has written several volumes of autobiographical fiction and poetry. Her work is characteristically imbued with strong feminist values, and provides intimate details of the tribulations she has endured as the wife of an alcoholic husband.

Daughter of a distinguished educator, Tikkanen, who writes in Swedish, found work early in her career at Helsinki's Swedish-language newspaper, *Hufvudstadsbladet,* and later obtained a teaching position in an upper school before becoming the director of an adult education institution. After her first marriage ended in divorce, she wed the well-known writer and artist Henrik Tikkanen (1924-1984), who was known as an extraordinarily talented but difficult man. Though devoted to her alcoholic and emotionally abusive husband, Tikkanen was also able to develop an understanding of how male domination affected her life and those of countless women of her time. She expressed these insights both in activist work as a leader of northern Europe's feminist movement, and perhaps even more influentially in her writing.

Critics agree that Tikkanen's novels and poems are highly autobiographical. Her novels *Nu imorron* and *Ingenmansland* describe the marriage between an alcoholic, unfaithful, and jealous husband and his loving but frustrated wife, who grows to realize that the unhealthy relationship undermines her own talents. According to George C. Schoolfield in *Encyclopedia of World Literature,* these books are a "somewhat fictionalized" portrayal of Tikkanen's own marriage. She went on to write *Vem bryr sej om Dori Mihailov?,* the story of a lonely and abused single mother, and then the novel that brought her international fame, *Män kan inte väldtas.* This book, translated into several languages and adapted as a film in 1978, tells the story of a divorcee who is raped by a man after she goes with him to his apartment. Bent on revenge, she later rapes him. *Love Story of the Century,* a collection of narrative prose poems, returns more directly to the story of Tikkanen's relationship with her husband. In Schoolfield's view, the book can be seen as an act of revenge against Henrik Tikkanen for his complaints against his wife. "Concentrating not only on the husband's drunkenness but his egocentricity," the critic observed, "the book . . . reached a huge audience of women who found it a reflection, in some measure, of their own marital lot." The book's "bitter story of an unbearable but evidently inescapable relationship," in Schoolfield's words, was especially popular in Germany.

During the 1980s, Tikkanen went on to explore other themes. *Mörkret som ger glädjen djup* is the fictionalized tale of the nineteenth century Finnish-Swedish poet Josef Julius Wecksell, who went mad in his twenties, and his intense relationship with his mother. *Sofias egen bok,* a work of nonfiction, presents the story of Tikkanen's youngest daughter, Sofia, who was diagnosed with Minimal Brain Dysfunction—a condition known in the U.S. as Attention Disorder/Hyperactivity Disorder (HDAD). At the time, the condition was little known and families obtained inadequate professional support; Tikkanen recounts Sofia's frequent seizures, extensive regimen of medications, and frustrating experiences with school, peers, and job. In 1998, Tikkanen updated Sofia's story with *Sofia vuxen med sitt MBD,* a book *World Literature Today* reviewer Margareta Mattsson deemed an "unsentimental presentation of a chronic condition, composed in an admirably clear and light style."

Tikkanen explores the childhood roots of her adult psyche in *Rödluvan,* which the author describes as a novel. She likens the book's domineering and demanding, but lovable, father to the wolf of the fairy tale, suggesting that the dynamic between him and the compliant wife taught the writer to acquiesce to male tyranny. In *Storfångaren,* Tikkanen writes of her exhilarating visit to Greenland after her husband's death, and of her passionate new love—a prominent Danish writer. Acknowledging the book's descriptive power and vitality, Schoolfield nevertheless found its intimate details "trying." The critic much preferred *Arnaía kastad i havet,* a poem cycle associating Tikkanen with the mythic character Arnaia, later renamed Penelope and wife of Odysseus. Arnai pursues a suitor, Amphinomus, who appears to be based on the Danish lover Tikkanen introduced in her previous book, but Arnaia refuses to accept a relationship constructed only on his terms and asserts her right to make her own decisions. "The result," observed Schoolfield, "is a cri de couer of great intensity" but also a book of lighthearted wit and ironic treatment of mythic themes. It is, in his opinion, one of Tikkanen's best works.

Personliga angelägenheter, which won Tikkanen the State Literature Committee's Suomi Prize, is yet another analysis of love. The book juxtaposes the story of a contemporary woman who is in love with a married man with the story, told through a diary, of her father's long-ago love affair and its tragic consequences. "Tikkanen's use of language is superb," commented Margareta Martin in *World Literature Today.*

BIOGRAPHICAL/CRITICAL SOURCES:

BOOKS

Encyclopedia of World Literature in the Twentieth Century, 3rd edition, St. James Press (Detroit, MI), 1999.

Wilson, Katharina M., Schleuter, Paul, and Schleuter, June, editors, *Women Writers of Great Britain and Europe: An Encyclopedia,* Garland (New York, NY), 1997.

Zuck, Virpi, editor, *Dictionary of Scandinavian Literature,* Greenwood Press (New York, NY), 1990.

PERIODICALS

Library Journal, March 1, 1984, Joyce Nower, review of *Love Story of the Century,* p. 495.

World Literature Today, autumn, 1990, George C. Schoolfield, review of *Storfångaren,* p. 655-656; autumn, 1993, George C. Schoolfield, review of *Arnia kastad i havet,* pp. 851-852; winter, 1998, Margareta Martin, review of *Personliga angelagenheter,* p. 157; spring, 1999, Margareta Mattsson, review of *Sofia vuxen med sitt MBD,* p. 345.*

TILLINGHAST, David

PERSONAL: Married; children: two sons. *Education:* Louisiana Polytechnic Institute (now Louisiana Tech University), B.A., 1961; University of Wisconsin, M.A., 1963; University of South Carolina at Columbia, Ph.D., 1974.

ADDRESSES: Office—Department of English, Clemson University, Clemson, SC 29634-1503.

CAREER: Mount Union College, Alliance, OH, instructor in English, 1963-65; Rollins College, Winter Park, FL, instructor in English, 1965-67; Nicholls State College (now University), Thibodaux, LA, assistant professor of English, 1968-71; Clemson University, Clemson, SC, assistant professor, 1975-84, associate professor, 1984-97, professor of English, 1997—. Louisiana Tech University, Fletcher Lecturer, 1986; guest lecturer at educational institutions, including Young Harris College, Wells College, Anderson College, and Washington College, Chestertown, MD; gives readings from his works.

AWARDS, HONORS: John Atherton scholar, Bread Loaf Writers Conference, 1973; first place award in poetry, Roger C. Peace Creative Writing Awards, and best in show award, Greenville Arts Festival, both Metropolitan Arts Council, Greenville, SC, 1984; Louisiana Writers Award, 1988; Lane-South Award, 1992; awards from South Carolina Fiction Project, 1995 and 1998.

WRITINGS:

(Editor) *Boiler Room,* South Carolina Arts Commission (Columbia, SC), 1975.

(Editor) *Ears Quickly,* South Carolina Arts Commission (Columbia, SC), 1976.

Women Hoping for Rain and Other Poems, State Street Press (Brockport, NY), 1987.

Work represented in anthologies, including *Anthology of Magazine Verse and Yearbook of American Poetry,* edited by Alan F. Pater, Monitor Book (Beverly Hills, CA), 1985; *Uncommonplace: An Anthology of Contemporary Louisiana Writers,* Louisiana State University Press (Baton Rouge, LA), 1998; and *From the Green Horseshoe: Poems by James Dickey's Students,* University of South Carolina Press (Columbia, SC). Contributor of short stories, poetry, and articles to periodicals, including *Antigonish Review, Poet Lore, Virginia Quarterly Review, South Carolina Review, Queen's Quarterly,* and *Wisconsin Review.*

SIDELIGHTS: David Tillinghast told *CA:* "My wife and I built a log cabin in the British Columbia wilderness and lived off the land for a year. Seven chapters of a manuscript on this experience have been published. We removed our two youngest boys from school when they were in the eighth and ninth grades, built a cabin in the Ozarks, and lived off the land. It was an enriching family year."

BIOGRAPHICAL/CRITICAL SOURCES:

PERIODICALS

Georgia Review, fall, 1988, review of *Women Hoping for Rain and Other Poems,* p. 624.
South Carolina Review, fall, 1989, review of *Women Hoping for Rain and Other Poems,* p. 141.
Virginia Quarterly Review, winter, 1988, review of *Women Hoping for Rain and Other Poems,* p. 27.

*   *   *

TIMBERG, Robert

PERSONAL: Male. *Education:* Naval Academy, 1964.

ADDRESSES: Office—c/o *Baltimore Sun*-Washington Bureau, 1627 "K" St. NW, Suite 1100, Washington, DC 20006.

CAREER: Journalist. *Baltimore Sun,* reporter, Deputy Washington bureau chief. *Military service:* Vietnam veteran.

WRITINGS:

The Nightingale's Song, Simon & Schuster (New York, NY), 1995.
John McCain: An American Odyssey, Simon & Schuster (New York, NY), 1999.

SIDELIGHTS: Robert Timberg's *The Nightingale's Song* surveys the lives of five Vietnam-era graduates of the Naval Academy at Annapolis—John McCain, James Webb, John Poindexter, Robert "Bud" McFarlane, and Oliver North. After the war, all of them entered political positions in Washington, DC. John McCain, who spent five and a half years in prison camps in North Vietnam, became a U.S. senator. James Webb, who wrote several military novels, became Secretary of the Navy during Ronald Reagan's presidency. John Poindexter, Bud McFarlane, and Oliver North, who all had distinguished service records, were all members of the National Security Council who became embroiled in the Iran-Contra scandal. Timberg's thesis is that these men were disgusted by the anti-war, anti-military reaction they received when they returned to the United States after the Vietnam War. Hungry for approval and praise, they found a home in the administration of President Ronald Reagan. According to Timberg, by honoring Vietnam veterans and glorifying the war they served in, president Ronald Reagan and the extreme right gave them the power they so desperately sought and allowed them to become involved in the Iran-Contra affair. "I remember thinking that perhaps Iran-Contra was at least in part the bill for Vietnam finally coming due," said Timberg, according to Lance Morrow in *Time.* A *Publishers Weekly* reviewer praised the book, calling it "sprawling but often engrossing."

Timberg, like the men he writes about, is a graduate of the Naval Academy and a Vietnam vet, and like his heroes, he was disgusted by the antiwar feelings of the American public during and after the Vietnam War. The book discusses the response of returned soldiers to this social climate. However, as Barbara Ehrenreich points out in *Nation,* Timberg does not distinguish between reactions of the elite, military-school-graduate members of the military—like Timberg and the men he writes about—and those of the ordinary "grunts" who were drafted against their will and who, in many cases, joined the antiwar protesters when they returned home. John McCain spoke for these elites when he said, "Nobody made me fly over Vietnam. Nobody drafts you into doing these kinds of things. That's what I was trained to do and that's what I wanted to do." As Ehrenreich noted, "War, just or unjust, is their business, and they were anxious not to miss this one."

Timberg also provides a fascinating account of life at the Naval Academy, where underclassmen survived at the whim of upperclassmen, who subjected them to rigorous and unending hazing. As a result, Ehrenreich remarked, "you have a public servant who is groveling, insecure, driven and willing to do almost anything a father figure asks, or seems merely to hint at." According to Timberg, this psychology is what made men like Oliver North so ready to become involved in scandal.

John McCain: An American Odyssey takes an in-depth look at senator John McCain, although according to Nathaniel Tripp in the *New York Times Book Review,* the book "pretty much consists of excerpts from [*The Nightingale's Song*]." Timberg describes McCain's childhood, education, and military career, including his captivity in Vietnam. During his imprisonment, which included thirty-one months in solitary confinement, as well as torture and starvation, McCain was offered the chance to be released early as part of a propaganda campaign by the North Vietnamese. As Lance Morrow wrote, "McCain, crippled and skeletal, spat in their faces and let loose such an outpouring of naval obscenity that the startled North Vietnamese dignitaries flew backward out of McCain's cell like tumbleweed." When McCain returned to the United States, as a war hero, he was taken up by Ronald and Nancy Reagan and entered the political scene. Timberg also describes McCain's two marriages, his involvement in a financial scandal, and his successful bid for a senate seat. But, Tripp remarked, "Timberg's effusive praise for those who served in Vietnam, peppered with his contempt for [1960s] draft dodgers, leaves the real John McCain once again as inscrutable to the reader as he was to his captors." However, Michael R. Beschloss wrote in *Washington Monthly* that this "dramatic volume" is written with "novelistic skillfulness."

BIOGRAPHICAL/CRITICAL SOURCES:

PERIODICALS

Air Power History, winter, 1996, p. 62.
Armed Forces and Society, summer, 1997, p. 687.
Books in Canada, March, 1998, p. 30.
Far Eastern Economic Review, December 28, 1995, p. 107.
Historian, winter, 1997, p. 446.
Los Angeles Times Book Review, July 16, 1995, p. 2.
Marine Corps Gazette, January, 1996, p. 74.
Nation, July 17, 1995, p. 99.
Naval War College Review, spring, 1996, p. 136.
New York Review of Books, October 21, 1999, p. 6.
New York Times (Late Edition), July 17, 1995, p. C13.
New York Times Book Review, August 6, 1995, p. 6; December 3, 1995, p. 82; September 29, 1996, p. 32; October 3, 1999, p. 17.
Publishers Weekly, May 15, 1995, p. 62.
Time, July 17, 1995, p. 61; December 25, 1995, p. 151.
Wall Street Journal, July 21, 1995, p. A8.
Washington Monthly, July-August, 1995, p. 58.
Wilson Quarterly, autumn, 1995, p. 90.*

*   *   *

TONDELLI, Pier Vittorio   1955-1991

PERSONAL: Born September 14, 1955, in Correggio, Italy; died January 16, 1991, in Correggio, Italy, from complications associated with AIDS; son of Brenno and Marta Tondelli. *Education:* Attended the University of Bologna, 1975-79. *Religion:* Catholic. *Avocational interests:* Pop culture and sexuality.

CAREER: Fiction writer, novelist and literary commentator of contemporary issues. *Military service:* Completed one year of military service with the Italian Army in Orvieto and Rome, Italy.

AWARDS, HONORS: Riccione-Ater Prize for Theater in 1985 for *La notte della vittoria.*

WRITINGS:

Altri libertini (title means "Other Libertines"), Feltrinelli (Milan, Italy), 1980.
Pao Pao, Feltrinelli (Milan, Italy), 1982.
Rimini, Bompiani (Milan, Italy), 1985.
Biglietti agli Amici (title means "Notes to Friends"), Baskerville (Bologna, Italy), 1986.
Camere separate, Bompiani (Bologna, Italy), 1989, translation by Simon Pleasance published as *Separate Rooms,* Serpent's Tail (New York, NY), 1992.
Un weekend postmoderno: Cronache dagli anni ottanta, Bompiani (Bologna, Italy), 1990.
L'abbandono: racconti dagli anni ottanta, edited by Fulvio Panzeri, Bompiani (Bologna, Italy), 1993.
Dinner Party, edited by Fulvio Panzeri, Bompiani (Bologna, Italy), 1994.

PLAYS

La notte della vittoria, first produced in Cesano Boscone at La Monaca Auditorium, January, 1986, revised as *Dinner Party,* produced in Rome, Italy at Sala Umberto, 1991.

OTHER

(Editor, author of introduction) *Giovanni Blues: Under 25 I,* Il lavoro editoriale (Ancona, Italy), 1986.
(Editor, author of afterward) *Belli e perversi: Under 25 II,* Transeuropa (Ancona, Italy), 1987.
(Editor) Gianni De Martino, *Hotel Oasis,* "Mouse to Mouse" series, Mondadori (Milan, Italy), 1988.
(Editor) Elisabetta Valentini, *Fotomodella,* "Mouse to Mouse" series, Mondadori (Milan, Italy), 1988.
(Editor) *Papergang: Under 25 III,* Transeuropa (Ancona, Italy), 1990.
(With Luciano Mannuzzi) *Sabato italiano* (motion picture treatment), Numero Uno Cinematografica, 1992.

Contributor to *Un Homme grand: Jack Kerouac à la confluence des cultures,* edited by Pierre Anctil, Louis Dupont, Remi Ferland, and Eric Waddell, Carleton University Press (Ottawa, Canada), 1990; contributor to periodicals, including *Linus,* and the monthly column "Culture Club" to *Rockstar.*

SIDELIGHTS: As if somehow aware he would be living a relatively short life, Pier Vittorio Tondelli maximized his experiences to the greatest extent possible during his thirty-six years. Although he chose not to politicize his homosexuality, it was the inspiration and peripheral subject or plot for much of his writing. In addition to sexual experimentation and identity, Tondelli was enthralled with and wrote about other aspects of contemporary pop culture in the 1970s and 1980s, including drugs, music, cinema, world travel, gangs, and aspects of urban life as experienced in many different countries and cultures. In his four novels, as well as in his various essays, articles, and notes, Tondelli attempted to depict the different rites of passages and outlooks thematically common among society's youth. However, he was a private individual and generally avoided overt comparisons to his own life's specific events and emotional realities. As praised by Christopher Concolino in *Dictionary of Literary Biography,* Tondelli's "interest in the contemporary cultural world at large, coupled with a strong sense of his own cultural origins, make Tondelli one of the keenest observers of popular culture among Italian writers of his generation."

Born on September 14, 1955, in a small, provincial community in Italy's Po River valley, Tondelli was part of a traditional Catholic family and lived a happy—albeit uneventful—childhood. Although a student of the classics during his secondary education, Tondelli was drawn to cinema, the arts, and American literature during his collegiate pursuits. As a student at the University of Bologna during the late 1970s, the experimental young man was well versed in the passionate ideologies of social reformation and generational evolution. An example of Tondelli's interests is evident in the subject of a term paper he submitted to his professor of semiotics, who happened to be internationally-acclaimed author Umberto Eco. Titled "La cultura del vino" (title means "The Culture of Wine"), Tondelli went into great detail about the history and literary associations associated with the libation. Despite Tondelli's obvious exuberance for the subject, Eco was not duly impressed. Another anecdote characterizing Tondelli's interest in non-intellectual pursuits happened on his first trip to New York. Apparently, according to Concolino, Tondelli "searched Manhattan for the per-

fect 'martini cocktail,' of which he had knowledge only through literary sources."

In terms of content, Tondelli has been aligned with Walt Whitman, Christopher Isherwood, and Allen Ginsberg. The works, characters, and writing styles of Henry Miller, Jack Kerouac, and W. H. Auden particularly influenced Tondelli. His non-literary influences included American and European movies from the 1970s and 1980s, rock-and-roll lyrics, comic book art, experimental theater, and contemporary painting. Concolino quoted Tondelli as saying that "'in spite of being a child of a larger Western culture, an incurable fan of pop and rock music and a consumer of American films and beat generation literature, it has taken me time to understand deep down inside that I am also profoundly Emilian.'" This realization allowed Tondelli a certain freedom from his quest for identity and belonging.

After he was through with his formal education, Tondelli focused on world travel. He became familiar with most of the major European cities, absorbing their cultural attributes as well as their seemingly limitless social opportunities. When he was twenty-four he was called to serve in the army, and completed a year in Orvieto and Rome with the military. This experience was the impetus for his second novel, *Pao Pao,* published in 1982. He resumed traveling after his military service, visiting Great Britain, Eastern Europe, and North Africa. He became familiar with discothèques, popular music, nightlife, and the general artistic milieu of nearly every place he visited. His vast traveling experiences and adventures are detailed throughout his work.

Tondelli's penchant for travel, entertainment, and constant adventure was somehow not inhibited by the fact that he did not make enough money as a freelance journalist to support his lifestyle. By the good graces and generosity of his friends, as well as a patron who offered financial support on the basis of Tondelli's literary talent and potential, Tondelli enjoyed a couple of years of living well beyond his earned means. It was not unusual, during his years after the army, to sleep in a different place every night. Eventually, he established residency in Florence and developed friendships that would later be depicted through his characters in *Rimini,* his third novel, published in 1985. *Rimini* was Tondelli's greatest commercial triumph, selling more than one hundred thousand copies almost immediately. However, some critics felt that it was not a spectacularly clever work. Italian critic Oreste Del Buono summarized its critical worth and appeal when he called it "romanzo di consumo" (light reading produced for the mass market). Nonetheless, it provided for Tondelli a comfortable living, and is in many ways similar to contemporary romance novels.

Even as he got older, Tondelli never lost his interest in youth culture. He set his personal interests into action during the 1980s when he agreed to serve in an editorial capacity for two enterprises that were formed for the explicit promotion of young authors and writers. In addition, he regularly contributed articles to *Linus,* a magazine geared toward a young audience. Also, he scribed a monthly column for *Rockstar* magazine that was entitled "Culture Club." These well-intended activities were not unusual for Tondelli, who was described as a kind, shy man, even though his writing was often daring and even lascivious. In fact, not unlike the controversies and fights about censorship that followed the likes of Henry Miller's novels, Tondelli's first book, *Altri libertini,* was, according to Concolino, "charged with obscenity upon publication and confiscated though Tondelli was later absolved of the charges." In the first of the text's six loosely-related chapters, Tondelli vividly describes prostitutes, drug users and pushers, gang members, mobsters, and other depraved aspects of urban life. The most controversial issues, however, revolved around the sexual exploits and experiences of his youthful characters. He purposefully wrote about the adventures and misadventures in a frenzied style, further enhancing the immediacy and intensity of youthful consciousness.

Perhaps the work that held the most meaning for Tondelli was his 1986 *Biglietti agli Amici.* Ironically, this short, pamphlet-type work was not intended for mass consumption, but was instead explicitly written for his close friends. He used some clever devices, such as dividing the work into twenty-four sections, with each section intended for one of twenty-four friends, and each section representing an hour in the day. The writing is casual and personal, and in many ways offers insight into some of Tondelli's personal concerns and feelings. One of the most notable topics Tondelli included was a concept he called "fading," which referred to "the waning of emotional intensity within a couple." Taken into context with his life and experiences, "fading" is considered to refer less to breaking up in relationships than to the process endured as a partner watches his lover confront an imminent mortality, usually due to AIDS.

With his later works, Tondelli raised the issue of social exclusion implicit in a homosexual lifestyle. No matter what levels of enlightenment a homosexual achieves during his lifetime, there seems always to exist an undercurrent of absent validation due to the lack of true social acceptance. This theme is best portrayed in the following excerpt from *Camere separate,* published in 1989. Leo, the main character, watches Thomas, his lover, as he clings to the last moments of his life. Thomas's family does not acknowledge Leo's pain or presence, nor do they include Leo in the process. Translated in English, the passage is as follows: "Leo understands that he has to go. At the final moment Thomas is given back to his family, to the same people who bore him; who are now, with hearts ravaged by suffering, trying to help him face death. There is no place for him in this parental regrouping. He didn't marry Thomas; didn't have children with him; neither of them legally bears the other's name, and there's not a single church registry on the face of the earth holding the signatures of those who witnessed their union."

The deep-seated hopelessness, as well as the commentary on harsh homosexual realities found in this passage, serves as a compelling argument that Tondelli is one of Italy's important contributors to the homosexual cause for societal edification. Concolino stated that "Tondelli's depiction of homosexual society makes visible what had been hidden from view, implicitly asserting that social relations among homosexuals are more complex and highly developed than the scant portrayals that literature historically has accorded them and advancing homosexuality as a cultural construct."

BIOGRAPHICAL/CRITICAL SOURCES:

BOOKS

Dictionary of Literary Biography, Volume 196: *Italian Novelists Since World War II, 1965-1995,* Gale (Detroit, MI), 1999.
Tondelli, Pier Vittorio, *Separate Rooms,* translated by Simon Pleasance, Serpent's Tail (New York, NY), 1992.*

*   *   *

TOOP, David 1949-

PERSONAL: Born 1949.

ADDRESSES: Agent—c/o Serpent's Tail, 180 Varick St., 10th Floor, New York, NY 10014.

CAREER: Musician, composer, and writer.

WRITINGS:

(Editor) *New/Rediscovered Musical Instruments,* foreword by Madeau Stewart, Quartz/Mirliton, 1974.

The Rap Attack: African Jive to New York Hip Hop, South End Press (Boston, MA), 1984, second edition published as *Rap Attack 2: African Rap to Global Hip Hop,* Serpent's Tail (London, England), 1991, Serpent's Tail (New York, NY), 1994, third edition published as *Rap Attack 3: African Rap to Global Hip Hop,* Serpent's Tail (New York, NY), 1999.

Ocean of Sound: Aether Talk, Ambient Sound, and Imaginary Worlds, Serpent's Tail (New York, NY), 1995.

Exotica: Fabricated Soundscapes in a Real World, Serpent's Tail (New York, NY), 1999.

Contributor to periodicals, including *Collusion, Face,* and London *Times.* Associated with *Musics,* late 1970s; contributing editor, *Wire.*

RECORDINGS AS COMPOSER

(With Nestor Figueras and Paul Durwell) *Cholagogues,* Bead (London, England), 1977.

(With Steve Beresford, Tonie Marshall, and John Zorn) *Deadly Weapons,* Nato (Chantenay-Villedieu, France), c. 1980.

(With Max Eastley) *Buried Dreams,* 1994.

Screen Ceremonies, Wire Editions, 1996.

SIDELIGHTS: David Toop is a musician, recording artist, composer, and writer who has published various works on music. His first book, *New/Rediscovered Musical Instruments,* which he produced as editor in 1974, features essays promoting innovations and breakthroughs in music. A *Times Literary Supplement* reviewer was unimpressed, dismissing the book as "depressing" and characterizing its contents as "scrapheap improvisations."

Toop's second book, *The Rap Attack: African Jive to New York Hip Hop,* traces the evolution of African and African-American music. A. D. Franklin, writing in *Choice,* found that Toop "expertly traces the development and influence of the hip hop culture from its street origins to its commercial exploitation with references to its African and Afro-American antecedents." Another reviewer, Barney Hoskyns, wrote in his *New Statesman* assessment that *The Rap Attack* constitutes an "excellent genealogy," and he added that Toop's "technical exposition is riveting." Robert M. Cleary, meanwhile, wrote in *Reference Services Review* that

The Rap Attack "extends the attempt to trace rap to its roots." Cleary declared that Toop's book "provides the most extensive background on the early days of rap."

The Rap Attack appeared in second and third editions as *Rap Attack 2: African Rap to Global Hip Hop* and *Rap Attack 3: African Rap to Global Hip Hop,* respectively. Chris Morris described *Rap Attack 2,* in his *Billboard* review, as "one of the very few books about rap to attempt a comprehensive genre overview," and he called it "the most in-depth study of the music currently available." Kwaku, reviewing *Rap Attack 3* in *Billboard,* observed that "the tome overwhelmingly concentrates on hip-hop as an African-American phenomenon."

Toop followed *The Rap Attack* with *Ocean of Sound: Aether Talk, Ambient Sound, and Imaginary Worlds,* which a *Whole Earth Review* critic described as a "dreamy attempt to set down an aesthetic for ambient music." Aaron Cohen, in his *Booklist* critique, wrote that Toop's study examines a range of music figures, including experimental composer John Cage, jazz trumpeter Miles Davis, and Beach Boys singer-songwriter Brian Wilson, and he deemed *Ocean of Sound* "a clear and direct book." John Diliberto, meanwhile, wrote in *Billboard* that "we are fortunate to have a writer with Toop's wit, knowledge, and easy readability to provide at least one path through these waters," and Mark Sinker stated in *New Statesman & Society* that "Toop knows far more, about a far broader range of music, than any other critic in the nonspecialist British press." In addition, Sinker declared that *Ocean of Sound* is "amorphously packed with seductive pleasures and immensely informative."

Exotica: Fabricated Soundscapes in a Real World, is a book described by Mike Thorne, in his *Times Literary Supplement* appraisal, as comprised of "disparate anecdotes and interviews, which Toop attempts to draw together under a central theme, of the introduction of the exotic into various genres of Western music." Thorne was less than impressed, contending that the book suffers from a "lack of coherent organization and presentation." But Rupa Huq, who reviewed *Exotica* in *New Statesman,* found the book "unusual and surprisingly rewarding." Huq, who noted that Toop produced *Exotica* in the wake of his wife's suicide, described the book as "an intensely personal memoir that reads simultaneously as a sober study and as if written on acid."

Toop's works as a composer and musician include *Deadly Weapons,* a recording on which he performed with such artists as Steve Beresford and Tonie Marshall. John Corbett noted in *Down Beat* that Toop plays "reverbed guitar" on the recording.

BIOGRAPHICAL/CRITICAL SOURCES:

PERIODICALS

Billboard, April 4, 1992, Chris Morris, review of *Rap Attack 2: African Rap to Global Hip Hop,* p. 53; May 4, 1996, John Diliberto, review of *Ocean of Sound: Aether Talk, Ambient Sound, and Imaginary Worlds,* p. 44; February 19, 2000, Kwaku, " 'Rap Attack' Returns with Global View."

Booklist, May 15, 1996, Aaron Cohen, review of *Ocean of Sound: Aether Talk, Ambient Sound, and Imaginary Worlds,* p. 1561.

Choice, October 6, 1985, A. D. Franklin, review of *The Rap Attack: African Jive to New York Hip Hop,* p. 1054.

Down Beat, February, 1994, John Corbett, review of *Deadly Weapons,* p. 60.

Reference Services Review, February, 1993, Robert M. Cleary, review of *The Rap Attack: African Jive to New York Hip Hop,* pp. 80-81.

New Statesman, November 30, 1984, Barney Hoskyns, "As Arthur Rimbaud Once Said," p. 36; May 31, 1999, Rupa Huq, review of *Exotica: Fabricated Soundscapes in a Real World,* p. 48.

New Statesman & Society, January 5, 1996, Mark Sinker, review of *Ocean of Sound: Aether Talk, Ambient Sound, and Imaginary Worlds.*

Times Literary Supplement, July 5, 1974, review of *New/Rediscovered Musical Instruments,* p. 706; January 7, 2000, Mike Thorne, review of *Exotica: Fabricated Soundscapes in a Real World,* p. 10.

Whole Earth Review, spring 1999, review of *Ocean of Sound: Aether Talk, Ambient Sound, and Imaginary Worlds,* p. 61.

OTHER

Hybrid, http://www.hybrid.alphalink.com.au (October 1, 2001).*

* * *

TRAUTMAN, Victoria B. 1959-
(Baxter Clare)

PERSONAL: Born November 28, 1959, in San Francisco, CA; daughter of Lowell Clare (a banker) and Mary Elizabeth (a librarian; maiden name, Newton) Trautman; companion of Anno O'Connor (a teacher). *Ethnicity:* "Caucasian." *Education:* Florida International University, B.S., 1988; California Polytechnic University, M.S., 1996.

ADDRESSES: Home and Office—500 Parkhill Rd., Pozo, CA 93453. *E-mail*—baxtertrautman@thegrid. net.

CAREER: Hearst Castle, San Simeon, CA, volunteer coordinator, 1989-94; Camp Roberts Army Reserve, Paso Robles, CA, wildlife biologist, 1992-98; self-employed wildlife consultant, San Luis Obispo, CA, 1997—. Pacific Wildlife Care, volunteer animal rehabilitator, 1997—.

WRITINGS:

(Under pseudonym Baxter Clare) *Bleeding Out* (mystery), Firebrand Books (Ithaca, NY), 1999.
Spirit of the Valley (nonfiction), Sierra Books (San Francisco, CA), 2000.

WORK IN PROGRESS: A sequel to *Bleeding Out,* for Firebrand Books (Ithaca, NY); research on American attitudes on death and aging.

SIDELIGHTS: Victoria B. Trautman told *CA:* "I write because it makes me feel whole. When I go too long without it, I get very irritable and restless, and that's when I know I have to get back to whatever I'm working on! I think my darker side, my not-so-nice alter ego fuels my fiction work, so when I don't give it an outlet I tend to get cranky. Conversely, nature fuels my nonfiction writing, and I get equally cranky when I lose touch with the gifts that nature offers every day.

"My schedule is such that, at least three days a week, I'm outdoors working, and I hold two days a week for writing. I get up before sunrise, make coffee, and write until sundown, with lots of dog and cat breaks in between. I need large blocks of time to become the character(s) I am describing. I think a lot about writing when I'm doing my other work (which pays the bills!) and will jot down quick sketches that I develop during my writing days."

* * *

TRENCH, Sally 1949-

PERSONAL: Born 1949; children: two, six stepchildren.

ADDRESSES: Agent—c/o Hodder Headline, 338 Euston Rd., London NW1 3BH, England.

CAREER: Social activist, 1968—; Project Spark (program designed to help troubled children assimilate into mainstream education), founder and director.

WRITINGS:

Bury Me in My Boots, Hodder & Stoughton (London, England), 1968.
Sally Trench's Book, Stein and Day (New York, NY), 1968.
Somebody Else's Children, Hodder & Stoughton (London, England), 1990.
Fran's War, Hodder & Stoughton (London, England) 1999.

SIDELIGHTS: From the age of sixteen, Sally Trench has been raising awareness of the plight of the homeless and other often-neglected members of humanity. Her social activism has been instrumental in getting aid to Bosnian children. Her books, from *Bury Me in My Boots* in which she wrote of her experiences with the homeless, to *Fran's War,* constitute an ardent dedication to the cause of social activism. *Bury Me In My Boots* is a journal of her thoughts and experiences living with the homeless. Trench comments on the inspiration behind the book in an interview for *America* conducted by James S. Torrens. "The book hit a nerve in England. I never wrote it to be published; I wrote it as a diary to keep me sane." Critic Colin Macinnes in *New Statesman* commented on the book's effectiveness. "Her portrait of London 'derries' . . . should remind anyone who thinks Mayhew's London has gone, that it has not—it's just less visible, swept under the carpet, which is our way with outcasts in the welfare-affluent age. She did not, I think, penetrate the beat world as effectively—though she did have the inspired idea of 'turning on' the beats to help the dossers."

Of her book *Somebody Else's Children, Times Educational Supplement* critic Victoria Neumark commented: "Ms. Trench is not a writer. Her book is as spiky as she herself sounds, full of sentimental phrases, abruptly told anecdotes, jarring leaps in narrative. But these do not mask her practical goodness. Here is someone who means it when she says she loves everyone." Trench's next book, *Fran's War,* presents the reader with a portrait of war-torn Bosnia painted by an adolescent girl growing up there. The inspiration for this story, said a reviewer for *Publishers Weekly,* is "the four years (1992-1996) the author spent as an activist in Bosnia, helping the destitute population survive the trauma of

the war." According to the reviewer, the details of the story survive Trench's writing defects to make her story powerful. "It is the slow accumulation of details that make the events in this plainspoken story come horrifyingly alive."

BIOGRAPHICAL/CRITICAL SOURCES:

PERIODICALS

America, December 17, 1994, James S. Torrens, "Getting to the Children in Bosnia: An Interview with Sally Trench," p. 6.
Booklist, October 1, 1999, Vanessa Bush, review of *Fran's War,* p. 339.
New Statesman, June 14, 1968, Colin Macinnes, "Marginal Lives," pp. 804-805.
Publishers Weekly, September 20, 1999, review of *Fran's War.*
Times Educational Supplement, October 26, 1990, Victoria Neumark, "Beating the Bureaucrats," p. R3.*

*   *   *

TSUKA, Kohei (Bong Woon Kim)   1948-

PERSONAL: Born April 24, 1948, in Iizuka City, Japan; married Naoko Ikoma; children: one daughter. *Education:* Attended Keio University.

ADDRESSES: Office—Villa Kamimuta, Room 401, Tabata, 6-3-18 Tabata, Kita-ku, Tokyo 114-0014, Japan; fax: 03-5-814-5178.

CAREER: Playwright and theater director. Waseda University Theater Club, writer and director, 1972; established and affiliated with Thukakoahei office, 1975-82; established Kitaku Thukakoahei Gikidan, 1994, and Oita City Thukakoahei Gikidan, 1996.

AWARDS, HONORS: Japanese Academy Award, 1983, for *Kamata March Song;* Yomiuri Literature Prize, 1990, for *The Tale of Hiryu '90.*

WRITINGS:

Kamata koshinkyoku (play), first produced in Tokyo, Japan, 1980, English adaptation by Gary Perlman produced as *The Fall Guy* in New York, NY, at Playhouse 91, 1995.

Other plays include *Red Beret for You,* 1969; *The Murder of Atami,* 1975; *For the Father Who Couldn't Die in the War,* 1976; *Introduction to Revolution,* 1977; *The Tale of Kiryu,* 1977; *Sun Is in Your Mind,* 1978; *Kamata March Song,* 1981; *A Stripper's Story,* 1984; *Town with Well,* 1985; *The Day They Bombed Hiroshima,* 1986; *Birth of a Star,* 1986; *My Country,* 1990; *Tell It to My Daughter,* 1990; *The Tale of Hiryu '90,* 1990; and *The Story of Ryoma,* 1992. Author of the novelization and the 1982 screenplay based on the stage play *The Fall Guy.* Also author of essays.

SIDELIGHTS: Japanese playwright Tsuka Kohei "has tapped into something deep in the national psyche" in his drama *Kamata koshinkyoku,* wrote *New York Times* theater critic Ben Brantley of the play's English debut in 1995. Originally produced in Tokyo in 1980, the play presents a self-absorbed film star so adulated by his admirers that one of them, the "fall guy" of the title, will do anything to protect the actor's safety and reputation. Indeed, Yasu even marries the star's pregnant mistress to keep the actor free from any scandal, and agrees to do extremely dangerous film stunts to ensure success for his hero's latest cinematic project. "The work is shaped by a logic that may baffle Western audiences," noted Brantley, "but as a social phenomenon . . . [it] exerts an undeniable fascination." Though *Back Stage* reviewer Irene Backalenick felt that the play lost too much in translation to succeed on the American stage, Brantley praised its probing of a complex theme: "the extent to which Yasu . . . and Konatsu . . . are willing to abase themselves for the many they both, in different ways, love."

BIOGRAPHICAL/CRITICAL SOURCES:

PERIODICALS

Back Stage, April 21, 1995, Irene Backalenick, review of *The Fall Guy,* p. 42.
New York Times, April 15, 1995, Ben Brantley, review of *The Fall Guy,* p. N- 11.*

*   *   *

TUCKER, Toba Pato 1935-

PERSONAL: Born July 1, 1935, in Bronx, NY; daughter of Joseph (a bread baker) and Rose (a homemaker; maiden name, Folbaum) Pato; children: Dena Suzanne Tucker. *Politics:* Democrat. *Religion:* Jewish. *Avocational interests:* Hiking, long-distance walking, cross-country skiing, white-water rafting, films, music, cooking, baking.

ADDRESSES: Office—P.O. Box 69-823, Los Angeles, CA 90069. *E-mail*—tobaphoto@aol.com.

CAREER: Photographer, with work exhibited throughout the United States. International Center of Photography, teacher, 1978-81; guest artist at schools and workshops; lecturer at museums, libraries, and universities. Work represented in collections, including those at Metropolitan Museum of Art, Museum of Modern Art, National Museum of the American Indian, Southwest Museum for Native American Art, Museum of Indian Arts and Culture, and Carnegie Museum of Natural History.

AWARDS, HONORS: First prize, Musee Francais de la Photographie, 1978; grant from National Endowment for the Arts, 1981; award from Agfa-Gevaert Corp., 1985; grants from New York State Council on the Arts, 1986 and 1987; awards from Polaroid Corp. and New York Foundation for the Arts, 1989; grants from Arkansas Endowment for the Humanities and Arkansas Arts Council, 1989 and 1990; awards from Grand Marnier Foundation, 1991 and 1992, Daniele Agostino Foundation, 1993, Judith S. Randal Foundation, 1994, and Horace W. Goldsmith Foundation, 1995 and 1996.

WRITINGS:

(Photographer and contributor) *Heber Springs Portraits: Continuity and Change in the World Disfarmer Photographed,* University of New Mexico Press (Albuquerque, NM), 1996.
(Photographer and contributor) *Pueblo Artists: Portraits,* Museum of New Mexico Press (Santa Fe, NM), 1998.
(Photographer and contributor) *Haudenosaunee: Portraits of the Firekeepers, the Onondaga Nation,* Syracuse University Press (Syracuse, NY), 1999.

Contributor to periodicals, including *Life, Native Peoples, Popular Photography, Camera Arts,* and *Modern Photography.*

WORK IN PROGRESS: Research on Alaskan songs and dances and a renewed interest in tradition; research on the Native American relocation to California in the 1950s.

SIDELIGHTS: Toba Pato Tucker told *CA:* "I am a documentary portrait photographer interested in recording continuity and change in American culture for history and artistic purposes. Although my work is not exclusively devoted to Native Americans, they have been my primary subjects.

"People often ask me why I photograph Native Americans, and I struggle to articulate my purpose. Collectively Native Americans are an ancient people striving to retain their traditional way of life and integrity while confronting modern society and the dominant culture. I wanted to record them for history and art at the end of the twentieth century, and I will now continue my work in the new millennium. As individuals, they emanate an air of quiet wisdom and are a compellingly handsome people with strength and inner dignity written on their faces. I believe that this dignity is inherent in all people, but Native Americans seem to epitomize it and give it a visible presence that I try to present in my portraits. Remarkably, they give me permission to do so, in spite of their usual reluctance to be photographed, because they know Native Americans have been exploited by the camera throughout history. It is by our collaboration—I with my camera, they with their permission and cooperation—that we create the essential images by which their future generations and the outside world will remember them.

"My first Native American portrait was made by chance on the street in Saint Paul, Minnesota. That was more than two decades ago, not long after I began photographing. As I printed the Chippewa Indian's image, his face came up in the developer and captivated me—it was mystical, his expression undefinable and unknown to me. The mystery of his persona, as revealed in that photograph, prompted my decision to photograph Native Americans.

"Since then I have photographed the Navajo Nation in the southwest, the Shinnecock and Montauk Indians on eastern Long Island, the Onondaga Nation, one of the Six Nations of the Iroquois confederacy in upstate New York, and the artists and artisans of the Pueblos in New Mexico and Arizona.

"I have also photographed the people in the community of Heber Springs, Arkansas, and related these new portraits to those made by Mike Disfarmer fifty years ago in his studio on Main Street.

"The text to my books of photographs are primarily written by prominent and eloquent members from within the communities I photograph, since I want the people to speak for themselves. In addition, there are contributions from distinguished authors empathetic to the material. Although I am a visual artist, I am inspired to write for my books and give an experiential account of the journey through the worlds I am privileged to photograph, recounting my impressions of the people and their landscape and the circumstances of creating the portraits."

V

van der STEEN, Mensje Francine
   See van KEULEN, Mensje

*   *   *

VAN DRAANEN, Wendelin

PERSONAL: Married; children: two sons. *Avocational interests:* Reading, running, and playing in a rock band.

ADDRESSES: Home—California. *Office*—c/o Author Mail, Random House/Knopf, 299 Park Ave., New York, NY 10171-0002.

CAREER: Writer. Has taught high school math and computer science.

AWARDS, HONORS: Edgar Award for Best Children's Mystery, and Best Book for Young Adults selection, American Library Association, both 1999, both for *Sammy Keyes and the Hotel Thief.*

WRITINGS:

How I Survived Being a Girl, HarperCollins, 1997.
Flipped, Knopf, 2001.

"SAMMY KEYES" SERIES

Sammy Keyes and the Hotel Thief, illustrated by Dan Yaccarino, Knopf, 1998.
Sammy Keyes and the Skeleton Man, illustrated by Dan Yaccarino, Knopf, 1998.
Sammy Keyes and the Sisters of Mercy, illustrated by Dan Yaccarino, Knopf, 1999.
Sammy Keyes and the Runaway Elf, illustrated by Dan Yaccarino, Knopf, 1999.

Sammy Keyes and the Curse of Moustache Mary, illustrated by Dan Yaccarino, Knopf, 2000.
Sammy Keyes and the Hollywood Mummy, illustrated by Dan Yaccarino, Knopf, 2001.

WORK IN PROGRESS: Another Sammy Keyes novel.

SIDELIGHTS: Wendelin Van Draanen is the author of the popular "Sammy Keyes" mystery series for young readers, featuring an indomitable tomboy with a penchant for landing herself in trouble. The misunderstood heroine, whose formal name is Samantha, often starts out as the primary suspect in some sort of minor crime and finds the real culprit through efforts to clear her own name. The junior-high schooler also combats some tough family and social situations with the same sense of humor and adventure. Van Draanen's first book in the series—only her second ever published—won the Edgar Award for Best Children's Mystery in 1999. "The audience I have in mind is the kid who's coming to a place where they have to make decisions on their own," the writer once commented. "I try to shed a little light on the merits of being good, heroic, and honest. I hope that kids come away from reading my work with a little more strength and belief in themselves and the sense that they *can* shape their own destiny."

Until she was in the fourth grade when her sister was born, Van Draanen grew up the sole daughter in a family with three children, having an older and a younger brother. The situation provided the inspiration for her intrepid, tomboy protagonists of her books, though the future author described her own juvenile persona as tentative and shy. "My parents immigrated to the United States, so there was always something 'foreign' about our family," Van Draanen once said. "I never really felt like I fit in unless I was with my family."

Still, she admitted to a daring streak when backed up by her siblings. "I did a lot of 'boy stuff,' " she recalled. "We spied on the neighbors, played in the school yard across the street—roller-skating, kickball, dodgeball, hide 'n' seek—we also loved to go swimming at the Plunge (community pool) and ride bikes. Indoor activities included reading (loved mysteries) and endless hours of chess. We also had chores, chores, chores!"

Like other shy children, Van Draanen found comfort in the world of books. She particularly enjoyed popular teen sleuth series, including *Nancy Drew,* the *Hardy Boys,* and *Encyclopedia Brown.* "My father would read to us at bedtime," she once noted. "He'd gather my brothers and me up in a bed and read from a collection of stories for children. We relished storytime and the way he read. My mother did this, too, but I remember the times with my father the best." Van Draanen remembered learning to read at an early age, thanks to one of her siblings. "I began to read by watching my older brother learn to read. I'd hang over his shoulder while he got help from my mother, and that's how I picked it up. My mother worked with all of us, teaching us reading and mathematics at a very early age. One of my favorite pictures of me as a young girl was taken at the age of about eighteen months—I'm sitting on the toilet, feet dangling, engrossed in a book that's in my lap."

Entering adolescence was a time of added uncertainty for Van Draanen, however. Her coming-of-age adventures would form the basis for the comical problems she later forces Sammy Keyes to suffer. "I liked elementary school, but beginning in junior high I felt terribly awkward and on the outskirts of social circles," she once commented. "I guess you'd call me a straight-A student. Academics were important in our family. I liked learning." She remained rather shy throughout her teens, and did not even have her first date until the night of her senior prom.

Van Draanen looked forward to an impressive career. "My parents were both chemists, so I was sure I'd become something scientific," she once said. "I really wanted to be a singer, but was much too shy to put that forward, so I stuck to science and math. I certainly did not want to be a writer! It seemed so dull!" But when she was in college, a catastrophe in her family would inadvertently open up a new door for her: their family business was destroyed by arson, and she took time off from school to help out. For a time, they were financially ruined, and Van Draanen was troubled by feelings of anger and helplessness. She began to have problems sleeping, and to help alleviate some of the stress,

she decided to write about the incident, with the hope of turning it into a screenplay.

Van Draanen discovered that writing was not only cathartic but enjoyable. What she found most rewarding, she would later note, was the ability to create a happy ending, to have her characters make positive gains through personal difficulties. Van Draanen would eventually find her vocation as a teacher of computer science to high schoolers, but she also had ten finished novels, each around four hundred pages long, by the mid-1990s. By then she had married and had begun a family of her own in California.

Van Draanen was inspired to try her hand at writing for children as a result of a chance gift. "My husband gave me *Dandelion Wine* (by Ray Bradbury) and told me it was one of his favorite books. I read it and it reminded me of all the wonderful mischief my brothers and I got into when we were young, and decided it would be fun to write a book like *Dandelion Wine* about my experiences growing up." The result was *How I Survived Being a Girl,* published in 1997. It is Van Draanen's first work for young readers before her "Sammy Keyes" series, and the works share a heroine with pointed similarities. Carolyn, the narrator of *How I Survived Being a Girl,* is a tomboy who feels herself somewhat alienated from the girls in her neighborhood and at school. She much prefers tagging along with her brothers and their friends, especially a neighbor boy named Charlie. During the summer of her twelfth year, Carolyn spies on neighbors, digs foxholes with Charlie, steals a book, and helps her brother with his paper route.

The setting of *How I Survived Being a Girl* is vague, but reviewers seemed to agree that Van Draanen placed her story at some point in the relatively recent past. Girls must still wear dresses to school, for instance, and are strongly discouraged from becoming newspaper carriers—official and unofficial biases that had vanished by the end of the 1970s. Carolyn manages to skirt the skirt issue by wearing shorts under hers; meanwhile, she derides her peers who play with dolls and wear frilly, impractical clothes. Yet as she begins a new school year in September, Carolyn finds that some of her attitudes are beginning to change. She sees Charlie in a new way, and starts to speak out and become more politically active. She even starts a petition drive to force some changes at her school. When a baby sister arrives in her family, this softens her attitude, too. "I tell her . . . how being a girl is actually all right once you figure out that you should break some of the rules instead of just living with them," says Carolyn at the end.

A *Publishers Weekly* reviewer called *How I Survived Being a Girl* an "energetic first novel" and "a sunny, funny look at a girl with a smart mouth and scabby knees." Writing in *School Library Journal,* Kathleen Odean found some fault with the premise that a new sibling can bring out an adolescent girl's feminine instincts. "Perhaps the unspecified time setting . . . makes it inevitable that she will be 'tamed a bit,' as she puts it," remarked Odean. Yet a *Kirkus Reviews* critic praised Van Draanen's style and the narrative voice of her alter ego, Carolyn. "Her irreverent narration is engaging," stated the reviewer about the book's heroine, "and she's refreshingly astute about family and neighborhood dynamics."

Van Draanen found that "I loved writing in the voice of a twelve-year-old so much that I haven't gone back, and have no desire to go back, to writing for adults," she once stated. She began writing a teen-detective story that would evolve into a popular and much-praised series. The first of these arrived in 1998 with *Sammy Keyes and the Hotel Thief.* Here, readers are introduced to the feisty, intelligent title character who lives with her grandmother in a seniors-only apartment building. Because of this, Sammy is forced to sneak around just to get to school; naturally, her social life is severely curtailed as well. Sammy lives with her grandmother, readers learn, because her mother, to whom she refers as "Lady Lana," has moved to Hollywood.

Sammy has some formidable enemies. One is the nosy Mrs. Graybill, who lives down the hall; another is a girl, Heather, who torments her daily at school. To keep herself amused at home, Sammy often observes the goings-on of the outside world with a pair of binoculars from her fifth-floor window. "Usually you just see people looking out their windows, pointing to stuff on the street or talking on the phone," Sammy states, "but sometimes you can see people yelling at each other, which is really strange because you can't *hear* anything."

Sammy is particularly fascinated by the shady Heavenly Hotel across the street, and one afternoon spots a fourth-floor resident moving about a room rather quickly. She then sees the man rifling through a purse while wearing gloves. As Sammy tells it: "And I'm trying to get a better look at his face through all his bushy brown hair and beard, when he stuffs a wad of money from the purse into his jacket pocket and then looks up. Right at me. For a second there I don't think he believed his eyes. He kind of leaned into the window and stared, and I stared right back through the binoculars. Then I did something really, really stupid. I waved."

The man flees the room, and she wonders whether she has just witnessed a crime and if she ought to tell someone about it. But her grandmother is making dinner, and she can't call 911 from the kitchen; getting to a police station is also problematic. Then, her grandmother calls her into the kitchen and reminds her to feed the cat. When the doorbell rings, Sammy is so agitated that she does not quietly make for the closet, as is her usual drill when an unexpected visitor arrives. "This time, though, I jumped. I jumped and yelped like a puppy. And all of a sudden my heart's pounding because I know who it is," Sammy panics. "It's the guy I saw at the Heavenly Hotel, come to shut me up for good."

Eventually, Sammy manages to tell the police, who fail to take her seriously at first. Meanwhile, Heather is plotting against her at school, but Sammy's cleverness uncovers the plot in time. She also learns that a burglar has indeed been stealing from purses in the neighborhood. Other characters in the book include a pair of comical detectives, her friend Marissa, a local DJ, and an eccentric astrologer who is also a robbery victim. They all help Sammy bring the thief to justice. "The solution will likely come as a surprise, and the sleuth delights from start to finish," asserted a *Publishers Weekly* contributor in a review of *Sammy Keyes and the Hotel Thief.* A *Horn Book* review by Martha V. Parravano described Van Draanen's protagonist as "one tough, smart, resourceful seventh grader," and compared the heroine and structure of the lighthearted detective novel to popular adult mystery writers such as Sue Grafton, who are adept at "making the investigator's character and private life at least as interesting and complex as the plot," noted Parravano.

Van Draanen followed the success of the first Sammy Keyes book with a second that same year, *Sammy Keyes and the Skeleton Man.* As it opens around Halloween time, Sammy still lives with her grandmother and is eagerly outfitting herself as the Marsh Monster for the holiday. While trick-or-treating, she and her friends bravely approach the "Bush House," a scary manse with wildly overgrown shrubbery. But then Sammy is nearly knocked down by a man wearing a skeleton costume and carrying a pillowcase. She and her friends advance and discover a fire in the house, and Sammy puts it out. They also find that a burglary has just taken place, and several valuable books are missing from the house.

Sammy, naturally, finds herself drawn into the drama and wants to solve the whodunit. She learns that the Bush House is neglected because its owners, the Le-Bard brothers, are feuding with one another. Once again, her cleverness helps her find a solution and also helps her keep one step ahead of Heather, who continues to plot against her. Sammy, for instance, sneaks into Heather's Halloween party and plants a baby monitor in her room—which provides Sammy with evidence that Heather has been making prank phone calls in Sammy's name. Yet Sammy's natural talent for making friends also helps her forge an unusual bond with Chauncy LeBard, and she even gets the two warring brothers to agree to talk. In the end, she unmasks the skeleton man and recovers the missing rarities. Martha V. Parravano, reviewing the story for *Horn Book,* praised it as a "highly readable mystery [that] hits the ground running." Critic Lynda Short also offered positive words in *School Library Journal:* "Readers will enjoy the mystery, hijinks, plotting, and adult comeuppance."

Van Draanen's third entry in the series, *Sammy Keyes and the Sisters of Mercy,* was published in 1999. Still walking that fine line between intellectual brilliance and juvenile delinquency, Sammy finds herself sentenced to twenty hours of detention, which she must fulfill by helping out at the local Roman Catholic church. One day, cleaning the windows of St. Mary's, she sees a girl she does not know and approaches her, but the girl vanishes and Sammy is suddenly alerted to the distress of Father Mayhew, who has just discovered his valuable ivory cross missing. Sammy, of course, is the first suspect in the theft. Yet other possible culprits surface as well, and in order to clear her own name, she resolves to catch the thief herself. On another day, she again sees the mysterious girl at the church's soup kitchen and eventually learns that she is homeless.

Again, Van Draanen tries to make Sammy a typical adolescent. There is more enmity with Heather, and she is determined to beat her foe in the local softball league championships. In the end, it is Sammy's offer to help a group of musical nuns who do missionary work out of an old school bus that helps solve the mystery of Father Mayhew's missing cross. "As always, quirky characters are Van Draanen's strength," remarked Kay Weisman in a *Booklist* review. An assessment from Jennifer Ralston in *School Library Journal* praised the main plot of *Sammy Keyes and the Sisters of Mercy* as well as the other story lines, both recurring and new. Ralston noted the story lines provide "depth and interest to an already engrossing mystery while capturing the angst of junior high school." Beth E. Anderson, reviewing it for *Voice of Youth Advocates,* commended Van Draanen's heroine. "Sammy is genuine, funny, devoted to her friends and blessed with a strength of char-

acter that lets her reach for a peaceful solution," Anderson wrote.

Van Draanen wrote another entry in the series that also appeared in 1999, *Sammy Keyes and the Runaway Elf.* Set during the Christmas season, Sammy is still in seventh grade and becomes involved in her community's holiday parade. She is assigned to the "Canine Calendar Float" and is charged with babysitting a famous Pomeranian, the calendar cover dog, Marique. Parade chaos ensues, however, when a trio of culprits dressed as the Three Kings throw cats onto the hound-laden float. The prized Marique vanishes, and its owner, wealthy Mrs. Landvogt, blackmails Sammy into finding Marique in order to avoid paying the fifty thousand dollar ransom demanded. An elfin girl, Elyssa, turns out to be a runaway, and Van Draanen weaves her plight and the dognapping together and ties it up with another, according to critics, satisfying conclusion. Once again, however, several suspects must first be eliminated and comical plot twists steered through. This time, Sammy manages to befriend the formidable Mrs. Graybill, too. Remarking upon Sammy's penchant for making friends both younger and much older than herself, *School Library Journal* reviewer Linda Bindner noted that "Van Draanen handles the relationships with style and sensitivity."

A fifth book in the series, *Sammy Keyes and the Curse of Moustache Mary,* was published in 2000, followed by *Sammy Keyes and the Hollywood Mummy* in 2001. Reviewing the latter title in *School Library Journal,* critic Wanda Meyers-Hines noted that it is "clever and fast-paced, and . . . filled with cliff-hanger chapter endings and characters with secrets." As with all of her books, Van Draanen finds that the complex plots seem to come to her slowly. "I get an idea and just let it stew and stew in my brain until it's boiling over," she once said. "Then I start writing and can't stop until the story's out." She conducts all of her research herself and then sits down to writing in her inimitable character's voice. "I need to be able to get into the 'Sammy-zone,' where I feel like I'm channeling her. I work best when the computer can just suck me in and trap me. That's when things start cookin'!"

The success of her career as an author led Van Draanen to give up her teaching job. "This is my first year as a full-time writer," she said in the summer of 2000. "All those years before I'd get up when my husband got ready for work (5:00 A.M.) and just stumble over to the computer to get in an hour or two before I had to get the kids up (I have a six year old and a nine year old) and go off to teach school. I still get up early with my husband and find that early morning is still my most productive time." She plans to continue writing for adolescents. "They're growing, they're changing, and they're receptive to making the world a better place," Van Draanen enthused. "They have big dreams that they want to reach for. I try to give them the strength to believe that—with determination, thought, and persistence—they can attain them. Growing up's not easy. Everyone feels awkward through adolescence, but when you're a kid it seems that you're the only one who's not fitting in. Everyone else seems to have it together, or be comfortable with themselves. It's not true, but that's how we feel when we're kids.

"It's my goal to get kids through those awkward years and onto adulthood safely. The choices they make in the areas of honesty, convictions, friendships, and compassion now will effect them their entire lives."

BIOGRAPHICAL/CRITICAL SOURCES:

BOOKS

Van Draanen, Wendelin, *Sammy Keyes and the Hotel Thief,* Knopf, 1998.

PERIODICALS

Booklist, September 1, 1998, p. 131; April 1, 1999, Kay Weisman, review of *Sammy Keyes and the Sisters of Mercy,* p. 1415; September 1, 1999, p. 146; March 1, 2001, Gillian Engberg, review of *Sammy Keyes and the Hollywood Mummy,* p. 1272.

Horn Book, July-August, 1998, Martha V. Parravano, review of *Sammy Keyes and the Hotel Thief,* pp. 498-499; November-December, 1998, Martha V. Parravano, review of *Sammy Keyes and the Skeleton Man,* p. 743.

Kirkus Reviews, December 1, 1996, review of *How I Survived Being a Girl.*

Publishers Weekly, January 6, 1997, review of *How I Survived Being a Girl,* p. 73; April 27, 1998, review of *Sammy Keyes and the Hotel Thief,* p. 67.

San Luis Obispo Tribune, September 27, 1999.

School Library Journal, February, 1997, Kathleen Odean, review of *How I Survived Being a Girl,* p. 106; July, 1998, p. 100; September, 1998, Lynda Short, review of *Sammy Keyes and the Skeleton Man,* p. 211; July, 1999, Jennifer Ralston, review of *Sammy Keyes and the Sisters of Mercy,* p. 101; September, 1999, Linda Bindner, review of *Sammy Keyes and the Runaway Elf,* p. 229; August, 2000, p. 190; February, 2001, Wanda Meyers-Hines, review of *Sammy Keyes and the Hollywood Mummy,*

p. 122; March, 2001, Sarah Flowers, review of *Sammy Keyes and the Hotel Thief,* p. 87.

Voice of Youth Advocates, April, 2000, Beth E. Anderson, review of *Sammy Keyes and the Sisters of Mercy,* pp. 40-41.

*　　*　　*

van KEULEN, Mensje 1946-
(Josien Meloen, Mensje Francina van der Steen)

PERSONAL: Born Mensje Francina van der Steen, June 10, 1946, in The Hague, Netherlands; married Lon van Keulen, a photographer (divorced); children: one son, Aldo. *Education:* Studied painting in London.

ADDRESSES: Home—Amsterdam, Netherlands. *Office*—c/o Uitgeverij Atlas, Postbus 13, 1000 AA Amsterdam, Netherlands.

CAREER: Novelist, poet, and artist; editor of literary magazine *Maatstaf,* 1973-81.

WRITINGS:

Bleekers zomer (novel; title means "Bleeker Is Summer"), Rap (Amsterdam, Netherlands), 1972.

Allemaal tranen (short stories; title means "Only Tears"), De Arbeiderspers (Amsterdam, Netherlands), 1972.

Van lieverlede (novel; title means "Little By Little"), De Arbeiderspers (Amsterdam, Netherlands), 1975.

Lotgevallen (poems; title means "Vicissitudes"), Rap (Amsterdam, Netherlands), 1977.

De avonturen van Anna Molino (poems; title means "The Adventures of Anna Molino"), De Arbeiderspers (Amsterdam, Netherlands), 1980.

Overspel (novel; title means "Adultery"), De Arbeiderspers (Amsterdam, Netherlands), 1982.

De ketting: verhalen, Der Arbeiderspers (Amsterdam, Netherlands), 1983.

Tommie Station, Querido (Amsterdam, Netherlands), 1985.

(With Adriaan van Dis and Thomas Verbogt) *Tropen jaren,* Veen (Utrecht, Netherlands), 1986.

Englebert (novel), De Arbeiderspers (Amsterdam, Netherlands), 1987.

De lach van Schreck (short stories; title means "The Laugh of Schreck"), De Arbeiderspers (Amsterdam, Netherlands), 1991.

Geheime dame, Atlas (Amsterdam, Netherlands), 1992.

De rode strik, Atlas (Amsterdam, Netherlands), 1994.
Olifanten op een web, Atlas (Amsterdam, Netherlands), 1997.

SIDELIGHTS: Trained as a visual artist, Mensje van Keulen worked as a magazine illustrator early in her career. Indeed, her first stories and poems appeared, with her drawings, in prominent literary magazines, and she served as editor of one of them, *Maatstaf,* from 1973 to 1981. Her first book, the novel *Bleekers zomer,* attracted positive notice and identified van Keulen as one of the post-World War II generation of writers who would bring realism back to Dutch literature. A contributor to *The Bloomsbury Guide to Women's Literature* considered van Keulen's work sober and pessimistic, concerned as it is with themes of suffering, doom, war, grief, and decay.

In addition to her work for adult readers, van Keulen is also respected as a children's author. She lives in Amsterdam.

BIOGRAPHICAL/CRITICAL SOURCES:

BOOKS

Buck, Claire, editor. *The Bloomsbury Guide to Women's Literature,* Prentice Hall (New York, NY), 1992.*

*   *   *

VOLKOVA, Bronislava 1946-

PERSONAL: Born May 15, 1946, in Decin, Czechoslovakia; daughter of Stefan Fischer (a machine engineer) and Margit Morenova (a violin virtuoso); married Robert Smith, 1995 (died, 1999). *Education:* Attended Leningrad State University, 1967-68, Moscow State University, 1972, University of Cologne, 1974 and 1975, and Harvard University and Massachusetts Institute of Technology, 1977-78; Charles University (Prague, Czechoslovakia), Ph.D., 1970, CSc., 1973. *Politics:* "None." *Religion:* "All." *Avocational interests:* "Semiotics, mysticism, collage, yoga, Qi-Gong, theater, dance."

ADDRESSES: Home—926 Commons Dr., Bloomington, IN 47401. *Office*—Indiana University, Slavic Department, Kirkwood Ave., BH 502, Bloomington, IN 47405. *E-mail*—volkova@indiana.edu.

CAREER: University of 17th of November, Prague, Czechoslovakia, assistant professor of Russian,

1973-74; Slavisches Institut der Universitat zu Koln, Cologne, West Germany, assistant professor of Slavic Languages, 1975; Slavisches Seminar der Philipps-Universitat Marburg, Marburg, West Germany, visiting professor of Slavic languages, 1976; Harvard University, Cambridge, MA, Mellon Faculty Fellow in Slavic Department, 1977-78; Indiana University, Bloomington, IN, visiting professor, 1978-80, assistant professor, 1982-86, associated professor, 1986-91, professor of Slavic languages and literatures, 1991—, adjunct professor of comparative literature, 1992—; University of Virginia, Charlottesville, VA, assistant professor of Slavic languages and literatures and general linguistics, 1980-82. CIEE Program, Prague, resident director; affiliated with Council on International Educational Exchange; has appeared on various radio and television programs in many countries, including England, Germany, U.S., and Czechoslovakia; given more than 100 papers, lectures and poetry readings.

MEMBER: International PEN Club, International Semiotic Society, Societas Linguistica Europea, Poets and Writers, Czechoslovak Society of Arts and Sciences, Association of Czech Writers.

AWARDS, HONORS: American Council of Learned Societies Award, 1988, for research in Canada and West Germany; George Gall Memorial Award, Systems Research Foundation, 1988, for "scholarly work in literature and for most significant contribution to modern poetry"; "Poet of Merit," American Poetry Association, 1989; IREX Award, 1989, for research in Czechoslovakia; Fulbright Award, 1990-91, for research in Czechoslovakia; numerous research grants and fellowships by Mellon, University of Virginia and Indiana University, 1980s and 1990s.

WRITINGS:

Emotive Signs in Language and Semantic Functioning of Derived Nouns in Russian, John Benjamins (Amsterdam, Netherlands), 1987.
A Feminist's Semiotic Odyssey through Czech Literature, Edwin Mellen (Lewiston, NY), 1997.

Contributor of reviews and other works to various publications, including *Folia Slavica, Slavic and East European Journal, Rocky Mountain Review of Language and Literature, Proceedings of the Semiotic Society of America,* and *World Literature Today.* Member of editorial board, *Kosmas,* 1995—.

POETRY

Motaky do usi peny, PmD (Munich, Germany), 1984, bilingual edition published as *Prison Notes Smuggled into the Ears of Seafoam / Motaky do usi peny,* Edwin Mellen (Lewiston, NY), 1999.

Dum v ohni (title means "House on Fire"), PmD (Munich, Germany), 1985.

Vzduch bez podpatku (title means "Air without Heels"), PmD (Munich, Germany), 1987.

Jista nepritomnost (title means "A Certain Absence"), PmD (Munich, Germany), 1990.

Promeny, Alfa-Omega (Prague), 1991, bilingual edition with author's collages published as *Promeny/Transformations,* Prague, 2000.

Zranitelnost zeme (title means "Vulnerability of Earth"), PmD (Munich, Germany), 1992.

(Translator of original Czech poetry, with the assistance of A. Durkin, W. Barnstone, L. Parrot and G. Orr), *The Courage of the Rainbow: Selected Poems* Sheep Meadow (New York, NY), 1993.

Hluchonema dlan (title means "The Deaf and Dumb Hand"), PmD (Munich, Germany), 1993.

Roztristene svety (title means "The Shattered Worlds"), Votobia (Olomouc, Czech Republic), 1995.

Contibutor of poems and stories in Czech, English, Spanish, French and German to various publications, including *Midwest Poetry Review, American Poetry Anthology, Best New Poets of 1988,* and *Massage Magazine.*

WORK IN PROGRESS: Entering Light/Vstup do svetla, poetry manuscript.

SIDELIGHTS: Bronislava Volkova told *CA* that "creative expression, experimentation, and love" are her primary motivations for writing; "new insights, and unpredictable encounters" are what particularly influence her work; and "solitude, nature, my vision, animals, and God" inspired her to write on her chosen subjects.

BIOGRAPHICAL/CRITICAL SOURCES:

PERIODICALS

Prague Post, July, 1994, Alan Levy, "Bronislava Volkova: The Poet as Healer."

W-Y

WAKEFIELD, Norm(an) 1934-

PERSONAL: Born November 9, 1934, in Dansville, NY; son of Francis and Edith Sophia Wakefield; married Winifred Townsend, February 2, 1963; children: Amy Wakefield Nappa, Joel, Jill Wakefield Wuellner, Jody Wakefield Brolsma, Annette. *Ethnicity:* "Anglo." *Education:* Attended Moody Bible Institute, 1960; Westmont College, B.A., 1963; Wheaton College, Wheaton, IL, M.A., 1968; Southern Baptist Theological Seminary, Ed.D., 1971. *Religion:* Protestant.

ADDRESSES: Home—3609 East Mercer Lane, Phoenix, AZ 85028. *E-mail*—winnor@juno.com.

CAREER: Biola University, La Mirada, CA, adjunct professor at Talbot School of Theology, 1985-90; Phoenix Seminary, Phoenix, AZ, professor of pastoral theology, 1991-2000. *Military service:* U.S. Navy, aviation electronics technician, 1955-57.

WRITINGS:

You Can Have a Happier Family, Regal (Glendale, CA), 1977.
Listening, Word Books (Waco, TX), 1981.
(With Larry Richards) *Basic Christian Values,* Zondervan (Grand Rapids, MI), 1981.
(With Larry Richards) *First Steps for New and Used Christians,* Zondervan (Grand Rapids, MI), 1981.
(With Larry Richards) *Fruit of the Spirit,* Zondervan (Grand Rapids, MI), 1981.
(With Larry Richards) *The Good Life,* Zondervan (Grand Rapids, MI), 1981.
Solving Problems before They Become Conflicts, Zondervan (Grand Rapids, MI), 1987.
(With Josh McDowell) *The Dad Difference,* Here's Life (San Bernardino, CA), 1989.

(With Josh McDowell) *Friend of the Lonely Heart,* Word Books (Dallas, TX), 1991.
(With Mike Nappa) *A Legacy of Joy,* Barbour Publishing (Ulrichville, OH), 1998.
(With Mike Nappa) *True Stories of Transformed Lives,* Tyndale (Wheaton, IL), 1999.
(With daughter, Judy Brolsma) *Men Are from Israel, Women Are from Moab,* Inter-Varsity Press (Downers Grove, IL), 2000.

SIDELIGHTS: Norm Wakefield told *CA:* "As I've grown older I've developed a heartfelt passion for life. One way this is expressed is in my eagerness to encourage others to find intimacy with our Lord, and among family and friends. I am blessed with an abundance of joy-filled friendships as well as a passion for individuals in their life challenges. An inward drive to leave behind a legacy of joy motivates me daily.

"Writing is one significant channel in which I can express this passion. For me the process begins with my own discoveries about life. As I gain insights I pass them on through the written page. The feedback and affirmation I receive helps me know that what I have written is targeting another's heart.

"The most recent book, *Men Are from Israel, Women Are from Moab,* arose from my deep admiration for the biblical account of Ruth and Boaz. Though they came from very diverse backgrounds, they found an attraction based on mutual respect and delight for the character qualities each possessed. These two individuals inspire us to a unity of spirit that transcends gender differences."

WALLACE, Christine 1960-

PERSONAL: Born 1960, in Sydney, Australia. *Education:* Australian National University, B.A.; University of Sydney, BEc.

ADDRESSES: Agent—c/o Pan Macmillan, Level 18, St. Martins Tower, 31 Market St., Sidney, New South Wales 2000, Australia.

CAREER: Biographer and journalist, c. 1993—.

WRITINGS:

Hewson: A Portrait, Sun Australia (Sydney, Australia), 1993.

Greer: Untamed Shrew, Macmillan, Pan Macmillan Australia (Sydney, Australia), 1997, published as *Germaine Greer: Untamed Shrew,* Faber & Faber (Boston, MA), 1998.

SIDELIGHTS: Born in Sydney in 1960, Christine Wallace is an Australian biographer and journalist who spent ten years reporting on federal politics from the Canberra Press Gallery. Her first book was *Hewson: A Portrait.* Wallace garnered more attention in 1998 with her second book, *Greer: Untamed Shrew,* the first full-length biography of the provocative feminist Germaine Greer. Greer exploded onto the scene with her manifesto, *The Female Eunuch,* in 1970. Greer's book renounced the sexual repression imposed on women by the institution of marriage and called for greater sexual freedom and the open pursuit of sexual pleasure for women: "The blessed are laid-back, into their bodies, in touch with themselves. They shrink from no penetration, they feel no invasion of self, they fear nothing and regret nothing, they defy jealousy. The regular recurrence of orgasm provides the proof that they are in the 'state of grace.' " Greer practiced her own theory with gusto.

Greer grew up in Australia in the 1950s, the product of an unhappy marriage between her parents, a homemaker and an advertising salesman (Greer later wrote a biography titled *Daddy, We Hardly Knew You,* 1989). She was marked by her difficult relationship with Catholicism, her parents, and her husband. After her education at Catholic schools Greer attended the University of Melbourne. After she graduated she moved to Sydney, where she mixed with a group of intellectuals and bohemians called the Push; this group helped form Greer's own brand of anarchistic pessimism. Before completing a Ph.D. in English from Cambridge, Greer worked as an actress and a journalist. She was an un-

known when her "dumb agent" suggested she write a book on "the fiftieth anniversary of female suffrage or some such bullshit," as quoted by the *Times Literary Supplement.* An infuriated tirade followed: "What are we talking about! Women didn't get the vote until there was nothing left worth voting for. And what do you think the vote accomplishes anyway?" The possibilities of that rage were recognized by an enterprising publisher; thus *The Female Eunuch* was born.

Wallace's biography of Greer is unauthorized; Greer was vitriolically opposed to Wallace's biography and called the journalist "a dung-eating beatle" and "flesh-eating bacteria." In fact, because the subject of the biography is still alive, *Greer* created a significant invasion-of-privacy debate after its Australian publication in 1997. Wallace relied on articles, speeches, and numerous interviews with academics, activists, and others (including Greer's mother) to describe not only Greer's life and work but also her intellectual context. Even-handed in describing Greer's childhood and youth, Wallace is unflinchingly harsh in evaluating Greer's work and political importance. She calls *The Female Eunuch* a testament to "hegemonic heterosexuality," and concludes that Greer opportunistically took advantage of the women's movement for her own self-promotion (Wallace writes that Greer was "only alive, truly alive, when her ego had an erection."). She contends that Greer derived her book from Black Panther Eldridge Cleaver's chapter "Allegory of the Black Eunuch" in his *Soul on Ice,* and describes *The Female Eunuch* as "politically naive." She further argues that Greer's blaming of women for male violence against them is a capitulation to men in language that "relied on traditional rhetorical ploys." But perhaps the most galling assertion to Greer is that the feminist was largely shaped by events in her personal life. Despite her biting criticism, Wallace still credits *The Female Eunuch* with awakening women to their sexual repression. Karl Miller wrote in the *Times Literary Supplement* that Wallace's book "is a more instructive book than Greer's clarion-call *The Female Eunuch,* though it has to be added that Greer's electric presence helps to account for its appeal."

BIOGRAPHICAL/CRITICAL SOURCES:

BOOKS

Greer, Germaine, *The Female Eunuch,* MacGibbon & Kee (London, England), 1970.

Wallace, Christine, *Greer: Untamed Shrew,* Macmillan, Pan Macmillan Australia, 1997.

PERIODICALS

Booklist, March 1, 1999, Mary Carroll, review of *Greer: Untamed Shrew,* p. 1134.

Library Journal, April 1, 1999, Carol Ann McAllister, review of *Greer: Untamed Shrew,* p. 108.

Melbourne Age, July 2, 1999, review of *Greer: Untamed Shrew.*

New York Times Book Review, May 9, 1999, Camile Paglia, review of *Greer: Untamed Shrew,* p. 19.

Publishers Weekly, February 15, 1999, review of *Greer: Untamed Shrew,* p. 96.

Times Literary Supplement, June 19, 1998, Karl Miller, "The Strine Quartet," pp. 15-16.*

*   *   *

WALLRAFF, Hans Günter   1942-

PERSONAL: Born October 1, 1942, in Burscheid, Germany; son of Josef and Johanna Wallraff; married Birgit Böll; children: two daughters.

ADDRESSES: Home—Thebaerstr 20, D-5000, Cologne, Germany. *Office*—c/o Kiepenheuer & Witsch, Rondorfer STR 5, 50968, Cologne, Germany.

CAREER: Freelance writer and investigative journalist. Book dealer, 1957-81; factory worker, 1963-66.

MEMBER: PEN.

WRITINGS:

(With Christian Geissler) *"Wir brauchen dich:" als Arbeiter in deutschen Industriebetrieben,* Rütten & Loening (München, Germany), 1966.

(With Arno Ploog) *Notstand unser,* Fischer (Frankfurt, Germany), 1967.

Nachspiele: Szenische Dokumentation, Edition Valtaire (Frankfurt, Germany), 1968.

13 unerwünschte Reportagen, Kiepenheuer and Witsch (Köln, Germany), 1969.

Industriereportagen: Als Arbeiter in deutschen Grossbetrieben, Rowohlt (Hamburg, Germany), 1970.

Unerwünschte Reportagen, Aufbau (Berlin, Germany), 1970.

Neue Reportagen, Untersuchungen und Lehrbeispiele, Kiepenheuer & Witsch (Köln, Germany), 1972.

(With Jens Hagen) *Was wollt ihr denn, ihr lebt ja noch: Chronik einer Industrieansiedlung,* Rowohlt (Reinbek bei Hamburg, Germany), 1973.

(With Bernt Engelmann) *Ihr da oben, wir da unten,* Kiepenheuer and Witsch (Köln, Germany), 1973.

(With Bernd Kuhlmann) *Wie hätten wir's denn gerne? Unternehmerstrategen proben d. Klassenkampf,* Hammer (Wuppertal, Germany), 1975.

(With Eckart Spoo) *Unser Faschismus nebenan: Griechenland gestern ein Lehrstück für morgen,* Kiepenheuer & Witsch (Köln, Germany), 1975.

Die Reportagen, Kiepenheuer & Witsch (Köln, Germany), 1976.

(With Hella Schlumberger) *Aufdeckung einer Verschwörung: die Spínola- Aktion,* Kiepenheuer and Witsch (Köln, Germany), 1976.

Befehlsverweigerung: die Bundeswehr und Industriereportagen, Kiepenheuer and Witsch (Köln, Germany), 1976.

(With Hella Schlumberger) *Die aufdeckung einer Verschwörung: figuren der seitgeschichte,* Kiepenheuer and Witsch (Köln, Germany), 1976.

Der Aufmacher: der Mann, der bei Bild Hans Esser war, Kiepenheuer and Witsch (Köln, Germany), 1977.

(With Heinrich Böll) *Berichte zure Geninnungslage der Nation,* Rowohlt (Reinbek bei Hamburg, Germany), 1977.

Wallraff, the Undesirable Journalist, Pluto Press (London, England), 1978.

(With R. Crumb) *Vorläufiger Lebenslauf nach Akten und Selbstaussagen des Stefan B.,* Giftzwerg Press (Heerhugowaard, Netherlands), 1978.

Verslaggever van BILD, Van Gennep (Amsterdam, Netherlands), 1978.

The Wallraff Reports, Overlook Press (Woodstock, NY), 1979.

Zeugen der Anklage: dei "Bild'beschreibung wird fortgesetzt, Kiepenheuer and Witsch (Köln, Germany), 1979.

(With Oren Schmuckler and Max von der Grün) *Unsere Fabrik,* C. J. Bucher (Luzern, Switzerland), 1979.

Von einem, der auszog und das Fürchten lernte, Zweitausendeins (Frankfurt, Germany), 1979.

(With Henrich Böll and Phillipe Ivernel) *Rapports,* F. Maspéro (Paris, France), 1980.

Das BILD-Handbuch bis zum Bildausfall, Konkret Literatur (Hamburg, Germany), 1981.

Zeugen der Anklage die "BILD-beschreibung wird fortgwsetzt, Kiepenheuer and Witsch (Köln, Germany), 1982.

Der Aufmacher: der Mann, der bei Bild Hans Esser war, Kiepenheuer and Witsch (Köln, Germany), 1982.

Die unheimliche Republik: politische Verfolgung in der Bundesrepublik, VSA- Verlag (Hamburg, Germany), 1982.

(With Eckart Spoo) *Unser Faschismus renbenan: Erfahrungen bei NATO-Partnern,* Rowohlt (Hamburg, Germany), 1982.

Nicaragua von innen, Konkret Literatur Verlag (Hamburg, Germany), 1983.

(With Jochen Busse and Gerhard Schmidt) *Is Was, Kanzler? Eine Bonner Klamotte,* Prometh (Köln, Germany), 1984.

Mein Lesebuch, Fischer Taschenbuch Verlag (Frankfurt, Germany), 1984.

Bericht vom Mittelpunkt der Welt: die Reportagen, Kiepenheuer and Witsch (Köln, Germany), 1984.

Bild-Störung: ein Handbuch, Kiepenheuer and Witsch (Köln, Germany), 1985.

Ganz unten, Kiepenheuer and Witsch (Köln, Germany), 1985, English translation published as *Lowest of the Low,* Pluto (London, England), 1986.

Enthüllungen: Recherchen, Reportagen und Reden vor Gericht, Zweitausendeins (Frankfurt, Germany), 1985.

Was wollt ihr denn, ihr lebt ja noch: Chronik einer Industrieansiedlung, W. Heyne (München, Germany), 1985.

Günter Wallraffs BILDerbuch, Steidl (Göttingen, Germany), 1985.

Predigt von unten, Steidl (Göttingen), 1986.

Reportagen 1963-1974: mir Materialien und einem Nachwort des Autors, Kiepenheuer und Witsch (Köln, Germany), 1987.

Vom Ende der Eiszeit und wie man Feuer macht: Aufsätze, Kritiken, Reden, Kiepeheuer and Witsch (Köln, Germany), 1987.

Akteneinsicht: Bericht zur Gesinnungslage des Staatsschutzes, Steidl (Göttingen, Germany), 1987.

Und macht euch die Erde untertan: eine Widerrede, Steidl (Göttingen, Germany), 1987.

Ganz unten: mit einer Dokumentation der Folgen, Kiepenheuer and Witsch (Köln, Germany), 1988.

(With Heinrich Böll, Elmar Schmähling, and Jürgen Fuchs) *Mein Tagebuch aus der Bundeswehr,* Kiepenheuer and Witsch (Köln, Germany), 1992.

Enthüllungen, Steidl (Göttingen, Germany), 1992.

ADAPTATIONS: The Man Inside (motion picture), New Line Home Video, based on Wallraff's true story of a man who infiltrated the most powerful newspaper in Western Europe and exposed it as a ruthless propaganda machine.

SIDELIGHTS: Born in Burscheid, Federal Republic of Germany in 1942, Hans Günter Wallraff has been a book dealer, factory worker, and freelance writer. Wallraff's most noted work is as an investigative journalist. Of his early exploits, he once chained himself to an Athens light pole to protest Greece's military regime. The result was arrest, imprisonment, and torture. Another time, Wallraff, disguised as a representative of rich, right-wing Germans, enticed Portugal's former president to Dusseldorf. Promising to lend support to a coup, Wallraff obtained enough confidential information from Antonio de Spinolo to have the man deported from Switzerland.

Perhaps Walraff's most daring investigative infiltration was inside the walls of West Germany's largest newspaper: *Bild.* Posing as a writer/journalist Wallraff, according to Serge d'Adesky, a reviewer in *The Progressive,* "gathered enough material for a book, *Der Aufmacher,* . . . which accused *Bild* of fabricating interviews, publishing sham photographs, cooperating with government intelligence agencies, and slandering public officials who do not share the paper's right-wing editorial policy." *Bild* responded with a five-part series "exposing" Wallraff as "an underground communist." A Hamburg court blocked further publication of *Der Aufmacher.* Wallraff's response, noted d'Adesky, was to "produce a second exposé" titled *Zeugen der Anklug.*

During the several years Wallraff worked in factories, he "had not become insensitive to the improprieties and abuses of factory life and thus was able to speak out against them" according to Albert J. Camigliano, a reviewer in *Monatshefte fur Deutshen Unterricht.* A reviewer in *National Review* called Wallraff "a militant reporter" when *Ganz unten,* a book that chronicled the lives of immigrant Turkish laborers, was released. Arthur Williams, a reviewer in *Modern Language Review,* described *Ganz unten* as "in important work" that "teachers and tutors will be eager to include in . . . their reading lists." Clive Davis, a reviewer in *New Statesman & Society,* called the book "an unremittingly bleak piece of work" reminiscent of *Black Like Me,* and noted that Wallraff hoped to bring attention and humanitarian aid to thousands of ill-used, "illegal" Turkish immigrants. Arlene Akiko Teraoka, a reviewer in *New German Critic,* complemented Wallraff for turning his investigative journalist "camera lens, at us" so that we may be "confronted and challenged, perhaps threatened, by the stark image of life 'ganz unten' in the Federal Republic of Germany." Anna K. Kuhn, a reviewer in *New German Critique,* noted that *Ganz unten* since its appearance in 1985 has been a runaway best seller. "To date," Kuhn stated, "it has been translated into eighteen languages," including French, Czech, Serbo-Croatian, Spanish, Portuguese, Chinese, and English. Considered Wallraff's most popular work, it has also become his most controversial. As Kuhn concluded, *Gans unten* "illustrat[ed] the pitfalls confronting even sympathetic members of a hegemonic culture when they try to [re]present and/or plead a minority cause."

BIOGRAPHICAL/CRITICAL SOURCES:

PERIODICALS

Modern Language Review, July 1989, Arthur Williams, review of *Ganz unten,* pp. 807-808.

Monatshefte fur Deutschen Unterricht, winter 1983, Albert J. Camigliano, "Günter Wallraff: B(e)aring the Facts," pp. 405-418.

National Review, June 20, 1986, "Social Bombshell," p. 42.

New German Critique, winter 1989, Arlene Akiko Teraoka, "Talking 'Turk': On Narrative Strategies and Cultural Stereotypes," pp. 104-128; winter 1989, Ann K. Kuhn, "Bourgeois Ideology and the (Mis)Reading of Günter Wallraff's *Ganz Unten,*" pp. 191-202.

New Statesman & Society, October 14, 1988, Clive Davis, "Ali's Pilgrimage," p. 33.

Progressive, September 1981, Serge d'Adesky, "Muckraking Master," p. 51.*

*　　*　　*

WARD, Jule DeJager 1942-

PERSONAL: Born September 8, 1942, in Detroit, MI; daughter of John (a drafter) and Margaret (a nurse; maiden name, Luger) DeJager; married John F. Ward, Jr., December 19, 1969; children: Kristin, Carrie, Betsy Ward Herald, John Brophy. *Ethnicity:* "Dutch." *Education:* St. Mary's College, B.A., 1967; DePaul University, M.A. (with distinction), 1985; University of Chicago, M.A., 1986, Ph.D., 1996. *Politics:* Democrat. *Religion:* Roman Catholic. *Avocational interests:* Teaching, writing.

ADDRESSES: Home—Chicago, IL. *Office*—DePaul University, 2350 Kenmore, Chicago, IL 60614. *E-mail*—juledej@aol.com.

CAREER: DePaul University, Chicago, IL, instructor in ethics and theology, 1993-2000. Active in religious education programs for people with "developmental delays"; consultant to Religion, Culture, and Family Project.

MEMBER: American Academy of Religion, Catholic Theological Society of America, Society for Christian Ethics, College Theological Society, Misericordia Family Association.

WRITINGS:

La Leche League: At the Crossroads of Medicine, Feminism, and Religion, University of North Carolina Press (Chapel Hill, NC), 2000.

(Contributor) Kay A. Reed, and Isabel Wollaston, editors, *Suffer the Little Children: Urban Violence and Sacred Space,* University of Birmingham, 2001.

WORK IN PROGRESS: Catholic Family Life: Chicago Style, 2002; research on family religious life in a comparative perspective.

SIDELIGHTS: Jule DeJager Ward told *CA:* "William James observed the religious experiences of those with whom he came in contact and those whom he read about. Then he shared his observations with us. Many of us recognize ourselves in James's now more than one-hundred-year-old insights about religious experience. I enjoy doing just what James did. I direct my observations more specifically toward how religious sensibility enlivens those parts of our lives we believe to be completely outside religion. There are so many practices and beliefs that we tend to label non-religious that, in reality, have everything to do with religion. Our actions reveal not just what we believe to be true about the present moment and our present place, but what we believe to be true about the universe and our place in it. Without always realizing it, humans place themselves within the broadest possible context in order to make both the big and the small decisions in their lives. Some of these are decisions about relationships: who to marry or what is a friend. Some are moral decisions: when is it okay to tell an untruth or whether abortion is murder. Some are simply what constitutes fun: what is the difference between an offensive film and an entertaining one. We also construct roles for ourselves through making these decisions. When I write, I try to look at how people make these decisions and what it means for their lives and the lives of those around them."

*　　*　　*

WARMOND, Ellen
See YPEREN, Pieternella Cornelia van

WARTENBERG, Thomas E.   1949-

PERSONAL: Born November 20, 1949, in Newark, NJ; son of Rolf and Hannah Wartenberg; married Wendy Berg (a lawyer), July 5, 1986; children: Jacob Benjamin. *Education:* Amherst College, B.A., 1971; Stanford University, M.A., 1973; Pittsburgh University, Ph.D., 1977. *Politics:* "Radical."

ADDRESSES: Home—136 Crescent St., Northampton, MA 01060. *Office*—Department of Philosophy, Mount Holyoke College, 50 College St., South Hadley, MA 01075; fax: 413-538-2579. *E-mail*—twartenb@mtholy oke.edu.

CAREER: Duke University, Durham, NC, assistant professor of philosophy, 1977-83; Hampshire College, Amherst, MA, visiting associate professor of philosophy, 1983-84; Mount Holyoke College, South Hadley, MA, professor of philosophy and film studies, 1986—.

WRITINGS:

The Forms of Power, Temple University Press (Philadelphia, PA), 1990.
Rethinking Power, SUNY Press, 1992.
Philosophy & Film, Routledge, 1995.
Unlike Couples, Westview, 1999.
What Is Art?, Harcourt (New York, NY), in press.

WORK IN PROGRESS: The Philosophy of Film; Narrative Film and Masculinity: A Reassessment; and *Can Films be Socially Critical?*

*   *   *

WEBER, Nan   1954-

PERSONAL: Born May 4, 1954, in Milwaukee, WI; daughter of Robert (a printer) and Florence (a homemaker; maiden name, Stivers) Weber; married Paul Boruff (a musician), August 5, 1992. *Ethnicity:* "White." *Education:* University of Wisconsin— Milwaukee, B.F.A., 1976; Salt Lake Community College, A.S. (Interpreting for the Deaf), 1997. *Avocational interests:* Independent production of videotapes and eight-millimeter films.

ADDRESSES: Home—467 South Post St., Salt Lake City, UT 84104-1229. *E-mail*—Nanner333@aol.com.

CAREER: Presenter of women's history performances, 1976—. Western Montana College, Dillon, elder-hostel instructor and onsite coordinator, 1992—.

MEMBER: Women Writing the West, Registry of Interpreters for the Deaf, Montana Performing Arts Consortium.

AWARDS, HONORS: Eagle Edit Award, Utah Film and Video Center, 1993, for the short videotape *Jumprope.*

WRITINGS:

Mattie: A Woman's Journey West (nonfiction), Homestead Publishing (Moose, WY), 1997.

Creator of videotapes, including *Jumprope.*

WORK IN PROGRESS: A manuscript about Maria Virgina and Joseph Alfred Slade, with sister Georgia Weber and Nelson Ober; research on prostitutes of western mining camps and on dude ranches of Montana.

*   *   *

WEITZMAN, David L.   1936-

PERSONAL: Born November 24, 1936, in Chicago, IL; son of Louis (a pharmacist) and Louise (Ottenheimer) Weitzman; children: Arin, Brooks, Peter. *Education:* Attended Art Institute of Chicago; Purdue University, B.S. (English), 1958; Northwestern University, M.A. (history), 1959. *Politics:* Liberal. *Religion:* Jewish.

ADDRESSES: Home—P.O. Box 456, Covelo, CA 95428. *Office*—Nancy Ellis Literary Services, P.O. Box 1564, Willits, CA 95490. *E-mail*—weitzman@ mcn.org.

CAREER: Freelance writer and illustrator. Former school teacher in the San Francisco Bay Area and in Round Valley, CA; instructor at University of California, Berkeley, Merritt College, and University of California Education Extension. Member of curriculum delegation to People's Republic of China, 1978; participant in museum education programs, film documentaries, and workshops. *Exhibitions:* Bedford Gallery, Walnut Creek, CA; Gallery 10, Sutter Creek, CA; Elizabeth Stone Gallery, Birmingham, MI; Janice Charach Epstein Museum, West Bloomfield, MI; Columbus Public Library, Columbus, OH; American Institute of Graphic Arts, New York City; Art Center of Battle Creek, Battle Creek, MI; College of Dupage, Glenn Ellen, IL; Slater Mill Historic Site, Pawtucket, RI; and Allen County Museum, Lima, OH. *Military service:* U.S. Air Force, 1959-63; became first lieutenant.

MEMBER: Society for Industrial Archeology.

AWARDS, HONORS: Distinguished Book designation, Association of Children's Librarians, and PEN Book Award, both 1982, both for *Windmills, Bridges, and Old Machines;* Bronze Medal, Leipzig International Book Design Exhibition, 1989, for *Superpower;* Books for the Teen Age designations, New York Public Library, 1994, for *Great Lives: Human Culture,* and 1996, for *Great Lives: Theatre;* Notable Social Studies Trade Books for Young People designation, Children's Book Council/National Council for the Social Studies, 1999, for *Locomotive.*

WRITINGS:

NONFICTION

Chinese Studies in Paperback (bibliography), Mc-Cutchan (Berkeley, CA), 1967.

(Coauthor) *Asia* (textbook), Addison-Wesley, 1969.

Asian Studies Curriculum Project, Field/Addison-Wesley, 1969.

(With Richard E. Gross) *The Human Experience* (textbook), Houghton, 1974.

Eggs and Peanut Butter: A Teacher's Scrapbook, Word Wheel (Menlo Park, CA), 1975.

The Brown Paper School Presents My Backyard History Book, illustrated by James Robertson, Little, Brown, 1975.

Underfoot: An Everyday Guide to Exploring the American Past, Scribner's, 1976.

Traces of the Past: A Field Guide to Industrial Archaeology, Scribner's, 1980.

A Day in Peking (textbook), Houghton, 1981.

Windmills, Bridges, and Old Machines: Discovering Our Industrial Past, Scribner's, 1982.

(With David King and Mariah Marvin) *United States History* (textbook), Addison-Wesley, 1984.

Industrial Eye, photographs by Jet Lowe, J. Wiley, 1987.

The Mountain Man and the President, illustrated by Charles Shaw, Raintree/Steck-Vaughn, 1992.

Great Lives: Theatre, Scribner's, 1994.

Great Lives: Human Culture, Scribner's, 1994.

(And illustrator) *Locomotive: Building an Eight-Wheeler,* Houghton, 1999.

FICTION; SELF-ILLUSTRATED

Superpower: The Making of a Steam Locomotive, Godine, 1987.

Thrashin' Time: Harvest Days in the Dakotas, Godine, 1991.

Old Ironsides: Americans Build a Fighting Ship, Houghton, 1997.

Pouring Iron: An Old Foundry Ghost Story, Houghton, 1998.

Rama and Sita: A Tale from Ancient Java, Godine, 2001.

OTHER

Working Shadows (fiction), Atheneum, 1996.

(Illustrator) Catherine Salton, *Rafael and the Noble Task* (fiction), HarperCollins, 2000.

Writer for video documentaries, with Terry Moyemont, *USS Constitution: Living the Legend* and, with Andy Fahrenwald, *Pouring Iron.*

WORK IN PROGRESS: Text and illustrations for *Model T* (working title), for Random House, 2002; *Rider in the Sky* (working title), with John Hulls, for Random House, 2002.

SIDELIGHTS: A creative and inspiring educator, David L. Weitzman has found an outlet for his curiosity about early American technology through writing and illustrating a number of highly praised books for children. Within the pages of such works as *Windmills, Bridges, and Old Machines: Discovering Our Industrial Past* and *Pouring Iron,* readers can learn about the development of crafts and their role in the development of modern industry. In addition to his writing, Weitzman is also an illustrator; his highly detailed drawings have appeared in exhibitions around the United States, and he has been involved in several film documentaries.

Born in 1936 in Chicago, Weitzman attended Purdue University, where he earned a degree in English before moving on to Northwestern for an advanced history degree. Fortunately for many young people in Weitzman's adopted state of California, after a three-year stint with the United States Air Force, he turned to teaching, spending over two decades moving between elementary, secondary, and college classrooms. His first books for a general audience, 1975's *The Brown Paper School Presents My Backyard History Book* and 1976's *Underfoot: An Everyday Guide to Exploring the American Past,* were the result of his work with young people in the classroom, where a project on discovering one's roots taught students to collect oral histories, search cemeteries and historic archives, and chart their lineage. As he explained to Herbert Mitgang in the *New York Times,* his interest in uncovering personal history began at home: "I began getting involved in my own family and then applied the techniques in the classroom. When I taught in the Bay area, many of my students were Blacks and Asians. Searching for their own pasts, the youngsters discovered much about themselves—and restored pride and understanding at home." *My Backyard History Book* contains directions for collecting and preserving family history, as well as indulging in such creative projects as making gravestone rubbings and learning to identify historic architecture. Calling the underlying concept "fresh," *Booklist* contributor Denise M. Wilms maintained that *My Backyard History Book* would inspire readers to "take interest in their own and their community's roots." *Underfoot* takes a more personal approach, as Weitzman walks readers through a search for local history, traveling from attics to cemeteries to the library stacks. "Although Weitzman appears to be self-taught, his amateur approach . . . has an engaging quality that might well keep many readers reading," noted a contributor to *Wilson Library Bulletin.*

Weitzman indulged in his love affair with industrial technology in 1982's *Windmills, Bridges, and Old Machines.* Dubbed "a kind of ode to the old machine, a sonnet to the sawmill or steam locomotive" by *New York Times Book Review* contributor Holcomb B. Noble, Weitzman's book follows the growth of technology from the paddle wheel to the wind mill to the saw mill to building the Erie Canal. Praising *Windmills, Bridges, and Old Machines* for its inclusion of photographs, easy-to-read diagrams, and numerous interesting facts, *Booklist* contributor Barbara Elleman cited the author's "chatty style and personal, enthusiastic approach" in increasing the book's readability. *School Library Journal* reviewer Jeffrey A. French commented that the volume's "description of old industries and machinery is notable for its breadth."

Weitzman has mixed a pinch of fiction with several handfuls of fact in such books as *Thrashin' Time: Harvest Days in the Dakotas* and *Pouring Iron: An Old Foundry Ghost Story.* In *Pouring Iron* readers are introduced to young Howard as he takes a tour of a nineteenth-century foundry near Sacramento, California. Through the people—and ghosts of former foundry workers—Howard meets, readers learn everything from the area's history to the building of the foundry to the manner in which iron was shaped. While *School Library Journal* contributor Shirley Wilton found confusing Weitzman's effort to mix "fact and fiction, past and present" in *Pouring Iron,* she deemed the mix a success in a similar work, the 1997 novel *Old Ironsides.*

In *Old Ironsides* Weitzman returns readers to the late eighteenth century, as the fledgling United States looks for a way to remove the threat to its merchant ships from pirates. John Aylwin, the son of a Boston shipbuilder, is at the center of the effort to construct a ship that would be able to withstand the effects of both piracy and warfare. That ship—a 1,500 ton frigate named the *USS Constitution* but dubbed "Old Ironsides"—became the first United States man-of-war. The story's text is "buoyed by precise pen-and-ink drawings that help readers grasp the scope of the project and understand how a ship is constructed," noted Elizabeth S. Watson in *Horn Book.* A *Kirkus Reviews* contributor also praised Weitzman's "captivating black-and-white" renderings, adding that the author/illustrator "has a draftsman's eye for detail." In *School Library Journal,* contributor Shirley Wilton commented favorably on the inclusion of an epilogue describing the *USS Constitution*'s decisive role in the War of 1812, adding that *Old Ironsides* "should find readers among young people interested in ships, in how things are made, or in American history."

Other books by Weitzman that focus on technology through a fictional lens include *Superpower: The Making of a Steam Locomotive,* first published in 1987, and 1999's *Locomotive: Building an Eight-Wheeler.* In both books Weitzman creates highly detailed drawings of the locomotive's construction and development, setting them within a historical framework. In *Superpower,* eighteen-year-old Ben starts work at the Lima, Ohio, locomotive works in the mid-1920s and becomes involved in the production of the new "Berkshire" steam locomotive. Along with Ben, readers learn every step of the manufacturing process, from drawings to foundry work to machine shop to assembly.

Locomotive draws young train buffs further back in time, as its author reveals the development of an 1870s wood-burning locomotive, this time without the fictional framework that some critics have argued detracts from the author's purpose. Praising Weitzman's discussion of the process in constructing the passenger locomotive, as well as his inclusion of sophisticated technical details, *School Library Journal* contributor Margaret Bush concluded that *Locomotive* "will be enjoyed most by readers with a strong mechanical bent." Bush's praise was echoed by a *Kirkus Reviews* writer who proclaimed *Locomotive* to be "a bull's-eye for meeting the desires of both railroad buffs and the mechanically inclined."

BIOGRAPHICAL/CRITICAL SOURCES:

PERIODICALS

Booklist, October 15, 1975, Denise M. Wilms, review of *The Brown Paper School Presents My Backyard History Book,* pp. 306-307; February 1, 1983, Barbara Elleman, *Windmills, Bridges, and Old Machines,* p. 728; April 15, 1991, Ann D. Carlson, review of *Windmills, Bridges, and Old Machines,* p. 1635; March 1, 1992, Deborah Abbott, review of *Thrashin' Time,* p. 1279; May 1, 1997, Susan Dove Lempke, review of *Old Ironsides,* p. 1498; December 15, 1998, John Peters, review of *Pouring Iron,* p. 752.

Bulletin of the Center for Children's Books, March, 1983, Zena Sutherland, review of *Windmills, Bridges, and Old Machines,* p. 139; June, 1997, Elizabeth Bush, review of *Old Ironsides,* pp. 377-378.

Choice, October, 1975, review of *Eggs and Peanut Butter,* p. 1052.

Five Owls, September-October, 1994, review of *Thrashin' Time,* p. 5.

Horn Book, May, 1997, Elizabeth S. Watson, review of *Old Ironsides,* p. 312.

Kirkus Reviews, February 15, 1997, review of *Old Ironsides,* p. 307; September, 1999, review of *Locomotive,* p. 1423.

New York Times, February 11, 1977, Herbert Mitgang, review of *Underfoot,* p. C25.

New York Times Book Review, November 16, 1975, Barbara Karlin, review of *The Brown Paper School Presents My Backyard History Book,* p. 31; February 6, 1983, Holcomb B. Noble, review of *Windmills, Bridges, and Old Machines,* p. 33; July 26, 1992, Verlyn Klinkenborg, review of *Thrashin' Time,* p. 19.

Publishers Weekly, November 30, 1998, review of *Pouring Iron,* p. 73; September 6, 1999, review of *Locomotive,* p. 103.

School Library Journal, January, 1976, Sandra Weir, review of *The Brown Paper School Presents My Backyard History Book,* pp. 42-43; August, 1983, Jeffrey A. French, review of *Windmills, Bridges, and Old Machines,* p. 72; January, 1988, French, review of *Superpower: The Making of a Steam Locomotive,* pp. 94-95; April, 1992, Lee Bock, review of *Thrashin' Time,* p. 144; April, 1995, Kristin Lott, review of *Human Culture,* p. 148; April, 1997, Shirley Wilton, review of *Old Ironsides,* p. 142; January, 1999, Wilton, review of *Pouring Iron,* p. 132; November, 1999, Margaret Bush, review of *Locomotive,* p. 178.

Wilson Library Bulletin, January, 1978, review of *Underfoot,* p. 371.

* * *

WELLMAN, Sam(uel) 1939-

PERSONAL: Born 1939, in KS; son of Leonard (a railworker) and Iris (a retail buyer; maiden name, Reinhold) Wellman; married Ruth Austin (a travel agent), 1972; children: Amy, Keith. *Education:* University of Nebraska, B.S., 1962; Princeton University, Ph.D., 1968. *Politics:* "American." *Religion:* Christian.

ADDRESSES: Home—Kansas. *Office*—c/o Author Mail, Chelsea House, 1974 Sproul Rd., Ste. 400, Broomall, PA 19008. *E-mail*—xnwriter7@hotmail.com.

CAREER: Writer.

WRITINGS:

BIOGRAPHIES; FOR YOUNG ADULTS

Michelle Kwan ("Female Sports Stars" series), Chelsea House (Philadelphia, PA), 1997.

Kristi Yamaguchi ("Female Figure Skating Legends" series), Chelsea House (Philadelphia, PA), 1999.

Mariah Carey ("Galaxy of Superstars" series), Chelsea House (Philadelphia, PA), 1999.

T. D. Jakes: Religious Leader ("Black Americans of Achievement" series), Chelsea House (Philadelphia, PA), 1999.

Ben Affleck ("Galaxy of Superstars" series), Chelsea House (Philadelphia, PA), 2000.

BIOGRAPHIES; "HEROES OF THE FAITH" SERIES

David Livingstone: Missionary and Explorer, Barbour (Uhrickville, OH), 1995.

Corrie ten Boom, Barbour (Uhrickville, OH), 1995.

Billy Graham: The Great Evangelist, Barbour (Uhrickville, OH), 1996.

John Bunyan: Author of the Pilgrim's Progress, Barbour (Uhrickville, OH), 1996.

C. S. Lewis: Author of Mere Christianity, Barbour (Uhrickville, OH), 1997.

John Wesley: Founder of the Methodist Church, Barbour (Uhrickville, OH), 1997.

Mother Teresa: Missionary of Charity, Barbour (Uhrickville, OH), 1997.

William Carey: Father of Missions, Barbour (Uhrickville, OH), 1997.

Amy Carmichael: A Life Abandoned to God, Barbour (Uhrickville, OH), 1998.

George Washington Carver: Inventor and Naturalist, Barbour (Uhrickville, OH), 1998.

Mary Slessor: Queen of Calabar, Barbour (Uhrickville, OH), 1998.

Gladys Aylward: Missionary in China, Barbour (Uhrickville, OH), 1998.

Florence Nightingale: Lady with the Lamp, Barbour (Uhrickville, OH), 1999.

Brother Andrew: God's Undercover Agent, Barbour (Uhrickville, OH), 1999.

Francis and Edith Schaeffer: Defenders of the Faith, Barbour (Uhrickville, OH), 2000.

BIOGRAPHIES; "YOUNG READERS CHRISTIAN LIBRARY" SERIES

Abraham Lincoln, illustrated by Ken Save, Barbour (Uhrickville, OH), 1995.

Christopher Columbus, illustrated by Ken Save, Barbour (Uhrickville, OH), 1995.

Billy Graham, illustrated by Ken Save, Barbour (Uhrickville, OH), 1997.

David, illustrated by Ken Landgraf, Barbour (Uhrickville, OH), 1999.

John Wesley: The Horseback Preacher, illustrated by Ken Landgraf, Barbour (Uhrickville, OH), 2000.

OTHER

Bible Promise Book for Fathers, Barbour (Uhrickville, OH), 1997.

Bible Promise Book for Kids, Barbour (Uhrickville, OH), 1997.

The Cabinet (textbook; "Your Government—How It Works" series), Chelsea House (Philadelphia, PA), 2000.

The Secretary of State, (textbook; "Your Government—How It Works" series), Chelsea House (Philadelphia, PA), 2001.

WORK IN PROGRESS: Biographical research on Abraham Lincoln, Aleksandr Solzhenitsyn, and Black Elk.

SIDELIGHTS: A prolific author of nonfiction books for young adults, Sam Wellman once commented: "Writing improved my life. Is there any self-contained activity that hones the thoughts like writing? Writing prose is like a debate with inner truths you didn't know you possessed. It was not until I attempted to become a writer that these inner truths surfaced and defeated many years of accumulated, very muddled values. The act of writing overhauled my thinking and values. But writing can be more than a self-improvement exercise. Writing can also be an effective method for communicating with others. And then there is writing for publication. . . ."

BIOGRAPHICAL/CRITICAL SOURCES:

PERIODICALS

Booklist, Hazel Rochman, review of *David Livingstone,* p. 338.

Children's Book Watch, July, 1996, review of *Christopher Columbus,* p. 2; November, 1998, review of *Billy Graham,* p. 5; December, 1998, review of *Michelle Kwan,* p. 2.

School Library Journal, January, 1999, Ann W. Moore, review of *C. S. Lewis* and *John Bunyan,* and Cindy Darling Codell, review of *Mother Teresa,* p. 157; February, 1999, Shirley Wilton, review of *John Wesley,* p. 113.

*   *   *

WELLS, Joel F(reeman) 1930-2001

OBITUARY NOTICE—See index for *CA* sketch: Born March 17, 1930, in Evansville, IN; died February 27, 2001, in Evanston, IL. Editor and author. Wells was the editor of the Catholic magazine *Critic* from 1964 to 1985. Also an author, he penned a number of self-help and humor books, including *Bodies and Souls,* published in 1961, and *Blithe Spirits* in 1962. Some of his later works include *How to Survive with Your Teenager* and *Coping in the 80s,* published in 1986. Additionally, Wells contributed articles and pieces of fiction to such publications as *National Catholic Reporter* and *New Republic.* He was founding editor of the Thomas More Press, and in 1982 was named Doctor of Letters by Rosary College.

OBITUARIES AND OTHER SOURCES:

PERIODICALS

Chicago Tribune, March 2, 2001, section 2, p. 11.

*   *   *

WESTERMANN, Kurt-Michael 1951-

PERSONAL: Born June 12, 1951, in Grosshansdorf, Germany; son of Jens (an author) and Ingeborg (a wea-ver) Westermann; married Elisabeth Vidotto, August 18, 1995; children: Mirko Köhnke. *Ethnicity:* "German." *Education:* University of Bremen, diploma in graphic design. *Politics:* "Critical left liberal." *Religion:* Evangelical Lutheran.

ADDRESSES: Home—Papenhuderstrasse 40, D-22087 Hamburg, Germany. *Office*—Mechitaristengasse 5/5, A-1070 Vienna, Austria; fax: 00-431-522-1594. *Agent*—Christian Brandstätter, Schwarzenbergstr. 5, A-1010 Vienna, Austria. *E-mail*—kurtwester@aol.com.

CAREER: Freelance graphic designer and photographer, Hamburg, Germany and Vienna, Austria, 1977—. Corbis (photography archive), member.

AWARDS, HONORS: Two awards from Austria's Art Directors Club, 1984 and 1986.

WRITINGS:

(Photographer) *Der Basar: Mittelpunkt des Lebens in der islamischen Welt: Geschichte und Gegenwart eines menschengerechten Stadtmodells,* text by Walter M. Weiss, C. Brandstätter (Vienna, Austria), 1994, published as *The Bazaar: Markets and Merchants of the Islamic World,* Thames & Hudson (New York, NY), 1998.

(Photographer) Walter M. Weiss, *Souks et bazars d'Orient: de Fès à Samarkand,* Arthaud (Paris, France), published as *Souks,* Flammarion (Paris, France), 1995.

(Photographer) Adolf Opel, *Ingeborg Bachmann in Ägypten: "Landschaft, für die Augen gemacht sind,"* Deuticke (Vienna, Austria), 1996.

(Photographer) *Marokko: magische Welt zwischen Atlas und Atlantik = al-Maghrib: al-'alam al-sihr i ma bayna jib al al-Atlas wa-al-Muh it al-Atlas i,* text by Walter M. Weiss, C. Brandstätter (Vienna, Austria), 1997.

(Photographer) *Ägypten: die Wiege der Götter,* text by Walter M. Weiss, C. Brandstätter (Vienna, Austria), 1998.

(Photographer) *Nationalpark Hohe Tauern: Paradies in den Alpen,* text by Barbara Sternthal, C. Brandstätter (Vienna, Austria), 2000.

Also author of other works, including travel books published by DuMont (Cologne, Germany), 1978—. Contributor to periodicals, including *Art, Die Zeit,* and *Geo.*

WORK IN PROGRESS: A portrait of ancient and modern Iran, for Brandstaetter (Vienna, Austria).

SIDELIGHTS: Kurt-Michael Westermann told *CA:* "At the beginning, all is curiosity! I have questions about the world and its life. I watch everyday life as a daydreamer. What we call reality intrigues me the most and prompts me to search for answers in the background, the personal interests, and the roots of individuals. I want to show the motivations for their style, based on the historical and social possibilities. I am a traveler, even when I am not on tour.

"A main feature of my work is the cultural world around the Mediterranean, in Europe and the Islamic world. I look for the poetic way of a foreign world, the world of the neighbor, and the clear facts of everyday life. I think this makes it possible to proceed with more understanding and more peace.

"As a photographer I seek the technical education to use the right equipment for the special style needed to interpret people's lives and the flair of their countries and the countryside in different ethnic worlds. I like the work of Steve McCurry, Erwin Blumenfeld, Kapuchinsky, Naghib Mahfous, and Gustave Flaubert."

BIOGRAPHICAL/CRITICAL SOURCES:

PERIODICALS

Booklist, September 1, 1998, review of *The Bazaar: Markets and Merchants of the Islamic World.*
Philadelphia Inquirer, December 6, 1998, Carlin Romano, review of *The Bazaar.*
Wall Street Journal, December 4, 1998, Raymond Sokolov, review of *The Bazaar.*

*   *   *

WHITAKER, Rick   1968-

PERSONAL: Born 1968, in St. Marys, OH. *Education:* Hunter College, B.A.

ADDRESSES: Home—Cooperstown, NY. *Office*—c/o Four Walls Eight Windows, 39 West 14th Street, Ste. 503, New York, NY 10011.

CAREER: Writer. Worked variously as an editorial assistant, Knopf, assistant to Paul Kellogg, general director of New York City Opera, and former managing editor, *The Philosophical Forum.*

WRITINGS:

Assuming the Position: A Memoir of Hustling, Four Walls Eight Windows (New York, NY), 1999.

Contributor of short stories to periodicals, including the *Quarterly* and *StoryQuarterly.* Contributor of book reviews to periodicals, including *New York Times Book Review, New York Observer* and *Ballet Review.*

SIDELIGHTS: Rick Whitaker is an American short story writer, critic and memoirist. Born in 1968 in Ohio, Whitaker moved to New York City in 1989 where he worked as an editorial assistant at Knopf and earned a degree in philosophy from Hunter College. He lives in Cooperstown, New York.

While Whitaker was working in New York City, he became addicted to drugs and soon became a male prostitute to earn money to support his burgeoning drug habit. He recounts his life as a hustler in his 1999 memoir *Assuming the Position: A Memoir of Hustling.* "Assuming the Position . . . which details his encounters with more than 100 clients over several years, must be one of the few examples of its genre to spice explicit sex with ruminations on Nietzsche and Wittgenstein," noted Jonathan Mandell in *New York.*

Assuming the Position elicited mixed reactions from critics. A critic for *Kirkus Reviews* called the memoir "flaccid," arguing that Whitaker's emotional catharsis would "be better achieved on a psychiatrist's couch." Philip Clark in *Lambda Book Report* found the book's "principal charm" was that the author admitted that his story was "neither glamorous nor out-of-the-ordinary," but nonetheless concluded that the memoir's "honesty never quite redeems its flat prose and narrative." A critic for *Publishers Weekly* pointed out that Whitaker was at his "most astute" when analyzing the psychological precursors to his hustling, including his parents' relationship and his own relationship with his father. The critic ultimately found, though, that these "relatively modest psychological insights" pale against the "far more compelling pulp narrative" of his exploits as a prostitute.

BIOGRAPHICAL/CRITICAL SOURCES:

PERIODICALS

Advocate, December 7, 1999, review of *Assuming the Position,* p. 22.
Kirkus Reviews, September 1, 1999, review of *Assuming the Position,* p. 1401.

Lambda Book Report, March, 2000, Philip Clark, review of *Assuming the Position,* p. 24.
New York, June 7, 1999, Jonathan Mandell, review of *Assuming the Position,* p. 24.
Publishers Weekly, August 16, 1999, review of *Assuming the Position,* p. 68.

OTHER

Pif, http://www.pifmagazine.com/ (September 18, 2001), Richard Weems, review of *Assuming the Position: A Memoir of Hustling.*
Salon, http://www.salon.com/ (September 18, 2001), Dennis Drabelle, review of *Assuming the Position.**

* * *

WHITTALL, Arnold (Morgan)   1935-

PERSONAL: Born November 11, 1935, in Shrewsbury, England. *Education:* Emmanuel College, Cambridge, England, B.A., 1959, Ph.D., 1964.

ADDRESSES: Office—c/o Faber & Faber, Inc., 53 Shore Rd., Winchester, MA 01890-2821.

CAREER: Musicologist. Nottingham University, Nottingham, England, lecturer, 1964-69; University College, Cardiff, Wales, lecturer, 1969-71, senior lecturer, 1971-75; King's College, London, England, reader, 1976—.

WRITINGS:

Schoenberg Chamber Music (booklet; "BBC Music Guides" series), University of Washington Press (Seattle, WA), 1972.
Music since the First World War, St. Martin's Press (New York, NY), 1977.
The Music of Britten and Tippett: Studies in Themes and Techniques, Cambridge University Press (New York, NY), 1982.
Romantic Music: A Concise History from Schubert to Sibelius, Thames & Hudson (New York, NY), 1987.
(With Jonathan Dunsby) *Music Analysis in Theory and Practice,* Yale University Press (New Haven, CT), 1988.
Musical Composition in the Twentieth Century, Oxford University Press (New York, NY), 1999.
Jonathan Harvey (booklet), Faber, 1999.

Contributor to music publications and journals.

SIDELIGHTS: Arnold Whittall is a music scholar and historian whose area of specialization is late nineteenth- and twentieth-century music. His analyses concentrate particularly on Wagner, Debussy, Schoenberg, Webern, and Britten. Whittall's *Music since the First World War,* published in 1977, covers sixty years of music, beginning with Nielsen. A *Choice* reviewer called it a book "to be studied rather than read." Andrew Clements, writing in *New Statesman,* found Whittall's examinations of Sibelius and Webern to be "particularly good" and called *Music since the First World War* "as good an introduction to twentieth-century music as anything currently available."

The Music of Britten and Tippett: Studies in Themes and Techniques is Whittall's comparison of the two great British composers Benjamin Britten and Michael Tippett. Whittall notes how the music of each changed over the years. Tippett became more unorthodox in his technique, while Britten's reserved approach became even more evident in his increasingly classical style. Britten, who was nine years younger than Tippett, died in 1976. His successes include the operas *Peter Grimes* and *A Midsummer Night's Dream.* Britten appealed to a wide audience, while Tippett had a smaller following until his revival of *The Midsummer Marriage* at Covent Garden in 1968 put him on an equal footing with his friend in popularity. When Britten died, Tippett wrote that he was "the most purely musical person I have ever met and I have ever known." Clements wrote in *New Statesman* that Whittall's study "is the first attempt to draw the expressive worlds of the two . . . into a single unified critique." David Matthews wrote in the *Times Literary Supplement* that Whittall's approach "is not partisan; he declines to play off one composer against the other, being, it would seem, an unqualified admirer of both. His method is for the most part analytical; he surveys the two composers whole output chronologically side by side, a few works at a time. His analyses are succinct and penetrating. Some of them are tantalizingly brief; this is almost inevitable in a book dealing with so much music."

Whittall addresses some of the challenges common to twentieth-century composers and demonstrates how Britten and Tippett have met them. One such issue is tonality. Matthews wrote that Whittall "traces each composer's changing attitude toward the tonal system which, as he puts it, 'may still seem to many the most natural, as well as the most appealing, which man is ever likely to devise.' " Whittall also addresses how closely each composer's work is modeled after that of Beethoven. Matthews said that "the more Tippett tries to get under Beethoven's skin, the less he is truly him-self; for Tippett's free-ranging genius and his love of improvisatory flights are essentially opposed to Beethoven's tautness. In fact it is Britten—who may have rejected Beethoven in adult life but who in early adolescence was as obsessively saturated with his music as Tippett was—who is the more genuinely Beethovenian composer, in purely musical terms at least."

The subject of Whittall's 1999 booklet, *Jonathan Harvey,* was described by Andrew Porter in the *Times Literary Supplement* as the composer who "writes technically adventurous music, drawing on the resources of computer and synthesizer at their musically most advanced. At the same time, he is a romantic, a mystic, a transcendental meditator." *Jonathan Harvey* contains thirty-five pages of Harvey's extensive answers to questions, Whittall's commentary on the development of Harvey's music, a list of works, and a discography. Porter called Whittall's choice of music examples "well chosen" and his description of Harvey's intentions, means of achieving them, and results "communicatively described."

BIOGRAPHICAL/CRITICAL SOURCES:

PERIODICALS

British Book Notes, November, 1982, review of *The Music of Britten and Tippett: Studies in Themes and Techniques,* p. 697.

Choice, March, 1978, review of *Music since the First World War,* p. 84; February, 1983, review of *The Music of Britten and Tippett,* p. 840.

Musical Quarterly, summer, 1984, Charles Fussell, review of *The Music of Britten and Tippett,* p. 413.

Music & Letters, February, 1989, Anthony Pople, review of *Music Analysis in Theory and Practice,* p. 76.

Music Educators Journal, February, 1979, review of *Schoenberg Chamber Music,* p. 28.

Music Review, August, 1990, A. F. Leighton Thomas, review of *Romantic Music,* p. 236.

New Statesman, January 27, 1978, Andrew Clements, review of *Music since the First World War,* pp. 124-125; September 24, 1982, Andrew Clements, review of *The Music of Britten and Tippett,* p. 22.

Notes, September, 1992, Alicyn Warren, review of *Music Analysis in Theory and Practice,* p. 154.

Times Literary Supplement, August 27, 1982, David Matthews, "Affirmations and Ambiguities," p. 917; November 19, 1999, Andrew Porter, review of *Jonathan Harvey,* p. 12.*

WIDMER, Urs 1938-

PERSONAL: Born May 21, 1938, in Basel, Switzerland. *Education:* Earned Ph.D.

ADDRESSES: Office—c/o Diogenes Verlag, Sprecherstr 8, 8032, Zurich, Switzerland.

WRITINGS:

1945 [Neunzehnhundertfünfundvierzig] oder die "Neue Sprache," Padagogisscher Verlag (Düsseldorf, Germany), 1966.

Alois, Diogenes (Zurich, Switzerland), 1968, published with *Die Amsel im Regen im Garten,* 1988.

(With Jürgen Becker) *WDR Hörspielbuch,* Westdeutscher Rundfunk (Cologne, Germany), 1969.

Die Amsel im Regen im Gerten, Diogenes (Zurich, Switzerland), 1971.

Der richterliche Eingriff in den Vertrag, Aku-Fotodruck (Zurich, Switzerland), 1971.

Das Normale und die Sehnsucht (essays), Diogenes (Zurich, Germany), 1972.

Die lange Nacht der Detektive: Kriminalstück in 3 Akten (play), Diogenes (Zurich, Germany), 1973.

Das Vermächtnis der Miss D. Awdrey-Gore, Diogenes (Zurich, Germany), 1974.

Die Forschungsreise, Diogenes (Zurich, Germany), 1974.

Stellung und Entwicklung der schweizerischen Papierindustrie im Lichte der wirtschaftlichen Integration Europas (thesis on the paper box industry), Peter Lang (Bern, Switzerland), 1974.

Schweizer Geschichten, Hallway (Stuttgart, Germany), 1975.

Das jüngst entjungferte Mädchen, Diogenes (Zurich, Switzerland), 1975.

Die gelben Männer (novel), Diogenes (Zurich, Switzerland), 1976.

Vom Fenster meinse Hauses aus, Diogenes (Zurich, Switzerland), 1977.

Nepal: Stück in der Basler Umgangssprache, Diogenes (Zurich, Switzerland), 1977.

(Coauthor) *Erklarung einiger Dinge,* Langewiesche-Brandt (Munich, Germany), 1978.

(With Max Zaugg) *Hand und Fuss,* Moon Press (The Hague, Netherlands), 1978.

(Coauthor) *Shakespeares Geschichten: alle Stücke von William Shakespeare,* Diogenes (Zurich, Switzerland), 1978.

Suomei und ihr Netz (textbook), R. Mayer (Munich, Germany), 1979.

(With Thomas Bodmer) *Das Urs Widmer Lesebuch,* Diogenes (Zurich, Switzerland), 1980.

Zust oder die Aufschneider: ein Traumspiel, Diogenes (Zurich, Switzerland), 1980.

Das enge Land (novel), Diogenes (Zurich, Switzerland), 1981.

Liebesnacht, Diogenes (Zurich, Switzerland), 1982.

Fernsehabend, Grasl (Baden, Germany), 1983.

Die gestohlene Schöpfung: ein Märchen, Diogenes (Zurich, Switzerland), 1984.

Indianersommer, Diogenes (Zurich, Switzerland), 1985.

(Coauthor) *Alltag-Knalltag: guten-Morgen-Satiren,* Fischer Tasenbuch (Frankfurt, Germany), 1985.

Nepal/Der neue Noah: zwie Stucke, Verlag der Autoren (Frankfurt, Germany), 1986.

Stan und Ollie in Deutschland (play), Verlag der Autoren (Frankfurt, Germany), 1987.

Das Verschwinden der Chinesen im neuen Jahr, Diogenes (Zurich, Switzerland), 1987.

(Contributor) *Paul Camenisch* (exhibition catalog), Editions Galerie Specht (Basel, Switzerland), 1987.

Auf auf ihr Hirten! Die Kuh haut ab!, Diogenes (Zurich, Switzerland), 1988.

Liebesnacht; die gestohlene Schöpfung; Indiansommer (collection), Verlag Volk und Welt (Berlin, Germany), 1988.

Der Kongress der Paläolepidopterolgen (novel), Diogenes (Zurich, Switzerland), 1989.

Das Fähnlein der sieben Aufrechten, K. Wagenbach (Berlin, Germany), 1989.

Das Paradies des vergessens (stories), Diogenes (Zurich, Switzerland), 1990.

(With others) *Josefine Mutzenbacher, oder, Die Geschichte einer Wienerischen Dirne von ihr selbst erzählt* (novel), Schneekluth (Munich, Germany), 1990.

(With Michael Ruetz) *Schweiz,* Süddeutscher (Munich, Germany), 1990.

Die sechste Puppe im Bauche der funften Puppe im Bauch der vierten und andere Überlegungen zur Literatur, Literaturverlag Droschl, 1991.

Der blaue Siphon (stories), Diogenes (Zurich, Switzerland), 1992.

Der Sprung in der Schüssel, Verlag der Autoren (Frankfurt, Germany), 1992.

(With Urs Rauber) *Jeanmarie: ein Stuck Scheiz,* Verlag der Autoren (Frankfurt, Germany), 1992.

Herz der Finsternis: mit dem "Dongo-Tagebuch" und dem "Up-river Book" sowie einem Nachwort im Anhang, Haffmans, 1992.

Liebesbrief für Mary, Diogenes (Zurich, Switzerland), 1993.

1945 nachgetragen: in den Trümmern von Darmstadt (history), E. Roether Verlag, 1995.

Im Kongo (novel), Diogenes (Zurich, Switzerland), 1996.

(With others) *Gesaenge der Haemmer,* O. Müller (Salzburg, Austria), 1996.

Top Dogs (play), Verlag der Autoren (Frankfurt, Germany), 1997.

(With others) *Der Pensionierte: Fragment eines Kriminalromans,* Diogenes (Zurich, Switzerland), 1997.

Urs Widmer, Edition Text + Kritik (Munich, Germany), 1998.

Vor uns die Sintflut, Diogenes (Zurich, Switzerland), 1998.

(Contributor) *Die schwarze Spinne: nach der Erzählung von Jeremias Gotthelf,* Verlag der Autoren (Frankfurt, Germany), 1998.

Der Geliebte der Mutter (novel), Diogenes (Zurich, Switzerland), 2000.

SIDELIGHTS: Urs Widmer of Switzerland produces fiction in a variety of formats. He writes plays, such as *Top Dogs,* in which the audience is challenged by actors portraying "themselves" as characters. As *Theatre Journal* critic Thomas Apple pointed out, the play "has to do with the personal and social consequences of hyperorganized workplaces populated by appropriately hyperorganized workers." In such prose works as *Das Paradies des Vergessens* and *Der blaue Siphon,* Widmer "cultivates the short form, mininovels in which he nevertheless compresses astonishingly complex plots," according to Sigrid Bauschinger, writing in *World Literature Today.* Reviewing *Das Paradies des Vergessens,* Bauschinger noted that in just one hundred pages, Widmer manages to fit three interconnected tales centered on a writer whose run-ins with his contentious publisher mirror the plots of his stories. That motif is taken up in *Der blaue Siphon,* in which a writer has visions of doom triggered by war memories. While brief, said Bauschinger, this book is also "filled with an astonishing array of plots and subplots," with a narrator "constantly [moving] among present, past, and future."

In 1996, Widmer published *Im Kongo,* a novel that employs World War II themes, as some of the author's previous works did. In reviewing the book for *German Quarterly,* Peter Arnds said that what interests him about German-language novels of the '80s and '90s "is the continuity of the Fascist experience from past to present that these novels share as a theme. If one applies this principle of continuity to Widmer's text, the central question is how the Swiss past, Switzerland's stance vis à vis Nazi Germany, resurfaces in the present as depicted [in the story]." The protagonist, Kuno, is introduced sitting in the Zaire jungle, writing his memoirs on a laptop computer. He recalls his past as a retirement-home employee in Zurich, where his own father and another elderly man reveal their roles in World War II. Kuno himself has Nazi ties—he is in the employ of a Nazi-sympathizer brewer who has sent him to Africa to learn why a brewing plant is failing. The novel takes a surrealistic turn as Kuno and other (white) characters are envisioned as black on their return to Zurich.

In this novel, the Congo functions as a metaphor, wrote Arnds. "In many ways it is the direct opposite of Switzerland, the jungle as opposed to a civilized place, the black continent as opposed to the white one, the freedom of an immense landscape versus the narrowness of a small country in the Alps. But upon closer inspection one finds that the Congo shows parallels with Switzerland." Specifically, "the parallel of the Swiss forest through which Jewish refugees tried to make their way into freedom with the deadly Zairian jungle is obvious. Often where Widmer speaks of atrocities in the Congo he simultaneously refers to Switzerland, its capture of refugees and their deportation back into Nazi Germany."

To Arnds, the extent to which "the violence of one historical period is connected to another becomes apparent if one looks at the theme of entrepreneurship in the novel. The jungle brewery . . . inscribes a line from colonialism via National Socialism to post-colonial business in the Third World." The beer produced "quenches the men's thirst—whether in the desert during the war or in the Congo jungle—and therefore fills them with energy to be violent, but it also seems to facilitate violence because it numbs them to the atrocities."

BIOGRAPHICAL/CRITICAL SOURCES:

PERIODICALS

German Quarterly, fall, 1998, "Into the Heart of Darkness: Switzerland, Hitler, Mobuto, and Joseph Conrad in Urs Widmer's Novel *Im Kongo,*" pp. 329- 342.

Theatre Journal, May, 1998, review of *Top Dogs,* p. 262.

World Literature Today, fall, 1991, review of *Das Paradies des Vergessens,* p. 698; spring, 1993, review of *Der blaue Siphon,* p. 370.

OTHER

Text + Kritik Heft 140: Urs Widmer, http://www.etk-muenchen.de/literatur/tuk/TUK140.html (March 12, 2001).

Urs Widmer, http://www.actufiches.ch/ (March 12, 2001).

Urs Widmer Der Geliebte der Mutter, http://www.new-books-in-german.com/aut2000/book05b.htm (March 12, 2001).*

*   *   *

WILLEMS, Paul 1936-

PERSONAL: Born 1936, in Belgium; son of Marie (a writer; maiden name, Gevers) Willems.

ADDRESSES: Office—c/o Editions Labor, quai du Commerce 29, 1000 Brussels, Belgium.

CAREER: Writer.

WRITINGS:

IN ENGLISH TRANSLATION

Four Plays of Paul Willems: Dreams and Reflections (includes translations of *Il pleut dans ma maison, Ville à viole,* and *Elle disait dormir pour mourir*), edited by Suzanne Burgoyne Dieckman, translated by Luc Deneulin, Garland (London, England), 1992 (also see below).

Paul Willems' The Drowned Land; and La Vita Breve (includes translation of *Le pas noyé*), translated by Donald Flanell Friedman and Suzanne Burgoyne, Peter Lang (New York, NY), 1994 (also see below).

OTHER

Tout est réel ici (title means "Everything Is Real Here"), 1941.

L'Herbe qui tremble (title means "Trembling Grass"), 1942.

Blessures (novel; title means "Wounds"), Gallimard (Paris, France), 1945.

La Cronique du cygne (novel; title means "Chronicle of the Swan"), Plon (Paris, France), 1949.

Le Bon Vin de M. Nuche (title means "Mr. Nuche's Good Wine"), 1949.

Peau d'ours (title means "Bearskin"), 1951.

Off et la lune (title means "Off and the Moon"), 1958.

La Plage aux anguilles (three-act play; title means "The Beach with Eels"), 1959.

Il pleut dans ma maison (three-act play; title means "It's Raining in My House"), Brepois (Brussels, Belgium), 1962.

Warna; ou, Le Poids de la neige (four-act play), 1963.

La Ville à viole (three-act play; title means "Sailing City"), Gallimard, 1967.

Le Soleil sur la mer (play; title means "Sunlight on the Sea"), 1970.

(Editor, with Robert de Smet) *Europalia 71-Nederlands, Pays-Bas, 17.9-17.10,* (Brussels, Belgium), 1971.

Les Miroirs d'Ostende (five-act play; title means "The Mirrors of Ostende"), 1974.

La Cathedrale de brume, Fata Morgana (Montpelier, France), 1983.

(With Paul Emond, Henri Ronse, and Frabrice van de Kerckhove) *Le Monde de Paul Willems: Textes, entretiens, études,* Editions Labor (Brussels, Belgium), 1984.

Le pas noyé, Fata Morgana (Montepelier, France), 1990.

Le Vase de Delft, et autres nouvelles (short stories), Editions Labor (Brussels, Belgium), 1995.

Théâtre (1954-1962), Musée de la littérature (Brussels, Belgium), 1995.

La Neige; suivi de, La Petit Chat vert; et, Histoire du garçon qui voulait décrocher la lune (plays), Editions Labor (Brussels, Belgium), 1996.

Elle disait dormir pour mourir (title means "She Confused Sleeping and Dying"), Rideau de Bruxelles (Brussels, Belgium), 2000.

Works also published in other volumes.

SIDELIGHTS: Paul Willems is a prolific Belgian writer who is probably best known, at least in his native land, for his many plays. Willems was born in 1912 near Antwerp and raised at the family estate, which, as Suzanne Burgoyne noted in her essay published in *New Theatre Vistas,* contained a "legendary ghost and gardens." Burgoyne affirmed that some of Willems's plays "bear the imprint of the chateau," and she added that "Willems celebrates nature as the source of intense sensory experiences which can open a passage to 'lost paradise.'"

In the early 1940s, Willems began as a writer with fiction and essays. By the end of the decade, however, he had completed his first play. During the ensuing decades he proved himself a master in producing plays that blur the distinction between the dream world and what is generally considered to be reality. Among his many stage writings are *Warna,* wherein an aging woman comes to dispute the passing of time, and *La Ville á viole,* which explores the tension between youth and maturity. These plays, as Donald F. Friedman wrote in *World Literature Today,* "evoke mysterious places, junctures of the known and the unknown, which offer a promise of reality other than the quotidian." Friedman described such plays as "both dark voyages and light," and he noted "a purity of poetic illumination that offers an approach to beatitude."

After establishing himself as a playwright, Willems continued to produce fiction. His collections include *Le Vase de Delft, et autres nouvelles,* which Henri Kops praised in *World Literature Today* for its "engaging originality." In his review, Kops acknowledged Willems as "the dean of Belgian letters."

BIOGRAPHICAL/CRITICAL SOURCES:

BOOKS

Oliva, Judy Lee, editor, *New Theatre Vistas: Modern Movements in International Theatre,* Garland (New York, NY), 1996.

PERIODICALS

World Literature Today, winter 1991, Donald Friedman, "Spaces of Dream, Protection, and Imprisonment in the Theater of Paul Willems," pp. 46-48; spring 1996, Henri Kops, review of *Le Vase de Delft et autres nouvelles,* p. 364.*

*   *   *

WILLIAMS, John A(lfred) 1925-
(J. Dennis Gregory, a pseudonym)

PERSONAL: Born December 5, 1925, in Jackson, MS; son of John Henry (a laborer) and Ola Mae Williams; married Carolyn Clopton, 1947 (divorced); married Lorrain Isaac, October 5, 1965; children: (first marriage) Gregory D., Dennis A.; (second marriage) Adam J. *Education:* Syracuse University, A.B., 1950, graduate study, 1950-51. *Avocational interests:* Travel (has visited Austria, Belgium, Cameroon, the Caribbean, Congo, Cuba, Cyprus, Denmark, Egypt, Ethiopia, France, Germany, Great Britain, Greece, Israel, Italy, Mexico, the Netherlands, Nigeria, Portugal, Senegal, Spain, the Sudan, Sweden, and Switzerland).

ADDRESSES: Home—693 Forest Ave., Teaneck, NJ 07666.

CAREER: Writer. Public relations department, Doug Johnson Associates, Syracuse, NY, 1952-54, and later with Arthur P. Jacobs Co.; Columbia Broadcasting System (CBS), Hollywood, CA, and New York, NY, staff member for radio and television special events pro-

John A. Williams

grams, 1954-55; Comet Press Books, New York, NY, publicity director, 1955-56; *Negro Market Newsletter,* New York, NY, publisher and editor, 1956-57; Abelard-Schuman Ltd., New York, NY, assistant to the publisher, 1957-58; American Committee on Africa, New York, NY, director of information, 1958; European correspondent for *Ebony* and *Jet* (magazines), Chicago, IL, 1958-59; Station WOV, New York, special events announcer, 1959; *Newsweek,* New York, NY, correspondent in Africa, 1964-65; National Education Television, narrator and co-producer of programs, 1965-66, interviewer on *Newsfront* program, 1968.

City College of the City University of New York, teacher and lecturer in writing, 1968-69; College of the Virgin Islands, lecturer in African-American literature, 1970; University of California, Santa Barbara, regents lecturer, 1972; Sarah Lawrence College, Bronxville, NY, guest writer, 1972-73; La Guardia Community College, City University of New York, distinguished professor of English, 1973-78; Rutgers University, professor of English, journalism, and creative writing, 1979-90, Paul Robeson Professor of English, 1990-

1994. Visiting professor, Macalester College, 1970, University of Hawaii, 1974, Boston University, 1978-79, University of Houston, 1993, and Bard College, 1994-95; distinguished visiting professor, Cooper Union, 1974-75; Exxon visiting professor, New York University, 1986-87. *Military service:* U.S. Navy, pharmacist's mate 3/C, active duty, 1943-46; served in the South Pacific.

MEMBER: Authors Guild, PEN, Poets and Writers, ASCAP.

AWARDS, HONORS: Award from National Institute of Arts and Letters, 1962; centennial medal for outstanding achievement from Syracuse University, 1970; Richard Wright-Jacques Roumain Award, 1973; National Endowment for the Arts grant, 1977; Lindback Award, Rutgers University, 1982, for distinguished teaching; Premio Casa Award, *U. S. Observer* (Santiago, Cuba), 1983; American Book Award, Before Columbus Foundation, 1983, for *!Click Song,* and 1998, for *Safari West;* New Jersey State Council on the Arts Award, 1985; Michael Award, New Jersey Literary Hall of Fame, 1987; named distinguished writer, Middle Atlantic Writers, 1987; Carter G. Woodson Award, Mercy College, 1989; inducted into the National Literary Hall of Fame, 1998; namesake of the John A. Williams Lecture Series, Rutgers University, 1999. LL.D. from Southeastern Massachusetts University, 1978, Syracuse University, 1995, and State University of New York, Old Westbury, 2001.

WRITINGS:

NOVELS

The Angry Ones, Ace Books (New York, NY), 1960, published as *One for New York,* Chatham Bookseller (Chatham, NJ), 1975.
Night Song, Farrar, Straus (New York, NY), 1961, film adaptation produced as *Sweet Love, Bitter,* Film 2 Associates, 1967.
Sissie, Farrar, Straus, 1963, published as *Journey Out of Anger,* Eyre & Spottiswoode (London, England), 1965.
The Man Who Cried I Am, Little, Brown (Boston, MA), 1967.
Sons of Darkness, Sons of Light: A Novel of Some Probability, Little, Brown (Boston, MA), 1969.
Captain Blackman, Doubleday (New York, NY), 1972.
Mothersill and the Foxes, Doubleday (New York, NY), 1975.
The Junior Bachelor Society, Doubleday (New York, NY), 1976, television mini-series adaptation produced as *The Sophisticated Gents,* Danny Wilson Productions, 1981.
!Click Song, Houghton Mifflin (Boston, MA), 1982.
The Berhama Account, New Horizon Press (Far Hills, NJ), 1985.
Jacob's Ladder, Thunder's Mouth (New York, NY), 1987.
Clifford's Blues, Coffee House (Minneapolis, MN), 1999.

NONFICTION

Africa: Her History, Lands, and People, Cooper Square (New York, NY), 1963, 3rd edition, 1969.
(Under pseudonym J. Dennis Gregory, with Harry J. Anslinger) *The Protectors: The Heroic Story of the Narcotics Agents, Citizens and Officials in Their Unending, Unsung Battles against Organized Crime in America and Abroad,* Farrar, Straus (New York, NY), 1964.
This Is My Country Too, New American Library (New York, NY), 1965.
The Most Native of Sons: A Biography of Richard Wright, Doubleday (New York, NY), 1970.
The King God Didn't Save: Reflections on the Life and Death of Martin Luther King, Jr., Coward-McCann (New York, NY), 1970.
Flashbacks: A Twenty-Year Diary of Article Writing, Doubleday (New York, NY), 1973.
Minorities in the City, HarperCollins (New York, NY), 1975.
(With Dennis A. Williams) *If I Stop I'll Die: The Comedy and Tragedy of Richard Pryor,* Thunder's Mouth, 1991.

EDITOR

The Angry Black (anthology), Lancer Books, 1962, 2nd edition published as *Beyond the Angry Black,* Cooper Square, 1966.
(With Charles F. Harris) *Amistad I,* Knopf (New York, NY), 1970.
(With Charles F. Harris) *Amistad II,* Knopf (New York, NY), 1971.
Yardbird # 1, Reed & Young (Berkeley, CA), 1979.
(With Gilbert H. Muller) *The McGraw-Hill Introduction to Literature,* McGraw-Hill (New York, NY), 1985, 2nd edition, 1994.
(With Michel Fabre) *Street Guide to African Americans in Paris,* CEAA (Paris, France), 1992, 2nd edition, 1994.
(With Gilbert H. Muller) *Bridges: Literature across Cultures,* McGraw-Hill (New York, NY), 1994.

(With Gilbert H. Muller) *Approaches to Literature,* McGraw-Hill (New York, NY), 1994.

(With Gilbert H. Muller) *Ways In: Approaches to Reading and Writing about Literature,* 1994.

OTHER

The History of the Negro People: Omowale—The Child Returns Home (television script; filmed in Nigeria), National Education Television, 1965.

The Creative Person: Henry Roth (television script; filmed in Spain), National Education Television, 1966.

Last Flight from Ambo Ber (play; first produced in Boston, 1981), American Association of Ethiopian Jews, 1984.

August Forty-five (play), produced at Rutgers University, 1991.

Safari West (poetry), Hochelaga (Montreal, Canada), 1998.

Vanqui (opera libretto), performed by Opera Columbus, 1999.

Works have been translated into several languages, including Swedish, Dutch, and French. Contributor to anthologies, including *Censored Books: Critical Viewpoints,* Scarecrow, 1993; *Black Southern Voices,* Penguin, 1993; *Calling the Wind,* HarperCollins, 1993; *Brotherman,* Ballantine, 1995; *Spooks, Spies, and Private Eyes,* Doubleday, 1996; *Cornerstones,* St. Martin's, 1996; *Anthology of African-American Literature,* Norton, 1997; and *Power, Race, and Gender in Academe,* Modern Language Association, 2000. Contributor of stories and articles to newspapers and magazines, including *Los Angeles Times, National Leader, Jet, Negro Digest, Yardbird, Holiday, Saturday Review, Ebony, Essence, Emerge, Nation,* and *New York.*

Editor and publisher, *Negro Market Newsletter,* 1956-57; contributing editor, *Herald-Tribune Book Week,* 1963-65; member of editorial board, *Audience,* 1970-72; contributing editor, *American Journal,* 1972-74; contributing editor, *Politicks,* 1977; contributing editor, *Journal of African Civilizations,* 1980-88.

WORK IN PROGRESS: Three.

SIDELIGHTS: John A. Williams, according to *Dictionary of Literary Biography* contributor James L. de Jongh, is "arguably the finest Afro-American novelist of his generation," although he "has been denied the full degree of support and acceptance some critics think his work deserves." Part of the reason for this, Williams believes, may be because of racial discrimination. In 1961, for instance, he was awarded a grant to the American Academy in Rome based on the quality of his novel *Night Song,* but the grant was rescinded by the awarding panel. Williams felt that this happened because he was black and because of rumors that he was about to marry a white woman, which he later did. However, Alan Dugan, "the poet who eventually was awarded the prize, courageously made public the issue at the presentation ceremony," explained Jeffrey Helterman, another *Dictionary of Literary Biography* commentator, and the resulting scandal caused the American Academy to discontinue its prize for literature for a time.

Williams's first three novels trace the problems facing blacks in a white society. The books *The Angry Ones, Night Song,* and *Sissie* relate attempts by black men and women to come to terms with a nation that discriminates against them. In *The Angry Ones,* for instance, the protagonist, Steve Hill, "struggles with various kinds of racial prejudice in housing and employment, but the focus [of the novel] is on his growing realization of the way his employers at Rocket Press destroy the dreams of would-be authors," explained Helterman. Like Williams himself, Hill perceives that he is being exploited by a white-dominated industry in which a black artist has no place. Williams has said that "the plain, unspoken fact is that the Negro is superfluous in American society as it is now constructed. Society must undergo a restructuring to make a place for him, or it will be called upon to get rid of him."

The Man Who Cried I Am, a novel that brought Williams international recognition, further explores the exploitation of blacks by a white society. The protagonist, Max Reddick, is a black writer living in Europe, as did Williams for a time. Max is married to a Dutch woman, and he is dying of cancer of the rectum. His chief literary rival and mentor is Harry Ames, a fellow black author, but one who "packages racial anger and sells it in his books," according to Helterman. While in Paris to attend Harry's funeral Max learns that Harry has in fact been murdered because he had uncovered a plot by the Western nations to prevent the unification of black Africa. Max himself unearths another conspiracy: America's genocidal solution to the race problem—code-named "King Alfred"—which closely resembles Hitler's "Final Solution." Finally Max, and a Malcolm X-like figure called Minister Q, are captured by the opposing forces and put to death. *The Man Who Cried I Am* escapes the protest novel format of most black literature by putting the situation on an epic scale. Jerry H. Bryant described the book in *Critique: Studies in Modern Fiction* as "Williams's adaptation of the rhetoric of black power to his own needs as a novelist," calling it "in a sense Williams's *Huckleberry Finn.* It reflects his deep skepticism over the capacity of America to live up to its professed ideals, and a development of deep pessimism about whites in particular and man in general." Such a novel had reviewers posing deep questions. "What purpose does the King Alfred portion of the novel serve?" asked Robert E. Fleming in *Contemporary Literature.* "In one sense, black people have been systematically killed off in the United States since their first introduction to its shores. Malnutrition, disease, poverty, psychological conditioning, and spiritual starvation have been the tools, rather than military operations and gas chambers, but the result has often been the same. King Alfred is not only a prophetic warning of what might happen here but a fictional metaphor for what has been happening and is happening still," he concluded.

The Man Who Cried I Am includes a character named Paul Durrell, who is obviously based on civil rights leader Martin Luther King. Durrell is presented in a negative light, and Williams's unfavorable opinion of Durrell's real-life counterpart became all the more evident in his 1970 nonfiction book, *The King God Didn't Save: Reflections on the Life and Death of Martin Luther King, Jr.* In this unflattering biography, Williams portrays Dr. King as a man who allowed himself to be manipulated by high-ranking federal agents and as a leader who was badly out of touch with the community he influenced so strongly. In addition to *The King God Didn't Save,* Williams published another biography in 1970. Intended for reading by a young adult audience, *The Most Native of Sons: A Biography of Richard Wright* relates the life of the radical black author whose work profoundly influenced Williams.

Williams's 1982 novel, *!Click Song,* details the careers of two writers, Paul Cummings and Cato Caldwell Douglass, friends who attended school on the GI Bill after World War II. Cummings is Jewish; it is his reaffirmation of his Jewishness that provides the theme for his novels, and his suicide opens the book. Douglass, on the other hand, is black; his problem, as Jervis Anderson indicated in the *New York Times Book Review,* is to overcome racism in the publishing industry. *Chicago Tribune Book World* contributor Seymour Krim compared the two characters: Cummings "was a more successful competitor, a novelist who had won a National Book Award and all the attention that goes with it, while Cato was forced to lecture for peanuts before Black Studies groups. A further irony is the fact that Cummings was a 'passed' Jew who had only recently declared his real name, Kaminsky, in an effort to purge

himself. Purge or not, his writing has gone downhill since his born-again declaration, while his earnings have gone up." Roy Hoffman, writing for the *Washington Post Book World* pointed out, however, that "as Paul's career skyrockets, his private life goes to shambles. As Cato's career runs into brick walls, his personal life grows ever more fulfilled, ever more radiant."

"*!Click Song* is at least the equal of Williams's other masterpiece, *The Man Who Cried I Am,*" stated de Jongh. "The emotional power, the fluid structuring of time, the resonant synthesis of fiction and history are similar. But the novelist's mastery is greater, for Williams's technique here is seamless and invisible," the reviewer concluded. Other critics have also celebrated Williams's work; Krim noted, "Unlike a James Baldwin or an Amiri Baraka, Williams is primarily a storyteller, which is what makes the reality of Black Rage become something other than a polemic in his hands. . . . Before [Cato Douglass's] odyssey is ended, we know in our bones what it is like to be a gifted black survivor in America today; we change skins as we read, so to speak, and the journey of living inside another is so intense that no white reader will ever again be able to plead ignorance."

Clifford's Blues, Williams's 1999 novel, tells the story of Clifford Pepperidge, a black, homosexual jazz pianist imprisoned at Dachau. His experiences are related to the reader through a diary he secretly keeps, which is framed by letters from 1986, telling the story of how the journal came to be published. Clifford, an American who left New Orleans to avoid Jim Crow laws and American racism, writes in his journal of those imprisoned in the camp—not only Jews, but Russians, Africans, gypsies, communists, and homosexuals. "Germany was once an expatriate haven where jazz musicians and blacks and gays . . . could enjoy the liberal freedom of cities like Berlin," explained Jo-Ann Reid in *Gay and Lesbian Review Worldwide.* "Ironically, the Germany he sought as an escape from segregated America would become a far worse prison." Dieter Lange, an SS Officer, takes Clifford on as a "house slave," using Clifford's piano performances to make his way up the Nazi hierarchy. The diary ends, ambiguously, on April 28, 1945, the date of the American liberation of Dachau. According to a reviewer in *Publishers Weekly,* "Williams creates a chillingly lifelike account of the treatment of black people by the Nazis." The reviewer concluded, Clifford's "diary, though fictional, is an eloquent testimony."

Although Williams's writing explores racial themes, he has stated that he dislikes being categorized as a black author. In his view, that label only facilitates the segregation of black writers and their work from the rest of American literature. In an interview with Shirley Horner, published in the *New York Times,* he confessed that he was "pessimistic" about the possibility that racial tensions in modern American society could ever be resolved. He added, however, that "it's the kind of pessimism that I would be delighted to be proved wrong, absolutely wrong." Commenting specifically on relations between blacks and Jews, he stated, "I don't think those days of black-Jewish cooperation were ever that glorious; it's nice to think that they were. . . . Blacks and Jews in 1993 are even less willing to learn from each other, so few people try." He explained that he and his wife, who is Jewish, had moved to Teaneck, New Jersey, because they thought that "the town would not be inhospitable to a mixed marriage." Asked if they had suffered many slights because of their marriage, Williams acknowledged, "We've had our share, as we expected we would. I'm sure that there are lots of things that go on because of our marriage that I'm totally unaware of. . . . In such a marriage, you both have to be strong in ways that are sometimes not very visible. A sense of humor helps."

When asked by his son Dennis Williams, in an interview in *Forkroads,* about his approach, Williams said, "Writing's become a way of life, and I'm not sure it's not also seeking shelter from storms—that could be a part of it. But I write practically every day. For me it's like putting on my pants. And if I'm not writing I'm taking notes while watching TV or something else, but my mind is always somewhere in the production of something or finishing something and sometimes starting something new." Later in the same interview, Williams commented on his greatest likes and dislikes about being a writer: "I most like language and ideas and weaving cloth from them as well as from experiences. I can't say I dislike anything about it, even now. I like the idea of being a writer. I am very proud to be a writer."

AUTOBIOGRAPHICAL ESSAY:

John A. Williams contributed the following autobiographical essay to *CA:*

I was out working on my serve one day during the summer of 1984, when this kid (actually he was a young man, a grad student in—what else—Business Ad) came strutting through the courts.

"Excuse me," he said. "Are you good, sir? I mean *good?*"

I paused. I am a teacher, so nothing much young people say or do astonishes me. "Not very," I said. "But I can hit with you if you like."

"I dunno," he said. He was short and stocky. Like me. "I have to tell you without bragging that I am a *very* good tennis player. So, I'll take a raincheck on the hitting, okay?"

I said okay and returned to my serve.

The ball was going in well; it had a slight kick and I was moving it to where I wanted it to go. From time to time I noticed that the kid was watching me from around the corner near the water fountain.

After about fifteen minutes he returned. "Would you mind," he asked, "if I cancelled the raincheck and we hit some?"

"Not at all," I said. "But I may have to pause for a breather now and then."

"That's okay."

We began to hit. He was astoundingly clumsy. He was barely getting to the ball which I was banging from corner to corner, deep, to keep him off me and to control the pace. He loved my short balls; he jumped on them with the speed and dexterity of a midget mastodon—but more often than not, he punched them into the net. Just before I reached that point when I could see the ball coming, know where it would land and what kind of spin was on it—but would be unable to get to it—he quit. He had an appointment. He thanked me and shook hands. He made some *pro forma* complimentary remarks about my age and agility and then left the courts as arrogantly as he'd entered them.

I've known people in publishing just like that kid all my writing life. They arrive in your space arrogant and filled with assumptions. Or you arrive in theirs in the person of a book, which is even better for them because you are then at a book-length remove from their actual presences. Their assumptions therefore are easier to act on. These assumptions—actually, they are polite indictments—include my being ornery, difficult and troublesome.

I may be each of these things at different times, as the situation demands, but I've never been any one of them without good reason. These assumptions are not based on my writing, but my person. Why?

People don't seem to recall the details of the beginnings of the legend of my irascibility, but every once in a while, even today, twenty-five years later, someone will sidle up to me and ask, "What *really* happened with the Prix de Rome?" For this is where the legend began.

I do not know what happened to make me the first recipient of the Prix de Rome, a fellowship to the American Academy in Rome, ever to be rejected. I simply do not know, though I have theories. I do know that after the rejection in 1962, for twelve years the Writing Fellowship to the American Academy in Rome, awarded in conjunction with the American Academy of Arts and Letters, was abolished. (Not quite, though. There was established, quite soon after, a Traveling Fellowship for Writers that paid up to $1,500 more than the Prix de Rome. The Rome Fellowship was reinstated in 1976.)

The details as I know them were simply that I was told that I had been the unanimous choice of the 1962 jurors to be awarded the Prix de Rome—an award, incidentally, I never heard of until someone called to tell me that, in effect, if I were free to spend a year in Rome, the award was mine. You do not apply for the Fellowship; it invades your space. The jurors were Louise Bogan, John Hersey, Dudley Fitts, Phyllis McGinley, John Cheever, S. J. Perelman, and Robert Coates.

In due course I went for what was until then the routine interview with the director of the Rome Academy, Richard Kimball. Shortly after, I was told why I had not after all been selected to go. I was too old. There had been a mistake. (How, why, when, where, who?) None of the reasons was solid. My publisher, Farrar, Straus and Cudahy, took up the battle, with Roger Straus and Robert Giroux leading the way.

I was thirty-six at the time. Rejections had not been uncommon in my life. All of this might have been swept under the rug had it not been for Alan Dugan, who was older than I and who replaced me, but who also announced that there was a "bug" in the operations of the two academies. The National Institute of Arts and Letters, which is associated with the American Academy of Arts and Letters, offered to me what amounted to a consolation prize of $2,000. I did not accept the prize until after the relationship between the American and Rome academies was, at least for public consumption, severed.

The rejection seems to have originated at the time of my interview with Kimball. He may have read the novel for which I was given the Fellowship, *Night Song* (1961). It was about jazz music, drugs, an interracial romance, and a protagonist shaped like Charlie Parker. I had a beard then—with far less gray in it than now—and I wore a cap. I still do. Between the book, which he could not have finished, and my appearance, an assumption was made. There seems to have emanated from Kimball's office the report that I was "bellicose" during the interview. The fact is, that if he had asked me to kiss his backside, I would have. I was that grateful.

If he was piqued about my depiction of interracial liaisons and assumed that I was involved in one and might have carried my mate to Rome, not only was it none of his business, but it was not, at that time, true. I was engaged to a woman from Los Angeles, one Thomasina Jones. Not many people knew this, so, I suppose, they might have made assumptions. There was also the word, coming from underground, that perhaps I might not "fit in at Rome," whatever large or small reference that may have had then.

Then there were the drugs. At least six Fellows of the Rome Academy told a researcher of the incident that they'd heard something about me in connection with drugs. The researcher was Dr. Blossom Kirschenbaum, who did her M.A. and then Ph.D. on the American Academy of Arts and Letters and the Writing Fellowship given by the American Academy of Arts and Letters. Neither thesis has been published.

"The general understanding," Kirschenbaum quotes a Fellow, "was that more than marijuana was involved." I was supposed to have "not only . . . used heroin but also . . . pushed the stuff."

So the slander went, snowballing along, leading Kirschenbaum to comment that, "Other writers, hearing his [my] name, recalling his exclusion from what had been intimated was a peer-group, while they would not necessarily envision sensational images, would recall a cloud; something had been wrong, and the something wrong was attached to his [my] name."

I had always insisted, and still do, that the rejection was as much social as racial. There had been other blacks in Rome, among them Ralph Ellison and the composer Ulysses Kay. When Kirschenbaum interviewed me in the spring of 1972, she remarked that Ellison had said or written that I accused him of a part of the conspiracy that led to my rejection.

I had not. I wrote immediately to him and denied that I'd ever accused him of anything whatsoever. He replied, said he was grateful that I'd written, and that "someone went to a lot of trouble to create that mischief," and that one day he hoped "to learn who it was."

I never heard from him again, although he told other people—Ishmael Reed, Quincy Troupe, and Steve Cannon, for example—that he and I *had* discussed the Prix de Rome business. But, in fact, we have never discussed it, and on the rare occasion when we've been thrown together, he's said nothing and neither have I. (During lunch one day during the summer of 1974 while I was at the University of Hawaii, Leon Edel remarked that Ellison had an "undue influence" upon the careers of younger black writers.)

From here we proceed to the assumption that a number of people base their knowledge of me on the "something" that was wrong all the way down to the least of the Old Boys. This, of course, implies a network. And why not? Going through Kirschenbaum's typescript, the names leaped out like flushed quail, the ones who offered the quotes, the commentary. They are book reviewers (a high-frequency network of its own), trustees of grants foundations, writers who are jealously supportive of good friends who are also writers. The connections are as knotted as the cords in a tennis net.

Kirschenbaum in her summary laments the fact that these events precluded my being able to enrich Rome with my presence, my wit, charm and humanity. I think she is right, and my publishers then believed as much, too. And why not? It was in part due to them that I got into the mess in the first place.

*

Young writers are naturally curious about how older writers got started, were first published, and this retelling leads back to Farrar, Straus. Although I had published a novel in a paperback edition in January 1960, I felt that I hadn't really been published at all; even though I'd done a number of short stories in the middle-to-late 1950s, I did not have any luck getting them in print. I did publish a few "Bop Fables" in the "Girlies" (they called them then), such as "The Bopper's Romeo and Juliet," "The Bopper's Hamlet," "Brubbie Desbeck Goes to Mars," etc. There were two stories I still like: "A Good Season" (which was supposed to be "Spring Song," one of a cycle of four stories) and "Son in the Afternoon," which I wrote in 1956. This one went out several times and came back almost as soon as I'd dropped if off at my agent, who was Candida Donadio.

Phoebe Lou Adams was handling fiction for *Atlantic,* and the story had been sent to her. It was returned with her note: " 'The Son' story is no go unless run with a picture of the author, who, believe me, had damn well better be black as the ace of spades. Since we can't manage that setup, there's no hope here." Her note was dated January 30, 1958, and clearly was not intended for my eyes.

Late in 1960, I thought I'd give the story one final try before consigning it to the files, and I sent it to Noonday Press. When I checked in a few weeks later, one of the editors, Elizabeth Pollet, told me they liked it, but wanted to hold it until their inventory went down. Would I mind? Certainly not, I assured her. Hers was the first decent response I got from the story at that time.

A few months passed and I checked in again to discover that Noonday had become a part of Farrar, Straus and Cudahy. Noonday would not be publishing stories any more, but, asked Pollet, did I have a novel?

Did I have a novel. I had one in the works, *Sissie,* and one that was completed and in the hands of Marc Jaffee and Arlene Donovan at Dell Books; it was to be another paperback original. It was called *Night Song.* Cecil Hemley, who was Pollet's boss, wanted to see that, too. He would become my editor, and he thought he could arrange with Dell to have FS&C do the novel first and Dell do the paperback as a two-book deal for me. All this, however, was in the speculative stage, as they'd not read *Sissie,* which I'd just delivered to them.

One gray day early in April (why I remember that it was gray may be the subject of the biography I hope my sons will one day write) Hemley called. They wanted to do both. The deal was on. On April 21, 1961, I signed a contract for $4,000 and Pollet, Hemley, and I went out to celebrate. I was going to be *published* at last. I was thirty-six years old. (Eventually Hemley, who was also a novelist, would bring Isaac Bashevis Singer and Susan Sontag to the firm. A couple of years later he left publishing for teaching. I gather there were differences between him and Giroux.)

Thus, FS&C was involved when the Prix de Rome business broke.

Hemley died suddenly in 1964. He was the first real editor I had. When I finished *Sissie* he set aside a complete day, and in his office overlooking Union Square Park, he read back to me the entire manuscript. Sounds that were dissonant came racing back; awkward scenes wobbled like soaked tennis balls. We cut a lot of stuff. From that day on I became a believer in "reading back aloud" as a major aid during the rewriting process. (Readings from work in progress serves the same purpose.)

It will be argued that had it not been for the Prix de Rome incident no one would have heard of me. There is truth in that argument—on the other hand, Rome did not make me a "hot property," either.

I did not come from that class and kind of people who either formulated what the Rome Academy represented or did Fellowships there. Folk from my class were seldom invited onto anyone's tennis court. My rejection served to strengthen my conviction (which is even stronger today) that there would not be any surcease from the wars of caste and class in the foreseeable future. A black person may be given a temporary pass to the courts, but it is only that. And if he overstays his time, he will be laughed at behind his back, jolted into a return to reality, or left to wither on the vine. Rome was reaffirmation.

*

I grew up in Syracuse, New York, "apple-knocker country," where summers are splendid and winters war against the psyche. Black people seem to have entered Syracuse history around 1769. My father's grandmother, Margaret Smallwood, was born there in 1820, and she married Gorman Williams in 1838.

My mother's grandfather was Anthony Jones, who was born in Mississippi in 1830 and died at the age of eighty-two in 1912. My mother, Ola (the only one in her family with an African name) who is now eighty-three, recalls as a child trying to chase a fly from beneath the netting that had been stretched over Grampa Tony's open coffin; she recalls church bells tolling beyond what she was used to counting. Grampa Tony had two wives and two sets of children; from the second came my grandfather, Joseph David Jones, who himself had two wives, but not the two sets of kids.

My mother was the eldest daughter of J. D. Jones. In the eastern region of Nigeria her name means Keeper of the Beautiful House; and in the western region, He Who Wants To Be Chief. Both terms apply to her. My mother left Mississippi in her late teens to work in Watertown, New York, "living in." When she'd paid off the expenses of her travel, she moved to Syracuse where she met my father, whom she used to refer to as a "sheik," or a "lounge lizard."

She and all her family always felt superior to my father and his family, who were black city folk, owning noth-

ing and subsisting on what was then called common labor. People on the land (Grampa Joe owned eighty-eight acres) could grow and raise things, and there were tasks they had to do. They did not have to wait for jobs to happen or for favors.

They married, John Henry and Ola Mae, and subsequently she became pregnant and, as was the norm then, returned home for my birth, my grandfather having sent the passage money for Ola only. My father worked his way south with a circus. He liked to wear starched white shirts, which no one wore in Hinds County, Mississippi, except on Sunday, for funerals or weddings.

Something happened and the sheriff came out to J. D. Jones's farm. His son-in-law was the only "strange nigger" around, so he must have done it, whatever it was. My grandfather (who did not like my father) "sammed" for the sheriff and for the first time my mother was ashamed of him.

But what was John Henry to do? He ran. Hid under the hay in a wagon going north. Went through a blockade and took a pitchfork tine through the meat of his shoulder without screaming and got away. He never traveled far from Syracuse after that. When I was a boy I used to play in the dimple left by that wound.

The section I lived in, the old Fifteenth Ward, was integrated. Not because of any goodness of heart, but because that was where the money ran out or where the relatives lived, and the rents were cheap. The men played touch football in the street or softball or baseball in the parks; everyone knew everyone else and you dared not get into too much trouble because there was always someone to tell your folks. And the squealers were black, Greek, Irish, Jewish, Italian, and down-at-the-heels WASP. About forty or fifty of us went to the schools together and over the years played ball and drank together. Something else happens during the teens: no more playing "Doctor" in the cellars or strip poker; no more playing "House." The beneficent neighbors turn watchful over their Greek, Irish, Jewish, Italian, and down-at-the-heels WASP daughters; things change.

It was no big thing. There were lots of black girls and, in the final analysis, we all moved through that period, went to war, to college, married and raised families, and discovered that what we had had, in whole or in part, was what now seems to have been very special. I have many, many friends still in Syracuse. Looking back, though, it is easy to see that the U.S. Government also played a part in the subsequent, temporary division be-

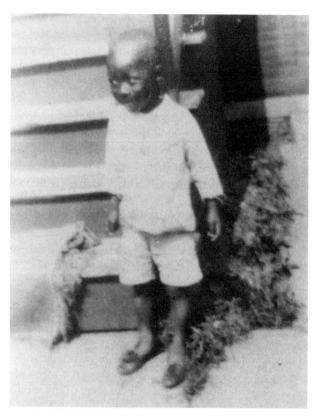

Williams, age three, Syracuse, New York, 1928

tween friends. It decided to build a housing project in the neighborhood, the Pioneer Homes. In the process, many sturdy homes were levelled, forcing folk to move to other neighborhoods. When the project opened, it was on a segregated basis.

All this was later, close to the end of innocence.

I was the eldest of four kids. There were good times along with the bad. At a period when both my parents were working, we had a baby-sitter. I shall be forever grateful to this horny kid (I can't think of her as being anything other than a kid), for she took a goatish, nine-year-old boy who was, clearly, more randy in mind than in body, and showed him whats and whyfors and wherefors. She appears briefly in *Mothersill and the Foxes* (1975).

I liked to read. I was the only kid in my class who was allowed to take four books from the public library every week because they knew I'd read and return them and ask for more. I stole a lot of books from The Syracuse Boys' Club, which was run by a saintly tall man named Frank Zerbe. It was completely integrated, whereas the YMCA closed its door to black boys. The Dunbar Center was run, when I was boy, by the gloriously named

Golden B. Darby. Dunbar was the second of my hangouts; it was a small two-story house across the street from Syracuse University's Medical School on South McBride Street. It would later move to South Townsend, just before World War II.

*

I think of my boyhood as a time that was on the cusp of change. I was two when Lindbergh made his flight to Paris. There were more horse-drawn wagons than cars; watering tanks were still on some corners when I left town—much, much later. The corner grocery store was still a fixture, although the A&P and The American Stores (now Acme) were edging in. Baseball was the undisputed king of sports; parades were huge and wondrous spectacles, always filled with vets from the Great War who wore silver helmets. When a plane flew into a huge cloud we never expected it to come out. And up on "The Hill" stood Syracuse University whose chimes rang down upon us every day, and whose students snake-danced downtown whooping and hollering on the eves of traditional football games with Colgate and Cornell.

I once knew the campus like the palm of my hand, for there were times—short periods to be sure—when I'd run away from home, grieved and angered because I'd been whipped. I slept under the well-tended groves of white fir trees that lined the hill up behind the stadium. In the morning I pilfered milk from doorsteps and boosted fresh fruit from peddlers' wagons. Oh, but they were always waiting for me when I returned home.

I do not recall too many of my father's relatives—some cousins, a couple of uncles, but no grandparents. But I can still recall my maternal grandfather's first visit. He shared my room and I was grateful because I was sure there were ghosts in it. Grampa was a stern, precise man with a controlled sense of humor. He wore celluloid collars and a straw hat. (It was summer.) And he seemed to be a favorite with the sisters in church, his second wife having died some years before his trip north. My grandly named Uncle Ulysses came too, but he stayed longer. I later learned that he had walked up and down in front of our house across the street for three days before my mother noticed something familiar about him. She called out, "Yoooo! Ul*ysees!* Is that you?"

Still later came my favorite aunt, Elizabeth, who had been known as Sammy; then came Florence, not quite my least favorite aunt, and others followed. We were a way-station, doing what families did in those days and still do. All the relatives who came drifted away into their own lives, taking up residence in Syracuse. Elizabeth married Fred Page, my favorite, now ailing uncle, even if by marriage, with whom I used to hunt. Fred worked at Simon's Texaco Gas Station and used to read the *Daily Forward.* His Yiddish was said to have been quite good. (Fred died in July, 1985.)

Religion was no big thing on my father's side of the family, but most certainly was on my mother's. We went to the African Methodist Episcopal Zion Church on East Fayette Street. It was, I think, the second oldest AME in the nation. It was still there in 1983. We went not only to church, but to Sunday School and vespers. I grew to like Sunday School, though, not out of any love for the teachers or the lessons, but to watch Miss Beverly. So I went early and placed myself on the steps of the church and waited. She played the organ for the Baptist church around the corner. Down the street she would come swinging, dressed to the nines and perfumed like the soft winds of heaven itself. She was a bit on the hefty side, Miss Beverly was, and down she would come, high heels beating a sexy tattoo on the walk, her hips a-rumble with motion. She was the only great thing about Sundays, for in the early afternoon, right after the Sunday dinner, we were sent to the Rescue Mission. Services were run by Amos Phipps, a Scot with a magnificent voice who also sang gospels on the radio. The Mission was also the home of reformed alcoholics who lived in another part of the building. So, in addition to Lindbergh and Babe Ruth, we had echoes of Billy Sunday and Aimee Semple McPherson.

My parents divorced when I was about eleven or twelve, and my father was unable to help provide support. By order of the Children's Court, we were shunted from Ola to John Henry every few months until, finally, we rebelled. I led the rebellion, of course; I was the eldest. I had several fights with my father (spurred on by Ola's reports of the dastardly relations he was carrying on with other women), all of which ended with me on the floor, lights flashing in my head. Finally, we were allowed to stay with my mother.

It was a bad time. The Depression was crunching everybody and everything; it was especially tough to men whose only work skill was strength. Today my mother says, though she didn't then, "There were no jobs. He couldn't help it." Both are alive, though at different ends of the country. My mother had one other marriage, but her husband died in 1975; my father has had several marriages. I think he regrets them all.

I was placed in charge of many things that I had no wish to be in charge of: my brother Joe, the baby, and my sisters, Ruth and Helen; of bringing in coal and wood, starting fires and keeping them going; of this and of that. I took on a variety of part-time jobs: taking out trash through neighborhoods and putting the cans back, cleaning up a bookstore once a week, delivering the famous black papers of the time, the *Chicago Defender,* the *Pittsburgh Courier,* the *Afro-American News,* and the local paper, the *Progressive Herald.* I ran errands for Mr. Jackson who ran an odds-and-ends shop (cigarettes were a penny each), and swiped lead fittings from the plumbing of the homes that were being demolished for the new project. I collected papers and rags and, together with the lead, sold them to the local junkman, always careful, of course, to place a few rocks between the papers or in the rags. Sometimes, I climbed the wall of his yard, picked out two or three hefty bags of rags and sold them back to him a couple of days later.

I hungered to be a great football player like Brud Holland of Cornell or Bernie Jefferson of Northwestern; or a great pole vaulter like Cornelius Wamerdam, or a sprinter like Jesse Owens or Marty Glickman. How I found the time to sandwich in the ball playing and the running amazes and amuses me now. Yet I did. I even found time to join the Dunbar Center Drum and Bugle Corps, which was under the supervision of Herbert Johnson, whom we called Hoppie. He also coached basketball and was the scoutmaster of Troop 47 to which I belonged. I was a Life Scout with the troop. I became so good with the bugle that they came to get me whenever a vet died so I could blow "Taps." And when I went into the Navy in 1943, I was the regimental bugler at Camp Robert Smalls, a segregated base at Great Lakes, Illinois, until my company finished boot training. When that was over, I went to Hospital Corps School in the first class of blacks ever admitted into it. The word was that the Navy and Marines badly needed medics. I was the school bugler until we finished the course. During my "professional" bugling career I was known, without great affection, as "Bugle Boy."

*

Over the years I have written about or drawn upon those three years I spent in the Navy. The closest I came to being killed during the war, when arms were raised specifically against *me,* not just a bunch of people climbing a beach or working through a tropical forest, was when Americans, sailors, placed a .45 to my head and almost pulled the trigger. No Japanese bomber pilot or rifleman or machine gunner ever did that.

The Williams family, 1932: (from left) sister Ruth, father John Henry, sister Helen, mother Ola Mae. Williams is in front of his father. Brother Joseph was in the hospital with pneumonia

It is enough to say that I did two years overseas and went from New Caledonia up the island chain to Guam where we were when the war ended, just when we were preparing for our third "push." I was a Pharmacist's Mate 3/C when it was over. Black servicemen the world over had to fight two battles: one with the Japanese or Germans or Italians, and the other with white American servicemen. It has always been that way; even with the Gillem Report, which called for military integration in 1948, with Korea and Vietnam, military racism continued. It is in the fabric of society and has yet to be pulled out. In *Captain Blackman* (1972) I tried to examine this. (I researched quite a bit for that novel, traveling to Italy, France, and around the country, digging out old records, tracking various military units and corresponding with individuals who "knew things.")

The Navy experience was invaluable even if wounding. But I traded my three years for almost five of education under the GI Bill of Rights.

Like millions of other ex-servicemen, I felt that the war intercepted a future of drudgery. I had had to drop out of high school to help with the family, working for the city hauling garbage or on gangs that built roads. I could almost look into the future and see my life shaped by jobs at Carrier Corporation, Easy Washer, New Process Gear, General Electric, or one of the several steel companies. And they would not be good jobs, either, for discrimination had always existed in these places.

All my family wondered what I was going to do. I surprised them when I said I was going back to school. Which I did. I finished high school in a semester and that summer (1946) worked as a coremaker in a foundry. My mother wanted me to take out a GI loan and buy a house. I told her I didn't want a house; I wanted an education. (She remembers this, though now with pride.)

I applied to Howard University. They turned me down. Because a couple of friends and former teammates were going to Morris Brown College in Atlanta, I thought I'd go too, and play ball. I went South that fall and worked out with the football team. But off campus I was never sure I was doing the *right* thing, or if I were sitting in the right place, or in the right line. I feared I would get into trouble and have to hurt someone and they, in turn of course, would hurt me fatally. I could not stay cooped up on campus. On the day classes began, I took the Jim Crow train back north to Cincinnati, where you could then move to other cars, and on to Syracuse where I enrolled at Syracuse University.

I had not the vaguest idea what I wanted to do or be. My family thought that, since I'd been a corpsman, I was qualified to study medicine. I thought about newspapering because I'd delivered all those papers. About all I was sure of was that I had to learn more about the world I lived in and how it worked, and about people and things. All the random reading I'd done as a kid thrust me in that direction.

For all of my boyhood the chimes had bonged down upon our neighborhood from Syracuse University's Crouse College of Fine Arts. No doubt, being enrolled there had been a subconscious desire for much of my life. The place was bulging at the seams with vets in 1946, and it was an exciting time for us and for all the younger students as well. It was there that I got the first hint from a freshman comp teacher that I could write. His name was Couchman. I heard of him many, many years ago; he'd left Syracuse to go to the University of Pennsylvania. He was the first person in any capacity to know who ever commended me on my writing. I'd done an essay about a landing, recalling what it was like and what it felt like that morning when the engines of your ship stopped throbbing and you could hear the waves rush and lap at its sides in the stillness. Then you

Oakland, California, 1945; Williams (left) on first night back from two years in the South Pacific

pressed toward the stairs that led topside, out of the stench of the hold and into the fresh morning air; you pushed and shoved with your unit to the cargo ropes where you climbed down them into the landing boats. There were the planes dive-bombing and the cruisers, battlewagons, destroyers and destroyer escorts cutting loose with their guns at the island. You got sprayed; the coxswains gunned their engines and tilted with their rudders to keep in line, and then you were off to the beach. The moment of utter and total nakedness came when the ramp was let down and ground itself into the sand.

Couchman wrote—I cannot remember what—but the words shot me out of myself toward whatever it is I now have become. (In April, 1985, shortly before speaking to a group of librarians in New York, I met a young woman whose husband is a fiction writer. His name was Jeff Couchman. I asked if her father-in-law had taught at Syracuse and then gone on to Penn. She said yes. His first name: Gordon. I explained what he'd meant to me and asked that she give him my regards. He's seventy-three now and doesn't travel much. I was

sure he wouldn't recall me. But I recalled him. Later I met Jeff Couchman and through him got in touch with his father. Gordon Couchman responded with a long and gracious letter. He remembered me. He's now retired but still very much the teacher and, I gather, a solid human being.)

Later, Daniel Curley became my writing teacher. He demanded, demanded, demanded work, always in that soft, disassociated voice. If he did not, then why do I now feel after all these years, that he did? (In support of my allegation, he himself wrote to me several years ago from the University of Illinois and mentioned that his students called him Mr. Cruely.) Leonard S. Brown was another of my favorite teachers who taught (and was said to be a character in) *Under the Volcano,* a novel whose structure I tried to emulate in *Sissie.* I did better with *The Man Who Cried I Am,* but with *!Click Song,* I think I finally succeeded, though on a wider time-scale.

My other interest was radio journalism. I was, at the time, the only black student. There were a few others in print: Bob Johnson, now executive editor of *Jet,* Rick Hurt, who went to the *Norfolk Journal and Guide,* Wendell Roye, and Ralph Matthews, Jr., whose dad was an editor of the *Afro-American.* In those days, none of us dared to think—we certainly did not believe—that white papers would ever hire blacks. Most of them were solidly status quo and we did not expect them to change. I went for radio because, if I got a job, no one would see me. Anyone could walk into a newspaper office and look over the staff; not necessarily in a radio station where rooms were soundproofed and the doors were topped with signs reading ON THE AIR! (STAY OUT!)

But I forgot about the people who did the hiring.

Although I still lived and worked in the community where I'd grown up, there was a mixed reaction to my going "Up on The Hill." A few others had left town to go to college—former teammates and buddies. The reaction I got was one of tolerant amusement, but from the older folk a sense of pride. In the bars where I hung out, I was called "Schoolboy." There seemed to be a bit of pride there, too.

Like others, I worked while attending classes, sometimes at night, sometimes after classes. And I was also writing for the local paper, the *Progressive Herald,* a black, Democratic weekly, the *Chicago Defender* under Enoch Waters, and the Associated Negro Press, which was run by Claude Barnett. The two white dailies, the *Syracuse Post Standard* and the *Syracuse Herald-Journal,* like nearly all the papers in the country, did not hire black staff, but I did do occasional pieces for them when it came to Black History week or a few things on the black community. Later, after I left graduate school, I did work with a white public relations firm, Doug Johnson Associates, and placed a pile of press releases with both papers, none with bylines.

When a sophomore, I'd married Carolyn Louise Clopton, whose family had come to Utica and then to Syracuse, via Aberdeen, Mississippi. That was 1947 and our first son came the following year. Work was as much a part of my life as college. I got one offer of a job in radio in LeMoyne, Tennessee, from a black station, and I was even willing to go South for it. But Carolyn was opposed to the move. Dennis, our second son, was born in 1951, as my time in college and graduate school ran out.

With all that was going on, however, with classes and jobs, I was writing and publishing poetry in a few places, and I felt that I was certainly to be a writer. This,

of course, was not bringing in the bread and milk, and so I returned to a foundry where I had worked and earned excellent wages during summers. The foundry was my first job out of graduate school, and the return to it served to break off most of my connections with friends at the university who were still studying. One of these friends, for a number of years, was Dennis John Lynds, a poet and fiction writer who today writes mainly mysteries.

Syracuse, the city, had undergone severe change; the old neighborhood had become a slum. All who were able moved away from it. Housing was tight—and restricted. We lived with my mother-in-law. It was she, in fact, who bought me my very first typewriter. When our son Dennis was on the way, my anger at those housing restrictions boiled over and I wrote a blistering letter to the veterans counselor of Onondaga County, a man named Harvey Smith. The next thing I knew we had an apartment in a brand new project, much of which had been given over to the housing of vets.

One of the characters in *The Junior Bachelor Society* (1976) works in a foundry and suffers a severe back injury. I hurt my back in the foundry so badly that I was forced to leave. I wore a brace and lived on Seconal for months. I really don't know just how we survived until I landed a job as a vegetable clerk in a Loblaw supermarket, which I took while awaiting a hoped-for appointment as a caseworker in the County Welfare Department. That came through in about six months.

On the job I became reacquainted with Bill Chiles, who'd been our caseworker during the Depression, when systems were wired black caseworkers to black families and white caseworkers to white and black families. There had been but two black caseworkers to handle the black community. Bill was by now a supervisor. He became much like a favorite uncle. (Fathers never confide totally in you; uncles often do.) He loved the Dodgers and Adlai Stevenson. He taught me more about the curves and fastballs of racism than any other person I've ever met. He taught me dedication, though we never discussed that; I simply watched him work his job. He taught me to cut open the spaces between the written lines of things and to perceive what was really being said. He played a good game of pool, KCMO (Kansas City, Missouri) style, which was where he'd come from. And he was a deeply religious man, a Catholic, who was respected by all the politicians in the county. In his way Bill did more for black people in Syracuse than they could ever dream of. He, more than any other person, taught me what being a man was about.

Williams, president of NAACP branch and president of Delta Zeta chapter, Alpha Phi Alpha Fraternity, Syracuse University, 1949

Through Bill's help I got transferred to the Children's Protective Service, and that provided some of the material I used in *Mothersill and the Foxes* (1975). Mothersill was the name of a 1920s seasick remedy, to cure the ups and downs, the downs and ups, for Mothersill considered himself to be great in bed, but in fact, his role in lovemaking was pretty much on a par with whatever bed was being used at the time. The job with CPS was tough. It was all child abuse—fathers buggering their sons or raping their daughters in and out of the boondocks outside Syracuse; kids getting bashed about for reasons that had more to do with their parents than anything they themselves could ever do. It was a horrendous, twenty-four-hour a day job. And I could not take it.

My marriage began to unravel while I was in CPS, and I found myself doing what I vowed never to do—leave

my kids. I never forgave my father for doing that, although I might have had he had any interest whatsoever in his grandsons. He had none. They sometimes passed in the street, I have been told, and he never even knew them.

I moved to another part of town and continued working and writing and learning to play tennis until my brother Joe flew East and together we drove to Los Angeles where he lived with my mother, sister Helen, and our stepfather, Albert Page. They'd all moved out there in 1948. Helen had had a bad marriage and two kids. With Joe's help, she was barely surviving. My other sister, Ruth, remained in the East recuperating from yet another bad marriage. Her husband, a preacher, had gone bonkers and tried to kill her and her four kids.

*

I'd not been in California since the war. I suffered badly out there. I couldn't always get a job and those I did get were short-lived and did not pay well. The daily papers were just then about to hire a single black reporter. Nothing in radio. In 1954, all was slick and slide, con and hustle, from Hollywood all the way to Watts. The black papers, all weeklies, were on the brink of disaster every seven days. Thing was out there, nobody wanted you if you knew anything, if you had talent, or if you knew more than they.

The big phrase of rejection in those days was that you were "over-qualified," and so it seemed to be with blacks as well as for whites. I once hooked up with a small-time black PR man (we handled publicity for NBC-TV and CBS-TV whenever there was a guest black actor on a show), and one day after watching me punch out a bunch of press releases he said, "You work like the white folks taught you." It was, obviously, a phrase I never forgot, but I am still afraid to examine its meaning too closely.

My mother and stepfather lived in Watts, which by 1965 would be called a ghetto. I never found it so. There were many substantial homes and churches, businesses and schools, and a vigorous sense of community. There I began to recover from my busted marriage and eventually worked for Golden State Mutual Life Insurance Company, where I wrote speeches for the officers, did PR and wrote advertising copy and edited a couple of company publications. I was also noodling around with my own work.

Being away from my kids gnawed at me, and I determined to get back East to New York where I could get to see them and have them spend time with me.

When I got back in the summer of 1955, I found a small, renovated kitchenette on West Eighty-fourth Street between Columbus and Amsterdam Avenues, which the *New York Post* had called "The Worst Block in Manhattan." It was pretty bad. I was afraid to go out in the morning to look for work and terrified at night when I had to return.

Nevertheless, through Dennis Lynds, who'd remained in Manhattan after finishing grad school, I applied for a job at a vanity press, Comet Press Books, then at 11 West Forty-second Street. I got the job, writing jacket copy and publicity. I moved to a studio apartment, actually a hotel, a couple of blocks away on Eighty-fifth Street between West End and Riverside Drive. The most important thing that happened, however, was that on the job I met Lorrain Isaac, who was the last of her family to get away from Hungary before Europe blew up. She came out when she was six and when I met her was a savvy New Yorker—though she lived in the Bronx. More about her later.

I loved living in New York instead of visiting it. I worked hard on my job, but on weekends I ran around a track at Roosevelt Park and Seventy-second Street, and I jogged around the reservoir in Central Park. People thought I was a nut. The jogging craze would not hit the city for another fifteen to twenty years.

I made $75 a week on my job, but I was able to see my kids and have them spend time with me. Dennis Lynds lived not far away, and I spent a great deal of time in the evening throwing darts in his kitchen on Seventy-third Street, and where he was writing and working and often entertaining people who were studying at the Actors Studio. Lynds and I talked about writing almost as much as we wrote, and he was a dedicated writer, snatching every moment he could to sit down at his Olympia.

On the job, another of the staff was Beverly Loo; she and Lori were good friends. Loo later left to join Farrar, Straus and Cudahy, and eventually to become a chief officer at McGraw-Hill, working very quietly until the Clifford Irving-Howard Hughes scam broke. I learned through Lori that Loo did not like blacks—but thought I was okay. In fact, I was okay enough then for her to ask me to coach her on how she should behave on dates—how far she should go, what she should give up, etc.

We—Lori and I—suspect that perhaps Loo had tipped off the boss that we were heavy into hanky-panky. We were, but one could not then consider it to have been

heavy. Lori was fired, almost without ceremony, and I lingered on in the job, trying to make best-sellers out of books that had been, even in conception, better than some of the books being published today. I thought I deserved a raise. I asked for it. And that was what the publishers—basically printers with spaces between jobs—wanted; they fired me. So, struggle. My ex-wife got on my case and Judge Leo Yehle, whom I'd known all my life, first as a ward of the court and then as an adviser for Childrens' Protective Service, fired off a summons for non-support, and the New York City cops descended. I appeared in court. The judge said pay up. I told him I had nothing to pay with and that he'd better jail me then and there. He gave me a couple of weeks, but I left to go to the Wiltwyck School for Boys, where author Claude Brown and heavyweight boxing champ Floyd Patterson had sojourned briefly as children. I had to run because I couldn't get a job and my unemployment checks had run out; they were $36 a week and my rent was $20. Had it not been for Lori's mother's kosher ground beef and other odds and ends, I would have been in a calamitous situation.

But, through all this, I *had* managed to rewrite a novel I called *One for New York,* which I'd begun in California, although then I had no title for it. When I thought it was safe, and I had had quite enough of Wiltwyck's staff—composed then of several people in my situation or worse—I returned to the city. A friend let me stay with him and I became involved in doing publicity for the company he was in and which was headed by Joseph Chaikin. My friend later died of diabetes.

I scrambled for work. I was, of course, still "overqualified." I don't know how I survived, but I managed to accumulate enough money to rent an empty storefront not far from where Lori lived. But I soon ran out of whatever work I was doing and in the dead of one night borrowed a car, loaded it up, and slipped out. I moved in unannounced with Lynds who was by then living on Lafayette Street in the Village. He was far more gracious about the intrusion than I would have been.

Writing made me whole; it kept me sane; it made me believe in *me* when there was ample evidence everywhere that no one else did. I behaved very badly during that time. Now I look back, sometimes with disgust, but mostly with wonder and surprise that I lasted through it. I held a series of part-time jobs, after failing to secure anything full time. One of these was at station WOV, where I broadcasted special events. It had taken almost eight years for me to land in a job I had been trained for.

Then I worked as an assistant to Lou Schwartz at Abelard-Schuman. It was an atrocious job and Schwartz, the president, had a personality to match. When I learned that all the editors working under me were earning twice to three times the money I was making, I asked for a raise. And got fired again.

The American Committee on Africa hired me as an information director and fund raiser; it was the most satisfying job I'd held since leaving college. There I met people like Tom M'Boya, Kwame Nkrumah, Eduardo Mondlane, Azikiwe, Bishop Joost de Blank of South Africa, and many other folk, most of them now assassinated, in exile, or imprisoned.

One for New York was being sent around by my agent, Candida Donadio, and was drawing fears from editors that readers in the South would not buy the book. Once when I got a good bite from New American Library, I rewrote the thing in twenty-four hours sitting naked on a towel in ninety-degree heat.

Lynds had moved out, on his way to a second marriage, and I was able to bring the kids down more often, but I was tiring of the grind, the constant rejections, which seemed a concerted attempt to rub me out. Lori and I had made some kind of peace, but that did not promise much for our future. I decided to get the hell out for a while. I got some stringing assignments from *Jet* and the Associated Negro Press and let Candida push the novel.

In the autumn of 1958, with more hope than money, I left for Spain and settled in a village south of Barcelona called Castelldefels, which was to figure in *Sissie* (1963) and *!Click Song* (1982).

There was much poverty in Spain then and people murmured about overthrowing Franco but of course never did. Soldiers and policemen were everywhere, even on the buses and trains. Yet I was respected, although also seen as an object of curiosity. How could I feel so at peace in a dictatorship and so miserable at home in a democracy? I had to return in the spring because the Associated Negro Press was not paying for my copy, and *Jet's* checks weren't long enough to cover my needs. I returned to New York sadder, wiser, and richer in ways I did not then understand.

*

Toward the end of the year, Jerry Gross of Ace Books (now at Dodd, Mead) bought *One for New York* as a paperback original, and changed the title to *The Angry Ones* (with my grudging acquiescence, for I wanted to *sell* the thing). In the meantime I had survived once again on nickel-and-dime jobs. The novel was published in January 1960, which was about the time Bayard Rustin called to ask me if I would be interested in running a rally in Madison Square Garden for the Sane Nuclear Policy Committee. Bayard had been on the board of The American Committee on Africa. I agreed, for the $1,500 I got from Ace had not lasted very long.

The rally took place May 9, 1960. We had brought together people like Eleanor Roosevelt with whom I had tea to discuss the rally, Alf Landon, Governor G. Mennen Williams, Mike Nichols and Elaine May, Norman Cousins, Walter Reuther, Tom Poston, Orson Bean, Harry Belafonte, Norman Thomas, and others. The rally was a smashing success. The Garden rocked. There was a magnificent spirit surging through it and it spilled out into a candlelight walk to the UN. All this was at the same time some members of the planning board were being subpoenaed to appear before the House Un-American Activities Committee.

That summer Candida got me a fellowship to the Bread Loaf Writers Conference and I went up there with a typewriter, prepared to work. I didn't, but I met a lot of people: the poet, John Engels, Arthur Roth, Ann McGovern, Richard Yates, Edward Lewis Wallant, Gloria Oden, Bob Rich, John Ciardi, Sylvester Leaks, Dudley Fitts, and others. The next year was 1961. And *Night Song* was published.

Through Carl Van Vechten I met Chester Himes about this time. He was a small, very handsome man whose speech was somewhat slurred because of a broken jaw he'd suffered as a boy. When he returned to Paris where he was living, we stayed in touch. Chester's predicament in those days, and for some time after, was that he had very little money. His trips to New York invariably had to do with trying to arrange the publication of a new book or an American edition of a book he'd done for Gallimard, for whom he was doing *policiers,* the Grave Digger Jones and Coffin Ed Johnson detective novels. Except that they were more than detective books. I did a lot of leg-work for Chester, seeking agents, calling former agents, checking bookstores to see which of his many books had been published here without his knowledge (there were always two or three), and I wrote letters for him and articles about him.

Chester had a great, raw sense of humor; he'd often crack up before he finished telling a joke or describing an incident. One of his favorites was about driving through Germany. The engine blew out of the back of his VW. As soon as he was able, Chester sat down and wrote to the VW people at Wolfsburg; he told them he was a writer, and if they did not replace his car at once, he would write about them and the lousy product they made. They didn't replace the car, but they did install a brand new engine. Chester had his first stroke—he was to have several others—when he was in Mexico in 1962. He never admitted that he'd had a stroke; he said he'd been bitten by a scorpion. I don't think he *ever* admitted that he was a stroke victim. He died at seventy-five in November 1984, in Spain where he'd moved about a decade earlier.

Sissie, which followed *Night Song,* had the bad fortune to come out at approximately the same time as James Baldwin's *Another Country.* It was a pity that so perceptive a reviewer as David Boroff, who much preferred my novel to Baldwin's, had to go and die.

I settled in with agent Carl Brandt, Jr. of Brandt and Brandt. Several editors sought me out (and I now regret somewhat that I didn't go with one or two of them). I was getting magazine assignments regularly. I was eating well and seeing my kids and even able to visit my mother and stepfather in Los Angeles where earlier I'd met Tommie Jones and was briefly engaged.

I'd done a quickie anthology for Lancer Books, a children's book on Africa, and was about to publish a book I wrote for Harry J. Anslinger, former federal commissioner of narcotics. I had no regular job, but I wasn't pressed to the wall anymore.

I had a friend at *Newsweek* who kept saying "Come on over," but, given my past experience with the media, I wasn't in any hurry. *Holiday* wanted me to do a big piece on what was going on around the country, a sort of "Travels with Mr. Charley," the other side of Steinbeck's *Travels with Charley* which had earlier appeared in the magazine.

By now my hunting buddy, Wendell Roye, who'd also gone to Syracuse University, was working with the U.S. Information Agency in Kano, Nigeria. By mail he urged me to come and take a look at Africa, and I thought, Well, why not? But first I did the *Holiday* assignment, driving around the country north, south, east, and west. Brandt arranged for me to meet some people—Bill Gulick in the Northwest, Shirley Ann Grau and Hodding Carter, Jr. in the South. The trip is recorded in *This Is My Country Too* (1965). *Newsweek* wanted to use me in Africa, and the Israeli Government Press Office was offering a junket, so I flew to London

and made my way slowly through Paris, where I visited Himes, then Rome, Athens, and on into Tel Aviv. It was January 1964, and Lori and I didn't know for sure where we were going together.

I wrote as I traveled and worked and sent in another draft of the *Holiday* piece from Ethiopia. I met the playwright Moshe Shamir (also a novelist) and the poet Yehuda Amichai in Israel, which in 1964 was a very stirring place to be. (Cuba in 1983 gave off the same vibrations.) I ran into my first black British troops on Cyprus where the Turks and Greeks were fighting. In Cairo I made contact with members of exiled groups from South Africa. Two of the people I knew were later implicated in the assassination of Tom M'Boya. With my pockets filled with toilet paper (Nasser's revenge?), I headed to Ethiopia where there was a border war with the Somalis. Ethiopians were not eating too well even then.

When I first arrived at the Ghion Hotel in Addis Ababa, I noticed that my white fellow passengers were being sent in one direction, while I was directed to another. I took one look at my room and returned to the desk. "I want to go where *they* went," I said. I got a chalet, and nicely laid out it was, too. Trying to cover the war was like being a character in Waugh's *Scoop.* There was confusion, rumor, or nothing. I couldn't get an interview with Selassie, but he did give one to a young white reporter from a small Missouri paper. I saw the emperor one day when returning from the cable office. My driver stopped. There was a Cadillac in front of us. On both sides of the road people who were working in the fields had stopped and as one, like wheatstalks in a wind, bent toward the emperor's car. Even my driver got out, pressed his palms together and bowed. He scowled at me because I didn't.

One night in the hotel restaurant I was feeling once again a keen sense of being *between* things—not African, not American—and I was distressed. Then two or three great bellows of laughter rolled through the room, unmistakably African-American laughter. I got up and went to the table from which these beautiful sounds were coming and asked if I could join the two men sitting there. I had never done anything like that before or since in my life.

I finished up what could be done in Addis Ababa and flew north to Asmara in search of a story about two American housewives who were flying around the world and were supposed to touch down up there.

I got a driver, headed for the other airport, and found it. There were military planes with American markings on them. We started in and were stopped at gunpoint. The driver spoke only Italian and Amharic. I waved my press card; the driver seemed to be saying it was all my fault. It dawned on me that there was fighting up here, and it was between Selassie's troops and the Eritrean rebels. And those soldiers holding rifles on me thought I was one of the rebels. I didn't understand them and they didn't understand me and I saw myself either dead or in a jail within moments. Just then there came tooling out of the base a dashing young flying officer (he had wings on his shirt) in a sporty little MG. "What's going on here?" he asked in flawless, American English.

I explained the situation to him, flashed all the paper I could muster. He had me unload my bag and place it in his car, and then he drove me back to the main airport. There I bought him cognacs until a plane came that would take me out of there. He was also somewhat suspicious. The plane was going to Khartoum, but I didn't care if it was going to the moon.

I can't say that things improved too much in West Africa, but the stay with Wendell Roye and his wife Ernestine was a break from hotel living and endless contact with officials. Down in Lagos I saw once again Chinua Achebe (I'd met him in New York in 1962) and then Cyprian Ekwensi, both premier novelists. They had harsh things to say about the way their books were being produced by Heinemann in its African Writers Series; both felt that they were considered more to be exotic happenings than serious writers. This was especially true with Amos Tutuola and his the *Palm Wine Drinkard.* (My impression today, though, is that Heinemann has done a rather good job of bringing Asian and African writers onto the literary scene.)

I left Lagos for the Eastern Region, then the Cameroons and what was then the Congo, where there were plenty of rifles young soldiers seemed all too willing to push into your face. It was therefore with some relief that I returned to Lagos and where a curious thing happened. One day a guy from USIA, where I stopped regularly on my beat, asked if I'd like to interview Malcolm X. The last I'd heard, he was in Mecca. This man gave me the date of Malcolm's arrival and the flight. I asked no questions about the source of this information, which turned out to be accurate.

I was staying downtown at the Bristol. Malcolm was to be at the Federal Palace, a bit out of town. I called and asked for Mr. Small—his "slave name." A Brit with a classy accent answered. I hung up. I had *meant* to ask for Mr. *Little.* I called again and Malcolm answered; his voice is still unforgettable. I introduced myself and he interrupted to ask, "Did you write a novel called *Sissie?*"

I said yes and he asked me to come right over. There was one other person with him, an African-American dressed in an *agbada.* I had the feeling that they thought no one, or at least very few people, knew they were there. We had more of a talk than an interview and this was because we were joined by a group of Pakistanis. Malcolm talked in riddles I understood, but they could not. He had a lot of cameras and took a lot of pictures. He was, for my money, everything I thought he might be. (Almost a year later I was back in Nigeria staying at the Federal Palace, when word came that he had been killed.)

I returned to Kano to spend a few days with Wendell and Ernestine and then flew to Amsterdam. There, where another buddy, S. P. Lomax—whose fine story, "Pollution," I used in the Lancer anthology I edited, *The Angry Black* (1962)—found me a place to stay for the month I was there. I met the Dutch publisher of *Night Song (Synkopen en de Nacht)* and my Dutch translator, who'd also translated Richard Wright, Margrit de Sabloniere. Another publisher there was bringing out *The Angry Black (De Zwarte Woede).* There was a small black expatriate community there then, far less frantic and more sure of itself than the one in Paris: Bill Hutson and Sam Middleton, painters; Lomax, Paul Carter Harrison, the playwright, and others in the Dutch performing arts.

It seems strange today, but then everywhere in Europe where blacks were living in any number, there was great suspicion about the presence of informers. This was also true in Amsterdam. The world for me was growing very strange. It was not possible to be a black American reporter in Africa without danger, and it was not possible to be just hanging around in a European city for a few weeks without being considered an agent, and this was a theme which, in part, I tried to utilize in *The Man Who Cried I Am.*

(It later developed that one of the people in the Amsterdam group, who'd traveled back and forth, New York to Amsterdam, over the years, "jumped, fell, or was pushed to his death," as the phrasing goes, in 1977. I don't suppose much would have been made of his death had it not happened that, quite soon after his body was discovered by a neighbor of his girlfriend with whom he'd been, representatives of the U.S. consulate reportedly showed up at her apartment and over her vigorous protests, claimed all his papers.)

An American feels that Europe is small. I rented a VW and pushed it down to Castelldefels with only a seven-hour stop in about a day and a half. And then drove back to Amsterdam with but one stop and took the *Rotterdam* out of Rotterdam to New York. Five days on the water gave me a chance to cool out, and I was doing well until I entered New York and discovered that the day before those three kids—Goodman, Chancy and Schwerner—were missing in Mississippi. I wonder if their murders still bother others as much as they still torment me.

The *Holiday* piece was scheduled to run soon, and New American Library was going to do the entire thing. (*Holiday* used about 20,000 words of a book about the trip, a book suggested by one of the magazine's editors.) I had lunch with my editor at NAL; he was E. L. Doctorow. We met at Al Sacht's and he was slightly apprehensive because of the things he'd heard about me. But, it was like love at second sight; we exchanged visits and were good friends.

Lori was packing to move to California. She gave me an ultimatum, (I had given her several, shaped more like pleadings) but I didn't want to get married, not just yet. I was having a grand time. Off she went and left me to my good times.

Newsweek (remember it was 1964) wanted to pull me into the New York office. But after so many years of not having to report to anyone, and using my time to write my things, I turned them down. I was too old to get fastened to a desk or beat in New York, and besides, I had a novel warming up, and the title would be *The Man Who Cried I Am.*

I was then living with a lady, and we were having problems. As a result, when I was asked to go to Nigeria and do a film for a series on National Educational Television that winter, I jumped at the chance.

I picked up another *Newsweek* press card—just in case—and returned to Nigeria where we shot the film from the script I'd written and was still writing as we moved through the country. In the old slave port of Badagry the largest mausoleum in the local cemetery belonged to a wealthy slave trader, a Nigerian, of the nineteenth century. His name was engraved on a wall. It was Aba Williams. Perhaps the most notable items in the film were the interviews with Achebe and Ekwensi.

Back in New York I found that my lady had not moved while I was gone, as I'd hoped; so I moved to Chelsea. In the summer of 1965, after trying to make amends by letter and phone, I went to Los Angeles to talk Lori into marrying me. After a couple of days of family chitchat, I borrowed my parents' car. "Where you goin', Johnny?" my stepfather asked. He was nosey without being malicious. My mother, I am sure, was just as curious.

"To Westwood," I said.

"Westwood," he echoed. "Ain't no colored people live in Westwood."

"I know," I said and drove off.

I brought Lori by to meet the folks and a couple of days later we flew down to Mexico City where we met José Donoso, a Brandt and Brandt client, and his wife, Maria Pilar. Lori and I had planned to drive to Acapulco. The Donosos wondered if we could drop them off in Cuernavaca, where they were staying. Once in the town, Lori and I decided to stay and we rented a villa in town for about $10 a day. We saw a lot of Pepe and Maria and also Carlos Fuentes.

I didn't manage to settle too much with Lori, but, since it was my turn to deliver ultimatums, I gave her a deadline by which time I'd book one or two passages to Europe, and flew back to New York. So, naturally she called about ten days later and asked if I'd be good enough to secure a cabin for two with outside windows.

I was now pretty well into *The Man Who Cried I Am* and Harry Sions, who'd been my editor at *Holiday* and who'd moved to Little, Brown, offered me a contract for it. Although many people insisted that Harry was self-centered and arrogant, I liked him. We had things in common. He was, he told me, Little, Brown's first Jewish editor. I was its first black novelist. I was forced to back away from Harry somewhat, however, when one day during a lunch he said "niggers" instead of "Negroes." Things were never quite the same after that. But I had a contract and was getting a second wife who had been approved by Greg and Dennis who'd known her for years. I also had to sublet my apartment, pack, and help Greg get ready for college; he was going to Syracuse.

In the midst of all this James Meredith showed up. I'd met him in Nigeria and we'd stayed in touch. He was a strange houseguest. When I write, I cannot listen to the radio, although other things don't disturb me to any great extent. Meredith would turn on the radio. I would request that he turn it off. When he did not, I got up and turned it off. He would come back and turn it on, only to cause me to turn if off again. Finally I told him that if he was going to stay those two or three days, he'd have to leave the goddamn radio alone or move out pronto. I think he moved out a day later. I don't know what Meredith was like before he pulled those three years at Ole Miss. Something happened to him and to my knowledge no one ever bothered to find out what.

Lori arrived and we got married, finished packing, found tenants and, the day before we were to leave on the *France,* I was abruptly hospitalized with a bleeding ulcer. I knew I was riding on peaks of tension and stress, but I liked life that way and thought I could do it forever. My body, fortunately, and not my head, told me I couldn't. We got away a month late and missed Chester Himes in Paris where we spent a few days checking out a new car and visiting friends. Lori had begun a journal a few days before we left the States, and she would continue it for the year we were away.

We drove to Spain, back to Barcelona and Castelldefels where we settled unknowingly a mile away from Philip and Fran Levine and their three sons. During the six months we were there we became good friends, often exchanging visits two or three times a day. Also in the village lived Hardie St. Martin. Bob Coover, whom we met once, lived in Tarragona, a couple of towns farther south. Thomas McGrath and his wife came through on a traveling fellowship that would not let them rest for long anywhere, and Edgar Bowers was a Levine house-guest for a few days. We were, in fact, inundated with poets.

Chip Chafetz and Sid Solomon at Cooper Square Press—for whom I'd done the juvenile book on Africa and an anthology I was still working on, *Beyond the Angry Black*—had given me the address of Henry Roth in Seville. Roth's magnificent novel, *Call It Sleep,* had been republished by Chip and Sid and then done in paperback by Peter Mayer at Avon. When Lori and I tired of the routine: work, get wood, light the fireplace, get butane, light the butane stove, cook, eat, sleep, do nothing at all, we took a trip around the country and stopped in to see Henry and Muriel Roth. It was a trip during which Lori got Franco's Revenge in Granada and I got it in Seville (far more severe than Nasser's Revenge). We had to prolong our stay in Seville while I went through chills and fevers. Henry practically made me get out of bed and walk. He loved to talk and walk and to bounce ideas and to have them bounced off him. When we parted, it was agreed that after their trip to Florence where they were going to visit Mario Matterassi, who was translating *Call It Sleep,* the Roths would stay with us when they returned to Spain. Henry was feeling quite good then; he'd just finished a story

for the *New Yorker.* (We read it months later in Amsterdam. It was simply great. It seems to have vanished. It was called "The Surveyor," and it proved beyond a doubt that Roth was still a supreme writer.)

In addition to working on *The Man* and the anthology, I was writing a piece for *Holiday,* "Black Man in Europe," so I was doing considerable interviewing on the trip and in other countries after we left Spain at the end of spring.

But, long before we left, the Roths had returned. I wanted to do a film about him and contacted NET, the forerunner of Public Television and for whom I'd done the film in Nigeria, *Omowale: The Child Returns Home.* Henry was nervous about the show when he returned, even though all the loose ends had not been worked out. When finally they were, a cameraman (the same one I'd worked with in Nigeria, Peter Winkler) and a director who was going to double as sound man arrived. The director knew nothing about Roth and treated him so discourteously—or tried to—(though I'm sure Henry never even noticed) that I was moved to battle him one night while Henry, Muriel, and Lori were finishing up coffee after dinner. (Peter was at our house afflicted with Franco's Revenge.) The director was not as eager as I, and so nothing came of it. Or the show. The first ten minutes had had to be reshot, we discovered when we returned to New York, because he'd blown the sound. We shot in three days or less, quick and dirty, as they say in the film business. *The Creative Person: Henry Roth* could not have been one of the better segments of the series.

The director, with the film in hand, returned to New York; Peter took his camera and went off to the French Riviera; the Roths moved into Barcelona. We returned to our routine.

After leaving Spain and the Levines, we journeyed around Europe and finally came to rest on the south side of Amsterdam—between Rooseveltlaan and Kennedylaan, not far from the heart of the old city. Many of the black artists had returned to the States, sensing that things had changed for the better. Sam Middleton stayed and is there today; he didn't trust the change of scenery back home. In short order I finished off the anthology and the *Holiday* piece and one or two other things. I also finished *The Man* and sent if off to Harry Sions and Carl Brandt, after which we argued by mail over two or three points basically having to do with *their* view of reality versus mine, as embodied in the book—a problem I always had with editors. However, I did do some touching up on the book and when that was completed, we took off on a trip to Scandinavia and back to Paris where we sold the car and prepared to return home on the *Rotterdam*. It had been a good year.

*

Another segment of my life was beginning now. The following year, 1967, *The Man* was published, in October, and Adam, who would grow to become my tennis coach, was born in November. I was forty-one, Lori, thirty-five. As usual, I had started work on another novel (and had collected notes for a third while in Europe) at about the same time I was able to see the end of a previous book. This for me had become routine. I called the work-in-progress *Sons of Darkness, Sons of Light.*

When *The Man* was about to be published, Claude Brown, whom I'd met in 1965, brought Toni Morrison to meet me. She'd done a review of *The Man* for *Life* (which was not published). Like Don L. Lee, she thought everything about the novel was great—except for the interracial liaisons and marriages depicted in it. Subsequently Toni asked if I would read a manuscript she was working on, and I agreed. I very much liked *The Bluest Eye* and kicked it over to Harry Sions who also liked it. But he wanted to see more of it. These reactions, Toni said, encouraged her to finish the novel. It was published three years later by Holt, Rinehart and Winston.

Lori and I had returned at a time when the nation was in a crisis situation. Rebellions were breaking out in city after city; the war in Vietnam wasn't going well. Was it going to be guns *and* butter, or guns *or* butter? Publishers eagerly sought works by black authors, and black editors as well, to nurse them. Close to the end of the decade there were over a dozen black editors working in New York; today there may be four.

Colleges and universities were also looking for bodies to hurl into the breach and, as a result, I began teaching writing at City College in 1968; there followed, in fits and starts, stints at several colleges and universities and at Rutgers. Those of us who landed in the academy or in publishing got there in largest measure because of events that took place not in offices or classrooms, but in the streets. But, by 1975, in both publishing and the academy, "The Black Thing" was on the way back to an unnoticed entity.

We had not yet arrived at that point when I delivered *Sons* to Harry Sions and we sat down to discuss a larger advance for the next book, which was to be about the

black soldier in Vietnam. This was a critical period for Lori and me. Greg was about to begin his senior year at Syracuse, Dennis was about to start Cornell, and Adam, that evidence of middle-aged ego, lay mewling and puking in his bedroom in our apartment at 35 West Ninety-second Street. It was impossible to raise money from the magazines to go to Vietnam to do articles (that would grow into a book) about black soldiers. The well-accepted line, fostered by feature-chasing articles, was that in the heat of battle a new democracy was being born, shared by white and black soldiers alike. My information didn't bear out the contention, so I suppose my view, not being popular, was certainly not to be encouraged.

Harry was opposed to giving me the advance I wanted and felt I deserved. His view was that my art could feed my family. (Sions was married, but had no children.) Still, because I was basically fond of him, and grateful for all he'd done, I let him know that Doubleday would give me the advance I wanted. Could he, would he, match it? Sions' response was to throw me out of his apartment—figuratively, of course. We never saw each other again. His sense that I'd betrayed him was so strong that he declined to have anything to do with *Sons of Darkness, Sons of Light:* Llewellyn Howland at Little, Brown was delegated to guide the novel through to publication in 1969. I still hear stories about how I "double-crossed" Sions.

The decade of the 1970s was my most productive as a writer. It also coincided with the period when I became a full-time teacher, the death of my stepfather, and our move from the Upper Westside of Manhattan to the suburb of Teaneck, New Jersey. During this time I edited or coedited four anthologies, two of them with Charles F. Harris, *Amistad 1* and *Amistad 2*. I wrote and published four nonfiction books including *The King God Didn't Save*, which *Time* savaged, but which, over the years, has won me many fans who managed to find the book somewhere. There were three published novels during this time, *Captain Blackman* (1972, which was to have been the Vietnam book); *Mothersill and the Foxes* (1975) and *The Junior Bachelor Society* (1976, which was made into an NBC-TV miniseries in 1981). During the late 1970s I wrote a pop novel, *The Berhama Account,* which was not published until 1985, three years after what I consider my very best novel, *!Click Song,* was published and, like so many of my other books, never found a paperback home.

But, if one is a writer, that is a last concern, I think. Even now, as *Berhama* is about to come out, and *The Man Who Cried I Am* is ready for reissue, another novel, halfway finished, sits in the typewriter. If I have my way, there will always be something sitting in the typewriter, or something finished and unpublished because a publisher reneged on a contract, a situation that seems far more commonplace than I could have imagined twenty-five years ago. (At present on the shelf there is a study I did of Richard Pryor-1983-84—for New American Library and which was rejected by the third editor on the project; the first quit NAL, the second quit, and the third rejected it out of hand.)

I like to switch-hit from fiction to nonfiction, and to have projects ready to go as soon as one is finished. I'm not sure I could ever get used to having more space between works than I now have. Much of my work has been produced since my marriage to Lori, which says a great deal for her and about our lives together. There are times when I am writing a novel and it feels like walking against a great wind, since my estimation of much of the long fiction that is around is not high at all. As a society we are not great readers. Good writing demands mental exertion and exertion generally is not in much demand, despite all the exercising going on. Still, next to writing a great poem, which I have not yet done, writing novels—always with an eye to doing something new with each one—most satisfies whatever is within me that demands such satisfaction.

My sons and daughters-in-law continue to be supportive ("Watch out for Grampa's back!") and if a writer is in any kind of family situation, he or she must have it. Basically, there isn't anything else except, perhaps, a little tennis now and again, preferably with the grandchildren.

POSTSCRIPT

John A. Williams contributed the following update to *CA* in 2001:

I no longer play tennis—not even close to the (in)frequency I used to. But, I should be out showing a couple of grandnieces who live just a few blocks away how to hold a racquet. I do ride a stationary bike ten—down from fifteen—miles a day, and sometimes haul out the bike our youngest son gave me about three years ago. I oil it up, put air in the tires, test the seat and tool around town after I've walked the bike up the hill from our house, usually on days when I am quite sure that I'm not yet ready to keel over while doing some serious pumping.

A number of people I mentioned in Volume 3 of *Contemporary Authors Autobiography Series (CAAS)* are now dead. Both my parents and my younger brother, Joe, and my uncle, Fred Page; Gordon Couchman, who'd moved to New York City; Wendell Jean Pierre, a long-time colleague at Rutgers; Seymour Krim, a friend from my days in Greenwich Village and beyond; Chester Himes; Candida Donadio, my first agent; Malcolm X; Jose Donoso, well met in Cuernavaca and Barcelona; Tom McGrath, also well met in Castelldefels; Sid Solomon and Henry (Chip) Chafetz, who held down the south end of "Books Row," at Fourth Avenue and Ninth Street in New York City, and had unearthed Henry Roth but rarely got credited for it; and Henry himself, as well as his wife, Muriel, among many others.

I had been teaching for twenty-six years, retiring from it in 1994. It paid the bills, was often very rewarding, and over the years many students became friends. Teaching's many challenges kept me on my toes. But it had its problems. Somewhat like publishing, educational institutions have changed, yet oddly in many ways, have remained the same. Increasingly, though, it seemed to me that many institutions tended to give students the idea that they were not necessarily bound to learn; that, in fact, it wasn't too bad a thing to cut classes or do the required work until the teacher gave you the look that said *You are a moving target for a big, fat F.* Also, my impression over the years was that many of my students concluded on first sight that, being a black teacher, I was very likely to go easy on handing out bad grades since I no doubt wished to keep teaching. They were partly correct, but only partly. It was true that the fence that had kept African-American teachers out of white institutions was slowly being lowered, but I *was* more or less inside the fence, and I was a serious teacher. More than one dean called me in to explain student complaints about their grades, which invariably were lower than their expectations. In two cases I left the schools rather than lower my standards to the deans'.

My summation on college teaching is in a small book published by the Modern Language Association of America, *Power, Race, and Gender in Academe* (2000). My contribution, "Through the Glass Looking," is one of ten. The collection was edited by Shirley Lim and Maria Herrera-Sober. This overview deals with a part of the fabric still being woven—or possibly fraying—in the American tapestry where double-talk, double standards, and double-cross, are in full bloom, this time specifically in academia.

Of course, so had publishing changed, too. The smaller houses got pushed off the range or swallowed by the

The author with his sons, Greg, Dannis, and Adam, 1996

newer and/or bigger guys. Editors played musical chairs again, leaving some gaps in the circle for new-comers whose views and loyalties were shaped by the money-makers that did not necessarily have to be liter-ary. Women writers in general gained much leverage in the past thirty-odd years, a number of them black; and a younger generation of black male writers came on the scene with somewhat less support than that received by the women, though I'm sure some would try to make a case for the opposite. The increase in African-American editors was best detected with a magnifying glass. And there were a few black publishing houses, some of which were around only long enough to take a deep breath.

In the earlier *CAAS* I mentioned my negative experi-ence at New American Library, in which two editors quit before I had finished the already contracted *If I Stop I'll Die: The Comedy and Tragedy of Richard Pryor,* and a third who promptly rejected the book. Thunder's Mouth Press, then relatively new on the block, agreed to publish it; they had already published my novel *Jacob's Ladder* in 1987. In 2001 TMP melted into Avalon. These events allowed me the singular pleasure of working with my son, the writer, Dennis, husband of Millicent and father of Margo and David (as opposed to Greg, my son, the educational consultant, husband of Lucia and father of John Gregory and Nancy, and my son, Adam, the musician who is not

married and has no children that I know of). Dennis published his first novel, *Them That's Not,* co-written with a boyhood friend, Spero Pines, in 1973. Our book on Pryor was published in 1991 after we'd done exten-sive research including, naturally, some of his perfor-mances. Reviews were few, but most were good. The British Oxford Film and Television early in 2001 dis-patched a couple of producers and a camera crew to the U.S. to shoot a documentary on African-American Comedy, in which a host of black comedians and their observers, including Dennis and his Dad, took part. It will be shown in 2002.

If I Stop I'll Die was our personal salute to Pryor. Over the years I'd interviewed and written about Dick Greg-ory and Bill Cosby. Richard Pryor had to be next. Den-nis had always loved Cosby, but that didn't stop him from getting into Pryor; we had a good time with him. From childhood, Dennis had been interested in writing, and before becoming a teacher at Cornell, from which he'd graduated, he'd done a stint at *Newsweek.* He's now an administrator-teacher at Georgetown Univer-sity and is working on his fourth novel. His others are *Crossover* (1992), and *Somebody's Child* (1997).

We had a good editor at TMP, Michael Schwartz; he stayed out of the way and let us roam where we would. Now and again he offered good ideas and trails to take along Pryor's life. These days, on the other hand, the number of editors who wish for writers to produce what they, the editors, desire, seems to have increased as much as the hands-off but listen-to-this-suggestion school of editors has decreased. This brings me to the current state of affairs as I've experienced them in publishing.

My last novel, *Clifford's Blues,* (1999), was rejected fifty-seven times, and when it was finally published, it was in a version from which I had removed (certainly not thrown away) just over 100 pages of the book. The travails and travels of the novel, whose lead character is a black gay inmate of the Dachau concentration camp, were sobering. One editor hit me with this in the rejection of it:

"I know the author is respectful of the sufferings of the inmates, but Cliff does not share them, and somehow his annoyance at the odd instance of racial prejudice is completely overshadowed by what we know is happening further east, in the face of the final solution.

"For this reason, I am not enthusiastic about taking this novel on. . . ."

Someone else suggested that "Black writers should stick to lynchings and discrimination in the U.S. and leave the Holocaust to the Jews and the Europeans."

Clifford (which Kirkus Reviews called a first novel) brought forth a certain, closeted censorship that was different from the "No one wants to read about prejudice" declaration that gave editors a pass on all but perhaps half a dozen black writers in the fifties. Neither I, nor any other black writer, was supposed to touch any element of the Holocaust. However, there *were* 25,000 Afro-Germans, who were sterilized, camped, killed, or left to fend for themselves in a Germany that had become murderously racist. Not very much at all has been written about them. (Hans Massaquoi's *Growing Up Black in Nazi Germany* was selling very well in Germany and the rest of Europe in the summer of 2001, but not in the U.S., though Massaquoi has been an American citizen for more than half a century.) And Afro-Europeans in countries occupied by Germany were of course camped, killed or closely watched. What led me to write the novel in the first place was seeing photos of two black inmates at the newly opened Dachau Museum in the spring of 1966. Channel 4 in England three years ago produced "Hitler's Forgotten Victims," about black Germans, but to my knowledge, it has not been shown in the States as the producer of the show told me it was scheduled to be.

The editorial comments above were not the only ones like them. One—editor or not—harms oneself by remembering only a single element of a connected history. As Richard L. Rubenstein said in his *The Cunning of History* (1975), "The parallels between the treatment of the slaves (I would have used enslaved) in transit from Africa to the New World and the death-camp inmates are unhappily instructive. . . ."

The huffing and puffing carried me right back to the late fifties when the editor of the *Atlantic Monthly* rejected my story, "Son in the Afternoon," because of a black young man's vengeful dallying with the white woman for whom his mother works. While "Son" has been widely anthologized, it ran into problems again in 1983. Little, Brown's *An Introduction to Fiction, Poetry and Drama,* third edition, carried this note concerning "Son": "This story, offered in the book's first edition, disappeared from the second edition because two or three instructors disliked it and reported that it struck their students speechless with embarrassment. In response to a larger demand from instructors who found teaching it well worth the risk, it is now restored. Emotionally charged, it has a black narrator who makes candid observations of both blacks and whites. We recommend it for assignment only if you know your class well and believe them capable of a free, frank discussion of it. If you use it, why not assign it together with another brief story, just so you'll have something to pass along in case of paralysis?"

To add to the "*Clifford* episodes," over the years three editors have lost manuscript copies of three of my books. And another editor "misplaced" and never found two additional manuscripts of mine, but that's my own fault, since this particular editor was widely reputed to have lost more manuscripts than were ever read. Not a single apology was offered, and I think I am being kind with my choice of verbs here; over the years nastier ones have often forced themselves into my consciousness.

Then there was the editor who angrily denied what I'd written about an American official's negative comments concerning Malcolm X when he was in Africa in 1964. (I was writing a commissioned book about X.) But I had a very solid source. I noted in the earlier *CAAS* that I had met Malcolm in West Africa that year. I knew there were U.S. efforts to minimize any effect he might be having wherever he visited. (I was made aware that X was coming. Better he should spend the time doing an interview with a guy from *Newsweek* than rousing the rabble in the marketplace.) The editor's words in heated defense of the official were, "I

Williams and his wife, Lori, in Innsbruck, Austria, 2001

know this man! He'd never say anything like that!" While I did get paid for it, my 1994 manuscript on Malcolm gathers dust somewhere in my work space.

That space is a large room, three steps down and off the kitchen, with windows on three sides. Lori's office is upstairs, where she copyedits for a number of publishers in the New York-New Jersey area. She has two windows. Her desk is always cluttered; mine is only a bit less so. The first floor of the house is empty after breakfast until lunchtime, after which it becomes empty again until just before dinner, when, over an occasional drink, we start throwing verbal haymakers at publishers and their editors. On occasion we'll take a brisk walk— Lori always walks briskly—or do other exercises together. I've talked her into using the stationary bike sometimes and when she does, she's on for five miles at a time.

Surveying my situation since 1986, in addition to works cited, I also published, in Canada, a small volume of

poetry, *Safari West* (1998); co-edited, with the Sorbonne's Michel Fabre, *A Street Guide to African Americans in Paris,* (1992, 1996); and managed to write and publish a number of articles, not including introductions and afterwords. Working with co-editor Gil Muller, we prepared a new edition of McGraw-Hill's *Ways In: Approaches to Reading and Writing About Literature* that will be out in 2002. I also completed my thirteenth novel, *Colleagues,* which is hunting down a publisher. While I am not sure what I'll do with the Malcolm X book, I am sure of my stride in *Over My Shoulder: Notes,* which is a memoir in progress.

In a change of pace, I wrote the libretto, most of it poetry, for the opera *Vanqui,* the name of the heroine. Composer Leslie Burrs wrote the music for the work that was commissioned by Opera Columbus and premiered in Columbus, Ohio, in 1999. And *Birdland* is another novel in progress.

As usual, my writing time is spent alternating between fiction and nonfiction, as I noted in the earlier piece. Otherwise, I am doing what Chester Himes once said: "Writers write." This is because I know I have writing to finish and some of it to pull together. Things like the country house in upstate New York need a touch here and there for continued use by the family. I believe cities are quite close to environmentally killing themselves and the people in them. Whatever space is not already owned or despoiled is where people will have to move. Lori and I think the country place is the most valuable thing we could ever leave our family, far better than words, which, after all, come after the fact. At seventy-six, that's the way it looks.

BIOGRAPHICAL/CRITICAL SOURCES:

BOOKS

Cash, Earl A., *Evolution of a Black Writer,* Third Press, 1975.

Contemporary Literary Criticism, Gale (Detroit, MI), Volume 5, 1976, Volume 13, 1980.

Dictionary of Literary Biography, Gale (Detroit, MI), Volume 2: *American Novelists since World War II,* 1978, Volume 33: *Afro-American Fiction Writers after 1955,* 1984.

Gayle, Addison, Jr., editor, *Black Expression: Essays by and about Black Americans in the Creative Arts,* Weybright and Talley, 1969, pp. 365-372.

Muller, Gilbert H., *John A. Williams,* Twayne (New York, NY), 1984.

O'Brien, John, editor, *Interviews with Black Writers,* Liveright (New York, NY), 1973, pp. 225-243.

PERIODICALS

Black Literature Forum, spring/summer, 1987, pp. 25-42.

Black World, June, 1975.

Bloomsbury Review, January/February, 1988, p. 10; October/November, 1991, p. 13.

Chicago Tribune Book World, April 18, 1982; November 17, 1985.

Contemporary Literature, spring, 1973.

Critic, April, 1963.

Critique: Studies in Modern Fiction, Volume 16, number 3, 1975.

Detroit News, June 6, 1982.

Forkroads, winter, 1995, Dennis A. Williams, "An Interview with John A. Williams," pp. 37-50.

Gay and Lesbian Review Worldwide, winter, 2000, Jo-Ann Reid, "Another Glimpse of Hell," p. 54.

Library Journal, November 1, 1961; September 15, 1967.

Los Angeles Times, June 19, 1996, Dick Adler, "Opening Doors for the Devil in a Blue Dress," p. E1.

Los Angeles Times Book Review, May 9, 1982; November 29, 1987.

Nation, September 18, 1976.

New Yorker, August 16, 1976.

New York Times, June 13, 1993.

New York Times Book Review, May 6, 1973, pp. 34-35; July 11, 1976; April 4, 1982; October 18, 1987; November 15, 1987.

Prairie Schooner, spring, 1976.

Publishers Weekly, November 11, 1974; February 1, 1999, p. 77.

Studies in Black Literature, spring, 1972, pp. 24-32.

Time, April 12, 1982.

Washington Post Book World, March 23, 1982; October 4, 1987.

* * *

WILLIS, Mary Pleshette

PERSONAL: Married; husband's name, Jack (a local television station CEO); children: Kate.

ADDRESSES: Home—New York, NY. *Office*—c/o Random House, 299 Park Ave., New York, NY 10171-0002.

CAREER: Writer.

AWARDS, HONORS: Emmy Award, for television afternoon special *Wanted: The Perfect Buy.*

WRITINGS:

Papa's Cord: A Novel, Knopf (New York, NY), 1999.

Also author of teleplays and pilots, including *Wanted: The Perfect Buy.*

WORK IN PROGRESS: A novel, *Night Fishing.*

SIDELIGHTS: Mary Pleshette Willis is an American novelist and television screenwriter. She worked as a writer for television, earning an Emmy Award for an afternoon special entitled *Wanted: The Perfect Buy,* before focusing on her first novel. She lives with her husband Jack, with whom she has a daughter, Kate, in New York.

Willis' first novel *Papa's Cord: A Novel* was published in 1999. The novel is the story of Josie Davidovitch, an upper-middle-class Jewish woman, who becomes engaged to athlete Gus Housman. Housman, however, suffers a paralyzing swimming accident before the wedding. Josie marries him anyway, and soon their story is published as a memoir and is optioned for a screenplay. Josie's authoritarian father then suffers a sudden illness and Josie must come to terms with her emotional past.

Critics were mixed in their assessment of *Papa's Cord.* "Despite the author's valiant effort to dissect a complex father-daughter relationship, stereotype triumphs over depth as the heroine acquires material wealth, worldly success and guilt," wrote a critic for *Publishers Weekly.* Molly Abramowitz in *Library Journal* concurred, arguing that stereotypical "portrayals of Jews and a superficial cast to the story leave much to be desired here." A *Kirkus Reviews* critic concluded that the world was a "literate soap opera, decently done but unremarkable." The critic for *Publishers Weekly,* however, found the portrayal of the adolescent-aged Josie a "more convincing take-charge" protagonist than the adult version and lauded Willis' "lucid descriptions" of New York.

BIOGRAPHICAL/CRITICAL SOURCES:

PERIODICALS

Kirkus Reviews, August 1, 1999, review of *Papa's Cord,* p. 1164.

Library Journal, August, 1999, Molly Abramowitz, review of *Papa's Cord,* p. 143.

Publishers Weekly, August 2, 1999, review of *Papa's Cord,* p. 71.*

WINDSOR, Allen
See SMITH, Warren Allen

*   *   *

WINICK, Judd 1970-

PERSONAL: Born February 12, 1970, in Long Island, NY; married Pam Ling, 2001. *Education:* University of Michigan, B.A., 1992.

ADDRESSES: Home—915 Cole St., No. 301, San Francisco, CA 94117. *E-mail*—judd@frumpy.com.

CAREER: Cartoonist, illustrator, and writer. AIDS educator and lecturer. Participant in MTV's *The Real World,* 1994; host of following television programs: (with Pam Ling) *MTV video Now What?: A Guide to Jobs, Money, and the Real World,* and *MTV's Real World-Road Rules Casting Special* and (co-host) *Best Fights of the Real World,* both 2000.

AWARDS, HONORS: Eisner Award nomination for best sequential story, 1998, for "Road Trip;" Eisner Award nominations, 1999, for talent deserving wider recognition, best humor artist/writer, and best original graphic novel, for *Pedro and Me;* notable graphic novel citation, Young Adult Library Services Association (YALSA), for *The Adventures of Barry Ween, Boy Genius;* GLAAD Media Award for best comic book, Bulletin Blue Ribbon Book citation, notable graphic novel citation, YALSA, *Publishers Weekly* Best Book citation, Américas Award for Children's and Young Adult Literature, National Association of Latin American Studies Programs, all for *Pedro and Me;* Bay Area Book Reviewers' Award, 2000, and Notable Children's Book selection and Gay Lesbian, Bisexual, Transgender Roundtable Nonfiction Honor Book, American Library Association, Robert F. Sibert Informational Book Honor Award, Quick Pick for Reluctant Readers selection, YALSA, all 2001, all for *Pedro and Me.*

WRITINGS:

SELF-ILLUSTRATED

Terminal Madness: The Complete Idiot's Guide Computer Cartoon Collection, Que (Indianapolis, IN), 1997.
The Adventures of Barry Ween, Boy Genius, ONI Press (Portland, OR), 1999.
The Adventures of Barry Ween, Boy Genius, 2.0, ONI Press (Portland, OR), 2000.

Judd Winick

Pedro and Me: Friendship, Loss, and What I Learned, Holt (New York, NY), 2000.
Frumpy the Clown: Freaking out the Neighbors, ONI Press (Portland, OR), 2001.
Frumpy the Clown: The Fat Lady Sings, ONI Press (Portland, OR), 2001.
The Adventures of Barry Ween, Boy Genius, 3.0, ONI Press (Portland, OR), 2001.

Author and illustrator of cartoon strip "Nuts and Bolts," published in *Michigan Daily,* 1988-92, and *San Francisco Examiner,* 1994, and collected in *Watching the Spin-Cycle: The Nuts and Bolts,* privately printed (Ann Arbor, MI). Author and illustrator of "Road Trip" comic strip, in *ONI Double Feature;* "Frumpy the Clown," syndicated, 1996-98; "The Adventures of Barry Ween, Boy Genius," Image Comics, 1999; "Green Lantern," DC Comics; and "Exiles," Marvel Comics. Illustrator, with others, of Jamie S. Rich's *Cut My Hair,* ONI Press, 2000, and for numerous titles in the "Complete Idiot's Guide" series, Que (Indianapolis, IN).

ADAPTATIONS: The Adventures of Barry Ween, Boy Genius was optioned for development as an animated television series by Platinum Studios.

WORK IN PROGRESS: A graphic novel.

SIDELIGHTS: The world became all too real for Judd Winick in 1993 as one of seven "stars" of MTV's *Real World III,* a pioneering reality-based television show. It was then that he met not only his future wife, Pam Ling, but also temporary housemate Pedro Zamora, a young man from Florida whose eventual death from AIDS would bring the tragic effects of that disease home to millions of young television viewers. Zamora, an AIDS activist, inspired Winick, a promising young cartoonist, to hit the lecture circuit for over a year after the filming of *The Real World* to speak with young people about AIDS-related issues. In 2000 Winick published a moving and honest graphic-novel account of his friendship with Zamora, *Pedro and Me: Friendship, Loss, and What I Learned.* Additionally, Winick is also a popular cartoonist, author, and illustrator of, among other things, the comic strip "Frumpy the Clown," which follows the trail of a chain-smoking, cynical clown who decides to move in with a typical suburban family, and "The Adventures of Barry Ween, Boy Genius," a series of comic books dealing with the misadventures of a cranky, obnoxious, brilliant, and foul-mouthed ten-year-old.

Born in 1970, Winick grew up in Dix Hill, Long Island, New York, "a grumpy, quasi-budding artist kid," as he admitted to Bill Jensen in *Newsday.* Schoolwork was not his favorite pastime at Half Hollow Hills East High School; instead, young Winick took refuge in reading comics and then in creating his own. By the time he was sixteen, he was already a professional cartoonist, selling a single-paneled strip, "Nuts and Bolts," to Anton Publications, which published newspapers in a three-state northeastern region.

When he graduated from high school and moved on to college at the University of Michigan, Winick studied drawing and art. He also continued his "Nuts and Bolts" strip, now expanded into four panels and running five days a week in the college paper, the *Michigan Daily.* Shortly before graduation, Winick's strips were collected in a privately printed edition, *Watching the Spin-Cycle: The Nuts and Bolts,* which sold out its thousand copies in a matter of two weeks. Encouraged by such a response, Winick landed a development contract with a syndicator to develop the cartoon as a national strip, but after a year of work in Boston, the "bottom dropped out," as Winick reported on his Web site. "[T]he syndicate decided that they were not going to pursue 'Nuts and Bolts' for syndication and were terminating the development contract."

Out of work, Winick returned temporarily to his parents' home, commuting into New York City for occasional illustration jobs and working on a development deal with Nickelodeon on an animated series based on "Nuts and Bolts." This deal also fell through and when, in August, 1993, Winick saw a newspaper ad for auditions for MTV's *The Real World,* to be shot in San Francisco, he jumped at the chance. The six-month-long audition process included doing a video, filling out a fifteen-page application, having in-person interviews with the producers, and being followed around for a day by a film crew. Finally, Winick, along with six others, were chosen for the cast of the reality show in which these seven—strangers from all over the United States—were put together in a house and filmed nonstop for half a year. One possible stumbling block came when producers asked Winick how he would feel about sharing quarters with another young man who was HIV positive. At that moment, Winick was forced to live up to his liberal PC convictions and confront the fears and ignorance they actually covered up. He told the producers there was no problem with that, but secretly he had his doubts, which he shared with friends. "Here I was, this weenie, open-minded, liberal New York Jew," Winick told Chad Jones in an *Oakland Tribune* interview. "I should have been fine with it, but I was really scared."

Winick and his fellow housemates gathered at a house on Lombard Street in San Francisco to be filmed cinema-verité style. The HIV-positive roommate turned out to be AIDS activist Pedro Zamora, a Cuban immigrant who had been diagnosed with AIDS as a teenager. Zamora wanted to be on the show to give a human face to the AIDS scourge, and he and Winick became fast friends. Together they and the others, including Asian-American medical student Pam Ling, confronted the day-to-day hassles of living together. During the filming of the show, Winick's cartoon strip, "Nuts and Bolts," was reprised in the local *San Francisco Examiner.*

Winick, who took the job on *The Real World* as a way to get free rent and live in San Francisco temporarily, quickly learned there was much more to the deal. He became known as the serious one of the group and the guy who could never get a date. This was his persona to an entire segment of Generation X viewers, the twenty-something audience MTV was hoping to reach. After filming for six months in 1993, the show began airing in 1994 and became one of the most popular in the series, not least because of Zamora's medical condition. It was not long after the show went on the air that Zamora became ill from AIDS complications. Winick agreed to take over his speaking engagements until Zamora could get back on his feet, but the activist never did. In August, 1994, Zamora was put in the hospital and died the following November, shortly after the final episode of *The Real World III* appeared on television.

Following Zamora's death, Winick continued to lecture about his friend and about AIDS education and prevention. For about a year and a half he devoted most of his time to this cause. It was, Winick explained on his Web site, "the most fulfilling and difficult time in my life."

By 1995 Winick needed to return to his cartooning career. He had, by this time, outgrown "Nuts and Bolts" and was ready to take on new challenges. Working as an illustrator, he began providing artwork for many of the "Complete Idiot's Guide" series, a collection of which were published as *Terminal Madness.* As a writer and illustrator, he worked on his first syndicated comic strip, "Frumpy the Clown," beginning in July of 1996. Stealing one of his favorite characters from "Nuts and Bolts," Winick gave the cynical clown a new home, with a suburban family mom, dad, children (Brad and Kim), and family dog. The children are ecstatic about their new member, Frumpy, but the parents, along with neighbors, wish only that he would go away. Winick depicts Frumpy and family embroiled in such quotidian tasks as getting the kids to school and fixing snacks, but all the while Frumpy attempts to enlighten the children about the dark truths lurking behind the bright lights of so-called reality, taking great delight in warping their young minds. Winick continued the strip for two years, with an initial syndication of thirty national papers. "Unfortunately," Winick noted on his Web site, "Frumpy ran into trouble." The clown's edginess ultimately cost readership in more family-oriented newspapers, and eventually syndication dwindled to a trickle. Also, and more importantly, Winick found the daily grind of turning out a comic strip less creative than he had imagined. "I found daily comic strips to be limiting," he noted, "not just in length and size formats or language, but creatively. I just didn't find the strip fulfilling."

It was about this time that Winick began work on a graphic novel about his friendship with Zamora, a project that would last over two years. Meanwhile, he also formed a relationship with ONI Press, and began work on a comic, "The Adventures of Barry Ween, Boy Genius." Barry is not your typical ten-year-old. Possessed of an IQ of 350, the youth delights in days spent on his own with the sitter heavily sedated, allowing him to work on his anti-terrorist equipment, or alternately build an atom smasher that fits under his bed. He gets into adventures with his pal Jeremy Ramirez, such as dealing with art thieves and time warps, repairing a stranded space ship of an alien on the run from intergalactic mobsters, and rescuing his buddy from the government. Popular with audiences already keen on the graphic format popularized by such works as *Maus* by Art Spiegelman, both "Barry Ween" and "Frumpy" were published in paperback collections by ONI Press.

Throughout 1999 Winick continued work on his graphic novel *Pedro and Me.* Armistead Maupin, the San Francisco-based author of *Tales of the City,* saw an early version of the work and encouraged Winick to push on and to be even more open and frank about his friendship with Zamora. Submitting the manuscript to his agent, Jill Kneerim, Winick was hopeful for early publication. But thirty publishers saw it, loved it, and failed to buy it. Then the manuscript was sent to editor Marc Aronson at Holt who was "very hands-off but provided lots of guidance," as Winick told Shannon Maughan in a *Publishers Weekly* interview. "He helped me work on the pacing, finding a moment here, a moment there, building a true beginning, middle and end." Eventually, through working with Aronson, Winick whittled down his manuscript to one hundred-eighty book pages. It was also decided to target the book at a young adult audience, the population most at risk for contracting AIDS.

Pedro and Me tells the twin stories of both Winick and Zamora. One young man came from Cuba in the Mariel Boatlift of 1968 that saw the immigration of 125,000 refugees from Castro's Cuba. Still in his early teens, Zamora watches his mother die of skin cancer in Florida; at seventeen he contracts the AIDS virus and soon thereafter becomes a major activist and AIDS educator. Meanwhile, Winick grows up safe and sound on Long Island, mowing lawns in the summer. As fellow cast members, Winick and Zamora grow to understand one another. Winick does not spare himself when he shows his own initial ignorance and fear of Zamora's disease, nor does he replay the events of *The Real World* house; rather he focuses on the friendship and what he learned from his brief time with Zamora. The story continues after the filming of *The Real World* is over, as Zamora becomes ill, and both Winick and Pam Ling take time out from their busy lives to be with him. It ends with the emotional deathbed scene with a gathering of friends.

Reviewers and critics had high praise for Winick's book and its message. Writing in the *Advocate,* a contributor called *Pedro and Me* a "touching remembrance" and a "cathartic experience," while a reviewer for *Publishers Weekly* described the graphic novel as "powerful and captivating," and felt that it struck "just the right balance of cool and forthrightness to attract a broad cross section of teens, twenty-somethings and beyond." The same writer noted the "deceptively simple" black and white comic-strip art that contains a "full spectrum of emotion," concluding that Winick's book was an "innovative and accessible approach" to a very difficult subject. *Booklist* contributor Stephanie Zvirin lauded the cartoonist's illustrations, noting that "facial expressions . . . count most" in a book filled with "great tenderness and a keen sense of loss." In a review for *School Library Journal,* Francisca Goldsmith commented that Winick does a "stellar job of marrying image to word to form a flowing narrative," and added: "This is an important book for teens and the adults who about them. Winick handles his topics with both sensitivity and a thoroughness that rarely coexist so seamlessly." "The vigorous comic-strip art, notable for its expressive depictions of real-life characters and variety of layout and perspective, does not diminish the seriousness of the subject matter," maintained Peter D. Sieruta in his *Horn Book* appraisal of *Pedro and Me.* Sieruta concluded, "In this warm and ultimately life-affirming remembrance, Winick gives the world a second chance to know Pedro and his message."

Reader response was equally positive, and Winick soon found he was once again a sought-after speaker at schools. "My hope is that people learn from Pedro the way I did," he noted in an interview for the *Advocate,* "that they have their stereotypes broken and learn about AIDS and the people who live with it—and that they are empowered by his accomplishments. Lastly, I hope they remember my friend. That's why I wrote and illustrated this in the first place."

But Winick has also attempted to move beyond the bounds of the world he first confronted in *The Real World.* While he hopes never to forget the message Zamora gave the world about AIDS and people with AIDS, he has other creative plans in the works, including a further graphic novel as well as writing for DC Comics' "Green Lantern" series. In his talks with students, Winick also encourages other budding cartoonists. "Develop a style," he tells cartoonist hopefuls on his Web site. "It's not necessary to be a jack of all trades. And get published! Any little paper that'll have you, or print them up yourself and give them away in comic stores. I don't believe in luck. Success comes when opportunity meets preparation."

BIOGRAPHICAL/CRITICAL SOURCES:

PERIODICALS

Advocate, February 1, 2000, review of *Pedro and Me,* p. 2; September 12, 2000, "Judd Remembers," p. 61.
Billboard, September 7, 1996, p. 100.
Booklist, September 15, 2000, Stephanie Zvirin, review of *Pedro and Me,* p. 230; December 1, 2000, p. 693.
Boston Herald, September 5, 2000.
Horn Book, November-December, 2000, Peter D. Sieruta, review of *Pedro and Me,* pp. 775-776.
Newsday, April 16, 2000, Bill Jensen, "From 'Real World' to Real World, Sort Of."
Oakland Tribune, September 6, 2000, Chad Jones, "Learning 'Real' Lessons."
Publishers Weekly, September 11, 2000, review of *Pedro and Me,* p. 92; September 18, 2000, Shannon Maughan, "That's What Friends Are For," p. 37.
Sacramento Bee, August 31, 2000.
San Francisco Chronicle, September 6, 2000.
School Library Journal, October, 2000, Francisca Goldsmith, review of *Pedro and Me,* p. 192.
TV Guide, July 29, 2000.
USA Today, September 18, 2000.

OTHER

Judd Winick Web site, http://www.juddwinick.com/ (May 14, 2001).
Fandom, http://www.fandom.com/ (May 13, 2001).

*   *   *

WOOLFSON, Jonathan

PERSONAL: Male. *Education:* Attended Oxford University, and Warburg Institute, London, England.

ADDRESSES: Office—Hertford College, Oxford University, Catte St., Oxford OX1 3BW, England.

CAREER: Oxford University, Oxford, England, lecturer in history and fellow of Hertford College.

AWARDS, HONORS: Fellow of British Academy.

WRITINGS:

Padua and the Tudors: English Students in Italy, 1485-1603 (monograph), James Clarke (Cambridge, England), 1998.

Also contributor of articles on Renaissance humanism, sixteenth-century universities, the collecting of antiquities, and the history of the book.

BIOGRAPHICAL/CRITICAL SOURCES:

PERIODICALS

Times Literary Supplement, April 23, 1999, Kate Lowe, "The Part Padua Played," p. 31.*

* * *

WURMBRAND, (Heinrich) Richard 1909-2001

OBITUARY NOTICE—See index for *CA* sketch: Born March 24, 1909, in Bucharest, Romania; naturalized United States citizen, 1971; died February 17, 2001, in Glendale, CA. Minister and author. Wurmbrand was an ordained Lutheran minister who created the International Christian Ministry to the Communist World, an organization for individuals of faith persecuted by Communist forces behind the Iron Curtain. Even after being arrested, imprisoned, and tortured fourteen years for spreading Christian ideals in Communist Romania, Wurmbrand continued on his mission to bring Christianity to others. Wurmbrand authored a number of books, many of which were translated into over fifty languages. Some of them include *Christ in the Communist Prisons,* his best-selling *Tortured for Christ,* which brought him international attention, *One Hundred Prison Meditations: Cries of Truth from Behind the Iron Curtain,* and *Marx and Satan.*

OBITUARIES AND OTHER SOURCES:

PERIODICALS

Daily Telegraph (London, England), February 23, 2001.
Guardian (London, England), March 16, 2001, p. 20.
Independent (London, England), February 23, 2001, p. 6.
Los Angeles Times, March 4, 2001, p. B6.
Times (London, England), April 24, 2001, p. 19.

XU, Meihong 1963(?)-

PERSONAL: Born c. 1963, in China; immigrated to the United States c. 1990; married Lin Cheng (a member of the People's Liberation Army; divorced); married Larry Engelmann (a journalist and professor), 1990 (divorced). *Education:* Institute of International Relations, Nanjing, China, B.A.

ADDRESSES: Home—San Jose, CA. *Office*—c/o Wiley Publishing, 605 Third Avenue, New York, NY 10158-0012.

CAREER: Author. *Military service:* People's Liberation Army, People's Republic of China, intelligence officer.

WRITINGS:

(With Larry Engelmann) *Daughter of China: A True Story of Love and Betrayal,* Wiley (New York, NY), 1999.

SIDELIGHTS: Meihong Xu's *Daughter of China: A True Story of Love and Betrayal* is a memoir of her service in the People's Liberation Army (PLA) in China and her meeting and marriage to Larry Engelmann, an American journalist, author, and teacher who was suspected of being a spy.

Xu left her farm village to join the PLA when she was seventeen. In 1981 she was chosen to train in espionage at the Nanjing military institute as part of an elite group of women known as the "twelve pandas." Lieutenant Xu married Lin Cheng, a member of the PLA, but because of their duties, they saw each other only twice a year. In 1988 Xu was sent to study at the Center for American Studies, a collaboration between Johns Hopkins University and Nanjing University. She represented herself as a student but was assigned to spy on Engelmann, who was suspected of being an agent. Xu was also charged with learning as much as possible about the United States so that her patron, a general, could create a replica of an American city to be used as a training ground for officers who would be sent to the United States. Xu took the name "Rose," and as she experienced the Western lifestyle, she became drawn to it and disenchanted with the Communist Party. The model city never came to be. *Washington Post Book World* reviewer Judith Shapiro said this "other mandate . . . stretches credibility."

Engelmann trusted Xu, and as they became close, Xu was certain he was not a spy. When the PLA discovered the friendship, Xu was arrested and interrogated for eight weeks. Her life was unexpectedly spared, but she was dismissed from the army and the Party and faced a bleak future in China. She had refused to disclose information that would incriminate anyone, including the general who was her mentor. Although Xu had never had a sexual relationship with Engelmann, she was pressured to bring false charges of rape against him. Engelmann was accused of that crime and forced to leave China. Xu went back to her husband, but eventually they divorced and she made the decision to escape. She contacted Engelmann, who offered to marry her and bring her to the United States.

Shapiro wrote that these events "are interspersed with well-crafted flashbacks. One vignette recounts a devastating incident in the collective memory of Meihong's village, when invading Japanese burned haystacks where the town's young girls lay hidden. A visit to a grandmother's grave introduces a tale of female infanticide, while a water buffalo glimpsed from a train evokes memories of a grandfather who longed to tend his fields but was forced to become a puppet for Communist propaganda." Shapiro called Engelmann's notation that their marriage ended in divorce and then continued to meet weekly to finish the book an "aching postscript."

Reviewing *Daughter of China* for *New Straits Times,* Chong Seck Chim recommended that readers struck by the quick dissolution of Xu and Engelmann's marriage might best "suspend judgment and just enjoy the book for what it's worth." In Chim's opinion, the most striking feature of *Daughter of China* is its portrait of peasant life and army training during those ultraconservative years. It is, Chim stated, "a breath-taking, firsthand account of man's cruelty to man." Another reviewer, Steven I. Levine, expressed some doubts about the book, calling it a "thrilling tear-jerker" but believing that "it is almost impossible to distinguish truth from fiction in a story told by a self-admitted accomplished liar."

A *Publishers Weekly* reviewer took *Daughter of China* much more seriously, stating that Xu's view of "the Cultural Revolution, the democracy movement, the Tiananmen Square massacre, and the hints of struggle among the top leadership will fascinate those familiar with Chinese politics."

BIOGRAPHICAL/CRITICAL SOURCES:

PERIODICALS

Library Journal, September 15, 1999, review of *Daughter of China: A True Story of Love and Betrayal,* p. 92.
New Straits Times, July 12, 2000, Chong Seck Chim, review of *Daughter of China: A True Story of Love and Betrayal.*
Publishers Weekly, September 27, 1999, review of *Daughter of China: A True Story of Love and Betrayal,* p. 81.
Times (London, England), June 30, 1999, Sue Ellicott, review of *Daughter of China: A True Story of Love and Betrayal,* p. 21.
Washington Post Book World, September 26, 1999, Judith Shapiro, review of *Daughter of China: A True Story of Love and Betrayal,* p. 4.*

*   *   *

YPEREN, Pieternella Cornelia van   1930- (Ellen Warmond)

PERSONAL: Born 1930.

ADDRESSES: Office—c/o Em Querido's Uitgeverij, Postbus 3879, 1001 AR, Amsterdam, Netherlands.

CAREER: Dutch poet; former dancer with Rotterdam Ballet Ensemble.

AWARDS, HONORS: Anna Bijns Prize for poetry, 1987.

WRITINGS:

AS ELLEN WARMOND

Proeftuin, D.A. Daamen (The Hague, Netherlands), 1953.
Naar men zegt: gedichten, Bakker (The Hague, Netherlands), 1955.
Weerszij van een vereld: gedichten, Bakker (The Hague, Netherlands), 1957.
Eeuwig duurt het langst, Querido (Amsterdam, Netherlands), 1961.
Paspoort voor niemandsland, Querido (Amsterdam, Netherlands), 1961.
Warmte, een woonplaats: gedichten, Querido (Amsterdam, Netherlands), 1961.
Het struisvogel-reservaat: gedichten, Querido (Amsterdam, Netherlands), 1963.

De huid als raakvlak, Querido (Amsterdam, Netherlands), 1964.

Testbeeld voor koud klimaat, Querido (Amsterdam, Netherlands), 1966.

Geen bloemen/geen bezoek, Querido (Amsterdam, Netherlands), 1968.

Van kwaad tot erger, Querido (Amsterdam, Netherlands), 1968.

Mens, Een inventaris, Querido (Amsterdam, Netherlands), 1969.

De groeten aan andersdenkenden, Querido (Amsterdam, Netherlands), 1970.

Saluutschot met knaldemper, Querido (Amsterdam, Netherlands), 1972.

Zie je me goed?, B. Bakker (The Hague, Netherlands), 1973.

The Shape of Houses: Women's Voices from Holland and Flanders, translated by Manfred Wolf, Two Windows Press (Berkeley, CA), 1974.

Uizicht op inzicht, Querido (Amsterdam, Netherlands), 1974.

Implosie, Querido (Amsterdam, Netherlands), 1976.

Gesloten spiegels, Querido (Amsterdam, Netherlands), 1979.

Tegenspeler tijd: een keuze uit de gedichten, Querido (Amsterdam, Netherlands), 1979.

Ordening, Querido (Amsterdam, Netherlands), 1981.

Uitzicht op inzicht, Querido (Amsterdam, Netherlands), 1983.

Saluutschot met knaldemper, Querido (Amsterdam, Netherlands), 1983.

Vragen stellen aan de stilte, Querido (Amsterdam, Netherlands), 1984.

Vluchtstroken van de taal, Querido (Amsterdam, Netherlands), 1988.

Persoonsbewijs voor inwoner, Querido (Amsterdam, Netherlands), 1991.

Kaalslag, Querido (Amsterdam, Netherlands), 1999.

Also contributor to *Change of Scene: Contemporary Dutch and Flemish Poems in English Translation.*

SIDELIGHTS: Once a dancer with the Rotterdam Ballet Ensemble, Dutch writer Pieternella Cornelia van Yperen (who writes under the name Ellen Warmond) is primarily known as a poet. She debuted with a small collection of poems titled *Proeftuin* in the early 1950s. Exploring such themes as fear, loneliness, and alienation, van Yperen endeavors to strike a balance between Western thought and Oriental philosophies. *Warmet, een woonplaats* is a set of poems in which van Yperen examines the "possibility of escaping" from Existential fears. Such themes can be found in her collections *Vragen stellen aan de stilte, Vlucht stroken van de taal* and *Persoonsbewijs voor inwoner.* van Yperen was the recipient of the Ann Bijns prize for poetry in 1987. Martinus Arnoud Bakker, a reviewer in *World Literature Today,* called *Persoonsbewijs voor inwoner* "representative of all sixteen books of verse" van Yperen had published to date. Bakker commented on van Yperen's evolution as a poet, noting, "though the fear made place for a growing awareness of love and trust, the images remained . . . concrete, even tangible." Bakker complemented van Yperen for her "unique ability to construct an image as solid as a rock."

BIOGRAPHICAL/CRITICAL SOURCES:

BOOKS

Bloomsbury Guide to Women's Literature, Prentice Hall General Reference (New York, NY), 1992.

Encyclopedia of Continental Women Writers, Garland Publishing (New York, NY), 1991.

PERIODICALS

World Literature Today, summer, 1992, Martinus Arnoud Bakker, review of *Persoonsbeqijs voor inwoner,* pp. 530-531.*